>**business**research**methods**

The McGraw-Hill/Irwin Series
in Operations and Decision Sciences

Business Statistics

Aczel and Sounderpandian: **Complete Business Statistics,** *Seventh Edition*

ALEKS Corporation: **ALEKS for Business Statistics,** *First Edition*

Alwan: **Statistical Process Analysis,** *First Edition*

Bowerman, O'Connell, and Murphree: **Business Statistics in Practice,** *Sixth Edition*

Bowerman, O'Connell, Orris, and Porter: **Essentials of Business Statistics,** *Third Edition*

Bryant and Smith: **Practical Data Analysis: Case Studies in Business Statistics,**
      Volumes I, II, and III*

Cooper and Schindler: **Business Research Methods,** *Eleventh Edition*

Doane: **LearningStats CD Rom,** *First Edition, 1.2*

Doane, Mathieson, and Tracy: **Visual Statistics,** *Second Edition, 2.0*

Doane and Seward: **Applied Statistics in Business and Economics,** *Third Edition*

Doane and Seward: **Essential Statistics in Business & Economics,** *Second Edition*

Gitlow, Oppenheim, Oppenheim, and Levine: **Quality Management,** *Third Edition*

Kutner, Nachtsheim, Neter, and Li: **Applied Linear Statistical Models,** *Fifth Edition*

Kutner, Nachtsheim, and Neter: **Applied Linear Regression Models,** *Fourth Edition*

Lind, Marchal, and Wathen: **Basic Statistics for Business and Economics,** *Seventh Edition*

Lind, Marchal, and Wathen: **Statistical Techniques in Business and Economics,** *Fourteenth Edition*

Olson and Shi: **Introduction to Business Data Mining,** *First Edition*

Orris: **Basic Statistics Using Excel and MegaStat,** *First Edition*

Wilson, Keating, and John Galt Solutions, Inc.: **Business Forecasting,** *Sixth Edition*

Zagorsky: **Business Information,** *First Edition*

Quantitative Methods and Management Science

Hillier and Hillier: **Introduction to Management Science,** *Fourth Edition*

Stevenson and Ozgur: **Introduction to Management Science with Spreadsheets,** *First Edition*

* Available only through McGraw-Hill's PRIMIS Online Assets Library.

>**business**research**methods**

Donald R. Cooper
Florida Atlantic University

Pamela S. Schindler
Wittenberg University

eleventhedition

BUSINESS RESEARCH METHODS

Published by McGraw-Hill/Irwin, a business unit of The McGraw-Hill Companies, Inc., 1221 Avenue of the Americas, New York, NY, 10020. Copyright © 2011, 2008, 2006, 2003, 2001, 1998, 1995, 1991 by The McGraw-Hill Companies, Inc. All rights reserved. No part of this publication may be reproduced or distributed in any form or by any means, or stored in a database or retrieval system, without the prior written consent of The McGraw-Hill Companies, Inc., including, but not limited to, in any network or other electronic storage or transmission, or broadcast for distance learning.

Some ancillaries, including electronic and print components, may not be available to customers outside the United States.

This book is printed on acid-free paper.

2 3 4 5 6 7 8 9 0 DOW/DOW 1 0 9 8 7 6 5 4 3 2 1

ISBN   978-0-07-337370-6
MHID   0-07-337370-2

Vice president and editor-in-chief: *Brent Gordon*
Editorial director: *Stewart Mattson*
Publisher: *Tim Vertovec*
Executive editor: *Richard T. Hercher, Jr.*
Director of development: *Ann Torbert*
Developmental editor: *Rebecca Mann*
Vice president and director of marketing: *Robin J. Zwettler*
Marketing director: *Sankha Basu*
Associate marketing manager: *Jaime Halteman*
Vice president of editing, design, and production: *Sesha Bolisetty*
Senior project manager: *Harvey Yep/Bruce Gin*
Senior buyer: *Carol A. Bielski*
Interior designer: *JoAnne Schopler*
Senior photo research coordinator: *Lori Kramer*
Photo researcher: *Keri Johnson*
Media project manager: *Cathy L. Tepper*
Cover design: *JoAnne Schopler*
Interior design: *JoAnne Schopler*
Typeface: *10/12 Times Roman*
Compositor: *MPS Limited, A Macmillan Company*
Printer: *R. R. Donnelley*

Library of Congress Cataloging-in-Publication Data

Cooper, Donald R.
    Business research methods / Donald R. Cooper, Pamela S. Schindler.—11th ed.
        p. cm.—(The McGraw-Hill/Irwin series in operations and decision sciences)
    Includes index.
    ISBN-13: 978-0-07-337370-6 (alk. paper)
    ISBN-10: 0-07-337370-2 (alk. paper)
    1. Industrial management—Research. I. Schindler, Pamela S. II. Title.
HD30.4.E47 2011
658.0072—dc22
                                                                            2010019201

To my sons, Ryan and Paul Cooper, and to Qian who encourages me in the journey of life.

Donald R. Cooper

To my husband, Bill, for his unwavering support, intuitive counsel, and enthusiasm for every challenge I tackle.

Pamela S. Schindler

walkthrough

Bringing Research to Life reveals research in the trenches.

Much of research activity isn't obvious or visible. These opening vignettes are designed to take the student behind the door marked RESEARCH. Through the activities of the principals at Henry & Associates, students learn about research projects, many that were revealed to the authors *off the record*. The characters and names of companies are fictional, but the research activities they describe are real–and happening behind the scenes in hundreds of firms every day.

>bringingresearchtolife

Jason Henry and Sara Arens, partners in Henry & Associates, are just wrapping up a Web-based briefing on the MindWriter project. Jason and Sara are in Boca Raton, Florida. Myra Wines, MindWriter's director of consumer affairs is participating from Atlanta, as are others, including Jean-Claude Malraison, MindWriter's general manager, who joined from Delhi, India, and Gracie Uhura, MindWriter's marketing manager, and her staff, who joined from a conference room in their Austin, Texas, facility.

"Based on the poll results that are on your screen, you have reached a strong consensus on your first priority. The research strongly supports that you should be negotiating stronger courier contracts to address the in-transit damage issues. Congratulations," concluded Jason.

"That wraps up our briefing, today. Sara and I are happy to respond to any e-mail questions any of you might have after reading the summary report that has been delivered to your e-mail. Our e-mail address is on screen, and it is also on the cover of the report. Myra, I'm handing control of the meeting back to you."

As Myra started to conclude the meeting, Sara was holding up a sign in front of Jason that read. "Turn off your microphone." Jason gave a thumbs-up sign and clicked off his mic.

"Thank you, Jason," stated Myra. "The research has clarified some critical issues for us and you have helped us focus on some probable solutions. This concludes the meeting. I'll be following up soon with an e-mail that contains a link to the recorded archive of this presentation, allowing you to share it with your staff. You will also be asked to participate in a brief survey when you close the Web-presentation window. I'd really appreciate your taking the three minutes it will take to complete the survey. Thank you all for attending."

As soon as the audience audio was disconnected, Myra indicated, "That went well, Jason. The use of the Q&A tool to obtain their pre-report ideas for action [is] a stroke of genius. When you posted the results as [a po]ll and had them indicate their first priority, they [were] all over the board. It helped them understand that

one purpose of the research and today's meeting was to bring them all together."

"Sara gets the credit for that stroke of genius," claimed Jason after removing his microphone and clicking on his speakerphone. "She is a strong proponent of interaction in our briefings. And she continually invents new ways to get people involved and keep them engaged."

"Kudos, Sara," exclaimed Myra. "Who gets the credit for simplifying the monthly comparison chart?"

"Those honors actually go to our intern, Sammye Grayson," shared Sara. "I told her while it was a suitable graph for the written report; it was much too complex a visual for the presentation. She did a great job. I'll pass on your praise."

"Well," asked Myra, "where do we go from here?"

"Jason and I will field any questions for the next week from you or your staff," explained Sara. "Then we will consider this project complete—until you contact us again."

"About that," Myra paused, "I've just received an e-mail from Jean-Claude. He wants to meet with you both about a new project he has in mind. He asks if he could pick you up at the Boca airport on Friday, about 2:30 P.M. He says his flying office will have you back in time for an early dinner."

Sara looked at her BlackBerry and indicated she was available. Jason looked at his own calendar and smiled across the desk at Sara. "Tell Jean-Claude we'll meet him at the airport. Any idea what this new project is about?"

"Not a clue!"

>chapter 13

Questionnaires and Instruments

>learningobjectives

After reading this chapter, you should understand . . .

1 The link forged between the management dilemma and the communication instrument by the management-research question hierarchy.

2 The influence of the communication method on instrument design.

3 The three general classes of information and what each contributes to the instrument.

4 The influence of question content, question wording, response strategy, and preliminary analysis planning on question construction.

5 Each of the numerous question design issues influencing instrument quality, reliability, and validity.

6 Sources for measurement questions.

7 The importance of pretesting questions and instruments.

Learning Objectives serve as memory flags.

Learning objectives serve as a road map as students start their journey into the chapter. Read first, these objectives subconsciously encourage students to seek relevant material, definitions, and exhibits.

Special tools for today's visual learner.

A transformation is taking place in many of our classrooms. During the last decade, more and more of our students have become visual—not verbal—learners. Verbal learners learn primarily from reading text. Visual learners need pictures, diagrams, and graphs to clarify and reinforce what the text relates.

Integrated research process exhibits reveal a rich and complex process in an understandable way.

Every textbook has exhibits. We use these tables and line drawings to bring key concepts to life and make complex concepts more understandable.

Within our array of exhibits is a very special series of **32 fully integrated research process exhibits.** Each exhibit in this series shares symbols, shapes, and colors with others in the series.

Exhibit 1-4 is the overview exhibit of the research process, to which all other exhibits related to the process will link.

Subsequent exhibits (like this one for survey design) show more detail in a part of this process.

Another exhibit in the series might layer the main process exhibit with additional information (like this exhibit from the ethics chapter).

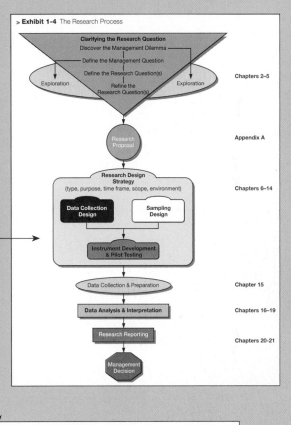

> **Exhibit 1-4** The Research Process

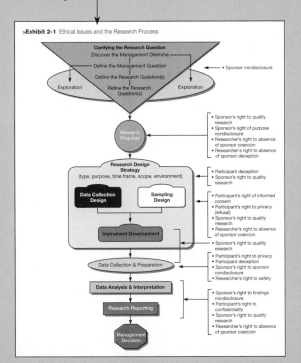

> **Exhibit 2-1** Ethical Issues and the Research Process

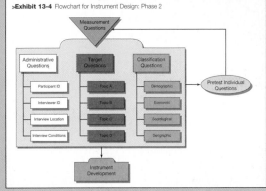

> **Exhibit 13-4** Flowchart for Instrument Design: Phase 2

Some topics deserve more attention—with their own chapter!

An emphasis on presentation.

Increasingly, researchers are making oral presentations of their findings though Web-driven technologies. We address this and other oral presentation formats and issues with a new chapter.

Qualitative research is mainstream.

Researchers increasingly admit that quantitative research can't reveal all they need to know to make smart business decisions. We capture the best of the current qualitative methods and reveal where and how they are used.

Help in moving from management dilemma to research design.

This is where talented people can steer research in the wrong or right direction. We devote a chapter to providing students with a methodology for making the right decisions more often.

Ethical issues get the attention they deserve.

Ethical issues abound in business research but may go unnoticed by students who need a framework to discuss and understand these issues. We devote a chapter to building that framework.

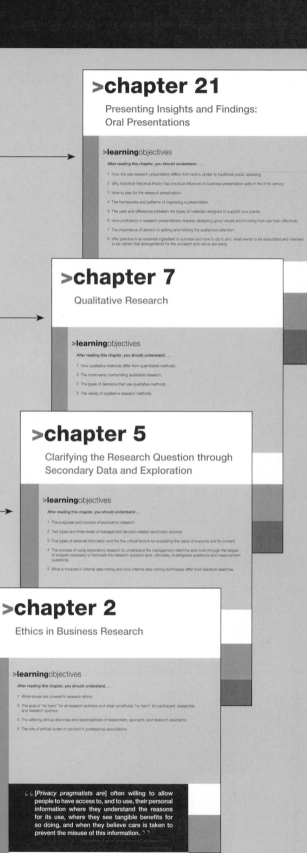

Students learn by and deserve the best examples.

Snapshots are research examples from the researcher's perspective.

Snapshots are like mini-cases: They help a student understand a concept in the text by giving a current example. As mini-cases they are perfect for lively class discussion. Each one focuses on a particular application of the research process as it applies to a particular firm and project. You'll find more than 60 of these timely research examples throughout the text.

Web addresses speed secondary data searches on companies involved with the example.

>snapshot

Is Your Research Project Leaving the Country?

Offshoring is defined as the movement of a process done at a company in one country to the same or another company in a different country. These processes in research often include IT (information technology), business, or knowledge processes. The primary reason to offshore research services is to lower the cost of the research. Offshoring tends to be more prevalent at larger research firms.

There are significant risks associated with offshoring research services, as Gordon Morris, global insights manager for Sony Ericsson (London, UK) discovered. During a global research project for the Experia X10 Android phone, sensitive business plans were shared with the contracted researchers. As a result of offshoring of some research services, information about the 2010 phone launch leaked several months early. "We estimate the potential damage caused by the leak at approximately £100 million," shared Morris. Leaks may be more likely to occur when offshoring is used because intellectual property standards, safe computing standards, and contract laws vary from country to country. Also, high employee turnover in some developing countries can also add to this risk.

In 2009 a new trade group was formed to encourage transparency in offshoring of research services: the Foundation for Transparency in Offshoring (FTO). A survey fielded to 850 U.S. and international research buyers and providers indicated that clients were more likely to think their projects did not involve offshoring than was actually true. Clients also were much more likely than research services suppliers to think clients should be told about offshoring. "Very few buyers have sufficient information to assess the relative strengths and risks associated with offshoring," said

Tom H. C. Anderson, FTO founder and chairman, and managing partner of the research consultancy Anderson Analytics. While not taking a stand for or against offshoring, the FTO encourages research companies to register their project practices and earn one of two seals: one seal certifies that the research organization that do offshore research services comply with the FTO disclosure standards, which are modeled after the EU's Safe Harbour Compliance Framework; the second seal identifies research organizations that do not offshore services at all.

FTO hopes that research buyers will look for the certification seals when purchasing research services. As Sonia Baldia, partner at Mayer Brown LLP and a legal expert on offshoring explained, "Clients absolutely need to know about any offshore subcontracting and the location in order to gauge risks and protect themselves."

www.offshoringtransparency.org

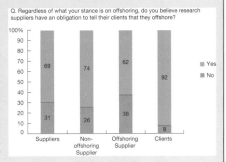

Q. Regardless of what your stance is on offshoring, do you believe research suppliers have an obligation to tell their clients that they offshore?

Human resources—American Society for Public Administration; Society for Human Resource Management.

Insurance—American Institute for Chartered Property Casualty Underwriters; American Society of Chartered Life Underwriters and Chartered Financial Consultants.

Management—Academy of Management; The Business Roundtable.

Real estate—National Association of Realtors.

Other professional associations' codes have detailed research sections: the American Marketing Association, the American Association for Public Opinion Research, the American Psychological Association, the American Political Science Association, the American Sociological Association, and the Society of Competitive Intelligence Professionals. These associations update their codes frequently.

Icons help students link parts of a richer, more complex example, told over a series of chapters.

MindWriter Some examples are so rich in detail that one Snapshot or exhibit just isn't sufficient. MindWriter is a computer laptop manufacturer that prides itself on customer service, especially when it comes to laptop repair at its CompleteCare center. Each time you see this icon in the text, you'll be learning more about the customer satisfaction research that Henry & Associates is doing.

The Closeup offers a more in-depth examination of a key example.

Sometimes you just need more time and space to showcase all the detail of an example. This glimpse of the Closeup from Chapter 20 reveals two pages from a complete annotated client research report.

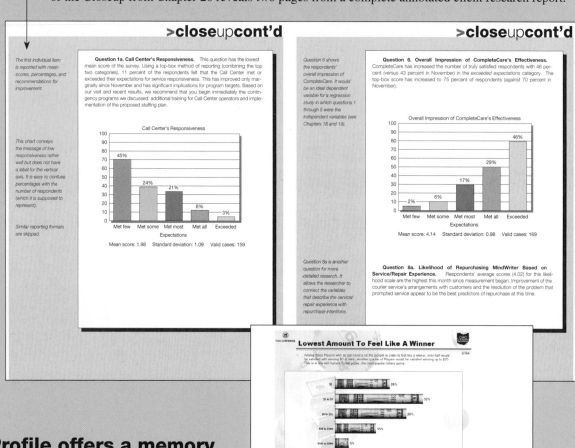

PicProfile offers a memory visual to enhance an example.

In research, as in life, sometimes a picture is worth more than words. Sometimes you need to see what is being described to fully understand the foundation research principle.

Psychological and Physical Foundations[41]

In his book *Clear and to the Point*, author Stephen Kosslyn argues that audience members of any presentation "should not have to search through a visual or conceptual haystack to find the needle you are talking about." Thus the process of **visualization** involves organizing and developing support materials that help the audience share in your understanding of the data. The composition and knowledge of the audience, the venue, and amount of time all influence choices in visualization.

Several psychological principles influence your audience's understanding of your findings. The **principle of relevance** infers that only information critical to understanding should be presented. Information that is presented verbally along with visual support will be perceived as more relevant than that mentioned only verbally without visual support. But the principle also indicates that we do not want to overwhelm the audience with too much information.

In the process of exploring your data, prior to developing a research presentation, you developed numerous tables, graphs, and textual summaries. Not all of these support materials, whether you use handouts, flip charts, or slides, can or should be used in most presentations due to time constraints. Any limitations in your audience's knowledge level (**principle of appropriate knowledge**) or their inability to process large amounts of information at one time (**principle of capacity limitations**) reduces the complexity of your support. In your attempt to share an understanding of the data, some support materials—for example, graphing techniques like box plots with which your audience may be unfamiliar—may instead create confusion or obscure the points you are trying to convey. A familiar visualization technique—a bar or column chart or table—would always convey information more quickly than an unfamiliar one. However, you can design even appropriate and familiar techniques in too complex a fashion by including unnecessary information. Your audience, after all, has only moments to digest visually what you may have been studying for days or weeks. Exhibit 21-9 summarizes data graphing techniques that are appropriate for oral presentations.

Learning aids cement the concepts.

Discussion questions that go one step further.

Five types of discussion questions reveal differing levels of understanding—from knowing a definition to applying a concept.

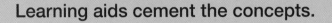

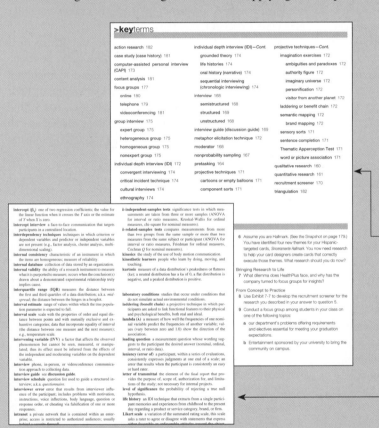

Key terms indexed at the end of the chapter and defined in the

Glossary reinforce the importance of learning the language of research.

Supplements offer the tools students and faculty ask for . . . and more.

On the book's Online Learning Center (www.mhhe.com/cooper11e), students will find cases and data sets, a research proposal, a sample student project, and supplemental material for several chapters, including templates for charting data. You'll also find 33 cases, nine of which are full video cases. Also, several written cases have video components included.

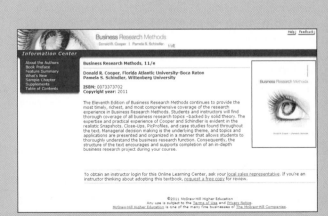

For undergraduate students just learning about research methods or graduate students advancing their research knowledge, with each new edition *Business Research Methods* promises—and has repeatedly delivered—not only a teachable textbook but a valued reference for the future. As a mark of its worldwide acceptance as an industry standard, *Business Research Methods* is now published in nine international editions and in four languages.

When you are creating an 11th edition, you don't want to tinker too much with what has made instructors want to teach with your textbook or researchers use it as a valuable shelf reference. But to ignore environmental changes would be irresponsible. We've tried to respond with clarity and purpose to changes in the business and government environments.

Leading

In this edition, you'll find a new chapter on oral presentations. Since the development of the data warehouse, identifying patterns and drawing meaningful conclusions from data has been as important as collecting primary data addressing specific problems. But business managers today are not always schooled in data analysis and interpretation. Thus, it becomes the job of the researcher to present data processes and conclusions in an understandable way. Also, advances in technology for presenting over the Web have made it possible to gather all the individuals who need to understand the research findings, often without leaving their offices, to hear the researcher explain the findings and conclusions. So, while presenting research findings in written reports is still the norm, the oral presentation of findings has taken on new significance—thus, the new chapter.

Responsive . . . to Students and Faculty

Snapshots, PicProfiles, and Closeups are the way we reveal what is timely and current in research. We wait until such issues are more mainstream before giving the topic a permanent place within the text. You'll find several of these new examples in this edition, dealing with Internet research, cloud computing, using Excel in data analysis and presentation, smartphone research, dirty data, gut hunches, wildcat surveys, and more. And you'll find research stories that relate to such organizations or brands as the Army, Netflix, Snausages, Best Buy, Blackstone Wines, Rypple, Twitter, Facebook, Ford, and Match.com, among numerous others.

Our process series of exhibits has expanded with the addition of Chapter 21 and the revision of Chapter 20. And

you'll find new and revamped exhibits in other chapters as well. Each is designed to make the process more understandable for students.

Chapter 19 got a fresh pair of eyes this edition. We hope you will find the enhanced clarity of concepts to your liking.

We've added a new type of discussion question—"From the Headlines"—to demonstrate to students that research is applicable to all types of scenarios. They are designed for faculty who enjoy using discussion examples in teaching research methods.

We've added research examples to the Instructor's Manual, for use in class discussion or testing. We continue to use chapter and end-of-text appendices for important information that, given the skills and knowledge of their students, an instructor might not always use. You'll find appendices related to a sample proposal, advanced search techniques, question development, the research industry, and more.

Fine-Tuned

Process Series of Exhibits   The core pedagogy of *Business Research Methods* is based on an understanding that student learners are of three types: visual, auditory, and kinesthetic. These exhibits offer a detailed, graphical map of the research process or a more detailed breakout of each subprocess, perfect for hands-on projects. Each of these exhibits is linked to others in the series with a consistent use of shape and color. You'll find 32 of these exhibits throughout the text.

Written Cases   Cases offer an opportunity to tell research stories in more depth and detail. You'll find cases about hospital services, lotteries, data mining, fundraising, new promotions, and website design, among other topics, featuring organizations like Akron Children's Hospital, Kelly Blue Book, Starbucks, Yahoo!, the American Red Cross, and more.

Video Cases   We are pleased to offer a first in video supplements, several short segments drawn from a two-hour metaphor elicitation technique (MET) interview. These segments should be invaluable in teaching students to conduct almost any type of individual depth interview and to explain the concept of researcher–participant rapport. Four of our video cases were written and produced especially to match the research process model in this text and feature noted companies: Lexus, Starbucks, Wirthlin Worldwide (now Harris Interactive), Robert Wood Johnson Foundation, GMMB, Visa, Bank One, Team One

Advertising, U.S. Tennis Association, Vigilante New York, and the Taylor Group. You can download video cases and video supplements from the Online Learning Center.

Web Exercises It is appropriate to do Web searches as part of a research methods course, so each chapter offers one or more exercises to stimulate your students to hone their searching skills. Due to the ever-changing nature of Web URLs, however, we offer these exercises in the instructor's manual, downloadable from the text website.

Sample Student Project Visualization of the finished deliverable is key to creating a strong research report. This detailed project sample is downloadable from the Online Learning Resource Center.

Collaborative

When we revise an edition, many individuals and companies contribute. Here are some who deserve special recognition and our gratitude.

- We would like to acknowledge the changes in Chapter 19, "Multivariate Analysis: An Overview," by Edye Cleary, a doctoral student in the School of Public Administration, Florida Atlantic University. She simplified numerous explanations and elaborated on others to make the material more student-friendly.

- To all those researchers who shared their projects, ideas, perspectives, and the love of what they do through e-mails and interviews and who helped us develop cases, Snapshots, PicProfiles, or Closeups, or provided new visuals: Andy Peytchev, Research Triangle Institute (RTI International); Jeffrey C. Adler, Centrac DC Marketing Research; Josh Mendelsohn, Chadwick Martin Bailey, Inc.; Ruth Stanat, SIS International Research; Sharon Starr, IPC, Inc.; Tom Anderson, Anderson Analytics; Jennifer Hirt-Marchand, Marcus Thomas LLC; Lance Jones, Keynote Systems; Keith Crosley, Proofpoint; Christopher Schultheiss, SuperLetter. com; Ryan Cooper, Lifetime TV; Hy Mariampolski, QualiData Research Inc; Julie Grabarkewitz and Paul Herrera, American Heart Association; Holly Ripans, American Red Cross; Mike Bordner and Ajay Gupta, Bank One; Laurie Laurant Smith, Arielle Burgess, Jill Grech, David Lockwood, and Arthur Miller, Campbell-Ewald; Francie Turk, Consumer Connections; Tom Krouse, Donatos Pizza; Annie Burns and Aimee Seagal, GMMB; Laura Light and Steve Struhl, Harris Interactive; Emil Vicale, Herobuilders.com; Adrian Chiu, NetConversions; Eric Lipp, Open Doors Organization; Stuart Schear, Robert Wood Johnson Foundation; Elaine Arkin,

consultant to RWJF; Colette Courtion, Starbucks; Mark Miller, Team One Advertising; Rebecca Conway, The Taylor Research Group; Scott Staniar, United States Tennis Association; Danny Robinson, Vigilante; Maury Giles, Wirthlin Worldwide; and Ken Mallon, Yahoo!; and numerous colleagues at IBM and Lenovo.

- To Rebecca Mann, our Developmental Editor, who facilitated the complex process and to our Executive Editor, Dick Hercher, who felt strongly enough about us as successful authors to support this revision.

- To the remainder of our McGraw-Hill team, for making the book a priority:
  - Project Manager: Harvey Yep
  - Marketing Manager: Jaime Halteman
  - Media Producer: Cathy Tepper
  - Production Supervisor: Carol Bielski
  - Designer: JoAnne Schopler
  - Photo Researcher: Keri Johnson
  - Photo Coordinator: Lori Kramer

- To our faculty reviewers for their insights, suggestions, disagreements, and challenges that encouraged us to look at our content in different ways: Scott Baker, Champlain College; Scott Bailey, Troy University; Robert Balik, Western Michigan University–Kalamazoo; John A. Ballard, College of Mount St. Joseph; Jayanta Bandyopadhyay, Central Michigan University; Larry Banks, University of Phoenix; Caroll M. Belew, New Mexico Highlands University; Jim Brodzinski, College of Mount St. Joseph; Taggert Brooks, University of Wisconsin–La Crosse; L. Jay Burks, Lincoln University; Marcia Carter, University of Southern New Hampshire; Raul Chavez, Eastern Mennonite University; Darrell Cousert, University of Indianapolis; David Dorsett, Florida Institute of Technology; Michael P. Dumler, Illinois State University; Kathy Dye, Thomas More College; Don English, Texas A&M University–Commerce; Antonnia Espiritu, Hawaii Pacific University; Hamid Falatoon, University of Redlands; Judson Faurer, Metropolitan State College of Denver; Eve Fogarty, New Hampshire College; Bob Folden, Texas A&M University–Commerce; Gary Grudintski, San Diego State University; John Hanke, Eastern Washington University; Alan G. Heffner, Silver Lake College; Lee H. Igel, New York University; Burt Kaliski, New Hampshire College; Jane Legacy, Southern New Hampshire University; Andrew Luna, State University of West Georgia; Andrew Lynch, Southern New Hampshire University; Iraj Mahdvi, National University; Judith McKnew, Clemson University; Rosemarie

Reynolds, Embry Riddle Aero University–Daytona; Randi L. Sims, Nova Southeastern University; Gary Stark, Northern Michigan University; Bruce Strom, University of Indianapolis; Cecelia Tempomi, Southwest Texas State University; Charles Warren, Salem State College; Dennis G. Weis, Alliant International University; Bill Wresch, University of Wisconsin-Oshkosh; and Robert Wright, University of Illinois at Springfield.

We are also indebted to dozens of students who identified areas of confusion so that we could make concepts more understandable, who participated in search tests, who worked on numerous research projects demonstrating where we needed to place more emphasis, and who reminded us with their questions and actions that many aspects of the research process operate below their learning radar.

Through this 11th edition, we hope you and your students discover, or rediscover, how stimulating, challenging, fascinating, and sometimes frustrating this world of research-supported decision making can be.

Pamela Schindler
Donald Cooper

>**brief**contents

>contents

>part III

The Sources and Collection of Data   267

>part IV
Analysis and Presentation of Data 399

>case index

>appendices

>part I

Introduction to Business Research

>chapter 1

Research in Business

>learningobjectives

After reading this chapter, you should understand . . .

1 What business research is and how it differs from decision support systems and business intelligence systems.

2 The trends affecting business research and the emerging hierarchy of research-based decision makers.

3 The different types of research studies used in business.

4 The distinction between good business research and that which falls short of professional quality.

5 The nature of the research process.

> ❝ This is a fantastic time to be entering the business world, because business is going to change more in the next 10 years than it has in the last 50. ❞
>
> Bill Gates, entrepreneur and founder of Microsoft

>**bringing**research**to**life

Myra Wines, director of consumer affairs for MindWriter, Inc., has been charged with the task of assessing MindWriter's CompleteCare program for servicing laptops. As a result, she sent several well-respected research firms a *request for proposal (RFP),* and she and her team are interviewing the last of those firms, Henry & Associates.

Newly promoted to her position, Wines has a TV journalism and government public relations background. She has been a MindWriter laptop owner since it came on the market decades earlier and has never personally experienced a problem. She wants a research supplier from whom she can learn, as well as one whom she can trust to do appropriate, high-quality research.

The last interviewee is Jason Henry, managing partners, Henry & Associates. H&A comes highly recommended by a professional colleague in a different industry. H&A has gained a reputation for merging traditional methodologies with some creative new approaches. Myra is interested in exploring the firm's methodology for customer satisfaction studies. As Wines approaches Henry in the waiting area, she extends her hand. "Welcome to MindWriter, Jason. I'm Myra Wines."

Henry rises, clasping Wines's hand in a firm hand shake. "Pleased to meet you, Myra."

Myra directs Jason's attention to a long corridor. "My team members are gathered in our conference room just down this hall. Let's join them, shall we?"

The interview process starts with Henry's short presentation on H&A and its capabilities. As the interview progresses, Henry shares some impressive results accomplished for former clients in noncompetitive industries. The last slide in his presentation features a top industry award H&A recently won for its customer satisfaction methodology.

During the Q&A that follows, Henry demonstrates current knowledge of the computer industry (he's obviously read numerous articles), confidence, and expertise, at a level that Wines initially had not expected given his relatively youthful appearance. At the conclusion of the interview, Wines is leaning toward hiring Henry & Associates, but wants to confer with her team.

The next day, Myra calls Jason at his office. "We've chosen Henry & Associates for the MindWriter CompleteCare assessment contract. Congratulations."

"Thank you," accepts Jason. "You've made the right choice."

"I've got two seats on a flight to Austin next Wednesday," shares Myra. "Can you join me? This will be my first look at the CompleteCare facility and my first face-to-face contact with its manager. I'd like someone along who can lay the groundwork for the project and understand the number crunching that's already been done."

The phone goes silent as Jason pauses to consult his BlackBerry. Two internal meetings will need to be shifted, but MindWriter is an important new client. "Yes, I can work that in as long as we're back by 7 p.m. I've got an evening commitment."

"Shouldn't be a problem," shares Myra. "Those seats I mentioned are on the corporate jet. We'll be back by 5:30. I'll meet you in the lobby at the county airstrip at 8 a.m. Wednesday then."

"A quick question," interrupts Jason before Myra can disconnect. "I need some idea of what's happening at this meeting."

"The meeting is to get you started. I'll introduce you to other people you will be working with and share more details about the concerns we have with the CompleteCare program," shares Myra.

"Fine. Can you arrange a third seat? It would be best to include Sara Arens from the very beginning. Her expertise will be crucial to the success of the assessment program."

"Yes, you mentioned her before. That shouldn't be a problem, but I'll check and get back to you."

"Then, Wednesday, Sara and I will plan on asking probing questions and listening to discover exactly what facts management has gathered, what the managers are concerned about, what the problem is from their point of view, what the problem really is at various levels of abstraction . . ."

"Listening to people. Discussing. Looking at things from different viewpoints. Those are things I am also very good at," shares Myra.

"Good. After we hear them out, we come to what H&A is good at: Measurement. Scaling. Project design. Sampling. Finding elusive insights. May I assume we'll be collaborating on the report of results?"

"Absolutely. I'll call you back within 10 minutes about that third seat."

> Why Study Business Research?

One of the dominant metaphors for understanding organizations is "reading." The art of reading situations is one of the skills that successful managers use to organize and manage their responsibilities. It is an intuitive process whereby a manager learns to "get a handle on a problem," and it occurs at an almost subconscious level. Although there is a mystique or magical power associated with this talent, skilled leaders and managers develop this trained knack for reading situations to allow them to properly diagnose and solve problems in organizational life. Everyone can learn to read organizations.

So it is with the research that drives decision making in organizations. Here, however, we take the theme for our book as "seeing." Seeing through to the truth needs patience more than activity. True "seeing" allows managers to break out of their traditional habits, look at the world through different eyes, to question old ways of finding solutions. To "see" is to find new ways to look at, think about, understand, and portray the world you see through your research lens.

Legendary photojournalist Henri Cartier-Bresson coined the phrase, "the decisive moment," meaning the moment when the subject and its significance come together for a split second. His talented, practiced eye recognized those fleeting moments. In our book, we also help you see the decisive moment through a trained capacity to plan, acquire, analyze, and disseminate insights that you mobilize to improve performance in your organizations.

You are about to begin your study of business research, both the process and the tools needed to reduce risk in managerial decision making. **Business research,** as we use it in this text, is a systematic inquiry that provides information to guide managerial decisions. More specifically, it is a process of planning, acquiring, analyzing, and disseminating relevant data, information, and insights to decision makers in ways that mobilize the organization to take appropriate actions that, in turn, maximize performance. A variety of different types of research projects are grouped under the label "business research," and we will explore them later in this chapter.

Assume for the moment that you are the manager of your favorite full-service restaurant. You are experiencing significant turnover in your waiter/waitress pool, and some long-time customers have commented that the friendly atmosphere, which has historically drawn them to your door, is changing. Where will you begin to try to solve this problem? Is this a problem for which research should be used?

Perhaps you are the head of your state's department of transportation, charged with determining which roads and bridges will be resurfaced or replaced in the next fiscal year. Usually you would look at the roads and bridges with the most traffic in combination with those representing the most economic disaster, if closed. However, the state's manager of public information has expressed concern about the potential for public outcry if work is once again directed to more affluent regions of the state. The manager suggests using research to assist in making your decision, because the decision is one with numerous operational, financial, and public relations ramifications. Should you authorize the recommended research?

As the opening vignette and the early decision scenarios reveal, decision makers can be found in every type of organization: businesses, not-for-profit organizations, and public agencies. Regardless of where these decision makers are found or whether their resources are abundant or limited, they all rely on information to make more efficient and effective use of their budgets. Thus, in this book, we will take the broadest perspective of managing and its resulting application to business research.

At no other time in our history has so much attention been placed on measuring and enhancing **return on investment (ROI).** At its most simplistic, when we measure ROI, we calculate the financial

Can you use social media research to discover a new pet food? Del Monte, the maker of Snausages, certainly thinks so. Using social media as a platform for launching discussions, Del Monte invited more than 300 dog lovers to its site and asked them a series of questions, including "What does your dog eat for breakfast?" "Would you buy more treats for your dog if they contained vitamins and minerals?" A large number of the participants indicated their dogs preferred eggs and bacon for breakfast. These dog owners also tried to use foods that were rich in omega3, antioxidants, and vitamins. Using this research, Del Monte created Snausages Breakfast Bites, shaped like fried eggs and bacon strips, and fortified to be nutritious with extra calcium, antioxidants, and Omega 3 and 6. It took just six weeks to bring this new snack food to market. Today you can find Snausages Breakfast Bites in every pet store in the country. **www.snausages.com**

return for all expenditures. Increasingly, organizational managers want to know what strategies and tactics capture the highest return. In the last dozen years, as technology has improved our measurement and tracking capabilities, managers have realized they need a better understanding of employees, stockholders, constituents, and customer behavior in order to influence the desired metrics. Business research plays an important role in this new measurement environment. Not only does it help managers choose better strategies and tactics, but business research expenditures are increasingly scrutinized for their contribution to ROI.

The research methods course recognizes that students preparing to manage any function—regardless of the setting—need training in a disciplined process for conducting an inquiry of a **management dilemma,** the problem or opportunity that requires a management decision. Several factors should stimulate your interest in studying research methods:[1]

1. *Information overload.* Although the Internet and its search engines present extensive amounts of information, the information's quality and credibility must be continuously evaluated. The ubiquitous access to information has brought about the development of knowledge communities and the need for organizations to leverage this knowledge universe for innovation—or risk merely drowning in data.

2. *Technological connectivity.* Individuals, public-sector organizations, and businesses are adapting to changes in work patterns (real-time and global), changes in the formation of relationships and communities, and the realization that geography is no longer a primary constraint.

3. *Shifting global centers of economic activity and competition.* The rising economic power of Asia and demographic shifts within regions highlight the need for organizations to expand their knowledge of consumers, suppliers, talent pools, business models, and infrastructures with which they are less familiar. This shift increases the value of research designs that can accommodate different norms, values, technologies, and languages.

4. *Increasingly critical scrutiny of big business.* The availability of information has made it possible for all a firm's stakeholders to demand inclusion in company decision making, while at the same time elevating the level of societal suspicion. Interconnected global systems of suppliers, producers, and customers have made the emergence and viability of megabusinesses not only possible, but likely.

5. *More government intervention.* As public-sector activities increase, in order to provide some minimal or enhanced level of social services, governments are becoming increasingly aggressive in protecting their various constituencies by posing restrictions on the use of managerial and business research tools (e.g., Do-Not-Call List, Spyware Act).

6. *Battle for analytical talent.* Managers face progressively complex decisions, applying mathematical models to extract meaningful knowledge from volumes of data and using highly sophisticated software to run their organizations. The shift to knowledge-intensive industries puts greater demand on a scarcity of well-trained talent with advanced analytical skills. The integration of global labor markets, with its infusion of new talent sources, is only a partial answer.

7. *Greater computing power and speed.*
   - *Lower-cost data collection.* Computers and telecommunications lowered the costs of data collection, drastically changing knowledge about consumers both at store and household levels; employees at the position, team, and department levels; suppliers and distributors at the transaction, division, and company levels; and equipment at the part, process, and production-run levels.
   - *Better visualization tools.* High-speed downloads of images allow us to help people visualize complex concepts; this enriches measurement capabilities.
   - *Powerful computations.* Sophisticated techniques of quantitative analysis are emerging to take advantage of increasingly powerful computing capabilities.
   - *More integration of data.* Computer advances permit business to create and manage large electronic storehouses of data that cross functional boundaries.
   - *Real-time access to knowledge.* Today's computers and software offer the power to collect and analyze data and customize reporting in real time for much quicker decision making.

8. *New perspectives on established research methodologies.* Older tools and methodologies once limited to exploratory research are gaining wider acceptance in dealing with a broader range of managerial problems.

To do well in such an environment, you will need to understand how to identify quality information and to recognize the solid, reliable research on which your high-risk managerial decisions can be based.

34

The percent of employees who never consider what their bosses, clients, or colleagues think before posting to a blog, discussion forum, or social network.

You will need to know how to conduct such research. Developing these skills requires understanding the scientific method as it applies to the decision-making environment. Many students will also need to hire research suppliers or write an effective RFP (request for proposal). To facilitate that goal, Appendix 1a, at the conclusion of this chapter, describes how the research industry works. Appendix A, at the end of the book, describes how to effectively plan and document research requests and proposals. Along with other reference material provided throughout the book, we address your needs as information collector, processor, evaluator, and user.

> Information and Competitive Advantage

Managers have access to information other than that generated by business research. Understanding the relationship between business research and these other information sources—decision support systems and business intelligence—is critical for understanding how information drives decisions relating to organizational mission, goals, strategies, and tactics.

Goals

A local bakery would have different goals than Nabisco, but each likely has goals related to sales (membership), market share, return on investment, profitability, customer acquisition, customer satisfaction, customer retention, employee productivity, production efficiency, maximization of stock price (or owner's equity), and so on—whether codified in a written plan or detailed only in an entrepreneur's brain. To assist in making increasingly complex decisions on goals, strategies, and tactics, managers turn first to information drawn from the decision support system, combined with that generated by business intelligence on competitive and environmental activity.

Decision Support

The need to complete one or many exchanges with its prospective customers, members, or constituents drives every organization. No matter how we define an *exchange*—a purchase, a vote, attendance at a function, a donation to a cause—each exchange, along with the strategic and tactical activities designed to complete it, generates numerous elements of data. If organized for retrieval, collectively these data elements constitute a **decision support system (DSS).** During the last two and one-half decades, advances in computer technology made it possible to share this collected transactional data among an organization's decision makers over an intranet or an extranet.

Today, sophisticated managers have developed DSSs, where data can be accessed in real time (as transactions are completed). Catalog managers (e.g., casual clothing retailer Lands' End) know exactly what tactics generate a transaction from a particular individual within their prospect and customer databases, as well as just how profitable each customer is to the company and an estimate of that customer's lifetime value to the company. Such managers have a distinct advantage in strategic and tactical planning over those without real-time access to transactional data.

Business Intelligence

Because no decision exists in a vacuum, the decision maker must have a broad knowledge of the firm's environment. A **business intelligence system (BIS)** is designed to provide the manager with ongoing information about events and trends in the technological, economic, political and legal, demographic, cultural, social, and, most critically, competitive arenas. Such information is compiled from a variety of sources, as is noted in Exhibit 1-1.

Often, data from a DSS or BIS stimulate the question Should we do business research? In the MindWriter example, this might be data collected about laptop problems needing repair; or, for our restaurant whose friendliness quotient is changing, it might be customer comments collected by the wait staff.

Strategy

Strategy is defined as the general approach an organization will follow to achieve its goals. In an earlier example, a restaurant was receiving comments that the friendly atmosphere was changing. This perception may have been the result of a change in strategy. Perhaps the restaurant decided to switch from an atmosphere where patrons were encouraged to linger over their meal (occupying a table for a long period of time while adding incremental revenues with each additional course) to a new strategy of turning each table in a shorter time frame by changing food preparation and the menu.

>Exhibit 1-1 Some Sources of Business Intelligence

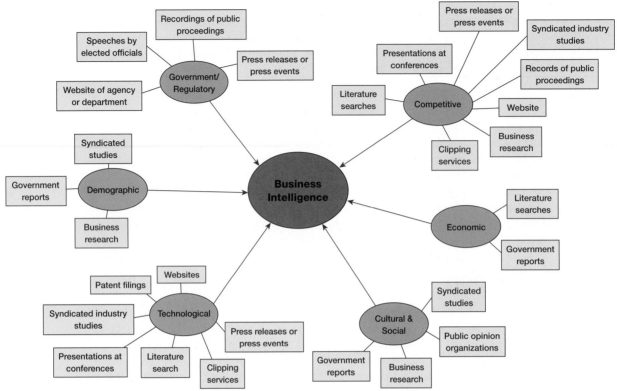

A firm usually implements more than one strategy at a time. With regard to training, one organization might train its data warehouse employees with mostly classroom activities, while another will use on-the-job training. Another strategy might describe how an organization handles maintenance on its equipment—rigorous periodic maintenance versus maintenance only when equipment breaks down. Microsoft recently completed a major corporate restructuring. It decided to tie its 600 managers' compensation, not to sales and profits, but to levels of customer satisfaction as measured by periodic customer satisfaction surveys.[2]

The discovery of opportunities and problems that influence strategic decisions is often the task of the BIS in combination with business research.

Tactics

Business research also contributes significantly to the design **tactics**—those specific, timed activities that execute a strategy. Business research also can be used to help a manager decide which of several tactics is likely to successfully execute the desired strategy. In our earlier example, our restaurant manager might have changed the menu (marketing tactic) to feature entrées that could be prepared faster (operations tactic) and delivered to a table more quickly. The manager might also have instituted a new training program (HR tactic) to implement a new zoned, table-coverage structure (operations tactic), along with a new sales-incentive program (HR tactic) that discouraged the wait staff from making small talk with patrons and rewarded teamwork and efficiency.

All of the above examples demonstrate the purposes of business research:

- To identify and define opportunities and problems.
- To define, monitor, and refine strategies.
- To define, monitor, and refine tactics.
- To improve our understanding of the various fields of management.[3]

> Hierarchy of Information-Based Decision Makers

Although not all organizations use business research to help make planning decisions, increasingly the successful ones do. Exhibit 1-2 shows an emerging hierarchy of organizations in terms of their use of business research.

In the top tier, organizations see research as the fundamental first step in any venture. They go beyond the tried-and-true methodologies and use creative combinations of research techniques to gain deep insights to aid in their sophisticated decision making. Some even develop their own proprietary methodologies. These firms may partner with a small group of outside research suppliers that have the expertise to use innovative combinations of research methods to address management dilemmas. These visionary managers can be found in research firms, service firms, nonprofit organizations, and product and service manufacturers and distributors. Minute Maid, the manufacturer that brings us fresh and frozen juice-based products, fosters decision making at this level. Its vice president of Consumer and Marketing Knowledge is a member of the firm's highest strategic planning team (see Exhibit 1-3).[4] Implementation and activation of the research are the critical stages of decision makers in this tier. Design Forum, an architectural and graphic design firm specializing in retail design and positioning for such firms as Lexus, Dunkin' Donuts, and McDonald's, is another firm operating at this level; every recommendation to each client is based on data drawn from the use of extensive research.

In the second tier of the hierarchy are those decision makers that rely periodically on research information. They usually turn to business research primarily when they perceive the risk of a particular strategy or tactic to be too great to proceed without it. They rely heavily on those methodologies that proved themselves in the last several decades of the 20th century—surveys and focus groups—often choosing the methodology before fully assessing its appropriateness to the dilemma at hand. This tier is occupied by many large, medium, and small organizations of all types. Some of the firms newly arrived to this tier are in transition from the base tier. They have realized that failing to collect information prior to decision making or failing to extract insight from information that has been collected in their DSS puts them at a distinct competitive disadvantage.

Finally, the base tier comprises those managers who primarily use instinct and intuition rather than research knowledge to facilitate their decisions. These firms may or may not have sophisticated DSSs

>**Exhibit 1-2** Hierarchy of Information-Based Decision Makers

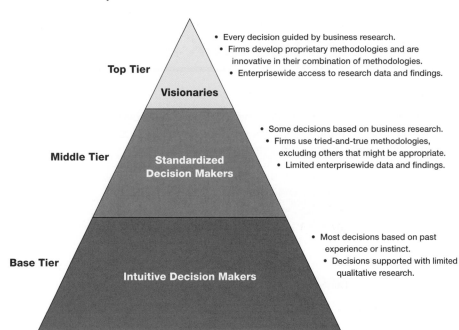

Mary Kay: Enticing Managers to Use Research-Based Decision Making

Cosmetics firm Mary Kay, like many companies facing rapidly changing technology, is in transition—from relying on instinct, anecdotal evidence, and qualitative data to relying on quality quantitative information. When Teri Burgess moved from a product marketing position at Mary Kay to director of marketing analysis, her task was to create a database from mounds of consumer data. Now that the database is as user-friendly as demanded, she faces a new task, and one surprisingly familiar to business researchers worldwide: enticing decision makers to rely on the insights available to them. "Part of the reluctance is cultural," shared Burgess. Without this information, seasoned managers have made the hard decisions: to discontinue once-popular products, to introduce new fashion colors, to position stable products for alternative benefits. "And part of it may be lack of motivation. Until upper management demands that managers support their ideas and proposals with information from research and the decision support system, no amount of training—in how the system works and can be helpful—will make it happen."

www.marykay.com

or BISs. They believe themselves to be so close to customers and distribution partners, as well as to employees and other stakeholders, that they rarely need business research. When they do collect information, they use a limited amount of qualitative research, often in the form of an informal group discussion or small number of individual interviews, to confirm their ideas. Especially in the business-to-business arena, they often rely on feedback filtered by members of the sales force. Following guidelines for adequate sampling or other procedures of scientific inquiry is not fundamental to this group. Larger firms that occupy this tier are influenced as much by organizational culture as by resources. Many small companies find themselves in this tier not because of an unwillingness to use business research but based on a perception that any more formalized research is too expensive to employ and that their resources won't accommodate this mode of decision making.

The trends of the past two decades, especially the technology that has been driving research methodologies of data collection and dissemination, make it likely that managers who do not prepare to advance up the hierarchy will be at a severe competitive disadvantage.

>Exhibit 1-3 Minute Maid and the Role of Research

Minute Maid's Consumer and Marketplace Knowledge team demonstrates that effective research doesn't end once the collected data are reported. Organizations in the top tier of research-based decision making see activation of strategies and tactics based on research-supported insights as the highest priority. **www.minutemaid.com**

Minute Maid CMK Mission

Our Mission Is To . . .

- Leverage consumer, customer and marketplace knowledge to identify, develop, and influence business strategies and tactics that will generate growth in operating income year after year

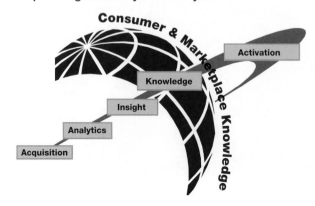

> The Research Process: A Preview

Writers usually treat the research study as a sequential process involving several clearly defined steps. Exhibit 1-4 models the sequence of the **research process.** No one claims that research requires completion of each step before going to the next. Recycling, circumventing, and skipping occur. Some steps are begun out of sequence, some are carried out simultaneously, and some may be omitted. Despite these variations, the idea of a sequence is useful for developing a project and for keeping the project orderly as it unfolds.

>**Exhibit 1-4** The Research Process

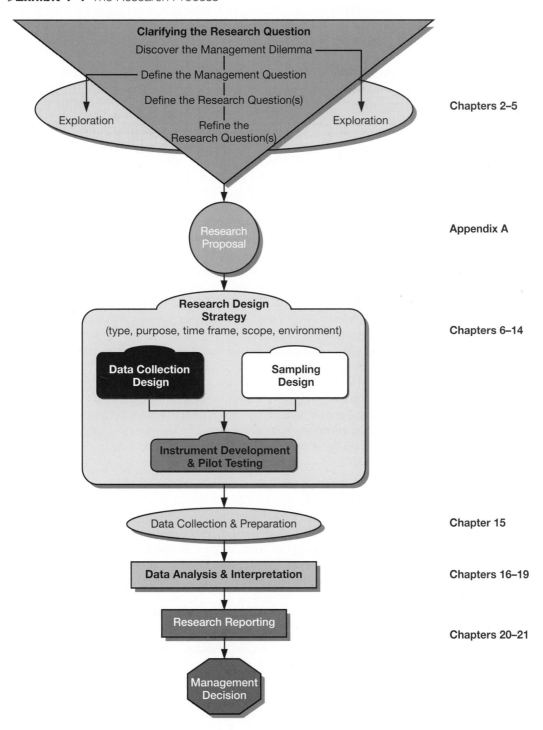

The research process begins much as the opening vignette suggests. You will notice that the top of the model is devoted to understanding the manager's problem—the management dilemma. A management dilemma triggers the need for a decision. For MindWriter, a growing number of complaints about post-purchase service started the process. In other situations, a controversy arises, a major commitment of resources is called for, or conditions in the environment signal the need for a decision. For MindWriter, the critical event could have been the introduction by a competitor of new technology that would revolutionize the battery life of laptops. Such events cause managers to reconsider their purposes or objectives, define a problem for solution, or develop strategies and tactics for solutions they have identified.

In every chapter, we will refer to this model as we discuss each step in the process. Our discussion of the questions that guide project planning and data gathering is also incorporated into the various elements of the model. In the chapters that follow, we discuss scientific research procedures and ethical conduct by showing their application to the pragmatic problems of managers. At a minimum, our objective is to make you a more intelligent consumer of research products prepared by others (see Appendix 1a) as well as to enable you to perform quality research for your own decisions and those to whom you report.

Exhibit 1-4 is an important organizing tool because it provides a framework for introducing how each process module is designed, connected to other modules, and then executed. Thus, it organizes the book.

Is Research Always Problem-Solving Based?

Researchers often are asked to respond to "problems" that managers needed to solve. **Applied research** has a practical problem-solving emphasis. Whether the problem is negative, like rectifying an inventory system that is resulting in lost sales, or an opportunity to increase stockholder wealth through acquiring another firm, problem solving is prevalent.

The problem-solving nature of applied research means it is conducted to reveal answers to specific questions related to action, performance, or policy needs. **Pure research** or **basic research** is also problem-solving based, but in a different sense. It aims to solve perplexing questions or obtain new knowledge of an experimental or theoretical nature that has little direct or immediate impact on action, performance, or policy decisions. Basic research in the business arena might involve a researcher who is studying the results of the use of coupons versus rebates as demand stimulation tactics, but not in a specific instance or in relation to a specific client's product. In another pure research scenario, researchers might study the influence on productivity of compensation systems that pay by piece-work versus salary-plus-bonus structures. Thus, both applied and pure research are problem-solving based, but applied research is directed much more to making immediate managerial decisions.

In answer to the question posed at the beginning of this section, Is research always problem-solving based? the answer is yes. Whether the typology is applied or pure, simple or complex, all research should provide an answer to some question. If managers always knew what was causing problems or offering opportunities in their realm of responsibility, there would be little need for applied research or basic research; intuition would be all that was necessary to make quality decisions.

> What Is Good Research?

Good research generates dependable data that are derived by professionally conducted practices and that can be used reliably for decision making. In contrast, poor research is carelessly planned and conducted, resulting in data that a manager can't use to reduce his or her decision-making risks. Good research follows the standards of the **scientific method:** systematic, empirically based procedures for generating replicable research.

We list several defining characteristics of the scientific method in Exhibit 1-5 and discuss below the managerial dimensions of each.

1. *Purpose clearly defined.* The purpose of the business research—the problem involved or the decision to be made—should be clearly defined and sharply delineated in terms as unambiguous as possible. Getting this in writing is valuable even in instances in which the same person serves as researcher and decision maker. The statement of the decision problem should include

>**Exhibit 1-5** What Actions Guarantee Good Business Research?

Characteristics of Research	What a Manager Should Look For in Research Done by Others or Include in Self-Directed Research	Chapter
Purpose clearly defined	• Researcher distinguishes between symptom of organization's problem, the manager's perception of the problem, and the research problem.	4, 5
Research process detailed	• Researcher provides complete research proposal.	4, Appendix A
Research design thoroughly planned	• Exploratory procedures are outlined with constructs defined. • Sample unit is clearly described along with sampling methodology. • Data collection procedures are selected and designed.	3, 4, 5, 6–14
High ethical standards applied	• Safeguards are in place to protect study participants, organizations, clients, and researchers. • Recommendations do not exceed the scope of the study. • The study's methodology and limitations sections reflect researcher's restraint and concern for accuracy.	2, 20, 21
Limitations frankly revealed	• Desired procedure is compared with actual procedure in report. • Desired sample is compared with actual sample in the report. • Impact on findings and conclusions is detailed.	6, 14, 15, 20, 21
Adequate analysis for decision maker's needs	• Sufficiently detailed findings are tied to collection instruments.	15–21
Findings presented unambiguously	• Findings are clearly presented in words, tables, and graphs. • Findings are logically organized to facilitate reaching a decision about the manager's problem. • Executive summary of conclusions is outlined. • Detailed table of contents is tied to the conclusions and findings presentation.	15–21
Conclusions justified	• Decision-based conclusions are matched with detailed findings.	15–21
Researcher's experience reflected	• Researcher provides experience/credentials with report.	20, 21

its scope, its limitations, and the precise meanings of all words and terms significant to the research. Failure of the researcher to do this adequately may raise legitimate doubts in the minds of research report readers as to whether the researcher has sufficient understanding of the problem to make a sound proposal attacking it.

2. *Research process detailed.* The research procedures used should be described in sufficient detail to permit another researcher to repeat the research. This includes the steps to acquire participants, informed consent, sampling methods and representativeness, and data gathering procedures. Except when secrecy is imposed, research reports should reveal with candor the sources of data and the means by which they were obtained. Omission of significant procedural details makes it difficult or impossible to estimate the validity and reliability of the data and justifiably weakens the confidence of the reader in the research itself as well as any recommendations based on the research.

3. *Research design thoroughly planned.* The procedural design of the research, and its choice among competing designs, should be clearly described and carefully planned to yield results that are as objective as possible. A survey of opinions or recollections ought not to be used when more reliable evidence is available from documentary sources or by direct observation. Bibliographic searches should be as thorough and complete as possible. Experiments should

have satisfactory controls, reducing threats to internal validity and enhancing the probability of external validity (generalizability). Direct observations should be recorded as soon as possible after the event. Efforts should be made to minimize the influence of personal bias in selecting and recording data.

4. *High ethical standards applied.* Researchers often work independently and have significant latitude in designing and executing projects. A research design that includes safeguards against causing mental or physical harm to participants and makes data integrity a first priority should be highly valued. Ethical issues in research reflect important moral concerns about the practice of responsible behavior in society.

    Researchers frequently find themselves precariously balancing the rights of their subjects against the scientific dictates of their chosen method. When this occurs, they have a responsibility to guard the welfare of the participants in the studies and also the organizations to which they belong, their clients, their colleagues, and themselves. Careful consideration must be given to those research situations in which there is a possibility for physical or psychological harm, exploitation, invasion of privacy, and/or loss of dignity. The research need must be weighed against the potential for these adverse effects. Typically, you can redesign a study, but sometimes you cannot. The researcher should be prepared for this dilemma.

5. *Limitations frankly revealed.* The researcher should report, with complete frankness, flaws in procedural design and estimate their effect on the findings. There are very few perfect research designs. Some of the imperfections may have little effect on the validity and reliability of the data; others may invalidate them entirely. A competent researcher should be sensitive to the effects of imperfect design. The researcher's experience in analyzing data should provide a basis for estimating the influence of design flaws. As a decision maker, you should question the value of research about which no limitations are reported.

6. *Adequate analysis for decision maker's needs.* Analysis of the data should be extensive enough to reveal its significance, what managers call insights. The methods of analysis used should be appropriate. The extent to which this criterion is met is frequently a good measure of the competence of the researcher. Adequate analysis of the data is the most difficult phase of research for the novice. The validity and reliability of data should be checked carefully. The data should be classified in ways that assist the researcher in reaching pertinent conclusions and clearly reveal the findings that have led to those conclusions. When statistical methods are used, appropriate descriptive and inferential techniques should be chosen, the probability of error should be estimated, and the criteria of statistical significance applied.

7. *Findings presented unambiguously.* Some evidence of the competence and integrity of the researcher may be found in the report itself. For example, language that is restrained, clear, and precise; assertions that are carefully drawn and hedged with appropriate reservations; and an apparent effort to achieve maximum objectivity tend to leave a favorable impression of the researcher with the decision maker. Generalizations that outrun the statistical findings or other evidence on which they are based, exaggerations, and unnecessary verbiage tend to leave an unfavorable impression. Such reports are not valuable to managers wading through the minefields of organizational decision making. Presentation of data should be comprehensive, reasonably interpreted, easily understood by the decision maker, and organized so that the decision maker can readily locate critical findings.

8. *Conclusions justified.* Conclusions should be limited to those for which the data provide an adequate basis. Researchers are often tempted to broaden the basis of induction by including personal experiences and their interpretations—data not subject to the controls under which the research was conducted. Equally undesirable is the all-too-frequent practice of drawing conclusions from a study of a limited population and applying them universally. Researchers also may be tempted to rely too heavily on data collected in a prior study and use it in the interpretation of a new study. Such practice sometimes occurs among research specialists who confine their work to clients in a small industry. These actions tend to decrease the objectivity of the research and weaken readers' confidence in the findings. Good researchers always specify the conditions under which their conclusions seem to be valid.

9. *Researcher's experience reflected.* Greater confidence in the research is warranted if the researcher is experienced, has a good reputation in research, and is a person of integrity. Were it possible for the reader of a research report to obtain sufficient information about the researcher, this criterion perhaps would be one of the best bases for judging the degree of confidence a piece of research warrants and the value of any decision based upon it. For this reason the research report should contain information about the qualifications of the researcher.

Good business research has an inherent value only to the extent that it helps management make better decisions to achieve organizational goals. Interesting information about consumers, employees, competitors, or the environment might be pleasant to have, but its value is limited if the information cannot be applied to a critical decision. If a study does not help management select more effective, more efficient, less risky, or more profitable alternatives than otherwise would be the case, its use should be questioned. Alternatively, management may have insufficient resources (time, money, or skill) to conduct an appropriate study or may face a low level of risk associated with the decision at hand. In these situations, it is valid to avoid business research and its associated costs in time and money. Business research finds its justification in the contribution it makes to the decision maker's task and to the bottom line.

> A Glimpse at Four Research Studies

From each of the following illustrations of management dilemmas, we can abstract the essence of research. How is it carried out? What can it do? What should it not be expected to do? As you read the four cases, be thinking about the possible range of situations for conducting research, and try answering these questions: (1) What is the decision-making dilemma facing the manager? (2) What must the researcher accomplish?

ClassicToys

You work for ClassicToys, a corporation that is considering the acquisition of a toy manufacturer. The senior vice president for development asks you to head a task force to investigate six companies that are potential candidates. You assemble a team composed of representatives from the relevant functional areas. Pertinent data are collected from public sources because of the sensitive nature of the project. You examine all of the following: company annual reports; articles in business journals, trade magazines, and newspapers; financial analysts' assessments; and company advertisements. The team members then develop summary profiles of candidate firms based on the characteristics gleaned from the sources. The final report highlights the opportunities and problems that acquisition of the target firm would bring to all areas of the business.

MedImage

You are the business manager for MedImage, a large group of physicians specializing in diagnostic imaging (MRI, nuclear, tomography, and ultrasound). A prominent health insurance organization has contacted you to promote a new cost-containment program. The doctors' committee to which you will make a recommendation will have a narrow enrollment window for their decision. If they choose to join, they will agree to a reduced fee schedule in exchange for easier filing procedures, quicker reimbursement, and listing on a physicians' referral network. If they decline, they will continue to deal with their patients and the insurance carrier in the current manner. You begin your investigation by mining data from patient files to learn how many are using this carrier, frequency of care visits, complexity of filings, and so on. You then consult insurance industry data to discover how many potential patients in your area use this care plan, or similar care plans with alternative insurance carriers, and the likelihood of a patient choosing or switching doctors to find one that subscribes to the proposed program. You attempt to confirm your data with information from professional and association journals. Based on this information, you develop a profile that details the number of patients, overhead, and potential revenue realized by choosing to join the plan.

MoreCoatings

MoreCoatings, a paint manufacturer, is having trouble maintaining profits. The owner believes inventory management is a weak area of the company's operations. In this industry, many paint colors, types of paint, and container sizes make it easy for a firm to accumulate large inventories and still be unable to fill customer orders. You look into the present warehousing and shipping operations and find excessive sales losses and delivery delays because of out-of-stock conditions. An informal poll of customers confirms your impression. You suspect the present inventory database and reporting system do not provide prompt, usable information needed for appropriate production decisions.

Based on this supposition, you familiarize yourself with the latest inventory management techniques. You ask the warehouse manager to take an inventory, and you review the incoming orders for the last year. In addition, the owner shows you the production runs of the last year and his method for assessing the need for a particular color or paint type. By modeling the last year of business using production, order, and inventory management techniques, you choose the method that provides the best theoretical profit. You run a pilot line using the new control methodology. After two months, the data show a much lower inventory and a higher order fulfillment rate. You recommend that the owner adopt the new inventory method.

York College

You work for York College's alumni association. It is eager to develop closer ties with its aging alumni to provide strong stimuli to encourage increased donations and to induce older, nontraditional students to return to supplement enrollment. The president's office is considering starting a retirement community geared toward university alumni and asks your association to assess the attractiveness of the proposal from an alumni viewpoint. Your director asks you to divide the study into four parts.

Phase 1

First you are to report on the number of alumni who are in the appropriate age bracket, the rate of new entries per year, and the actuarial statistics for the group. This information allows the director to assess whether the project is worth continuing.

Phase 2

Your early results reveal a sufficient number of alumni to make the project feasible. The next step in the study is to describe the social and economic characteristics of the target alumni group. You review gift statistics, analyze job titles, and assess home location and values. In addition, you review files from the last five years to see how alumni responded when they were asked about their income bracket. You are able to describe the alumni group for your director when you finish.

Phase 3

It is evident that the target alumni can easily afford a retirement community as proposed. The third phase of the study is to explain the characteristics of alumni who would be interested in a university-related retirement community. For this phase, you engage the American Association of Retired Persons (AARP) and a retirement community developer. In addition, you search for information on senior citizens from the federal government. From the developer you learn what characteristics of retirement community planning and construction are most attractive to retirees. From the AARP you learn about the main services and features that potential retirees look for in a retirement community. From government publications you become familiar with existing regulations and recommendations for operating retirement communities and uncover a full range of descriptive information on the typical retirement community dweller. You make an extensive report to both the alumni director and the university president. The report covers the number of eligible alumni, their social and economic standings, and the characteristics of those who would be attracted by the retirement community.

Phase 4

The report excites the college president. She asks for one additional phase to be completed. She needs to predict the number of alumni who would be attracted to the project so that she can adequately plan the size of the community. At this point, you call on the business school's research methods class for help in designing a questionnaire for the alumni. By providing telephones and funding, you arrange for the class to conduct a survey among a random sample of the eligible alumni population. In addition, you have the class devise a second questionnaire for alumni who will become eligible in the next 10 years. Using the data collected, you can predict the initial demand for the community and estimate the growth in demand over the next 10 years. You submit your final report to the director and the president.

What Dilemma Does the Manager Face?

The manager's predicament is fairly well defined in the four cases. Let's see how carefully you read and understood them. In the ClassicToys study, the manager, the senior vice president for development, must make a proposal to the president or possibly the board of directors about whether to acquire a toy manufacturer and, if one is to be acquired, which one of the six under consideration is the best candidate. In MedImage, the physicians in the group must decide whether to join the proposed managed health care plan of one of their primary insurers. In the MoreCoatings study, the owner of the paint manufacturer must decide whether to implement a new inventory management system. At York College, the president must propose to the board of directors whether to fund the development of a retirement community. How did you do? If you didn't come to these same conclusions, reread the cases before proceeding to catch what you missed.

In real life, management dilemmas are not always so clearly defined. In the MoreCoatings study, rather than pinpointing the problem as one of inventory management, the paint manufacturer's owner could have faced several issues: (1) a strike by the teamsters impacting inventory delivery to retail and wholesale customers; (2) the development of a new paint formula offering superior coverage but requiring a relatively scarce ingredient to manufacture, thereby affecting production rates; (3) a fire that destroyed the primary loading dock of the main shipping warehouse in the Midwest; (4) the simultaneous occurrence of all three events. As the research process begins with a manager's decision-making task, accurately defining the dilemma is paramount but often difficult. We outline the research process that begins this activity at the end of this chapter and address it in detail in Chapter 4.

The Types of Research Studies Represented by the Four Examples

All four studies qualify as applied research and can be classified as reporting, descriptive, explanatory, or predictive.

Reporting

At the most elementary level, a **reporting study** provides a summation of data, often recasting data to achieve a deeper understanding or to generate statistics for comparison. The task may be quite simple and the data readily available. At other times, the information may be difficult to find. A reporting study calls for knowledge and skill with information sources and gatekeepers of information sources. Such a study usually requires little inference or conclusion drawing. In the ClassicToys study, the researcher needs to know what information should be evaluated in order to value a company. In the study of management, this knowledge would be acquired primarily in courses in financial management, accounting, and marketing. Knowing the type of information needed, the researcher in the ClassicToys study identifies sources of information, such as trade press articles and annual reports. Because of the possible effect of the toy manufacturer evaluation on the stock prices of the conglomerate instigating the study and each toy company, only public sources are used. Other reporting studies of a less sensitive nature might have the researcher interviewing source gatekeepers. In the York College study, for example, interviewing the director of local retirement facilities might have revealed other sources to include in the search. Such an expert is considered a gatekeeper. Early in your career, identifying gatekeepers for your firm and industry is critical to success as a manager.

Purists might argue that reporting studies do not qualify as research, although such carefully gathered data can have great value. A research design does not have to be complex and require inferences for a project to be called research. In the early part of your career, you will likely be asked to perform a number of reporting studies. Many managers consider the execution of such studies an excellent way for new employees to become familiar with their employer and its industry.

Descriptive

A **descriptive study** tries to discover answers to the questions *who, what, when, where,* and, sometimes, *how.* The researcher attempts to describe or define a subject, often by creating a profile of a group of problems, people, or events. Such studies may involve the collection of data and the creation of a distribution of the number of times the researcher observes a single event or characteristic (known as a **research variable**), or they may involve relating the interaction of two or more variables. In Med-Image, the researcher must present data that reveal who is affiliated with the insurer, who uses managed health care programs (both doctors and patients), the general trends in the use of imaging technology in diagnosing illness or injury severity, and the relationship of patient characteristics, doctor referrals, and technology-use patterns.

Descriptive studies may or may not have the potential for drawing powerful inferences. Organizations that maintain databases of their employees, customers, and suppliers already have significant data to conduct descriptive studies using internal information. Yet many firms that have such data files do not mine them regularly for the decision-making insight they might provide. In the opening vignette, Myra Wines could mine numerous company databases for insight into the nature and number of service-related problems arising after purchase and, similarly, for information about product use inquiries. A database generated by warranty registration cards could reveal significant data concerning purchaser characteristics, as well as purchase location and product use behavior. A descriptive study, however, does not explain *why* an event has occurred or why the variables interact the way they do.

The descriptive study is popular in research because of its versatility across management disciplines. In not-for-profit corporations and other organizations, descriptive investigations have a broad appeal to the administrator and policy analyst for planning, monitoring, and evaluating. In this context, *how* questions address issues such as quantity, cost, efficiency, effectiveness, and adequacy.[5]

Explanatory

Academics debate the relationship between the next two types of studies, explanatory and predictive, in terms of which precedes the other. Both types of research are grounded in theory, and theory is created to answer why and how questions. For our purposes, an **explanatory study** goes beyond description and attempts to explain the reasons for the phenomenon that the descriptive study only observed. Research that studies the relationship between two or more variables is also referred to as a *correlational study*. The researcher uses theories or at least hypotheses to account for the forces that caused a certain phenomenon to occur. In MoreCoatings, believing the problem with paint stockouts is the result of inventory management, the owner asks the researcher to detail warehousing and shipping processes. It would be a descriptive study if it had stopped here. But if problems in the processes could be linked with sales losses due to an inability to make timely deliveries to retail or wholesale customers, then an explanatory study would emerge. The researcher tests this hypothesis by modeling the last year of business using the relationships between processes and results.

Predictive

If we can provide a plausible explanation for an event after it has occurred, it is desirable to be able to predict when and in what situations the event will occur. A **predictive study,** the fourth type, is just as rooted in theory as explanation. NATA, a national trade association for the aviation industry, may be interested in explaining the radiation risks from the sun and stars for flight crews and passengers. The variables might include altitude, proximity of air routes to the poles, time of year, and aircraft shielding. Perhaps the relations among the four variables explain the radiation risk variable. This type of study often calls for a high order of inference making. Why, for example, would a flight at a specified altitude at one time of year not produce so great a radiation risk to the airliner's occupants as the same flight in another season? The answer to such a question would be valuable in planning air routes. It also would contribute to the development of a better theory of the phenomenon. In business research, prediction is found in studies conducted to evaluate specific courses of action or to forecast current and future values.

The researcher is asked to predict the success of the proposed retirement facility for alumni for York College based on the number of applicants for residency the project will attract. This prediction will be based on the explanatory hypothesis that alumni frequent programs and projects sponsored by the institution because of an association they maintain between their college experience and images of youthfulness and mental and physical stimulation.

Yahoo!: Banner Ads Move CPG

Product managers of consumer packaged goods (CPG) are facing increasing pressure for strong return-on-investment metrics for media buys, yet they still heavily rely on advertising recall or click stream analysis. "The thinking is that no one goes online to search out information on paper towels. But that doesn't mean that Internet ads can't significantly lift in-store sales," explained Ken Mallon, Yahoo's director of insights products. What was needed were new metrics that could showcase Internet ads' targeting efficiency and sales responsiveness. Yahoo teamed its extensive database of Internet visitors with the ACNielsen Homescan panel (126,000 global households that provide extensive demographic and lifestyle data and allow their purchases to be tracked). What resulted is *Yahoo! Consumer Direct powered by ACNielsen.* More than 40 percent of active Internet users use broadband or high-speed Internet access. This enables such households to be tested for exposure to standard media banner ads and also to the more interactive rich-media ads that are increasing on the Internet. For each advertiser, *Consumer Direct* tracks two metrics on each test group: effectiveness of ad targeting (Are the visitors being exposed to the ads most likely to purchase?) and persuasiveness of the advertising (What percentage of households exposed to the advertising actually purchase the advertised product?). Yahoo then compares this information to that on a group not exposed to the banner ads. Yahoo, with the assistance of Dynamic Logic, also provides advertisers with five more metrics critical for CPG success: ad awareness, brand awareness, brand favorability, message association with advertiser, and purchase intent.

"Using the browsing patterns of high-purchase households in the *Consumer Direct* research to model behavior, we then apply this knowledge to the Yahoo! database to identify 10 million households that exhibit similar browsing behavior," explained Mallon. These Yahoo visitors see ads to which they are most likely to respond. Every *Consumer Direct* CPG client has experienced sales lift.

www.yahoo.com; www.acnielsen.com; www.dynamiclogic.com

Finally, we would like to be able to control a phenomenon once we can explain and predict it. Being able to replicate a scenario and dictate a particular outcome is the objective of **control.** In the York College study, if we assume that the college proceeds with its retirement community and enjoys the predicted success, the president will find it attractive to be able to build a similar facility to serve another group of alumni and duplicate that success.

Control is a logical outcome of prediction. The complexity of the phenomenon and the adequacy of the prediction theory, however, largely decide success in a control study. At York College, if a control study were done of the various promotional approaches used with alumni to stimulate images of youthfulness, the promotional tactics that drew the largest number of alumni applications for residency could be identified. Once known, this knowledge could be used successfully with different groups of alumni only if the researcher could account for and control all other variables influencing applications.

Any of the four types of studies—reporting, descriptive, explanatory, or predictive—can properly be called research. We also can conclude from the various examples that research is a systematic inquiry aimed at providing information to solve managerial problems.

>summary

1 Research is any organized inquiry carried out to provide information for solving problems. This includes reporting, descriptive, explanatory, and predictive studies. We emphasize the last three in this book. Business research is a systematic inquiry that provides information to guide decisions. More specifically, it is a process of determining, acquiring, analyzing and synthesizing, and disseminating relevant data, information, and insights to decision makers in ways that mobilize the organization to take appropriate actions that, in turn, maximize performance. If organized for retrieval, data

collected from the day-to-day operations of the organization constitute a decision support system (DSS). A business intelligence system (BIS) is designed to provide the manager with ongoing information about events and trends in the technological, economic, political and legal, demographic, cultural, social, and, most critically, competitive arenas. Research studies are used to supplement DSS and BIS.

2 The managers of tomorrow will need to know more than any managers in history. Business research will be a major contributor to that knowledge. Managers will find knowledge of research methods to be of value in many strategic and tactical situations. They may need to conduct research either for themselves or for others. As buyers of research services, managers will need to be able to judge research quality. Finally, they may become research specialists themselves.

   Not all managers have established research as a priority in their process of decision making. Consequently, a hierarchy of research-based decision makers is emerging. The top tier contains those managers who use research as a fundamental step in all decisions and who use creative vision to establish proprietary methodologies. The middle tier includes those managers who occasionally turn to research but only rely on the tried-and-true methods. The bottom tier is those managers who by choice or economic circumstance choose to rely on intuition and judgment rather than business research.

3 The research process is a model for the development and interpretation of research studies. Although many researchers perceive the research study as a sequential process involving several clearly defined steps, no one claims that research requires completion of each step before going to the next. Recycling, circumventing, and skipping occur. Some steps are begun out of sequence, some are carried out simultaneously, and some may be omitted. Despite these variations, the idea of a sequence is useful for developing a project and for keeping the project orderly as it unfolds.

4 What characterizes good research? Generally, one expects good research to be purposeful with a clearly defined focus and plausible goals; with defensible, ethical, and repeatable procedures; and with evidence of objectivity. The reporting of procedures—their strengths and weaknesses—should be complete and honest. Appropriate analytical techniques should be used; conclusions drawn should be limited to those clearly justified by the findings; and reports of findings and conclusions should be clearly presented and professional in tone, language, and appearance. Managers should always choose a researcher who has an established reputation for quality work. The research objective and its benefits should be weighed against potentially adverse effects.

5 Research is any organized inquiry carried out to provide information for solving problems. This includes reporting, descriptive, explanatory, and predictive studies. Reporting studies provide a summation of data, often recasting data to achieve a deeper understanding or to generate statistics for comparison. A descriptive study tries to discover answers to the questions *who, what, when, where,* and, sometimes, *how.* An explanatory study attempts to explain the reasons for the phenomenon that the descriptive study only observed. A predictive study attempts to predict when and in what situations an event will occur. Studies may also be described as applied research or basic research. Applied research applies research to discovering solutions for immediate problems or opportunities. Basic (or pure) research aims to solve perplexing questions or obtain new knowledge of an experimental or theoretical nature that has little direct or immediate impact on action, performance, or policy decisions.

>**key**terms

applied research 12

business intelligence system (BIS) 7

business research 4

control 20

custom researcher 24

decision support system (DSS) 7

descriptive study 18

explanatory study 19

full-service researchers 24

management dilemma 5

omnibus researcher 27

omnibus study 27

predictive study 19

proprietary methodology 24

pure research (basic research) 12

reporting study 18

research process 11

research variable 19

return on investment (ROI) 4

scientific method 12

specialty researchers 26

strategy 7

syndicated data provider 27

tactics 8

>**discussion**questions

Terms in Review

1 What is business research? Why should there be any question about the definition of research?

2 What is the difference between applied research and basic or pure research? Use a decision about how a salesperson is to be paid, by commission or salary, and describe the question that would guide applied research versus the question that would guide pure research.

3 Distinguish between an explanatory and predictive research study.

4 Distinguish between a reporting study and a descriptive study.

Making Research Decisions

5 A sales force manager needs to have information in order to decide whether to create a custom motivation program or purchase one offered by a consulting firm. What are the dilemmas the manager faces in selecting either of these alternatives?

6 The new president of an old established company is facing a problem. The company is currently unprofitable and is, in the president's opinion, operating inefficiently. The company sells a wide line of equipment and supplies to the dairy industry. Some items it manufactures and many it wholesales to dairies, creameries, and similar plants. Because the industry is changing in several ways, survival will be more difficult in the future. In particular, many equipment companies are bypassing the wholesalers and selling directly to dairies. In addition, many of the independent dairies are being taken over by large food chains. How might business research help the new president make the right decisions?

7 You have received a business research report done by a consultant for your firm, a life insurance company. The study is a survey of customer satisfaction based on a sample of 600. You are asked to comment on its quality. What will you look for?

8 As area sales manager for a company manufacturing and marketing outboard engines, you have been assigned the responsibility of conducting a research study to estimate the sales potential of your products in the domestic (U.S. or Canadian) market. Discuss key issues and concerns arising from the fact that you, the manager, are also the researcher.

Bringing Research to Life

9 What evidence is presented in the Bringing Research to Life vignette of efforts to understand the management dilemma?

From Concept to Practice

10 Apply the principles in Exhibit 1-4 to the research scenario in question 8.

From the Headlines

11 Toyota had a major problem with unexplained acceleration in several of its top models in 2010. It closed down production and stopped sales of multiple models. What types of research might Toyota have conducted to make these decisions?

>**cases***

 Data Development Inc.

 Ohio Lottery: Innovative Research Design Drives Winning

HeroBuilders.com

* You will find a description of each case in the Case Abstracts section of this textbook. Check the Case Index to determine whether a case provides data, the research instrument, video, or other supplementary material. Written cases are downloadable from the text website (www.mhhe.com/cooper11e). All video material and video cases are available from the Online Learning Center. The film reel icon indicates a video case or video material relevant to the case.

How the Research Industry Works

The picture of the research industry is one of extremes. Very large suppliers account for the largest portion of the sales in the industry, but smaller firms and one-person shops dominate when you look at the number of research firms. Exhibit 1a-1 provides an overview of the suppliers within the research industry.

Internal Research Suppliers[1]

Not all decision makers rely on research to make decisions. Those firms that do are likely to have an internal research department or an individual who coordinates research initiatives. The structure and scope of these operations are as diverse as the management dilemmas that they research. They range from one-person operations, in which the individual primarily coordinates the hiring of external research suppliers, to small-staffed operations that do some survey or qualitative studies, to large-staffed divisions that more closely approximate the structures of research companies.

Historically, in the 1960s, as business research entered a new era of quantification and respectability, the number of firms with internal research departments grew. The research function gained acceptance as a formal part of the organization. When the decade of the 1970s arrived, researchers were often assigned to a particular functional area (e.g., marketing or human resources), and they reported directly to the executive in charge of that area. The researcher's influence at the strategic level was constrained by the rather narrow definition of their role—order takers who reacted to the demand for research projects and reports. This perception of a researcher's role as having limited strategic contribution continued through the 1990s. The results of one Advertising Research Foundation (ARF) study in 1999 indicated that "according to the CEOs surveyed, the accuracy and actionability of the information provided by research was thought to be low."[2]

In a 2001 quantitative study conducted with the aid of the Cambridge Group, ARF sought to identify ways to redefine the research function, thereby making it more

>**Exhibit 1a-1** Who Conducts Business Research?

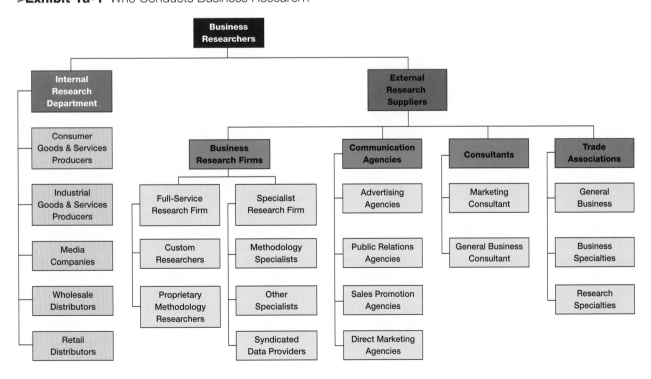

relevant to senior management. The opinions of CEOs, senior-level managers, and researchers at over 100 Fortune 500 companies were solicited to discover the core competencies possessed by an ideal management decision support function and to learn which decisions and activities were most important for research support. While results from executives revealed generally positive ratings for research, a gap still existed between researchers and senior-level managers and CEOs on their perceptions of researchers' role. Based on the executive's responses, research began to expand into such areas as providing actionable insights, reducing risk in marketplace actions, and improving return on investment.[3] This evolution of the research industry is consistent with scholar and consultant Philip Kotler's contention that, as costs rise, CEOs and board members demand greater accountability for decisions and expenditures.[4]

For budget, equipment, facilities, and expertise reasons, the trend in the industry is clearly not to staff large internal research departments. In poor economic times, many firms eliminate their internal research operations altogether, feeling that such services are expendable or are readily available from external suppliers. In some ways the growth in prominence of the role of information technology manager or officer (those that manage the DSS and BIS functions) has forced the researcher to an even more subordinate staff role. While both information technology management and research are critical, in most organizations the two functions have little directly to do with one another.

External Research Suppliers

Within the category "research specialists," more than 2,000 research firms operate in the United States.[5]

Research Firms

Full-Service Firms **Full-service researchers** include some of the largest research firms in the world and some of the smallest. Exhibit 1a-2 identifies some of the largest firms. Full-service firms are often involved in research planning for their clients from the moment of discovery of the management dilemma or, at the very least, from the definition of the management question. Such firms usually have expertise in both quantitative and qualitative methodologies, and they often have at their disposal multifaceted facilities capable of serving a wide variety of research designs, including both fieldwork and laboratory operations. Some are capable of working in worldwide venues, while others offer their services to only one industry or one geographic region. While these firms may have one or more areas of noteworthy expertise, they are truly multidimensional in terms of both research planning and execution. In a research environment where clients increasingly demand managerial insights, not just research reporting, these firms are often a combination of research

and consulting operations. NFO WorldGroup is an example of a full-service research firm. It describes itself as "marketing minds who specialize in research."[6] Taylor Nelson Sofres Intersearch is another full-service firm. It describes its approach as follows: "We combine category knowledge with research expertise in our cross-functional research teams."[7]

Custom Researchers Such phrases as "ad hoc research" or "custom-designed research" are often used to describe custom full-service research firms. A **custom researcher** crafts a research design unique to the decision maker's dilemma. In essence, such research firms start each project from ground zero. This does not mean, however, that they fail to apply lessons learned from previous projects. What is implied is that such firms do not assume that a given methodology is appropriate for each client's research, even if the research to be done is in an arena in which the research firm has considerable expertise: for example, customer satisfaction or copy testing or product evaluation or employee motivation research. While a custom researcher might not always be a full-service research firm, by definition, a full-service researcher would always fit into the custom research category. Taylor Nelson Sofres Intersearch (TNS) describes its custom research operations this way: "[Our custom research capability] allows us to design approaches that truly meet [the client's] needs if proprietary research solutions do not."[8]

Proprietary Methodology Researchers A **proprietary methodology** is a research program or technique that is owned by a single firm. It may be a slight twist on an established methodology or may be a method developed by that firm. Firms often brand these methodologies to establish distinction in the minds of prospective clients, as ACNielsen did with its Homescan® syndicated panel. Proprietary methodologies often grow from significant expertise in a given methodology or a given industry and develop over many years and thousands of client projects.

With the development of its customer engagement methodology, The Gallup Organization has reinvented itself using the proprietary research model, moving from public opinion pollster and custom researcher to research-based consulting firm. Although Gallup is capable of doing and still does custom research, it captures a significant portion of its revenue from management consulting based on proprietary methodologies. One of its proprietary methodologies is called *Q12*. This survey methodology uses 12 questions to measure customer engagement. Gallup uses these same questions with all clients, so Q12 serves as a benchmark diagnostic for its subsequent consulting work. Gallup has copyrighted its questions and the survey instrument that incorporates them to guarantee that its intellectual property remains protected. Having

>**Exhibit 1a-2** Some of the World's Largest Research Companies

Organization	Type of Research	Research Revenue, 2008	
		U.S. ($ millions)	Worldwide ($ millions)
The Nielsen Co. www.nielsen.com	The global leader in providing services in marketing and consumer information, TV and other media measurement, online intelligence, mobile measurement, trade shows, and business publications. Has multiple divisions, including Nielsen Claritas, Nielsen BASES, and Scarborough Research.	$2,231.0	$4,575.0
The Kantar Group www.kantargroup.com	Provides worldwide media research and measurement for media owners, agencies, and advertisers.	918.5	3,616.1
TNS www.tnsglobal.com	Provides customer research, omnibus studies, and attitudinal polling in a variety of industries, as well as drug sample monitoring.	361.6	1,738.4
IMS Health Inc. www.imshealth.com	Provides information solutions to the pharmaceutical and health care industries.	842.0	1,487.5
IRI www.infores.com	Provides UPC scanner-based business solutions to the consumer packaged-good (CPG) Industry	454.0	725.0
Arbitron Inc. www.arbitron.com	Provides information services used to develop the local marketing strategies of the electronic media and their advertisers and agencies.	364.4	368.8
GfK USA www.gfk.com	Provides both custom and syndicated research, as well as research based consulting, and analytical customer-relationship management (CRM) services around the world; noted for its RoperASW and MediaMark divisions with specialties in media audience measurement.	313.1	797.2
Ipsos www.ipsos-na.com	Explores market potential and market trends, tests products and advertising, studies audiences and their perceptions of various media, and measures public opinion trends around the globe.	307.6	442.1
Synovate www.synovate.com	Provides global marketing research and consulting to business, government, and associations.	245.0	959.7
Maritz Research www.maritz.com	Provides large-scale, custom-designed research studies that produce critical marketing information in the areas of customer choice, customer experience, and customer loyalty.	197.4	230.7
J.D. Power and Associates www.jdpower.com	Conducts independent surveys of customer satisfaction, quality, and buyer behavior; best known for its marketing information for the automotive and hospitality industries.	188.6	272.2
Harris Interactive Inc. www.harrisinteractive.com	A worldwide market research and consulting firm, best known for the Harris Poll and for its pioneering use of the Internet to conduct scientifically accurate research.	137.1	221.8
comScore Inc. www.comscore.com	A leader in online behavior measurement, providing a global cross section of 2 million Internet users who provide their browsing and transaction behavior, including online and offline purchasing. It also provides Internet audience measurement for advertising agencies, publishers, marketers, and financial analysts, and reports details of online media usage, visitor demographics, and online buying power for home, work, and university audiences across 100 local U.S. markets and for 37 countries.	100.9	117.4
Burke Inc. www.burke.com	Recently rated #1 in the industry in customer satisfaction, this full-service marketing research firm is noted for its use of advanced analytical techniques and technology to provide decision support services across all major industry sectors. Burke is also known for providing marketing research and consumer insights education through the Burke Institute, which has trained participants through more than 3,000 public and in-house customized marketing research seminars in 39 countries.	50.8	60.4

Source: Data were developed from the companies' websites and from "Honomichl Top 50," *Marketing News* (American Marketing Association), June 30, 2009; for references: http://www.marketingpower.com/ResourceLibrary/MarketingNews/Pages/2009/43/6-30-09%20pages/Honomichl_Top_50_Report.aspx.

a proprietary research methodology allows Gallup to charge its clients significant premiums for its research and consulting services.[9] Without proprietary methodologies, all research firms essentially offer the same research services—although we accept that some perform such services with far more skill and expertise than others.

Specialty Research Firms

Specialty researchers represent the largest number of research firms and tend to dominate the small research firms operated by a single researcher or a very small staff. These firms may establish a specialty in one or several different arenas:

- *Methodology.* The firms (methodology specialists) may conduct only one type of research (e.g., survey research, customer satisfaction research, ad copy testing, packaging evaluation, focus groups, retail mystery shopping, or retail design research).
- *Process.* The firms usually contribute to only a portion of the research process (e.g., sample recruiting, telephone interviewing, or fielding a Web survey).
- *Industry.* The firms become experts in one or a few industries (e.g., pharmaceutical research or entertainment research or telecommunications research).
- *Participant group.* The firms become experts in a particular participant group (e.g., Latino-Americans or children or doctors or country club golfers).
- *Geographic region.* The firms may operate in only one region of a country—as is true for many mystery shopping firms—or a single country or group of countries.

One large group in this specialty research category includes firms that conduct focus groups. These firms not only offer the trained moderators who manage the small-group discussions, many of whom hold a PhD in psychology, but also provide the sample screening procedures, the specially designed facilities, and the technical communications equipment for making this qualitative research as insightful as possible. Specialty researchers may also perform a subset of a methodology specialty. For example, numerous firms offer focus group moderators but not the focus group facilities. Others provide the recruiting of focus group participants and the facilities but not the moderators.

Firms doing observation studies comprise another subset of specialty researchers. These researchers are often found studying retail shoppers, tracing their footsteps or recording the amount of time a shopper spends reading labels or interacting with displays. Envirosell and Design Forum both do observation studies: Envirosell's research is designed to make retail environments and processes more productive; Design Forum uses research to create the external and internal environment that establishes and reinforces the retailer's image. Ethnography is a type of study that combines observation and communication studies. The Context-Based Research Group describes itself as "an ethnographic research and consulting firm." It combines the backgrounds and skills of cultural anthropologists (more than 3,000 around the world) with the communications and business strategy discipline experts to serve a diverse client base, including retailers, software manufacturers, food manufacturers, hotels, pharmaceutical companies, and even proponents of social causes.[10]

Firms providing Web page optimization research and Web performance metrics are an emerging group of methodology specialists. Such firms as Yahoo!, NetIQ (with WebTrends), and NetConversions are examples of methodology specialists in metrics related to Web content development.

One of Britain's fastest-growing research firms MORInsight is a specialist in employee research. It claims "MORInsight contains benchmarking data from over 200 employee surveys covering a wide range of subjects from job satisfaction to employee engagement and advocacy."[11] Mercer HR Consulting, with offices in more than 41 countries, also specializes in employee research. Mercer claims, "Advancements in quantification and measurement now make it possible to enhance this process by linking what employees say to what they actually do—and measuring the impact on business performance."[12] IBM's operations research specialists were able to design and introduce a new Web-based procurement auction process for Mars, Incorporated, that paid for itself in increased cost savings in just one year and wins accolades from suppliers for "increased efficiency, transparency, and fairness."[13]

Collectively, specialty researchers often assist other research firms to complete projects. One large group in the process specialist category is the sampling specialist. These firms provide the screening and recruiting of probability samples for a wide range of survey studies, as well as studies employing in-depth interviews, laboratory and in-home product testing, laboratory experiments, home ethnographies, and so on. Survey Sampling Inc. is one of the largest suppliers of samples for telephone, mail, and online surveys and also offers specialty samples for industrial and health care research.[14] Greenfield Online specializes in assisting research firms by providing online samples that fulfill a variety of characteristics. Greenfield claims to have compiled the largest panel of opt-in participants in the online community. It has also partnered with Microsoft to build recruited online samples drawn from MSN.com membership.[15]

With the increase of online research, many researchers—especially internal research departments and small custom research firms—want to offer this methodology but do not have the capability to field such a study themselves. Qualtrics Labs, with its array of software and service products (surveypro.com for designing and fielding simple surveys, QuestionPro.com for more complex surveys,

PerfectSurveys.com for intranet and e-mail surveys) promises researchers without online capabilities the ability to deliver professional-quality online survey results.[16] Training Technologies Inc. also designs, fields, tracks, and posts survey results for those researchers without the necessary technical capabilities.[17]

Syndicated Data Providers

When managers want comparative performance and opinion data, pitting themselves against their competitors in sales, market share, share of voice, image as a corporate citizen or employer, or salary and benefit levels, they turn to researchers that are syndicated data providers. For a substantial fee, often millions of dollars per year, managers subscribe to receive the periodic data as well as the interpretation of these data. A **syndicated data provider** tracks the change of one or more measures over time, usually in a given industry. For example, a syndicated data provider might track product movements through various retail outlets and wholesale environments. The tracking of sales performance measures during promotional events such as coupon drops, distribution of product samples, special events (e.g., the appearance of a celebrity at a charity event), and advertising is often the key to successful strategic planning. These research firms are also responsible for providing decision makers with measures of price elasticity. In consumer packaged goods, the first research company to provide scanner-based tracking through grocery outlets was Information Resources Inc. (IRI), in 1987.[18] Other firms providing syndicated research are noted in Exhibit 1a-3.

Each syndicated data provider determines the frequency of data collection and reporting based on the needs of the members in the syndicate. Although some studies provide data monthly or weekly, not all such studies are done as frequently as sales tracking studies. Some syndicated data are collected only once per year or once every few years. Other syndicated data are collected several times per year during designated collection periods. One example is the tracking of media consumption. Nielsen Media Research is well known for its *People Meter* research that mechanically records and then reveals the viewing habits of a panel of television watchers. Data are collected four times per year during so-called *sweep weeks*. These are times when the TV networks often substitute special programming for their regular shows to increase viewership. Advertising rates for the whole season of advertising slots are determined by a show's audience size and composition during a sweep week. Arbitron collects similar data on radio listening habits. Typically the firm subscribing to the syndicate has full access to its data and the composite data, but not to an individual competitor's data.

Omnibus Researchers

Sometimes the decision maker needs the answer to one or a few questions to make a quick tactical decision, such as when it faces a crisis caused by a product recall or the indictment of a company executive for fraud. Within the world of survey research, several research firms provide such a service, some even with a 24- to 48-hour turnaround. Exhibit 1a-4 offers some examples. An **omnibus researcher** fields research studies, often by survey, at regular, predetermined intervals. An **omnibus study** combines one or a few questions from several decision makers who need information from the same population. Typically, the manager pays by the number of questions, usually between $700 and $1,500 per question. Many omnibus studies are still done by phone, but as online participants increasingly mirror the general population, an increasing number are being offered via the Internet. NOP World (NOP) uses a representative sample of 1,000 adults for its Telebus study.[19] NOP contacts participants during the weekend and provides the decision maker with feedback on Monday morning. For a firm facing a public relations crisis, the quick turnaround is invaluable, and the data are available at a fraction of the cost of a custom-designed study. NOP does omnibus studies with automobile drivers, parents, youths, and other population segments in Great Britain, using telephone and online surveys as well as face-to-face interviews. Medical Marketing Research Inc. conducts omnibus studies with physicians in all the medical specialties, while TNS offers the PhoneBus survey, interviewing 1,000 to 2,000 participants twice per week, with results within four days.[20]

Communication Agencies

It is difficult for an advertising agency to recommend advertising in a particular medium (e.g., television) or on a particular program (e.g., *Survivor* or *CSI*) without fully understanding the demographics and lifestyles of the viewing audiences of each show. This explains why advertising, public relations, sales promotion, and direct marketing agencies are heavy users of syndicated research data, especially from media industry suppliers. It is even more difficult to develop a creative strategy without research on target audience knowledge, motivations, attitudes, and behavior. Agencies are also voracious consumers and providers of custom and proprietary research. Within communication agency circles, there is some debate on whether a research division within an agency can maintain the objectivity needed to do custom research or whether, with conflicting demands from numerous clients, an internal research operation can be efficient and timely, so clients sometimes request that the research needed by these communication specialists be done by an external supplier.

Some agencies do extensive basic research to identify influences on ad recall and ad wear-out, on ad placement effectiveness, on the effectiveness of various creative approaches (e.g., celebrity endorser versus animated product as spokesperson), on the effectiveness of communication

>Exhibit 1a-3 Some Syndicated Data Providers

Company	Syndicated Service	What It Measures
ACNielsen en-us.nielsen.com	Scantrack Homescan	Provides sales tracking across grocery, drug, and mass merchandisers. Provides consumer panel service for tracking retail purchases and motivations.
Yahoo! and ACNielsen www.yahoo.com	Internet Confidence Index	Measures (quarterly) the confidence levels in Internet products and services.
Scarborough Research (a service of Arbitron Inc. and VNU) www.scarborough.com		Provides a syndicated study to print and electronic media, new media companies, outdoor media, sports teams and leagues, agencies, advertisers, and Yellow Pages on local, regional, and national levels—including local market shopping patterns, demographics, media usage, and lifestyle activities.
Millward Brown www.millwardbrown.com	IntelliQuest www.intelliquest.com	Provides studies enabling clients to understand and improve the position of their technology, brands, products, media, or channels.
Information Resources www.infores.com	BehaviorScan	Collects store tracking data used with consumer panel data to track advertising influence in consumer packaged goods.
Nielsen Media Research www.nielsenmedia.com	National People Meter	Provides audience estimates for all national program sources, including broadcast networks, cable networks, Spanish-language networks, and national syndicators.
GfK NOP www.gfkamerica.com	Starch Ad Readership Studies	Provides raw readership scores collected via individual depth interview; records the percent of readers who saw the ad and read the copy. The ad is ranked not only against other ads in the issue but also against other ads in its product category over the last two years.
CSA TMO www.csa-fr.com	OPERBAC	Provides continuous tracking of banking insurance and credit purchases in European markets.
DoubleClick www.doubleclick.com	Diameter	Provides online audience measurement services for Web publishers, advertisers, and agencies.
Nielsen//NetRatings www.nielsen-netratings.com		Measures audience data using actual click-by-click Internet user behavior measured through a comprehensive real-time meter installed on individual computers worldwide (home and work).
Taylor Nelson Sofres Intersearch www.tns-i.com	Global eCommerce	Measures e-commerce activity in 27 countries, providing insights into 37 marketplaces via interviews.
ORC International www.orc.co.uk	NHS Talkback	Measures employee opinion for NHS Trusts in the United Kingdom via phone surveys.
J.D. Power Associates www.jdpower.com	PowerReport, PowerGram, etc.	Publishes in-depth analytical reports on automotive, travel, health, and other industries.
BMRB www.bmrb.co.uk	Youth TGI	A biannual survey of youth aged 7–19 on purchase and media consumption habits and lifestyle behaviors.

Source: This table was developed from descriptions published on each company's website. All sites were accessed in January 2010.

>Exhibit 1a-4 Some Omnibus Studies

Company	Sample Size	Sample Characteristics	Turnaround (from question to delivery)	Details
IPSOS MORI CAPibus-GB www.capibus.com	1,000–1,200	Adults, face-to-face, in home survey	10 days (avg.)	Multiple questions allowed; fielded most weeks.
NewsPoll Research *Adult Online Omnibus* www.newspoll.com.au	1,200	Adults, 18–64, in Australia		Multiple questions; conducted every two weeks.
British Market Research Bureau *Telephone Omnibus* www.bmrb.co.uk	2,000	Adults, 16 years of age and older, in United Kingdom	7 days	By phone, from Friday through Sunday; up to six precoded questions, £525.
Synovate Synovate Data Gage www.synovate.com	5,000 to 110,000 in 5,000 increments	Adults	1 month	By mail; questions that will fit on 3½" by 8½" two-sided card.
Synovate TeenNation www.synovate.com	500	Teens, 12 to 17 years of age	1 week	Online interviews; can incorporate graphic images.
AcuPoll Omnibus www.acupoll.com	Varies	Adults	7 days, USA; 10 days, Europe	Online; several times monthly.

Source: This table was constructed from descriptions published on each company's website and accessed January 19, 2007.

strategies (e.g., humor, violence, or sexuality in advertising), on the ROI for various media buys, and on the comparative effectiveness of different action stimulants (such as coupons versus samples), to name a few. For direct marketing agencies every single client's project is actually an experiment, with the offer, the action stimulants, the creative strategy, or even the mailing envelope modified in split-sample tests. All agencies do extensive copy testing as a development tool in building a campaign and effectiveness testing with postplacement recall, knowledge, and behavior measures. Such measures combine custom research with syndicated research to explain why a campaign was a success.

Consultants Business consultants offer a wide range of services at the strategic and tactical levels. All are involved in doing extensive secondary data research for their clients. Such consultants may also be major influencers in research design, both of custom research and the selection of proprietary models. Even when they don't do the actual data collection themselves, they are often involved in the interpretation of results. Depending on the size of the firm, some consultancies conduct both qualitative studies (notably focus groups and expert interviews) and quantitative studies (usually through surveys) on knowledge, attitudes,

opinions, and motivations as they seek new opportunities or solutions to their client's problems.

For example, a study of middle-level managers by consultancy Accenture indicates that 50 percent of managers feel that the information that is collected isn't valuable to them. One-third of managers said that it takes a long time to get the right data, and 57 percent said that compiling information from multiple sources is a tough part of their jobs. Almost 59 percent said they are missing data that might be valuable for decision making because it "exists elsewhere in the company and just cannot be found." Only 16 percent of managers said they store valuable data in a collaborative workplace, and as many as 42 percent use the wrong information in decision making at least once a week.[21]

Trade Associations Generally, trade associations have as their purpose to promote, educate, and lobby for the interests of their members. Although many commission pure research that advances trade interests, not all conduct or supply research services.

A List of Business Sources Check the comprehensive list of business sources available for download from the text website.

>chapter 2

Ethics in Business Research

>learningobjectives

After reading this chapter, you should understand. . .

1 What issues are covered in research ethics.

2 The goal of "no harm" for all research activities and what constitutes "no harm" for participant, researcher, and research sponsor.

3 The differing ethical dilemmas and responsibilities of researchers, sponsors, and research assistants.

4 The role of ethical codes of conduct in professional associations.

> " [*Privacy pragmatists are*] often willing to allow people to have access to, and to use, their personal information where they understand the reasons for its use, where they see tangible benefits for so doing, and when they believe care is taken to prevent the misuse of this information. "
>
> Humphrey Taylor, chairman of The Harris Poll®,
> Harris Interactive

>**bringing**research**to**life

Jason Henry has returned to the office following a proposal presentation designed to capture a research project from a potential new business. Sara Arens, Jason's partner, and Jason had worked together many hours on the project proposal. Both had hopes that the project would represent an entrée to significant new business for Henry and Associates.

"How did the proposal meeting go with MicroPeripheral this morning," inquired Sara as Jason dropped into a chair across from Sara's desk.

"It didn't," flatly stated Jason.

"Well, we had a good proposal, but we can't win every contract," commiserated Sara. "Do we know why?"

"Oh, we could have had the contract," claimed Jason. "I just decided the contract wasn't right for Henry and Associates."

"Now you've got my attention," said Sara, leaning forward. "That would have been a small piece of business now, but being a research supplier to such a large computer peripheral manufacturer showed definite possibilities for a lucrative long-term relationship. What went wrong?"

"According to its president, Bill Henderson," explained Jason as he and Sara walked back to Jason's office, "MicroPeripheral (MP) has taken a near-lead position in peripherals for laptop computing, but peripherals are volatile. Peripherals grow smaller every month and have to be sold more cheaply. Henderson needed a detailed market report that MP could very well afford to pay for, but he really wanted something we couldn't deliver."

"The proposal we developed was for a detailed market study," puzzled Sara.

"Yes, but he had in mind an entirely different study than we proposed. He proposed hiring a headhunter to set up interviews for a mythical senior diversification manager position within a mythical company—he called it a disguised study. He wanted us to provide the focus group facility for the interviews so that we could use our equipment to digitally record every interview."

"I fail to see how this would have given him the market data he needed," stated Sara, now clearly confused.

"According to Henderson, another CEO had tried this ploy and been able to attract competitors' employees to be interviewed. Every interview added greatly to the firm's understanding of the competition and the market. But then they hit the jackpot. One of the candidates was a key exec from the major competitor. On the basis of that interview and the information the duped executive innocently revealed, the company decided to shut down its California production line and open production in Mexico for a smaller, faster, cheaper version of its main product. The advance notice permitted the firm to steal significant market share."

"He had the gall to suggest we participate in this fraud?"

"Henderson assured me that it wasn't illegal, but I didn't stick around to hear more. I literally grabbed our proposal from the desk top—the one with the Henry and Associates logo boldly marked on the front—and walked out."

"So I imagine you've been on the phone since you returned," surmised Sara.

"I called every single research firm whose logo was visible in the array of proposals on Henderson's desk. They were all most appreciative," said Jason, smiling for the first time.

"And it's likely," smiled Sara, "that Henderson will soon find all his other proposals will be withdrawn."

> What Are Research Ethics?

As in other aspects of business, all parties in research should exhibit ethical behavior. **Ethics** are norms or standards of behavior that guide moral choices about our behavior and our relationships with others. The goal of ethics in research is to ensure that no one is harmed or suffers adverse consequences from research activities. This objective is usually achieved. However, unethical activities are pervasive and include violating nondisclosure agreements, breaking participant confidentiality, misrepresenting results, deceiving people, using invoicing irregularities, avoiding legal liability, and more.

The recognition of ethics as a problem for economic organizations is repeatedly revealed in surveys. Despite an increase in awareness of formal ethics programs and the presence of written ethical codes of conduct (83 percent), one survey reports that although 52 percent of U.S. workers claim to have observed at least one type of ethical misconduct, only 55 percent of those observing misconduct reported the violation (a decline of 10 percent from a similar study done two years before). Strong-ethical-culture organizations were 1.6 times as likely to report incidents as weak-ethical-culture organizations. Such lack of action raises questions about the effectiveness of codes of conduct and reporting systems.[1]

There is no single approach to ethics. Advocating strict adherence to a set of laws is difficult because of the unforeseen constraint put on researchers. Because of Germany's war history, for example, the government forbids many types of medical research. Consequently, the German people do not benefit from many advances in biotechnology and may have restricted access to genetically altered drugs in the future. Alternatively, relying on each individual's personal sense of morality is equally problematic. Consider the clash between those who believe death is deliverance from a life of suffering and those who value life to the point of preserving it indefinitely through mechanical means. Each value system claims superior knowledge of moral correctness.

Clearly, a middle ground between being completely code governed or relying on ethical relativism is necessary. The foundation for that middle ground is an emerging consensus on ethical standards for researchers. Codes and regulations guide researchers and sponsors. Review boards and peer groups help researchers examine their research proposals for ethical dilemmas. Many design-based ethical problems can be eliminated by careful planning and constant vigilance. In the end, responsible research anticipates ethical dilemmas and attempts to adjust the design, procedures, and protocols during the planning process rather than treating them as an afterthought. Ethical research requires personal integrity from the researcher, the project manager, and the research sponsor.

Because integrity in research is vital, we are discussing its components early in this book and emphasizing ethical behavior throughout our coverage. Our objective is to stimulate an ongoing exchange about values and practical research constraints in the chapters that follow. This chapter is organized around the theme of ethical treatment of participants, clients, research sponsors, and other researchers. We also highlight appropriate laws and codes, resources for ethical awareness, and cases for application. Exhibit 2-1 relates each ethical issue under discussion to the research process introduced in Chapter 1.

> Ethical Treatment of Participants

When ethics are discussed in research design, we often think first about protecting the rights of the participant, or subject. Whether data are gathered in an experiment, interview, observation, or survey, the participant has many rights to be safeguarded. In general, research must be designed so that a participant does not suffer physical harm, discomfort, pain, embarrassment, or loss of privacy. To safeguard against these, the researcher should follow three guidelines:[2]

1. Explain study benefits.
2. Explain participant rights and protections.
3. Obtain informed consent.

>**Exhibit 2-1** Ethical Issues and the Research Process

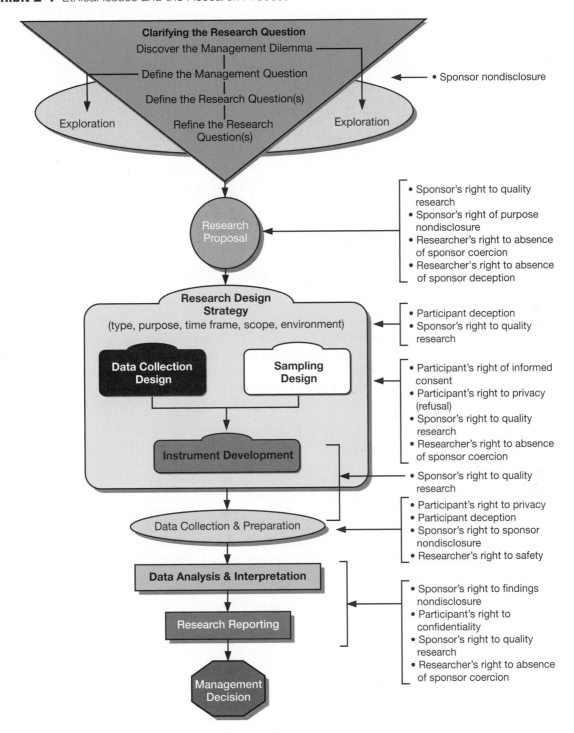

Benefits

Whenever direct contact is made with a participant, the researcher should discuss the study's benefits, being careful to neither overstate nor understate the benefits. An interviewer should begin an introduction with his or her name, the name of the research organization, and a brief description of the purpose and benefit of the research. This puts participants at ease, lets them know to whom they are speaking,

Engendering Trust Online

With the Internet a growing source of research information, participants in such research deserve to know how the information they share will be used. According to Truste.org, "As an Internet user, you have a right to expect online privacy and the responsibility to exercise choice over how your personal information is collected, used, and shared by websites." Truste.org offers its trustmarks to Internet sites that follow its privacy guidelines:

- *Adoption and implementation of a privacy policy* that takes into account consumer anxiety over sharing personal information online.

- *Notice and disclosure* of information collection and use practices.
- *Choice and consent,* giving users the opportunity to exercise control over their information.
- *Data security and quality and access* measures to help protect the security and accuracy of personally identifiable information.

www.truste.org

and motivates them to answer questions truthfully. In short, knowing why one is being asked questions improves cooperation through honest disclosure of purpose. Inducements to participate, financial or otherwise, should not be disproportionate to the task or presented in a fashion that results in coercion.

Sometimes the actual purpose and benefits of your study or experiment must be concealed from the participants to avoid introducing bias. The need for concealing objectives leads directly to the problem of deception.

Deception

Deception occurs when the participants are told only part of the truth or when the truth is fully compromised. Some believe this should never occur. Others suggest two reasons for deception: (1) to prevent biasing the participants before the survey or experiment and (2) to protect the confidentiality of a third party (e.g., the sponsor). Deception should not be used in an attempt to improve response rates.

The benefits to be gained by deception should be balanced against the risks to the participants. When possible, an experiment or interview should be redesigned to reduce reliance on deception. In addition, the participants' rights and well-being must be adequately protected. In instances where deception in an experiment could produce anxiety, a subject's medical condition should be checked to ensure that no adverse physical harm follows. The American Psychological Association's ethics code states that the use of deception is inappropriate unless deceptive techniques are justified by the study's expected scientific, educational, or applied value and equally effective alternatives that do not use deception are not feasible.[3] And, finally, the participants must have given their informed consent before participating in the research.

Informed Consent

Securing **informed consent** from participants is a matter of fully disclosing the procedures of the proposed survey or other research design before requesting permission to proceed with the study. There are exceptions that argue for a signed consent form. When dealing with children, the researcher is wise to have a parent or other person with legal standing sign a consent form. When doing research with medical or psychological ramifications, the researcher is also wise to obtain a signed consent form. If there is a chance the data could harm the participant or if the researchers offer only limited protection of confidentiality, a signed form detailing the types of limits should be obtained. For most business research, oral consent is sufficient. An example of how informed-consent procedures are implemented

Researchers have special ethical responsibilities when using children as participants. GMI Global Youth Panel offers direct access to kids and is fully compliant with the Children's Online Privacy Protection Act (COPPA). COPPA federal regulations ensure that proper parental permission is obtained prior to initiating membership on the panel. Besides providing informed consent, parents are often interviewed during the selection process to ensure that if their child is chosen, he or she is mature enough to handle the activities planned and has the verbal and physical capabilities necessary. Researchers who work with children want the child to perceive participation as an enjoyable—and sometimes even an exciting—experience.
www.gmi-mr.com/global-panels/

is shown in Exhibit 2-2. In this example, a university research center demonstrates how it adheres to the highest ethical standards for survey procedures.[4]

In situations where participants are intentionally or accidentally deceived, they should be debriefed once the research is complete.

Debriefing Participants

Debriefing involves several activities following the collection of data:

- Explanation of any deception.
- Description of the hypothesis, goal, or purpose of the study.
- Poststudy sharing of results.
- Poststudy follow-up medical or psychological attention.

First, the researcher shares the truth of any deception with the participants and the reasons for using deception in the context of the study's goals. In cases where severe reactions occur, follow-up medical or psychological attention should be provided to continue to ensure the participants remain unharmed by the research.

>Exhibit 2-2 Informed-Consent Procedures for Surveys

Content
Surveys conducted by the Indiana University Center for Survey Research contain the following informed-consent components in their introductions:

1. Introduce ourselves—interviewer's name and Indiana University Center for Survey Research.
2. Briefly describe the survey topic (e.g., barriers to health insurance).
3. Describe the geographic area we are interviewing (e.g., people in Indiana) or target sample (e.g., aerospace engineers).
4. Tell who the sponsor is (e.g., National Endowment for the Humanities).
5. Describe the purpose(s) of the research (e.g., satisfaction with services received/provided by a local agency).
6. Give a "good-faith" estimate of the time required to complete the interview.
7. Promise anonymity and confidentiality (when appropriate).
8. Tell the participant the participation is voluntary.
9. Tell the participant that item-nonresponse is acceptable.
10. Ask permission to begin.

Sample Introduction
Hello, I'm [fill in NAME] from the Center for Survey Research at Indiana University. We're surveying Indianapolis area residents to ask their opinions about some health issues. This study is sponsored by the National Institutes of Health and its results will be used to research the effect of community ties on attitudes toward medical practices. The survey takes about 40 minutes. Your participation is anonymous and voluntary, and all your answers will be kept completely confidential. If there are any questions that you don't feel you can answer, please let me know and we'll move to the next one. So, if I have your permission, I'll continue.

Sample Conclusion
The participant is given information on how to contact the principal investigator. For example: John Kennedy is the principal investigator for this study. Would you like Dr. Kennedy's address or telephone number in case you want to contact him about the study at any time?

Even when research does not deceive the participants, it is a good practice to offer them follow-up information. This retains the goodwill of the participant, providing an incentive to participate in future research projects. For surveys and interviews, participants can be offered a brief report of the findings. Usually, they will not request additional information. Occasionally, however, the research will be of particular interest to a participant. A simple set of descriptive charts or data tables can be generated for such an individual.

For experiments, all participants should be debriefed in order to put the experiment into context. Debriefing usually includes a description of the hypothesis being tested and the purpose of the study. Participants who were not deceived still benefit from the debriefing session. They will be able to understand why the experiment was created. The researchers also gain important insight into what the participants thought about during and after the experiment. This may lead to modifications in future research designs. Like survey and interview participants, participants in experiments and observational studies should be offered a report of the findings.

To what extent do debriefing and informed consent reduce the effects of deception? Research suggests that the majority of participants do not resent temporary deception and may have more positive feelings about the value of the research after debriefing than those who didn't participate in the study.[5] Nevertheless, deception is an ethically thorny issue and should be addressed with sensitivity and concern for research participants.

Rights to Privacy

Privacy laws in the United States are taken seriously. All individuals have a right to privacy, and researchers must respect that right. The importance of the right to privacy is illustrated with an example.

># >**snap**shot

Google: Tracking Search Patterns

According to Nielsen/NetRatings and SearchEngineWatch.com, Internet users in the United States spent about 26.5 hours a month online and executed 214 million searches a day, 91 million of them on Google. Google tracks searches by time of day, originating IP address, and sites on which the user clicked. Even though queries come from more than 100 countries, patterns emerge. Google provides these aggregate patterns on its website Google Zeitgeist, but it protects its raw data from prying eyes in compliance with its privacy policy. It knows, for example, that networking sites *Bebo* and *MySpace* generated the most Google searches and that Paris Hilton earned the top spot on searches on Google News. We are vitally interested in understanding the world around us, shown by the fact that ". . . 'oil spill' was one of the top 'topic searches' following the BP rig explosion." What makes Google tracking a researcher's goldmine is its ability to predict future trends as well as mirror current trends. Businesses are interested not only in these predictive capabilities but also because searches reveal things about individuals that they wouldn't willingly talk about with researchers. So, while Google publishes some of its aggregate trends on its Zeitgeist website, it is just beginning to explore how to use the more detailed data for its own business-development purposes.

www.google.com/intl/en/press/zeitgeist/index.html;

www.netratings.com; www.searchenginewatch.com

An employee of MonsterVideo, a large video company, is also a student at the local university. For a research project, this student and his team members decide to compare the video-viewing habits of a sample of customers. Using telephone interviews, the students begin their research. After inquiring about people's viewing habits and the frequency of rentals versus purchases, the students move on to the types of films people watch. They find that most participants answer questions about their preferences for children's shows, classics, best-sellers, mysteries, and science fiction. But the cooperation ceases when the students question the viewing frequency of pornographic movies. Without the guarantee of privacy, most people will not answer these kinds of questions truthfully, if at all. The study then loses key data.

The privacy guarantee is important not only to retain validity of the research but also to protect participants. In the previous example, imagine the harm that could be caused by releasing information on the viewing habits of certain citizens. Clearly, the confidentiality of survey answers is an important aspect of the participants' right to privacy. Once the guarantee of **confidentiality** is given, protecting that confidentiality is essential. The researcher protects participant confidentiality in several ways:

- Obtaining signed nondisclosure documents.
- Restricting access to participant identification.
- Revealing participant information only with written consent.
- Restricting access to data instruments where the participant is identified.
- Not disclosing data subsets.

Researchers should restrict access to information that reveals names, telephone numbers, addresses, or other identifying features. Only researchers who have signed nondisclosure, confidentiality forms should be allowed access to the data. Links between the data or database and the identifying information file should be weakened. Individual interview response sheets should be inaccessible to everyone except the editors and data entry personnel. Occasionally, data collection instruments should be destroyed once the data are in a data file. Data files that make it easy to reconstruct the profiles or identification of individual participants should be carefully controlled. For very small groups, data should not be made available because it is often easy to pinpoint a person within the group. Employee-satisfaction survey feedback in small units can be easily used to identify an individual through descriptive statistics alone. These last two protections are particularly important in human resources research.[6]

Has Trust Trumped Privacy?

Since e-commerce rang up its first sale, privacy advocates have been telling business that privacy is an important issue among online browsers and purchasers. An early Harris Poll survey conducted for *BusinessWeek* showed more than one-third of U.S. adults would be uncomfortable with their online actions being profiled, while 82 percent would be uncomfortable with online activities being merged with personally identifiable information such as income, driver's license number, credit data, and medical status. Researcher Alan Westin, president and publisher of *Privacy & American Business*, identified three different groups related to privacy: *privacy fundamentalists* (26 percent who feel they have lost their privacy and fear further erosion), *privacy pragmatists* (64 percent who are willing to share personal information when they understand the reasons for its use or see tangible benefits from sharing), and *privacy unconcerned* (10 percent for whom privacy is not an overriding concern). Even in the face of the inappropriate release of large private information data bases by government, financial institutions, and retailers entrusted with the information, a new study by ChoiceStream supports this narrowing of adults' privacy concerns. While two-thirds of adults still worry about the protection of personal identity information online, 57 percent are willing to trade privacy for personalization of content to providers they trust. And, not surprising, younger adults (ages 18–34) are more willing than the older adults to share their click patterns and their personal information.

www.clickstream.com; www.harrisinteractive.com

But privacy is more than confidentiality. A **right to privacy** means one has the right to refuse to be interviewed or to refuse to answer any question in an interview. Potential participants have a right to privacy in their own homes, including not admitting researchers and not answering telephones. And they have the right to engage in private behavior in private places without fear of observation. To address these rights, ethical researchers do the following:

- Inform participants of their right to refuse to answer any questions or participate in the study.
- Obtain permission to interview participants.
- Schedule field and phone interviews.
- Limit the time required for participation.
- Restrict observation to public behavior only.

Data Collection in Cyberspace

Some ethicists argue that the very conduct that results in resistance from participants—interference, invasiveness in their lives, denial of privacy rights—has encouraged researchers to investigate topics online that have long been the principal commodity of offline investigation. The novelty and convenience of communicating by computer has led researchers to cyberspace in search of abundant sources of data. Whether we call it the "wired society," "digital life," "computer-mediated communication," or "cyberculture," the growth of cyberstudies causes us to question how we gather data online, deal with participants, and present results.

In a special ethics issue of *Information Society*, scholars involved in cyberspace research concluded:

All participants agree that research in cyberspace provides no special dispensation to ignore ethical precepts. Researchers are obligated to protect human subjects and "do right" in electronic venues as in more conventional ones. Second, each participant recognizes that cyberspace poses complex ethical issues that may lack exact analogs in other types of inquiry. The ease of covert observation, the occasional blurry distinction between public and private venues, and the difficulty of obtaining the informed consent of subjects make cyber-research particularly vulnerable to ethical breaches by even the most scrupulous scholars. Third, all recognize that because research procedures or activities may be permissible or not precluded by law or policy, it does not follow that they are necessarily ethical or allowable. Fourth, all agree that the individual researcher has the ultimate responsibility for assuring that inquiry is not only done honestly, but done with ethical integrity.[7]

Issues relating to cyberspace in research also relate to data mining. The information collection devices available today were once the tools of the spy, the science fiction protagonist, or the superhero. Smart cards, biometrics (finger printing, retinal scans, facial recognition), electronic monitoring (closed circuit television, digital camera monitoring), global surveillance, and genetic identification (DNA) are just some of the technological tools being used by today's organizations to track and understand employees, customers, and suppliers. The data mining of all this information, collected from advanced and not necessarily obvious sources, offers infinite possibilities for research abuse.

The amount, in millions, that employers will lose this year due to employee fraud.

Data Mining Ethics

The primary ethical data-mining issues in cyberspace are privacy and consent. (See Exhibit 2-3.) Smart cards, those ubiquitous credit card–sized devices that embed personal information on a computer chip that is then matched to purchase, employment, or other behavior data, offer the researcher implied consent to participant surveillance. But the benefits of card use may be enough to hide from an unsuspecting user the data-mining purpose of the card. For example, The Kroger Co., one of the largest grocers in the United States, offers significant discounts for enrollment in its Kroger Plus Shopper's Card program.[8] Retailers, wholesalers, medical and legal service providers, schools, government agencies, and resorts, to name a few, use smart cards or their equivalent. In most instances, participants provide, although sometimes grudgingly, the personal information requested by enrollment procedures. But in others, enrollment is mandatory, such as when smart cards are used with those convicted of crimes and sentenced to municipal or state correction facilities or those attending specific schools. In some instances, mandatory sharing of information is initially for personal welfare and safety—such as when you admit yourself for a medical procedure and provide detailed information about medication or prior surgery. But in others, enrollment is for less critical but potentially attractive monetary benefits—for

>**Exhibit 2-3** The Seven Basic Principles of the U.S. Safe Harbor Agreement

Companies that comply with this voluntary U.S. data privacy pact are granted immunity from legal action under the EU's data protection directive.

- *Notice.* Companies must notify consumers/participants about what information is being collected, how that information will be used, whom that information will be shared with, and how individuals can contact the organization with any inquiries or complaints.

- *Choice.* Consumers/participants must be provided with an opt-out mechanism for any secondary uses of data and for disclosures to third parties. For sensitive information, participants must opt in before providing data that will be shared.

- *Access.* Individuals must have access to personal information about themselves that an organization holds and be able to correct, amend, or delete that information where it is inaccurate, except where the burden or expense of providing access would be disproportionate to the risks to the individual's privacy.

- *Security.* Organizations must take reasonable precautions to protect personal information from loss, misuse, and unauthorized access, disclosure, alteration, and destruction.

- *Onward transfer.* Companies disclosing personal data to a third party must, with certain exceptions, adhere to the notice and choice principles. A third party must subscribe to the safe-harbor principles.

- *Data integrity.* Reasonable steps must be taken to ensure that data collected are reliable, accurate, complete, and current.

- *Enforcement.* Companies must ensure there are readily available and affordable independent mechanisms to investigate consumer complaints, obligations to remedy problems, procedures to verify compliance with safe-harbor principles, and sufficiently rigorous sanctions to ensure compliance.

Source: Diane Bowers, "Privacy and the Research Industry in the U.S.," *ESOMAR Research World,* no. 7, July–August 2001, pp. 8–9 (http://www.esomar.nl/PDF/DataPrivacyUpdateUSA.pdf); Lori Enos, "Microsoft to Sign EU Privacy Accord," www.EcommerceTimes.com, May 16, 2001 (http://www.newsfactor.com/perl/story/9752.html); U.S. Department of Commerce, "Safe Harbor Overview," accessed November 30, 2002 (http://www.export.gov/safeharbor/sh_overview.html).

example, free car care services when a smart card is included with the keys to a new vehicle. The bottom line is that the organization collecting the information gains a major benefit: the potential for better understanding and competitive advantage.

European Union

General privacy laws may not be sufficient to protect the unsuspecting in the cyberspace realm of data collection. The 15 European Union (EU) countries started the new century by passing the European Commission's Data Protection Directive. Under the directive, commissioners can prosecute companies and block websites that fail to live up to its strict privacy standards. Specifically, the directive prohibits the transmission of names, addresses, ethnicity, and other personal information to any country that fails to provide adequate data protection. This includes direct mail lists, hotel and travel reservations, medical and work records, and orders for products, among a host of others.[9] U.S. industry and government agencies have resisted regulation of data flow. But the EU insists that it is the right of all citizens to find out what information about themselves is in a database and correct any mistakes. Few U.S. companies would willingly offer such access due to the high cost;[10] a perfect example of this reluctance is the difficulty individuals have correcting erroneous credit reports, even when such information is based on stolen personal identity or credit card transactions.

Yet questions remain regarding the definition of specific ethical behaviors for cyber-research, the sufficiency of existing professional guidelines, and the issue of ultimate responsibility for participants. If researchers are responsible for the ethical conduct of their research, are they solely responsible for the burden of protecting participants from every conceivable harm?

> Ethics and the Sponsor

There are also ethical considerations to keep in mind when dealing with the research client or sponsor. Whether undertaking product, market, personnel, financial, or other research, a sponsor has the right to receive ethically conducted research.

Information can make or break a business on one of the world's busiest avenues, Wall Street. That's why you need a researcher that can extract information while keeping results strictly confidential. Seaport Surveys is one such firm. It specializes in executive recruiting, as well as business-to-business interviewing and executive focus groups in the greater New York area.

www.seaportsurveys.com

Confidentiality

Some sponsors wish to undertake research without revealing themselves. They have a right to several types of confidentiality, including sponsor nondisclosure, purpose nondisclosure, and findings nondisclosure.

Companies have a right to dissociate themselves from the sponsorship of a research project. This type of confidentiality is called **sponsor nondisclosure.** Due to the sensitive nature of the management dilemma or the research question, sponsors may hire an outside consulting or research firm to complete research projects. This is often done when a company is testing a new product idea, to prevent potential consumers from being influenced by the company's current image or industry standing, or if a company is contemplating entering a new market, it may not wish to reveal its plans to competitors. In such cases, it is the responsibility of the researcher to respect this desire and devise a plan that safeguards the identity of the research sponsor.

Purpose nondisclosure involves protecting the purpose of the study or its details. A research sponsor may be testing a new idea that is not yet patented and may not want the competition to know of its plans. It may be investigating employee complaints and may not want to spark union activity, or the sponsor might be contemplating a new public stock offering, in which advance disclosure would spark the interest of authorities or cost the firm thousands or millions of dollars. Finally, even if a sponsor feels no need to hide its identity or the study's purpose, most sponsors want the research data and findings to be confidential, at least until the management decision is made. Thus sponsors usually demand and receive **findings nondisclosure** between themselves or their researchers and any interested but unapproved parties.

The Sponsor–Researcher Relationship

In an organizational setting, the researcher should look on the sponsoring manager as a client. An effective sponsor–researcher relationship is not achieved unless both fulfill their respective obligations and several critical barriers are overcome.

The obligations of managers are to specify their problems and provide researchers with adequate background information and access to company information gatekeepers. It is usually more effective if managers state their problems in terms of the decision choices they must make rather than the information they want. If this is done, both manager and researcher can jointly decide what information is needed.

Researchers also have obligations. Organizations expect them to develop a creative research design that will provide answers to important business questions. Not only should researchers provide data analyzed in terms of the problem specified, but they also should point out the limitations that affect the results. In the process, conflict may arise between what the decision maker wants and what the researcher can provide ethically or thinks should be provided. The sponsor wants certainty and simple, explicit recommendations, while the researcher often can offer only probabilities and hedged interpretations. This conflict is inherent in their respective roles and has no simple resolution. However, a workable balance can usually be found if each person is sensitive to the demands, ethical constraints, and restrictions imposed on the other.

Among the sources of manager–researcher conflict are:

- Knowledge gap between the researcher and the manager.
- Job status and internal, political coalitions to preserve status.
- Unneeded or inappropriate research.
- The right to quality research.

Knowledge Gap

Some conflicts between decision makers and researchers are traced to management's limited exposure to research. Managers seldom have either formal training in research methodology, the various aspects of research ethics, or research expertise gained through experience. And, due to the explosive growth of research technology in recent years, a knowledge gap has developed between managers and research specialists as more sophisticated investigative techniques have come into use. Thus, the research specialist removes the manager from his or her comfort zone: the manager must now put his or her faith, and sometimes his or her career, in the hands of the research specialist's knowledge and adherence to ethical standards.

Job Status and Internal Coalitions

In addition, managers often see research people as threats to their personal status. Managers still view management as the domain of the "intuitive artist" who is the master in this area. They may believe a request for research assistance implies they are inadequate to the task. These fears are often justified. The researcher's function is to test old ideas as well as new ones. To the insecure manager, the researcher is a potential rival.

The researcher will inevitably have to consider the corporate culture and political situations that develop in any organization. Members strive to maintain their niches and may seek ascendancy over their colleagues. Coalitions form and people engage in various self-serving activities, both overt and covert. As a result, research is blocked, or the findings or objectives of the research are distorted for an individual's self-serving purposes. To allow one's operations to be probed with a critical eye may be to invite trouble from others competing for promotion, resources, or other forms of organizational power.

Unneeded or Inappropriate Research

Not every managerial decision requires research. Business research has an inherent value only to the extent that it helps management make better decisions. Interesting information about consumers, employees, or competitors might be pleasant to have—but its value is limited if the information cannot be applied to a critical decision. If a study does not help management select more efficient, less risky, or more profitable alternatives than otherwise would be the case, the researcher has an ethical responsibility to question its use.

Right to Quality Research

An important ethical consideration for the researcher and the sponsor is the sponsor's **right to quality research**. This right entails:

- Providing a research design appropriate for the research question.
- Maximizing the sponsor's value for the resources expended.
- Providing data-handling and data-reporting techniques appropriate for the data collected.

From the proposal through the design to data analysis and final reporting, the researcher guides the sponsor on the proper techniques and interpretations. Often sponsors will have heard about a sophisticated data-handling technique and will want it used even when it is inappropriate for the problem at hand. The researcher should guide the sponsor so that this does not occur. The researcher should propose the design most suitable for the problem. The researcher should not propose activities designed to maximize researcher revenue or minimize researcher effort at the sponsor's expense.

Finally, we have all heard the remark, "You can lie with statistics." It is the researcher's responsibility to prevent that from occurring. The ethical researcher always follows the analytical rules and conditions for results to be correct. The ethical researcher reports findings in ways that minimize the drawing of false conclusions. The ethical researcher also uses charts, graphs, and tables to show the data objectively, despite the sponsor's preferred outcomes.

Sponsor's Ethics

Occasionally, research specialists may be asked by sponsors to participate in unethical behavior. Compliance by the researcher would be a breach of ethical standards. Some examples to be avoided are:

- Violating participant confidentiality.
- Changing data or creating false data to meet a desired objective.

- Changing data presentations or interpretations.
- Interpreting data from a biased perspective.
- Omitting sections of data analysis and conclusions.
- Making recommendations beyond the scope of the data collected.

Let's examine the effects of complying with these types of coercion. A sponsor may offer a promotion, future contracts, or a larger payment for the existing research contract; or the sponsor may threaten to fire the researcher or tarnish the researcher's reputation. For some researchers, the request may seem trivial and the reward high. But imagine for a moment what will happen to the researcher who changes research results. Although there is a promise of future research, can the sponsor ever trust that researcher again? If the researcher's ethical standards are for sale, which sponsor might be the highest bidder next time? Although the promise of future contracts seems enticing, it is unlikely to be kept. Each coercive reward or punishment has an equally poor outcome. The "greater than" contracted payment is a payoff. The threats to one's professional reputation cannot be carried out effectively by a sponsor who has tried to purchase you. So the rewards for behaving unethically are illusory.

What's the ethical course? Often, it requires confronting the sponsor's demand and taking the following actions:

- Educate the sponsor to the purpose of research.
- Explain the researcher's role in fact finding versus the sponsor's role in decision making.
- Explain how distorting the truth or breaking faith with participants leads to future problems.
- Failing moral suasion, terminate the relationship with the sponsor.

> Researchers and Team Members

Another ethical responsibility of researchers is their team's safety as well as their own. In addition, the responsibility for ethical behavior rests with the researcher who, along with assistants, is charged with protecting the anonymity of both the sponsor and the participant.

Safety

It is the researcher's responsibility to design a project so that the safety of all interviewers, surveyors, experimenters, or observers is protected. Several factors may be important to consider in ensuring a researcher's **right to safety.** Some urban areas and undeveloped rural areas may be unsafe for research assistants. If, for example, the researcher must personally interview people in a high-crime district, it is reasonable to provide a second team member to protect the researcher. Alternatively, if an assistant feels unsafe after visiting a neighborhood by car, an alternate researcher should be assigned to the destination.[11] It is unethical to require staff members to enter an environment where they feel physically threatened. Researchers who are insensitive to these concerns face both research and legal risks—the least of which involves having interviewers falsify instruments.

Ethical Behavior of Assistants

Researchers should require ethical compliance from team members just as sponsors expect ethical behavior from the researcher. Assistants are expected to carry out the sampling plan, to interview or observe participants without bias, and to accurately record all necessary data. Unethical behavior, such as filling in an interview sheet without having asked the participant the questions, cannot be tolerated. The behavior of the assistants is under the direct control of the responsible researcher or field

One consequence of the financial crisis was multiple home foreclosures. In some neighborhoods, these abandoned properties have changed the very landscape of safety for residents and visitors alike. Methodologies that would require researchers to visit such neighborhoods would need to be carefully assessed. If a visit was deemed crucial to the research, significant safeguards would need to be in place.

supervisor. If an assistant behaves improperly in an interview or shares a participant's interview sheet with an unauthorized person, it is the researcher's responsibility. Consequently, all assistants should be well trained and supervised.

Protection of Anonymity

As discussed previously, researchers and assistants protect the confidentiality of the sponsor's information and the anonymity of the participants. Each researcher handling data should be required to sign a confidentiality and nondisclosure statement.

> Professional Standards

Various standards of ethics exist for the professional researcher. Many corporations, professional associations, and universities have a **code of ethics.** The impetus for these policies and standards can be traced to two documents: the Belmont Report of 1979 and the *Federal Register* of 1991.[12] Society or association guidelines include ethical standards for the conduct of research. One comprehensive source contains 51 official codes of ethics issued by 45 associations in business, health, and law.[13] The business section of this source consists of ethics standards for:

Accounting—American Institute of Certified Public Accountants.

Advertising—American Association of Advertising Agencies; Direct Marketing Association.

Banking—American Bankers Association.

Engineering—American Association of Engineering Societies; National Society of Professional Engineers.

Financial planning—Association for Investment Management and Research; Certified Financial Planner Board of Standards/Institute of Certified Financial Planners; International Association for Financial Planning.

>**snap**shot

Is Your Research Project Leaving the Country?

Offshoring is defined as the movement of a process done at a company in one country to the same or another company in a different country. These processes in research often include IT (information technology), business, or knowledge processes. The primary reason to offshore research services is to lower the cost of the research. Offshoring tends to be more prevalent at larger research firms.

There are significant risks associated with offshoring research services, as Gordon Morris, global insights manager for Sony Ericsson (London, UK) discovered. During a global research project for the Experia X10 Android phone, sensitive business plans were shared with the contracted researchers. As a result of offshoring of some research services, information about the 2010 phone launch leaked several months early. "We estimate the potential damage caused by the leak at approximately £100 million," shared Morris. Leaks may be more likely to occur when offshoring is used because intellectual property standards, safe computing standards, and contract laws vary from country to country. Also, high employee turnover in some developing countries can also add to this risk.

In 2009 a new trade group was formed to encourage transparency in offshoring of research services: the Foundation for Transparency in Offshoring (FTO). A survey fielded to 850 U.S. and international research buyers and providers indicated that clients were more likely to think their projects did not involve offshoring than was actually true. Clients also were much more likely than research services suppliers to think clients should be told about offshoring. "Very few buyers have sufficient information to assess the relative strengths and risks associated with offshoring," said Tom H. C. Anderson, FTO founder and chairman, and managing partner of the research consultancy Anderson Analytics. While not taking a stand for or against offshoring, the FTO encourages research companies to register their project practices and earn one of two seals: one seal certifies that the research organizations that do offshore research services comply with the FTO disclosure standards, which are modeled after the EU's Safe Harbour Compliance Framework; the second seal identifies research organizations that do not offshore services at all.

FTO hopes that research buyers will look for the certification seals when purchasing research services. As Sonia Baldia, partner at Mayer Brown LLP and a legal expert on offshoring explained, "Clients absolutely need to know about any offshore subcontracting and the location in order to gauge risks and protect themselves."

www.offshoringtransparency.org

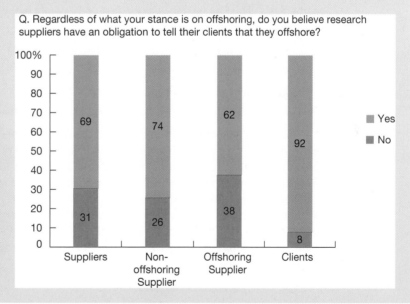

Q. Regardless of what your stance is on offshoring, do you believe research suppliers have an obligation to tell their clients that they offshore?

Human resources—American Society for Public Administration; Society for Human Resource Management.

Insurance—American Institute for Chartered Property Casualty Underwriters; American Society of Chartered Life Underwriters and Chartered Financial Consultants.

Management—Academy of Management; The Business Roundtable.

Real estate—National Association of Realtors.

Other professional associations' codes have detailed research sections: the American Marketing Association, the American Association for Public Opinion Research, the American Psychological Association, the American Political Science Association, the American Sociological Association, and the Society of Competitive Intelligence Professionals. These associations update their codes frequently.

We commend professional societies and business organizations for developing standards. However, without enforcement, standards are ineffectual. Effective codes (1) are regulative, (2) protect the public interest and the interests of the profession served by the code, (3) are behavior-specific, and (4) are *enforceable.* A study that assessed the effects of personal and professional values on ethical consulting behavior concluded:

> The findings of this study cast some doubt on the effectiveness of professional codes of ethics and corporate policies that attempt to deal with ethical dilemmas faced by business consultants. A mere codification of ethical values of the profession or organization may not counteract ethical ambivalence created and maintained through reward systems. The results suggest that unless ethical codes and policies are consistently reinforced with a significant reward and punishment structure and truly integrated into the business culture, these mechanisms would be of limited value in actually regulating unethical conduct.[14]

Federal, state, and local governments also have laws, policies, and procedures in place to regulate research on human beings. The U.S. government began a process that covers all research having federal support. Initially implemented in 1966, the Institutional Review Boards (IRBs) engage in a risk assessment and benefit analysis review of proposed research. The Department of Health and Human Services (HHS) translated the federal regulations into policy. Most other federal and state agencies follow the HHS-developed guidelines. Exhibit 2-4 describes some characteristics of the IRB process.

The current review requirement has been relaxed so that research that is routine no longer needs to go through the complete process.[15] Each institution receiving funding from HHS or doing research for HHS is required to have its own IRB to review research proposals. Many institutions require all research, whether funded or unfunded by the government, to undergo review by the local IRB. The IRBs concentrate on two areas. First is the guarantee of obtaining complete, informed consent from participants. This can be traced to the first of 10 points in the Nuremberg Code.[16] Complete informed consent has four characteristics:

1. The participant must be competent to give consent.
2. Consent must be voluntary.
3. Participants must be adequately informed to make a decision.
4. Participants should know the possible risks or outcomes associated with the research.

The second item of interest to the IRB is the risk assessment and benefit analysis review. In the review, risks are considered when they add to the normal risk of daily life. Significantly, the only benefit considered is the immediate importance of the knowledge to be gained. Possible long-term benefits from applying the knowledge that may be gained in the research are not considered.[17]

Other federal legislation that governs or influences the ways in which research is carried out are the Right to Privacy laws. Public Law 95-38 is the Privacy Act of 1974. This was the first law guaranteeing Americans the right to privacy. Public Law 96-440, the Privacy Protection Act of 1980, carries the right to privacy further. These two laws are the basis for protecting the privacy and confidentiality of the participants and the data.

> Resources for Ethical Awareness

There is optimism for improving ethical awareness. According to the Center for Business Ethics at Bentley College, over a third of Fortune 500 companies have ethics officers, a substantial rise. Almost 90 percent of business schools have ethics programs, up from a handful several years ago.[18] Exhibit 2-5 provides a list of recommended resources for business students, researchers, and managers. The Center for Ethics and Business at Loyola Marymount University provides an online environment for discussing issues related to the necessity, difficulty, costs, and rewards of conducting business ethically. Its website offers a comprehensive list of business and research ethics links.[19]

>**Exhibit 2-4** Characteristics of the Institutional Review Board (IRB) Process

Step	Process	Examples
Purpose	A committee is established to review and approve research involving human subjects.	Review minimizes potential research-related risks and requires full disclosure so that participants can make informed decisions about whether or not to participate.
Applications	Determine the level of participant involvement in your study and select appropriate forms.	• Involves human subjects. • Does not involve human subjects. • Analyzes coded (secondary) data. • Analyzes biological specimens.
Initial Review	Center level review (previously exempt research).	• Research involving watching public behavior of children, in which the investigator does not take part in the activities, can be reviewed at the center level. • Research conducted in established or commonly accepted educational settings, involving normal educational practices, such as (1) research on regular and special education instructional strategies, or (2) research on the effectiveness of or the comparison among instructional techniques, curricula, or classroom management methods. (Surveys or interviews cannot be center level reviewed.)
	Expedited review.	Research on individual or group behavior characteristics (such as studies of perception, motivation, communication, cultural beliefs or practices, and social behavior) or research employing survey, interview, oral history, focus group, program evaluation, human factors evaluation or quality assurance methodologies when the research does not qualify for center level review.
	Full review.	Research involving physically intrusive procedures; where previous experience has been shown to create a potential of risk to subjects; that may result in a significant level of psychological or physical stress.
Prepare IRB Materials	An IRB submission form and research protocol.	Submissions are often accompanied by: • Informed-consent forms. • Completed informed consent form checklists. • Evidence of approval by cooperative IRBs at other sites. • Data collection instruments. • Certification of translation for consents or instruments to be used with non-English-speaking subjects. • Brochure/recruitment materials.
Continuing Review	Research approved for limited period of time (e.g., one year).	Beyond time period, research cannot continue without IRB approval: A continuation request is submitted.
Revision	The principal investigator submits in writing any changes he or she intends to make to the study to the IRB.	Revision to the research protocol (e.g., changes to the informed consent form, survey instruments used, or number and nature of subjects).
IRB Actions	Approve Pending	Approve as submitted. Pending: (1) Researcher clarifies an aspect of the study, provides additional information, or discusses the potential risks and benefits of the study, or (2) makes minor changes to the informed consent document(s) or the research protocol.
	Disapprove	Disapprove: Proposed research places the participants at risks that outweigh the benefit or value of the gained knowledge; study raises unacceptable ethical questions.

Source: Based on Nova Southeastern University's review information: http://www.nova.edu/irb/process.html#init_review.

>**Exhibit 2-5** Resources for Ethical Awareness

Journals and Magazines
Business Ethics; www.business-ethics.com/.
Business Ethics Quarterly; https://secure.pdcnet.org/pdc/bvdb.nsf/journal?openform&journal=pdc_beq.
Business and Society; (IASB Journal); http://bas.sagepub.com/.
Business and Society Review; http://www.wiley.com/bw/journal.asp?ref=0045-3609.
Electronic Journal of Business Ethics and Organizational Studies (EJBO); http://ejbo.jyu.fi/.
Ethics Newsline; www.globalethics.org/newsline/.
Ethikos; www.ethikos.com/.
International Business Ethics Review Newsletter; http://businessethicsonline.info/.
Journal of the Center for Business Ethics at Bentley College; http://www.bentley.edu/cbe/.
Journal of Business Ethics; www.springerlink.com/content/100281/.
Journal of Business Ethics; http://www.ingentaconnect.com/content/klu/busi.

Research, Training, and Conferences
Applied Research Ethics National Association (ARENA) Boston, MA (617-423-4412; www.primr.org/).
Business ethics conferences, The Conference Board, New York, NY (212-759-0900; www.conference-board.org).
Center for Business Ethics, Bentley College, Waltham, MA (781-891-2000; www.bentley.edu/cbe/).
Center for Ethical Business Culture, University of St. Thomas, Minneapolis, MN (800-328 6819 Ext. 2-4120; www.cebcglobal.org/).
Center for Ethics and Business, Loyola Marymount University, Los Angeles, CA (310-338-2700; www.ethicsandbusiness.org).
Center for Professional and Applied Ethics, University of North Carolina at Charlotte, Charlotte, NC (704-687-2850; http://ethics.uncc.edu/).
Center for the Study of Ethics in the Professions, Illinois Institute of Technology, Chicago, IL (312-567-3017; www.iit.edu/departments/csep/).
Council of American Survey Research Organization (CASRO), Port Jefferson, NY (631-928-6954; www.casro.org).
Dartmouth College Ethics Institute, Hanover, NH (603-646-1263; www.dartmouth.edu/~ethics/).
Edmond J. Safra Foundation Center for Ethics, Harvard University, Cambridge, MA (617-495-1336; www.ethics.harvard.edu/).
Electronic Privacy Information Center, Washington, DC (202-483-1140; www.epic.org).
Ethics Corps Training for Business Leaders, Josephson Institute of Ethics, Marina del Rey, CA (310-306-1868; www.josephsoninstitute.org).
Ethics Resource Center, Washington, DC (202-737-2258; www.ethics.org).
European Business Ethics Network, Breukelen, The Netherlands (32 016 32 37 79; www.eben.org).
Graduate Research Ethics Education Workshop, Association of Practical and Professional Ethics, Indiana University, Bloomington, IN (812-855-6450; http://www.indiana.edu/~appe/).
Institute for Business and Professional Ethics, DePaul University, Chicago, IL (312-362-6624; http://commerce.depaul.edu/ethics/).
International Association for Business and Society (www.iabs.net/).
Marketing Research Association, Rocky Hill, CT (860-257-4008; www.mra-net.org).
Markkula Center for Applied Ethics, Santa Clara University, Santa Clara, CA (408-554-5319; www.scu.edu/ethics/practicing/focusareas/business/).

>**Exhibit 2-5** Resources for Ethical Awareness (*concluded*)

Research, Training, and Conferences (*cont.*)
Teaching Research Ethics, Poynter Center, Indiana University, Bloomington, IN (812-855-0621; http://www.indiana.edu/~poynter/).
The Beard Center for Leadership in Ethics, Palumbo-Donahue School of Business Administration, Duquesne University, Pittsburgh. PA (412-396-5475; www.business.duq.edu/Beard/corporate.html).
The Carol and Lawrence Ziklin Center for Business Ethics Research, The Wharton School, University of Pennsylvania, Philadelphia, A (215-898-1166; www.zicklincenter.org/).
World Association of Public Opinion Research (WAPOR), Lincoln, NE (402-458-2030; www.unl.edu/WAPOR/).
World Association of Research Professionals (ESOMAR), Amsterdam, The Netherlands (31 20 589 78 00; www.esomar.org/).

>summary

1 Ethics are norms or standards of behavior that guide moral choices about our behavior and our relationships with others. Ethics differ from legal constraints, in which generally accepted standards have defined penalties that are universally enforced. The goal of ethics in research is to ensure that no one is harmed or suffers adverse consequences from research activities.

   As research is designed, several ethical considerations must be balanced:

• Protect the rights of the *participant* or subject.

• Ensure the *sponsor* receives ethically conducted and reported research.

• Follow ethical standards when *designing research*.

• Protect the *safety* of the researcher and team.

• Ensure the *research team* follows the design.

2 In general, research must be designed so that a participant does not suffer physical harm, discomfort, pain, embarrassment, or loss of privacy. Begin data collection by explaining to participants the benefits expected from the research. Explain that their rights and well-being will be adequately protected and say how that will be done. Be certain that interviewers obtain the informed consent of the participant.

The use of deception is questionable; when it is used, debrief any participant who has been deceived.

3 Many *sponsors* wish to undertake research without revealing themselves. Sponsors have the right to demand and receive confidentiality between themselves and the researchers. Ethical researchers provide sponsors with the research design needed to solve the managerial question. The ethical researcher shows the data objectively, despite the sponsor's preferred outcomes.

   The research team's safety is the responsibility of the researcher. Researchers should require ethical compliance from team members in following the research design, just as sponsors expect ethical behavior from the researcher.

4 Many corporations and research firms have adopted a code of ethics. Several professional associations have detailed research provisions. Of interest are the American Association for Public Opinion Research, the American Marketing Association, the American Political Science Association, the American Psychological Association, and the American Sociological Association. Federal, state, and local governments have laws, policies, and procedures in place to regulate research on human beings.

>keyterms

code of ethics 44

confidentiality 37

debriefing 35

deception 34

ethics 32

informed consent 34

nondisclosure:

   findings 41

   purpose 41

   sponsor 41

right to privacy 38

right to quality 42

right to safety 43

>discussionquestions

Making Research Decisions

1 **A Competitive Coup in the In-Flight Magazine.** When the manager for market intelligence of AutoCorp, a major automotive manufacturer, boarded the plane in Chicago, her mind was on shrinking market share and late product announcements. As she settled back to enjoy the remains of a hectic day, she reached for the in-flight magazine. It was jammed into the seat pocket in front of her.

Crammed into this already tiny space was a report with a competitor's logo, marked "Confidential—Restricted Circulation." It contained a description of new product announcements for the next two years. Not only was it intended for a small circle of senior executives, but it also answered the questions she had recently proposed to an external research firm.

The proposal for the solicited research could be canceled. Her research budget, already savaged, could be saved. She was home free, legally and career-wise.

She foresaw only one problem. In the last few months, AutoCorp's newly hired ethicist had revised the firm's Business Conduct Guidelines. They now required company employees in possession of a competitor's information to return it or face dismissal. But it was still a draft and not formally approved. She had the rest of the flight to decide whether to return the document to the airline or slip it into her briefcase.

a What are the most prudent decisions she can make about her responsibilities to herself and others?

b What are the implications of those decisions even if there is no violation of law or regulation?

2 **Free Waters in Miro Beach: Boaters Inc. versus City Government.**[20] The city commissioners of Miro Beach proposed limits on boaters who anchor offshore in waterfront areas of the St. Lucinda River adjoining the city. Residents had complained of pollution from the live-aboard boaters. The parking lot of boats created an unsightly view.

The city based its proposed ordinance on research done by the staff. The staff did not hold graduate degrees in either public or business administration, and it was not known if staff members were competent to conduct research. The staff requested a proposal from a team of local university professors who had conducted similar work in the past. The research cost was $10,000. After receiving the proposal, the staff chose to do the work itself and not expend resources for the project. Through an unidentified source, the professors later learned their proposal contained enough information to guide the city's staff and suggested data collection areas that might provide information that could justify the boaters' claims.

Based on the staff's one-time survey of waterfront litter, "pump-out" samples, and a weekly frequency count of boats, an ordinance was drafted and a public workshop was held. Shortly after, a group of concerned boat owners formed Boaters Inc., an association to promote boating, raise funds, and lobby

the commission. The group's claims were that the boaters (1) spent thousands of dollars on community goods and services, (2) did not create the litter, and (3) were being unjustly penalized because the commission's fact finding was flawed.

With the last claim in mind, the boaters flooded the city with public record requests. The clerks reported that some weeks the requests were one per day. Under continued pressure, the city attorney hired a private investigator (PI) to infiltrate Boaters Inc. to collect information. He rationalized this on the grounds that the boaters had challenged the city's grant applications in order to "blackmail the city into dropping plans to regulate the boaters."

The PI posed as a college student and worked for a time in the home of the boater organization's sponsor while helping with mailings. Despite the PI's inability to corroborate the city attorney's theory, he recommended conducting a background investigation on the organization's principal, an employee of a tabloid newspaper. (The FBI, on request of city or county police organizations, generally performs background investigations.)

The PI was not a boating enthusiast and soon drew suspicion. Simultaneously, the organization turned up the heat on the city by requesting what amounted to 5,000 pages of information—"studies and all related documents containing the word 'boat.'" Failing to get a response from Miro Beach, the boaters filed suit under the Florida Public Records Act. By this time, the city had spent $20,000.

The case stalled, went to appeal, and was settled in favor of the boaters. A year later, the organization's principal filed an invasion of privacy and slander suit against the city attorney, the PI, and the PI's firm. After six months, the suit was amended to include the city itself and sought $1 million in punitive damages.

a What are the most prudent decisions the city can make about its responsibilities to itself and others?

b What are the implications of those decisions even if there is no violation of law or regulation?

3 **The High Cost of Organizational Change.** It was his first year of college teaching, and there were no summer teaching assignments for new hires. But the university was kind enough to steer him to an aviation firm, Avionics Inc., which needed help creating an organizational assessment survey. The assignment was to last five weeks, but it paid about the same as teaching all summer. The work was just about as perfect as it gets for an organizational behavior specialist. Avionics Inc.'s vice president, whom he met the first day, was cordial and smooth. The researcher would report to a senior manager who was coordinating the project with the human resources and legal departments.

It was soon apparent that in the 25-year history of Avionics Inc., there had never been an employee survey. This was understandable given management's lack of concern for employee complaints. Working conditions had deteriorated without management intervention, and government inspectors counted the number of heads down at desks as an index of performance. To make matters worse, the engineers were so disgruntled that word of unionization had spread like wildfire. A serious organizing effort was planned before the VP could approve the survey.

Headquarters dispatched nervous staffers to monitor the situation and generally involve themselves with every aspect of the questionnaire. Shadowed, the young researcher began to feel apprehension turn to paranoia. He consoled himself, however, with the goodwill of 500 enthusiastic, cooperative employees who had pinned their hopes for a better working environment to the results of this project.

The data collection was textbook perfect. No one had asked to preview the findings or had shown any particular interest. In the fifth week, he boarded the corporate jet with the VP and senior manager to make a presentation at headquarters. Participants at the headquarters location were invited to attend. Management was intent on heading off unionization by showing its confidence in the isolated nature of "a few engineers' complaints." They had also promised to engage the participants in action planning over the next few days.

An hour into the flight, the Avionics Inc. VP turned from his reading to the young researcher and said, "We have seen your results, you know. And we would like you to change two key findings. They are not all that critical to this round of fixing the 'bone orchard,' and you'll have another crack at it as a real consultant in the fall."

"But that would mean breaking faith with your employees . . . people who trusted me to present the results objectively. It's what I thought you wanted . . ."

"Yes, well, look at it this way," replied the VP. "All of your findings we can live with except these two. They're an embarrassment to senior management. Let me put it plainly. We have government contracts into the foreseeable future. You could retire early with consulting income from this place. Someone will meet us on the runway with new slides. What do you say?"

a What are the most prudent decisions Avionics Inc. can make about its responsibilities to itself and others?

b What are the implications of those decisions even if there is no violation of law or regulation?

4 Data-Mining Ethics and Company Growth Square Off. SupplyCo. is a supplier to a number of firms in an industry. This industry has a structure that includes suppliers, manufacturers, distributors, and consumers. Several companies are involved in the manufacturing process—from processed parts to creation of the final product—with each firm adding some value to the product.

By carefully mining its customer data warehouse, SupplyCo. reveals a plausible new model for manufacturing and distributing industry products that would increase the overall *The scenario in the Cummins Engines video case has some of the same properties as this ethical dilemma.* efficiency of the industry system, reduce costs of production (leading to greater industry profits and more sales for SupplyCo.), and result in greater sales and profits for some of the industry's manufacturers (SupplyCo.'s customers).

On the other hand, implementing the model would hurt the sales and profits of other firms that are also SupplyCo.'s customers but which are not in a position (due to manpower, plant, or equipment) to benefit from the new manufacturing/distribution model. These firms would lose sales, profits, and market share and potentially go out of business.

Does SupplyCo. have an obligation to protect the interests of *all* its customers and to take no action that would harm any of them, since SupplyCo. had the data within its warehouse only because of its relationship with its customers? (It would betray some of its customers if it were to use the data in a manner that would cause these customers harm.) Or does it have a more powerful obligation to its stockholders and employees to aggressively pursue the new model that research reveals would substantially increase its sales, profits, and market share against competitors?

a What are the most prudent decisions SupplyCo. Can make about its responsibilities to itself and others?

b What are the implications of those decisions even if there is no violation of law or regulation?

From the Headlines

5 Assume you were contracted as a research supplier to Apple during the development of the iPad, introduced in 2010. What ethical issues would have influenced your firm's behavior in its involvement with this project?

>cases*

 Akron Children's Hospital

Proofpoint: Capitalizing on a Reporter's Love of Statistics

 Cummins Engines

* You will find a description of each case in the Case Abstracts section of this textbook. Check the Case Index to determine whether a case provides data, the research instrument, video, or other supplementary material. Written cases are downloadable from the text website (www.mhhe.com/cooper11e). All video material and video cases are available from the Online Learning Center. The film reel icon indicates a video case or video material relevant to the case.

>chapter 3

Thinking Like a Researcher

>learningobjectives

After reading this chapter, you should understand...

1. The terminology used by professional researchers employing scientific thinking.

2. What you need to formulate a solid research hypothesis.

3. The need for sound reasoning to enhance business research results.

> ❝ Brand communities play a pivotal role for a brand connecting with its consumers, and as one of our Never Ending Friending focus group respondent notes: "I want brands to be my friends," which means that consumers would like to have common ideas, conversations and benefits delivered to them on their own terms. ❞
>
> Judit Nagy, vice president, consumer insights,
> MySpace/Fox Interactive Media

Truly effective research is more likely to result when a marketing research supplier works collaboratively with its client throughout the research process. However, not all clients are trained in research methodology, and some come from backgrounds other than marketing. The supplier needs to understand the client's background in order to effectively develop the collaboration. We rejoin Henry and Associates as Jason Henry strives to profile the research knowledge, if any, of his client's representative—Myra Wines—the individual with whom he will be working on the MindWriter CompleteCare laptop servicing assessment project.

"Myra, have you had any experience with research suppliers?" asks Jason.

"Some. Actually, I worked for one of your competitors for a short time after college, on a project with the U.S. Army. That project helped me decide that research wasn't my life's work—not that it wasn't and isn't an important field and an important part of my new responsibilities."

"No need to apologize. Some of us have what it takes and others don't."

"Actually, there wasn't anything missing in my ability to observe data, or build rapport with study participants, or find insights," shares Myra. "The project made all the papers; you probably read about it."

"Refresh my memory."

"The death rate near one Army munitions testing area was unexplainably high. Local activists were trying to shut it down, fearing it was an environmental hazard. The Army had a vested interest in keeping it open. Besides, it didn't think the civilian deaths had anything to do with the firing range. U.S. Senator Sly forced the Army to investigate. Since the Army thought it had a public relations job on its hands, my firm was a logical choice; PR campaigns were a specialty.

"The firing range was a played-out mine, strip-mined until it was worse than a moonscape. The area had once been a prosperous mining region, where the people were known for fearlessly and proudly going out to dig and produce. The nearest town was so severely economically depressed that, for the pitifully few jobs the Army provided, the folks welcomed the military in to bomb their backyard to cinders.

"The cannon the Army was testing was impressive. Troops armed it with 3-inch shells, put on ear protectors and goggles, and lobbed shells into the range. There would be a tremendous flash and boom, and the shells would go roaring and soaring out of sight. We would soon hear a tremendous boom coming back to us and see dust and ash kicked up several hundred feet. We were all very happy not to be downrange. When we went downrange later, we found a huge crater and a fused puddle of iron, but nothing else but slag and molten rocks.

"There was one problem. About every 20th shell would be a dud. It would fly off and land, and maybe kick up some dust, but explode it would not.

"On paper, this was not supposed to be a problem. The Army sent an officious second lieutenant to brief us. He showed us reports that the Army had dropped such duds from hundred-foot platforms, from helicopters, had applied torches to them—everything—and had discovered them to be completely inert. The only thing he claimed would ignite one of these duds was to drop another live bomb on it.

"Regrettably, this proved not to be the case. My team had barely finished its initial briefing when in the middle of the night we heard one of these so-called duds explode. We rushed out at dawn and, sure enough, found a new crater, molten slag, molten rock, and so forth. It was quite a mystery.

"Our team took shifts doing an all-night observation study. During my two-hour stint, my partner and I saw people with flashlights moving around in there.

"We didn't know if the people were military or civilian. We learned later that locals were coming in at night, intending to crack open the bombs and scavenge for copper wire or anything they thought was salvageable. Except, of course, their actions occasionally ignited one of the beauties and erased any evidence of a crime being committed by vaporizing the perpetrators on the spot.

"Part of our research was to measure public sentiment about the firing range among the locals. During our stay in the area, we discovered the locals were involved in every kind of thrill sport. It was not unusual to see a 50-mile auto race with four ambulances on hand on the edge of the oval, to cart off the carnage to the surgical hospital in the next county. I saw men leap into cars with threadbare tires, loose wheels, malfunctioning brakes, with brake fluid and transmission fluid drooling all over the track. They could wheel their cars out onto the track on a tire they knew was thin as tissue, and if it blew out and put them in the hospital, their reaction was 'Some days you can't win for losin'.' Nobody thought anything of this. If we asked, their answer was, 'I'll go when my number is up,' or 'It's not in my hands.'

"Their attitude made sense, from a cultural-economic view. That attitude had permitted the men to go down in the mines year after year. Even the local sheriff wouldn't stop their daredevil behavior. 'They are going to die anyway,' he was overheard remarking. 'We all are going to die. People die every month that never go out on that dirt track.' Of course, unlike driving a car, messing with a potentially live bomb didn't leave much to skill but left everything to chance.

"The Army had considered an educational campaign to keep the scavengers out but, given our findings, decided it couldn't deal with such thinking by applying logic. Instead, it changed its procedure. The troops would now fire the shells in the morning and spend the afternoon finding the duds, to which they attached kerosene lanterns. At dusk, a fighter-bomber would fly over the area and bomb the lanterns—and the duds—to a molecular state. It was neat and it worked. And the death rate of the locals dropped dramatically."

As Myra finished her story, Jason asks, "It sounds like a successful project. By studying the locals' attitudes and behavior, you could discard the alternative of the education campaign. Why did you decide research wasn't for you?"

"My boss didn't like the idea that I broke confidentiality and told a local reporter what the locals were doing. I'd seen someone's dad or brother blown to pieces and felt I had to act. My dismissal taught me one of the rules of good research—the client always gets to choose whether to use, or release, the findings of any study."

> The Language of Research

When we do research, we seek to know what is in order to understand, explain, and predict phenomena. We might want to answer the question "What will be the department's reaction to the new flexible work schedule?" or "Why did the stock market price surge higher when all normal indicators suggested it would go down?" When dealing with such questions, we must agree on definitions. Which members of the department: clerical or professional? What kind of reaction? What are normal indicators? These questions require the use of concepts, constructs, and definitions.

Concepts

To understand and communicate information about objects and events, there must be a common ground on which to do it. Concepts serve this purpose. A **concept** is a generally accepted collection of meanings or characteristics associated with certain events, objects, conditions, situations, and behaviors. Classifying and categorizing objects or events that have common characteristics beyond any single observation creates concepts. When you think of a spreadsheet or a warranty card, what comes to mind is not a single example but your collected memories of all spreadsheets and warranty cards, from which you abstract a set of specific and definable characteristics.

We abstract such meanings from our experiences and use words as labels to designate them. For example, we see a man passing and identify that he is running, walking, skipping, crawling, or hopping. These movements all represent concepts. We also have abstracted certain visual elements by which we identify that the moving object is an adult male, rather than an adult female or a truck or a horse. We use numerous concepts daily in our thinking, conversing, and other activities.

Sources of Concepts

Concepts that are in frequent and general use have been developed over time through shared language usage. We acquire them through personal experience. Ordinary concepts make up the bulk of communication even in research, but we often run into difficulty trying to deal with an uncommon concept or a newly advanced idea. One way to handle this problem is to borrow from other languages (e.g., *gestalt*) or to borrow from other fields (e.g., from art, *impressionism*). The concept of gravitation is borrowed from physics and used in marketing in an attempt to explain why people shop where they do. The concept of distance is used in attitude measurement to describe degree of variability between the attitudes of two or more persons. Threshold is used effectively to describe a concept about the way we perceive.

Sometimes we need to adopt new meanings for words (make a word cover a different concept) or develop new labels for concepts. The recent broadening of the meaning of *model* is an example of the first instance; the development of concepts such as *sibling* and *status-stress* is an example of the second. When we adopt new meanings or develop new labels, we begin to develop a specialized jargon or terminology. Jargon no doubt contributes to efficiency of communication among specialists, but it excludes everyone else.

Importance to Research

In research, special problems grow out of the need for concept precision and inventiveness. We design hypotheses using concepts. We devise measurement concepts by which to test these hypothetical statements. We gather data using these measurement concepts. The success of research hinges on (1) how clearly we conceptualize and (2) how well others understand the concepts we use. For example, when we survey people on the question of customer loyalty, the questions we use need to tap faithfully the attitudes of the participants. Attitudes are abstract, yet we must attempt to measure them using carefully selected concepts.

The challenge is to develop concepts that others will clearly understand. We might, for example, ask participants for an estimate of their family's total income. This may seem to be a simple, unambiguous concept, but we will receive varying and confusing answers unless we restrict or narrow the concept by specifying:

- Time period, such as weekly, monthly, or annually.
- Before or after income taxes.
- For head of family only or for all family members.
- For salary and wages only or also for dividends, interest, and capital gains.
- Income in kind, such as free rent, employee discounts, or food stamps.

Constructs

Concepts have progressive levels of abstraction—that is, the degree to which the concept does or does not have something objective to refer to. *Table* is an objective concept. We can point to a table, and we have images of the characteristics of all tables in our mind. An abstraction like *personality* is much more difficult to visualize. Such abstract concepts are often called constructs. A **construct** is an image or abstract idea specifically invented for a given research and/or theory-building purpose. We build

>Exhibit 3-1 Constructs Composed of Concepts in a Job Redesign

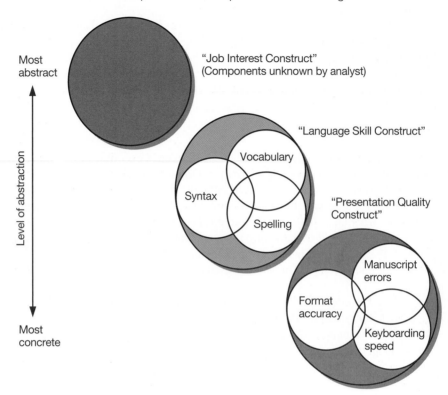

constructs by combining the simpler, more concrete concepts, especially when the idea or image we intend to convey is not subject to direct observation. When Jason and Myra tackle MindWriter's research study, they will struggle with the construct of *satisfied service customer.*

Concepts and constructs are easily confused. Consider this example: Heather is a human resource analyst at CadSoft, an architectural software company that employs technical writers to write product manuals, and she is analyzing task attributes of a job in need of redesign. She knows the job description for technical writer consists of three components: presentation quality, language skill, and job interest. Her job analysis reveals even more characteristics.

Exhibit 3-1 illustrates some of the concepts and constructs Heather is dealing with. The concepts at the bottom of the exhibit (format accuracy, manuscript errors, and keyboarding speed) are the most concrete and easily measured. We are able to observe keyboarding speed, for example, and even with crude measures agree on what constitutes slow and fast keyboarders. Keyboarding speed is one concept in the group that defines a construct that the human resource analyst calls "presentation quality." Presentation quality is really not directly observable. It is a nonexistent entity, a "constructed type," used to communicate the combination of meanings presented by the three concepts. Heather uses it only as a label for the concepts she has discovered are related empirically.

Concepts at the next level in Exhibit 3-1 are vocabulary, syntax, and spelling. Heather also finds them to be related. They form a construct that she calls "language skill." She has chosen this term because the three concepts together define the language requirement in the job description. Language skill is placed at a higher level of abstraction in the exhibit because two of the concepts it comprises, vocabulary and syntax, are more difficult to observe and their measures are more complex.

Heather has not yet measured the last construct, "job interest." It is the least observable and the most difficult to measure. It will likely be composed of numerous concepts—many of which will be quite abstract. Researchers sometimes refer to such entities as **hypothetical constructs** because they can be inferred only from the data; thus, they are presumed to exist but must await further testing to see what they actually consist of. If research shows the concepts and constructs in this example to be interrelated, and if their connections can be supported, then Heather will have the beginning of a

conceptual scheme. In graphic form, it would depict the relationships among the knowledge and skill requirements necessary to clarify the job redesign effort.

Definitions

Confusion about the meaning of concepts can destroy a research study's value without the researcher or client even knowing it. If words have different meanings to the parties involved, then the parties are not communicating well. Definitions are one way to reduce this danger.

Researchers struggle with two types of definitions: dictionary definitions and operational definitions. In the more familiar dictionary definition, a concept is defined with a synonym. For example, a customer is defined as a patron; a patron, in turn, is defined as a customer or client of an establishment; a client is defined as one who employs the services of any professional and, loosely, as a patron of any shop.[1] Circular definitions may be adequate for general communication but not for research. In research, we measure concepts and constructs, and this requires more rigorous definitions.

Operational Definitions

An **operational definition** is a definition stated in terms of specific criteria for testing or measurement. These terms must refer to empirical standards (i.e., we must be able to count, measure, or in some other way gather the information through our senses). Whether the object to be defined is physical (e.g., a can of soup) or highly abstract (e.g., achievement motivation), the definition must specify the characteristics and how they are to be observed. The specifications and procedures must be so clear that any competent person using them would classify the object in the same way.

During her research project with the military, Myra observed numerous shells that, when fired, did not explode on impact. She knew the Army attached the operational definition "a shell that does not explode on impact" to the construct dud shell. But if asked, Myra would have applied the operational term *dud shell* only to "a shell that, once fired from a cannon, could not be made to explode by any amount of manipulation, human or mechanical." Based on her operational definition, the town's residents rarely encountered "duds" during their excursions onto the firing range.

Suppose college undergraduates are classified by class. No one has much trouble understanding such terms as *freshman, sophomore,* and so forth. But the task may not be that simple if you must determine which students fall in each class. To do this, you need operational definitions.

Operational definitions may vary, depending on your purpose and the way you choose to measure them. Here are two different situations requiring different definitions of the same concepts:

1. You conduct a survey among students and wish to classify their answers by their class levels. You merely ask them to report their class status and you record it. In this case, class is freshman, sophomore, junior, or senior; and you accept the answer each respondent gives as correct. This is a rather casual definition process but nonetheless an operational definition. It is probably adequate even though some of the respondents report inaccurately.

2. You make a tabulation of the class level of students from the university registrar's annual report. The measurement task here is more critical, so your operational definition needs to be more precise. You decide to define class levels in terms of semester hours of credit completed by the end of the spring semester and recorded in each student's record in the registrar's office:

Freshman	Fewer than 30 hours' credit
Sophomore	30 to 59 hours' credit
Junior	60 to 89 hours' credit
Senior	90 or more hours' credit

Those examples deal with relatively concrete concepts, but operational definitions are even more critical for treating abstract ideas. Suppose one tries to measure a construct called "consumer

Using Scientific Definitions to Shape Political Debate over BioMed

When politics trumps science in defining critical research terminology, legislators intentionally or unwittingly fail to communicate information accurately. This could be critical in discovering products for breakthrough cures, tracking the progression of diseases (thus affecting decisions about hospital staffing and insurance), and finding better ways to test new drugs to discover their various applications.

One example is The National Academies, which advises the federal government and public on scientific issues. It has "created voluntary guidelines for embryonic stem cell research." These guidelines also "provide a comprehensive definition of terms that are accepted by every major research body in the U.S." Because stem-cell research and human cloning are such volatile political issues, the federal government hasn't proposed countrywide guidelines. As a result, individual states opportunistically exploit scientific terminology and fill the void with altered definitions that operationally join humans with embryos and add overarching definitions of human cloning.

Another example relates to the Kansas House of Representatives, which has two bills in process. H.B. 2098 claims "to define terms related to human cloning." The companion bill, H.B. 2255, seeks to ban public funding for *somatic cell nuclear transfer* (SCNT), the bill's term for creating cloned embryonic stem cells. Opponents of embryonic stem-cell research (who contend that embryos are human beings and wish to ban such research) find the definition credible. While "68 percent of Kansans support *somatic cell nuclear transfer*, there is also strong opposition to *reproductive cloning*." Thus, by combining both techniques in the public's mind in a single operational definition, opponents aim to ban SCNT.

Paul Terranova, vice chancellor for research at Kansas University Medical Center, is critical of the many scientific inaccuracies in the definitions used in both bills. When politics collide with science, should politics triumph?

www.kumc.edu; www.kslegislature.org

socialization." We may intuitively understand what this means, but to attempt to measure it among consumers is difficult. We would probably develop questions on skills, knowledge, and attitudes; or we may use a scale that has already been developed and validated by someone else. This scale then operationally defines the construct.

Whether you use a definitional or operational definition, its purpose in research is basically the same—to provide an understanding and measurement of concepts. We may need to provide operational definitions for only a few critical concepts, but these will almost always be the definitions used to develop the relationships found in hypotheses and theories.

Variables

In practice, the term **variable** is used as a synonym for *construct,* or the property being studied. In this context, a variable is a symbol of an event, act, characteristic, trait, or attribute that can be measured and to which we assign categorical values.[2]

For purposes of data entry and analysis, we assign numerical value to a variable based on the variable's properties. For example, some variables, said to be *dichotomous,* have only two values, reflecting the presence or absence of a property: employed–unemployed or male–female have two values, generally 0 and 1. When Myra Wines observed the cannon shells, they were exploded or unexploded. Variables also take on values representing added categories, such as the demographic variables of race or religion. All such variables that produce data that fit into categories are said to be discrete, because only certain values are possible. An automotive variable, for example, where "Chevrolet" is assigned a 5 and "Honda" is assigned a 6, provides no option for a 5.5.

Income, temperature, age, and a test score are examples of *continuous* variables. These variables may take on values within a given range or, in some cases, an infinite set. Your test score may range from 0 to 100, your age may be 23.5, and your present income could be $35,000. The procedure for assigning values to variables is described in detail in Chapter 11.

>**Exhibit 3-2** Independent and Dependent Variables: Synonyms

Independent Variable	Dependent Variable
Predictor	Criterion
Presumed cause	Presumed effect
Stimulus	Response
Predicted from…	Predicted to…
Antecedent	Consequence
Manipulated	Measured outcome

Independent and Dependent Variables

Researchers are most interested in relationships among variables. For example, does a newspaper coupon (independent variable) influence product purchase (dependent variable), or can a salesperson's ethical standards influence her ability to maintain customer relationships? As one writer notes:

> There's nothing very tricky about the notion of independence and dependence. But there is something tricky about the fact that the relationship of independence and dependence is a figment of the researcher's imagination until demonstrated convincingly. Researchers hypothesize relationships of independence and dependence: They invent them, and then they try by reality testing to see if the relationships actually work out that way.[3]

Many textbooks use the term *predictor variable* as a synonym for **independent variable (IV).** This variable is manipulated by the researcher, and the manipulation causes an effect on the dependent variable. We recognize that there are often several independent variables and that they are probably at least somewhat "correlated" and therefore not independent among themselves. Similarly, the term *criterion variable* is used synonymously with **dependent variable (DV).** This variable is measured, predicted, or otherwise monitored and is expected to be affected by manipulation of an independent variable. Exhibit 3-2 lists some terms that have become synonyms for *independent variable* and *dependent variable*.

In each relationship, there is at least one independent variable (IV) and one dependent variable (DV). It is normally hypothesized that, in some way, the IV "causes" the DV to occur. It should be noted, however, that although it is easy to establish whether an IV influences a DV, it is much harder to show that the relationship between an IV and DV is a causal relationship (see also Chapter 6). In Exhibit 3-3a, this relationship is illustrated by an arrow pointing from the independent variable to the dependent variable. For simple relationships, all other variables are considered extraneous and are ignored.

Moderating or Interaction Variables

In actual study situations, however, such a simple one-to-one relationship needs to be conditioned or revised to take other variables into account. Often, we can use another type of explanatory variable that is of value here: the **moderating variable** (MV). A moderating or interaction variable is a second independent variable that is included because it is believed to have a significant contributory or contingent effect on the original IV–DV relationship. The arrow pointing from the moderating variable to the arrow between the IV and DV in Exhibit 3-3a shows the difference between an IV directly impacting the DV and an MV affecting the relationship between an IV and the DV. For example, one might hypothesize that in an office situation:

> The introduction of a four-day working week (IV) will lead to higher productivity (DV), especially among younger workers (MV).

In this case, there is a differential pattern of relationship between the four-day week and productivity that results from age differences among the workers. Hence, after introduction of a four-day working week, the productivity gain for younger workers is higher than that for older workers. It should be noted that the effect of the moderating or interaction variable is the "surplus" of the combined occurrence of introducing a four-day working week and being a younger worker. For example, let's assume that the

>Exhibit 3-3 Relationships among Types of Variables

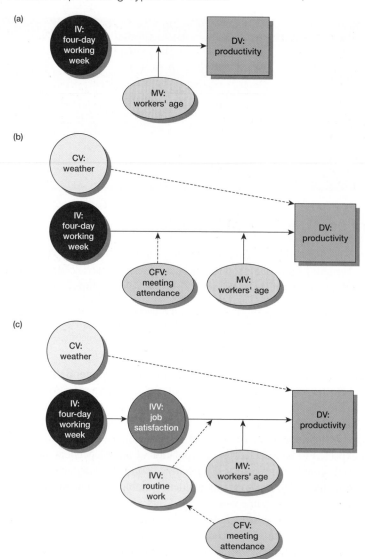

productivity of younger workers is 12 percentage points higher than that for older workers, and that the productivity of workers having a four-day working week is 6 percentage points higher than those of workers having a five-day working week. If the productivity of a younger worker having a four-day working week is only 18 percentage points higher than the productivity of a older worker with a five-day working week, there is no interaction effect, because the 18 percentage points are the sum of the main effects. There would be an interaction effect if the productivity of the younger worker on a four-day week was, say, 25 percentage points higher than the productivity of the older worker on a five-day week.

Whether a given variable is treated as an independent or moderating variable depends on the hypothesis under investigation. If you were interested in studying the impact of the length of the working week, you would make the length of week the IV. If you were focusing on the relationship between age of worker and productivity, you might use working week length as an MV.

Extraneous Variables

An almost infinite number of **extraneous variables** (EVs) exists that might conceivably affect a given relationship. Some can be treated as IVs or MVs, but most must either be assumed or excluded from the study. Fortunately, an infinite number of variables has little or no effect on a given situation. Most can

Forrester Research: Can an Auto Dealership Go Lean?

Not all research is driven by a specific client problem. Some firms specialize in researching emerging issues when the issue is more idea than reality. Forrester Research is one such research firm. As senior analyst Mark Bunger explains, research problems often come from taking an issue in one field and transplanting it into another arena. "The genesis of Forrester's 'Making Auto Retail Lean' study was a book I was reading by James Womack and Daniel Jones, *Lean Thinking: Banish Waste and Create Wealth in Your Corporation*." In their book the authors describe lean thinking as the "elimination of unnecessary waste in business" and explain that if lean principles are applied to the whole product cycle, from suppliers to customers, firms can demonstrate significant increases in productivity and sales. "I knew lean principles were being applied in the manufacturing of cars. I wondered if such principles were applied at the level of the auto dealership and with what effect." Bunger's question led Forrester to launch a study that had Bunger and his team of research associates conducting hour-long phone interviews with vendors of products and services related to supply chain enhancement (e.g., IBM), followed by a 15-minute, 20-question phone survey of 50 auto dealer CEOs. Bunger also visited dealers in his immediate area to flesh out ideas from the phone interviews. Data revealed that "dealers have the wrong cars 40 percent of the time." Yet if they applied the lean principles so effective for car manufacturers, they could lower their demand chain–related costs up to 53 percent.

The Forrester study followed a fairly standard model for the firm: approximately two weeks to define and refine the problem—a stage that involves significant secondary data analysis; two to four weeks for data collection—a stage that involves selecting at least two sample segments (usually "experts" and users; for this study, vendors and dealers); and 2 to 30 hours to prepare a brief or report. Forrester's research is purchased by subscription. Subscribing companies related to the automotive industry have "whole-view" access to any report on any study that Forrester develops at an approximate cost of $7,000 per *seat*. When a subscriber wants numerous people to have direct access to Forrester research, a firm's subscription could be worth several million dollars.

Should auto dealers go lean? What reasoning approaches did you use to reach your conclusion? What concepts and constructs are embedded in this example? What hypotheses could you form from this example?

www.forrester.com

safely be ignored because their impact occurs in such a random fashion as to have little effect. Others might influence the DV, but their effect is not at the core of the problem we investigate. Still, we want to check whether our results are influenced by them. Therefore, we include them as **control variables** (CVs) in our investigation to ensure that our results are not biased by not including them. Taking the example of the effect of the four-day working week again, one would normally think that weather conditions, the imposition of a local sales tax, the election of a new mayor, and thousands of similar events and conditions would have little effect on working week and office productivity.

Extraneous variables can also be **confounding variables** (CFVs) to our hypothesized IV–DV relationship, similar to moderating variables. You may consider that the kind of work being done might have an effect on the impact of working week length on office productivity. This might lead you to introducing time spent in a meeting to coordinate the work as a confounding variable (CFV). In our office example, we would attempt to control for type of work by studying the effect of the four-day working week within groups attending meetings with different intensity. In Exhibit 3-3b, weather is shown as an extraneous variable; the broken line indicates that we included it in our research because it might influence the DV, but we consider the CV as irrelevant for the investigation of our research problem. Similarly we included the type of work as a CFV.

Intervening Variables

The variables mentioned with regard to causal relationships are concrete and clearly measurable—that is, they can be seen, counted, or observed in some way. Sometimes, however, one may not be completely satisfied by the explanations they give. Thus, while we may recognize that a four-day working week results in higher productivity, we might think that this is not the whole story—that working week length affects some **intervening variable** (IVV) that, in turn, results in higher productivity. An IVV is a conceptual mechanism through which the IV and MV might affect the DV. The IVV can be defined as a factor that theoretically affects the DV but cannot be observed or has not been measured; its effect must be inferred from the effects of the independent and moderator variables on the observed phenomenon.[4]

In the case of the working week hypothesis, one might view the intervening variable (IVV) to be job satisfaction, giving a hypothesis such as:

The introduction of a four-day working week (IV) will lead to higher productivity (DV) by increasing job satisfaction (IVV).

55

The percent of executives who admitted that their companies do not have an official policy for social networks.

Here we assume that a four-day working week increases job satisfaction; similarly, we can assume that attending internal meetings is an indicator negatively related to the routine character of work. Exhibit 3-3c illustrates how theoretical constructs, which are not directly observed, fit into our model.

Propositions and Hypotheses

We define a **proposition** as a statement about observable phenomena (concepts) that may be judged as true or false. When a proposition is formulated for empirical testing, we call it a **hypothesis.** As a declarative statement about the relationship between two or more variables, a hypothesis is of a tentative and conjectural nature.

Hypotheses have also been described as statements in which we assign variables to cases. A **case** is defined in this sense as the entity or thing the hypothesis talks about. The variable is the characteristic, trait, or attribute that, in the hypothesis, is imputed to the case.[5] For example, we might create the following hypothesis:

Brand Manager Jones (case) has a higher-than-average achievement motivation (variable).

If our hypothesis was based on more than one case, it would be a generalization. For example:

Brand managers in Company Z (cases) have a higher-than-average achievement motivation (variable).

Descriptive Hypotheses

Both of the preceding hypotheses are examples of **descriptive hypotheses.** They state the existence, size, form, or distribution of some variable. Researchers often use a research question rather than a descriptive hypothesis. For example:

Descriptive Hypothesis Format	Research Question Format
In Detroit (case), our potato chip market share (variable) stands at 13.7 percent.	What is the market share for our potato chips in Detroit?
American cities (cases) are experiencing budget difficulties (variable).	Are American cities experiencing budget difficulties?
Eighty percent of Company Z stockholders (cases) favor increasing the company's cash dividend (variable).	Do stockholders of Company Z favor an increased cash dividend?
Seventy percent of the high school–educated males (cases) scavenge in the Army firing range for salvageable metals (variable).	Do a majority of high school–educated male residents scavenge in the Army firing range for salvageable metals?

Either format is acceptable, but the descriptive hypothesis format has several advantages:

- It encourages researchers to crystallize their thinking about the likely relationships to be found.
- It encourages them to think about the implications of a supported or rejected finding.
- It is useful for testing statistical significance.

Relational Hypotheses

The research question format is less frequently used with a situation calling for **relational hypotheses.** These are statements that describe a relationship between two variables with respect to some case. For example, "Foreign (variable) cars are perceived by American consumers (case) to be of better quality (variable) than domestic cars." In this instance, the nature of the relationship between the two variables ("country of origin" and "perceived quality") is not specified. Is there only an implication that the variables occur in some predictable relationship, or is one variable somehow responsible for the other? The first interpretation (unspecified relationship) indicates a correlational relationship; the second (predictable relationship) indicates an explanatory, or causal, relationship.

Correlational hypotheses state that the variables occur together in some specified manner without implying that one causes the other. Such weak claims are often made when we believe there are more basic causal forces that affect both variables or when we have not developed enough evidence to claim a stronger linkage. Here are three sample correlational hypotheses:

Young women (under 35 years of age) purchase fewer units of our product than women who are 35 years of age or older.

The number of suits sold varies directly with the level of the business cycle.

People in Atlanta give the president a more favorable rating than do people in St. Louis.

By labeling these as correlational hypotheses, we make no claim that one variable causes the other to change or take on different values.

With **explanatory (causal) hypotheses,** there is an implication that the existence of or a change in one variable causes or leads to a change in the other variable. As we noted previously, the causal variable is typically called the independent variable (IV) and the other the dependent variable (DV). Cause means roughly to "help make happen." So the IV need not be the sole reason for the existence of or change in the DV. Here are four examples of explanatory hypotheses:

An increase in family income (IV) leads to an increase in the percentage of income saved (DV).

Exposure to the company's messages concerning industry problems (IV) leads to more favorable attitudes (DV) by employees toward the company.

Loyalty to a particular grocery store (IV) increases the probability of purchasing the private brands (DV) sponsored by that store.

An increase in the price of salvaged copper wire (IV) leads to an increase in scavenging (DV) on the Army firing range.

In proposing or interpreting causal hypotheses, the researcher must consider the direction of influence. In many cases, the direction is obvious from the nature of the variables. Thus, one would assume that family income influences savings rate rather than the reverse. This also holds true for the Army example. Sometimes our ability to identify the direction of influence depends on the research design. In the worker attitude hypothesis, if the exposure to the message clearly precedes the attitude measurement, then the direction of exposure to attitude seems clear. If information about both exposure and attitude was collected at the same time, the researcher might be justified in saying that different attitudes led to selective message perception or nonperception. Store loyalty and purchasing of store brands appear to be interdependent. Loyalty to a store may increase the probability of one's buying the store's private brands, but satisfaction with the store's private brand may also lead to greater store loyalty.

The Role of the Hypothesis

In research, a hypothesis serves several important functions:

- It guides the direction of the study.
- It identifies facts that are relevant and those that are not.
- It suggests which form of research design is likely to be most appropriate.
- It provides a framework for organizing the conclusions that result.

Unless the researcher curbs the urge to include additional elements, a study can be diluted by trivial concerns that do not answer the basic questions posed by the management dilemma. The virtue of the hypothesis is that, if taken seriously, it limits what shall be studied and what shall not. To consider specifically the role of the hypothesis in determining the direction of the research, suppose we use this:

Husbands and wives agree in their perceptions of their respective roles in purchase decisions.

The hypothesis specifies who shall be studied (married couples), in what context they shall be studied (their consumer decision making), and what shall be studied (their individual perceptions of their roles).

The nature of this hypothesis and the implications of the statement suggest that the best research design is a communication-based study, probably a survey or interview. We have at this time no other practical means to ascertain perceptions of people except to ask about them in one way or another. In addition, we are interested only in the roles that are assumed in the purchase or consumer decision-making situation. The study should not, therefore, involve itself in seeking information about other types of roles husbands and wives might play. Reflection upon this hypothesis might also reveal that husbands and wives disagree on their perceptions of roles, but the differences may be explained in terms of additional variables, such as age, social class, background, personality, and other factors not associated with their difference in gender.

What Is a Strong Hypothesis?   A strong hypothesis should fulfill three conditions:

- Adequate for its purpose.
- Testable.
- Better than its rivals.

The conditions for developing a strong hypothesis are developed more fully in Exhibit 3-4.

>**Exhibit 3-4** Checklist for Developing a Strong Hypothesis

Criteria	Interpretation
Adequate for Its Purpose	❑ Does the hypothesis reveal the original problem condition?
	❑ Does the hypothesis clearly identify facts that are relevant and those that are not?
	❑ Does the hypothesis clearly state the condition, size, or distribution of some variable in terms of values meaningful to the research problem (descriptive)?
	❑ Does the hypothesis explain facts that gave rise to the need for explanation (explanatory)?
	❑ Does the hypothesis suggest which form of research design is likely to be most appropriate?
	❑ Does the hypothesis provide a framework for organizing the conclusions that result?
Testable	❑ Does the hypothesis use acceptable techniques?
	❑ Does the hypothesis require an explanation that is plausible given known physical or psychological laws?
	❑ Does the hypothesis reveal consequences or derivatives that can be deduced for testing purposes?
	❑ Is the hypothesis simple, requiring few conditions or assumptions?
Better Than Its Rivals	❑ Does the hypothesis explain more facts than its rivals?
	❑ Does the hypothesis explain a greater variety or scope of facts than its rivals?
	❑ Is the hypothesis one that informed judges would accept as being the most likely?

Radio Chips versus Retinal Scans: Which Theory Offers the Best Protection?

When the first confirmed case of bovine spongiform encephalopathy (BSE—known as "mad cow" disease) was discovered in a Washington state dairy cow in December 2003, numerous countries banned U.S. beef imports, bringing the $3.2 billion export industry to a standstill. That year, the United States Department of Agriculture (USDA) performed random tests on approximately 0.03 percent of all slaughtered cattle, about 20,000 cows of the nearly 40 million head of cattle slaughtered annually. In comparison, western European countries tested 10 million cows and Japan tested each of its 1.2 million slaughtered cows.

Theories are essential to a researcher's quest to explain and predict phenomena while creating business opportunities and informing public policy. One USDA theory is that the best way to identify sources of cattle-born disease is to monitor a cow from birth to slaughter. Thus, the USDA wanted a national livestock database. After evaluating the options, the USDA proposed another theory: Cows tagged with radio frequency identification devices (RFID) would create the most accurate database.

About the size of a quarter, the RFID tag is stapled to the base of the animal's ear. It is programmed with a numeric code that is scanned by a stationary or handheld device when a cow reaches a new location in the production process. As cows move from farm to feeding lot to slaughterhouse, each animal's origin and location can be updated in the national database.

But RFID tags can be damaged, dislodged, or tampered with. Slaughterhouses need additional safeguards to be certain these devices don't end up in the meat. "All you need is one chip in someone's burger and you've got a problem," says Brian Bolton, vice president of marketing for Optibrand. This Colorado company offers a different theory for the best identification and tracking: A camera that records the unique vascular patterns in a cow's retina at each stage of the beef production chain is the most reliable. With retinal scanning, Bolton says, "the tracking technology is contained in the handheld reader. It takes a tiny picture of a cow's retina and then links it to that animal's computerized record." Meatpacker Swift & Co., the nation's third-largest beef processor, has been using Optibrand's devices for several years. Retinal scan wands also read RFID tags, access global positioning receivers, and stamp each scan with a location record. However, retinal scanning is not always practical because scans must be taken about an inch from an animal's eye.

In addition to RFID and retinal scanning, beef producers and processors implement other tracking systems, thus implementing their own theories. Some use implantable computer chips and others use DNA matching systems. While still preferring RFID technology, the USDA's director of national animal identification, John F. Wiemers, concedes, "We think there's room for all these technologies."

Which tracking theory do you favor? What are the most important variables you would consider in justifying your decision?

www.usda.gov; www.optibrand.com; http://www.jbsswift.com/

Theory

Hypotheses play an important role in the development of theory. How theory differs from hypothesis may cause confusion. We make the general distinction that the difference between theory and hypothesis is one of degree of complexity and abstraction. In general, theories tend to be complex and abstract and to involve multiple variables. Hypotheses, on the other hand, tend to be more simple, limited-variable statements involving concrete instances.

A person not familiar with research uses the term *theory* to express the opposite of *fact*. In this sense, theory is viewed as being speculative or "ivory tower." One hears that managers need to be less theoretical or that some idea will not work because it is too theoretical. This is an incorrect picture of the relationship between fact and theory to the researcher. In truth, fact and theory are each necessary for the other to be of value. Our ability to make rational decisions, as well as to develop scientific knowledge, is measured by the degree to which we combine fact and theory. We all operate on the basis of theories we hold. In one sense, theories are the generalizations we make about variables and the relationships among them. We use these generalizations to make decisions and predict outcomes. For example, it is midday and you note that the outside natural light is dimming, dark clouds are moving rapidly in from the west, the breeze is freshening, and the air temperature is cooling. Would your understanding of the relationship among these variables (your weather theory) lead you to predict that something decidedly wet will probably occur in a short time?

>Exhibit 3-5 Traditional Product Life Cycle

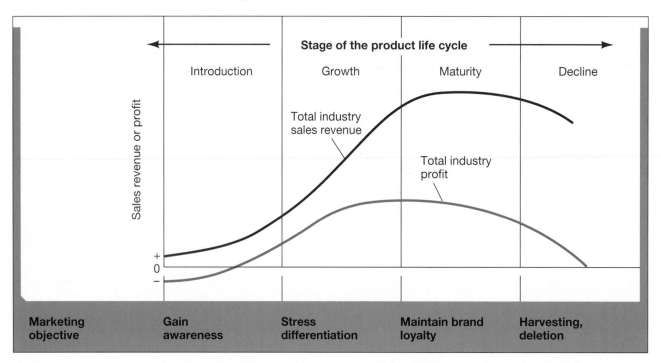

Source: Adapted from Roger Kerin, Eric Berkowitz, Steven Hartley, and William Rudelius, *Marketing*, 7th ed. (Burr Ridge, IL: McGraw-Hill, 2003), p. 295.

A **theory** is a set of systematically interrelated concepts, definitions, and propositions that are advanced to explain and predict phenomena (facts). In this sense, we have many theories and use them continually to explain or predict what goes on around us. To the degree that our theories are sound and fit the situation, we are successful in our explanations and predictions.

In marketing, the product life cycle describes the stages that a product category goes through in the marketplace.[6] The generalized product life cycle has four stages (although the length and shape of product life cycles differ): introduction, growth, maturity, and decline (Exhibit 3-5). In each stage, many concepts, constructs, and hypotheses describe the influences that change revenue and profit. Definitions are also needed for communicating about the claims of the theory and its consistency in testing to reality.

For example, in the growth stage, companies spend heavily on advertising and promotion to create product awareness. In the early period of this stage these expenditures may be made to fuel *primary demand* (construct), improving product class awareness rather than brand awareness. Also, high pricing may reflect *skimming* (concept) to help the company recover developmental costs. The product manager may alternatively use low pricing, or *penetration pricing* (concept), to build unit volume. In the growth stage, sales increase rapidly because many consumers are trying or actually using the product; and those who tried (were satisfied) and bought again—*repeat purchasers* (concept)—are swelling the ranks. If the company is unable to attract repeat purchasers, this usually means death for the product (proposition). The maturity stage is a good time for the company in terms of generating cash (proposition). The costs of developing the product and establishing its position in the marketplace are paid and it tends to be profitable. Firms will often try to use *extension strategies* (constructs). These are attempts to delay the decline stage of the product life cycle by introducing new versions of the product. In the decline stage, "products will consume a disproportionate share of management time and financial resources relative to their potential future worth"[7] (hypothesis). To make this hypothesis fully testable, we would need operational definitions for disproportionate share, time, resources, and future worth.

The challenge for the researcher in this example is to build more comprehensive theories to explain and predict how modifying the product and other variables will benefit the firm.

Models

The term *model* is used in business research and other fields of business to represent phenomena through the use of analogy. A **model** is defined here as a representation of a system that is constructed to study some aspect of that system or the system as a whole. Models differ from theories in that a theory's role is explanation whereas a model's role is representation.

Early models (and even those created as recently as the 1990s for mainframe computers) were enormously expensive and often incomprehensible to all but their developers. Modeling software, such as Excel, has made modeling more inexpensive and accessible.

Models allow researchers and managers to characterize present or future conditions: the effect of advertising on consumer awareness or intention to purchase, a product distribution channel, brand switching behavior, an employee training program, and many other aspects of business. A model's purpose is to increase our understanding, prediction, and control of the complexities of the environment.

Exhibit 3-6 provides an example of a *maximum-flow* model used in management science. In this example, a European manufacturer of automobiles needs an increased flow of shipping to its Los Angeles distribution center to meet demand. However, the primary distribution channel is saturated and alternatives must be sought. Although this is a geographic model, more sophisticated network, mathematical, and path diagrams are subsequently created so that researchers can create hypotheses about the nature, relationship, and direction of causality among variables.

Descriptive, predictive, and normative models are found in business research.[8] *Descriptive models* are used frequently for more complex systems, such as the one in Exhibit 3-6. They allow visualization of numerous variables and relationships. *Predictive* models forecast future events (e.g., the Fourt and Woodlock model could be used to forecast basketball shoes for a market segment).[9] *Normative* models are used chiefly for control, informing us about what actions should be taken. Models may also be static, representing a system at one point in time, or dynamic, representing the evolution of a system over time.

Models are developed through the use of inductive and deductive reasoning, which we suggested previously is integral to accurate conclusions about business decisions. As illustrated in Exhibit 3-7, a model may originate from empirical observations about behavior based on researched facts and relationships among variables. Inductive reasoning allows the modeler to draw conclusions from the

>**Exhibit 3-6** A Distribution Network Model

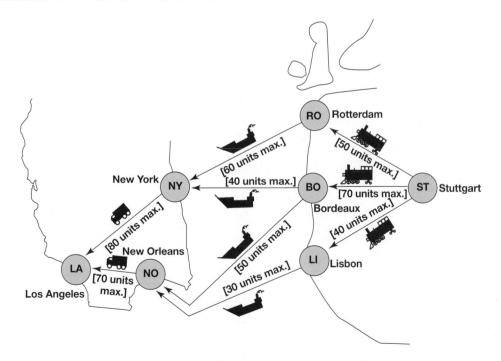

>**Exhibit 3-7** The Role of Reasoning in Model Development

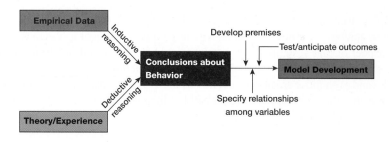

facts or evidence in planning the dynamics of the model. The modeler may also use existing theory, managerial experience, judgment, or facts deduced from known laws of nature. In this case, deductive reasoning serves to create particular conclusions derived from general premises.

Models are an important means of advancing theories and aiding decision makers. Because the inputs are often unknown, imprecise, or temporal estimates of complex variables, creating and using models in the decision-making process can be a time-consuming endeavor.

> Research and the Scientific Method

Good business research is based on sound reasoning. Competent researchers and astute managers alike practice thinking habits that reflect **sound reasoning**—finding correct premises, testing the connections between their facts and assumptions, making claims based on adequate evidence. In the reasoning process, induction and deduction, observation, and hypothesis testing can be combined in a systematic way. In this chapter we illustrate how this works and why careful reasoning is essential for producing scientific results.

If the tools of thinking are the mind of science, then the **scientific attitude** is the spirit. The scientific attitude unleashes the creative drive that makes discovery possible. The portraits of scientists involved in some of the most spectacular discoveries of the last century—Crick, Watson, and Pauling (who developed the foundations of DNA structure), and others—are the stories of imagination, intuition, curiosity, suspicion, anguish, the rage to know, and self-doubt. A good business researcher must also possess these essential predispositions. Each must exercise imagination in the discovery process in capturing the most essential aspect of the problem, or in selecting a technique that reveals the phenomenon in its most natural state.

Curiosity in its many forms characterizes the persistent effort to understand relationships. For example, consider the Hawthorne studies discovering a relationship between the seemingly unrelated entities of productivity and levels of light in the workplace. Exemplars like Weber, Taylor, Fayol, Gulick, Mayo, Maslow, McGregor, Argyris, Simon, Likert, Katz, and Kahn (among others in organizational studies) have all typified the curiosity to ask questions with the passion not to quit and a discomfort with existing answers. From applied researchers addressing managers' practical needs to academics fascinated with the construction of grand theories, the attitude of science is the enabling spirit of discovery.

The **scientific method,** as practiced in business research, guides our approach to problem solving. The essential tenets of the scientific method are:

- Direct observation of phenomena.
- Clearly defined variables, methods, and procedures.
- Empirically testable hypotheses.
- The ability to rule out rival hypotheses.
- Statistical rather than linguistic justification of conclusions.
- The self-correcting process.

>**snap**shot

Business and Battlefield: Scientific Evidence Supports "Gut-Hunches"

A team of researchers at Leeds University Business School conducted studies on how intuition and hunches result from the way our brains store, process, and retrieve information on a subconscious level.[a] Their research is important to executives and managers, who often claim that hunches are preferred over deliberate analysis when a quick decision is required. Gerald Hodgkinson, the lead researcher remarked, "People usually experience true intuition when they are under severe time pressure or in a situation of information overload or acute danger, where conscious analysis of the situation may be difficult or impossible."[b]

If we consider the analogy of the business executive attempting to avoid fatal decisions in a fast-moving, turbulent environment with a soldier scanning the landscape for any evidence of improvised explosive devices (IEDs) in a treacherous neighborhood, then the importance to organizations comes into focus. This aspect of decision-making research seeks to understand how to channel and fine-tune intuitive skills. Being able to identify when managers and executives switch from an intuitive mode to deliberate analysis, and why, may shed light on which decisions are likely to be correct for their environments.

In an article on the importance of hunches in battle, Benedict Carey described how hunches were critical to military survival in threat environments like Iraq and Afghanistan, especially clearing roads of IEDs. Fighting a war-within-a-war, insurgents and U.S. bomb teams have improved their IED tactics: insurgents by better placing, concealing, and detonating and U.S. teams with better recognition and diffusion. Reduced casualties, it was found, could be attributed to some soldiers who could sense danger in a life-or-death situation well before others.[c]

Army research psychologist Steven Burnett led a study involving approximately 800 military men and women that focused on how some soldiers see what others miss. They found that two types of personnel are particularly good at spotting anomalies: those with hunting backgrounds and those from tough urban neighborhoods, where knowing what gang controls a block is a survival necessity. These latter troops also seemed to have innate "threat-assessment" abilities.[d]

Martin P. Paulus, a psychiatrist at the University of California, San Diego found that the brains of elite military units appear to record apparent threats differently from the average enlistee.[e] When presented with the sight of angry faces, Navy Seals show significantly higher activation in the insula (the brain location that collects sensations from around the body and interprets them cohesively) than regular soldiers.

Not long ago, management academics thought of hunches and intuition as folklore, or as just feelings. Feelings have "little to do with rational decision making, or that got in the way of it," said Dr. Antonio Damasio, director of the Brain and Creativity Institute.[f] Notwithstanding that hunches are still not part of scientific orthodoxy,[g] they are supported by strong evidence in neuroscience and psychology.

The technical evidence is complicated but fascinating. Here is a glimpse.

> Each of us was born with two brains—the cranial brain between our ears, and a second brain with just as many neurons and neurotransmitters as the first, but located in the sheaths of tissue lining our stomach, small intestine, and colon. During early fetal development the same clump of embryonic tissue constituted both our primary brain and our gut brain. In later development the two brains separated yet remained connected (and in communication) through the vagus nerve extending from the brain stem through the enteric nervous system, otherwise known as our gut brain.[h]

Receptors for the gut that process serotonin (a neurotransmitter) are identical to those found in the bilateral part of the brain where intuitive thinking is believed to originate. Professor Wolfgang Prinz of the Max Planck Institute in Munich reveals that our gut brain "may be the source for unconscious decisions which the main brain later claims as conscious decisions of its own."[i]

There is a lot of research to support gut brain intuition; however, a few examples are illustrative.[j] At the Institute of Noetic Sciences, researchers showed how the human gut reacts to emotionally alarming information seconds before the conscious mind is aware of the information. Previous experiments found similar evidence of reaction times four to seven seconds before conscious awareness of emotionally disturbing images.[k] In another study by Professor Ronald Rensink of the University of British Columbia, one-third of the subjects could sense changes in the patterns of a series of images before the actual changes occurred.[l] "It's like a gut feeling," said Rensink. "It's like using the force. The point of this is that these kinds of feelings are often correct."[m]

Stephen Jay Gould, the eminent paleontologist, biologist, and historian of science said, "Science . . . progresses by hunch, vision, and intuition."[n] Let's not forget the hunches.

An important term in this list is *empirical.* Empirical testing or **empiricism** is said "to denote observations and propositions based on sensory experience and/or derived from such experience by methods of inductive logic, including mathematics and statistics."[10] Researchers using this approach attempt to describe, explain, and make predictions by relying on information gained through observation. This book is fundamentally concerned with empiricism—with the design of procedures to collect factual information about hypothesized relationships that can be used to decide if a particular understanding of a problem and its possible solution are correct.

The scientific method, and scientific inquiry generally, is described as a puzzle-solving activity.[11] For the researcher, puzzles are solvable problems that may be clarified or resolved through reasoning processes. The steps that follow represent one approach to assessing the validity of conclusions about observable events.[12] They are particularly appropriate for business researchers whose conclusions result from empirical data. The researcher:

1. Encounters a curiosity, doubt, barrier, suspicion, or obstacle.

2. Struggles to state the problem—asks questions, contemplates existing knowledge, gathers facts, and moves from an emotional to an intellectual confrontation with the problem.

3. Proposes a hypothesis, a plausible explanation, to explain the facts that are believed to be logically related to the problem.

4. Deduces outcomes or consequences of the hypothesis—attempts to discover what happens if the results are in the opposite direction of that predicted or if the results support the expectations.

5. Formulates several rival hypotheses.

6. Devises and conducts a crucial empirical test with various possible outcomes, each of which selectively excludes one or more hypotheses.

7. Draws a conclusion (an inductive inference) based on acceptance or rejection of the hypotheses.

8. Feeds information back into the original problem, modifying it according to the strength of the evidence.

Clearly, reasoning is pivotal to much of the researcher's success: gathering facts consistent with the problem, proposing and eliminating rival hypotheses, deducing outcomes, developing crucial empirical tests, and deriving the conclusion.

Sound Reasoning for Useful Answers

Every day we reason with varying degrees of success and communicate our meaning in ordinary language or, in special cases, in symbolic, logical form. Our meanings are conveyed through one of two types of discourse: exposition or argument. **Exposition** consists of statements that describe without attempting to explain. **Argument** allows us to explain, interpret, defend, challenge, and explore meaning. Two types of argument of great importance to research are deduction and induction.

Deduction

Deduction is a form of argument that purports to be conclusive—the conclusion must necessarily follow from the reasons given. These reasons are said to imply the conclusion and represent a proof. This is a much stronger and different bond between reasons and conclusions than is found with induction. For a deduction to be correct, it must be both true and valid:

- Premises (reasons) given for the conclusion must agree with the real world (true).
- The conclusion must necessarily follow from the premises (valid).

A deduction is valid if it is impossible for the conclusion to be false if the premises are true. Logicians have established rules by which one can judge whether a deduction is valid. Conclusions are not logically justified if one or more premises are untrue or the argument form is invalid. A conclusion may

This Synovate ad reinforces
that one trait—curiosity—is
necessary for someone to be
a good researcher.
www.synovate.com

still be a true statement, but for reasons other than those given. For example, consider the following simple deduction:

All employees at BankChoice can be trusted to observe the ethical code.	(Premise 1)
Sara is an employee of BankChoice.	(Premise 2)
Sara can be trusted to observe the ethical code.	(Conclusion)

If we believe that Sara can be trusted, we might think this is a sound deduction. But this conclusion cannot be accepted as a sound deduction unless the form of the argument is valid and the premises are true. In this case, the form is valid, and premise 2 can be confirmed easily. However, more than a billion dollars each year in confirmed retail employee theft will challenge the premise "All employees can be trusted to observe an ethical code." And instances of employee fraud among professionals make any specific instance questionable. If one premise fails the acceptance test, then the conclusion is not a sound deduction. This is so even if we still have great confidence in Sara's honesty. Our conclusion, in this case, must be based on our confidence in Sara as an individual rather than on a general premise that all employees of BankChoice are ethical.

As researchers, we may not recognize how much we use deduction to understand the implications of various acts and conditions. For example, in planning a survey, we might reason as follows:

Inner-city household interviewing is especially difficult and expensive.	(Premise 1)
This survey involves substantial inner-city household interviewing.	(Premise 2)
The interviewing in this survey will be especially difficult and expensive.	(Conclusion)

On reflection, it should be apparent that a conclusion that results from deduction is, in a sense, already "contained in" its premises.[13]

Induction

Inductive argument is radically different. There is no such strength of relationship between reasons and conclusions in induction. In **induction** you draw a conclusion from one or more particular facts or pieces of evidence. The conclusion explains the facts, and the facts support the conclusion. To illustrate, suppose your firm spends $1 million on a regional promotional campaign and sales do not increase. This is a fact—sales did not increase during or after the promotional campaign. Under such circumstances, we ask, "Why didn't sales increase?"

One likely answer to this question is a conclusion that the promotional campaign was poorly executed. This conclusion is an induction because we know from experience that regional sales should go up during a promotional event. Also we know from experience that if the promotion is poorly executed, sales will not increase. The nature of induction, however, is that the conclusion is only a hypothesis. It is one explanation, but there are others that fit the facts just as well. For example, each of the following hypotheses might explain why sales did not increase:

- Regional retailers did not have sufficient stock to fill customer requests during the promotional period.
- A strike by the employees of our trucking firm prevented stock from arriving in time for the promotion to be effective.
- A category-five hurricane closed all our retail locations in the region for the 10 days during the promotion.

In this example, we see the essential nature of inductive reasoning. The inductive conclusion is an inferential jump beyond the evidence presented—that is, although one conclusion explains the fact of no sales increase, other conclusions also can explain the fact. It may even be that none of the conclusions we advanced correctly explain the failure of sales to increase.

For another example, let's consider the situation of Tracy Nelson, a salesperson at the Square Box Company. Tracy has one of the poorest sales records in the company. Her unsatisfactory performance prompts us to ask the question "Why is she performing so poorly?" From our knowledge of Tracy's sales practices, the nature of box selling, and the market, we might conclude (hypothesize) that her problem is that she makes too few sales calls per day to build a good sales record. Other hypotheses might also occur to us on the basis of available evidence. Among these hypotheses are the following:

- Tracy's territory does not have the market potential of other territories.
- Tracy's sales-generating skills are so poorly developed that she is not able to close sales effectively.
- Tracy does not have authority to lower prices and her territory has been the scene of intense price-cutting by competitive manufacturers, causing her to lose many sales to competitors.
- Some people just cannot sell boxes, and Tracy is one of those people.

Each of the above hypotheses is an induction we might base on the evidence of Tracy's poor sales record, plus some assumptions or beliefs we hold about her and the selling of boxes. All of them have some chance of being true, but we would probably have more confidence in some than in others. All require further confirmation before they gain our confidence. Confirmation comes with more evidence. The task of research is largely to (1) determine the nature of the evidence needed to confirm or reject hypotheses and (2) design methods by which to discover and measure this other evidence.

Researchers often use observation when evaluating toys and children. Apply deductive reasoning to this image. Develop your own conclusions concerning what will happen next.

Combining Induction and Deduction

Induction and deduction are used together in research reasoning. Dewey describes this process as the "double movement of reflective thought."[14] Induction occurs when we observe a fact and ask, "Why is this?" In answer to this question, we advance a tentative explanation (hypothesis). The hypothesis is plausible if it explains the event or condition (fact) that prompted the question. Deduction is the process by which we test whether the hypothesis is capable of explaining the fact. The process is illustrated in Exhibit 3-8:

1. You promote a product but sales don't increase. (Fact 1)

2. You ask the question "Why didn't sales increase?" (Induction)

3. You infer a conclusion (hypothesis) to answer the question: The promotion was poorly executed. (Hypothesis)

4. You use this hypothesis to conclude (deduce) that sales will not increase during a poorly executed promotion. You know from experience that ineffective promotion will not increase sales. (Deduction 1)

This example, an exercise in circular reasoning, points out that one must be able to deduce the initiating fact from the hypothesis advanced to explain that fact. A second critical point is also illustrated in Exhibit 3-8. To test a hypothesis, one must be able to deduce from it other facts that can then be investigated. This is what research is all about. We must deduce other specific facts or events from the hypothesis and then gather information to see if the deductions are true. In this example:

5. We deduce that a well-executed promotion will result in increased sales. (Deduction 2)

6. We run an effective promotion, and sales increase. (Fact 2)

>Exhibit 3-8 Why Didn't Sales Increase?

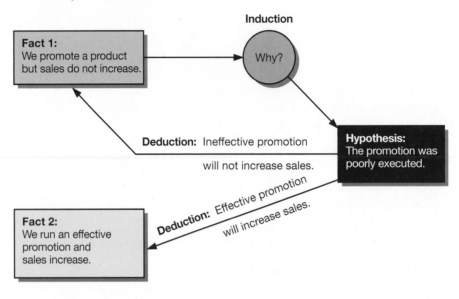

>Exhibit 3-9 Why Is Tracy Nelson's Performance So Poor?

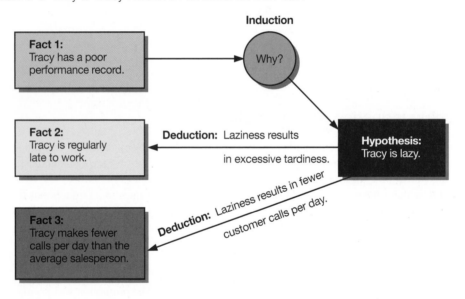

How would the double movement of reflective thought work when applied to Tracy Nelson's problem? The process is illustrated in Exhibit 3-9. The initial observation (fact 1) leads to hypothesis 1 that Tracy is lazy. We deduce several other facts from the hypothesis. These are shown as fact 2 and fact 3. We use research to find out if fact 2 and fact 3 are true. If they are found to be true, they confirm our hypothesis. If they are found to be false, our hypothesis is not confirmed, and we must look for another explanation.

In most research, the process may be more complicated than these examples suggest. For instance, we often develop multiple hypotheses by which to explain the problem in question. Then we design a study to test all the hypotheses at once. Not only is this more efficient, but it is also a good way to reduce the attachment (and potential bias) of the researcher for any given hypothesis.

>summary

1 Scientific methods and scientific thinking are based on concepts, the symbols we attach to bundles of meaning that we hold and share with others. We invent concepts to think about and communicate abstractions. We also use higher-level concepts—constructs—for specialized scientific explanatory purposes that are not directly observable. Concepts, constructs, and variables may be defined descriptively or operationally. Operational definitions must specify adequately the empirical information needed and how it will be collected. In addition, they must have the proper scope or fit for the research problem at hand.

   Concepts and constructs are used at the theoretical levels; variables are used at the empirical level. Variables accept numerals or values for the purpose of testing and measurement. They may be classified as explanatory, independent, dependent, moderating, extraneous, and intervening.

2 Propositions are of great interest in research because they may be used to assess the truth or falsity of relationships among observable phenomena. When we advance a proposition for testing, we are hypothesizing. A hypothesis describes the relationships between or among variables. A good hypothesis is one that can explain what it claims to explain; is testable; and has greater range, probability, and simplicity than its rivals. Sets of inter-related concepts, definitions, and propositions that are advanced to explain and predict phenomena are called theories. Models differ from theories in that models are analogies or representations of some aspect of a system or of the system as a whole. Models are used for description, prediction, and control.

3 Scientific inquiry is grounded in the inference process. This process is used for the development and testing of various propositions largely through the double movement of reflective thinking. Reflective thinking consists of sequencing induction and deduction in order to explain inductively (by hypothesis) a puzzling condition. In turn, the hypothesis is used in a deduction of further facts that can be sought to confirm or deny the truth of the hypothesis.

   Researchers think of the doing of science as an orderly process that combines induction, deduction, observation, and hypothesis testing into a set of reflective thinking activities. Although the scientific method consists of neither sequential nor independent stages, the problem-solving process that it reveals provides insight into the way research is conducted.

>keyterms

argument 70

case 62

concept 54

conceptual scheme 57

construct 55

deduction 70

empiricism 70

exposition 70

hypothesis 62

   correlational 63

   descriptive 62

   explanatory (causal) 63

   relational 63

hypothetical construct 56

induction 72

model 67

operational definition 57

proposition 62

scientific attitude 68

scientific method 68

sound reasoning 68

theory 66

variable 58

   control 61

   confounding (CFV) 61

   dependent (DV) (criterion variable) 59

   extraneous (EV) 60

   independent (IV) (predictor variable) 59

   intervening (IVV) 62

   moderating (MV) 59

>discussionquestions

Terms in Review

1 Distinguish among the following sets of items, and suggest the significance of each in a research context:

 a Concept and construct.

 b Deduction and induction.

 c Operational definition and dictionary definition.

 d Concept and variable.

 e Hypothesis and proposition.

 f Theory and model.

 g Scientific method and scientific attitude.

2 Describe the characteristics of the scientific method.

3 Below are some terms commonly found in a management setting. Are they concepts or constructs? Give two different operational definitions for each.

 a First-line supervisor.

 b Employee morale.

 c Assembly line.

 d Overdue account.

 e Line management.

 f Leadership.

 g Union democracy.

 h Ethical standards.

4 In your company's management development program, there was a heated discussion between some people who claimed, "Theory is impractical and thus no good," and others who claimed, "Good theory is the most practical approach to problems." What position would you take and why?

5 An automobile manufacturer observes the demand for its brand increasing as per capita income increases. Sales increases also follow low interest rates, which ease credit conditions. Buyer purchase behavior is seen to be dependent on age and gender. Other factors influencing sales appear to fluctuate almost randomly (competitor advertising, competitor dealer discounts, introductions of new competitive models).

 a If sales and per capita income are positively related, classify all variables as dependent, independent, moderating, extraneous, or intervening.

 b Comment on the utility of a model based on the hypothesis.

Making Research Decisions

6 You observe the following condition: "Our female sales representatives have lower customer defections than do our male sales representatives."

 a Propose the concepts and constructs you might use to study this phenomenon.

 b How might any of these concepts and/or constructs be related to explanatory hypotheses?

7 You are the office manager of a large firm. Your company prides itself on its high-quality customer service. Lately complaints have surfaced that an increased number of incoming calls are being misrouted or dropped. Yesterday, when passing by the main reception area, you noticed the receptionist fiddling with his hearing aid. In the process, a call came in and would have gone unanswered if not for your intervention. This particular receptionist had earned an unsatisfactory review three months earlier for tardiness. Your inclination is to urge this 20-year employee to retire or to fire him, if retirement is rejected, but you know the individual is well liked and seen as a fixture in the company.

 a Pose several hypotheses that might account for dropped or misrouted incoming calls.

 b Using the double movement of reflective thought, show how you would test these hypotheses.

Bringing Research to Life

8 Identify and classify all the variables in the Army's dud shell research.

9 What was Myra's hypothesis for the Army's dud shell research? What was the Army's hypothesis?

From Concept to Practice

10 Using Exhibits 3-1 and 3-9 as your guides, graph the inductions and deductions in the following statements. If there are gaps, supply what is needed to make them complete arguments.

 a Repeated studies indicate that economic conditions vary with—and lag 6 to 12 months behind—the changes in the national money supply. Therefore, we may conclude the money supply is the basic economic variable.

 b Research studies show that heavy smokers have a higher rate of lung cancer than do nonsmokers; therefore, heavy smoking causes lung cancer.

 c Show me a person who goes to church regularly, and I will show you a reliable worker.

From the Headlines

11 That investment manager Bernard Madoff's hedge fund Ascot Partners was a giant scam will likely be *the* finance story remembered from the last decade. It is estimated that Madoff stole an estimated $50 billion from noteworthy individuals and institutional investors, and he covered the crime by creating fictional financial statements for each investor. If you were an institutional investor, how might employing scientific attitude and scientific method have protected your organization from this Ponzi scheme?

>cases*

Campbell-Ewald: R-E-S-P-E-C-T Spells Loyalty

Open Doors: Extending Hospitality to Travelers with Disabilities

HeroBuilders.com

* You will find a description of each case in the Case Abstracts section of this textbook. Check the Case Index to determine whether a case provides data, the research instrument, video, or other supplementary material. Written cases are downloadable from the text website (www.mhhe.com/cooper11e). All video material and video cases are available from the Online Learning Center.

>chapter 4

The Research Process: An Overview

>learningobjectives

After reading this chapter, you should understand. . .

1 Research is decision- and dilemma-centered.

2 The clarified research question is the result of careful exploration and analysis and sets the direction for the research project.

3 How value assessments and budgeting influence the process for proposing research and, ultimately, research design.

4 What is included in research design, data collection, data analysis, and reporting.

5 Research process problems to avoid.

> " Learning to ask empowering questions—especially in moments of crisis—is a critical skill that will ultimately shape the meanings you create. "
>
> Anthony Robbins, founder,
> Robbins Research International, Inc.

We rejoin Henry and Associates' Jason Henry as he works on the MindWriter CompleteCare customer satisfaction project. At this stage in the MindWriter research process, Jason Henry's task is to help MindWriter's project director, Myra Wines, define the correct information to collect. Jason Henry's partner Sara Arens, Henry, and Wines have just spent the day at the CompleteCare facility in Austin and with other MindWriter managers who are influential to CompleteCare's success. They spent part of their time with Gracie Uhura, MindWriter's marketing manager.

On the return flight from Austin, Jason Henry and MindWriter's Myra Wines are discussing their trip. "That went really well," she says.

"There are going to be a few problems," disagrees Jason.

"Gracie wants the sun, the sky, and the moon. She, like most managers, wants to know the demographic characteristics of her users . . . their job descriptions . . . their salaries . . . their ethnicities . . . their education. Wants to know the perception of MindWriter; wants to know their satisfaction with the purchase channel and with CompleteCare service, too."

"And your point is?" asks Myra.

"You and Gracie need to keep your eye on the bottom line. You can bet someone will want to know how you and Gracie can justify asking all these questions. They will ask, 'What is going to be the payoff in knowing the ethnicity of customers?' And if you or Gracie can't explain the justification for needing the information, if one of you can't establish that the dollar benefit of knowing is at least as great as the dollar cost of finding out, the question will get struck from the developing research."

"Is there no way we can justify knowing everything Gracie wants to know?" inquires Myra.

"We can do a pilot study by survey of a few hundred customers and see if the ethnic background, or the salary level, or any other item that Gracie cares about is a good indicator of satisfaction, willingness to make a repeat purchase, postpurchase service satisfaction, and so forth. If it is, maybe more extensive measurement can be justified."

"So you feel we need to propose an exploratory study to whittle down the information to critical items, followed by a larger study."

"A pilot study could help in other ways, too. Gracie wants to know the customers' perceptions of MindWriter's overall quality. But we have to ask ourselves, 'Are these customers really qualified to form independent opinions, or will they simply be parroting what they have read in the computer magazines or what a dealer told them?' A pilot study of a few hundred users can help determine if it is really useful to ask them their overall impression of the product.

"However, with the repair problem, we can be reasonably sure that CompleteCare customers know their own minds when it comes to evaluating their firsthand experience with MindWriter's service department."

"Today's tour of the CompleteCare facility really helped me understand the context of management's concern," comments Myra. "Did you or Sara have a chance to look over any of the customer letters from the service department?"

Jason digs into his briefcase and extracts a small sheaf of photocopies. "Yes, and Sara had reviewed transcriptions, too, on service center phone conversations. She pulled a few for us. One person writes, 'My MindWriter was badly damaged on arrival. I could not believe its condition when I unpacked it.' And here, 'The service technicians seemed to be unable to understand my complaint, but once they understood it, they performed immediate repairs.' You and I will collaborate to boil down these, and possibly dozens more like them, to a couple of representative questions that can be pilot-tested for clarity, consistency, and representativeness. You don't want MindWriter to pay for everything Gracie says she wants, just what she wants that has a payoff and is researchable."

> The Research Process

Writers usually treat the research task as a sequential process involving several clearly defined steps. No one claims that research requires completion of each step before going to the next. Recycling, circumventing, and skipping occur. Some steps are begun out of sequence, some are carried out simultaneously, and some may be omitted. Despite these variations, the idea of a sequence is useful for developing a project and for keeping the project orderly as it unfolds.

Exhibit 4-1 models the sequence of the **research process.** We refer to it often as we discuss each step in subsequent chapters. Our discussion of the questions that guide project planning and data gathering

>Exhibit 4-1 The Research Process

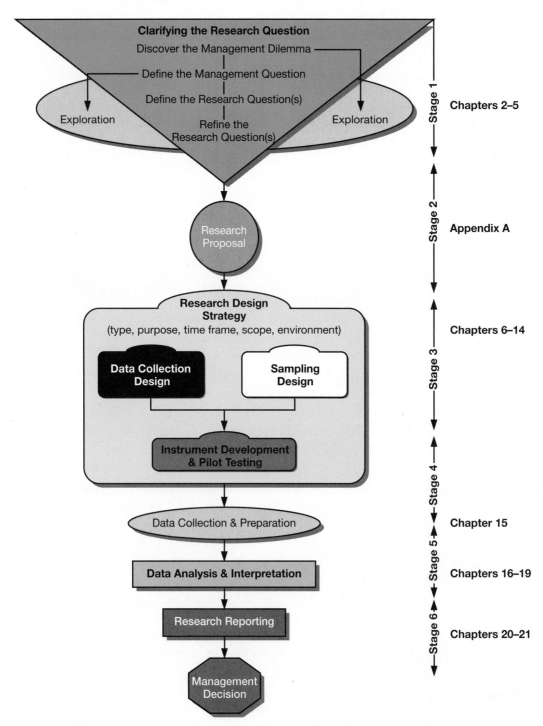

Stage 1	**Chapters 2–5**
Stage 2	**Appendix A**
Stage 3	**Chapters 6–14**
Stage 4	**Chapter 15**
Stage 5	**Chapters 16–19**
Stage 6	**Chapters 20–21**

is incorporated into the model (see the elements within the pyramid in Exhibit 4-1). Exhibit 4-1 also organizes this chapter and introduces the remainder of the book.

The research process begins much as the vignette suggests. A management dilemma triggers the need for a decision. For MindWriter, a growing number of complaints about postpurchase service started the process. In other situations, a controversy arises, a major commitment of resources is called for, or conditions in the environment signal the need for a decision. For MindWriter, the critical event could have been the introduction by a competitor of new technology that would revolutionize the processing speed of laptops. Such events cause managers to reconsider their purposes or objectives, define a problem for solution, or develop strategies for solutions they have identified.

In our view of the research process, the management question—its origin, selection, statement, exploration, and refinement—is the critical activity in the sequence. Throughout the chapter we emphasize problem-related steps. A familiar quotation from Albert Einstein, no less apt today than when it was written, supports this view:

> The formulation of a problem is far more often essential than its solution, which may be merely a matter of mathematical or experimental skill. To raise new questions, new possibilities, to regard old problems from a new angle requires creative imagination and marks real advance in science.[1]

Whether the researcher is involved in basic or applied research, a thorough understanding of the management question is fundamental to success in the research enterprise.

> Stage 1: Clarifying the Research Question

A useful way to approach the research process is to state the basic dilemma that prompts the research and then try to develop other questions by progressively breaking down the original question into more specific ones. You can think of the outcome of this process as the **management–research question hierarchy.** Exhibit 4-2 follows the MindWriter example through the process.

The process begins at the most general level with the **management dilemma.** This is usually a symptom of an actual problem, such as:

- Rising costs.
- The discovery of an expensive chemical compound that would increase the efficacy of a drug.
- Increasing tenant move-outs from an apartment complex.
- Declining sales.
- Increasing employee turnover in a restaurant.
- A larger number of product defects during the manufacture of an automobile.
- An increasing number of letters and phone complaints about postpurchase service (as in MindWriter; see Exhibit 4-2).

The management dilemma can also be triggered by an early signal of an opportunity or growing evidence that a fad may be gaining staying power—like the growing interest in hybrid cars—indicated by the number of broadcast news segments and print stories over an extended period of time.

Identifying management dilemmas is rarely difficult (unless the organization fails to track its performance factors—like sales, profits, employee turnover, manufacturing output and defects, on-time deliveries, customer satisfaction, etc.). However, choosing one dilemma on which to focus may be difficult. Choosing incorrectly will direct valuable resources (time, manpower, money, and equipment) on a path that may not provide critical decision-making information (the purpose of good research). As a manager, only practice makes you proficient. For new managers, or established managers facing new responsibilities, developing several management-research question hierarchies, each starting with a different dilemma, will assist in the choice process. In all figures related to the research process model, in this and subsequent chapters, we use an inverted pyramid to represent the management-research question hierarchy.

>Exhibit 4-2 Formulating the Research Question for MindWriter

To move from the management dilemma to the management question and subsequent research questions takes exploratory research. Such research may include examining previous studies, reviewing published studies and organizational records, and interviewing experts or information gatekeepers.

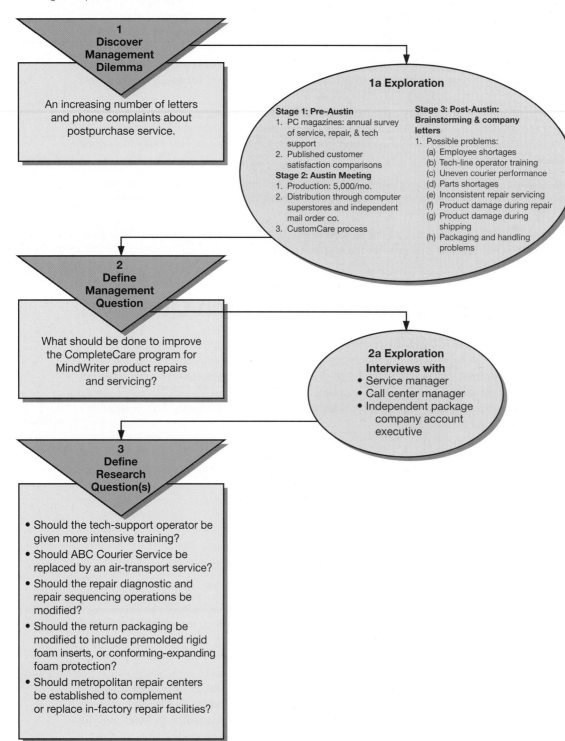

>**snap**shot

Should Companies Hire Teens?

According to the U.S. Bureau of Labor Statistics, 32.6 percent of teens nationwide worked during the summer of 2008, another year of decreased participation in the labor force. With the economy in recession, it's no wonder that teen employment is down along with overall employment.

For the summer of 2008, according to the Bureau of Labor Statistics, teens had an unemployment rate of 23.6 percent, an increase of more than 9 percent from just two years ago and almost three times the unemployment rate for adults. Economists think that teen unemployment may be significantly understated by the number of teens who felt locked out of the job market and did not actively seek employment.

Let's assume you are a manager of an organization that is questioning whether it should hire teen workers. A study sponsored by The Conference Board, Partnership for 21st Century Skills, Society for Human Resource Management, and Corporate Voices for Working Families, "Are They Really Ready to Work?" reports the opinions of more than 400 U.S. executives and human resource professions. Their unfavorable opinion was that "far too many young people are inadequately prepared to be successful in the workplace." Assessing teens with a Workforce Readiness Report Card, "10 skills that a majority of employer respondents rate as 'very important' to workforce success are on the Deficiency List." The report further defines the problem of teen workplace skills: "At the high school level, well over one-half of new entrants are deficiently prepared in the most important skills—Oral and Written Communications, Professionalism/Work Ethic, and Critical Thinking/Problem Solving."

You remember how important work was in building self-confidence and independence, so you don't want to write off all teens, but you are also concerned that supporting a "hire

teens" initiative might be counter-productive to your own job advancement if the study proves to be true. What research could you do to help formulate your recommendation on whether your organization should or should not hire teen workers?

www.bls.gov

Subsequent stages of the hierarchy take the manager and his or her research collaborator through various brainstorming and exploratory research exercises to define the following:

- **Management question**—a restatement of the manager's dilemma(s) in question form.
- **Research questions**—the hypothesis that best states the objective of the research; the question(s) that focuses the researcher's attention.
- **Investigative questions**—questions the researcher must answer to satisfactorily answer the research question; what the manager feels he or she needs to know to arrive at a conclusion about the management dilemma.
- **Measurement questions**—What participants in research are asked or what specifically is observed in a research study.

The definition of the management question sets the research task. A poorly defined management question will misdirect research efforts. In Chapter 5 we explore this critical stage in more detail in our search to clarify the research question.

Covering Kids: The Management-Research Question Hierarchy

Robert Wood Johnson Foundation (RWJF), a health care philanthropy, sponsors the Covering Kids initiative for one reason: Millions of children in low- to moderate-income families who are eligible for the State Children's Health Insurance Program (SCHIP) are not enrolled. RWJF initially became involved because it was concerned that the federal government and the states were not actively or effectively publicizing Medicaid and SCHIP. The initial goal of RWJF's involvement was to make eligible families aware of SCHIP and Medicaid and encourage enrollment. To this end, RWJF obtained the services of advertising agency GMMB, research firm Wirthlin Worldwide, and veteran social marketer Elaine Bratic Arkin.

The Foundation initially asked, "What must be done to enroll the largest percentage of eligible children in Medicaid and SCHIP?" Before GMMB could move forward, the team needed to determine whether the communication program needed to correct misconceptions, communicate benefits, overcome perceived process complexities, or do some combination of these. Early exploratory research sought answers to "What keeps eligible families from taking advantage of the prescription and doctor-visit programs of SCHIP and Medicaid?" The team also asked, "Is a negative stigma attached to participation in government health care programs?" When research indicated the answer to this question was "No," subsequent efforts focused on identifying other critical factors that discouraged families from enrolling. After research revealed that most working parents did not realize their children were eligible for a government program, the management question was refined to "What must be communicated to parents of eligible children to get them to enroll their children in these programs?"

Ultimately a creative combination of research design and data analysis revealed: (1) the winning communications framework:

Being a good parent means raising happy, healthy children, and enrolling a program offering low-cost or free health care is a smart choice for families, and (2) every communication must give working parents an easy, foolproof way to determine if their children are eligible while reinforcing the logic that making the call to enroll their children would address parents' innate desire to be good parents.

www.wirthlin.com; www.gmmb.com; www.rwjf.org

> Stage 2: Proposing Research
Resource Allocation and Budgets

General notions about research budgets have a tendency to single out data collection as the most costly activity. Data collection requires substantial resources but perhaps less of the budget than clients expect. Employees must be paid, training and travel must be provided, and other expenses incurred must be paid; but this phase of the project often takes no more than one-third of the total research budget. The geographic scope and the number of observations required do affect the cost, but much of the cost is relatively independent of the size of the data-gathering effort. Thus, a guide might be that (1) project planning; (2) data gathering; and (3) analysis, interpretation, and reporting each shares about equally in the budget.

> **Exhibit 4-3** Proposing Research

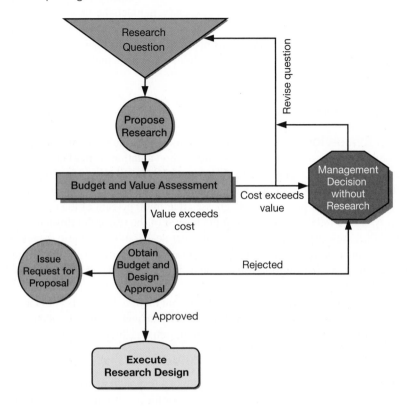

   Without budgetary approval, many research efforts are terminated for lack of resources (see Exhibit 4-3). A budget may require significant development and documentation as in grant and contract research, or it may require less attention as in some in-house projects or investigations funded out of the researcher's own resources. The researcher who seeks funding must be able not only to persuasively justify the costs of the project but also to identify the sources and methods of funding. One author identifies three types of budgets in organizations where research is purchased and cost containment is crucial:

- *Rule-of-thumb budgeting* involves taking a fixed percentage of some criterion. For example, a percentage of the prior year's sales revenues may be the basis for determining the marketing research budget for a manufacturer.

- *Departmental or functional area budgeting* allocates a portion of total expenditures in the unit to research activities. Government agencies, not-for-profits, and the private sector alike will frequently manage research activities out of functional budgets. Units such as human resources, marketing, or engineering then have the authority to approve their own projects.

- *Task budgeting* selects specific research projects to support on an ad hoc basis. This type is the least proactive but does permit definitive cost-benefit analysis.[2]

Valuing Research Information

There is a great deal of interplay between budgeting and value assessment in any management decision to conduct research. An appropriate research study should help managers avoid losses and increase sales or profits; otherwise, research can be wasteful. The decision maker wants a firm cost estimate for a project and an equally precise assurance that useful information will result from the study. Even if the researcher can give good cost and information estimates, the managers still must judge whether the benefits outweigh the costs.

Conceptually, the value of applied research is not difficult to determine. In a business situation, the research should produce added revenues or reduce expenses in much the same way as any other investment of resources. One source suggests that the value of research information may be judged in terms of "the difference between the result of decisions made with the information and the result that would be made without it."[3] While such a criterion is simple to state, its actual application presents difficult measurement problems.

Evaluation Methods

Ex Post Facto Evaluation   If there is any measurement of the value of research, it is usually an after-the-fact event. Twedt reports on one such effort, an evaluation of marketing research done at a major corporation.[4] He secured "an objective estimate of the contribution of each project to corporate profitability." He reports that most studies were intended to help management determine which one of two (or more) alternatives was preferable. He guesses that in 60 percent of the decision situations, the correct decision would have been made *without* the benefit of the research information. In the remaining 40 percent of the cases, the research led to the correct decision. Using these data, he estimates that the return on investment in marketing research in this company was 3.5 times for the year studied. However, he acknowledges the return-on-investment figure was inflated because only the direct research costs were included.

This effort at cost-benefit analysis is commendable even though the results come too late to guide a current research decision. Such analysis may sharpen the manager's ability to make judgments about future research proposals. However, the critical problem remains, that of project evaluation *before* the study is done.

Prior or Interim Evaluation   A proposal to conduct a thorough management audit of operations in a company may be a worthy one, but neither its costs nor its benefits are easily estimated in advance. Such projects are sufficiently unique that managerial experience seldom provides much aid in evaluating such a proposal. But even in these situations, managers can make some useful judgments. They may determine that a management audit is needed because the company is in dire straits and management does not understand the scope of its problems. The management information need may be so great as to ensure that the research is approved. In such cases, managers may decide to control the research expenditure risk by doing a study in stages. They can then review costs and benefits at the end of each stage and give or withhold further authorization.

Option Analysis   Some progress has been made in the development of methods for assessing the value of research when management has a choice between well-defined options. Managers can conduct a formal analysis with each alternative judged in terms of estimated costs and associated benefits and with managerial judgment playing a major role.

If the research design can be stated clearly, one can estimate an approximate cost. The critical task is to quantify the benefits from the research. At best, estimates of benefits are crude and largely reflect an orderly way to estimate outcomes under uncertain conditions. To illustrate how the contribution of research is evaluated in such a decision situation, we must digress briefly into the rudiments of decision theory.

Decision Theory   When there are alternatives from which to choose, a rational way to approach the decision is to try to assess the outcomes of each action. The case of two choices will be discussed here, although the same approach can be used with more than two choices.

Two possible actions (A_1 and A_2) may represent two different ways to organize a company, provide financing, produce a product, and so forth. The manager chooses the action that affords the best outcome—the action choice that meets or exceeds whatever criteria are established for judging alternatives. Each criterion is a combination of a **decision rule** and a **decision variable.** The decision variable might be "direct dollar savings," "contribution to overhead and profits," "time required for completion of the project," and so forth. For MindWriter, the decision variable might be number of postservice complaints or the level of postservice satisfaction. Usually the decision variable is expressed in dollars, representing sales, costs, some form of profits or contribution, or some other quantifiable measure. The decision rule may be "choose the course of action with the lowest loss possibility" or perhaps "choose the alternative that provides the greatest annual net profit." For MindWriter, the decision rule might be "choose the alternative that provides the highest level of postservice satisfaction."

The alternative selected (A_1 versus A_2) depends on the decision variable chosen and the decision rule used. The evaluation of alternatives requires that (1) each alternative is explicitly stated, (2) a decision variable is defined by an outcome that may be measured, and (3) a decision rule is determined by which outcomes may be compared.

The Research Proposal

Exhibit 4-1 depicts the research proposal as an activity that incorporates decisions made during early project planning phases of the study, including the management–research question hierarchy and exploration. The proposal thus incorporates the choices the investigator makes in the preliminary steps, as depicted in Exhibit 4-3.

A written proposal is often required when a study is being suggested. This is especially true if an outside research supplier will be contracted to conduct the research. The written proposal ensures that the parties concur on the project's purpose, the proposed methods of investigation, the extent of analysis, and the timing of each phase as well as of delivery of results. Budgets are spelled out, as are other responsibilities and obligations. The proposal may serve the purpose of a legally binding contract.

A research proposal also may be oral, wherein all aspects of the research are discussed but not codified in writing. This is more likely when a manager directs his or her own research or the research activities of subordinates. We describe detailed research proposals in Appendix A, and you will find a sample proposal on the text website.

> Stage 3: Designing the Research Project
Research Design

The **research design** is the blueprint for fulfilling objectives and answering questions. Selecting a design may be complicated by the availability of a large variety of methods, techniques, procedures, protocols, and sampling plans. For example, you may decide on a secondary data study, case study, survey, experiment, or simulation. If a survey is selected, should it be administered by mail, computer, telephone, the Internet, or personal interview? Should all relevant data be collected at one time or at regular intervals? What kind of structure will the questionnaire or interview guide possess? What question wording should be employed? Should the responses be scaled or open-ended? How will reliability and validity be achieved? Will characteristics of the interviewer influence responses to the measurement questions? What kind of training should the data collectors receive? Is a sample or a census to be taken? What types of sampling should be considered? These questions represent only a few of the decisions that have to be made when just one method is chosen.

Although selecting an appropriate design may be complicated by this range of options, the creative researcher actually benefits from this confusing array of options. The numerous combinations spawned by the abundance of tools may be used to construct alternative perspectives on the same problem. By creating a design using diverse methodologies, researchers are able to achieve greater insight than if they followed the most frequently used method or the method receiving the most media attention. Although pursuing research on a single research problem from a multimethod, multistudy strategy is not currently the norm, such designs are getting increasing attention from researchers and winning numerous industry awards for effectiveness. The advantages of several competing designs should be considered before settling on a final one.

>picprofile

Kraft research won well-deserved recognition for research that helped diagnose and improve sales of sliced cheese by 11.8 percent with a 14.5 percent increase in base volume. Kraft started by sending ethnographers from Strategic Frame-working to interview moms aged 25 to 64 who were fixing sandwiches in their kitchens. Focus groups then reinforced that moms feel good about giving their kids cheese because of its nutritional value, but that moms would choose a lower-priced cheese, even though their kids preferred Kraft. A subsequent phone survey by Market Facts revealed that moms would buy the pricier Kraft slices due to its extra calcium. Two TV commercials were tested using the "good-taste-plus-the-calcium-they-need" message. The tests revealed that the commercial showing kids scarfing down the gooey sandwiches where the Dairy Fairy delivered the calcium message outperformed a more serious commercial with the same message. Subsequent copy-testing research by Millward Brown Group revealed that the dual message (taste-preferred/calcium) was heard. **www.kraft.com; www.strategicframeworking.com; www.marketfacts.com; www.millwardbrown.com**

Jason's preference for MindWriter is to collect as much information as possible from an exploration of company records, interviews with company managers of various departments, and multiple phone surveys with CompleteCare service program users. Financial constraints, however, might force Mind-Writer to substitute a less expensive methodology: a self-administered study in the form of a postcard sent to each CompleteCare program user with his or her returned laptop, followed by phone contact with those who don't return the postcard.

Sampling Design

Another step in planning the research project is to identify the **target population** (those people, events, or records that contain the desired information and can answer the measurement questions) and then determine whether a sample or a census is desired. Taking a **census** requires that the researcher examine or count all elements in the target population. A **sample** examines a portion of the target population, and the portion must be carefully selected to represent that population. If sampling is chosen, the researcher must determine which and how many people to interview, which and how many events to observe, or which and how many records to inspect. When researchers undertake sampling studies, they are interested in estimating one or more population values (such as the percent of satisfied service customers who will buy new MindWriter laptops when the need arises) and/or testing one or more statistical hypotheses (e.g., that highly satisfied CompleteCare service customers will be far more likely to repurchase the MindWriter brand of laptops).

If a study's objective is to examine the attitudes of U.S. automobile assemblers about quality improvement, the population may be defined as the entire adult population of auto assemblers employed by the auto industry in the United States. Definition of the terms *adult* and *assembler* and the relevant job descriptions included under "assembly" and "auto industry" may further limit the population under study. The investigator may also want to restrict the research to readily identifiable companies in the market, vehicle types, or assembly processes.

The sampling process must then give every person within the target population a known nonzero chance of selection if probability sampling is used. If there is no feasible alternative, a nonprobability approach may be used. Jason knows that his target population comprises MindWriter customers who have firsthand experience with the CompleteCare program. Given that a list of CompleteCare program users (a sample frame) is readily available each month, a probability sample is feasible.

Pilot Testing

The data-gathering phase of the research process typically begins with pilot testing. Pilot testing may be skipped when the researcher tries to condense the project time frame.

A **pilot test** is conducted to detect weaknesses in design and instrumentation and to provide proxy data for selection of a probability sample. It should, therefore, draw subjects from the target population and simulate the procedures and protocols that have been designated for data collection. If the study is a survey to be executed by mail, the pilot questionnaire should be mailed. If the design calls for observation by an unobtrusive researcher, this behavior should be practiced. The size of the pilot group may range from 25 to 100 subjects, depending on the method to be tested, but the respondents do not have to be statistically selected. In very small populations or special applications, pilot testing runs the risk of exhausting the supply of respondents and sensitizing them to the purpose of the study. This risk is generally overshadowed by the improvements made to the design by a trial run.

There are a number of variations on pilot testing. Some of them are intentionally restricted to data collection activities. One form, *pretesting,* may rely on colleagues, respondent surrogates, or actual respondents to refine a measuring instrument. This important activity has saved countless survey studies from disaster by using the suggestions of the respondents to identify and change confusing, awkward, or offensive questions and techniques. One interview study was designed by a group of college professors for EducTV, an educational television consortium. In the pilot test, they discovered that the wording of nearly two-thirds of the questions was unintelligible to the target group, later found to have a median eighth-grade education. The revised instrument used the respondents' language and was successful. Pretesting may be repeated several times to refine questions, instruments, or procedures.

> Stage 4: Data Collection and Preparation

The gathering of data may range from a simple observation at one location to a grandiose survey of multinational corporations at sites in different parts of the world. The method selected will largely determine how the data are collected. Questionnaires, standardized tests, observational forms, laboratory notes, and instrument calibration logs are among the devices used to record raw data.

But what are data? One writer defines **data** as the facts presented to the researcher from the study's environment. First, data may be further characterized by their abstractness, verifiability, elusiveness, and closeness to the phenomenon.[5] As *abstractions,* data are more metaphorical than real. For example, the growth in GDP cannot be observed directly; only the effects of it may be recorded. Second, data are processed by our senses—often limited in comparison to the senses of other living organisms. When sensory experiences consistently produce the same result, our data are said to be trustworthy because they may be *verified.* Third, capturing data is *elusive,* complicated by the speed at which events occur and the time-bound nature of observation. Opinions, preferences, and attitudes vary from one milieu to another and with the passage of time. For example, attitudes about spending during the late 1980s differed dramatically one decade later within the same population, due to the sustained prosperity within the final four years of the millennium. Finally, data reflect their truthfulness by *closeness to the phenomena*. **Secondary data** have had at least one level of interpretation inserted between the event and its recording. **Primary data** are sought for their proximity to the truth and control over error. These cautions remind us to use care in designing data collection procedures and generalizing from results.

Data are edited to ensure consistency across respondents and to locate omissions. In the case of survey methods, editing reduces errors in the recording, improves legibility, and clarifies unclear and inappropriate responses. Edited data are then put into a form that makes analysis possible. Because it is impractical to place raw data into a report, alphanumeric codes are used to reduce the responses to a more manageable system for storage and future processing. The codes follow various decision rules that the researcher has devised to assist with sorting, tabulating, and analyzing. Personal computers have made it possible to merge editing, coding, and data entry into fewer steps even when the final analysis may be run on a larger system.

> Stage 5: Data Analysis and Interpretation

Managers need information, not raw data. Researchers generate information by analyzing data after its collection. **Data analysis** usually involves reducing accumulated data to a manageable size, developing summaries, looking for patterns, and applying statistical techniques. Scaled responses on questionnaires and experimental instruments often require the analyst to derive various functions, as well as to explore relationships among variables. Further, researchers must interpret these findings in light of the client's research question or determine if the results are consistent with their hypotheses and theories. Increasingly, managers are asking research specialists to make recommendations based on their interpretation of the data.

A modest example involves a market research firm that polls 2,000 people from its target population for a new generation of wallet-sized portable telephones. Each respondent will be asked four questions:

1. "Do you prefer the convenience of Pocket-Phone over existing cellular telephones?"
2. "Are there transmission problems with Pocket-Phone?"
3. "Is Pocket-Phone better suited to worldwide transmission than your existing cellular phone?"
4. "Would cost alone persuade you to purchase Pocket-Phone?"

The answers will produce 8,000 pieces of raw data. Reducing the data to a workable size will yield eight statistics: the percentage of yes and no answers to each question. When a half-dozen demographic questions about the respondents are added, the total amount of data easily triples. If the researcher scaled the four key questions rather than eliciting yes-no responses, the analysis would likely require more powerful statistical analysis than summarization.

> Stage 6: Reporting the Results

Finally, it is necessary to prepare a report and transmit the findings and recommendations to the manager for the intended purpose of decision making. The researcher adjusts the style and organization of the report according to the target audience, the occasion, and the purpose of the research. The results of applied research may be communicated via conference call, letter, written report, oral presentation, or some combination of any or all of these methods. Reports should be developed from the manager's or information user's perspective. The

49
The percent of hiring managers who discovered a lie on a résumé.

sophistication of the design and sampling plan or the software used to analyze the data may help to establish the researcher's credibility, but in the end, the manager's foremost concern is solving the management dilemma. Thus, the researcher must accurately assess the manager's needs throughout the research process and incorporate this understanding into the final product, the research report.

The management decision maker occasionally shelves the research report without taking action. Inferior communication of results is a primary reason for this outcome. With this possibility in mind, a research specialist should strive for:

- Insightful adaptation of the information to the client's needs.
- Careful choice of words in crafting interpretations, conclusions, and recommendations.

Occasionally, organizational and environmental forces beyond the researcher's control argue against the implementation of results. Such was the case in a study conducted for the Association of American Publishers, which needed an ad campaign to encourage people to read more books. The project, costing $125,000, found that only 13 percent of Americans buy general-interest books in stores. When the time came to commit $14 million to the campaign to raise book sales, the membership's interest had faded and the project died.[6]

At a minimum, a research report should contain the following:

- An *executive summary* consisting of a synopsis of the problem, findings, and recommendations.
- An *overview of the research:* the problem's background, literature summary, methods and procedures, and conclusions.
- A section *on implementation strategies* for the recommendations.
- A *technical appendix* with all the materials necessary to replicate the project.

> Research Process Issues

Although it is desirable for research to be thoroughly grounded in management decision priorities, studies can wander off target or be less effective than they should be.

The Favored-Technique Syndrome

Some researchers are method-bound. They recast the management question so that it is amenable to their favorite methodology—a survey, for example. Others might prefer to emphasize the case study, while still others wouldn't consider either approach. Not all researchers are comfortable with experimental designs. The past reluctance of most social scientists to use experimental designs is believed to have retarded the development of scientific research in that arena.

The availability of technique is an important factor in determining how research will be done or whether a given study can be done. Persons knowledgeable about and skilled in some techniques but not in others are too often blinded by their special competencies. Their concern for technique dominates the decisions concerning what will be studied (both investigative and measurement questions) and how (research design).

Since the advent of total quality management (TQM), numerous, standardized customer satisfaction questionnaires have been developed. Jason may have done studies using these instruments for any number of his clients. Myra should be cautious. She must not let Jason steamroll her into the use of an instrument he has developed for another client, even though he might be

A focus group is a favored technique, one that is useful for many types of research but also not suited to research problems that need different types of data. As this iThink ad points out, focus groups are especially useful when you want respondents candid thoughts, especially now that online focus groups are more common.

very persuasive about its success in the past. Such a technique might not be appropriate for Mind-Writer's search to resolve postpurchase service dissatisfaction.

Company Database Strip-Mining

The existence of a pool of information or a database can distract a manager, seemingly reducing the need for other research. As evidence of the research-as-expense-not-investment mentality mentioned in Chapter 1, managers frequently hear from superiors, "We should use the information we already have before collecting more." Modern management information systems are capable of providing massive volumes of data. This is not the same as saying modern management information systems provide substantial knowledge.

Each field in a database was originally created for a specific reason, a reason that may or may not be compatible with the management question facing the organization. The MindWriter service department's database, for example, probably contains several fields about the type of problem, the location of the problem, the remedy used to correct the problem, and so forth. Jason and Sara can accumulate facts concerning the service, and they can match each service problem with a particular MindWriter model and production sequence (from a production database), and, using yet another database (generated from warranty registration), they can match each problem to a name and address of an owner. But, having done all that, they still aren't likely to know how a particular owner uses his or her laptop or how satisfied an owner was with MindWriter's postpurchase service policies and practices.

Mining management information databases is fashionable, and all types of organizations increasingly value the ability to extract meaningful information. While such data mining is often a starting point in decision-based research, rarely will such activity answer all management questions related to a particular management dilemma.

Unresearchable Questions

Not all management questions are researchable, and not all research questions are answerable. To be researchable, a question must be one for which observation or other data collection can provide the answer. Many questions cannot be answered on the basis of information alone.

Questions of value and policy often must be weighed in management decisions. In the MetalWorks study, management may be asking, "Should we hold out for a liberalization of the seniority rules in our new labor negotiations?" While information can be brought to bear on this question, such additional considerations as "fairness to the workers" or "management's right to manage" may be important to the decision. It may be possible for many of these questions of value to be transformed into questions of fact. Concerning "fairness to the workers," one might first gather information from which to estimate the extent and degree to which workers will be affected by a rule change; then one could gather opinion statements by the workers about the fairness of seniority rules. Even so, substantial value elements remain. Questions left unanswered include "Should we argue for a policy that will adversely affect the security and well-being of older workers who are least equipped to cope with this adversity?" Even if a question can be answered by facts alone, it might not be researchable because currently accepted and tested procedures or techniques are inadequate.

Ill-Defined Management Problems

Some categories of problems are so complex, value-laden, and bound by constraints that they prove to be intractable to traditional forms of analysis. These questions have characteristics that are virtually the opposite of those of well-defined problems. One author describes the differences like this:

> To the extent that a problem situation evokes a high level of agreement over a specified community of problem solvers regarding the referents of the attributes in which it is given, the operations that are permitted, and the consequences of those operations, it may be termed unambiguous or well defined with respect to that community. On the other hand,

to the extent that a problem evokes a highly variable set of responses concerning referents of attributes, permissible operations, and their consequences, it may be considered ill-defined or ambiguous with respect to that community.[7]

Another author points out that ill-defined research questions are least susceptible to attack from quantitative research methods because such problems have too many interrelated facets for measurement to handle with accuracy.[8] Yet another authority suggests there are some research questions of this type for which methods do not presently exist or, if the methods were to be invented, still might not provide the data necessary to solve them.[9] Novice researchers should avoid ill-defined problems. Even seasoned researchers will want to conduct a thorough exploratory study before proceeding with the latest approaches.

Politically Motivated Research

It is important to remember that a manager's motivations for seeking research are not always obvious. Managers might express a genuine need for specific information on which to base a decision. This is the ideal scenario for quality research. Sometimes, however, a research study may not really be desirable but is authorized anyway, chiefly because its presence may win approval for a certain manager's pet idea. At other times, research may be authorized as a measure of personal protection for a decision maker in case he or she is criticized later. In these less-than-ideal cases, the researcher may find it more difficult to win the manager's support for an appropriate research design.

>summary

1 Research originates in the decision process. A manager needs specific information for setting objectives, defining tasks, finding the best strategy by which to carry out the tasks, or judging how well the strategy is being implemented.

 A dilemma-centered emphasis—the problem's origin, selection, statement, exploration, and refinement—dominates the sequence of the research process. A management dilemma can originate in any aspect of an organization. A decision to do research can be inappropriately driven by the availability of coveted tools and databases. To be researchable, a problem must be subject to observation or other forms of empirical data collection.

2 How one structures the research question sets the direction for the project. A management problem or opportunity can be formulated as a hierarchical sequence of questions. At the most general level is the management dilemma. This is translated into a management question and then into a research question—the major objective of the study. In turn, the research question is further expanded into investigative questions. These questions represent the various facets of the problem to be solved, and they influence research design, including design strategy, data collection planning, and sampling. At the most specific level are measurement questions that are answered by respondents in a survey or answered about each subject in an observational study.

 Exploration of the problem is accomplished through familiarization with the available literature, interviews with experts, focus groups, or some combination. Revision of the management or research questions is a desirable outcome of exploration and enhances the researcher's understanding of the options available for developing a successful design.

3 Budgets and value assessments determine whether most projects receive necessary funding. Their thorough documentation is an integral part of the research proposal. Proposals are required for many research projects and should, at a minimum, describe the research question and the specific task the research will undertake.

4 Decisions concerning the type of study, the means of data collection, measurement, and sampling plans must be made when planning the design. Most researchers undertake sampling studies because of an interest in estimating population values or testing a statistical hypothesis. Carefully constructed delimitations are essential for specifying an appropriate probability sample. Nonprobability samples are also used.

 Pilot tests are conducted to detect weaknesses in the study's design, data collection instruments, and procedures. Once the researcher is satisfied that the plan is sound, data collection begins. Data are collected, edited, coded, and prepared for analysis.

 Data analysis involves reduction, summarization, pattern examination, and the statistical evaluation of hypotheses.

A written report describing the study's findings is used to transmit the results and recommendations to the intended decision maker. By cycling the conclusions back into the original problem, a new research iteration may begin, and findings may be applied.

5 Several research process problems can diminish the value of research. Included in these are using a technique that is inappropriate for the information needed just because it is familiar or the researcher has experience with it; attempting to substitute data mining for research; focusing on an unresearchable question; failing to correctly define the management problem; and conducting politically motivated rather than management dilemma-motivated research.

>**key**terms

census 88

data 89

data analysis 90

decision rule 86

decision variable 86

investigative questions 83

management dilemma 81

management question 83

management–research question hierarchy 81

measurement questions 83

pilot test 89

primary data 90

research design 87

research process 80

research question(s) 83

sample 88

secondary data 90

target population 88

>**discussion**questions

Terms in Review

1 Some questions are answerable by research and others are not. Using some management problems of your choosing, distinguish between them.

2 Discuss the problems of trading off exploration and pilot testing under tight budgetary constraints. What are the immediate and long-term effects?

3 A company is experiencing a poor inventory management situation and receives alternative research proposals. Proposal 1 is to use an audit of last year's transactions as a basis for recommendations. Proposal 2 is to study and recommend changes to the procedures and systems used by the materials department. Discuss issues of evaluation in terms of:

   a Ex post facto versus prior evaluation.

   b Evaluation using option analysis and decision theory.

Making Research Decisions

4 Confronted by low productivity, the president of Oaks International Inc. asks a research company to study job satisfaction in the corporation. What are some of the important reasons that this research project may fail to make an adequate contribution to the solution of management problems?

5 Based on an analysis of the last six months' sales, your boss notices that sales of beef products are declining in your chain's restaurants. As beef entrée sales decline, so do profits. Fearing beef sales have declined due to several newspaper stories reporting *E. coli* contamination discovered at area grocery stores, he suggests a survey of area restaurants to see if the situation is pervasive.

   a What do you think of this research suggestion?

   b How, if at all, could you improve on your boss's formulation of the research question?

Bringing Research to Life

6 What are the benefits to MindWriter if Henry and Associates implements a pilot study?

7 How can MindWriter's existing database of service complaints be used to accumulate service problem information in advance of the proposed research. What information should be sought?

From Concept to Practice

8 Using Exhibit 4-1 and case examples from some research company's website, discover how favored technique approaches to research design dominate many firms' activities.

9 Using Exhibit 4-1, find a case study of a research example in which a clear statement of the management dilemma leads to a precise and actionable research. (Hint: Visit research company websites—see Appendix 1a for company ideas—or use a search engine to find examples.)

From the Headlines

10 By some estimates, it costs approximately $55,000 to generate an application (APP) for the Apple iPod. Just offering an APP is not a guarantee of success. The most successful APPs, sold as downloads, have to offer true functional value. Apple takes weeks to review an APP proposal; only with Apple's approval can an APP be officially offered for the iPod. If you were Apple, what research would you want to see within the proposal to approve a new APP for the iPod?

>cases*

 Akron Children's Hospital

Calling Up Attendance

 Covering Kids with Health Care

 Donatos: Finding the New Pizza

 Goodyear's Aquatred

HeroBuilders.com

Inquiring Minds Want to Know—NOW!

Lexus SC 430

Mastering Teacher Leadership

NCRCC: Teeing Up a New Strategic Direction

 Ohio Lottery: Innovative Research Design Drives Winning

Ramada Demonstrates Its *Personal Best*™

State Farm: Dangerous Intersections

USTA: Come Out Swinging

* You will find a description of each case in the Case Abstracts section of this textbook. Check the Case Index to determine whether a case provides data, the research instrument, video, or other supplementary material. Written cases are downloadable from the text website (www.mhhe.com/cooper11e). All video material and video cases are available from the Online Learning Center. The film reel icon indicates a video case or video material relevant to the case.

>chapter 5

Clarifying the Research Question through Secondary Data and Exploration

>learningobjectives

After reading this chapter, you should understand...

1 The purposes and process of exploratory research.

2 Two types and three levels of management decision-related secondary sources.

3 Five types of external information and the five critical factors for evaluating the value of a source and its content.

4 The process of using exploratory research to understand the management dilemma and work through the stages of analysis necessary to formulate the research question (and, ultimately, investigative questions and measurement questions).

5 What is involved in internal data mining and how internal data-mining techniques differ from literature searches.

> **Companies are certainly aware of data mining, but most companies are not making effective use of the data collected. They are not so good at analyzing it or applying these insights to the business.**
>
> Gregory Piatetsky-Shapiro, president
> Kdnuggets

>**bringing**research**to**life

Henry & Associates' Jason Henry and Sara Arens are fully into exploration for the MindWriter CompleteCare project. We join them as they discuss where they've been and where they are going in the process of defining the research question.

Jason Henry presses the intercom button. "Sara, have you had a chance to summarize the transcripts from the CompleteCare call center?"

"Those, as well as the summary of the complaint letters," responds Sara as she strolls through the door to Jason's office.

Jason jerks at the closeness of her voice. "It's unnerving how you anticipate what I want before I ask for it."

"Not so tough," chuckles Sara, enjoying seeing the unflappable Jason look a little shaken. "You did tell me you wanted them first thing this morning. And it is 8:05."

"What about those articles on measuring customer satisfaction in technological products?"

"I'm human, Jason, not a robotic search engine. That's the next thing on my BlackBerry to-do list."

"It seems logical that there might be special issues related to computers or other technical products when it comes to measuring satisfaction."

"But we both know that logic often doesn't have a thing to do with reality. Do you want me to brief you on what I've discovered from the complaint correspondence and the transcripts, or would you rather read the summary?"

"No, just leave it. I've set up an 8:30 phone interview with Sam Turnbull, the manager of the CompleteCare repair program. I need a few more minutes to review the questions I drafted last night."

"Fine. This call transcript was particularly interesting," shares Sara as she hands the transcript across the desk. "You might want to ask about this particular case. I'm sure he'll remember it."

"I'll just go start my search on whether technical products have differing measurement issues for satisfaction than the other industries we've studied."

"Um, hm . . ." Jason responds as he peruses the transcript. Then he glances up and stops Sara before she glides out the door. "While you are at it, see if there is an industrywide study on laptop satisfaction, something we might use as a benchmark. And anything you can find about the special problems associated with laptop construction, operation, use patterns, or repairs."

"I'm on it."

> A Search Strategy for Exploration

Exploration is particularly useful when researchers lack a clear idea of the problems they will meet during the study. Through exploration researchers develop concepts more clearly, establish priorities, develop operational definitions, and improve the final research design. Exploration may also save time and money. If the problem is not as important as first thought, more formal studies can be canceled.

Exploration serves other purposes as well. The area of investigation may be so new or so vague that a researcher needs to do an exploration just to learn something about the dilemma facing the manager. Important variables may not be known or thoroughly defined. Hypotheses for the research may be needed. Also, the researcher may explore to be sure it is practical to do a formal study in the area.

Despite its obvious value, researchers and managers alike give exploration less attention than it deserves. There are strong pressures for quick answers. Moreover, exploration is sometimes linked to old biases about qualitative research: subjectiveness, nonrepresentativeness, and nonsystematic design. More realistically, exploration may save both time and money and should not be slighted.

The exploratory phase search strategy usually comprises one or more of the following:

- Discovery and analysis of secondary sources.
  - Published studies (usually focused on the results of surveys or on case studies featuring one or a few incidents).
  - Document analysis.
  - Retrieval of information from organization's database(s).
- Interviews with those knowledgeable about the problem or its possible solutions (called **expert interviews**).
- Interviews with individuals involved with the problem (called **individual depth interviews,** or IDIs).
- Group discussions with individuals involved with the problem or its possible solutions (including informal groups, as well as formal techniques such as focus groups or brainstorming).

As the exploration process modeled with the management-research question hierarchy suggests (see Exhibit 5-1), exploration of secondary sources may be useful at any stage of the hierarchy. But most researchers find a review of secondary sources critical to moving from management question to research question. In moving from management question to research question, the researcher uses both internal and external secondary sources. Although most marketers would explore their internal archives first, here we will address external sources first.

In this **exploratory research** phase of your project, your objective is to accomplish the following:

- Expand your understanding of the management dilemma by looking for ways others have addressed and/or solved problems similar to your management dilemma or management question.
- Gather background information on your topic to refine the research question.
- Identify information that should be gathered to formulate investigative questions.
- Identify sources for and actual questions that might be used as measurement questions.
- Identify sources for and actual sample frames (lists of potential participants) that might be used in sample design.

In most cases the exploration phase will begin with a **literature search**—a review of books as well as articles in journals or professional literature that relate to your management dilemma. This review should include high-quality Web-published materials. A literature search requires the use of the library's online catalog and one or more bibliographic databases or indexes. For some topics, it may be useful to consult a handbook or specialized encyclopedia first to establish a list of key terms, people, or events that have influenced your topic and also to determine what the major publications are and who

>**Exhibit 5-1** Integration of Secondary Data into the Research Process

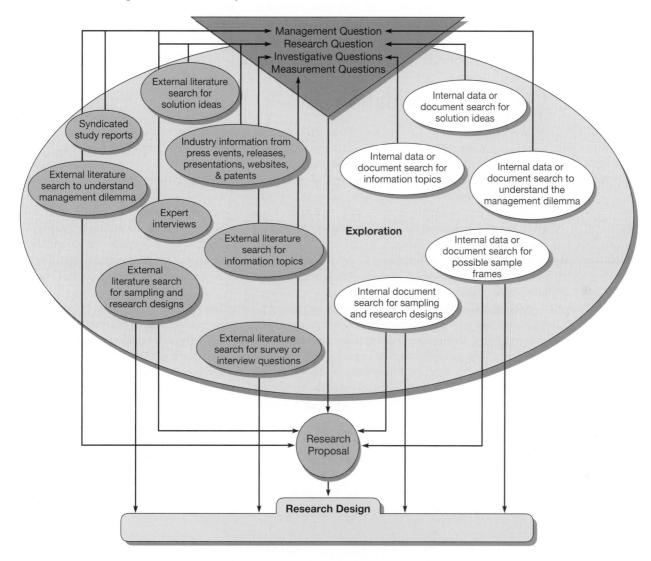

the foremost authors are. Other reference materials will be incorporated into your search strategy as needed. In general, this literature search has five steps:

1. Define your management dilemma or management question.

2. Consult encyclopedias, dictionaries, handbooks, and textbooks to identify key terms, people, or events relevant to your management dilemma or management question.

3. Apply these key terms, names of people, or events in searching indexes, bibliographies, and the Web to identify specific secondary sources.

4. Locate and review specific secondary sources for relevance to your management dilemma.

5. Evaluate the value of each source and its content.

The result of your literature search may be a solution to the management dilemma. In such a case, no further research is necessary. Often, however, the management question remains unresolved, so the decision to proceed generates a research proposal (see Appendix A). The resulting proposal covers at minimum a statement of the research question and a brief description of the proposed research methodology. The proposal summarizes the findings of the exploratory phase of the research, usually with a bibliography of secondary sources that have led to the decision to propose a formal research study.

In this chapter we will concentrate on the exploration phase of the project and focus on finding, selecting, and evaluating information in both printed and electronic formats. In some instances, researchers will discover the answer to their management dilemma in the results of a secondary search. A great exploration of secondary sources pays dividends—big ones—if a costly research project is deemed unnecessary.

Levels of Information

As you explore your problem or topic, you may consider many different types of information sources, some much more valuable than others. Information sources are generally categorized into three levels: (1) primary sources, (2) secondary sources, and (3) tertiary sources.

Primary sources are original works of research or raw data without interpretation or pronouncements that represent an official opinion or position. Included among the primary sources are memos; letters; complete interviews or speeches (in audio, video, or written transcript formats); laws; regulations; court decisions or standards; and most government data, including census, economic, and labor data. Primary sources are always the most authoritative because the information has not been filtered or interpreted by a second party. Other internal sources of primary data are inventory records, personnel records, purchasing requisition forms, statistical process control charts, and similar data.

Secondary sources are interpretations of primary data. Encyclopedias, textbooks, handbooks, magazine and newspaper articles, and most newscasts are considered secondary information sources. Indeed, nearly all reference materials fall into this category. Internally, sales analysis summaries and investor annual reports would be examples of secondary sources, because they are compiled from a variety of primary sources. To an outsider, however, the annual report is viewed as a primary source, because it represents the official position of the corporation. A firm searching for secondary sources can search either internally or externally, as Exhibit 5-2 depicts.

>Exhibit 5-2 Secondary Sources for Developing the Question Hierarchy

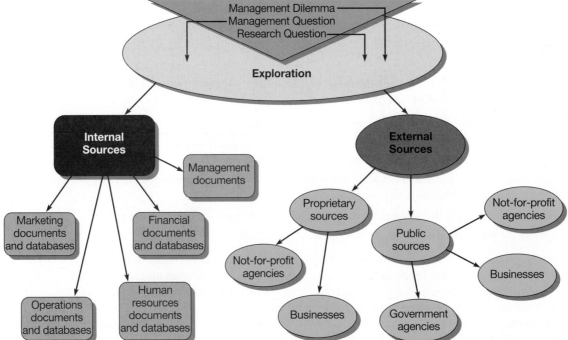

Blogs: Gold Mine or Land Mine?

Internet designers conceived a worldwide-accessible collection of documents, rather like a gargantuan library. What they could not foresee was the suppressed desire of millions to play the role of reporter, columnist, anchor, or analyst. Many blogs, defined as frequent, chronological publication of personal thoughts and Web links, started as personal online journals. Newer ones, however, show more influential agendas. While the Internet has influenced research in numerous visible ways—how we collect data, process data, even report data—one unexpected influence of the Internet is this new and growing source of data. And it isn't a source we can take lightly.

Technorati's latest State of the Blogosphere Report tracked its 50 millionth blog, with more than 175,000 new ones created daily, as well as 1.6 million postings per day, or about 18.6 posts per second. English (41 percent) and Japanese (31 percent) language posts dominate the blogosphere. According to the PEW Internet & American Life Project, 39 percent of U.S. adults read blogs, up from 17 percent in only two years. With the aid of search engines and RSS aggregators, a savvy company can monitor, respond to, and critique the ideas of these vocal and influential individuals. Companies worried about disgruntled or careless employees revealing emerging product ideas or financial or legal strategies to competitors are establishing strict blogging policies. Forward-thinking companies are launching their own blogs, for both external and internal audiences, to encourage open, free-wheeling conversations about their brands, products, employment policies, and problem-solving approaches. And researchers are challenged to spot emerging trends by mining this vast array of ideas and opinions traveling on the net at hyperspeed.

Using the source evaluation process, how would you evaluate blog data?

http://technorati.com; www.pewinternet.org

Tertiary sources may be interpretations of a secondary source but generally are represented by indexes, bibliographies, and other finding aids (e.g., Internet search engines).

From the beginning, it is important to remember that all information is not of equal value. As the source levels indicate, primary sources have more value than secondary sources, and secondary sources have more value than tertiary sources. In the opening vignette, Sara has read the MindWriter CompleteCare call center transcripts (a primary source), and Jason suggests that she also check for articles

The U.S. Government is the world's largest source of data and information used by managers in all types of organizations. Learning how to navigate this government portal is a critical skill.
www.usa.gov

Crossing the Deception Line?

Most business intelligence activities are designed to help firms deal with the risks of operating in challenging environments. Nowhere is the issue of deception more in the news forefront than in the arena of business intelligence, an arena filled with actions designed to unearth the practices and processes of suppliers, competitors, employees, and even directors.

One recent example in the news involves the actions of an intelligence firm, Diligence, Inc. Diligence was hired by well-known Washington, D.C., lobbying firm Barbour Griffith & Rogers (BGR) to discover competitive information for one of its clients, a Russian conglomerate, about that firm's archrival IPOC International Growth Fund Ltd. (IPOC). The task as described here is not inherently deceitful. Worldwide, employees are charged with such tasks on a daily basis. You could approach such a task in numerous ways: conduct a comprehensive literature search, talk with industry experts, interview former employees, monitor competitor publications, or attend presentations by their executives, and so forth. Diligence chose a covert use of deception to achieve its task.

Diligence first discovered that IPOC was the client of a reputable accounting firm KPMG. Diligence researched KPMG's employees, seeking an individual who might leak audit information. The search revealed the identity of a British-born accountant. Diligence sent an employee, masquerading as a British intelligence officer needing assistance on a matter of top British national security, to recruit the assistance of the accountant. After several weeks of luncheon meetings, the Diligence employee started inquiring about IPOC's audit. Ultimately, the KPMG employee shared proprietary information with the supposed undercover British security agent. KPMG sued Diligence and the case was settled out of court with Diligence paying KPMG $1.7 million. IPOC's lawsuit against Diligence and its client is still pending.

Most of us recognize the demarcation between deception and fraud. But what if in a casual social conversation with an acquaintance over lunch you inadvertently reveal what some firm wants to know? Some researchers say that deception is never appropriate. Other researchers claim that deception is appropriate to mask the sponsor's identity and the purpose of the research. Where do you stand on the issue of deception in business intelligence gathering?

www.businessweek.com

related to laptop manufacture, repair, and satisfaction (all secondary sources). Sara's summary of the transcript and letters is a secondary source. Henry & Associates' program for MindWriter will hinge on Jason's understanding of the current laptop repair scenario. If the information is essential to solving the management dilemma, it is wise to verify it in a primary source. That's why Sara wants Jason to ask CompleteCare's manager (primary source) for his take on the facts related to the disturbing call transcript she found.

Types of Information Sources

There are dozens of types of information sources, each with a special function. In this section we describe five of the information types used most by researchers at this phase of the project. We provide a list of key business information sources on your text CD.

Indexes and Bibliographies

Indexes and **bibliographies** are the mainstay of any library because they help you identify and locate a single book or journal article from among the millions published. The single most important bibliography in any library is its online catalog. As with all other information types, there are many specialized indexes and bibliographies unique to business topics. These can be very useful in a literature search to find authors and titles of prior works on the topic of interest.

Skill in searching bibliographic databases is essential for the business researcher. For the novice or less skilled, we provide two appendices at the end of this chapter. The first, "Bibliographic Database

Searches," reviews the process of searching. The second, "Advanced Searches," reveals the more advanced techniques of skilled searchers.

Dictionaries

Dictionaries are so ubiquitous that they probably need no explanation. We all use them to verify spelling or grammar usage or to define terms. In business, as in every field, there are many specialized dictionaries that define words, terms, or jargon unique to a discipline. Most of these specialized dictionaries include in their word lists information on people, events, or organizations that shape the discipline. They are also an excellent place to find acronyms. A growing number of dictionaries and *glossaries* (terms in a specialized field, area, or topic plus their definitions) are now available on the Web. Information from dictionaries and glossaries may be used to identify key terms for a search of an online or printed database.

Encyclopedias

Marketers use an **encyclopedia** to find background or historical information on a topic or to find names or terms that can enhance search results in other sources. For example, you might use an encyclopedia to find the date that Microsoft introduced Windows and then use that date to draw more information from an index to the time period. Encyclopedias are also helpful in identifying the experts in a field and the key writings on any topic. One example of an encyclopedia is the *Online TDM Encyclopedia* published by the Victoria Transportation Policy Institute.

> The *Online TDM Encyclopedia* is a comprehensive source of information about innovative management solutions to transportation problems. The Encyclopedia provides detailed information on dozens of Transportation Demand Management (TDM) strategies, plus chapters on their planning, evaluation and implementation. It can help you view transportation problems from a new perspective, and expand the range of possible solutions to apply.[1]

Another example drawn from the area of finance is the *Encyclopedia of Private Equity and Venture Capital,* published by VC Experts, Inc., a provider of expertise and opportunity in private equity and venture capital.[2]

Handbooks

A **handbook** is a collection of facts unique to a topic. Handbooks often include statistics, directory information, a glossary of terms, and other data such as laws and regulations essential to a field. The best handbooks include source references for the facts they present. The *Statistical Abstract of the United States* is probably the most valuable and frequently used handbook available. It contains an extensive variety of facts, an excellent and detailed index, and a gateway to even more in-depth data for every table included. One handbook with which students and managers alike are familiar is the *Occupational Outlook Handbook* published by the U.S. Bureau of Labor Statistics. In it you can find details about many business occupations.[3] Many handbooks are quite specialized, such as the one published by the Potato Association of America. It reveals not only consumption patterns but also potato growing and processing statistics.[4]

One of the most important handbooks, especially in the business-to-business arena, is the *North American Industry Classification System, United States (NAICS).* Jointly designed with Canada and Mexico to provide comparability in business statistics throughout North America, especially as new businesses and new business sectors develop, this classification system of all businesses replaced the Standard Industrial Classification in 1997. Its next revision is in 2009.[5]

Directories

Directories are used for finding names and addresses as well as other data. Although many are available and useful in printed format, directories in digitized format that can be searched by certain characteristics or sorted and then downloaded are far more useful. Many are available free through the Web,

Surfing the Deep Web

According to Rider University librarian Robert Lackie, "Although many popular search engines boast about their ability to index information on the Web, some of the Web's information is invisible to their searching spiders." Why is it invisible? Searchwise's president Chris Sherman explains, "The most basic reason is that there are no links pointing to a page that a search engine spider can follow. Or, a page may be made up of data types that search engines don't index—graphics, CGI scripts, or Macromedia Flash, for example." Today, non-HTML pages, dynamically created pages, and even scripted pages that were invisible a few years ago are now regularly found by search engines Google, Yahoo!, and more. What those search engines still cannot "see" is the content of specialized searchable databases on the Web (e.g., specialized government databases) and those the search engines *choose* to exclude because they view them as of little use to the searching public. BrightPlanet, a compiler of more than 35,000 searchable databases—the largest on the Internet—estimates that the invisible Web may be as much as 500 times the size of the searchable Web.

Lackie suggests we access this hidden content with just a few tools: directories and portals, searchable sites (some of which likely are available through your university library), free Web databases, and a few general and many specialized search engines. Here is just a sample:

> **Librarians' Internet Index** (http://lii.org/)—This directory maintained by librarians offers 20,000 entries, organized into 14 main topics and nearly 300 related topics.

Direct Search (www.freepint.com/)—This search tool offers access to a compilation of links to the search interfaces of resources.

InfoMine (http://infomine.ucr.edu)—This directory offers a scholarly resource collection that includes tens of thousands of sites.

About.com (http://www.about.com/)—This portal amasses its content by the passionate interests of 570 expert guides; more than 34 million people visit its neatly organized content of thousands of topics, including Invisible Web.

CompletePlanet (http://www.completeplanet.com/)—BrightPlanet's site contains more than 70,000 searchable databases and specialty search engines.

FindArticles (http://www.findarticles.com/)—This specialized database contains more than 10 million articles from "leading academic, industry and general interest publications."

Super Searchers Web Page (http://www.infotoday.com/supersearchers/)—This site indexes a growing collection of links to subject-specific Web resources in global business, primary research, mergers/acquisitions, news, investment, business, entrepreneurial research, and legal information resources.

AOL Video (http://video.aol.com/)—This audio/video search engine indexes multimedia formats, including Windows Media, Real, QuickTime, and MP3s.

Never stop your information search until you've looked for specialized databases that might be invisible. Such sources could be hiding a treasure trove of information perfect for your particular research question.

but the most comprehensive directories are proprietary (i.e., must be purchased). An especially useful directory available in most libraries in either print or electronic format is the *Encyclopedia of Associations* (called *Associations Unlimited* on the Web), which provides a list of public and professional organizations plus their locations and contact numbers.[6] New York AMA Communications Services, Inc., publishes the *Green Book, a Guide for Buyers of Marketing Research Services.*[7]

Evaluating Information Sources

A researcher using secondary sources, especially if drawn from the Internet, will want to conduct a **source evaluation.** Marketers should evaluate and select information sources based on five factors that can be applied to any type of source, whether printed or electronic. These are:

- *Purpose*—the explicit or hidden agenda of the information source.
- *Scope*—the breadth and depth of topic coverage, including time period, geographic limitations, and the criteria for information inclusion.
- *Authority*—the level of the data (primary, secondary, tertiary) and the credentials of the source author(s).

- *Audience*—the characteristics and background of the people or groups for whom the source was created.
- *Format*—how the information is presented and the degree of ease of locating specific information within the source.

Sara is about to embark on an Internet search for various types of information. Exhibit 5-3 summarizes the critical questions she should ask when applying these source evaluation factors to the evaluation of Internet sources she discovers.

>**Exhibit 5-3** Evaluating Websites as Information Sources

Evaluation Factor	Questions to Answer
Purpose	• Why does the site exist?
	• How evident is the purpose it is trying to convey?
	• Does it achieve its purpose?
	• How does its purpose affect the type and bias of information presented?
Authority	• What are the credentials of the author or institution or organization sponsoring the site?
	• Does the site give you a means of contacting anyone for further information?
	• Who links to this site?
	• If facts are supplied, where do they come from?
Scope	• How old is the information?
	• How often is it updated?
	• How much information is available?
	• Is it selective or comprehensive?
	• What are the criteria for inclusion?
	• If applicable, what geographic area or time period or language does it cover?
	• How does the information presented compare with that on similar sites?
	• Is it a series of links only (a metasite), or is there added value?
	• What is the nature of the added value?
	• What information did you expect to find that was missing?
	• Is the site self-contained, or does it link to other websites?
Audience	• Whom does the site cater to?
	• What level of knowledge or experience is assumed?
	• How does this intended audience affect the type and bias of the information?
Format	• How quickly can you find needed information?
	• How easy is the site to use? Is it intuitive?
	• Does it load quickly?
	• Is the design appealing?
	• Are there navigation buttons?
	• Is there a site map or search button?
	• Is there an easily identifiable Help button?
	• Is Help helpful?
	• Are pages in ASCII or graphic format?
	• Is the information downloadable into a spreadsheet or word processing program, if desired?

The purpose of early exploration is to help the researcher understand the management dilemma and develop the management question. Later stages of exploration are designed to develop the research question and ultimately the investigative and measurement questions.

> Mining Internal Sources

The term **data mining** describes the process of discovering knowledge from databases stored in data marts or data warehouses. The purpose of data mining is to identify valid, novel, useful, and ultimately understandable patterns in data.[8] Similar to traditional mining, where we search beneath the surface for valuable ore, data mining searches large databases for indispensable information for managing an organization. Both require sifting a large amount of material to discover a profitable vein. Data mining is a useful tool, an approach that combines exploration and discovery with confirmatory analysis.

An organization's own internal historical data are often an underutilized source of information in the exploratory phase. Due to employee turnover, the researcher may lack knowledge that such historical data exist; or, based on time or budget constraints and the lack of an organized archive, the researcher may choose to ignore such data. Although digging through data archives can be as simplistic as sorting through a file containing past patient records or inventory shipping manifests, or rereading company reports and management-authored memos that have grown dusty with age, we will concentrate the remainder of our discussion on more sophisticated structures and techniques.

A **data warehouse** is an electronic repository for databases that organizes large volumes of data into categories to facilitate retrieval, interpretation, and sorting by end users. The data warehouse provides an accessible archive to support dynamic organizational intelligence applications. The key words here are *dynamically accessible.* Data warehouses that offer archaic methods for data retrieval are seldom used. Data in a data warehouse must be continually updated to ensure that managers have access to data appropriate for real-time decisions. In a data warehouse, the contents of departmental computers are duplicated in a central repository where standard architecture and consistent data definitions are applied. These data are available to departments or cross-functional teams for direct analysis or through intermediate storage facilities or **data marts** that compile locally required information. The entire system must be constructed for integration and compatibility among the different data marts.

The more accessible the databases that comprise the data warehouse, the more likely a researcher will use such databases to reveal patterns. Thus, researchers are more likely to mine electronic databases than paper ones. It will be useful to remember that data in a data warehouse were once primary data, collected for a specific purpose. When researchers data-mine a company's data warehouse, all the data contained within that database have become secondary data. The patterns revealed will be used for purposes other than those originally intended. For example, in an archive of sales invoices, we have a wealth of data about what was sold, how much of each item or service, at what price level, to whom, and where and when and how the products were shipped. Initially the company generated the sales invoice to facilitate the process of getting paid for the items shipped. When a researcher mines that sales invoice archive, the search is for patterns of sales, by product, category, region of the country or world, price level, shipping methods, and so forth. Therefore, data mining forms a bridge between primary and secondary data.

Numerous companies build large consumer purchase behavior databases by collecting purchases made via store-owned credit programs or frequent purchase cards not linked directly with payment plans. Studying such data can reveal the likely success of a new product introduction or the sales lift effect of a coupon drop.

>snapshot

How Will Cloud Computing Affect Research?

Cloud computing refers to "a computing environment where data and services reside in scalable data centers accessible over the Internet."[a] Most of us are unaware of this cloud, but we may be using it if we subscribe to a Web-based e-mail service such as G-mail. Of course, the influence of cloud computing extends much farther. While cloud computing is different than SaaS (software as a service, where organizations access applications via the Internet but their data, documents, etc., reside on their own computers), many expanding clouds include both the infrastructure for data warehousing along with unique and customizable applications. Amazon, Dell, Google, IBM, Microsoft, HP, Yahoo, and Salesforce.com are some of the bigger players, but the cloud is dense with smaller players, too.

Amazon's Elastic Compute Cloud, known as Amazon EC2, claims to change "the economics of computing by allowing [the organization] to pay only for [server] capacity that [it] actually uses."[b] What that means for research is that data mined from all research sources (customer transactions, employee evaluations, financial records, surveys, etc.) may no longer be resident on an individual organization's servers, but rather resident on the Web. We can already see this occuring with sites such as SurveyMonkey.com. A company can design and field multiple online surveys, and the data from each is collected and resident with SurveyMonkey (or potentially outsourced to another cloud provider). SurveyMonkey allows you to analyse the data online as the survey progresses—in real time—and share access to that data or its analysis with anyone.

The big advantage of cloud computing is that it is "paid for only when it is activated and can scale as large or small as needed at the time it is needed."[c] As Salesforce.com claims for its cloud, Force.com, "There's no hardware to purchase, scale, and maintain, no operating systems, database servers, or application servers to install, no consultants and staff to manage it all, and no need for upgrades."[d] Its second strength is collaboration through widely dispersed access that many feel stimulates innovation. For example, with Microsoft's cloud, called Live Mesh, "users can place documents [including data] into the 'mesh,' which is essentially an online storage locker, and then access them from [anywhere]."[e]

The cloud's biggest perceived weakness is security and lack of control of proprietary information. Adam Selipesky, Amazon.com's vice president for product management and developer relations, speaking on cloud computing, indicates that companies are "starting to come to terms with the idea of data leaving their four walls, but [many are] not there yet."[f]

aws.amazon.com/ec2/; www.mesh.com; www.SurveyMonkey .com; www.salesforce.com/platform/

Traditional database queries are unidimensional and historical—for example, "How much beer was sold during December in the Sacramento area?" In contrast, data mining attempts to discover patterns and trends in the data and to infer rules from these patterns. For example, an analysis of retail sales by Sacramento FastShop identified products that are often purchased together—like beer and diapers—although they may appear to be unrelated. With the rules discovered from the data mining, a manager is able to support, review, and/or examine alternative courses of action for solving a management dilemma, alternatives that may later be studied further in the collection of new primary data.

Evolution of Data Mining

The complex algorithms used in data mining have existed for more than two decades. The U.S. government has employed customized data-mining software using neural networks, fuzzy logic, and pattern recognition to spot tax fraud, eavesdrop on foreign communications, and process satellite imagery.[9] Until recently, these tools have been available only to very large corporations or agencies due to their high costs. However, this is rapidly changing.

In the evolution from *business data* to *information,* each new step has built on previous ones. For example, large database storage is crucial to the success of data mining. The four stages listed in Exhibit 5-4 were revolutionary because each allowed new management questions to be answered accurately and quickly.[10]

The process of extracting information from data has been done in some industries for years. Insurance companies often compete by finding small market segments where the premiums paid greatly

>Exhibit 5-4 The Evolution of Data Mining

Evolutionary Step	Investigative Question	Enabling Technologies	Characteristics
Data Collection (1960s)	"What was my average total revenue over the last five years?"	Computers, tapes, disks	Retrospective, static data delivery
Data Access (1980s)	"What were unit sales in California last December?"	Relational databases (RDBMS), structured query language (SQL), ODBC	Retrospective, dynamic data delivery at record level
Data Navigation (1990s)	"What were unit sales in California last December? Drill down to Sacramento."	Online analytic processing (OLAP), multidimensional databases, data warehouses	Retrospective, dynamic data delivery at multiple levels
Data Mining (2000)	"What's likely to happen to Sacramento unit sales next month? Why?"	Advanced algorithms, multiprocessor computers, massive databases	Prospective, proactive information delivery

outweigh the risks. They then issue specially priced policies to a particular segment with profitable results. However, two problems have limited the effectiveness of this process: getting the data has been both difficult and expensive, and processing it into information has taken time—making it historical rather than predictive. Now, instead of incurring high data collection costs to resolve management questions, secondary data are available to assist the manager's decision making. It was State Farm Insurance's ability to mine its extensive nationwide database of accident locations and conditions at intersections that allowed it to identify high-risk intersections and then plan a primary data study to determine alternatives to modify such intersections.

Functional areas of management and select industries are currently driving data-mining projects: marketing, customer service, administrative/financial analysis, sales, manual distribution, insurance, fraud detection, and network management.[11] Data-mining technology provides two unique capabilities to the researcher or manager: pattern discovery and prediction.

Pattern Discovery

Data-mining tools can be programmed to sweep regularly through databases and identify previously hidden patterns. An example of pattern discovery is the detection of stolen credit cards based on analysis of credit card transaction records. MasterCard processes 12 million transactions daily and uses data mining to detect fraud.[12] Other uses include finding retail purchase patterns (used for inventory management), identifying call center volume fluctuations (used for staffing), and locating anomalous data that could represent data entry errors (used to evaluate the need for training, employee evaluation, or security).

Predicting Trends and Behaviors

A typical example of a predictive problem is targeted marketing. Using data from past promotional mailings to identify the targets most likely to maximize return on investment can make future mailings more effective. Bank of America and Mellon Bank both use data-mining software to pinpoint marketing programs that attract high-margin, low-risk customers. Bank of America focuses on credit lines and retail lending; Mellon Bank has used data mining to optimize its home equity line of credit marketing to existing customers.[13] Other predictive problems include forecasting bankruptcy and loan default and finding population segments with similar responses to a given stimulus. Data-mining tools also can be used to build risk models for a specific market, such as discovering the top 10 most significant buying trends each week.

33

The percent of financial executives who have full confidence in their current risk strategies.

>**snap**shot

Mining the Web for Feelings?

Data mining, or pattern extraction from large amounts of data, is great for sifting through numbers, but can it interpret "feelings"?

Alex Wright asked this question in a recent *New York Times* article about the explosion of blogs and social networks with the accompanying deluge of opinions.[a] Bloggers can have a huge impact in influencing views on politics, business, entertainment, and sports. Since blogging and networking are about expressing and listening to opinion, tools for emotive text analysis are essential. The problem for analysts is to extract human emotion from reviews and recommendations and translate them into usable data.

The emerging field of *sentiment analysis and opinion mining* provides us with a means of applying a computational treatment to opinion, sentiment, and subjectivity in textual form. Its goal is to decode a speaker or writer's attitude on some topic. This might be an evaluation, the writer's affective state, or the emotional effect the writer creates in readers. A business might ask, for example, "Are our preliminary product reviews positive or negative?" Or, "Are blog posts running in favor of a particular policy position that affects environmental costs?"

How does it work? Software scans for keywords and categorizes a statement as positive or negative, using a simple binary assignment ("success" is good, "failure" is bad). But, as Wright explains, the simplicity "fails to capture the subtleties that bring human language to life: irony, sarcasm, slang and other idiomatic expressions."[b] The difficulty for most sentiment algorithms is the reliance on simple keywords to express complex feelings about a product, movie, or service. It is the cultural factors, linguistic shading, and contexts that make turning written text into digitized sentiment difficult.[c]

Bo Pang, one of the first academics and software developers in the field explains that to understand the true intent of a statement, filters for intensity and subjectivity should be added to polarity (good-bad/positive-negative). Intensity refers to the level of emotion being expressed and subjectivity is the degree of source impartiality.[d] Multi-way scales are also used to expand polarity scaling, sometimes with 3- to 5-star ratings.[e]

As businesses look to the field of sentiment analysis to automate filtering, understanding, and identifying relevant emotional content, they venture beyond traditional fact-based services. One such subscription service responded to the demand to find trends in opinions about products, services, or news topics. It allows customers to monitor blogs, news articles, online forums, and social networking sites. Other services track business topics, newspaper editorials, movie releases, and Twitter.[f]

What broader ethical issues involving questions of privacy and vulnerability to manipulation do you see? How are your answers reconciled with the potential economic impact of sentiment analysis?

Data-Mining Process

Data mining, as depicted in Exhibit 5-5, involves a five-step process:[14]

- *Sample:* Decide between census and sample data.
- *Explore:* Identify relationships within the data.
- *Modify:* Modify or transform data.
- *Model:* Develop a model that explains the data relationships.
- *Assess:* Test the model's accuracy.

To better visualize the connections between the techniques just described and the process steps listed in this section, you may want to download a demonstration version of data-mining software from the Internet.

Sample

Exhibit 5-5 suggests that the researcher must decide whether to use the entire data set or a sample of the data.[15] If the data set in question is not large, if the processing power is high, or if it is important to understand patterns for every record in the database, sampling should not be done. However, if the data warehouse is very large (terabytes of data), the processing power is limited, or speed is more important

>Exhibit 5-5 Data-Mining Process

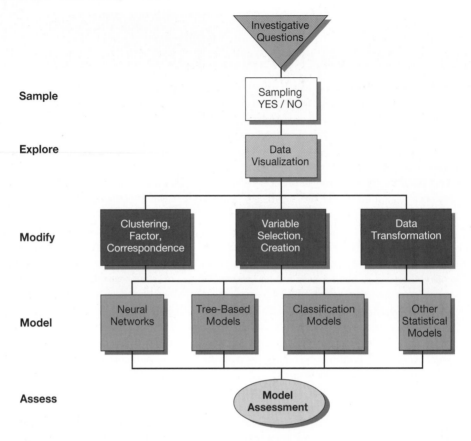

than complete analysis, it is wise to draw a sample. In some instances, researchers may use a data mart for their sample—with local data that are appropriate for their geography. Alternatively, the researcher may select an appropriate sampling technique. Since fast turnaround for decisions is often more important than absolute accuracy, sampling is appropriate.

If general patterns exist in the data as a whole, these patterns will be found in the sample. If a niche is so tiny that it is not represented in a sample yet is so important that it influences the big picture, it will be found using exploratory data analysis (EDA), which we explore in Chapter 16.

Explore

After the data are sampled, the next step is to explore them visually or numerically for trends or groups. Both visual and statistical exploration (data visualization) can be used to identify trends. The researcher also looks for outliers to see if the data need to be cleaned, cases need to be dropped, or a larger sample needs to be drawn.

Modify

Based on the discoveries in the exploration phase, the data may require modification. Clustering, fractal-based transformation, and the application of fuzzy logic are completed during this phase as appropriate. A data reduction program, such as factor analysis, correspondence analysis, or clustering, may be used. If important constructs are discovered, new factors may be introduced to categorize the

$1 Million Data Analysis Prize Improves Netflix Movie Predictions

Netflix Inc., the world's largest online movie rental service, with more than 11 million members, offers subscriber access to more than 100,000 DVDs and Blu-ray titles on the company's website. Netflix distributes by mail and DVDs are returned at the subscribers' convenience with prepaid mailers.[a] It also partners with consumer electronics leaders to stream movies and TV episodes directly to members' TV sets.

A customer's title selection is aided by Cinematch software that generates recommendations based on a customer's film-viewing habits. Accurate recommendations increase Netflix's customer base and service satisfaction, so the company started a contest in October 2006, offering a $1 million prize to the first contestant that could improve the predictions by at least 10 percent, as measured by predicted versus actual one-through-five-star ratings by customers.[b] Contestants dealt with a huge data set—100 million movie ratings—and the challenge of modeling on a large scale. After three years and entries from more than 50,000 contestants, a seven-man team of statisticians, machine-learning experts, and computer engineers from the United States, Austria, Canada, and Israel won by developing powerful algorithms that improve Netflix's existing software by more than 10 percent.[c]

It was not one insight, mathematical algorithm, or construct that helped the team exceed the Netflix goal; instead it was the power of collaboration.[d] Moreover, the contest went well beyond refining movie predictions. It received serious media coverage as a leading example of "prize economics" and the "crowd-sourcing of innovation." Prize economics involves creating a contest to spawn a new innovation at a lower cost than in-house research, while crowd-sourcing refers to combining the conventional wisdom of groups synergistically to accomplish a task.

Predictive recommendation systems will increasingly become a common tool to help find practical information and valuable products among the numerous offerings competing for our attention on the Web, according to Lester Mackey, an early contestant and Ph.D. candidate at the Statistical Artificial Intelligence Lab at the University of California, Berkeley. "A lot of these techniques will propagate across the Internet," he predicted.[e]

What variables do you think the contestants would have found most valuable within the Netflix data warehouse?

www.netflix.com

data into these groups. In addition, variables based on combinations of existing variables may be added, recoded, transformed, or dropped.

At times, descriptive segmentation of the data is all that is required to answer the investigative question. However, if a complex predictive model is needed, the researcher will move to the next step of the process.

Model

Once the data are prepared, construction of a model begins. Modeling techniques in data mining include neural networks as well as decision tree, sequence-based, classification and estimation, and genetic-based models.

Assess

The final step in data mining is to assess the model to estimate how well it performs. A common method of assessment involves applying a portion of data that was not used during the sampling stage. If the model is valid, it will work for this "holdout" sample. Another way to test a model is to run the model against known data. For example, if you know which customers in a file have high loyalty and your model predicts loyalty, you can check to see whether the model has selected these customers accurately.

> The Question Hierarchy: How Ambiguous Questions Become Actionable Research

The process we call the management-research question hierarchy is designed to move the researcher through various levels of questions, each with a specific function within the overall business research process. This multistep process is presented in Exhibit 5-6 and in the example in Exhibit 5-7. The role of exploration in this process is depicted in Exhibit 5-8.

The Management Question

Management questions are the restatement of the management dilemma in question form. The management questions that evolve from the management dilemma are too numerous to list, but we can categorize them (see Exhibit 5-9). No matter how the management question is defined, many research directions can be taken. A specific question can lead to many studies. Therefore, it is the joint responsibility of the researcher and the marketer to choose the most productive project.

Assume, for example, a business researcher is hired to help the new management of a bank. The president is concerned about erosion of the bank's profitability (the management dilemma) and wants to turn this situation around. BankChoice is the oldest and largest of three banks in a city with a population of about 80,000. Profits have stagnated in recent years. The president and the researcher discuss the problem facing the organization and settle on this management question: "How can we improve our profit picture?"

The management question does not specify what kind of business research is to be done. This question is strictly managerial in thrust. It implies that the bank's management faces the task of developing a strategy for increasing profits. The question is broad. Notice that it doesn't indicate whether management should increase profits via increased deposits, downsizing of personnel, outsourcing of the payroll function, or some other means.

>**Exhibit 5-6** Management–Research Question Hierarchy

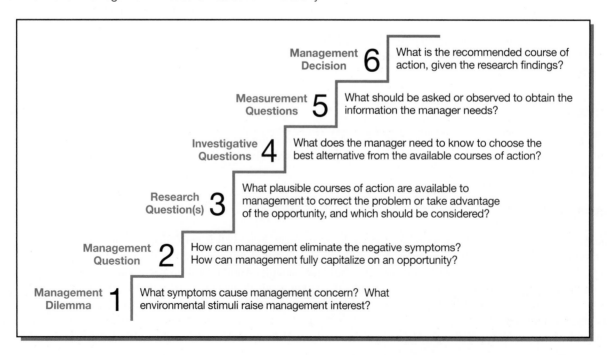

>**Exhibit 5-7** SalePro's Management–Research Question Hierarchy

Declining sales is one of the most common symptoms serving as a stimulus for a research project, especially a continuing pattern that is unexplained. SalePro, a large manufacturer of industrial goods, faces this situation. Exploration (1) reveals that sales, in fact, should not be declining in the South and Northeast. Environmental factors there are as favorable as in the growing regions. Subsequent exploration (2, 3) leads management to believe that the problem is in one of three areas: salesperson compensation, product formulation, or trade advertising. Further exploration (4) has SalePro management narrowing the focus of its research to alternative ways to alter the sales compensation system, which (5) leads to a survey of all sales personnel in the affected regions.

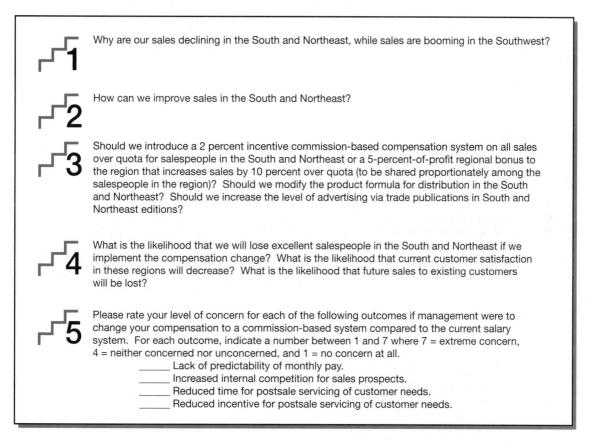

Further discussion between the bank president and the business researcher shows there are really two questions to be answered. The problem of low deposit growth is linked to concerns of a competitive nature. While lowered deposits directly affect profits, another part of the profit weakness is associated with negative factors within the organization that are increasing customer complaints. The qualified researcher knows that the management question as originally stated is too broad to guide a definitive business research project. As a starting point, the broadly worded question is fine, but BankChoice will want to refine its management question into these more specific subquestions:

- How can we improve deposits?
- How can we improve internal operations that currently result in customer complaints?

This separation of the management question into two subquestions may not have occurred without a discussion between the researcher and the manager.

Exploration

BankChoice has done no formal business research in the past. It has little specific information about competitors or customers and has not analyzed its internal operations. To move forward in the

>Exhibit 5-8 Formulating the Research Question

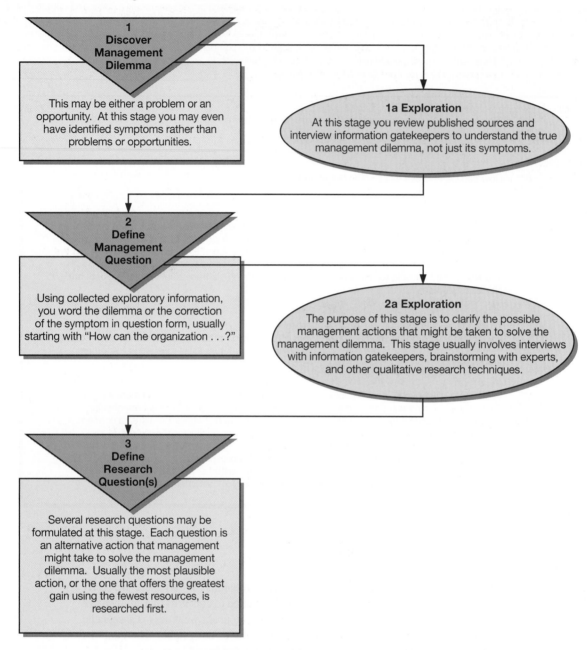

management-research question hierarchy and define the research question, the client needs to collect some exploratory information on:

- What factors are contributing to the bank's failure to achieve a stronger growth rate in deposits?
- How well is the bank doing regarding customer satisfaction and financial condition compared to industry norms and competitors?

Small-group discussions are conducted among employees and managers, and trade association data are acquired to compare financial and operating statistics from company annual reports and end-of-year division reports. From the results of these two exploratory activities, it is obvious that BankChoice's operations are not as progressive as its competitors' but it has its costs well in line. So the revised

>**Exhibit 5-9** Types of Management Questions

Categories	General Question	Sample Management Questions
Choice of Purpose or Choice of Objectives	• What do we want to achieve?	• Should we reposition brand X as a therapeutic product from its current cosmetic positioning? • What goals should XYZ try to achieve in its next round of distributor negotiations?
Generalization and Evaluation of Solutions (choices between concrete actions to solve problems or take advantage of opportunities)	• How can we achieve the ends that we seek?	• How can we achieve our 5-year goal of doubling sales and profits? • What should be done to improve the CompleteCare program for product repairs and servicing?
Troubleshooting or Control (monitoring or diagnosing ways an organization is failing to meet its goals)	• How well is our marketing program meeting its goals? • Why is our marketing program not meeting its goals?	• What is our product line's sales-to-promotion cost ratio? • Why does our department have the lowest sales-to–Web page visit ratio? • Why does our product line have the lowest off-shelf display occasions in the industry?

management question becomes What should be done to make the bank more competitive? The process of exploration will be critical in helping BankChoice identify its options.

In addition to solving problems, marketers are likely to be looking for opportunities in the marketplace. So let's look at another case, TechByte. This company is interested in enhancing its position in a given technology that appears to hold potential for future growth. This interest or need might quickly elicit a number of questions:

- How fast might this technology develop?
- What are the likely applications of this technology?
- What companies now possess this technology, and which ones are likely to make a major effort to obtain the technology?
- How much will the new technology absorb in resources?
- What are the likely payoffs?

In the above exploration of opportunities, researchers would probably begin with specific books and periodicals. They would be looking only for certain aspects in this literature, such as recent developments, predictions by informed individuals about the prospects of the technology, identification of those involved in the area, and accounts of successful ventures or failures by others in the field. After becoming familiar with the literature, researchers might seek interviews with scientists, engineers, and product developers who are well known in the field. They would give special attention to those who represent the two extremes of opinion in regard to the prospects of the technology. If possible, they would talk with persons having information on particularly thorny problems in development and application. Of course, much of the information will be confidential and competitive. However, skillful investigation can uncover many useful indicators. BankChoice ultimately decides to conduct a survey of local residents. Two hundred residents complete questionnaires, and the information collected is used to guide repositioning of the bank.

In the opening MindWriter vignette, Sara takes on the task of discovering published PC industry studies on service and technical support, as well as published customer satisfaction comparisons among technical companies and products. Meanwhile, at MindWriter, Myra Wines is searching company archives for prior studies on customer satisfaction. Jason has realized from reviewing Sara's summary of customer correspondence that Henry & Associates needs more knowledge on product design,

CompleteCare's practices, and product handling; so Jason plans a second exploratory process starting with an expert interview with MindWriter's Sam Turnbull.

An unstructured exploration allows the researcher to develop and revise the management question and determine what is needed to secure answers to the proposed question.

The Research Question

Using his or her understanding of the basic theoretical concepts, the researcher's task is to assist the manager in formulating a research question that fits the need to resolve the management dilemma. A **research question** best states the objective of the business research study. It is a more specific manage-ment question that must be answered. It may be more than one question or just one. A business research process that answers this more specific question provides the manager with the information necessary to make the decision he or she is facing. Incorrectly defining the research question is the fundamental weakness in the business research process. Time and money can be wasted studying an alternative that won't help the manager rectify the original dilemma.

Meanwhile, at BankChoice the president has agreed to have the business research be guided by the following research question: should BankChoice position itself as a modern, progressive institution (with appropriate changes in services and policies) or maintain its image as the oldest, most reliable institution in town?

Fine-Tuning the Research Question

The term *fine-tuning* might seem to be an odd usage for research, but it creates an image that most researchers come to recognize. Fine-tuning the question is precisely what a skillful practitioner must do after the exploration is complete. At this point, a clearer picture of the management and research questions begins to emerge (see Exhibit 5-10, p. 118). After the researcher does a preliminary review of the literature, a brief exploratory study, or both, the project begins to crystallize in one of two ways:

1. It is apparent that the question has been answered and the process is finished.
2. A question different from the one originally addressed has appeared.

The research question does not have to be materially different, but it will have evolved in some fashion. This is not cause for discouragement. The refined research question(s) will have better focus and will move the business research forward with more clarity than the initially formulated question(s).

In addition to fine-tuning the original question, the researcher should address other research question–related activities in this phase to enhance the direction of the project:

1. Examine the variables to be studied. Are they satisfactorily defined? Have operational definitions been used where appropriate?
2. Review the research questions with the intent of breaking them down into specific second- and third-level questions.
3. If hypotheses (tentative explanations) are used, be certain they meet the quality tests mentioned in Chapter 3.
4. Determine what evidence must be collected to answer the various questions and hypotheses.
5. Set the scope of the study by stating what is not a part of the research question. This will establish a boundary to separate contiguous problems from the primary objective.

Investigative Questions

Investigative questions represent the information that the decision maker needs to know; they are the questions the researcher must answer to satisfactorily arrive at a conclusion about the research question. To study the market, the researcher working on the BankChoice project develops two major investigative questions. Each question has several subquestions. These questions provide insight into the lack of deposit growth:

1. What is the public's position regarding financial services and their use?
   a. What specific financial services are used?
   b. How attractive are various services?
   c. What bank-specific and environmental factors influence a person's use of a particular service?
2. What is the bank's competitive position?
   a. What are the geographic patterns of our customers and of our competitors' customers?
   b. What demographic differences are revealed among our customers and those of our competitors?
   c. What descriptive words or phrases does the public (both customers and noncustomers) associate with BankChoice? With BankChoice's competitors?
   d. How aware is the public of BankChoice's promotional efforts?
   e. What opinion does the public hold of BankChoice and its competitors?
   f. How does growth in services compare among competing institutions?

Return again to the MindWriter situation. What does management need to know to choose among the different packaging specifications? As you develop your information needs, think broadly. In developing your list of investigative questions, include:

- *Performance considerations* (such as the relative costs of the options, the speed of packing serviced laptops, and the arrival condition of test laptops packaged with different materials).
- *Attitudinal issues* (such as perceived service quality based on packaging materials used).
- *Behavioral issues* (such as employees' ease of use in packing with the considered materials).

> **close**up MindWriter

Proposing Research for MindWriter and the Exploration Phase

>**Exhibit 5-10** Proposal for MindWriter CompleteCare Satisfaction Research

When last we checked, Sara and Jason were preparing a proposal for Gracie Uhura, product manager at MindWriter Corporation. Sara decided to exclude the "executive summary" for two reasons: The proposal is short and the essentials will be contained in the cover letter. The proposal follows the components discussed in this chapter. It is an appropriate adaptation for an internal, small-scale study. The module "qualification of researcher" was not needed because MindWriter's employee solicited the proposal; Sara had prejudged the researcher's qualifications.

Repair Process Satisfaction Proposal
MindWriter Corporation CompleteCare Program

Problem Statement

MindWriter Corporation has recently created a service and repair program, CompleteCare, for its portable/laptop/notebook computers. This program promises to provide a rapid response to customers' service problems.

　　MindWriter is currently experiencing a shortage of trained technical operators in its telephone center. The package courier, contracted to pick up and deliver customers' machines to CompleteCare, has provided irregular execution. MindWriter has also experienced parts availability problems for some machine types.

　　Recent phone logs at the call center show complaints about CompleteCare; it is unknown how representative these complaints are and what implications they may have for satisfaction with MindWriter products.

　　Management desires information on the program's effectiveness and its impact on customer satisfaction to determine what should be done to improve the CompleteCare program for MindWriter product repair and servicing.

Research Objectives

The purpose of this research is to discover the level of satisfaction with the CompleteCare service program. Specifically, we intend to identify the component and overall levels of satisfaction with CompleteCare. Components of the repair process are important targets for investigation because they reveal:

　　(1) How customer tolerance levels for repair performance affect overall satisfaction, and

　　(2) Which process components should be immediately improved to elevate the overall satisfaction of those MindWriter customers experiencing product failures.

　　We will also discover the importance of types of product failure on customer satisfaction levels.

Importance/Benefits

High levels of user satisfaction translate into positive word-of-mouth product endorsements. These endorsements influence the purchase outcomes for (1) friends and relatives and (2) business associates.

　　Critical incidents, such as product failures, have the potential to either undermine existing satisfaction levels or preserve and even increase the resulting levels of product satisfaction. The outcome of the episode depends on the quality of the manufacturer's response.

　　An extraordinary response by the manufacturer to such incidents will preserve and enhance user satisfaction levels to the point that direct and indirect benefits derived from such programs will justify their costs.

　　This research has the potential for connecting to ongoing MindWriter customer satisfaction programs and measuring the long-term effects of CompleteCare (and product failure incidents) on customer satisfaction.

Research Design

Exploration: Qualitative. We will augment our knowledge of CompleteCare by interviewing the service manager, the call center manager, and the independent package company's account executive. Based on a thorough inventory of CompleteCare's internal external processes, we propose to develop a mail survey.

Questionnaire Design. A self-administered questionnaire (postcard size) offers the most cost-effective method for securing feedback on the effectiveness of CompleteCare. The introduction on the postcard will be a variation of MindWriter's current advertising campaign.

　　Some questions for this instrument will be based on the investigative questions we presented to you previously, and others will be drawn from the executive interviews. We anticipate a maximum of 10 questions. A new five-point expectation scale, compatible with your existing customer satisfaction scales, is being designed.

(continued)

>closeupcont'd

>Exhibit 5-10 Proposal for MindWriter CompleteCare Satisfaction Research (*concluded*)

Although we are not convinced that open-ended questions are appropriate for postcard questionnaires, we understand that you and Mr. Malraison like them. A comments/suggestions question will be included. In addition, we will work out a code block that captures the call center's reference number, model, and item(s) serviced.

Logistics. The postal arrangements are: box rental, permit, and "business reply" privileges to be arranged in a few days. The approval for a reduced postage rate will take one to two weeks. The budget section itemizes these costs.

Pilot Test. We will test the questionnaire with a small sample of customers using your tech-line operators. This will contain your costs. We will then revise the questions and forward them to our graphics designer for layout. The instrument will then be submitted to you for final approval.

Evaluation of Nonresponse Bias. A random sample of 100 names will be secured from the list of customers who do not return the questionnaire. Call center records will be used for establishing the sampling frame. Nonresponders will be interviewed on the telephone and their responses compared statistically to those of the responders.

Data Analysis

We will review the postcards returned and send you a weekly report listing customers who are dissatisfied (score a "1" or "2") with any item of the questionnaire or who submit a negative comment. This will improve your timeliness in resolving customer complaints. Each month, we will provide you with a report consisting of frequencies and category percentages for each question. Visual displays of the data will be in bar chart/histogram form. We propose to include at least one question dealing with overall satisfaction (with CompleteCare and/or MindWriter). This overall question would be regressed on the individual items to determine each item's importance. A performance grid will identify items needing improvement with an evaluation of priority. Other analyses can be prepared on a time and materials basis.

The open-ended questions will be summarized and reported by model code. If you wish, we also can provide content analysis for these questions.

Results: Deliverables

1. Development and production of a postcard survey. MindWriter employees will package the questionnaire with the returned merchandise.
2. Weekly exception reports (transmitted electronically) listing customers who meet the dissatisfied customer criteria.
3. Monthly reports as described in the data analysis section.
4. An ASCII diskette with each month's data shipped to Austin by the fifth working day of each month.

Budget

Card Layout and Printing. Based on your card estimate, our designer will lay out and print 2,000 cards in the first run ($500). The specifications are as follows: 7-point Williamsburg offset hi-bulk with one-over-one black ink. A gray-scale layer with a MindWriter or CompleteCare logo can be positioned under the printed material at a nominal charge. The two-sided cards measure 4¼ by 5½.

This allows us to print four cards per page. The opposite side will have the business reply logo, postage paid symbol, and address.

Cost Summary

Interviews	$ 1,550.00
Travel costs	2,500.00
Questionnaire development	1,850.00
Equipment/supplies	1,325.00
Graphics design	800.00
Permit fee (annual)	75.00
Business reply fee (annual)	185.00
Box rental (annual)	35.00
Printing costs	500.00
Data entry (monthly)	430.00
Monthly data files (each)	50.00
Monthly reports (each)	1,850.00
Total start-up costs	$11,150.00
Monthly run costs	$ 1,030.00*

*An additional fee of $0.21 per card will be assessed by the post office for business reply mail. At approximately a 30 percent return rate, we estimate the monthly cost to be less than $50.

PROPOSAL FOR MINDWRITER RESEARCH

Two days after their Austin trip, at 1 p.m. sharp, Sara ushers Myra into a round Henry & Associates' conference room.

Inside, Jason has posted paper to the curved walls.

Across the top of the first sheet, Sara has written, "Satisfaction with the service department." Today they focus on the easiest task and leave the customer profile pilot study for later. Besides, Gracie Uhura, marketing manager for MindWriter, is pressed for answers on whether the CompleteCare repair program enhances customer satisfaction and thus brand loyalty. If she is responsive on the smaller project, Henry & Associates is sure it will get the OK for the more ambitious one.

Jason and Myra pull two chairs in front of the first blank panel, at first staring in silence at its blankness.

As Jason begins to talk, Sara summarizes his ideas on the panels. He has learned a lot about MindWriter. Beginning with a visit to the Internet and an intense search through MindWriter's archives before their Austin trip, followed by the meetings in Austin, he knows the product is sold through computer superstores and independent mail-order companies. He also has learned that MindWriter ships about 5,000 portable/laptop computers per month. The product is successful yet constrained by the same supply shortages as the rest of the industry. Personal computer magazines have been consulted for their annual surveys on service, repair, and technical support. Overall customer satisfaction comparisons have been obtained from published sources.

Myra approaches the second blank panel and summarizes the information learned from the Austin trip under the label "CompleteCare Process." When customers experience a malfunction, they call an 800 number. The call center answers service, support, and ordering questions. Technical representatives are trained to:

- Take the name, phone, address, and MindWriter model number.
- Listen to the customer and ask questions to detect the nature of the problem.
- Attempt to resolve the problem if they can walk the customer through corrective steps.

If unable to resolve the problem, the representative provides a return authorization code and dispatches a package courier to pick up the unit before 5 p.m. The unit is delivered to Austin for service the next morning. The CompleteCare repair facility calls the customer if the repair information is incomplete. The unit is repaired by the end of that day and picked up by the courier. The call center then updates its database with service record information. If all goes well, the customer receives the repaired unit by 10:00 a.m. the following morning, 48 hours after MindWriter received the customer's original problem call.

As Myra sits down, Jason begins to rough out the known "problems" on a third panel. There are employee shortages at the call center and difficulties getting the new technical representatives trained. The courier is inconsistent in executing its pickup and delivery contract. MindWriter is experiencing parts availability problems for some models. And, occasionally, units are returned to the customer either not fixed or damaged in some way. Jason brainstorms that the service area is not doing an adequate job. But Myra asserts that problems could be in the original packing, in handling, or even from activities related to taking the boxes on and off the shipping pallets.

Their brainstorming results in a restatement of the management question: What should be done to improve the CompleteCare program (MindWriter's program for product repairs and servicing)? After further discussion, Myra, Sara, and Jason brainstorm the following research and investigative questions.

RESEARCH QUESTIONS

1. Should the technical representative be given more intensive training?
2. Should ABC Courier Service be replaced with an overnight air-transport service?
3. Should the repair-diagnostic and repair-sequencing operations be modified?
4. Should the return packaging be modified to include premolded rigid foam inserts, conforming-expanding foam protection, or some other configuration?
5. Should metropolitan repair centers be established to complement or replace in-factory repair facilities?

INVESTIGATIVE QUESTIONS

1. How well is the call center helping the customers? Is it helping the customers with instructions? What percentage of customers' technical problems is the center solving without callbacks? How long do customers wait on the phone?
2. How good is the transportation company? Does it pick up and deliver the laptops responsively? How long do customers wait for pickup? Delivery? Are the laptops damaged due to package handling? What available packaging alternatives are cost-effective?
3. How good is the repair group? What is the sequencing of the repair program, diagnostics through completion? Is the repair complete? Are customers' problems resolved? Are new repair problems emerging? Are customers' repair-time expectations being met?
4. (Do this set of questions on your own. See discussion question 8 at the end of this chapter.)
5. What is the overall satisfaction with CompleteCare and with the MindWriter product?

Myra now has enough information to go back to Gracie Uhura at MindWriter. In particular, Myra wants to know whether she and Jason have translated Gracie's management question in a way that will adequately fulfill Gracie's need for information.

(continued)

>**close**up**cont'd**

Even though Jason had a phone interview with Sam Turnbull, MindWriter's service manager, Myra and Jason may also want to interview the call center manager and the independent package company's account executive to determine if they are on the right track with their investigative questions. These people will be able to answer some investigative questions. The rest of the investigative questions will need to be translated into measurement questions to ask customers. If Myra and Jason are comfortable with the additional information from their interviews (and any additional customer letters), Henry and Associates can then develop a questionnaire for CompleteCare customers.

Jason, Sara, and Myra wrap up their session discussing preliminary plans and timing. Jason wants a pilot test with a limited number of customers. Afterward, he will revise the questions, set up the logistics, and then roll out the business research program. Sampling will be a critical matter. If Gracie's budget is large, they

can use a probability sample from the customer list that MindWriter generates every week. This will make telephone interviews possible. If a less expensive alternative is needed, however, they can propose that a questionnaire postcard survey be included with every laptop as it is returned to the customer. They also would do random sampling from the list of customers who do not respond. Nonresponders would be interviewed on the telephone. This way Myra and Jason can be assured of a cost-effective questionnaire with correction for nonresponse bias (an error that develops when an interviewer cannot locate or involve the targeted participant).

Myra, Sara, and Jason devise a tentative schedule (see Exhibit 5-11) before calling to arrange the follow-up interviews. They want to give Gracie target dates for completion of the exploratory phase and the instrument and pilot test, as well as a deadline for the first month's results.

>**Exhibit 5-11** A Gantt Chart of the MindWriter Project

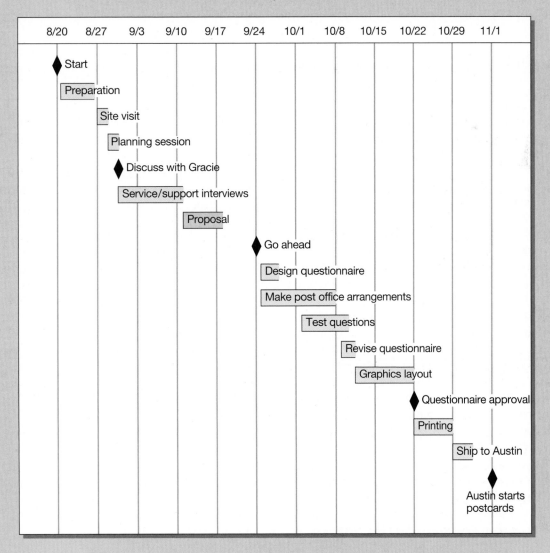

Measurement Questions

Measurement questions are the actual questions that researchers use to collect data in a study. They could become questions on a survey or elements on an observation checklist.

Measurement questions should be outlined by the completion of the project planning activities but usually await pilot testing for refinement. Two types of measurement questions are common in business research:

- Predesigned, pretested questions.
- Custom-designed questions.

Predesigned measurement questions are questions that have been formulated and tested previously by other researchers, are recorded in the literature, and may be applied literally or be adapted for the project at hand. Some studies lend themselves to the use of these readily available measurement devices. Such questions provide enhanced validity and can reduce the cost of the project. Often, however, the measurement questions must be custom tailored to the investigative questions. The resources for developing **custom-designed measurement questions**—questions formulated specifically for the project at hand—are the collective insights from all the activities in the business research process completed to this point, particularly insights from exploration. Later, during the pilot testing phase of the research process, these custom-designed questions will be refined.

We discuss measurement questions only briefly here; a more complete discussion begins in Chapter 11.

>summary

1 The exploratory phase of the research process uses information to expand understanding of the management dilemma, look for ways others have addressed and/or solved problems similar to the management dilemma or management question, and gather background information on the topic to refine the research question. Exploration of the problem is accomplished through familiarization with the available literature, interviews with experts and other individual depth interviews, and group discussions or some combination of these. Revision of the management or research questions is a desirable outcome of exploration and enhances the researcher's understanding of the options available for developing a successful design.

2 Researching secondary sources is complex and challenging. There are two categories of sources available (external and internal) and three types of sources (primary, secondary, and tertiary). Primary sources are original works of research or raw data without interpretation. Secondary sources are interpretations of primary data. Tertiary sources may be interpretations of secondary sources or, more commonly, finding aids such as indexes, bibliographies, and Internet search engines.

3 There are generally five types of information sources used in most literature searches, including indexes and bibliographies, dictionaries, encyclopedias, handbooks, and directories. Each is useful to an exploratory phase literature search in a variety of ways. One of the harder tasks associated with

using secondary sources is evaluating the quality of the information. Five factors to consider when evaluating the quality of the source are purpose, scope, authority, audience, and format.

4 How one structures the research question sets the direction for the project. A management problem or opportunity can be formulated as a hierarchical sequence of questions. At the base level is the management dilemma. This is translated into a management question and then into a research question—the major objective of the study. In turn, the research question is further expanded into investigative questions. These questions represent the various facets of the problem to be solved, and they influence research design, including design strategy, data collection planning, and sampling. At the most specific level are measurement questions that are answered by respondents in a survey or answered about each subject in an observational study.

5 Managers faced with current decisions requiring immediate attention often overlook internal data in a company's data warehouse. Data mining refers to the process of discovering knowledge from databases. Data-mining technology provides two unique capabilities to the researcher or manager: pattern discovery and the prediction of tends and behaviors. Data-mining tools perform exploratory and confirmatory statistical analyses to discover and validate relationships. Data mining involves a five-step process: sample, explore, modify, model, and assess.

>**key**terms

>**discussion**questions

Terms in Review

1 Explain how each of the five evaluation factors for a secondary source influences its management decision-making
value.

   a Purpose

   b Scope

   c Authority

   d Audience

   e Format

2 Define the distinctions between primary, secondary, and
tertiary sources in a secondary search.

3 What problems of secondary data quality must researchers
face? How can they deal with them?

Making Research Decisions

4 Below are a number of requests that a research staff assistant might receive. What specific tools or services would
you expect to use to find the requisite information? (Hint:
Use the appendices at the end of this chapter and the
sources list on the Online Learning Center.)

   a Has the FTC published any recent statements (within the
last year) concerning its position on quality stabilization?

   b I need a list of the major companies located in Greens-
boro, North Carolina.

   c Please get me a list of the directors of General Motors,
Microsoft, and Morgan Stanley & Co.

   d Is there a trade magazine that specializes in the flooring
industry?

   e I would like to track down a study of small-scale service
franchising that was recently published by a bureau of
business research at one of the southern universities.
Can you help me?

5 Confronted by low sales, the president of Oaks International Inc. asks a research company to study the activities
of the customer relations department in the corporation.
What are some of the important reasons that this research
project may fail to make an adequate contribution to the
solution of management problems?

6 You have been approached by the editor of *Gentlemen's
Magazine* to carry out a research study. The magazine
has been unsuccessful in attracting shoe manufacturers
as advertisers. When the sales reps tried to secure advertising from shoe manufacturers, they were told men's
clothing stores are a small and dying segment of their
business. Since *Gentlemen's Magazine* goes chiefly to
men's clothing stores, the manufacturers reasoned that
it was, therefore, not a good vehicle for their advertising.
The editor believes that a survey (via mail questionnaire)
of men's clothing stores in the United States will probably show that these stores are important outlets for
men's shoes and are not declining in importance as shoe
outlets. He asks you to develop a proposal for the study
and submit it to him. Develop the management–research
question hierarchy that will help you to develop a specific
proposal.

7 Develop the management–research question hierarchy for
a management dilemma you face at work or with an organization to which you volunteer.

8 How might you use data mining if you were a human resources officer or a supervising manager?

Bring Research to Life

9 Using the MindWriter postservicing packaging alternative as the research question, develop appropriate investigative questions within the question hierarchy by preparing an exhibit similar to Exhibit 5-8.

10 Using Exhibits 5-6, 5-8, 5b-1, and 5b-2, state the research question and describe the search plan that Jason should have conducted before his brainstorming sessions with Myra Wines. What government sources should be included in Jason's search?

11 Using the "uneven courier performance" problem or the "product damaged during repair" problem (see the Closeup on page 118), develop some exploration activities that would let Jason or Myra proceed to develop a more refined research question dealing with this problem.

From Concept to Practice

12 Develop the management–research question hierarchy (Exhibits 5-6 and 5-8), citing management dilemma, management question, and research question(s), for each of the following:

a The president of a home health care services firm.

b The vice president of investor relations for an auto manufacturer.

c The retail advertising manager of a major metropolitan newspaper.

d The chief of police in a major city.

From the Headlines

13 In May 2007, TJX Co., the parent company of T.J. Maxx and other retailers, announced in a Securities and Exchange Commission filing that more than 45 million credit and debit card numbers had been stolen from its IT systems. The company had taken some measures over a period of a few years to protect customer data through obfuscation and encryption. But TJX didn't apply these policies uniformly across its IT systems. As a result, it still had no idea of the extent of the damage caused by the data breach. If you were TJX, what data-mining research could you do to evaluate the safety of your customer's personal data?

>cases*

A Gem of a Study

 Akron Children's Hospital

Calling Up Attendance

 Donatos: Finding the New Pizza

HeroBuilders.com

Inquiring Minds Want to Know—NOW!

Mastering Teacher Leadership

NCRCC: Teeing Up and New Strategic Direction

 Ohio Lottery: Innovative Research Design Drives Winning

Ramada Demonstrates Its *Personal Best™*

State Farm: Dangerous Intersections

 USTA: Come Out Swinging

* You will find a description of each case in the Case Abstracts section of this textbook. Check the Case Index to determine whether a case provides data, the research instrument, video, or other supplementary material. Written cases are downloadable from the text website (www.mhhe.com/cooper11e). All video material and video cases are available from the Online Learning Center. The film reel icon indicates a video case or video material relevant to the case.

Bibliographic Database Searches

Searching a Bibliographic Database

In a *bibliographic database,* each record is a bibliographic citation to a book or a journal article. In your university library, the online catalog is an example of a bibliographic database.

There are several bibliographic databases available to business researchers. Some of the more popular and comprehensive business bibliographic databases are:

- Proquest (from Proquest Information and Learning, formerly *ABI/Inform*).
- Business and Industry (from Gale Group).
- Business Source Complete (from EBSCO).
- Dow Jones Facftiva.
- Lexis-Nexis Universe (from a division of Reed Elsevier).

Most of these databases offer numerous purchase options both in the amount and type of coverage. Some include abstracts, short summaries of the articles cited. Nearly all of these databases include the contents of around two-thirds of the indexed journals in full text, although the amount and the specific titles may vary widely from database to database. Full-text options vary from an exact image of the page to ASCII text only or text plus graphics. Search options also vary considerably from database to database. For these reasons, most libraries supporting business programs offer more than one business periodical database.

The process of searching bibliographic databases and retrieving results is basic to all databases.

1. Select a database appropriate to your topic.
2. Construct a **search query** (also called a *search statement*).
   - Review and evaluate search results.
   - Modify the search query, if necessary.
3. Save the valuable results of your search.
4. Retrieve articles not available in the database.
5. Supplement your results with information from Web sources.

Select a Database Most of us select the most convenient database without regard to its scope, but considering the database contents and its limitations and criteria for inclusion at the beginning of your search will probably save you time in the long run. Remember that a library's online catalog is a bibliographic database that will help identify books and perhaps other media on a topic. While journal or periodical titles are listed in a library's online catalog, periodical or journal articles are rarely included. Use books for older, more comprehensive information. Use periodical articles for more current information or for information on very specific topics. A librarian can suggest one or more appropriate databases for the topic you are researching.

Save Results of Search While the temptation to print may be overwhelming, remember that if you download your results, you can cut and paste quotations, tables, and other information into your proposal without rekeying. In either case, make sure you keep the bibliographic information for your footnotes and bibliography. Most databases offer the choice of marking the records and printing or downloading them all at once or printing them one by one.

Retrieve Articles For articles not available in full text online, retrieval will normally require the additional step of searching the library's online catalog (unless there is a link from the database to the catalog) to determine if the desired issue is available and where it is located. Many libraries offer a document delivery service for articles not available. Some current articles may be available on the Web or via a fee-based service.

World Wide Web Search Process

The World Wide Web is a vast information, business, and entertainment resource that would be difficult, if not foolish, to overlook. Millions of pages of data are publicly available, and the size of the Web doubles every few months.[1] But searching and retrieving reliable information on the Web is a great deal more problematic than searching a bibliographic database. There are no standard database fields, no carefully defined subject hierarchies

>Exhibit 5a-1 Web Search Process Compared to Bibliographic Search Process

Bibliographic Search Process	Web Search Process
1. Select a database appropriate to your topic.	1. Select a search engine or directory.*
2. Construct a search query.	2. Determine your search options.*
• Review and evaluate search results.	3. Construct a search query.*
• Modify the search query, if necessary.	• Review and evaluate search results.
3. Save those valuable results of your search.	• Modify the search query, if necessary.
4. Retrieve articles not available in the database.	4. Save those valuable results of your search.*
5. Supplement your results with information from Web sources.	5. Supplement your results with information from non-Web sources.*

*Denotes a variation.

(called *controlled vocabulary*), no cross-references, no synonyms, no selection criteria, and, in general, no rules. There are dozens of search engines and they all work differently, but how they work is not always easy to determine. Nonetheless, the convenience of the Web and the extraordinary amount of information to be found on it are compelling reasons for using it as an information source.

As you can see in Exhibit 5a-1, the basic steps to searching the Web are similar to those outlined for searching a bibliographic database. As you approach the Web, you start at the same point: focusing on your management question. Are you looking for a known item (e.g., IBM's website or that of the American Marketing Association)? Are you looking for information on a specific topic? If you are looking for a specific topic, what are its parameters? For example, if your topic is managed health care, are you hoping to find statistics, marketing ideas, public policy issues, accounting standards, or evidence of its impact on small business?

There are perfectly legitimate reasons to browse for information, and with its hypertext linking system, the Web is the ultimate resource for browsing. The trick is to browse and still stay focused on the topic at hand. In the browse mode you do not have any particular target. You follow hypertext links from site to site for the sheer joy of discovery. This is somewhat analogous to window shopping at the mall or browsing the bookshelves in the library. It may or may not be fruitful. And browsing is not likely to be efficient. Researchers often work on tight deadlines, because managers often cannot delay critical decisions. Therefore, researchers rarely have the luxury of undirected browsing.

Below we detail those steps in the Web search process that pose altered behavior for searches.

Select a Search Engine or Directory
A search for specific information or for a specific site that will help you solve your management question requires a great deal more skill and knowledge than browsing. Start by selecting one or more Internet search engines. Web search engines vary considerably in the following ways:

- The types of Internet sources they cover (http, telnet, Usenet, ftp, etc.).
- The way they search Web pages (every word? titles or headers only?).
- The number of pages they include in their indexes.
- The search and presentation options they offer.
- The frequency with which they are updated.

Furthermore, some information publicly indexable via the Web is not retrievable at all using current Web search engines. Among the material open to the public, but not indexed by search engines, are the following:[2]

- Pages that are proprietary (i.e., fee-based) and/or password-protected, including the contents of bibliographic and other databases. Some password-protected databases, such as the Thomas Register, are actually free and available to the public after initial registration.
- Pages accessible only through a search form (databases), including such highly popular Web resources as library catalogs, e-commerce catalogs (such as Lands' End, Amazon.com, and similar offerings), and the Security and Exchange Commission's EDGAR catalog of SEC filings. If you want to find the price of a book at Amazon.com, you first will have to find the Amazon.com page and then search the database for the title.
- Poorly designed framed pages.
- Some non-HTML or nonplain-text pages, especially PDF graphics files, for which no text alternative is offered. These pages cannot be retrieved using any current search engine.

- Pages excluded by the Robots Exclusion Standard (usually implemented with a robots.txt file). This standard is used by Web administrators to tell indexing robots that certain pages are off-limits. An outstanding example of this is the U.S. government's extensive information resource called GPO Access (described later).

The search engine, portal, or directory you select may well be determined by how comprehensive you want your results to be.[3] If you want to use some major sites only, then start with a directory such as Yahoo! If, however, you are interested in gathering comments and opinions that are the focus of usenet groups, then use a more inclusive search engine such as Northern Light (http://www.northernlight.com). At least within the publicly indexable pages, one approach emphasizes selectivity, and the other, comprehensiveness. If you are interested in comprehensiveness, use more than one search engine. You are likely to yield very different and perhaps better results using additional search engines.

What is the difference between a search engine, a portal, and a directory? Directories rely on human intervention to select, index, and categorize Web contents. Subject directories build an index based on Web pages or web sites, but not on words within a page. Presenting a series of subject categories that are then further subdivided, Yahoo! (http://www.yahoo.com/) was the first Web subject directory and is still one of the most popular choices for finding information on the Web. The reason is that most users are satisfied with a few good sites rather than a long list of possibilities.

A search engine's different software components allow it to search and retrieve Web pages. These include:

- Software that automatically sends robots, sometimes called spiders, out to comb the Web, going from server to server to build an index of the words, pages, and files that are publicly indexable.
- Algorithms that determine how those pages will be selected and prioritized for display.
- User interface software that determines the search options available to the user.

Robots may be sent to roam the Web on a daily basis or on a six-week basis, so it is possible that some newer pages may not be included in the index developed by a particular search engine. Most search engines try for at least a monthly update of their indexes. Some robots may search only the upper-level pages and totally ignore valuable pages buried within a site.

The algorithm used by the search engine can have an enormous impact on the type and quantity of information retrieved. Search algorithms determine whether every word is to be included or only the top 50 or so words,

whether more weight will be given to words in metadata or titles or in words used frequently, and so on. The possibilities are limitless and are the major reason that results from one search may vary considerably from those of another search.

A **portal** is, as the name suggests, a gateway to the Web. A portal often includes a directory, a search engine, and other user features such as news and weather. Most Internet service providers (ISPs) are portals to the Web. The AOL home page is an example. This portal uses information based on past user search behavior to determine what to offer on the opening screen. Therefore, some valuable search engines, indexes, directories, and more may be relegated to an "other search aids" category. If as a researcher your behavior differs from the majority pattern, you have to be more knowledgeable about search strategies to bypass the frontline strategies offered by the portal. Several ISP portals now offer subscribers the option of customizing the portal with user-chosen search engines and secondary sources. Most of the major search engines are now actually portals to the Web that include their own search engine. Specialized portals are increasingly popular. One such portal is the Annual Report Service, a collection of links to a large number of company annual reports (www.annualreportservice.com).

Determine Search Options Nearly all search services have a Help button that will lead you to information about the search protocols and options of that particular search engine. How does the search engine work? Can you combine terms using Boolean operators (AND, OR, NOT) or other connectors? How do you enter phrases? truncate terms? determine output display? limit by date or other characteristic? Some search engines provide a basic and an advanced search option. How do they differ?

Construct a Search Query and Enter Search Term(s) The Web is not a database, nor does it have a controlled vocabulary. Therefore, you must be as specific as possible, using the keywords in your management question and any variations you can think of. It is up to you to determine synonyms, variant spellings, and broader or narrower terms that will help you retrieve the information you need. This may involve some trial and error. For instance, a general term (such as *business*) would be useless in a search engine that purports to index every word in every document.

Save Results of Search If you have found good information, you will want to keep it for future reference so that you can cite it in your proposal or refer to it later in the development of your investigative questions. If you do not keep documents, you may have to reconstruct your search. At a future time, given that some portion of the Web is revised and updated daily, those same documents may no longer be available.

Supplement Results with Information from Non-Web Sources
There is still a great deal of information in books, journals, and other print sources that is not available on the Web. Although many novice researchers start and end here, the more sophisticated researcher knows a Web search is just one of many important options.

Searching for Specific Types of Information on the Web

Once you have defined your topic and established your search terms, you need to determine whether you are looking for a specific site (known item) or an address of a person or institution (who), a geographic place name and location (where), or a topic (what).

Known-Item Searches
In the same way that search protocols for the library's online catalog vary between a known-item (author or exact title) and a more general keyword search, the way you query the Web for an exact item also varies from a more general query. A trend among search engines is to establish algorithms that will yield more precise results. One of the first to follow this trend was the search engine Google (http://www.google.com/), which debuted in 1998. Google and others like it help you retrieve the most precise results from known-item searches by creating an algorithm that interprets a link to a site as a vote for that site. The sites that receive the most votes (links) rise to the top of the results list in a known-item search. The Google system also emphasizes the importance of the linking page in its algorithm.

Who Searches
In the *who* searches, you are looking for an e-mail address, a phone number, a street address, or a Web address of a person or institution. For this type of information, you will first need to identify a database containing the information you need and then search that database according to its search protocols. At this writing, almost all Web search engines and portal sites partner with infoUSA (http://www.infoUSA.com/) to supply the phone number databases for their white and yellow page services.[4]

Where Searches
A *where* option comprises the mapping services that help you locate an address on a map or discover the route from one place to another. Mapping services are databases tied to geographic information systems (GISs). One popular site is MapQuest (http://www.mapquest.com).

What Searches
As we have already noted, search engines vary considerably in the way they work and in their size. If you are searching for a very unusual term, select one of the more comprehensive search engines, such as Northern Light (http://www.northernlight.com/) or AltaVista (http://altavista.com/). Generally, it is more efficient to start with a directory such as Yahoo! or one of the more specialized directories on the Web. Some especially good specialized sites are the Argus Clearinghouse (http://www.clearinghouse.net/), featuring subject guides on dozens of topics prepared by librarians and other specialists, and INFOMINE Scholarly Internet Resource Collections from the University of California housed at University of California–Riverside (http://infomine.ucr.edu/). See Exhibit 5a-2 for a selection of business-related websites.

Since the Web was introduced to the world in 1992, Web technology has been seeking ways to make the contents more accessible. The dynamic nature of the Web, its lightning growth rate, the ephemeral nature of some Web pages, the different skill levels and interests of users, and the lack of standards make this an enormous challenge. Trends indicate that the Web will continue to grow and that we will continue to apply new technologies to tapping the information available on this vast and unique resource.[5] Already, some search engines are better able to identify key resources. Efforts are under way to adopt standardized metatags in the coding to describe the contents of Web pages. Some search engines are using expert systems to learn more about the information requester. This is already being used extensively to target advertisements and is being used more frequently to "select" from among several options the information source that will be delivered to the requester. More efforts are being made to index a larger portion of the Web content; at the same time, efforts are also under way to improve the relevancy of the results delivered for any one search.

Government Information

Government publications, especially those of the U.S. government, are mandatory resources for many business research projects. The agencies of the U.S. government, considered as a whole, are the largest publishing body in the world. The government collects and provides access to a wide variety of social, economic, and demographic data. In addition, government laws and regulations, court decisions, policy papers, and studies all have a potential impact on business. Additionally, the government provides directories, maps, and other information sources. Specialists are available throughout the government to provide individual assistance.

Searching for government information is a complicated task that usually requires some knowledge of how

>Exhibit 5a-2 Selected Websites for General Business Research

Site ID	Site URL	Sponsor
Advertising World	http://advertising.utexas.edu/world/	Department of Advertising, University of Texas, Austin
Annual Reports Online	http://www.zpub.com/sf/arl/	Annual Reports Library, San Francisco
BizLink, Your On-line Business Resource	http://www.plcmc.org/bizlink/	Public Library of Charlotte and Mecklenburg County
Business and Economics Resources Online	http://lcweb.loc.gov/rr/business/beonline/	Library of Congress
Electronic Commerce	http://onlinebusiness.about.com	About.com Inc.
ENTERWeb (Enterprise Development Website)	http://www.enterweb.org/	ENTERWeb
Guide to Labor-Oriented Internet Resources	http://www.irle.berkeley.edu/library/	Institute of Industrial Relations Library, University of California, Berkeley
Hoover's Online	http://www.hoovers.com	Hoover's, Inc.
Industry Research Desk	http://www.virtualpet.com/industry/rdindex2.htm	Polsen Enterprises Research Services
MSU-CIBER International Business Resources on the WWW	http://globaledge.msu.edu/	Michigan State University Center for International Business Education and Research
Rutgers Accounting Web	http://accounting.rutgers.edu/	Accounting Research Center, Rutgers University
Tax and Accounting Sites Directory	http://www.taxsites.com/	Schmidt Enterprises
Thomas Register of American Manufacturers	http://www.thomasnet.com	Thomas Publishing Co.
WorkIndex ("gateway to human resource solutions")	http://hronline.com/	*Human Resource Executive Magazine,* in cooperation with the Cornell School of Industrial Relations

government functions. In recent years, the U.S. government has been working aggressively to make its information available, not only through the Depository Library Program but also through the development of electronic resources. As a result, information that used to be tucked into the farthest corners of the library is now readily available and searchable on the Web. In many libraries, the entire government documents collection is included in the library's catalog, with links to Internet resources. In the remainder of this appendix, we examine three of the most useful government information types. A list of selected government resources on the Web is included in Exhibit 5a-3.

Government Organization Two of the most useful resources regarding government organization are:

- *U.S. Government Manual* (published annually); http://www.gpoaccess.gov/gmanual/ (updated annually).
- *Congressional Directory* (published annually); http://www.gpoaccess.gov/cdirectory/ (updated regularly).

The *U.S. Government Manual* describes the functions of every government agency and is particularly useful for identifying key personnel and agency contacts,

>Exhibit 5a-3 A List of Selected Government Sources

Source	Internet
Economic Indicators	http://www.economicindicators.gov/
Economic Statistics Briefing Room (current economic statistics)	http://www.whitehouse.gov/briefing-room
EDGAR Database of Corporate Information (SEC filings)	http://www.sec.gov/edgar.shtml
FedBizOpps (Federal Business Opportunities) (a listing of government procurement, sales, and contract awards)	http://www.fedbizopps.gov
FedStats	http://www.fedstats.gov
FirstGov: Business	http://www.usa.gov/Business/Business_Gateway.shtml
GPO Access	http://www.gpoaccess.gov/index.html
Stat-USA (U.S. Department of Commerce)	http://www.stat-usa.gov/
Thomas (U.S. Congress on the Internet)	http://thomas.loc.gov
U.S. Bureau of Economic Analysis	http://www.bea.gov/
U.S. Bureau of Labor Statistics	http://stats.bls.gov/
U.S. Bureau of the Census	http://www.census.gov/
U.S. Department of Commerce	http://www.commerce.gov/
U.S. Department of Labor	http://www.dol.gov/
U.S. Patent and Trademark Office	http://www.uspto.gov/
U.S. Small Business Administration	http://www.sbaonline.sba.gov/

including those at the local and regional levels. Generally very knowledgeable and helpful, these people are invaluable in any research project for their ability to cut through red tape and to answer questions pertinent to their agencies.

The *Congressional Directory* lists members of Congress and congressional committees, as well as key personnel throughout the U.S. government.

Laws, Regulations, and Court Decisions

Government information regarding these key areas and other legal information can be obtained by consulting GPO Access (http://www.gpoaccess.gov/). GPO Access is the government's official and real-time site for finding government information. Included at this site is the complete *Monthly Catalog of U.S. Government Publications.* Use it to identify the full range of government publications, printed and electronic, issued in or after 1994.

Especially valuable on GPO Access are the databases covering laws, regulations, and congressional debates and publications. The key databases for laws and regulations are:

- *Congressional Bills*—provides texts of varying versions of bills. Only a small portion of this collection

ever becomes law, but the topics can reveal trends of interest to business researchers.

- *Public Laws*—provides the texts of laws as they are passed; covers 1994 to the present. The printed version of this source is called *U.S. Statutes at Large.*

- *U.S. Code*—a codification of laws currently in effect and as revised over time. It is also available in libraries as a printed document.

- *Federal Register*—"the official daily publication for rules, proposed rules, and notices of federal agencies and organizations, as well as executive orders and other presidential documents";[6] covers 1995 to the present. It is also available in libraries as a printed or microfiche document.

- *Code of Federal Regulations (CFR)*—"a codification of the general and permanent rules originally published in the *Federal Register* by the executive departments and agencies of the federal government."[7] A printed version is available in libraries.

GPO Access includes other valuable databases, including the Supreme Court decisions from 1937 to the present, the *Economic Report of the President,* the U.S. Budget,

Commerce Business Daily (CBDNet), and GAO reports. New databases are added regularly.

Many libraries have created local gateways to GPO Access that help speed information retrieval (http://www.gpoaccess.gov/). GPO Access offers dozens of fields to search, and they can be searched independently or together. Searching each database independently provides more flexibility and more precise searching options because some fields are unique to a particular database. In general, search options are similar to those for other databases. Use the search hints for each file for more details and special search possibilities.

Government Statistics Information regarding government statistics may be obtained by consulting the following sources:

- *Statistical Abstract of the United States* (http://www.census.gov/prod/www/abs/statab.html).

- FedStats (http://www.fedstats.gov).

- U.S. Bureau of the Census (http://www.census.gov/).

The government collects statistics on just about every topic imaginable—from crimes to hospital beds, from teachers to tax revenue, from steel production to flower imports. For any statistical inquiry, start with the *Statistical Abstract of the United States.* This annual compendium compiles statistics issued by nearly every government agency as well as additional data from selected nongovernment organizations. Many are time-series tables covering several years or even decades. All tables indicate the source of the statistics. These sources can then be consulted if desired for even more comprehensive data. Check the library's catalog or ask the librarian to find these more specialized resources. Some may be available via FedStats.

FedStats is an online compilation of statistics provided by more than 70 U.S. agencies, including the Census Bureau, the Bureau of Labor Statistics, and the Federal Bureau of Investigation. Use the search option or the directory option to find the needed statistical tables. An especially useful feature of FedStats is the state and regional statistical data option.

No discussion of government statistical information would be complete without an examination of the U.S. Bureau of the Census. The Census Bureau is probably most well known for the Decennial Census of Population and Housing. The first such census was taken in 1790 to meet the constitutional mandate for apportioning seats in

Congress. It has been taken in every year ending in zero since that date. Now it is used not only to apportion seats in the House of Representatives but also for allocation of federal aid to states and for a myriad of other purposes. The decennial census asks a certain core of questions of everyone. These are known as the "100 percent questions." While these questions may vary slightly from census to census, data on age, race, gender, relationship, and Hispanic origin are fairly constantly collected. A longer questionnaire is sent to a sample of the population. Data from its additional questions, used in conjunction with the data from the 100 percent questions, are used by government agencies at all levels; local planners; business and industry; schools; and social service agencies, among others, for planning; grant writing; economic development; and many other purposes.

To make census information easier to understand, the Census Bureau, in cooperation with local planning agencies, has created a multilevel mapping system. The entire country is mapped into small units called *blocks*. Data from the 100 percent questions are available for all blocks, but sample data are not. Both 100 percent–question data and sample data are available for census tracts (groups of blocks) and for larger mapped units such as cities, metropolitan statistical areas, counties, and states. Tracts are especially valuable to local-level researchers because their boundaries remain mostly constant from census to census, thus allowing comparison. In cases where there is population growth, tracts may be split from one census to another and therefore may need to be added together to achieve comparable statistics. Metropolitan statistical areas, defined by the Office of Management and Budget, consist of a large population nucleus together with adjacent communities having a high degree of social and economic integration with that core. Metropolitan statistical areas comprise one or more entire counties, except in New England, where cities and towns are the basic geographic units.

In addition to the decennial census, the Census Bureau conducts the economic census in years ending in two and seven, covering all areas of the economy from the national to the local level. Both the decennial census and the economic census are supplemented by numerous survey reports, including the new American Community Survey, initiated to provide more up-to-date information on American communities. In fact, the Census Bureau has proposed using the American Community Survey—instead of the long (sample) questionnaire used through 2000—in the next decennial census. For an overview of the many report topics available, see the "Subjects A–Z" listing on the Census Bureau website (http://www.census.gov/).

>appendix5b

Advanced Searches

In advanced searches, you use your knowledge of the database to make the search more productive.

Limiters in Periodical Databases

- Date
- Full text
- Periodical title
- Peer review (scholarly journals)

The Search Query

Use the keywords from your management question to prepare a query for the databases. Bibliographic databases, including the library's online catalog, all have similar search options, usually a basic keyword search, an advanced search, and a way to choose a subject from a browse list. Like all databases, bibliographic databases consist of several standard fields.

Standard Search Fields for Monographs

- Author
- Title
- Subject headings
- Publisher
- Series

Limiters in Book Catalogs

- Language
- Date of publication
- Type of publication

In most bibliographic databases, all searches are keyword searches, but it is possible to search for a specific author or title or series (a known-item search) by limiting your results to a specific field of the bibliographic record. This is especially important if you are researching a prolific author such as Peter Drucker, who may have many works both by and about him. If you do not limit or narrow your search to a specific field, then you will do a general keyword search of all the records in the database. Because of the size of most databases, single-word searches generally yield results that are not very useful unless the single word is very unique. Instead, examine your management question for all relevant keywords and variations and establish a more precise search query using the connectors described as follows.

Standard Search Fields for Periodical Databases

- Author
- Title
- Subject headings
- Publisher
- Abstract
- Company name
- NAICS code

Limiters in Periodical Databases

- Date
- Full text
- Periodical Title
- Peer review (scholarly journals)

The most important thing to remember about search engines for the Web or for databases is that they do not all work alike. In fact, they have widely varying search protocols. What you do not know can act against you. So, if finding good information is important to you, take a couple of minutes to determine what special features and search options are used. For instance, if you enter a multi-word term, what happens? Does the database search your term as a phrase? Or does it insert a connector such as *AND* or *OR* between each word? How does it handle stopwords (*the, in,* and other similar small words)? The results will vary considerably in these three scenarios.

>**Exhibit 5b-1** Review of Advanced Search Options

Expanding Your Search		Narrowing Your Search	
OR	**AND**	**Phrases**	
Use **OR** to search for plurals, synonyms, or spelling variations. Either or both terms will be present in results. • woman **OR** women • business **OR** corporation • international **OR** foreign	Use **AND** to require that all terms you specify be present in the results. • child **AND** advertising	Use a term consisting of two or more words. Some phrases require double quotes to enclose the phrase, while others do not. • human resource management • "human resource management"	
Truncation	**NOT**	**ADJ**	
Symbols (?, *, !) that replace one or more characters or letters in a word or at the end of a word. • electr* (retrieves electricity, electric, electrical) • child? (retrieves children, childish, child's)	Use **NOT** to eliminate terms from your search. But use **NOT** with care. It is easy to eliminate the good with the unwanted. • medicine **NOT** nursing • Caribbean **NOT** Cuba	ADJ requires the first term specified to immediately precede the last term specified. • six **ADJ** sigma	
		Limiters	
	Conditions **(date, publication type, language)** for limiting your search. Most databases also offer *field limiting,* limiting the occurrences of your search to a specific database field, such as the author field, title, etc. Some bibliographic databases offer the convenience of limiting the search results to peer-reviewed articles or to articles only available in full text. Use the latter with care as some significant articles may be overlooked even though they are available in the library.		

Search Strategy Options

Basic Searches If you have a unique term, try a basic search with that term. Most bibliographic databases will present the results list in reverse date order; that is, the most recently published items will appear first. Review the list of items your search has retrieved. Are there too many? not enough? very relevant or not very relevant? If they meet the Goldilocks test of "just right," then you can move on to the next step (saving results).

Advanced Searches If you have retrieved too few or no relevant items, or if you have retrieved hundreds of items, you should consider modifying your search query. Start with the most relevant items you find in the results list. Then do one of the following:

- Search for the cited works (the bibliography) of the full-text articles.

- Search for other works by the author or authors of the relevant citations.

- Check the subject headings assigned to the articles. Are there any more precise terms or synonyms that would improve your search results? More importantly, are there pairs of terms that appear in all of the most relevant items? Is there a thesaurus with the database that defines or expands the terminology used in the subject headings?

As a result of your examination of the relevant citations and any background preparation you have done in other sources such as encyclopedias, you should now have one or more concepts and synonyms for each concept. You can now use Boolean operators or connectors (see Exhibit 5b-1) to combine terms or sets of terms to expand or narrow your search. There are four basic Boolean operators or connectors: OR, AND, NOT, and ADJ.

Think of your management question as a series of key concepts. For example, your management question might be How can I design an appropriate or awareness program to prevent sexual harassment lawsuits in my company? In this example, concept A would be *training;* concept B would be *harassment;* concept C would be *lawsuits.* In the most basic of keyword searches, you could use a keyword search with the operator AND to combine them:

training AND harassment AND lawsuits

If your search results are inadequate, you might need to expand your search statement with synonyms connected with the operator OR. For our sample management question, your search would look like Exhibit 5b-2. If your search results are too numerous, you'd need to limit your search.

>Exhibit 5b-2 Advanced Searching Process

Step 1: Build a list of synonyms for each concept in the management question.				
Concept A	Operator	Concept B	Operator	Concept C
training	AND	sex* harassment	AND	lawsuit
awareness		wom*n		law
behavior		female		courts
professional		gender		legal
development		men		

Step 2: Create and search with a concept group by combining each term in a column with **OR.** Put each concept group in parentheses. Then combine each concept group with **AND.**

(training OR awareness OR behavior OR professional development) AND (sex* harassment OR wom*n OR men OR female OR gender) AND (lawsuit OR legal OR law OR courts)

>part II

The Design of Business Research

>chapter 6

Research Design: An Overview

>**learning**objectives

After reading this chapter, you should understand . . .

1 The basic stages of research design.

2 The major descriptors of research design.

3 The major types of research designs.

4 The relationships that exist between variables in research design and the steps for evaluating those relationships.

> 66 Most human beings and most companies don't like to make choices. And they particularly don't like to make a few choices that they really have to live with. 99
>
> Alan Lafley, former president and chairman of the board,
> Procter & Gamble

"So what has you frowning at the coffee pot so early on this beautiful morning," greets Jason Henry, as he encounters his partner Sara Arens staring at the coffee machine. "I believe the statisticians have confirmed that 'A watched pot never boils.'"

"I'm just debating whether I need another cup before joining you for the debriefing on our new project," shares Sara. "My mind has been running on overdrive since yesterday." Sara pours herself a generous cup and tops off Jason's cup as well. "Let's move to the conference room. I have lots of information to share with you."

"The meeting didn't turn out quite like we expected. Not just another project from a former client. What I faced yesterday was, well, a syndicate of businesses—representatives from Sun Microsystems, Best Buy, AT&T; even some major health institutions were in the group, to name just a few. In a nutshell, they want us to design and conduct the definitive study on the effectiveness of work–life balance employee programs," exclaims Sara, grinning widely.

"Work-life balance programs—those are the ones that track employee performance, but not their time on the job, that give employees a lot more control over when and where they work, right?" asks Jason. "Weren't you just talking about these programs being profiled in the article you read last week in . . ."

". . . in *BusinessWeek*," interrupts Sara. "The exciting thing about the study is that they are so open on methodology. They want us to design the ultimate study. We will have access to data from those organizations that have implemented such programs—possibly enabling ex post facto studies. There were retailers, hospitals, manufacturers, high-technology companies present, almost every type of organization you could want in such a ground-breaking study.

Several of the companies are real believers in work–life balance initiatives and are rolling out implementation of programs from division to division. As a result, they have some divisions in which the programs are not yet implemented. And these organizations cross continental boundaries. We'll have to work with cross-cultural issues as well as workplace culture issues. And several other organizations within the syndicate are interested in implementing such work–life balance initiatives but have agreed not to implement programs until the research is in place to monitor changes in attitudes, perceptions, and behaviors."

"Ah, so that work we did in Europe and China last year, where the workplace cultures had such a significantly different impact, will pay dividends on this next project. So you are thinking control studies?" questions Jason.

"Well, we certainly have the opportunity to set up such field experiments," claimed Sara. "But initially I'm thinking a multiphase descriptive communication study, too, maybe combining qualitative research to get at deeper feelings and motivations for work environment change with surveys to generate statistical measures of pre- and postattitudes, but also some longitudinal monitoring studies—and some of these could be observation research. We have so many options that we will need some exploratory work to help us focus. Some of the companies had done some preimplementation descriptive research on morale and some longitudinal measures on performance changes. I think we should digest those reports before we make any decisions about design. They promised to overnight the reports—we may have some this morning, but we should have the bulk of them tomorrow."

"We could start our interns on a literature search now," suggested Jason.

"That's a good idea," comments Sara. "I'm sure the reports that are coming will direct us to some background research, but from the comments that were shared, it also appears that several of the initiatives started as brainstorms of C-level executives and some companies just floated the initiatives without any research at all. Now they are thinking that in order to justify further investment they need to understand better why some initiatives have boosted performance significantly, while others have had lesser success or no success—that gives credence to a causal/explanatory study."

". . . and, whether they can expect such incremental change to be ongoing or increase or diminish over time," analyses Jason. "They really need a predictive study to know whether an organization should expect specific performance changes with the implementation of unique initiatives in different workplace cultures."

"So when do they want us to present our recommended design?"

"I've set up a meeting for that presentation in four weeks. Your schedule was free on both Thursday and Friday that week," shared Sara. "They want us both there along with representatives of any suppliers that we plan to use."

> What Is Research Design?

The topics covered by the term *research design* are wide-ranging, as depicted in Exhibit 6-1. This chapter introduces a classification of research designs and provides an overview of the most important design types (exploratory, descriptive, and causal). We refer you to subsequent chapters for a more thorough coverage of the unique features of qualitative studies, observational studies, surveys, and experiments. Our objective here is not for you to acquire the details of research design in one reading

>Exhibit 6-1 Design in the Research Process

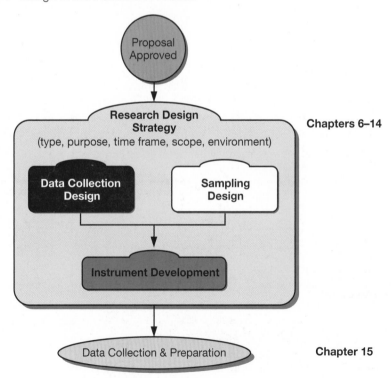

but for you to understand its scope and to get a glimpse of the available options for tailoring a design to an organization's particular research needs.

There are many definitions of research design, but no single definition imparts the full range of important aspects.

- Research design constitutes the blueprint for the collection, measurement, and analysis of data.
- Research design aids the researcher in the allocation of limited resources by posing crucial choices in methodology.[1]
- Research design is the plan and structure of investigation so conceived as to obtain answers to research questions. The plan is the overall scheme or program of the research. It includes an outline of what the investigator will do from writing hypotheses and their operational implications to the final analysis of data.[2]
- Research design expresses both the structure of the research problem—the frame-work, organization, or configuration of the relationships among variables of a study—and the plan of investigation used to obtain empirical evidence on those relationships.[3]

These definitions differ in detail, but together they give the essentials of **research design:**

- An activity- and time-based plan.
- A plan always based on the research question.
- A guide for selecting sources and types of information.
- A framework for specifying the relationships among the study's variables.
- A procedural outline for every research activity.

At its core, research is a project and project management tools such as **critical path method (CPM)** can be used to depict sequential and simultaneous steps and estimate scheduling and timetables for each activity or phase of the research, as is done in Exhibit 6-2. The pathway from start to end that takes the longest time to complete is called the *critical path*. Any delay in an activity along this path will delay the end of the entire project. We introduced you to an alternative scheduling tool, the Gantt chart, in Chapter 5 (see Exhibit 5-11). Before you develop a schedule, however, you need to know precisely what research you plan to do.

>**Exhibit 6-2** CPM Schedule of Research Design.

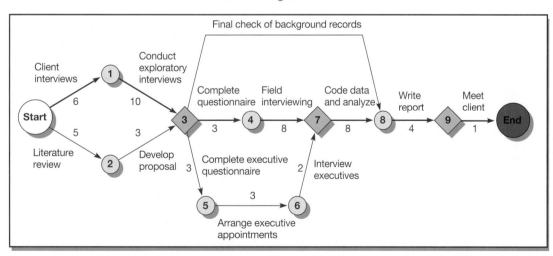

Milestones:
3 Proposal approval
7 Interviews completed
9 Final report completed

Critical Path:
S–1–3–4–7–8–9–E

Time to Completion:
40 working days

>**Exhibit 6-3** Descriptors of Research Design

Category	Options
The degree to which the research question has been crystallized	• Exploratory study • Formal study
The method of data collection	• Monitoring • Communication study
The power of the researcher to produce effects in the variables under study	• Experimental • Ex post facto

The purpose of the study	• Reporting
	• Descriptive
	• Causal
	  • Explanatory
	  • Predictive

The time dimension	• Cross-sectional • Longitudinal
The topical scope—breadth and depth—of the study	• Case • Statistical study
The research environment	• Field setting • Laboratory research • Simulation
The participants' perceptions of research activity	• Actual routine • Modified routine

Classification of Designs

Early in any research study, one faces the task of selecting the specific design to use. A number of different design dimensions exist, but, unfortunately, no simple classification system defines all the variations that must be considered. Exhibit 6-3 groups research design issues using eight different descriptors.[4] A brief discussion of these descriptors illustrates their nature and contribution to research.

Degree of Research Question Crystallization

A study may be viewed as exploratory or formal. The essential distinctions between these two options are the degree of structure and the immediate objective of the study. **Exploratory studies** tend toward loose structures with the objective of discovering future research tasks. The immediate purpose of exploration is usually to develop hypotheses or questions for further research. The **formal study** begins where the exploration leaves off—it begins with a hypothesis or research question and involves precise procedures and data source specifications. The goal of a formal research design is to test the hypotheses or answer the research questions posed.

The exploratory–formal study dichotomy is less precise than some other classifications. All studies have elements of exploration in them, and few studies are completely uncharted. The sequence discussed in Chapter 4 (see Exhibit 4-1 and the model on the inside front cover) suggests that more formalized studies contain at least an element of exploration before the final choice of design. More detailed consideration of exploratory research is found later in this chapter.

Method of Data Collection

This classification distinguishes between monitoring and communication processes. We use the term *communication* to contrast with *monitoring* because collecting data by questioning encompasses more than the survey method. **Monitoring** includes studies in which the researcher inspects the activities of a subject or the nature of some material without attempting to elicit responses from anyone. Traffic counts at an intersection, license plates recorded in a restaurant parking lot, a search of the library collection, an observation of the actions of a group of decision makers, the State Farm Dangerous Intersection Study—all are examples of monitoring. In each case the researcher notes and records the information available from observations. Monitoring for MindWriter might include "following" a computer through the repair process, documenting each activity or interaction between CompleteCare and call center employees and the damaged laptop.

In the **communication study,** the researcher questions the subjects and collects their responses by personal or impersonal means. The collected data may result from (1) interview or telephone conversations, (2) self-administered or self-reported instruments sent through the mail, left in convenient locations, or transmitted electronically or by other means, or (3) instruments presented before and/or after a treatment or stimulus condition in an *experiment.* Sara and Jason propose a communication study, using a response card inserted in the packaging of laptops returned after CompleteCare servicing.

76

The percent of mobile phone subscribers worldwide who use SMS text messaging.

Researcher Control of Variables

In terms of the researcher's ability to manipulate variables, we differentiate between experimental and ex post facto designs. In an **experiment,** the researcher attempts to control and/or manipulate the variables in the study. It is enough that we can cause variables to be changed or held constant in keeping with our research objectives. Experimental design is appropriate when one wishes to discover whether certain variables produce effects in other variables. Experimentation provides the most powerful support possible for a hypothesis of causation.

With an **ex post facto design,** investigators have no control over the variables in the sense of being able to manipulate them. They can only report what has happened or what is happening. It is important that the researchers using this design not influence the variables; to do so introduces bias. The researcher is limited to holding factors constant by judicious selection of subjects according to strict sampling procedures and by statistical manipulation of findings. MindWriter is planning an ex post facto design.

The Purpose of the Study

The essential difference between the various studies in this grouping—reporting, descriptive, and causal-explanatory or causal-predictive—lies in their objectives. A **reporting study** provides a summation of data, often recasting data to achieve a deeper understanding or to generate statistics for comparison. In a study of crime, for example, a reporting study might tally the number of employee thefts that take place in shopping malls versus free-standing stores. If the research is concerned with finding out *who, what, where, when,* or *how much,* then the study is **descriptive.** Descriptive research on employee theft would measure the types of theft committed (clothing vs. electronics vs. housewares), how often, when (time of year, time of day, day of week), where (receiving dock, stockroom, sales floor), and by whom (gender, age, years of service, departmental assignment). If a study is concerned with learning why—that is, how one variable produces changes in another—it is **causal-explanatory.** In a causal-explanatory study, we try to explain relationships among variables—for instance, why the crime rate is higher in mall A than in mall B or why male employees steal more than female employees. A **causal-predictive** study attempts to predict an effect on one variable by manipulating another variable while holding all other variables constant. In our crime example, researchers using a causal-predictive study might be interested in whether installation of video surveillance cameras on the receiving dock and in stockrooms would reduce employee theft in mall stores. At the outset, the MindWriter project is descriptive, although subsequent studies might be causal.

The Time Dimension

Cross-sectional studies are carried out once and represent a snapshot of one point in time. **Longitudinal studies** are repeated over an extended period. The advantage of a longitudinal study is that it can track changes over time. Jason and Sara's proposal describes a longitudinal study, with satisfaction measurements taken continuously over several months and reported monthly.

In longitudinal studies of the *panel* variety, the researcher may study the same people over time. In marketing, panels are set up to report consumption data on a variety of products. These data, collected from national samples, provide a major data bank on relative market share, consumer response to new products, and new promotional methods. Other longitudinal studies, such as *cohort groups,* use different subjects for each sequenced measurement. The service industry might have looked at the needs of aging baby boomers by sampling 40- to 45-year-olds in 1990 and 50- to 55-year-olds in 2000. Although each sample would be different, the population of 1945 to 1950 cohort survivors would remain the same.

Some types of information once collected cannot be collected a second time from the same person without the risk of bias. The study of public awareness of an advertising campaign over a six-month period would require different samples for each measurement.

While longitudinal research is important, the constraints of budget and time impose the need for cross-sectional analysis. Some benefits of a longitudinal study can be revealed in a cross-sectional study by adroit questioning about past attitudes, history, and future expectations. Responses to these kinds of questions should be interpreted with care, however.

The Topical Scope

The statistical study differs from the case study in several ways. **Statistical studies** are designed for breadth rather than depth. They attempt to capture a population's characteristics by making inferences from a sample's characteristics. Hypotheses are tested quantitatively. Generalizations about findings are presented based on the representativeness of the sample and the validity of the design. MindWriter plans a statistical study.

Case studies place more emphasis on a full contextual analysis of fewer events or conditions and their interrelations. Although hypotheses are often used, the reliance on qualitative data makes support or rejection more difficult. An emphasis on detail provides valuable insight for problem solving, evaluation, and strategy. This detail is secured from multiple sources of information. It allows evidence to be verified and avoids missing data. Remember the proposed monitoring study for MindWriter? If MindWriter tracked one or more laptops, this could serve as a case study of the CompleteCare program.

Although case studies have been maligned as "scientifically worthless" because they do not meet minimal design requirements for comparison,[5] they have a significant scientific role. It is known that "important scientific propositions have the form of universals, and a universal can be falsified by a single counterinstance."[6] Thus, a single, well-designed case study can provide a major challenge to a theory and provide a source of new hypotheses and constructs simultaneously. Discovering new hypotheses to correct postservice complaints would be the major advantage of tracking a given number of damaged MindWriter laptops through the case study design.

The Research Environment

Designs also differ as to whether they occur under actual environmental conditions (**field conditions**) or under staged or manipulated conditions (**laboratory conditions**).

To simulate is to replicate the essence of a system or process. **Simulations** are increasingly used in research, especially in operations research. The major characteristics of various conditions and relationships in actual situations are often represented in mathematical models. Role-playing and other behavioral activities may also be viewed as simulations. A simulation for MindWriter might involve an arbitrarily damaged laptop being tracked through the call center and the CompleteCare program, monitoring results at each workstation. Another popularly used simulation is the retail service study involving "mystery shoppers."

Participants' Perceptual Awareness

The usefulness of a design may be reduced due to a **participant's perceptual awareness** when people in a disguised study perceive that research is being conducted. Participants' perceptual awareness influences the outcomes of the research in subtle ways or more dramatically as we learned from the pivotal Hawthorne studies of the late 1920s. Although there is no widespread evidence of attempts by participants or respondents to please researchers through successful hypothesis guessing or evidence of the prevalence of sabotage, when participants believe that something out of the ordinary is happening, they may behave less naturally. There are three levels of perception:

1. Participants perceive no deviations from everyday routines.
2. Participants perceive deviations, but as unrelated to the researcher.
3. Participants perceive deviations as researcher-induced.[7]

The "mystery shopper" scenario is the perfect example of the final level of perceptual awareness noted in the preceding list. If a retail sales associate knows she is being observed and evaluated—with consequences in future compensation, scheduling, or work assignment—she is likely to change her performance. In all research environments and control situations, researchers need to be vigilant to effects that may alter their conclusions. Participants' perceptions serve as a reminder to classify one's study by type, to examine validation strengths and weaknesses, and to be prepared to qualify results accordingly.

> Exploratory Studies

Exploration is particularly useful when researchers lack a clear idea of the problems they will meet during the study. Through exploration researchers develop concepts more clearly, establish priorities, develop operational definitions, and improve the final research design. Exploration may also save time and money. If the problem is not as important as first thought, more formal studies can be canceled.

Exploration serves other purposes as well. The area of investigation may be so new or so vague that a researcher needs to do an exploration just to learn something about the dilemma facing the manager. Important variables may not be known or thoroughly defined. Hypotheses for the research may be needed. Also, the researcher may explore to be sure it is practical to do a formal study in the area. A federal government agency, the Office of Industry Analysis, proposed that research be done on how executives in a given industry made decisions about raw material purchases. Questions were planned asking how (and at what price spreads) one raw material was substituted for another in certain manufactured products. An exploration to discover if industry executives would divulge adequate information about their decision making on this topic was essential for the study's success.

Despite its obvious value, researchers and managers alike give exploration less attention than it deserves. There are strong pressures for quick answers. Moreover, exploration is sometimes linked to old biases about qualitative research: subjectiveness, nonrepresentativeness, and nonsystematic design. More realistically, exploration saves time and money and should not be slighted.

Qualitative Techniques

The objectives of exploration may be accomplished with different techniques. Both qualitative and quantitative techniques are applicable, although exploration relies more heavily on **qualitative techniques.** One author creates a verbal picture to differentiate the two:

> Quality is the essential character or nature of something; quantity is the amount. Quality is the what; quantity the how much. Qualitative refers to the meaning, the definition or analogy or model or metaphor characterizing something, while quantitative assumes the meaning and refers to a measure of it . . . The difference lies in Steinbeck's [1941] description of the Mexican Sierra, a fish from the Sea of Cortez. One can count the spines on the dorsal fin of a pickled Sierra, 17 plus 15 plus 9. "But," says Steinbeck, "if the Sierra strikes hard on the line so that our hands are burned, if the fish

Cheskin Knows Teens

All great research starts with a question. When Pepsi, GM, and Purple Moon needed a realistic and strategic understanding of the teen population to help guide product development and communications strategies, they turned to Cheskin. A 50-year-old consulting and strategic research firm, Cheskin designed a research approach that looks at teens the way they look at themselves.

- Cheskin sends cameras out to hundreds of teens, asking them to photograph their lives as they really are.
- Cheskin researchers interview friends together, asking them about their dreams, fears, cares, and concerns.
- Cheskin interviews experts who have built careers on understanding teen psyche.
- Cheskin researchers visit common teen hangouts, observing how teens act when away from adults.

As a result, Cheskin identified five main types of teenagers. Then the researchers designed a new model that tracks the relative influence of these teen types over time, to accurately predict how trends move through the teen population. "We identify youth by their social cliques instead of by demographic constructs, and create portraits you'll recognize in the street." This project is now an annual study of teen culture and behavior.

www.cheskin.com

sounds and nearly escapes and finally comes in over the rail, his colors pulsing and his tail beating the air, a whole new relational externality has come into being." Qualitative research would define the being of fishing, the ambiance of a city, the mood of a citizen, or the unifying tradition of a group.[8]

When we consider the scope of qualitative research, several approaches are adaptable for exploratory investigations of management questions:

- Individual depth interviews (usually conversational rather than structured).
- Participant observation (to perceive firsthand what participants in the setting experience).
- Films, photographs, and videotape (to capture the life of the group under study).
- Projective techniques and psychological testing (such as a Thematic Apperception Test, projective measures, games, or role-playing).
- Case studies (for an in-depth contextual analysis of a few events or conditions).
- Street ethnography (to discover how a cultural subgroup describes and structures its world at the street level).
- Elite or expert interviewing (for information from influential or well-informed people in an organization or community).
- Document analysis (to evaluate historical or contemporary confidential or public records, reports, government documents, and opinions).
- Proxemics and kinesics (to study the use of space and body-motion communication, respectively).[9]

When these approaches are combined, four exploratory techniques emerge with wide applicability for the management researcher:

1. Secondary data analysis.
2. Experience surveys.
3. Focus groups.
4. Two-stage designs.

Secondary Data Analysis

The first step in an exploratory study is a search of the secondary literature. Studies made by others for their own purposes represent **secondary data.** It is inefficient to discover anew through the collection of **primary data** or original research what has already been done and reported at a level sufficient for management to make a decision.

Within secondary data exploration, a researcher should start first with an organization's own data archives. Reports of prior research studies often reveal an extensive amount of historical data or decision-making patterns. By reviewing prior studies, you can identify methodologies that proved successful and unsuccessful. Solutions that didn't receive attention in the past due to different environmental circumstances are revealed as potential subjects for further study. The researcher needs to avoid duplication in instances when prior collected data can provide sufficient information for resolving the current decision-making dilemma. While MindWriter's CompleteCare program is newly introduced, it is likely that one or more studies of the previous servicing practices and policies revealed customer attitudes on which MindWriter based the design of the current program.

The second source of secondary data is published documents prepared by authors outside the sponsor organization. There are tens of thousands of periodicals and hundreds of thousands of books on all aspects of business. Data from secondary sources help us decide what needs to be done and can be a rich source of hypotheses. Special catalogs, subject guides, and electronic indexes—available in most libraries—will help in this search. In many cases you can conduct a secondary search from your home or office using a computer, an online service, or an Internet gateway. Regarding MindWriter, thousands of articles have been written on customer service, and an Internet search using the keyword *customer service* reveals tens of thousands of hits.

If one is creative, a search of secondary sources will supply excellent background information as well as many good leads. Yet if we confine the investigation to obvious subjects in bibliographic sources, we will often miss much of the best information. Suppose the Copper Industry Association is interested in estimating the outlook for the copper industry over the next 10 years. We could search through the literature under the headings "copper production" and "copper consumption." However, a search restricted to these two topics would miss more than it finds. When a creative search of the copper industry is undertaken, useful information turns up under the following reference headings: mines and minerals; nonferrous metals; forecasting; planning; econometrics; consuming industries such as automotive and communications; countries where copper is produced, such as Chile; and companies prominent in the industry, such as Anaconda and Kennecott.

We provide a detailed list of secondary sources on the text website.

Experience Survey

While published data are a valuable resource, it is seldom that more than a fraction of the existing knowledge in a field is put into writing. A significant portion of what is known on a topic, while in writing, may be proprietary to a given organization and thus unavailable to an outside searcher. Also, internal data archives are rarely well organized, making secondary sources, even when known, difficult to locate. Thus, we will profit by seeking information from persons experienced in the area of study, tapping into their collective memories and experiences.

When we interview persons in an **experience survey,** we should seek their ideas about important issues or aspects of the subject and discover what is important across the subject's range of knowledge. The investigative format we use should be flexible enough so that we can explore various avenues that emerge during the interview.

- What is being done?

- What has been tried in the past without success? With success?

- How have things changed?

- What are the change-producing elements of the situation?

- Who is involved in decisions and what role does each person play?

- What problem areas and barriers can be seen?

- What are the costs of the processes under study?

- Whom can we count on to assist and/or participate in the research?

- What are the priority areas?

The product of such questioning may be a new hypothesis, the discarding of an old one, or information about the practicality of doing the study. Probing may show whether certain facilities are available, what factors need to be controlled and how, and who will cooperate in the study.

Discovery is more easily carried out if the researcher can analyze cases that provide special insight. Typical of exploration, we are less interested in getting a representative cross section than in getting information from sources that might be insightful. Assume we study StarAuto's automobile assembly plant. It has a history of declining productivity, increasing costs, and growing numbers of quality defects. People who might provide insightful information include:

- *Newcomers to the scene*—employees or personnel who may have been recently transferred to this plant from similar plants.

- *Marginal or peripheral individuals*—persons whose jobs place them on the margin between contending groups. First-line supervisors and lead workers are often neither management nor worker but something in between.

- *Individuals in transition*—recently promoted employees who have been transferred to new departments.

- *Deviants and isolates*—those in a given group who hold a different position from the majority, as well as workers who are happy with the present situation, highly productive departments and workers, and loners of one sort or another.

- *"Pure" cases* or cases that show extreme examples of the conditions under study—the most unproductive departments, the most antagonistic workers, and so forth.

- *Those who fit well and those who do not*—the workers who are well established in their organizations versus those who are not, those executives who fully reflect management views and those who do not.

- *Those who represent different positions in the system*—unskilled workers, assemblers, superintendents, and so forth.[10]

Jason and Sara plan to interview three managers during the early phase of their research for Mind-Writer: the managers of (1) the service facility, (2) the call center, and (3) the contract courier service. Their emphasis should be not only on finding out what has been done in the past but also on discovering the parameters of feasible change. They might want to expand their interviews to include long-term employees of the various departments, as their views are likely to be different from those of their managers. Because postpurchase service problems might be directly related to product design, expanding their experience survey to individuals associated with engineering and production should also be considered.

Focus Groups

Focus groups became widely used in research during the 1980s and are used for increasingly diverse research applications today.[11] A **focus group** is a group of people (typically 6 to 10 participants), led by a trained moderator, who meet for 90 minutes to 2 hours. The facilitator or moderator uses group dynamics principles to focus or guide the group in an exchange of ideas, feelings, and experiences on a specific topic.

One topical objective of a focus group might be a new product or product concept, a new employee motivation program, or improved production-line organization. The basic output of the session is a list of ideas and behavioral observations, with recommendations by the moderator. These ideas and observations are often used for later quantitative testing. In exploratory research, the qualitative data that focus groups produce may be used for enriching all levels of research questions and hypotheses and comparing the effectiveness of design options. The most common application of focus group research continues to be in the consumer arena. However, corporations are using focus group results for diverse exploratory applications.

MindWriter could use focus groups involving employees (of the call center and service departments) to determine changes and provide an analysis of change ideas. It may want focus groups with customers (both dissatisfied and satisfied) to uncover what has occurred in their different experiences. In another application, when a large title insurance company was developing a computerized help system, it ran focus groups with

Meet Nick. Zoomerang Sample Member Nº 2,487,103. He's a dad. An anthropologist. A poker player. And a sucker for coming-of-age movies. He's ready to tell you all about that—and more than 500 other aspects of his life, opinions, preferences, and tastes.

He's one of more than 2.5 million people who make up Zoomerang Sample—the fastest, smartest way to reach your target consumers with pinpoint accuracy. Whether you're doing an online survey or an online focus group, with Zoomerang Sample you'll stay in touch with the evolving tastes and preferences of your target market. So you can draw sharper insights and make more informed decisions. Just ask Nick.

1(888) 760-3182 or visit us at info.zoomerang.com/easysample

Z *zoomerang*

Zoomerang and Zoomerang Sample are part of MarketTools, Inc. Zoomerang Sample is sourced from MarketTools' ZoomPanel of more than 2.5 million participants.

How do you get inside the mind of a potential respondent? Zoomerang has compiled a sample frame of more than 2.5 million people with diverse interests who are willing to share their opinions during focus groups or through surveys. **www.zoomerang.com**

The Ohio Lottery Initiates a Two-Stage Study

What motivates a lottery player to play? What is the understanding of the payout or odds and how relevant is this understanding to making a purchase? Are purchases of lottery tickets routine or impulsive? Are purchases perceived as recreation or gambling? How is winning defined? What is the influence of in-store promotion and signage? Is playing perceived as chance or skill? What is the significance of the dollar value of the ticket?

In 2005, the Ohio Lottery sponsored a study conducted by Marcus Thomas LLC with the services of MRSI. The first phase used a qualitative methodology, the metaphorical elicitation technique (MET), to elicit emotions, feelings, and motivations surrounding lottery play. This technique required participants to bring images that were evocative of their lottery experience to a scheduled interview. Such images are usually photographs or pictures from print publications. An individual depth interview of approximately 90 minutes extracts the meaning of each picture. Twenty-five MET interviews were conducted in three cities.

Phase two was a detailed, online survey taking approximately 39 minutes. The questions developed for the survey were drawn from the experience with the MET interviews. All 1,505 (1,305 players and 200 nonplayers) participants completed the survey by accessing a secure website between July 22 and July 31, 2005. The quantitative study verified the lessons from the MET analysis—that messaging should emphasize fun, the rush experienced while learning whether the dream of the win will come true, and the low-risk nature of the entertainment. Detailed analysis of the data has also enabled the Ohio Lottery to understand the segments of lottery players.

To learn more about this study, and see sample questions and data displays, read the case *Ohio Lottery: Innovative Research Design Drives Winning* on your text CD.

www.marcusthomasllc.com; www.mrsi.com.

its branch office administrators to discover their preferences for distributing files on the company's **intranet** (a company's proprietary network—behind a security "firewall" that limits access to authorized users only). In other cases, a small college used focus groups to develop a plan to attract more freshmen applications, and a blood center used a focus group to improve blood donations.[12]

Two-Stage Design

A useful way to design a research study is as a **two-stage design.** With this approach, exploration becomes a separate first stage with limited objectives: (1) clearly defining the research question and (2) developing the research design.

In arguing for a two-stage approach, we recognize that much about the problem is not known but should be known before effort and resources are committed. In these circumstances, one is operating in unknown areas, where it is difficult to predict the problems and costs of the study. Proposals that acknowledge the practicality of this approach are particularly useful when the research budget is inflexible. A limited exploration for a specific, modest cost carries little risk for both sponsor and researcher and often uncovers information that reduces the total research cost.

An exploratory study is finished when the researchers have achieved the following:

- Established the major dimensions of the research task.
- Defined a set of subsidiary investigative questions that can be used as guides to a detailed research design.
- Developed several hypotheses about possible causes of a management dilemma.
- Learned that certain other hypotheses are such remote possibilities that they can be safely ignored in any subsequent study.
- Concluded additional research is not needed or is not feasible.

Wildcat Survey—Problem or Opportunity?

A *wildcat survey* is executed when business managers bypass their internal research departments and, using online survey software, launch their own survey. This is a growing phenomenon, according to Ruth Stanat, president and CEO of SIS International Research, and is most frequently done "to control costs and gain immediate feedback."

But there are drawbacks, most notably loss of control of internal sample panels; duplication of contact and sample fatigue; and insufficient training in question development and data analysis, leading to poor data quality and weak data insights. "If [sample respondents] feel bombarded by our surveys," shared Sharon Starr, director of market research for IPC Inc., "they will start to ignore surveys at best, or resent the company for wasting their time at worst. The company's image will suffer if the company looks disunified and out of control."

The availability of seemingly simple survey solutions from firms like Zoomerang and SurveyMonkey has magnified the problem. Jeffrey C. Adler, president of Centrac DC Marketing Research, likens it to trying to fix a broken switch on his own furnace. "I could have gone to Home Depot and purchased the switch myself, theoretically saving a lot of money. However, I was smart enough to recognize that changing the switch was not my area of expertise. How big would the savings have been if I wired the thing myself and caused damage to the furnace or burned down the house?" Adler argues that when end-users

work through research departments or specialists, they are paying for expertise in *using* the tools. He laments that managers recognize this easily with an electrician or a surgeon; but fail to recognize this with research specialists.

Some in the industry think research specialists have, in part, created the problem by not providing knowledge and insights to the manager about the practice of research itself. By not educating that manager about how research is done, that manager is less able to distinguish greater from lesser quality research. If research buyers or sponsors understood the real challenges of research in a specific project, it is argued, they would have a greater appreciation for the art and science of research.

"There is an opportunity for research departments to extend an olive branch to other parts of the business by providing best practices, templates, and even resources for self-executed projects," suggests Josh Mendelsohn, vice president of Chadwick Martin Bailey Inc. "I certainly wish everyone had the time/budget to do full-fledged research projects in every case, but sometimes the business need doesn't justify the cost/time it takes to do something the right way. By providing assistance, the validity issues are likely to go away and redundancies are going to be less. And research [divisions] then become more of a business partner to be consulted than an internal vendor to be battled with."

**www.sismarketresearch.com; www.ipc.org; www.centracdc
.com; www.cmbinfo.com**

> Descriptive Studies

In contrast to exploratory studies, more formalized studies are typically structured with clearly stated hypotheses or investigative questions. Formal studies serve a variety of research objectives:

1. Descriptions of phenomena or characteristics associated with a subject population (the *who, what, when, where,* and *how* of a topic).

2. Estimates of the proportions of a population that have these characteristics.

3. Discovery of associations among different variables.

The third study objective is sometimes labeled a *correlational study,* a subset of descriptive studies. A descriptive study may be simple or complex; it may be done in many settings. Whatever the form, a descriptive study can be just as demanding of research skills as the causal study, and we should insist on the same high standards for design and execution.

The simplest descriptive study concerns a univariate question or hypothesis in which we ask about, or state something about, the size, form, distribution, or existence of a variable. In the account analysis at BankChoice (introduced in Chapters 4 and 5) we might be interested in developing a profile of savers. We first may want to locate them in relation to the main office. The question might be, What percentage of the savers live within a two-mile radius of the office? Using the hypothesis format, we might predict, 60 percent or more of the savers live within a two-mile radius of the office.

We may also be interested in securing information about other variables, such as the relative size of accounts, the number of accounts for minors, the number of accounts opened within the last six

>picprofile

months, and the amount of activity (number of deposits and withdrawals per year) in accounts. Data on each of these variables, by themselves, may have value for management decisions. Bivariate relationships between these or other variables may be of even greater interest. Cross-tabulations between the distance from the account owner's residence or employment to the branch and account activity may suggest that differential rates of activity are related to account owner location. A cross-tabulation of account size and gender of account owner may also show interrelation. Such findings do not imply a causal relationship. In fact, our task is to determine if the variables are independent (or unrelated) and if they are not, then to determine the strength or magnitude of the relationship. Neither procedure tells us which variable is the cause. For example, we might be able to conclude that gender and account size are related but not that gender is a causal factor in account size.

Descriptive studies are often much more complex than this example. One study of savers began as described and then went into much greater depth. Part of the study included an observation of account records that revealed a concentration of nearby savers. Their accounts were typically larger and more active than those whose owners lived at a distance. A sample survey of savers provided information on stages in the family life cycle, attitudes toward savings, family income levels, and other matters. Correlation of this information with known savings data showed that women owned larger accounts. Further investigation suggested that women with larger accounts were often widowed or working single women who were older than the average account holder. Information about their attitudes and savings practices led to new business strategies at the bank.

Some evidence collected led to causal questions. The correlation between nearness to the office and the probability of having an account at the office suggested the question, Why would people who live far from the office have an account there? In this type of question a hypothesis makes its greatest contribution by pointing out directions that the research might follow. It might be hypothesized that:

1. Distant savers (operationally defined as those with addresses more than two miles from the office) have accounts at the office because they once lived near the office; they were "near" when the account decision was made.

2. Distant savers actually live near the office, but the address on the account is outside the 2-mile radius; they are "near," but the records do not show this.

3. Distant savers work near the office; they are "near" by virtue of their work location.

4. Distant savers are not normally near the office but responded to a promotion that encouraged savers to bank via computer; this is another form of "nearness" in which this concept is transformed into one of "convenience."

When these hypotheses were tested, it was learned that a substantial portion of the distant savers could be accounted for by hypotheses 1 and 3. The conclusion: Location was closely related to saving at a given association. The determination of cause is not so simple, however, and these findings still fall within the definition of a descriptive study.

MindWriter could benefit from a descriptive study that profiles satisfied service customers versus dissatisfied ones. Service customer characteristics could then be matched with specific types of service problems, which could lead to identifying changes in product design or customer service policies.

> Causal Studies

The correlation between location and probability of account holding at BankChoice might look like strong evidence to many, but the researcher with scientific training will argue that correlation (simultaneous occurrence) is not causation. The essence of the disagreement seems to lie in the concept of cause.

The essential element of **causation** is that A "produces" B or A "forces" B to occur. Empirically, we can never demonstrate an A-B causality with certainty. The reason is that we do not "demonstrate" such causal linkages deductively. Unlike deductive conclusions, empirical conclusions are inferences— inductive conclusions. As such, they are statements of the probability that A "produces" B based on what we observe and measure.

In Chapter 3 we discussed the example of sales failing to increase following a promotion. Having ruled out other causes for the flat sales, we were left with one inference that *was probably but not certainly* the cause: a poorly executed promotion.

Meeting the ideal standard of causation requires that one variable *always* causes another and no other variable has the same causal effect. The *method of agreement,* proposed by John Stuart Mill in the 19th century, states, "When two or more cases of a given phenomenon have one and only one condition in common, then that condition may be regarded as the cause (or effect) of the phenomenon."[13] Thus, if we can find Z and only Z in every case where we find C, and no others (A, B, D, or E) are found with Z, then we can conclude that C and Z are causally related. Exhibit 6-4 illustrates this method.

An example of the method of agreement might be the problem of occasional high absenteeism on Mondays in a factory. A study of two groups with high absenteeism (No. 1 and No. 2 in Exhibit 6-4)

>**Exhibit 6-4** Mill's Method of Agreement

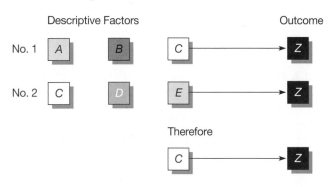

shows no common job, department, demographic, or personal characteristics *(A, B, D, and E)*. However, membership in a camping club *(C)* is common across both groups. The conclusion is that club membership is associated with high absenteeism *(Z)*.

The method of agreement helps rule out some variables as irrelevant. In Exhibit 6-3, *A, B, D,* and *E* are unlikely to be causes of *Z*. However, there is an implicit assumption that there are no variables to consider other than *A, B, C, D,* and *E*. One can never accept this supposition with certainty because the number of potential variables is infinite. In addition, while *C* may be the cause, it may instead function only in the presence of some other variable not included.

The *negative canon of agreement* states that where the absence of *C* is associated with the absence of *Z*, there is evidence of a causal relationship between *C* and *Z*. Together with the method of agreement, this forms the basis for the method of difference: "If there are two or more cases, and in one of them observation *Z* can be made, while in the other it cannot; and if variable *C* occurs when observation *Z* is made, and does not occur when observation *Z* is not made; then it can be asserted that there is a causal relationship between *C* and *Z*."[14]

Using our MindWriter example, if Jason and Sara were to discover that a particular servicing problem repeatedly occurred only when a single employee was involved in the servicing of customers' laptops and never when that employee was absent, an assumption of causation might be made. The method of difference is illustrated in Exhibit 6-5. Although these methods neither ensure discovery of all relevant variables nor provide certain proof of causation, they help advance our understanding of causality by eliminating inadequate causal arguments.[15]

While no one can ever be certain that variable *A* causes variable *B* to occur, one can gather some evidence that increases the belief that *A* leads to *B*. In testing causal hypotheses, we seek three types of evidence:

1. Covariation between *A* and *B*.
   - Do we find that *A* and *B* occur together in the way hypothesized (symmetrical relationship)?
   - When *A* does not occur, is there also an absence of *B*?
   - When there is more or less of *A*, does one also find more or less of *B*?

2. Time order of events moving in the hypothesized direction.
   - Does *A* occur before *B*?

3. No other possible causes of *B*.
   - Can one determine that *C, D,* and *E* do not covary with *B* in a way that suggests possible causal connections?

In addition to these three conditions, successful inference-making from experimental designs must meet two other requirements. The first is referred to as **control.** All factors, with the exception of the independent variable, must be held constant and not confounded with another variable that is not part of the study. Second, each person in the study must have an equal chance for exposure to each level of the independent variable. This is **random assignment** of subjects to groups.

>Exhibit 6-5 Mill's Method of Difference

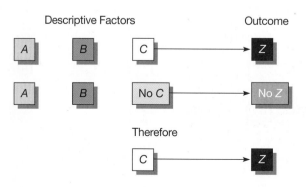

If we consider the possible relationships that can occur between two variables, we can conclude there are three possibilities:

- Symmetrical
- Reciprocal
- Asymmetrical[16]

A **symmetrical relationship** is one in which two variables fluctuate together, but we assume the changes in neither variable are due to changes in the other. Symmetrical conditions are most often found when two variables are alternate indicators of another cause or independent variable. We might conclude that a correlation between low work attendance and active participation in a company camping club is the result of (dependent on) another factor, such as a lifestyle preference.

A **reciprocal relationship** exists when two variables mutually influence or reinforce each other. This could occur if the reading of an advertisement leads to the use of a brand of product. The usage, in turn, sensitizes the person to notice and read more of the advertising of that particular brand.

Most research analysts look for **asymmetrical relationships.** With these we postulate that changes in one variable (the independent variable, or IV) are responsible for changes in another variable (the dependent variable, or DV). The identification of the IV and DV is often obvious, but sometimes the choice is not clear. In these latter cases we evaluate independence and dependence on the basis of:

1. *The degree to which each variable may be altered.* The relatively unalterable variable is the independent variable (IV) (e.g., age, social status, present manufacturing technology).

2. *The time order between the variables.* The independent variable (IV) precedes the dependent variable (DV).

Exhibit 6-6 describes the four types of asymmetrical relationships: stimulus-response, property-disposition, disposition-behavior, and property-behavior. Experiments usually involve

>**Exhibit 6-6** Four Types of Asymmetrical Causal Relationships

Relationship Type	Nature of Relationship	Examples
Stimulus-Response	An event or change results in a response from some object.	• A change in work rules leads to a higher level of worker output. • A change in government economic policy restricts corporate financial decisions. • A price increase results in fewer unit sales.
Property-Disposition	An existing property causes a disposition.	• Age and attitudes about saving. • Gender and attitudes toward social issues. • Social class and opinions about taxation.
Disposition-Behavior	A disposition causes a specific behavior.	• Opinions about a brand and its purchase. • Job satisfaction and work output. • Moral values and tax cheating.
Property-Behavior	An existing property causes a specific behavior.	• Stage of the family life cycle and purchases of furniture. • Social class and family savings patterns. • Age and sports participation.

Definitions: A *stimulus* is an event or force (e.g., drop in temperature, crash of stock market, product recall, or explosion in factory). A *response* is a decision or reaction. A *property* is an enduring characteristic of a subject that does not depend on circumstances for its activation (e.g., age, gender, family status, religious affiliation, ethnic group, or physical condition). A *disposition* is a tendency to respond in a certain way under certain circumstances (e.g., attitudes, opinions, habits, values, and drives). A *behavior* is an action (e.g., consumption practices, work performance, interpersonal acts, and other kinds of performance).

stimulus-response relationships. Property-disposition relationships are often studied in business and social science research.

Unfortunately, most research studies cannot be carried out experimentally by manipulating variables. Yet we still are interested in the question of causation. Instead of manipulating and/or controlling exposure to an experimental variable, we study subjects who have been exposed to the independent factor and those who have not and compare the results. This is known in research as ex post facto design. More will be said about this and other aspects of experimentation in Chapter 9.

Causal inferences are going to be made. Although they may be neither permanent nor universal, these inferences allow us to build knowledge of presumed causes over time. Such empirical conclusions provide us with successive approximations to the truth.

>summary

1 If the direction of a research project is not clear, it is often wise to follow a two-step research procedure. The first stage is exploratory, aimed at formulating hypotheses and developing the specific research design. The general research process contains three major stages: (1) exploration of the situation, (2) collection of data, and (3) analysis and interpretation of results.

2 A research design is the strategy for a study and the plan by which the strategy is to be carried out. It specifies the methods and procedures for the collection, measurement, and analysis of data. Unfortunately, there is no simple classification of research designs that covers the variations found in practice. Some major descriptors of designs are

- Exploratory versus formalized.
- Monitoring versus communication study.
- Experimental versus ex post facto.
- Descriptive versus causal.
- Cross-sectional versus longitudinal.
- Case versus statistical.
- Field versus laboratory versus simulation.
- Subjects perceive no deviations, some deviations, or researcher-induced deviations.

3 Exploratory research is appropriate for the total study in topic areas where the developed data are limited. In most other studies, exploration is the first stage of a project and is used to orient the researcher and the study. The objective of exploration is the development of hypotheses, not testing.

Formalized studies, including descriptive and causal, are those with substantial structure, specific hypotheses to be tested, or research questions to be answered. Descriptive studies are those used to describe phenomena associated with a subject population or to estimate proportions of the population that have certain characteristics.

Causal studies seek to discover the effect that a variable(s) has on another (or others) or why certain outcomes are obtained. The concept of causality is grounded in the logic of hypothesis testing, which, in turn, produces inductive conclusions. Such conclusions are probabilistic and thus can never be demonstrated with certainty. Current ideas about causality as complex processes improve our understanding over Mill's canons, though we can never know all the relevant information necessary to prove causal linkages beyond a doubt.

4 The relationships that occur between two variables may be symmetrical, reciprocal, or asymmetrical. Of greatest interest to the research analyst are asymmetrical relationships, which may be classified as any of the following types:

- Stimulus-response
- Property-disposition
- Disposition-behavior
- Property-behavior

We test causal hypotheses by seeking to do three things. We (1) measure the covariation among variables, (2) determine the time order relationships among variables, and (3) ensure that other factors do not confound the explanatory relationships.

The problems of achieving these aims differ somewhat in experimental and ex post facto studies. Where possible, we try to achieve the ideal of the experimental design with random assignment of subjects, matching of subject characteristics, and manipulation and control of variables. Using these methods and techniques, we measure relationships as accurately and objectively as possible.

>**key**terms

>**discussion**questions

Terms in Review

1 Distinguish between the following:

   a Exploratory and formal studies.

   b Experimental and ex post facto research designs.

   c Descriptive and causal studies.

2 Establishing causality is difficult, whether conclusions have been derived inductively or deductively.

   a Explain and elaborate on the implications of this statement.

   b Why is ascribing causality more difficult when conclusions have been reached through induction?

   c Correlation does not imply causation. Illustrate this point with examples from business.

3 Using yourself as the subject, give an example of each of the following asymmetrical relationships:

   a Stimulus-response

   b Property-disposition

   c Disposition-behavior

   d Property-behavior

4 Why not use more control variables rather than depend on randomization as the means of controlling extraneous variables?

5 Researchers seek causal relationships by either experimental or ex post facto research designs.

   a In what ways are these two approaches similar?

   b In what ways are they different?

Making Research Decisions

6 You have been asked to determine how hospitals prepare and train volunteers. Since you know relatively little about this subject, how will you find out? Be as specific as possible.

7 You are the administrative assistant for a division chief in a large holding company that owns several hotels and theme parks. You and the division chief have just come from the CEO's office, where you were informed that the guest complaints related to housekeeping and employee attitude are increasing. Your on-site managers have mentioned some tension among the workers but have not considered it unusual. The CEO and your division chief instruct you to investigate. Suggest at least three different types of research that might be appropriate in this situation.

8 Propose one or more hypotheses for each of the following variable pairs, specifying which is the IV and which is the DV. Then develop the basic hypothesis to include at least one moderating variable or intervening variable.

   a The Index of Consumer Confidence and the business cycle.

   b Level of worker output and closeness of worker
   supervision.

   c Level of employee theft and the presence of video surveillance cameras.

Bringing Research to Life

9 Using the eight design descriptors, profile the MindWriter
CompleteCare satisfaction study as described in this and
preceding chapters.

From Concept to Practice

10 Use the eight design descriptors in Exhibit 6-3 to profile
the research described in the chapter Snapshots.

From the Headlines

11 On Thursday, May 28, 2009, in a presentation to financial
analysts, the CEO of P&G announced a break from tradition. It would release Tide Basics, a value-oriented version
of its leading Tide detergent. P&G holds the leading market
share position in more than 40 consumer-good categories;
most of its brands are premium, not value, brands. What
research might P&G have done that led to this decision?

12 P&G announced May 28, 2009, that it would move its
IAMS pet food division from Vandalia (OH) to Mason (OH).
The move affected 240 workers, who were offered positions to join the 2,000 workers already occupying the pet
food division headquarters in Mason. A company statement indicated, "We're doing this to increase productivity,
collaboration, and access to P&G's resources/expertise."
P&G also told employees that it was beginning a separate,
multi-month study on how to increase collaboration and
efficiencies with the 250 employees still working in its pet
food research and development complex located in Lewisburg (OH). What research might be included in the multi-
month study to determine the future of the Lewisburg R&D
facility and its employees?

>cases*

A Gem of a Study

Calling Up Attendance

Campbell-Ewald Pumps Awareness
into the American Heart Association

Covering Kids with Health Care

Donatos: Finding the New Pizza

Goodyear's Aquatred

Inquiring Minds Want to
Know—NOW!

Ohio Lottery: Innovative Research
Design Drives Winning

Open Doors: Extending Hospitality
to Travelers with Disabilities

Proofpoint: Capitalizing on a
Reporter's Love of Statistics

Ramada Demonstrates Its *Personal
Best*™

Starbucks, Bank One, and Visa
Launch Starbucks Card Duetto Visa

State Farm: Dangerous Intersections

Volkswagen's Beetle

* You will find a description of each case in the Case Abstracts section of this textbook. Check the Case Index to
determine whether a case provides data, the research instrument, video, or other supplementary material. Written cases
are downloadable from the text website (www.mhhe.com/cooper11e). All video material and video cases are available from the Online Learning Center. The film reel icon indicates a video case or video material relevant to the case.

>chapter 7

Qualitative Research

>**learning**objectives

After reading this chapter, you should understand . . .

1 How qualitative methods differ from quantitative methods.

2 The controversy surrounding qualitative research.

3 The types of decisions that use qualitative methods.

4 The variety of qualitative research methods.

> 66 It is better to think of the Web . . . as the sounds of independent voices, just like the street corner soapbox preacher or that friend of yours who always recommends the best books. 99
>
> David Meerman Scott, marketing strategist and author,
> The New Rules of Marketing and PR

"Welcome back," Jason comments as he stops by Sara Arens's office. "Any problems?"

"Thanks. Glad to be back. Moderating the Atlanta HealthPlus frozen-food groups was rather like slipping on comfortable shoes. It really helped to observe the Webcast of the San Francisco and Detroit groups just last week. I'll be starting the report preparation for HealthPlus shortly."

"Sara, I'm lucky to have someone I can count on with the extensive qualitative research experience that you have," compliments Jason.

"Thanks," smiles Sara. "I see that the transcripts from the San Francisco group arrived in my absence. The Detroit ones should be here this afternoon, with Atlanta arriving by Wednesday. I'm just unearthing my observation notes from San Francisco now, so I can compare them with the transcripts.

"We captured some critical comments that I'm sure will be helpful in developing the new HealthPlus ad campaign," shares Sara as she extracts the desired transcripts from the file folders on her desk. From the size of the stack, she'll be doing a fair amount of reading in the next few days. "HealthPlus was right when it surmised that consumers are skeptical that something healthy can taste good. But we've also learned there are some triggers we can use in the advertising to get them to embrace the idea of eating healthy."

"HealthPlus certainly seems well positioned given the growing concern over rampant obesity, especially among youth," observes Jason. "I'll look forward to your insights."

"Do you know if Sam has started N6 yet?" asks Sara.

"Is N6 the new software that provides the preliminary analysis on the focus group transcript content?" asks Jason. At Sara's affirmative nod, he responds, "Then, yes, our eager intern has the San Francisco transcript in process."

"Good to hear," comments Sara. "He thinks this newest version of NUD*IST is impressive. And it does save us a lot of time."

"By the way, the Atlanta facility was equipped with the newest version of FocusVision's VideoMarker, for marking the focus group video. That's the first time I've used the marking feature as a moderator. The facility promised me the marked CD by early next week. It's going to save a lot of time in preparing the client presentation."

Jason smiles. Sara's enthusiasm appears strong for anything digital or electronic. "Well, it looks like you have things well in hand, Sara. I'll want you in the preliminary project meeting with LeapFrog at 4."

"Right," comments Sara as she looks up from sorting note files and transcripts, "the learning-toy producer that wants concept testing—I'll be there."

> What Is Qualitative Research?

Managers basically do business research to understand how and why things happen. If the manager needs to know only what happened, or how often things happened, quantitative research methodologies would serve the purpose. But to understand the different meanings that people place on their experiences often requires research techniques that delve more deeply into people's hidden interpretations, understandings, and motivations. Qualitative research is designed to tell the researcher how (process) and why (meaning) things happen as they do.

Qualitative research includes an "array of interpretive techniques which seek to describe, decode, translate, and otherwise come to terms with the meaning, not the frequency, of certain more or less naturally occurring phenomena in the social world."[1] Qualitative techniques are used at both the data collection and data analysis stages of a research project. At the data collection stage, the array of techniques includes focus groups, individual depth interviews (IDIs), case studies, ethnography, grounded theory, action research, and observation. During analysis, the qualitative researcher uses content analysis of written or recorded materials drawn from personal expressions by participants, behavioral observations, and debriefing of observers, as well as the study of artifacts and trace evidence from the physical environment. Observation as a methodology deserves special attention and is covered in detail in Chapter 8.

Qualitative research aims to achieve an in-depth understanding of a situation, whether it explains why a person entering a Kroger grocery proceeds down each aisle in turn or heads for the rear of the store and chooses only alternate aisles thereafter or explains why some advertisements make us laugh and contribute to our commitment to a brand while others generate outrage and boycotts. Judith Langer, a noted qualitative researcher, indicates that qualitative research is ideal if you want to extract feelings, emotions, motivations, perceptions, consumer "language," or self-described behavior.[2] Exhibit 7-1 offers some examples of appropriate uses of qualitative research in business.

Qualitative research draws data from a variety of sources, including the following:[3]

- People (individuals or groups).
- Organizations or institutions.
- Texts (published, including virtual ones).
- Settings and environments (visual/sensory and virtual material).
- Objects, artifacts, media products (textual/visual/sensory and virtual material).
- Events and happenings (textual/visual/sensory and virtual material).

In this chapter we will focus on the qualitative methods that draw data from people and organizations. The next chapter focuses on observation studies, which many authors consider an important contribution to qualitative data and which also contribute to the last four categories.

> Qualitative versus Quantitative Research
The Controversy

Qualitative research methodologies have roots in a variety of disciplines, including anthropology, sociology, psychology, linguistics, communication, economics, and semiotics. Historically, qualitative methodologies have been available much longer—some as early as the 19th century—than the quantitative tools marketers rely on so heavily. Possibly because of their origins, qualitative methods don't enjoy the unqualified endorsement of upper management. Many senior managers maintain that qualitative data are too subjective and susceptible to human error and bias in data collection and interpretation. They believe such research provides an unstable foundation for expensive and critical business decisions. The fact that results cannot be generalized from a qualitative study to a larger population is considered a fundamental weakness.

Increasingly, however, managers are returning to these techniques as quantitative techniques fall short of providing the insights needed to make those ever-more-expensive business

What Does Cyberspace Offer for Performance Review Research?

Many successful leaders *understand* that performance feedback is important. They know how meaningful it was to them in their personal and career growth. As a result, many successful organizations have 360-degree formal feedback systems. Employees have traditionally received this feedback through periodic surveys completed by subordinates, peers, and supervisors.

An Accenture study, however, shows many middle managers value informal feedback, because the traditional formal review process generates less specific feedback than desired and is not timely in its delivery. So with Generation Y moving into management roles, can human resources (HR) leverage its love of the Web as a way to enhance informal performance review?

Employees comfortable with the Web are already using it to vent publicly about their job on sites like glassdoor.com and jobvent.com. Others create Google discussion groups or a Web forum to discuss what they like and what they don't like about their company, their industry, and even their boss. Some companies are using these anonymous tirades to identify and address workplace issues.

Social networks have long been used in the hiring process. According to Kenexa, a human resource company that studies human behavior and team dynamics in the workplace, and offers software, business processes and consulting, "more than 30 percent of the employees being hired in private organizations

come through employee referrals—the highest from any one particular source."[a] Is it a logical extension, then, to see if networking can be leveraged for performance review?

Rypple is a company stepping into the social-networking-for-performance-reviews space, taking a page from Facebook and Twitter, to make performance appraisal research more useful. What's a Rypple? Think of it as a Tweet with a purpose. With Rypple you can ask a question like, "What can I do to make YOU more effective in your role?" or "What can I do to help us be more effective in reaching our division's goals?" Using contacts from existing sources like Outlook, Yahoo, Hotmail, Gmail, or Facebook, you select prospects to receive a brief message requesting feedback. The message contains a link to a short online form where the contact types in his or her response (called a rypple) to the single question. Feedback is aggregated, quickly returned, and semi-anonymous (restricted to those contacts to whom you sent your message).[b] Rypple indicates 50 percent of those asked for feedback will provide it.

Daniel Portillo, the senior director of personnel at Mozilla, makers of the Firefox browser, tried it. "It's impossible to develop if you're not getting constructive criticism."[c] He discovered "people are direct, but not malicious."[d]

www.rypple.com; www.kenexa.com; www.glassdoor.com; www.jobvent.com; www.mozilla.com

decisions. Managers deal with the issue of trustworthiness of qualitative data through exacting methodology:[4]

- Carefully using literature searches to build probing questions.
- Thoroughly justifying the methodology or combination of methodologies chosen.
- Executing the chosen methodology in its natural setting (field study) rather than a highly controlled setting (laboratory).
- Choosing sample participants for relevance to the breadth of the issue rather than how well they represent the target population.
- Developing and including questions that reveal the exceptions to a rule or theory.
- Carefully structuring the data analysis.
- Comparing data across multiple sources and different contexts.
- Conducting peer-researcher debriefing on results for added clarity, additional insights, and reduced bias.

The Distinction

To understand the distinctions between qualitative and quantitative methodologies, let's define the latter. **Quantitative research** attempts precise measurement of something. In business research, quantitative methodologies usually measure consumer behavior, knowledge, opinions, or attitudes. Such

>Exhibit 7-1 Some Appropriate Uses for Qualitative Research

Decision Arena	Questions to be Answered
Job Analysis	• Does the current assignment of tasks generate the most productivity? • Does the advancement through different job levels incorporate the necessary training to foster the strongest performance?
Advertising Concept Development	• What images should we use to connect with our target customers' motivations?
Productivity Enhancement	• What actions could we take to boost worker productivity without generating worker discontent?
New Product Development	• What would our current market think of a proposed product idea? • We need new products, but what should they be to take advantage of our existing customer-perceived strengths? • Which products will create the greatest synergy with our existing products in terms of ROI and distribution partner growth?
Benefits Management	• Should our compensation plan be more flexible and customizable? • How do employees perceive wellness-prevention programs as compared to corrective health programs in terms of value?
Retail Design	• How do consumers prefer to shop in our store? Do they shop with a defined purpose, or are they affected by other motives?
Process Understanding	• What steps are involved in cleaning a wood floor? How is our product perceived or involved in this process?
Market Segmentation	• Why does one demographic or lifestyle group use our product more than another? • Who are our customers and how do they use our product to support their lifestyle? • What is the influence of culture on product choice?
Union Representation	• How do various departments perceive the current effort to unionize our plant? Where and what are the elements of discontent?
Sales Analysis	• Why have once-loyal customers stopped buying our service?

methodologies answer questions related to how much, how often, how many, when, and who. Although the survey is not the only methodology of the quantitative researcher, it is considered a dominant one.

The purpose of qualitative research is based on "researcher immersion in the phenomenon to be studied, gathering data which provide a detailed description of events, situations and interaction between people and things, [thus] providing depth and detail."[5] Quantitative research is often used for theory testing (Will a $1-off instant coupon or a $1.50 mail-in rebate generate more sales for Kellogg's Special K?), requiring that the researcher maintain a distance from the research to avoid biasing the results. Qualitative research—sometimes labeled *interpretive research* because it seeks to develop understanding through detailed description—often builds theory but rarely tests it.

Besides the purpose of the research, this process sets up several key distinctions between qualitative and quantitative research, elaborated in Exhibit 7-2, including level of researcher involvement; sampling methodology and size; data collection processes, including participant preparation and researcher and research sponsor involvement; data type and preparation; data analysis and timing; processes for reaching insights and meaning; time frame of insight discovery; and the level of data security.[6]

Unlike the case with quantitative data, both the researcher and research sponsor often have more significant involvement in collecting and interpreting qualitative data. The researcher may serve as

>Exhibit 7-2 Qualitative versus Quantitative Research

	Qualitative	Quantitative
Focus of Research	• Understand and interpret	• Describe, explain, and predict
Researcher Involvement	• High—researcher is participant or catalyst	• Limited; controlled to prevent bias
Research Purpose	• In-depth understanding; theory building	• Describe or predict; build and test theory
Sample Design	• Nonprobability; purposive	• Probability
Sample Size	• Small	• Large
Research Design	• May evolve or adjust during the course of the project • Often uses multiple methods simultaneously or sequentially • Consistency is not expected • Involves longitudinal approach	• Determined before commencing the project • Uses single method or mixed methods • Consistency is critical • Involves either a cross-sectional or a longitudinal approach
Participant Preparation	• Pretasking is common	• No preparation desired to avoid biasing the participant
Data Type and Preparation	• Verbal or pictorial descriptions • Reduced to verbal codes (sometimes with computer assistance)	• Verbal descriptions • Reduced to numerical codes for computerized analysis
Data Analysis	• Human analysis following computer or human coding; primarily nonquantitative • Forces researcher to see the contextual framework of the phenomenon being measured—distinction between facts and judgments less clear • Always ongoing during the project	• Computerized analysis—statistical and mathematical methods dominate • Analysis may be ongoing during the project • Maintains clear distinction between facts and judgments
Insights and Meaning	• Deeper level of understanding is the norm; determined by type and quantity of free-response questions • Researcher participation in data collection allows insights to form and be tested during the process	• Limited by the opportunity to probe respondents and the quality of the original data collection instrument • Insights follow data collection and data entry, with limited ability to reinterview participants
Research Sponsor Involvement	• May participate by observing research in real time or via taped interviews	• Rarely has either direct or indirect contact with participant
Feedback Turnaround	• Smaller sample sizes make data collection faster for shorter possible turnaround • Insights are developed as the research progresses, shortening data analysis	• Larger sample sizes lengthen data collection; Internet methodologies are shortening turnaround but inappropriate for many studies • Insight development follows data collection and entry, lengthening research process; interviewing software permits some tallying of responses as data collection progresses
Data Security	• More absolute given use of restricted access facilities and smaller sample sizes	• Act of research in progress is often known by competitors; insights may be gleaned by competitors for some visible, field-based studies

Source: This exhibit was developed from material extracted from Judith Langer, *The Mirrored Window: Focus Groups from a Moderator's Point of View* (Ithaca, NY: Paramount Market Publishing, 2001); Hy Mariampolski, *Qualitative Market Research: A Comprehensive Guide* (Thousand Oaks, CA: Sage Publications, 2001); and David Carson, Audrey Gilmore, Chad Perry, and Kjell Gronhaug, *Qualitative Marketing Research* (Thousand Oaks, CA: Sage Publications, 2001).

a participant or a catalyst, as a participant observer, or as a group interview moderator. The research sponsor may observe (in some cases via Webcast of interviews directly to the sponsor's desktop computer), influence interview questions, and add interpretations and insights during the process. By contrast, with large quantitative studies, the researcher who interprets the data and draws conclusions from it is rarely the data collector and often has no contact at all with the participant.

Since researchers are immersed in the participant's world, any knowledge they gain can be used to adjust the data extracted from the next participant. In quantitative research, identical data are desired from all participants, so evolution of methodology is not acceptable.

Quantitative data often consist of participant responses that are coded, categorized, and reduced to numbers so that these data may be manipulated for statistical analysis. One objective is the quantitative tally of events or opinions, called *frequency of response.* Qualitative data are all about texts. Detailed descriptions of events, situations, and interactions, either verbal or visual, constitute the data. Data may be contained within transcriptions of interviews or video focus groups, as well as in notes taken during those interactions. But by definition they generate reams of words that need to be coded and analyzed by humans for meaning. While computer software is increasingly used for the coding process in qualitative research, at the heart of the qualitative process is the researcher—and his or her experience—framing and interpreting the data.[7]

Qualitative studies with their smaller sample sizes offer an opportunity for faster turnaround of findings. While speed should never be the primary reason for choosing a methodology, qualitative data may be especially useful to support a low-risk decision that must be made quickly.

Multimillion-dollar strategies may lose their power if the competitor reacts too quickly. Data security is therefore of increasing concern. Both group and individual interviewing, the mainstay techniques of qualitative research, can be conducted in highly secure environments. In comparison, once a quantitative survey or field observation or experiment is started, it is quickly common knowledge among a research sponsor's competitors. Although the data might not be known, the area of inquiry often can be determined. For example, in a test market—an experimental quantitative design—a research sponsor's competitors can often observe and extract insights right along with the sponsor.

> The Process of Qualitative Research

The process of developing a qualitative project is similar to the research process introduced in Chapter 1. However, three key distinctions suggested in the previous sections do affect the research process: (1) the level of question development in the management-research question hierarchy prior to the commencing of qualitative research, (2) the preparation of the participant prior to the research experience, and (3) the nature and level of data that come from the debriefing of interviewers or observers.

The qualitative researcher starts with an understanding of the manager's problem, but the management-research question hierarchy is rarely developed prior to the design of research methodology. Rather, the research is guided by a broader question more similar in structure to the management question. Exhibit 7-3 introduces the modifications to the research process.

Much of qualitative research involves the deliberate preparation of the participant, called preexercises or **pretasking.** This step is important due to the desire to extract detail and meaning from the participant. A variety of creative and mental exercises draw participants' understanding of their own thought processes and ideas to the surface. Some of these include:

- Placing the product or medium for in-home use (with instructions to use the product or medium—e.g., a magazine—repeatedly over the preparation period before the interview).

- Having the participants bring visual stimuli (e.g., family photos of areas or rooms in their homes that they hate to clean or have trouble decorating, or a favorite item of clothing).

- Having the participants prepare a visual collage (e.g., taking pictures over several weeks, with a one-time-use camera, of their children's favorite outfits for different purposes or situations or cutting pictures out of magazines that reflect how they feel when using a particular product or brand).

- Having the participants keep detailed diaries of behavior and perceptions (e.g., a record of their step-by-step experience preparing a meal using a particular product).

>**Exhibit 7-3** Qualitative Research and the Research Process

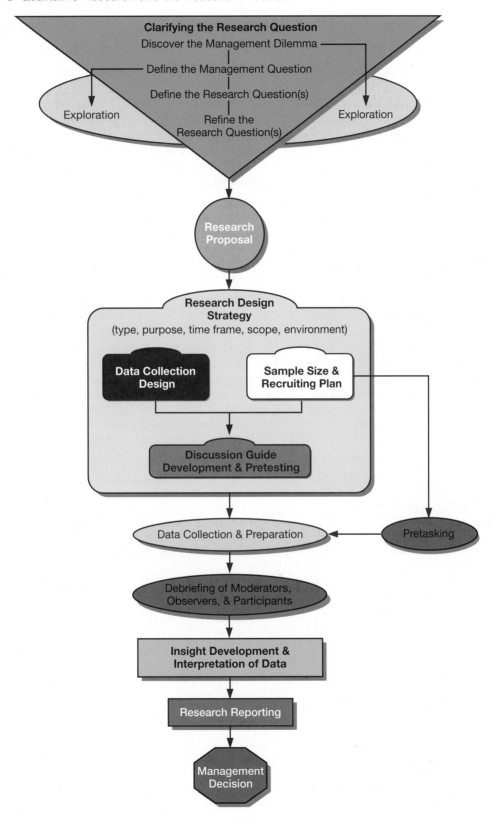

- Having the participants draw a picture of an experience (e.g., what they felt like when they last shopped in a particular store).
- Having the participants write a dialog of a hypothetical experience (e.g., how a conversation between the participant and a sales associate would progress when a complaint was not resolved).[8]

Pretasking is rarely used in observation studies and is considered a major source of error in quantitative studies.

In quantitative research, unless a researcher is collecting his or her own data, interviewers or data collectors are rarely involved in the data interpretation or analysis stages. Although data collectors contribute to the accuracy of data preparation, their input is rarely, if ever, sought in the development of data interpretations. In qualitative studies, due to the higher level of involvement of both the sponsor and the interviewer/data collector, these parties in the process are often debriefed or interviewed, with their insight adding richness to the interpretation of the data. Exhibit 7-4 provides an example of research question formation for a qualitative project.

>Exhibit 7-4 Formulating the Qualitative Research Question

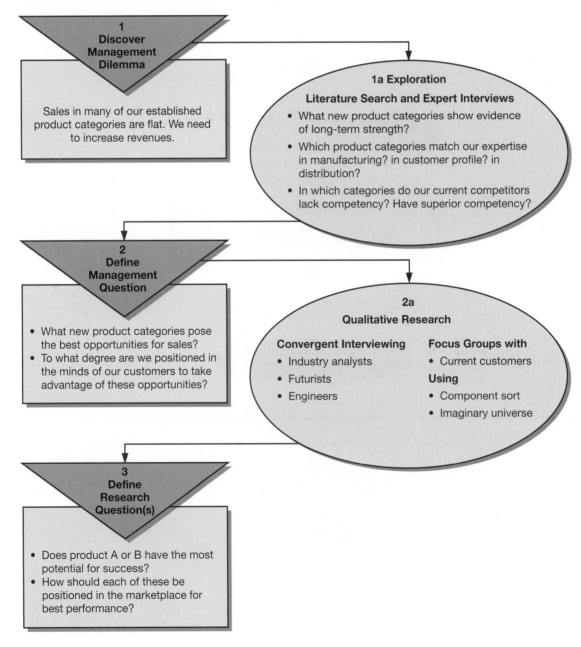

>**pic**profile

When Anderson Analytics wants to help its research participants delve into their deepest thoughts on a research topic, they use projective techniques that employ a colorful cast of characters. Participants choose one from the cast that most closely represents them or another they are trying to describe. They then attribute attitudes, feelings, emotions, and perceptions to the character. "The added bonus of the characters is that some of the characters elicit similar responses [across research projects], so we have some idea on benchmarking," shares Anderson Analytics managing partner Tom Anderson. "For instance the heavier male character with the guitar is often thought of as an outsider, 'poser' wanting desperately to fit in, generally not well liked." **www.andersonanalytics.com**

> Qualitative Research Methodologies

The researcher chooses a qualitative methodology based on the project's purpose; its schedule, including the speed with which insights are needed; its budget; the issue(s) or topics(s) being studied; the types of participants needed; and the researcher's skill, personality, and preferences.

Sampling

One general sampling guideline exists for qualitative research: Keep sampling as long as your breadth and depth of knowledge of the issue under study are expanding; stop when you gain no new knowledge or insights. That said, sample sizes for qualitative research vary by technique but are generally small. A study might include just two or three focus groups or a few dozen individual depth interviews. However unusual, one AT&T study, conducted to develop its 800 Reasons ad campaign for using AT&T long-distance service, used thousands of structured interviews in dozens of cities over several weeks. These interviews provided numerous reasons why businesses used the AT&T 800 service, and each of these "reasons" became the focus of a television and/or magazine ad in the multi-ad campaign.[9]

Qualitative research involves **nonprobability sampling**—where little attempt is made to generate a representative sample. Several types of nonprobability sampling are common:

- *Purposive sampling.* Researchers choose participants arbitrarily for their unique characteristics or their experiences, attitudes, or perceptions; as conceptual or theoretical categories of participants develop during the interviewing process, researchers seek new participants to challenge emerging patterns.

- *Snowball sampling.* Participants refer researchers to others who have characteristics, experiences, or attitudes similar to or different from their own.

- *Convenience sampling.* Researchers select any readily available individuals as participants.

Hamilton Beach: Right Blend(er) for Mexico, but Not for Europe

Hamilton Beach/Proctor Silex (HB/PS) is a small-kitchen-appliance powerhouse in the United States. HB/PS sold one in every four such appliances in the United States, and more than 40 million appliances last year, so a global marketing strategy seemed a logical extension. But focus groups told the company differently. In Mexico, focus groups confirmed that the brand was considered quality and that the criteria American consumers used to select an appliance would be mirrored by the Mexicans. But the story was very different in Europe. There, focus groups revealed that HB/PS's lack of brand awareness wouldn't be nearly as much of a problem as its "clunky," "sturdy" designs. Europeans wanted aesthetically pleasing shapes and color in the appliances they chose for their homes, not the "professional," "institutional," or "large-capacity" products that Americans were buying.

BGIGlobal, part of SYNOVATE, the ninth-largest research firm in the world, coordinated the focus groups in Europe. Product displays similar to those found in European retailers encouraged arriving participants to explore the products that would later be discussed and dissected. During the group interview, participants were encouraged to provide a detailed narrative of their last purchase within the small-kitchen-appliance category. HB/PS needed to understand the criteria driving the process and where decisions took place. The discussion guide driving the focus groups in both countries was similar. But in Europe, the first group reinforced for David Israel, HB/PS's international marketing manager, the value of the focus group methodology—its flexibility. As participants raised each new, startling issue, notes began flowing to the moderator, encouraging participants to travel down paths that the discussion guide hadn't anticipated. The focus groups helped HB/PS understand that it wasn't ready for the European market—at least not until its product designers redefined the product lines.

www.bgiglobal.com; www.hamiltonbeach.com

Interviews

The **interview** is the primary data collection technique for gathering data in qualitative methodologies. Interviews vary based on the number of people involved during the interview, the level of structure, the proximity of the interviewer to the participant, and the number of interviews conducted during the research.

62

The percent of wealthy consumers reporting that the state of the economy has changed their view of luxury purchases . . . that flaunting luxury is insensitive.

An interview can be conducted individually (individual depth interview, or IDI) or in groups. Exhibit 7-5 compares the individual and the group interview as a research methodology. Both have a distinct place in qualitative research.

Interviewing requires a trained interviewer (often called a **moderator** for group interviews) or the skills gained from experience. These skills include making respondents comfortable, probing for detail without making the respondent feel harassed, remaining neutral while encouraging the participant to talk openly, listening carefully, following a participant's train of thought, and extracting insights from hours of detailed descriptive dialogue. Skilled interviewers learn to use their personal similarities with *or* differences from their interviewee to mine for information; similarities are used to convey sympathy and understanding, while differences are used to demonstrate eagerness to understand and empathize.

In quantitative research we are more interested in the data collector's following a prescribed procedure, whereas in qualitative research the individual conducting the interview needs a fuller understanding of the dilemma and how the insights will be used. So a skilled interviewer must be a "quick-study," someone who can grasp an understanding of an issue without necessarily having prior experience with the product or service or being a technical expert.

The researcher chooses either an **unstructured interview** (no specific questions or order of topics to be discussed, with each interview customized to each participant; generally starts with a participant narrative) or a **semistructured interview** (generally starts with a few specific questions and then

>**Exhibit 7-5** A Comparison of Individual Depth Interviews and Group Interviews

Individual Interview	Group Interview
Research Objective • Explore life of individual in depth • Create case histories through repeated interviews over time • Test a survey	• Orient the researcher to a field of inquiry and the language of the field • Explore a range of attitudes, opinions, and behaviors • Observe a process of consensus and disagreement • Add contextual detail to quantitative findings
Topic Concerns • Detailed individual experiences, choices, biographies • Sensitive issues that might provoke anxiety	• Issues of public interest or common concern • Issues where little is known or of a hypothetical nature
Participants • Time-pressed participants or those difficult to recruit (e.g., elite or high-status participants) • Participants with sufficient language skills (e.g., those older than seven) • Participants whose distinctions would inhibit participation	• Participants whose backgrounds are similar or not so dissimilar as to generate conflict or discomfort • Participants who can articulate their ideas • Participants who offer a range of positions on issues

follows the individual's tangents of thought with interviewer probes) or a **structured interview** (often uses a detailed interview guide similar to a questionnaire to guide the question order and the specific way the questions are asked, but the questions generally remain open-ended). Structured interviews permit more direct comparability of responses; question variability has been eliminated and thus answer variability is assumed to be real. Also, in the structured interview, the interviewer's neutrality has been maintained.

Most qualitative research relies on the unstructured or semistructured interview. The unstructured and semistructured interviews used in qualitative research are distinct from the structured interview in several ways. They:

- Rely on developing a dialog between interviewer and participant.
- Require more interviewer creativity.
- Use the skill of the interviewer to extract more and a greater variety of data.
- Use interviewer experience and skill to achieve greater clarity and elaboration of answers.

Many interviews are conducted face-to-face, with the obvious benefit of being able to observe and record nonverbal as well as verbal behavior. An interview, however, can be conducted by phone or online. Phone and online interviews offer the opportunity to conduct more interviews within the same time frame and draw participants from a wider geographic area. These approaches also save the travel expenses of moving trained interviewers to participants, as well as the travel fees associated with bringing participants to a neutral site. Using interviewers who are fresher and more comfortable in conducting an interview—often from their home or office—should increase the quality of the interview. Also, depending on the group from which participants are drawn, there may be insufficient numbers to conduct group interviews in any one market, forcing the use of phone or online techniques.

Interviewer Responsibilities

The interviewer needs to be able to extract information from a willing participant who often is not consciously aware that he or she possesses the information desired. The actual interviewer is usually responsible for generating the **interview** or **discussion guide,** the list of topics to be discussed (unstructured

>Exhibit 7-6 The Interview Question Hierarchy

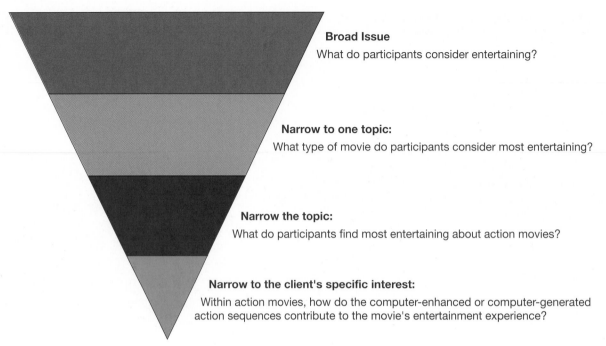

Broad Issue
What do participants consider entertaining?

Narrow to one topic:
What type of movie do participants consider most entertaining?

Narrow the topic:
What do participants find most entertaining about action movies?

Narrow to the client's specific interest:
Within action movies, how do the computer-enhanced or computer-generated action sequences contribute to the movie's entertainment experience?

Source: This graphic was adapted from one developed by Judith Langer and published in *The Mirrored Window: Focus Group from a Moderator's Point of View* (Ithaca, NY: Paramount Market Publishing, 2001), www.paramountbooks.com.

interview) or the questions to be asked (semistructured) and in what order (structured). In building this guide, many interviewers employ a hierarchical questioning structure, depicted in Exhibit 7-6. Broader questions start the interview, designed to put participants at ease and give them a sense that they have a lot to contribute, followed by increasingly more specific questions to draw out detail.

The interviewer is often responsible for generating the screening questions used to recruit participants for the qualitative research. This preinterview uses a device similar to a questionnaire, called a **recruitment screener.** Exhibit 7-7 provides the various elements necessary for a comprehensive recruitment screener. Each question is designed to reassure the researcher that the person who has the necessary information and experiences, as well as the social and language skills to relate the desired information, is invited to participate. Data gathered during the recruitment process are incorporated into the data analysis phase of the research, as recruitment data provide additional context for participants' expressions.

In general, then, the interviewer is a consultant with wide-ranging responsibilities:[10]

- Recommends the topics and questions.
- Controls the interview, but also plans—and may manage—the locations and facilities for the study.
- Proposes the criteria for drawing the sample participants.
- Writes the recruitment screener and may recruit participants.
- Develops the various pretasking exercises.
- Prepares any research tools (e.g., picture sorts or written exercises) to be used during the interview.
- Supervises the transcription process.
- Helps analyze the data and draw insights.
- Writes or directs the writing of the client report, including extracting video clips for the oral report.

>**Exhibit 7-7** What Is Included in a Recruitment Screener?

For best effect, qualitative research takes creative, articulate, expressive individuals. Finding appropriate participants is the task of the researcher. Here are some common elements addressed at this phase of the research.

Type of Information	Description
Heading	Include project name, date of interviews, identity of screener.
Screening Requirements	Specify conditions that must be met to extend a prospect an offer to participate; may include quotas for various demographic, lifestyle, attitudinal, or usage questions.
Identity Information	Include name of prospect, address, phone, e-mail.
Introduction	Describe purpose of study in a motivational way. Completely "blind" studies do not motivate participation.
Security Questions	Reveal possible participant overparticipation or conflicts of interest; similar information on spouse or immediate family members.
Demographic Questions	Determine match for age, gender, ethnicity or race, income, geography, employment status, or occupation.
Product/Brand Usage/Purchase Questions	Establish frequency of use, purchase, loyalty, etc.
Lifestyle Questions	Establish the participant's daily life experiences, as well as those of the person with whom the participant shares his or her life.
Attitudinal and Knowledge Questions	Look for breadth in perceptions, attitudes, opinions, knowledge.
Articulation and Creative Questions	Seek evidence that participant can articulate his or her ideas and form and express opinions; scenarios might include problem–solution questions or ask participant to confront an unusual challenge. ("What could you do with a brick?")
Offer/Termination	Invite participation, discuss compensation and pretasking, set up interview, or indicate that the person is not right for the current study but may be right for future studies.

Projective Techniques

Because researchers are often looking for hidden or suppressed meanings, **projective techniques** can be used within the interview structures. Some of these techniques include:[11]

- **Word or picture association**   Participants are asked to match images, experiences, emotions, products and services, even people and places, to whatever is being studied. *"Tell me what you think of when you think of Kellogg's Special K cereal."*

- **Sentence completion**   Participants are asked to complete a sentence. *"Complete this sentence: People who buy over the Internet…"*

- **Cartoons or empty balloons**   Participants are asked to write the dialog for a cartoonlike picture. *"What will the customer comment when she sees the salesperson approaching her in the new-car showroom."*

- **Thematic Apperception Test**   Participants are confronted with a picture (usually a photograph or drawing) and asked to describe how the person in the picture feels and thinks.

- **Component sorts**   Participants are presented with flash cards containing component features and asked to create new combinations.

- **Sensory sorts**   Participants are presented with scents, textures, and sounds, usually verbalized on cards, and asked to arrange them by one or more criteria.

• **Laddering or benefit chain**	Participants are asked to link functional features to their physical and psychological benefits, both real and ideal.
• **Imagination exercises**	Participants are asked to relate the properties of one thing/person/brand to another. *"If Crest toothpaste were a college, what type of college would it be?"*
• **Imaginary universe**	Participants are asked to assume that the brand and its users populate an entire universe; they then describe the features of this new world.
• **Visitor from another planet**	Participants are asked to assume that they are aliens and are confronting the product for the first time; they then describe their reactions, questions, and attitudes about purchase or retrial.
• **Personification**	Participants are asked to imagine inanimate objects with the traits, characteristics and features, and personalities of humans. *"If brand X were a person, what type of person would brand X be?"*
• **Authority figure**	Participants are asked to imagine that the brand or product is an authority figure and to describe the attributes of the figure.
• **Ambiguities and paradoxes**	Participants are asked to imagine a brand as something else (e.g., a Tide dog food or Marlboro cereal), describing its attributes and position.
• **Semantic mapping**	Participants are presented with a four-quadrant map where different variables anchor the two axes; they then spatially organize health insurance options, product components, or organizations within the four quadrants.
• **Brand mapping**	Participants are presented with different brands and asked to talk about their perceptions, usually in relation to several criteria. They may also be asked to spatially place each brand on one or more semantic maps.
• **Metaphor elicitation technique**	Participants are pretasked to collect images that reveal how they feel about a research topic; during an IDI, participants discuss each image and create a collage of their images, with emotions, thoughts, or perceptions noted near each image.

Paper-based exercises often draw out less verbal members of a group. Projective techniques can dissipate tension caused by sensitive topics or can be useful when a change of focus in the interview is imminent. A well-trained interviewer is required if the research demands that one or more of these techniques be included within an individual depth interview or group interview. These techniques are also time-consuming to apply, lengthening the time frame of the individual or group interview. They also lengthen the data analysis time.

Individual Depth Interviews

An **individual depth interview (IDI)** is an interaction between an individual interviewer and a single participant. Individual depth interviews generally take between 20 minutes (telephone interviews) and 2 hours (prescheduled, face-to-face interviews) to complete, depending on the issues or topics of interest and the contact method used. Some techniques such as *life histories* may take as long as five hours. Participants are usually paid to share their insights and ideas; $1 per minute is the budgeting rule of thumb for general consumers, but much higher rates are demanded by participants representing highly skilled professionals.[12]

IBM's High-Touch Strategy Is Research-Driven

When Samuel Palmisano became chairman and chief executive of IBM, industry analysts didn't expect this 30-year IBM loyalist to rock the boat. But he started a research program that resulted in a very aggressive reorganization. The IBM strategy isn't quite so novel—create a strong connection between IBM and its customer—as is the extensive research behind it. Palmisano wanted his employees to talk to customers about their most troubling business problems. Rather than send the sales force to do that job, IBM formed teams: the sales executive in charge of the corporate account, a representative from the services division, a person from the software unit, and someone from the IBM research labs. These teams became known as "four in a box." But what each team was asked to do was think outside the box:

figure out how IBM might help customers solve their pesky problems. And what resulted from all those customer interviews? A reorganization of the $89 billion company into 12 industry groups (e.g., banking, insurance, automobiles, utilities, consumer packaged goods, telecommunications, life sciences, etc.) rather than its previous three divisions (software, services, and research). The shift is under way to make IBM an executive-level consulting firm rather than a technology services company. The reorganization has IBM's labs, which used to focus on making machines calculate faster and more efficiently, refocusing on modeling patterns of human behavior to help solve business problems.

www.ibm.com

Interviewees are often provided with advance materials via mail, fax, or the Internet. Recently, advances in technology have encouraged the use of detailed visual and auditory aids during interviews, creating the methodology known as **computer-assisted personal interviews (CAPIs)**. CAPIs often use a structured or semistructured individual depth interview.

Several unstructured individual depth interviews are common in business research, including oral histories, cultural interviews, life histories, critical incident technique, and sequential (or chronologic) interviewing. Exhibit 7-8 describes these techniques and provides examples.

Managing the Individual Depth Interview

Participants for individual depth interviews are usually chosen not because their opinions are representative of the dominant opinion but because their experiences and attitudes will reflect the full scope of the issue under study. Participants for individual depth interviews also need to be verbally articulate, in order to provide the interviewer with the richness of desired detail. Primary Insights Inc. developed its *CUE* methodology to help marketers understand the performance cues that consumers use to judge a product. It uses purposive sampling to recruit individuals "with a specific interest in and aptitude for analytical thinking and discovering how things work." *CUE* combines in-home product use with a diary preexercise, followed by individual depth interviews that extract what the participant saw, felt, heard, smelled, and sensed when interacting with the product. What evolves is a hierarchy of sensory cues that clients may use when modifying products to improve customer satisfaction.[13]

Individual depth interviews are usually recorded (audio and/or video) and transcribed to provide the researcher with the rich detail that the methodology is used for. Interviewers are also themselves debriefed to get their personal reactions to participant attitudes, insights, and the quality of the interview. Individual depth interviews use extensive amounts of interviewer time, in both conducting interviews and evaluating them, as well as facility time when premises are occupied for interviews. And while some respondents feel more comfortable discussing sensitive topics or sharing their own observations, behaviors, and attitudes with a single person, others are more forthcoming in group situations.

>**Exhibit 7-8** Types of Research Using IDIs

Types	How Research Is Conducted	How Research Is Used
Oral History *(narrative)*	Ask participants to relate their personal experiences and feelings related to historical events or past behavior.	To develop products, for example, books. *[September 11, 2001: Stories from 55 Broad Street* by Eddie T. Deerfield and Thomas T. Noland Jr. (editors); *An Album of Memories: Personal Histories from the Greatest Generation* by Tom Brokaw.]
Cultural Interviews	Ask a participant to relate his or her experiences with a culture or subculture, including the knowledge passed on by prior generations and the knowledge participants have or plan to pass on to future generations.	To determine product positioning or advertising creation. (E.g., how people use baking soda leads to positioning the product as not just a baking ingredient but also a deodorizer, toothpaste substitute, etc.)
Life Histories	Extract from a single participant memories and experiences from childhood to the present day regarding a product or service category, brand, or firm. Participants are encouraged to share how the significant people in their lives talked about or were involved with the organization, how their attitudes or preferences have changed over their lives with respect to the organization, and how their perceptions and preferences have been altered by their various life experiences.	To determine positioning for company prior to an I.D. or name change. (E.g., Frosted Flakes and Tony the Tiger—ad spots where adults feel they must appear in disguise because they eat a "child's cereal.")
Critical Incident Technique	The participant describes: • What led up to the incident. • Exactly what he or she did or did not do that was especially effective or ineffective. • The outcome or result of this action and why this action was effective or what more effective action might have been expected.	To evaluate manufacturing processes, personal sales and telemarketing sales programs, compensation or incentive programs, or other management-related incidents.
Convergent Interviewing *(convergent and divergent interviewing)*	Experts serve as participants in a sequential series of IDIs; researcher refines the questions with each interview in order to converge on the central issues or themes in a topic area.	To develop appropriate questions for all types of research (in exploratory research).
Sequential Interviewing *(chronologic interviewing)*	Approach the participant with questions formed around an anticipated series of activities that did or might have happened, in order to have the participant recall the detail of his or her own experience.	To determine store design, advertising development, and product design; it is used to extract details related to shopping behavior, advertising consumption behavior, and product use behavior.
Ethnography	Interviewer and participant collaborate in a field-setting participant observation and unstructured interview.	To determine product redesign, advertising development, positioning, distribution selection; to discover reactions and attitudes of striking employees.
Grounded Theory	Using a structured interview, each subsequent interview is adjusted based on the findings and interpretations from each previous interview, with the purpose to develop general concepts or theories with which to analyze the data.	To determine product design or redesign and advertising and promotion development.

Source: This exhibit was developed from Hy Mariampolski, *Qualitative Market Research: A Comprehensive Guide* (Thousand Oaks, CA: Sage Publications, 2001), p. 53; David Carson, Audrey Gilmore, Chad Perry, and Kjell Gronhaug, *Qualitative Marketing Research* (Thousand Oaks, CA: Sage Publications, 2001), pp. 84–89 and 152–157; Anselm Strauss and Julia Corbin, *Basics of Qualitative Research: Techniques and Procedure for Producing Grounded Theory* (Thousand Oaks, CA: Sage Publications, 1998).

Group Interviews

A **group interview** is a data collection method using a single interviewer with more than one research participant. Group interviews can be described by the group's size or its composition.

Group interviews vary widely in size: *dyads* (two people), *triads* (three people), *minigroups* (two to six people), small groups (focus groups—6 to 10 people—unarguably the most well known of group interview techniques), or *supergroups* (up to 20 people). The smaller groups are usually used when the overall population from which the participants are drawn is small, when the topic or concept list is extensive or technical, or when the research calls for greater intimacy. Dyads also are used when the special nature of a friendship or other relationship (e.g., spouses, superior–subordinate, siblings) is needed to stimulate frank discussion on a sensitive topic. Dyads and triads are also used frequently with young children who have lower levels of articulation or more limited attention spans and are thus more difficult to control in large groups. A supergroup is used when a wide range of ideas is needed in a short period of time and when the researcher is willing to sacrifice a significant amount of participant interaction for speed.

In terms of composition, groups can be **heterogeneous** (consisting of different individuals; variety of opinions, backgrounds, actions) or **homogeneous** (consisting of similar individuals; commonality of opinions, backgrounds, actions). Groups also can comprise **experts** (individuals exceptionally knowledgeable about the issues to be discussed) or **nonexperts** (those who have at least some desired information but at an unknown level).

Driven by the belief that the data extracted will be richer because of the interaction, group interviews are one of the few research techniques in which the participants are encouraged to interact. However, given time constraints, group interviews permit spending only limited time extracting detail from each participant.[14] This problem is magnified when a group interview is structured to cover numerous questions or topics.

Another drawback of the group interview is the increased difficulty recruiting, arranging, and coordinating group discussions. But this aggravation—which can be subcontracted to a specialist research supplier—is deemed a small price to pay for the insights that often are revealed by group interaction.

Interviewers are tested by the challenge of managing the group's conversation while avoiding interjecting themselves into the group's process. It is also the moderator's job to control the extrovert or dominant personality and ensure meaningful contributions from all others, including the most introverted or private thinkers. When control is not maintained, some members' opinions may be suppressed and valuable insights lost. Sometimes an individual will be more honest with a neutral interviewer than with a group of peers. One example is a group of small-business owners being unwilling to divulge competitive strengths and weaknesses. A skilled researcher can anticipate which topics are more likely to obtain good results with an individual or a group interview.

A group interview's structure and process include moderator interaction with the group and probing of the group to clarify responses. As a result, the moderator may create bias in the results by sending verbal and nonverbal signals that some responses are more favorable than others. The moderator might also direct discussion down paths that are least likely to help the client. Only training, and subsequent experience, can overcome these potential weaknesses of group interviews.

The skilled researcher helps the sponsor determine an appropriate number of group interviews to conduct. The number of groups is determined by

- The *scope* of the issue(s) being studied: The broader the issue(s), the more groups needed.
- The number of *distinct market segments* of interest: The larger the number and the greater the distinctions, the more groups needed.
- The *number of new ideas or insights* desired: The larger the number, the more groups needed.
- The *level of detail* of information: The greater the level of detail, the more groups needed.
- The *level of geographic or ethnic distinctions* in attitudes or behavior: The greater these influences, the more groups needed.
- The *homogeneity of the groups:* The less homogeneity, the more groups needed.

The general rule is: Keep conducting group interviews until no new insights are gained. Often a limited number of groups will suffice, or sometimes the number might grow to 8 or even 12.

Problems within Focus Groups

Founder and principal researcher Robert W. Kahle of Kahle Research Solutions Inc., in his book *Dominators, Cynics, and Wallflowers*, dissects typical focus group participants to illuminate ways to modify their problem behaviors. DOMINATORS are all-knowing, quick to answer, and choose a seat location in order to challenge the moderator for control. CYNICS display negative behaviors and deride the ideas of others. HOSTILES have an agenda of their own and seek corrective action; they are often angry and combative. INTOXICATEDS are under the influence of something, fidgety and incoherent. PROSELYTIZERS cannot accept that others hold opposing opinions and try to persuade others to their opinion. BLATHERERS offer long, off-topic answers and ignore moderator cues. JOKERS find every comment source material for a new joke, story, or comical facial expression. FOLLOWERS tend to repeat others' opinions. WALLFLOWERS withdraw both physically and verbally. Finally, CO-MODERATORS often engage participants before a discussion starts, ask questions of their own, and seek to befriend or support other participants.

Why is each of these behaviors a problem and how would you handle each of these problem participants?

www.kahleresearch.com; www.paramountbooks.com

It is often preferable, depending on the topic, to run separate group interviews for different subsets of the target population. For example, a study on nutritional advice may begin with separate consumer and physician groups to determine the best ways to provide the advice. This type of homogeneous grouping tends to promote more intense discussion and freer interaction.[15]

Researchers caution against forming groups solely on demographic descriptors, favoring "natural" groups (like families, co-workers, church members, etc.) where the participants share an affinity base.[16] For customer groups, however, consideration should be given to such factors as gender, ethnicity, employment status, and education, because culture is a primary determinant of perception. In a recent exploratory study of discount shoppers, the attitudes about the economy and personal finances expressed by East Coast respondents and West Coast respondents diverged widely. The research sponsor was able to use information from group interviews to build a strategy tailored to each geographic area.[17]

Regardless of group composition, it is the moderator who sets the tone of the group. Homogenous groups often discover their similarities early and get along well. But with heterogeneous groups, the moderator must provide the ice-breaker activities that get the participants interacting with each other. As with individual depth interviews, the moderator is responsible for developing the recruitment screener and the group discussion guide. Exhibit 7-9 summarizes the facilitators and inhibitors of individual participation in group interviews.

>**Exhibit 7-9** Factors Influencing Participant Contributions in Group Interviews

Positive/Facilitators	
Recognition/Ego Enhancement	Moderator's expressed appreciation for participant contributions that contribute to issue understanding; participant's open agreement with other participant comments.
Personal contribution	Participant's desire to be, and perception that his or her contributions are, helpful.
Validation	Participant's need to have his or her feelings, attitudes, or ideas validated.
Catharsis/Load-sharing	Participant's need to share something negative or bothersome with others.
Personal Growth	Participant's desire to increase knowledge or understanding through new perspectives; participant's desire for new experiences.
Socialization	Participant's desire to meet new people and make new friends in a "safe" environment.
Expectations	Participant's accurate understanding of the purpose of the group discussion.
Extrinsic Rewards	Participant's value perception of fee for participation.
Negative/Inhibitors	
Use of Abstract Terminology	Moderator or participant's use of terminology or unfamiliar jargon.
Ego Threats	Participant's challenging another participant's knowledge of the subject.
Political Correctness	Participant's withholding comments for fear that his or her contributions might be perceived as disrespectful of another's knowledge or opinions.
Ego Defense	Participant's withholding a comment for fear that it will make him or her appear unintelligent or that the opinion will be unpopular with the group.
Memory Decay	Participant's failure to remember incidents or details of incidents.
Embellishment	Participant's creative additions to memories of behaviors in order to participate fully or inflate status.
Inarticulation/Rambling Accounts	Participant's inability to express ideas quickly or concisely.
Confusion	Participant's lack of understanding of the issue under discussion.
Reticence	Participant's need to be invited to participate (rather than actively volunteering comments).
Time	Participant's concern about other obligations.
Dominating/Monopolizing	Participant's attempting to take leadership or the spotlight, thus blocking contributions of others.

A closer look at one of the best known of group interviews, the focus group, may clarify these distinctions.

Focus Groups

The term *focus group* was first coined by R. K. Merton in his 1956 book, *The Focused Interview*. The **focus group** is a panel of people (typically made up of 6 to 10 participants), led by a trained moderator, who meet for 90 minutes to two hours. The facilitator or moderator uses group dynamics principles to focus or guide the group in an exchange of ideas, feelings, and experiences on a specific topic. You'll find a sample focus group discussion guide in Appendix B.

Focus groups are often unique in research due to the research sponsor's involvement in the process. Most facilities permit the sponsor to observe the group and its dynamics in real time, drawing his or her own insights from the conversations and nonverbal signals he or she observes. Many facilities also allow the client to supply the moderator with new topics or questions that are generated by those observing in real time. This option is generally not available in an individual depth interview, other group interviews, or survey research.

Focus groups typically last about two hours but may run from one to three hours. Facilities usually provide for the group to be isolated from distractions. Thus, the famous, or infamous, mirrored window allows those who are interested to observe the group while they avoid interfering with the group dynamics. Some facilities allow for product preparation and testing, as well as other creative exercises.

Fewer and lengthier focus groups are becoming common. As sessions become longer, activities are needed to bring out deeper feelings, knowledge, and motivations. Besides the creativity sessions that employ projective techniques or involve the participants in writing or drawing sessions, or creating visual compilations, other common activities within focus groups include:[18]

- *Free association.* "What words or phrases come to mind when you think of X?"
- *Picture sort.* Participants sort brand labels or carefully selected images related to brand personality on participant-selected criteria.
- *Photo sort.* Photographs of people are given to the group members, who are then asked: "Which of these people would... ?" or "Which of these people would not... ?"
- *Role play.* Two or more members of the group are asked to respond to questions from the vantage point of their personal or assigned role.

Focus groups are often used as an exploratory technique but may be a primary methodology. In two such cases, a small college used focus groups to develop a plan to attract more freshmen applications, and a blood center used a focus group to improve blood donations.[19] Focus groups are especially valuable in the following scenarios:[20]

- Obtaining general background about a topic or issue.
- Generating research questions to be explored via quantitative methodologies.
- Interpreting previously obtained quantitative results.
- Stimulating new ideas for products and programs.
- Highlighting areas of opportunity for specific managers to pursue.
- Diagnosing problems that managers need to address.
- Generating impressions and perceptions of brands and product ideas.
- Generating a level of understanding about influences in the participant's world.

Groups best enable the exploration of surprise information and new ideas. Agendas can be modified as the research team moves on to the next focus group. Even within an existing focus group, an adept facilitator can build on the ideas and insights of previous groups, getting to a greater depth of understanding. However, because they are qualitative devices, with limited sampling accuracy, results from focus groups should not be considered a replacement for quantitative analyses.

In the opening vignette, Sara Arens was involved in conducting and analyzing focus groups for a frozen-food manufacturer. Sara's partner Jason is involved with assessing the CompleteCare service program for MindWriter. For the latter project Jason and Sara could use focus groups involving employees (of the call center and service departments) to determine suggestions for improvements and provide an analysis of proposed improvements. MindWriter may want focus groups with CompleteCare customers (both dissatisfied and satisfied customers but restricted to separate groups) to reveal the scope of attitudes and experiences not documented within complaints.

Other Venues for Focus Group Interviews

Although the following venues are most frequently used with focus groups, they can be used with other sizes and types of group interviews.

Hallmark: Qualitative Research Enriches Sinceramente Hallmark

U.S. census data show a sharp rise in the number of people who identify themselves as Hispanic, including many households where Spanish is the primary language spoken at home. Today 35.3 million people are included in this group, a 58 percent increase over the prior census figure. To better reflect the specific needs of today's Latino consumers, Hallmark enhanced its commitment to the Hispanic market and launched a new brand of culturally relevant greeting cards called *Hallmark en Español.* Recently, Hallmark expanded its commitment by launching *Sinceramente Hallmark,* a line of more than 2,500 cards for everyday occasions and holidays.

Hallmark's early research used online focus groups to create new messages for the line extension. The creative team, which includes Hispanic artists and writers, talked extensively to Hispanic consumers to gain insights into relevant designs and messages. While the extensive line includes year-round products for birthdays, love, weddings, and anniversaries, it also contains cards for special days of celebration, like *Quinceañera* (a special celebration of a girl's 15th birthday) and Dia de los Reyes (a celebration of the arrival of the three wise men in Bethlehem), among others. *Sinceramente Hallmark* includes bilingual cards, combining Spanish and English words—reflecting how many Hispanics speak—as well as digital cards available from the Hallmark website. The top five markets for Hispanic card sales are (1) Los Angeles, (2) Miami, (3) Chicago, (4) New York, and (5) San Francisco.

www.hallmark.com

Cover: May God bless you, Quinceañera.
Let your light shine before men in such a way that they may see your good works, and glorify your Father who is in heaven. Matthew 5:16 (NASB).
Inside: You have the light of the Lord within you . . . the light that can be seen in everything about you . . . And today you begin the radiant life of a lovely woman! Happy Birthday.

Telephone Focus Groups   In traditional focus groups, participants meet face-to-face, usually in specialized facilities that enable respondents to interact in a comfortable setting while being observed by a sponsoring client. However, often there is a need to reach people that face-to-face groups cannot attract. With modern telephone conferencing facilities, **telephone focus groups** can be particularly effective in the following situations:

- When it is difficult to recruit desired participants—members of elite groups and hard-to-find respondents such as experts, professionals, physician specialists, high-level executives, and store owners.

- When target group members are rare, "low incidence," or widely dispersed geographically—directors of a medical clinic, celebrities, early adopters, and rural practitioners.

- When issues are so sensitive that anonymity is needed but respondents must be from a wide geographic area—people suffering from a contagious disease, people using nonmainstream products, high-income individuals, competitors.

- When you want to conduct only a couple of focus groups but want nationwide representation.

FocusVision's VideoMarker

Extracting insights from data, conveying those insights to decision makers, and implementing strategies and tactics based on those insights is a constant challenge for most researchers. "The power to convince decision makers is often locked in the footage of such interviews," shares Peter Houlahan, president and COO of FocusVision. FocusVision, a company that provides more than 280 facilities worldwide with services for videoconference focus groups and individual depth interviews (IDIs), developed new technology for this purpose: *VideoMarker*. Clients plug in their laptop (in a viewing room or their office via videostreaming technology). While watching the event, when they see footage they want to mark, they click on the "VideoMark" button above the video area on their PC. A pop-up textbox allows the client to enter a note. The note is automatically coded with a time mark and the name of its creator. When the event is complete, video of the entire project and all notes are archived for immediate access (by password) and recorded on a CD-ROM that is sent to the client. Researchers can then create video clips to share with colleagues via e-mail, embed in documents or PowerPoint presentations, or group together into highlight reels. "The capability to show actual footage when presenting research results is especially relevant when clients aren't present to watch behind a one-way mirror or when they participate via videoconferencing or videostreaming,"

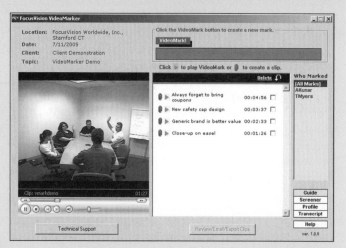

offers Houlahan. One pharmaceutical company arranged to interview patients in more than seven hours of focus groups. With *VideoMarker*, researchers captured the highlights, which were then—with the patients' consent—incorporated into IDI research with physicians. "These research highlights were the key motivational tool used to persuade doctors to change how they prescribed the company's product."

www.focusvision.com

Telephone focus groups are usually shorter than traditional groups, averaging about one hour. Participants could be in their own offices or homes or be brought to a central location with the necessary equipment. Telephone focus groups are usually less expensive than face-to-face focus groups—by up to 40 percent.

In contrast to face-to-face groups, heterogeneous telephone groups can be productive. People in traditional superior-subordinate roles can be mixed as long as they are not from the same city. A telephone focus group is less likely to be effective under the following conditions:

- When participants need to handle a product.
- When an object of discussion cannot be sent through the mail in advance.
- When sessions will run long.
- When the participants are groups of young children.

Online Focus Groups
An emerging technique for exploratory research is to approximate group dynamics using e-mail, websites, Usenet newsgroups, or an Internet chat room. It is possible to do "live" voice chats online, reducing or eliminating the cost associated with telephone focus groups. Posting questions to a newsgroup with an interest in the research problem can generate considerable discussion. However, online discussions are not confidential unless they take place on an intranet. Although online forum discussions are unlikely to reflect the average participants, they can be a good way of getting in touch with populations that have special interests (e.g., BMW club members, little league coaches, or "power computer users"). **Online focus groups** have also proved to be

effective with teens and young adults, as well as technically employed segments of the market, those essentially comfortable with computer use. They are especially valuable when a computer-based application, such as software or a game, is the topic of group discussion. The technology permits use of visual images of materials (e.g., ads or product concepts) but retains the barrier between the group and the moderator. Online focus groups are a trade-off. What you gain in speed and access, you give up in insights extracted from group dynamics, the flexibility to use nonverbal language as a source of data, and the moderator's ability to use physical presence to influence openness and depth of response.

Videoconferencing Focus Groups **Videoconferencing** is another technology used with group interviews. Many researchers anticipate growth for this methodology. Like telephone focus groups, videoconferencing enables significant savings. By reducing the travel time for the moderator and the client, coordinating such groups can be accomplished in a shorter time. However, videoconferencing retains the barrier between the moderator and participants, although less so than the telephone focus group. Since large corporations and universities are more likely to have their own internal videoconferencing facilities, most videoconferencing focus groups will tend to occur within this setting, thus reducing the breadth of participants to those who can access these specialized facilities.

Recording, Analyzing, and Reporting Group Interviews

In face-to-face settings, some moderators use large sheets of paper on the wall of the group room to record trends; others use a personal notepad. Facility managers produce both video- and audiotapes to enable a full analysis of the interview. The verbal portion of the group interview is transcribed along with moderator debriefing sessions and added to moderator notes. These are analyzed across several focus group sessions using **content analysis.** This analytical process provides the research sponsor with a qualitative picture of the respondents' concerns, ideas, attitudes, and feelings. The preliminary profile of the content of a group interview is often done with computer software in content analysis (for example, N6, mentioned in the opening vignette). Such software searches for common phrasing and words, context, and patterns of expression on digitized transcripts.

> Combining Qualitative Methodologies

Case Study[21]

The **case study,** also referred to as the *case history,* is a powerful research methodology that combines individual and (sometimes) group interviews with record analysis and observation. Researchers extract information from company brochures, annual reports, sales receipts, and newspaper and magazine articles, along with direct observation (usually done in the participant's "natural" setting), and combine it with interview data from participants. The objective is to obtain multiple perspectives of a single organization, situation, event, or process at a point in time or over a period of time. Case study methodology—or the written report from such a research project, often called a *case analysis* or *case write-up*—can be used to understand particular processes. For example, one study might evaluate new product development processes for similarities, especially the use of outside consultants, ideational techniques, and computer simulation. Another study might examine in detail the purchaser's response to a stimulus like a display. The results of the research could be used to experiment with modifications of the new product development process or with display selection and placement processes to generate higher-value transactions. The research problem is usually a how and why problem, resulting in a descriptive or explanatory study.

Researchers select the specific organizations or situations to profile because these examples or subjects offer critical, extreme, or unusual cases. Researchers most often choose multiple subjects, rather than a single subject, to study because of the opportunity for cross-case analysis. In studying multiple subjects, a deeper understanding of the subject emerges. When multiple units are chosen, it is because they offer similar results for predictable reasons (literal replication) or contrary results for predictable reasons (theoretical replication). While theoretical sampling seems to be common, a minimum of 4 cases with a maximum of 15 seems to be favored.

In the case study, interview participants are invited to tell the story of their experience, with those chosen representing different levels within the same organization or different perspectives of the same situation or process to permit depth of perspective. The flexibility of the case study approach and the emphasis on understanding the context of the subject being studied allow for a richness of understanding sometimes labeled *thick description.*

During analysis, a single case analysis is always performed before any cross-case analysis is conducted. The emphasis is on what differences occur, why, and with what effect. Prescriptive inferences about best practices are concluded after completing case studies on several organizations or situations and are speculative in nature.

Students are quite familiar with studying cases as a means of learning business principles. *In Search of Excellence,* a book by Tom Peters and Robert Waterman, was developed using case study methodology.[22] Other similar studies profiled in books written on Procter & Gamble and Disney have also used this methodology. In the business arena, such case studies have examined changes in new product development, sales processes, hiring practices, and training programs.

Action Research

Managers conduct research in order to gain insights to make decisions in specific scenarios. **Action research** is designed to address complex, practical problems about which little is known—thus no known heuristics exist. So the scenario is studied; a corrective action is determined, planned, and implemented; the results of the action are observed and recorded; and the action is assessed as effective or not. The process is repeated until a desired outcome is reached, but along the way much is learned about the processes and about the prescriptive actions being studied. Action researchers investigate the effects of applied solutions. Whatever theories are developed are validated through practical application.[23]

Suppose a restaurant that had never received a customer complaint earns its first challenge by a disgruntled diner. If no general rule existed about how to treat unhappy patrons, the organization could study the situation and come up with alternative actions. It might:

- Ignore the problem. (Its lack of experience would prevent it from knowing that negative word of mouth—negative buzz—would be the likely result.)
- Do whatever is necessary to replace the unsatisfactory meal within the shortest period of time.
- Accept the current circumstance as uncorrectable, apologize to the customer, and remedy the situation by picking up the table's full dining tab and offering the customer a free meal to get him or her back in the restaurant another day.

In action research, one of those alternatives would be chosen and implemented, and then the results recorded. Was the customer happy when he or she left? Did the customer return to dine another evening or never return again? Over the next three months, what was the customer's full revenue value? If the customer didn't return, the next time a disgruntled customer voiced dissatisfaction, a different action would be chosen, implemented, and then assessed in comparison to the first option's results.

> Merging Qualitative and Quantitative Methodologies

Triangulation is the term used to describe the combining of several qualitative methods or combining qualitative with quantitative methods. Because of the controversy described earlier, qualitative studies may be combined with quantitative ones to increase the perceived quality of the research, especially when a quantitative study follows a qualitative one and provides validation for the qualitative findings. Four strategies for combining methodologies are common in business research:[24]

1. Qualitative and quantitative studies can be conducted simultaneously.

2. A qualitative study can be ongoing while multiple waves of quantitative studies are done, measuring changes in behavior and attitudes over time.

3. A qualitative study can precede a quantitative study, and a second qualitative study then might follow the quantitative study, seeking more clarification.

4. A quantitative study can precede a qualitative study.

An example of the first strategy would be the combination of a public opinion poll at the time focus groups are being held to discover ways to sway a particular public's opinion. For the second strategy, we might collect life histories while multiple waves of questionnaires are measuring the response to differing promotional tactics. For the third, we could perform a qualitative study to identify peoples' behaviors and perceptions with respect to furniture shopping processes and interior decorating; then we could use that information to develop a quantitative study to measure the actual frequency of behaviors and attitudes. And, fourth, we might survey people's behavior and attitudes toward a brand and find we need some IDIs to explain findings that are unclear.

Many researchers recognize that qualitative research compensates for the weaknesses of quantitative research and vice versa. These forward thinkers believe that the methodologies complement rather than rival each other.

>summary

1 Qualitative research includes an array of interpretive techniques that seek to describe, decode, translate, and otherwise come to terms with the meaning, not the frequency, of certain more or less naturally occurring phenomena in the social world. Qualitative research methodologies differ from quantitative methodologies based on the focus of the research; its purpose; researcher involvement; sampling design; sample size; research design, including participant pretasking; data source, type, and preparation; methods of data analysis; level of insights and meaning extracted; research sponsor involvement; speed of the research; and data security. A qualitative methodology may be used alone to address organizational problems or in combination with other qualitative or quantitative methodologies.

2 While qualitative research is being used increasingly because of the methodologies' ability to generate deeper understanding, it still is perceived by many senior-level executives as a stepchild of quantitative data collection. This is primarily due to qualitative research's use of nonprobability sampling, the smaller sample sizes involved, and the nonprojectability of the results to a broader, target population.

3 Qualitative research is designed to tell the researcher how (process) and why (meaning) things happen as they do. In business planning and decision making, qualitative methodologies are used in market segmentation; advertising creative development; new product development, especially concept testing; sales analysis; sales development; package design; brand development and assessment, especially understanding brand value; positioning; retail design; and understanding various processes, including consumers' decision-making processes. In data analysis, qualitative research uses content analysis of written or recorded materials drawn from personal expressions by participants, behavioral observations, and debriefing of observers, as well as the study of artifacts and trace evidence from the physical environment.

4 Qualitative methodologies used in decision making evolved from techniques used in anthropology, sociology, psychology, linguistics, communication, economics, and semiotics. Common among these strategies are the individual depth interview (IDI) and the group interview, as well as observation, ethnography, action research, and grounded theory. Within group interviews, the focus group is the most widely used methodology.

Qualitative research often uses projective techniques, designed to encourage the participant to reveal in detail deeply suppressed attitudes, opinions, feelings, and experiences. Among these techniques are word or picture association, sentence completion, cartoons or empty balloons, the Thematic Apperception Test, imagination exercises, and sorting exercises. Participant preparation and the actual qualitative sessions themselves often include various creativity sessions and exercises.

>**key**terms

>**discussion**questions

Terms in Review

1 How does qualitative research differ from quantitative research?

2 How do data from qualitative research differ from data in quantitative research?

3 Why do senior executives feel more comfortable relying on quantitative data than qualitative data? How might a qualitative research company lessen the senior-level executive's skepticism?

4 Distinguish between structured, semistructured, and unstructured interviews.

Making Research Decisions

5 Assume you are a manufacturer of small kitchen electrics, like Hamilton Beach/Proctor Silex, and you want to determine if some innovative designs with unusual shapes and colors developed for the European market could be successfully marketed in the U.S. market. What qualitative research would you recommend, and why?

6 Assume you are Hallmark. (See the Snapshot on page 179.) You have identified four new themes for your Hispanic-targeted cards, *Sinceramente Hallmark*. You now need research to help your card designers create cards that correctly execute those themes. What research should you do now?

Bringing Research to Life

7 What dilemma does HealthPlus face, and why has the company turned to focus groups for insights?

From Concept to Practice

8 Use Exhibit 7-7 to develop the recruitment screener for the research you described in your answer to question 5.

9 Conduct a focus group among students in your class on one of the following topics:

  a our department's problems offering requirements and electives essential for meeting your graduation expectations.

  b Entertainment sponsored by your university to bring the community on campus.

From the Headlines

10 NCR Corporation, known as a world leader in ATMs, point-of-sale (POS) retail checkout scanners, and check-in kiosks at airports, announced in June 2009 that it would move its world headquarters from Dayton (OH) to Duluth (GA), a suburb of Atlanta, after more than 125 years. An employer of 1,200 mostly high-salaried, professional workers in Dayton, NCR was enticed to move by Georgia's offer of more than $56.9 million in tax credits; its fast-growing, educated 25- to 34-year-old population cohort; international offices for 10 European state governments; and the busiest international airport (Atlanta) in the world.

a What qualitative research might NCR have done to reach this decision?

b NCR will use its move to Georgia to downsize its world headquarters workforce. What qualitative research could help NCR determine which of its 1,200 employees will be offered positions in Duluth?

>cases*

 Akron Children's Hospital

 Covering Kids with Health Care

 Lexus SC 430

NCRCC: Teeing Up a New Strategic Direction

 Ohio Lottery: Innovative Research Design Drives Winning

Open Doors: Extending Hospitality to Travelers with Disabilities

Ramada Demonstrates Its *Personal Best*™

 Starbucks, Bank One, and Visa Launch Starbucks Card Duetto Visa

 USTA: Come Out Swinging

*You will find a description of each case in the Case Abstracts section of this textbook. Check the Case Index to determine whether a case provides data, the research instrument, video, or other supplementary material. Written cases are downloadable from the text website (www.mhhe.com/cooper11e). All video material and video cases are available from the Online Learning Center. The film reel icon indicates a video case or video material relevant to the case.

>chapter 8

Observation Studies

>learningobjectives

After reading this chapter, you should understand . . .

1 When observation studies are most useful.

2 The distinctions between monitoring nonbehavioral and behavioral activities.

3 The strengths of the observation approach in research design.

4 The weaknesses of the observation approach in research design.

5 The three perspectives from which the observer–participant relationship may be viewed in observation studies.

6 The various designs of observation studies.

> 66 Once a pattern becomes predictable, the brain starts to ignore it. We get bored; attention is a scare resource, so why waste it on something that's perfectly predictable. 99
>
> *Jonah Lehrer, neuroscientist and author,*
> How We Decide

"How's the HomeExtravaganza project coming?" asks Jason as he sticks his head into Sara Arens's office.

"I finished reviewing the proposals yesterday and selected MarketViews as the subcontractor to do the observation study," responds Sara. "MarketViews will start a week after the checklist is finalized—that's the next step."

"You've obviously determined how the observation study will interact with the larger shopper motivation study we're doing. Fill me in."

"You indicated last week that early survey feedback is that customer confusion related to merchandise location and availability may be a contributing factor to declining repeat visits and sales. The observation study will identify specific types of shopper confusion in the store and the sales associates' response to that confusion."

"I was in the store in Boca just this week for the first time," remarks Jason. "The extensive product display is impressive, but a little overwhelming—and the store is mammoth, as well. I was certainly wishing I'd worn my Nikes!

"Even though HomeExtravaganza uses greeters and its advertising promises lots of helpful associates, the motivation study is logging complaints that the associates aren't as helpful as they need to be," continues Jason.

"MarketViews recommends participant observation to determine just what form associate help is taking."

"I've used MarketViews before with good results."

"I'm meeting with MarketViews' project director this afternoon to rough out the checklist. So I'm taking an early lunch and plan to visit the store one more time," explains Sara. "We want to select specific locations for the interactions to take place and specific behaviors . . . like walking the customer to the aisle location versus giving directions to the location, finding the item in the aisle versus leaving the customer at the aisle entry. And I've come prepared," says Sara as she comes from behind her desk wearing her Reebok running shoes.

"I'll leave you to your own observation study then," remarks Jason.

> The Uses of Observation

Much of what we know comes from observation. We notice co-workers' reactions to political intrigue, the sounds of the assembly area, the smell of perfume, the taste of office coffee, the smoothness of the vice president's marble desk, and a host of other stimuli. While such observation may be a basis for knowledge, the collection processes are often haphazard.

Observation qualifies as scientific inquiry when it is conducted specifically to answer a research question, is systematically planned and executed, uses proper controls, and provides a reliable and valid account of what happened. The versatility of observation makes it an indispensable primary source method and a supplement for other methods. Many academics have a limited view of observation, relegating it to a minor technique of field data collection. This ignores its potential for forging business decisions and denies its historic stature as a creative means of obtaining primary data. Exhibit 8-1 depicts the use of observation in the research process.

In Chapter 6, we said that research designs are classified by the *approach* used to gather primary data: We can *observe,* or we can *communicate.* Exhibit 8-2 describes the conditions under which observation is an appropriate method for data collection. It also contrasts those conditions with ones from the communication modes discussed in Chapter 7—interviews—and Chapter 10—surveys (see Exhibit 8-2).

>**Exhibit 8-1** Observation and the Research Process

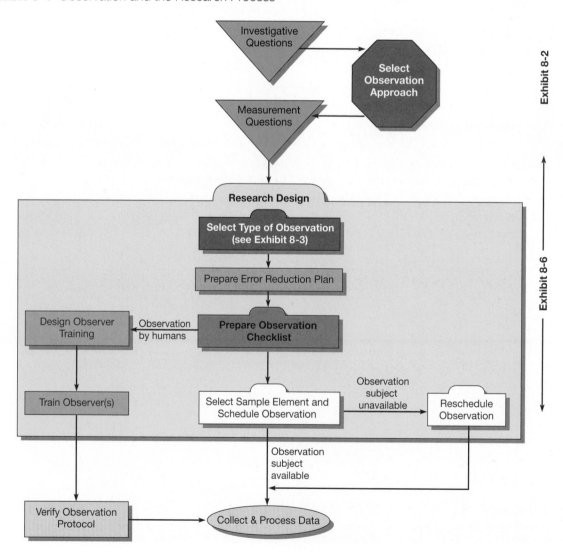

>**Exhibit 8-2** Selecting the Data Collection Method

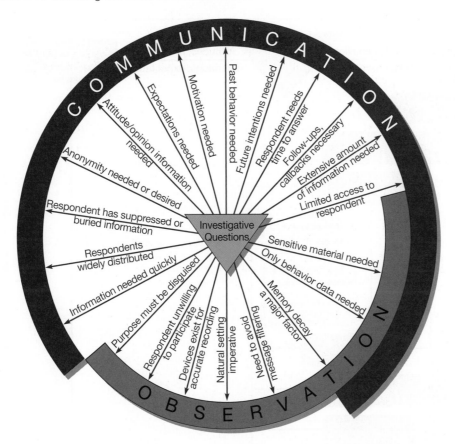

Besides collecting data visually, observation involves listening, reading, smelling, and touching. Behavioral scientists define observation in terms of animal or human behavior, but this too is limiting. As used in this text, **observation** includes the full range of monitoring behavioral and nonbehavioral activities and conditions, which, as shown in Exhibit 8-3, can be classified roughly as follows:

Nonbehavioral Observation

• Record analysis
• Physical condition analysis
• Physical process analysis

Behavioral Observation:

• Nonverbal analysis
• Linguistic analysis
• Extralinguistic analysis
• Spatial analysis

Nonbehavioral Observation

A prevalent form of observation research is **record analysis.** This may involve historical or current records and public or private records. They may be written, printed, sound-recorded, photographed, or videotaped. Historical statistical data are often the only sources used for a study. Analysis of current

>**Exhibit 8-3** Selecting an Observation Approach

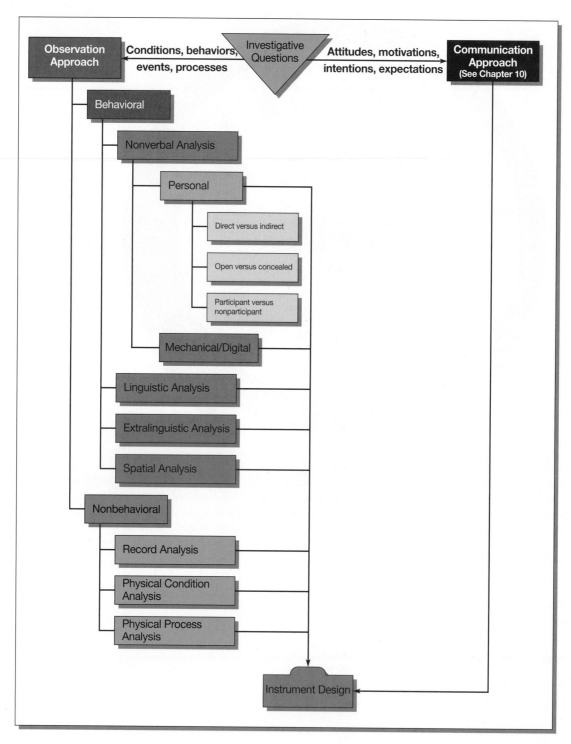

financial records and economic data also provides a major data source for studies. Other examples of this type of observation are the *content analysis* (described in Chapter 15) of competitive advertising and the analysis of personnel records.

Physical condition analysis is typified by store audits of merchandise availability, studies of plant safety compliance, analysis of inventory conditions, and analysis of financial statements. **Process** or **activity analysis** includes time/motion studies of manufacturing processes and analysis of traffic flows in a distribution system, paperwork flows in an office, and financial flows in the banking system.

Behavioral Observation

The observational study of persons can be classified into four major categories.[1] **Nonverbal behavior** is the most prevalent of these and includes body movement, motor expressions, and even exchanged glances. At the level of gross body movement, one might study how a salesperson travels a territory. At a fine level, one can study the body movements of a worker assembling a product or time-sample the activity of a department's workforce to discover the share of time each worker spends in various ways. More abstractly, one can study body movement as an indicator of interest or boredom, anger or pleasure in a certain environment. Motor expressions such as facial movements can be observed as a sign of emotional states. Eyeblink rates are studied as indicators of interest in advertising messages. Exchanged glances are of interest in studies of interpersonal behavior.

Linguistic behavior is a second frequently used form of behavior observation. One simple type familiar to most students is the tally of "ahs" or other annoying sounds or words a professor makes or uses during a class. More serious applications are the study of a sales presentation's content or the study of what, how, and how much information is conveyed in a training situation. A third form of linguistic behavior involves interaction processes that occur between two people or in small groups. Bales has proposed one widely used system for classifying such linguistic interactions.[2]

Behavior also may be analyzed on an extralinguistic level. Sometimes **extralinguistic behavior** is as important a means of communication as linguistic behavior. One author has suggested there are four dimensions of extralinguistic activity.[3] They are (1) *vocal,* including pitch, loudness, and timbre; (2) *temporal,* including the rate of speaking, duration of utterance, and rhythm; (3) *interaction,* including the tendencies to interrupt, dominate, or inhibit; and (4) *verbal stylistic,* including vocabulary and pronunciation peculiarities, dialect, and characteristic expressions. These dimensions could add substantial insight to the linguistic content of the interactions between supervisors and subordinates or salespeople and customers.

A fourth type of behavior study involves **spatial relationships,** especially how a person relates physically to others. One form of this study, *proxemics,* concerns how people organize the territory about them and how they maintain discrete distances between themselves and others. A study of how salespeople physically approach customers and a study of the effects of crowding in a workplace are examples of this type of observation.

Often in a study, the researcher will be interested in two or more of these types of information and will require more than one observer. In these forms of behavior study, it is also important to consider the relationship between observers and participants.

3

The number of minutes the average cubicle dweller works before being interrupted by phone, e-mail, instant message, or social networking activities.

> Evaluation of the Observation Method

Observation is the only method available to gather certain types of information. The study of records, mechanical processes, and young children, as well as other inarticulate participants, falls into this category. Another value of observation is that we can collect the original data at the time they occur. We need not depend on reports by others. Every respondent filters information no matter how well intentioned he or she is. Forgetting occurs and there are reasons why the respondent may not want to report fully and fairly. Observation overcomes many of these deficiencies of questioning.

A third strength is that we can secure information that most participants would ignore either because it is so common and expected or because it is not seen as relevant. For example, if you are observing buying activity in a store, there may be conditions important to the research study that the shopper does not notice or consider important, such as: What is the weather? What is the day of the week or the time of the day? How heavy is customer traffic? What is the level of promotional activity in competing stores? We can expect to learn only a few of the answers to these questions from most participants.

The fourth advantage of observation is that it alone can capture the whole event as it occurs in its natural environment. Whereas the environment of an experiment may seem contrived to participants, and the number and types of questions limit the range of responses gathered from respondents, observation is less restrictive than most primary collection methods. Also, the limitations on the length of data collection activities imposed by surveys or experiments are relaxed for observation. You may be interested in all the conditions surrounding a confrontation at a bargaining session between union and management representatives. These sessions may extend over time, and any effort to study the unfolding of the negotiation is facilitated by observation. Questioning could seldom provide the insight of observation for many aspects of the negotiation process.

Finally, participants seem to accept an observational intrusion better than they respond to questioning. Observation is less demanding of them and normally has a less biasing effect on their behavior than does questioning. In addition, it is also possible to conduct disguised and unobtrusive observation studies much more easily than disguised questioning.

The observation method has some research limitations. The observer normally must be at the scene of the event when it takes place, yet it is often impossible to predict where and when the event will occur. One way to guard against missing an event is to observe for prolonged periods until it does occur, but this strategy brings up a second disadvantage. Observation is a slow and expensive process that requires either human observers or costly surveillance equipment.

A third limitation of observation is that its most reliable results are restricted to information that can be learned by overt action or surface indicators. To go below the surface, the observer must make inferences. Two observers will probably agree on the nature of various surface events, but the inferences they draw from such data are much more variable.

Fourth, the research environment is more likely suited to subjective assessment and recording of data than to controls and quantification of events. When control is exercised through active intervention by the researchers, their participation may threaten the validity of what is being assessed. Even when sample sizes are small, the observation records can be disproportionately large and difficult to analyze.

Fifth, observation is limited as a way to learn about the past. It is similarly limited as a method by which to learn what is going on in the present at some distant place. It is also difficult to gather information on such topics as intentions, attitudes, opinions, or preferences. Nevertheless, any consideration of the merits of observation confirms its value when used with care and understanding.

> The Observer–Participant Relationship

Interrogation presents a clear opportunity for interviewer bias. The problem is less pronounced with observation but is still real. The relationship between observer and participant may be viewed from three perspectives:

- Whether the observation is direct or indirect.
- Whether the observer's presence is known or unknown to the participant.
- What role the observer plays.

>**snap**shot

People Meters Go Personal

Television networks and stations measure audience viewing patterns to assist in making numerous decisions, among them program continuation or discontinuation, program location on the schedule, and advertising rates. They share this viewer data with advertisers, who then use the data to make network, station, and program selections. Nielson Media Research partially collects its television viewer data for both broadcast and cable with electronic devices labeled "People Meters." The People Meter measures three things: the tuning of the TV set (on, off, time); what channel/station is being tuned; and who is watching (via assigned code buttons). Additionally, households in the 53 largest markets have set-tuning meters that measure and transmit set-tuning data on a daily basis. There are 5,000 households in the national sample and more than 20,000 households in various local samples used to represent more than 102 million TV households in the United States. To supplement the People Meter data, more than 1.6 million households provide written viewership diaries during four measurement periods known as "sweeps." Sweeps, usually two weeks long, occur in November, February, May, and July of each year.

As a result of an increase in media consumption outside the home, since May 2000 Nielsen Media Research and Arbitron have been testing a Portable People Meter (PPM system), pictured here, for media measurement in radio, television, and cable TV. People who accept an invitation to join a panel agree to carry a PPM with them wherever they go throughout the day. Media companies send out an inaudible signal attached to each program, which the PPM accepts. When a panel member returns home, he or she puts the PPM in a docking station for transmission.

Participants are known to modify behavior when undisguised and unconcealed observation is used. Adaptations to normal behavior are rarely sustained over time. So Nielsen

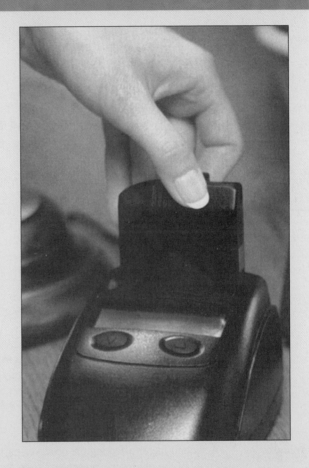

Media extends the time of observation to reduce this error source. Which part of Nielsen's research design employs observation techniques?

www.nielsenmedia.com; www.arbitron.com

Directness of Observation

Direct observation occurs when the observer is physically present and personally monitors what takes place. This approach is very flexible because it allows the observer to react to and report subtle aspects of events and behaviors as they occur. He or she is also free to shift places, change the focus of the observation, or concentrate on unexpected events if they occur. A weakness of this approach is that observers' perception circuits may become overloaded as events move quickly, and observers must later try to reconstruct what they were not able to record. Also, observer fatigue, boredom, and distracting events can reduce the accuracy and completeness of observation.

Indirect observation occurs when the recording is done by mechanical, photographic, or electronic means. For example, a special camera that takes one frame every second may be mounted in a department of a large store to study customer and employee movement. Indirect observation is less flexible than direct observation but is also much less biasing and may be less erratic in accuracy. Another advantage of indirect observation is that the permanent record can be reanalyzed to include

>snapshot

New Mexico's Longitudinal Observation Study of Seatbelt Use

Researchers Barbara F. Chatterjee and Isaac Romero, with the New Mexico Department of Health, reported seatbelt observation studies conducted in four phases over a 20-year period. Initially intended to support campaigns for state laws requiring child car seats (1982–1984) and car seat belt use, the study was ultimately expanded to shoulder belt usage (1985–1993) in five cities representing 40 percent of the New Mexico population. Observed were vehicle passengers (driver and front outboard passenger) and a separate analysis for cars and trucks (including pickups, vans, SUVs). In the study's third phase (1994–1997), it was expanded to cover 17 cities and 80 percent of the population. Observations were typically conducted after each enforcement campaign, "Operation Buckled Down." Observations consisted of 100 observations per site, usually collected within one hour on same day of week and time of day. Data were collected using 100 vehicles per/site times 55 sites. Nine to 19 sites were assigned to each observer. In the fourth phase (1998–present), they improved their

methodology from a convenience sample to a stratified random sample, consistent with National Highway Traffic Safety Administration protocols. Using the universe of public highway segments, they accounted for 60 percent of all vehicle miles traveled in the state (108 roadway segments, 27 in each of four county groups).

The observers, who used an elaborate checklist, were required to monitor all passenger vehicles and trucks less than 10,000 pounds, identify their survey station with a sign, and map lanes and traffic flow and direction. In high-volume sites, data recorders replaced paper forms from previous phases of the study. Observers, including retired law enforcement officers and others, received from four to six hours of training. Using multiple methods, comparisons from different studies, and rigorous reliability checks, the researchers saw seatbelt use improve from approximately 20 percent in 1983 to 90 percent by 2004.

www.atsip.org

many different aspects of an event. Electronic recording devices, which have improved in quality and declined in cost, are being used more frequently in observation research.

Concealment

A second factor affecting the observer-participant relationship concerns whether the participant should know of the observer's presence. When the observer is known, there is a risk of atypical activity by the participant. The initial entry of an observer into a situation often upsets the activity patterns of the participants, but this influence usually dissipates quickly, especially when participants are engaged in some absorbing activity or the presence of observers offers no potential threat to the participants' self-interest. The potential bias from participant awareness of observers is always a matter of concern, however.

Observers use **concealment** to shield themselves from the object of their observation. Often, technical means such as one-way mirrors, hidden cameras, or microphones are used. These methods reduce the risk of observer bias but bring up a question of ethics. Hidden observation is a form of spying, and the propriety of this action must be reviewed carefully.

A modified approach involves partial concealment. The presence of the observer is not concealed, but the objectives and participant of interest are. A study of selling methods may be conducted by sending an observer with a salesperson who is making calls on customers. However, the observer's real purpose may be hidden from both the salesperson and the customer (e.g., she may pretend she is analyzing the display and layout characteristics of the stores they are visiting).

Participation

The third observer-participant issue is whether the observer should participate in the situation while observing. A more involved arrangement, **participant observation,** exists when the observer enters the social setting and acts as both an observer and a participant. Sometimes he or she is known as an observer to some or all of the participants; at other times the true role is concealed. While reducing the potential for bias, this again raises an ethical issue. Often participants will not have given their consent and will not have knowledge of or access to the findings. After being deceived and having their privacy invaded, what further damage could come to the participants if the results became public? This issue needs to be addressed when concealment and covert participation are used.

Participant observation makes a dual demand on the observer. Recording can interfere with participation, and participation can interfere with observation. The observer's role may influence the way others act. Because of these problems, participant observation is used less in business research than, say, in anthropology or sociology. It is typically restricted to cases in which nonparticipant observation is not practical—for example, a study of the functioning of a traveling auditing team.

> Conducting an Observation Study
The Type of Study

Observation is found in almost all research studies, at least at the exploratory stage. Such data collection is known as **simple observation.** Its practice is not standardized, as one would expect, because of the discovery nature of exploratory research. The decision to use observation as the major data collection method may be made as early as the moment the researcher moves from research questions to investigative questions. The latter specify the outcomes of the study—the specific questions the researcher must answer with collected data. If the study is to be something other than exploratory, **systematic observation** employs standardized procedures, trained observers, schedules for recording, and other devices for the observer that mirror the scientific procedures of other primary data methods. Systematic studies vary in the emphasis placed on recording and encoding observational information:

> At one end of the continuum are methods that are unstructured and open-ended. The observer tries to provide as complete and nonselective a description as possible. On the other end of the continuum are more structured and predefined methods that itemize, count, and categorize behavior. Here the investigator decides beforehand which behavior will be recorded and how frequently observations will be made. The investigator using structured observation is much more discriminating in choosing which behavior will be recorded and precisely how [it is] to be coded.[4]

One author classifies observation studies by the degree of structure in the environmental setting and the amount of structure imposed on the environment by the researcher,[5] as reflected in Exhibit 8-4. The researcher conducting a class 1, completely unstructured study would be in a natural or field setting endeavoring to adapt to the culture. A typical example would be an ethnographic study in which the researcher, as a participant-observer, becomes a part of the culture and describes in great detail everything surrounding the event or activity of interest. Donald Roy, in the widely used case in organizational behavior, "Banana Time," took a punch press job in a factory to describe the rituals that a small work group relied on to make their highly repetitive, monotonous work bearable.[6] With other purposes in mind, business researchers may use this type of study for hypothesis generation.

Class 4 studies—completely structured research—are at the opposite end of the continuum from completely unstructured field investigations. The research purpose of class 4 studies is to test hypotheses; therefore, a definitive plan for observing specific, operationalized behavior is known in advance. This requires a measuring instrument, called an **observation checklist,** which is analogous to a questionnaire. Exhibit 8-5 shows the parallels between survey design and checklist development. Checklists

>**Exhibit 8-4** Classification of Observation Studies

Research Class	Environment	Purpose	Research Tool
1. Completely unstructured	Natural setting	Generate hypotheses	
2. Unstructured	Laboratory	↓	
3. Structured	Natural setting		Observation checklist
4. Completely structured	Laboratory	Test hypotheses	Observation checklist

>**Exhibit 8-5** Flowchart for Observation Checklist Design

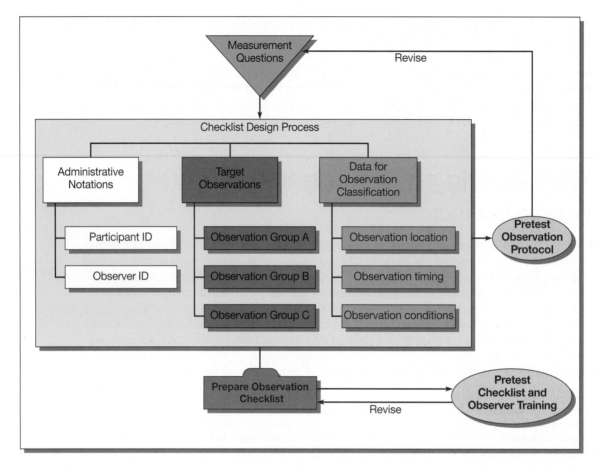

should possess a high degree of precision in defining relevant behavior or acts and have mutually exclusive and exhaustive categories. The coding is frequently closed, thereby simplifying data analysis. The participant groups being observed must be comparable and the laboratory conditions identical. The classic example of a class 4 study was Bales's investigation into group interaction.[7] Many team-building, decision-making, and assessment center studies follow this structural pattern.

The two middle classes of observation studies emphasize the best characteristics of either researcher-imposed controls or the natural setting. In class 2, the researcher uses the facilities of a laboratory—videotape recording, two-way mirrors, props, and stage sets—to introduce more control into the environment while simultaneously reducing the time needed for observation. In contrast, a class 3 study takes advantage of a structured observational instrument in a natural setting.

Content Specification

Specific conditions, events, or activities that we want to observe determine the observational reporting system (and correspond to measurement questions). To specify the observation content, we should include both the major variables of interest and any other variables that may affect them. From this cataloging, we then select those items we plan to observe. For each variable chosen, we must provide an operational definition if there is any question of concept ambiguity or special meanings. Even if the concept is a common one, we must make certain that all observers agree on the measurement terms by which to record results. For example, we may agree that variable W will be reported by count, while variable Y will be counted and the effectiveness of its use judged qualitatively.

Observation may be at either a *factual* or an *inferential* level. Exhibit 8-6 shows how we could separate the factual and inferential components of a salesperson's presentation. This table is suggestive only. It does not include many other variables that might be of interest, including data on customer

>**Exhibit 8-6** Content of Observation: Factual versus Inferential

Factual	Inferential
Introduction/identification of salesperson and customer.	Credibility of salesperson. Qualified status of customer.
Time and day of week.	Convenience for the customer. Welcoming attitude of the customer.
Product presented.	Customer interest in product.
Selling points presented per product.	Customer acceptance of selling points per product.
Number of customer objections raised per product.	Customer concerns about features and benefits.
Salesperson's rebuttal of objection.	Effectiveness of salesperson's rebuttal attempts.
Salesperson's attempt to restore controls.	Effectiveness of salesperson's control attempt. Consequences for customer who prefers interaction.
Length of interview.	Customer's/salesperson's degree of enthusiasm for the interview.
Environmental factors interfering with the interview.	Level of distraction for the customer.
Customer purchase decision.	General evaluation of sales presentation skill.

purchase history; company, industry, and general economic conditions; the order in which sales arguments are presented; and specific words used to describe certain product characteristics. The particular content of observation will also be affected by the nature of the observation setting.

Observer Training

There are a few general guidelines for the qualification and selection of observers:

- *Concentration:* Ability to function in a setting full of distractions.
- *Detail-oriented:* Ability to remember details of an experience.
- *Unobtrusive:* Ability to blend with the setting and not be distinctive.
- *Experience level:* Ability to extract the most from an observation study.

An obviously attractive observer may be a distraction in some settings but ideal in others. The same can be said for the characteristics of age or ethnic background.

If observation is at the surface level and involves a simple checklist or coding system, then experience is less important. Inexperience may even be an advantage if there is a risk that experienced observers may have preset convictions about the topic. Regardless, most observers are subject to fatigue, halo effects, and **observer drift,** which refers to a decay in reliability or validity over time that affects the coding of categories.[8] Only intensive videotaped training relieves these problems.

The observers should be thoroughly versed in the requirements of the specific study. Each observer should be informed of the outcomes sought and the precise content elements to be studied. Observer trials with the instrument and sample videotapes should be used until a high degree of reliability is apparent in their observations. When there are interpretative differences between observers, they should be reconciled.

Data Collection

The data collection plan specifies the details of the task. In essence it answers the questions *who, what, when, how,* and *where.*

Who?

What qualifies a participant to be observed? Must each participant meet a given criterion—those who initiate a specific action? Who are the contacts to gain entry (in an ethnographic study), the

>snapshot

Walmart Boosts RFID Technology for Observation

A consortium of 36 consumer packaged-goods (CPG) manufacturers, research companies, and universities have been working to change the way consumers generate and deliver purchase and consumption information, as well as how this information is integrated with detailed supply chain management information. If the Auto ID Center gets its way, all future CPGs will contain radio frequency identification (RFID) smart labels that will send signals to Internet databases and track a specific product unit from manufacturing through warehousing, retail display, and storage and potentially through consumer storage and consumption and the recycling center. Walmart recently gave the new technology a boost by directing its 100 top suppliers to start using RFID technology as early as January 2005. By its sheer size, Walmart's dictate could transform how observation studies in CPG are done. Goodyear, the world's largest tire manufacturer, also announced that its tires shipped to Walmart in 2005 would contain an RFID microchip within the tire itself, which could also relay tire information to drivers about inflation and wear to improve vehicle safety.

From a research perspective, the opportunities seem enormous. Store shelf and display locations could be evaluated for promotional effectiveness, especially when combined with shopper card information. Average age of inventory could be known to the day or hour by matching the RFID location information with shipping and receiving documents. Product recalls

could be handled with efficiency. While bar codes currently provide similar information to that promised by RFID tags, they must be scanned to be read. RFID tags need no such intervention but transmit continuously until disabled. Technically, if the tag on the product is not disabled at the time of purchase, the RFID tag could transmit location information from a consumer's car, home, or refrigerator. Such signals broadcast from a consumer's home or car would require compliance, similar to the way consumers volunteer to be part of ACNielsen's *Homescan* panel today. But according to Katherine Albrecht, founder of consumer action group CASPIAN, "Supermarket cards and retail surveillance devices are merely the opening volley of the marketers' war against consumers. If consumers fail to oppose these practices now, our long-term prospects may look like something from a dystopian science fiction novel."

The main driver of the RFID movement is supply chain savings. According to one analyst, Walmart could save $8.4 billion a year by 2007 by perfecting its inventory management with the information provided by the tags. It also has the possibility of reducing theft, which is another large savings.

http://walmartstores.com/; www.goodyear.com;

www.nocards.org; www.nielsen.com;

http://trolleyscan.com

intermediary to help with introductions, the contacts to reach if conditions change or trouble develops? Who has responsibility for the various aspects of the study? Who fulfills the ethical responsibilities to the participants?

What?

The characteristics of the observation must be set as sampling elements and units of analysis. This is achieved when event-time dimension and "act" terms are defined. In **event sampling,** the researcher records selected behavior that answers the investigative questions. In **time sampling,** the researcher must choose among a time-point sample, continuous real-time measurement, or a time-interval sample. For a time-point sample, recording occurs at fixed points for a specified length. With continuous measurement, behavior or the elapsed time of the behavior is recorded. Like continuous measurement, time-interval sampling records every behavior in real time but counts the behavior only once during the interval.[9]

Assume the observer is instructed to observe a quality control inspection for 10 minutes out of each hour (a duration of two minutes each for five times). Over a prolonged period, if the samples are drawn randomly, time sampling can give a good estimate of the pattern of activities. In a time-interval sampling of workers in a department, the outcome may be a judgment of how well the department is being supervised. In a study of sales presentations using continuous real-time sampling, the research outcome may be an assessment of a given salesperson's effectiveness or the effectiveness of different types of persuasive messages.

>**snap**shot

SizeUSA

Few observation studies can approach the sheer size and comprehensiveness of SizeUSA, a digital observation study designed to make apparel, furniture, and car shopping more enjoyable. With obesity on the rise (20 percent of U.S. adults meet the government's definition for *obese*, with two-thirds being "overweight"), it's not surprising that manufacturers and retailers from Liz Claiborne to Steelcase to Ford to JCPenney's might need new insights. This may be in part because manufacturer's sizing was previously based on a 1941 study. But it was technology that made the three-dimensional scanning of American bodies possible. The Body Measurement System uses four cameras to register more than 200,000 data points on a body. These data points become coordinates for measuring from one data point to another. The resulting 200 body measurements take less than one minute. The study, sponsored by more than 30 manufacturers, retailers, and universities, scanned more than 10,000 adults. As a result, apparel manufacturers are reassessing garment specifications. Will it be long before car seats take on new dimensions, booths in restaurants expand for those with more ample proportions, casket builders redesign their products, or buying patterns for stocking retail shelves show a new understanding of regional differences in body shape?

www.sizeusa.com/

Other important dimensions are defined by acts. What constitutes an *act* is established by the needs of the study. It is the basic unit of observation. Any of the following could be defined as an act for an observation study:

- A single expressed thought.
- A physical movement.
- A facial expression.
- A motor skill.

Although acts may be well defined, they often present difficulties for the observer. A single statement from a sales presentation may include several thoughts about product advantages, a rebuttal to an objection about a feature, or some remark about a competitor. The observer is hard-pressed to sort out each thought, decide whether it represents a separate unit of observation, and then record it quickly enough to follow continued statements.

When?

Is the time of the study important, or can any time be used? In a study of out-of-stock conditions in a supermarket, the exact times of observation may be important. Inventory is shipped to the store on certain days only, and buying peaks occur on other days. The likelihood of a given product being out of stock is a function of both time-related activities.

When Physicians and Their Patients Are Research Subjects

When Akron Children's Hospital asked Marcus Thomas LLC to renew its brand promise, Marcus Thomas chose an observation study to guide its work. To peel down to the emotional core driving parents' hospital selection decision, Marcus Thomas negotiated permission to shadow physicians and parents during testing, diagnosis, and treatment of the child patients.

When physicians and patients are the subjects of research, ethical issues abound. But the observation study was "the best way to reveal the core emotional experiences and motivations for parents' decisions," according to Jennifer Hirt-Marchand, vice president and director of research for Marcus Thomas. So firm researchers spent days in the hospital watching interactions among patients, parents, physicians, nurses, and other staff. They were careful to respect the sensitivity of the subject and the environment they observed. "While parents were unbelievably cooperative, the researchers tried to be as unobtrusive as possible," said Robin Segbers, Marcus Thomas's manager of planning.

Listening to physician conversations with parents and child patients revealed to researchers a core brand promise that Akron Children's Hospital could embody and that would influence parents to choose Akron Children's for acute care (i.e., requiring more than three consecutive days of hospitalization):

Akron Children's Hospital focuses ALL of the hospital's resources (energy, creativity, state-of-the-art technology, compassion, technical skill, competence, etc.) toward the simple goal of helping every child reach his or her full potential.

This observation study was phase one of research that subsequently included focus groups and telephone surveys. An ad campaign built on the findings of this research succeeded in increasing occupancy at Akron Children's by 11 percent. For more information, read the case. "Akron Children's Hospital: Part A and Part B."

www.akronchildrens.org; www.marcusthomasllc.com

How?

Will the data be directly observed? If there are two or more observers, how will they divide the task? How will the results be recorded for later analysis? How will the observers deal with various situations that may occur—when expected actions do not take place or when someone challenges the observer in the setting?

Where?

Within a spatial confine, where does the act take place? In a retail traffic pattern study, the proximity of a customer's pause space to a display or directional sign might be recorded. Must the observation take place in a particular location within a larger venue? The location of the observation, such as a sales approach observation within a chain of retail stores, can significantly influence the acts recorded.

Observers face unlimited variations in conditions. Fortunately, most problems do not occur simultaneously. When the plans are thorough and the observers well trained, observation research is quite successful.

> Unobtrusive Measures

Up to this point, our discussion has focused on direct observation as a traditional approach to data collection. Like surveys and experiments, some observation studies—particularly participant observation—require the observer to be physically present in the research situation. This contributes to a **reactivity response,** a phenomenon in which participants alter their behavior in response to the researcher.

Webb and his colleagues have given us an insight into some very innovative observational procedures that can be both nonreactive and inconspicuously applied. Called **unobtrusive measures,**

>closeup

Designing the Observation Study

The design of a behavioral observation study follows the same pattern as other research. Once the researcher has specified the investigative questions, it is often apparent that the best way to conduct the study is through observation. Guidance for conducting a behavioral observation and translating the investigative question(s) into an observation checklist is the subject of this Closeup. We first review the procedural steps and then explain how to create a checklist.

Most studies that use behavioral observation follow a general sequence of steps that parallel the research process. (See Exhibit 8-1.) Here we adapt those steps to the terminology of the observation method:

- Define the content of the study.
- Develop a data collection plan that identifies the observational targets, sampling strategy, and acts (operationalized as a checklist or coding scheme).
- Secure and train observers.
- Collect the data.
- Analyze the data.

In this chapter's Bringing Research to Life, we recount an incident in which Sara Arens is subcontracting a behavioral observation study to MarketViews, a specialty research firm. The client, HomeExtravaganza, is experiencing declining repeat visits at its new superstore units. Preliminary results from a periodic survey indicate that customer confusion in the megastore is discouraging customers from returning, so an observation study is planned to see how employees and store design elements contribute to or solve the problem. The research questions might be:

- What do employees do to reduce or eliminate customer confusion?
- What do employees do that contributes to customer confusion?
- Which design elements diffuse customer confusion?
- Which design elements contribute to customer confusion?

Further assume that the survey indicates that customers who feel confused and cited this confusion as their reason for not returning had entered the store looking for a variety of merchandise, stocked in various locations throughout the vast store. They described their hopelessness as evolving from the experience of not knowing where to start the process of searching. Such customers showed no particular similarities or differences in terms of ethnic background, age, or education level. Some had the assistance of greeters or floor assistance associates, while others did not.

The observation targets will be twofold: shoppers entering the store through the main entrance and employees serving as greeters and floor assistance associates. Customers who request assistance from the main-entrance greeter or who consult the directional location signs will be the primary target. If they approach a floor assistance associate, the employee will also become a target.

Survey research reveals some inconsistency by time of day and type of merchandise sought, so MarketViews plans to sample during four primary day parts—early morning, midday, afternoon, and early evening—as well as at all three "directional locations," where signage describing the store and the shopper's current "You are here" location is noted.

Notes taken by Sara during a tour of the store help to identify the acts to record. During their subsequent meeting, it is decided that MarketViews will record the customer's seeking of assistance, either personal or signage; his or her consulting of the directional signage and its location; the customer's path to the desired merchandise; and whether a purchase is completed. The assistance acts of the floor assistance associate will also be recorded. These are determined to be assistance versus no assistance, pointing plus verbal direction, verbal direction only, providing the customer with a store copy-sheet directional map on which the associate marks the location of the merchandise and the path to get there, inquiry to other staff for location assistance, passing the customer to another floor assistance associate, accompanying the customer to the correct aisle, accompanying the customer to actual merchandise shelf location, and providing verbal assistance to selection of the appropriate product from the array of products provided.

It is determined that a checklist will be created and tested by MarketViews, with any necessary changes occurring after the test. The checklist developed is shown in Exhibit 8-7. The foremost concern is that either the customer or the associate will discover that he or she is being observed and will change behavior. Human observers will be used to trace the path of observational targets. By means of the store's security cameras, researchers will record customers flowing through the main entrance and past the greeter location and stopping at directional location signs. Counts of brochure store maps distributed from the directional signage locations and copysheet directional maps used by floor assistance associates will also be used as a measure of customers seeking directional assistance.

(continued)

>**close**up**cont'd**

>**Exhibit 8-7** Sample Checklist for HomeExtravaganza Study

Time_____ Day: M T W Th F Sa Su Date_____ Store No. _____ Observer #_____

Target Customer Interception Location: ❑ Main Entry ❑ Directional Location Sign: ❑ #1
❑ #2
❑ #3

Target Shopper Characteristics: ❑ Male ❑ Female
❑ Child ❑ Child-teen+ ❑ Adult ❑ Senior

Shopper Companion(s): ❑ Alone ❑ With others: ❑ other adult No. _____ M No. _____ F
❑ child/children No. _____

Shopping Cart Used: ❑ No ❑ Yes

Greeter verbal interaction with target: ❑ No ❑ Yes Greeter No. _____
Action ❑ Point to directional sign
❑ Verbal directions

Floor Assistance Associate Interaction: ❑ No ❑ Yes Interception location: Aisle# _____ Crossway# _____
Associate # _____
Assistance given: ❑ No ❑ Yes Action: ❑ Verbal direction only
❑ Verbal direction plus pointing
❑ Store directional copy-map with marked mdse location
❑ Store directional copy-map with mdse location & path
❑ Inquire of other staff
❑ Pass customer to another FAA
❑ Accompany customer to aisle location
❑ Accompany customer to mdse shelf location
❑ Product selection assistance offered

Directional Sign Interaction: ❑ No ❑ Yes Sign location: ❑ #1
❑ #2
❑ #3

Purchase: ❑ No ❑ Yes: Item Sought Assistance For: ❑ No ❑ Yes

Customer Path:

these approaches encourage creative and imaginative forms of indirect observation, archival searches, and variations on simple and contrived observation.[10] Of particular interest are measures involving indirect observation based on **physical traces** that include *erosion* (measures of wear) and *accretion* (measures of deposit).

Natural erosion measures are illustrated by the frequency of replacement of vinyl floor tile in front of museum exhibits as an indicator of exhibit popularity. The study of wear and tear on book pages is a measure of library book use. Counting the remaining brochures in a car dealer's display rack after a favorable magazine review suggests consumer interest.

Physical traces also include natural accretion such as discovering the listenership of radio stations by observing car radio settings as autos are brought in for service. Another type of unobtrusive study involves estimating liquor and magazine consumption by collecting and analyzing family trash. An interesting application compared beer consumption reports acquired through interviews with the findings of sampled trash. If the interview data were valid, the consumption figures for the area were at 15 percent. However, the validity was questioned when the beer can count from trash supported a 77 percent consumption rate.[11]

William Rathje is a professor of archaeology at Stanford University and founder of the Garbage Project in Tucson. His study of trash, refuse, rubbish, and litter resulted in the subdiscipline that the *Oxford English Dictionary* has termed *garbology*. By excavating landfills, he has gained insight into human behavior and cultural patterns—sometimes sorting the contents of up to 150 coded categories. His previous studies have shown that "people will describe their behavior to satisfy cultural expectations, like the mothers in Tucson who unanimously claimed they made their baby food from scratch, but whose garbage told a very different tale."[12]

Physical trace methods present a strong argument for use based on their ability to provide low-cost access to frequency, attendance, and incidence data without contamination from other methods or reactivity from participants. They are excellent "triangulation" devices for cross-validation. Thus, they work well as supplements to other methods. Designing an unobtrusive study can test a researcher's creativity, and one must be especially careful about inferences made from the findings. Erosion results may have occurred because of wear factors not considered, and accretion material may be the result of selective deposit or survival.

>summary

1 Observation is one of the few options available for studying records, mechanical processes, lower animals, small children, and complex interactive processes. We can gather data as the event occurs and can come closer to capturing the whole event than with interrogation. On the other hand, we have to be present to catch the event or have some recording device on the scene to do the job.

2 Observation includes a variety of monitoring situations that cover nonbehavioral and behavioral activities.

3 The strengths of observation as a data collection method include:

- Securing information about people or activities that cannot be derived from experiments or surveys.
- Avoiding participant filtering and forgetting.
- Securing environmental context information.
- Optimizing the naturalness of the research setting.
- Reducing obtrusiveness.

4 Observation may be limited by:

- The difficulty of waiting for long periods to capture the relevant phenomena.
- The expense of observer costs and equipment.
- The reliability of inferences from surface indicators.
- The problems of quantification and disproportionately large records.
- The limitation on presenting activities and inferences about cognitive processes.

5 We can classify observation in terms of the observer-participant relationship. This relationship may be viewed from three perspectives: (1) Is the observation direct or indirect? (2) Is the observer's presence known or unknown? (3) Is the observer a participant or nonparticipant?

6 The design of an observation study follows the same general pattern as other research. Observation studies fall into four general types based on the degree of structure and

the nature of the observational environment. The researcher must define the content of the study; develop a data collection plan that identifies participants, sampling strategy, and "acts" (often operationalized as a checklist or coding scheme); secure and train observers; and launch the study.

Unobtrusive measures offer an unusual and creative approach to reducing reactivity in observation research by indirect observation and other methods. Measures of erosion and accretion serve as ways to confirm the findings from other methods or operate as singular data sources.

>**key**terms

>**discussion**questions

Terms in Review

1 Compare the advantages and disadvantages of the survey to those of observation. Under which circumstances could you make a case for using observation?

2 What ethical risks are involved in observation? In the use of unobtrusive measures?

3 Based on present or past work experience, suggest problems that could be resolved by using observation-based data.

4 Distinguish between the following:

   a The relative value of communication and observation.

   b Nonverbal, linguistic, and extralinguistic analysis.

   c Factual and inferential observation.

Making Research Decisions

5 The observer–participant relationship is an important consideration in the design of observation studies. What kind of relationship would you recommend in each of the following cases?

   a Observations of professional conduct in the classroom by the student author of a course evaluation guide.

   b Observation of retail shoppers by a researcher who is interested in determining customer purchase time by type of goods purchased.

   c Observation of a focus group interview by a client.

   d Effectiveness of individual farmworker organizers in their efforts to organize employees of grape growers.

6 Assume you are the manufacturer of modular office systems and furniture as well as office organization elements (desktop and wall organizers, filing systems, etc.). Your company has been asked to propose an observation study to examine the use of office space by white-collar and managerial workers for a large insurance company. This study will be part of a project to improve office efficiency and paperwork flow. It is expected to involve the redesign of office space and the purchase of new office furniture and organization elements.

   a What are the varieties of information that might be observed?

   b Select a limited number of content areas for study, and operationally define the observation acts that should be measured.

7 Develop a checklist to be used by observers in the previous study.

   a Determine how many observers you need, and assign two or three to a specific observation task.

   b Compare the results of your group members' checklists for stability of recorded perceptions.

8 You wish to analyze the pedestrian traffic that passes a given store in a major shopping center. You are interested in determining how many shoppers pass by this store, and you would like to classify these shoppers on various relevant dimensions. Any information you secure should be obtainable from observation alone.

    a What other information might you find useful to observe?

    b How would you decide what information to collect?

    c Devise the operational definitions you would need.

    d What would you say in your instructions to the observers you plan to use?

    e How might you sample this shopper traffic?

Bringing Research to Life

9 Develop the investigative questions that should have guided Sara's observation study of HomeExtravaganza.

From Concept to Practice

10 Using Exhibit 8-3, identify the type of study described in each of the Snapshots featured in this chapter.

From the Headlines

11 Amazon's Kindle, its electronic book, magazine, and newspaper reader, has been far more successful than its SONY competitor. This could be at least somewhat influenced by the "Oprah factor"; the Kindle was first introduced on the *Oprah* show and strongly endorsed by the mega-mogul. But the original Kindle had some physical problems—button placement and page-turn speed among them. Correcting these problems resulted in the Kindle2, released in 2009 to glowing reviews. What observation research might have been used in the redesign of the original kindle?

>cases*

 Akron Children's Hospital

 Envirosell

Net Conversions Influence Kelley Blue Book

State Farm: Dangerous Intersections

* You will find a description of each case in the Case Abstracts section of the textbook. Check the Case Index to determine whether a case provides data, the research instrument, video, or other supplementary material. Written cases are downloadable from the text website (www.mhhe.com/cooper11e). All video material and video cases are available from the Online Learning Center. The film reel icon indicates a video case or video material relevant to the case.

>chapter 9

Experiments

>learningobjectives

After reading this chapter, you should understand . . .

1 The uses for experimentation.

2 The advantages and disadvantages of the experimental method.

3 The seven steps of a well-planned experiment.

4 Internal and external validity with experimental research designs.

5 The three types of experimental designs and the variations of each.

> “ There is no such thing as a failed experiment, only experiments with unexpected outcomes. ”
>
> Richard Buckminster Fuller, engineer and architect

Jason slides into a seat next to Sara at the conference lunch table. Sara glances his way and nods briefly but keeps her attention on the man to her left. He is describing some of the finer details of the Point of Purchase Advertising Institute's groundbreaking experiment to put display materials on a directly comparative basis with other audited advertising and sales promotion activities. Sara had just attended his presentation during the morning session of the conference.

As he stops speaking, Sara introduces Jason, "Doug Adams, I'd like you to meet my colleague, Jason Henry. Jason, Doug is vice president and cofounder of Prime Consulting Group, Inc. [Prime]."

Jason extends his hand across Sara's plate, "Pleased to meet you, Doug. Prime took the lead on that POP [point-of-purchase] industry experiment, right? Sorry I missed your presentation, but Sara," Jason nods to Sara, "suggested we divide and conquer—to cover more sessions."

Doug returns Jason's smile and handshake. "It seems to be the topic of conversation at this table at the moment, so maybe you'll get some of the content here," welcomes Doug. "I was just explaining how we needed a methodology that could separate out other sales influencers, like price, local advertising, media-delivered coupons, or a secondary stocking location in order to measure the sales lift generated by the POP material. For example, if Frito-Lay offered Doritos at $2.49, reduced from $2.99, plus it stocked a secondary location near the soft-drink aisle, Frito-Lay could track the sales lift. If sales increased even more when a Doritos sign was posted over the secondary stock location, then the power of the POP could be determined."

"Your session was generating all the buzz as I entered the dining room," comments Jason. "How many types of POP were assessed?"

"Ultimately, 20 different types," shares Doug. "Several different message types—for example, brand name, photo, price, retail savings, thematic . . . like a movie tie-in . . . or generic . . . like the summer barbeque season—and numerous locations."

"Like regular shelf stocking location, end-cap, front lobby . . . ?" asks Jason. At Doug's affirmative nod Jason asks, "How did you keep the manufacturers from distorting the experiment?"

To give Doug a chance to take a bite, Sara supplies, "Prime used a double-blind audit tracking procedure using observation, coupled with sales tracking through more than 250 supermarkets from the IRI panel of stores and 120 convenience stores from six retailers with Nielsen's Market Decisions program. The manufacturers didn't know which stores were involved."

"And did the POP create the sales lift the retailers expected?" asks Jason.

"Not only were we able to calculate sales lift for each type of promotion," shares Doug, "but we were also able to calculate a full cost-per-thousand [CPM] estimate, including the cost of manufacturing, delivering and installing the point-of-purchase material. TV, radio, and in-store ads are still quoting CPM exposures without the cost of the ad."

"If grocery and convenience stores buy in, this will be a large piece of business for one or several firms," comments Sara. "What's been the reaction?"

"When a retailer, who has been relying on his gut instinct to accept or reject POP materials for his store, sees that the same material can cause a 20 to 40 percent lift in store sales, he's bound to be receptive. We think it's going to be a major new research initiative," smiles Doug. "Are you interested?"

> What Is Experimentation?

Why do events occur under some conditions and not under others? Research methods that answer such questions are called *causal* methods. (Recall the discussion of causality in Chapter 6.) Ex post facto research designs, in which a researcher interviews respondents or observes what is or what has been, also have the potential for discovering causality. The distinction between these methods and experimentation is that the researcher is required to accept the world as it is found, whereas an experiment allows the researcher to alter systematically the variables of interest and observe what changes follow.

In this chapter we define experimentation and discuss its advantages and disadvantages. An outline for the conduct of an experiment is presented as a vehicle to introduce important concepts. The questions of internal and external validity are also examined: Does the experimental treatment determine the observed difference, or was some extraneous variable responsible? And how can one generalize the results of the study across times, settings, and persons? The chapter concludes with a review of the most widely accepted designs, a section on test markets, and a Closeup example.

Experiments are studies involving intervention by the researcher beyond that required for measurement. The usual intervention is to manipulate some variable in a setting and observe how it affects the subjects being studied (e.g., people or physical entities). The researcher manipulates the independent or explanatory variable and then observes whether the hypothesized dependent variable is affected by the intervention.

An example of such an intervention is the study of bystanders and thieves.[1] In this experiment, participants were asked to come to an office where they had an opportunity to see a person steal some money from a receptionist's desk. A confederate of the experimenter, of course, did the stealing. The major hypothesis concerned whether people observing a theft will be more likely to report it (1) if they are alone when they observe the crime or (2) if they are in the company of someone else.

There is at least one **independent variable (IV)** and one **dependent variable (DV)** in a causal relationship. We hypothesize that in some way the IV "causes" the DV to occur. The independent or explanatory variable in our example was the state of either being alone when observing the theft or being in the company of another person. The dependent variable was whether the subjects reported observing the crime. The results suggested that bystanders were more likely to report the theft if they observed it alone rather than in another person's company.

On what grounds did the researchers conclude that people who were alone were more likely to report crimes observed than people in the company of others? Three types of evidence form the basis for this conclusion. First, there must be an agreement between independent and dependent variables. The presence or absence of one is associated with the presence or absence of the other. Thus, more reports of the theft (DV) came from lone observers (IV_1) than from paired observers (IV_2).

Second, beyond the correlation of independent and dependent variables, the time order of the occurrence of the variables must be considered. The dependent variable should not precede the independent variable. They may occur almost simultaneously, or the independent variable should occur before the dependent variable. This requirement is of little concern since it is unlikely that people could report a theft before observing it.

The third important support for the conclusion comes when researchers are confident that other extraneous variables did not influence the dependent variable. To ensure that these other variables are not the source of influence, researchers control their ability to confound the planned comparison. Under laboratory conditions, standardized conditions for control can be arranged. The crime observation experiment was carried out in a laboratory set up as an office. The entire event was staged without the observers' knowledge. The receptionist whose money was to be stolen was instructed to speak and act in a specific way. Only the receptionist, the observers, and the "criminal" were in the office. The same process was repeated with each trial of the experiment.

Although such controls are important, further precautions are needed so that the results achieved reflect only the influence of the independent variable on the dependent variable.

> An Evaluation of Experiments

Advantages

When we elaborated on the concept of cause in Chapter 6, we said causality could not be proved with certainty but the probability of one variable being linked to another could be established convincingly. The experiment comes closer than any primary data collection method to accomplishing this goal. The foremost advantage is the researcher's ability to manipulate the independent variable. Consequently, the probability that changes in the dependent variable are a function of that manipulation increases. Also, a control group serves as a comparison to assess the existence and potency of the manipulation.

The second advantage of the experiment is that contamination from extraneous variables can be controlled more effectively than in other designs. This helps the researcher isolate experimental variables and evaluate their impact over time. Third, the convenience and cost of experimentation are superior to other methods. These benefits allow the experimenter opportunistic scheduling of data collection and the flexibility to adjust variables and conditions that evoke extremes not observed under routine circumstances. In addition, the experimenter can assemble combinations of variables for testing rather than having to search for their fortuitous appearance in the study environment.

Fourth, **replication**—repeating an experiment with different subject groups and conditions—leads to the discovery of an average effect of the independent variable across people, situations, and times. Fifth, researchers can use naturally occurring events and, to some extent, **field experiments** (a study of the dependent variable in actual environmental conditions) to reduce subjects' perceptions of the researcher as a source of intervention or deviation in their everyday lives.

Disadvantages

The artificiality of the laboratory is arguably the primary disadvantage of the experimental method. However, many subjects' perceptions of a contrived environment can be improved by investment in the facility. Second, generalization from nonprobability samples can pose problems despite random assignment. The extent to which a study can be generalized from college students to managers or executives is open to question. And when an experiment is unsuccessfully disguised, volunteer subjects

Online Dating Industry Claims Vs. Kissing a Lot of Frogs

Internet dating is big business, as current and projected revenues show (see the accompanying figure). From the Chemistry.com website to actual chemical testing, people seek compatibility matches using methods such as hour-long surveys and even DNA samples[a] in order to identify their genetic soul mate. Each of several popular Internet dating sites claims that its method is more scientifically valid than the competition.[b] The proof of effectiveness, however, should make research methods students cringe.

Estimated Online Dating Revenues (Billions)[c]

Chemistry.com's Helen Fisher studied the neural receptors of people in love and linked her results to six specific chemicals that were subsequently represented on a 56-item questionnaire.[d] Despite a 28,000-person sample drawn from its website, there was no compelling evidence beyond the old adage that those of like mind (having the same goals) have a better chance of attracting something permanent.

Markus Frind, chief executive and founder of Plenty of Fish.com, says his site produces 800,000 relationships each year, but creates about 100,000 marriages during that time—a figure based on "some study I found online." He adds, "I don't want to pay $200,000 to a research company to find out how many marriages I have per year."[e] The site's psychologist, James Houran, claims that those meeting through the site were more satisfied with their relationship than those using any other system.[f]

Historically, Match.com counted member self-reports of marriages. Later it claimed in press releases that it "is credited with more marriages than any other site." This was based on the results of a 2004 survey of 4,743 couples registered on WeddingChannel.com for whom Match.com was the primary connection. Match.com's media kit also claimed 12 marriages per day have their roots with the site. The company now says that was imprecise.[g]

eHarmony, known for its patented 258-item questionnaire, chose Harris Interactive to research some of the most interesting claims. In 2005, Harris Interactive estimated that 90 people a day married as a result of the site. By 2007, the number had swelled to 236 people per day. Using these data and Centers for Disease Control and Prevention (CDC) and Census Bureau comparisons, and adjusting for those married in the 20 to 54 age group, eHarmony claimed credit for 2 percent of marriages in the country.[h] eHarmony also claimed that couples who met through its site were "happier" than those who met in other ways (a control group).[i] Psychology professor Jeffrey Lohr and two psychology graduates at the University of Arkansas challenged this finding with evidence that eHarmony couples had been married only six months (honeymoon effect), whereas the control group had been married about two years.[j]

"You have to kiss a lot of frogs before you find your handsome prince," may continue to be equally valid advice if the online dating industry does not use more rigorous methods to justify its claims.

www.chemistry.com; www.match.com; www.PlentyofFish.com

are often those with the most interest in the topic. Third, despite the low costs of experimentation, many applications of experimentation far outrun the budgets for other primary data collection methods. Fourth, experimentation is most effectively targeted at problems of the present or immediate future. Experimental studies of the past are not feasible, and studies about intentions or predictions are difficult. Finally, management research is often concerned with the study of people. There are limits to the types of manipulation and controls that are ethical.

> Conducting an Experiment[2]

In a well-executed experiment, researchers must complete a series of activities to carry out their craft successfully. Although the experiment is the premier scientific methodology for establishing causation, the resourcefulness and creativeness of the researcher are needed to make the experiment live up to its potential. In this section, and as we introduce Exhibit 9-1, we discuss seven activities the researcher must accomplish to make the endeavor successful:

1. Select relevant variables.
2. Specify the treatment levels.
3. Control the experimental environment.
4. Choose the experimental design.
5. Select and assign the subjects.
6. Pilot test, revise, and test.
7. Analyze the data.

Selecting Relevant Variables

Throughout the book we have discussed the idea that a research problem can be conceptualized as a hierarchy of questions starting with a management problem. The researcher's task is to translate an amorphous problem into the question or hypothesis that best states the objectives of the research. Depending on the complexity of the problem, investigative questions and additional hypotheses can be created to address specific facets of the study or data that need to be gathered. Further, we have mentioned that a **hypothesis** is a relational statement because it describes a relationship between two or more variables. It must also be **operationalized,** a term we used earlier in discussing how concepts are transformed into variables to make them measurable and subject to testing.

Consider the following research question as we work through the seven points listed above:

Does a sales presentation that describes product benefits in the introduction of the message lead to improved retention of product knowledge?

Since a hypothesis is a tentative statement—a speculation—about the outcome of the study, it might take this form:

Sales presentations in which the benefits module is placed in the introduction of a 12-minute message produce better retention of product knowledge than those where the benefits module is placed in the conclusion.

The researchers' challenges at this step are to:

1. Select variables that are the best operational representations of the original concepts.
2. Determine how many variables to test.
3. Select or design appropriate measures for them.

The researchers would need to select variables that best operationalize the concepts *sales presentation, product benefits, retention,* and *product knowledge.* The product's classification and the nature of the intended audience should also be defined. In addition, the term *better* could be operationalized statistically by means of a significance test.

The number of variables in an experiment is constrained by the project budget, the time allocated, the availability of appropriate controls, and the number of subjects being tested. For statistical reasons, there must be more subjects than variables.[3]

The selection of measures for testing requires a thorough review of the available literature and instruments. In addition, measures must be adapted to the unique needs of the research situation without compromising their intended purpose or original meaning.

Specifying Treatment Levels

In an experiment, participants experience a manipulation of the independent variable, called the **experimental treatment.** The **treatment levels** of the independent variable are the arbitrary or natural groups the researcher makes within the independent variable of an experiment. For example, if salary is hypothesized to have an effect on employees' exercising of stock purchase options, it might be divided into high, middle, and low ranges to represent three levels of the independent variable.

>**Exhibit 9-1** Experimentation in the Research Process

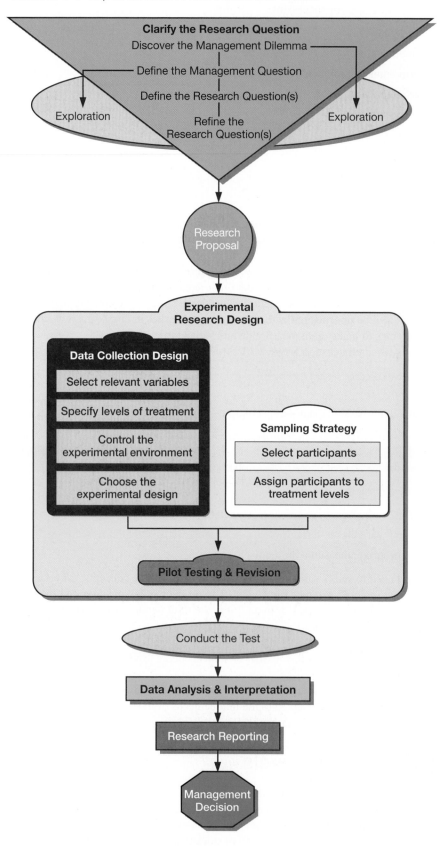

>**Exhibit 9-2** Experiment of Placement of Benefits Module within Sales Presentation

Hypothesis: Sales presentations in which the benefits module is placed in the introduction of a 12-minute message produce better retention of product knowledge by the customer than those in which the benefits module is placed in the conclusion.

$$\text{Effect} = DV_1 - DV_2$$

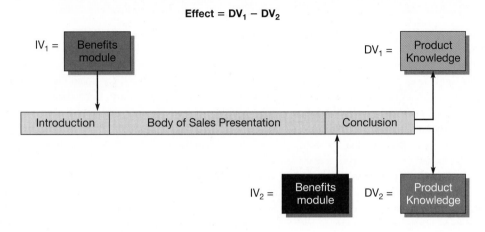

The levels assigned to an independent variable should be based on simplicity and common sense. In the sales presentation example, the experimenter should not select 8 minutes and 10 minutes as the starting points to represent the two treatment levels if the average message about the product is 12 minutes long. Similarly, if the benefits module is placed in the first and second minutes of the presentation, observable differences may not occur because the levels are too close together. Thus, in the first trial, the researcher is likely to position the midpoint of the benefits module the same interval from the end of the introduction as from the end of the conclusion (see Exhibit 9-2).

Under an entirely different hypothesis, several levels of the independent variable may be needed to test order-of-presentation effects. Here we use only two. Alternatively, a **control group** could provide a base level for comparison. The control group is composed of subjects who are not exposed to the independent variable(s), in contrast to those who receive the experimental treatment.

Controlling the Experimental Environment

In our sales presentation experiment, extraneous variables can appear as differences in age, gender, race, dress, communications competence, and many other characteristics of the presenter, the message, or the situation. These have the potential for distorting the effect of the treatment on the dependent variable and must be controlled or eliminated. However, at this stage, we are principally concerned with **environmental control,** holding constant the physical environment of the experiment. The introduction of the experiment to the subjects and the instructions would likely be videotaped for consistency. The arrangement of the room, the time of administration, the experimenter's contact with the subjects, and so forth, must all be consistent across each administration of the experiment.

Other forms of control involve subjects and experimenters. When subjects do not know if they are receiving the experimental treatment, they are said to be **blind.** When the experimenters do not know if they are giving the treatment to the experimental group or to the control group, the experiment is said to be **double blind.** Both approaches control unwanted complications such as subjects' reactions to expected conditions or experimenter influence.

Choosing the Experimental Design

Unlike the general descriptors of research design that were discussed in Chapter 6, experimental designs are unique to the experimental method. They serve as positional and statistical plans to designate relationships between experimental treatments and the experimenter's observations or measurement

Does the Subject Line Influence E-mail Open Rates?

E-mail has become a popular way to communicate with employees, customers, suppliers, and other alliance partners, so getting those e-mails opened is important business. Ben Chestnut, a partner in Rocket Science Group LLC, shares that open rates vary widely due to a large number of factors and that companies can only track those e-mails that are written in HTML. "When an e-mail has an image that is downloaded, we can track the download. Or if an e-mail contains a link, we can track that someone clicked on the link." Thus, open rates for e-mail studies could be understated by excluding those who actually read text-only e-mails.

Rocket Science Group recently ran a study on its e-mail design product MailChimp to discover if high-open-rate e-mails had significantly different subject lines than low-open-rate e-mails. MailChimp offers templates that could be modified if information warranted. Chestnut started with campaigns that e-mailed more than 100 people (more than 40 million pieces of e-mail). These campaigns were sorted by open rates to identify which fit into two groups of interest: those with high open rates (60–87 percent) and those with low open rates (1–14 percent). From each group he drew a sample (20) and compared the subject lines. "The difference seemed to be in the expectations that were set for each e-mail," explained Chestnut. Promotional offers—discount coupons or percentage-off savings—on subject lines were a signal that the e-mail was one designed to sell. If the recipient had opted in for only informative e-mail (e.g., a newsletter), then they would not be expecting or welcome a hard-sell e-mail. Two conclusions drawn from the study included: (1) that e-mails should specify the content in the e-mail subject line (surprisingly, not all do) and (2) that the mailer should always honor the parameters of its negotiated relationship with the intended e-mail receiver. How would you evaluate this study?

www.rocketsciencegroup.com; www.mailchimp.com

points in the temporal scheme of the study. In the conduct of the experiment, the researchers apply their knowledge to select one design that is best suited to the goals of the research. Judicious selection of the design improves the probability that the observed change in the dependent variable was caused by the manipulation of the independent variable and not by another factor. It simultaneously strengthens the generalizability of results beyond the experimental setting.

Selecting and Assigning Participants

The participants selected for the experiment should be representative of the population to which the researcher wishes to generalize the study's results. This may seem self-evident, but we have witnessed several decades of experimentation with college sophomores that contradict that assumption. In the sales presentation example, corporate buyers, purchasing managers, or others in a decision-making capacity would provide better generalizing power than undergraduate college students *if* the product in question was targeted for industrial use rather than to the consumer.

The procedure for random sampling of experimental subjects is similar in principle to the selection of respondents for a survey. The researcher first prepares a sampling frame and then assigns the subjects for the experiment to groups using a randomization technique. Systematic sampling may be used if the sampling frame is free from any form of periodicity that parallels the sampling ratio. Since the sampling frame is often small, experimental subjects are recruited; thus, they are a self-selecting sample. However, if randomization is used, those assigned to the experimental group are likely to be similar to those assigned to the control group. **Random assignment** to the groups is required to make the groups as comparable as possible with respect to the dependent variable. Randomization does not guarantee that if a pretest of the groups was conducted before the treatment condition, the groups would be pronounced identical; but it is an assurance that those differences remaining are randomly distributed. In our example, we would need three randomly assigned groups—one for each of the two treatments and one for the control group.

When it is not possible to randomly assign subjects to groups, matching may be used. **Matching** employs a nonprobability quota sampling approach. The object of matching is to have each experimental and control subject matched on every characteristic used in the research. This becomes more cumbersome as the number of variables and groups in the study increases. Since the characteristics of concern are only those that are correlated with the treatment condition or the dependent variable, they are easier to identify, control, and match.[4] In the sales presentation experiment, if a large part of the sample was composed of businesswomen who had recently completed communications training, we would not want the characteristics of gender, business experience, and communication training to be disproportionately assigned to one group.

Some authorities suggest a **quota matrix** as the most efficient means of visualizing the matching process.[5] In Exhibit 9-3, one-third of the subjects from each cell of the matrix would be assigned to each of the three groups. If matching does not alleviate the assignment problem, a combination of matching, randomization, and increasing the sample size would be used.

Pilot Testing, Revising, and Testing

The procedures for this stage are similar to those for other forms of primary data collection. Pilot testing is intended to reveal errors in the design and improper control of extraneous or environmental conditions. Pretesting the instruments permits refinement before the final test. This is the researcher's best opportunity to revise scripts, look for control problems with laboratory conditions, and scan the environment for factors that might confound the results. In field experiments, researchers are sometimes caught off guard by events that have a dramatic effect on subjects: the test marketing of a competitor's product announced before an experiment, or a reduction in force, reorganization, or merger before a crucial organizational intervention. The experiment should be timed so that subjects are not sensitized to the independent variable by factors in the environment.

Analyzing the Data

If adequate planning and pretesting have occurred, the experimental data will take an order and structure uncommon to surveys and unstructured observational studies. It is not that data from experiments are easy to analyze; they are simply more conveniently arranged because of the levels of the treatment

45

The percent of Americans eating out less in 2009 in order to save money.

>**Exhibit 9-3** Quota Matrix Example

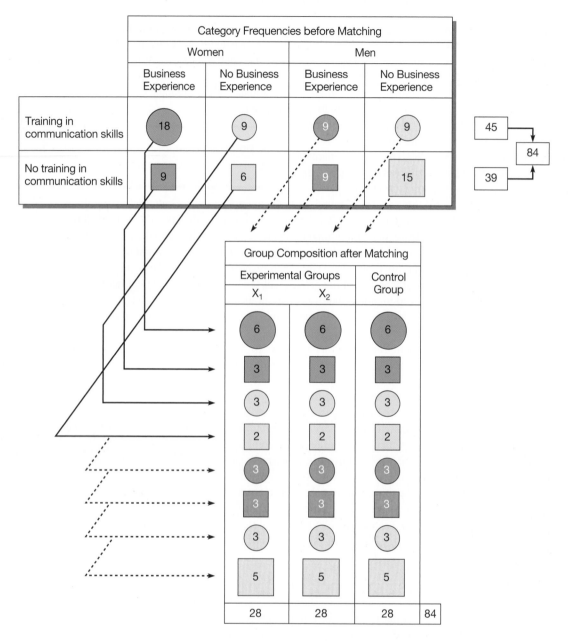

condition, pretests and posttests, and the group structure. The choice of statistical techniques is commensurately simplified.

Researchers have several measurement and instrument options with experiments. Among them are:

- Observational techniques and coding schemes.
- Paper-and-pencil tests.
- Self-report instruments with open-ended or closed questions.
- Scaling techniques (e.g., Likert scales, semantic differentials, Q-sort).
- Physiological measures (e.g., galvanic skin response, EKG, voice pitch analysis, eye dilation).

> Validity in Experimentation

Even when an experiment is the ideal research design, it is not without problems. There is always a question about whether the results are true. We have previously defined validity as whether a measure accomplishes its claims. Although there are several different types of validity, here only the two major varieties are considered: **internal validity**—do the conclusions we draw about a demonstrated experimental relationship truly imply cause?—and **external validity**—does an observed causal relationship generalize across persons, settings, and times?[6] Each type of validity has specific threats we need to guard against.

Internal Validity

Among the many threats to internal validity, we consider the following seven:

- History
- Maturation
- Testing
- Instrumentation
- Selection
- Statistical regression
- Experimental mortality

History

During the time that an experiment is taking place, some events may occur that confuse the relationship being studied. In many experimental designs, we take a control measurement (O_1) of the dependent variable before introducing the manipulation (X). After the manipulation, we take an after-measurement (O_2) of the dependent variable. Then the difference between O_1 and O_2 is the change that the manipulation has caused.

A company's management may wish to find the best way to educate its workers about the financial condition of the company before this year's labor negotiations. To assess the value of such an effort, managers give employees a test on their knowledge of the company's finances (O_1). Then they present the educational campaign (X) to these employees, after which they again measure their knowledge level (O_2). This design, known as a pre-experiment because it is not a very strong design, can be diagrammed as follows:

$$O_1 \qquad X \qquad O_2$$
Pretest   Manipulation   Posttest

Between O_1 and O_2, however, many events could occur to confound the effects of the education effort. A newspaper article might appear about companies with financial problems, a union meeting might be held at which this topic is discussed, or another occurrence could distort the effects of the company's education test.

Maturation

Changes also may occur within the subject that are a function of the passage of time and are not specific to any particular event. These are of special concern when the study covers a long time, but they may also be factors in tests that are as short as an hour or two. A subject can become hungry, bored, or tired in a short time, and this condition can affect response results.

Testing

The process of taking a test can affect the scores of a second test. The mere experience of taking the first test can have a learning effect that influences the results of the second test.

Instrumentation

This threat to internal validity results from changes between observations in either the measuring instrument or the observer. Using different questions at each measurement is an obvious source of potential trouble, but using different observers or interviewers also threatens validity. There can even be an instrumentation problem if the same observer is used for all measurements. Observer experience, boredom, fatigue, and anticipation of results can all distort the results of separate observations.

Selection

An important threat to internal validity is the differential selection of subjects for experimental and control groups. Validity considerations require that the groups be equivalent in every respect. If subjects are randomly assigned to experimental and control groups, this selection problem can be largely overcome. Additionally, matching the members of the groups on key factors can enhance the equivalence of the groups.

Statistical Regression

This factor operates especially when groups have been selected by their extreme scores. Suppose we measure the output of all workers in a department for a few days before an experiment and then conduct the experiment with only those workers whose productivity scores are in the top 25 percent and bottom 25 percent. No matter what is done between O_1 and O_2, there is a strong tendency for the average of the high scores at O_1 to decline at O_2 and for the low scores at O_1 to increase. This tendency results from imperfect measurement that, in effect, records some persons abnormally high and abnormally low at O_1. In the second measurement, members of both groups score more closely to their long-run mean scores.

Experiment Mortality

This occurs when the composition of the study groups changes during the test. Attrition is especially likely in the experimental group, and with each dropout the group changes. Because members of the control group are not affected by the testing situation, they are less likely to withdraw. In a compensation incentive study, some employees might not like the change in compensation method and may withdraw from the test group; this action could distort the comparison with the control group that has continued working under the established system, perhaps without knowing a test is under way.

All the threats mentioned to this point are generally, but not always, dealt with adequately in experiments by random assignment. However, five additional threats to internal validity are independent of whether or not one randomizes.[7] The first three have the effect of equalizing experimental and control groups.

1. *Diffusion or imitation of treatment.* If people in the experimental and control groups talk, then those in the control group may learn of the treatment, eliminating the difference between the groups.

2. *Compensatory equalization.* Where the experimental treatment is much more desirable, there may be an administrative reluctance to deprive the control group members. Compensatory actions for the control groups may confound the experiment.

3. *Compensatory rivalry.* This may occur when members of the control group know they are in the control group. This may generate competitive pressures, causing the control group members to try harder.

4. *Resentful demoralization of the disadvantaged.* When the treatment is desirable and the experiment is obtrusive, control group members may become resentful of their deprivation and lower their cooperation and output.

5. *Local history.* The regular history effect already mentioned impacts both experimental and control groups alike. However, when one assigns all experimental persons to one group session and all control people to another, there is a chance for some idiosyncratic event to confound results. This problem can be handled by administering treatments to individuals or small groups that are randomly assigned to experimental or control sessions.

External Validity

Internal validity factors cause confusion about whether the experimental treatment (X) or extraneous factors are the source of observation differences. In contrast, external validity is concerned with the interaction of the experimental treatment with other factors and the resulting impact on the ability to generalize to (and across) times, settings, or persons. Among the major threats to external validity are the following interactive possibilities:

- Reactivity of testing on X.
- Interaction of selection and X.
- Other reactive factors.

The Reactivity of Testing on X

The reactive effect refers to sensitizing subjects via a pretest so that they respond to the experimental stimulus (X) in a different way. A before-measurement of a subject's knowledge about the ecology programs of a company will often sensitize the subject to various experimental communication efforts that might be made about the company. This before-measurement effect can be particularly significant in experiments where the IV is a change in attitude.

Interaction of Selection and X

The process by which test subjects are selected for an experiment may be a threat to external validity. The population from which one selects subjects may not be the same as the population to which one wishes to generalize results. Suppose you use a selected group of workers in one department for a test of the piecework incentive system. The question may remain as to whether you can extrapolate those results to all production workers. Or consider a study in which you ask a cross section of a population to participate in an experiment but a substantial number refuse. If you conduct the experiment only with those who agree to participate (self-selection), can the results be generalized to the total population?

Other Reactive Factors

The experimental settings themselves may have a biasing effect on a subject's response to X. An artificial setting can obviously produce results that are not representative of larger populations. Suppose the workers who are given the incentive pay are moved to a different work area to separate them from the control group. These new conditions alone could create a strong reactive condition.

If subjects know they are participating in an experiment, there may be a tendency to role-play in a way that distorts the effects of X. Another reactive effect is the possible interaction between X and subject characteristics. An incentive pay proposal may be more effective with persons in one type of job, with a certain skill level, or with a certain personality trait.

Problems of internal validity can be solved by the careful design of experiments, but this is less true for problems of external validity. External validity is largely a matter of generalization, which, in a logical sense, is an inductive process of extrapolating beyond the data collected. In generalizing, we estimate the factors that can be ignored and that will interact with the experimental variable. Assume that the closer two events are in time, space, and measurement, the more likely they are to follow the same laws. As a rule of thumb, first seek internal validity. Try to secure as much external validity as is compatible with the internal validity requirements by making experimental conditions as similar as possible to conditions under which the results will apply.

> Experimental Research Designs

The many experimental designs vary widely in their power to control contamination of the relationship between independent and dependent variables. The most widely accepted designs are based on this characteristic of control: (1) preexperiments, (2) true experiments, and (3) field experiments (see Exhibit 9-4).

Preexperimental Designs

All three preexperimental designs are weak in their scientific measurement power—that is, they fail to control adequately the various threats to internal validity. This is especially true of the after-only study.

After-Only Study

This may be diagrammed as follows:

$$
\begin{array}{cc}
X & O \\
\text{Treatment or manipulation} & \text{Observation or measurement} \\
\text{of independent variable} & \text{of dependent variable}
\end{array}
\qquad (1)
$$

An example is an employee education campaign about the company's financial condition without a prior measurement of employee knowledge. Results would reveal only how much the employees know after the education campaign, but there is no way to judge the effectiveness of the campaign. How well do you think this design would meet the various threats to internal validity? The lack of a pretest and control group makes this design inadequate for establishing causality.

>**Exhibit 9-4** Key to Design Symbols

X	An *X* represents the introduction of an experimental stimulus to a group. The effects of this independent variable(s) are of major interest.
O	An *O* identifies a measurement or observation activity.
R	An *R* indicates that the group members have been randomly assigned to a group.
E	An *E* represents the effect of the experiment and is presented as an equation.

The *X*s and *O*s in the diagram are read from left to right in temporal order.

$$O \quad X \quad O \quad O$$
Time →

When multiple *X*s and *O*s appear vertical to each other, this indicates that the stimuli and/or the observations take place simultaneously.

$$X \quad O$$
$$O$$
Time →
q

Parallel rows that are not separated by dashed lines indicate that comparison groups have been equalized by the randomization process.

$$X \quad O$$
$$O$$

Those separated with a dashed line have not been so equalized.

$$O \quad X \quad O$$
$$----$$
$$O$$

One-Group Pretest–Posttest Design

This is the design used earlier in the educational example. It meets the various threats to internal validity better than the after-only study, but it is still a weak design. How well does it control for history? Maturation? Testing effect? The others?

$$\underset{\text{Pretest}}{O} \qquad \underset{\text{Manipulation}}{X} \qquad \underset{\text{Posttest}}{O} \qquad\qquad (2)$$

Static Group Comparison

This design provides for two groups, one of which receives the experimental stimulus while the other serves as a control. In a field setting, imagine this scenario. A forest fire or other natural disaster is the experimental treatment, and psychological trauma (or property loss) suffered by the residents is the measured outcome. A pretest before the forest fire would be possible, but not on a large scale

T.G.I. Friday's Experiments with Smaller Portions

According to *New York Times* writer Andrew Martin, "Americans are eating about 12 percent more calories a day than they did in the mid-1980s . . . [and the] percentage of Americans who are overweight, meanwhile, increased to 66 percent in 2004 from 47 percent in the late 1970s. Hardly anyone believes it is a coincidence that Americans became fatter at the same time they began eating out more than ever and restaurants super-sized their portions."

On the heels of the push-back from the "super-size" ex-posé and barrage of dietary and health-related ad campaigns, Richard Snead, president and chief executive officer of Carlson Restaurants Worldwide, parent of T.G.I. Friday's restaurants says, "We are listening." Gambling on the proposition that smaller portions help people lose weight or maintain their self-concept, Friday's launched an experiment: T.G.I. Friday's is adding in all its restaurants a six-entree Right Portion, Right Price menu. Snead contends, "No matter what your lifestyle choice,

you don't have to sacrifice taste. Smaller portions at smaller prices meet all lifestyle choices."

But will the experiment pay off? Adjusting portion size is problematic because customers connect large quantities of food with value. When the Ruby Tuesday's chain reduced some of its portions in 2004, consumers complained. The restaurant returned to the original fare after five months. Olive Garden and Red Lobster chains acknowledge the resistance of customers to smaller portions. Burger King used this larger-is-more-value perception in a recent ad campaign appealing to males. The actor, complaining he is too hungry to settle for "chick food," runs for the close-by Whooper. John Glass, an analyst at CIBC World Markets, cites unattractive financial consequences to portion downsizing: "A lower check drags down comp-store sales. What you hope is, you offset the check with higher traffic." Mr. Glass added, "It's been a difficult sell on Wall Street."

www.tgifridays.com

(as in the California fires). Moreover, timing of the pretest would be problematic. The control group, receiving the posttest, would consist of residents whose property was spared.

$$
\begin{array}{cc}
X & O_1 \\
\rule{2em}{0.4pt} & \rule{2em}{0.4pt} \\
 & O_2
\end{array}
\qquad (3)
$$

The addition of a comparison group creates a substantial improvement over the other two designs. Its chief weakness is that there is no way to be certain that the two groups are equivalent.

True Experimental Designs

The major deficiency of the preexperimental designs is that they fail to provide comparison groups that are truly equivalent. The way to achieve equivalence is through matching and random assignment. With randomly assigned groups, we can employ tests of statistical significance of the observed differences.

A Nose for Problem Odors

Ever wonder how consumer product companies test the effectiveness of their creations? At Hill Top Research Inc., researchers use a variety of devices—including the human nose. In one deodorant study subjects were brought to a test site that contained a *hot room*. Researchers applied the product being tested to each subject's armpit, followed by the insertion of a cotton pad under each arm, which subjects retained by pressing their arms to their sides. Researchers then led subjects to the *hot room*—where temperatures are warm enough to make anyone sweat. When the subjects exit the room after the defined period of time, the cotton pad was removed for analysis. Then the odor detective did his or her job. A cup with a small hole in the bottom was placed against the subject's armpit (to assure uniform distance between nose and pit), and then the detective positioned her nose near the hole and inhaled. With a successful formulation, the odor detective would not detect a strong or offensive odor.

What are some of the variables a researcher would need to control in this study? What sources of error must be controlled?

www.hill-top.com

It is common to show an X for the test stimulus and a blank for the existence of a control situation. This is an oversimplification of what really occurs. More precisely, there is an X_1 and an X_2, and sometimes more. The X_1 identifies one specific independent variable, while X_2 is another independent variable that has been chosen, often arbitrarily, as the control case. Different levels of the same independent variable may also be used, with one level serving as the control.

Pretest–Posttest Control Group Design

This design consists of adding a control group to the one-group pretest–posttest design and assigning the subjects to either of the groups by a random procedure (R). The diagram is:

$$R \quad O_1 \quad X \quad O_2$$
$$R \quad O_3 \qquad O_4 \tag{4}$$

The effect of the experimental variable is

$$E = (O_2 - O_1) - (O_4 - O_3)$$

In this design, the seven major internal validity problems are dealt with fairly well, although there are still some difficulties. Local history may occur in one group and not the other. Also, if communication exists between people in test and control groups, there can be rivalry and other internal validity problems.

Maturation, testing, and regression are handled well because one would expect them to be felt equally in experimental and control groups. Mortality, however, can be a problem if there are different dropout rates in the study groups. Selection is adequately dealt with by random assignment.

The record of this design is not as good on external validity, however. There is a chance for a reactive effect from testing. This might be a substantial influence in attitude change studies where pretests introduce unusual topics and content. Nor does this design ensure against reaction between selection and the experimental variable. Even random selection may be defeated by a high decline rate by subjects. This would result in using a disproportionate share of people who are essentially volunteers and who may not be typical of the population. If this occurs, we will need to replicate the experiment several times with other groups under other conditions before we can be confident of external validity.

Posttest-Only Control Group Design

In this design, the pretest measurements are omitted. Pretests are well established in classical research design but are not really necessary when it is possible to randomize. The design is:

$$R \quad X \quad O_1$$
$$R \qquad O_2 \tag{5}$$

A Job Enrichment Quasi-Experiment[8]

One theory of job attitudes holds that "hygiene" factors, which include working conditions, pay, security, status, interpersonal relationships, and company policy, can be a major source of dissatisfaction among workers but have little positive motivational power. This theory says that the positive motivator factors are intrinsic to the job; they include achievement, recognition for achievement, the work itself, responsibility, and growth or advancement.[9]

A study of the value of job enrichment as a builder of job satisfaction was carried out with laboratory technicians, or "experimental officers" (EOs), at British Chemical. The project was a multiple group time series quasi-experiment. The project is diagrammed at the end of this "Closeup."

Two sections of the department acted as experimental groups and two sections acted as control groups. It is not clear how these groups were chosen, but there was no mention of random assignment. One of the experimental groups and one of the control groups worked closely together, while the other two groups were separated geographically and were engaged in different research. Hygiene factors were held constant during the research, and the studies were kept confidential to avoid the tendency of participants to act in artificial ways.

A before-measurement was made using a job reaction survey instrument. This indicated the EOs typically had low morale, and many wrote of their frustrations. All EOs were asked to write monthly progress reports, and these were used to assess the

quality of their work. The assessment was made against eight specifically defined criteria by a panel of three managers who were not members of the department. These assessors were never told which laboratory technicians were in the experimental group and which were in the control group.

The study extended over a year, with the treatments introduced in the experimental groups at the start of the 12-month study period. Changes were made to give experimental group EOs important chances for achievement; these changes also made the work more challenging. Recognition of achievement was given, authority over certain aspects was increased, new managerial responsibilities were assigned to the senior EOs, added advancements were given to others, and the opportunity for self-initiated work was provided. After about six months, these same changes were instituted with one of the control groups, while the remaining group continued for the entire period as a control. Several months of EO progress reports were available as a prior baseline for evaluation. The results of this project are shown in Exhibit 9-5.

$$O\ O\ O\ X\ O\ O\ O\ O\ O\ O\ O\ O\ O\ O\ O$$

$$O\ O\ O\ O\ O\ O\ O\ O\ X\ O\ O\ O\ O\ O\ O$$

$$O\ O\ O\ O\ O\ O\ O\ O\ O\ O\ O\ O\ O\ O\ O$$

>**Exhibit 9-5** Assessment of EOs' Monthly Reports

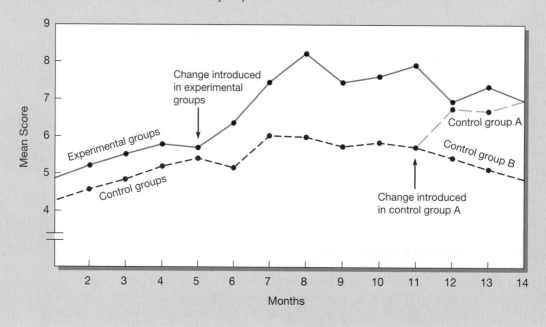

The experimental effect is measured by the difference between O_1 and O_2:

$$E = (O_2 - O_1)$$

The simplicity of this design makes it more attractive than the pretest–posttest control group design. Internal validity threats from history, maturation, selection, and statistical regression are adequately controlled by random assignment. Since the participants are measured only once, the threats of testing and instrumentation are reduced, but different mortality rates between experimental and control groups continue to be a potential problem. The design reduces the external validity problem of testing interaction effect.

Field Experiments: Quasi- or Semi-Experiments[10]

Under field conditions, we often cannot control enough of the extraneous variables or the experimental treatment to use a true experimental design. Because the stimulus condition occurs in a natural environment, a field experiment is required.

A modern version of the bystander and thief field experiment, mentioned at the beginning of the chapter, involves the use of electronic article surveillance to prevent shrinkage due to shoplifting. In a proprietary study, a shopper came to the optical counter of an upscale mall store and asked to be shown special designer frames. The salesperson, a confederate of the experimenter, replied that she would get them from a case in the adjoining department and disappeared. The "thief" selected two pairs of sunglasses from an open display, deactivated the security tags at the counter, and walked out of the store.

Thirty-five percent of the subjects (store customers) reported the theft upon the return of the salesperson. Sixty-three percent reported it when the salesperson asked about the shopper. Unlike previous studies, the presence of a second customer did not reduce the willingness to report a theft.

This study was not possible with a control group, a pretest, or randomization of customers; but the information gained was essential and justified a compromise of true experimental designs. We use the preexperimental designs previously discussed or quasi-experiments to deal with such conditions. In a quasi-experiment, we often cannot know when or to whom to expose the experimental treatment. Usually, however, we can decide when and whom to measure. A quasi-experiment is inferior to a true experimental design but is usually superior to preexperimental designs. In this section, we consider a few common quasi-experiments.

Nonequivalent Control Group Design

This is a strong and widely used quasi-experimental design. It differs from the pretest–posttest control group design, because the test and control groups are not randomly assigned. The design is diagrammed as follows:

$$\begin{array}{ccc} O_1 & X & O_2 \\ \hline & & \\ O_3 & & O_4 \end{array} \qquad (6)$$

There are two varieties. One is the *intact equivalent design,* in which the membership of the experimental and control groups is naturally assembled. For example, we may use different classes in a school, membership in similar clubs, or customers from similar stores. Ideally, the two groups are as alike as possible. This design is especially useful when any type of individual selection process would be reactive.

The second variation, the *self-selected experimental group design,* is weaker because volunteers are recruited to form the experimental group, while nonvolunteer subjects are used for control. Such a design is likely when subjects believe it would be in their interest to be a subject in an experiment—say, an experimental training program.

Comparison of pretest results $(O_1 - O_3)$ is one indicator of the degree of equivalence between test and control groups. If the pretest results are significantly different, there is a real question about the groups' comparability. On the other hand, if pretest observations are similar between groups, there is more reason to believe internal validity of the experiment is good.

Separate Sample Pretest–Posttest Design

This design is most applicable when we cannot know when and to whom to introduce the treatment but we can decide when and whom to measure. The basic design is:

$$
\begin{array}{cccc}
R & O_1 & (X) & \\
R & & X & O_2
\end{array}
\qquad (7)
$$

The bracketed treatment (X) is irrelevant to the purpose of the study but is shown to suggest that the experimenter cannot control the treatment.

This is not a strong design because several threats to internal validity are not handled adequately. History can confound the results but can be overcome by repeating the study at other times in other settings. In contrast, it is considered superior to true experiments in external validity. Its strength results from its being a field experiment in which the samples are usually drawn from the population to which we wish to generalize our findings.

We would find this design more appropriate if the population were large, if a before-measurement were reactive, or if there were no way to restrict the application of the treatment. Assume a company is planning an intense campaign to change its employees' attitudes toward energy conservation. It might draw two random samples of employees, one of which is interviewed about energy use attitudes before the information campaign. After the campaign the other group is interviewed.

Group Time Series Design

A time series design introduces repeated observations before and after the treatment and allows subjects to act as their own controls. The single treatment group design has before-after measurements as the only controls. There is also a multiple design with two or more comparison groups as well as the repeated measurements in each treatment group.

The time series format is especially useful where regularly kept records are a natural part of the environment and are unlikely to be reactive. The time series approach is also a good way to study unplanned events in an ex post facto manner. If the federal government were to suddenly begin price controls, we could still study the effects of this action later if we had regularly collected records for the period before and after the advent of price control.

The internal validity problem for this design is history. To reduce this risk, we keep a record of possible extraneous factors during the experiment and attempt to adjust the results to reflect their influence.

>summary

1 Experiments are studies involving intervention by the researcher beyond that required for measurement. The usual intervention is to manipulate a variable (the independent variable) and observe how it affects the subjects being studied (the dependent variable).

   An evaluation of the experimental method reveals several advantages: (1) the ability to uncover causal relationships, (2) provisions for controlling extraneous and environmental variables, (3) convenience and low cost of creating test situations rather than searching for their appearance in business situations, (4) the ability to replicate findings and thus rule out idiosyncratic or isolated results, and (5) the ability to exploit naturally occurring events.

2 Some advantages of other methods that are liabilities for the experiment include (1) the artificial setting of the laboratory, (2) generalizability from nonprobability samples,

(3) disproportionate costs in select business situations, (4) a focus restricted to the present and immediate future, and (5) ethical issues related to the manipulation and control of human subjects.

3 Consideration of the following activities is essential for the execution of a well-planned experiment:

   a Select relevant variables for testing.

   b Specify the treatment levels.

   c Control the environmental and extraneous factors.

   d Choose an experimental design suited to the hypothesis.

   e Select and assign subjects to groups.

   f Pilot test, revise, and conduct the final test.

   g Analyze the data.

4 We judge various types of experimental research designs by how well they meet the tests of internal and external validity. An experiment has high internal validity if one has confidence that the experimental treatment has been the source of change in the dependent variable. More specifically, a design's internal validity is judged by how well it meets seven threats. These are history, maturation, testing, instrumentation, selection, statistical regression, and experiment mortality.

External validity is high when the results of an experiment are judged to apply to some larger population. Such an experiment is said to have high external validity regarding that population. Three potential threats to external validity are testing reactivity, selection interaction, and other reactive factors.

5 Experimental research designs include (1) preexperiments, (2) true experiments, and (3) quasi-experiments. The main distinction among these types is the degree of control that the researcher can exercise over validity problems. Three preexperimental designs were presented in the chapter. These designs represent the crudest form of experimentation and are undertaken only when nothing stronger is possible. Their weakness is the lack of an equivalent comparison group; as a result, they fail to meet many internal validity criteria. They are the (1) after-only study, (2) one-group pretest–posttest design, and (3) static group comparison.

Two forms of the true experiment were also presented. Their central characteristic is that they provide a means by which we can ensure equivalence between experimental and control groups through random assignment to the groups. These designs are (1) pretest–posttest control group and (2) posttest-only control group.

The classical two-group experiment can be extended to multigroup designs in which different levels of the test variable are used as controls rather than the classical nontest control.

Between the extremes of preexperiments, with little or no control, and true experiments, with random assignment, there is a gray area in which we find quasi-experiments. These are useful designs when some variables can be controlled, but equivalent experimental and control groups usually cannot be established by random assignment. There are many quasi-experimental designs, but only three were covered in this chapter: (1) nonequivalent control group design, (2) separate sample pretest–posttest design, and (3) group time series design.

>keyterms

blind 213	experimental treatment 211	matching 215
control group 213	external validity 217	operationalized 211
dependent variable (DV) 208	field experiment 209	quota matrix 215
double blind 213	hypothesis 211	random assignment 215
environmental control 213	independent variable (IV) 208	replication 209
experiment 208	internal validity 217	treatment levels 211

>discussionquestions

Terms in Review

1 Distinguish between the following:

 a Internal validity and external validity.

 b Preexperimental design and quasi-experimental design.

 c History and maturation.

 d Random sampling, randomization, and matching.

 e Environmental variables and extraneous variables.

2 Compare the advantages of experiments with the advantages of survey and observational methods.

3 Why would a noted business researcher say, "It is essential that we always keep in mind the model of the controlled experiment, even if in practice we have to deviate from an ideal model"?

4 What ethical problems do you see in conducting experiments with human subjects?

5 What essential characteristics distinguish a true experiment from other research designs?

Making Research Decisions

6 A lighting company seeks to study the percentage of defective glass shells being manufactured. Theoretically, the percentage of defectives is dependent on temperature, humidity, and the level of artisan expertise. Complete

historical data are available for the following variables on a daily basis for a year:

a Temperature (high, normal, low).

b Humidity (high, normal, low).

c Artisan expertise level (expert, average, mediocre).

Some experts feel that defectives also depend on production supervisors. However, data on supervisors in charge are available for only 242 of the 365 days. How should this study be conducted?

7 Describe how you would operationalize variables for experimental testing in the following research question: What are the performance differences between 10 microcomputers connected in a local-area network (LAN) and one minicomputer with 10 terminals?

8 A pharmaceuticals manufacturer is testing a drug developed to treat cancer. During the final stages of development the drug's effectiveness is being tested on individuals for different (1) dosage conditions and (2) age groups. One of the problems is patient mortality during experimentation. Justify your design recommendations through a comparison of alternatives and in terms of external and internal validity.

a Recommend the appropriate design for the experiment.

b Explain the use of control groups, blinds, and double blinds if you recommend them.

9 You are asked to develop an experiment for a study of the effect that compensation has on the response rates secured from personal interview subjects. This study will involve 300 people who will be assigned to one of the following conditions: (1) no compensation, (2) $1 compensation, and (3) $3 compensation. A number of sensitive issues will be explored concerning various social problems, and the 300 people will be drawn from the adult population. Describe your design. You may find Appendix 9a valuable for this question.

10 What type of experimental design would you recommend in each of the following cases? Suggest in some detail how you would design each study:

a A test of three methods of compensation of factory workers. The methods are hourly wage, incentive pay, and weekly salary. The dependent variable is direct labor cost per unit of output.

b A study of the effects of various levels of advertising effort and price reduction on the sale of specific branded grocery products by a retail grocery chain.

c A study to determine whether it is true that the use of fast-paced music played over a store's public address system will speed the shopping rate of customers without an adverse effect on the amount spent per customer.

Bringing Research to Life

11 Design an experiment for the opening vignette.

From Concept to Practice

12 Using Exhibit 9-4, diagram an experiment described in one of the Snapshots in this chapter using research design symbols.

From the Headlines

13 Much Internet advertising is priced based on click-through activity. A prospect is shown an ad on a host website based on search words he or she might have entered in a search engine such as Google or Bing. If the prospect clicks directly on the ad they see on the host website to visit the advertiser's site, the ad is considered effective and the advertiser must pay the host website for the ad. But research in 2009 revealed that while all prospects do not click on the ad they are shown on a host website, many do visit the advertiser's site. They simply key in the advertiser's URL directly into their browser or search engine. How would you design an experiment to determine if non-click-through ads displayed on your host website were actually effective in getting a prospect to an advertiser's website?

>cases*

McDonald's Tests Catfish Sandwich	NetConversions Influences Kelley Blue Book

* You will find a description of each case in the Case Abstracts section of the textbook. Check the Case Index to determine whether a case provides data, the research instrument, video, or other supplementary material. Written cases are downloadable from the text website (www.mhhe.com/cooper11e). All video material and video cases are available from the Online Learning Center.

>appendix9a

Complex Experimental Designs

Earlier in the chapter, we discussed true experimental designs in their most frequently used forms, but researchers often require an extension of the basic design for sophisticated experiments and market tests. Extensions differ from the traditional designs in (1) the number of different experimental stimuli that are considered simultaneously by the experimenter and (2) the extent to which assignment procedures are used to increase precision.

Before we consider the types of variations, there are some commonly used terms that should be defined. *Factor* is widely used to denote an independent variable. Factors are divided into treatment levels, which represent various subgroups. A factor may have two or more levels, such as (1) male and female; (2) large, medium, and small; or (3) no training, brief training, and extended training. These levels should be defined operationally.

Factors also may be classified by whether the experimenter can manipulate the levels associated with the participant. *Active factors* are those the researcher can manipulate by causing a participant to receive one level or another. Treatment is used to denote the different levels of active factors. With the second type, the *blocking factor,* the experimenter can only identify and classify the participant on an existing level. Gender, age group, customer status, and ethnicity are examples of blocking factors, because the participant comes to the experiment with a preexisting level of each.

Up to this point, the assumption is that experimental participants are people, but this is often not so. A broader term is *test unit;* it can refer equally well to an individual, product type, geographic market, medium of information dissemination, and innumerable other entities.[*]

Completely Randomized Design

The basic form of the true experiment is a completely randomized design. To illustrate its use, and that of more complex designs, consider a decision now facing the pricing manager at the Top Cannery. He would like to know what the ideal difference in price is between Top's private brand of canned vegetables and national brands such as Del Monte and Stokely's.

[*]Check this website for examples of industrial experiments: http://www.statsoft.com/.

It is possible to set up an experiment on price differentials for canned green beans. Eighteen company stores and three price spreads (treatment levels) of 7 cents, 12 cents, and 17 cents between the company brand and national brands are used for the study. Six of the stores are assigned randomly to each of the treatment groups. The price differentials are maintained for a period, and then a tally is made of the sales volumes and gross profits of the canned green beans for each group of stores.

This design can be diagrammed as follows:

$$\begin{array}{cccc} R & O_1 & X_1 & O_2 \\ R & O_3 & X_3 & O_4 \\ R & O_5 & X_5 & O_6 \end{array} \quad \text{(A1)}$$

Here, O_1, O_3, and O_5 represent the total gross profits for canned green beans in the treatment stores for the month before the test. X_1, X_3, and X_5 represent 7-cent, 12-cent, and 17-cent treatments, while O_2, O_4, and O_6 are the gross profits for the month after the test started.

We assume that the randomization of stores to the three treatment groups was sufficient to make the three store groups equivalent. When there is reason to believe this is not so, we must use a more complex design.

Randomized Block Design

If there is a single major extraneous variable, the randomized block design is used. Random assignment is still the basic way to produce equivalence among treatment groups, but the researcher may need additional assurances. First, if the sample being studied is very small, it is risky to depend on random assignment alone to guarantee equivalence. Small samples, such as the 18 company stores, are typical in field experiments because of high costs or because few test units are available. Another reason for blocking is to learn whether treatments bring different results among various groups of participants.

Consider again the canned green beans pricing experiment. Assume there is reason to believe that lower-income families are more sensitive to price differentials than are higher-income families. This factor could seriously distort our results unless we stratify the stores by customer income. Therefore, each of the 18 stores is assigned to

229

one of three income blocks and randomly assigned, within blocks, to the price difference treatments. The design is shown in the following table.

Active Factor: Price Difference	Blocking Factor: Customer Income			
		High	Medium	Low
7 cents	R	X_1	X_1	X_1
12 cents	R	X_2	X_2	X_2
17 cents	R	X_3	X_3	X_3

(A2)

Note: The O's have been omitted. The horizontal rows no longer indicate a time sequence, but various levels of the blocking factor. However, before-and-after measurements are associated with each of the treatments.

In this design, one can measure both main effects and interaction effects. The *main effect* is the average direct influence that a particular treatment of the independent variable (IV) has on the dependent variable (DV), independent of other factors. The *interaction effect* is the influence of one factor or variable on the effect of another. The main effect of each price difference is discovered by calculating the impact of each of the three treatments averaged over the different blocks. Interaction effects occur if you find that different customer income levels have a pronounced influence on customer reactions to the price differentials. (See Chapter 17, "Hypothesis Testing.")

Whether the randomized block design improves the precision of the experimental measurement depends on how successfully the design minimizes the variation within blocks and maximizes the variation between blocks. If the response patterns are about the same in each block, there is little value to the more complex design. Blocking may be counterproductive.

Latin Square Design

The Latin square design may be used when there are two major extraneous factors. To continue with the pricing example, assume we decide to block on the size of store and on customer income. It is convenient to consider these two blocking factors as forming the rows and columns of a table. We divide each factor into three levels to provide nine groups of stores, each representing a unique combination of the two blocking variables. Treatments are then randomly assigned to these cells so that a given treatment appears only once in each row and column. Because of this restriction, a Latin Square must have the same number

of rows, columns, and treatments. The design looks like the following table.

Store Size	Customer Income		
	High	Medium	Low
Large	X_3	X_1	X_2
Medium	X_2	X_3	X_1
Small	X_1	X_2	X_3

(A3)

Treatments can be assigned by using a table of random numbers to set the order of treatment in the first row. For example, the pattern may be 3, 1, 2 as shown above. Following this, the other two cells of the first column are filled similarly, and the remaining treatments are assigned to meet the restriction that there can be no more than one treatment type in each row and column.

The experiment takes place, sales results are gathered, and the average treatment effect is calculated. From this, we can determine the main effect of the various price spreads on the sales of company and national brands. The cost information allows us to discover which price differential produces the greatest margin.

A limitation of the Latin square is that we must assume there is no interaction between treatments and blocking factors. Therefore, we cannot determine the interrelationships among store size, customer income, and price spreads. This limitation exists because there is not an exposure of all combinations of treatments, store sizes, and customer income groups. Such an exposure would require a table of 27 cells, while this one has only 9. If one is not especially interested in interaction, the Latin square is much more economical.

Factorial Design

One commonly held misconception about experiments is that the researcher can manipulate only one variable at a time. This is not true; with factorial designs, you can deal with more than one treatment simultaneously. Consider again the pricing experiment. The president of the chain might also be interested in finding the effect of posting unit prices on the shelf to aid shopper decision making. The following table can be used to design an experiment that includes both the price differentials and the unit pricing.

Unit Price Information?	Price Spread		
	7 Cents	12 Cents	17 Cents
Yes	X_1Y_1	X_1Y_2	X_1Y_3
No	X_2Y_1	X_2Y_2	X_2Y_3

(A4)

This is known as a 2 × 3 factorial design in which we use two factors: one with two levels and one with three levels of intensity.* The version shown here is completely randomized, with the stores being randomly assigned to one of six treatment combinations. With such a design, it is possible to estimate the main effects of each of the two independent variables and the interactions between them. The results can help to answer the following questions:

1. What are the sales effects of the different price spreads between company and national brands?

2. What are the sales effects of using unit-price marking on the shelves?

3. What are the sales effect interrelations between price spread and the presence of unit-price information?

*We describe factorial designs used with conjoint analysis in Chapter 19.

Covariance Analysis

We have discussed direct control of extraneous variables through blocking. It is also possible to apply some degree of indirect statistical control on one or more variables through analysis of covariance. Even with randomization, one may find that the before-measurement shows an average knowledge-level difference between experimental and control groups. With covariance analysis, one can adjust statistically for this before-difference. Another application might occur if the canned green beans pricing experiment were carried out with a completely randomized design, only to reveal a contamination effect from differences in average customer income levels. With covariance analysis, one can still do some statistical blocking on average customer income after the experiment has been run.†

†We discuss the statistical aspects of covariance analysis with analysis of variance (ANOVA) in Chapter 17.

>appendix9b

Test Markets

This section examines traditional and emerging designs for test marketing, including the characteristics of six test market types and the strengths and weaknesses of each type.

A *test market* is a controlled experiment conducted in a carefully chosen marketplace (e.g., website, store, town, or other geographic location) to measure marketplace response and predict sales or profitability of a product. The objective of a market test study is to help marketing managers introduce new products or services, add products to existing lines, identify concepts with potential, or relaunch enhanced versions of established brands. By testing the viability of a product, managers reduce the risks of failure. Complex experimental designs are often required to meet the controlled experimental conditions of test markets. They also are used in other research in which control of extraneous variables is essential.

The successful introduction of new products is critical to a firm's financial success. Failures not only create significant losses for companies but also hurt the brand and company reputation. According to ACNielsen, the failure rate for new products approaches 70 percent.[1] Estimates from other sources vary between 40 and 90 percent depending on whether the products are in consumer or industrial markets. Product failure may be attributable to many factors, especially inadequate research. Test-marketed products, typically evaluated in consumer industries, enjoy a significantly higher success rate because managers can reduce their decision risk through reality testing. They gauge the effectiveness of pricing, packaging, promotions, distribution channels, dealer response, advertising copy, media usage patterns, and other aspects of the marketing mix. Test markets also help managers evaluate improved versions of existing products and services.

Test Market Selection

There are several criteria to consider when selecting test market locations. As we mentioned earlier, one of the primary advantages of a carefully conducted experiment is external validity or the ability to generalize to (and across) times, settings, or persons. The location and characteristics of participants should be *representative* of the market in which the product will compete. This requires consideration of the product's target competitive environment, market size, patterns of media coverage, distribution channels, product usage, population size, housing, income, lifestyle attributes, age, and ethnic characteristics. Not even "typical" all-American cities are ideal for all market tests. Kimberly-Clark's Depend and Poise brand products for bladder control could not be adequately tested in a college town. Cities that are overtested create problems for market selection because savvy participants' prior experiences cause them to respond atypically.

Multiple locations are often required for optimal demographic balance. Sales may vary by region, necessitating test sites that have characteristics equivalent to those of the targeted national market. Several locations may also be required for experimental and control groups.

Media coverage and *isolation* are additional criteria for locating the test. Although the test location may not be able to duplicate precisely a national media plan, it should adequately represent the planned promotion through print and broadcast coverage. Large metropolitan areas produce media spillover that may contaminate the test area. Advertising is wasted as the media alerts distributors, retailers, and consumers in adjacent areas about the product. Competitors are warned more quickly about testing activities and the test loses it competitive advantage. In 2002, Dairy Queen (DQ) Corp., which has 5,700 stores throughout the world, began testing electronic irradiated burgers at the Hutchinson and Spicer locations in Minnesota. No quick-service restaurant chains provide irradiated burgers, although McDonald's and Burger King also researched this option. DQ originally focused information about the test at the store level rather than with local media. When the *Minneapolis Star Tribune* ran a story about the test, DQ had to inform all Minnesota store operators about the article, although all operators had known about the planned test. The article created awareness for anti-irradiation activists and the potential for demonstrations—an unplanned consequence of the test market.[2] Although relatively isolated communities are more desirable because their remoteness aids controlling critical promotional features of the test, in this instance media spillover and unintended consequences of unplanned media coverage became a concern.

The *control of distribution* affects test locations and types of test markets. Cooperation from distributors is essential for market tests conducted by the product's manufacturer. The distributor should sell exclusively in the test market to avoid difficulties arising from out-of-market warehousing, shipping, and inventory control. When distributors in the city are either unavailable or uncooperative, a controlled test, in which the research firm manages distribution, should be considered.

Types of Test Markets

There are six major types of test markets: standard, controlled, electronic, simulated, virtual, and Web-enabled. In this section, we discuss their characteristics, advantages and disadvantages, and future uses.

Standard Test Market
The *standard test market* is a traditional test of a product and/or marketing mix variables on a limited geographic basis. It provides a real-world test for evaluating products and marketing programs on a smaller, less costly scale. The firm launching the product selects specific sales zones, test market cities, or regions that have characteristics comparable to those of the intended consumers of the product. The firm performs the test through its existing distribution channels, using the same elements as used in a national rollout. Exhibit 9b-1 shows some U.S. cities commonly used as test markets.

Standard test markets benefit from using actual distribution channels and discovering the amount of trade support necessary to launch and sustain the product. High costs ($1 million is typical, ranging upward to $30 million) and long time (12 to 18 months for a go/no-go decision) are disadvantages. The loss of secrecy when the test exposes the concept to the competition further complicates the usefulness of traditional tests.

In March 2000, in an affluent suburb of Indianapolis, Shell Oil Co. test-marketed the first robotic gas pump that allows drivers to serve themselves without leaving their cars. The innovation, which uses a combination of robotics, sensors, and cameras to guide the fuel nozzle into a vehicle's gas tank, took eight years to develop. Its features allow a parent to stay with children while pumping gas and enable a driver to avoid exposure to gas fumes or the risk of spillage, static fire, or even bad weather. Unfortunately, the product requires a coded computer chip containing vehicle information that must be placed on the windshield and a special, spring-loaded gas cap, which costs $20. The introduction could hardly have been more ill-timed. Just as gasoline prices began their upward advance and the end of winter removed the incentive for staying behind the wheel, Shell planned to charge an extra $1 per fill-up.[3]

Controlled Test Markets
The term *controlled test market* refers to real-time forced distribution tests conducted by a specialty research supplier that guarantees distribution of the test product through outlets in selected cities. The test locations represent a proportion of the marketer's total store sales volume. The research firm typically handles the retailer sell-in process and all distribution activities for the client during the market test. The firm offers financial incentives for distributors to obtain shelf space from nationally prominent retailers and provides merchandising, inventory, pricing, and stocking control. Using scanner-based, survey, and other data sources, the research service gathers sales, market share, and consumer demographics data, as well as information on first-year volumes.

Companies such as ACNielsen Market Decisions and Information Resources Inc. give consumer packaged-goods

The SmartPump is a robotic gas pump that dispenses fuel without the customer ever getting out of the car. Customers pay an additional $1 for the service.

www.shell.com

>Exhibit 9b-1 Test Market Cities

Source: Acxiom Corporation, a database services company, released its first "Mirror on America" May 24, 2004, ranking America's top 150 Metropolitan Statistical Areas (MSAs) on overall consumer test market characteristics. "Which American City Provides the Best Consumer Test Market?" http://www.acxiom.com/default.aspx?ID=2521&Country_Code=USA. Also see http://www.bizjournals.com/phoenix/stories/2000/11/20/daily5.html and http://celebrity-network.net/trc/business.htm.

(CPG) manufacturers the ability to evaluate sales potential while reducing the risks of new or relaunched products prior to a national rollout. Market Decisions, for example, has over 25 small to medium-size test markets available nationwide. Typically, consumers experience all the elements associated with the first-year marketing plan, including media advertising and consumer and trade promotions. Manufacturers with a substantial commitment to a national rollout also have the opportunity to "fast-track" products during a condensed time period (three to six months) before launch.[4]

Controlled test markets cost less than traditional ones (although they may reach several million dollars per year). They reduce the likelihood of competitor monitoring and provide a streamlined distribution function through the sponsoring research firm. Their drawbacks include the number of markets evaluated, the use of incentives—which distort trade cost estimates—and the evaluation of advertising.

> *Consumer packaged goods are consumer goods packaged by manufacturers and not sold unpackaged (in bulk) at the retail level (e.g., food, drinks, personal care products)*

Electronic Test Markets

An *electronic test market* is a test system that combines store distribution services, consumer scanner panels, and household-level media delivery in specifically designated markets. Retailers and cable TV operators have cooperative arrangements with the research firm in these markets. Electronic test markets, previously used with consumer packaged-goods brands, have the capability to measure marketing mix variables that drive trial and repeat purchases by demographic segment for both CPG and non-CPG brands. Information Resources Inc. (IRI), for example, offers a service called BehaviorScan, which is also known as a *split-cable test* or *single-source test,* that combines scanner-based consumer panels with sophisticated broadcasting systems. IRI uses a combination of Designated Market Area–level cut-ins on broadcast networks and local cable cut-ins to assess the effect of the advertising that the household panel views. IRI and ACNielsen collect supermarket, drugstore, and mass merchandiser scanner data used in such systems. The BehaviorScan service makes use of these data with respondents who are then exposed to different commercials with various advertising weights.[5]

IRI's TV system operates as a within-market TV advertising testing service. The five BehaviorScan markets are Eau Claire, Wisconsin; Cedar Rapids, Iowa; Midland, Texas; Pittsfield, Massachusetts; and Grand Junction, Colorado. As small markets, with populations of 75,000 to 215,000, they provide lower marketing support costs than other test markets and offer appropriate experimental controls over the test conditions. Although several thousand households may be used, by assigning every local cable subscriber a cell, the service can indiscernibly deliver different TV commercials to each cell and evaluate the effect of the advertising on the panelists' purchasing behavior. For a control, nonpanelist households in the cable cell are interviewed by telephone.

BehaviorScan tracks the actual purchases of a household panel through bar-coded products at the point of purchase. Participants show their identification card at a participating store and are also asked to "report purchases from non-participating retailers, including mass merchandisers and supercenters, by using a handheld scanner at home."[6] Computer programs link the household's purchases with television viewing data to get a refined estimate (± 10 percent) of the product's national sales potential in the first year. Consider the observation of a Frito-Lay senior vice president:

> BehaviorScan is a critical component of Frito-Lay's go-to-market strategy for a couple of reasons. First, it gives us absolutely the most accurate read on the sales potential of a new product, and a well-rounded view of consumer response to all elements of the marketing mix. Second, BehaviorScan TV ad testing enables us to significantly increase our return on our advertising investment.[7]

The advantages of electronic test markets are apparent from the quality of strategic information provided but suffer from an artifact of their identification card data collection strategy: participants may not be representative.

Simulated Test Markets A *simulated test market (STM)* occurs in a laboratory research setting designed to simulate a traditional shopping environment using a sample of the product's consumers. STMs do not occur in the marketplace but are often considered a pretest before a full-scale market test. STMs are designed to determine consumer response to product initiatives in a compressed time period. A computer model, containing assumptions of how the new product would sell, is augmented with data provided by the participants in the simulation.

STMs have common characteristics: (1) Consumers are interviewed to ensure that they meet product usage and demographic criteria; (2) they visit a research facility where they are exposed to the test product and may be shown commercials or print advertisements for target and competitive products; (3) they shop in a simulated store environment (often resembling a supermarket aisle); (4) those not purchasing the product are offered free samples;

(5) follow-up information is collected to assess product reactions and to estimate repurchase intentions; and (6) researchers combine the completed computer model with consumer reactions in order to forecast the likely trial purchase rates, sales volume, and adoption behavior prior to market entry.

When in-store variations are used, research suppliers select three to five cities representing the market where the product will be launched. They choose a mall with a high frequency of targeted consumers. In the mall, a simulated store in a vacant facility is stocked with products from the test category. Intercept interviews qualify participants for a 15-minute test during which participants view an assortment of print or television advertisements and are asked to recall salient features. Measures of new product awareness are obtained. With "dollars" provided by the research firm, participants may purchase the test product or any of the competing products. Advertising awareness, packaging, and adoption are assessed with a computer model, as in the laboratory setting. Purchasers may be offered additional opportunities to buy the product at a reduced price in the future.

STMs were widely adopted in the 1970s by global manufacturers as an alternative to standard test markets, which were considered more expensive, slower, and less protected. Although STM models continue to work somewhat well in today's mass-market world, their effectiveness will diminish in the next decade as the one-to-one marketing environment becomes more diverse. To obtain forecast accuracy at the individual level, not just trial or repeat probabilities, STMs require individualized marketing plans to estimate different promotional and advertising factors for each person.[8]

M/A/R/C Research, Inc., has what it calls its *Assessor* model with many features that address the deficiencies of previous STM forecasting models. For example, instead of a comparison of consumer reactions to historical databases, individual consumer preferences and current experiences with existing brands help to define the fit for the new product environment. A competitive context pertinent to each consumer's unique set of alternatives plays a prominent role in new product assessment. Important user segments (e.g., parent brand users, heavy users, or teenagers) are analyzed separately to capture distinct behaviors. According to M/A/R/C, the results of three different models (attitudinal preference models; a trial, repeat, depth-of-repeat model; and a behavioral decision model) are merged to reduce the influence of bias. From an accuracy standpoint, over 90 percent of the validated Assessor forecasts are within 10 percent of the actual, in-market sales volume figures.[9] Realistically, plus or minus 10 percent represents a level of precision that many firms are not willing to accept.

STMs offer several benefits. The cost ($50,000 to $150,000) is one-tenth of the cost of a traditional test

Is Current Test Marketing Representative?

With 70 percent of new product introductions failing, the test market, a long-standing experimental research tradition in the marketing research of consumer goods, is under attack. A test market involves placing a new product in a sample of stores, usually in two or more cities, and then monitoring sales performance under different promotion, pricing, and physical placement conditions. Nonproponents claim the racial diversity of the U.S. population is not well reflected in several U.S. cities often chosen to provide crucial evidence of product viability. Cedar Rapids (Iowa), Columbus (Ohio), Little Rock (Arkansas), and Evansville (Indiana), four popular test market locations, are primarily populated by non-Hispanic white households. Yet 22.9 percent of U.S. households claimed a different ethnic background in the Census Bureau's 2000 decennial census. Information Resources, Inc.

(IRI), whose *BehaviorScan* syndicated research uses similar cities, claims household demographics are only one criterion for site choice. Valerie Skala, IRI's vice president of Analytic Product Management and Development, claims "category and brand purchase patterns, as well as representative retail development," are more important. Test marketing site choice is also determined by cost and availability of retailers willing to stock the new product. IRI and VNU's ACNielsen Market Decisions have contracts with retailers that facilitate immediate placement, eliminating the need to negotiate placement with each store's corporate office. Does the absence of comparable demographics in test markets render the test market methodology faulty?

www.nielsen.com; http://us.infores.com/

market, competitor exposure is minimized, time is reduced to six to eight months, and modeling allows the evaluation of many marketing mix variables. The inability to measure trade acceptance and its lack of broad-based consumer response are its drawbacks.

Virtual Test Markets

A *virtual test market* uses a computer simulation and hardware to replicate the immersion of an interactive shopping experience in a three-dimensional environment. Essential to the immersion experience is the system's ability to render realistically product offerings in real time. Other features of interactive systems are the ability to explore (navigate in the virtual world) and manipulate the content in real time. In virtual test markets, the participants move through a store and display area containing the product. They handle the product by touching its image and examine it dimensionally with a rotation device to inspect labels, prices, usage instructions, and packaging. Purchases are made by placing the product in a shopping cart. Data collected include time spent by product category, frequency and time with product manipulation, and order quantity and sequence, as well as video feedback of participant behavior.

An example of a virtual environment application reveals it as an inexpensive research tool:

Goodyear conducted a study of nearly 1,000 people. . . . Each respondent took a trip through a number of different virtual tire stores stocked with a variety of brands and models. . . . Goodyear found the results of the test valuable on several fronts. First, the research revealed the extent to which shoppers in different market segments valued

the Goodyear brand over competing brands. Second, the test suggested strategies for repricing the product line.[10]

Virtual test markets are part of a family of virtual technology techniques dating back to the early 1990s. The term *Virtual Shopping*® was registered by Allison Research Technologies (ART) in the mid-90s.[11] ART's interfaces create a detailed virtual environment (supermarket, bar/tavern, convenience store, fast-food restaurant, drugstore, computer store, car dealership, and so forth) for participant interaction. Consumers use a display interface to point out what products are appealing or what they might purchase. Products, in CPG and non-CPG categories, are arrayed just as in an actual store. Data analysis includes the current range of sophisticated research techniques and simulated test market methodologies.[12] Improvements in virtual reality technology are creating opportunities for multisensory shopping. Current visual and auditory environments are being augmented with additional modes of sensory perception such as touch, taste, and smell.

A hybrid market test that bridges virtual environments and Internet platforms begins to solve the difficult challenge of product design teams: concept selection. A traditional reliance on expensive physical prototypes may be resolved with virtual prototypes. Virtual prototypes were discovered to provide results comparable to those of physical ones, cost less to construct, and allow Web researchers to explore more concepts. In some cases, however, the computer renderings make virtual prototypes look better in virtual reality and score lower in physical reality—specially when comparisons are made with commercially available products.[13]

Web-Enabled Test Markets   Manufacturers have found an efficient way to test new products, refine old ones, survey customer attitudes, and build relationships. *Web-enabled test markets* are product tests using online distribution. They are primarily used by large CPG manufacturers that seek fast, cost-effective means for estimating new product demand. Although they offer less control than traditional experimental design, Procter & Gamble test-marketed Dryel, the home dry-cleaning product, for more than three years on 150,000 households in a traditional fashion while Drugstore.com tested the online market before its launch in 1999, taking less than a week and surveying about 100 people. Procter & Gamble now conducts 40 percent of its 6,000 product tests online. The company's annual research budget is about $140 million, but it believes that figure can be halved by shifting research projects to the Internet.[14]

In 2000, when P&G geared up to launch Crest Whitestrips, a home tooth-bleaching kit, its high retail price created uncertainty. After an eight-month campaign offering the strips solely through the product's dedicated website, it sold 144,000 whitening kits online. Promoting the online sale, P&G ran TV spots, placed advertisements in lifestyle magazines, and sent e-mails to customers who signed up to receive product updates (12 percent of whom subsequently made a purchase). Retailers were convinced to stock the product, even at the high price. By timing the introduction with additional print and TV ad campaigns, P&G sold nearly $50 million worth of Crest Whitestrips kits three months later.[15] P&G's success has been emulated by its competitors and represents a growing trend. General Mills, Quaker, and a number of popular start-ups have followed, launching online test-marketing projects of their own.

>chapter 10

Surveys

>**learning**objectives

After reading this chapter, you should understand...

1 The process for selecting the appropriate and optimal communication approach.

2 What factors affect participation in communication studies.

3 The major sources of error in communication studies and how to minimize them.

4 The major advantages and disadvantages of the three communication approaches.

5 Why an organization might outsource a communication study.

> " There once was a demographic survey done to determine if money was connected to happiness, and Ireland was the only place where this did not turn out to be true. "
>
> Fiona Shaw, Irish actress and theater director

>**bringing**research**to**life

Henry and Associates has been asked by Albany Outpatient Laser Clinic Inc. to develop a survey to assess patient satisfaction. As part of the exploratory phase, Sara has been reviewing documentation provided by the clinic. Complaint letters were included in the documentation.

"Jason, you'll enjoy this one," Sara comments as she joins him for their meeting to discuss the Albany Outpatient Laser Clinic patient satisfaction project. She extends the letter and smiles widely.

"Is that the letter that clinic administrator George Bowlus promised he'd send over this morning?" Sara nods as she passes it across the desk.

Edna Koogan, P. A., Attorney at Law
P. O. Box 8219-2767
Albany, New York 12212-2767

Dr. Edith Coblenz, M.D.
3456 Barshoot Building
Albany, New York 12212

Dear Edith,

I want you to have my side of this morning's incident at the Albany Outpatient Laser Clinic Inc. I am sure you have by now heard from the business manager and the admissions director and possibly the anesthetist. You are a stockholder in the center, I know, and as your former lawyer and current patient, I thought I owed you a warning and explanation.

You told me to report to the center at 7 a.m. for a workup in preparation for eye surgery tomorrow. I caught a cab and was there at 6:55 promptly. I identified myself as your patient, and at once the receptionist called someone from the back room and said, "Ms. Koogan's personal physician is Dr. Coblenz," which is, of course, not true, as you are my eye doctor. But I was too cold to argue since they had left us standing in the snow until 7:10.

A fellow insisted on taking my glasses and medications with him "for a workup." As soon as he disappeared with my glasses a second admissions clerk appeared and handed me a "questionnaire" to fill out. It appeared to be a photocopy of a photocopy of a photocopy and was very faintly printed in small gray type on a light gray sheet. When I pointed out that I was about to be admitted for treatment of glaucoma, a leading cause of blindness, she told me, "Do the best you can." When I objected emphatically, she seemed taken aback. I suppose most of her 80-year-old patients are more compliant, but I guess I am an intractable old attorney.

Was I wrong to object to the questionnaire being too faint and the type too small? Am I the first glaucoma patient who has ever been treated at the Laser Center? One would think they would understand you can't ask someone blind in one eye to fill out such a questionnaire, especially without her glasses. The clerk finally, grudgingly, asked me to sit by her side, so she could help me.

There were several questions about my name, address, age, and occupation. Then she wanted to know the name of the admitting physician and then the phone number (but not the name) of the physician who was most familiar with my health. I said the admitting physician was an eye doctor and the physician most familiar with my health was a GP, and asked, which did she want the phone number for, the eye doctor or the GP? She admonished me to try and "get over that bad attitude." Then she told me to go fill out the form as best I could.

Dr. Edith Coblenz, M.D.   Page 2

A very nice patient (hemorrhoids, no vision problems) offered to help me. She began reading the questionnaire and came to the item "Past Medical History: Yes or No." She didn't think this made any sense, and neither did I, because everyone has a past medical history, and no one would answer no; but after a while we decided that it meant I should answer yes or no to all of the questions underneath, such as: Did I have diabetes? Did I have heart disease? When we came to "Have you ever had or been treated for the flu?" we could not decide if it meant, have I ever had the flu? Or have I had flu recently (I had flu six months ago, but is that "recent"?) so we asked the receptionist. She became almost speechless and said she would get me some help.

After a while the "help" appeared—a nurse who wanted to measure my blood pressure and induce me to take a blue pill, which she said would be good for my "nerves." I refused and pointed out rather curtly that this was not a gulag but an admissions department, a place of business, for crying out loud, where they ought to be able to handle a little criticism from someone trained to elicit accurate information.

By then several nice people had pitched in to help me with the questionnaire. But this made it even harder to decide on the answers, because we understood so many of the questions differently and couldn't agree. When we came to "Are all your teeth intact?" One man thought it meant, "Do you have false teeth?" And another thought it meant, "Do you have any broken dentures?" But a woman who assured me her son is a dentist said it meant, "Do you have any loose teeth?" We couldn't decide how to settle this issue.

Then there was the question "Do you have limited motion of your neck?" and by then everyone was enjoying the incongruity of these questions. Of course I have limited motion of the neck. Doesn't everyone? We decided to save that question for later clarification.

After all of the yes-no questions there came various other stumpers, such as "Please list your current medications." The problem is, of course, that I have purple eye drops and yellow eye drops, but the young man had taken them away from me "for a workup," so I had no way of accurately answering the questions. I was pretty sure one of them was glucagon, so I guessed and put that down, but then I had second thoughts and scratched it out. (When I got home, I checked and it was betagan, not glucagon.)

There were four of us working on the questionnaire by then, and we were laughing and crowing and having a high time and discharging our anxieties, which further annoyed the admissions clerk. So she called the anesthetist, a stuck-up young fellow who said he had written the questionnaire himself and had never had any problems with it. That is when I told him, if he had not had any problems with this questionnaire, this proved it was better to be lucky than smart.

He said he was going to overlook my "attitude" because he knew I was old and anxious about the coming operation. I told him I was going to take my business somewhere else because of the bilaterality problem. "What is that?" he asked. I said, I have two eyes, and if anyone as dumb as him went after me with a laser, he would probably cut the wrong eye.

I caught a cab and sent my neighbor back for my glasses. As your lawyer, I urge you not to further involve yourself with such fools.

Edna

"It would seem that Albany Clinic might need help. With questionnaire development," comments Jason.   Sara responds sarcastically, "You think?"

> Characteristics of the Communication Approach

Research designs can be classified by the approach used to gather primary data. There are two alternatives. We can observe conditions, behavior, events, people, or processes. Or we can *communicate* with people about various topics, including participants' attitudes, motivations, intentions, and expectations. The researcher determines the appropriate data collection approach largely by identifying the types of information needed—investigative questions the researcher must answer. As researchers we learn

>**Exhibit 10-1** Data Collection Approach: Impact on the Research Process

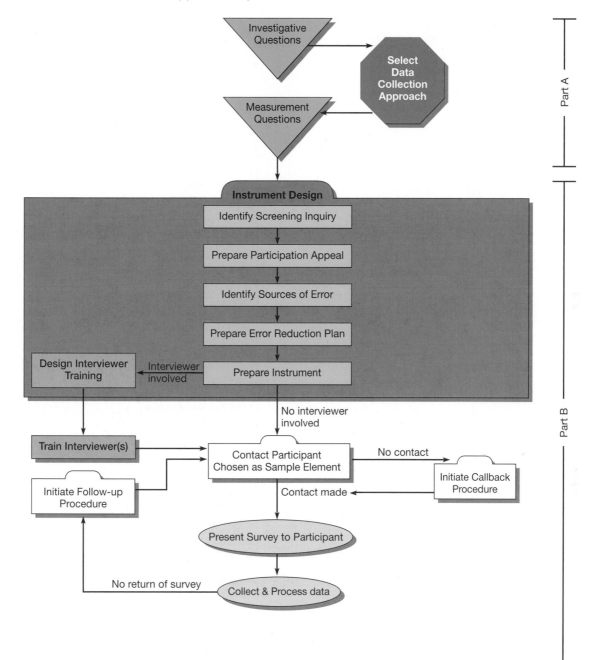

much about opinions and attitudes by communication-based research; observation techniques are incapable of revealing such critical elements. This is also true of intentions, expectations, motivations, and knowledge. Information about past events is often available only through surveying or interviewing people who remember the events. Thus, the choice of a communication versus an observation approach may seem an obvious one, given the directions in which investigative questions may lead. The characteristics of the sample unit—specifically, whether a participant can articulate his or her ideas, thoughts, and experiences—also play a role in the decision. Part A of Exhibit 10-1 shows the relationship of these decisions to the research process detailed in Chapter 4. Part B indicates how the researcher's choice of a communication approach affects the following:

- The creation and selection of the measurement questions (to be explored in Chapters 11 and 12).

- Instrument design (to be discussed in Chapter 13), which incorporates attempts to reduce error and create participant-screening procedures.

>**Exhibit 10-2** Selecting a Communication Data Collection Method

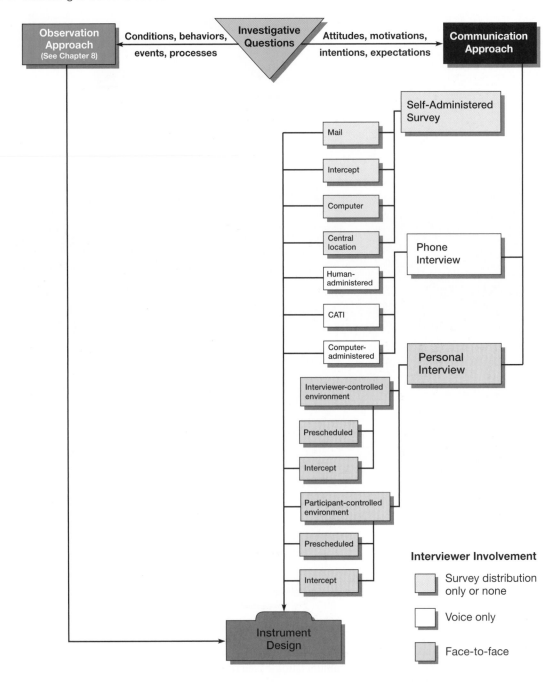

- Sampling issues (explored in Chapters 14), which drive contact and callback procedures.
- Data collection processes, which create the need for follow-up procedures (when self-administered instruments are used) and possible interviewer training (when personal or telephone surveying methods are used).

In this chapter we focus on the choices the researcher must make once the communication approach has been chosen (Exhibit 10-2). We discuss the characteristics and applications of the various communication approaches as well as their individual strengths and weaknesses (summarized in Exhibit 10-5).

The **communication approach** involves surveying or interviewing people and recording their responses for analysis. A **survey** is a measurement process used to collect information during a highly structured interview—sometimes with a human interviewer and other times without. Questions are carefully chosen or crafted, sequenced, and precisely asked of each participant. The goal of the survey is to derive comparable data across subsets of the chosen sample so that similarities and differences can be found. When combined with statistical probability sampling for selecting participants, survey findings and conclusions are projectable to large and diverse populations.

The great strength of the survey as a primary data collecting approach is its versatility. Abstract information of all types can be gathered by questioning others. Additionally, a few well-chosen questions can yield information that would take much more time and effort to gather by observation. A survey that uses the telephone, mail, a computer, e-mail, or the Internet as the medium of communication can expand geographic coverage at a fraction of the cost and time required by observation.

The bad news for communication research is that all communication research has some error. Understanding the various sources of error helps researchers avoid or diminish such error.

Error in Communication Research

As depicted in Exhibit 10-3, there are three major sources of error in communication research: measurement questions and survey instruments, interviewers, and participants. Researchers cannot help a

>**Exhibit 10-3** Sources of Error in Communication Research

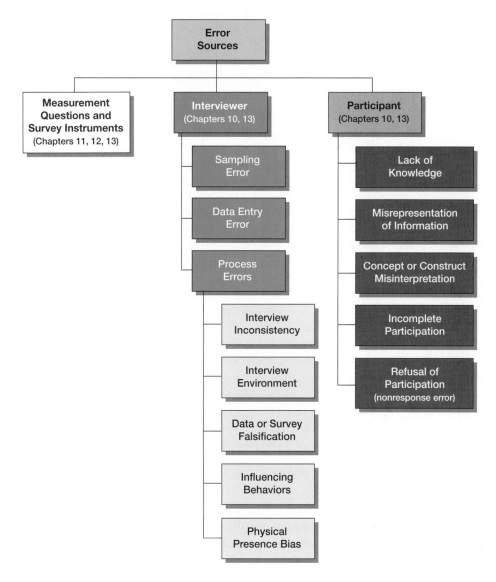

business decision maker answer a research question if they (1) select or craft inappropriate questions, (2) ask them in an inappropriate order, or (3) use inappropriate transitions and instructions to elicit information. We will spend considerable time in Chapters 11, 12, and 13 discovering ways to avoid these sources of error.

Interviewer Error

From the introduction to the conclusion of the interview, there are many points where the interviewer's control of the process can affect the quality of the data. **Interviewer error,** a major source of sampling error and response bias, is caused by numerous actions:

- *Failure to secure full participant cooperation (sampling error).* The sample is likely to be biased if interviewers do not do a good job of enlisting participant cooperation. While instrument error was evident in the Albany Clinic study, there is also a question of whether the distributor of the survey (the receptionist) contributed to the lack of data quality in the data collected from Edna. Toward the end of the communication, there is some doubt about the seriousness with which questions were answered. Stressing the importance of the information for the upcoming surgery and having a receptionist trained to serve as question interpreter/ prober could reduce this type of error.

- *Failure to record answers accurately and completely (data entry error).* Error may result from an interview recording procedure that forces the interviewer to summarize or interpret partici- pant answers or that provides insufficient space to record verbatim answers as provided by the participant.

- *Failure to consistently execute interview procedures.* The precision of survey estimates will be reduced and there will be more error around estimates to the extent that interviewers are inconsistent in ways that influence the data. In the Albany Clinic study, providing different definitions (of diseases) to different clinic patients completing the medical history would create bias.

- *Failure to establish appropriate interview environment.* Answers may be systematically inac- curate or biased when interviewers fail to appropriately train and motivate participants or fail to establish a suitable interpersonal setting.[1] Since the Albany Clinic study asked for factual rather than attitudinal data, interviewer-injected bias would have been limited. If the clinic had required the admissions clerk (who insulted Edna by referring to her negative attitude) to also conduct a postsurgery interview on patient satisfaction, the results of the latter study may have been influenced by interviewer bias.

- *Falsification of individual answers or whole interviews.* Perhaps the most insidious form of interviewer error is cheating. Surveying is difficult work, often done by part-time employees, usually with only limited training and under little direct supervision. At times, falsification of an answer to an overlooked question is perceived as an easy solution to counterbalance the incom- plete data. This easy, seemingly harmless first step can be followed by more pervasive forgery. It is not known how much of this occurs, but it should be of constant concern to research direc- tors as they develop their data collection design and to those organizations that outsource survey projects.

- *Inappropriate influencing behavior.* It is also obvious that an interviewer can distort the results of any survey by inappropriate suggestions, directions, or verbal probes; by word emphasis and question rephrasing; by tone of voice; or by body language, facial reaction to an answer, or other nonverbal signals. These activities, whether intentional or merely due to carelessness, are widespread. This problem was investigated using a simple questionnaire and participants who then reported on the interviewers. The conclusion was "The high frequency of deviations from instructed behavior is alarming."[2]

- *Physical presence bias.* Interviewers can influence participants in unperceived subtle ways. Older interviewers are often seen as authority figures by young participants, who modify their responses accordingly. Some research indicates that perceived social distance between interviewer and participant has a distorting effect, although the studies do not fully agree on just what this relationship is.[3]

In light of the numerous studies on the various aspects of interview bias, the safest course for researchers is to recognize the constant potential for response error.

Participant Error

Three broad conditions must be met by participants to have a successful survey:

- The participant must possess the information being targeted by the investigative questions.
- The participant must understand his or her role in the interview as the provider of accurate information.
- The participant must have adequate motivation to cooperate.

Thus, participants cause error in two ways: whether they respond (willingness) and how they respond.

Participation-Based Errors   Three factors influence participation:[4]

- The participant must believe that the experience will be pleasant and satisfying.
- The participant must believe that answering the survey is an important and worthwhile use of his or her time.
- The participant must dismiss any mental reservations that he or she might have about participation.

Whether the experience will be pleasant and satisfying depends heavily on the interviewer in personal and telephone surveys. Typically, participants will cooperate with an interviewer whose behavior reveals confidence and who engages people on a personal level. Effective interviewers are differentiated not by demographic characteristics but by these interpersonal skills. By confidence, we mean that most participants are immediately convinced they will want to participate in the study and cooperate fully with the interviewer. An engaging personal style is one in which the interviewer instantly establishes credibility by adapting to the individual needs of the participant. For the survey that does not employ human interpersonal influence, convincing the participant that the experience will be enjoyable is the task of a prior notification device or the study's written introduction.

For the participant to think that answering the survey is important and worthwhile, some explanation of the study's purpose is necessary, although the amount of disclosure will vary based on the sponsor's objectives. In personal or phone surveys the researcher will provide the interviewer with instructions for discovering what explanation is needed and supplying it. Usually, the interviewer states the purpose of the study, tells how the information will be used, and suggests what is expected of the participant. Participants should feel that their cooperation will be meaningful to themselves and to the survey results. When this is achieved, more participants will express their views willingly.

As depicted in Exhibit 10-4, the quality and quantity of information secured depend heavily on the ability and willingness of participants to cooperate. Potential participants often have reservations about being interviewed that must be overcome. They may suspect the interviewer has an illegitimate purpose. They may view the topic as too sensitive and thus the interview as potentially embarrassing or intrusive. Or they may feel inadequate or fear the questioning will belittle them. Previous encounters with businesses that have attempted to disguise their sales pitch or fund-raising activities as a research survey can also erode participants' willingness to cooperate. In personal and phone interviews, participants often react more to their feelings about the interviewer than to the content of the questions.

At the core of a survey or interview is an interaction between two people or between a person and a questionnaire. In the interaction the participant is asked to provide information. While he or she has hope of some minimal personal reward—in the form of compensation for participation or enhanced

>Exhibit 10-4 Factors Influencing Participant Motivation

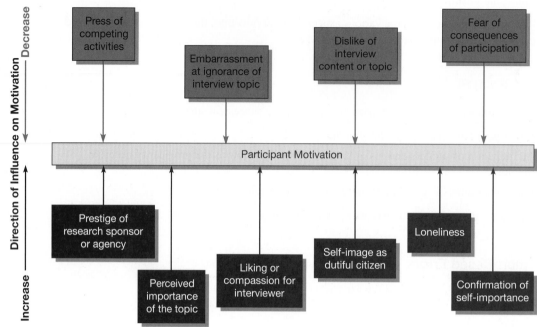

Source: Influenced by Robert L. Kahn and Charles F. Cannell, "Interviewing," in David L. Sills, ed., *International Encyclopedia of the Social Sciences*, vol. 8, p. 153. Copyright © 1968 by Crowell Collier and Macmillan, Inc.

status or knowledge—he or she has little hope of receiving any immediate or direct benefit from the data extracted. Thus, participant motivation is a responsibility of the researcher and the interviewer. Studies of reactions to many surveys show that participants can be motivated to participate in personal and phone interviews and, in fact, can even enjoy the experience. In one study, more than 90 percent of participants said the interview experience was interesting, and three-fourths reported they were willing to be interviewed again.[5] In intercept/self-administered studies, the interviewer's primary role is to encourage participation as the participant completes the questionnaire on his or her own. Taking away Edna's glasses, along with the natural anxiety associated with eye surgery, would not have encouraged Edna's participation. However, the "required" nature of the information (we assume surgery would not commence without prior completion of the questionnaire) guaranteed Edna's participation, no matter how grudgingly given.

By failing to respond or refusing to respond, participants create a nonrepresentative sample for the study overall or for a particular item or question in the study. In surveys, **nonresponse error** occurs when the responses of participants differ in some systematic way from the responses of nonparticipants. This occurs when the researcher (1) cannot locate the person (the predesignated sample element) to be studied or (2) is unsuccessful in encouraging that person to participate. This is an especially difficult problem when you are using a probability sample of subjects. Many studies have shown that better-educated individuals and those more interested in the topic participate in surveys. A high percentage of those who reply to a given survey have usually replied to others, while a large share of those who do not respond are habitual nonparticipants.[6]

Researchers are not without actions to avoid or diminish the error discussed above. We will explore these options in detail in Chapters 11 through 14. Despite its challenges, communicating with research participants—and the use of the survey—is the principal method of marketing research.

Response-Based Errors   **Response error** is generated in two ways: when the participant fails to give a correct answer or fails to give the complete answer. The interviewer can do little about the

Starwood Hotels Measures the Power of Comments

Many hotels do continuous monitoring of guest satisfaction through room-placed survey cards. Starwood Hotels and Resorts, parent company for Westin, Sheraton, Four Points by Sheraton, St. Regis, W Hotels, and The Luxury Collection hotel chains, has added a slightly different twist to such efforts. Starwood and their marketing research partner Anderson Analytics are developing models to predict a customer's likelihood of return to a brand. The method involves incorporating quantitative overall satisfaction scores and analysis of a customer's write-in responses, called *verbatims*. The first foray into such analysis sampled more than 30,000 surveys with verbatims drawn from more than 5 million surveys over a five-year period. Tom Anderson, managing partner for Anderson Analytics, revealed that "assigning interpretive codes to those verbatims needed to be a joint process between managers of various hotel functions and researchers." Analysis using SPSS software revealed

one key discovery: a guest who complains during his or her stay *and* has his or her complaint satisfactorily resolved is no more likely to give a low return-to-brand score on the survey than is a guest who never experiences a problem. Analysis also discovered key words and phrases in verbatims that are indicative of greater likelihood of a high return-to-brand score. SPSS estimates that firms ignore almost 80 percent of existing data in their warehouses because such data are in the form of verbatims. Marrying quantitative scores with the power of customer comments should give Starwood a far more complete picture and the power to make every guest's stay a positively remarkable one.

www.andersonanalytics.com; www.starwoodhotels.com; www.spss.com

participant's information level. Screening questions qualify participants when there is doubt about their ability to answer. The most appropriate applications for communication research are those where participants are uniquely qualified to provide the desired information. Questions can be used to inquire about characteristics of a participant, such as his or her household income, age, sexual preference, ethnicity, or family lifecycle stage. Questions can also be asked that reveal information exclusively internal to the participant. We include here items such as the participant's lifestyle, attitudes, opinions, expectations, knowledge, motivations, and intentions.

If we ask participants to report on events that they have not personally experienced, we need to assess the replies carefully. If our purpose is to learn what the participant understands to be the case, it is legitimate to accept the answers given. But if our intent is to learn what the event or situation actually was, we must recognize that the participant is reporting secondhand data and the accuracy of the information declines.

In the study of MindWriter's CompleteCare program, only those individuals who have experienced difficulty with their laptops and gone through the program have direct knowledge of the service process. Although some associates and family members are likely to have some secondhand knowledge of the experience, no one but the actual laptop owners is likely to give as clear a picture of what works and what doesn't with CompleteCare. The laser patient, Edna, on the other hand, had a totally different experience when she went for surgery to correct her vision. Answers to many questions on the patient survey might have been known by a caregiver, especially since Edna was experiencing eye problems serious enough to warrant surgery. And the clinic's admissions department could have been

45

The percent of smartphone users who check their e-mail before they get dressed.

confident that such information was as accurate as it would have been if given by Edna herself. Since inaccuracy is a correctable source of error, a family or group member should not be asked about another member's experience unless there is no other way to get the information directly. We should not depend on secondhand sources if a more direct source can be found.

Participants also cause error by responding in such a way as to unconsciously or consciously misrepresent their actual behavior, attitudes, preferences, motivations, or intentions (*response bias*). Participants create response bias when they modify their responses to be socially acceptable or to save face or reputation with the interviewer (*social desirability bias*), and sometimes even in an attempt to appear rational and logical.

One major cause of response bias is *acquiescence*—the tendency to be agreeable. On the participant's part, acquiescence may be a result of lower cognitive skills or knowledge related to a concept or construct, language difficulties, or perceived level of anonymity. However, researchers can contribute to acquiescence by the speed with which they ask questions (the faster questions are asked, the more acquiescence) and the placement of questions in an interview (the later the question, the more acquiescence.)[7]

Sometimes participants may not have an opinion on the topic of concern. Under this circumstance, their proper response should be "don't know" or "have no opinion." Some research suggests that most participants who chose the don't-know response option actually possess the knowledge or opinion that the researcher seeks.[8] Participants may choose the option because they may want to shorten the time spent in the participation process, may be ambivalent or have conflicting opinions on the topic, may feel they have insufficient information to form a judgment—even though they actually have taken a position—don't believe that the response choices match their position, or don't possess the cognitive skills to understand the response options. If they choose the don't-know option for any of these reasons, studies suggest that probing for their true position will increase both reliability and validity of the data. However, forcing a participant to express some opinion he or she does not hold by withholding a don't-know option makes it difficult for researchers to know the reliability of the answers.

Participants may also interpret a question or concept differently from what was intended by the researcher. This occurs when the researcher uses words that are unfamiliar to the participant. Thus, the individual answers a question that is different from the one the researcher intended to ask. This problem is reflected in Edna's letter concerning the clinic's survey.

Regardless of the reasons, each source of participant-initiated error diminishes the value of the data collected. It is difficult for a researcher to identify such occasions. Thus, communicated responses should be accepted for what they are—statements by individuals that reflect varying degrees of truth and accuracy.

Choosing a Communication Method

Once the sponsor or researcher has determined that surveying or interviewing is the appropriate data-collection approach, various means may be used to secure information from individuals. A researcher can conduct a semistructured interview or survey by personal interview or telephone or can distribute a self-administered survey by mail, fax, computer, e-mail, the Internet, or a combination of these. As noted in Exhibit 10-5, although there are commonalities among these approaches, several considerations are unique to each.

In the last two decades of the 20th century and the first decade of the 21st century, a revolution—albeit a quiet one—was under way in survey research. Driven by changing technology and the need to make research more responsible to the bottom line and ROI objectives, the paper-and-pencil survey standard of the prior 60 years was replaced by a new computerized standard. Whether it goes by the name of "computer-assisted data collection" (CADAC), "computer-assisted survey information collection" (CASIC), or "computer-assisted interviewing" (CAI), the trend is growing. Although less obvious in the public sector (the U.S. government is the largest survey researcher in the world, and paper-and-pencil approaches still hold prominence there), in the private sector of survey research with households and organizations, the computer's influence on this methodology is far-reaching. It influences all the various data collection practices.

>**Exhibit 10-5** Comparison of Communication Approaches

	Self-Administered Survey	Telephone Survey	Survey via Personal Interview
Description	Questionnaires are: a. Mailed, faxed, or couriered to be self-administered—with return mechanism generally included (denoted below as a). b. Computer-delivered via intranet, Internet, and online services—computer stores/forwards completed instruments automatically (denoted below as b). c. People are intercepted in a central location and studied via paper or computerized instrument—without interviewer assistance: e.g., restaurant and hotel comment cards (denoted below as c).	People selected to be part of the sample are interviewed on the telephone by a trained interviewer.	People selected to be part of the sample are interviewed in person by a trained interviewer.
Advantages	• Allows contact with otherwise inaccessible participants (e.g., CEOs). • Incentives may be used to increase response rate. • Often lowest-cost option. • Expanded geographic coverage without increase in costs (a). • Requires minimal staff (a). • Perceived as more anonymous (a). • Allows participants time to think about questions (a). • More complex instruments can be used (b). • Fast access to the computer-literate (b). • Rapid data collection (b, c). • Participant who cannot be reached by phone (voice) may be accessible (b, c). • Sample frame lists viable locations rather than prospective participants (b, c). • Visuals may be used (b, c).	• Lower costs than personal interview. • Expanded geographic coverage without dramatic increase in costs. • Uses fewer, more highly skilled interviewers. • Reduced interviewer bias. • Fastest completion time. • Better access to hard-to-reach participants through repeated callbacks. • Can use computerized random dialing. • CATI—computer-assisted telephone interviewing: Responses can be entered directly into a computer file to reduce error and cost.	• Good cooperation from participants. • Interviewer can answer questions about survey, probe for answers, use follow-up questions, and gather information by observation. • Special visual aids and scoring devices can be used. • Illiterate and functionally illiterate participants can be reached. • Interviewer can prescreen participant to ensure he or she fits the population profile. • CAPI—computer-assisted personal interviewing: Responses can be entered into a portable microcomputer to reduce error and cost.
Disadvantages	• Low response rate in some modes. • No interviewer intervention available for probing or explanation (a). • Cannot be long or complex (a). • Accurate mailing lists needed (a). • Often participants returning survey represent extremes of the population—skewed responses (a). • Anxiety among some participants (b). • Directions/software instruction needed for progression through the instrument (b). • Computer security (b). • Need for low-distraction environment for survey completion (c).	• Response rate is lower than for personal interview. • Higher costs if interviewing geographically dispersed sample. • Interview length must be limited. • Many phone numbers are unlisted or not working, making directory listings unreliable. • Some target groups are not available by phone. • Responses may be less complete. • Illustrations cannot be used.	• High costs. • Need for highly trained interviewers. • Longer period needed in the field collecting data. • May be wide geographic dispersion. • Follow-up is labor-intensive. • Not all participants are available or accessible. • Some participants are unwilling to talk to strangers in their homes. • Some neighborhoods are difficult to visit. • Questions may be altered or participant coached by interviewers.

> Self-Administered Surveys

The **self-administered questionnaire** is ubiquitous in modern living. You have experienced service evaluations of hotels, restaurants, car dealerships, and transportation providers. Often, a short questionnaire is left to be completed by the participant in a convenient location or is packaged with a product. User registrations, product information requests in magazines, warranty cards, the MindWriter CompleteCare study, and the Albany Clinic study are examples of self-administered surveys. Self-administered **mail surveys** are delivered not only by the U.S. Postal Service but also via fax and courier service. Other delivery modalities include *computer-delivered* and *intercept* studies.

Evaluation of the Self-Administered Survey

Nowhere has the computer revolution been felt more strongly than in the area of the self-administered survey. Computer-delivered self-administered questionnaires (also labeled **computer-assisted self-interviews, or CASIs**) use organizational intranets, the Internet, or online services to reach their participants. Participants may be targeted (as when BizRate, an online e-business rating service, sends an e-mail to a registered e-purchaser to participate in a survey following the completion of their order) or self-selecting (as when a computer screen pop-up window offers a survey to an individual who clicks on a particular website or when a potential participant responds to a postcard or e-mail inquiry looking for participants). The questionnaire and its managing software may be resident on the computer or its network, or both may be sent to the participant by mail—**disk-by-mail (DBM) survey.** A 2006 PEW-Internet study found that 73 percent[9] of U.S. households are actively online, with 27 percent[10] accessing the Internet wirelessly from a place other than home or work. Although women and men both use search engines and use the Internet for information, men are more likely to use the Internet for entertainment, while women use it for maintaining connections.[11] Is it any wonder, then, that researchers have embraced computer-delivered self-administered surveys? See Exhibit 10-6.

Intercept surveys—at malls, conventions, state fairs, vacation destinations, even busy city street corners—may use a traditional paper-and-pencil questionnaire or a computer-delivered survey via a kiosk. The respondent participates without interviewer assistance, usually in a predetermined environment, such as a room in a shopping mall. All modes have special problems and unique advantages (as shown in Exhibit 10-5).

Because computer-delivered surveys, especially those delivered via the Internet, are in their infancy, much of what researchers know about self-administered surveys has been learned from experiments conducted with mail surveys and from personal experience. So as we explore the strengths and weaknesses of the various self-administered survey methods, we will start with this body of knowledge.

Costs

Self-administered surveys of all types typically cost less than surveys via personal interviews. This is true of mail surveys, as well as of both computer-delivered and intercept surveys. Telephone and mail costs are in the same general range, although in specific cases either may be lower. The more geographically dispersed the sample, the more likely it is that self-administered surveys via computer or mail will be the low-cost method. A mail or computer-delivered study can cost less because it is often a one-person job. And computer-delivered studies (including those that employ interviewer-participant interaction) eliminate the cost of printing surveys, a significant cost of both mail studies and personal interviewing employing paper-and-pencil surveys. The most significant cost savings with computer-delivered surveys involve the much lower cost of pre- and postnotification (often done by mail or phone when other self-administered surveys are involved), as well as the lower per-participant survey delivery cost of very large studies.[12]

Sample Accessibility

One asset to using mail self-administered surveys is that researchers can contact participants who might otherwise be inaccessible. Some groups, such as major corporate executives and physicians, are

>**Exhibit 10-6** The Web as a Survey Research Venue

Web Advantages	Example
Short turnaround of results; results are tallied as participants complete surveys.	A soft-drink manufacturer got results from a Web survey in just five days.
Ability to use visual stimuli.	• Florida's tourism office used eye movement tracking to enhance its website and improve its billboard and print ads. • One major advertising agency is conducting Web research using virtual supermarket aisles that participants wander through, reacting to client products and promotions. • LiveWorld has developed a packaging study showing more than 75 images of labels and bottle designs.
Ability to do numerous surveys over time.	A printer manufacturer did seven surveys in six months during the development of one of its latest products.
Ability to attract participants who wouldn't participate in another research project, including international participants.	An agricultural equipment manufacturer did a study using two-way pagers provided free to farmers to query users about its equipment—participants usually unavailable by phone or PC.
Participants feel anonymous.	Anonymity was the necessary ingredient for a study on impotence conducted by a drug manufacturer.
Shortened turnaround from questionnaire draft to execution of survey.	A Hewlett-Packard survey using Greenfield Online's QuickTake took two weeks to write, launch, and field—not the standard three months using non-Web venues.

Web Disadvantages (and emerging solutions)	Example
Recruiting the right sample is costly and time-consuming; unlike phone and mail sample frames, no lists exist. (Firms like Greenfield Online and Survey Samples Inc. now provide samples built from panels of Internet users who have indicated an interest in participating in online surveys.)	TalkCity, working for Whitton Associates and Fusion5, set up a panel of 3,700 teens for a survey to test new packaging for a soft drink using phone calls, referrals, e-mail lists, banner ads, and website visits. It drew a sample of 600 for the research. It cost more than $50,000 to set up the list.
Converting surveys to the Web can be expensive. (Firms like Qualtric Labs with its SurveyPro software and Apian with its Perseus software for wireless surveys and intranet surveys have made the process of going from paper to Internet much easier.)	LiveWorld's teen study cost $50,000 to $100,000 to set up, plus additional fees with each focus group or survey. The total price tag was several hundred thousand dollars.
It takes technical as well as research skill to field a Web survey. (Numerous firms now offer survey hosting services.)	A 10- to 15-minute survey can take up to five days of technical expertise to field and test.
While research is more compatible with numerous browsers, the technology isn't perfect. (Some survey hosting services use initial survey screen questions that identify the browser and system specifications and deliver the survey in the format most compatible with the participant's system.)	A well-known business magazine did a study among a recruited sample only to have the survey abort on question 20 of a longer study.

Source: These examples are drawn from the personal experience of the authors, as well as from Noah Shachtman, "Why the Web Works as a Market Research Tool," *AdAge.com*, Summer 2001 (http://adage.com/tools2001).

difficult to reach in person or by phone, as gatekeepers (secretaries, office managers, and assistants) limit access. But researchers can often access these special participants by mail or computer. When the researcher has no specific person to contact—say, in a study of corporations—the mail or computer-delivered survey may be routed to the appropriate participant. Additionally, the computer-delivered survey can often reach samples that are identified in no way other than their computer and Internet use, such as the users of a particular online game or those who have shopped with a particular online retailer.

Time Constraints

Although intercept studies still pressure participants for a relatively quick response, in a mail survey the participant can take more time to collect facts, talk with others, or consider replies at length than is possible in a survey employing the telephone or in a personal interview. Computer-delivered studies, especially those accessed via e-mail links to the Internet, often have time limitations on both access and completion once started. And once started, computer-delivered studies usually cannot be interrupted by the participant to seek information not immediately known. One recent computer-delivered study sponsored by Procter & Gamble, however, asked of participants (who used skin moisturizers) the actual duration of time that the participant spent applying the product to various skin areas following a bath or shower. These questions came in the middle of a fairly lengthy survey. The participant was encouraged to discontinue the survey, time his or her moisturizer application following the next bath or shower, and return to the survey via a link and personal code with detailed responses.[13]

Anonymity

Mail surveys are typically perceived as more impersonal, providing more anonymity than the other communication modes, including other methods for distributing self-administered questionnaires. Computer-delivered surveys still enjoy that same perceived anonymity, although increased concerns about privacy may erode this perception in the future.[14]

Topic Coverage

A major limitation of self-administered surveys concerns the type and amount of information that can be secured. Researchers normally do not expect to obtain large amounts of information and cannot probe deeply into topics. Participants will generally refuse to cooperate with a long and/or complex mail, computer-delivered, or intercept questionnaire unless they perceive a personal benefit. Returned mail questionnaires with many questions left unanswered testify to this problem, but there are also many exceptions. One general rule of thumb is that the participant should be able to answer the questionnaire in no more than 10 minutes—similar to the guidelines proposed for telephone studies. On the other hand, one study of the general population delivered more than a 70 percent response to a questionnaire calling for 158 answers.[15] Several early studies of computer-delivered surveys show that participants indicate some level of enjoyment with the process, describing the surveys as interesting and amusing.[16] The novelty of the process, however, is expected to decline with experience, and recent declines in Web and e-mail survey response rates seem to be supporting this expectation.

Maximizing Participation in the Self-Administered Survey

To maximize the overall probability of response, attention must be given to each point of the survey process where the response may break down.[17] For example:

- The wrong address, e-mail or postal, can result in nondelivery or nonreturn.
- The envelope or fax cover sheet may look like junk mail and be discarded without being opened, or the subject line on e-mail may give the impression of spam and not encourage that the e-mail be opened.
- Lack of proper instructions for completion may lead to nonresponse.
- The wrong person may open the envelope or receive the fax or e-mail and fail to call it to the attention of the right person.
- A participant may find no convincing explanation or inducement for completing the survey and thus discard it.
- A participant may temporarily set the questionnaire aside or park it in his or her e-mail in-box and fail to complete it.
- The return address may be lost, so the questionnaire cannot be returned.

Thus, efforts should be directed toward maximizing the overall probability of response. One approach, the Total Design Method (TDM), suggests minimizing the burden on participants by designing questionnaires that:[18]

- Are easy to read.
- Offer clear response directions.
- Include personalized communication.
- Provide information about the survey via advance notification.
- Encourage participants to respond.[19]

More than 200 methodological articles have been published on efforts to improve response rates. Few approaches consistently showed positive response rates.[20] However, several practical suggestions emerge from the conclusions:[21]

- Preliminary or advance notification of the delivery of a self-administered questionnaire increases response rates.
- Follow-ups or reminders after the delivery of a self-administered questionnaire increase response rates.
- Clearly specified return directions and devices (e.g., response envelopes, especially postage-stamped) improve response rates.
- Monetary incentives for participation increase response rates.
- Deadline dates do not increase response rates but do encourage participants to respond sooner.
- A promise of anonymity, although important to those who do respond, does not increase response rates.
- An appeal for participation is essential.

Self-Administered Survey Trends

Computer surveying is surfacing at trade shows, where participants complete questionnaires while making a visit to a company's booth. Continuous tabulation of results provides a stimulus for attendees to visit a particular exhibit as well as gives the exhibitor detailed information for evaluating the productivity of the show. This same technology easily transfers to other situations where large groups of people congregate.

Companies are now using intranet capabilities to evaluate employee policies and behavior. Ease of access to electronic mail systems makes it possible for both large and small organizations to use computer surveys with both internal and external participant groups. Many techniques of traditional mail surveys can be easily adapted to computer-delivered questionnaires (e.g., follow-ups to nonparticipants are more easily executed and are less expensive).

It is not unusual to find registration procedures and full-scale surveying being done on World Wide Web sites. University sites are asking prospective students about their interests, and university departments are evaluating current students' use of online materials. A short voyage on the Internet reveals organizations using their sites to evaluate customer service processes, build sales-lead lists, evaluate planned promotions and product changes, determine supplier and customer needs, discover interest in job openings, evaluate employee attitudes, and more. Advanced and easier-to-use software for designing Web questionnaires is no longer a promise of the future—it's here.

The **Web-based questionnaire,** a measurement instrument both delivered and collected via the Internet, has the power of computer-assisted telephone interview systems, but without the expense of network administrators, specialized software, or additional hardware. As a solution for Internet or intranet websites, you need only a personal computer and Web access. Most software products are wizard driven with design features that allow custom survey creation and modification.

Two primary options are proprietary solutions offered through research firms and off-the-shelf software designed for researchers who possess the knowledge and skills we describe here and in Chapters 11, 12, and 13. With fee-based services, you are guided (often online) through problem formulation, questionnaire design, question content, response strategy, and wording and sequence of questions. The supplier's staff generates the questionnaire HTML code, hosts the survey at their server, and provides data consolidation and reports. Off-the-shelf software is a strong alternative. *PC Magazine* reviewed six packages containing well-designed user interfaces and advanced data preparation features.[22] The advantages of these software programs are:

- Questionnaire design in a word processing environment.
- Ability to import questionnaire forms from text files.
- A coaching device to guide you through question and response formatting.
- Question and scale libraries.
- Automated publishing to a Web server.
- Real-time viewing of incoming data.
- Ability to edit data in a spreadsheet-type environment.
- Rapid transmission of results.
- Flexible analysis and reporting mechanisms.

Ease of use is not the only influence pushing the popularity of web-based instruments. Cost is a major factor. A Web survey is much less expensive than conventional survey research. Although fees are based on the number of completions, the cost of a sample of 100 might be one-sixth that of a conventional telephone interview. Bulk mailing and e-mail data collection have also become more cost-effective because any instrument may be configured as an e-mail questionnaire.

The computer-delivered survey has made it possible to use many of the suggestions for increasing participation. Once the computer-delivered survey is crafted, the cost of redelivery via computer is very low. Preliminary notification via e-mail is both more timely and less costly than notification for surveys done by phone or mail. The click of a mouse or a single keystroke returns a computer-delivered study. Many computer-delivered surveys use color, even color photographs, within the survey structure. This is not a cost-effective option with paper surveys. And video clips—never an option with a

>**snap**shot

Are Cell Phones and Smartphones Ready for Research?

According to a 2008 National Institutes of Health study of 13,083 U.S. households, about 18.4 percent of adults live in wireless-phone-only households. This number is more than four times the number of such households in early 2004. Among households that had both landlines and mobile phones, the 2008 study revealed that 14.5 percent received "all or almost all" calls via their mobile phones even if they had a landline. With landline phone coverage on decline in many developed countries, researchers are using sampling techniques and survey design to address issues and take advantage of the opportunities that wireless phones offer.

According to Andy Peytchev, PhD, survey methodologist with Research Triangle Institute (RTI International) in North Carolina, multimethod phone studies, where some participants are reached via landlines and others via cell phones, are becoming the norm rather than the exception to achieve a national probability sample. Landline data can be weighted according to census population parameters. But not all problems can be fixed by weighting. "Youth landline responses versus youth cell phone responses, for example, are different. We don't know exactly why, just that they are different. You would have potential for undercoverage errors if you just used cell phones or landlines."

Cell phone surveys offer unique challenges. Many participants want to know why they are being contacted on their cell phone. So RTI International has changed its standard phone introduction. Interviewers inform cell phone participants that they know they are being contacted via their cell phone and why. RTI International also offers cell phone respondents an incentive to continue the survey that is sufficient to show its appreciation and recognize the cost of cell phone minute charges. Cell phone surveys also require additional questions. RTI International trains its interviewers to inquire, "Are you driving right now?" If participants are driving, surveyors ask for an alternative time to contact the participant, and then disconnect the call. Interviewers may also ask cell phone participants whether they are in a safe place.

Little research has been done on self-administered smartphone surveys, but Peytchev is interested in the opportunities. Smartphone surveys can include images—both those the participants take and share and those shared by the researcher. But Peytchev cautions, "Images can distort the meaning of the question. Everything you present to the participant is seen as information." And images collected from participants have to be analyzed and interpreted. Some RTI experiments have revealed that participants are reluctant to complete text-box responses and that if such a response device is included, cell phone participants are more likely to choose nonsense answers to avoid texting. This adds a new twist to survey research on the age-old issue of just what questions to ask.

www.rti.org; www.cdc.gov/nchs/

mail survey—are possible with a computer-delivered survey. In addition, e-currencies have simplified the delivery of monetary and other incentives. However, employing all the stimulants for participation cannot overcome technology snafus. These glitches are likely to continue to plague participation as long as researchers and participants use different computer platforms, operating systems, and software.

While web- and e-mail-based self-administered surveys have certainly caught the lion's share of business attention in the last few years, the tried-and-true methods of telephone and personal interviews still have their strengths—and their advocates in the research community.

> Survey via Telephone Interview

The **telephone survey** is still the workhorse of survey research. With the high level of telephone service penetration in the United States and the European Union, access to participants through low-cost, efficient means has made telephone interviewing a very attractive alternative for researchers. Nielsen Media Research uses thousands of calls each week to determine television viewing habits, and Arbitron does the same for radio listening habits. Pollsters working with political candidates use telephone surveys to assess the power of a speech or a debate during a hotly contested campaign. Numerous firms field phone omnibus studies each week. Individual questions in these studies are used to capture every-thing from people's feeling about the rise in gasoline prices to the power of a celebrity spokesperson in an advertising campaign or the latest teenage fashion trend.

Evaluation of the Telephone Interview

Of the advantages that telephone interviewing offers, probably none ranks higher than its moderate cost. One study reports that sampling and data collection costs for telephone surveys can run from 45 to 64 percent lower than costs for comparable personal interviews.[23] Much of the savings comes from cuts in travel costs and administrative savings from training and supervision. When calls are made from a single location, the researcher may use fewer, yet more skilled, interviewers. Telephones are

>picprofile

RTI International Call Center Services employs hundreds of interviewers, institutional contractors, quality control monitors, team leaders, and supervisors in its state-of-the-art call center in Raleigh, North Carolina. The call center typically conducts between 10 and 30 different data collection efforts concurrently, and operates seven days per week using the latest in voice-over-Internet-protocol technology as well as sophisticated call systems. Call center staff come from all walks of life. Many are students or others who work as interviewers part-time in the evenings and on weekends. RTI International conducts rigorous training with all telephone staff on standardized interviewing techniques, strategies for gaining participant cooperation, and the use of its computer-assisted telephone interviewing system. www.rti.org

especially economical when callbacks to maintain precise sampling requirements are necessary and participants are widely scattered. Long-distance service options make it possible to interview nationally at a reasonable cost.

Telephone interviewing can be combined with immediate entry of the responses into a data file by means of terminals, personal computers, or voice data entry. This brings added savings in time and money. The **computer-assisted telephone interview (CATI)** is used in research organizations throughout the world. A CATI facility consists of acoustically isolated interviewing carrels organized around supervisory stations. The telephone interviewer in each carrel has a personal computer or terminal that is networked to the phone system and to the central data processing unit. A software program that prompts the interviewer with introductory statements, qualifying questions, and precoded questionnaire items drives the survey. These materials appear on the interviewer's monitor. CATI works with a telephone number management system to select numbers, dial the sample, and enter responses. One facility, the Survey Research Center at the University of Michigan, consists of 60 carrels with 100 interviewers working in shifts from 8 a.m. to midnight (EST) to call nationwide. When fully staffed, it produces more than 10,000 interview hours per month.[24]

Another means of securing immediate response data is the **computer-administered telephone survey.** Unlike CATI, there is no human interviewer. A computer calls the phone number, conducts the interview, places data into a file for later tabulation, and terminates the contact. The questions are voice-synthesized, and the participant's answers and computer timing trigger continuation or disconnect. Several modes of computer-administered surveys exist, including *touch-tone data entry (TDE); voice recognition (VR),* which recognizes a limited vocabulary—usually yes/no responses; and *automatic speech recognition (ASR)* for recognizing and recording a wide range of verbal responses. CATI is often compared to the self-administered questionnaire and offers the advantage of enhanced participant privacy. One study showed that the noncontact rate for this electronic survey mode is similar to that for other telephone interviews when a random phone list is used. It also found that rejection of this mode of data collection affects the refusal rate (and thus nonresponse error) because people hang up more easily on a computer than on a human.[25] The **noncontact rate** is a ratio of potential but unreached contacts (no answer, busy, answering machine or voice mail, and disconnects but not refusals) to all potential contacts.

The **refusal rate** refers to the ratio of contacted participants who decline the interview to all potential contacts. New technology, notably call-filtering systems in which the receiver can decide whether a call is answered based on caller identity, is expected to increase the noncontact rate associated with telephone surveys. The 2003 CMOR Respondent Cooperation and Industry Image Study reported that although survey refusal rates have been growing steadily over several years, the rate "took a sharper than usual increase" this year. The study also noted that "positive attitudes [about participating in surveys] are declining, while negative perceptions are increasing."[26]

When compared to either personal interviews or mail self-administered surveys, the use of telephones brings a faster completion of a study, sometimes taking only a day or so for the fieldwork. When compared to personal interviewing, it is also likely that interviewer bias, especially bias caused by the physical appearance, body language, and actions of the interviewer, is reduced by using telephones.

Finally, behavioral norms work to the advantage of telephone interviewing. If someone is present, a ringing phone is usually answered, and it is the caller who decides the purpose, length, and termination of the call.[27]

There are also disadvantages to using the telephone for research. A skilled researcher will evaluate the use of a telephone survey to minimize the effect of these disadvantages:

- Inaccessible households (no telephone service or no/low contact rate).
- Inaccurate or nonfunctioning numbers.
- Limitation on interview length (fewer measurement questions).
- Limitations on use of visual or complex questions.
- Ease of interview termination.
- Less participant involvement.
- Distracting physical environment.

In several polls related to the public's understanding of the Do Not Call registry, Harris Interactive found that although the registry was working to reduce undesired telemarketing calls (91 percent reported fewer or no calls), there was still confusion about whether survey calls were restricted. In one study, Harris found that 42 percent of U.S. adults erroneously thought registering for the national Do Not Call registry would ban telephone survey calls as well. Five years later, Harris found that 63 percent of those who actually registered did not know whether survey researchers were allowed to call, while only 24 percent knew that registration would not block survey calls. Since the Do Not Call registry was established, 70 percent of those who are registered have been surveyed by phone. But many (29 percent) still do not know that registration expires and must be renewed. What's the true measure of success of this program? That fully 96 percent have renewed or will renew their registration.

www.harrisinteractive.com

Farewell, Old Friend.

There are now more than 50 million consumer phone numbers in the National Do Not Call Registry – and it's growing every day. To complicate matters, almost half* of all Americans incorrectly believe that telephone survey calls are now banned by the Do Not Call rules.

The future of telephone survey work is in doubt. But there is no doubt that viable, accurate data collection alternatives exist.

Call Harris Interactive today to learn more – we'll be happy to answer the phone.

*42% of all U.S. adults think that the registry applies to calls to conduct surveys about products and services – *The Harris Poll®* – September 4, 2003

www.harrisinteractive.com/DNC **Tel 877.919.4765**
©2005, Harris Interactive Inc. All rights reserved. EOE M/F/D/V 04.05

HarrisInteractive®
MARKET RESEARCH

Inaccessible Households

Approximately 94 percent of all U.S. households have access to telephone service.[28] On the surface, this should make telephone surveys a prime methodology for communication studies. However, several factors reduce such an enthusiastic embrace of the methodology. Rural households and households with incomes below the poverty line remain underrepresented in telephone studies, with phone access below 75 percent.[29] More households are using filtering devices and services to restrict access, including caller ID, privacy manager, Tele-Zapper, and unlisted numbers (estimated between 22 and 30 percent of all household phone numbers).[30] Meanwhile, the number of inaccessible individuals continues to increase as cellular/wireless phone use increases. From 1985 to 2007, the number of U.S.

wireless telecommunication subscribers grew from 203.6 thousand[31] to 233 million.[32] Many of these numbers are unlisted or possess screening or filtering services. Additionally, people's use of phone modems to access the Internet makes household lines ring busy for long periods of time. Recent FCC filings indicate that fewer than 15 percent of U.S. households have second telephone lines, required for simultaneous Internet access.[33] Effective May 2004 federal wireless local-number portability legislation made it possible for subscribers to take their wired phone number to their wireless phone service (or the reverse) or to shift their wireless service between carriers without losing their wireless number. Thus, the guidelines for identifying the physical location of a phone by its number—and, in turn, the location of its owner—no longer apply.[34]

These causes of variations in participant availability by phone can be a source of bias. A random dialing procedure is designed to reduce some of this bias. **Random dialing** normally requires choosing phone exchanges or exchange blocks and then generating random numbers within these blocks for calling.[35] Of course, just reaching a household doesn't guarantee its participation.

Inaccurate or Nonfunctioning Numbers

One source says the highest incidence of unlisted numbers is in the West, in large metropolitan areas, among nonwhites, and for persons between 18 and 34 years of age.[36] Several methods have been developed to overcome the deficiencies of directories; among them are techniques for choosing phone numbers by using random dialing or combinations of directories and random dialing.[37] However, increasing demand for multiple phone lines by both households and individuals has generated new phone area codes and local exchanges. This too increases the inaccuracy rate.

Limitation on Interview Length

A limit on interview length is another disadvantage of the telephone survey, but the degree of this limitation depends on the participant's interest in the topic. Ten minutes has generally been thought of as ideal, but interviews of 20 minutes or more are not uncommon. One telephone survey sponsored by Kraft lasted approximately 30 minutes. It was designed to judge the willingness of sample issue recipients to subscribe to a prototype magazine, *food&family*. The survey also measured the effectiveness of the sample issue of the magazine to deliver purchase intent for Kraft products featured in the recipes contained therein.[38] In another study, interviews ran for one and a half hours in a survey of long-distance services.[39]

Limitations on Use of Visual or Complex Questions

The telephone survey limits the complexity of the survey and the use of complex scales or measurement techniques that is possible with personal interviewing, CASI, or WWW surveys. For example, in personal interviews, participants are sometimes asked to sort or rank an array of cards containing different responses to a question. For participants who cannot visualize a scale or other measurement device that the interview is attempting to describe, one solution has been to employ a nine-point scaling approach and to ask the participant to visualize it by using the telephone dial or keypad.[40] In telephone interviewing it is difficult to use maps, illustrations, and other visual aids. In some instances, however, interviewers have supplied these prior to a prescheduled interview via fax, e-mail, or the Internet.

Ease of Interview Termination

Some studies suggest that the response rate in telephone studies is lower than that for comparable face-to-face interviews. One reason is that participants find it easier to terminate a phone interview. Telemarketing practices may also contribute. Public reaction to investigative reports of wrongdoing and unethical behavior within telemarketing activities places an added burden on the researcher, who must try to convince a participant that the phone interview is not a pretext for soliciting contributions (labeled *frugging*—fund-raising under the guise of research) or selling products (labeled *sugging*—sales under the guise of research).

Less Participant Involvement

Telephone surveys can result in less thorough responses, and persons interviewed by phone find the experience to be less rewarding than a personal interview. Participants report less rapport with telephone interviewers than with personal interviewers. Given the growing costs and difficulties of personal interviews, it is likely that an even higher share of surveys will be by telephone in the future. Thus, it behooves researchers using telephone surveys to attempt to improve the enjoyment of the interview. One authority suggests:

> We need to experiment with techniques to improve the enjoyment of the interview by the participant, maximize the overall completion rate, and minimize response error on specific measures. This work might fruitfully begin with efforts at translating into verbal messages the visual cues that fill the interaction in a face-to-face interview: the smiles, frowns, raising of eyebrows, eye contact, etc. All of these cues have informational content and are important parts of the personal interview setting. We can perhaps purposefully choose those cues that are most important to data quality and participant trust and discard the many that are extraneous to the survey interaction.[41]

Changes in the Physical Environment

Replacement of home or office phones with cellular and wireless phones also raises concerns. In regard to telephone surveys, researchers are concerned about the changing environment in which such surveys might be conducted, the resulting quality of data collected under possibly distracting circumstances—at a busy intersection, in the midst of weekly shopping in a congested grocery aisle, at the local high school basketball tournament—and the possible increase in refusal rates.

Telephone Survey Trends

Future trends in telephone surveying bear watching. Answering machines or voice-mail services pose potentially complex response rate problems since they are estimated to have substantial penetration in American households. Previous research discovered that most such households are accessible; the subsequent contact rate was greater in answering-machine households than in no-machine households and about equal with busy-signal households. Other findings suggested that (1) individuals with answering machines were more likely to participate, (2) machine use was more prevalent on weekends than on weekday evenings, and (3) machines were more commonplace in urban than in rural areas.

Voice-mail options offered by local phone service providers have less market penetration but are gaining increasing acceptance. Questions about the sociodemographics of users and nonusers and the relationship of answering-machine/voice-mail technology to the rapid changes in the wireless market remain to be answered.[42] Caller identification technology, the assignment of facsimile machines or computer modems to dedicated phone lines, and technology that identifies computer-automated dialers and sends a disconnect signal in response are all expected to have an impact on the noncontact rate of phone interviews.

The variations among the 60 telephone companies' services and the degree of cooperation that will be extended to researchers are also likely to affect noncontact rates. There is also concern about the ways in which random dialing can be made to deal with nonworking and ineligible numbers.[43] But arguably no single threat poses greater danger than the government-facilitated Do Not Call registry initiated in 2003 by the Federal Trade Commission.[44] More than 107.4 million U.S. household and cell numbers are now registered.[45] Although currently survey researchers are exempt from its restrictions, customer confusion about the distinction between research and telemarketing is likely to cause an increase in the nonresponse rate. Telemarketers might be the catalyst, but legitimate research will suffer.

>**snap**shot

Voice Adds Depth to Survey

Do telephone surveys and interviews fit in today's Web-survey dominant research landscape? Anderson Analytics, a Stamford (CT) business intelligence and marketing research company, recently teamed up with BigEars, a New Zealand-based company specializing in fully automated telephone surveys and interviews, to conduct a survey among college students about their cell phones. The hybrid study employed both an online survey and the automated telephone survey method.

The BigEars operates much like a Web-based survey tool. The difference is that the respondent answers over the phone, typically via an 800 number. "By eliminating the human interviewer from the call, we allow the caller to participate whenever it suits them, rather than when it suits us," shared Tom Anderson, managing partner of Anderson Analytics.

The survey results indicated that the main advantage of using telephone surveys is its ability to encourage longer and more robust responses to open-ended questions. According to Mark Forsyth, managing director of BigEars, "Talking isn't work." Answers given to open-ended questions over the phone were 15 percent longer than answers typed in the parallel online

survey. In addition, the voice recording offered opportunities for in-depth qualitative analysis; emotion and inflection in individual voice clips were used to examine the outliers in the study. "Being able to listen to the actual voices of the students, rather than simply coding or reading their responses, allows for a whole new dimension of analysis and confidence in the findings" said Tom Anderson.

"With this new hybrid methodology, if you want reaction to an event or transaction, such as a visit to a store, you can capture your data immediately, while it's fresh in the person's mind," said Jesse Chen, senior consultant and developer at Anderson Analytics. "Some people are more comfortable on the Web, and some are more comfortable on the phone—by catering to these differences you can broaden participation."

So how do college students feel about their cell phones? You can see the top-line report at http://www.andersonanalytics .com/reports/AndersonAnalyticsBigEars.ppt.

www.andersonanalytics.com; www.yourbigears.com

> Survey via Personal Interview

A **survey via personal interview** is a two-way conversation between a trained interviewer and a participant. With her poor eyesight and the problems of question clarity, a personal interview, rather than the intercept/self-administered questionnaire, might have been a preferable communication method for Edna at the Albany Outpatient Laser Clinic.

Evaluation of the Personal Interview Survey

There are real advantages as well as clear limitations to surveys via personal interview. The greatest value lies in the depth of information and detail that can be secured. It far exceeds the information secured from telephone and self-administered studies via mail or computer (both intranet and Internet). The interviewer can also do more things to improve the quality of the information received than is possible with another method.

The absence of assistance in interpreting questions in the Albany Clinic study was a clear weakness that would have been improved by the presence of an interviewer. Interviewers can note conditions of the interview, probe with additional questions, and gather supplemental information through observation. Edna was obviously in good spirits and very relaxed after she and her fellow patients had critiqued the questionnaire. This attitude would have been observed and noted by an interviewer. Of course, we're hopeful that the interviewer would correctly interpret laughter as a sign of humor and not as a negative attitude, as did the admissions clerk.

Human interviewers also have more control than other kinds of communication studies. They can prescreen to ensure the correct participant is replying, and they can set up and control interviewing

Aleve: Personal Interviews Provide Relief

Bayer Consumer Care inherited Aleve, a long-duration over-the-counter painkiller, from Procter & Gamble in 1996. Since its launch in 1994, P&G hadn't been able to move Aleve beyond a 6 percent market share. Bayer chose CLT Research Associates to identify potential Aleve users. CLT conducted in-home interviews with a random sample of 800 men and women aged 18 to 75 who had used a nonprescription pain reliever in the past year. The research revealed that 24 percent of those interviewed could be defined as "pain-busters" (heavy users of analgesics who were likely to try new products to gain relief). More than one-third of those identified as pain-busters had tried Aleve. Bayer's task was to use the research to identify a strategy to get pain-busters to choose Aleve when they faced their analgesic-stocked medicine cabinet.

First, Moskowitz Jacobs Inc. had 249 participants rate various statements about Aleve. Statements that promised "control over pain" or "freedom to do the things you want" were

discovered as important emotional triggers for consumers interested in minimizing the number of pills they took to relieve pain—Aleve's differential benefit. Next Bayer managers analyzed syndicated data from Medioscope, Nielsen Panel Data, MRI, and Simmons and conducted a series of focus groups moderated by Viewpoints Consulting Inc. to flesh out findings. The sum of this research revealed Aleve users were more likely to suffer from arthritis and back pain than the average analgesic user. This helped Bayer define the benefit of Aleve as "liberation from tough pain, making a dramatic difference in the quality of life." The resulting Dramatic Difference ad campaign boosted the subsequent year's sales by 16 percent. Aleve has been so successful (27.5 percent increase in 2006) that by 2008 Bayer will have doubled its production of the drug.

www.aleve.com; www.cltresearch.com; www.smrb.com; http://acnielsen.com

conditions. They can use special scoring devices and visual materials, as is done with a **computer-assisted personal interview (CAPI).** Interviewers also can adjust the language of the interview as they observe the problems and effects the interview is having on the participant.

With such advantages, why would anyone want to use any other survey method? Probably the greatest reason is that personal interviewing is costly, in terms of both money and time. A survey via personal interview may cost anywhere from a few dollars to several hundred dollars for an interview with a hard-to-reach person. Costs are particularly high if the study covers a wide geographic area or has stringent sampling requirements. An exception to this is the survey via **intercept interview** that targets participants in centralized locations such as retail malls or, as with Edna, in a doctor's office. Intercept interviews reduce costs associated with the need for several interviewers, training, and travel. Product and service demonstrations also can be coordinated, further reducing costs. Their cost-effectiveness, however, is offset when representative sampling is crucial to the study's outcome. The intercept survey would have been a possibility in the Albany Clinic study, although more admissions clerks would likely have been needed if volunteers were not available to perform this task. You will find tips on intercept surveys on the text website.

Costs have risen rapidly in recent years for most communication methods because changes in the social climate have made personal interviewing more difficult. Many people today are reluctant to talk with strangers or to permit strangers to visit in their homes. Interviewers are reluctant to visit unfamiliar neighborhoods alone, especially for evening interviewing. Finally, results of surveys via personal interviews can be affected adversely by interviewers who alter the questions asked or in other ways bias the results. As Edna and her friends discussed the Albany Clinic survey, they each applied their own operational definitions to the concepts and constructs being asked. This confusion created a bias that might have been eliminated by a well-trained interviewer. Interviewer bias, identified as one of the three major sources of error in Exhibit 10-3, was discussed earlier in this chapter. If we are to overcome these deficiencies, we must appreciate the conditions necessary for interview success.

> Selecting an Optimal Survey Method

The choice of a communication method is not as complicated as it might first appear. By comparing your research objectives with the strengths and weaknesses of each method, you will be able to choose one that is suited to your needs. The summary of advantages and disadvantages of personal interviews, telephone interviews, and self-administered questionnaires presented in Exhibit 10-5 should be useful in making such a comparison.

When your investigative questions call for information from hard-to-reach or inaccessible participants, the telephone interview, mail survey, or computer-delivered survey should be considered. However, if data must be collected very quickly, the mail survey would likely be ruled out because of lack of control over the returns. Alternatively, you may decide your objective requires extensive questioning and probing; then the survey via personal interview should be considered.

If none of the choices turns out to be a particularly good fit, it is possible to combine the best characteristics of two or more alternatives into a *hybrid* survey. Although this decision will incur the costs of the combined modes, the flexibility of tailoring a method to your unique needs is often an acceptable trade-off.

In the MindWriter study, Jason Henry plans to insert a postcard questionnaire (a self-administered survey delivered via courier) in each laptop returned by the CompleteCare repair service. But this plan is not without problems. Not all customers will return their questionnaires, creating nonresponse bias. The postcard format doesn't permit much space for encouraging customer response. Alerting customers to the importance of returning the response card by phone (to announce courier delivery of a repaired laptop) might improve the research design, but it would be too costly when 10,000 units are processed monthly. Participants would not be in the best frame of mind if they received a damaged laptop; dissatisfaction could lead to a decreased response rate and an increase in call center contacts. Jason's proposal contains a follow-up procedure—telephoning nonparticipants to obtain their answers when response cards are not returned. This will likely decrease nonresponse error. When most of the study participants are answering measurement questions without assistance, telephone interviewing creates the possibility of interviewer bias at an unknown level for at least part of the data.

In the Albany Clinic study, the researcher could have taken several actions to improve the quality of the data. Distributing the questionnaire to the patient's eye doctor or to the patient (by mail) prior to arrival would have increased the accuracy of identifying medications, diagnoses, hospitalizations, and so forth. The patient's eye doctor was in the best position to encourage compliance with the collection process but was not consulted. Having the patient bring the completed questionnaire to the admissions procedure, where the admissions clerk could review the completed instrument for accuracy and completeness, would have given the researcher the opportunity to clarify any confusion with the questions, concepts, and constructs. Finally, pretesting the instrument with a sample of patients would have revealed difficulties with the process and operational definitions. Edna's concerns could have been eliminated before they surfaced.

Ultimately, all researchers are confronted by the practical realities of cost and deadlines. As Exhibit 10-5 suggests, on the average, surveys via personal interview are the most expensive communication method and take the most field time unless a large field team is used. Telephone surveys are moderate in cost and offer the quickest option, especially when CATI is used. Questionnaires administered by e-mail or the Internet are the least expensive. When your desired sample is available via the Internet, the Internet survey may prove to be the least expensive communication method with the most rapid (simultaneous) data availability. The use of the computer to select participants and reduce coding and processing time will continue to improve the cost-to-performance profiles of this method in the future.

Most of the time, an optimal method will be apparent. However, managers' needs for information often exceed their internal resources. Such factors as specialized expertise, a large field team, unique facilities, or a rapid turnaround prompt managers to seek assistance from research vendors of survey-related services.

Outsourcing Survey Services

Commercial suppliers of research services vary from full-service operations to specialty consultants. When confidentiality is likely to affect competitive advantage, the manager or staff will sometimes prefer to bid only a phase of the project. Alternatively, the organization's staff members may possess such unique knowledge of a product or service that they must fulfill a part of the study themselves. Regardless, the exploratory work, design, sampling, data collection, or processing and analysis may be contracted separately or as a whole. Most organizations use a request for proposal (RFP) to describe their requirements and seek competitive bids (see the sample RFP in Appendix A).

Research firms also offer special advantages that their clients do not typically maintain in-house. Centralized-location interviewing or computer-assisted telephone facilities may be particularly desirable for certain research needs. A professionally trained staff with considerable experience in similar management problems is another benefit. Data processing and statistical analysis capabilities are especially important for some projects. Other vendors have specially designed software for interviewing and data tabulation.[46] Panel suppliers provide another type of research service, with emphasis on longitudinal survey work.[47] By using the same participants over time, a **panel** can track trends in attitudes toward issues or products, product adoption or consumption behavior, and a myriad of other research interests. Suppliers of panel data can secure information from personal and telephone interviewing techniques as well as from the mail, the Web, and mixed-modes surveys. Diaries are a common means of chronicling events of research interest by the panel members. These are mailed back to the research organization. Point-of-sale terminals and scanners aid electronic data collection for panel-type participant groups. And mechanical devices placed in the homes of panel members may be used to evaluate media usage. ACNielsen, Yankelovich Partners, The Gallup Organization, and Harris Interactive all manage extensive panels.

>summary

1 The communication approach involves surveying or interviewing people and recording their responses for analysis. Communication is accomplished via personal interviews, telephone interviews, or self-administered surveys, with each method having its specific strengths and weaknesses. The optimal communication method is the one that is instrumental for answering your research question and dealing with the constraints imposed by time, budget, and human resources. The opportunity to combine several survey methodologies makes the use of the mixed mode desirable in many projects.

2 Successful communication requires that we seek information the participant can provide and that the participant understand his or her role and be motivated to play that role. Motivation, in particular, is a task for the interviewer. Good rapport with the participant should be established quickly, and then the technical process of collecting data should begin. The latter often calls for skillful probing to supplement the answers volunteered by the participant. Simplicity of directions and instrument appearance are additional factors to consider in encouraging response in self-administered communication studies.

3 Two factors can cause bias in interviewing. One is nonresponse. It is a concern with all surveys. Some studies show that the first contact often secures less than 20 percent of the designated participants. Various methods are useful for increasing this representation, the most effective being

making callbacks until an adequate number of completed interviews have been secured. The second factor is response error, which occurs when the participant fails to give a correct or complete answer. The interviewer also can contribute to response error. The interviewer can provide the main solution for both of these two types of errors.

4 The self-administered questionnaire can be delivered by the U.S. Postal Service, facsimile, a courier service, a computer, or an intercept. Computer-delivered self-administered questionnaires use organizational intranets, the Internet, or online services to reach their participants. Participants may be targeted or self-selecting. Intercept studies may use a traditional questionnaire or a computerized instrument in environments where interviewer assistance is minimal.

Telephone interviewing remains popular because of the diffusion of telephone service in households and the low cost of this method compared with personal interviewing. Long-distance telephone interviewing has grown. There are also disadvantages to telephone interviewing. Many phone numbers are unlisted, and directory listings become obsolete quickly. There is also a limit on the length and depth of interviews conducted using the telephone.

The major advantages of personal interviewing are the ability to explore topics in great depth, achieve a high degree of interviewer control, and provide maximum interviewer flexibility for meeting unique situations. However, this method is costly and time-consuming, and its flexibility can result in excessive interviewer bias.

5 Outsourcing survey services offers special advantages to managers. A professionally trained research staff, centralized-location interviewing, focus group facilities, and computer-assisted facilities are among them. Specialty firms offer software and computer-based assistance for telephone and personal interviewing as well as for mail and mixed modes. Panel suppliers produce data for longitudinal studies of all varieties.

>**key**terms

communication approach 242

computer-administered telephone survey 257

computer-assisted personal interview (CAPI) 262

computer-assisted self-interview (CASI) 250

computer-assisted telephone interview (CATI) 257

disk-by-mail (DBM) survey 250

intercept interview 262

interviewer error 244

mail survey 250

noncontact rate 257

nonresponse error 246

panel 264

random dialing 259

refusal rate 257

response error 246

self-administered questionnaire 250

survey 242

survey via personal interview 261

telephone survey 255

Web-based questionnaire 254

>**discussion**questions

Terms in Review

1 Distinguish among response error, interviewer error, and nonresponse error.

2 How do environmental factors affect response rates in personal interviews? How can we overcome these environmental problems?

Making Research Decisions

3 Assume you are planning to interview shoppers in a shopping mall about their views on increased food prices and what the federal government should do about them. In what different ways might you try to motivate shoppers to cooperate in your survey?

4 In recent years, in-home personal interviews have grown more costly and more difficult to complete. Suppose, however, you have a project in which you need to talk with people in their homes. What might you do to hold down costs and increase the response rate?

5 In the following situations, decide whether you would use a personal interview, telephone survey, or self-administered questionnaire. Give your reasons.

    a A survey of the residents of a new subdivision on why they happened to select that area in which to live. You also wish to secure some information about what they like and do not like about life in the subdivision.

    b A poll of students at Metro University on their preferences among three candidates who are running for president of the student government.

    c A survey of 58 wholesale grocery companies, scattered over the eastern United States, on their personnel management policies for warehouse personnel.

    d A survey of financial officers of the Fortune 500 corporations to learn their predictions for the economic outlook in their industries in the next year.

    e A study of applicant requirements, job tasks, and performance expectations as part of a job analysis of student work-study jobs on a college campus of 2,000 students, where 1,500 are involved in the work-study program.

6 You decide to take a telephone survey of 40 families in the 721-exchange area. You want an excellent representation of all subscribers in the exchange area. Explain how you will carry out this study.

7 You plan to conduct a mail survey of the traffic managers of 1,000 major manufacturing companies across the country. The study concerns their company policies regarding the payment of moving expenses for employees who are transferred. What might you do to improve the response rate of such a survey?

8 A major corporation agrees to sponsor an internal study on sexual harassment in the workplace. This is in response to concerns expressed by its female employees. How would you handle the following issues:

a The communication approach (self-administered, telephone, personal interview, and/or mixed).

b The purpose: Fact finding, awareness, relationship building, and/or change.

c Participant motivation.

d Minimization of response and nonresponse error.

Bringing Research to Life

9 Define the appropriate communication study for the Albany Outpatient Laser Clinic.

From Concept to Practice

10 Using Exhibit 10-1 as your guide, graph the communication study you designed in question 9.

From the Headlines

11 How might Apple use the survey methodology to evaluate the success of its iPad?

>cases*

 Akron Children's Hospital

 Campbell-Ewald Pumps Awareness into the American Heart Association

Can Research Rescue the Red Cross?

 Covering Kids with Health Care

 Data Development

 Donatos: Finding the New Pizza

Inquiring Minds Want to Know—NOW!

 Lexus SC 430

Mastering Teacher Leadership

NCRCC: Teeing Up and New Strategic Direction

 Ohio Lottery: Innovative Research Design Drives Winning

Proofpoint: Capitalizing on a Reporter's Love of Statistics

 Starbucks, Bank One, and Visa Launch Starbucks Duetto Visa

 USTA: Come Out Swinging

*You will find a description of each case in the Case Abstracts section of the textbook. Check the Case Index to determine whether a case provides data, the research instrument, video, or other supplementary material. Written cases are downloadable from the text website (www.mhhe.com/cooper11e). All video material and video cases are available from the Online Learning Center. The film reel icon indicates a video case or video material relevant to the case.

>part III

The Sources and Collection of Data

>chapter 11

Measurement

>**learning**objectives

After reading this chapter, you should understand . . .

1 The distinction between measuring objects, properties, and indicants of properties.

2 The similarities and differences between the four scale types used in measurement and when each is used.

3 The four major sources of measurement error.

4 The criteria for evaluating good measurement.

66 The only man who behaved sensibly was my tailor; he took my measurement anew every time he saw me, while all the rest went on with their old measurements and expected them to fit me. 99

George Bernard Shaw,
playwright and essayist

The executive director of Glacier Symphony gestures broadly at the still snowcapped Canadian Rockies. "It has been three very happy years for me here, though not easy ones since I let corporate America intrude on our idyllic existence."

"You mean the MindWriter people?" prompts Jason Henry. "The ones who flew me up here? My clients and your benefactor?"

"Please, don't misunderstand," says the executive director as she propels Jason across a manicured lawn toward the refreshment tent. "When I rented them a part of our compound for use in corporate education, they quite generously insisted that I avail myself of some of their training for midlevel managers."

"They said you were having trouble with attendance?" ventures Jason. "Tell me what you do here."

"We offer one of the most outstanding summer music festivals in the country—maybe the continent. We present several concerts each week, all summer long, with evening performances on both Friday and Saturday. During the week, rehearsals are open to music patrons and students. And, of course, our skilled musicians enhance their own skills by networking with each other.

"During the winter my artistic directors prepare the next summer's program and hire the musicians, coordinating closely with me on the budget. This is quite complicated, because most of our musicians spend only two weeks with us. Fully 600 performing artists from many parts of the continent are part of this orchestra over the course of a summer festival.

"Colleges in British Columbia send me their music scholarship students for summer employment as dishwashers, waiters, cleaners, and the like. It is a special opportunity for them, rubbing shoulders

with their idols and learning to enhance their own performance skills in the process."

"So your problem is. . . ?" urges Jason again.

"My problem is patronage, specifically the lack of commitment of the local residents of Glacier to consistently support their Glacier Symphony Festival. Do you realize how rare it is for a town this size to have more than 600 performing musicians in a summer? You would think the residents would be as ecstatic as our dishwashers!"

"Do you know why they are less than supportive?" inquires Jason, glad they have finally arrived at the reason MindWriter had asked him to divert his homebound flight from San Francisco to British Columbia.

"Well, some of the residents have communicated with us informally," comments the director, somewhat hesitantly.

"And they said . . . ?" urges Jason, more than a little impatiently, remembering why he so values his partner for usually handling this phase of exploratory research.

"One commented: 'I've never heard this music before—why can't the performers play something I'll recognize.' Another, 'Where were the video screens? And the special visual effects?' And another: 'Why would I want to spend more than an hour watching a stage full of people sitting in chairs?'"

"Hold on," says Jason, making a note in his PalmPilot. "I can see your orchestra is striking a sour note." Jason smiles, chuckling at his own wit, while the director remains stoic. "MindWriter uses an extensive program for measuring customer satisfaction, and . . ."

"Ah, yes, measuring customer satisfaction," interrupts the director, "second only to cash flow for the MindWriter folks. The care and frequency with which they measure customer satisfaction in the MindWriter seminars here dumbfounds me. Throughout each seminar they host here, morning, afternoon, or evening, everyone breaks for coffee and is required to fill out a critique of the speaker. The results are tabulated by the time the last coffee cup has been collected, and the seminar leader has been given feedback. Is he or she presenting material too slowly or too quickly? Are there too many jokes or not enough? Are concrete examples being used often enough? Do the participants want a hard copy of the slides? They measure attitudinal data six times a day and even query you about the meals, including taste, appearance, cleanliness and speed, friendliness, and accuracy of service."

"Understandable," observes Jason. "Your scholarship students have frequent contact with the residents, both here and in town, right? We might use them to collect some more formal data," brainstorms Jason to himself.

"Jason," interjects the director, "were you ever a musician?"

"No," explains Jason, "my interests ran more toward statistics than Schubert."

"Then you wouldn't realize that while musicians could talk about music—and the intricacies of performing music—for hours with each other, once a resident exclaims little or no interest, our scholarship students would likely tune them out."

"It is just as well," comments Jason, now resigned to getting more involved in Glacier Symphony's problem than he had first assumed would be necessary. "Untrained interviewers and observers can be highly unreliable and inaccurate in measuring and reporting behavior," says Jason. "Have you tried a suggestion box?"

"No, but I do send reminder postcards for each concert."

"Not quite the same thing," murmurs Jason as he hands the director his business card. "As a devotee of the MindWriter way, I'm sure you have a current satisfaction survey for concert goers in your files." At her nod, Jason continues: "Send it to me. At MindWriter's request and at its expense, I'll revise it for you. I'll work out the collection and analysis details on my flight home and be in touch next week."

The director, smiling and shaking Jason's hand, responds, "I'll ask one of our scholarship students to drive you back to the community airport, then. You're bound to have a lot in common."

> The Nature of Measurement

In everyday usage, measurement occurs when an established index verifies the height, weight, or other feature of a physical object. How well you like a song, a painting, or the personality of a friend is also a measurement. To measure is to discover the extent, dimensions, quantity, or capacity of something, especially by comparison with a standard. We measure casually in daily life, but in research the requirements are rigorous.

Measurement in research consists of assigning numbers to empirical events, objects or properties, or activities in compliance with a set of rules. This definition implies that measurement is a three-part process:

1. Selecting observable empirical events
2. Developing a set of **mapping rules:** a scheme for assigning numbers or symbols to represent aspects of the event being measured
3. Applying the mapping rule(s) to each observation of that event.[1]

You recall the term *empirical*. Researchers use an empirical approach to describe, explain, and make predictions by relying on information gained through observation.

Assume you are studying people who attend an auto show where prototypes for new models are on display. You are interested in learning the male-to-female ratio among attendees. You observe those who enter the show area. If a person is female, you record an F; if male, an M. Any other symbols such as 0 and 1 or # and % also may be used if you know what group the symbol identifies. Exhibit 11-1 uses this example to illustrate the three components.

>**Exhibit 11-1** Characteristics of Measurement

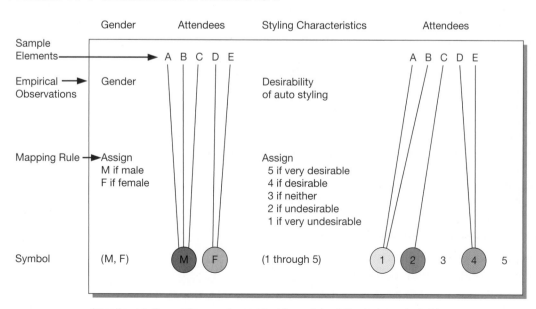

Attendees A, B, and C are male, and find the auto's styling to be undesirable.
Attendees D and E are female and find the auto's styling desirable.

Researchers might also want to measure the styling desirability of a new concept car at this show. They interview a sample of visitors and assign, with a different mapping rule, their opinions to the following scale:

What is your opinion of the styling of the concept CS?

Very desirable   5   4   3   2   1   Very undesirable

All measurement theorists would call the rating scale in Exhibit 11-1 a form of measurement, but some would challenge whether classifying males and females is a form of measurement. Their argument is that measurement must involve quantification—that is, "the assignment of numbers to objects to represent amounts or degrees of a property possessed by all of the objects."[2] This condition was met when measuring opinions of car styling. Our approach endorses the more general view that "numbers as symbols within a mapping rule" can reflect both qualitative and quantitative concepts.

The goal of measurement—indeed, the goal of "assigning numbers to empirical events in compliance with a set of rules"—is to provide the highest-quality, lowest-error data for testing hypotheses, estimation or prediction, or description. Researchers deduce from a hypothesis that certain conditions should exist. Then they measure for these conditions in the real world. If found, the data lend support to the hypothesis; if not, researchers conclude the hypothesis is faulty. An important question at this point is, "Just what does one measure?"

The object of measurement is a *concept*, the symbols we attach to bundles of meaning that we hold and share with others. We invent higher-level concepts—*constructs*—for specialized scientific explanatory purposes that are not directly observable and for thinking about and communicating abstractions. Concepts and constructs are used at theoretical levels; variables are used at the empirical level. *Variables* accept numerals or values for the purpose of testing and measurement. Concepts, constructs, and variables may be defined descriptively or operationally. An *operational definition* defines a variable in terms of specific measurement and testing criteria. It must specify adequately the empirical information needed and how it will be collected. In addition, it must have the proper scope or fit for the research problem at hand. We review these terms with examples in Exhibit 11-2.

What Is Measured?

Variables being studied in research may be classified as objects or as properties. **Objects** include the concepts of ordinary experience, such as tangible items like furniture, laundry detergent, people, or automobiles. Objects also include things that are not as concrete, such as genes, attitudes, and peer-group pressures. **Properties** are the characteristics of the object. A person's *physical properties* may be stated in terms of weight, height, and posture, among others. *Psychological properties* include attitudes and intelligence. *Social properties* include leadership ability, class affiliation, and status. These and many other properties of an individual can be measured in a research study.

In a literal sense, researchers do not measure either objects or properties. They measure indicants of the properties or indicants of the properties of objects. It is easy to observe that A is taller than B and that C participates more than D in a group process. Or suppose you are analyzing members of a sales force of several hundred people to learn what personal properties contribute to sales success. The properties are age, years of experience, and number of calls made per week. The indicants in these cases are so accepted that one considers the properties to be observed directly.

In contrast, it is not easy to measure properties of constructs like "lifestyles," "opinion leadership," "distribution channel structure," and "persuasiveness." Since each property cannot be measured directly, one must infer its presence or absence by observing some indicant or pointer measurement. When you begin to make such inferences, there is often disagreement about how to develop an operational definition for each indicant.

25

The percent of corporations using or planning to use *cloud computing*—using software and server space via Internet sources.

Not only is it a challenge to measure such constructs, but a study's quality depends on what measures are selected or developed and how they fit the circumstances. The nature of measurement scales, sources of error, and characteristics of sound measurement are considered next.

>Exhibit 11-2 Review of Key Terms

Concept: a bundle of meanings or characteristics associated with certain events, objects, conditions, situations, or behaviors.

Classifying and categorizing objects or events that have common characteristics beyond any single observation creates concepts. When you think of a spreadsheet or a warranty card, what comes to mind is not a single example but your collected memories of all spreadsheets and warranty cards from which you abstract a set of specific and definable characteristics.

Construct: an image or idea specifically invented for a given research and/or theory-building purpose.

We build constructs by combining the simpler, more concrete concepts, especially when the idea or image we intend to convey is not subject to direct observation. When Jason and Sara prepare the measurement instrument for MindWriter's research study, they will wrestle with the construct of a "satisfied service customer" and its meaning.

Variable: an event, act, characteristic, trait, or attribute that can be measured and to which we assign numerals or values; a synonym for the construct or the property being studied.

The numerical value assigned to a variable is based on the variable's properties. For example, some variables, said to be *dichotomous,* have only two values, reflecting the presence or absence of a property: employed-unemployed or male-female have two values, generally 0 and 1. Variables also take on values representing added categories, such as the demographic variables of race and religion. All such variables that produce data that fit into categories are *discrete* variables, since only certain values are possible. An automotive variable, for example, where "Chevrolet" is assigned a 5 and "Honda" is assigned a 6 provides no option for a 5.5. Income, temperature, age, and a test score are examples of *continuous* variables. These variables may take on values within a given range or, in some cases, an infinite set. Your test score may range from 0 to 100, your age may be 23.5, and your present income could be $35,000.

Operational definition: a definition for a construct stated in terms of specific criteria for testing or measurement; refers to an empirical standard (we must be able to count, measure, or gather information about the standard through our senses).

Researchers deal with two types of definitions: dictionary definitions and operational definitions. In the more familiar dictionary definition, a concept is defined with a synonym. For example, a customer is defined as a patron; a patron, in turn, is defined as a customer or client of an establishment. When we measure concepts and constructs, we require the more rigorous definition offered by an operational definition. Whether the object being defined is physical (e.g., a can of soup) or highly abstract (e.g., an attitude toward packaging), the operational definition must specify the characteristics and how they are to be observed or counted. The specifications and procedures must be so clear that any competent person using them would classify the objects in the same way. For example: *For our study, a can of peaches will be any container—metal, glass, plastic, or composite—that weighs at least 12 ounces and is purchased at a grocery, drug, convenience, or mass merchandiser within the Detroit, Michigan, Consolidated Metropolitan Statistical Area (CMSA).*

> Measurement Scales

In measuring, one devises some mapping rule and then translates the observation of property indicants using this rule. For each concept or construct, several types of measurement are possible; the appropriate choice depends on what you assume about the mapping rules. Each one has its own set of underlying assumptions about how the numerical symbols correspond to real-world observations.

Mapping rules have four assumptions:

1. Numbers are used to classify, group, or sort responses. No order exists.

2. Numbers are ordered. One number is greater than, less than, or equal to another number.

3. Differences between numbers are ordered. The difference between any pair of numbers is greater than, less than, or equal to the difference between any other pair of numbers.

4. The number series has a unique origin indicated by the number zero. This is an absolute and meaningful zero point.

>**Exhibit 11-3** Measurement Scales

Type of Scale	Characteristics of Data	Basic Empirical Operation	Example
Nominal	Classification (mutually exclusive and collectively exhaustive categories), but no order, distance, or natural origin	Determination of equality	Gender (male, female)
Ordinal	Classification and order, but no distance or natural origin	Determination of greater or lesser value	Doneness of meat (well, medium well, medium rare, rare)
Interval	Classification, order, and distance, but no natural origin	Determination of equality of intervals or differences	Temperature in degrees
Ratio	Classification, order, distance, and natural origin	Determination of equality of ratios	Age in years

Combinations of these characteristics of classification, order, distance, and origin provide four widely used classifications of measurement scales:[3] (1) nominal, (2) ordinal, (3) interval, and (4) ratio. Let's preview these measurement scales before we discuss their technical details. Suppose your professor asks a student volunteer to taste-test six candy bars. The student begins by evaluating each on a chocolate–not chocolate scale; this is a nominal measurement. Then the student ranks the candy bars from best to worst; this is an ordinal measurement. Next, the student uses a 7-point scale that has equal distance between points to rate the candy bars with regard to some taste criterion (e.g., crunchiness); this is an interval measurement. Finally, the student considers another taste dimension and assigns 100 points among the six candy bars; this is a ratio measurement.

The characteristics of these measurement scales are summarized in Exhibit 11-3. Deciding which type of scale is appropriate for your research needs should be seen as a part of the research process, as shown in Exhibit 11-4.

Nominal Scales

In business research, nominal data are widely used. With **nominal scales,** you are collecting information on a variable that naturally or by design can be grouped into two or more categories that are mutually exclusive and collectively exhaustive. If data were collected from the symphony patrons at the Glacier compound, patrons could be classified by whether they had attended prior symphony per-

formances or this was their first time. Every patron would fit into one of the two groups within the variable *attendance.*

The counting of members in each group is the only possible arithmetic operation when a nominal scale is employed. If we use numerical symbols within our mapping rule to identify categories, these numbers are recognized as labels only and have no quantitative value. The number 23, we know, does not imply a sequential count of players or a skill level; it is only a means of identification. Of course, you might want to argue about a jersey number representing a skill level if it is LeBron James wearing jersey 23.

Religious Preferences	
Mapping Rule A	**Mapping Rule B**
1 = Baptist	1 = Christian
2 = Catholic	2 = Muslim
3 = Protestant	3 = Hindu
4 = Scientology	4 = Buddhist
5 = Unitarian-Universalist	5 = Jewish
6 = Jewish	6 = Other
7 = Secular/nonreligious/agnostic/atheist	

>**Exhibit 11-4** Moving from Investigative to Measurement Questions

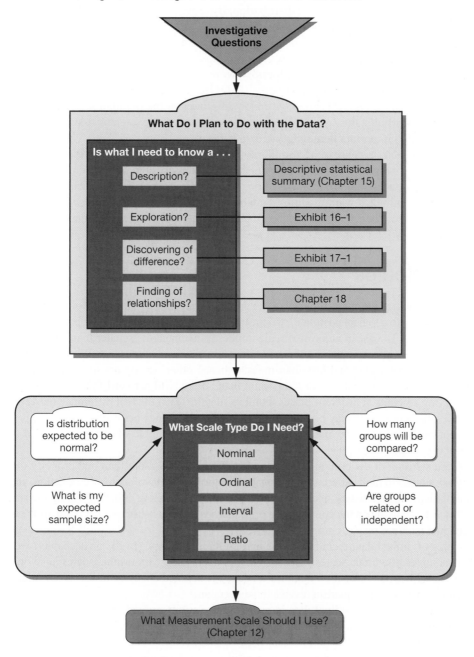

Nominal classifications may consist of any number of separate groups if the groups are mutually exclusive and collectively exhaustive. Thus, one might classify the students in a course according to their expressed religious preferences. Mapping rule A given in the table is not a sound nominal scale because its categories are not mutually exclusive or collectively exhaustive. Mapping rule B meets the minimum requirements; it covers all the major religions and offers an "other" option. Nominal scales are the least powerful of the four data types. They suggest no order or distance relationship and have no arithmetic origin. The scale wastes any information a sample element might share about varying degrees of the property being measured.

Since the only quantification is the number count of cases in each category (the frequency distribution), the researcher is restricted to the use of the mode as the measure of central tendency.[4] The *mode* is the most frequently occurring value. You can conclude which category has the most members, but that is all. There is no generally used measure of *dispersion* for nominal scales. Dispersion describes how scores cluster or scatter in a distribution. By cross-tabulating nominal variables with other variables, you can begin to discern patterns in data.

Although nominal data are statistically weak, they are still useful. If no other scale can be used, one can almost always classify a set of properties into a set of equivalent classes. Nominal measures are especially valuable in exploratory work where the objective is to uncover relationships rather than secure precise measurements. This type of scale is also widely used in survey and other research when data are classified by major subgroups of the population. Classifications such as respondents' marital status, gender, political orientation, and exposure to a certain experience provide insight into important demographic data patterns.

Jason visited Glacier because of his familiarity with MindWriter's extensive research into customer satisfaction. His visit revealed Glacier's need for some exploratory nominal data on symphony patrons. Patrons could be divided into groups—based on their appreciation of the conductor (favorable, unfavorable), on their attitude toward facilities (suitable, not suitable), on their perception of the program (clichéd, virtuoso), on their level of symphony support (financial support, no financial support)—and then analyzed.

Ordinal Scales

Ordinal scales include the characteristics of the nominal scale plus an indication of order. Ordinal data require conformity to a logical postulate, which states: If *a* is greater than *b* and *b* is greater than *c*, then *a* is greater than *c*.[5] The use of an ordinal scale implies a statement of "greater than" or "less than" (an equality statement is also acceptable) without stating how much greater or less. While ordinal measurement speaks of greater-than and less-than measurements, other descriptors may be used—"superior to," "happier than," "poorer than," or "important than." Like a rubber yardstick, an ordinal scale can stretch varying amounts at different places along its length. Thus, the real difference between ranks 1 and 2 on a satisfaction scale may be more or less than the difference between ranks 2 and 3. An ordinal concept can be extended beyond the three cases used in the simple illustration of $a > b > c$. Any number of cases can be ranked.

Another extension of the ordinal concept occurs when there is more than one property of interest. We may ask a taster to rank varieties of carbonated soft drinks by flavor, color, carbonation, and a combination of these characteristics. We can secure the combined ranking either by asking the respondent to base his or her ranking on the combination of properties or by constructing a combination ranking of the individual rankings on each property.

Examples of ordinal data include attitude and preference scales. (In the next chapter, we provide detailed examples of attitude scales.) Because the numbers used with ordinal scales have only a rank meaning, the appropriate measure of central tendency is the median. The *median* is the midpoint of a distribution. A percentile or quartile reveals the dispersion.

Correlational analysis of ordinal data is restricted to various ordinal techniques. Measures of statistical significance are technically confined to a body of statistics known as *nonparametric methods*, synonymous with *distribution-free statistics*.[6]

Researchers differ about whether more powerful tests are appropriate for analyzing ordinal measures. Because nonparametric tests are abundant, simple to calculate, have good statistical power,[7] and do not require that the researcher accept the assumptions of parametric testing, we advise their use with nominal and ordinal data. It is understandable, however, that because parametric tests (such as the *t*-test or analysis of variance) are versatile, accepted, and understood, they will be used with ordinal data when researchers can demonstrate that those data approach the assumptions necessary for interval level analysis.

Interval Scales

Interval scales have the power of nominal and ordinal data plus one additional strength: They incorporate the concept of equality of interval (the scaled distance between 1 and 2 equals the distance between 2 and 3). Calendar time is such a scale. For example, the elapsed time between 3 and

6 a.m. equals the time between 4 and 7 a.m. One cannot say, however, that 6 a.m. is twice as late as 3 a.m., because "zero time" is an arbitrary zero point. Centigrade and Fahrenheit temperature scales are other examples of classical interval scales. Both have an arbitrarily determined zero point, not a unique origin.

Researchers treat many attitude scales as interval, as we illustrate in the next chapter. When a scale is interval and the data are relatively symmetric with one mode, you use the arithmetic mean as the measure of central tendency. You can compute the average time of a TV promotional message or the average attitude value for different age groups in an insurance benefits study. The standard deviation is the measure of dispersion. The product-moment correlation, t-tests, F-tests, and other parametric tests are the statistical procedures of choice for interval data.[8]

When the distribution of scores computed from interval data leans in one direction or the other (skewed right or left), we often use the median as the measure of central tendency and the interquartile range as the measure of dispersion. The reasons for this are discussed in Chapter 15, Appendix 15a.

Ratio Scales

Ratio scales incorporate all of the powers of the previous scales plus the provision for absolute zero or origin. Ratio data represent the actual amounts of a variable. Measures of physical dimensions such as weight, height, distance, and area are examples. In the behavioral sciences, few situations satisfy the requirements of the ratio scale—the area of psychophysics offering some exceptions. In business research, we find ratio scales in many areas. There are money values, population counts, distances, return rates, productivity rates, and amounts of time (e.g., elapsed time in seconds before a customer service representative answers a phone inquiry).

Swatch's *BeatTime*—a proposed standard global time introduced at the 2000 Olympics that may gain favor as more of us participate in cross-time-zone chats (Internet or otherwise)—is a ratio scale. It offers a standard time with its origin at 0 beats (12 midnight in Biel, Switzerland, at the new Biel Meridian timeline). A day is composed of 1,000 beats, with a "beat" worth 1 minute, 26.4 seconds.[9]

With the Glacier project, Jason could measure a customer's age, the number of years he or she has attended, and the number of times a selection has been performed in the Glacier summer festival. These measures all generate ratio data. For practical purposes, however, the analyst would use the same statistical techniques as with interval data.

All statistical techniques mentioned up to this point are usable with ratio scales. Other manipulations carried out with real numbers may be done with ratio-scale values. Thus, multiplication and division can be used with this scale but not with the others mentioned. Geometric and harmonic means are measures of central tendency, and coefficients of variation may also be calculated for describing variability.

Researchers often encounter the problem of evaluating variables that have been measured on different scales. For example, the choice to purchase a product by a consumer is a nominal variable, and cost is a ratio variable. Certain statistical techniques require that the measurement levels be the same. Since the nominal variable does not have the characteristics of order, distance, or point of origin, we cannot create them

In measurement, a researcher needs to know precisely what is being measured. As this SAS ad indicates, not having a good view of the big picture is unacceptable.
www.sas.com

>**snap**shot

Measurement of TiVo Households: Skipped Ads vs. Most Watched

Doesn't it seem odd that some of the most popular shows on TV have the least watched ads? From TiVo research we discover that, "nearly all of the television shows that won 2009 Emmys showed higher levels of ad-skipping than the averages for their respective genres."[a] Sitcoms had a 66 percent level of ad-skipping in contrast to the 88 percent who fast-forwarded through "MadMen" ads and the 73 percent of the audiences who skipped over ads for all TV dramas.[b] According to Todd Juenger, TiVo's vice president for audience research and measurement, people who watch hit shows are more likely to skip ads because they are more involved in the show than other viewers.[c]

Madison Avenue media planners have long counseled companies to avoid buying ads in the fourth quarter of the Super Bowl, even understanding that part of the appeal of the Super Bowl is watching the ads. However, such advice is now being reassessed after the second championship in consecutive years was won in the final moments of play.[d] NBC's broadcast of commercials in the last quarter of Super Bowl XLIII had strong viewer numbers. Two of the most-watched ads on TiVo DVRs were the final ads in the game: Bud Light Lime beer and GoDaddy.com, the website registration firm. These ads were broadcast after the Arizona Cardinals touchdown and before the Pittsburgh Steelers reclaimed the lead and won. "There are two reasons a commercial gets a high rating [in a TiVo household]," Mr. Juenger said. "Either [the show] is rewound often and watched repeatedly or [the ad] happens to be in the middle of [compelling programming that is watched over and over].[e]

Those who sat on the edge of their seats for the end of Super Bowl XLIII helped rank it as the second-most-watched Super Bowl. For those rewatching the end of the fourth quarter, suggest some hypotheses that explain ad-skipping. What measures would you use to test your hypotheses?

www.tivo.com

---

artificially after the fact. The ratio-based salary variable, on the other hand, can be reduced. Rescaling product cost into categories (e.g., high, medium, low) simplifies the comparison. This example may be extended to other measurement situations—that is, converting or rescaling a variable involves reducing the measure from the more powerful and robust level to a lesser one.[10] The loss of measurement power with this decision means that lesser-powered statistics are then used in data analysis, but fewer assumptions for their proper use are required.

In summary, higher levels of measurement generally yield more information. Because of the measurement precision at higher levels, more powerful and sensitive statistical procedures can be used. As we saw with the candy bar example, when one moves from a higher measurement level to a lower one, there is always a loss of information. Finally, when we collect information at higher levels, we can always convert, rescale, or reduce the data to arrive at a lower level.

> Sources of Measurement Differences

The ideal study should be designed and controlled for precise and unambiguous measurement of the variables. Since complete control is unattainable, error does occur. Much error is systematic (results from a bias), while the remainder is random (occurs erratically). One authority has pointed out several sources from which measured differences can come.[11]

Assume you are conducting an ex post facto study of corporate citizenship of a multinational manufacturer. The company produces family, personal, and household care products. The participants are residents of a major city. The study concerns the Prince Corporation, a large manufacturer with its headquarters and several major facilities located in the city. The objective of the study is to discover the public's opinions about the company's approach to health, social welfare, and the environment. You also want to know the origin of any generally held adverse opinions.

Ideally, any variation of scores among the respondents would reflect true differences in their opinions about the company. Attitudes toward the firm as an employer, as an ecologically sensitive organization,

or as a progressive corporate citizen would be accurately expressed. However, four major error sources may contaminate the results: (1) the respondent, (2) the situation, (3) the measurer, and (4) the data collection instrument.

Error Sources

The Respondent

Opinion differences that affect measurement come from relatively stable characteristics of the respondent. Typical of these are employee status, ethnic group membership, social class, and nearness to manufacturing facilities. The skilled researcher will anticipate many of these dimensions, adjusting the design to eliminate, neutralize, or otherwise deal with them. However, even the skilled researcher may not be as aware of less obvious dimensions. The latter variety might be a traumatic experience a given participant had with the Prince Corporation, its programs, or its employees. Respondents may be reluctant to express strong negative (or positive) feelings, may purposefully express attitudes that they perceive as different from those of others, or may have little knowledge about Prince but be reluctant to admit ignorance. This reluctance to admit ignorance of a topic can lead to an interview consisting of "guesses" or assumptions, which, in turn, create erroneous data.

Respondents may also suffer from temporary factors like fatigue, boredom, anxiety, hunger, impatience, or general variations in mood or other distractions; these limit the ability to respond accurately and fully. Designing measurement scales that engage the participant for the duration of the measurement is crucial.

Situational Factors

Any condition that places a strain on the interview or measurement session can have serious effects on the interviewer-respondent rapport. If another person is present, that person can distort responses by joining in, by distracting, or by merely being there. If the respondents believe anonymity is not ensured, they may be reluctant to express certain feelings. Curbside or intercept interviews are unlikely to elicit elaborate responses, while in-home interviews more often do.

The Measurer

The interviewer can distort responses by rewording, paraphrasing, or reordering questions. Stereotypes in appearance and action introduce bias. Inflections of voice and conscious or unconscious prompting with smiles, nods, and so forth, may encourage or discourage certain replies. Careless mechanical processing—checking of the wrong response or failure to record full replies—will obviously distort findings. In the data analysis stage, incorrect coding, careless tabulation, and faulty statistical calculation may introduce further errors.

The Instrument

A defective instrument can cause distortion in two major ways. First, it can be too confusing and ambiguous. The use of complex words and syntax beyond participant comprehension is typical. Leading questions, ambiguous meanings, mechanical defects (inadequate space for replies, response-choice omissions, and poor printing), and multiple questions suggest the range of problems. Many of these problems are the direct result of operational definitions that are insufficient, resulting in an inappropriate scale being chosen or developed.

A more elusive type of instrument deficiency is poor selection from the universe of content items. Seldom does the instrument explore all the potentially important issues. The Prince Corporation study might treat company image in areas of employment and ecology but omit the company management's civic leadership, its support of local education programs, its philanthropy, or its position on minority issues. Even if the general issues are studied, the questions may not cover enough aspects of each area of concern. Although we might study the Prince Corporation's image as an employer in terms of salary and wage scales, promotion opportunities, and work stability, perhaps such topics as working conditions, company management relations with organized labor, and retirement and other benefit programs should also be included.

> The Characteristics of Good Measurement

What are the characteristics of a good measurement tool? An intuitive answer to this question is that the tool should be an accurate counter or indicator of what we are interested in measuring. In addition, it should be easy and efficient to use. There are three major criteria for evaluating a measurement tool: validity, reliability, and practicality.

- *Validity* is the extent to which a test measures what we actually wish to measure.
- *Reliability* has to do with the accuracy and precision of a measurement procedure.
- *Practicality* is concerned with a wide range of factors of economy, convenience, and interpretability.[12]

In the following sections, we discuss the nature of these qualities and how researchers can achieve them in their measurement procedures.

Validity

Many forms of **validity** are mentioned in the research literature, and the number grows as we expand the concern for more scientific measurement. This text features two major forms: external and internal validity.[13] The *external validity* of research findings is the data's ability to be generalized across persons, settings, and times; we discussed this in reference to experimentation in Chapter 9, and more will be said in Chapter 14 on sampling.[14] In this chapter, we discuss only internal validity. **Internal validity** is further limited in this discussion to the ability of a research instrument to measure what it is purported to measure. Does the instrument really measure what its designer claims it does?

One widely accepted classification of validity consists of three major forms: (1) content validity, (2) criterion-related validity, and (3) construct validity (see Exhibit 11-5).[15]

>**Exhibit 11-5** Summary of Validity Estimates

Types	What Is Measured	Methods
Content	Degree to which the content of the items adequately represents the universe of all relevant items under study.	• Judgmental • Panel evaluation with content validity ratio
Criterion-Related Concurrent Predictive	Degree to which the predictor is adequate in capturing the relevant aspects of the criterion. Description of the present; criterion data are available at the same time as predictor scores. Prediction of the future; criterion data are measured after the passage of time.	• Correlation • Correlation • Correlation
Construct	Answers the question, "What accounts for the variance in the measure?"; attempts to identify the underlying construct(s) being measured and determine how well the test represents it (them).	• Judgmental • Correlation of proposed test with established one • Convergent-discriminant techniques • Factor analysis • Multitrait-multimethod analysis

Content Validity

The **content validity** of a measuring instrument is the extent to which it provides adequate coverage of the investigative questions guiding the study. If the instrument contains a representative sample of the universe of subject matter of interest, then content validity is good. To evaluate the content validity of an instrument, one must first agree on what elements constitute adequate coverage. In the Prince Corporation study, we must decide what knowledge and attitudes are relevant to the measurement of corporate public image and then decide which forms of these opinions are relevant positions on these topics. In the Glacier study, Jason must first determine what factors are influencing customer satisfaction before determining if published indexes can be of value. If the data collection instrument adequately covers the topics that have been defined as the relevant dimensions, we conclude the instrument has good content validity.

A determination of content validity involves judgment. First, the designer may determine it through a careful definition of the topic, the items to be scaled, and the scales to be used. This logical process is often intuitive and unique to each research designer.

A second way is to use a panel of persons to judge how well the instrument meets the standards. The panel independently assesses the test items for an instrument as essential, useful but not essential, or not necessary. "Essential" responses on each item from each panelist are evaluated by a content validity ratio, and those meeting a statistical significance value are retained. In both informal judgments and this systematic process, "content validity is primarily concerned with inferences about test construction rather than inferences about test scores."[16]

It is important not to define content too narrowly. If you were to secure only superficial expressions of opinion in the Prince Corporation attitude survey, it would probably not have adequate content coverage. The research should delve into the processes by which these attitudes came about. How did the respondents come to feel as they do, and what is the intensity of feeling? The same would be true of MindWriter's evaluation of service quality and satisfaction. It is not enough to know a customer is dissatisfied. The manager charged with enhancing or correcting the program needs to know what processes, employees, parts, and time sequences within the CompleteCare program have led to that dissatisfaction.

Criterion-Related Validity

Criterion-related validity reflects the success of measures used for prediction or estimation. You may want to predict an outcome or estimate the existence of a current behavior or time perspective. An attitude scale that correctly forecasts the outcome of a purchase decision has predictive validity. An observational method that correctly categorizes families by current income class has concurrent validity. Although these examples appear to have simple and unambiguous validity criteria, there are difficulties in estimating validity. Consider the problem of estimating family income. There is a knowable true income for every family, but we may find the figure difficult to secure. Thus, while the criterion is conceptually clear, it may be unavailable.

A researcher may want to develop a preemployment test that will predict sales success. There may be several possible criteria, none of which individually tells the full story. Total sales per salesperson may not adequately reflect territory market potential, competitive conditions, or the different profitability rates of various products. One might rely on the sales manager's overall evaluation, but how unbiased and accurate are such impressions? The researcher must ensure that the validity criterion used is itself "valid." Any criterion measure must be judged in terms of four qualities: (1) relevance, (2) freedom from bias, (3) reliability, and (4) availability.[17]

A criterion is *relevant* if it is defined and scored in the terms we judge to be the proper measures of salesperson success. If you believe sales success is adequately measured by dollar sales volume achieved per year, then it is the relevant criterion. If you believe success should include a high level of penetration of large accounts, then sales volume alone is not fully relevant. In making this decision, you must rely on your judgment in deciding what partial criteria are appropriate indicants of salesperson success.

Freedom from bias is attained when the criterion gives each salesperson an equal opportunity to score well. The sales criterion would be biased if it did not show adjustments for differences in territory potential and competitive conditions.

A *reliable* criterion is stable or reproducible. An erratic criterion (using monthly sales, which are highly variable from month to month) can hardly be considered a reliable standard by which to judge performance on a sales employment test. Finally, the information specified by the criterion must be *available*. If it is not available, how much will it cost and how difficult will it be to secure? The amount of money and effort that should be spent on development of a criterion depends on the importance of the problem for which the test is used.

Once there are test and criterion scores, they must be compared in some way. The usual approach is to correlate them. For example, you might correlate test scores of 40 new salespeople with first-year sales achievements adjusted to reflect differences in territorial selling conditions.

Construct Validity

In attempting to evaluate **construct validity,** we consider both the theory and the measuring instrument being used. If we were interested in measuring the effect of trust in cross-functional teams, the way in which "trust" was operationally defined would have to correspond to an empirically grounded theory. If a known measure of trust was available, we might correlate the results obtained using this measure with those derived from our new instrument. Such an approach would provide us with preliminary indications of *convergent* validity (the degree to which scores on one scale correlate with scores on other scales designed to assess the same construct). If Jason were to develop a customer satisfaction index for Glacier and, when compared, the results revealed the same indications as a predeveloped, established index, Jason's instrument would have convergent validity. Similarly, if Jason developed an instrument to measure satisfaction with the CompleteCare program and the derived measure could be confirmed with a standardized customer satisfaction measure, convergent validity would exist.

Returning to our preceding example, another method of validating the trust construct would be to separate it from other constructs in the theory or related theories. To the extent that trust could be separated from bonding, reciprocity, and empathy, we would have completed the first steps toward *discriminant* validity (the degree to which scores on a scale *do not* correlate with scores from scales designed to measure different constructs).

We discuss the three forms of validity separately, but they are interrelated, both theoretically and operationally. Predictive validity is important for a test designed to predict product success. In developing such a test, you would probably first list the factors (constructs) that provide the basis for useful prediction. For example, you would advance a theory about the variables in product success—an area

>**Exhibit 11-6** Understanding Validity and Reliability

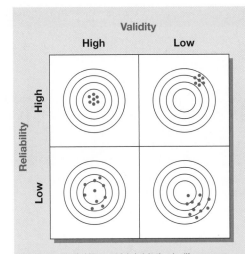

Let's use an archer's bow and target as an analogy.

High reliability means that repeated arrows shot from the same bow would hit the target in essentially the same place—although not necessarily the intended place (first row of the graphic). If we had a bow with high validity as well, then every arrow would hit the bull's-eye (upper left panel). If reliability is low or decreases for some reason, arrows would be more scattered (lacking similarity or closeness, like those shown in the second row).

High validity means that the bow would shoot true every time. It would not pull to the right or send an arrow careening into the woods. Arrows shot from a high-validity bow will be clustered around a central point (the bull's eye), even when they are dispersed by reduced reliability (lower left graphic). Low-validity shots are distorted, rather like a flawed bow pulling our arrows to the right (second column of the graphic). We wouldn't hit the bull's-eye we were aiming at because the low-validity bow—like the flawed data collection instrument—would not perform as planned. When low validity is compounded by low reliability, the pattern of arrows is not only off the bull's-eye but also dispersed (lower right graphic).

for construct validity. Finally, in developing the specific items for inclusion in the success prediction test, you would be concerned with how well the specific items sample the full range of each construct (a matter of content validity). Looking at Exhibit 11-6, we can better understand the concepts of validity and reliability by using an archer's bow and target as an analogy.

Reliability

A measure is reliable to the degree that it supplies consistent results. **Reliability** is a necessary contributor to validity but is not a sufficient condition for validity. The relationship between reliability and validity can be simply illustrated with the use of a bathroom scale. If the scale measures your weight correctly (using a concurrent criterion such as a scale known to be accurate), then it is both reliable and valid. If it consistently overweighs you by six pounds, then the scale is reliable but not valid. If the scale measures erratically from time to time, then it is not reliable and therefore cannot be valid. So if a measurement is not valid, it hardly matters if it is reliable—because it does not measure what the designer needs to measure in order to solve the research problem. In this context, reliability is not as valuable as validity, but it is much easier to assess.

Reliability is concerned with estimates of the degree to which a measurement is free of random or unstable error. Reliable instruments can be used with confidence that transient and situational factors are not interfering. Reliable instruments are robust; they work well at different times under different conditions. This distinction of time and condition is the basis for frequently used perspectives on reliability—stability, equivalence, and internal consistency (see Exhibit 11-7).

Stability

A measure is said to possess **stability** if you can secure consistent results with repeated measurements of the same person with the same instrument. An observation procedure is stable if it gives the same reading on a particular person when repeated one or more times. It is often possible to repeat observations on a subject and to compare them for consistency. When there is much time between measurements, there is a chance for situational factors to change, thereby affecting the observations. The change would appear incorrectly as a drop in the reliability of the measurement process.

>Exhibit 11-7 Summary of Reliability Estimates

Type	Coefficient	What Is Measured	Methods
Test–Retest	Stability	Reliability of a test or instrument inferred from examinee scores; same test is administered twice to same subjects over an interval of less than six months.	Correlation
Parallel Forms	Equivalence	Degree to which alternative forms of the same measure produce same or similar results; administered simultaneously or with a delay. Interrater estimates of the similarity of judges' observations or scores.	Correlation
Split-Half, KR20, Cronbach's Alpha	Internal consistency	Degree to which instrument items are homogeneous and reflect the same underlying construct(s).	Specialized correlational formulas

Stability measurement in survey situations is more difficult and less easily executed than in observational studies. Although you can observe a certain action repeatedly, you usually can resurvey only once. This leads to a test–retest arrangement—with comparisons between the two tests to learn how reliable they are. Some of the difficulties that can occur in the test–retest methodology and cause a downward bias in stability include:

- *Time delay between measurements*—leads to situational factor changes (also a problem in observation studies).
- *Insufficient time between measurements*—permits the respondent to remember previous answers and repeat them, resulting in biased reliability indicators.
- *Respondent's discernment of a study's disguised purpose*—may introduce bias if the respondent holds opinions related to the purpose but not assessed with current measurement questions.
- *Topic sensitivity*—occurs when the respondent seeks to learn more about the topic or form new and different opinions before the retest.

A suggested remedy is to extend the interval between test and retest (from two weeks to a month). While this may help, the researcher must be alert to the chance that an outside factor will contaminate the measurement and distort the stability score. Consequently, stability measurement through the test–retest approach has limited applications. More interest has centered on equivalence.

Equivalence

A second perspective on reliability considers how much error may be introduced by different investigators (in observation) or different samples of items being studied (in questioning or scales). Thus, while stability is concerned with personal and situational fluctuations from one time to another, **equivalence** is concerned with variations at one point in time among observers and samples of items. A good way to test for the equivalence of measurements by different observers is to compare their scoring of the same event. An example of this is the scoring of Olympic figure skaters by a panel of judges.

In studies where a consensus among experts or observers is required, the similarity of the judges' perceptions is sometimes questioned. How does a panel of supervisors render a judgment on merit raises, a new product's packaging, or future business trends? *Interrater reliability* may be used in these cases to correlate the observations or scores of the judges and render an index of how consistent their ratings are. In Olympic figure skating, a judge's relative positioning of skaters (determined by establishing a rank order for each judge and comparing each judge's ordering for all skaters) is a means of measuring equivalence.

The major interest with equivalence is typically not how respondents differ from item to item but how well a given set of items will categorize individuals. There may be many differences in response between two samples of items, but if a person is classified the same way by each test, then the tests have good equivalence.

One tests for item sample equivalence by using alternative or *parallel forms* of the same test administered to the same persons simultaneously. The results of the two tests are then correlated. Under this condition, the length of the testing process is likely to affect the subjects' responses through fatigue, and the inferred reliability of the parallel form will be reduced accordingly. Some measurement theorists recommend an interval between the two tests to compensate for this problem. This approach, called *delayed equivalent forms,* is a composite of test-retest and the equivalence method. As in test-retest, one would administer form X followed by form Y to half the examinees and form Y followed by form X to the other half to prevent "order-of-presentation" effects.[18]

The researcher can include only a limited number of measurement questions in an instrument. This limitation implies that a sample of measurement questions from a content domain has been chosen and another sample producing a similar number will need to be drawn for the second instrument. It is frequently difficult to create this second set. Yet if the pool is initially large enough, the items may be randomly selected for each instrument. Even with more sophisticated procedures used by publishers of standardized tests, it is rare to find fully equivalent and interchangeable questions.[19]

Internal Consistency

A third approach to reliability uses only one administration of an instrument or test to assess the **internal consistency** or homogeneity among the items. The *split-half* technique can be used when the measuring tool has many similar questions or statements to which the participant can respond. The instrument is administered and the results are separated by item into even and odd numbers or into randomly selected halves. When the two halves are correlated, if the results of the correlation are high, the instrument is said to have high reliability in an internal consistency sense. The high correlation tells us there is similarity (or homogeneity) among the items. The potential for incorrect inferences about high internal consistency exists when the test contains many items—which inflates the correlation index.

The Spearman-Brown correction formula is used to adjust for the effect of test length and to estimate reliability of the whole test.[20]

Practicality

The scientific requirements of a project call for the measurement process to be reliable and valid, while the operational requirements call for it to be practical. **Practicality** has been defined as *economy, convenience, and interpretability.*[21] Although this definition refers to the development of educational and psychological tests, it is meaningful for business measurements as well.

Economy

Some trade-off usually occurs between the ideal research project and the budget. Data are not free, and instrument length is one area where economic pressures dominate. More items give more reliability, but in the interest of limiting the interview or observation time (and therefore costs), we hold down the number of measurement questions. The choice of data collection method is also often dictated by economic factors. The rising cost of personal interviewing first led to an increased use of telephone surveys and subsequently to the current rise in Internet surveys. In standardized tests, the cost of test materials alone can be such a significant expense that it encourages multiple reuse. Add to this the need for fast and economical scoring, and we see why computer scoring and scanning are attractive.

Convenience

A measuring device passes the convenience test if it is easy to administer. A questionnaire or a measurement scale with a set of detailed but clear instructions, with examples, is easier to complete correctly than one that lacks these features. In a well-prepared study, it is not uncommon for the interviewer instructions to be several times longer than the interview questions. Naturally, the more complex the concepts and constructs, the greater is the need for clear and complete instructions. We can also make the instrument easier to administer by giving close attention to its design and layout. Although reliability and validity dominate our choices in design of scales here and later in Chapter 12, administrative difficulty should play some role. A long completion time, complex instructions, participant's perceived difficulty with the survey, and their rated enjoyment of the process also influence design. Layout issues include crowding of material, poor reproductions of illustrations, and the carryover of items from one page to the next or the need to scroll the screen when taking a Web survey. Both design and layout issues make completion of the instrument more difficult.

Interpretability

This aspect of practicality is relevant when persons other than the test designers must interpret the results. It is usually, but not exclusively, an issue with standardized tests. In such cases, the designer of the data collection instrument provides several key pieces of information to make interpretation possible:

- A statement of the functions the test was designed to measure and the procedures by which it was developed.
- Detailed instructions for administration.
- Scoring keys and instructions.
- Norms for appropriate reference groups.
- Evidence about reliability.
- Evidence regarding the intercorrelations of subscores.
- Evidence regarding the relationship of the test to other measures.
- Guides for test use.

>summary

1 Although people measure things casually in daily life, research measurement is more precise and controlled. In measurement, one settles for measuring properties of the objects rather than the objects themselves. An event is measured in terms of its duration. What happened during it, who was involved, where it occurred, and so forth, are all properties of the event. To be more precise, what are measured are indicants of the properties. Thus, for duration, one measures the number of hours and minutes recorded. For what happened, one uses some system to classify types of activities that occurred. Measurement typically uses some sort of scale to classify or quantify the data collected.

2 There are four scale types. In increasing order of power, they are nominal, ordinal, interval, and ratio. Nominal scales classify without indicating order, distance, or unique origin. Ordinal data show magnitude relationships of more than and less than but have no distance or unique origin. Interval scales have both order and distance but no unique origin. Ratio scales possess classification, order, distance, and unique origin.

3 Instruments may yield incorrect readings of an indicant for many reasons. These may be classified according to error

sources: (a) the respondent or participant, (b) situational factors, (c) the measurer, and (d) the instrument.

4 Sound measurement must meet the tests of validity, reliability, and practicality. Validity reveals the degree to which an instrument measures what it is supposed to measure to assist the researcher in solving the research problem. Three forms of validity are used to evaluate measurement scales. Content validity exists to the degree that a measure provides an adequate reflection of the topic under study. Its determination is primarily judgmental and intuitive. Criterion-related validity relates to our ability to predict some outcome or estimate the existence of some current condition. Construct validity is the most complex and abstract. A measure has construct validity to the degree that it conforms to predicted correlations of other theoretical propositions.

A measure is reliable if it provides consistent results. Reliability is a partial contributor to validity, but a measurement tool may be reliable without being valid. Three forms of reliability are stability, equivalence, and internal consistency. A measure has practical value for the research if it is economical, convenient, and interpretable.

>**key**terms

interval scale 277

mapping rules 270

measurement 270

nominal scale 274

objects 272

ordinal scale 276

practicality 285

properties 272

ratio scale 277

reliability 283

    equivalence 284

    internal consistency 285

    stability 283

validity 280

    construct 282

    content 281

    criterion-related 281

    internal 280

>**discussion**questions

Terms in Review

1 What can we measure about the four objects listed below? Be as specific as possible.

   a Laundry detergent

   b Employees

   c Factory output

   d Job satisfaction

2 What are the essential differences among nominal, ordinal, interval, and ratio scales? How do these differences affect the statistical analysis techniques we can use?

3 What are the four major sources of measurement error? Illustrate by example how each of these might affect measurement results in a face-to-face interview situation.

4 Do you agree or disagree with the following statements? Explain.

   a Validity is more critical to measurement than reliability.

   b Content validity is the most difficult type of validity to determine.

   c A valid measurement is reliable, but a reliable measurement may not be valid.

   d Stability and equivalence are essentially the same thing.

Making Research Decisions

5 You have data from a corporation on the annual salary of each of its 200 employees.

   a Illustrate how the data can be presented as ratio, interval, ordinal, and nominal data.

   b Describe the successive loss of information as the presentation changes from ratio to nominal.

6 Below are listed some objects of varying degrees of abstraction. Suggest properties of each of these objects that can be measured by each of the four basic types of scales.

   a Store customers.

   b Voter attitudes.

   c Hardness of steel alloys.

   d Preference for a particular common stock.

   e Profitability of various divisions in a company.

7 You have been asked by the head of marketing to design an instrument by which your private, for-profit school can evaluate the quality and value of its various curricula and courses. How might you try to ensure that your instrument has:

   a Stability?

   b Equivalence?

   c Internal consistency?

   d Content validity?

   e Predictive validity?

   f Construct validity?

8 A new hire at Mobil Oil, you are asked to assume the management of the *Mobil Restaurant Guide.* Each restaurant striving to be included in the guide needs to be evaluated. Only a select few restaurants may earn the five-star status. What dimensions would you choose to measure to apply the one to five stars in the *Mobil Restaurant Guide?*

9 You have been asked to develop an index of student morale in your department.

   a What constructs or concepts might you employ?

   b Choose several of the major concepts, and specify their dimensions.

   c Select observable indicators that you might use to measure these dimensions.

   d How would you compile these various dimensions into a single index?

   e How would you judge the reliability and/or validity of these measurements?

Bringing Research to Life

10 Given that Glacier Symphony has previously measured its customer satisfaction by survey, how might Jason assess the internal validity of the Glacier questionnaire?

From Concept to Practice

11 Using Exhibit 11-3 and one of the case questionnaires on your text CD, match each question to its appropriate scale type. For each scale type not represented, develop a measurement question that would be of that scale type.

From the Headlines

12 As part of its bankruptcy restructuring, on June 3, 2009, General Motors (GM) launched an ad campaign that revealed glimmers of a streamlined GM: fewer brands (Cadillac, Buick, Chevrolet, GMC) and fewer models within each brand.

a What research would you have done to determine which vehicle models GM should retain and which it should drop?

b What would you have measured and with what type of measurement scale?

>cases*

Campbell-Ewald: R-E-S-P-E-C-T Spells Loyalty

 Ohio Lottery: Innovative Research Design Drives Winning

 Data Development

 Pebble Beach Co.

Donatos: Finding the New Pizza

Ramada Demonstrates Its *Personal Best*™

NCRCC: Teeing Up and New Strategic Direction

 USTA: Come Out Swinging

NetConversions Influences Kelley Blue Book

Yahoo!: *Consumer Direct* Marries Purchase Metrics to Banner Ads

*You will find a description of each cash in the Case Abstracts section of the textbook. Check the Case Index to determine whether a case provides data, the research instrument, video, or other supplementary material. Written cases are downloadable from the text website (www.mhhe.com/cooper11e). All video material and video cases are available from the Online Learning Center. The film reel icon indicates a video case or video material relevant to the case.

>chapter 12

Measurement Scales

>learningobjectives

After reading this chapter, you should understand . . .

1 The nature of attitudes and their relationship to behavior.

2 The critical decisions involved in selecting an appropriate measurement scale.

3 The characteristics and use of rating, ranking, sorting, and other preference scales.

> 66 Any measurement must take into account the position of the observer. There is no such thing as measurement absolute, there is only measurement relative. 99
>
> Jeanette Winterson,
> journalist and author

They board the sleek corporate jet in Palm Beach and are taken aft to meet with the general manager of MindWriter, who is seated at a conference table that austerely holds one sheaf of papers and a white telephone.

"I'm Jean-Claude Malraison," the general manager says. "Myra, please sit here . . . and you must be Jason Henry. On the flight up from Caracas I read your proposal for the CompleteCare project. I intend to sign your contract if you answer one question to my satisfaction about the schedule.

"I took marketing research in college and didn't like it, so you talk fast, straight, and plainly unless we both decide we need to get technical. If the phone rings, ignore it and keep talking. When you answer my one question, I'll put you off the plane in the first Florida city that has a commercial flight back to . . . to . . ."

"This is Palm Beach, Jean-Claude," says the steward.

"What I don't like is that you are going to hold everything up so you can develop a scale for the questionnaire. Scaling is what I didn't like in marketing research. It is complicated and it takes too much time. Why can't you use some of the scales our marketing people have been using? Why do you have to reinvent the wheel?" The manager is looking toward Myra.

"Our research staff agrees with us that it would be inappropriate to adapt surveys developed for use in our consumer products line," says Myra smoothly.

"OK. Computers are not the same as toaster ovens and VCRs. Gotcha. Jason, what is going to be different about the scales you intend to develop?"

"When we held focus groups with your customers, they continually referred to the need for your product service to 'meet expectations' or 'exceed expectations.' The hundredth time we heard this we realized . . ."

"It's our company credo, 'Underpromise and exceed expectations.'"

"Well, virtually none of the scales developed for customer satisfaction deal with expectations. We want a scale that ranges in five steps from 'Met few expectations' to 'Exceeded expectations,' but we don't know what to name the in-between intervals so that the psychological spacing is equal between increments. We think 'Met many expectations' and 'Met most expectations' and 'Fully met expectations' will be OK, but we want to be sure."

"You are not being fussy here, are you, Jason?"

"No. Because of the way you are running your service operation, we want great precision and reliability."

"Justify that, please, Myra."

"Well, Jean-Claude, besides setting up our own repair force, we have contracted with an outside organization to provide repairs in certain areas, with the intention after six months of comparing the performance of the inside and outside repair organizations and giving the future work to whoever performs better. We feel that such an important decision, which involves the job security of MindWriter employees, must have full credibility."

"I can accept that. Good." The manager scribbles his signature on the contract. "You'll receive this contract in three days, after it has wended its way past the paper pushers. Meantime, we'll settle for a handshake. Nice job, so far, Myra. You seem to have gotten a quick start with MindWriter. Congratulations, Jason.

"Turn the plane around and put these folks out where they got on. They can start working this afternoon . . . . Gosh, is that the beach out there? It looks great. I've got to get some sun one of these days."

"You do look pale," says Myra, sympathetically.

"*Fais gaffe, tu m'fais mal!*" he mutters under his breath.

This chapter covers procedures that will help you understand measurement scales so that you might select or design measures that are appropriate for your research. We concentrate here on the problems of measuring more complex constructs, like attitudes. Conceptually, we start this process by revisiting the research process (see Exhibit 12-1) to understand where the act of scaling fits in the process.

Scales in business research are generally constructed to measure behavior, knowledge, and attitudes. Attitude scales are among the most difficult to construct, so we will use attitudes to develop your understanding of scaling.

> The Nature of Attitudes

Jason is properly concerned about attitude measurement for the MindWriter study. But what is an attitude? There are numerous definitions, but one seems to capture the essence: An **attitude** is a learned, stable predisposition to respond to oneself, other persons, objects, or issues in a consistently favorable or unfavorable way.[1] Important aspects of this definition include the learned nature of attitudes, their relative permanence, and their association with socially significant events and objects. Because an attitude is a *predisposition,* it would seem that the more favorable one's attitude is toward a product or service, the more likely that the product or service will be purchased. But, as we will see, that is not always the case.

Let's use Myra as an example to illustrate the nature of attitudes:

1. She is convinced that MindWriter has great talent, terrific products, and superior opportunities for growth.
2. She loves working at MindWriter.
3. She expects to stay with the firm and work hard to achieve rapid promotions for greater visibility and influence.

The first statement is an example of a *cognitively* based attitude. It represents Myra's memories, evaluations, and beliefs about the properties of the object. A *belief* is an estimate (probability) about the truth of something. In this case, it is the likelihood that the characteristics she attributes to her work environment are true. The statement "I think the cellular market will expand rapidly to incorporate radio and video" is also derived from cognition and belief. The second statement above is an *affectively* based attitude. It represents Myra's feelings, intuition, values, and emotions toward the object. "I love the Yankees" and "I hate corn flakes" are other examples of emotionally oriented attitudes. Finally, researchers recognize a third component, *conative* or *behaviorally* based attitudes. The concluding statement reflects Myra's expectations and behavioral intentions toward her firm and the instrumental behaviors necessary to achieve her future goals.

The Relationship between Attitudes and Behavior

The attitude–behavior relationship is not straightforward, although there may be close linkages. Attitudes and behavioral intentions do not always lead to actual behaviors; and although attitudes and behaviors are expected to be consistent with each other, that is not always the case. Moreover, behaviors can influence attitudes. For example, marketers know that a positive experience with a product or service reinforces a positive attitude or makes a customer question a negative attitude. This is one reason that restaurants where you have a bad dining experience may give you a coupon for a free meal on your next visit. They know a bad experience contributes mightily to formation of negative attitudes.

Business researchers treat attitudes as *hypothetical constructs* because of their complexity and the fact that they are inferred from the measurement data, not actually observed. These qualifications

>Exhibit 12-1 The Scaling Process

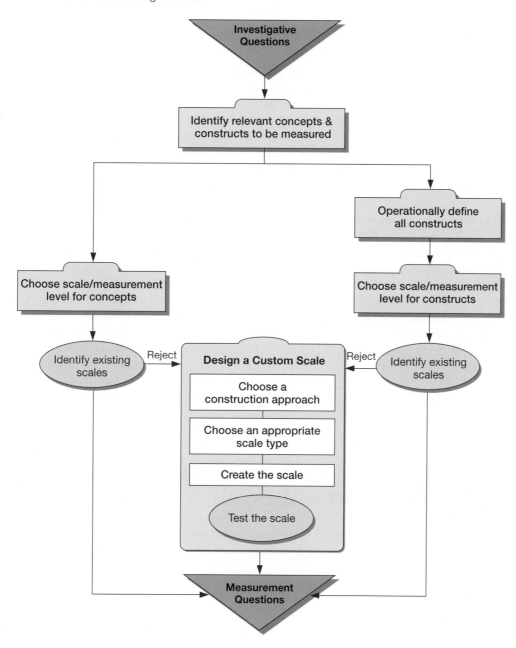

cause researchers to be cautious about the ways certain aspects of measured attitudes predict behavior. Several factors have an effect on the applicability of attitudinal research:

- Specific attitudes are better predictors of behavior than general ones.
- Strong attitudes (strength is affected by *accessibility* or how well the object is remembered and brought to consciousness, how extreme the attitude is, or the degree of confidence in it) are better predictors of behavior than weak attitudes composed of little intensity or topical interest.
- Direct experiences with the attitude object (when the attitude is formed, during repeated exposure, or through reminders) produce behavior more reliably.
- Cognitive-based attitudes influence behaviors better than affective-based attitudes.
- Affective-based attitudes are often better predictors of consumption behaviors.

- Using multiple measurements of attitude or several behavioral assessments across time and environments improves prediction.
- The influence of reference groups (interpersonal support, urges of compliance, peer pressure) and the individual's inclination to conform to these influences improves the attitude-behavior linkage.[2]

Researchers measure and analyze attitudes because attitudes offer insights about behavior. Many of the attitude measurement scales used have been tested for reliability and validity, but often we craft unique scales that don't share those standards. An example is an instrument that measures attitudes about a particular tourist attraction, product, or candidate, as well as the person's intention to visit, buy, or vote. Neither the attitude nor the behavioral intent instrument, alone or together, is effective in predicting the person's actual behavior if it has not been designed carefully. Nevertheless, managers know that the measurement of attitudes is important because attitudes reflect past experience and shape future behavior.

Attitude Scaling

Attitude scaling is the process of assessing an attitudinal disposition using a number that represents a person's score on an attitudinal continuum ranging from an extremely favorable disposition to an extremely unfavorable one. **Scaling** is the "procedure for the assignment of numbers (or other symbols) to a property of objects in order to impart some of the characteristics of numbers to the properties in question."[3] Procedurally, we assign numbers to indicants of the properties of objects. Thus, one assigns a number scale to the various levels of heat and cold and calls it a thermometer. To measure the temperature of the air, you know that a property of temperature is that its variation leads to an expansion or contraction of mercury. A glass tube with mercury provides an indicant of temperature change by the rise or fall of the mercury in the tube. Similarly, your attitude toward your university could be measured on numerous scales that capture indicators of the different dimensions of your awareness, feelings, or behavioral intentions toward the school.

34

The percent of workers who are considered truly loyal.

> Selecting a Measurement Scale

Selecting and constructing a measurement scale requires the consideration of several factors that influence the reliability, validity, and practicality of the scale:

- Research objectives.
- Response types.
- Data properties.
- Number of dimensions.
- Balanced or unbalanced.
- Forced or unforced choices.
- Number of scale points.
- Rater errors.

Research Objectives

Researchers' objectives are too numerous to list (including, but not limited to, studies of attitude, attitude change, persuasion, awareness, purchase intention, cognition and action, actual and repeat purchase). Researchers, however, face two general types of scaling objectives:

- To measure characteristics of the participants who participate in the study.
- To use participants as judges of the objects or indicants presented to them.

Assume you are conducting a study of customers concerning their attitudes toward a change in corporate identity (a company logo and peripherals). With the first study objective, your scale would measure the customers' orientation as favorable or unfavorable. You might combine each person's answers to form an indicator of overall orientation. The emphasis in this first study is on measuring attitudinal differences among people. With the second objective, you might use the same data, but you are now interested in how satisfied people are with different design options. Each participant is asked to choose the object he or she favors or the preferred solution. Participants judge which object has more of some characteristic or which design solution is closest to the company's stated objectives.

Response Types

Measurement scales fall into one of four general types: rating, ranking, categorization, and sorting. A **rating scale** is used when participants score an object or indicant without making a direct comparison to another object or attitude. For example, they may be asked to evaluate the styling of a new automobile on a 7-point rating scale. **Ranking scales** constrain the study participant to making comparisons and determining order among two or more properties (or their indicants) or objects. Participants may be asked to choose which one of a pair of cars has more attractive styling. A *choice* scale requires that participants choose one alternative over another. They could also be asked to rank-order the importance of comfort, ergonomics, performance, and price for the target vehicle. **Categorization** asks participants to put themselves or property indicants in groups or categories. Asking auto show attendees to identify their gender or ethnic background or to indicate whether a particular prototype design would appeal to a youthful or mature driver would require a category response strategy. **Sorting** requires that participants sort cards (representing concepts or constructs) into piles using criteria established by the researcher. The cards might contain photos or images or verbal statements of product features such as various descriptors of the car's performance.

Data Properties

Decisions about the choice of measurement scales are often made with regard to the data properties generated by each scale. In Chapter 11, we said that we classify scales in increasing order of power; scales are nominal, ordinal, interval, or ratio. Nominal scales classify data into categories without indicating order, distance, or unique origin. Ordinal data show relationships of *more than* and *less than* but have no distance or unique origin. Interval scales have both order and distance but no unique origin. Ratio scales possess all four properties' features. The assumptions underlying each level of scale determine how a particular measurement scale's data will be analyzed statistically.

Number of Dimensions

Measurement scales are either *unidimensional* or *multidimensional*. With a **unidimensional scale,** one seeks to measure only one attribute of the participant or object. One measure of an actor's star power is his or her ability to "carry" a movie. It is a single dimension. Several items may be used to measure this dimension and by combining them into a single measure, an agent may place clients along a linear continuum of star power. A **multidimensional scale** recognizes that an object might be better described with several dimensions than on a unidimensional continuum. The actor's *star power* variable might be better expressed by three distinct dimensions—ticket sales for last three movies, speed of attracting financial resources, and column-inch/amount-of-TV coverage of the last three films.

Balanced or Unbalanced

A **balanced rating scale** has an equal number of categories above and below the midpoint. Generally, rating scales should be balanced, with an equal number of favorable and unfavorable response choices. However, scales may be balanced with or without an indifference or midpoint option. A balanced scale might take the form of "very good—good—average—poor—very poor." An **unbalanced rating scale** has an unequal number of favorable and unfavorable response choices. An example of an unbalanced scale that has only one unfavorable descriptive term and four favorable terms is "poor—fair—good—very good—excellent." The scale designer expects that the mean ratings will be near "good" and that there will be a symmetrical distribution of answers around that point, but the scale does not allow participants who are unfavorable to express the intensity of their attitude.

The use of an unbalanced rating scale can be justified in studies in which researchers know in advance that nearly all participants' scores will lean in one direction or the other. Raters are inclined to score attitude objects higher if the objects are very familiar and if they are ego-involved.[4] Brand-loyal customers are also expected to respond favorably. When researchers know that one side of the scale is not likely to be used, they try to achieve precision on the side that will most often receive the participant's attention. Unbalanced scales are also considered when participants are known to be either "easy raters" or "hard raters." An unbalanced scale can help compensate for the error of *leniency* created by such raters.

Forced or Unforced Choices

An **unforced-choice rating scale** provides participants with an opportunity to express no opinion when they are unable to make a choice among the alternatives offered. A **forced-choice rating scale** requires that participants select one of the offered alternatives. Researchers often exclude the response choice "no opinion," "undecided," "don't know," "uncertain," or "neutral" when they know that most participants have an attitude on the topic. It is reasonable in this circumstance to constrain participants so that they focus on alternatives carefully and do not idly choose the middle position. However, when many participants are clearly undecided and the scale does not allow them to express their uncertainty, the forced-choice scale biases results. Researchers discover such bias when a larger percentage of participants express an attitude than did so in previous studies on the same issue. Some of this bias is attributable to participants providing meaningless responses or reacting to questions about which they have no attitudes (see Chapter 13). This affects the statistical measures of the mean and median, which shift toward the scale's midpoint, making it difficult to discern attitudinal differences throughout the instrument.[5] Understanding neutral answers is a challenge for researchers. In a customer satisfaction study that focused on the overall satisfaction question with a company in the electronics industry, an unforced scale was used. Study results, however, revealed that 75 percent of those in the "neutral" participant group could be converted to brand loyalists if the company excelled (received highly favorable ratings) on only 2 of the 26 other scaled questions in the study.[6] Thus, the participants in the neutral group weren't truly neutral, and a forced-choice scale would have revealed the desired information.

Number of Scale Points

What is the ideal number of points for a rating scale? Academics and practitioners often have dogmatic reactions to this question, but the answer is more practical: A scale should be appropriate for its purpose. For a scale to be useful, it should match the stimulus presented and extract information proportionate to the complexity of the attitude object, concept, or construct. A product that requires little effort or thought to purchase, is habitually bought, or has a benefit that fades quickly (low-involvement products) can be measured generally with a simple scale. A 3-point scale (better than average—average—worse than average) is probably sufficient for a deodorant, a fast-food burger, gift-wrapping, or a snack. There is little support for choosing a scale with 5 or more points in this instance. But when the product is complex, plays an important role in the consumer's life, and is costly (e.g., financial services, luxury goods, automobiles, and other high-involvement products), a scale with 5 to 11 points should be considered.

As we noted in Chapter 11, the characteristics of reliability and validity are important factors affecting measurement decisions. First, as the number of scale points increases, the *reliability* of the measure increases.[7] Second, in some studies, scales with 11 points may produce more *valid* results than 3-, 5-, or 7-point scales.[8] Third, some constructs require greater measurement sensitivity and the opportunity to extract more variance, which additional scale points provide. Fourth, a larger number of

Online surveys are increasingly common due in large part to their speed in data collection. They also offer versatility for use with various types of measurement scales; flexibility in containing not only verbal but graphical, photographic, video, and digital elements; access to difficult-to-contact or inaccessible participants; and lower cost of large-sample completion. The visual appearance of the measurement scale is very important in getting the participant to click through to completion. This invitation from Nortel Networks and the opening screen of the questionnaire are designed to encourage participation. Informative, Inc., fielded this survey for Nortel Networks (designed to evaluate Nortel's website). The first screen of the questionnaire indicates two strategies: a multiple-choice, single-response strategy incorporating forced choice, and a multi-item rating grid that does not force choice (notice the NA column). If you look closely, you can also see a scroll bar on the first screen. Some designers will put only one question to a screen in Web questionnaires believing that participants who have to scroll may not fully complete the survey. This survey was designed for a technical audience, so that was not as much a concern. **www.nortelnetworks.com**

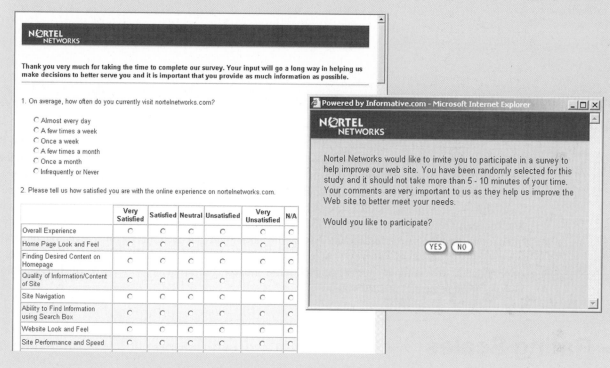

scale points are needed to produce accuracy when using single-dimension versus multiple-dimension scales.[9] Finally, in cross-cultural measurement, the cultural practices may condition participants to a standard metric—a 10-point scale in Italy, for example. Exhibit 12-2 previews the scales discussed in this chapter along with the characteristics of scale types described in Chapter 11.

Rater Errors

The value of rating scales depends on the assumption that a person can and will make good judgments. Before accepting participants' ratings, we should consider their tendencies to make errors of central tendency and halo effect.[10] Some raters are reluctant to give extreme judgments, and this fact accounts for the **error of central tendency.** Participants may also be "easy raters" or "hard raters," making what is called an **error of leniency.** These errors most often occur when the rater does not know the object or property being rated. To address these tendencies, researchers can:

- Adjust the strength of descriptive adjectives.
- Space the intermediate descriptive phrases farther apart.
- Provide smaller differences in meaning between the steps near the ends of the scale than between the steps near the center.
- Use more points in the scale.

>Exhibit 12-2 Characteristics of Scale Types

Characteristic	Dichotomous	Multiple Choice	Checklist	Rating	Ranking	Free Response
Type of Scale	Nominal	Nominal, ordinal, or ratio	Nominal	Ordinal or interval	Ordinal	Nominal or ratio
Usual Number of Answer Alternatives Provided	2	3 to 10	10 or fewer	3 to 7	10 or fewer	None
Desired Number of Participant Answers	1	1	10 or fewer	1 per item	7 or fewer	1
Used to Provide . . .	Classification	Classification, order, or specific numerical estimate	Classification	Order or distance	Order	Classification, (of idea), order, or specific numerical estimate

The **halo effect** is the systematic bias that the rater introduces by carrying over a generalized impression of the subject from one rating to another. An instructor expects the student who does well on the first question of an examination to do well on the second. You conclude a report is good because you like its form, or you believe someone is intelligent because you agree with him or her. Halo is especially difficult to avoid when the property being studied is not clearly defined, is not easily observed, is not frequently discussed, involves reactions with others, or is a trait of high moral importance.[11] Ways of counteracting the halo effect include having the participant rate one trait at a time, revealing one trait per page (as in an Internet survey, where the participant cannot return to change his or her answer), or periodically reversing the terms that anchor the endpoints of the scale, so positive attributes are not always on the same end of each scale.

> Rating Scales

In Chapter 11, we said that questioning is a widely used stimulus for measuring concepts and constructs. For example, a researcher asks questions about participants' attitudes toward the taste of a soft drink. The responses are "thirst quenching," "sour," "strong bubbly," "orange taste," and "syrupy." These answers alone do not provide a means of discerning the degree of favorability and thus would be of limited value to the researcher. However, with a properly constructed scale, the researcher could develop a taste profile for the target brand. We use rating scales to judge properties of objects without reference to other similar objects. These ratings may be in such forms as "like—dislike," "approve—indifferent—disapprove," or other classifications using even more categories.

Examples of rating scales we discuss in this section are shown in Exhibit 12-2. Since this exhibit amplifies the overview presented in this section, we will refer you to the exhibit frequently.[12]

Simple Attitude Scales

The **simple category scale** (also called a *dichotomous scale*) offers two mutually exclusive response choices. In Exhibit 12-3 they are "yes" and "no," but they could just as easily be "important" and "unimportant," "agree" and "disagree," or another set of discrete categories if the question were different. This response strategy is particularly useful for demographic questions or where a dichotomous response is adequate.

When there are multiple options for the rater but only one answer is sought, the **multiple-choice, single-response scale** is appropriate. Our example has five options. The primary alternatives should encompass 90 percent of the range, with the "other" category completing the participant's list. When there is no possibility for an "other" response or exhaustiveness of categories is not critical, the "other" response may be omitted. Both the multiple-choice, single-response scale and the simple category scale produce nominal data.

A variation, the **multiple-choice, multiple-response scale** (also called a *checklist*), allows the rater to select one or several alternatives. In the example in Exhibit 12-3, we are measuring seven items with one question, and it is possible that all seven sources for home design were consulted. The cumulative feature of this scale can be beneficial when a complete picture of the participant's choice is desired, but it may also present a problem for reporting when research sponsors expect the responses to sum to 100 percent. This scale generates nominal data.

Simple attitude scales are easy to develop, are inexpensive, and can be designed to be highly specific. They provide useful information and are adequate if developed skillfully. There are also weaknesses. The design approach is subjective. The researcher's insight and ability offer the only assurance that the items chosen are a representative sample of the universe of attitudes about the attitude object. We have no evidence that each person will view all items with the same frame of reference as will other people. Although such scales are frequently used, there has been a great effort to develop construction techniques that overcome some of their deficiencies.

Likert Scales

The **Likert scale,** developed by Rensis Likert (pronounced Lick-ert), is the most frequently used variation of the summated rating scale. **Summated rating scales** consist of statements that express either a favorable or an unfavorable attitude toward the object of interest. The participant is asked to agree or disagree with each statement. Each response is given a numerical score to reflect its degree of attitudinal favorableness, and the scores may be summed to measure the participant's overall attitude. Summation is *not* necessary and in some instances may actually be misleading, as our caution below clearly shows.

>**Exhibit 12-3** Sample Rating Scales

Simple Category Scale (dichotomous) data: nominal	"I plan to purchase a MindWriter laptop in the next 12 months." ☐ Yes ☐ No
Multiple-Choice, Single-Response Scale data: nominal	"What newspaper do you read most often for financial news?" ☐ *East City Gazette* ☐ *West City Tribune* ☐ Regional newspaper ☐ National newspaper ☐ Other (specify: _____)
Multiple-Choice, Multiple-Response Scale (checklist) data: nominal	"Check *any* of the sources you consulted when designing your new home:" ☐ Online planning services ☐ Magazines ☐ Independent contractor/builder ☐ Developer's models/plans ☐ Designer ☐ Architect ☐ Other (specify: _____)
Likert Scale Summated Rating data: interval	"The Internet is superior to traditional libraries for comprehensive searches." STRONGLY AGREE (5)　　AGREE (4)　　NEITHER AGREE NOR DISAGREE (3)　　DISAGREE (2)　　STRONGLY DISAGREE (1)

>**Exhibit 12-3** Cont'd

Semantic Differential Scale
data: interval

> Lands' End Catalog
>
> FAST ___ : ___ : ___ : ___ : ___ : ___ : ___ SLOW
> HIGH QUALITY ___ : ___ : ___ : ___ : ___ : ___ : ___ LOW QUALITY

Numerical Scale
data: ordinal or*
interval

> EXTREMELY
> FAVORABLE   5   4   3   2   1   EXTREMELY
>   UNFAVORABLE
>
> Employee's cooperation in teams ___
> Employee's knowledge of task ___
> Employee's planning effectiveness ___

Multiple Rating List Scale
data: ordinal or
interval

> "Please indicate how important or unimportant each service characteristic is":
>
> | | IMPORTANT | | | | | UNIMPORTANT | |
> |------------------------------|---|---|---|---|---|---|---|
> | Fast, reliable repair | 7 | 6 | 5 | 4 | 3 | 2 | 1 |
> | Service at my location | 7 | 6 | 5 | 4 | 3 | 2 | 1 |
> | Maintenance by manufacturer | 7 | 6 | 5 | 4 | 3 | 2 | 1 |
> | Knowledgeable technicians | 7 | 6 | 5 | 4 | 3 | 2 | 1 |
> | Notification of upgrades | 7 | 6 | 5 | 4 | 3 | 2 | 1 |
> | Service contract after warranty | 7 | 6 | 5 | 4 | 3 | 2 | 1 |

Constant-Sum Scale
data: ratio

> "Taking all the supplier characteristics we've just discussed and now considering *cost*, what is their relative importance to you (dividing 100 units between)":
>
> Being one of the lowest-cost suppliers
> All other aspects of supplier performance
> Sum   100

Stapel Scale
data: ordinal or*
interval

> (Company Name)
>
> | +5 | +5 | +5 |
> | +4 | +4 | +4 |
> | +3 | +3 | +3 |
> | +2 | +2 | +2 |
> | +1 | +1 | +1 |
> | Technology Leader | Exciting Products | World-Class Reputation |
> | −1 | −1 | −1 |
> | −2 | −2 | −2 |
> | −3 | −3 | −3 |
> | −4 | −4 | −4 |
> | −5 | −5 | −5 |

Graphic Rating Scale
data: ordinal or*
interval or ratio

> "How likely are you to recommend CompleteCare to others?" (Place an X at the position along the line that best reflects your judgment.)
>
> VERY LIKELY |———————————————| VERY UNLIKELY
>
> (alternative with graphic)

* In Chapter 11 we noted that researchers differ in the ways they treat data from certain scales. If you are unable to establish the linearity of the measured variables or you cannot be confident that you have equal intervals, it is proper to treat data from these scales as ordinal.

Measuring Respect

Campbell-Ewald, an award-winning integrated communications agency headquartered in Detroit, believes it is good business to treat customers with respect—and the agency can prove it. As part of a major research initiative to discover why customer relationship management (CRM) solutions were falling short of expectations, Campbell-Ewald mailed more than 5,000 surveys to adults 18 or older who were customers in each of three business sectors: insurance, automotive, and retail. The goal? To answer the question "Does respect influence customer loyalty and, thereby, purchasing?" With partner research company Synovate and Campbell-Ewald clients, three surveys were developed. Each included 27 to 29 attitudinal statements that queried the adults on how they defined respect and the importance of respect to purchase behavior in each sector. Customers responded to the statements using a 5-point scale (strongly agree to strongly

disagree). Using analysis of the results, Campbell-Ewald validated the relevance of its five "People Principles," which, in turn, have helped clients like General Motors, Continental Airlines, and Farmers Insurance incorporate respectful behavior into their business practices. The five "People Principles" of respect are:

- Appreciate me.
- Intentions don't matter; actions do.
- Listen; then you'll know what I said.
- It's about me, not about you.
- Admit it—you goofed!

How would you operationalize the construct of respect?

To learn more about this research, read the case: "Campbell-Ewald: R-E-S-P-E-C-T Spells Loyalty."

www.campbell-ewald.com; www.synovate.com

In Exhibit 12-3, the participant chooses one of five levels of agreement. This is the traditional Likert scale because it meets Likert's rules for construction and testing. The numbers indicate the value to be assigned to each possible answer, with 1 the least favorable impression of Internet superiority and 5 the most favorable. Likert scales also use 7 and 9 scale points. Technically, this is known as a Likert-type scale since its construction is often less rigorous. However, the advantages of the 7- and 9- point scales are a better approximation of a normal response curve and extraction of more variability among respondents. The values for each choice are normally not printed on the instrument, but they are shown in Exhibit 12-4 to illustrate the scoring system.

The Likert scale has many advantages that account for its popularity. It is easy and quick to construct.[13] Conscientious researchers are careful that each item meets an empirical test for discriminating ability between favorable and unfavorable attitudes. Likert scales are probably more reliable and provide a greater volume of data than many other scales. The scale produces interval data.

Originally, creating a Likert scale involved a procedure known as *item analysis*. In the first step, a large number of statements were collected that met two criteria: (1) Each statement was relevant to the attitude being studied; (2) each was believed to reflect a favorable or unfavorable position on that attitude. People similar to those who are going to be studied were asked to read each statement and to state the level of their agreement with it, using a 5-point scale. A scale value of 1 indicated a strongly unfavorable attitude (strongly disagree). The other intensities were 2 (disagree), 3 (neither agree nor disagree), 4 (agree), and 5 (strongly agree), a strongly favorable attitude (see Exhibit 12-3). To ensure consistent results, the assigned numerical values are reversed if the statement is worded negatively (1 is always strongly unfavorable and 5 is always strongly favorable). Each person's responses are then added to secure a total score. The next step is to array these total scores and select some portion representing the highest and lowest total scores (generally defined as the top and bottom 10 to 25 percent of the distribution). The middle group (50 to 80 percent of participants) are excluded from the subsequent analysis.

The two extreme groups represent people with the most favorable and least favorable attitudes toward the attitude being studied. These extremes are the two criterion groups by which individual items are evaluated. **Item analysis** assesses each item based on how well it discriminates between those persons whose total score is high and those whose total score is low. It involves calculating the mean scores for each scale item among the low scorers and high scorers. The mean scores for the high-score

>Exhibit 12-4 Evaluating a Scale Statement by Item Analysis

For the statement "My digital camera's features are exciting," we select the data from the bottom 25 percent of the distribution (low total score group) and the top 25 percent (high total score group). There are 73 people in each group. The remaining 50 percent of the middle of the distribution is not considered for this analysis.

Response Categories	Low Total Score Group				High Total Score Group			
	X	f	fX	$X(fX)$	X	f	fX	$X(fX)$
① {Strongly agree	5	3	15	75	5	22	110	550
Agree	4	4	16	64	4	30	120	480
Undecided	3	29	87	261	3	15	45	135
Disagree	2	22	44	88	2	4	8	16
Strongly disagree}	1	15	15	15	1	2	2	2
Total		73	177	503 ← ②→		73	285	1,183
		n_L	ΣX_L	$\Sigma X(fX)_L$		n_H	ΣX_H	$\Sigma X(fX)_H$

$$\bar{X}_L = \frac{177}{73} = 2.42 \quad \longleftarrow ③ \longrightarrow \quad \bar{X}_H = \frac{285}{73} = 3.90$$

$$\Sigma(X_L - \bar{X}_L)^2 = 503 - \frac{(177)^2}{73} \quad \longleftarrow ④ \longrightarrow \quad \Sigma(X_H - \bar{X}_H)^2 = 1,183 - \frac{(285)^2}{73}$$

$$= 73.84 \qquad\qquad\qquad\qquad\qquad = 70.33$$

$$t = \frac{\bar{X}_H - \bar{X}_L}{\sqrt{\dfrac{\Sigma(X_H - \bar{X}_H)^2 + \Sigma(X_L - \bar{X}_L)^2}{n(n-1)}}} \quad \longleftarrow ⑤$$

$$= \frac{3.90 - 2.42}{\sqrt{\dfrac{70.33 + 73.84}{73(73-1)}}}$$

$$= 8.92 \quad \longleftarrow ⑥$$

Legend:

① For each of the response categories, the scale's value (X) is multiplied by the frequency or number of participants (f) who chose that value. These values produce the product (fX). This number is then multiplied by X. For example, there are 3 participants in the low-score group who scored a 5 (strongly agreed with the statement): $(fX) = (3)(5) = 15$; $(X)(fX) = (5)(15) = 75$.

② The frequencies and products are summed.

③ A mean score for each group is computed.

④ Deviation scores are computed, squared, and summed as required by the formula.

⑤ The data are tested in a modified t-test that compares high- and low-scoring groups for the item. Notice the mean scores in the numerator of the formula.

⑥ The calculated value is compared with a criterion, 1.75. If the calculated value (in this case, 8.92) is equal to or exceeds the criterion, the statement is said to be a good discriminator of the measured attitude. (If it is less than the criterion, we would consider it a poor discriminator of the target attitude and delete it from the measuring instrument.) We then select the next measurement item and repeat the process.

and low-score groups are then tested for statistical significance by computing t values. (In evaluating response patterns of the high and low groups to the statement "My digital camera's features are exciting," we secure the results shown in Exhibit 12-4.) After finding the t values for each statement, they are rank-ordered, and those statements with the highest t values are selected. The 20 to 25 items that have the highest t values (statistically significant differences between mean scores) are selected for inclusion in the final scale.[14] Researchers have found that a larger number of items for each attitude object improve the reliability of the scale. As an approximate indicator of a statement's discrimination power, one authority also suggests using only those statements whose *t* value is 1.75 or greater, provided there are 25 or more subjects in each group.[15]

Although item analysis is helpful in weeding out attitudinal statements that do not discriminate well, the summation procedure causes problems for researchers. The following example on website banner ads shows that the same summated score can mean different things:

1. This banner ad provides the relevant information I expect.
2. I would bookmark this site to use in the future.
3. This banner ad is annoying.
4. I would click for deeper links to discover more details.

If a 5-point scale is used, the maximum favorable score would be 20 (assuming 5 is assigned to the strongly agree response and question 3, a negation, is reverse-scored). Approximately one-half of the statements are worded favorably and the other half unfavorably to safeguard against halo effects. The problem of summation arises because different patterns are concealed by the same total score. One participant could find the website's ad relevant, worth returning to, and somewhat pleasing but not desire deeper information, whereas another could find the ad annoying but have favorable attitudes on the other three questions, thereby producing the same total score.

Semantic Differential Scales

The **semantic differential (SD) scale** measures the psychological meanings of an attitude object using bipolar adjectives. Researchers use this scale for studies such as brand and institutional image. The method consists of a set of bipolar rating scales, usually with 7 points, by which one or more participants rate one or more concepts on each scale item. The SD scale is based on the proposition that an object can have several dimensions of connotative meaning. The meanings are located in multidimensional property space, called *semantic space.* Connotative meanings are suggested or implied meanings, in addition to the explicit meaning of an object. For example, a roaring fire in a fireplace may connote *romantic* as well as its more explicit meaning of *burning flammable material within a brick kiln.* One restaurant trying to attract patrons on slow Tuesday evenings offered a special Tuesday menu and called it "down home cooking." Yankee pot roast, stew, and chicken pot pie, although not its usual cuisine, carried the connotative meaning of *comfort foods* and brought patrons into the restaurant, making Tuesday one of the busiest nights of the week. Advertisers, salespeople, and product and package designers have long known that they must use words, shapes, associations, and images to activate a person's connotative meanings.

Osgood and his associates developed the semantic differential method to measure the psychological meanings of an object to an individual.[16] They produced a list of 289 bipolar adjective pairs, which were reduced to 76 pairs and formed into rating scales for attitude research. Their analysis allowed them to conclude that semantic space is multidimensional rather than unidimensional. Three factors contributed most to meaningful judgments by participants: (1) evaluation, (2) potency, and (3) activity. These concepts from the historical thesaurus study (Exhibit 12-5) illustrate the wide applicability of the technique to persons, abstract concepts, events, institutions, and physical objects.[17]

Results of the thesaurus study are shown in Exhibit 12-5.

Researchers have followed a somewhat different approach to SD scales than did the original study advocates. They have developed their own adjectives or phrases and have focused on the evaluative dimension more often (which might help explain the popularity of the Likert scale). The positive benefit is that the scales created have been adapted to specific management questions. One study explored a retail store image using 35 pairs of words or phrases classified into eight groups. These word pairs were especially created for the study. Excerpts from this scale are presented in Exhibit 12-6. Other categories of scale items were "general characteristics of the company," "physical characteristics of the store," "prices charged by the store," "store personnel," "advertising by the store," and "your friends and the store." Since the scale pairs are closely associated with the characteristics of the store and its use, one could develop image profiles of various stores.

The semantic differential has several advantages. It is an efficient and easy way to secure attitudes from a large sample. These attitudes may be measured in both direction and intensity. The total set of responses provides a comprehensive picture of the meaning of an object and a measure of the person

>**Exhibit 12-5** Results of the Thesaurus Study

Evaluation (E)	Potency (P)	Activity (A)
Good–bad	Hard–soft	Active–passive
Positive–negative	Strong–weak	Fast–slow
Optimistic–pessimistic	Heavy–light	Hot–cold
Complete–incomplete	Masculine–feminine	Excitable–calm
Timely–untimely	Severe–lenient	
	Tenacious–yielding	

Subcategories of Evaluation			
Meek Goodness	**Dynamic Goodness**	**Dependable Goodness**	**Hedonistic Goodness**
Clean–dirty	Successful–unsuccessful	True–false	Pleasurable–painful
Kind–cruel	High–low	Reputable–disreputable	Beautiful–ugly
Sociable–unsociable	Meaningful–meaningless	Believing–skeptical	Sociable–unsociable
Light–dark	Important–unimportant	Wise–foolish	Meaningful–meaningless
Altruistic–egotistical	Progressive–regressive	Healthy–sick	
Grateful–ungrateful	Clean–dirty		
Beautiful–ugly			
Harmonious–dissonant			

Source: Adapted from Charles E. Osgood, G. J. Suci, and P. H. Tannenbaum, *The Measurement of Meaning* (Urbana: University of Illinois Press, 1957), table 5, pp. 52–61.

>**Exhibit 12-6** Adapting SD Scales for Retail Store Image Study

Convenience of Reaching the Store from Your Location		
Nearby	___: ___: ___: ___: ___: ___: ___:	Distant
Short time required to reach store	___: ___: ___: ___: ___: ___: ___:	Long time required to reach store
Difficult drive	___: ___: ___: ___: ___: ___: ___:	Easy drive
Difficult to find parking place	___: ___: ___: ___: ___: ___: ___:	Easy to find parking place
Convenient to other stores I shop	___: ___: ___: ___: ___: ___: ___:	Inconvenient to other stores I shop

Products Offered		
Wide selection of different kinds of products	___: ___: ___: ___: ___: ___: ___:	Limited selection of different kinds of products
Fully stocked	___: ___: ___: ___: ___: ___: ___:	Understocked
Undependable products	___: ___: ___: ___: ___: ___: ___:	Dependable products
High quality	___: ___: ___: ___: ___: ___: ___:	Low quality
Numerous brands	___: ___: ___: ___: ___: ___: ___:	Few brands
Unknown brands	___: ___: ___: ___: ___: ___: ___:	Well-known brands

Source: Robert F. Kelly and Ronald Stephenson, "The Semantic Differential: An Information Source for Designing Retail Patronage Appeals," *Journal of Marketing* 31 (October 1967), p. 45.

>**Exhibit 12-7** Steps in Constructing an SD Scale

1. Select the concepts: nouns, noun phrases, or nonverbal stimuli such as visual sketches. Concepts are chosen by judgment and reflect the nature of the investigative question. In the MindWriter study, one concept might be "Call Center accessibility."

2. Select bipolar word pairs or phrase pairs appropriate to your needs. If the traditional Osgood adjectives are used, several criteria guide your selection:

   • Three bipolar pairs are required when using evaluation, potency, and activity. Scores on these individual items can be averaged, by factor, to improve their reliability.

   • The scale should be relevant to the concepts being judged. Choose adjectives that allow connotative perceptions to be expressed. Irrelevant concept-scale pairings yield neutral midpoint values that convey little information.

   • Scales should be stable across raters and concepts. A pair such as "large–small" may be interpreted as denotative when judging a physical object such as "automobile" but may be used connotatively with abstract concepts such as "product quality."

   • Scales should be linear between polar opposites and pass through the origin. A pair that fails this test is "rugged–delicate," which is nonlinear on the evaluation dimension. When used separately, both adjectives have favorable meanings.*

3. Create the scoring system and assign a weight to each point on the scale. The negative signs in the original scoring procedure ($-3, -2, -1, 0, +1, +2, +3$) were found to produce coding errors, and the 0 point is arbitrary. Most SD scales have 7 points: 7, 6, 5, 4, 3, 2, and 1.

4. As with Likert scales, about half of the adjective pairs are randomly reversed to minimize the halo effect.

*Charles E. Osgood, G. J. Suci, and P. H. Tannenbaum, *The Measurement of Meaning* (Urbana: University of Illinois Press, 1957).

>**Exhibit 12-8** SD Scale for Analyzing Industry Association Candidates

	Analyze (candidate) for current position:									
(E)	Sociable	(7): ____: ____: ____: ____: ____: ____: ____:	(1) Unsociable
(P)	Weak	(1): ____: ____: ____: ____: ____: ____: ____:	(7) Strong
(A)	Active	(7): ____: ____: ____: ____: ____: ____: ____:	(1) Passive
(E)	Progressive	(7): ____: ____: ____: ____: ____: ____: ____:	(1) Regressive
(P)	Yielding	(1): ____: ____: ____: ____: ____: ____: ____:	(7) Tenacious
(A)	Slow	(1): ____: ____: ____: ____: ____: ____: ____:	(7) Fast
(E)	True	(7): ____: ____: ____: ____: ____: ____: ____:	(1) False
(P)	Heavy	(7): ____: ____: ____: ____: ____: ____: ____:	(1) Light
(A)	Hot	(7): ____: ____: ____: ____: ____: ____: ____:	(1) Cold
(E)	Unsuccessful	(1): ____: ____: ____: ____: ____: ____: ____:	(7) Successful

doing the rating. It is a standardized technique that is easily repeated but escapes many problems of response distortion found with more direct methods. It produces interval data. Basic instructions for constructing an SD scale are found in Exhibit 12-7.

In Exhibit 12-8 we see a scale being used by a panel of corporate leaders evaluating candidates for a high-level position in their industry's lobbying association. The selection of the concepts is driven by the characteristics they believe the candidate must possess to be successful in advancing their agenda. There are three candidates.

Based on the panel's requirements, we choose 10 scales to score the candidates. The letters along the left side, which show the relevant attitude dimension, would be omitted from the actual scale, as would the numerical values shown. Note that the evaluation, potency, and activity scales are mixed.

>Exhibit 12-9 Graphic Representation of SD Analysis

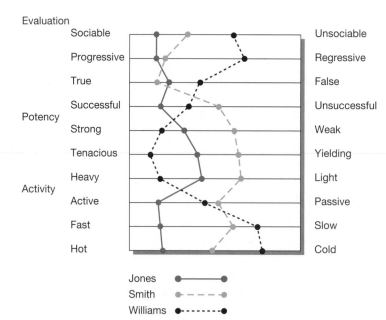

Evaluation	
Sociable	Unsociable
Progressive	Regressive
True	False
Potency	
Successful	Unsuccessful
Strong	Weak
Tenacious	Yielding
Activity	
Heavy	Light
Active	Passive
Fast	Slow
Hot	Cold

Jones ●———●
Smith ●– – –●
Williams ●·······●

To analyze the results, the set of evaluation (E) values is averaged, as are those for the potency (P) and activity (A) dimensions.

The data are plotted in a "snake diagram" in Exhibit 12-9. Here the adjective pairs are reordered so that evaluation, potency, and activity descriptors are grouped together, with the ideal factor reflected by the left side of the scale.

Numerical/Multiple Rating List Scales

Numerical scales have equal intervals that separate their numeric scale points, as shown in Exhibit 12-3. The verbal anchors serve as the labels for the extreme points. Numerical scales are often 5-point scales but may have 7 or 10 points. The participants write a number from the scale next to each item. If numerous questions about a product's performance were included in the example, the scale would provide both an absolute measure of importance and a relative measure (ranking) of the various items rated. The scale's linearity, simplicity, and production of ordinal or interval data make it popular for managers and researchers. When evaluating a new product concept, purchase intent is frequently measured with a 5- to 7-point numerical scale, with the anchors being "definitely would buy" and "definitely would not buy."

A **multiple rating list scale** (Exhibit 12-3) is similar to the numerical scale but differs in two ways: (1) It accepts a circled response from the rater, and (2) the layout facilitates visualization of the results. The advantage is that a mental map of the participant's evaluations is evident to both the rater and the researcher. This scale produces interval data.

Stapel Scales

The **Stapel scale** is used as an alternative to the semantic differential, especially when it is difficult to find bipolar adjectives that match the investigative question. In the example in Exhibit 12-3 there are three attributes of corporate image. The scale is composed of the word (or phrase) identifying the image dimension and a set of 10 response categories for each of the three attributes.

Fewer response categories are sometimes used. Participants select a plus number for the characteristic that describes the attitude object. The more accurate the description, the larger is the positive number. Similarly, the less accurate the description, the larger is the negative number chosen.

Ratings range from +5 to −5, with participants selecting a number that describes the store very accurately to very inaccurately. Like the Likert, SD, and numerical scales, Stapel scales usually produce interval data.

Constant-Sum Scales

A scale that helps the researcher discover proportions is the **constant-sum scale.** With a constant-sum scale, the participant allocates points to more than one attribute or property indicant, such that they total a constant sum, usually 100 or 10. In the Exhibit 12-3 example, two categories are presented that must sum to 100. In the restaurant example, the participant distributes 100 points among four categories:

> You have 100 points to distribute among the following characteristics of the Dallas Steakhouse. Indicate the relative importance of each attribute:
>
> _____ Food Quality
> _____ Atmosphere
> _____ Service
> _____ Price
> 100 TOTAL

Up to 10 categories may be used, but both participant precision and patience suffer when too many stimuli are proportioned and summed. A participant's ability to add is also taxed in some situations; thus, this is not a response strategy that can be effectively used with children or the uneducated. The advantage of the scale is its compatibility with percent (100 percent) and the fact that alternatives that are perceived to be equal can be so scored—unlike the case with most ranking scales. The scale is used to record attitudes, behavior, and behavioral intent. The constant-sum scale produces interval data.

Graphic Rating Scales

The **graphic rating scale** was originally created to enable researchers to discern fine differences. Theoretically, an infinite number of ratings are possible if participants are sophisticated enough to differentiate and record them. They are instructed to mark their response at any point along a continuum. Usually, the score is a measure of length (millimeters) from either endpoint. The results are treated as interval data. The difficulty is in coding and analysis. This scale requires more time than scales with predetermined categories.

Never_____X_____Always

Other graphic rating scales (see Exhibit 12-3) use pictures, icons, or other visuals to communicate with the rater and represent a variety of data types. Graphic scales are often used with children, whose more limited vocabulary prevents the use of scales anchored with words.

> Ranking Scales

In ranking scales, the participant directly compares two or more objects and makes choices among them. Frequently, the participant is asked to select one as the "best" or the "most preferred." When there are only two choices, this approach is satisfactory, but it often results in ties when more than two choices are found. For example, assume participants are asked to select the most preferred among three or more models of a product. In response, 40 percent choose model A, 30 percent choose model B, and 30 percent choose model C. Which is the preferred model? The analyst would be taking a risk to suggest that A is most preferred. Perhaps that interpretation is correct, but 60 percent of the participants chose some model other than A. Perhaps all B and C voters would place A last, preferring either B or C to A. This ambiguity can be avoided by using some of the techniques described in this section.

>**Exhibit 12-10** Ranking Scales

Paired-Comparison Scale data: ordinal	"For each pair of two-seat sports cars listed, place a check beside the one you would most prefer if you had to choose between the two." ___ BMW Z4 M Coupe ___ Chevrolet Corvette Z06 ___ Porsche Cayman S ___ Porsche Cayman S ___ Chevrolet Corvette Z06 ___ Porsche Cayman S ___ BMW Z4 M Coupe ___ Dodge Viper SRT10 ___ Chevrolet Corvette Z06 ___ Dodge Viper SRT10 ___ Dodge Viper SRT10 ___ BMW Z4 M Coupe
Forced Ranking Scale data: ordinal	"Rank the radar detection features in your order of preference. Place the number 1 next to the most preferred, 2 by the second choice, and so forth." ___ User programming ___ Cordless capability ___ Small size ___ Long-range warning ___ Minimal false alarms
Comparative Scale data: ordinal	"Compared to your previous hair dryer's performance, the new one is": SUPERIOR ABOUT THE SAME INFERIOR — — — — — 1 2 3 4 5

Using the **paired-comparison scale,** the participant can express attitudes unambiguously by choosing between two objects. Typical of paired comparisons would be the sports car preference example in Exhibit 12-10. The number of judgments required in a paired comparison is $[(n)(n-1)/2]$, where n is the number of stimuli or objects to be judged. When four cars are evaluated, the participant evaluates six paired comparisons $[(4)(3)/2 = 6]$.

In another example we might compare packaging design proposals considered by a brand manager (see Exhibit 12-11). Generally, there are more than two stimuli to judge, resulting in a potentially tedious task for participants. If 15 suggestions for design proposals are available, 105 paired comparisons would be made.

Reducing the number of comparisons per participant without reducing the number of objects can lighten this burden. You can present each participant with only a sample of the stimuli. In this way, each pair of objects must be compared an equal number of times. Another procedure is to choose a few objects that are believed to cover the range of attractiveness at

Assume you are asked by Galaxy Department Stores to study the shopping habits and preferences of teen girls. Galaxy is seeking a way to compete with specialty stores that are far more successful in serving this market segment. Galaxy is considering the construction of an intrastore boutique catering to these teens. What measurement issues would determine your construction of measurement scales?

>**Exhibit 12-11** Response Patterns of 200 Heavy Users' Paired Comparisons on Five
Alternative Package Designs

Paired-comparison data may be treated in several ways. If there is substantial consistency, we will find that if A is preferred to B, and B to C, then A will be consistently preferred to C. This condition of transitivity need not always be true but should occur most of the time. When it does, take the total number of preferences among the comparisons as the score for that stimulus. Assume a manager is considering five distinct packaging designs. She would like to know how heavy users would rank these designs. One option would be to ask a sample of the heavy-users segment to pair-compare the packaging designs. With a rough comparison of the total preferences for each option, it is apparent that B is the most popular.

	Designs				
	A	**B**	**C**	**D**	**E**
A	—	164*	138	50	70
B	36	—	54	14	30
C	62	146	—	32	50
D	150	186	168	—	118
E	130	170	150	82	—
Total	378	**666**	510	178	268
Rank order	3	**1**	2	5	4

*Interpret this cell as 164 of 200 customers preferred suggested design B (column) to design A (row).

equal intervals. All other stimuli are then compared to these few standard objects. If 36 automobiles are to be judged, four may be selected as standards and the others divided into four groups of eight each. Within each group, the eight are compared to each other. Then the 32 are individually compared to each of the four standard automobiles. This reduces the number of comparisons from 630 to 240.

Paired comparisons run the risk that participants will tire to the point that they give ill-considered answers or refuse to continue. Opinions differ about the upper limit, but five or six stimuli are not unreasonable when the participant has other questions to answer. If the data collection consists only of paired comparisons, as many as 10 stimuli are reasonable. A paired comparison provides ordinal data.

The **forced ranking scale,** shown in Exhibit 12-10, lists attributes that are ranked relative to each other. This method is faster than paired comparisons and is usually easier and more motivating to the participant. With five items, it takes 10 paired comparisons to complete the task, and the simple forced ranking of five is easier. Also, ranking has no transitivity problem where A is preferred to B, and B to C, but C is preferred to A—although it also forces a false unidimensionality.

A drawback to forced ranking is the number of stimuli that can be handled by this method. Five objects can be ranked easily, but participants may grow careless in ranking 10 or more items. In addition, rank ordering produces ordinal data since the distance between preferences is unknown.

Often the manager is interested in benchmarking. This calls for a standard by which other programs, processes, brands, point-of-sale promotions, or people can be compared. The **comparative scale** is ideal for such comparisons if the participants are familiar with the standard. In the Exhibit 12-10 example, the standard is the participant's previous hair dryer. The new dryer is being assessed relative to it. The provision to compare yet other dryers to the standard is not shown in the example but is nonetheless available to the researcher.

Some researchers treat the data produced by comparative scales as interval data since the scoring reflects an interval between the standard and what is being compared. We would treat the rank or position of the item as ordinal data unless the linearity of the variables in question could be supported.

Paired Comparison Increases Hospitality

Should Northwest Airlines, Marriott, or Alaskan Airlines attempt to attract the business of Americans with disabilities? If so, what would it take to capture the segment? Eric Lipp, executive director of the Open Doors Organization (ODO), an advocacy organization for those with disabilities, sponsored a study to find out. High on his agenda was providing an incentive to the travel industry to make accommodations to attract the 22 million adults with disabilities who have traveled in the last two years on 63 million trips—and who may want to travel more. "We now estimate that Americans with disabilities currently spent $13.2 billion in travel expenditures and that amount would at least double [to $27.2 billion] if travel businesses were more attuned to the needs of those with disabilities."

ODO hired Harris Interactive, a global market research and consulting firm best known for The Harris Poll and for pioneering the Internet method to conduct scientifically accurate market research. Harris Interactive conducted a hybrid study via both online and phone surveys to determine the magnitude of the disability travel segment, its purchasing power, and the accommodations the segment needed to increase travel. "Those with disabilities can't all be reached with one method," explained Laura Light, project director with Harris Interactive. "The nature of their physical limitation might preclude one method or the other."

And how did the firm evaluate all the possible accommodations—from Braille safety cards on airplanes to a designated person to handle problems in a hotel? Harris Interactive used its proprietary *COMPASS*™ methodology, which uses paired comparisons as a measurement tool. "*COMPASS*™ saves the participant time and energy," explained Light. "Even with a long list, *COMPASS*™ can be done quickly." In the ODO study, *COMPASS*™ was used twice: once to measure 17 possible airline accommodations and once to measure 23 possible hotel accommodations. By having each participant evaluate only a portion of the large number of accommodation pairs rather than the full list (136 for airline accommodations and 253 for hotel accommodations), each question was answered in under four minutes. By using this process with all members of the sample, Harris Interactive is able to rank-order the items and measure the magnitude of difference between items. This makes it easier for Delta, Marriott, or Alaskan Airlines to make the right choices about accommodations for those with disabilities.

www.opendoorsnfp.org; www.harrisinteractive.com

To learn more about this research, read the case "Open Doors: Extending Hospitality to Travelers with Disabilities."

> Sorting

Q-sorts require sorting of a deck of cards into piles that represent points along a continuum. The participant—or judge—groups the cards based on his or her response to the concept written on the card. Researchers using Q-sort resolve three special problems: item selection, structured or unstructured choices in sorting, and data analysis. The basic Q-sort procedure involves the selection of a set of verbal statements, phrases, single words, or photos related to the concept being studied. For statistical stability, the number of cards should not be less than 60; and for convenience, not be more than 120. After the cards are created, they are shuffled, and the participant is instructed to sort the cards into a set of piles (usually 7 to 11), each pile representing a point on the judgment continuum. The left-most pile represents the concept statements, which are "most valuable," "favorable," "agreeable," and so forth. The right-most pile contains the least favorable cards. The researcher asks the participant to fill the center, or neutral, pile with the cards about which the participant is indecisive. In the case of a *structured* sort, the distribution of cards allowed in each pile is predetermined. With an *unstructured* sort, only the number of piles will be determined. Although the distribution of cards in most structured sorts resembles a normal distribution, there is some controversy about analyzing the data as ranking (ordinal data) versus interval data.

The purpose of sorting is to get a conceptual representation of the sorter's attitude toward the attitude object and to compare the relationships between people. The relative ranking of concepts allows researchers to derive clusters of individuals possessing similar preferences. By researchers varying

>**close**up

MindWriter Scaling

Jason has been working on scaling for Mind-Writer's CompleteCare project for a week when the request comes to Myra Wines to report her progress to MindWriter's general manager. He has narrowed the choice to the three scales in Exhibit 12-12: a Likert scale, a numerical rating scale with two verbal anchors, and a hybrid expectation scale. All are 5-point scales that are presumed to measure at the interval level.

He needs a statement that can accompany the scale for preliminary evaluation. Returning to their list of investigative questions, he finds a question that seems to capture the essence of the repair process: Are customers' problems resolved? Translated into an assertion for the scale, the statement becomes "Resolution of problem that prompted service/repair." He continues to labor over the wording of the verbal anchors. Appropriate versions of the investigative question are constructed, and then the scales are added.

After consulting with MindWriter's research staff, Myra and Jason discuss the advantages of the scales. Myra suggests it is unlikely that CompleteCare would meet none of the customers' expectations. And, with errors of leniency, "none" should be replaced by the term "few" so that the low end of the scale would be more relevant. Jason has read a *Marketing News* article that

said Likert scales and scales similar to MindWriter's numerical scale frequently produced a heavy concentration of 4s and 5s—a common problem in customer satisfaction research.

Others suggest a 7-point scale to remedy this, but Jason thinks the term "exceeded" on the expectation scale could compensate for scores that cluster on the positive end.

Now ready for a pilot test, Jason decides to compare the expectation scale with MindWriter's numerical rating scale. (The Likert scale requires that they create more potential items than they had room for on the postcard.) Using the CompleteCare database, names, addresses, and phone numbers are selected, and 30 customers are chosen at random from those who have had recent service. Jason chooses the delayed equivalent forms method for reliability testing (see Chapter 11). Jason administers the expectation scale followed by the numerical scale to half of the participants and the numerical scale followed by the expectation scale to the other half. Each half sample experiences a time delay. No "order-of-presentation" effects are found. Subsequently, Jason correlates the numerical satisfaction scores with the expectation scores and plots the results, shown in Exhibit 12-13.

On the problem resolution question, the participants' scores from the satisfaction scale and those from the expectation scale

>**Exhibit 12-12** Alternative Scales Considered for MindWriter

Likert Scale				
The problem that prompted service/repair was resolved.				
Strongly Disagree	Disagree	Neither Agree nor Disagree	Agree	Strongly Agree
1	2	3	4	5

Numerical Scale (MindWriter's Favorite)				
To what extent are you satisfied that the problem that prompted service/repair was resolved?				
Very Dissatisfied				Very Satisfied
1	2	3	4	5

Hybrid Expectation Scale				
Resolution of the problem that prompted service/repair.				
Met Few Expectations	Met Some Expectations	Met Most Expectations	Met All Expectations	Exceeded Expectations
1	2	3	4	5

>closeupcont'd

>Exhibit 12-13 Plot of MindWriter Scale Evaluation

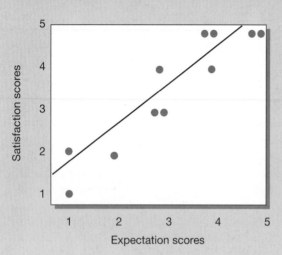

are positively correlated. The correlation index is .90 (1.00 is a perfect positive correlation). This reveals the equivalence of both scales. On another reliability issue, stability, a check of the test-retest reliability over a one-week interval produces a correlation index of .93 for the expectation scale, but the MindWriter satisfaction scale has a lower index ($r = .75$). This implies that the expectation scale is more likely to produce stable and consistent results. Finally, as shown in the plot, the data for the resolution question measured on both scales are linear (they cluster around a straight line). It is logical to conclude that the expectation scale, which was originally thought to have advantages, performs well in initial tests and is a good replacement for MindWriter's existing scale.

The decision is made. They will use the new hybrid expectation scale for the MindWriter research on the CompleteCare service program.

the instructions, the technique can be used to describe products, services, behavioral intentions, and a host of other applications. In the example below, participants are asked to complete a structured sort of cards containing the names of magazines. The scale values and the number of cards in each pile are predetermined, although the distribution in this case represents a normal statistical distribution.

What magazines do you want Singapore Airlines to carry for its in-flight service?

Most Preferred										Least Preferred	
10	9	8	7	6	5	4	3	2	1	0	(scale value)
3	4	7	10	13	16	13	10	7	4	3	(number of cards per pile)

> Cumulative Scales

Total scores on **cumulative scales** have the same meaning. Given a person's total score, it is possible to estimate which items were answered positively and negatively. A pioneering scale of this type was the scalogram. **Scalogram analysis** is a procedure for determining whether a set of items forms a unidimensional scale.[18] A scale is unidimensional if the responses fall into a pattern in which endorsement of the item reflecting the extreme position results in endorsing all items that are less extreme.

Assume we are surveying opinions regarding a new style of running shoe. We have developed a preference scale of four items:

1. The Airsole is good-looking.
2. I will insist on Airsole next time because it is great-looking.
3. The appearance of Airsole is acceptable to me.
4. I prefer the Airsole style to other styles.

Participants indicate whether they agree or disagree. If these items form a unidimensional scale, the response patterns will approach the ideal configuration shown in Exhibit 12-14. Item 2 is the most

>**Exhibit 12-14** Ideal Scalogram Response Pattern*

	Item			
2	**4**	**1**	**3**	**Participant Score**
X	X	X	X	4
—	X	X	X	3
—	—	X	X	2
—	—	—	X	1
—	—	—	—	0

*X = agree; — = disagree.

extreme position of the four attitude statements. A participant who agrees with item 2 will agree with all four items. The items are ordered in the scalogram left to right from most to least extreme. If each agreement renders a score of 1, a score of 4 indicates all statements are agreed upon and represents the most favorable attitude. Persons with a score of 3 should disagree with item 2 but agree with all others, and so on. According to scalogram theory, this pattern confirms that the universe of content (attitude toward the appearance of this running shoe) is scalable.

The scalogram and similar procedures for discovering underlying structure are useful for assessing attitudes and behaviors that are highly structured, such as social distance, organizational hierarchies, and evolutionary product stages.[19] The scalogram is used much less often today, but retains potential for specific applications.

>summary

1 Managers know that the measurement of attitudes is an important aspect of strategy and often the best tool available because attitudes reflect past experience and shape future behavior. Attitudes are learned, stable predispositions to respond to oneself, other persons, objects, or issues in a consistently favorable or unfavorable way. Attitudes are generally thought to be composed of three components: affective, cognitive, and behavioral intentions.

2 Selecting and constructing a measurement scale requires the consideration of several factors that influence the reliability, validity, and practicality of the scale. Two broad research objectives are to measure characteristics of the individuals who participate in studies and to use participants as judges of the objects or indicants presented to them. Measurement scales fall into one of four general response types: rating, ranking, categorization, and sorting. The properties of data are classified in increasing order of power—nominal, ordinal, interval, or ratio—which determines how a particular measurement scale's data will be analyzed statistically. Measurement scales are either unidimensional or multidimensional. A balanced rating

scale has an equal number of categories above and below the midpoint, whereas an unbalanced rating scale has an unequal number of favorable and unfavorable response choices. An unforced-choice rating scale provides participants with an opportunity to express no opinion when they are unable to make a choice among the alternatives offered. A forced-choice scale requires that they select one of the offered alternatives. The ideal number of points for a rating scale should match the stimulus presented and extract information proportionate to the complexity of the attitude object. The value of rating scales depends on the assumption that a rater can and will make good judgments. Errors of central tendency, halo effect, and leniency adversely affect a precise understanding of the measurement.

3 Rating scales have several uses, design features, and requirements. The simple category scale offers two mutually exclusive response choices. The multiple-choice, single-response scale offers the rater several options, including "other." The multiple-choice, multiple-response scale (also called a checklist) allows the rater to select one or several alternatives, thereby providing a cumulative feature.

The Likert scale consists of a series of statements, and the participant is asked to agree or disagree with each statement. Summation is possible with this scale although not necessary and in some instances undesirable.

The semantic differential (SD) scale measures the psychological meanings of an attitude object. Researchers use this scale for studies of brand and institutional image. The method consists of a set of bipolar rating scales, usually with 7 points, by which one or more participants rate one or more concepts on each scale item. The Stapel scale is used as an alternative to the semantic differential, especially when it is difficult to find bipolar adjectives that match the investigative question. Participants select a plus number for the characteristic that describes the attitude object. Ratings range from +5 to −5, and participants select a number that describes the object very accurately to very inaccurately.

Numerical scales have equal intervals that separate their numeric scale points. Verbal anchors serve as the labels for the extreme points. Numerical scales are often 5-point scales but may have 7 or 10 points. A multiple rating list scale is similar to the numerical scale but accepts a circled response from the rater, and the layout allows visualization of the results.

A scale that helps the researcher discover proportions is the constant-sum scale. The participant distributes 100 points among up to 10 categories. The graphic rating scale was originally created to enable researchers to discern fine differences. Raters check their response at any point

along a continuum. Other graphic rating scales use pictures, icons, or other visuals to communicate with children or others whose limited vocabulary prevents the use of scales anchored with words.

Ranking scales allow the participant to compare two or more objects and make choices among them. Frequently, the participant is asked to select one as the "best" or the "most preferred." When there are only two choices, as with the paired-comparison scale, the participant can express attitudes unambiguously by choosing between two objects. The forced ranking scale lists attributes that are ranked relative to each other. This method is faster than paired comparisons and more user-friendly. Often the researcher is interested in benchmarking. This calls for a standard by which training programs, processes, brands, point-of-sale purchases, or people can be compared. The comparative scale is ideal for such comparisons if the participants are familiar with the standard.

Q-sorts are a form of scaling that requires sorting of a deck of cards into piles that represent points along a continuum. The purpose of sorting is to get a conceptual representation of the sorter's attitude toward the attitude object and to compare the relationships between people. Given a person's total score, it is possible to estimate which items were answered positively and negatively on cumulative scales. A pioneering cumulative scale was the scalogram, a procedure for determining whether a set of items forms a unidimensional scale.

>**key**terms

attitude 292

balanced rating scale 295

categorization 295

comparative scale 309

constant-sum scale 307

cumulative scale 312

error of central tendency 297

error of leniency 297

forced-choice rating scale 296

forced ranking scale 309

graphic rating scale 307

halo effect (error) 298

item analysis 301

Likert scale 299

multidimensional scale 295

multiple-choice, multiple-response scale 299

multiple-choice, single-response scale 298

multiple rating list scale 306

numerical scale 306

paired-comparison scale 308

Q-sort 310

ranking scale 295

rating scale 295

scaling 294

scalogram analysis 312

semantic differential (SD) scale 303

simple category scale 298

sorting 295

Stapel scale 306

summated rating scale 299

unbalanced rating scale 296

unforced-choice rating scale 296

unidimensional scale 295

>discussionquestions

Terms in Review

1 Discuss the relative merits of and problems with:

   a Rating and ranking scales.

   b Likert and differential scales.

   c Unidimensional and multidimensional scales.

Making Research Decisions

2 Assume you are Menu Foods and you planned a major research study just prior to the largest pet food recall in our history. You plan to proceed with the study and feel you must add one or more questions to measure the consumer's confidence that your firm will be able to recover. Draft a scale for each of the following types that will measure that confidence.

   a Constant-sum scale.

   b Likert-type summated scale.

   c Semantic differential scale.

   d Stapel scale.

   e Forced ranking scale.

3 An investigative question in your employee satisfaction study seeks to assess employee "job involvement." Create a measurement question that uses the following scales:

   a A graphic rating scale.

   b A multiple rating list.

   Which scale do you recommend and why?

4 You receive the results of a paired-comparison preference test of four soft drinks from a sample of 200 persons. The results are as follows:

	Koak	Zip	Pabze	Mr. Peepers
Koak	—	50*	115	35
Zip	150	—	160	70
Pabze	85	40	—	45
Mr. Peepers	165	130	155	—

*Read as 50 persons preferred Zip to Koak.

   a How do these brands rank in overall preference in this sample?

   b Develop an interval scale for these four brands.

5 One of the problems in developing rating scales is the choice of response terms to use. Below are samples of some widely used scaling codes. Do you see any problems with them?

   a Yes—Depends—No

   b Excellent—Good—Fair—Poor

   c Excellent—Good—Average—Fair—Poor

   d Strongly Approve—Approve—Uncertain—Disapprove—Strongly Disapprove

6 You are working on a consumer perception study of four brands of bicycles. You will need to develop measurement questions and scales to accomplish the tasks listed below. Be sure to explain which data levels (nominal, ordinal, interval, ratio) are appropriate and which quantitative techniques you will use.

   a Prepare an overall assessment of all the brands.

   b Provide a comparison of the brands for each of the following dimensions:

      (1) Styling

      (2) Durability

      (3) Gear quality

      (4) Brand image

7 Below is a Likert-type scale that might be used to evaluate your opinion of the educational degree program in which you are enrolled. There are five response categories: Strongly Agree, Agree, Neither Agree nor Disagree, Disagree, and Strongly Disagree. If Strongly Agree (SA) represents the most positive attitude, how would you value the items below? Record your answers to the items.

   a This program is not very challenging. SA A N D SD

   b The general level of teaching is good. SA A N D SD

   c I really think I am learning a lot from this program. SA A N D SD

   d Students' suggestions are given little attention here. SA A N D SD

   e This program does a good job of preparing one for a career. SA A N D SD

   f This program is below my expectations. SA A N D SD

   In what two different ways could such responses be used? What would be the purpose of each?

Bringing Research to Life

8 What is the basis of Jason and Myra's argument for the need of an arbitrary scale to address customer expectations?

From Concept to Practice

9 Using the response strategies within Exhibit 12-1 or 12-10, which would be appropriate and add insight to understanding the various indicants of student demand for the academic program in which the students are enrolled?

From the Headlines

10 According to *BusinessWeek,* the U.S. workforce is becoming a temporary workforce. Even full-time workers are often contract employees without health, vacation, or other benefits. What measurement scale(s) would be appropriate to measure this trend?

>cases*

 Akron Children's Hospital

Calling Up Attendance

Campbell-Ewald: R-E-S-P-E-C-T Spells Loyalty

 Cummins Engines

 Donatos: Finding the New Pizza

Inquiring Minds Want to Know—NOW!

Mastering Teacher Leadership

NCRCC: Teeing Up and New Strategic Direction

 Ohio Lottery: Innovative Research Design Drives Winning

 Pebble Beach Co.

Ramada Demonstrates Its *Personal Best*™

 USTA: Come Out Swinging

 Volkswagen's Beetle

Yahoo!: *Consumer Direct* Marries Purchase Metrics to Banner Ads

* You will find a description of each case in the Case Abstracts section of this textbook. Check the Case Index to determine whether a case provides data, the research instrument, video, or other supplementary material. Written cases are downloadable from the text website (www.mhhe.com/cooper11e). All video material and video cases are available from the Online Learning Center. The film reel icon indicates a video case or video material relevant to the case.

>chapter 13

Questionnaires and Instruments

>learningobjectives

After reading this chapter, you should understand . . .

1 The link forged between the management dilemma and the communication instrument by the management-research question hierarchy.

2 The influence of the communication method on instrument design.

3 The three general classes of information and what each contributes to the instrument.

4 The influence of question content, question wording, response strategy, and preliminary analysis planning on question construction.

5 Each of the numerous question design issues influencing instrument quality, reliability, and validity.

6 Sources for measurement questions.

7 The importance of pretesting questions and instruments.

> 66 Research that asks consumers what they did and why is incredibly helpful. Research that asks consumers what they are going to do can often be taken with a grain of salt. 99
>
> Al Ries, author, co-founder and chairman
> Ries & Ries

The questionnaire is the most common data collection instrument in business research. Crafting one is part science and part art. To start, a researcher needs a solid idea of what type of analysis will be done for the project. Based on this desired analysis plan, the researcher identifies the type of scale that is needed. In Chapter 10, Henry and Associates had captured a new project for Albany Outpatient Laser Clinic. We join Jason Henry and Sara Arens as they proceed through the questionnaire creation process for this new project.

"How is the Albany questionnaire coming?" asks Jason as he enters Sara's office.

"The client approved the investigative questions this morning. So we are ready to choose the measurement questions and then write the questionnaire," shares Sara, glancing up from her computer screen. "I was just checking our bank of pretested questions. I'm looking for questions related to customer satisfaction in the medical field."

"If you are already searching for appropriate questions, you must have the analysis plan drafted. Let me see the dummy tables you developed," requests Jason. "I'll look them over while you're scanning."

Sara hands over a sheaf of pages. Each has one or more tables referencing the desired information variables. Each table indicates the statistical diagnostics that would be needed to generate the table.

As the computer finishes processing, Sara scans the revealed questions for appropriate matches to Albany's information needs. "At first glance, it looks like there are several multiple-choice scales and ranking questions we might use. But I'm not seeing a rating scale for overall satisfaction. We may need to customize a question just for Albany."

"Custom designing a question is expensive. Before you make that choice," offers Jason, "run another query using *CardioQuest* as a keyword. A few years ago, I did a study for that large cardiology specialty in Orlando. I'm sure it included an overall satisfaction scale. It might be worth considering."

Sara types *CardioQuest* and *satisfaction,* and then waits for the computer to process her request. "Sure enough, he's right again," murmurs Sara. "How do you remember all the details of prior studies done eons ago?" she asks, throwing the purely hypothetical question at Jason. But Sara swivels to face Jason, all senses alert when she hears his muffled groan.

Jason frowns as he comments, "You have far more analytical diagnostics planned than would be standard for a project of this type and size, Sara. For example, are Tables 2, 7, and 10 really necessary?" Jason pauses but doesn't allow time for Sara to answer. "To stay within budget, we are going to have to whittle down the analysis phase of the project to what is essential. Let's see if we can reduce the analysis plan to something that we both can live with. Now, walk me through what you think you'll reveal by three-way cross-tabulating these two attitudinal variables with the education variable."

>Exhibit 13-1 Overall Flowchart for Instrument Design

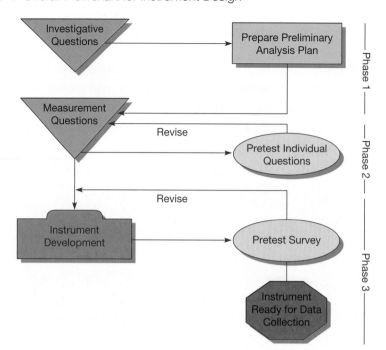

New researchers often want to draft questions immediately. Their enthusiasm makes them reluctant to go through the preliminaries that make for successful surveys. Exhibit 13-1 is a suggested flowchart for instrument design. The procedures followed in developing an instrument vary from study to study, but the flowchart suggests three phases. Each phase is discussed in this chapter, starting with a review of the research question hierarchy.

> Phase 1: Revisiting the Research Question Hierarchy

The management-research question hierarchy is the foundation of the research process and also of successful instrument development (see Exhibit 13-2). By this stage in a research project, the process of moving from the general management dilemma to specific measurement questions has traveled through the first three question levels:

1. *Management question*—the dilemma, stated in question form, that the manager needs resolved.

2. *Research question(s)*—the fact-based translation of the question the researcher must answer to contribute to the solution of the management question.

3. *Investigative questions*—specific questions the researcher must answer to provide sufficient detail and coverage of the research question. Within this level, there may be several questions as the researcher moves from the general to the specific.

4. *Measurement questions*—questions participants must answer if the researcher is to gather the needed information and resolve the management question.

In the Albany Outpatient Laser Clinic study, the eye surgeons would know from experience the types of medical complications that could result in poor recovery. But they might be far less knowledgeable about what medical staff actions and attitudes affect client recovery and perception of well-being. Coming up with an appropriate set of information needs in this study will take the guided

>**Exhibit 13-2** Flowchart for Instrument Design: Phase 1

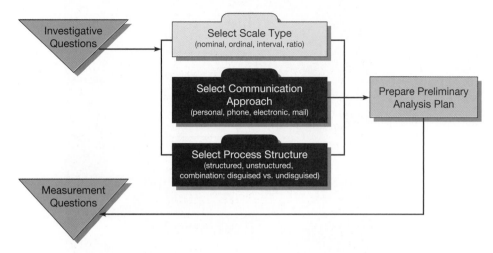

expertise of the researcher. Significant exploration would likely have preceded the development of the investigative questions. In the project for MindWriter, exploration was limited to several interviews and data mining of company service records because the concepts were not complicated and the researchers had experience in the industry.

Normally, once the researcher understands the connection between the investigative questions and the potential measurement questions, a strategy for the survey is the next logical step. This proceeds to getting down to the particulars of instrument design. The following are prominent among the strategic concerns:

1. What type of scale is needed to perform the desired analysis to answer the management question?
2. What communication approach will be used?
3. Should the questions be structured, unstructured, or some combination?
4. Should the questioning be undisguised or disguised? If the latter, to what degree?

Technology has also affected the survey development process, not just the method of the survey's delivery. Today's software, hardware, and Internet and intranet infrastructures allow researchers to (1) write questionnaires more quickly by tapping question banks for appropriate, tested questions, (2) create visually driven instruments that enhance the process for the participant, (3) use questionnaire software that eliminates separate manual data entry, and (4) build questionnaires that save time in data analysis.[1]

Type of Scale for Desired Analysis

The analytical procedures available to the researcher are determined by the scale types used in the survey. As Exhibit 13-2 clearly shows, it is important to plan the analysis before developing the measurement questions. Chapter 12 discussed nominal, ordinal, interval, and ratio scales and explained how the characteristics of each type influence the analysis (statistical choices and hypothesis testing). We demonstrate how to code and extract the data from the instrument, select appropriate descriptive measures or tests, and analyze the results in Chapters 15 through 19. In this chapter, we are most interested in asking each question in the right way and in the right order to collect the appropriate data for desired analysis.

Communication Approach

As discussed in Chapter 10, communication-based research may be conducted by personal interview, telephone, mail, computer (intranet and Internet), or some combination of these (called *hybrid studies*). Decisions regarding which method to use as well as where to interact with the participant (at home, at

More than half of the Fortune 500 companies use the feedback capabilities of Vovici. This recent merger of award-winning *WebSurveyor* (now *EFM Feedback*) and *Perseus* (now *EFM Community*) software solutions offers an Enterprise Feedback Management approach, combining survey development and deployment, analysis, and reporting components. The Vovici website contains survey templates, sample questionnaires, and sample questions for a variety of survey needs. **www.vovici.com**

a neutral site, at the sponsor's place of business, etc.) will affect the design of the instrument. In personal interviewing and computer surveying, it is possible to use graphics and other questioning tools more easily than it is in questioning done by mail or phone. The different delivery mechanisms result in different introductions, instructions, instrument layout, and conclusions. For example, researchers may use intercept designs, conducting personal interviews with participants at central locations like shopping malls, stores, sports stadiums, amusement parks, or county fairs. The intercept study poses several instrument challenges. You'll find tips for intercept questionnaire design on the text website.

In the MindWriter example, these decisions were easy. The dispersion of participants, the necessity of a service experience, and budget limitations all dictated a mail survey in which the participant received the instrument either at home or at work. Using a telephone survey, which in this instance is the only way to follow up with nonparticipants, could, however, be problematic. This is due to memory decay caused by the passage of time between return of the laptop and contact with the participant by telephone.

Jason and Sara have several options for the Albany study. Clearly a self-administered study is possible, because all the participants are congregating in a centralized location for scheduled surgery. But given the importance of some of the information to medical recovery, a survey conducted via personal interview might be an equally valid choice. We need to know the methodology before we design the questionnaire, because some measurement scales are difficult to answer without the visual aid of seeing the scale.

Disguising Objectives and Sponsors

Another consideration in communication instrument design is whether the purpose of the study should be disguised. A **disguised question** is designed to conceal the question's true purpose. Some degree of disguise is often present in survey questions, especially to shield the study's sponsor. We disguise the sponsor and the objective of a study if the researcher believes that participants will respond differently than they would if both or either was known.

The accepted wisdom among researchers is that they must disguise the study's objective or sponsor in order to obtain unbiased data. The decision about when to use disguised questions within surveys may be made easier by identifying four situations where disguising the study objective is or is not an issue:

• Willingly shared, conscious-level information.

• Reluctantly shared, conscious-level information.

- Knowable, limited-conscious-level information.
- Subconscious-level information.

In surveys requesting conscious-level information that should be willingly shared, either disguised or undisguised questions may be used, but the situation rarely requires disguised techniques.

Example: Have you attended the showing of a foreign language film in the last six months?

In the MindWriter study, the questions revealed in Exhibit 13-12 ask for information that the participant should know and be willing to provide.

Sometimes the participant knows the information we seek but is reluctant to share it for a variety of reasons. When we ask for an opinion on some topic on which participants may hold a socially unacceptable view, we often use projective techniques. (See Chapter 7.) In this type of disguised question, the survey designer phrases the questions in a hypothetical way or asks how other people in the participant's experience would answer the question. We use projective techniques so that participants will express their true feelings and avoid giving stereotyped answers. The assumption is that responses to these questions will indirectly reveal the participants' opinions.

Example: Have you downloaded copyrighted music from the Internet without paying for it? (nonprojective)

Example: Do you know people who have downloaded copyrighted music from the Internet without paying for it? (projective)

Not all information is at the participant's conscious level. Given some time—and motivation—the participant can express this information. Asking about individual attitudes when participants know they hold the attitude but have not explored why they hold the attitude may encourage the use of disguised questions. A classic example is a study of government bond buying during World War II.[2] A survey sought reasons why, among people with equal ability to buy, some bought more war bonds than others. Frequent buyers had been personally solicited to buy bonds, while most infrequent buyers had not received personal solicitation. No direct *why* question to participants could have provided the answer to this question because participants did not know they were receiving differing solicitation approaches.

Example: What is it about air travel during stormy weather that attracts you?

In assessing buying behavior, we accept that some motivations are subconscious. This is true for attitudinal information as well. Seeking insight into the basic motivations underlying attitudes or consumption practices may or may not require disguised techniques. Projective techniques (such as sentence completion tests, cartoon or balloon tests, and word association tests) thoroughly disguise the study objective, but they are often difficult to interpret.

Example: Would you say, then, that the comment you just made indicates you would or would not be likely to shop at Galaxy Stores? (survey probe during personal interview)

In the MindWriter study, the questions were direct and undisguised, as the specific information sought was at the conscious level. The MindWriter questionnaire is Exhibit 13-12, p. 345. Customers knew they were evaluating their experience with the service and repair program at MindWriter; thus the purpose of the study and its sponsorship were also undisguised. While the sponsor of the Albany Clinic study was obvious, any attempt by a survey to reveal psychological factors that might affect recovery and satisfaction might need to use disguised questions. The survey would not want to unnecessarily upset a patient before or immediately following surgery, because that might in itself affect attitude and recovery.

Preliminary Analysis Plan

Researchers are concerned with adequate coverage of the topic and with securing the information in its most usable form. A good way to test how well the study plan meets those needs is to develop "dummy" tables that display the data one expects to secure. Each **dummy table** is a cross-tabulation

>Exhibit 13-3 Dummy Table for American Eating Habits

Age	Use of Convenience Foods				
	Always Use	Use Frequently	Use Sometimes	Rarely Use	Never Use
18–24					
25–34					
35–44					
45–54					
55–64					
65+					

between two or more variables. For example, in the biennial study of what Americans eat conducted by *Parade* magazine,[3] we might be interested to know whether age influences the use of convenience foods. The dummy table shown in Exhibit 13-3 would match the age ranges of participants with the degree to which they use convenience foods. The preliminary analysis plan serves as a check on whether the planned measurement questions (e.g., the rating scales on use of convenience foods and on age) meet the data needs of the research question. This also helps the researcher determine the type of scale needed for each question (e.g., ordinal data on frequency of use and on age)—a preliminary step to developing measurement questions for investigative questions.

In the opening vignette, Jason and Sara use the development of a preliminary analysis plan to determine whether the project could be kept on budget. The number of hours spent on data analysis is a major cost of any survey. Too expansive an analysis plan can reveal unnecessary questions. *The guiding principle of survey design is always to ask only what is needed.*

> Phase 2: Constructing and Refining the Measurement Questions

Drafting or selecting questions begins once you develop a complete list of investigative questions and decide on the collection processes to be used. The creation of a survey question is not a haphazard or arbitrary process. It is exacting and requires paying significant attention to detail and simultaneously addressing numerous issues. Whether you create or borrow or license a question, in Phase 2 (see Exhibit 13-4) you generate specific measurement questions considering subject content, the wording of each question (influenced by the degree of disguise and the need to provide operational definitions for constructs and concepts), and response strategy (each producing a different level of data as needed for your preliminary analysis plan). In Phase 3 you must address topic and question sequencing. We discuss these topics sequentially, although in practice the process is not linear. For this discussion, we assume the questions are structured.

The order, type, and wording of the measurement questions, the introduction, the instructions, the transitions, and the closure in a quality questionnaire should accomplish the following:

- Encourage each participant to provide accurate responses.
- Encourage each participant to provide an adequate amount of information.
- Discourage each participant from refusing to answer specific questions.
- Discourage each participant from early discontinuation of participation.
- Leave the participant with a positive attitude about survey participation.

>**Exhibit 13-4** Flowchart for Instrument Design: Phase 2

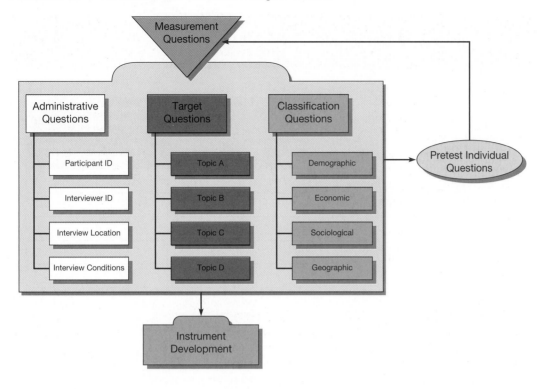

Question Categories and Structure

Questionnaires and **interview schedules** (an alternative term for the questionnaires used in personal interviews) can range from those that have a great deal of structure to those that are essentially unstructured. Questionnaires contain three categories of measurement questions:

- Administrative questions.
- Classification questions.
- Target questions (structured or unstructured).

Administrative questions identify the participant, interviewer, interview location, and conditions. These questions are rarely asked of the participant but are necessary for studying patterns within the data and identify possible error sources. **Classification questions** usually cover sociological-demographic variables that allow participants' answers to be grouped so that patterns are revealed and can be studied. These questions usually appear at the end of a survey (except for those used as *filters* or *screens,* questions that determine whether a participant has the requisite level of knowledge to participate). **Target questions** address the investigative questions of a specific study. These are grouped by topic in the survey. Target questions may be **structured** (they present the participants with a fixed set of choices; often called *closed questions*) or **unstructured** (they do not limit responses but do provide a frame of reference for participants' answers; sometimes referred to as *open-ended questions*).

In the Albany Clinic study, some questions will need to be unstructured because anticipating medications and health history for a wide variety of individuals would be a gargantuan task for a researcher and would take up far too much paper space.

Question Content

Question content is first and foremost dictated by the investigative questions guiding the study. From these questions, questionnaire designers craft or borrow the target and classification questions that will

A Survey Cold as Ice

One December, 1.5 million North Carolinians lost power due to a storm that covered the state with more than an inch of ice that coated tree limbs and brought down power lines. After seven years of repeated natural disasters (two hurricanes, a record-setting flood, a major snowstorm, and drought), North Carolina needed to assess the true cost of this latest disaster and see how the state's residents used weather predictions to prepare for it. It is the state's responsibility to determine the effectiveness of its communication initiatives. The state decided to use a survey.

Odum Institute (at the University of North Carolina–Chapel Hill), which maintains one of the nation's largest archives of polling data, and RTI International (a nonprofit "dedicated to conducting research that improves the human condition") stepped in. They conducted a telephone survey of 457 households in 36 counties—those counties included in North Carolina's application for federal disaster assistance. The goal was to give decision makers and the public information that would be useful in preparing for the state's next natural disaster.

RTI knew its analysis plan needed to reveal not only the direct costs of dealing with the disaster but also the indirect costs, like missed work, damage to residences, spoiled food, or hotel accommodations. It also knew that residents' satisfaction with emergency response would influence their actions during the next disaster. And RTI needed to measure attitudes about prevention. Would willingness to prevent a reoccurrence of lost power by burying power lines increase with number of days of power lost?

Shown in the right column is one dummy table for the RTI study for North Carolina, including the aggregate data that were collected. What types of measurement scales would be necessary to complete this table?

> **Overall Satisfaction**

	Power Supplier Response Satisfaction Rating		
Days without Power	**Municipal Power**	**Duke Power**	**Progress Energy**
	7.6	6.6	6.5
1			
2			
3			
Etc.			

Eighty percent of households indicated a willingness to take preventive actions—including 47 percent that were willing to pay extra on their monthly bill to bury power lines. But one of the more significant findings was that the municipal power companies responded more quickly and earned a higher performance rating from customers than did Duke Power and Progress Energy. On a 10-point satisfaction scale ("I was satisfied with my electric power company's response to the ice storm") where 5 was "neither agree nor disagree," municipals earned a 7.6 while the nonmunicipal electric providers earned 6.6 and 6.5, respectively. Each day without power led to a decline in the household's satisfaction level—and the governor and local politicians suffered a similar fate. This survey had a margin of error of ±4.7 percent.

www.rti.org

be asked of participants. Four questions, covering numerous issues, guide the instrument designer in selecting appropriate question content:

- Should this question be asked (does it match the study objective)?
- Is the question of proper scope and coverage?
- Can the participant adequately answer this question as asked?
- Will the participant willingly answer this question as asked?

Exhibit 13-5 summarizes these issues related to constructing and refining measurement questions that are described here and detailed in Appendix 13a: "Crafting Effective Measurement Questions."

>**Exhibit 13-5** A Summary of the Major Issues Related to Measurement Questions

Issue Category	Fundamental Issue
Question Content	
1. Purposeful versus interesting	Does the question ask for data that will be merely interesting or truly useful in making a decision?
2. Incomplete or unfocused	Will the question reveal what the decision maker needs to know?
3. Double-barreled questions	Does the question ask the participant for too much information? Would the desired single response be accurate for all parts of the question?
4. Precision	Does the question ask precisely what the decision maker needs to know?
5. Time for thought	Is it reasonable to assume that the participant can frame an answer to the question?
6. Participation at the expense of accuracy	Does the question pressure the participant for a response regardless of knowledge or experience?
7. Presumed knowledge	Does the question assume the participant has knowledge he or she may not have?
8. Recall and memory decay	Does the question ask the participant for information that relates to thoughts or activity too far in the participant's past to be remembered?
9. Balance (general vs. specific)	Does the question ask the participant to generalize or summarize behavior that may have no discernable pattern?
10. Objectivity	Does the question omit or include information that will bias the participant's response?
11. Sensitive information	Does the question ask the participant to reveal embarrassing, shameful, or ego-related information?
Question Wording	
12. Shared vocabulary	Does the question use words that have no meaning or a different meaning for the participant?
13. Unsupported assumption	Does the question assume a prior experience, a precondition, or prior knowledge that the participant does not or may not have?
14. Frame of reference	Is the question worded from the participant's, rather than the researcher's, perspective?
15. Biased wording	Does the question contain wording that implies the researcher's desire for the participant to respond in one way versus another?
16. Personalization vs. projection	Is it necessary for the participant to reveal personal attitudes and behavior, or may the participant project these attitudes and behaviors to someone like him or her?
17. Adequate alternatives	Does the question provide a mutually exhaustive list of alternatives to encompass realistic or likely participant attitudes and behaviors?
Response Strategy Choice	
18. Objective of the study	Is the question designed to classify or label attitudes, conditions, and behaviors or to reveal them?
19. Level of information	Does the participant possess the level of information appropriate for participation in the study?
20. Thoroughness of prior thought	Has the participant developed an attitude on the issue being asked?
21. Communication skill	Does the participant have sufficient command of the language to answer the question?
22. Participant motivation	Is the level of motivation sufficient to encourage the participant to give thoughtful, revealing answers?

Question Wording

It is frustrating when people misunderstand a question that has been painstakingly written. This problem is partially due to the lack of a shared vocabulary. The difficulty of understanding long and complex sentences or involved phraseology aggravates the problem further. Our dilemma arises from the requirements of question design (the need to be explicit, to present alternatives, and to explain meanings). All contribute to longer and more involved sentences.[4]

The difficulties caused by question wording exceed most other sources of distortion in surveys. They have led one social scientist to conclude:

> To many who worked in the Research Branch it soon became evident that error or bias attributable to sampling and to methods of questionnaire administration were relatively small as compared with other types of variations—especially variation attributable to different ways of wording questions.[5]

Although it is impossible to say which wording of a question is best, we can point out several areas that cause participant confusion and measurement error. The diligent question designer will put a survey question through many revisions before it satisfies these criteria:[6]

- Is the question stated in terms of a shared vocabulary?
- Does the question contain vocabulary with a single meaning?
- Does the question contain unsupported or misleading assumptions?
- Does the question contain biased wording?
- Is the question correctly personalized?
- Are adequate alternatives presented within the question?

In the vignette, Sara's study of the prior survey used by the Albany Laser Clinic illustrated several of these problems. One question asked participants to identify their "referring physician" and the "physician most knowledgeable about your health." This question was followed by one requesting a single phone number. Participants didn't know which doctor's phone number was being requested. By offering space for only one number, the data collection instrument implied that both parts of the question might refer to the same doctor. Further, the questions about past medical history did not offer clear directions. One question asked participants about whether they had "had the flu recently," yet made no attempt to define whether *recently* was within the last 10 days or the last year. Another asked "Are your teeth intact?" Prior participants had answered by providing information about whether they wore false teeth, had loose teeth, or had broken or chipped teeth—only one of which was of interest to the doctor performing surgery. To another question ("Do you have limited motion of your neck?"), all respondents answered yes. Sara could only conclude that a talented researcher did not design the clinic's previously used questionnaire. Although the Albany Outpatient Laser Clinic survey did not reveal any **leading questions,** these can inject significant error by implying that one response should be favored over another. One classic hair care study asked, "How did you like Brand X when it lathered up so nicely?" Obviously, the participant was supposed to factor in the richness of the lather in evaluating the shampoo.

The MindWriter questionnaire (see Exhibit 13-12) simplified the process by using the same response strategy for each factor the participant was asked to evaluate. The study basically asks, "How did our CompleteCare service program work for you when you consider each of the following factors?" It accomplishes this by setting up the questioning with "Take a moment to tell us how well we've served you." Because the sample includes CompleteCare users only, the underlying assumption that participants have used the service is acceptable. The language is appropriate for the participant's likely level of education. And the open-ended question used for "comments" adds flexibility to capture any unusual circumstances not covered by the structured list.

Target questions need not be constructed solely of words. Computer-assisted, computer-administered, and Web surveys and interview schedules, and to a lesser extent printed surveys, often incorporate visual images as part of the questioning process.

Response Strategy

A third major decision area in question design is the degree and form of structure imposed on the participant. The various response strategies offer options that include **unstructured response** (or *open-ended response,* the free choice of words) and **structured response** (or *closed response,* specified alternatives provided). Free responses, in turn, range from those in which the participants express themselves extensively to those in which participants' latitude is restricted by space, layout, or instructions to choose one word or phrase, as in a fill-in question. Closed responses typically are categorized as dichotomous, multiple-choice, checklist, rating, or ranking response strategies.

Several situational factors affect the decision of whether to use open-ended or closed questions.[7] The decision is also affected by the degree to which these factors are known to the interviewer. The factors are:

- Objectives of the study.
- Participant's level of information about the topic.
- Degree to which participant has thought through the topic.
- Ease with which participant communicates.
- Participant's motivation level to share information.

All of the strategies that are described in this section are available for use on Web questionnaires. However, with the Web survey you are faced with slightly different layout options for response, as noted in Exhibit 13-6. For the multiple-choice or dichotomous response strategies, the designer chooses between radio buttons and drop-down boxes. For the checklist or multiple response strategy, the designer must use the checkbox. For rating scales, designers may use pop-up windows that contain the scale and instructions, but the response option is usually the radio button. For ranking questions, designers use radio buttons, drop-down boxes, and textboxes. For the free response question, the designer chooses either the one-line textbox or the scrolled textbox. Web surveys and other computer-assisted surveys can return participants to a given question or prompt them to complete a response when they click the "submit" button; this is especially valuable for checklists, rating scales, and ranking questions. You may wish to review Exhibits 12-3 and 12-10. These provide other question samples.

Free-Response Question

Free-response questions, also known as *open-ended questions,* ask the participant a question and either the interviewer pauses for the answer (which is unaided) or the participant records his or her ideas in his or her own words in the space provided on a questionnaire. Survey researchers usually try to reduce the number of such questions because they pose significant problems in interpretation and are costly in terms of data analysis.

Dichotomous Question

A topic may present clearly dichotomous choices: something is a fact or it is not; a participant can either recall or not recall information; a participant attended or didn't attend an event. **Dichotomous questions** suggest opposing responses, but this is not always the case. One response may be so unlikely that it would be better to adopt the middle-ground alternative as one of the two choices. For example, if we ask participants whether a product is underpriced or overpriced, we are not likely to get many selections of the former choice. The better alternatives to present to the participant might be "fairly priced" or "overpriced."

In many two-way questions, there are potential alternatives beyond the stated two alternatives. If the participant cannot accept either alternative in a dichotomous question, he or she may convert the question to a multiple-choice or rating question by writing in his or her desired alternative. For example,

>Exhibit 13-6 Internet Survey Response Options

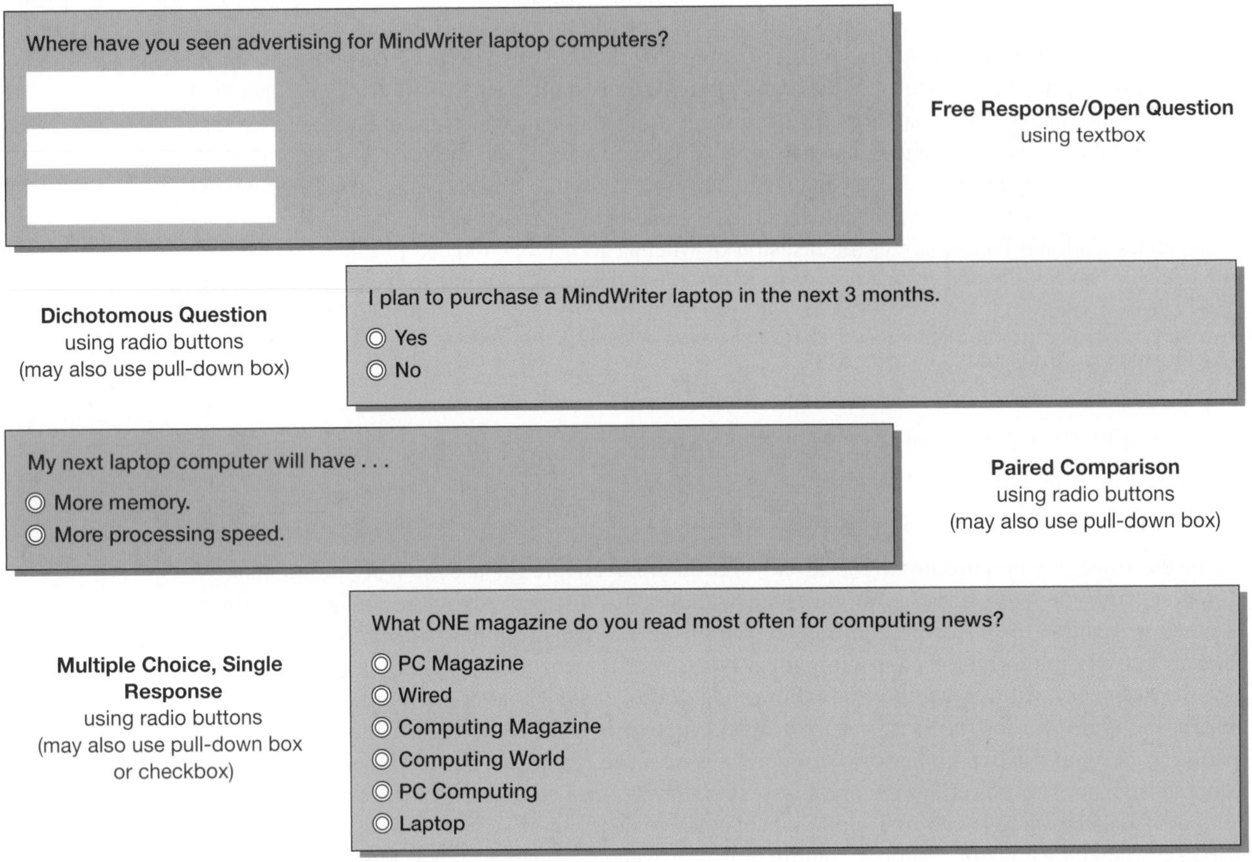

Where have you seen advertising for MindWriter laptop computers?

Free Response/Open Question
using textbox

Dichotomous Question
using radio buttons
(may also use pull-down box)

I plan to purchase a MindWriter laptop in the next 3 months.

○ Yes
○ No

My next laptop computer will have . . .

○ More memory.
○ More processing speed.

Paired Comparison
using radio buttons
(may also use pull-down box)

Multiple Choice, Single Response
using radio buttons
(may also use pull-down box
or checkbox)

What ONE magazine do you read most often for computing news?

○ PC Magazine
○ Wired
○ Computing Magazine
○ Computing World
○ PC Computing
○ Laptop

the participant may prefer an alternative such as "don't know" to a yes-no question or prefer "no opinion" when faced with a favor-oppose option. In other cases, when there are two opposing or complementary choices, the participant may prefer a qualified choice ("yes, if X doesn't occur," or "sometimes yes and sometimes no," or "about the same"). Thus, two-way questions may become multiple-choice or rating questions, and these additional responses should be reflected in your revised analysis plan. Dichotomous questions generate nominal data.

60

The percent of businesses hit annually by cyber-crime.

Multiple-Choice Question

Multiple-choice questions are appropriate when there are more than two alternatives or when we seek gradations of preference, interest, or agreement; the latter situation also calls for rating questions. Although such questions offer more than one alternative answer, they request that the participant make a single choice. Multiple-choice questions can be efficient, but they also present unique design and analysis problems.

One type of problem occurs when one or more responses have not been anticipated. Assume we ask whether retail mall security and safety rules should be determined by the (1) store managers, (2) sales associates who work at the mall, (3) federal government, or (4) state government. The union has not been mentioned in the alternatives. Many participants might combine this alternative with "sales

>**Exhibit 13-6** (Cont'd)

What ONE magazine do you read most often for computing news?

Please select your answer	V
PC Magazine	V
Wired	
Computing Magazine	
Computing World	
PC Computing	
Laptop	

Multiple Choice, Single Response
using pull–down box

Checklist
using checkbox
(may also use radio buttons)

Which of the following computing magazines did you look at in the last 30 days?

☐ PC Magazine
☑ Wired
☐ Computing Magazine
☐ Computing World
☐ PC Computing
☐ Laptop

Please indicate the importance of each of the characteristics in choosing your next laptop. [Select one answer in each row. Scroll to see the complete list of options.]

	Very Important		Neither Important nor Unimportant		Not at all Important	
Fast reliable repair service	◉	○	○	○	○	V
Service at my location	○	○	◉	○	○	
Maintenance by the manufacturer	◉	○	○	○	○	
Knowledgeable technicians	◉	○	○	○	○	
Notification of upgrades	○	○	○	○	◉	∧

Rating Grid
(may also use checkboxes)
Requires a single response per line. The longer the list, the more likely the participant must scroll.

Ranking Question
using pull-down box
(may also use textboxes, in which ranks are entered)
[This question asks for a limited ranking of only three of the listed elements.]

From the list below, please choose the three most important service options when choosing your next laptop.

Fast reliable repair service	— V
Service at my location	—
Maintenance by the manufacturer	1
Knowledgeable technicians	2
Notification of upgrades	3
	— V

associates," but others will view "unions" as a distinct alternative. Exploration prior to drafting the measurement question attempts to identify the most likely choices.

A second problem occurs when the list of choices is not exhaustive. Participants may want to give an answer that is not offered as an alternative. This may occur when the desired response is one that combines two or more of the listed individual alternatives. Many participants may believe the store management *and* the sales associates acting jointly should set store safety rules, but the question does not include this response. When the researcher tries to provide for all possible options, choosing from the list of alternatives can become exhausting. We guard against this by discovering the major choices through exploration and pretesting (discussed in detail in Appendix 13b). We may also add the category "Other (please specify)" as a safeguard to provide the participant with an acceptable alternative

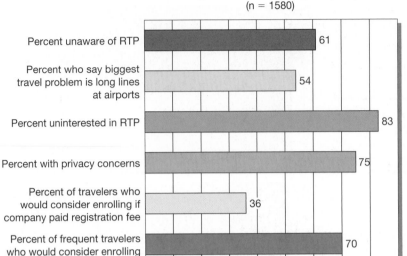

Travel Issues and Transportation Security Administration's Registered Traveler Program (RTP)
(n = 1580)

for all other options. In our analysis of responses to a pretested, self-administered questionnaire, we may create a combination alternative.

Yet another problem occurs when the participant divides the question of store safety into several questions, each with different alternatives. Some participants may believe rules dealing with air quality in stores should be set by a federal agency while those dealing with aisle obstructions or displays should be set by store management and union representatives. Still others may want store management in conjunction with a sales associate committee to make rules. To address this problem, the instrument designer would need to divide the question. Pretesting should reveal if a multiple-choice question is really a **double-barreled question.**

Another challenge in alternative selection occurs when the choices are not mutually exclusive (the participant thinks two or more responses overlap). In a multiple-choice question that asks students, "Which one of the following factors was most influential in your decision to attend Metro U?" these response alternatives might be listed:

1. Good academic reputation.
2. Specific program of study desired.
3. Enjoyable campus life.
4. Many friends from home attend.
5. High quality of the faculty.
6. Opportunity to play collegiate-level sports.

Some participants might view items 1 and 5 as overlapping, and some may see items 3 and 4 in the same way.

It is also important to seek a fair balance in choices when a participant's position on an issue is unknown. One study showed that an off-balance presentation of alternatives biases the results in favor of the more heavily offered side.[8] If four gradations of alternatives are on one side of an issue and two are offered reflecting the other side, responses will tend to be biased toward the better-represented side. However, researchers may have a valid reason for using an unbalanced array of alternatives. They may be trying to determine the degree of positive (or negative) response, already knowing which side of an issue most participants will choose based on the selection criteria for participation.

It is necessary in multiple-choice questions to present reasonable alternatives—particularly when the choices are numbers or identifications. If we ask, "Which of the following numbers is closest to the number of students enrolled in American colleges and universities today?" these choices might be presented:

1. 75,000
2. 750,000
3. 7,500,000
4. 25,000,000
5. 75,000,000

It should be obvious to most participants that at least three of these choices are not reasonable, given general knowledge about the population of the United States and about the colleges and universities in their hometowns. (The estimated 2006 U.S. population is 298.4[9] million based on the 2000 census of 281.4 million. The Ohio State University has more than 59,000[10] students.)

The order in which choices are given can also be a problem. Numeric alternatives are normally presented in order of magnitude. This practice introduces a bias. The participant assumes that if there is a list of five numbers, the correct answer will lie somewhere in the middle of the group. Researchers are assumed to add a couple of incorrect numbers on each side of the correct one. To counteract this tendency to choose the central position, put the correct number at an extreme position more often when you design a multiple-choice question.

Order bias with nonnumeric response categories often leads the participant to choose the first alternative (**primacy effect**) or the last alternative (**recency effect**) over the middle ones. Primacy effect dominates in visual surveys—self-administered via Web or mail—while recency effect dominates in oral surveys—phone and personal interview surveys.[11] Using the *split-ballot technique* can counteract this bias: Different segments of the sample are presented alternatives in different orders. To implement this strategy in face-to-face interviews, the researcher would list the alternatives on a card to be handed to the participant when the question is asked. Cards with different choice orders can be alternated to ensure positional balance. The researcher would leave the choices unnumbered on the card so that the participant replies by giving the response category itself rather than its identifying number. It is a good practice to use cards like this any time there are four or more choice alternatives. This saves the interviewer reading time and ensures a more valid answer by keeping the full range of choices in front of the participant. With computer-assisted surveying, the software can be programmed to rotate the order of the alternatives so that each participant receives the alternatives in randomized order (for nonordered scales) or in reverse order (for ordered scales).

In most multiple-choice questions, there is also a problem of ensuring that the choices represent a one-dimensional scale—that is, the alternatives to a given question should represent different aspects of the same conceptual dimension. In the college selection example, the list included features associated with a college that might be attractive to a student. This list, although not exhaustive, illustrated aspects of the concept "college attractiveness factors within the control of the college." The list did not mention other factors that might affect a school attendance decision. Parents and peer advice, local alumni efforts, and one's high school adviser may influence the decision, but these represent a different conceptual dimension of "college attractiveness factors"—those not within the control of the college.

Multiple-choice questions usually generate nominal data. When the choices are numeric alternatives, this response structure may produce at least interval and sometimes ratio data. When the choices represent ordered but unequal, numerical ranges (e.g., a question on family income: <$20,000; $20,000–$100,000; >$100,000) or a verbal rating scale (e.g., a question on how you prefer your steak prepared: well done, medium well, medium rare, or rare), the multiple-choice question generates ordinal data.

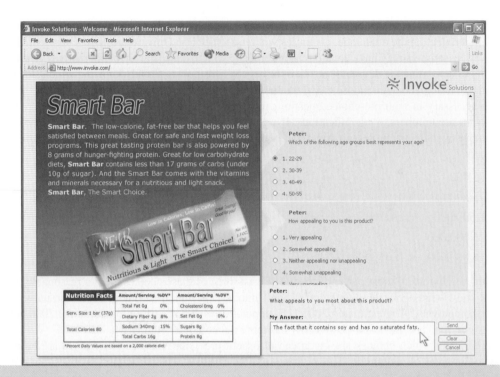

Checklist

When you want a participant to give multiple responses to a single question, you will ask the question in one of three ways: the checklist, rating, or ranking strategy. If relative order is not important, the **checklist** is the logical choice. Questions like "Which of the following factors encouraged you to apply to Metro U? (Check all that apply)" force the participant to exercise a dichotomous response (yes, encouraged; no, didn't encourage) to each factor presented. Of course, you could have asked for the same information with a series of dichotomous selection questions, one for each individual factor, but this would have been both time- and space-consuming. Checklists are more efficient. Checklists generate nominal data.

Rating Question

Rating questions ask the participant to position each factor on a companion scale, either verbal, numeric, or graphic. "Each of the following factors has been shown to have some influence on a student's choice to apply to Metro U. Using your own experience, for each factor please tell us whether the factor was 'strongly influential,' 'somewhat influential,' or 'not at all influential.'" Generally, rating-scale structures generate ordinal data; some carefully crafted scales generate interval data.

It is important to remember that the researcher should represent only one response dimension in rating-scale response options. Otherwise, effectively, you present the participant with a double-barreled question with insufficient choices to reply to both aspects.

Example A: How likely are you to enroll at Metro University?

(Responses with more than one dimension, ordinal scale)

(a) extremely likely to enroll

(b) somewhat likely to enroll

(c) not likely to apply

(d) will not apply

Example B: How likely are you to enroll at Metro University?

(Responses within one dimension, interval scale)

(a) extremely likely to enroll

(b) somewhat likely to enroll

(c) neither likely nor unlikely to enroll

(d) somewhat unlikely to enroll

(e) extremely unlikely to enroll

Ranking Question

When relative order of the alternatives is important, the **ranking question** is ideal. "Please rank-order your top three factors from the following list based on its influence in encouraging you to apply to Metro U. Use 1 to indicate the most encouraging factor, 2 the next most encouraging factor, etc." The checklist strategy would provide the three factors of influence, but we would have no way of knowing the importance the participant places on each factor. Even in a personal interview, the order in which the factors are mentioned is not a guarantee of influence. Ranking as a response strategy solves this problem.

One concern surfaces with ranking activities. How many presented factors should be ranked? If you listed the 15 brands of potato chips sold in a given market, would you have the participant rank all 15 in order of preference? In most instances it is helpful to remind yourself that while participants may have been selected for a given study due to their experience or likelihood of having desired information, this does not mean that they have knowledge of all conceivable aspects of an issue, but only of some. It is always better to have participants rank only those elements with which they are familiar. For this reason, ranking questions might appropriately follow a checklist question that identifies the objects of familiarity. If you want motivation to remain strong, avoid asking a participant to rank more than seven items even if your list is longer. Ranking generates ordinal data.

All types of response strategies have their advantages and disadvantages. Several different strategies are often found in the same questionnaire, and the situational factors mentioned earlier are the major guides in this matter. There is a tendency, however, to use closed questions instead of the more flexible open-ended type. Exhibit 13-7 summarizes some important considerations in choosing between the various response strategies.

Sources of Existing Questions

The tools of data collection should be adapted to the problem, not the reverse. Thus, the focus of this chapter has been on crafting an instrument to answer specific investigative questions. But inventing, refining, and pretesting questions demands considerable time and effort. For some topics, a careful review of the related literature and an examination of existing instrument sourcebooks can shorten

>Exhibit 13-7 Summary of Scale Types

Type	Restrictions	Scale Items	Data Type
Rating Scales			
Simple Category Scale	Needs mutually exclusive choices.	One or more	Nominal
Multiple Choice Single-Response Scale	Needs mutually exclusive choices; may use exhaustive list or "other."	Many	Nominal
Multiple Choice Multiple-Response Scale (checklist)	Needs mutually exclusive choices; needs exhaustive list or "other."	Many	Nominal
Likert Scale	Needs definitive positive or negative statements with which to agree/disagree.	One or more	Interval
Likert-type Scale	Needs definitive positive or negative statements with which to agree/disagree.	One or more	Ordinal or interval
Semantic Differential Scale	Needs words that are opposites to anchor the graphic space.	One or more	Interval
Numerical Scale	Needs concepts with standardized or defined meanings; needs numbers to anchor the end-points or points along the scale; score is a measurement of graphical space from one anchor.	One or many	Ordinal or interval
Multiple Rating List Scale	Needs words that are opposites to anchor the end-points on the verbal scale.	Up to 10	Ordinal or interval
Fixed (Constant) Sum Scale	Participant needs ability to calculate total to some fixed number, often 100.	Two or more	Ratio
Stapel Scale	Needs verbal labels that are operationally defined or standard.	One or more	Ordinal or interval
Graphic Rating Scale	Needs visual images that can be interpreted as positive or negative anchors; score is a measurement of graphical space from one anchor.	One or more	Ordinal, interval, or ratio
Ranking Scales			
Paired Comparison Scale	Number is controlled by participant's stamina and interest.	Up to 10	Ordinal
Forced Ranking Scale	Needs mutually exclusive choices.	Up to 10	Ordinal
Comparative Scale	Can use verbal or graphical scale.	Up to 10	Ordinal

this process. Increasingly, companies that specialize in survey research maintain a question bank of pretested questions. In the opening vignette, Sara was accessing Henry and Associates' question bank.

A review of literature will reveal instruments used in similar studies that may be obtained by writing to the researchers or, if copyrighted, may be purchased through a clearinghouse. Instruments also are available through compilations and sourcebooks. While these tend to be oriented to social science applications, they are a rich source of ideas for tailoring questions to meet a manager's needs. Several compilations are recommended; we have suggested them in Exhibit 13-8.[12]

Borrowing items from existing sources is not without risk. It is quite difficult to generalize the reliability and validity of selected questionnaire items or portions of a questionnaire that have been taken

>**Exhibit 13-8** Sources of Questions

Printed Sources		
Author(s)	**Title**	**Source**
William Bearden and R. Netemeyer	*Handbook of Marketing Scales: Multi-Item Measures for Marketing and Consumer Behavior Research*	London: Sage Publications, Inc., 2001
Alec Gallup and George H. Gallup, eds.	*The Gallup Poll Cumulative Index: Public Opinion, 1935–1997*	Wilmington, DE: Scholarly Resources, 1999
John P. Robinson, Philip R. Shaver, and Lawrence S. Wrightsman	*Measures of Personality and Social-Psychological Attitudes*	San Diego, CA: Academic Press, 1990, 1999
John Robinson, Phillip R. Shaver, and L. Wrightsman	*Measures of Political Attitudes*	San Diego, CA: Academic Press, 1990, 1999
George H. Gallup Jr., ed.	*The Gallup Poll: Public Opinion 1998*	Wilmington, DE: Scholarly Resources, 1998
Gordon Bruner and Paul Hensel	*Marketing Scales Handbook: A Compilation of Multi-Item Measure V.II*	Chicago, IL: American Marketing Association, 1996, 1998
Elizabeth H. Hastings and Philip K. Hastings, eds.	*Index to International Public Opinion 1986–1987*	Westport, CT: Greenwood Publishing Group, September 1988
Elizabeth Martin, Diana McDuffee, and Stanley Presser	*Sourcebook of Harris National Surveys: Repeated Questions 1963–1976*	Chapel Hill, NC: Institute for Research in Social Science, 1981
Philip E. Converse, Jean D. Dotson, Wendy J. Hoag, and William H. McGee III, eds.	*American Social Attitudes Data Sourcebook, 1947–1978*	Cambridge, MA: Harvard University Press, 1980
Philip K. Hastings and Jessie C. Southwick, eds.	*Survey Data for Trend Analysis: An Index to Repeated Questions in the U.S. National Surveys Held by the Roper Public Opinion Research Center*	Williamsburg, MA: Roper Public Opinion Center, 1975
National Opinion Research Center	*General Social Surveys 1972–2000: Cumulative Code Book*	Ann Arbor, MI: ICPSR, 2000
John P. Robinson, Robert Athanasiou, and Kendra B. Head	*Measures of Occupational Attitudes and Occupational Characteristics*	Ann Arbor, MI: Institute for Social Research, University of Michigan, 1968.
Web Sources		
Interuniversity Consortium for Political and Social Research (general social survey)	www.icpsr.umich.edu/	
iPoll (contains more than 500,000 questions in its searchable database)	www.ropercenter.uconn.edu/	
Survey Research Laboratory, Florida State University	www.fsu.edu/~survey/	
The Odum Institute (houses the Louis Harris Opinion Polls)	http://www.irss.unc.edu/odum/jsp/content_node.jsp?nodeid=7	
Kaiser Family Foundation Health Poll Search	www.kff.org/kaiserpolls/healthpoll.cfm	
Polling the Nations (more than 14,000 surveys)	www.orspub.com	

out of the original context. Researchers whose questions or instruments you borrow may not have reported sampling and testing procedures needed to judge the quality of the measurement scale. Just because Jason has a satisfaction scale in the question bank used for the CardioQuest survey does not mean the question will be appropriate for the Albany Outpatient Laser Clinic. Sara would need to know the intended purpose of the CardioQuest study and the time of construction, as well as the results of pretesting, to determine the reliability and validity of its use in the Albany study. Even then she would be wise to pretest the question in the context of her Albany survey.

Language, phrasing, and idioms can also pose problems. Questions tend to age or become outdated and may not appear (or sound) as relevant to the participant as freshly worded questions. Integrating previously used and customized questions is problematic. Often adjacent questions in one question-naire are relied on to carry context. If you select one question from a contextual series, the borrowed question is left without its necessary meaning.[13] Whether an instrument is constructed with designed questions or adapted with questions borrowed or licensed from others, pretesting is expected.

> Phase 3: Drafting and Refining the Instrument

As depicted in Exhibit 13-9, Phase 3 of instrument design—drafting and refinement—is a multistep process:

1. Develop the participant-screening process (done especially with personal or phone surveys, but also with early notification procedures with e-mail and Web surveys), along with the introduction.

>Exhibit 13-9 Flowchart for Instrument Design: Phase 3

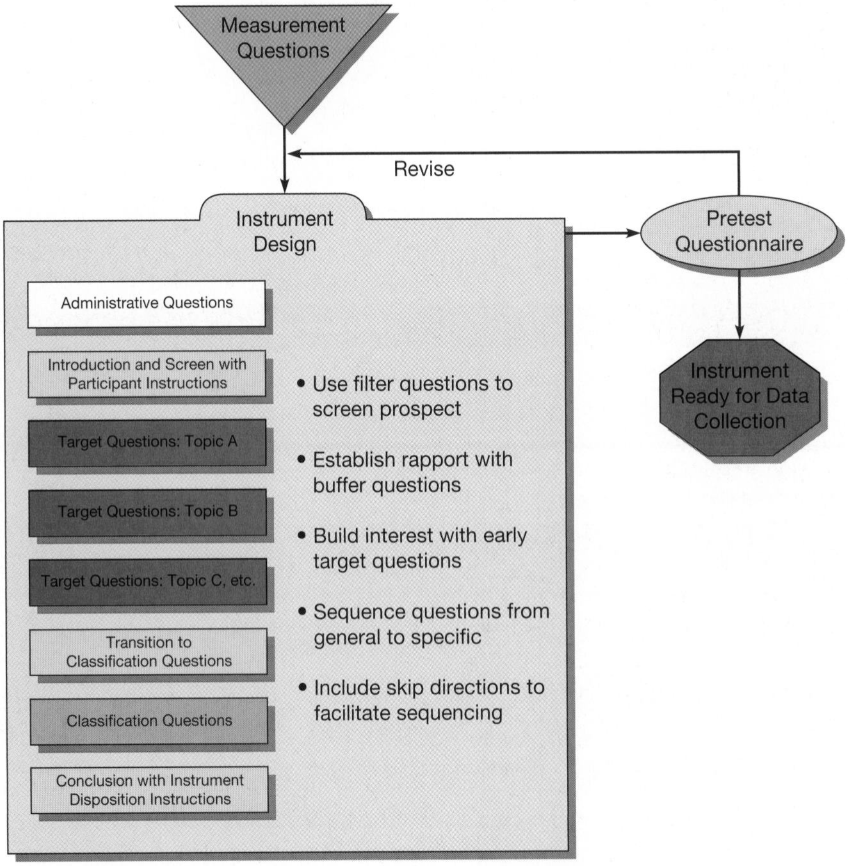

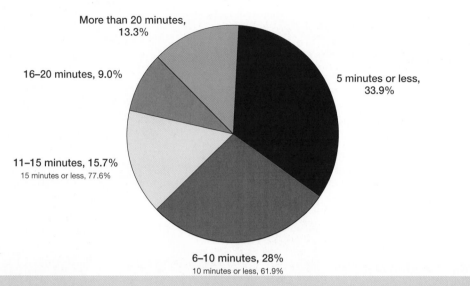

Maximum Online Survey Length Prior to Abandonment

More than 20 minutes, 13.3%

16–20 minutes, 9.0%

11–15 minutes, 15.7%
15 minutes or less, 77.6%

6–10 minutes, 28%
10 minutes or less, 61.9%

5 minutes or less, 33.9%

>**pic**profile

As marketing resistance rises and survey cooperation declines, survey length is of increasing concern. InsightExpress studied the Web survey process and revealed that people taking Web surveys prefer shorter to longer surveys, consistent with what we know about phone and intercept survey participants. While 77 percent were likely to complete a survey that took 15 minutes or less, almost one in three participants needed a survey to be 5 minutes or less for full completion. As participating in online surveys loses its novelty, prospective participants are likely to become even more reluctant to give significant time to the survey process. Therefore, it is critical that researchers ask only what is necessary. **www.insightexpress.com**

2. Arrange the measurement question sequence:
   a. Identify groups of target questions by topic.
   b. Establish a logical sequence for the question groups and questions within groups.
   c. Develop transitions between these question groups.

3. Prepare and insert instructions for the interviewer—including termination instructions, skip directions, and probes for the participants.

4. Create and insert a conclusion, including a survey disposition statement.

5. Pretest specific questions and the instrument as a whole.

Participant Screening and Introduction

The introduction must supply the sample unit with the motivation to participate in the study. It must reveal enough about the forthcoming questions, usually by revealing some or all of the topics to be covered, for participants to judge their interest level and their ability to provide the desired information. In any communication study, the introduction also reveals the amount of time participation is likely to take. The introduction also reveals the research organization or sponsor (unless the study is disguised) and possibly the objective of the study. In personal or phone interviews as well as in e-mail and Web surveys, the introduction usually contains one or more **screen questions** or filter questions to determine if the potential participant has the knowledge or experience necessary to participate in the study. At a minimum, a phone or personal interviewer will provide his or her first name to help establish critical rapport with the potential participant. Additionally, more than two-thirds of phone surveys contain a statement that the interviewer is "not selling anything."[14] Exhibit 13-10 provides a sample introduction and other components of a telephone study of nonparticipants to a self-administered mail survey.

Does Cupid Deserve a Place in the Office Cubicle?

As a manager, should you encourage or discourage office romance? Spherion Inc., a leading recruiting and staffing company, recently sponsored its latest Spherion® Workplace Snapshot survey. "The results of this survey confirm what we know intuitively—that many workers find opportunities for romance where they work," shared John Heins, senior vice president and chief human resources officer at Spherion.

The workplace romance findings were collected using the Harris Interactive QuickQuery online omnibus, an online survey fielded two to three times per week. A U.S. sample of 1,588 employed adults, aged 18 or older, were polled in a three-day period in January. Results were weighted to bring them in line with the actual U.S. population.

According to the survey, nearly 40 percent of workers (30 percent of women, 47 percent of men) would consider dating a co-worker or have done so. Approximately 25 percent (27 percent of men, 23 percent of women) of such romances result in marriage. While 41 percent of workers (47 percent of women, 36 percent of men) think an office romance will jeopardize their job security or advancement, 42 percent conduct their romance openly. "The new wrinkle is the explosion of online venues such as blogs, YouTube, and social networking sites, which provide very public means for personal news to be shared," commented Heins. "Becoming a target of gossip on the Internet does have the potential to affect career advancement and security."

Only 16 percent of workers' employers have a policy regarding workplace romance. Although most of us will spend one-third of each day at work, Boswell Group's founding psychoanalyst Kerry Sulkowicz reminds us that "if there's any reporting relationship between the two [people involved], the less powerful person will be the one asked to change jobs or leave."

www.spherion.com; harrisinteractive.com; www.boswellgroup.com

Measurement Question Sequencing

The design of survey questions is influenced by the need to relate each question to the others in the instrument. Often the content of one question (called a **branched question**) assumes other questions have been asked and answered. The psychological order of the questions is also important; question sequence can encourage or discourage commitment and promote or hinder the development of researcher-participant rapport.

The basic principle used to guide sequence decisions is this: the nature and needs of the participant must determine the sequence of questions and the organization of the interview schedule. Four guidelines are suggested to implement this principle:

1. The question process must quickly awaken interest and motivate the participant to participate in the interview. Put the more interesting topical target questions early. Leave classification questions (e.g., age, family size, income) not used as filters or screens to the end of the survey.

2. The participant should not be confronted by early requests for information that might be considered personal or ego-threatening. Put questions that might influence the participant to discontinue or terminate the questioning process near the end.

>**Exhibit 13-10** Sample Components of Communication Instruments

Component	Example
Introduction	Good evening. May I please speak with (name of participant)? Mr. (participant's last name), I'm (your name), calling on behalf of MindWriter Corporation. You recently had your MindWriter laptop serviced at our CompleteCare Center. Could you take five minutes to tell us what you thought of the service provided by the center?
Transition	The next set of questions asks about your family and how you enjoy spending your nonworking or personal time.
Instructions for... a. Terminating (following filter or screen question)	I'm sorry, today we are only talking with individuals who eat cereal at least three days per week, but thank you for speaking with me. (Pause for participant reply.) Good-bye.
b. Participant discontinue	Would there be a time I could call back to complete the interview? (Pause; record time.) We'll call you back then at (repeat day, time). Thank you for talking with me this evening. Or: I appreciate your spending some time talking with me. Thank you.
c. Skip directions (between questions or groups of questions)	3. Did you purchase boxed cereal in the last 7 days? ❏ Yes ❏ No (skip to question 7)
d. Disposition instructions	A postage-paid envelope was included with your survey. Please refold your completed survey and mail it to us in the postage-paid envelope.
Conclusion a. Phone or personal interview	That's my last question. Your insights and the ideas of other valuable customers will help us to make the CompleteCare program the best it can be.
b. Self-administered (usually precedes the disposition instructions)	Thank you for talking with us this evening. (Pause for participant reply). Good evening. Thank you for sharing your ideas about the CompleteCare program. Your insights will help us serve you better.

3. The questioning process should begin with simple items and then move to the more complex, as well as move from general items to the more specific. Put taxing and challenging questions later in the questioning process.

4. Changes in the frame of reference should be small and should be clearly pointed out. Use transition statements between different topics of the target question set.

Awaken Interest and Motivation

We awaken interest and stimulate motivation to participate by choosing or designing questions that are attention-getting and not controversial. If the questions have human-interest value, so much the better. It is possible that the early questions will contribute valuable data to the major study objective, but their major task is to overcome the motivational barrier.

Sensitive and Ego-Involving Information

Regarding the introduction of sensitive information too early in the process, two forms of this error are common. Most studies need to ask for personal classification information about participants. Participants normally will provide these data, but the request should be made at the end of the survey. If made at the start of the survey, it often causes participants to feel threatened, dampening their interest and motivation to continue. It is also dangerous to ask any question at the start that is too personal. For example, participants in one survey were asked whether they suffered from insomnia. When the question was asked immediately after the interviewer's introductory remarks, about 12 percent of those interviewed admitted to having insomnia. When a matched sample was asked the same question after two **buffer questions** (neutral questions designed chiefly to establish rapport with the participant), 23 percent admitted suffering from insomnia.[15]

One of the attractions of using a Web survey is the ease with which participants follow branching questions immediately customized to their response patterns. In this survey, participants were shown several pictures of a prototype vehicle. Those who responded to question 2 by selecting one or more of the attributes in the checklist question were sequenced to a version of question 3 that related only to their particular responses to question 2. Note also that in question 3 the researcher chose not to force an answer, allowing the participant to indicate he or she had no opinion ("Don't know") on the issue of level of importance.

2. Which of the following attributes do you like about the automobile you just saw? (Select all that apply.)
- ☑ Overall appeal
- ☑ Headroom
- ☐ Design
- ☐ Color
- ☑ Height from the ground
- ☐ Other [_____]
- ☐ None of the above

[Next Question]

3. For those items that you selected, how important is each? (Provide one answer for each attribute.)

	Extremely important		Neither important nor not important		Not at all important	Don't know
a) Overall appeal	○	○	○	○	○	○
b) Height from the ground	○	○	○	○	○	○
c) Headroom	○	○	○	○	○	○

Simple to Complex

Deferring complex questions or simple questions that require much thought can help reduce the number of "don't know" responses that are so prevalent early in interviews.

General to Specific

The procedure of moving from general to more specific questions is sometimes called the *funnel approach.* The objectives of this procedure are to learn the participant's frame of reference and to extract the full range of desired information while limiting the distortion effect of earlier questions on later ones. This process may be illustrated with the following series of questions:

1. How do you think this country is getting along in its relations with other countries?
2. How do you think we are doing in our relations with Iran?
3. Do you think we ought to be dealing with Iran differently than we are now?
4. (If yes) What should we be doing differently?
5. Some people say we should get tougher with Iran and others think we are too tough as it is; how do you feel about it?[16]

The first question introduces the general subject and provides some insight into the participant's frame of reference. The second question narrows the concern to a single country, while the third and fourth seek views on how the United States should deal with Iran. The fifth question illustrates a specific opinion area and would be asked only if this point of toughness had not been covered in earlier responses. Question 4 is an example of a branched question; the response to the previous question determines whether or not question 4 is asked of the participant. You might find it valuable to refer to Exhibit 7-6, "The Interview Question Hierarchy," page 170.

>**Exhibit 13-11** Question Sequencing

Question	Percent Answering Yes	
	A. Asked First	B. Asked First
A. Should the United States permit its citizens to join the French and British armies?	45%	40%
B. Should the United States permit its citizens to join the German army?	31	22

There is also a risk of interaction whenever two or more questions are related. Question-order influence is especially problematic with self-administered questionnaires, because the participant is at liberty to refer back to questions previously answered. In an attempt to "correctly align" two responses, accurate opinions and attitudes may be sacrificed. Computer-administered and Web surveys have largely eliminated this problem.

The two questions shown in Exhibit 13-11 were asked in a national survey at the start of World War II.[17] Apparently, some participants who first endorsed enlistment with the Allies felt obliged to extend this privilege to joining the German army. When the decision was first made against joining the German army, a percentage of the participants felt constrained from approving the option to join the Allies.

Question Groups and Transitions

The last question-sequencing guideline suggests arranging questions to minimize shifting in subject matter and frame of reference. Participants often interpret questions in the light of earlier questions and miss shifts of perspective or subject unless they are clearly stated. Participants fail to listen carefully and frequently jump to conclusions about the import of a given question before it is completely stated. Their answers are strongly influenced by their frame of reference. Any change in subject by the interviewer may not register with them unless it is made strong and obvious. Most questionnaires that cover a range of topics are divided into sections with clearly defined transitions between sections to alert the participant to the change in frame of reference. Exhibit 13-12 provides a sample of a transition in the MindWriter CompleteCare study when measurement questions changed from service-related questions to personal and family-related questions.

Instructions

Instructions to the interviewer or participant attempt to ensure that all participants are treated equally, thus avoiding building error into the results. Two principles form the foundation for good instructions: clarity and courtesy. Instruction language needs to be unfailingly simple and polite.

Instruction topics include those for:

- *Terminating an unqualified participant*—defining for the interviewer how to terminate an interview when the participant does not correctly answer the screen or filter questions.

- *Terminating a discontinued interview*—defining for the interviewer how to conclude an interview when the participant decides to discontinue.

- *Moving between questions on an instrument*—defining for an interviewer or participant how to move between questions or topic sections of an instrument (*skip directions*) when movement is dependent on the specific answer to a question or when branched questions are used.

- *Disposing of a completed questionnaire*—defining for an interviewer or participant completing a self-administered instrument how to submit the completed questionnaire.

In a self-administered questionnaire, instructions must be contained within the survey instrument. This may be as simple as "Click the submit button to send your answers to us." Personal interviewer instructions sometimes are in a document separate from the questionnaire (a document thoroughly discussed during interviewer training) or are distinctly and clearly marked (highlighted, printed in colored ink, or boxed on the computer screen or in a pop-up window) on the data collection instrument itself. Sample instructions are presented in Exhibit 13-12.

Instrument Design for MindWriter

MindWriter

Replacing an imprecise management question with specific measurement questions is an exercise in analytical reasoning. We described that process incrementally in the MindWriter features in Chapters 3, 4, and 13. In Chapter 3, Jason's fact finding at MindWriter resulted in the ability to state the management dilemma in terms of management, research, and investigative questions. Adding context to the questions allowed Jason and Sara to construct the proposal described in Appendix A. In Chapter 12, they returned to the list of investigative questions and selected one question to use in testing their scaling approach. Here is a brief review of the steps Jason and Sara have taken so far and the measurement questions that have resulted.

SYNOPSIS OF THE PROBLEM

MindWriter Corporation's new service and repair program for laptop computers, CompleteCare, was designed to provide a rapid response to customers' service problems. Management has received several complaints, however. Management needs information on the program's effectiveness and its impact on customer satisfaction. There is also a shortage of trained technical operators in the company's telephone center. The package courier is uneven in executing its pickup and delivery contract. Parts availability problems exist for some machine types. Occasionally, customers receive units that either are not fixed or are damaged in some way.

Management question: What should be done to improve the CompleteCare program for MindWriter laptop repairs and servicing to enhance customer satisfaction?

RESEARCH QUESTIONS

1. Should the technical representatives be given more intensive training?

2. Should ABC Courier Service be replaced by an overnight air transport?

3. Should the repair diagnostic and repair sequencing operations be modified?

4. Should the return packaging be modified to include premolded rigid foam inserts, conforming-expanding foam protection, or neither?

5. Should metropolitan repair centers be established to complement or replace in-factory repair facilities?

INVESTIGATIVE QUESTIONS

a. Are customers' expectations being met in terms of the time it takes to repair the systems? What is the

customers' overall satisfaction with the CompleteCare service program and the MindWriter product?

b. How well is the call center helping customers? Is it helping them with instructions? What percentage of customers' technical problems is it solving without callbacks or subsequent repairs? How long must customers wait on the phone?

c. How good is the transportation company? Does it pick up and deliver the system responsively? How long must customers wait for pickup and delivery? Are the laptops damaged due to package handling?

d. How good is the repair group? What problems are most common? What repair processes are involved in fixing these problems? For what percentage of laptops is the repair completed within the promised time limit? Are customers' problems fully resolved? Are there new problems with the newer models? How quickly are these problems diagnosed?

e. How are repaired laptops packaged for return shipping? What is the cost of alternative rigid foam inserts and expandable-foam packaging? Would new equipment be required if the packaging were changed? Would certain shipping-related complaints be eliminated with new packaging materials?

The extensive scope of the research questions and resulting measurement questions forced MindWriter to reassess the scope of the desired initial research study, to determine where to concentrate its enhancement efforts. Management chose a descriptive rather than a prescriptive scope.

MEASUREMENT QUESTIONS

The measurement questions used for the self-administered package insert instrument are shown in Exhibit 13-12.[18] The first investigative question in (a), above, is addressed in survey items 3, 5, and 8a, while the second question is addressed in items 6 and 8a. Of the investigative questions in (b), the first two are addressed as "responsiveness" and "technical competence" with telephone assistance in the questionnaire. The second two investigative questions in (b) may be answered by accessing the company's service database. The questionnaire's three-part question on courier service parallels investigative question (c). Specific service deficiencies will be recorded in the "Comments/Suggestions" section. Investigative questions under (d) and (e) are covered with questionnaire items 3, 4, and 5. Because service deficiencies reflected in item 5 may be attributed to both the repair facility and the courier, the reasons (items 1, 2, 3, 4,

>**close**up**cont'd**

and comments) will be cross-checked during analysis. Questionnaire item 6 uses the same language as the last investigative question in (a). Questionnaire item 7 is an extension of item 6 but attempts to secure an impression of behavioral intent to use CompleteCare again. Finally, the last item will make known the extent to which change is needed in CompleteCare by revealing repurchase intention as linked to product and service experience.

>**Exhibit 13-12** Measurement Questions for the MindWriter Study

	Met **few** expectations 1	Met **some** expectations 2	Met **most** expectations 3	Met **all** expectations 4	**Exceeded** expectations 5

MindWriter personal computers offer you ease of use and maintenance. When you need service, we want you to rely on **CompleteCare,** wherever you may be. That's why we're asking you to take a moment to tell us how well we've served you.

1. Telephone assistance with your problem:
   - a. Responsiveness — 1 2 3 4 5
   - b. Technical competence — 1 2 3 4 5
2. The courier service's effectiveness:
   - a. Arrangements — 1 2 3 4 5
   - b. Pickup speed — 1 2 3 4 5
   - c. Delivery speed — 1 2 3 4 5
3. Speed of the overall repair process. — 1 2 3 4 5
4. Resolution of the problem that prompted service/repair. — 1 2 3 4 5
5. Condition of your MindWriter on arrival. — 1 2 3 4 5
6. Overall impression of CompleteCare's effectiveness. — 1 2 3 4 5
7. Likelihood of using CompleteCare on another occasion.
   (1 = very unlikely   3 = neither likely nor unlikely   5 = very likely) — 1 2 3 4 5
8. Likelihood of repurchasing a MindWriter based on:
   (1 = very unlikely   3 = neither likely nor unlikely   5 = very likely)
   - a. Service/repair experience — 1 2 3 4 5
   - b. Product performance — 1 2 3 4 5

Comments/Suggestions: _____

How may we contact you to follow up on any problems you have experienced?

Last Name ___ First Name ___ (___) Phone ___

City ___ State ___ Zip ___

Service Code

Source: ©Cooper Research Group, Inc., 2000. Used by permission. See reference note 18.

Conclusion

The role of the conclusion is to leave the participant with the impression that his or her involvement has been valuable. Subsequent researchers may need this individual to participate in new studies. If every interviewer or instrument expresses appreciation for participation, cooperation in subsequent studies is more likely. A sample conclusion is shown in Exhibit 13-12.

Overcoming Instrument Problems

There is no substitute for a thorough understanding of question wording, question content, and question sequencing issues. However, the researcher can do several things to help improve survey results, among them:

- Build rapport with the participant.
- Redesign the questioning process.

- Explore alternative response strategies.
- Use methods other than surveying to secure the data.
- Pretest all the survey elements. (See Appendix 13b.)

Build Rapport with the Participant

Most information can be secured by direct undisguised questioning if rapport has been developed. Rapport is particularly useful in building participant interest in the project, and the more interest participants have, the more cooperation they will give. One can also overcome participant unwillingness by providing some material compensation for cooperation. This approach has been especially successful in mail surveys and is increasingly used in Web surveys.

The assurance of confidentiality also can increase participants' motivation. One approach is to give discrete assurances, both by question wording and by interviewer comments and actions, that all types of behavior, attitudes, and positions on controversial or sensitive subjects are acceptable and normal. Where you can say so truthfully, guarantee that participants' answers will be used only in combined statistical totals (aggregate data), not matched to an individual participant. If participants are convinced that their replies contribute to some important purpose, they are more likely to be candid, even about taboo topics. If a researcher's organization uses an Institutional Review Board to review surveys before use, the board may require an instruction indicating that any response—in fact, participation—is voluntary. This is especially important where surveys are used with internal publics (employees).

Redesign the Questioning Process

You can redesign the questioning process to improve the quality of answers by modifying the administrative process and the response strategy. We might show that confidentiality is indispensable to the administration of the survey by using a group administration of questionnaires, accompanied by a ballot-box collection procedure. Even in face-to-face interviews, the participant may fill in the part of the questionnaire containing sensitive information and then seal the entire instrument in an envelope. Although this does not guarantee confidentiality, it does suggest it.

We can also develop appropriate questioning sequences that will gradually lead a participant from "safe" questions to those that are more sensitive. As already noted in our discussion of disguised questions, indirect questioning (using projective techniques) is a widely used approach for securing opinions on sensitive topics. The participants are asked how "other people" or "people around here" feel about a topic. It is assumed the participants will reply in terms of their own attitudes and experiences, but this outcome is hardly certain. Indirect questioning may give a good measure of the majority opinion on a topic but fail to reflect the views either of the participant or of minority segments.

With certain topics, it is possible to secure answers by using a proxy code. When we seek family income groups, we can hand the participant a card with income brackets like these:

A. Under $25,000 per year.

B. $25,000 to $49,999 per year.

C. $50,000 to $74,999 per year.

D. $75,000 and over per year.

The participant is then asked to report the appropriate bracket as either A, B, C, or D. For some reason, participants are more willing to provide such an obvious proxy measure than to verbalize actual dollar values.

Explore Alternative Response Strategies

When drafting the original question, try developing positive, negative, and neutral versions of each type of question. This practice dramatizes the problems of bias, helping you to select question wording that minimizes such problems. Sometimes use an extreme version of a question rather than the expected one.

Minimize nonresponses to particular questions by recognizing the sensitivity of certain topics. In a self-administered instrument, for example, asking a multiple-choice question about income or age, where incomes and ages are offered in ranges, is usually more successful than using a free-response question (such as "What is your age, please?_____").

The Value of Pretesting

The final step toward improving survey results is **pretesting,** the assessment of questions and instruments before the start of a study (see Exhibits 13-1, 13-2, and 13-9). There are abundant reasons for pretesting individual questions, questionnaires, and interview schedules: (1) discovering ways to increase participant interest, (2) increasing the likelihood that participants will remain engaged to the completion of the survey, (3) discovering question content, wording, and sequencing problems, (4) discovering target question groups where researcher training is needed, and (5) exploring ways to improve the overall quality of survey data.

> Most of what we know about pretesting is prescriptive. According to contemporary authors, there are no general principles of good pretesting, no systematization of practice, no consensus about expectations, and we rarely leave records for each other. How a pretest was conducted, what investigators learned from it, how they redesigned their questionnaire on the basis of it—these matters are reported only sketchily in research reports, if at all.[19]

Nevertheless, pretesting not only is an established practice for discovering errors but also is useful for training the research team. Ironically, professionals who have participated in scores of studies are more likely to pretest an instrument than is a beginning researcher hurrying to complete a project. Revising questions five or more times is not unusual. Yet inexperienced researchers often underestimate the need to follow the design-test-revise process. We devote Appendix 13b to pretesting.

>summary

1 The instrument design process starts with a comprehensive list of investigative questions drawn from the management-research question hierarchy. Instrument design is a three-phase process with numerous issues within each phase: (a) developing the instrument design strategy, (b) constructing and refining the measurement questions, and (c) drafting and refining the instrument.

2 Several choices must be made in designing a communication study instrument. Surveying can be a face-to-face interview, or it can be much less personal, using indirect media and self-administered questionnaires. The questioning process can be unstructured, as in an IDI, or the questions can be clearly structured. Responses may be unstructured and open-ended or structured with the participant choosing from a list of possibilities. The degree to which the objectives and intent of the questions should be disguised must also be decided.

3 Instruments obtain three general classes of information. Target questions address the investigative questions and are the most important. Classification questions concern participant characteristics and allow participants' answers to be grouped for analysis. Administrative questions identify the participant, interviewer, and interview location and conditions.

4 Question construction involves three critical decision areas. They are (a) question content, (b) question wording, and (c) response strategy. Question content should pass the following tests: Should the question be asked? Is it of proper scope? Can and will the participant answer adequately?

Question wording difficulties exceed most other sources of distortion in surveys. Retention of a question should be confirmed by answering these questions: Is the question stated in terms of a shared vocabulary? Does the vocabulary have a single meaning? Does the question contain misleading assumptions? Is the wording biased? Is it correctly personalized? Are adequate alternatives presented?

The study's objective and participant factors affect the decision of whether to use open-ended or closed questions. Each response strategy generates a specific level of data, with available statistical procedures for each scale type influencing the desired response strategy. Participant factors include level of information about the topic, degree to which the topic has been thought through, ease of communication, and motivation to share information. The decision is also affected by the interviewer's perception of participant factors.

Both dichotomous response and multiple-choice questions are valuable, but on balance the latter are preferred if only because few questions have only two possible answers. Checklist, rating, and ranking strategies are also common.

5 Question sequence can drastically affect participant willingness to cooperate and the quality of responses. Generally, the sequence should begin with efforts to awaken the participant's interest in continuing the interview. Early questions should be simple rather than complex, easy rather than difficult, nonthreatening, and obviously germane to the announced objective of the study. Frame-of-reference changes should be minimal, and questions should be sequenced so that early questions do not distort replies to later ones.

6 Sources of questions for the construction of questionnaires include the literature on related research and sourcebooks of scales and questionnaires. Borrowing items has attendant risks, such as time and situation-specific problems or reliability and validity. Incompatibility of language and idiom also needs to be considered.

>**key**terms

administrative question 325	dummy table 323	rating question 334
branched question 340	free-response question 329	recency effect 333
buffer question 341	interview schedule 325	screen question (filter question) 339
checklist 334	leading question 328	structured response 329
classification question 325	multiple-choice question 330	target question 325
dichotomous question 329	pretesting 347	structured, 325
disguised question 322	primacy effect 333	unstructured, 325
double-barreled question 332	ranking question 335	unstructured response 329

>**discussion**questions

Terms in Review

1 Distinguish between:

   a Direct and indirect questions.

   b Open-ended and closed questions.

   c Research, investigative, and measurement questions.

   d Alternative response strategies.

2 Why is the survey technique so popular? When is it not appropriate?

3 What special problems do open-ended questions have? How can these be minimized? In what situations are open-ended questions most useful?

4 Why might a researcher wish to disguise the objective of a study?

5 One of the major reasons why survey research may not be effective is that the survey instruments are less useful than they should be. What would you say are the four possible major faults of survey instrument design?

6 Why is it desirable to pretest survey instruments? What information can you secure from such a pretest? How can you find the best wording for a question on a questionnaire?

7 One design problem in the development of survey instruments concerns the sequence of questions. What suggestions would you give to researchers designing their first questionnaire?

8 One of the major problems facing the designer of a survey instrument concerns the assumptions made. What are the major "problem assumptions"?

Making Research Decisions

9 Following are six questions that might be found on questionnaires. Comment on each as to whether or not it is a

good question. If it is not, explain why. (Assume that no lead-in or screening questions are required. Judge each question on its own merits.)

   a Do you read *National Geographic* magazine regularly?

   b What percentage of your time is spent asking for information from others in your organization?

   c When did you first start chewing gum?

   d How much discretionary buying power do you have each year?

   e Why did you decide to attend Big State University?

   f Do you think the president is doing a good job now?

10 In a class project, students developed a brief self-administered questionnaire by which they might quickly evaluate a professor. One student submitted the following instrument. Evaluate the questions asked and the format of the instrument.

Professor Evaluation Form

1. Overall, how would you rate this professor?

   ☐ Good   ☐ Fair   ☐ Poor

2. Does this professor

   a. Have good class delivery? _____

   b. Know the subject? _____

   c. Have a positive attitude toward the subject? _____

   d. Grade fairly? _____

   e. Have a sense of humor? _____

   f. Use audiovisuals, case examples, or other classroom aids? _____

   g. Return exams promptly? _____

3. What is the professor's strongest point? _____

4. What is the professor's weakest point? _____

5. What kind of class does the professor teach? _____

6. Is this course required? _____

7. Would you take another course from this professor? _____

11 Assume the American Society of Training Directors is studying its membership in order to enhance member benefits and attract new members. Below is a copy of a cover letter and mail questionnaire received by a member of the society. Please evaluate the usefulness and tone of the letter and the questions and format of the instrument.

Dear ASTD Member:

The ASTD is evaluating the perception of value of membership among its members. Enclosed is a short questionnaire and a return envelope. I hope you will take a few minutes and fill out the questionnaire as soon as possible, because the sooner the information is returned to me, the better.

Sincerely,

Director of Membership

Questionnaire

Directions: Please answer as briefly as possible.

1. With what company did you enter the field of training?

   _____

2. How long have you been in the field of training?

   _____

3. How long have you been in the training department of the company with which you are presently employed?

   _____

4. How long has the training department in your company been in existence? _____

5. Is the training department a subset of another department? If so, what department? _____

6. For what functions (other than training) is your department responsible? _____

7. How many people, including yourself, are in the training department of your company (local plant or establishment)?

   _____

8. What degrees do you hold and from what institutions?

   Major _____ Minor _____

9. Why were you chosen for training? What special qualifications prompted your entry into training?

   _____

   _____

10. What experience would you consider necessary for an individual to enter into the field of training with your company? Include both educational requirements and actual experience.

   _____

   _____

   _____

Bringing Research to Life

12 Design the introduction of the Albany Outpatient Laser Clinic survey, assuming it will continue to be a self-administered questionnaire.

13 To evaluate whether presurgery patient attitudes affect recovery and ultimate patient satisfaction with the Albany Outpatient Laser Clinic, design a question for the self-administered survey. (You may wish to review the opening vignettes in this chapter and Chapter 9.)

From Concept to Practice

14 Using Exhibits 13-1, 13-4, and 13-9, develop the flowchart for the Albany Outpatient Laser Clinic study in the opening vignette.

From the Headlines

15 One of Kraft's hallmark brands is Jell-O. During May 2009, the Jell-O Sugar Free Pudding cups line was getting a makeover with the introduction of two new flavors: Boston Cream Pie and Cinnamon Roll.

a What survey research would you have done to determine whether to introduce these new flavors?

b Design the questionnaire for the survey research you would have done.

>cases*

 Akron Children's Hospital

Calling Up Attendance

Campbell-Ewald: R-E-S-P-E-C-T Spells Loyalty

Can Research Rescue the Red Cross?

Inquiring Minds Want to Know—NOW!

Mastering Teacher Leadership

NCRCC: Teeing Up and New Strategic Direction

 Ohio Lottery: Innovative Research Design Drives Winning

 Pebble Beach Co.

Proofpoint: Capitalizing on a Reporter's Love of Statistics

 Starbucks, Bank One, and Visa Launch Starbucks Duetto Visa

 USTA: Come Out Swinging

Volkswagen's Beetle

* You will find a description of each case in the Case Abstracts section of the textbook. Check the Case index to determine whether a case provides data, the research instrument, video, or other supplementary material. Written cases are downloadable from the text website (www.mhhe.com/cooper11e). All video material and video cases are available from the Online Learning Center. The film reel icon indicates a video case or video material relevant to the case.

>**appendix**13a

Crafting Effective Measurement Questions

Numerous issues influence whether the questions we ask on questionnaires generate the decision-making data that managers sorely need. Each of the issues summarized in Exhibit 13-5 is developed more fully here.

Question Content

Should This Question Be Asked?

Purposeful versus Interesting Questions that merely produce "interesting information" cannot be justified on either economic or research grounds. Challenge each question's function. Does it contribute significant information toward answering the research question? Will its omission limit or prevent the thorough analysis of other data? Can we infer the answer from another question? A good question designer knows the value of learning more from fewer questions.

Is the Question of Proper Scope and Coverage?

Incomplete or Unfocused We can test this content issue by asking, Will this question reveal all we need to know? We sometimes ask participants to reveal their motivations for particular behaviors or attitudes by asking them, Why? This simple question is inadequate to probe the range of most causal relationships. When studying product use behavior, for example, we learn more by directing two or three questions on product use to the heavy-use consumer and only one question to the light user.

Questions are also inadequate if they do not provide the information you need to interpret responses fully. If you ask about the Albany Clinic's image for quality patient care, do different groups of patients or those there for the first versus the third time have different attitudes? To evaluate relative attitudes, do you need to ask the same question about other companies? In the original Albany Clinic survey, participants were asked, "Have you ever had or been treated for a recent cold or flu?" If participants answer yes, what exactly have they told the researcher that would be of use to the eye surgeon? Wouldn't it be likely that the surgeon is interested in medication taken to treat colds or flu within, say, the prior 10 days? This question

also points to two other problems of scope and coverage: the double-barreled question and the imprecise question.

Double-Barreled Questions Does the question request so much content that it should be broken into two or more questions? While reducing the overall number of questions in a study is highly desirable, don't try to ask double-barreled questions. The Albany Clinic question about flu ("Have you ever had or been treated for a recent cold or flu?") fires more than two barrels. It asks four questions in all (Ever had cold? Ever had flu? Been treated for cold? Been treated for flu?).

Here's another common example posed to menswear retailers: "Are this year's shoe sales and gross profits higher than last year's?" Couldn't sales be higher with stagnant profits, or profits higher with level or lower sales? This second example is more typical of the problem of double-barreled questions.

A less obvious double-barreled question is the question we ask to identify a family's or a group's TV station preference. Since a single station is unlikely, a better question would ask the station preference of each family member separately or, alternatively, screen for the group member who most often controls channel selection on Monday evenings during prime time. Also, it's highly probable that no one station would serve as an individual's preferred station when we cover a wide range of time (8 to 11 p.m.). This reveals another problem, the imprecise question.

Precision To test a question for precision, ask, Does the question ask precisely what we want and need to know? We sometimes ask for a participant's income when we really want to know the family's total annual income before taxes in the past calendar year. We ask what a participant purchased "last week" when we really want to know what he or she purchased in a "typical 7-day period during the past 90 days." The Albany Clinic's patients were asked for cold and flu history during the time frame "ever." It is hard to imagine an adult who has never experienced a cold or flu and equally hard to assume an adult hasn't been treated for one or both at some time in his or her life.

A second precision issue deals with common vocabulary between researcher and participant. To test your question for this problem, ask, Do I need to offer operational definitions of concepts and constructs used in the question?

Can the Participant Answer Adequately?

Time for Thought   Although the question may address the topic, is it asked in such a way that the participant will be able to frame an answer, or is it reasonable to assume that the participant can determine the answer? This is also a question that drives sample design, but once the ideal sample unit is determined, researchers often assume that participants who fit the sample profile have all the answers, preferably on the tips of their tongues. To frame a response to some questions takes time and thought; such questions are best left to self-administered questionnaires.

Participation at the Expense of Accuracy   Participants typically want to cooperate in interviews; thus they assume giving any answer is more helpful than denying knowledge of a topic. Their desire to impress the interviewer may encourage them to give answers based on no information. A classic illustration of this problem occurred with the following question:[1] "Which of the following statements most closely coincides with your opinion of the Metallic Metals Act?" The response pattern shows that 70 percent of those interviewed had a fairly clear opinion of the Metallic Metals Act; however, there is no such act. The participants apparently assumed that if a question was asked, they should provide an answer. Given reasonable-sounding choices, they selected one even though they knew nothing about the topic.

To counteract this tendency to respond at any cost, *filter* or *screen questions* are used to qualify a participant's knowledge. If the MindWriter service questionnaire is distributed via mail to all recent purchasers of MindWriter products, we might ask, "Have you required service for your laptop since its purchase?" Only those for whom service was provided could supply the detail and scope of the responses indicated in the investigative question list. If such a question is asked in a phone interview, we would call the question a *screen,* because it is being used to determine whether the person on the other end of the phone line is a qualified sample unit. This same question asked on a computer-administered questionnaire would likely *branch* or *skip* the participant to a series of classification questions.

Assuming that participants have prior knowledge or understanding may be risky. The risk is getting many answers that have little basis in fact. The Metallic Metals Act illustration may be challenged as unusual, but in another case a Gallup report revealed that 45 percent of the persons surveyed did not know what a "lobbyist in Washington" was and 88 percent could not give a correct description of "jurisdictional strike."[2] This points to the need for operational definitions as part of question wording.

Presumed Knowledge   The question designer should consider the participants' information level when determining the content and appropriateness of a question. In some studies, the degree of participant expertise can be substantial, and simplified explanations are inappropriate and discourage participation. In asking the public about gross margins in menswear stores, we would want to be sure the "general-public" participant understands the nature of "gross margin." If our sample unit were a merchant, explanations might not be needed. A high level of knowledge among our sample units, however, may not eliminate the need for operational definitions. Among merchants, gross margin per unit in dollars is commonly accepted as the difference between cost and selling price; but when offered as a percentage rather than a dollar figure, it can be calculated as a percentage of unit selling price or as a percentage of unit cost. A participant answering from the "cost" frame of reference would calculate gross margin at 100 percent; another participant, using the same dollars and the "selling price" frame of reference, would calculate gross margin at 50 percent. If a construct is involved and differing interpretations of a concept are feasible, operational definitions may still be needed.

Recall and Memory Decay   The adequacy problem also occurs when you ask questions that overtax participants' recall ability. People cannot recall much that has happened in their past, unless it was dramatic. Your mother may remember everything about your arrival if you were her first child: the weather, time of day, even what she ate prior to your birth. If you have several siblings, her memory of subsequent births may be less complete. If the events surveyed are of incidental interest to participants, they will probably be unable to recall them correctly even a short time later. An unaided recall question, "What radio programs did you listen to last night?" might identify as few as 10 percent of those individuals who actually listened to a program.[3]

Balance (General versus Specific)   Answering adequacy also depends on the proper balance between generality and specificity. We often ask questions in terms too general and detached from participants' experiences. Asking for average annual consumption of a product may make an unrealistic demand for generalization on people who do not think in such terms. Why not ask how often the product was used last week or last month? Too often participants are asked to recall individual use experiences over an extended time and to average them for us. This is asking participants to do the researcher's work and encourages substantial response errors. It may also contribute to a higher refusal rate and higher discontinuation rate.

There is a danger in being too narrow in the time frame applied to behavior questions. We may ask about movie attendance for the last seven days, although this is too short a time span on which to base attendance estimates. It may be better to ask about attendance, say, for the last 30 days.

>**Exhibit 13a-1** A Test of Alternative Response Strategies

A. What is your favorite brand of ice cream? _____
B. Some people have a favorite brand of ice cream, while others do not have a favorite brand. In which group are you? (please check)
    ❑ I do not have a favorite brand of ice cream.
    ❑ I have a favorite brand of ice cream.
  What is your favorite (if you have a favorite)? _____

>**Exhibit 13a-2** Results of Alternative Response Strategies Test

Response	Version A	Version B
Named a favorite brand	77%*	39%*
Named a favorite flavor rather than a brand	19	18
Had no favorite brand	4	43
Total	100%	100%
	n = 57	*n* = 56

*Significant difference at the 0.001 level.

There are no firm rules about this generality-specificity problem. Developing the right level of generality depends on the subject, industry, setting, and experience of the question designer.

Objectivity The ability of participants to answer adequately is also often distorted by questions whose content is biased by what is included or omitted. The question may explicitly mention only the positive or negative aspects of the topic or make unwarranted assumptions about the participant's position. Consider Exhibit 13a-1, an experiment in which two forms of a question were asked. Fifty-seven randomly chosen graduate business students answered version A, and 56 answered version B. Their responses are shown in Exhibit 13a-2. The probable cause of the difference in level of brand preference expressed is that A is an unsupported assumption. It assumes and suggests that everyone has a favorite brand of ice cream and will report it. Version B indicates the participant need not have a favorite.

A deficiency in both versions is that about one participant in five misinterpreted the meaning of the term *brand*. This misinterpretation cannot be attributed to low education, low intelligence, lack of exposure to the topic, or quick or lazy reading of the question. The subjects were students who had taken at least one course in marketing in which branding was prominently treated.*

Will the Participants Answer Willingly?

Sensitive Information Even if participants have the information, they may be unwilling to give it. Some

topics are considered too sensitive to discuss with strangers. These vary from person to person, but one study suggests the most sensitive topics concern money matters and family life.[4] More than one-fourth of those interviewed mentioned these as the topics about which they would be "least willing to answer questions." Participants of lower socioeconomic status also included political matters in this "least willing" list.

Participants also may be unwilling to give correct answers for ego reasons. Many exaggerate their incomes, the number of cars they own, their social status, and the amount of high-prestige literature they read. They also minimize their age and the amount of low-prestige literature they read. Many participants are reluctant to try to give an adequate response. Often this will occur when they see the topic as irrelevant to their own interests or to their perception of the survey's purpose. They participate halfheartedly, often answer with "don't know," give negative replies, give stereotypical responses, or refuse to be interviewed.

You can learn more about crafting questions dealing with sensitive information by reading "Measuring Attitudes on Sensitive Subjects" on the text website.

Question Wording

Shared Vocabulary Because surveying is an exchange of ideas between interviewer and participant, each must understand what the other says, and this is possible only if the vocabulary used is common to both parties.[5] Two problems arise. First, the words must be simple enough to allow adequate communication with persons of limited education. This is dealt with by reducing the level of word difficulty to simple English words and phrases (more is said about this in the section on word clarity).

Word confusion difficulties are discussed later in this appendix.

Technical language is the second issue. Even highly educated participants cannot answer questions stated in unfamiliar technical terms. Technical language also poses difficulties for interviewers. In one study of how corporation executives handled various financial problems, interviewers had to be conversant with technical financial terms. This necessity presented the researcher with two alternatives—hiring people knowledgeable in finance and teaching them interviewing skills or teaching financial concepts to experienced interviewers.[6] This vocabulary problem also exists in situations where similar or identical studies are conducted in different countries and multiple languages.

A great obstacle to effective question wording is the choice of words. Questions to be asked of the public should be restricted to the 2,000 most common words in the English language.[7] Even the use of simple words is not enough. Many words have vague references or meanings that must be gleaned from their context. In a repair study, technicians were asked, "How many radio sets did you repair last month?" This question may seem unambiguous, but participants interpreted it in two ways. Some viewed it as a question of them alone; others interpreted "you" more inclusively, as referring to the total output of the shop. There is also the possibility of misinterpreting "last month," depending on the timing of the questioning. Using "during the last 30 days" would be much more precise and unambiguous. Typical of the many problem words are these: *any, could, would, should, fair, near, often, average,* and *regular.* One author recommends that after stating a question as precisely as possible, we should test each word against this checklist:

- Does the word chosen mean what we intend?
- Does the word have multiple meanings? If so, does the context make the intended meaning clear?
- Does the word chosen have more than one pronunciation? Is there any word with similar pronunciation with which the chosen word might be confused?
- Is a simpler word or phrase suggested or possible?[8]

We cause other problems when we use abstract concepts that have many overtones or emotional qualifications.[9] Without concrete referents, meanings are too vague for the researcher's needs. Examples of such words are *business, government,* and *society.*

Shared vocabulary issues are addressed by using the following:

- Simple rather than complex words.
- Commonly known, unambiguous words.
- Precise words.
- Interviewers with content knowledge.

Unsupported Assumptions Unwarranted assumptions contribute to many problems of question wording. A metropolitan newspaper, *Midwest Daily,* conducted a study in an attempt to discover what readers would like in its redesigned lifestyle section. One notable question asked readers: "Who selects your clothes? You or the man in your life?" In this age of educated, working, independent women, the question managed to offend a significant portion of the female readership. In addition, *Midwest Daily* discovered that many of its female readers were younger than researchers originally assumed and the only man in their lives was their father, not the spousal or romantic relationship alluded to by the questions that followed. Once men reached this question, they assumed that the paper was interested in serving only the needs of female readers. The unwarranted assumptions built into the questionnaire caused a significantly smaller response rate than expected and caused several of the answers to be uninterpretable.

Frame of Reference Inherent in word meaning problems is also the matter of a frame of reference. Each of us understands concepts, words, and expressions in light of our own experience. The U.S. Bureau of the Census wanted to know how many people were in the labor market. To learn whether a person was employed, it asked, "Did you do any work for pay or profit last week?" The researchers erroneously assumed there would be a common frame of reference between the interviewer and participants on the meaning of *work.* Unfortunately, many persons viewed themselves primarily or foremost as homemakers or students. They failed to report that they also worked at a job during the week. This difference in frame of reference resulted in a consistent underestimation of the number of people working in the United States.

In a subsequent version of the study, this question was replaced by two questions, the first of which sought a statement on the participant's major activity during the week. If the participant gave a nonwork classification, a second question was asked to determine if he or she had done any work for pay besides this major activity. This revision increased the estimate of total employment by more than 1 million people, half of them working 35 hours or more per week.[10]

The frame of reference can be controlled in two ways. First, the interviewer may seek to learn the frame of reference used by the participant. When asking participants to evaluate their reasons for judging a retail store as unattractive, the interviewer must learn the frames of reference they use. Is the store being evaluated in terms of its particular features and layout, the failure of management to respond to a complaint made by the participant, the preference of the participant for another store, or the participant's recent difficulty in returning an unwanted item?

>**Exhibit 13a-3** Split Test of Alternative Question Wording

Should the United States do any of the following at this time?
    A. Increase our armed forces further, even if it means more taxes.

Should the United States do any of the following at this time?
    B. Increase our armed forces further, even if you have to pay a special tax.

Eighty-eight percent of those answering question A thought the armed forces should be increased, while only 79 percent of those answering question B favored increasing the armed forces.

Source: Hadley Cantril, ed., *Gauging Public Opinion* (Princeton, NJ: Princeton University Press, 1944), p. 48.

Second, it is useful to specify the frame of reference for the participant. In asking for an opinion about the new store design, the interviewer might specify that the question should be answered based on the participant's opinion of the layout, the clarity and placement of signage, the ease of finding merchandise, or another frame of reference.

Biased Wording

Bias is the distortion of responses in one direction. It can result from many of the problems already discussed, but word choice is often the major source. Obviously such words or phrases as *politically correct* or *fundamentalist* must be used with great care. Strong adjectives can be particularly distorting. One alleged opinion survey concerned with the subject of preparation for death included the following question: "Do you think that decent, low-cost funerals are sensible?" Who could be against anything that is *decent* or *sensible?* There is a question about whether this was a legitimate survey or a burial service sales campaign, but it shows how suggestive an adjective can be.

Congressional representatives have been known to use surveys as a means of communicating with their constituencies. Questions are worded, however, to imply the issue stance that the representative favors. Can you tell the representative's stance in the following question?

> *Example:* Would you have me vote for a balanced budget if it means higher costs for the supplemental Social Security benefits that you have already earned?

We can also strongly bias the participant by using prestigious names in a question. In a historic survey on whether the war and navy departments should be combined into a single defense department, one survey said, "General Eisenhower says the army and navy should be combined," while the other version omitted his name. Given the first version (name included), 49 percent of the participants approved of having one department; given the second version, only 29 percent favored one department.[11] Just imagine using Michael Jordan's or Shaq O'Neill's name in a survey question asked of teen boys interested in basketball. The power of aspirational reference groups to sway opinion and attitude is well established in advertising; it shouldn't be underestimated in survey design.

We also can bias response through the use of superlatives, slang expressions, and fad words. These are best excluded unless they are critical to the objective of the question. Ethnic references should also be stated with care.

Personalization

How personalized should a question be? Should we ask, "What would you do about...?" Or should we ask, "What would people with whom you work do about...?" The effect of personalization is shown in a classic example reported by Cantril.[12] A split test—in which a portion of the sample received one question, with another portion receiving a second question—was made of a question concerning attitudes about the expansion of U.S. armed forces in 1940, as noted in Exhibit 13a-3.

These and other examples show that personalizing questions changes responses, but the direction of the influence is not clear. We cannot tell whether personalization or no personalization is superior. Perhaps the best that can be said is that when either form is acceptable, we should choose that which appears to present the issues more realistically. If there are doubts, then split survey versions should be used (one segment of the sample should get one question version, while a second segment should receive the alternative question version).

Adequate Alternatives

Have we adequately expressed the alternatives with respect to the purpose of the question? It is usually wise to express each alternative explicitly to avoid bias. This is illustrated well with a pair of questions that were asked of matched samples of participants.[13] The question forms that were used are noted in Exhibit 13a-4.

Often the above issues are simultaneously present in a single question. Exhibit 13a-5 reveals several questions drawn from actual mail surveys. We've identified the problem issues and suggest one solution for improvement.

>Exhibit 13a-4 Expressing Alternatives

The way a question is asked can influence the results. Consider these two alternative questions judging companies' images in the community in the face of layoffs:

   A. Do you think most manufacturing companies that lay off workers during slack periods could arrange things to avoid layoffs and give steady work right through the year?
   B. Do you think most manufacturing companies that lay off workers in slack periods could avoid layoffs and provide steady work right through the year, or do you think layoffs are unavoidable?

The Results:

When Asked...	A	B
Company could avoid layoffs	63%	35%
Could not avoid layoffs	22	41
No opinion	15	24

Source: Hadley Cantril, ed., *Gauging Public Opinion* (Princeton, NJ: Princeton University Press, 1944), p. 48.

While the suggested improvement might not be the only possible solution, it does correct the issues identified. What other solutions could be applied to correct the problems identified?

Response Strategy

The objectives of the study; characteristics of participants, especially their level of information, level of motivation to participate, and ease of communication; the nature of the topic(s) being studied; the type of scale needed; and your analysis plan dictate the response strategy. Examples of the strategies described in Chapter 13 and discussed in detail in Chapters 11 and 12 are found in Exhibit 13-6.

Objective of the Study If the objective of the question is only to classify the participant on some stated point of view, then the closed question will serve well. Assume you are interested only in whether a participant approves or disapproves of a certain corporate policy. A closed question will provide this answer. This response strategy ignores the full scope of the participant's opinion and the events that helped shape the attitude at its foundation. If the objective is to explore this wider territory, then an open-ended question (free-response strategy) is preferable.

Open-ended questions are appropriate when the objective is to discover opinions and degrees of knowledge. They are also appropriate when the interviewer seeks sources of information, dates of events, and suggestions or when probes are used to secure more information. When the topic of a question is outside the participant's experience, the open-ended question may offer the better way to learn his or her level of information.

Closed questions are better when there is a clear frame of reference, the participant's level of information is predictable, and the researcher believes the participant understands the topic.

Open-ended questions also help to uncover certainty of feelings and expressions of intensity, although well-designed closed questions can do the same.

Thoroughness of Prior Thought If a participant has developed a clear opinion on the topic, a closed question does well. If an answer has not been thought out, an open-ended question may give the participant a chance to ponder a reply, and then elaborate on and revise it.

Communication Skill Open-ended questions require a stronger grasp of vocabulary and a greater ability to frame responses than do closed questions.

Participant Motivation Experience has shown that closed questions typically require less motivation and answering them is less threatening to participants. But the response alternatives sometimes suggest which answer is appropriate; for this reason, closed questions may be biased.

While the open-ended question offers many advantages, closed questions are generally preferable in large surveys. They reduce the variability of response, make fewer demands on interviewer skills, are less costly to administer, and are much easier to code and analyze. After adequate exploration and testing, we can often develop closed questions that will perform as effectively as open-ended questions in many situations. Experimental studies suggest that closed questions are equal or superior to open-ended questions in many more applications than is commonly believed.[14]

>**Exhibit 13a-5** Reconstructing Questions

Problem/Solution	Poor Measurement Question	Improved Measurement Question

Problems: Checklist appears to offer options that are neither exhaustive nor mutually exclusive. Also, it doesn't fully address the content needs of understanding why people choose a hotel when they travel for personal reasons versus business reasons.
 	
Solution: Organize the alternatives. Create subsets within choices; use color or shading to highlight subsets. For coding ease, expand the alternatives so the participant does not frequently choose "Other."
	If your purpose for THIS hotel stay included personal pleasure, for what ONE purpose specifically?
	❑ Visit friend/relative
	❑ Weekend escape
	❑ Sporting event
	❑ Sightseeing
	❑ Family event
	❑ Vacation
	❑ Other: _____
		Which reason BEST explains your purpose for THIS personal pleasure hotel stay?
		❑ Dining
		❑ Shopping
		❑ Entertainment
		   …was this for a… ❑ Sport-related event?
		                        ❑ Theater, musical, or other performance?
		                        ❑ Museum or exhibit?
		❑ Visit friend/relative
		   …was this for a special event? ❑ YES ❑ NO
		❑ Vacation
		   …was this primarily for… ❑ Sightseeing?
		                        ❑ Weekend escape?
		❑ Other:_____

Problems: Double-barreled question; no time frame for the behavior; "frequently" is an undefined construct for eating behavior; depending on the study's purpose, "order" is not as powerful a concept for measurement as others (e.g., purchase, consume, or eat)
 	
Solution: Split the questions; expand the response alternatives; clearly define the construct you want to measure.
	When you eat out, do you frequently order appetizers and dessert?
	❑ YES ❑ NO
		Considering your personal eating experiences away from home in the last 30 days, did you purchase an appetizer or dessert more than half the time?
		
		                More Than Less Than
		                Half the Time Half the Time
		Purchased
		  an appetizer ❑ ❑
		  a dessert ❑ ❑
		❑ Purchased neither appetizers nor desserts.

Problem: Nonspecific time frame; likely to experience memory decay; nonspecific screen (not asking what you really need to know to qualify a participant). **Solution:** Replace "ever" with a more appropriate time frame; screen for the desired behavior.	Have you ever attended a college basketball game? ❑ YES ❑ NO	In the last six months, have you been a spectator at a basketball game played by college teams on a college campus? ❑ YES ❑ NO
Problem: Question faces serious memory decay as a coat may not be purchased each year; isn't asking if the coat was a personal purchase or for someone else; nor do you know the type of coat purchased; nor do you know whether the coat was purchased for full price or at a discount. **Solution:** Limit the time frame; specify the coat type.	How much did you pay for the last coat you purchased?	Did you purchase a dress coat for your personal use in the last 60 days? ❑ YES ❑ NO Thinking of this dress coat, how much did you pay? (to the nearest dollar) $ _____.00 Was this coat purchase made at a discounted price? ❑ YES ❑ NO

Pretesting Options and Discoveries

Pretesting is a critical activity for successful development of a survey. We explore here the purposes and methods for effectively pretesting questions and instruments.

Pretesting Options

There are various types of pretesting that can be used to refine an instrument. They range from obtaining informal reviews by colleagues to creating conditions similar to those of the final study.

Researcher Pretesting

Designers typically test informally in the initial stages and build more structure into the tests along the way. Fellow instrument designers can do the first-level pretest. One way to accomplish this is to have researchers divided into teams. One team writes the survey, while the other critically reviews it. The reviewers' and researchers' many differences of opinion are likely to create numerous suggestions for improvement. Usually at least two or three drafts can be effectively developed by bringing research colleagues into the process.

Participant Pretesting

Participant pretests require that the questionnaire be field-tested by sample participants or participant surrogates (individuals with characteristics and backgrounds similar to those of the desired participants).

Field pretests involve distributing the test instrument exactly as the actual instrument will be distributed. Most studies use two or more pretests. National projects may use one trial to examine local reaction and another to check for regional differences. Although many researchers try to keep pretest conditions and times close to what they expect for the actual study, personal interview and telephone limitations make it desirable to test in the evenings or on weekends in order to interview people who are not available for contact at other times.

Test mailings are useful, but it is often faster to use a substitute procedure. In the MindWriter example, the managers who were interviewed in the exploratory study were later asked to review the pilot questionnaire. The interviewers left them alone and returned later. Upon their return, they went over the questions with each manager. They explained that they wanted the manager's reactions to question clarity and ease of answering. After several such interviews, the instrument was revised and the testing process was repeated with customers. With minor revision, the questionnaire was reproduced and prepared for insertion into the computer packing material.

Collaborative Pretests

Different approaches taken by interviewers and the participants' awareness of those approaches affect the pretest. If the researcher alerts participants to their involvement in a preliminary test of the questionnaire, the participants are essentially being enlisted as collaborators in the refinement process. Under these conditions, detailed probing of the parts of the question, including phrases and words, is appropriate. Because of the time required for probing and discussion, it is likely that only the most critical questions will be reviewed. The participant group may therefore need to be conscripted from colleagues and friends to secure the additional time and motivation needed to cover an entire questionnaire. If friends or associates are used, experience suggests that they introduce more bias than strangers, argue more about wording, and generally make it more difficult to accomplish other goals of pretesting such as timing the length of questions or sections.[1]

Occasionally, a highly experienced researcher may improvise questions during a pretest. When this occurs, it is essential to record the interview or take detailed notes so that the questionnaire may be reconstructed later. Ultimately, a team of interviewers would be required to follow the interview schedule's prearranged sequence of questions. Only experienced investigators should be free to depart from the interview schedule during a pretest and explore participants' answers by adding probes.

Noncollaborative Pretests

When the researcher does not inform the participant that the activity is a pretest, it is still possible to probe for reactions but without the cooperation and commitment of time provided by collaborators. The comprehensiveness of the effort also suffers because of flagging cooperation.

The virtue of this approach is that the questionnaire can be tested under conditions approaching those of the final study. This realism is similarly useful for training interviewers.

Pretesting Discoveries

Participant Interest

An important purpose of pretesting is to discover participants' reactions to the questions. If participants do not find the experience stimulating when an interviewer is physically present, how will they react on the phone or in the self-administered mode? Pretesting helps discover where repetitiveness or redundancy is bothersome or what topics were not covered that the participant expected. An alert interviewer will look for questions or groups of questions that the participant perceives to be sensitive or threatening or topics about which the participant knows nothing.

Meaning

Questions that we borrow or adapt from the work of others carry an authoritativeness that may prompt us to avoid pretesting them, but they are often most in need of examination. Are they still timely? Is the language relevant? Do they need context from adjacent questions? Newly constructed questions should be similarly checked for meaningfulness to the participant. Does the question evoke the same meaning as that intended by the researcher? How different is the researcher's frame of reference from that of the average participant? Words and phrases that trigger a "what do you mean?" response from the participant need to be singled out for further refinement.

Question Transformation

Participants do not necessarily process every word in the question. They also may not share the same definitions for the terms they hear. When this happens, participants modify the question to make it fit their own frame of reference or simply change it so that it makes sense to them. Probing is necessary to discover how participants have transformed the question when this is suspected.[2]

Continuity and Flow

In self-administered questionnaires, questions should read effortlessly and flow from one to another and from one section to another. In personal and telephone interviews, the sound of the question and its transition must be fluid as well. A long set of questions with 9-point scales that worked well in a mail instrument would not be effective on the telephone unless you were to ask participants to visualize the scale as the touch keys on their phone. Moreover, transitions that may appear redundant in a self-administered questionnaire may be exactly what needs to be heard in personal or telephone interviewing.

Question Sequence

Question arrangement can play a significant role in the success of the instrument. Research authorities recommend starting with stimulating questions and placing sensitive questions last. Since questions concerning income and family life are most likely to be refused, this is good advice for building trust before getting to classification questions that might lead to a refusal situation. However, interest-building questions need to be tested first to be sure they are stimulating. Pretesting with a large enough sample of participants permits some experimentation with question sequence.

Skip Instructions

In interviews and questionnaires, skip patterns and their contingency sequences may not work as envisioned on paper. Skip instructions are designed to route or sequence the participant to another question contingent on his or her answer to the previous question (*branched questions*). Pretesting in the field helps to identify problems with skip instructions or symbols (e.g., box-and-arrow schematic) that the designers may not have thought of. By correcting these instructions in the revision stage, we also avoid problems with flow and continuity.

Variability

Making sure that question alternatives cover the range of possible participant answers is an important purpose of pretesting. With 25 to 100 participants in the pretest sample, statistical data on the proportion of participants answering yes or no or marking "strongly agree" to "strongly disagree" can supplement the qualitative assessment provided by the pretest interviewers. This information is useful for sample size calculations and for getting preliminary indications of reliability problems with scaled questions. When researchers use a very small pretest sample of participants, pretesting cannot provide definitive quantitative conclusions. Small samples can, however, deliver an early warning about survey questions that may not discriminate among participants or can identify sections of the survey where meaningful subgrouping may occur in the final sample.

Length and Timing

Most draft questionnaires or interview schedules suffer from lengthiness. By timing each question and section, the researcher is in a better position to make decisions about modifying or cutting material. In personal and telephone interviews, labor is a project expense. Thus, if the budget influences the final length of the questionnaire, an accurate estimate of elapsed time is essential. Videotaped or audiotaped pretests may also be used for this purpose. Their function in reducing errors in data recording is widely accepted.

When Surveying Doesn't Work

Sometimes surveying will not secure the information needed. A classic example concerns a survey conducted to discover magazines read by participants. An unusually high rate was reported for prestigious magazines, and an unusually low rate was reported for tabloid magazines. The study was revised so that the subjects, instead of being interviewed, were asked to contribute their old magazines to a charity drive (an observation study). The collection gave a more realistic estimate of readership of both types of magazines.[3]

Most researchers have found that the survey is a very powerful tool in their research methods arsenal. It is only a matter of careful attention to detail and practice that will have you joining their ranks.

>chapter 14

Sampling

>learningobjectives

After reading this chapter, you should understand . . .

1 The two premises on which sampling theory is based.

2 The characteristics of accuracy and precision for measuring sample validity.

3 The five questions that must be answered to develop a sampling plan.

4 The two categories of sampling techniques and the variety of sampling techniques within each category.

5 The various sampling techniques and when each is used.

> " The proof of the pudding is in the eating. By a small sample we may judge of the whole piece. "
>
> Miguel de Cervantes Saavedra, author

>**bringing**research**to**life

Researchers comprise a fairly small professional community. Within a given company, other than those that specialize in research, few trained researchers may be found, making collaboration necessary. Researchers from different companies often share their experiences at professional conferences in an attempt to advance the industry as a whole. As a result, researchers are often privy to each other's successes as well as their failures. They use each other's mistakes to improve their own projects. We join Jason and Sara as they are discussing sampling for a new project with Glacier Symphony.

"The ideal participant is thoughtful, articulate, rational, and, above all, cooperative. Real people, however, are fractious, stubborn, ill-informed, and even perverse. Nevertheless, they are who you have to work with," muses Jason as he and Sara hammer out the details of the Glacier Symphony sampling plan.

"Sam Champion, marketing director for CityBus," shares Sara, "certainly had sampling problems. He allowed a novice researcher—Eric Burbidge—to do the sampling to determine where the company could most effectively promote its new daily route schedule. Its big problem was a small budget and riders from two separate cities, where two different papers had substantial circulations—and just as substantial advertising rates. CityBus was hoping to advertise in only one paper. But the newspapers didn't have circulation figures for specific news vending boxes. Champion told the tale at the last MRA luncheon.

"It seems Burbidge was inexperienced enough to try to answer CityBus's question of which newspaper to use for ads by conducting a survey on one bus that runs between the two cities during evening rush hour. Burbidge boards the bus on route 99 and tells the driver he's from headquarters and there to do an official survey during the evening ride." Sara pauses for effect and lowers her voice to mimic a base frog. "I need to test my hypothesis that readership of newspapers on route 99 is equally divided between the *East City Gazette* and the *West City Tribune*."

Jason, now interested, interrupts, "He said that to a busload of passengers?"

"Well, no, the passengers hadn't yet boarded. The way Champion told the story, Burbidge barged his way to the front of the line and rapped his clipboard on the door to gain entry before any of the passengers could board. He said that to the driver.

"Anyway, Burbidge distributes his questionnaires, and the passengers diligently complete them and bring them forward to where Burbidge sits at the front of the bus. And then they start to play paper-ball hockey in the aisle of the bus."

"Paper-ball hockey?" questions Jason.

"Evidently they wad the newspapers they have been reading while waiting for the bus into balls and bat them through the legs of self-appointed goalies at each end of the bus aisle. Anyway, the driver tells Burbidge that since East City Club plays hockey that night that when he cleans out the bus most of the newspapers will be the *East City Gazette*. The riders evidently like to study the night's pro game in advance, so newsstand sales are brisk in the terminal, but only for the newspaper that does the better job of covering the sport *du jour*. Of course the next night, the riders would be buying the *West City Tribune* because it does a better job of covering pro basketball.

"Burbidge is upset and mumbles something about the survey asking for the paper most recently purchased. The driver tells him not to sweat it. 'They buy the *Gazette* before hockey and the *Trib* before basketball … but of course in the morning they bring the paper that is dropped on their doorstep.'

"Burbidge is now mumbling that by choosing route 99, and choosing hockey night, he has totally distorted his results.

"The driver, who is Champion's favorite dart opponent, is thoroughly enjoying Burbidge's discomfort because he was acting like such an ass at the beginning. So the driver tells Burbidge, 'I know from reading the CityBus newsletter that by the time you announce the new routes and schedules, we will be finished with hockey and basketball and into the baseball season. And, of course, most of these folks on the 5:15 bus are East City folks, while most on the 5:45 bus are West City folks, so your outcome will naturally be affected by choosing the 5:15 any time of the year.'

"Burbidge, fully exasperated, asks the driver, 'Is there anything else you would care to share with me?'

"The driver evidently couldn't hide his grin when he says, 'The riders on the 5:45 usually don't read the newspaper much at all. They've been watching sports in the terminal bar while waiting for the bus. Most aren't feeling any pain—if you get my meaning—and can't read the small newsprint as I don't turn on the overhead lights.'"

Sara pauses, allowing Jason to ask, "Is there a lesson to this story, Sara?"

"Well, we've been talking about having the student musicians distribute and collect surveys at each Friday evening's performance. I'm wondering if Glacier Symphony has any demographic data from previous surveys that might shed some light on concert attendees. I'd hate to systematically bias our sample, like Burbidge did. Since we won't be present to collect the data—like he was—we might never know."

> The Nature of Sampling

Most people intuitively understand the idea of sampling. One taste from a drink tells us whether it is sweet or sour. If we select a few ads from a magazine, we usually assume our selection reflects the characteristics of the full set. If some members of our staff favor a promotional strategy, we infer that others will also. These examples vary in their representativeness, but each is a sample.

The basic idea of **sampling** is that by selecting some of the elements in a population, we may draw conclusions about the entire population. A **population element** is the individual participant or object on which the measurement is taken. It is the unit of study. Although an element may be a person, it can just as easily be something else. For example, each staff member questioned about an optimal promotional strategy is a population element, each advertising account analyzed is an element of an account population, and each ad is an element of a population of advertisements. A **population** is the total collection of elements about which we wish to make some inferences. All office workers in the firm compose a population of interest; all 4,000 files define a population of interest. A **census** is a count of all the elements in a population. If 4,000 files define the population, a census would obtain information from every one of them. We call the listing of all population elements from which the sample will be drawn the **sample frame.**

For CityBus, the population of interest is all riders of affected routes in the forthcoming route restructuring. In studying customer satisfaction with the CompleteCare service operation for MindWriter, the population of interest is all individuals who have had a laptop repaired while the CompleteCare program has been in effect. The population element is any one individual interacting with the service program.

Why Sample?

There are several compelling reasons for sampling, including (1) lower cost, (2) greater accuracy of results, (3) greater speed of data collection, and (4) availability of population elements.

Lower Cost

The economic advantages of taking a sample rather than a census are massive. Consider the cost of taking a census. In 2000, due to a Supreme Court ruling requiring a census rather than statistical sampling techniques, the U.S. Bureau of the Census increased its 2000 Decennial Census budget estimate by $1.723 billion, to $4.512 billion.[1] Is it any wonder that researchers in all types of organizations ask, Why should we spend thousands of dollars interviewing all 4,000 employees in our company if we can find out what we need to know by asking only a few hundred?

Greater Accuracy of Results

Deming argues that the quality of a study is often better with sampling than with a census. He suggests, "Sampling possesses the possibility of better interviewing (testing), more thorough investigation of missing, wrong, or suspicious information, better supervision, and better processing than is possible with complete coverage."[2] Research findings substantiate this opinion. More than 90 percent of the total survey error in one study was from nonsampling sources and only 10 percent or less was from random sampling error.[3] The U.S. Bureau of the Census, while mandated to take a census of the population every 10 years, shows its confidence in sampling by taking sample surveys to check the accuracy of its census. The U.S. Bureau of the Census knows that in a census, segments of the population are seriously undercounted. Only when the population is small, accessible, and highly variable is accuracy likely to be greater with a census than a sample.

Greater Speed of Data Collection

Sampling's speed of execution reduces the time between the recognition of a need for information and the availability of that information. For every disgruntled customer that the MindWriter CompleteCare program generates, several prospective customers will move away from MindWriter to a competitor's laptop. So fixing the problems within the CompleteCare program will not only keep current customers coming back but also discourage prospective customers from defecting to competitive brands due to negative word of mouth.

Availability of Population Elements

Some situations require sampling. Safety is a compelling marketing appeal for most vehicles. Yet we must have evidence to make such a claim. So we crash-test cars to test bumper strength or efficiency of airbags to prevent injury. In testing for such evidence, we destroy the cars we test. A census would mean complete destruction of all cars manufactured. Sampling is also the only process possible if the population is infinite.

Sample versus Census

The advantages of sampling over census studies are less compelling when the population is small and the variability within the population is high. Two conditions are appropriate for a census study: a census is (1) *feasible* when the population is small and (2) *necessary* when the elements are quite different from each other.[4] When the population is small and variable, any sample we draw may not be representative of the population from which it is drawn. The resulting values we calculate from the sample are incorrect as estimates of the population values. Consider North American manufacturers of stereo components. Fewer than 50 companies design, develop, and manufacture amplifier and loudspeaker products at the high end of the price range. The size of this population suggests a census is feasible. The diversity of their product offerings makes it difficult to accurately sample from this group. Some companies specialize in speakers, some in amplifier technology, and others in compact-disc transports. Choosing a census in this situation is appropriate.

What Is a Good Sample?

The ultimate test of a sample design is how well it represents the characteristics of the population it purports to represent. In measurement terms, the sample must be valid. Validity of a sample depends on two considerations: accuracy and precision.

Ford Reenergizes by Changing Sampling Strategy

In the midst of financial crisis in the automobile industry, Ford's James Farley decided his research was excluding a very important sample unit: the dealer. With dealers controlling 75 percent of advertising expenditures for the auto giant, Farley thought excluding them as research subjects was suicidal. So he recruited 30 of the most influential dealers to fly to Detroit to provide information and critique the creative proposals of the Ford ad agency, Team Detroit.

Farmington Hills (MI) full-service research firm Morpace put the dealers through an intensive focus group experience. The dealers were soon challenged with questions. "Which incentives work and which don't?" "What does the Ford brand mean to you?" "What is wrong with Ford's advertising?" In subsequent sessions, the dealers were asked to critique ad slogans and branding strategies, recommending those that best capture the Ford experience. The dealers left the 72-hour marathon session enthusiastic about the direction Ford was taking and with

significant buy-in for the next ad campaign. Farley's actions gave voice to its dealers with its altered research sampling strategy.

www.ford.com; www.morpace.com; www.teamdetroit.com

Accuracy

Accuracy is the degree to which bias is absent from the sample. When the sample is drawn properly, the measure of behavior, attitudes, or knowledge (the measurement variables) of *some* sample elements will be *less than* (thus, underestimate) the measure of those same variables drawn from the population. Also, the measure of the behavior, attitudes, or knowledge of *other* sample elements will be *more than* the population values (thus, overestimate them). Variations in these sample values offset each other, resulting in a sample value that is close to the population value. For these offsetting effects to occur, however, there must be enough elements in the sample, and they must be drawn in a way that favors neither overestimation nor underestimation.

For example, assume you were asked to test the level of brand recall of the "counting sheep" creative approach for the Serta mattress company. Hypothetically, you could measure via sample or census. You want a measure of brand recall in combination with message clarity: "Serta mattresses are *so comfortable* you'll feel the difference the minute you lie down." In the census, 52 percent of participants who are TV viewers correctly recalled the brand and message. Using a sample, 70 percent recalled the brand and correctly interpreted the message. With both results for comparison, you would know that your sample was biased, as it significantly overestimated the population value of 52 percent. Unfortunately, in most studies taking a census is not feasible, so we need an estimate of the amount of error.[5]

An accurate (unbiased) sample is one in which the underestimators offset the overestimators. **Systematic variance** has been defined as "the variation in measures due to some known or unknown influences that 'cause' the scores to lean in one direction more than another."[6] Homes on the corner of the block, for example, are often larger and more valuable than those within the block. Thus, a sample that selects only corner homes will cause us to overestimate home values in the area. Burbidge learned that in selecting bus route 99 for his newspaper readership sample, the time of the day, day of the week, and season of the year of the survey dramatically reduced the accuracy and validity of his sample.

Increasing the sample size can reduce systematic variance as a cause of error. However, even the large size won't reduce error if the list from which you draw your participants is biased. The classic example of a sample with systematic variance was the *Literary Digest* presidential election poll in 1936, in which more than 2 million people participated. The poll predicted Alfred Landon would defeat Franklin Roosevelt for the presidency of the United States. Your memory is correct; we've never had a president named Alfred Landon. We discovered later that the poll drew its sample from telephone owners, who were in the middle and upper classes—at the time, the bastion of the Republican Party—while Roosevelt appealed to the much larger working class, whose members could not afford to own phones and typically voted for the Democratic Party candidate.

Serta Counting Sheep

Precision

A second criterion of a good sample design is precision of estimate. Researchers accept that no sample will fully represent its population in all respects. However, to interpret the findings of research, we need a measure of how closely the sample represents the population. The numerical descriptors that describe samples may be expected to differ from those that describe populations because of random fluctuations inherent in the sampling process. This is called **sampling error** (or *random sampling error*) and reflects the influence of chance in drawing the sample members. Sampling error is what is left after all known sources of systematic variance have been accounted for. In theory, sampling error consists of random fluctuations only, although some unknown systematic variance may be included when too many or too few sample elements possess a particular characteristic. Let's say Jason draws a sample from an alphabetical list of MindWriter owners who are having their laptops currently serviced by the CompleteCare program. We insert a survey response card in a sample of returned laptops. Assume 80 percent of those surveyed had their laptops serviced by Max Jensen. Also assume from the exploratory study that Jensen had more complaint letters about his work than any other technician. Arranging the list of laptop owners currently being serviced in an alphabetical listing would have failed to *randomize* the sample frame. If Jason drew the sample from that listing, he would actually have increased the sampling error.

Precision is measured by the standard error of estimate, a type of standard deviation measurement; the smaller the standard error of estimate, the higher is the precision of the sample. The ideal sample design produces a small standard error of estimate. However, not all types of sample design provide estimates of precision, and samples of the same size can produce different amounts of error.

Types of Sample Design

The researcher makes several decisions when designing a sample. These are represented in Exhibit 14-1. The sampling decisions flow from two decisions made in the formation of the management-research question hierarchy: the nature of the management question and the specific investigative questions that evolve from the research question. These decisions are influenced by requirements of the project and its objectives, level of risk the researcher can tolerate, budget, time, available resources, and culture.

In the discussion that follows, we will use three examples:

- The CityBus study introduced in the vignette at the beginning of this chapter.
- The continuing MindWriter CompleteCare customer satisfaction study.
- A study of the feasibility of starting a dining club near the campus of Metro University.

The researchers at Metro U are exploring the feasibility of creating a dining club whose facilities would be available on a membership basis. To launch this venture, they will need to make a substantial

>Exhibit 14-1 Sampling Design within the Research Process

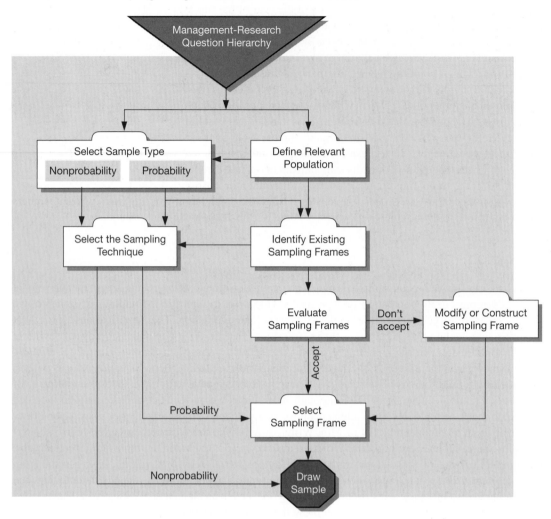

investment. Research will allow them to reduce many risks. Thus, the research question is, Would a membership dining club be a viable enterprise? Some investigative questions that flow from the research question include:

1. Who would patronize the club, and on what basis?

2. How many would join the club under various membership and fee arrangements?

3. How much would the average member spend per month?

4. What days would be most popular?

5. What menu and service formats would be most desirable?

6. What lunch times would be most popular?

7. Given the proposed price levels, how often per month would each member have lunch or dinner?

8. What percent of the people in the population say they would join the club, based on the projected rates and services?

We use the last three investigative questions for examples and focus specifically on questions 7 and 8 for assessing the project's risks. First, we will digress with other information and examples on sample design, coming back to Metro U in the next section.

In decisions of sample design, the representation basis and the element selection techniques, as shown in Exhibit 14-2, classify the different approaches.

>**Exhibit 14-2** Types of Sampling Designs

Element Selection	Representation Basis	
	Probability	**Nonprobability**
Unrestricted	Simple random	Convenience
Restricted	Complex random	Purposive
	Systematic	Judgment
	Cluster	Quota
	Stratified	Snowball
	Double	

Representation

The members of a sample are selected using probability or nonprobability procedures.

Nonprobability sampling is arbitrary and subjective; when we choose subjectively, we usually do so with a pattern or scheme in mind (e.g., only talking with young people or only talking with women). Each member of the population does not have a known chance of being included. Allowing interviewers during a mall-intercept study to choose sample elements "at random" (meaning "as they wish" or "wherever they find them") is not random sampling. Although we are not told how Burbidge selected the riders of bus route 99 as his sample, it's clear that he did not use probability sampling techniques.

Early Internet samples had all the drawbacks of nonprobability samples. Those individuals who frequented the Internet were not representative of most target markets or audiences, because far more young, technically savvy men frequented the Internet than did any other demographic group. As Internet use increases and gender discrepancies diminish, many such samples now closely approximate non-Internet samples. Of increasing concern, however, is what the Bureau of the Census labels the "great digital divide"—low-income and ethnic subgroups' underrepresentation in their use of the Internet compared to the general population. Additionally, many Internet samples were, and still are, drawn substantially from panels. These are composed of individuals who have self-selected to become part of a pool of individuals interested in participating in online research. There is much discussion among professional researchers about whether Internet samples should be treated as probability or nonprobability samples. Some admit that any sample drawn from a panel is more appropriately treated as a nonprobability sample; others vehemently disagree, citing the success of such well-known panels as NielsenMedia's People Meter panels for TV audience assessment and IRI's BehaviorScan panel for tracking consumer packaged goods. As you study the differences here, you should draw your own conclusion.

Key to the difference between nonprobability and probability samples is the term *random*. In the dictionary, random is defined as "without pattern" or as "haphazard." In sampling, random means something else entirely. **Probability sampling** is based on the concept of random selection—a controlled procedure that assures that each population element is given a known nonzero chance of selection. This procedure is never haphazard. Only probability samples provide estimates of precision. When a researcher is making a decision that will influence the expenditure of thousands, if not millions, of dollars, an estimate of precision is critical. Also, only probability samples offer the opportunity to generalize the findings to the population of interest from the sample population. Although exploratory research does not necessarily demand this, explanatory, descriptive, and causal studies do.

Element Selection

Whether the elements are selected individually and directly from the population—viewed as a single pool—or additional controls are imposed, element selection may also classify samples. If each sample element is drawn individually from the population at large, it is an unrestricted sample. Restricted sampling covers all other forms of sampling.

Creating Samples: Then and Now

With more and more research being done via the Internet, what's the future of the probability sample? This is just one of the questions we asked Linda Piekarski, a 20-plus-year veteran with Survey Sampling, Inc. (SSI), a firm that compiles samples for probability and nonprobability research.

Sampling has changed a lot in the last 5 to 10 years, but it's all part of an evolution that firms like SSI have seen before. "In the 1950s probability samples were drawn based on addresses. Teams of female researchers would go door-to-door in neighborhoods, verifying that the address was occupied. And clients would get paper lists of addresses for their samples." But, gradually, those researchers didn't find people at home—they were off working at their own careers—so the telephone became the primary means of contact. "Today, because researchers haven't done a good job of educating the public about the value of research and the difference between research and telemarketing,

we are having the same problems with phone contact. People lead busy lives. More and more researchers have trouble making contact via phone. Even when they do, today's privacy technology (phone companies' privacy management and caller-ID services, answering machines, voice mail, and Tele-zappers) increasingly makes survey completion difficult." As a result, many researchers have turned to permission-based samples (panels) via the Internet. SSI has developed its own e-mail based permission population composed of thousands of individuals for research purposes only. "And we protect their identities and their e-mail addresses so they don't get spammed." But Piekarski worries about the validity and reliability of the information drawn with such samples. "As accessible as these people are, it's still not a probability sample."

www.surveysampling.com

> Steps in Sampling Design

There are several questions to be answered in securing a sample. Each requires unique information. While the questions presented here are sequential, an answer to one question often forces a revision to an earlier one.

1. What is the target population?
2. What are the parameters of interest?
3. What is the sampling frame?
4. What is the appropriate sampling method?
5. What size sample is needed?

What Is the Target Population?

The definition of the population may be apparent from the management problem or the research question(s), but often it is not. Is the population for the dining club study at Metro University defined as "full-time day students on the main campus of Metro U"? Or should the population include "all persons employed at Metro U"? Or should townspeople who live in the neighborhood be included? Without knowing the target market chosen for the new venture, it is not obvious which of these is the appropriate sampling population.

There also may be confusion about whether the population consists of individuals, households, or families, or a combination of these. If a communication study needs to measure income, then the definition of the population element as individual or household can make quite a difference. In an observation study, a sample population might be nonpersonal: displays within a store or any ATM a bank owns or all single-family residential properties in a community. Good operational definitions are critical in choosing the relevant population.

Assume the Metro University Dining Club is to be solely for the students and employees on the main campus. The researchers might define the population as "all currently enrolled students and employees on the main campus of Metro U." However, this does not include family members. They may want to revise the definition to make it "current students and employees of Metro U, main campus, and their families."

In the nonprobability sample, Burbidge seems to have defined his relevant population as any rider of the CityBus system. He presumes he has an equal need to determine newspaper readership of both regular and infrequent CityBus riders so that he might reach them with information about the new route structure, maps, and schedules. He can, however, easily reach regular riders by distributing information about the new routes via display racks on the bus for a period before the new routes are implemented. Infrequent riders, then, are the real population of interest of his newspaper readership study.

What Are the Parameters of Interest?

Population parameters are summary descriptors (e.g., incidence proportion, mean, variance) of variables of interest in the population. **Sample statistics** are descriptors of those same relevant variables computed from sample data. Sample statistics are used as estimators of population parameters. The sample statistics are the basis of our inferences about the population. Depending on how measurement questions are phrased, each may collect a different level of data. Each different level of data also generates different sample statistics. Thus, choosing the parameters of interest will actually dictate the sample type and its size.

Asking Metro U affiliates to reveal their frequency of eating on or near campus (less than 5 times per week, greater than 5 but less than 10 times per week, or greater than 10 times per week) would provide an ordinal data estimator. Of course, we could ask the question differently and obtain an absolute count of eating experiences and that would generate ratio data. In MindWriter, the rating of service by CompleteCare on a 5-point scale would be an example of an interval data estimator. Asking the CityBus riders about their number of days of ridership during the past seven days would result in ratio data. Exhibit 14-3 indicates population parameters of interest for our three example studies.

When the variables of interest in the study are measured on interval or ratio scales, we use the sample mean to estimate the population mean and the sample standard deviation to estimate the population standard deviation. When the variables of interest are measured on nominal or ordinal scales, we use the sample proportion of incidence to estimate the population proportion and the pq to estimate the population variance. The **population proportion of incidence** "is equal to the number of elements in the population belonging to the category of interest, divided by the total number of elements in the

>**Exhibit 14-3** Example Population Parameters

Study	Population Parameter of Interest	Data Level & Measurement Scale
CityBus	Frequency of ridership within 7 days	Ordinal (more than 10 times, 6 to 10 times, 5 or fewer times)
		Ratio (absolute number of rides)
MindWriter	Perceived quality of service	Interval (scale of 1 to 5, with 5 being "exceeded expectations")
	Proportion by gender of Laptop 9000 customers with problems	Nominal (percent female, male)
Metro U	Frequency of eating on or near campus within the last 30 days	Ratio (actual eating experiences)
	Proportion of students/employees expressing interest in dining club	Nominal (interested, not interested)

New Product Research Blind Spot

"There has always been a gap in new product research," claims Jim Lane, senior VP, Alliance Research, "between the time a new product is introduced and when it is possible to extract customer information." The reason? Although new product marketers can track store sales audit data, locating purchasers to conduct attitudinal studies often lags as much as six months. Alliance Research combines its proprietary techniques for attitude measurement with parent company Catalina Marketing Corp.'s point-of-sale (POS) promotional system to develop a sample frame of purchasers of new products to participate in an interactive-voice-response (IVR) survey. Purchasers receive an invitation printed on the red-trimmed coupons that accompany their register receipts. For participation, Alliance compensates each respondent with up to $5, with current participation rates comparable to those for telephone studies. By inviting participants at the time of first purchase, the six-month wait for attitudinal data is history. Now this critical information is available to brand and marketing managers within weeks of a new product's hitting the shelf.

In what circumstances and why might immediate feedback not be an accurate measure of a new product's reception?

www.catalinamarketing.com

population."[7] Proportion measures are necessary for nominal data and are widely used for other measures as well. The most frequent proportion measure is the percentage. In the Metro U study, examples of nominal data are the proportion of a population that expresses interest in joining the club (e.g., 30 percent; therefore p is equal to 0.3 and q, those not interested, equals 0.7) or the proportion of married students who report they now eat in restaurants at least five times a month. The CityBus study seeks to determine whether East City or West City has the most riders on bus route 99. MindWriter might want to know if men or women have experienced the most problems with laptop model 9000. These measures for CityBus and MindWriter would result in nominal data.

There may also be important subgroups in the population about whom we would like to make estimates. For example, we might want to draw conclusions about the extent of dining club use that could be expected from married students versus single students, residential students versus commuter students, and so forth. Such questions have a strong impact on the nature of the sampling frame we accept (we would want the list organized by these subgroups, or within the list each characteristic of each element would need to be noted), the design of the sample, and its size. Burbidge should be more interested in reaching infrequent rather than regular CityBus riders with the newspaper advertising he plans; to reach frequent riders CityBus could use on-bus signs or distribute paper schedules rather than using more expensive newspaper ads. And in the MindWriter study, Jason may be interested in comparing the responses of those who experienced poor service and those who experienced excellent service through the CompleteCare program.

What Is the Sampling Frame?

The sampling frame is closely related to the population. It is the list of elements from which the sample is actually drawn. Ideally, it is a complete and correct list of population members only. Jason should find limited problems obtaining a sampling frame of CompleteCare service users, as MindWriter has maintained a database of all calls coming into the call center and all serial numbers of laptops serviced.

As a practical matter, however, the sampling frame often differs from the theoretical population. For the dining club study, the Metro U directory would be the logical first choice as a sampling frame. Directories are usually accurate when published in the fall, but suppose the study is being done in the spring. The directory will contain errors and omissions because some people will have withdrawn or left since the directory was published, while others will have enrolled or been hired. Usually university directories don't mention the families of students or employees. Just how much inaccuracy one can tolerate in choosing a sampling frame is a matter of judgment. You might use the directory anyway, ignoring the fact that it is not a fully accurate list. However, if the directory is a year old, the amount of error might be unacceptable. One way to make the sampling frame for the Metro U study more representative of the population would be to secure a supplemental list of the new students and employees as well as a list of the withdrawals and terminations from Metro U's registrar and human resources databases. You could then add and delete information from the original directory. Or, if their privacy policies permit, you might just request a current listing from each of these offices and use these lists as your sampling frame.

A decade ago, Chinese families with a home phone were envied. By June 2009, China's cellular telephone users exceeded 679 million, within a population of 1.3 billion. Business or personal phone listings are inadequate for developing sampling frames when in a 30 month period cellular users are expected to grow by 34 million.

A greater distortion would be introduced if a branch campus population were included in the Metro U directory. This would be an example of a too inclusive frame—that is, a frame that includes many elements other than the ones in which we are interested. A university directory that includes faculty and staff retirees is another example of a too inclusive sampling frame.

Often you have to accept a sampling frame that includes people or cases beyond those in whom you are interested. You may have to use a telephone directory to draw a sample of business telephone numbers. Fortunately, this is easily resolved. You draw a sample from the larger population and then use a screening procedure to eliminate those who are not members of the group you wish to study.

The Metro U dining club survey is an example of a sampling frame problem that is readily solved. Often one finds this task much more of a challenge. Suppose you need to sample the members of an ethnic group, say, Asians residing in Little Rock, Arkansas. There is probably no directory of this population. Although you may use the general city directory, sampling from this too inclusive frame would be costly and inefficient, because Asians represent only a small fraction of Little Rock's population. The screening task would be monumental. Since ethnic groups frequently cluster in certain neighborhoods, you might identify these areas of concentration and then use a reverse area telephone or city directory, which is organized by street address, to draw the sample. Burbidge had a definite problem, because no sample frame of CityBus riders existed. Although some regular riders used monthly passes, infrequent riders usually paid cash for their fares. It might have been possible for Burbidge to anticipate this and to develop over time a listing of customers. Bus drivers could have collected relevant contact information over a month, but the cost of contacting customers via phone or mail would have been much more expensive than the self-administered intercept approach Burbidge chose for data collection. One sampling frame available to Burbidge was a list of bus routes. This list would have allowed him to draw a probability sample using a cluster sampling technique. We discuss more complex sampling techniques later in this chapter.

The sampling issues we have discussed so far are fairly universal. It is not until we begin talking about sampling frames and sampling methods that international research starts to deviate. International researchers often face far more difficulty in locating or building sample frames. Countries differ in how each defines its population; this affects census and relevant population counts.[8] Some countries purposefully oversample to facilitate the analysis of issues of particular national interest; this means we need to be cautious in interpreting published aggregate national figures.[9] These distinctions and difficulties may lead the researcher to choose nonprobability techniques or different probability techniques than they would choose if doing such research in the United States or other developed countries. In a study that is fielded in numerous countries at the same time, researchers may use different sampling methodologies, resulting in hybrid studies that will need care to be combined. It is common practice to weight sample data in cross-national studies to develop sample data that are representative.[10] Choice of sampling methods is often dictated by culture as much as by communication and technology infrastructure. Just as all advertising campaigns would not be appropriate in all parts of the world, all sampling techniques would not be appropriate in all subcultures. Our discussion in this text focuses more on domestic than international research. We believe it is easier to learn the principles of research in an environment that you know versus one in which many students can only speculate. Yet we also believe that ethnic and cultural sensitivity should influence every decision of researchers, whether they do research domestically or internationally.

What Is the Appropriate Sampling Method?

The researcher faces a basic choice: a probability or nonprobability sample. With a probability sample, a researcher can make probability-based confidence estimates of various parameters that cannot be made with nonprobability samples. Choosing a probability sampling technique has several consequences. A researcher must follow appropriate procedures so that:

- Interviewers or others cannot modify the selections made.
- Only the selected elements from the original sampling frame are included.
- Substitutions are excluded except as clearly specified and controlled according to predetermined decision rules.

Despite all due care, the actual sample achieved will not match perfectly the sample that is originally drawn. Some people will refuse to participate, and others will be difficult, if not impossible, to find. Thus, no matter how careful we are in replacing those who refuse or are never located, sampling error is likely to rise.

With personnel records available at a university and a population that is geographically concentrated, a probability sampling method is possible in the dining club study. University directories are generally available, and the costs of using a simple random sample would not be great here. Then, too, since the researchers are thinking of a major investment in the dining club, they would like to be highly confident they have a representative sample. The same analysis holds true for MindWriter: A sample frame is readily available, making a probability sample possible and likely.

Although the probability cluster sampling technique was available to him, it is obvious that Burbidge chose nonprobability sampling, arbitrarily choosing bus route 99 as a judgment sample and attempting to survey everyone riding the bus during the arbitrary times in which he chose to ride. What drove him to this decision is likely what makes researchers turn to nonprobability sampling in other situations: ease, speed, and cost.

What Size Sample Is Needed?

Much folklore surrounds this question. The most pervasive myths are (1) a sample must be large or it is not representative and (2) a sample should bear some proportional relationship to the size of the population from which it is drawn. With nonprobability samples, researchers confirm these myths using the number of subgroups, rules of thumb, and budget considerations to settle on a sample size. In probability sampling, how large a sample should be is a function of the variation in the population parameters under study and the estimating precision needed by the researcher. Some principles that influence sample size include:

- The greater the dispersion or variance within the population, the larger the sample must be to provide estimation precision.
- The greater the desired precision of the estimate, the larger the sample must be.
- The narrower or smaller the error range, the larger the sample must be.

># **close**up

Keynote Systems Tests the Power of Search

Twice yearly Keynote Systems evaluates the performance of five search engines, including market leader Google, AOL Search, Yahoo! Search, Ask.com, and MSN Search. Keynote, a "worldwide leader in services that improve online business performance and communications technologies," uses an online panel to perform "interactive Web site tests to assess user experience," profiling not only how people use search engines, but why they search as they do. Keynote allocates participants and experimental treatments as in Exhibit 14-4: 2,000 people are randomly drawn from more than 160,000 panel members and invited to participate via e-mail. They are assigned randomly to five groups of 400; each group is assigned a particular search engine. Whether participants have any experience with that particular engine is not a criterion for assignment. Each group is assigned a series of search tasks, starting with a general task— Think about anything you would like to search for; go and search that—to more specific tasks—find a local establishment, a product, an image, and a news item. Each search engine-allocated group essentially performs the same series of tasks. From their activities, Keynote generates 250,000 metrics (including time involved in the search, whether the search was successful, etc.). It matches these metrics to survey data used to measure satisfaction, perceived difficulty, and specific frustrations. From this combined data it develops several indices.

"One of the things we noted from a series of such tests was that Google repeatedly received rave reviews, even in instances where performance measures told a different story," shares senior research consultant Lance Jones. With almost 60 percent

market share, Google has strong recognition and tends to set the bar in search site design. Is its brand that powerful that it can influence attitudes even in the face of conflicting performance experience? If the brand is not a factor, which search engine would produce the most satisfying and useful results, the best sponsored results, and the best presentation and design? Keynote wanted to design an experiment that would show the power of the search engine brand. To do that, they needed to remove brand identity from the search results. Its solution was to design a generic-appearing search engine website and results format page, feeding actual search results into its generic format.

For the brand power test (Exhibit 14-5) 2,000 participants were again divided into five groups and assigned one search engine. This time, however, half the participants were assigned to a branded group ($n = 200$) and would see the results with a text line "Results brought to you by Yahoo/Google/Ask, etc."; the other half ($n = 200$) would see the same results but without the brand notation line ($n = 200$). All five search engines were tested using the tasks performed in the standard twice-annual test, but all the results seen by participants were actually generated using the assigned search engine, then fed into the generic results presentation. "The results pages were delivered live and participants would have perceived no difference in elapsed time, as the results were delivered within milliseconds of what the standard search would have delivered," explained Jones. The test produced 1,600 queries that generated 12 distinct metrics.

>**Exhibit 14-4** Participant Allocation in Search Engine Test

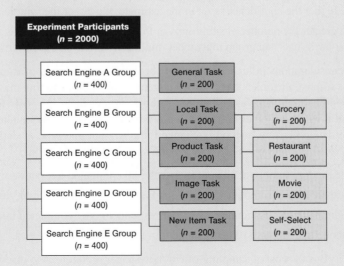

>Exhibit 14-5 Participant Allocation in Brand Power Test

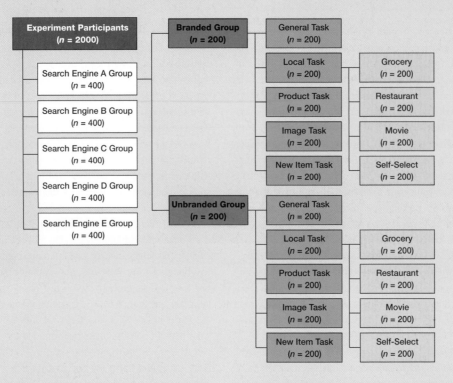

Is a brand powerful? Here are some sample results for Google; keep in mind that the branded group and the unbranded group saw the exact same results pages. On the unbranded group, the calculated Google results satisfaction score was 732 (on a 1,000-point scale), while the branded group delivered an 800; Google's sponsored results satisfaction was 763 (unbranded) compared to 809 (branded); full design satisfaction was 753 (unbranded) compared to 806 (branded). Evaluate the design of this sample.

www.keynote.com

- The higher the confidence level in the estimate, the larger the sample must be.
- The greater the number of subgroups of interest within a sample, the greater the sample size must be, as each subgroup must meet minimum sample size requirements.

Cost considerations influence decisions about the size and type of sample and the data collection methods. Almost all studies have some budgetary constraint, and this may encourage a researcher to use a nonprobability sample. Probability sample surveys incur list costs for sample frames, callback costs, and a variety of other costs that are not necessary when nonprobability samples are used. But when the data collection method is changed, the amount and type of data that can be obtained also change. Note the effect of a $2,000 budget on sampling considerations:

Simple random sampling: $25 per interview; 80 completed interviews.

Geographic cluster sampling: $20 per interview; 100 completed interviews.

Self-administered questionnaire: $12 per respondent; 167 completed instruments.

Telephone interviews: $10 per respondent; 200 completed interviews.[11]

For CityBus the cost of sampling riders' newspaper preferences to discover where to run the route-reconfiguration announcements must be significantly less than the cost of running ads in both East City and West City dailies. Thus, the nonprobability judgment sampling procedure that Burbidge used was logical from a budget standpoint. The investment required to open the dining club at Metro U also justifies the more careful probability approach taken by the students. For MindWriter, an investment in CompleteCare has already been made; Jason needs to be highly confident that his recommendations to change CompleteCare procedures and policies are on target and thoroughly supported by the data collected. These considerations justify MindWriter's probability sampling approach.

> Probability Sampling

Simple Random Sampling

The unrestricted, simple random sample is the purest form of probability sampling. Since all probability samples must provide a known nonzero probability of selection for each population element, the **simple random sample** is considered a special case in which each population element has a known and equal chance of selection.

$$\text{Probability of selection} = \frac{\text{Sample size}}{\text{Population size}}$$

The Metro U dining club study has a population of 20,000. If the sample size is 300, the probability of selection is 1.5 percent (300/20,000 = 0.015). In this section, we use the simple random sample to build a foundation for understanding sampling procedures and choosing probability samples. The simple random sample is easy to implement with automatic dialing (random dialing) and with computerized voice response systems. However, it requires a list of population elements, can be time-consuming and expensive, and can require larger sample sizes than other probability methods. Exhibit 14-6 provides an overview of the steps involved in choosing a random sample.

Complex Probability Sampling

Simple random sampling is often impractical. Reasons include (1) it requires a population list (sampling frame) that is often not available; (2) it fails to use all the information about a population, thus

>**Exhibit 14-6** How to Choose a Random Sample

Selecting a *random sample* is accomplished with the aid of computer software, a table of random numbers, or a calculator with a random number generator. Drawing slips out of a hat or Ping-Pong balls from a drum serves as an alternative *if every element in the sampling frame has an equal chance of selection.* Mixing the slips (or balls) and returning them between every selection ensures that every element is just as likely to be selected as any other.

A table of random numbers (such as Appendix D, Exhibit D-10) is a practical solution when no software program is available. Random number tables contain digits that have no systematic organization. Whether you look at rows, columns, or diagonals, you will find neither sequence nor order. Exhibit C-10 in Appendix C is arranged into 10 columns of five-digit strings, but this is solely for readability.

Assume the researchers want a sample of 10 from a population of 95 elements. How will the researcher begin?

1. *Assign each element within the sampling frame a unique number* from 01 to 95.

2. *Identify a random start from the random number table.* Drop a pencil point-first onto the table with closed eyes. Let's say the pencil dot lands on the eighth column from the left and 10 numbers down from the top of Exhibit C-10, marking the five digits 05067.

3. *Determine how the digits in the random number table will be assigned to the sampling frame* to choose the specified sample size (researchers agree to read the first two digits in this column downward until 10 are selected).

4. Select the sample elements from the sampling frame (05, 27, 69, 94, 18, 61, 36, 85, 71, and 83 using the above process. (The digit 94 appeared twice and the second instance was omitted; 00 was omitted because the sampling frame started with 01.)

Other approaches to selecting digits are endless: horizontally right to left, bottom to top, diagonally across columns, and so forth. Computer selection of a simple random sample will be more efficient for larger projects.

resulting in a design that may be wasteful; and (3) it may be expensive to implement in both time and money. These problems have led to the development of alternative designs that are superior to the simple random design in statistical and/or economic efficiency.

A more efficient sample in a statistical sense is one that provides a given precision (standard error of the mean or proportion) with a smaller sample size. A sample that is economically more efficient is one that provides a desired precision at a lower dollar cost. We achieve this with designs that enable us to lower the costs of data collecting, usually through reduced travel expense and interviewer time.

In the discussion that follows, four alternative probability sampling approaches are considered: (1) systematic sampling, (2) stratified sampling, (3) cluster sampling, and (4) double sampling.

Systematic Sampling

A versatile form of probability sampling is **systematic sampling.** In this approach, every kth element in the population is sampled, beginning with a random start of an element in the range of 1 to k. The kth element, or **skip interval,** is determined by dividing the sample size into the population size to obtain the skip pattern applied to the sampling frame. This assumes that the sample frame is an accurate list of the population; if not, the number of elements in the sample frame is substituted for population size.

$$k = \text{Skip interval} = \frac{\text{Population size}}{\text{Sample size}}$$

The major advantage of systematic sampling is its simplicity and flexibility. It is easier to instruct field workers to choose the dwelling unit listed on every kth line of a listing sheet than it is to use a random numbers table. With systematic sampling, there is no need to number the entries in a large personnel file before drawing a sample. To draw a systematic sample, do the following:

- Identify, list, and number the elements in the population.
- Identify the skip interval (k).
- Identify the random start.
- Draw a sample by choosing every kth entry.

Invoices or customer accounts can be sampled by using the last digit or a combination of digits of an invoice or customer account number. Time sampling is also easily accomplished. Systematic sampling would be an appropriate technique for MindWriter's CompleteCare program evaluation.

Systematic sampling can introduce subtle biases. A concern with systematic sampling is the possible *periodicity* in the population that parallels the sampling ratio. In sampling restaurant sales of dessert by drawing days of the year, a skip interval of 7 would bias results, no matter which day provides the random start. A less obvious case might involve a survey in an area of apartment buildings where the typical pattern is eight apartments per building. A skip interval of 8 could easily oversample some types of apartments and undersample others.

Another difficulty may arise when there is a *monotonic trend* in the population elements. That is, the population list varies from the smallest to the largest element or vice versa. Even a chronological list may have this effect if a measure has trended in one direction over time. Whether a systematic sample drawn under these conditions provides a biased estimate of the population mean or proportion depends on the initial random draw. Assume that a list of 2,000 commercial banks is created, arrayed from the largest to the smallest, from which a sample of 50 must be drawn for analysis. A skip interval of 40 beginning with a random start at 16 would exclude the 15 largest banks and give a small-size bias to the findings.

The only protection against these subtle biases is constant vigilance by the researcher. Some ways to avoid such bias include:

- Randomize the population before sampling (e.g., order the banks by name rather than size).
- Change the random start several times in the sampling process.
- Replicate a selection of different samples.

Although systematic sampling has some theoretical problems, from a practical point of view it is usually treated as a simple random sample. When similar population elements are grouped within the sampling frame, systematic sampling is statistically more efficient than a simple random sample. This might occur if the listed elements are ordered chronologically, by size, by class, and so on. Under these conditions, the sample approaches a proportional stratified sample. The effect of this ordering is more pronounced on the results of cluster samples than for element samples and may call for a proportional stratified sampling formula.[12]

Stratified Sampling

Most populations can be segregated into several mutually exclusive subpopulations, or strata. The process by which the sample is constrained to include elements from each of the segments is called **stratified random sampling.** University students can be divided by their class level, school or major, gender, and so forth. After a population is divided into the appropriate strata, a simple random sample can be taken within each stratum. The results from the study can then be weighted (based on the proportion of the strata to the population) and combined into appropriate population estimates.

> The average number of text messages sent per day by American teens.
>
> # 80

There are three reasons a researcher chooses a stratified random sample: (1) to increase a sample's statistical efficiency, (2) to provide adequate data for analyzing the various subpopulations or strata, and (3) to enable different research methods and procedures to be used in different strata.[13]

Stratification is usually more efficient statistically than simple random sampling and at worst it is equal to it. With the ideal stratification, each stratum is homogeneous internally and heterogeneous with other strata. This might occur in a sample that includes members of several distinct ethnic groups. In this instance, stratification makes a pronounced improvement in statistical efficiency.

It is also useful when the researcher wants to study the characteristics of certain population subgroups. Thus, if one wishes to draw some conclusions about activities in the different classes of a student body, stratified sampling would be used. Similarly, if a restaurant were interested in testing menu changes to attract younger patrons while retaining its older, loyal customers, stratified sampling using age and prior patronage as descriptors would be appropriate. Stratification is also called for when different methods of data collection are applied in different parts of the population, a research design that is becoming increasingly common. This might occur when we survey company employees at the home office with one method but must use a different approach with employees scattered throughout the country.

If data are available on which to base a stratification decision, how shall we go about it?[14] The ideal stratification would be based on the primary variable under study. If the major concern were to learn how often per month patrons would use the Metro U dining club, then one would like to stratify on this expected number of use occasions. The only difficulty with this idea is that if we knew this information, we would not need to conduct the study. We must, therefore, pick a variable for stratifying that we believe will correlate with the frequency of club use per month, something like days at work or class schedule as an indication of when a sample element might be near campus at mealtimes.

Researchers often have several important variables about which they want to draw conclusions. A reasonable approach is to seek some basis for stratification that correlates well with the major variables. It might be a single variable (class level), or it might be a compound variable (class by gender). In any event, we will have done a good stratifying job if the stratification base maximizes the difference among strata means and minimizes the within-stratum variances for the variables of major concern.

The more strata used, the closer you come to maximizing interstrata differences (differences between strata) and minimizing intrastratum variances (differences within a given stratum). You must base the decision partially on the number of subpopulation groups about which you wish to draw separate conclusions. Costs of stratification also enter the decision. The more strata you have, the higher the cost of the research project due to the cost associated with more detailed sampling. There is little to be gained in estimating population values when the number of strata exceeds six.[15]

The size of the strata samples is calculated with two pieces of information: (1) how large the total sample should be and (2) how the total sample should be allocated among strata. In deciding how to allocate a total sample among various strata, there are proportionate and disproportionate options.

Proportionate versus Disproportionate Sampling

In **proportionate stratified sampling,** each stratum is properly represented so that the sample size drawn from the stratum is proportionate to the stratum's share of the total population. This approach is more popular than any of the other stratified sampling procedures. Some reasons for this include:

- It has higher statistical efficiency than a simple random sample.
- It is much easier to carry out than other stratifying methods.
- It provides a self-weighting sample; the population mean or proportion can be estimated simply by calculating the mean or proportion of all sample cases, eliminating the weighting of responses.

On the other hand, proportionate stratified samples often gain little in statistical efficiency if the strata measures and their variances are similar for the major variables under study.

Any stratification that departs from the proportionate relationship is **disproportionate stratified sampling.** There are several disproportionate allocation schemes. One type is a judgmentally determined disproportion based on the idea that each stratum is large enough to secure adequate confidence levels and error range estimates for individual strata. The following table shows the relationship between proportionate and disproportionate stratified sampling.

Stratum	Population	Proportionate Sample	Disproportionate Sample
Male	45%	45%	35%
Female	55	55	65

A researcher makes decisions regarding disproportionate sampling, however, by considering how a sample will be allocated among strata. One author states,

> In a given stratum, take a larger sample if the stratum is larger than other strata; the stratum is more variable internally; and sampling is cheaper in the stratum.[16]

If one uses these suggestions as a guide, it is possible to develop an optimal stratification scheme. When there is no difference in intrastratum variances and when the costs of sampling among strata are equal, the optimal design is a proportionate sample.

While disproportionate sampling is theoretically superior, there is some question as to whether it has wide applicability in a practical sense. If the differences in sampling costs or variances among strata are large, then disproportionate sampling is desirable. It has been suggested that "differences of several-fold are required to make disproportionate sampling worthwhile."[17]

The process for drawing a stratified sample is:

- Determine the variables to use for stratification.
- Determine the proportions of the stratification variables in the population.
- Select proportionate or disproportionate stratification based on project information needs and risks.
- Divide the sampling frame into separate frames for each stratum.
- Randomize the elements within each stratum's sampling frame.
- Follow random or systematic procedures to draw the sample from each stratum.

Cluster Sampling

In a simple random sample, each population element is selected individually. The population can also be divided into groups of elements with some groups randomly selected for study. This is **cluster sampling.** Cluster sampling differs from stratified sampling in several ways, as indicated in Exhibit 14-7.

>**Exhibit 14-7** Comparison of Stratified and Cluster Sampling

Stratified Sampling	Cluster Sampling
1. We divide the population into a few subgroups.	1. We divide the population into *many* subgroups.
• Each subgroup has *many* elements in it.	• Each subgroup has *few* elements in it.
• Subgroups are selected according to some criterion that is related to the variables under study.	• Subgroups are selected according to some criterion of ease or availability in data collection.
2. We try to secure *homogeneity* within subgroups.	2. We try to secure *heterogeneity* within subgroups.
3. We try to secure *heterogeneity* between subgroups.	3. We try to secure *homogeneity* between subgroups.
4. We randomly choose *elements* from within each subgroup.	4. We randomly choose several *subgroups* that we then typically study in depth.

Two conditions foster the use of cluster sampling: (1) the need for more economic efficiency than can be provided by simple random sampling and (2) the frequent unavailability of a practical sampling frame for individual elements.

Statistical efficiency for cluster samples is usually lower than for simple random samples chiefly because clusters often don't meet the need for heterogeneity and, instead, are homogeneous. For example, families in the same block (a typical cluster) are often similar in social class, income level, ethnic origin, and so forth. Although statistical efficiency in most cluster sampling may be low, economic efficiency is often great enough to overcome this weakness. The criterion, then, is the net relative efficiency resulting from the trade-off between economic and statistical factors. It may take 690 interviews with a cluster design to give the same precision as 424 simple random interviews. But if it costs only $5 per interview in the cluster situation and $10 in the simple random case, the cluster sample is more attractive ($3,450 versus $4,240).

A low-cost, frequently used method, the area cluster sample may use geographic sample units (e.g., city blocks).

Area Sampling   Much research involves populations that can be identified with some geographic area. When this occurs, it is possible to use **area sampling,** the most important form of cluster sampling. This method overcomes the problems of both high sampling cost and the unavailability of a practical sampling frame for individual elements. Area sampling methods have been applied to national populations, county populations, and even smaller areas where there are well-defined political or natural boundaries.

Suppose you want to survey the adult residents of a city. You would seldom be able to secure a listing of such individuals. It would be simple, however, to get a detailed city map that shows the blocks of the city. If you take a sample of these blocks, you are also taking a sample of the adult residents of the city.

Design   In designing cluster samples, including area samples, we must answer several questions:

1. How homogeneous are the resulting clusters?
2. Shall we seek equal-size or unequal-size clusters?
3. How large a cluster shall we take?
4. Shall we use a single-stage or multistage cluster?
5. How large a sample is needed?

1. When clusters are homogeneous, this contributes to low statistical efficiency. Sometimes one can improve this efficiency by constructing clusters to increase intracluster variance. In the dining club study, researchers might have chosen a course as a cluster, choosing to sample all students in that course if it enrolled students of all four class years. Or maybe they could choose a departmental office that had faculty, staff, and administrative positions as well as student workers. In area sampling to increase intracluster variance, researchers could combine into a single cluster adjoining blocks that contain different income groups or social classes.

2. A cluster sample may be composed of clusters of equal or unequal size. The theory of clustering is that the means of sample clusters are unbiased estimates of the population mean. This is more often true when clusters are naturally equal, such as households in city blocks. While one can deal with clusters of unequal size, it may be desirable to reduce or counteract the effects of unequal size. There are several approaches to this:

- Combine small clusters and split large clusters until each approximates an average size.
- Stratify clusters by size and choose clusters from each stratum.
- Stratify clusters by size and then subsample, using varying sampling fractions to secure an overall sampling ratio.[18]

3. There is no *a priori* answer to the ideal cluster size question. Comparing the efficiency of differing cluster sizes requires that we discover the different costs for each size and estimate the different variances of the cluster means. Even with single-stage clusters (where the researchers interview or observe every element within a cluster), it is not clear which size (say, 5, 20, or 50) is superior. Some have found that in studies using single-stage area clusters, the optimal cluster size is no larger than the typical city block.[19]

4. Concerning single-stage or multistage cluster designs, for most large-scale area sampling, the tendency is to use multistage designs. Several situations justify drawing a sample within a cluster, in preference to the direct creation of smaller clusters and taking a census of that cluster using one-stage cluster sampling:[20]

- Natural clusters may exist as convenient sampling units yet, for economic reasons, may be larger than the desired size.
- We can avoid the cost of creating smaller clusters in the entire population and confine subsampling to only those large natural clusters.
- The sampling of naturally compact clusters may present practical difficulties. For example, independent interviewing of all members of a household may be impractical.

5. The answer to how many subjects must be interviewed or observed depends heavily on the specific cluster design, and the details can be complicated. Unequal clusters and multistage samples are the chief complications, and their statistical treatment is beyond the scope of this book.[21] Here we will treat only single-stage sampling with equal-size clusters (called *simple cluster sampling*). It is analogous to

simple random sampling. We can think of a population as consisting of 20,000 clusters of one student each, or 2,000 clusters of 10 students each, and so on. Assuming the same specifications for precision and confidence, we should expect that the calculation of a probability sample size would be the same for both clusters.

Double Sampling

It may be more convenient or economical to collect some information by sample and then use this information as the basis for selecting a subsample for further study. This procedure is called **double sampling, sequential sampling,** or **multiphase sampling.** It is usually found with stratified and/or cluster designs. The calculation procedures are described in more advanced texts.

Double sampling can be illustrated by the dining club example. You might use a telephone survey or another inexpensive survey method to discover who would be interested in joining such a club and the degree of their interest. You might then stratify the interested respondents by degree of interest and subsample among them for intensive interviewing on expected consumption patterns, reactions to various services, and so on. Whether it is more desirable to gather such information by one-stage or two-stage sampling depends largely on the relative costs of the two methods.

Because of the wide range of sampling designs available, it is often difficult to select an approach that meets the needs of the research question and helps to contain the costs of the project. To help with these choices, Exhibit 14-8 may be used to compare the various advantages and disadvantages

>**Exhibit 14-8** Comparison of Probability Sampling Designs

Type	Description	Advantages	Disadvantages
Simple Random *Cost: High* Use: Moderate	Each population element has an equal chance of being selected into the sample. Sample drawn using random number table/generator.	Easy to implement with automatic dialing (random-digit dialing) and with computerized voice response systems.	Requires a listing of population elements. Takes more time to implement. Uses larger sample sizes. Produces larger errors.
Systematic *Cost: Moderate* Use: Moderate	Selects an element of the population at the beginning with a random start, and following the sampling skip interval selects every kth element.	Simple to design. Easier to use than the simple random. Easy to determine sampling distribution of mean or proportion.	Periodicity within the population may skew the sample and results. If the population list has a monotonic trend, a biased estimate will result based on the start point.
Stratified *Cost: High* Use: Moderate	Divides population into subpopulations or strata and uses simple random on each stratum. Results may be weighted and combined.	Researcher controls sample size in strata. Increased statistical efficiency. Provides data to represent and analyze subgroups. Enables use of different methods in strata.	Increased error will result if subgroups are selected at different rates. Especially expensive if strata on the population have to be created.
Cluster *Cost: Moderate* Use: High	Population is divided into internally heterogeneous subgroups. Some are randomly selected for further study.	Provides an unbiased estimate of population parameters if properly done. Economically more efficient than simple random. Lowest cost per sample, especially with geographic clusters. Easy to do without a population list.	Often lower statistical efficiency (more error) due to subgroups being homogeneous rather than heterogeneous.
Double (sequential or multiphase) *Cost: Moderate* Use: Moderate	Process includes collecting data from a sample using a previously defined technique. Based on the information found, a subsample is selected for further study.	May reduce costs if first stage results in enough data to stratify or cluster the population.	Increased costs if indiscriminately used.

of probability sampling. Nonprobability sampling techniques are covered in the next section. They are used frequently and offer the researcher the benefit of low cost. However, they are not based on a theoretical framework and do not operate from statistical theory; consequently, they produce selection bias and nonrepresentative samples. Despite these weaknesses, their widespread use demands their mention here.

> Nonprobability Sampling

Any discussion of the relative merits of probability versus nonprobability sampling clearly shows the technical superiority of the former. In probability sampling, researchers use a random selection of elements to reduce or eliminate sampling bias. Under such conditions, we can have substantial confidence that the sample is representative of the population from which it is drawn. In addition, with probability sample designs, we can estimate an error range within which the population parameter is expected to fall. Thus, we can reduce not only the chance for sampling error but also estimate the range of probable sampling error present.

With a subjective approach like nonprobability sampling, the probability of selecting population elements is unknown. There are a variety of ways to choose persons or cases to include in the sample. Often we allow the choice of subjects to be made by field workers on the scene. When this occurs, there is greater opportunity for bias to enter the sample selection procedure and to distort the findings of the study. Also, we cannot estimate any range within which to expect the population parameter. Given the technical advantages of probability sampling over nonprobability sampling, why would anyone choose the latter? There are some practical reasons for using the less precise methods.

Practical Considerations

We may use nonprobability sampling procedures because they satisfactorily meet the sampling objectives. Although a random sample will give us a true cross section of the population, this may not be the objective of the research. If there is no desire or need to generalize to a population parameter, then there is much less concern about whether the sample fully reflects the population. Often researchers have more limited objectives. They may be looking only for the range of conditions or for examples of dramatic variations. This is especially true in exploratory research in which one may wish to contact only certain persons or cases that are clearly atypical. Burbidge would have likely wanted a probability sample if the decision resting on the data was the actual design of the new CityBus routes and schedules. However, the decision of where and when to place advertising announcing the change is a relatively low-cost one in comparison.

Additional reasons for choosing nonprobability over probability sampling are cost and time. Probability sampling clearly calls for more planning and repeated callbacks to ensure that each selected sample member is contacted. These activities are expensive. Carefully controlled nonprobability sampling often seems to give acceptable results, so the investigator may not even consider probability sampling. Burbidge's results from bus route 99 would generate questionable data, but he seemed to realize the fallacy of many of his assumptions once he spoke with bus route 99's driver—something he should have done during exploration prior to designing the sampling plan.

While probability sampling may be superior in theory, there are breakdowns in its application. Even carefully stated random sampling procedures may be subject to careless application by the people involved. Thus, the ideal probability sampling may be only partially achieved because of the human element.

It is also possible that nonprobability sampling may be the only feasible alternative. The total population may not be available for study in certain cases. At the scene of a major event, it may be infeasible to attempt to construct a probability sample. A study of past correspondence between two companies must use an arbitrary sample because the full correspondence is normally not available.

In another sense, those who are included in a sample may select themselves. In mail surveys, those who respond may not represent a true cross section of those who receive the questionnaire. The receivers of the questionnaire decide for themselves whether they will participate. In Internet surveys those who volunteer don't always represent the appropriate cross section—that's why screening questions are used before admitting a participant to the sample. There is, however, some of this self-selection in almost all surveys because every respondent chooses whether to be interviewed.

Methods

Convenience

Nonprobability samples that are unrestricted are called **convenience samples.** They are the least reliable design but normally the cheapest and easiest to conduct. Researchers or field workers have the freedom to choose whomever they find: thus, the name "convenience." Examples include informal pools of friends and neighbors, people responding to a newspaper's invitation for readers to state their positions on some public issue, a TV reporter's "person-on-the-street" intercept interviews, or the use of employees to evaluate the taste of a new snack food.

Although a convenience sample has no controls to ensure precision, it may still be a useful procedure. Often you will take such a sample to test ideas or even to gain ideas about a subject of interest. In the early stages of exploratory research, when you are seeking guidance, you might use this approach. The results may present evidence that is so overwhelming that a more sophisticated sampling procedure is unnecessary. In an interview with students concerning some issue of campus concern, you might talk to 25 students selected sequentially. You might discover that the responses are so overwhelmingly one-sided that there is no incentive to interview further.

Purposive Sampling

A nonprobability sample that conforms to certain criteria is called *purposive sampling*. There are two major types—judgment sampling and quota sampling.

Judgment sampling occurs when a researcher selects sample members to conform to some criterion. In a study of labor problems, you may want to talk only with those who have experienced on-the-job discrimination. Another example of judgment sampling occurs when election results are predicted from only a few selected precincts that have been chosen because of their predictive record in past elections. Burbidge chose bus route 99 because the current route between East City and West City led him to believe that he could get a representation of both East City and West City riders.

When used in the early stages of an exploratory study, a judgment sample is appropriate. When one wishes to select a biased group for screening purposes, this sampling method is also a good choice. Companies often try out new product ideas on their employees. The rationale is that one would expect the firm's employees to be more favorably disposed toward a new product idea than the public. If the product does not pass this group, it does not have prospects for success in the general market.

Quota sampling is the second type of purposive sampling. We use it to improve representativeness. The logic behind quota sampling is that certain relevant characteristics describe the dimensions of the population. If a sample has the same distribution on these characteristics, then it is likely to be representative of the population regarding other variables on which we have no control. Suppose the student body of Metro U is 55 percent female and 45 percent male. The sampling quota would call for sampling students at a 55 to 45 percent ratio. This would eliminate distortions due to a nonrepresentative gender ratio. Burbidge could have improved his nonprobability sampling by considering time-of-day and day-of-week variations and choosing to distribute surveys to bus route 99 riders at various times, thus creating a quota sample.

In most quota samples, researchers specify more than one control dimension. Each should meet two tests: it should (1) have a distribution in the population that we can estimate and (2) be pertinent to the topic studied. We may believe that responses to a question should vary depending on the gender of the respondent. If so, we should seek proportional responses from both men and women. We may also feel that undergraduates differ from graduate students, so this would be a dimension. Other dimensions, such as the student's academic discipline, ethnic group, religious affiliation, and social group affiliation, also may be chosen. Only a few of these controls can be used. To illustrate, suppose we consider the following:

Gender: Two categories—male, female.

Class level: Two categories—graduate, undergraduate.

College: Six categories—arts and science, agriculture, architecture, business, engineering, other.

Religion: Four categories—Protestant, Catholic, Jewish, other.

Fraternal affiliation: Two categories—member, nonmember.

Family social-economic class: Three categories—upper, middle, lower.

In an extreme case, we might ask an interviewer to find a male undergraduate business student who is Catholic, a fraternity member, and from an upper-class home. All combinations of these six factors would call for 288 such cells to consider. This type of control is known as *precision control.* It gives greater assurance that a sample will be representative of the population. However, it is costly and too difficult to carry out with more than three variables.

When we wish to use more than three control dimensions, we should depend on *frequency* control. With this form of control, the overall percentage of those with each characteristic in the sample should match the percentage holding the same characteristic in the population. No attempt is made to find a combination of specific characteristics in a single person. In frequency control, we would probably find that the following sample array is an adequate reflection of the population:

	Population	Sample
Male	65%	67%
Married	15	14
Undergraduate	70	72
Campus resident	30	28
Independent	75	73
Protestant	39	42

Quota sampling has several weaknesses. First, the idea that quotas on some variables assume a representativeness on others is argument by analogy. It gives no assurance that the sample is representative of the variables being studied. Often, the data used to provide controls might be outdated or inaccurate. There is also a practical limit on the number of simultaneous controls that can be applied to ensure precision. Finally, the choice of subjects is left to field workers to make on a judgmental basis. They may choose only friendly looking people, people who are convenient to them, and so forth.

Despite the problems with quota sampling, it is widely used by opinion pollsters and marketing and business researchers. Probability sampling is usually much more costly and time-consuming. Advocates of quota sampling argue that although there is some danger of systematic bias, the risks are usually not that great. Where predictive validity has been checked (e.g., in election polls), quota sampling has been generally satisfactory.

Snowball

This design has found a niche in recent years in applications where respondents are difficult to identify and are best located through referral networks. It is also especially appropriate for some qualitative studies. In the initial stage of **snowball sampling,** individuals are discovered and may or may not be selected through probability methods. This group is then used to refer the researcher to others who possess similar characteristics and who, in turn, identify others. Similar to a reverse search for bibliographic sources, the "snowball" gathers subjects as it rolls along. Various techniques are available for selecting a nonprobability snowball with provisions for error identification and statistical testing. Let's consider a brief example.

The high end of the U.S. audio market is composed of several small firms that produce ultra-expensive components used in recording and playback of live performances. A risky new technology for improving digital signal processing is being contemplated by one firm. Through its contacts with a select group of recording engineers and electronics designers, the first-stage sample may be identified for interviewing. Subsequent interviewees are likely to reveal critical information for product development and marketing.

Variations on snowball sampling have been used to study drug cultures, teenage gang activities, power elites, community relations, insider trading, and other applications where respondents are difficult to identify and contact.

>summary

1 Sampling is based on two premises. One is that there is enough similarity among the elements in a population that a few of these elements will adequately represent the characteristics of the total population. The second premise is that although some elements in a sample underestimate a population value, others overestimate this value. The result of these tendencies is that a sample statistic such as the arithmetic mean is generally a good estimate of a population mean.

2 A good sample has both accuracy and precision. An accurate sample is one in which there is little or no bias or systematic variance. A sample with adequate precision is one that has a sampling error that is within acceptable limits for the study's purpose.

3 In developing a sample, five procedural questions need to be answered:

   a What is the target population?

   b What are the parameters of interest?

   c What is the sampling frame?

   d What is the appropriate sampling method?

   e What size sample is needed?

4 A variety of sampling techniques are available. They may be classified by their representation basis and element selection techniques.

Element Selection	Representation Basis	
	Probability	**Nonprobability**
Unrestricted	Simple random	Convenience
Restricted	Complex random	Purposive
	• Systematic	• Judgment
	• Cluster	• Quota
	• Stratified	Snowball
	• Double	

Probability sampling is based on random selection—a controlled procedure that ensures that each population element is given a known nonzero chance of selection. The simplest type of probability approach is simple random sampling. In this design, each member of the population has an equal chance of being included in a sample. In contrast, nonprobability selection is "not random." When each sample element is drawn individually from the population at large, this is unrestricted sampling. Restricted sampling covers those forms of sampling in which the selection process follows more complex rules.

5 Complex sampling is used when conditions make simple random samples impractical or uneconomical. The four major types of complex random sampling discussed in this chapter are systematic, stratified, cluster, and double sampling. Systematic sampling involves the selection of every kth element in the population, beginning with a random start between elements from 1 to k. Its simplicity in certain cases is its greatest value.

Stratified sampling is based on dividing a population into subpopulations and then randomly sampling from each of these strata. This method usually results in a smaller total sample size than would a simple random design. Stratified samples may be proportionate or disproportionate.

In cluster sampling, we divide the population into convenient groups and then randomly choose the groups to study. It is typically less efficient from a statistical viewpoint than the simple random because of the high degree of homogeneity within the clusters. Its great advantage is its savings in cost—if the population is dispersed geographically—or in time. The most widely used form of clustering is area sampling, in which geographic areas are the selection elements.

At times it may be more convenient or economical to collect some information by sample and then use it as a basis for selecting a subsample for further study. This procedure is called double sampling.

Nonprobability sampling also has some compelling practical advantages that account for its widespread use. Often probability sampling is not feasible because the population is not available. Then, too, frequent breakdowns in the application of probability sampling discount its technical advantages. You may find also that a true cross section is often not the aim of the researcher. Here the goal may be the discovery of the range or extent of conditions. Finally, nonprobability sampling is usually less expensive to conduct than is probability sampling.

Convenience samples are the simplest and least reliable forms of nonprobability sampling. Their primary virtue is low cost. One purposive sample is the judgmental sample, in which one is interested in studying only selected types of subjects. The other purposive sample is the quota sample. Subjects are selected to conform to certain predesignated control measures that secure a representative cross section of the population. Snowball sampling uses a referral approach to reach particularly hard-to-find respondents.

>keyterms

area sampling 382

census 364

cluster sampling 380

convenience sample 385

disproportionate stratified sampling 380

double sampling 383

judgment sampling 385

multiphase sampling 383

nonprobability sampling 369

population 364

population element 364

population parameters 371

population proportion of incidence 371

probability sampling 369

proportionate stratified sampling 380

quota sampling 385

sample frame 364

sample statistics 371

sampling 364

sampling error 367

sequential sampling 383

simple random sample 377

skip interval 378

snowball sampling 386

stratified random sampling 379

systematic sampling 378

systematic variance 366

>discussionquestions

Terms in Review

1 Distinguish between:

  a Statistic and parameter.

  b Sample frame and population.

  c Restricted and unrestricted sampling.

  d Simple random and complex random sampling.

  e Convenience and purposive sampling.

  f Sample precision and sample accuracy.

  g Systematic and error variance.

  h Variable and attribute parameters.

  i Proportionate and disproportionate samples.

2 Under what kind of conditions would you recommend:

  a A probability sample? a nonprobability sample?

  b A simple random sample? a cluster sample? a stratified sample?

  c A disproportionate stratified probability sample?

3 You plan to conduct a survey using unrestricted sampling. What subjective decisions must you make?

4 Describe the differences between a probability sample and a nonprobability sample.

5 Why would a researcher use a quota purposive sample?

Making Research Decisions

6 Your task is to interview a representative sample of attendees for the large concert venue where you work. The new season schedule includes 200 live concerts featuring all types of musicians and musical groups. Since neither the number of attendees nor their descriptive characteristics are known in advance, you decide on nonprobability sampling. Based on past seating configurations, you can calculate the number of tickets that will be available for each of the 200 concerts. Thus, collectively, you will know the number of possible attendees for each type of music. From attendance research conducted at concerts held by the Glacier Symphony during the previous two years, you can obtain gender data on attendees by type of music. How would you conduct a reasonably reliable nonprobability sample?

7 Your large firm is about to change to a customer-centered organization structure, in which employees who have rarely had customer contact will now likely significantly influence customer satisfaction and retention. As part of the transition, your superior wants an accurate evaluation of the morale of the firm's large number of computer technicians. What type of sample would you draw if it was to be an unrestricted sample?

Bringing Research to Life

8 Design an alternative nonprobability sample that will be more representative of infrequent and potential riders for the CityBus project.

9 How would you draw a cluster sample for the CityBus project?

From Concept to Practice

10 Using Exhibit 14-8 as your guide, for each sampling technique describe the sample frame for a study of employers' skill needs in new hires using the industry in which you are currently working or wish to work.

From the Headlines

11 During the 2010 Super Bowl, the Snicker's candy bar campaign was voted the best ad by women 18 or older, men 18 or older, and youth 17 or younger. This ad features a neighborhood football game in which one player, who has flagging energy, is repeatedly tackled. His teammates tell him, "You play like Betty White!" The octogenarian actress and comedian appears in the ad being tackled. If you were AdBowl.com, how would you draw the sample to measure the best Super Bowl ad among the three groups of interest?

>cases*

 Akron Children's Hospital

Calling Up Attendance

 Campbell-Ewald Pumps Awareness into the American Heart Association

Campbell-Ewald: R-E-S-P-E-C-T Spells Loyalty

Can Research Rescue the Red Cross?

 Goodyear's Aquatred

Inquiring Minds Want to Know—NOW!

 Ohio Lottery: Innovative Research Design Drives Winning

 Pebble Beach Co.

 Starbucks, Bank One, and Visa Launch Starbucks Card Duetto Visa

State Farm: Dangerous Intersections

The Catalyst for Women in Financial Services

 USTA: Come Out Swinging

 Volkswagen's Beetle

* You will find a description of each case in the Case Abstracts section of the textbook. Check the Case Index to determine whether a case provides data, the research instrument, video, or other supplementary material. Written cases are downloadable from the text website (www.mhhe.com/cooper11e). All video material and video cases are available from the Online Learning Center. The film reel icon indicates a video case or video material relevant to the case.

Determining Sample Size

Basic Concepts for Sampling

In the Metro University Dining Club study, we explore probability sampling and the various concepts used to design the sampling process.

Exhibit 14a-1 shows the Metro U dining club study population ($N = 20,000$) consisting of five subgroups based on their preferred lunch times. The values 1 through 5 represent the preferred lunch times of 11 a.m., 11:30 a.m., 12 noon, 12:30 p.m., and 1 p.m. The frequency of response (f) in the population distribution, shown beside the population subgroup, is what would be found if a census of the elements was taken. Normally, population data are

unavailable or are too costly to obtain. We are pretending omniscience for the sake of the example.

Point Estimates

Now assume we sample 10 elements from this population without knowledge of the population's characteristics. We use a sampling procedure from a statistical software program, a random number generator, or a table of random numbers. Our first sample ($n_1 = 10$) provides us with the frequencies shown below sample n_1 in Exhibit 14a-1. We also calculate a mean score, $X_1 = 3.0$, for this sample. This mean would place the average preferred lunch time at 12 noon. The mean is a *point estimate* and our best predictor

>**Exhibit 14a-1** Random Samples of Preferred Lunch Times

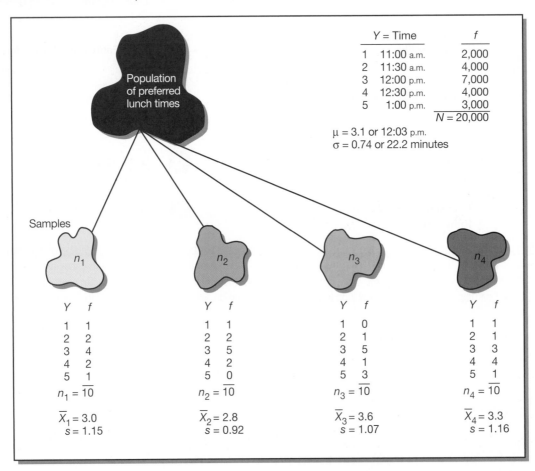

of the unknown population mean, μ (the arithmetic average of the population). Assume further that we return the first sample to the population and draw a second, third, and fourth sample by the same procedure. The frequencies, means, and standard deviations are as shown in the exhibit. As the data suggest, each sample shares some similarities with the population, but none is a perfect duplication because no sample perfectly replicates its population.

Interval Estimates

We cannot judge which estimate is the true mean (accurately reflects the population mean). However, we can estimate the interval in which the true μ will fall by using any of the samples. This is accomplished by using a formula that computes the *standard error of the mean*.

$$\sigma_{\bar{X}} = \frac{\sigma}{\sqrt{n}}$$

where

$\sigma_{\bar{x}}$ = standard error of the mean or the standard deviation of all possible $\bar{X}$ s

σ = population standard deviation

n = sample size

The standard error of the mean measures the standard deviation of the distribution of sample means. It varies directly with the standard deviation of the population from which it is drawn (see Exhibit 14a-2): If the standard deviation is reduced by 50 percent, the standard error will also be reduced by 50 percent. It also varies inversely with the square root of the sample size. If the square root of the sample size is doubled, the standard error is cut by one-half, provided the standard deviation remains constant.

Let's now examine what happens when we apply sample data (n_1) from Exhibit 14a-1 to the formula. The sample standard deviation from sample n will be used as an unbiased estimator of the population standard deviation.

$$\sigma_{\bar{X}} = \frac{s}{\sqrt{n}}$$

where

s = standard deviation of the sample, n_1

n_1 = 10

$\bar{X}_1$ = 3.0

s_1 = 1.15

Substituting into the equation:

$$\sigma_{\bar{X}} = \frac{s}{\sqrt{n}} = \frac{1.15}{\sqrt{10}} = .36$$

Estimating the Population Mean

How does this improve our prediction of μ from X? The standard error creates the interval range that brackets the point estimate. In this example, μ is predicted to be 3.0 or 12 noon (the mean of n_1) ±0.36. This range may be visualized on a continuum (see diagram at bottom of page).

We would expect to find the true μ between 2.64 and 3.36—between 11:49 a.m. and 12:11 p.m. (if 2 = 11:30 a.m. and 0.64 = (30 minutes) = 19.2 minutes, then 2.64 = 11:30 a.m. + 19.2 minutes, or 11:49 a.m.). Since we assume omniscience for this illustration, we know the population average value is 3.1. Further, because standard errors have characteristics like other standard scores, we have 68 percent confidence in this estimate—that is, one standard error encompasses ±1 Z or 68 percent of the area under the normal curve (see Exhibit 14a-3). Recall that the area under the curve also represents the confidence estimates that we make about our results. The combination of the interval range and the degree of confidence creates the *confidence interval*. To improve confidence to 95 percent, multiply the standard error of 0.36 by ± 1.96 (Z), since 1.96 Z covers 95 percent of the area under the curve (see Exhibit 14a-4). Now, with 95 percent confidence, the interval in which we would find the true mean increases to ± 0.70 (from 2.3 to 3.7 or from 11:39 a.m. to 12:21 p.m.).

Parenthetically, if we compute the standard deviation of the distribution of sample means in Exhibit 14a-1, [3.0, 2.8, 3.6, 3.3], we will discover it to be 0.35. Compare this to the standard error from the original calculation (0.36). The result is consistent with the second definition of the standard error: the standard deviation of the distribution of sample means (n_1, n_2, n_3, and n_4). Now let's return to the dining club example and apply some of these concepts to the researchers' problem.

If the researchers were to interview all the students and employees in the defined population, asking them, How many times per month would you eat at the club? they would get a distribution something like that shown in part A of Exhibit 14a-5. The responses would range from zero to as many as 30 lunches per month with a μ and σ.

However, they cannot take a census, so μ and σ remain unknown. By sampling, the researchers find the mean to be 10.0 and the standard deviation to be 4.1 eating experiences (how often they would eat at the club per month). In part C of Exhibit 14a-5, three observations about this sample distribution are consistent with our earlier illustration. First,

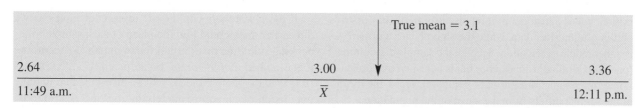

True mean = 3.1

2.64	3.00	3.36
11:49 a.m.	$\bar{X}$	12:11 p.m.

>Exhibit 14a-2 Effects on Standard Error of Mean of Increasing Precision

	Reducing the Standard Deviation by 50%	Quadrupling the Sample
$\sigma_{\bar{x}} = \dfrac{s}{\sqrt{n}}$	$\sigma_{\bar{x}} = \dfrac{0.74}{\sqrt{10}} = 0.234$	$\sigma_{\bar{x}} = \dfrac{0.8}{\sqrt{25}} = 0.16$
	$\sigma_{\bar{x}} = \dfrac{0.37}{\sqrt{10}} = 0.117$	$\sigma_{\bar{x}} = \dfrac{0.8}{\sqrt{100}} = 0.08$

where
$\sigma_{\bar{x}}$ = standard error of the mean
$\sigma_{\bar{x}}$ = standard deviation of the sample
n = sample size

Note: A 400 percent increase in sample size (from 25 to 100) would yield only a 200 percent increase in precision (from 0.16 to 0.08). Researchers are often asked to increase precision, but the question should be, At what cost? Each of those additional sample elements adds both time and cost to the study.

>Exhibit 14a-3 Confidence Levels and the Normal Curve

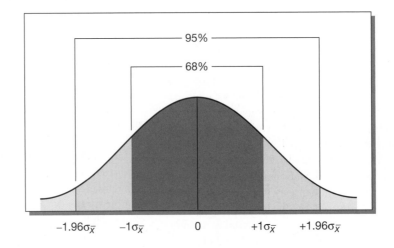

>Exhibit 14a-4 Standard Errors Associated with Areas under the Normal Curve

Standard Error (Z)	Percent of Area*	Approximate Degree of Confidence
1.00	68.27	68%
1.65	90.10	90
1.96	95.00	95
3.00	99.73	99

*Includes both tails in a normal distribution.

it is shown as a histogram; it represents a frequency distribution of empirical data, while the smooth curve of part A is a theoretical distribution. Second, the sample distribution (part C) is similar in appearance but is not a perfect duplication of the population distribution (part A). Third, the mean of the sample differs from the mean of the population.

If the researchers could draw repeated samples as we did earlier, they could plot the mean of each sample to secure the solid line distribution found in part B. According to the *central limit theorem,* for sufficiently large samples ($n = 30$), the sample means will be distributed around the population mean approximately in a normal distribution.

>**Exhibit 14a-5** A Comparison of Population Distribution, Sample Distribution, and Distribution of Sample Means of Metro U Dining Club Study

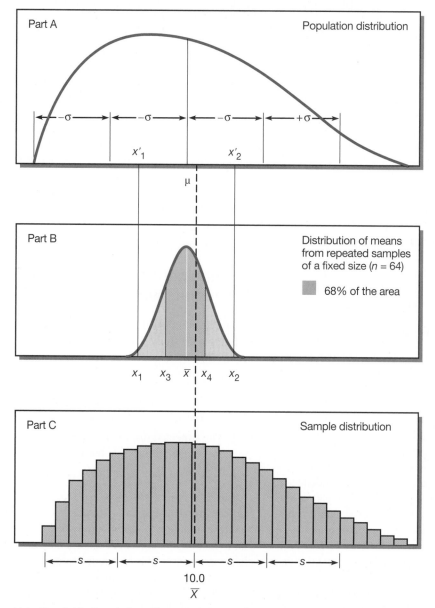

Note: The distributions in these figures are not to scale, but this fact is not critical to our understanding of the dispersion relationship depicted.

Even if the population is not normally distributed, the distribution of sample means will be normal if there is a large enough set of samples.

Estimating the Interval for the Metro U Dining Club Sample

Any sample mean will fall within the range of the distribution extremes shown in part B of Exhibit 14a-5. We also know that about 68 percent of the sample means in this distribution will fall between x_3 and x_4 and 95 percent will fall between x_1 and x_2.

If we project points x_1 and x_2 up to the population distribution (part A of Exhibit 14a-5) at points x'_1 and x'_2, we see the interval where any given mean of a random sample of 64 is likely to fall 95 percent of the time. Since we will not know the population mean from which to measure the standard error, we infer that there is also a 95 percent chance that the population mean is within two standard errors of the sample mean (10.0). This inference enables us to find the sample mean, mark off an interval around it, and state a confidence likelihood that the population mean is within this bracket.

Because the researchers are considering an investment in this project, they would want some assurance that the population mean is close to the figure reported in any sample they take. To find out how close the population mean is to the sample mean, they must calculate the standard error of the mean and estimate an interval range within which the population mean is likely to be.

Given a sample size of 64, they still need a value for the standard error. Almost never will one have the value for the standard deviation of the population (σ), so we must use a proxy figure. The best proxy for σ is the standard deviation of the sample (s). Here the standard deviation ($s = 4.1$) was obtained from a pilot sample:

$$\sigma_{\bar{X}} = \frac{s}{\sqrt{n}} = \frac{4.1}{\sqrt{64}} = 0.51$$

If one standard error of the mean is equal to 0.51 visit, then 1.96 standard errors (95 percent) are equal to 1.0 visit. The students can estimate with 95 percent confidence that the population mean of expected visits is within 10.0 ± 1.0 visit, or from 9.0 to 11.0 mean visits per month. We discuss pilot tests as part of the pretest phase in Chapter 13.

Changing Confidence Intervals

The preceding estimate may not be satisfactory in two ways. First, it may not represent the degree of confidence the researchers want in the interval estimate, considering their financial risk. They might want a higher degree of confidence than the 95 percent level used here. By referring to a table of areas under the normal curve, they can find various other combinations of probability. Exhibit 14a-6 summarizes some of those more commonly used. Thus, if the students want a greater confidence in the probability of including the population mean in the interval range, they can move to a higher standard error, say, $X \pm 3\sigma_X$. Now the population mean lies somewhere between $10.0 \pm 3 (0.51)$ or from 8.47 to 11.53. With 99.73 percent confidence, we can say this interval will include the population mean.

We might wish to have an estimate that will hold for a much smaller range, for example, 10.0 ± 0.2. To secure this smaller interval range, we must either (1) accept a lower level of confidence in the results or (2) take a sample large enough to provide this smaller interval with the higher desired confidence level.

If one standard error is equal to 0.51 visit, then 0.2 visit would be equal to 0.39 standard error ($0.2/0.51 = 0.39$). Referring to a table of areas under the normal curve (Appendix C, Exhibit C-1), we find that there is a 30.3 percent chance that the true population mean lies within ± 0.39 standard error of 10.0. With a sample of 64, the sample mean would be subject to so much error variance that only 30 percent of the time could the researchers expect to find the population mean between 9.8 and 10.2. This is such a low level of confidence that the researchers would normally move to the second alternative; they would increase the sample size until they could secure the desired interval estimate and degree of confidence.

Calculating the Sample Size for Questions Involving Means

Before we compute the desired sample size for the Metro U dining club study, let's review the information we will need:

1. The *precision* desired and how to quantify it:
   a. The *confidence level* we want with our estimate.
   b. The *size of the interval estimate*.
2. The expected *dispersion in the population* for the investigative question used.
3. Whether a finite population adjustment is needed.

The researchers have selected two investigative question constructs as critical—"frequency of patronage" and "interest in joining"—because they believe both to be crucial to making the correct decision on the Metro U dining club opportunity. The first requires a point estimate, the second a proportion. By way of review, decisions needed and decisions made by Metro U researchers are summarized in Exhibit 14a-7.

>**Exhibit 14a-6** Estimates Associated with Various Confidence Levels in the Metro U Dining Club Study

Approximate Degree of Confidence	Interval Range of Dining Visits per Month
68%	μ is between 9.48 and 10.52 visits
90	μ is between 9.14 and 10.86 visits
95	μ is between 8.98 and 11.02 visits
99	μ is between 8.44 and 11.56 visits

>**Exhibit 14a-7** Metro U Sampling Design Decision on "Meal Frequency" and "Joining" Constructs

Sampling Issues	Metro U Decisions	
	"Meal Frequency" (interval, ratio data)	**"Joining"** (nominal, ordinal data)
1. The precision desired and how to quantify it:		
• The confidence researcher wants in the estimate (selected based on risk)	95% confidence ($Z = 1.96$)	95% confidence ($Z = 1.96$)
• The size of the interval estimate the researcher will accept (based on risk)	±0.5 meal per month	±0.10 (10 percent)
2. The expected range in the population for the question used to measure precision:	0 to 30 meals	0 to 100%
Measure of Central Tendency		
• Sample mean	10	
• Sample proportion of population with the given attribute being measured		30%
Measure of Dispersion		
• Standard deviation	4.1	
• Measure of sample dispersion		$pq = 0.30(0.70) = 0.21$
3. Whether a finite population adjustment should be used	No	No
4. Estimate of standard deviation of population:		
• Standard error of mean	0.5/1.96 = 0.255	
• Standard error of the proportion		0.10/1.96 = 0.051
5. Sample size calculation	See formula (p. 396)	See formula (p. 396)
6. Calculated sample size	$n = 259*$	$n = 81$

*Because both investigative questions were of interest, the researcher would use the larger of the two sample sizes calculated, $n = 259$ for the study.

Precision

With reference to precision, the 95 percent confidence level is often used, but more or less confidence may be needed in light of the risks of any given project. Similarly, the size of the interval estimate for predicting the population parameter from the sample data should be decided. When a smaller interval is selected, the researcher is saying that precision is vital, largely because inherent risks are high. For example, on a 5-point measurement scale, one-tenth of a point is a very high degree of precision in comparison to a 1-point interval. Given that a patron could eat up to 30 meals per month at the dining club (30 days times 1 meal per day), anything less than one meal per day would be asking for a high degree of precision in the Metro U study. The high risk of the Metro U study warrants the 0.5 meal precision selected.

Population Dispersion

The next factor that affects the size of the sample for a given level of precision is the population dispersion. The smaller the possible dispersion, the smaller will be the sample needed to give a representative picture of population members. If the population's number of meals ranges from 18 to 25, a smaller sample will give us an accurate estimate of the population's average meal consumption. However, with a population dispersion ranging from 0 to 30 meals consumed, a larger sample is needed for the same degree of confidence in the estimates. Since the true population dispersion of estimated meals per month eaten at Metro U dining club is unknowable, the standard deviation of the sample is used as a proxy figure. Typically, this figure is based on any of the following:

- Previous research on the topic.
- A pilot test or pretest of the data instrument among a sample drawn from the population.
- A rule of thumb (one-sixth of the range based on six standard deviations within 99.73 percent confidence).

If the range is from 0 to 30 meals, the rule-of-thumb method produces a standard deviation of 5 meals. The researchers want more precision than the rule-of-thumb method provides, so they take a pilot sample of 25 and find the standard deviation to be 4.1 meals.

Population Size

A final factor affecting the size of a random sample is the size of the population. When the size of the sample exceeds 5 percent of the population, the finite limits of the population constrain the sample size needed. A correction factor is available in that event.

The sample size is computed for the first construct, meal frequency, as follows:

$$\sigma_{\bar{X}} = \frac{s}{\sqrt{n}}$$

$$\sqrt{n} = \frac{s}{\sigma_{\bar{X}}}$$

$$n = \frac{s^2}{\sigma_{\bar{X}}}$$

$$n = \frac{(4.1)^2}{(0.255)^2}$$

$$n = 258.5 \text{ or } 259$$

where

$$\sigma_{\bar{X}} = 0.255 \ (0.51/1.96)$$

If the researchers are willing to accept a larger interval range (± 1 meal), and thus a larger amount of risk, then they can reduce the sample size to $n = 65$.

Calculating the Sample Size for Questions Involving Proportions

The second key question concerning the dining club study was What percentage of the population says it would join the dining club, based on the projected rates and services? In business, we often deal with proportion data. An example is a CNN poll that projects the percentage of people who expect to vote for or against a proposition or a candidate. This is usually reported with a margin of error of ± 5 percent.

In the Metro U study, a pretest answers this question using the same general procedure as before. But instead of the arithmetic mean, with proportions, it is p (the proportion of the population that has a given attribute)[1]—in this case, interest in joining the dining club. And instead of the standard deviation, dispersion is measured in terms of $p \times q$ (in which q is the proportion of the population not having the attribute, and $q = (1 - p)$. The measure of dispersion of the sample statistic also changes from the standard error of the mean to the standard error of the proportion σ_p.

We calculate a sample size based on these data by making the same two subjective decisions—deciding on an acceptable interval estimate and the degree of confidence. Assume that from a pilot test, 30 percent of the students and employees say they will join the dining club. We decide to estimate the true proportion in the population within 10 percentage points of this figure ($p = 0.30 \pm 0.10$). Assume further that we want to be 95 percent confident that the population parameter is within ± 0.10 of the sample proportion. The calculation of the sample size proceeds as before:

$\pm 0.10 =$ desired interval range within which the population proportion is expected (subjective decision)

$1.96\sigma_p =$ 95 percent confidence level for estimating the interval within which to expect the population proportion (subjective decision)

$\sigma_p = 0.051 =$ standard error of the proportion (0.10/1.96)

$pq =$ measure of sample dispersion (used here as an estimate of the population dispersion)

$n =$ sample size

$$\sigma_p = \sqrt{\frac{pq}{n}}$$

$$n = \frac{pq}{\sigma_p^2}$$

$$n = \frac{0.3 \times 0.7}{(0.051)^2}$$

$$n = 81$$

The sample size of 81 persons is based on an infinite population assumption. If the sample size is less than 5 percent of the population, there is little to be gained by using a finite population adjustment. The students interpreted the data found with a sample of 81 chosen randomly from the population as: We can be 95 percent confident that 30 percent of the respondents would say they would join the dining club with a margin of error of ± 10 percent.

Previously, the researchers used pilot testing to generate the variance estimate for the calculation. Suppose this is not an option. Proportions data have a feature concerning the variance that is not found with interval or ratio data. The pq ratio can never exceed 0.25. For example, if $p = 0.5$, then $q = 0.5$, and their product is 0.25. If either p or q is greater than 0.5, then their product is smaller than

0.25 (0.4 × 0.6 = 0.24, and so on). When we have no information regarding the probable *p* value, we can assume that *p* = 0.5 and solve for the sample size.

$$n = \frac{pq}{\sigma_p^2}$$

$$n = \frac{(0.50)(0.50)}{(0.51)^2}$$

$$n = \frac{0.25}{(0.051)^2}$$

$$n = 96$$

where

pq = measure of dispersion
n = sample size
σ_p = standard error of the proportion

If we use this maximum variance estimate in the dining club example, we find the sample size needs to be 96 persons in order to have an adequate sample for the question about joining the club.

When there are several investigative questions of strong interest, researchers calculate the sample size for each such variable—as we did in the Metro U study for "meal frequency" and "joining." The researcher then chooses the calculation that generates the largest sample. This ensures that all data will be collected with the necessary level of precision.

>part IV

Analysis and Presentation of Data

>chapter 15

Data Preparation and Description

>learningobjectives

After reading this chapter, you should understand...

1 The importance of editing the collected raw data to detect errors and omissions.

2 How coding is used to assign numbers and other symbols to answers and to categorize responses.

3 The use of content analysis to interpret and summarize open questions.

4 Problems with and solutions for "don't know" responses and missing data.

5 The options for data entry and manipulation.

>   ❝ The goal is to transform data into information, and information into insight. ❞

Carly Fiorina, former president and chairwoman,
Hewlett-Packard Co.

>**bringing**research**to**life

Laypeople often think that data need only to be tallied to be presented. But a trained researcher understands that data are rarely ready to be tallied after they are collected. Data entry, if it doesn't happen simultaneously with the survey process, adds days to the process, as does checking the data for accuracy. Myra Wines, MindWriter's primary contact with Henry and Associates, arrives early for a meeting she requested with Jason and interrupts a data session on another of Jason's projects. She has a vested interest in what Jason is working on, and she is about to offer Henry and Associates a new project.

"Is my being early for our meeting a problem?" asks Myra as she moves past a pile of computer printouts stacked precariously high just inside the door to Jason's office. "Might the industrious team in your outer office be studying my MindWriter Project 2 data?"

"Not yet," comments Jason as he waves Myra to an empty chair. "Just give me one second." He quickly writes two notes on Post-its and slaps one on a pencil sketch of a graph and attaches the other to a histogram. "Sammye, you want to come get these?" Jason calls to one of the team members in the outer office.

Meanwhile, Myra chooses an available chair and waits. She is here to convince Jason to take on yet another project for MindWriter. This one has a short turnaround. Turning his attention to Myra, Jason extracts a folder lying on the credenza behind him. "Actually those worker bees are new members of my staff, graduate students from the university. They're assigned to the City Center for Performing Arts project," shares Jason. "It's because of your recommendation that we got the job. I thought you knew."

"Of course I knew. I've been serving on CCPA's board for two years. Will you be presenting the preliminary analysis at the next meeting this Friday?"

"As in day after tomorrow?" asks Jason. "Only in our dreams! The preliminary analysis you see them working on is strictly for us. Although we may develop presentation charts that might be presented to the Center Board, it is just as likely that none of the material you see stacked here will end up in the report as is. We are nowhere near ready to write the client report. We just finished cleaning the data file yesterday.

This morning I ran a full set of frequencies. Jill, David, and Sammye started their preliminary analysis … uh, 90 minutes ago."

"So I guess I'll have to wait until you have something more solid to learn even a briefing on what you've found so far?" inquires Myra, smiling.

"Ah," smiles Jason in return, "you've learned H&A's process fairly well." Myra grins and then modifies her position in the chair, leaning slightly toward Jason. Just before she speaks, Jason observes, "Oh, no! You're changing into your 'It's time to get down to business' posture. So what's the new project you want to discuss … and the impossible deadline you need me to meet?"

"Just hear me out, Jason. MindWriter's LT3000 product group has decided it needs to use 'superiority in custom-designed systems' as its claim in a new ad campaign, but legal says we don't have enough data to support the claim. The ad agency we have chosen has a short window of opportunity. We need supporting data within 10 days." Myra holds up her hand to stop the objection she anticipates from Jason. "We know you don't have time to collect new primary data and analyze it in 10 days … so I brought the next best thing. I've got three boxes of miscellaneous records in my trunk …"

"Let's go see what you brought me," Jason groans good-naturedly as he unfolds himself from his chair. "Then we'll see if this project is even feasible." As he passes through the outer office, Jason motions for one of the students to follow; then in an aside to Myra he said, "Myra, meet David Chesley. You're just lucky that my new interns are all so eager that they will enjoy juggling two projects at one time."

> Introduction

Once the data begin to flow, a researcher's attention turns to data analysis. This chapter focuses on the first phases of that process, data preparation and description. **Data preparation** includes editing, coding, and data entry and is the activity that ensures the accuracy of the data and their conversion from raw form to reduced and classified forms that are more appropriate for analysis. Preparing a descriptive statistical summary is another preliminary step leading to an understanding of the collected data. It is during this step that data entry errors may be revealed and corrected. Exhibit 15-1 reflects the steps in this phase of the research process.

> Editing

The customary first step in analysis is to edit the raw data. **Editing** detects errors and omissions, corrects them when possible, and certifies that maximum data quality standards are achieved. The editor's purpose is to guarantee that data are:

- Accurate.
- Consistent with the intent of the question and other information in the survey.
- Uniformly entered.

>**Exhibit 15-1** Data Preparation in the Research Process

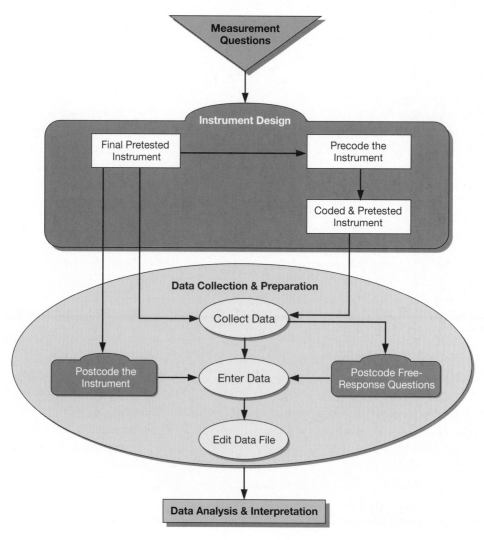

- Complete.
- Arranged to simplify coding and tabulation.

In the following question asked of adults 18 or older, one respondent checked two categories, indicating that he was a retired officer and currently serving on active duty.

Please indicate your current military status:

☑ Active duty	☐ Reserve	☑ Retired
☐ National Guard	☐ Separated	☐ Never served in the military

The editor's responsibility is to decide which of the responses is both consistent with the intent of the question or other information in the survey and most accurate for this individual participant.

Field Editing

In large projects, field editing review is a responsibility of the field supervisor. It, too, should be done soon after the data have been gathered. During the stress of data collection in a personal interview and paper-and-pencil recording in an observation, the researcher often uses ad hoc abbreviations and special symbols. Soon after the interview, experiment, or observation, the investigator should review the reporting forms. It is difficult to complete what was abbreviated or written in shorthand or noted illegibly if the entry is not caught that day. When entry gaps are present from interviews, a callback should be made rather than guessing what the respondent "probably would have said." Self-interviewing has no place in quality research.

A second important control function of the field supervisor is to validate the field results. This normally means he or she will reinterview some percentage of the respondents, at least on some questions, verifying that they have participated and that the interviewer performed adequately. Many research firms will recontact about 10 percent of the respondents in this process of data validation.

Central Editing

At this point, the data should get a thorough editing. For a small study, the use of a single editor produces maximum consistency. In large studies, editing tasks should be allocated so that each editor deals with one entire section. Although the latter approach will not identify inconsistencies between answers in different sections, the problem can be handled by identifying questions in different sections that might point to possible inconsistency and having one editor check the data generated by these questions.

Sometimes it is obvious that an entry is incorrect—for example, when data clearly specify time in days (e.g., 13) when it was requested in weeks (you expect a number of 4 or less)—or is entered in the wrong place. When replies are inappropriate or missing, the editor can sometimes detect the proper answer by reviewing the other information in the data set. This practice, however, should be limited to the few cases where it is obvious what the correct answer is. It may be better to contact the respondent for correct information, if time and budget allow. Another alternative is for the editor to strike out the answer if it is inappropriate. Here an editing entry of "no answer" or "unknown" is called for.

Another problem that editing can detect concerns faking an interview that never took place. This "armchair interviewing" is difficult to spot, but the editor is in the best position to do so. One approach is to check responses to open-ended questions. These are most difficult to fake. Distinctive response patterns in other questions will often emerge if data falsification is occurring. To uncover this, the editor must analyze as a set the instruments used by each interviewer.

Here are some useful rules to guide editors in their work:

- Be familiar with instructions given to interviewers and coders.
- Do not destroy, erase, or make illegible the original entry by the interviewer; original entries should remain legible.
- Make all editing entries on an instrument in some distinctive color and in a standardized form.
- Initial all answers changed or supplied.
- Place initials and date of editing on each instrument completed.

How Dirty Is the Dirty Data Problem?

Dirty data, data that is "misleading, incorrect, without generalized formatting, contains spelling or punctuation errors, is input incorrectly, or is falsified by the respondent"[a] is a major business problem. In this era of online data collection, data becomes dirty when duplicate data is created, like when a respondent "accidentally double clicks the 'submit' button on forms [or surveys], or [in a web click-through study] revisits a page which has 'expired' and refreshes it."[b] Data becomes dirty when it is outdated, like when a prospective customer moves or changes his or her phone number or e-mail address. Dirty data can also result when there is a "disconnect between data in computer systems and data embedded in paper or non-machine-readable electronic documents."[c]

Where might dirty data be a problem? Try your doctor's office when she is trying to diagnose your illness or condition. Or your favorite restaurant is trying to decide what item to drop from its menu. Or a manufacturer is trying to identify machine maintenance practices creating faulty parts. Or a human relations manager trying to distinguish which training regimen is having the most positive impact on the organization's bottom line. Craig Focardi, writing in *Mortgage Banking,* describes lenders as subsisting on a "diet of missing, incomplete, and inaccurate data elements for loan origination." He likens it to a "water-bucket brigade, where water is lost as water buckets pass from hand to hand."[d] He believes that poor-quality data was a contributing cause to the current mortgage liquidity crisis in the United States. "During the summer of 2007, subprime mortgage funding liquidity disappeared in part because subprime lenders and mortgage investors lacked the data to accurately reassess and reprice credit, collateral, and prepayment risks."

To tackle the data-quality issue it helps to categorize dirty data problems into four categories: invalid data, incomplete data, inconsistent data, and incorrect data.[e] *Invalid data* is data that contains entry errors, like a nonexistent postal code. *Incomplete data* is missing data that is needed to make a decision; deleting data from one database due to a disk crash or losing the link between databases in a data warehouse can create incomplete data, as can having data become a battleground in an internal turf war—"everyone clinging to [its] own little piece of the data store, nobody willing to share."[f] *Inconsistent data* is often seen only from the big-picture perspective; data from one database might make little or no sense when seen from the perspective of data in a separate but connected database. This might be due to data protocols, like naming a corporation: IBM could be entered as IBM, I.B.M., or International Business Machines in

the "supplier" field of multiple databases, preventing those databases from being correctly merged or preventing a researcher from discovering patterns relating to each supplier. *Incorrect data* is just wrong; it most often occurs when data is lost, or falsified, or when data, like a customer order, is not entered at all.

The basic steps for dealing with bad data are the same: detecting it and removing or correcting it. But some experts suggest a third step: determining how much error to tolerate.[g] If the bad data exists in critical areas, like patient blood test results or a firm's accounts receivables, it is likely worth the organization's time and effort to correct it. If the dirty data is in the notes section of a salesman's contact management file, it might not warrant such time and effort. The problem has gotten so bad that some companies have hired data stewards—a person charged with keeping it's company's data clean.[h]

According to research and advisory firm Gartner Inc., 25 percent of critical data in the world's top 1000 companies is and will continue to be flawed.[i] Other estimates suggest that number could be as high as 30 percent.[j] Dun & Bradstreet Corp., which helps companies clean their supplier files, estimates most companies show 20 percent duplicate supplier records.[k] A PricewaterhouseCoopers study indicated that poor data management cost global businesses "more than $1.4 billion per year in billing, accounting and inventory snafus."[l] The distinguished British Computer Society's Roger Needham Award–winning professor, Wenfei Fan, estimates that "dirty data costs U.S. businesses as much as $611 billion—and U.S. customers as much as $2.5 billion a year."[m]

Most experts agree that a first step is to establish data protocols, simplistic rules for how data is entered, like what items (pants, slacks, or trousers) are called or how dates are entered (March 20, 2010 or 20 March 10). Other suggestions include backing up data regularly, controlling access to data via security mechanisms, designing user interfaces that prevent the input of invalid data, and using error detection and correction software when transmitting data.[n] The president of Tigris Consulting adds, "you need to be very careful when pulling data from different systems together to make sure that it's the right field name, the right format and that semantically, [the data] means what you want it to mean."[o] But most data experts believe the situation won't improve until top management makes clean data a priority.

www.tigris.com; www.gartner.com; www.dnb.com;
www.pwc.com; www.bcs.org; www.mortgagebankingmagazine.com

>**snap**shot

CBS: Some Labs Are Extraordinary

Visitors to Las Vegas have an opportunity to determine the direction of CBS programming by visiting the CBS Television City Research Center in the MGM Grand Hotel and Casino. According to Andrew Wing, president of ACNielsen Entertainment, what makes Las Vegas an ideal location for a research lab is the cross section of the American population and the large number of international citizens among its 36 million visitors each year. In a typical screening with 250 people, individuals represent more than 40 states and every conceivable lifestyle. Participants watch a 30- to 45-minute segment of a new or proposed program, without commercial interruptions, followed by a survey process lasting 15 minutes. Each seat is equipped with a computer touch screen linked to ACNielsen Entertainment's proprietary Nielsen ReelResearch Internet site. Participants share feedback on the show and personal demographics in real time, while network executives observe participants and their feedback from remote offices around the country. The facility, designed by GES, also provides focus group capabilities, used for follow-up interviews along with other research initiatives. Participants are compensated with a chance to win a home theater system, as well as a $10 coupon that they may redeem on program-logo T-shirts, caps, pins, key chains, and even computer software in the CBS Television City store. Arising out of a temporary test conducted in 1991, the research facility today operates 12 hours per day year-round. So on your next visit to the City of Lights, when the slots or big-name entertainers lose appeal, entertain yourself with research.

What are some of the advantages to having touch-screen data entry?

www.nielsen.com; www.viad.com

> Coding

Coding involves assigning numbers or other symbols to answers so that the responses can be grouped into a limited number of categories. In coding, *categories* are the partitions of a data set of a given variable (e.g., if the variable is *gender,* the partitions are *male* and *female*). *Categorization* is the process of using rules to partition a body of data. Both closed- and open-response questions must be coded.

The categorization of data sacrifices some data detail but is necessary for efficient analysis. Most statistical and banner/table software programs work more efficiently in the *numeric* mode. Instead of entering the word *male* or *female* in response to a question that asks for the identification of one's gender, we would use numeric codes (e.g., 0 for male and 1 for female). Numeric coding simplifies the researcher's task in converting a nominal variable, like gender, to a "dummy variable," a topic we discuss in Chapter 19. Statistical software also can use alphanumeric codes, as when we use M and F, or other letters, in combination with numbers and symbols for gender.

Codebook Construction

A **codebook,** or *coding scheme,* contains each variable in the study and specifies the application of coding rules to the variable. It is used by the researcher or research staff to promote more accurate and more efficient data entry. It is also the definitive source for locating the positions of variables in the data file during analysis. In many statistical programs, the coding scheme is integral to the data file. Most codebooks—computerized or not—contain the question number, variable name, location of the variable's code on the input medium (e.g., spreadsheet or SPSS data file), descriptors for the response options, and whether the variable is alphabetic or numeric. An example of a paper-based codebook is shown in Exhibit 15-2. Pilot testing of an instrument provides sufficient information about the variables to prepare a codebook. A preliminary codebook used with pilot data may reveal coding problems that will need to be corrected before the data for the final study are collected and processed.

>Exhibit 15-2 Sample Codebook of Questionnaire Items

Question	Variable Number	Code Description	Variable Name
_____	1	Record number	RECNUM
_____	2	Respondent number	RESID
1	3	5 digit zip code 99999 = Missing	ZIP
2	4	2 digit birth year 99 = Missing	BIRTH
3	5	Gender 1 = Male 2 = Female 9 = Missing	GENDER
4	6	Marital status 1 = Married 2 = Widow(er) 3 = Divorced 4 = Separated 5 = Never married 9 = Missing	MARITAL
5	7	Own–Rent 1 = Own 2 = Rent 3 = Provided 9 = Missing	HOUSING
6		Reason for purchase 1 = Mentioned 0 = Not mentioned	
	8	Bought home	HOME
	9	Birth of child	BIRTHCHD
	10	Death of relative or friend	DEATH
	11	Promoted	PROMO
	12	Changed job/career	CHGJOB
	13	Paid college expenses	COLLEXP
	14	Acquired assets	ASSETS
	15	Retired	RETIRED
	16	Changed marital status	CHGMAR
	17	Started business	STARTBUS
	18	Expanded business	EXPBUS
	19	Parent's influence	PARENT
	20	Contacted by agent	AGENT
	21	Other	OTHER

Coding Closed Questions

The responses to closed questions include scaled items for which answers can be anticipated. Closed questions are favored by researchers over open-ended questions for their efficiency and specificity. They are easier to code, record, and analyze. When codes are established in the instrument design phase of the research process, it is possible to precode the questionnaire during the design stage. With computerized survey design, and computer-assisted, computer-administered, or online collection of data, precoding is necessary as the software tallies data as they are collected. **Precoding** is particularly helpful for manual data entry (e.g., from mail or self-administered surveys) because it makes the intermediate step of completing a *data entry coding sheet* unnecessary. With a precoded

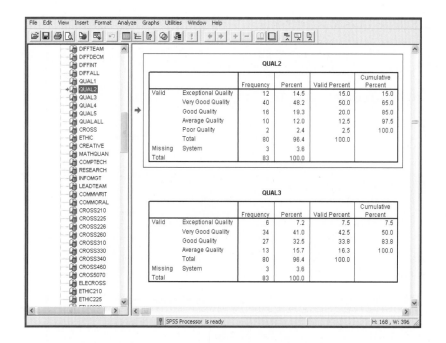

The researcher here requested a frequency printout of all variables when 83 cases had been entered. SPSS presents them sequentially in one document. The left frame indicates all the variables included in this particular output file. Both variables Qual2 and Qual3 indicate 3 missing cases. This would be a cautionary flag to a good researcher. During editing the researcher would want to verify that these are true instances where participants did not rate the quality of both objects, rather than data entry errors.
www.spss.com

instrument, the codes for variable categories are accessible directly from the questionnaire. A participant, interviewer, field supervisor, or researcher (depending on the data collection method) is able to assign the appropriate code on the instrument by checking, circling, or printing it in the proper coding location.

Exhibit 15-3 shows questions in the sample codebook. When precoding is used, editing precedes data processing. Note question 4, in which the respondent may choose between five categories of marital status and enter the number of the item best representing present status in the coding portion of the questionnaire. This code is later transferred to an input medium for analysis.

Coding Open-Ended Questions

One of the primary reasons for using open-ended questions is that insufficient information or lack of a hypothesis may prohibit preparing response categories in advance. Researchers are forced to categorize responses after the data are collected. Other reasons for using open-ended responses include the need to measure sensitive or disapproved behavior, discover salience or importance, or encourage natural modes of expression.[1] Also, it may be easier and more efficient for the participant to write in a known short answer rather than read through a long list of options. Whatever the reason for their use, analyzing enormous volumes of open-ended questions slows the analysis process and increases the opportunity for error. The variety of answers to a single question can be staggering, hampering postcollection categorization. Even when categories are anticipated and precoded for open-ended questions, once data are collected, researchers may find it useful to reassess the predetermined categories. One example is a 7-point scale in which the researcher offered the participant three levels of agreement, three levels of disagreement, and one neutral position. Once the data are collected, if these finer nuances of agreement do not materialize, the editor may choose to recategorize the data into three levels: one level of agreement, one level of disagreement, and one neutral position.

Exhibit 15-3, question 6, illustrates the use of an open-ended question for which advance knowledge of response options was not available. The answer to "What prompted you to purchase your most recent life insurance policy?" was to be filled in by the participant as a short-answer essay. After preliminary evaluation, response categories (shown in the codebook, Exhibit 15-2) were created for that item.

>Exhibit 15-3 Sample Questionnaire Items

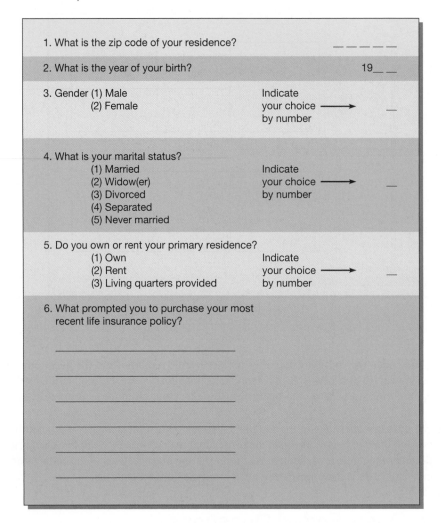

Coding Rules

Four rules guide the pre- and postcoding and categorization of a data set. The categories within a single variable should be:

- Appropriate to the research problem and purpose.
- Exhaustive.
- Mutually exclusive.
- Derived from one classification dimension.

Researchers address these issues when developing or choosing each specific measurement question. One of the purposes of pilot testing of any measurement instrument is to identify and anticipate categorization issues.

Appropriateness

Appropriateness is determined at two levels: (1) the best partitioning of the data for testing hypotheses and showing relationships and (2) the availability of comparison data. For example, when actual age is obtained (ratio scale), the editor may decide to group data by age ranges to simplify pattern discovery within the data. The number of age groups and breadth of each range, as well as the endpoints in each range, should be determined by comparison data—for example, U.S. census age ranges, a customer database that includes age ranges, or the age data available from Fox TV used for making an advertising media buy.

Exhaustiveness

Researchers often add an "other" option to a measurement question because they know they cannot anticipate all possible answers. A large number of "other" responses, however, suggests the measurement scale the researcher designed did not anticipate the full range of information. The editor must determine if "other" responses appropriately fit into established categories, if new categories must be added, if "other" data will be ignored, or if some combination of these actions will be taken.

Although the exhaustiveness requirement for a single variable may be obvious, a second aspect is less apparent. Does one set of categories—often determined before the data are collected—fully capture all the information in the data? For example, responses to an open-ended question about family economic prospects for the next year may originally be categorized only in terms of being "optimistic" or "pessimistic." It may also be enlightening to classify responses in terms of other concepts such as the precise focus of these expectations (income or jobs) and variations in responses between family heads and others in the family.

Mutual Exclusivity

Another important rule when adding categories or realigning categories is that category components should be mutually exclusive. This standard is met when a specific answer can be placed in one and only one cell in a category set. For example, in a survey, assume that you asked participants for their occupation. One editor's categorization scheme might include (1) professional, (2) managerial, (3) sales, (4) clerical, (5) crafts, (6) operatives, and (7) unemployed. As an editor, how would you code a participant's answer that specified "salesperson at Gap and full-time student" or maybe "elementary teacher and tax preparer"? According to census data, it is not unusual for adults in our society to have more than one job. Here, operational definitions of the occupations categorized as "professional," "managerial," and "sales" should help clarify the situation. But the editor facing this situation also would need to determine how the second-occupation data are handled. One option would be to add a second-occupation field to the data set; another would be to develop distinct codes for each unique multiple-occupation combination.

Single Dimension

The problem of how to handle an occupation entry like "unemployed salesperson" brings up a fourth rule of category design. The need for a category set to follow a single classificatory principle means every option in the category set is defined in terms of one concept or construct. Returning to the occupation example, the person in the study might be both a salesperson and unemployed. The "salesperson" label expresses the concept *occupation type;* the response "unemployed" is another dimension concerned with *current employment status* without regard to the respondent's normal occupation. When a category set encompasses more than one dimension, the editor may choose to split the dimensions and develop an additional data field; "occupation" now becomes two variables: "occupation type" and "employment status."

Using Content Analysis for Open Questions

Increasingly text-based responses to open-ended measurement questions are analyzed with content analysis software. **Content analysis** measures the semantic content or the *what* aspect of a message. Its breadth makes it a flexible and wide-ranging tool that may be used as a stand-alone methodology or as a problem-specific technique. Trend-watching organizations like the BrainReserve, the Naisbitt Group, SRI International, and Inferential Focus use variations on content analysis for selected projects, often spotting changes from newspaper or magazine articles before they can be confirmed statistically. The Naisbitt Group's content analysis of 2 million local newspaper articles compiled over a 12-year period resulted in the publication of *Megatrends.*

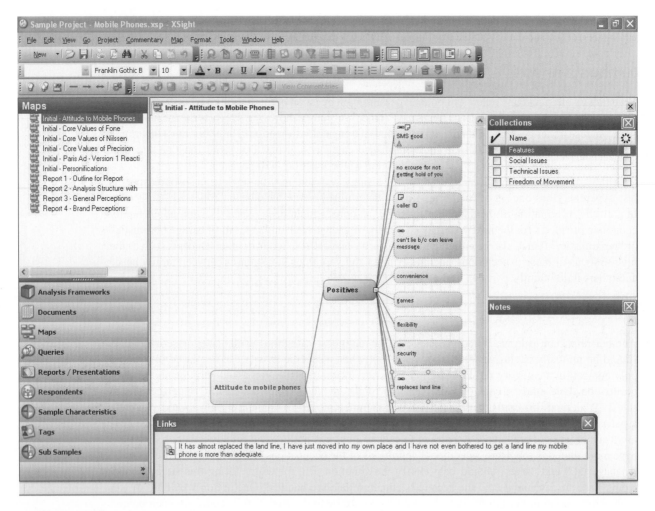

>picprofile

QSR International has released version two of its qualitative research software program XSight. Based on Microsoft XP guidelines and with tools to test theories, map your analysis, and report findings, XSight was originally designed as a sophisticated and portable workspace for market researchers. Today the program is used in a range of other industries that deal with unstructured information, including HR, law, and tourism. This screen demonstrates XSight's new "maps" function. Just like a flip chart or white board, "maps" give you the space to organize your thoughts and represent the connections between them visually. What makes XSight "maps" unique is that they can be underpinned with live links to supporting information, such as participant quotes. **www.qsrinternational.com**

Types of Content

Content analysis has been described as "a research technique for the objective, systematic, and quantitative description of the manifest content of a communication."[2] Because this definition is sometimes confused with simply counting obvious message aspects such as words or attributes, more recent interpretations have broadened the definition to include latent as well as manifest content, the symbolic meaning of messages, and qualitative analysis. One author states:

> In any single written message, one can count letters, words, or sentences. One can categorize phrases, describe the logical structure of expressions, ascertain associations, connotations, denotations, elocutionary forces, and one can also offer psychiatric, sociological, or political interpretations. All of these may be simultaneously valid. In short, a message may convey a multitude of contents even to a single receiver.[3]

Content analysis follows a systematic process for coding and drawing inferences from texts. It starts by determining which units of data will be analyzed. In written or verbal texts, data units are of four types: syntactical, referential, propositional, or thematic. Each unit type is the basis for coding texts into mutually exclusive categories in our search for meaning.

- *Syntactical* units can be words, phrases, sentences, or paragraphs; words are the smallest and most reliable data units to analyze. Although we can certainly count these units, we are more interested in the meaning their use reveals. In content analysis we might determine the words that are most commonly used to describe product A versus its competitor, product B. We ask, Are these descriptions for product A more likely to lead to favorable opinions and thus to preference and ultimately selection, compared to the descriptions used for product B?

- *Referential* units are *described* by words, phrases, and sentences; they may be objects, events, persons, and so forth, to which a verbal or textual expression refers. Participants may refer to a product as a "classic," a "power performer," or "ranked first in safety"—each word or phrase may be used to describe different objects, and it is the object that the researcher codes and analyzes in relation to the phrase.

- *Propositional* units are *assertions* about an object, event, person, and so on. For example, a researcher assessing advertising for magazine subscriptions might conclude, "Subscribers who respond to offer A will save $15 over the single issue rate." It is the assertion of savings that is attached to the text of this particular ad claim.

- *Thematic* units are *topics* contained within (and across) texts; they represent higher-level abstractions inferred from the text and its context. The responses to an open-ended question about purchase behavior may reflect a temporal theme: the past ("I never purchased an alternative brand before you changed the package"), the present ("I really like the new packaging"), or the future ("I would buy the product more often if it came in more flavors"). We could also look at the comments as relating to the themes or topics of "packaging" versus a product characteristic, "flavors."

> **55**
> The percent of white-collar workers who answer work-related calls or e-mail after work hours.

As with all other research methodologies, the analytical use of content analysis is influenced by decisions made prior to data collection. Content analysis guards against selective perception of the content, provides for the rigorous application of reliability and validity criteria, and is amenable to computerization.

What Content Is Analyzed?

Content analysis may be used to analyze written, audio, or video data from experiments, observations, surveys, and secondary data studies. The obvious data to be content-analyzed include transcripts of focus groups, transcripts of interviews, and open-ended survey responses. But researchers also use content analysis on advertisements, promotional brochures, press releases, speeches, Web pages, historical documents, and conference proceedings, as well as magazine and newspaper articles. In competitive intelligence and the marketing of political candidates content analysis is a primary methodology.

Example

Let's look at an informal application of content analysis to a problematic open question. In this example, which we are processing without the use of content analysis software, suppose employees in the sales department of a manufacturing firm are asked, "How might company–customer relations be improved?" A sample of the responses yields the following:

- We should treat the customer with more respect.
- We should stop trying to speed up the sales process when the customer has expressed objections or concerns.

>Exhibit 15-4 Open Question Coding Example (before revision)

Question: "How can company–customer relations be improved?"

Locus of Responsibility	Mentioned	Not Mentioned
A. Company	_____	_____
B. Customer	_____	_____
C. Joint Company-Customer	_____	_____
F. Other	_____	_____

- We should have software that permits real-time tracking of a customer's order.
- Our laptops are outdated. We can't work with the latest software or access information quickly when we are in the field.
- My [the sales department] manager is rude with customers when he gets calls while I'm in the field. He should be transferred or fired.
- Management should stop pressuring us to meet sales quotas when our customers have restricted their open-to-buy status.

The first step in analysis requires that the units selected or developed help answer the research question. In our example, the research question is concerned with learning who or what the sales force thinks is a source for improving company–customer relations. The first pass through the data produces a few general categories in one concept dimension: source of responsibility, shown in Exhibit 15-4. These categories are mutually exclusive. The use of "other" makes the category set exhaustive. If, however, many of the sample participants suggested the need for action by other parties—for example, the government or a trade association—then including all those responses in the "other" category would ignore much of the richness of the data. As with coding schemes for numerical responses, category choices are very important.

Since responses to this type of question often suggest specific actions, the second evaluation of the data uses propositional units. If we used only the set of categories in Exhibit 15-4, the analysis would omit a considerable amount of information. The second analysis produces categories for action planning:

- Human relations.
- Technology.
- Training.
- Strategic planning.
- Other action areas.
- No action area identified.

How can we categorize a response suggesting a combined training-technology process? Exhibit 15-5 illustrates a combination of alternatives. Taking the categories of the first list of the action areas makes it possible to get an accurate frequency count of the joint classification possibilities for this question.

Using available software, the researcher can spend much less time coding open-ended responses and capturing categories. Software also eliminates the high cost of sending responses to outside coding firms. What used to take a coding staff several days may now be done in a few hours.

Content analysis software applies statistical algorithms to open-ended question responses. This permits stemming, aliasing, and exclusion processes. *Stemming* uses derivations of common root words to create aliases (e.g., using *searching, searches, searched,* for *search*). *Aliasing* searches for synonyms (*wise* or *smart* for *intelligent*). *Exclusion* filters out trivial words (*be, is, the, of*) in the search for meaning.[4]

>**Exhibit 15-5** Open Question Coding (after revision)

Question: "How can company–customer relations be improved?"

Locus of Responsibility	Frequency (*n* = 100)
A. Management	
1. Sales manager	10
2. Sales process	20
3. Other	7
5. No action area identified	3
B. Salesperson	
1. Training	15
C. Customer	
1. Buying processes	12
2. Other	8
3. No action area identified	5
D. Environmental conditions	
E. Technology	20
F. Other	

When you are using menu-driven programs, an autocategorization option creates manageable categories by clustering terms that occur together throughout the textual data set. Then, with a few keystrokes, you can modify categorization parameters and refine your results. Once your categories are consistent with the research and investigative questions, you select what you want to export to a data file or in tab-delimited format. The output, in the form of tables and plots, serves as modules for your final report. Exhibit 15-6 shows a plot produced by a content analysis of the MindWriter complaints data. The distances between pairs of terms reveal how likely it is that the terms occur together, and the colors represent categories.

"Don't Know" Responses

The **"don't know" (DK) response** presents special problems for data preparation. When the DK response group is small, it is not troublesome. But there are times when it is of major concern, and it may even be the most frequent response received. Does this mean the question that elicited this response is useless? The answer is, It all depends. Most DK answers fall into two categories.[5] First, there is the legitimate DK response when the respondent does not know the answer. This response meets our research objectives; we expect DK responses and consider them to be useful.

In the second situation, a DK reply illustrates the researcher's failure to get the appropriate information. Consider the following illustrative questions:

1. Who developed the Managerial Grid concept?
2. Do you believe the new president's fiscal policy is sound?
3. Do you like your present job?
4. Which of the various brands of chewing gum do you believe has the best quality?
5. How often each year do you go to the movies?

>Exhibit 15-6 Proximity Plot of MindWriter Customer Complaints

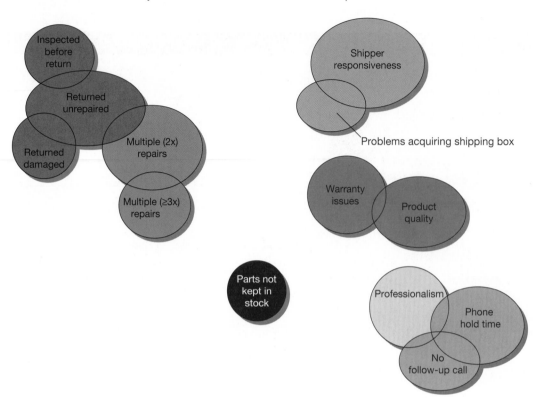

It is reasonable to expect that some legitimate DK responses will be made to each of these questions. In the first question, the respondents are asked for a level of information that they often will not have. There seems to be little reason to withhold a correct answer if known. Thus, most DK answers to this question should be considered as legitimate. A DK response to the second question presents a different problem. It is not immediately clear whether the respondent is ignorant of the president's fiscal policy or knows the policy but has not made a judgment about it. The researchers should have asked two questions: In the first, they would have determined the respondent's level of awareness of fiscal policy. If the interviewee passed the awareness test, then a second question would have secured judgment on fiscal policy.

In the remaining three questions, DK responses are more likely to be a failure of the questioning process, although some will surely be legitimate. The respondent may be reluctant to give the information. A DK response to question 3 may be a way of saying, "I do not want to answer that question." Question 4 might also elicit a DK response in which the reply translates to "This is too unimportant to talk about." In question 5, the respondents are being asked to do some calculation about a topic to which they may attach little importance. Now the DK may mean "I do not want to do that work for something of so little consequence."

Dealing with Undesired DK Responses

The best way to deal with undesired DK answers is to design better measurement questions. Researchers should identify the questions for which a DK response is unsatisfactory and design around it. Interviewers, however, often inherit this problem and must deal with it in the field. Several actions are then possible. First, good interviewer–respondent rapport will motivate respondents to provide more usable answers. When interviewers recognize an evasive DK response, they can repeat the question or probe for a more definite answer. The interviewer may also record verbatim any elaboration by the respondent and pass the problem on to the editor.

>**Exhibit 15-7** Handling "Don't Know" Responses

Question: Do you have a productive relationship with your present salesperson?

Years of Purchasing	Yes	No	Don't Know
Less than 1 year	10%	40%	38%
1–3 years	30	30	32
4 years or more	60	30	30
Total	100%	100%	100%
	n = 650	*n* = 150	*n* = 200

If the editor finds many undesired responses, little can be done unless the verbatim comments can be interpreted. Understanding the real meaning relies on clues from the respondent's answers to other questions. One way to do this is to estimate the allocation of DK answers from other data in the questionnaire. The pattern of responses may parallel income, education, or experience levels. Suppose a question concerning whether customers like their present salesperson elicits the answers in Exhibit 15-7. The correlation between years of purchasing and the "don't know" answers and the "no" answers suggests that most of the "don't knows" are disguised "no" answers.

There are several ways to handle "don't know" responses in the tabulations. If there are only a few, it does not make much difference how they are handled, but they will probably be kept as a separate category. If the DK response is legitimate, it should remain as a separate reply category. When we are not sure how to treat it, we should keep it as a separate reporting category and let the research sponsor make the decision.

Missing Data

Missing data are information from a participant or case that is not available for one or more variables of interest. In survey studies, missing data typically occur when participants accidentally skip, refuse to answer, or do not know the answer to an item on the questionnaire. In longitudinal studies, missing data may result from participants dropping out of the study, or being absent for one or more data collection periods. Missing data also occur due to researcher error, corrupted data files, and changes in the research or instrument design after data were collected from some participants, such as when variables are dropped or added. The strategy for handling missing data consists of a two-step process: the researcher first explores the pattern of missing data to determine the mechanism for *missingness* (the probability that a value is missing rather than observed) and then selects a missing-data technique.

Examine the sample distribution of variables from the MindWriter dataset shown in Exhibit 15-8. These data were collected on a 5-point interval scale. There are no missing data in variable 1A, although it is apparent that a range of 6 and a maximum value of 7 invalidate the calculated mean or average score. Variables 1B and 2B have one case missing but values that are within range. Variable 2A is missing four cases, or 27 percent of its data points. The last variable, 2C, has a range of 6, two missing values, and three values coded as "9." A "9" is often used as a DK or missing-value code when the scale has a range of less than 9 points. In this case both blanks and 9s are present—a coding concern. Notice that the fifth respondent answered only two of the five questions and the second respondent had two miscoded answers and one missing value. Finally, using descriptive indexes of shape, discussed in Appendix 15a, you can find three variables that depart from the symmetry of the normal distribution. They are skewed (or pulled) to the left by a disproportionately small number of 1s and 2s. And one variable's distribution is peaked beyond normal dimensions. We have just used the minimum and maximum values, the range, and the mean and have already discovered errors in coding, problems with respondent answer patterns, and missing cases.

>Exhibit 15-8 MindWriter Data Set: Missing and Out-of-Range Data

Case	1A	1B	2A	2B	2C
1	5.0	5.0	5.0	5.0	9.0
2	7.0	3.0		4.0	9.0
3	5.0	5.0	5.0	5.0	5.0
4	5.0	5.0	4.0		
5	1.0			2.0	
6	5.0	5.0	5.0	5.0	9.0
7	5.0	5.0	5.0	5.0	5.0
8	4.0	3.0	3.0	3.0	3.0
9	4.0	4.0	5.0	5.0	5.0
10	4.0	5.0		4.0	5.0
11	2.0	5.0	4.0	4.0	5.0
12	6.0	4.0	3.0	3.0	4.0
13	5.0	5.0		3.0	5.0
14	5.0	5.0	5.0	5.0	5.0
15	5.0	4.0	5.0	5.0	4.0
Valid	15	14	11	14	13
Missing	0	1	4	1	2
Mean	4.53	4.50	4.45	4.14	5.61
Range	6	2	2	3	6
Minimum	1	3	3	2	3
Maximum	7	5	5	5	9

Mechanisms for Dealing with Missing Data

By knowing what caused the data to be missing, the researcher can select the appropriate missing-data technique and thus avoid introducing bias in subsequent analysis. There are three basic types of missing data:

- Data missing completely at random (MCAR)—the probability that a particular variable is missing is NOT dependent on the variable itself and is NOT dependent on another variable in the data set (e.g., a participant inadvertently skips a question).
- Data missing at random (MAR)—the probability that a particular variable is missing is NOT dependent on the variable itself but is dependent on another variable in the data set (e.g., the answer to the first question of a branched-question set might cause missing data to the second question within the branched-question set).
- Data missing but not missing at random (NMAR)—when missing data are not predictable from other variables in the data set.

Three techniques are used to salvage data sets with missing data:

- *Listwise deletion*—cases with missing data on one variable are deleted from the sample for all analyses of that variable.

- *Pairwise deletion*—missing data are estimated using all cases that have data for each variable or pair of variables; the estimation replaces the missing data.
- *Predictive replacement*—missing data are predicted from observed values on another variable; the observed value is used to replace the missing data.

Listwise deletion is the default option for MCAR and is used by most statistical packages like SPSS and SAS. No bias is introduced because only fully complete cases are used as a sample for the variable. However, if data are MAR, not MCAR, then bias may be introduced, especially if a large number of cases are omitted from the sample. For example, in a survey if men were more likely than women to be responsible for missing data on the variable relating to training preference, then deleting men from the sample biases any analysis of training preferences toward women's training preference.

Pairwise deletion assumes data are MCAR. This technique, although used historically by linear models, has the potential for introducing bias.

Predictive replacement assumes data are MAR. One common option available on most statistical packages is the use of a mean or other central tendency score as the replacement for the missing data. This practice reduces the variability of the data, which can introduce bias.

When data are NMAR, the missing data are factored into the analysis as a separate category of data on that variable.

> Data Entry

Data entry converts information gathered by secondary or primary methods to a medium for viewing and manipulation. Keyboarding remains a mainstay for researchers who need to create a data file immediately and store it in a minimal space on a variety of media. However, researchers have profited from more efficient ways of speeding up the research process, especially from bar coding and optical character and mark recognition.

Alternative Data Entry Formats

Keyboarding

A full-screen editor, with which an entire data file can be edited or browsed, is a viable means of data entry for statistical packages like SPSS or SAS. SPSS offers several data entry products, including Data Entry Builder™, which enables the development of forms and surveys, and Data Entry Station™, which gives centralized entry staff, such as telephone interviewers or online participants, access to the survey. Both SAS and SPSS offer software that effortlessly accesses data from databases, spreadsheets, data warehouses, or data marts.

Database Development For large projects, database programs serve as valuable data entry devices. A **database** is a collection of data organized for computerized retrieval. Programs allow users to define data fields and link files so that storage, retrieval, and updating are simplified. The relationship between *data fields, data records, files,* and *databases* is illustrated in Exhibit 15-9. A company's orders serve as an example of a database. Ordering information may be kept in several files: salesperson's customer files, customer financial records, order production records, and order shipping documentation. The data are separated so that authorized people can see only those parts pertinent to their needs. However, the files may be linked so that when, say, a customer changes his or her shipping address, the change is entered once and all relevant files are updated. Another database entry option is e-mail data capture. It has become popular with those using e-mail-delivered surveys. The e-mail survey can be delivered to a specific respondent whose e-mail address is known. Questions are completed on the screen, returned via e-mail, and incorporated into a database.[6] An intranet can also capture data. When participants linked by a network take an online survey by completing a database form, the data are captured in a database in a network server for later or real-time analysis.[7] ID and password requirements can keep unwanted participants from skewing the results of an online survey.

>Exhibit 15-9 Data Fields, Records, Files, and Databases

Data fields represent single elements of information (e.g., an answer to a particular question) from all participants in a study. Data fields can contain numeric, alphabetic, or symbolic information. A **data record** is a set of data fields that are related to one case or participant (e.g., the responses to one completed survey). Records represent rows in a data file or spreadsheet program worksheet. **Data files** are sets of records (e.g., responses from all participants in a single study) that are grouped together for storage on diskettes, disks, tapes, CD-ROM, or optical disks. *Databases* are made up of one or more data files that are interrelated. A database might contain all customer survey information collected quarterly for the past 10 years.

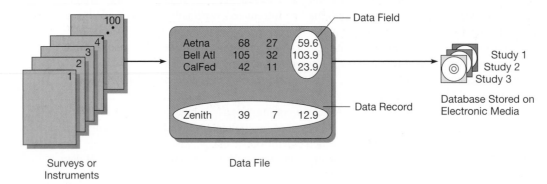

Researchers consider database entry when they have large amounts of potentially linked data that will be retrieved and tabulated in different ways over time. Another application of a database program is as a "front-end" entry mechanism. A telephone interviewer may ask the question "How many children live in your household?" The computer's software has been programmed to accept any answer between 0 and 20. If a "P" is accidentally struck, the program will not accept the answer and will return the interviewer to the question. With a precoded online instrument, some of the editing previously discussed is done by the program. In addition, the program can be set for automatic conditional branching. In the example, an answer of 1 or greater causes the program to prompt the questioner to ask the ages of the children. A 0 causes the age question to be automatically skipped. Although this option is available whenever interactive computing is used, front-end processing is typically done within the database design. The database will then store the data in a set of linked files that allow the data to be easily sorted. Descriptive statistics and tables—the first steps in exploring data—are readily generated from within the database.

Spreadsheet Spreadsheets are a specialized type of database for data that need organizing, tabulating, and simple statistics. They also offer some database management, graphics, and presentation capabilities. Data entry on a **spreadsheet** uses numbered rows and lettered columns with a matrix of thousands of cells into which an entry may be placed. Spreadsheets allow you to type numbers, formulas, and text into appropriate cells. Many statistics programs for personal computers and also charting and graphics applications have data editors similar to the Excel spreadsheet format shown in Exhibit 15-10. This is a convenient and flexible means for entering and viewing data.

Optical Recognition

If you use a PC image scanner, you probably are familiar with **optical character recognition (OCR)** programs that transfer printed text into computer files in order to edit and use it without retyping. There are other related applications. **Optical scanning** of instruments—the choice of testing services—is efficient for researchers. Examinees darken small circles, ellipses, or spaces between sets of parallel lines to indicate their answers. A more flexible format, **optical mark recognition (OMR)** uses a spreadsheet-style interface to read and process user-created forms. Optical scanners process the marked-sensed questionnaires and store the answers in a file. This method, most often associated with standardized and preprinted forms, has been adopted by researchers for data entry and preprocessing due to its speed (10 times faster than keyboarding), cost savings on data entry, convenience in charting and reporting data, and improved accuracy. It reduces the number of times data are handled, thereby reducing the number of errors that are introduced.

>Exhibit 15-10 Data Entry Using Spreadsheets

Each row is a record (a single participant's responses). Each column is a variable measured in the survey. In this survey, questions 1, 3, and 5 are nominal variables that have two response categories. Question 6 uses multiple columns because it is a multipart rating question using a 1-to-5 scale. This is a typical way of coding variables in a spreadsheet before they are imported by SPSS (assuming you are using a spreadsheet instead of the SPSS Data Editor to start your study). Note that each participant is assigned an identification number (case ID). After running preliminary frequencies, having a case ID data field enables you to quickly find and correct suspect data like odd value codes or missing cases.

Case ID	Q1	Q2	Q3	Q4	Q5	Q6a	Q6b	Q6c	Q6d	Q6e	Q6f
0001	1	2	1	10	2	1	2	1	1	4	4
0002	2	5	2	7	1	2	2	3	2	4	5
0003	1	2	1	6	2	2	4	3	4	4	4
0004	1	2	1	1	1	3	4	4	4	5	4
0005	2	6	2	8	2	3	5	4	2	5	1
0006	2	1	2	8	2	3	5	2	2	3	1
0007	1	3	1	8	1	2	5	3	5	3	3
0008	2	4	2	5	2	3	3	4	5	1	3
0009	1	2	1	9	1	3	2	4	5	2	5
0010	2	2	2	9	2	4	2	5	5	3	5
0011	2	5	2	9	1	4	1	1	3	1	5
0012	1	2	1	9	1	2	2	2	3	2	2
0013	2	1	2	3	2	5	3	3	4	2	1
0014	1	6	1	2	2	3	4	4	5	5	2
0015	2	4	2	3	1	1	4	3	1	5	3
0016	2	3	2	4	2	5	5	5	2	5	4
0017	1	3	1	6	1	5	5	2	1	1	4
0018	2	3	2	5	2	5	5	2	2	2	3

Other techniques include direct-response entry, of which voting procedures used in several states are an example. With a specially prepared punch card, citizens cast their votes by pressing a pen-shaped instrument against the card next to the preferred candidate. This opens a small hole in a specific column and row of the card. The cards are collected and placed directly into a card reader. This method also removes the coding and entry steps. Another governmental application is the 1040EZ form used by the Internal Revenue Service. It is designed for computerized number and character recognition. Similar character recognition techniques are employed for many forms of data collection. Again, both approaches move the response from the question to data analysis with little handling.

Voice Recognition

The increase in computerized random dialing has encouraged other data collection innovations. **Voice recognition** and voice response systems are providing some interesting alternatives for the telephone interviewer. Upon getting a voice response to a randomly dialed number, the computer branches into a questionnaire routine. These systems are advancing quickly and will soon translate recorded voice responses into data files.

Digital

Telephone keypad response, frequently used by restaurants and entertainment venues to evaluate customer service, is another capability made possible by computers linked to telephone lines. Using the telephone keypad (touch-tone), an invited participant answers questions by pressing the appropriate number. The computer captures the data by decoding the tone's electrical signal and storing the numeric or alphabetic answer in a data file. Although not originally designed for collecting survey data, software components within Microsoft Windows 7 have advanced speech recognition functionality, enabling people to enter and edit data by speaking into a microphone.[8]

Seeking Clean Netnography Data

In content analysis, researchers analyze anecdotal information to determine the major themes of comments. Researchers are increasingly using feedback data posted on the Web or internally in intranet chat rooms to capture such content. Postings come in the form of product reviews, company evaluations, employee experiences, message board and newsgroup postings, as well as chat room dialogues and discussion forum postings.

Selecting such data for analysis takes some careful screening. When using net postings, Chrysanthos Dellarocas of Massachusetts Institute of Technology recommends that the researcher extract information from sites that are able to authenticate the identity of participants; this reduces or prevents unfair ratings and discriminatory behavior. Some opinion sites use financial incentives to encourage postings, which may encourage the posting of numerous comments from a single individual, thus introducing bias. Dina Mayzlin of the Yale School of Management suggests selecting comments from a larger number of sites, rather than selecting large numbers of comments from a single site; such dispersion reduces bias. In cleaning such data, Zhilin Yang of City University of Hong Kong and Robin Peterson at New Mexico State University suggest that researchers screen messages to detect irrelevant anecdotes, duplication, requests for messages to be posted, and spam messages, all of which if left in the data set would inject bias.

If you would like to try collecting and screening such data, some useful sites include ZDnet.com, Bizrate.com, Amazon.com, eBay.com, Elance.com, Complaints.com, reviewcentre.com, and Epinion.com.

Field interviewers can use mobile computers or notebooks instead of clipboards and pencils. With a built-in communications modem, wireless LAN (or local area network), or cellular link, their files can be sent directly to another computer in the field or to a remote site. This lets supervisors inspect data immediately or simplifies processing at a central facility. This is the technology that Nielsen Media is using with its portable People Meter.

Bar Code   Since adoption of the Universal Product Code (UPC) in 1973, the bar code has developed from a technological curiosity to a business mainstay. After a study by McKinsey & Company, the Kroger grocery chain pilot-tested a production system and bar codes became ubiquitous in that industry.[9]

Bar-code technology is used to simplify the interviewer's role as a data recorder. When an interviewer passes a bar-code wand over the appropriate codes, the data are recorded in a small, lightweight unit for translation later. In the large-scale processing project Census 2000, the Census Data Capture Center used bar codes to identify residents. Researchers studying magazine readership can scan bar codes to denote a magazine cover that is recognized by an interview participant.

The **bar code** is used in numerous applications: point-of-sale terminals, hospital patient ID bracelets, inventory control, product and brand tracking, promotional technique evaluation, shipment tracking, marathon runners, rental car locations (to speed the return of cars and generate invoices), and tracking of insects' mating habits. The military uses two-foot-long bar codes to label boats in storage. The codes appear on business documents, truck parts, and timber in lumberyards. Federal Express shipping labels use a code called *Codabar*. Other codes, containing letters as well as numbers, have potential for researchers.

On the Horizon

Even with these time reductions between data collection and analysis, continuing innovations in multimedia technology are being developed by the personal computer business. The capability to integrate visual images, streaming video, audio, and data may soon replace video equipment as the preferred method for recording an experiment, interview, or focus group. A copy of the response data could be extracted for data analysis, but the audio and visual images would remain intact for later evaluation. Although technology will never replace researcher judgment, it can reduce data-handling errors, decrease time between data collection and analysis, and help provide more usable information.

>summary

1 The first step in data preparation is to edit the collected raw data to detect errors and omissions that would compromise quality standards. The editor is responsible for making sure the data are accurate, consistent with other data, uniformly entered, and ready for coding. In survey work, it is common to use both field and central editing.

2 Coding is the process of assigning numbers and other symbols to answers so that we can classify the responses into categories. Categories should be appropriate to the research problem, exhaustive of the data, mutually exclusive, and unidimensional. The reduction of information through coding requires that the researcher design category sets carefully, using as much of the data as possible. Codebooks are guides to reduce data entry error and serve as a compendium of variable locations and other information for the analysis stage. Software developments in survey construction and design include embedding coding rules that screen data as they are entered, identifying data that are not entered correctly.

3 Closed questions include scaled items and other items for which answers are anticipated. Precoding of closed items avoids tedious completion of coding sheets for each response. Open-ended questions are more difficult to code since answers are not prepared in advance, but they do encourage disclosure of complete information. A systematic method for analyzing open-ended questions is content analysis. It uses preselected sampling units to produce frequency counts and other insights into data patterns.

4 "Don't know" replies are evaluated in light of the question's nature and the respondent. While many DKs are legitimate, some result from questions that are ambiguous or from an interviewing situation that is not motivating. It is better to report DKs as a separate category unless there are compelling reasons to treat them otherwise. Missing data occur when respondents skip, refuse to answer, or do not know the answer to a questionnaire item, drop out of the study, or are absent for one or more data collection periods. Researcher error, corrupted data files, and changes to the instrument during administration also produce missing data. Researchers handle missing data by first exploring the data to discover the nature of the pattern and then selecting a suitable technique for replacing values by deleting cases (or variables) or estimating values.

5 Data entry is accomplished by keyboard entry from precoded instruments, optical scanning, real-time keyboarding, telephone pad data entry, bar codes, voice recognition, OCR, OMR, and data transfers from electronic notebooks and laptop computers. Database programs, spreadsheets, and editors in statistical software programs offer flexibility for entering, manipulating, and transferring data for analysis, warehousing, and mining.

>**key**terms

>**discussion**questions

Terms in Review

1 Define or explain:

   a Coding rules.

   b Spreadsheet data entry.

   c Bar codes.

   d Precoded instruments.

   e Content analysis.

   f Missing data.

   g Optical mark recognition.

2 How should the researcher handle "don't know" responses?

Making Research Decisions

3 A problem facing shoe store managers is that many shoes eventually must be sold at markdown prices. This prompts us to conduct a mail survey of shoe store managers in

which we ask, What methods have you found most successful for reducing the problem of high markdowns? We are interested in extracting as much information as possible from these answers to better understand the full range of strategies that store managers use. Establish what you think are category sets to code 500 responses similar to the 14 given here. Try to develop an integrated set of categories that reflects your theory of markdown management. After developing the set, use it to code the 14 responses.

a Have not found the answer. As long as we buy style shoes, we will have markdowns. We use PMs on slow merchandise, but it does not eliminate markdowns. (*PM* stands for "push-money"—special item bonuses for selling a particular style of shoe.)

b Using PMs before too old. Also reducing price during season. Holding meetings with salespeople indicating which shoes to push.

c By putting PMs on any slow-selling items and promoting same. More careful check of shoes purchased.

d Keep a close watch on your stock, and mark down when you have to—that is, rather than wait, take a small markdown on a shoe that is not moving at the time.

e Using the PM method.

f Less advance buying—more dependence on in-stock shoes.

g Sales—catch bad guys before it's too late and close out.

h Buy as much good merchandise as you can at special prices to help make up some markdowns.

i Reducing opening buys and depending on fill-in service. PMs for salespeople.

j Buy more frequently, better buying, PMs on slow-moving merchandise.

k Careful buying at lowest prices. Cash on the buying line. Buying closeouts, FDs, overstock, "cancellations." (*FD* stands for "factory-discontinued" style.)

l By buying less "chanceable" shoes. Buy only what you need, watch sizes, don't go overboard on new fads.

m Buying more staple merchandise. Buying more from fewer lines. Sticking with better nationally advertised merchandise.

n No successful method with the current style situation. Manufacturers are experimenting, the retailer takes the markdowns—cuts gross profit by about 3 percent—keep your stock at lowest level without losing sales.

4 Select a small sample of class members, work associates, or friends and ask them to answer the following in a paragraph or two: What are your career aspirations for the next five years? Use one of the four basic units of content analysis to analyze their responses. Describe your findings as frequencies for the unit of analysis selected.

Bringing Research to Life

5 What data preparation process was Jason doing during data entry?

6 Data entry followed data collection in the research profiled during the opening vignette. What concerned Jason about this process?

From Concept to Practice

7 Choose one of the cases from the text website that has an instrument (check the Case Abstracts section for a listing of all cases and an abstract for each). Code the instrument for data entry.

From the Headlines

8 Your responses to the latest U.S. Census were used for two purposes. First, the Census Bureau tallied each response to produce an official population count. Second, it produced a 1-in-20 sub-sample used for analysis by researchers. For those younger than 65, the estimates from the sample are similar to the full count. For those over age 65, the estimates disagree by as much as 15 percent. The sample data suggest that there are more very old men than very old women. And, the error jumbles the correlation between age and employment, age and marital status, and, possibly, other correlations as well. The Census Bureau has refused to correct the data.

a Should the data in the 1-in-20 micro-sample be used to study people aged 65 and over?

b What's the source of the problem? Programming error, coding error, or manipulating the data to protect the identity of each individual?

>cases*

Inquiring Minds Want to Know—NOW!	**NCRCC: Teeing Up and New Strategic Direction**
Mastering Teacher Leadership	**NetConversions Influences Kelley Blue Book**

* You will find a description of each case in the Case Abstracts section of this textbook. Check the Case Index to determine whether a case provides data, the research instrument, video, or other supplementary material. Written cases are downloadable from the text website (www.mhhe.com/cooper11e). All video material and video cases are available from the Online Learning Center.

>appendix15a

Describing Data Statistically

In the first part of the chapter, we discussed how responses from participants are edited, coded, and entered. Creating numerical summaries of this process provides valuable insights to analysts about their effectiveness. In this appendix, we review concepts from your introductory statistics course that offer descriptive tools for cleaning data, discovering problems, and summarizing distributions. A distribution (of data) is an array of value counts from lowest to highest value of a variable, resulting from the tabulation of incidence. Descriptive statistical measures are used to depict the center, spread, and shape of distributions and are helpful as preliminary tools for data description. We will define these measures and describe their use as *descriptive statistics* after introducing a sample data set and an overview of basic concepts.

Reviewing Statistical Concepts

The LCD (liquid crystal display) TV market is an interesting market to watch because of the changes in technology and marketing. Currently the major players in this market are Sharp, LG Electronics/Zenith, Samsung, Sony, Dell, and Panasonic. Only a few other brands earn a noticeable market share. Sharp products currently represent the largest percentage of unit sales. Let's assume we are interested in evaluating annual unit sales increases of several manufacturers. We survey nine manufacturers and we find a *frequency distribution* (an ordered array of all values for a variable) of annual percentage of unit sales increases: 5, 6, 6, 7, 7, 7, 8, 8, 9. From these unit sales scores, we construct a table for arraying the data. It presents value codes from lowest to highest value, with columns for count, percent, percent for missing values, and cumulative percent. An example is presented in Exhibit 15a-1.

The table arrays data by assigned numerical value, in this case the actual percentage unit sales increase recorded (far-left column). To discover how many manufacturers were in each unit sales increase category, you would read the frequency column. For example, at the intersection of the frequency column and the second row, there are two companies that posted a 6 percent annual unit sales increase. In the percentage column, you see what percentage of TV manufacturers in the survey gave a response for each level of unit sales increase. The three manufacturers who

had unit sales increases of 7 percent represent 33.3 percent of the total number of manufacturers surveyed (3/9 × 100). The cumulative percentage reveals the number of manufacturers that provided a response and *any others that preceded it* in the table. For this example, LCD TV percentage unit sales increases between 5 and 7 percent represent 66.7 percent. The cumulative percentage column is helpful primarily when the data have an underlying order. If, in part B, we create a code for source of origin (foreign = 1, domestic = 2) to each of the nine LCD TV manufacturers, the cumulative percentage column would provide the proportion. The *proportion* is the percentage of elements in the distribution that met a criterion. In this case, the criterion is the origin of manufacture.

In Exhibit 15a-2, the bell-shaped curve that is superimposed on the distribution of annual unit sales increases (percent) for LCD TV manufacturers is called the *normal distribution.* The distribution of values for any variable that has a normal distribution is governed by a mathematical equation. This distribution is a symmetrical curve and reflects a frequency distribution of many natural phenomena such as the height of people of a certain gender and age.

Many variables of interest that researchers will measure will have distributions that approximate a *standard normal distribution.* A standard normal distribution is a special case of the normal distribution in which all values are given standard scores. This distribution has a mean of 0 and a standard deviation of 1. For example, a manufacturer that had an annual unit sales increase of 7 percent would be given a standard score of zero since 7 is the mean of the LCD TV distribution. A *standard score* (or *Z score*) tells you how many units a case (a manufacturer in this example) is above or below the mean. The Z score, being standardized, allows us to compare the results of different normal distributions, something we do frequently in research. Assume that Zenith has an annual unit sales increase of 9 percent. To calculate a standard score for this manufacturer, you would find the difference between the value and the mean and divide by the standard deviation of the distribution shown in Exhibit 15a-1.

$$\text{Zenith's standard score} = \frac{\text{Value} - \text{Mean}}{\text{Standard deviation}} = \frac{9 - 7}{1.22}$$

$$= 1.64$$

>Exhibit 15a-1 Annual Percentage Unit Sales Increases for LCD TV Manufacturers

A

Unit Sales Increase (%)	Frequency	Percentage	Cumulative Percentage
5	1	11.1	11.1
6	2	22.2	33.3
7	3	33.3	66.7
8	2	22.2	88.9
9	1	11.1	100.0
Total	9	100.0	

B

Company Origin	Unit Sales Increase (%)	Frequency	Percentage	Cumulative Percent
Origin, foreign (1)	6	1	11.1	11.1
	7	2	22.2	33.3
	8	2	22.2	55.5
Origin, domestic (2)	5	1	11.1	66.6
	6	1	11.1	77.7
	7	1	11.1	88.8
	9	1	11.1	100.0
	Total	9	100.0	

>Exhibit 15a-2 Histogram of Annual Unit Sales Increase (%)

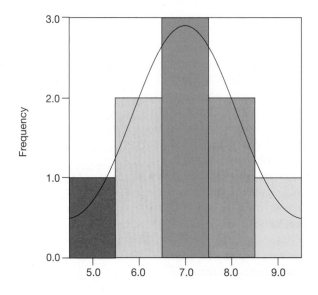

>**Exhibit 15a-3** Characteristics of Distributions

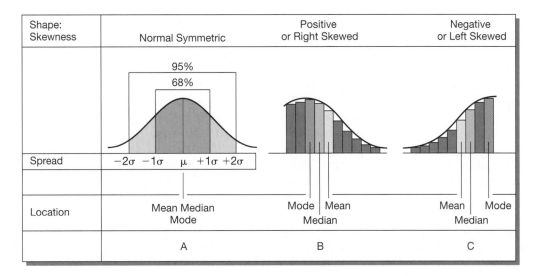

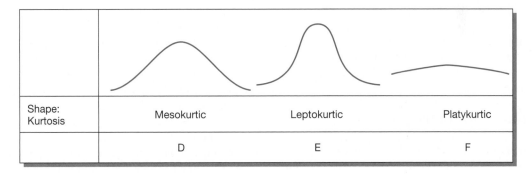

The standard normal distribution, shown in part A of Exhibit 15a-3, is a standard of comparison for describing distributions of sample data. It is used with inferential statistics that assume normally distributed variables.

We will come back to this exhibit in a moment. Now let's review some descriptive tools that reveal the important characteristics of distributions. The characteristics of central tendency, variability, and shape are useful tools for summarizing distributions. Their definitions, applications, and formulas fall under the heading of *descriptive statistics*. The definitions will be familiar to most readers.

Measures of Central Tendency

Summarizing information such as that from our collected data of LCD TV manufacturers often requires the description of "typical" values. Suppose we want to know the typical percentage unit sales increase for these companies. We might define *typical* as the average response (mean); the middle value, when the distribution is sorted from lowest to highest (median); or the most frequently occurring value (mode). The common measures of *central tendency* (or center) include the mean, median, and mode.

The *mean* is calculated by the following formula:

$$\overline{X} = \frac{\sum_{i=1}^{n} X_i}{n}$$

For the unit sales increase variable, the distribution of responses is 5, 6, 6, 7, 7, 7, 8, 8, 9. The arithmetic average, or mean (the sum of the nine values divided by 9), is

$$\frac{5 + 6 + 6 + 7 + 7 + 8 + 8 + 9}{9}$$

$$= 7 \text{ (an average 7\% unit sales increase)}$$

The *median* is the midpoint of the distribution. Half of the observations in the distribution fall above and the other half fall below the median. When the distribution has an even number of observations, the median is the average of the two middle scores. The median is the most appropriate locator of center for ordinal data and has resistance to extreme scores, thereby making it a preferred measure for interval and ratio data when their distributions are not normal. The median is sometimes symbolized by *M* or *mdn*.

From the sample distribution for the percentage unit sales increase variable, the median of the nine values is 7:

$$5 \quad 6 \quad 6 \quad 7 \quad \mathbf{7} \quad 7 \quad 8 \quad 8 \quad 9$$

If the distribution had 10 values, the median would be the average of the values for the fifth and sixth cases.

The *mode* is the most frequently occurring value. There may be *more than one* mode in a distribution. When there is more than one score that has the highest yet equal frequency, the distribution is bimodal or multimodal. There may be *no* mode in a distribution if every score has an equal number of observations. The mode is the location measure of central tendency for nominal data and a point of reference along with the median and mean for examining spread and shape of distributions. In our LCD TV percentage unit sales increase example, the most frequently occurring value is 7. As revealed in the frequency distribution in Exhibit 15a-2, there are three companies that have unit sales increases of 7 percent.

Notice in Exhibit 15a-3, part A, that the mean, median, and mode are the same in a normal distribution. When these measures of central tendency diverge, the distribution is no longer normal.

Measures of Variability

The common measures of *variability,* alternatively referred to as *dispersion* or *spread,* are the variance, standard deviation, range, interquartile range, and quartile deviation. They describe how scores cluster or scatter in a distribution.

The *variance* is a measure of score dispersion about the mean. If all the scores are identical, the variance is 0. The greater the dispersion of scores, the greater the variance. Both the variance and the standard deviation are used with interval and ratio data. The symbol for the sample variance is s^2, and that for the population variance is the Greek letter sigma, squared (σ^2). The variance is computed by summing the squared distance from the mean for all cases and dividing the sum by the total number of cases minus 1:

$$\text{Variance} = s^2 = \frac{\text{Sum of the squared distances from mean for all cases}}{(\text{Number of cases} - 1)}$$

$$s^2 = \frac{\sum_{i=1}^{n}(X_i - \overline{X})^2}{n - 1}$$

For the percentage unit sales increase variable, we would compute the variance as

$$s^2 = \frac{\begin{matrix}(5 - 7)^2 + (6 - 7)^2 + (6 - 7)^2 \\ + (7 - 7)^2 + (7 - 7)^2 + (7 - 7)^2 \\ + (8 - 7)^2 + (8 - 7)^2 + (9 - 7)^2\end{matrix}}{8} = 1.5$$

The *standard deviation* summarizes how far away from the average the data values typically are. It is perhaps the most frequently used measure of spread because it improves interpretability by removing the variance's square and expressing the deviations in their original units (e.g., sales in dollars, not dollars squared). It is also an important concept for descriptive statistics because it reveals the amount of variability within the data set. Like the mean, the standard deviation is affected by extreme scores. The symbol for the sample standard deviation is *s,* and that for a population standard deviation is *σ*. Alternatively, it is labeled *std. dev.* You can calculate the standard deviation by taking the square root of the variance:

$$s = \sqrt{s^2}$$

The standard deviation for the percentage unit sales increase variable in our example is 1.22:

$$1.22 = \sqrt{1.5}$$

The *range* is the difference between the largest and smallest scores in the distribution. The percentage annual unit sales increase variable has a range of 4 (9 − 5 = 4). Unlike the standard deviation, the range is computed from only the minimum and maximum scores; thus, it is a very rough measure of spread. With the range as a point of comparison, it is possible to get an idea of the homogeneity (small std. dev.) or heterogeneity (large std. dev.) of the distribution. For a homogeneous distribution, the ratio of the range to the standard deviation should be between 2 and 6. A number above 6 would indicate a high degree of heterogeneity. In the percentage unit sales increase example, the ratio is 4/1.22 = 3.28. The range provides useful but limited information for all data. It is mandatory for ordinal data.

The *interquartile range (IQR)* is the difference between the first and third quartiles of the distribution. It is also called the *midspread*. Ordinal or ranked data use this measure in conjunction with the median. It is also used with interval and ratio data when asymmetrical distributions are suspected or for exploratory analysis. Recall the following relationships: the minimum value of the distribution is the 0 percentile; the maximum, the 100th percentile. The first quartile (Q_1) is the 25th percentile; the median, Q_2, is the 50th percentile. The third quartile (Q_3) is the 75th percentile. For the percentage unit sales increase data, the quartiles are

$$\underset{\quad Q_1 \quad\quad Q_2 \quad\quad Q_3 \quad\quad Q_4}{5 \quad 6 \quad 6 \quad 7 \quad \mathbf{7} \quad 7 \quad 8 \quad 8 \quad 9}$$

The quartile deviation, or semi-interquartile range, is expressed as

$$Q = \frac{Q_1 - Q_3}{2}$$

The *quartile deviation* is always used with the median for ordinal data. It is helpful for interval and ratio data when the distribution is stretched (or skewed) by extreme values. In a normal distribution, the median plus one quartile deviation (Q) on either side encompasses 50 percent of the observations. Eight Qs cover approximately the range. Q's relationship with the standard deviation is constant ($Q = .6745s$) when scores are normally distributed. For our annual percentage unit sales increase example, the quartile deviation is 1 [$(6 - 8)/2 = 1$].

Measures of Shape

The measures of shape, skewness and kurtosis, describe departures from the symmetry of a distribution and its relative flatness (or peakedness), respectively. They use deviation scores ($X - \bar{X}$). *Deviation scores* show us how far any observation is from the mean. The company that posted a percentage unit sales increase of 9 has a deviation score of 2 ($9 - 7$). The measures of shape are often difficult to interpret when extreme scores are in the distribution. Generally, shape is best communicated through visual displays. (Refer to the graphics in Exhibit 15a-3, parts B through F.) From a practical standpoint, the calculation of skewness and kurtosis is easiest with spreadsheet or statistics software.

Skewness is a measure of a distribution's deviation from symmetry. In a symmetrical distribution, the mean, median, and mode are in the same location. A distribution that has cases stretching toward one tail or the other is called *skewed*. As shown in Exhibit 15a-3, part B, when the tail stretches to the right, to larger values, it is positively skewed. In part C, scores stretching toward the left, toward smaller values, skew the distribution negatively. Note the relationship between the mean, median, and mode in asymmetrical distributions. The symbol for skewness is *sk*.

$$sk = \frac{n}{(n-1)(n-2)} \Sigma \left(\frac{x_i - \bar{x}}{s}\right)^3$$

where s is the sample standard deviation (the unbiased estimate of sigma).

When a distribution approaches symmetry, *sk* is approximately 0. With a positive skew, *sk* will be a positive number; with negative skew, *sk* will be a negative number. The calculation of skewness for our annual percentage unit sales increase data produces an index of 0 and reveals no skew.

As illustrated in the lower portion of Exhibit 15a-3, *kurtosis* is a measure of a distribution's peakedness (or flatness). Distributions that have scores that cluster heavily or pile up in the center (along with more observations than normal in the extreme tails) are peaked or *leptokurtic*. Flat distributions, with scores more evenly distributed and tails fatter than a normal distribution, are called *playkurtic*. Intermediate or *mesokurtic* distributions approach normal—neither too peaked nor too flat. The symbol for kurtosis is *ku*.

$$ku = \left[\frac{n(n+1)}{(n-1)(n-2)(n-3)} \Sigma \left(\frac{x_i - \bar{x}}{s}\right)^4\right] - \frac{3(n-1)^2}{(n-2)(n-3)}$$

where s is the sample standard deviation (the unbiased estimate of sigma).

The value of *ku* for a normal or mesokurtic distribution is close to 0. A leptokurtic distribution will have a positive value, and the playkurtic distribution will be negative. As with skewness, the larger the absolute value of the index, the more extreme is the characteristic. In the annual percentage unit sales increase example, the kurtosis is calculated as -0.29, which suggested a very slight deviation from a normally shaped curve with some flattening contributed by smaller-than-expected frequencies of the value 7 in the example distribution.

>chapter 16

Exploring, Displaying, and Examining Data

>learningobjectives

After reading this chapter, you should understand . . .

1 That exploratory data analysis techniques provide insights and data diagnostics by emphasizing visual representations of the data.

2 How cross-tabulation is used to examine relationships involving categorical variables, serves as a framework for later statistical testing, and makes table-based analysis using one or more control variables an efficient tool for data visualization and decision making.

> 66 As data availability continues to increase, the importance of identifying/filtering and analyzing relevant data can be a powerful way to gain an information advantage over our competition. 99
>
> Tom H.C. Anderson, founder & managing partner
> Anderson Analytics, LLC

>**bringing**research**to**life

Myra and Jason are wrapping up their review of the materials Myra delivered for MindWriter's latest partnership with Henry and Associates. Jason, knowing Myra is eager to hear any tidbits on the City Center for Performing Arts project, escorts her through the outer office. Sammye, Henry and Associates newest intern, is busy poring over cross-tabs. He decides it is the perfect time to text Sammye on the rules of data confidentiality he broached with the interns last week.

"Sammye Grayson, meet Myra Wines from Mind-Writer. We'll be working with her on a short-turnaround project during the next week." Sammye rises to shake Myra's extended hand, as Jason asks, innocently, "Anything interesting on those initial cross-tabs?"

Myra smiles, raises an expressive eyebrow, and waits for Sammye's response.

Sammye hesitates and then, looking at Jason for some signal of why he asked the question in the presence of a different client, responds, "Three of the early cross-tabs appeared to show some support for the board's assumptions about the alcohol issue—on whether current patrons endorse the selling of beer and wine during intermissions. But we're not far enough into the data to say which of the board's assumptions are fully correct and which might have to be modified based on the patterns emerging within subgroups of the sample."

Jason raises a hand to stop the detailed answer to his question. Sammye knows from the look on his face that she's done something wrong.

"I shouldn't have answered your question," blurts Sammye. "I walked right into the trap you set, eyes wide open."

Myra jumps in before Jason can respond. "I've seen Jason do this once before to an intern, so you should feel like one of the team. And, no, you shouldn't have responded—confidentiality is rule number one—and as a client, I appreciate it. No harm done this time, though. What Jason failed to tell you is I'm on CCPA's board and part of the project team. Before Jason stopped you, things were getting interesting. Please continue."

Sammye, getting a nod from Jason, shares, "We'll probably have to do some recoding of the age and race variables for the patterns to emerge clearly. The team is also interested in the differences between ethnic groups in future performance preferences. We've also finished coding each patron's address with its GPS (Geographic Positioning System) code. The preliminary mapping begins tomorrow; Jason hired a master's candidate in geography to provide the mapping. I've scheduled a conference call for... (Sammye flips her desk calendar pages to the following week)... Friday of next week with Jackson Murray and other members of the CCPA project team."

"When the board approved your proposed analysis plan," queries Myra, "I don't remember seeing any reference to those boxlike diagrams with tails I see on that graph you just handed to Jason."

"Most of what the team will be doing the next three days," intervenes Jason, "involves more graphical displays than statistical ones. Right now we're just getting a sense of what the data are telling us. We'll decide what, if any, new analyses to add to the proposed plan by this Friday. It's this early work that lays the groundwork for the more sophisticated analyses that follow. There isn't anything glamorous about it, but without it we might miss some crucial findings."

Jason pauses for effect and then says, "By the way, that 'little diagram' is called a boxplot. I actually did several during the preliminary analysis phase for MindWriter's CompleteCare study. I didn't give them to you because I would have had to explain how to interpret them and..."

"...and anything you have to explain isn't clear enough," finishes Myra.

> Exploratory Data Analysis

The convenience of data entry via spreadsheet, optimal mark recognition (OMR), or the data editor of a statistical program makes it tempting to move directly to statistical analysis. That temptation is even stronger when the data can be entered and viewed in real time. Why waste time finding out if the data confirm the hypothesis that motivated the study? Why not obtain descriptive statistical summaries (based on our discussion in Appendix 15a) and then test hypotheses?

Exploratory data analysis is both a data analysis perspective and a set of techniques. In this chapter, we will present unique and conventional techniques including graphical and tabular devices to visualize the data. Exhibit 16-1 reminds you of the importance of data visualization as an integral element in the data analysis process and as a necessary step prior to hypothesis testing. In Chapter 3, we said research conducted scientifically is a puzzle-solving activity as well as an attitude of curiosity, suspicion, and imagination essential to discovery. It is natural, then, that exploration and examination of the data would be an integral part of our data analysis perspective.

In **exploratory data analysis (EDA)** the researcher has the flexibility to respond to the patterns revealed in the preliminary analysis of the data. Thus, patterns in the collected data guide the data analysis or suggest revisions to the preliminary data analysis plan. This flexibility is an important attribute of this approach. When the researcher is attempting to prove causation, however, confirmatory data analysis is required. **Confirmatory data analysis** is an analytical process guided by classical statistical inference in its use of significance testing and confidence.[1]

One authority has compared exploratory data analysis to the role of police detectives and other investigators and confirmatory analysis to that of judges and the judicial system. The former are involved

As this ad from Radius Global Market Research, formerly Data Development Worldwide, suggests, "pushing data, into a template gets the job done." But the company argues that it isn't an effective way to analyze data. Every project deserves a research question-specific data analysis plan. The way the data from a particular project are massaged is often determined by the skill of the researcher—just as the skill of the potter determines the design of the pot.
www.radius-global.com

>**Exhibit 16-1** Data Exploration, Examination, and Analysis in the Research Process

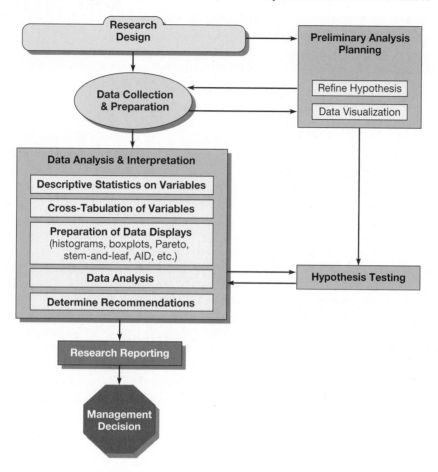

in the search for clues and evidence; the latter are preoccupied with evaluating the strength of the evidence that is found. Exploratory data analysis is the first step in the search for evidence, without which confirmatory analysis has nothing to evaluate.[2] Consistent with that analogy, EDA shares a commonality with exploratory designs, not formalized ones. Because it doesn't follow a rigid structure, it is free to take many paths in unraveling the mysteries in the data—to sift the unpredictable from the predictable.

A major contribution of the exploratory approach lies in the emphasis on visual representations and graphical techniques over summary statistics. Summary statistics, as you will see momentarily, may obscure, conceal, or even misrepresent the underlying structure of the data. When numerical summaries are used exclusively and accepted without visual inspection, the selection of confirmatory models may be based on flawed assumptions.[3] For these reasons, data analysis should begin with visual inspection. After that, it is not only possible but also desirable to cycle between exploratory and confirmatory approaches.

Frequency Tables, Bar Charts, and Pie Charts[4]

Several useful techniques for displaying data are not new to EDA. They are essential to any examination of the data. For example, a **frequency table** is a simple device for arraying data. An example is presented in Exhibit 16-2. It arrays data by assigned numerical value, with columns for percent, valid percent (percent adjusted for missing data), and cumulative percent. Ad recall, a nominal variable, describes the ads that participants remembered seeing or hearing without being prompted by the researcher or the measurement instrument. Although there are 100 observations,

Internet-Age Researchers: Building Critical Transferable Skills

According to *New York Times* columnist Steve Lohr, in the digital age statisticians "are changing the image of the profession as a place for dronish number-nerds. They are finding themselves increasingly in demand—and even cool."[a] Lohr asserts that the rapid ascendancy of statisticians, who can earn $125,000 in their first year after getting a doctorate, is the result of the recent explosion of digital data. With Web-based data expanding rapidly, up to fivefold by 2012,[b] there are myriad opportunities for exploration and problem solving.

Google's chief economist, Hal Varian, explains the importance of the Internet's free and ubiquitous data this way: "The ability to take data—to be able to understand it, to process it, to extract value from it, to visualize it, to communicate it—that's going to be a hugely important skill in the next decades...."[c]

While statisticians are in high demand, Varian emphasizes the need for managers to understand data themselves. In old organizations, you had an "army of people digesting data and feeding it to decision makers at the top." Today, it is essential that people can access, understand, and communicate insights from data analysis that affect everyday decisions. Using statistical models, multivariate analysis, and data mining, Internet-age

statisticians operate as "bridge scientists" engaged in the quest to find meaningful patterns in information while they advance business opportunities and identify risks.

So where are the newly fashionable "number-nerds" going? Even in a bad economy, Wall Street, finance, pharmaceuticals, insurance, research labs, and the government are hiring. Many of those being hired are part of multi-billion-dollar acquisitions. Keeping pace with the expanding market for "business intelligence" software, SPSS offers software and data tools designed to help countless companies understand their consumers. SPSS was acquired by IBM for $1.2 billion. IBM also offered nearly $5 billion for the purchase of Cognos. Additionally, Oracle purchased Hyperion Solutions for roughly $3.3 billion, while SAP purchased Business Objects for $4.8 billion. And Microsoft bought Farecast.com for $115 million to support its new venture, Bing Travel, that reveals if you should purchase an airline ticket now or wait for a time closer to your desired flight's departure.[d]

So, dive into data analysis and learn as much as you can. It's a skill that is much in demand.

www.google.com; www.SAP.com; www.spss.com

the small number of media placements make the variable easily tabled. The same data are presented in Exhibit 16-3 using a pie chart and a bar chart. The values and percentages are more readily understood in this graphic format, and visualization of the media placements and their relative sizes is improved.

>Exhibit 16-2 A Frequency Table of Ad Recall

Value Label	Value	Frequency	Percent	Valid Percent	Cumulative Percent
TV program A	1	10	10.0	10.0	10.0
TV program B	2	8	8.0	8.0	18.0
TV program C	3	7	7.0	7.0	25.0
TV program D	4	13	13.0	13.0	38.0
Radio program A	5	24	24.0	24.0	62.0
Radio program B	6	4	4.0	4.0	66.0
Radio program C	7	11	11.0	11.0	77.0
Magazine A	8	6	6.0	6.0	83.0
Magazine B	9	7	7.0	7.0	90.0
Outdoor billboard	10	10	10.0	10.0	100.0
Total		100	100.0	100.0	

Valid cases 100 Missing cases 0

>**Exhibit 16-3** Nominal Variable Displays (Ad Recall)

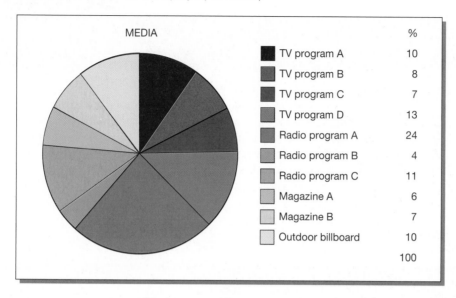

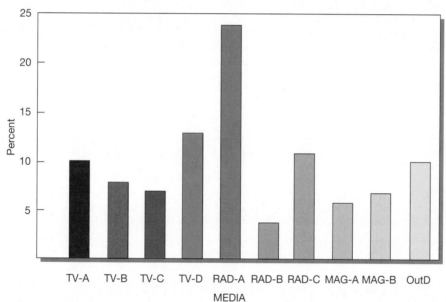

When the variable of interest is measured on an interval-ratio scale and is one with many potential values, these techniques are not particularly informative. Exhibit 16-4 (page 438) is a condensed frequency table of the average annual purchases of PrimeSell's top 50 customers. Only two values, 59.9 and 66, have a frequency greater than 1. Thus, the primary contribution of this table is an ordered list of values. If the table were converted to a bar chart, it would have 48 bars of equal length and two bars with two occurrences. Bar charts do not reserve spaces for values where no observations occur within the range. Constructing a pie chart for this variable would also be pointless.

Histograms

The histogram is a conventional solution for the display of interval-ratio data. **Histograms** are used when it is possible to group the variable's values into intervals. Histograms are constructed with bars (or asterisks) that represent data values, where each value occupies an equal amount of area within the

Using Tables to Understand Data

Because the researcher's primary job is to discover the message revealed by the data, he or she needs every tool to reveal the message. Authors Sally Bigwood and Melissa Spore in their book *Presenting Numbers, Tables, and Charts* suggest that the table is the ultimate tool for extracting knowledge from data.

The presence of any number within a table is for comparison with a similar number—from last year, from another candidate, from another machine, against a goal, and so forth. Using the author's rules for table creation, a researcher exploring data by constructing a table should:

• *Round numbers.*	• Rounded numbers can be most easily compared, enabling us to more easily determine the ratio or relationship of one number to another. • If precision is critical to the number (e.g., you are researching taxes or design specifications or drug interactions), don't round the numbers.

• *Arrange the numbers to reveal patterns.*	• Order numbers from largest to smallest number.
	  • In a vertically arranged table, order the largest number at the top.
	  • In a horizontal arrangement, order the largest numbers on the left.
	
	• When looking for changes over time, order the numbers by year, from most distant (left or top) to most recent.

• *Use averages, totals, or percentages to achieve focus.*	• An average provides a point for comparison. • Don't use an average if the raw data reveal a bimodal distribution. • Totals emphasize the big picture. • Percentages show proportionate relationships more easily than raw data.
• *Compare like scales in a single table.*	• Convert numbers to a common scale when the numbers reflect different scales (e.g., grams versus ounces of cereal consumption; monthly salary data versus hourly wage data).
• *Choose simplicity over complexity.*	• Several smaller tables reveal patterns better rather than one large, complex table. • Complex tables are used as a convenient reference source for multiple elements of data.
• *Use empty space and design to guide the eye to numbers that must be compared and to make patterns and exceptions stand out.*	• Design a table with a smaller number of columns than rows. • Single-space numbers that must be compared. • Use gridlines to group numbers within a table; avoid gridlines between numbers that must be compared. • Use empty space to create gutters between numbers in simple tables. • Right-align column headers and table numbers.

• *Summarize each data display.*	• Write a phrase or sentence that summarizes your interpretation of the data presented; don't leave interpretation to chance.
	  • Summary statements might be used as the title of a table or chart in the final research report.
	  • The summary need not mention any numbers.

• *Label and title tables for clarity of message.*	• Titles should be comprehensive: Include what (subject of the title or message), where (if data have a geographic base), when (date or time period covered), and unit of measure. • Include common information in the title: It lengthens a title but shortens the table's column headings. • Avoid abbreviations in column headings unless well known by your audience. • Avoid footnotes; if used, use symbols—like the asterisk—rather than numbers (numbers used as footnotes can be confused with the content numbers of the table). • For reference, provide an undertable source line for later reference.

>**close**up**cont'd**

AN EXAMPLE

Assume you were determining whether to expand into western Europe with distribution facilities to service online purchases.

We start with a table that presents data from a study of online shopping and purchasing behavior in selected countries in western Europe. The data were collected by research leader Synovate and SPA Market Research-UK and published by eMarketer.com in their digital newsletter. The data are ordered alphabetically by country.

What data might you need to help your make your decision about distribution facilities? Can you determine the average transaction size? If you don't know the conversion rate of the euro to the dollar, can you interpret the table? Should you put your investment in the U.K. with its frequent purchasers or elsewhere?

Online Spending and Purchases by Internet Users in Select Countries in Western Europe, September 2006 (average)		
	Spending	**Purchases**
Belgium	Eur 790	6
Denmark	Eur 1159	11
France	Eur 509	8
Germany	Eur 521	10
Italy	Eur 454	7
Netherlands	Eur 681	7
Norway	Eur 1406	7
Spain	Eur 452	5
Sweden	Eur 1013	9
United Kingdom	Eur 1201	18

Source: Synovate and SPA Market Research-UK for the European Interactive Advertising Association (EIAA), January 2007.

80134   www.eMarketer.com

The next table recasts the data using Bigwood and Spore's guidelines. First the table title has changed; now the six-month period on which the spending data are based is more obvious. We've also changed the column headers to reflect that each is an average, and we have right-justified the headers and the numbers. We've arranged the table by Average Spending (euro) in descending order and interpreted the euro column by adding a dollar conversion column. We might not need the right-most column if we were euro spenders ourselves but, if we are more familiar with another currency, the addition of this column helps us interpret the data. With this arrangement, the Scandinavian countries are looking more attractive, as is the U.K.

Western European Six-Month Online Spending and Purchases			
	Average Spending (Euros)	**Average Number of Purchases**	**Average Spending (Dollars)***
Norway	1406	7 biggest spenders	1,823.58
United Kingdom	1201	18	1,557.70
Denmark	1159	11	1,503.22
Sweden	1013	9	1,313.86
Belgium	790	6	1,024.63
Netherlands	681	7	883.26
Germany	521	10	675.74
France	509	8	660.17
Italy	454	7	588.84
Spain	452	5 smallest spenders	586.24

Source: Synovate and SPA Market Research-UK for the European Interactive Advertising Association (EIAA), January 2007.

*1 euro = 1.2967 dollars.

This next recasting offers a simple addition: the average of the columns. The table is now ordered by the Average Number of Purchases within the six-month period studied. This presentation allows the interpreter of the data to determine which countries are buying above the average for western Europe and which are buying below that average. Germany starts to emerge as a purchaser country, but look at the Average Spending column. If you were distributing high-value merchandise, would Germany look attractive?

Western European Six-Month Online Spending and Purchases		
	Average Spending (Euros)	**Average Number of Purchases**
United Kingdom	1201	18 Most frequent buyers
Denmark	1159	11
Germany	521	10
Sweden	1013	9
France	509	8 Average frequency buyers
Norway	1406	7
Netherlands	681	7
Italy	454	7
Belgium	790	6
Spain	452	5 least frequent buyers
Average	818.6	8.8

Source: Synovate and SPA Market Research-UK for the European Interactive Advertising Association (EIAA), January 2007.

Finally, we offer a recasting of the data based on a newly calculated column, Average Transaction (Euro). Germany doesn't look so attractive now.

One last note on tables: as a researcher you want to strive for consistency. If you are ordering from most to least, choose this arrangement for every table.

Western European Six-Month Online Spending and Purchases			
	Average Spending (Euros)	**Average Number of Purchases**	**Average Transaction (Euros)**	**Average Transaction (Dollars)***
Norway	1406	7	201 specialty shoppers	261
Belgium	790	6	132	171
Sweden	1013	9	113	146
Denmark	1159	11	105	137
Netherlands	681	7	97	126
Spain	452	5	90	117
United Kingdom	1201	18	67	87
Italy	454	7	65	84
France	509	8	64	83
Germany	521	10	52 bargain hunters	68

Source: Synovate and SPA Market Research-UK for the European Interactive Advertising Association (EIAA), January 2007.

*1 euro = 1.2967 dollars.

>closeupcont'd

Unlike previous tables, this last table is ordered from least to most. If you were blurry-eyed from studying numerous tables, you might quickly glance at the table, see Germany at the top, and misinterpret the data. Consistency across all tables in a study can help prevent such errors.

After recasting the data in various tables, where would you put your distribution center?

Western European Six-Month Online Spending and Purchases				
	Average Spending (Euros)	Average Number of Purchases	Average Transaction (Euros)	Average Transaction (Dollars)*
Germany	521	10	52	68
France	509	8	64	83
Italy	454	7	65	84
United Kingdom	1201	18	67	87
Spain	452	5	90	117
Netherlands	681	7	97	126
Denmark	1159	11	105	137
Sweden	1013	9	113	146
Belgium	790	6	132	171
Norway	1406	7	201	261

Source: Synovate and SPA Market Research-UK for the European Interactive Advertising Association (EIAA), January 2007.

*1 euro = 1.2967 dollars.

enclosed area. Data analysts find histograms useful for (1) displaying all intervals in a distribution, even those without observed values, and (2) examining the shape of the distribution for skewness, kurtosis, and the modal pattern. When looking at a histogram, one might ask: Is there a single hump (a mode)? Are subgroups identifiable when multiple modes are present? Are straggling data values detached from the central concentration?[5]

The values for the average annual purchases variable presented in Exhibit 16-4 were measured on a ratio scale and are easily grouped. Other variables possessing an underlying order are similarly appropriate for histograms. A histogram would not be used for a nominal variable like ad recall (Exhibit 16-3) that has no order to its categories.

A histogram of the average annual purchases is shown in Exhibit 16-5. The midpoint for each interval for the variable of interest, average annual purchases, is shown on the horizontal axis; the frequency or number of observations in each interval, on the vertical axis. We erect a vertical bar above the midpoint of each interval on the horizontal scale. The height of the bar corresponds with the frequency of observations in the interval above which it is erected. This histogram was constructed with intervals 20 increments wide, and the last interval contains only two observations, 206.9 and 218.2. These values are found in PrimeSell's average annual purchases frequency table (Exhibit 16-4). Intervals with 0 counts show gaps in the data and alert the analyst to look for problems with spread. When the upper tail of the distribution is compared with the frequency table, we find three extreme values (183.2, 206.9, and 218.2). Along with the peaked midpoint and reduced number of observations in the upper tail, this histogram warns us of irregularities in the data.

>Exhibit 16-4 Average Annual Purchases of PrimeSell's Top 50 Customers

Value	Frequency	Percent	Cumulative Percent	Value	Frequency	Percent	Cumulative Percent
54.9	1	2	2	75.6	1	2	54
55.4	1	2	4	76.4	1	2	56
55.6	1	2	6	77.5	1	2	58
56.4	1	2	8	78.9	1	2	60
56.8	1	2	10	80.9	1	2	62
56.9	1	2	12	82.2	1	2	64
57.8	1	2	14	82.5	1	2	66
58.1	1	2	16	86.4	1	2	68
58.2	1	2	18	88.3	1	2	70
58.3	1	2	20	102.5	1	2	72
58.5	1	2	22	104.1	1	2	74
59.9	2	4	26	110.4	1	2	76
61.5	1	2	28	111.9	1	2	78
62.6	1	2	30	118.6	1	2	80
64.8	1	2	32	123.8	1	2	82
66.0	2	4	36	131.2	1	2	84
66.3	1	2	38	140.9	1	2	86
67.6	1	2	40	146.2	1	2	88
69.1	1	2	42	153.2	1	2	90
69.2	1	2	44	163.2	1	2	92
70.5	1	2	46	166.7	1	2	94
72.7	1	2	48	183.2	1	2	96
72.9	1	2	50	206.9	1	2	98
73.5	1	2	52	218.2	1	2	100
				Total	50	100	

>Exhibit 16-5 Histogram of PrimeSell's Top 50 Customers' Average Annual Purchases

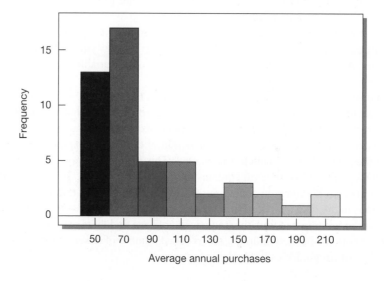

Stem-and-Leaf Displays[6]

The **stem-and-leaf display** is a technique that is closely related to the histogram. It shares some of the histogram's features but offers several unique advantages. It is easy to construct by hand for small samples or may be produced by computer programs. In contrast to histograms, which lose information by grouping data values into intervals, the stem-and-leaf presents actual data values that can be inspected directly, without the use of enclosed bars or asterisks as the representation medium. This feature reveals the distribution of values within the interval and preserves their rank order for finding the median, quartiles, and other summary statistics. It also eases linking a specific observation back to the data file and to the subject that produced it.

Visualization is the second advantage of stem-and-leaf displays. The range of values is apparent at a glance, and both shape and spread impressions are immediate. Patterns in the data—such as gaps where no values exist, areas where values are clustered, or outlying values that differ from the main body of the data—are easily observed.

To develop a stem-and-leaf display for the data in Exhibit 16-4, the first digits of each data item are arranged to the left of a vertical line. Next, we pass through the average annual purchases percentages in the order they were recorded and place the last digit for each item (the unit position, 1.0) to the right of the vertical line. Note that the digit to the right of the decimal point is ignored. The last digit for each item is placed on the horizontal row corresponding to its first digit(s). Now it is a simple matter to rank-order the digits in each row, creating the stem-and-leaf display shown in Exhibit 16-6.

Each line or row in this display is referred to as a *stem,* and each piece of information on the stem is called a *leaf.* The first line or row is

5 | 4 5 5 6 6 6 7 8 8 8 8 9

The meaning attached to this line or row is that there are 12 items in the data set whose first digit is five: 54, 55, 55, 56, 56, 56, 57, 58, 58, 58, 58, and 59. The second line,

6 | 1 2 4 6 6 7 9 9

shows that there are eight average annual purchase values whose first digit is six: 61, 62, 64, 66, 66, 67, 69, and 69.

When the stem-and-leaf display shown in Exhibit 16-6 is turned upright (rotated 90 degrees to the left), the shape is the same as that of the histogram shown in Exhibit 16-5.

>**Exhibit 16-6** A Stem-and-Leaf Display of PrimeSell's Average Annual Purchases Data

5	4 5 5 6 6 6 7 8 8 8 8 9
6	1 2 4 6 6 7 9 9
7	0 2 2 3 5 6 7 8
8	0 2 2 6 8
9	
10	2 4
11	0 1 8
12	3
13	1
14	0 6
15	3
16	3 6
17	
18	3
19	
20	6
21	8

>Exhibit 16-7 Pareto Diagram of MindWriter Repair Complaints

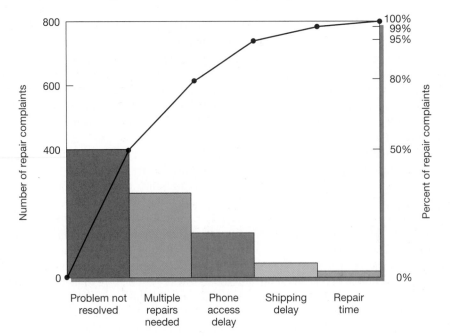

Pareto Diagrams

Pareto diagrams derive their name from a 19th-century Italian economist. In quality management, J. M. Juran first applied this concept by noting that only a vital few defects account for most problems evaluated for quality and that the trivial may explain the rest. Historically, this has come to be known as the 80/20 rule—that is, an 80 percent improvement in quality or performance can be expected by eliminating 20 percent of the causes of unacceptable quality or performance.

The **Pareto diagram** is a bar chart whose percentages sum to 100 percent. The data are derived from a multiple-choice, single-response scale; a multiple-choice, multiple-response scale; or frequency counts of words (or themes) from content analysis. The respondents' answers are sorted in decreasing importance, with bar height in descending order from left to right. The pictorial array that results reveals the highest concentration of improvement potential in the fewest number of remedies. An analysis of MindWriter customer complaints is depicted as a Pareto diagram in Exhibit 16-7. The cumulative frequency line in this exhibit shows that the top two problems (the repair did not resolve the customer's problem, and the product was returned multiple times for repair) accounted for 80 percent of the perceptions of inadequate repair service.

Boxplots[7]

The **boxplot,** or *box-and-whisker plot*, is another technique used frequently in exploratory data analysis.[8] A boxplot reduces the detail of the stem-and-leaf display and provides a different visual image of the distribution's location, spread, shape, tail length, and outliers. Boxplots are extensions of the **five-number summary** of a distribution. This summary consists of the median, the upper and lower quartiles, and the largest and smallest observations. The median and quartiles are used because they are particularly **resistant statistics**. Resistance is a characteristic that "provides insensitivity to localized misbehavior in data."[9] Resistant statistics are unaffected by outliers and change only slightly in response to the replacement of small portions of the data set.

Recall the discussion of the mean and standard deviation in Appendix 15a. Now assume we take a data set [5,6,6,7,7,7,8,8,9] and calculate its mean. The mean of the set is 7; the standard deviation 1.22. If the 9 is replaced with 90, the mean becomes 16 and the standard deviation increases to 27.78. The mean is now two times larger than most of the numbers in the distribution, and the standard deviation is more than 22 times its original size. Changing only one of nine values has disturbed the location and spread summaries to the point where they no longer represent the other eight values. Both the mean and the standard deviation are considered **nonresistant statistics**; they are susceptible to the effects of extreme values in the tails of the distribution and do not represent typical values well under conditions of asymmetry. The standard deviation is particularly problematic because it is computed from the squared deviations from the mean.[10] In contrast, the median and quartiles are highly resistant to change. When we changed the 9 to 90, the median remained at 7 and the lower and upper quartiles stayed at 6 and 8, respectively. Because of the nature of quartiles, up to 25 percent of the data can be made extreme without perturbing the median, the rectangular composition of the plot, or the quartiles themselves. These characteristics of resistance are incorporated into the construction of boxplots.

Boxplots may be constructed easily by hand or by computer programs. The basic ingredients of the plot are:

1. The rectangular plot that encompasses 50 percent of the data values.
2. A center line (or other notation) marking the median and going through the width of the box.
3. The edges of the box, called *hinges.*
4. The "whiskers" that extend from the right and left hinges to the largest and smallest values.[11]

These values may be found within 1.5 times the **interquartile range (IQR)** from either edge of the box. These components and their relationships are shown in Exhibit 16-8.

When you are examining data, it is important to separate legitimate outliers from errors in measurement, editing, coding, and data entry. **Outliers**, data points that exceed +1.5 the interquartile range, reflect unusual cases and are an important source of information for the study. They are displayed or given special statistical treatment, or other portions of the data set are sometimes shielded from their effects. Outliers that are entry mistakes should be corrected or removed during editing.

Exhibit 16-9 summarizes several comparisons that are of help to the analyst. Boxplots are an excellent diagnostic tool, especially when graphed on the same scale. The upper two plots in the exhibit are both symmetric, but one is larger than the other. Larger box widths are sometimes used when the second variable, from the same

65

The percent boost in company revenue created by best practices in data quality.

>**Exhibit 16-8** Boxplot Components

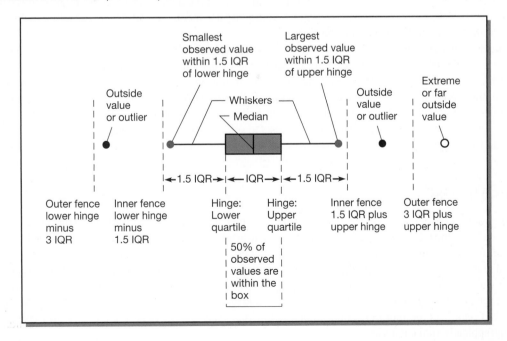

>**Exhibit 16-9** Diagnostics with Boxplots

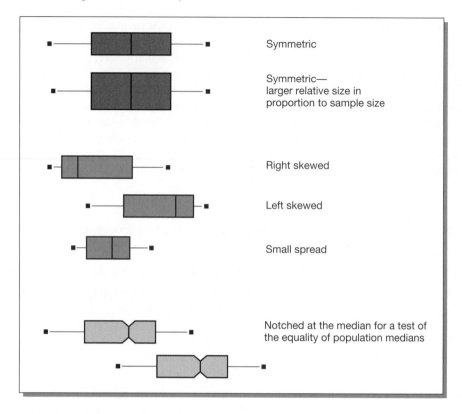

measurement scale, comes from a larger sample size. The box widths should be proportional to the square root of the sample size, but not all plotting programs account for this.[12] Right- and left-skewed distributions and those with reduced spread are also presented clearly in the plot comparison. Finally, groups may be compared by means of multiple plots. One variation, in which a notch at the median marks off a confidence interval to test the equality of group medians, takes us a step closer to hypothesis testing.[13] Here the sides of the box return to full width at the upper and lower confidence intervals. When the intervals do not overlap, we can be confident, at a specified confidence level, that the medians of the two populations are different.

In Exhibit 16-10, multiple boxplots compare five sectors of PrimeSell's customers by their average annual purchases data. The overall impression is one of potential problems for the analyst: unequal variances, skewness, and extreme outliers. Note the similarities of the profiles of finance and retailing in contrast to the high-tech and insurance sectors. If hypothesis tests are planned, further examination of this plot for each sector would require a stem-and-leaf display and a five-number summary. From this, we could make decisions on the types of tests to select for confirmatory analysis (see Chapters 17, 18, and 19).

Mapping

Increasingly, participant data are being attached to their geographic dimension as Geographic Information System (GIS) software and coordinate measuring devices have become more affordable and easier to use. Essentially a GIS works by linking data sets to each other with at least one common data field (e.g., a household's street address). The GIS allows the researcher to connect target and classification variables from a survey to specific geographic-based databases like U.S. Census data, to develop a richer understanding of the sample's attitudes and behavior. When radio frequency identification (RFID) data become more prevalent, much behavioral data will be able to connect with these new geographically rich databases.

>**Exhibit 16-10** Boxplot Comparison of Customer Sectors

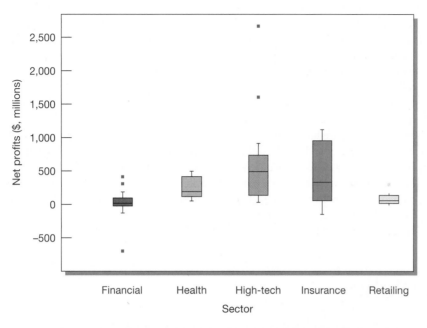

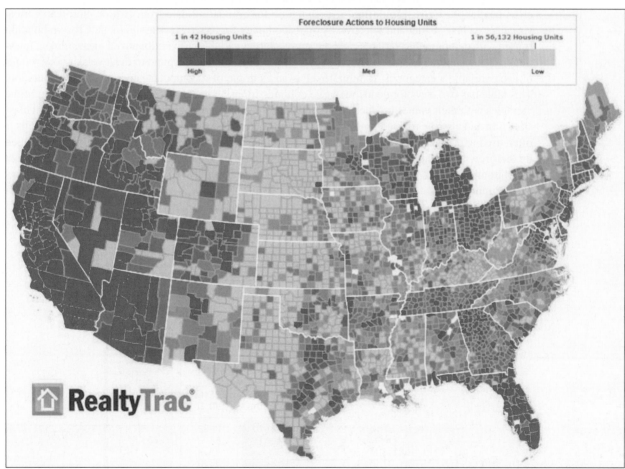

Sometimes there is no better way to display data than with a map. In 2009, home foreclosures in the United States hit an all-time high. But different parts of the country were affected differently by the subprime mortgage crisis. At a quick glance, when geospatial data are mapped, you can tell which states were most affected. This map from RealtyTrac shows home foreclosure listings, by state.

www.realtytrac.com/trendcenter

The most common way to display such data is with a map. Colors and patterns denoting knowledge, attitude, behavior, or demographic data arrays are superimposed over street maps (finest-level GIS), block-group maps, or county, state, or country maps to help identify the best locations for stores based on demographic, psychographic, and life-stage segmentation data. Florists array promotional response information geographically and use the map to plan targeted promotions. Consumer and business-to-business researchers use mapping of data on ownership, usage level, and price sensitivity in plotting geographic rollouts of new products. Although this is an attractive option for exploratory analysis, it does take specialized software and hardware, as well as the expertise to operate it. Students are encouraged to take specialized courses on GIS to expand their skill set in this growing area.

Throughout this section we have exploited the visual techniques of exploratory data analysis to look beyond numerical summaries and gain insight into the patterns of the data. Few of the approaches have stressed the need for advanced mathematics, and all have an intuitive appeal for the analyst. When the more common ways of summarizing location, spread, and shape have conveyed an inadequate picture of the data, we have used more resistant statistics to protect us from the effects of extreme scores and occasional errors. We have also emphasized the value of transforming the original scale of the data during preliminary analysis rather than at the point of hypothesis testing.

> Cross-Tabulation

Depending on the management question, we can gain valuable insights by examining the data with cross-tabulation. **Cross-tabulation** is a technique for comparing data from two or more categorical variables such as gender and selection by one's company for an overseas assignment. Cross-tabulation is used with demographic variables and the study's target variables (operationalized measurement questions). The technique uses tables having rows and columns that correspond to the levels or code values of each variable's categories. Exhibit 16-11 is an example of a computer-generated cross-tabulation. This table has two rows for gender and two columns for assignment selection. The combination of the variables with their values produces four cells. Each **cell** contains a count of the cases of the joint classification and also the row, column, and total percentages. The number of row cells and column cells is often used to designate the size of the table, as in this 2 × 2 table. The cells are individually identified by their row and column numbers, as illustrated. Row and column totals, called **marginals,** appear at the bottom and right "margins" of the table. They show the counts and percentages of the separate rows and columns.

>Exhibit 16-11 SPSS Cross-Tabulation of Gender by Overseas Assignment Opportunity

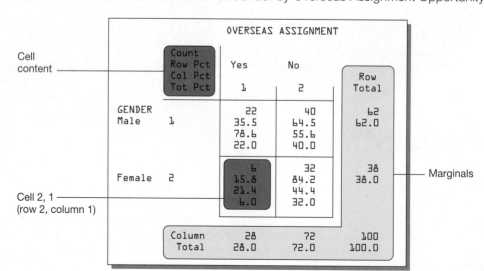

Empowering Excel

When developing data displays, some research analysts turn not to heavy duty statistical software packages like SPSS or SAS, but to the spreadsheet on their desktop. Two enterprising professors from Pennsylvania State University, Gary L. Lilien and Arvind Rangaswamy, have teamed to developed Microsoft Excel plug-ins that empower the spreadsheet to create some commonly desired displays with just a few mouse clicks. "With this software product, users will be able to use the power of world-class analytics from within Excel, an interface with which they are already comfortable," claims their website.

Each plug-in offers a unique template for data entry where the charting directions are embedded. Once the data are entered, a series of windows guides the user through the process of creating the display, such as the GE Matrix shown here. The user can practice the techniques on sample data from real companies or enter his or her own data.

The plug-ins currently facilitate displays for forecasting, conjoint analysis, customer choice analysis, customer lifetime value analysis, GE Portfolio Matrix plotting, positioning analysis, resource allocation analysis, new-product and service design, and segmentation/targeting analysis—all common analytical exercises for managers involved in marketing engineering. Thanks to Lilien and Rangaswamy, some sophisticated display techniques have been significantly simplified.

www.mktgeng.com

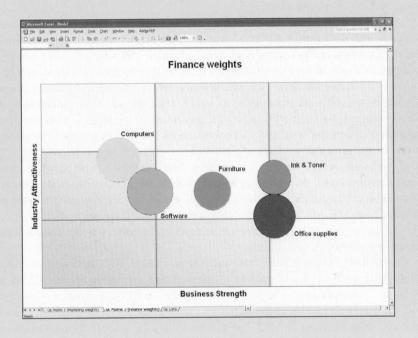

Cross-tabulation is a first step for identifying relationships between variables. When tables are constructed for statistical testing, we call them **contingency tables,** and the test determines if the classification variables are independent of each other (see chi-square in Chapter 17). Of course, tables may be larger than 2×2.

The Use of Percentages

Percentages serve two purposes in data presentation. First, they simplify the data by reducing all numbers to a range from 0 to 100. Second, they translate the data into standard form, with a base of 100, for relative comparisons. In a sampling situation, the number of cases that fall into a category is meaningless unless it is related to some base. A count of 28 overseas assignees has little meaning unless we

>Exhibit 16-12 Comparison of Percentages in Cross-Tabulation Studies by Overseas Assignment

Study 1

		OVERSEAS ASSIGNMENT		
Count Row Pct Col Pct Tot Pct		Yes 1	No 2	Row Total
GENDER Male	1	22 35.5 78.6 22.0	40 64.5 55.6 40.0	62 62.0
Female	2	6 15.8 21.4 6.0	32 84.2 44.4 32.0	38 38.0
Column Total		28 28.0	72 72.0	100 100.0

Study 2

		OVERSEAS ASSIGNMENT		
Count Row Pct Col Pct Tot Pct		Yes 1	No 2	Row Total
GENDER Male	1	225 25.0 62.5 15.0	675 75.0 59.2 45.0	900 60.0
Female	2	135 22.5 37.5 9.0	465 77.5 40.8 31.0	600 40.0
Column Total		360 24.0	1140 76.0	1500 100.0

know it is from a sample of 100. Using the latter as a base, we conclude that 28 percent of this study's sample has an overseas assignment.

Although the above is useful, it is even more useful when the research problem calls for a comparison of several distributions of data. Assume the previously reported data were collected five years ago and the present study had a sample of 1,500, of which 360 were selected for overseas assignments. By using percentages, we can see the relative relationships and shifts in the data (see Exhibit 16-12).

With two-dimension tables, the selection of a row or column will accentuate a particular distribution or comparison. This raises the question about which direction the percentages should be calculated. Most computer programs offer options for presenting percentages in both directions and interchanging the rows and columns of the table. But in situations in which one variable is hypothesized to be the presumed cause, is thought to affect or predict a response, or is simply antecedent to the other variable, we label it the independent variable. Percentages should then be computed in the direction of this variable. Thus, if the independent variable is placed on the row, select row percentages; if it is on the column, select column percentages. In which direction should the percentages run in the previous example? If only the column percentages are reported, we imply that assignment status has some effect on gender. This is implausible. When percentages are reported by rows, the implication is that gender influences selection for overseas assignments.

Care should be taken in interpreting percentages from tables. Consider again the data in Exhibit 16-12. From the first to the second study, it is apparent that the percentage of females selected for overseas assignments rose from 15.8 to 22.5 percent of their respective samples. This should not be confused with the percentage within each sample who were women with overseas assignments, a number which increased from 6 percent (Study 1) to 9 percent (Study 2). Among all overseas selectees, in the first study 21.4 percent were women, while in the second study, 37.5 percent were women. Similar comparisons can be made for the other categories. The tables verify an increase in women with overseas assignments, but we cannot conclude that their gender had anything to do with the increase.

Percentages are used by virtually everyone dealing with numbers—but often incorrectly. The following guidelines, if used during analysis, will help to prevent errors in reporting:[14]

- *Averaging percentages.* Percentages cannot be averaged unless each is weighted by the size of the group from which it is derived. Thus, a simple average will not suffice; it is necessary to use a weighted average.

- *Use of too large percentages.* This often defeats the purpose of percentages—which is to simplify. A large percentage is difficult to understand and is confusing. If a 1,000 percent increase is experienced, it is better to describe this as a 10-fold increase.

- *Using too small a base.* Percentages hide the base from which they have been computed. A figure of 60 percent when contrasted with 30 percent would appear to suggest a sizable difference.

>snapshot

Extensive Research Launches Starbucks Card Duetto™ Visa

BusinessWeek recognized the Starbucks Card Duetto™ Visa as one of the important new products of 2003. In fact, it was the only financial product on the list. Starbucks Card Duetto™ Visa is a multifunction card that combines the features of a prepaid stored-value card, known as the Starbucks Card, with a regular credit card. Starbucks, in conjunction with Visa and Bank One (now Chase), did extensive research to determine if the proposed new payment option had appeal. Focus groups were used to determine the level of potential consumer confusion with the multifunction card, determine card attractiveness, and refine messaging. A series of online surveys were conducted both before and after the launch of the product to determine market receptivity. A press release about the partnership about eight months before launch generated news coverage resulting in traffic to Starbucks' website. Early purchase intent was determined by those Starbucks customers who took initiative and signed up via the website to be prenotified by e-mail when the card became available. Among the postlaunch research

questions guiding measurement of return on marketing investment (ROMI) are:

- Does the card enhance the Starbucks customer experience (how satisfied is each customer, and do customers feel appreciated)?
- Did the card prove valuable to all partners: Starbucks, Chase, and Visa?
- Did card activity, which is linked to charitable donations, permit Starbucks to give back to the communities in which it operates in a significant way?

If you were in charge of this research, what would you be looking for during exploratory data analysis?

www.chase.com; usa.visa.com; www.starbucks.com

To learn more about this research, read the case and download the video "Starbucks, Bank One, and Visa Launch the Starbucks Card Duetto™ Visa" from the Online Learning Center.

Yet if there are only three cases in the one category and six in the other, the differences would not be as significant as they have been made to appear with percentages.

- *Percentage decreases can never exceed 100 percent.* This is obvious, but this type of mistake occurs frequently. The higher figure should always be used as the base or denominator. For example, if a price was reduced from $1 to $.25, the decrease would be 75 percent (75/100).

Other Table-Based Analysis

The recognition of a meaningful relationship between variables generally signals a need for further investigation. Even if one finds a statistically significant relationship, the questions of why and under what conditions remain. The introduction of a **control variable** to interpret the relationship is often necessary. Cross-tabulation tables serve as the framework.

Statistical packages like Minitab, SAS, and SPSS have among their modules many options for the construction of *n*-way tables with provision for multiple control variables. Suppose you are interested in creating a cross-tabulation of two variables with one control. Whatever the number of values in the primary variables, the control variable with five values determines the number of tables. For some applications, it is appropriate to have five separate tables; for others, it might be preferable to have adjoining tables or have the values of all the variables in one. Management reports are of the latter variety. Exhibit 16-13 presents an example in which all three variables are handled under the same banner. Programs such as this one can handle far more complex tables and statistical information.[15]

An advanced variation on *n*-way tables is **automatic interaction detection (AID).** AID is a computerized statistical process that requires that the researcher identify a dependent variable and a set of predictors or independent variables. The computer then searches among up to 300 variables for the best single division of the data according to each predictor variable, chooses one, and splits the sample using a statistical test to verify the appropriateness of this choice.

Exhibit 16-14 shows the tree diagram that resulted from an AID study of customer satisfaction with MindWriter's CompleteCare repair service. The initial dependent variable is the overall impression of

>Exhibit 16-13 SPSS Cross-Tabulation with Control and Nested Variables

	Control Variable					
	Category 1			Category 2		
	Nested Variable			Nested Variable		
	cat 1	cat 2	cat 3	cat 1	cat 2	cat 3
Stub...	Cells...					

	SEX OF EMPLOYEE			
	MALES		FEMALES	
	MINORITY CLASSIFICATION		MINORITY CLASSIFICATION	
	WHITE	NONWHITE	WHITE	NONWHITE
EMPLOYMENT CATEGORY				
CLERICAL	16%	7%	18%	7%
OFFICE TRAINEE	7%	3%	17%	2%
SECURITY OFFICER	3%	3%		
COLLEGE TRAINEE	7%	0%	1%	
EXEMPT EMPLOYEE	6%	0%	0%	
MBA TRAINEE	1%	0%	0%	
TECHNICAL	1%			

>Exhibit 16-14 Automatic Interaction Detection Example (MindWriter's Repair Satisfaction)

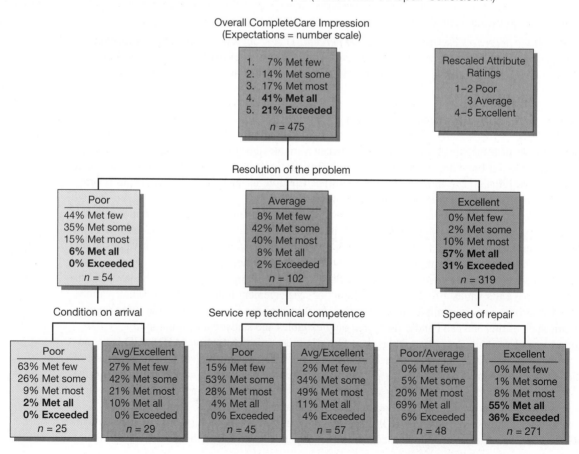

the repair service. This variable was measured on an interval scale of 1 to 5. The variables that contribute to perceptions of repair effectiveness were also measured on the same scale but were rescaled to ordinal data for this example (1–2 = poor, 3 = average, and 4–5 = excellent). The top box shows that 62 percent of the respondents rated the repair service as excellent (41% + 21%). The best predictor of repair effectiveness is "resolution of the problem."

On the left side of the tree, customers who rated "resolution of the problem" as poor have fewer expectations being met or exceeded than the average for the sample (6 percent versus 62 percent). A poor rating on "condition on arrival" exacerbates this, reducing the total satisfied group to 2 percent. From this example you can see that the researcher separately studied (applied AID to) each subgroup to find the variable that when split again makes the next largest contribution to understanding the consumers' evaluation process—and to the reduction of unexplained variation in each subsample. This analysis alerts decision makers at MindWriter to the best- and worst-case scenarios for the CompleteCare service, how to recover during a problematic month, and which "key drivers," or independent variables influencing the process, should receive corrective resources.

>summary

1 Exploratory data analysis (EDA) provides a perspective and set of tools to search for clues and patterns in the data. EDA augments rather than supplants traditional statistics. In addition to numerical summaries of location, spread, and shape, EDA uses visual displays to provide a complete and accurate impression of distributions and variable relationships.

Frequency tables array data from lowest to highest values with counts and percentages. They are most useful for inspecting the range of responses and their repeated occurrence. Bar charts and pie charts are appropriate for relative comparisons of nominal data. Histograms are optimally used with continuous variables where intervals group the responses. The Pareto diagram is a bar chart whose percentages sum to 100 percent. The causes of the problem under investigation are sorted in decreasing importance, with bar height descending from left to right. Stem-and-leaf displays and boxplots are EDA techniques that provide visual representations of distributions. The former present actual data values using a histogram-type device that allows inspection of spread and shape. Boxplots use the five-number summary to convey a detailed picture of a distribution's main body, tails, and outliers. Both stem-and-leaf displays and boxplots rely on resistant statistics to overcome the limitations of descriptive measures that are subject to extreme scores.

2 The examination of relationships involving categorical variables employs cross-tabulation. The tables used for this purpose consist of cells and marginals. The cells may contain combinations of count, row, column, and total percentages. The tabular structure is the framework for later statistical testing. Computer software for cross-classification analysis makes table-based analysis with one or more control variables an efficient tool for data visualization and later decision making. An advanced variation on *n*-way tables is automatic interaction detection (AID).

>**key**terms

>discussionquestions

Terms in Review

1 Define or explain:

a Marginals.

b Pareto diagram.

c Nonresistant statistics.

d Lower control limit.

e The five-number summary.

Making Research Decisions

2 Suppose you were preparing two-way tables of percentages for the following pairs of variables. How would you run the percentages?

a Age and consumption of breakfast cereal.

b Family income and confidence about the family's future.

c Marital status and sports participation.

d Crime rate and unemployment rate.

3 You study the attrition of entering college freshmen (those students who enter college as freshmen but don't stay to graduate). You find the following relationships between attrition, aid, and distance of home from college. What is your interpretation? Consider all variables and relationships.

	Aid		Home Near Receiving Aid		Home Far Receiving Aid	
	Yes (%)	No (%)	Yes (%)	No (%)	Yes (%)	No (%)
Drop Out	25	20	5	15	30	40
Stay	75	80	95	85	70	60

4 A local health agency is experimenting with two appeal letters, A and B, with which to raise funds. It sends out 400 of the A appeal and 400 of the B appeal (each subsample is divided equally among working-class and middle-class neighborhoods). The agency secures the results shown in the following table.

a Which appeal is the best?

b Which class responded better to which letter?

c Is appeal or social class a more powerful independent variable?

	Appeal A		Appeal B	
	Middle Class (%)	Working Class (%)	Middle Class (%)	Working Class (%)
Contribution	20	40	15	30
No Contribution	80	60	85	70
	100	100	100	100

5 Assume you have collected data on sales associates of a large retail organization in a major metropolitan area. You analyze the data by type of work classification, education level, and whether the workers were raised in a rural or urban setting. The results are shown here. How would you interpret them?

Annual Retail Employee Turnover per 100 Employees

	High Education		Low Education			
	Salaried	Hourly Wage	Salaried	Hourly Wage	Salaried	Hourly Wage
Rural	8	16	6	14	18	18
Urban	12	16	10	12	19	20

Bringing Research to Life

6 Identify the variables being cross-tabulated by Sammye. Identify some plausible reasons why such an exploration would be a good idea.

From Concept to Practice

7 Use the data in Exhibit 16-5 to construct a stem-and-leaf display.

a Where do you find the main body of the distribution?

b How many values reside outside the inner fence(s)?

From the Headlines

8 Asustek, the Taiwanese manufacturer that basically invented the *netbook* category, has been researching more radical design ideas, including a classy wrist-top computer, the Waveface Ultra. It is made from a bendable display that can connect to the Internet, make phone calls, and crunch data. Essentially, it's a bracelet that acts like a smartphone.

a How might you use such a device to display stimuli for respondents?

b What is the interactive data exchange potential for researchers?

>cases*

Agri Comp

NCRCC: Teeing Up and New
Strategic Direction

Mastering Teacher Leadership

Proofpoint: Capitalizing on a
Reporter's Love of Statistics

*You will find a description of each case in the Case Abstracts section of this textbook. Check the Case Index to determine whether a case provides data, the research instrument, video, or other supplementary material. Written cases are downloadable from the text website (www.mhhe.com/cooper11e). All video material and video cases are available from the Online Learning Center.

>cases*

>chapter 17

Hypothesis Testing

>learningobjectives

After reading this chapter, you should understand . . .

1 The nature and logic of hypothesis testing.

2 What a statistically significant difference is.

3 The six-step hypothesis testing procedure.

4 The differences between parametric and nonparametric tests and when to use each.

5 The factors that influence the selection of an appropriate test of statistical significance.

6 How to interpret the various test statistics.

> ❝ Don't confuse "hypothesis" and "theory."
> The former is a possible explanation; the
> latter, the correct one. The establishment
> of theory is the very purpose of science. ❞
>
> Martin H. Fischer, professor emeritus physiology,
> University of Cincinnati

"Sara, I'd like to meet with you about verifying the gender and age differences on the alcohol issue for Center City for Performing Arts Association." Jason makes his way through the cluttered outer office, stepping around piles of printouts, topped with sketched graphs or detailed cross-tabulated tables with handwritten notes.

Moments later, Sara enters, carrying the cross-tabulated data to which Jason had referred.

Jason smiles, waiting for her to settle. "So what have you got?"

"There is definitely a difference in attitude about serving alcohol during intermission at performances. But it doesn't appear to be quite what the CCPA board expected."

"How so?"

"Well, the younger patrons seem somewhat divided, while those between 35 and 54 are against and those 55 and over are strongly in favor."

"What was your original hypothesis?"

"Based on your meeting notes from the project session with the CCPA board, I formulated the hypothesis that there would be a difference on the alcohol issue based on age," shares Sara. "But I assumed that the younger the patrons, the more in favor of alcohol they would be. The numbers just aren't supporting that. And I'm not so sure that age is the right variable to look at."

Jason extends his hand across his desk. "Let me see the statistics on age."

"And I've got the stats on gender too," offers Sara.

"Are those in line with your hypothesis?"

"Not really," shares Sara. "Men and women are all over the place. I hypothesized that men would be in favor while women would be against. That's just not panning out."

Jason glances at the printout, pleased to see that her interpretation of the statistics is correct. "Looks like you have some work yet, to determine the pockets of resistance. Since the sample split—wasn't it 57 percent in favor to 43 percent against?—we don't want to recommend that CCPA proceed *without* being able to tell the board the likely direction of potential trouble.

"Sometimes our preliminary analysis plan can take us only so far," comments Jason. "Let's talk about what tests you plan to run now."

> Introduction

In Chapters 15 and 16, we discussed the procedures for data preparation and preliminary analysis. The next step for many studies is hypothesis testing.

Just as your understanding of scientific reasoning was important in the last two chapters, recollection of the specific differences between induction and deduction is fundamental to hypothesis testing. Inductive reasoning moves from specific facts to general, but tentative, conclusions. We can never be absolutely sure that inductive conclusions are flawless. With the aid of probability estimates, we can qualify our results and state the degree of confidence we have in them. Statistical inference is an application of inductive reasoning. It allows us to reason from evidence found in the sample to conclusions we wish to make about the population.

Inferential statistics is the second of two major categories of statistical procedures, the other being descriptive statistics. We used descriptive statistics in Chapter 14 when describing distributions. Under the heading **inferential statistics,** two topics are discussed in this book. The first, estimation of population values, was used with sampling in Chapter 14, but we will return to it here briefly. The second, testing statistical hypotheses, is the primary subject of this chapter. There are more examples of hypothesis tests in this chapter than most students will need for a term project or early assignments in their research careers. A section on nonparametric techniques in Appendix C provides further study for readers with a special interest in nominal and ordinal variables.

After you have detailed your hypotheses in your preliminary analysis planning, the purpose of hypothesis testing is to determine the accuracy of your hypotheses due to the fact that you have collected a sample of data, not a census. Exhibit 17-1 reminds you of the relationships among your design strategy, data collection activities, preliminary analysis, and hypothesis testing.

We evaluate the accuracy of hypotheses by determining the statistical likelihood that the data reveal true differences—not random sampling error. We evaluate the importance of a statistically significant difference by weighing the practical significance of any change that we measure.

Although there are two approaches to hypothesis testing, the more established is the classical or sampling-theory approach. **Classical statistics** are found in all of the major statistics books and are widely used in research applications. This approach represents an objective view of probability in which the decision making rests totally on an analysis of available sampling data. A hypothesis is established; it is rejected or fails to be rejected, based on the sample data collected.

The second approach is known as **Bayesian statistics,** which are an extension of the classical approach. They also use sampling data, but they go beyond to consider all other available information. This additional information consists of subjective probability estimates stated in terms of degrees of belief. These subjective estimates are based on general experience rather than on specific collected data. Various decision rules are established, cost and other estimates can be introduced, and the expected outcomes of combinations of these elements are used to judge decision alternatives.

Statistical Significance

Following classical statistics approach, we accept or reject a hypothesis on the basis of sampling information alone. Since any sample will almost surely vary somewhat from its population, we must judge whether the differences are statistically significant or insignificant. A difference has **statistical significance** if there is good reason to believe the difference does not represent random sampling fluctuations only. For example, Honda, Toyota, Chrysler, Nissan, Ford, and other auto companies produce hybrid vehicles using an advanced technology that combines a small gas engine with an electric motor. The vehicles run on an electric motor at slow speeds but shift to both the gasoline motor and the electric motor at city and higher freeway speeds. Their advertising strategies focus on fuel economy. Let's say that the hybrid Toyota has maintained an average of about 60 miles per gallon (mpg) with a standard deviation of 10 mpg. Suppose researchers discover by analyzing all production vehicles that the mpg is now 61. Is this difference statistically significant from 60? Of course it is, because the difference is based on a *census* of the vehicles and there is no sampling involved. It has been demonstrated conclusively that the population average has moved from 60 to 61 mpg. Although it is of statistical

>**Exhibit 17-1** Hypothesis Testing and the Research Process

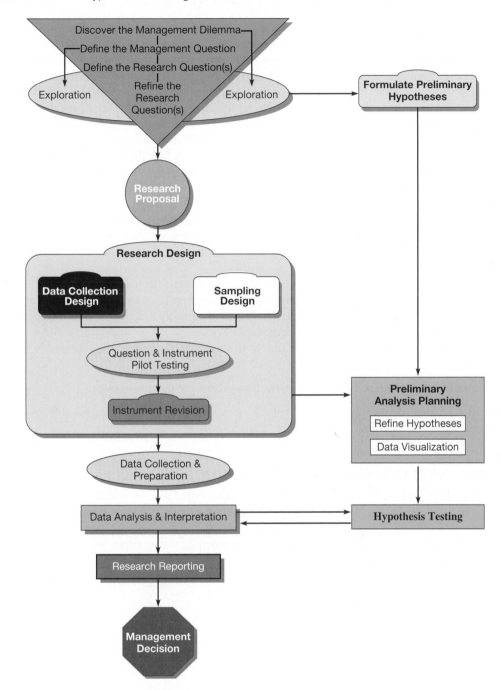

significance, whether it is of **practical significance** is another question. If a decision maker judges that this variation has no real importance, then it is of little practical significance.

Since it would be too expensive to analyze all of a manufacturer's vehicles frequently, we resort to sampling. Assume a sample of 25 cars is randomly selected and the average mpg is calculated to be 64. Is this statistically significant? The answer is not obvious. It is significant if there is good reason to believe the average mpg of the total population has moved up from 60. Since the evidence consists of only a sample, consider the second possibility: that this is only a random sampling error and thus is not significant. The task is to decide whether such a result from this sample is or is not statistically significant. To answer this question, one needs to consider further the logic of hypothesis testing.

The Logic of Hypothesis Testing

In classical tests of significance, two kinds of hypotheses are used. The **null hypothesis** is used for testing. It is a statement that no difference exists between the parameter (a measure taken by a census of the population or a prior measurement of a sample of the population) and the statistic being compared to it (a measure from a recently drawn sample of the population). Analysts usually test to determine whether there has been no change in the population of interest or whether a real difference exists. Why not state the hypothesis in a positive form? Why not state that any difference between the sample statistic and the population parameter is due to some reason? Unfortunately, this type of hypothesis cannot be tested definitively. Evidence that is consistent with a hypothesis stated in a positive form can almost never be taken as conclusive grounds for accepting the hypothesis. A finding that is consistent with this type of hypothesis might be consistent with other hypotheses too, and thus it does not demonstrate the truth of the given hypothesis.

For example, suppose a coin is suspected of being biased in favor of heads. The coin is flipped 100 times and the outcome is 52 heads. It would not be correct to jump to the conclusion that the coin is biased simply because more than the expected number of 50 heads resulted. The reason is that 52 heads is consistent with the hypothesis that the coin is fair. On the other hand, flipping 85 or 90 heads in 100 flips would seem to contradict the hypothesis of a fair coin. In this case there would be a strong case for a biased coin.

In the hybrid-vehicle example, the null hypothesis states that the population parameter of 60 mpg has not changed. A second, **alternative hypothesis** holds that there has been a change in average mpg (i.e., the sample statistic of 64 indicates the population value probably is no longer 60). The alternative hypothesis is the logical opposite of the null hypothesis.

The hybrid-car example can be explored further to show how these concepts are used to test for significance:

- The null hypothesis (H_0): There has been no change from the 60 mpg average.

The alternative hypothesis (H_A) may take several forms, depending on the objective of the researchers. The H_A may be of the "not the same" or the "greater than" or "less than" form:

- The average mpg has changed from 60.
- The average mpg has increased (decreased) from 60.

These types of alternative hypotheses correspond with two-tailed and one-tailed tests. A **two-tailed test,** or *nondirectional test,* considers two possibilities: the average could be more than 60 mpg, or it could be less than 60. To test this hypothesis, the regions of rejection are divided into two tails of the distribution. A **one-tailed test,** or *directional test,* places the entire probability of an unlikely outcome into the tail specified by the alternative hypothesis. In Exhibit 17-2, the first diagram represents a nondirectional hypothesis, and the second is a directional hypothesis of the "greater than" variety.

>Exhibit 17-2 Two- and One-Tailed Tests at the 5 percent Level of Significance

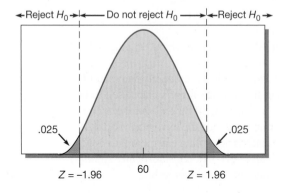
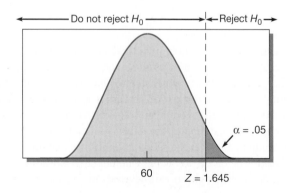

Toyota Prius, 2010 Car of the Year, is the preeminent hybrid gas-electric car. It inspires a cult-like devotion which has translated into unprecedented satisfaction rates in user studies. It produces an EPA fuel economy of 51 mpg city and 60 mpg highway. Its 'harmony' ad campaign, featuring 100 actors representing 1,000,000 images of people portraying grass, leaves, sun, cloud, flowers, and butterflies created almost as big a sensation as the 3rd generation car. **www.prius.com**

Hypotheses for Exhibit 17-2 may be expressed in the following form:

Null H_0: $\mu = 60$ mpg
Alternative H_A: $\mu \neq 60$ mpg (not the same case)

Or

Null H_0: $\mu \leq 60$ mpg
Alternative H_A: $\mu > 60$ mpg (greater than case)

Or

Null H_0: $\mu \geq 60$ mpg
Alternative H_A: $\mu < 60$ mpg (less than case)

In testing these hypotheses, adopt this decision rule: take no corrective action if the analysis shows that one cannot reject the null hypothesis. Note the language "cannot reject" rather than "accept" the null hypothesis. It is argued that a null hypothesis can never be proved and therefore cannot be "accepted." Here, again, we see the influence of inductive reasoning. Unlike deduction, where the connections between premises and conclusions provide a legitimate claim of "conclusive proof," inductive conclusions do not possess that advantage. Statistical testing gives only a chance to (1) disprove (reject) or (2) fail to reject the hypothesis. Despite this terminology, it is common to hear "accept the null" rather than the clumsy "fail to reject the null." In this discussion, the less formal *accept* means "fail to reject" the null hypothesis.

If we reject a null hypothesis (finding a statistically significant difference), then we are accepting the alternative hypothesis. In either accepting or rejecting a null hypothesis, we can make incorrect decisions. A null hypothesis can be accepted when it should have been rejected or rejected when it should have been accepted.

These problems are illustrated with an analogy to the American legal system.[1] In our system of justice, the innocence of an indicted person is presumed until proof of guilt beyond a reasonable doubt can be established. In hypothesis testing, this is the null hypothesis; there should be no difference between the presumption of innocence and the outcome unless contrary evidence is furnished. Once evidence establishes beyond reasonable doubt that innocence can no longer be maintained, a just conviction is required. This is equivalent to rejecting the null hypothesis and accepting the alternative hypothesis. Incorrect decisions or errors are the other two possible outcomes. We can unjustly convict an innocent person, or we can acquit a guilty person.

>**snap**shot

Direct-to-Consumer Ads under Heavy Fire

Direct-to-consumer (D-to-C) pharmaceutical ads have drawn a lot of criticism since 1997 Food and Drug Administration (FDA) regulations permitted such tactics. Proponents of legislation to disallow the practice fear such ads "unfairly influence important health care decisions" by causing patients to pressure doctors and thus encourage doctors to prescribe unnecessary prescriptions. The chairman of the American Medical Association believes such advertising may create an adversarial relationship between doctor and patient. He wants to know if the ads "improve the quality of care enough to make it worth the increased costs of the medicines being advertised." One democratic legislator believes "taxpayers would not have to subsidize excessive advertising that leads to higher prices at the pharmacy counter."

Ipsos-NPD tracks this issue for the pharmaceutical industry with its monthly PharmTrends® panel, comprising 16,000 U.S. households. Panel members are measured for ad recall,

prescriptions filled, physician recommendations for over-the-counter (OTC) products, and OTC products purchased, as well as condition being treated. Panel findings reveal that advertising "has encouraged higher levels of script fulfillment per year among consumers who reported that they were aware of advertising." Additionally, such advertising is credited with reminding patients to refill prescriptions. In its February InstaVue omnibus mail survey of 26,000 adults, 47 percent had seen pharmaceutical advertising in the past year, 25 percent indicated D-to-C ads encouraged them to call/visit their doctors to discuss the pharmaceutical advertised, and 15 percent reported asking for the very drug advertised.

How would you determine if this research confirmed or refuted that "pharmaceutical ads undermine quality of care"?

www.ipsos-npd.com

>**Exhibit 17-3** Comparison of Statistical Decisions to Legal Analogy

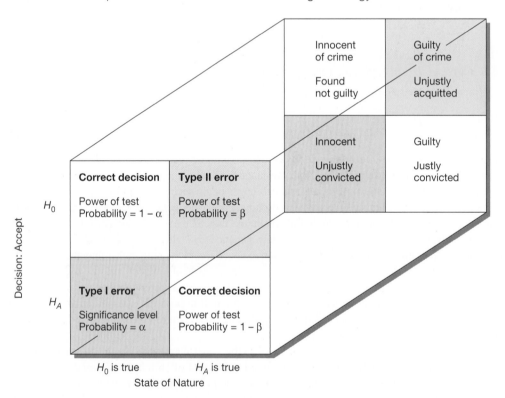

Exhibit 17-3 compares the statistical situation to the legal one. One of two conditions exists in nature—either the null hypothesis is true or the alternative hypothesis is true. An indicted person is innocent or guilty. Two decisions can be made about these conditions: one may accept the null hypothesis or reject it (thereby accepting the alternative). Two of these situations result in correct decisions; the other two lead to decision errors.

When a **Type I error** (α) is committed, a true null hypothesis is rejected; the innocent person is unjustly convicted. The value is called *the level of significance* and is the probability of rejecting the true null. With a **Type II error** (β), one fails to reject a false null hypothesis; the result is an unjust acquittal, with the guilty person going free. In our system of justice, it is more important to reduce the probability of convicting the innocent than that of acquitting the guilty. Similarly, hypothesis testing places a greater emphasis on Type I errors than on Type II errors. Next we shall examine each of these errors in more detail.

Type I Error

Assume the hybrid manufacturer's problem is complicated by a consumer testing agency's assertion that the average city mpg has changed. Assume the population mean is 50 mpg, the standard deviation of the population is 10 mpg, and the size of the sample is 25 vehicles. With this information, one can calculate the standard error of the mean ($\sigma_{\bar{x}}$) (the standard deviation of the distribution of sample means). This hypothetical distribution is pictured in Exhibit 17-4. The standard error of the mean is calculated to be 2 mpg:

$$\sigma_{\bar{x}} = \frac{\sigma}{\sqrt{n}} = \frac{10}{\sqrt{25}} = 2$$

>**Exhibit 17-4** Probability of Making a Type I Error Given H_0 Is True

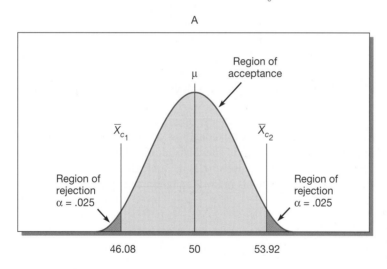

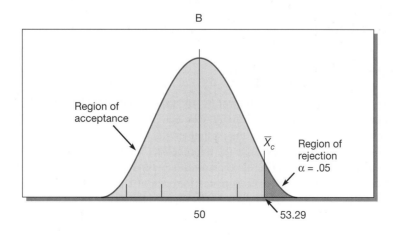

If the decision is to reject H_0 with a 95 percent confidence interval ($\alpha = .05$), a Type I error of .025 in each tail is accepted (this assumes a two-tailed test). In part A of Exhibit 17-4, see the **regions of rejection** indicated by the shaded areas. The area between these two regions is known as the **region of acceptance.** The dividing points between the rejection and acceptance areas are called **critical values.** Since the distribution of sample means is normal, the critical values can be computed in terms of the standardized random variable,[2] where

$Z = 1.96$ (significance level $= .05$)

$\overline{X}_c =$ the critical value of the sample mean

$\mu =$ the population value stated in $H_0 = 50$

$\sigma_{\overline{X}} =$ the standard error of a distribution of means of samples of 25

Thus, the critical values for the test of the null hypothesis (that the mpg has not changed) are computed as follows:

$$Z = \frac{\overline{X} - \mu}{\sigma_{\overline{X}}}$$

$$-1.96 = \frac{\overline{X}_c - 50}{2}$$

$$\overline{X}_c = 46.08$$

$$1.96 = \frac{\overline{X}_c - 50}{2}$$

$$\overline{X}_c = 53.92$$

If the probability of a Type I error is 5 percent ($\alpha = .05$), the probability of a correct decision if the null hypothesis is true is 95 percent. By changing the probability of a Type I error, you move critical values either closer to or farther away from the assumed parameter of 50. This can be done if a smaller or larger α error is desired and critical values are moved to reflect this. You can also change the Type 1 error and the regions of acceptance by changing the size of the sample. For example, if you take a sample of 100, the critical values that provide a Type I error of .05 are 48.04 and 51.96.

The alternative hypothesis concerned a change in either direction from 50, but the manufacturer is interested only in increases in mpg. For this, one uses a one-tailed (greater than) H_A and places the entire region of rejection in the upper tail of the distribution. One can accept a 5 percent α risk and compute a new critical value (X_c). (See Appendix D, Exhibit D-1, to find the Z value of 1.645 for the area of .05 under the curve.) Substitute this in the Z equation and solve for $\overline{X}_c$:

$$Z = 1.645 = \frac{\overline{X}_c - 50}{2}$$

$$\overline{X}_c = 53.29$$

This new critical value, the boundary between the regions of acceptance and rejection, is pictured in part B of Exhibit 17-4.

Type II Error

The manufacturer would commit a Type II error (β) by accepting the null hypothesis ($\mu = 50$) when in truth it had changed. This kind of error is difficult to detect. The probability of committing a β error depends on five factors: (1) the true value of the parameter, (2) the α level we have selected, (3) whether a one- or two-tailed test was used to evaluate the hypothesis, (4) the sample standard deviation, and (5) the size of the sample. We secure a different β error if the new β moves from 50 to 54 rather than only to 52. We must compute separate β error estimates for each of a number of assumed new population parameters and $\overline{X}_c$ values.

>**Exhibit 17-5** Probability of Making a Type II Error

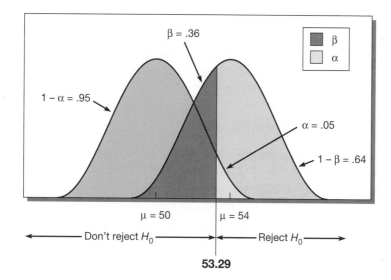

To illustrate, assume μ has actually moved to 54 from 50. Under these conditions, what is the probability of our making a Type II error if the critical value is set at 53.29? (See Exhibit 17-5.) This may be expressed in the following fashion:

$$P(A_2)S_1 = \alpha = .05 \text{ (assume a one-tailed alternative hypothesis)}$$

$$P(A_1)S_2 = \beta = ?$$

$$\sigma_{\bar{X}} = \frac{\sigma}{\sqrt{n}} = \frac{10}{\sqrt{25}} = 2$$

$$Z = \frac{\bar{X} - \mu}{\sigma_{\bar{X}}} = \frac{53.29 - 54}{2} = -.355$$

Using Exhibit D-1 in Appendix D, we interpolate between .35 and .36 Z scores to find the .355 Z score. The area between the mean and Z is .1387. β is the tail area, or the area below the Z, and is calculated as

$$\beta = .50 - .1387 = .36$$

This condition is shown in Exhibit 17-5. It is the percent of the area where we would *not* reject the null (H_0:$\mu = 50$) when, in fact, it was false because the true mean was 54. With an α of .05 and a sample of 25, there is a 36 percent probability of a Type II (β) error if the μ is 54. We also speak of the **power of the test**—that is (1 − β). For this example, the power of the test equals 64 percent (1 − .36)—that is, we will correctly reject the false null hypothesis with a 64 percent probability. A power of 64 percent is less than the 80 percent minimum percentage recommended by statisticians.

There are several ways to reduce a Type II error. We can shift the critical value closer to the original μ of 50; but to do this, we must accept a bigger α. Whether to take this action depends on the evaluation of the relative α and β risks. It might be desirable to enlarge the acceptable α risk because a worsening of the mileage would probably call for increased efforts to stimulate efficiency. Committing a Type I error would mean only that we engaged in efforts to stimulate efficiency when the situation had not worsened. This act probably would not have many adverse effects even if mpg had not increased.

A second way to reduce Type II error is to increase sample size. For example, if the sample were increased to 100, the power of the test would be much stronger:

$$\sigma_{\bar{X}} = \frac{\sigma}{\sqrt{n}} = \frac{10}{\sqrt{100}} = 1$$

$$Z = \frac{\bar{X} - \mu}{\sigma_{\bar{X}}} = \frac{53.29 - 54}{1} = -.71$$

$$\beta = .50 - .2612 = .24$$

This would reduce the Type II error to 24 percent and increase the power of the test to 76 percent.

A third method seeks to improve both α and β errors simultaneously and is difficult to accomplish. We know that measuring instruments, observations, and recording produce error. By using a better measuring device, tightening the observation and recording processes, or devising a more efficient sample, we can reduce the variability of observations. This diminishes the standard error of estimate and in turn reduces the sampling distributions' spread. The net effect is that there is less tail area in the error regions.

Statistical Testing Procedures

Testing for statistical significance follows a relatively well-defined pattern, although authors differ in the number and sequence of steps. One six-stage sequence is as follows:

1. *State the null hypothesis.* Although the researcher is usually interested in testing a hypothesis of change or differences, the null hypothesis is always used for statistical testing purposes.

2. *Choose the statistical test.* To test a hypothesis, one must choose an appropriate statistical test. There are many tests from which to choose, and there are at least four criteria that can be used in choosing a test. One is the power efficiency of the test. A more powerful test provides the same level of significance with a smaller sample than a less powerful test. In addition, in choosing a test, one can consider how the sample is drawn, the nature of the population, and (importantly) the type of measurement scale used. For instance, some tests are useful only when the sequence of scores is known or when observations are paired; other tests are appropriate only if the population has certain characteristics; still other tests are useful only if the measurement scale is interval or ratio. More attention is given to test selection later in the chapter.

3. *Select the desired level of significance.* The choice of the **level of significance** should be made before we collect the data. The most common level is .05, although .01 is also widely used. Other levels such as .10, .025, or .001 are sometimes chosen. The exact level to choose is largely determined by how much risk one is willing to accept and the effect that this choice has on β risk. The larger the α, the lower is the β.

4. *Compute the calculated difference value.* After the data are collected, use the formula for the appropriate significance test to obtain the calculated value. Although the computation typically results from a software program, we illustrate the procedures in this chapter to help you visualize what is being done.

5. *Obtain the critical test value.* After we compute the calculated t, χ^2, or other measure, we must look up the critical value in the appropriate table for that distribution (or it is provided with the software calculation). The critical value is the criterion that defines the region of rejection from the region of acceptance of the null hypothesis.

6. *Interpret the test.* For most tests if the calculated value is larger than the critical value, we reject the null hypothesis and conclude that the alternative hypothesis is supported (although it is by no means proved). If the critical value is larger, we conclude we have failed to reject the null.[3]

Probability Values (*p* Values)

According to the "interpret the test" step of the statistical test procedure, the conclusion is stated in terms of rejecting or not rejecting the null hypothesis based on a reject region selected before the test is conducted. A second method of presenting the results of a statistical test reports the extent to which the test statistic disagrees with the null hypothesis. This method has become popular because analysts want to know what percentage of the sampling distribution lies beyond the sample statistic on the curve, and most statistical computer programs report the results of statistical tests as probability values (*p* values). The *p* **value** is the probability of observing a sample value as extreme as, or more extreme than, the value actually observed, given that the null hypothesis is true. This area represents the probability of a Type I error that must be assumed if the null hypothesis is rejected. The *p* value is compared to the

significance level (α), and on this basis the null hypothesis is either rejected or not rejected. If the p value is less than the significance level, the null hypothesis is rejected (if p value < α, reject the null). If p is greater than or equal to the significance level, the null hypothesis is not rejected (if p value > α, don't reject the null).

Statistical data analysis programs commonly compute the p value during the execution of a hypothesis test. The following example will help illustrate the correct way to interpret a p value.

In part B of Exhibit 17-4 the critical value was shown for the situation in which the manufacturer was interested in determining whether the average mpg had increased. The critical value of 53.29 was computed based on a standard deviation of 10, sample size of 25, and the manufacturer's willingness to accept a 5 percent α risk. Suppose that the sample mean equaled 55. Is there enough evidence to reject the null hypothesis? If the p value is less than .05, the null hypothesis will be rejected. The p value is computed as follows.

The standard deviation of the distribution of sample means is 2. The appropriate Z value is

$$Z = \frac{\overline{X} - \mu}{\sigma_{\overline{X}}}$$

$$Z = \frac{55 - 50}{2}$$

$$Z = 2.5$$

The p value is determined using the standard normal table. The area between the mean and a Z value of 2.5 is .4938. For this one-tailed test, the p value is the area above the Z value. The probability of observing a Z value at least as large as 2.5 is only .0062 (.5000 − .4938 = .0062) if the null hypothesis is true.

This small p value represents the risk of rejecting a true null hypothesis. It is the probability of a Type I error if the null hypothesis is rejected. Since the p value (p = .0062) is smaller than α = .05, the null hypothesis is rejected. The manufacturer can conclude that the average mpg has increased. The probability that this conclusion is wrong is .0062.

> Tests of Significance

This section provides an overview of statistical tests that are representative of the vast array available to the researcher. After a review of the general types of tests and their assumptions, the procedures for selecting an appropriate test are discussed. The remainder of the section contains examples of parametric and nonparametric tests for one-sample, two-sample, and k-sample cases. Readers needing a comprehensive treatment of significance tests are referred to the suggested readings for this chapter.

Types of Tests

There are two general classes of significance tests: parametric and nonparametric. **Parametric tests** are more powerful because their data are derived from interval and ratio measurements. **Nonparametric tests** are used to test hypotheses with nominal and ordinal data. Parametric techniques are the tests of choice if their assumptions are met. Assumptions for parametric tests include the following:

- The observations must be independent—that is, the selection of any one case should not affect the chances for any other case to be included in the sample.
- The observations should be drawn from normally distributed populations.
- These populations should have equal variances.
- The measurement scales should be at least interval so that arithmetic operations can be used with them.

The researcher is responsible for reviewing the assumptions pertinent to the chosen test. Performing diagnostic checks on the data allows the researcher to select the most appropriate technique. The normality of a distribution may be checked in several ways. We have previously discussed the measures of location, shape, and spread for preliminary analysis and considered graphic techniques for exploring data patterns and examining distributions. Another diagnostic tool is the **normal probability plot.** This plot compares the observed values with those expected from a normal distribution.[4] If the data display the characteristics of normality, the points will fall within a narrow band along a straight line. An example is shown in the upper left panel of Exhibit 17-6.

An alternative way to look at this is to plot the deviations from the straight line. These are shown in a

28

The amount, in billions, saved by North American companies by having employees use a company purchasing card.

>**Exhibit 17-6** Probability Plots and Tests of Normality

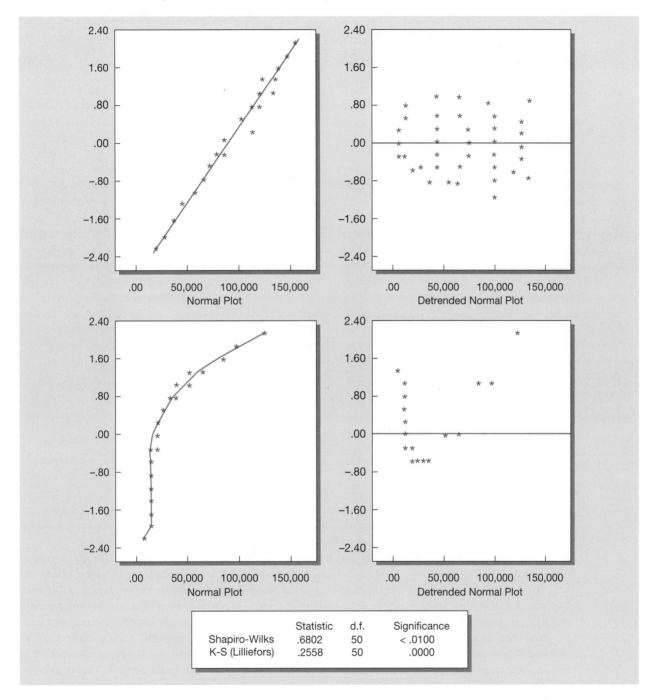

	Statistic	d.f.	Significance
Shapiro-Wilks	.6802	50	< .0100
K-S (Lilliefors)	.2558	50	.0000

"detrended" plot in the upper right panel of the figure. Here we would expect the points to cluster without pattern around a straight line passing horizontally through 0. In the bottom two panels of Exhibit 17-6, there is neither a straight line in the normal probability plot nor a random distribution of points about 0 in the detrended plot. Visually, the bottom two plots tell us the variable is not normally distributed. In addition, two separate tests of the hypothesis that the data come from normal distributions are rejected at a significance level of less than .01.[5]

If we wished to check another assumption—say, one of equal variance—a spread-and-level plot would be appropriate. Statistical software programs often provide diagnostic tools for checking assumptions. These may be nested within a specific statistical procedure, such as analysis of variance or regression, or provided as a general set of tools for examining assumptions.

Testing a Hypothesis of Unrealistic Drug Use in Movies

Are American teens exposed to unrealistic drug usage or to unrealistic consequences from such use? Mediascope, a nonprofit organization concerned with responsible depictions of social and health issues in the media, recently completed for the Office of National Drug Control Policy a content analysis of the top 200 rental movies to determine their depiction of substance use. The researchers used the Entertainment Merchants Association's most popular (top 100) home video titles based on rental income during two sequential years. Movies were categorized as follows: action adventure, comedy, or drama. Data were also collected on each title's Motion Picture Association of America (MPAA) rating (G, PG, PG-13, or R). Although technically teens should have been excluded from R-rated titles (which made up 48 percent of the overall sample), the study included all 20 of the most popular teen movies as identified in a prior independent study.

Trained coders watched all 200 movies, paying particular attention to alcohol, tobacco, illicit drugs, over-the-counter medicines, prescription medicines, inhalants, and unidentified pills. Coders ignored substances administered by medical personnel in a hospital or health-related scenario. Substance use included explicit portrayals of consumption. Substance appearance was noted when evidence of materials or paraphernalia was noted without any indication of use. Coders identified dominant messages about substance use and the consequences of use. Coders also noted scenes depicting illicit drug use or those depicting use by characters known to be under 18. Prevalence of use was determined by counting the characters in each movie and determining not only the percentage of characters using drugs but also whether the character had a major or minor role. Coders profiled characters by age, gender, and ethnicity, as well as other characteristics. Frequency of substance abuse was determined for each five-minute interval of each movie, with the presence or absence of various substances noted, starting with the completion of the title credits and ending when the final credits began. How would the last movie you watched have fared under this scrutiny?

www.mediacampaign.org; www.mediascope.org; www.vsda.org

Parametric tests place different emphasis on the importance of assumptions. Some tests are quite robust and hold up well despite violations. For others, a departure from linearity or equality of variance may threaten the validity of the results.

Nonparametric tests have fewer and less stringent assumptions. They do not specify normally distributed populations or equality of variance. Some tests require independence of cases; others are expressly designed for situations with related cases. Nonparametric tests are the only ones usable with nominal data; they are the only technically correct tests to use with ordinal data, although parametric tests are sometimes employed in this case. Nonparametric tests may also be used for interval and ratio data, although they waste much of the information available. Nonparametric tests are also easy to understand and use. Parametric tests have greater efficiency when their use is appropriate, but even in such cases nonparametric tests often achieve an efficiency as high as 95 percent. This means the nonparametric test with a sample of 100 will provide the same statistical testing power as a parametric test with a sample of 95.

How to Select a Test

In attempting to choose a particular significance test, the researcher should consider at least three questions:

- Does the test involve one sample, two samples, or *k* (more than two) samples?
- If two samples or *k* samples are involved, are the individual cases independent or related?
- Is the measurement scale nominal, ordinal, interval, or ratio?

Additional questions may arise once answers to these are known: What is the sample size? If there are several samples, are they of equal size? Have the data been weighted? Have the data been transformed? Often such questions are unique to the selected technique. The answers can complicate the selection, but once a tentative choice is made, standard statistics textbooks will provide further details.

Decision trees provide a more systematic means of selecting techniques. One widely used guide from the Institute for Social Research starts with questions about the number of variables, nature of the variables (continuous, discrete, dichotomous, independent, dependent, and so forth), and level of measurement. It goes through a tree structure asking detailed questions about the nature of the relationships being searched, compared, or tested. More than 130 solutions to data analysis problems are paired with commonly asked questions.[6]

An expert system offers another approach to choosing appropriate statistics. Capitalizing on the power and convenience of personal computers, expert system programs provide a comprehensive search of the statistical terrain just as a computer search of secondary sources does. Most programs ask about your research objectives, the nature of your data, and the intended audience for your final report. When you are not 100 percent confident of your answers, you can bracket them with an estimate of the degree of your certainty. One such program, Statistical Navigator™ covers various categories of statistics from exploratory data analysis through reliability testing and multivariate data analysis. In response to your answers, a report is printed containing recommendations, rationale for selections, references, and the statistical packages that offer the suggested procedure.[7] SPSS and SAS include coaching and help modules with their software.

Selecting Tests Using the Choice Criteria

In the next section, we use the three questions discussed in the last section (see bullets) to develop a classification of the major parametric and nonparametric tests and measures. Because parametric tests are preferred for their power when their assumptions are met, we discuss them first in each of the subsections: one-sample tests, two-sample tests, k- (more-than-two) sample tests. This is shown in Exhibit 17-7.[8] To illustrate the application of the criteria to test selection, consider that your testing situation involves two samples, the samples are independent, and the data are interval. The figure suggests the t-test of differences as the appropriate choice. The most frequently used of the tests listed in Exhibit 17-7 are covered next. For additional examples see Appendix C.

>**Exhibit 17-7** Recommended Statistical Techniques by Measurement Level and Testing Situation

Measurement Scale	One-Sample Case	Two-Samples Tests Related Samples	Two-Samples Tests Independent Samples	k-Samples Tests Related Samples	k-Samples Tests Independent Samples
Nominal	• Binomial • χ^2 one-sample test	• McNemar	• Fisher exact test • χ^2 two-samples test	• Cochran Q	• χ^2 for k samples
Ordinal	• Kolmogorov-Smirnov one-sample test • Runs test	• Sign test • Wilcoxon matched-pairs test	• Median test • Mann-Whitney U • Kolmogorov-Smirnov • Wald-Wolfowitz	• Friedman two-way ANOVA	• Median extension • Kruskal-Wallis one-way ANOVA
Interval and Ratio	• t-test • Z test	• t-test for paired samples	• t-test • Z test	• Repeated-measures ANOVA	• One-way ANOVA • n-way ANOVA

One-Sample Tests

One-sample tests are used when we have a single sample and wish to test the hypothesis that it comes from a specified population. In this case we encounter questions such as these:

- Is there a difference between observed frequencies and the frequencies we would expect, based on some theory?
- Is there a difference between observed and expected proportions?
- Is it reasonable to conclude that a sample is drawn from a population with some specified distribution (normal, Poisson, and so forth)?
- Is there a significant difference between some measures of central tendency ($\overline{X}$) and its population parameter (μ)?

A number of tests may be appropriate in this situation. The parametric test is discussed first.

Parametric Tests

The **Z test** or **t-test** is used to determine the statistical significance between a sample distribution mean and a parameter.

The **Z distribution** and **t distribution** differ. The *t* has more tail area than that found in the normal distribution. This is a compensation for the lack of information about the population standard deviation. Although the sample standard deviation is used as a proxy figure, the imprecision makes it necessary to go farther away from 0 to include the percentage of values in the *t* distribution necessarily found in the standard normal.

When sample sizes approach 120, the sample standard deviation becomes a very good estimate of the population standard deviation (σ); beyond 120, the *t* and *Z* distributions are virtually identical. Some typical real-world applications of the one-sample test are:

- Finding the average monthly balance of credit card holders compared to the average monthly balance five years ago.
- Comparing the failure rate of computers in a 20-hour test of quality specifications.
- Discovering the proportion of people who would shop in a new district compared to the assumed population proportion.
- Comparing the average product revenues this year to last year's revenues.

Example   To illustrate the application of the *t*-test in the one-sample case, consider again the hybrid-vehicle problem mentioned earlier. With a sample of 100 vehicles, the researchers find that the mean miles per gallon for the car is 52.5 mpg, with a standard deviation of 14. Do these results indicate the population mean might still be 50?

In this problem, we have only the sample standard deviation (*s*). This must be used in place of the population standard deviation (σ). When we substitute *s* for σ, we use the *t* distribution, especially if the sample size is less than 30. We define *t* as

$$t = \frac{\overline{X} - \mu}{s/\sqrt{n}}$$

This significance test is conducted by following the six-step procedure recommended earlier:

1. *Null hypothesis.*

$$H_0: = 50 \text{ miles per gallon (mpg)}$$
$$H_A: > 50 \text{ mpg (one-tailed test)}$$

2. *Statistical test.* Choose the *t*-test because the data are ratio measurements. Assume the underlying population is normal and we have randomly selected the sample from the population of production vehicles.

3. *Significance level.* Let $\alpha = .05$, with $n = 100$.
4. *Calculated value.*

$$t = \frac{52.5 - 50}{14\sqrt{100}} - \frac{2.5}{1.4} = 1.786 \qquad \text{d.f.} = n - 1 = 99$$

5. *Critical test value.* We obtain this by entering the table of critical values of t (see Appendix C, Exhibit C-2, at the back of the book), with 99 degrees of freedom (d.f.) and a level of significance value of .05. We secure a critical value of about 1.66 (interpolated between d.f. $= 60$ and d.f. $= 120$ in Exhibit D-2).

6. *Interpretation.* In this case, the calculated value is greater than the critical value (1.786 > 1.66), so we reject the null hypothesis and conclude that the average mpg has increased.

Nonparametric Tests

In a one-sample situation, a variety of nonparametric tests may be used, depending on the measurement scale and other conditions. If the measurement scale is nominal (classificatory only), it is possible to use either the binomial test or the chi-square (χ^2) one-sample test. The binomial test is appropriate when the population is viewed as only two classes, such as male and female, buyer and nonbuyer, and successful and unsuccessful, and all observations fall into one or the other of these categories. The binomial test is particularly useful when the size of the sample is so small that the χ^2 test cannot be used.

Chi-Square Test

Probably the most widely used nonparametric test of significance is the **chi-square (χ^2) test.** It is particularly useful in tests involving nominal data but can be used for higher scales. Typical are cases where persons, events, or objects are grouped in two or more nominal categories such as "yes–no," "favor–undecided–against," or class "A, B, C, or D."

Using this technique, we test for significant differences between the *observed* distribution of data among categories and the *expected* distribution based on the null hypothesis. Chi-square is useful in cases of one-sample analysis, two independent samples, or k independent samples. It must be calculated with actual counts rather than percentages.

In the one-sample case, we establish a null hypothesis based on the expected frequency of objects in each category. Then the deviations of the actual frequencies in each category are compared with the hypothesized frequencies. The greater the difference between them, the less is the probability that these differences can be attributed to chance. The value of χ^2 is the measure that expresses the extent of this difference. The larger the divergence, the larger is the χ^2 value.

The formula by which the χ^2 test is calculated is

$$\chi^2 = \sum_{i=1}^{k} \frac{(O_i - E_i)^2}{E_i}$$

in which

O_i = observed number of cases categorized in the ith category

E_i = expected number of cases in the ith category under H_0

k = the number of categories

There is a different distribution for χ^2 for each number of degrees of freedom (d.f.), defined as $(k - 1)$ or the number of categories in the classification minus 1:

$$\text{d.f.} = k - 1$$

With chi-square contingency tables of the two-samples or k-samples variety, we have both rows and columns in the cross-classification table. In that instance, d.f. is defined as rows minus 1 $(r - 1)$ times columns minus 1 $(c - 1)$:

$$\text{d.f.} = (r - 1)(c - 1)$$

In a 2×2 table there is 1 d.f., and in a 3×2 table there are 2 d.f. Depending on the number of degrees of freedom, we must be certain the numbers in each cell are large enough to make the χ^2 test appropriate. When d.f. $= 1$, each expected frequency should be at least 5 in size. If d.f. > 1, then the χ^2 test should not be used if more than 20 percent of the expected frequencies are smaller than 5 or when any expected frequency is less than 1. Expected frequencies can often be increased by combining adjacent categories. Four categories of freshmen, sophomores, juniors, and seniors might be classified into upper class and lower class. If there are only two categories and still there are too few in a given class, it is better to use the binomial test.

Assume a survey of student interest in the Metro University Dining Club (discussed in Chapter 15) is taken. We have interviewed 200 students and learned of their intentions to join the club. We would like to analyze the results by living arrangement (type and location of student housing and eating arrangements). The 200 responses are classified into the four categories shown in the accompanying table.

Living Arrangement	O Intend to Join	Number Interviewed	Percent (no. interviewed/200)	E = Expected Frequencies (percent × 60)
Dorm/fraternity	16	90	45	27
Apartment/rooming house, nearby	13	40	20	12
Apartment/rooming house, distant	16	40	20	12
Live at home	15	30	15	9
Total	60	200	100	60

Do these variations indicate there is a significant difference among these students, or are they sampling variations only? Proceed as follows:

1. *Null hypothesis.* $H_0: O_i = E_i$. The proportion in the population who intend to join the club is independent of living arrangement. In $H_A: O_i \neq E_i$, the proportion in the population who intend to join the club is dependent on living arrangement.

2. *Statistical test.* Use the one-sample χ^2 to compare the observed distribution to a hypothesized distribution. The χ^2 test is used because the responses are classified into nominal categories and there are sufficient observations.

3. *Significance level.* Let $\alpha = .05$.

4. *Calculated value.*

$$\chi^2 = \sum_{i=1}^{k} \frac{(O_i - E_i)^2}{E_i}$$

Calculate the expected distribution by determining what proportion of the 200 students interviewed were in each group. Then apply these proportions to the number who intend to join the club. Then calculate the following:

$$\chi^2 = \frac{(16-27)^2}{27} + \frac{(13-12)^2}{12} + \frac{(16-12)^2}{12} + \frac{(15-9)^2}{9}$$

$$= 4.48 + 0.08 + 1.33 + 4.0$$

$$= 9.89$$

$$\text{d.f.} = (4-1)(2-1) = 3$$

5. *Critical test value.* Enter the table of critical values of χ^2 (see Exhibit D-3), with 3 d.f., and secure a value of 7.82 for $\alpha = .05$.

6. *Interpretation.* The calculated value (9.89) is greater than the critical value (7.82), so the null hypothesis is rejected and we conclude that intending to join is dependent on living arrangement.

Research beyond the Clip

You're McDonald's and you just announced that you are closing 300 stores in the United States. How is this playing in newspapers across America? Is the reporting balanced? Or maybe you're BP (formerly British Petroleum), and you've just invested millions to change your corporate identification and logo and to reposition your firm as the "environmentally friendly" energy conglomerate through executive presentations and advertising. How is the press treating the story? Is the spin positive or negative? Where is the story appearing? Is your key message getting through? The Burrelle's Information Services division of Burrelle's/Luce (B/L) offers one of the longest established "clipping" services used by public relations managers to answer questions like these.

"The most basic research we provide clients is the ad-equivalent value of the news clips," shared Sharon Miller, account executive for B/L. The client notifies B/L that it plans to distribute a press release. Staff at B/L scan the desired print and Internet sources for news of the client—"clips." "For print and online publications, the actual space that the story occupies is physically measured. Then, that space is multiplied by the ad rate for identical space in that medium—the ad equivalent." Burrelle's also delivers an assessment of the coverage of key messages the client tried to convey, as well as the tone of the story and the firm's prominence in any story—did the firm get mentioned in the headline or the lead paragraph, or was it the focus of more than half of the article? Managers can obtain comparative analysis evaluating their firm's news coverage against that of other firms in their industry or against ROI investment criteria through online reporting via B/L's secure Insight platform. If you were a public relations professional, how would you test the hypothesis that your coverage for any given event was more positive than that of your competition?

www.burrellesluce.com

Two-Independent-Samples Tests

The need to use **two-independent-samples tests** is often encountered in business research. We might compare the purchasing predispositions of a sample of subscribers from two magazines to discover if they are from the same population. Similarly, a test of distribution methods from two channels or the market share movements from two competing products could be compared.

Parametric Tests

The Z and t-tests are frequently used parametric tests for independent samples, although the F test also can be used.

The Z test is used with large sample sizes (exceeding 30 for both independent samples) or with smaller samples when the data are normally distributed and population variances are known. The formula for the Z test is

$$Z = \frac{(\overline{X}_1 - \overline{X}_2) - (\mu_1 - \mu_2)0}{\sqrt{\dfrac{S_1^2}{n_1} + \dfrac{S_2^2}{n_2}}}$$

With small sample sizes, normally distributed populations, and the assumption of equal population variances, the t-test is appropriate:

$$t = \frac{(\overline{X}_1 - \overline{X}_2) - (\mu_1 - \mu_2)0}{\sqrt{S_p^2 \left(\dfrac{1}{n_1} + \dfrac{1}{n_2}\right)}}$$

where

$(\mu_1 - \mu_2)$ is the difference between the two population means.

S_p^2 is associated with the pooled variance estimate:

$$S_p^2 = \frac{(n_1 - 1)S_1^2 + (n_2 - 1)S_2^2}{n_1 + n_2 - 2}$$

To illustrate this application, consider a problem that might face a manager at KDL, a media firm that is evaluating account executive trainees. The manager wishes to test the effectiveness of two methods for training new account executives. The company selects 22 trainees, who are randomly divided into two experimental groups. One receives type A and the other type B training. The trainees are then assigned and managed without regard to the training they have received. At the year's end, the manager reviews the performances of employees in these groups and finds the following results:

	A Group	B Group
Average hourly sales	$X_1 = \$1,500$	$X_2 = \$1,300$
Standard deviation	$s_1 = 225$	$s_2 = 251$

Following the standard testing procedure, we will determine whether one training method is superior to the other:

1. *Null hypothesis.*

    H_0: There is no difference in sales results produced by the two training methods.

    H_A: Training method A produces sales results superior to those of method B.

2. *Statistical test.* The *t*-test is chosen because the data are at least interval and the samples are independent.

3. *Significance level.* $\alpha = .05$ (one-tailed test).

4. *Calculated value.*

$$t = \frac{(1,500 - 1,300) - 0}{\sqrt{\frac{(10)(225)^2 + (10)(251)^2}{20}\left(\frac{1}{11} + \frac{1}{11}\right)}}$$

$$= \frac{200}{101.63} = 1.97$$

There are $n - 1$ degrees of freedom in each sample, so total d.f. is

$$\text{d.f.} = (11 - 1) + (11 - 1) = 20$$

5. *Critical test value.* Enter Appendix D, Exhibit D-2 with d.f. = 20, one-tailed test, $\alpha = .05$. The critical value is 1.725.

6. *Interpretation.* Since the calculated value is larger than the critical value (1.97 > 1.725), reject the null hypothesis and conclude that training method A is superior.

Nonparametric Tests

The chi-square (χ^2) test is appropriate for situations in which a test for differences between samples is required. It is especially valuable for nominal data but can be used with ordinal measurements. When parametric data have been reduced to categories, they are frequently treated with χ^2 although this results in a loss of information. Preparing to solve this problem is the same as presented earlier although the formula differs slightly:

$$\chi^2 = \sum_i \sum_j \frac{(O_{ij} - E_{ij})^2}{E_{ij}}$$

in which

O_{ij} = observed number of cases categorized in the *ij*th cell

E_{ij} = expected number of cases under H_0 to be categorized in the *ij*th cell

Suppose MindWriter is implementing a smoke-free workplace policy and is interested in whether smoking affects worker accidents. Since the company has complete reports on on-the-job accidents, a sample of names of workers is drawn from those who were involved in accidents during the last year. A similar sample from among workers who had no reported accidents in the last year is drawn. Members of both groups are interviewed to determine if each is a nonsmoker or smoker and, if a smoker, whether the person classifies himself or herself as a heavy or moderate smoker. The results appear in the following table, with expected values calculated as shown.

On-the-Job Accident

Cell Designation Count Expected Values	Yes	No	Total
Smoker	1,1	1,2	
Heavy smoker	127	4	16
	8.24	7.75	
	2,1	2,2	
Moderate	9	6	15
	7.73	7.27	
	3,1	3,2	
Nonsmoker	13	22	35
	18.03	16.97	
Column Total	34	32	66

The testing procedure is:

1. *Null hypothesis.*

   H_0: There is no relationship in on-the-job accident occurrences between smokers and nonsmokers.

   H_A: There is a relationship in on-the-job accident occurrences between smokers and nonsmokers.

2. *Statistical test.* x^2 is appropriate, but it may waste some of the data because the measurement appears to be ordinal.

3. *Significance level.* $\alpha = .05$, with d.f. $= (3 - 1)(2 - 1) = 2$

4. *Calculated value.* The expected distribution is provided by the marginal totals of the table. If there is no relationship between accidents and smoking, there will be the same proportion of smokers in both accident and nonaccident groups. The numbers of expected observations in each cell are calculated by multiplying the two marginal totals common to a particular cell and dividing this product by *n*. For example,

$$\frac{34 \times 16}{66} = 8.24, \text{ the expected value in cell (1,1)}$$

$$x^2 = \frac{(12 - 8.24)^2}{8.24} + \frac{(4 - 7.75)^2}{7.75} + \frac{(9 - 7.73)^2}{7.73} + \frac{(6 - 7.72)^2}{7.72}$$

$$+ \frac{(13 - 18.03)^2}{18.03} + \frac{(22 - 16.97)^2}{16.97}$$

$$= 7.01$$

5. *Critical test value.* Turn to Appendix D, Exhibit D-3, and find the critical value 7.01 with $\alpha = .05$ and d.f. $= 2$.

6. *Interpretation.* Since the calculated value is greater than the critical value, the null hypothesis is rejected.

For chi-square to operate properly, data must come from random samples of multinomial distributions, and the expected frequencies should not be too small. We previously noted the traditional cautions that expected frequencies (E_i) below 5 should not compose more than 20 percent of the cells, and that no cell should have an E_i of less than 1. Some research has argued that these restrictions are too severe.[9]

>Exhibit 17-8 Comparison of Corrected and Noncorrected Chi-Square Results Using SPSS Procedure Cross-Tab

```
                     INCOME BY POSSESSION OF MBA

                              MBA
                   Count
                              Yes      No
                                                   Row
                              1        2           Total
           INCOME    ─────────────────────────

                     High 1    30       30          60
                                                    60.0

                     Low 2     10       30          40
                                                    40.0

                     Column    40       60          100
                     Total     40.0     60.0        100.0

Chi-Square                          Value     D.F.      Significance

Pearson                             6.25000     1        .01242
Continuity Correction               5.25174     1        .02192
Likelihood Ratio                    6.43786     1        .01117
Mantel-Haenszel                     6.18750     1        .01287
Minimum Expected Frequency: 16.000
```

In another type of χ^2, the 2×2 table, a correction known as *Yates' correction for continuity* is applied when sample sizes are greater than 40 or when the sample is between 20 and 40 and the values of E_i are 5 or more. (We use this correction because a continuous distribution is approximating a discrete distribution in this table. When the E_i's are small, the approximation is not necessarily a good one.) The formula for this correction is

$$\chi^2 = \frac{n\left(|AD - BC| - \frac{n}{2}\right)^2}{(A + B)(C + D)(A + C)(B + D)}$$

where the letters represent the cells designated as

A	B
C	D

When the continuity correction is applied to the data shown in Exhibit 17-8, a χ^2 value of 5.25 is obtained. The observed level of significance for this value is .02192. If the level of significance had been set at .01, we would accept the null hypothesis. However, had we calculated χ^2 without correction, the value would have been 6.25, which has an observed level of significance of .01242. Some researchers may be tempted to reject the null at this level. (But note that the critical value of χ^2 at .01 with 1 d.f. is 6.64. See Appendix D, Exhibit D-3.) The literature is in conflict regarding the merits of Yates' correction, but if nothing else, this example suggests one should take care when interpreting 2×2 tables.[10] To err on the conservative side would be in keeping with our prior discussion of Type I errors.

The Mantel-Haenszel test and the likelihood ratio also appear in Exhibit 17-8. The former is used with ordinal data; the latter, based on maximum likelihood theory, produces results similar to Pearson's chi-square.

Two-Related-Samples Tests

The **two-related-samples tests** concern those situations in which persons, objects, or events are closely matched or the phenomena are measured twice. One might compare the consumption of husbands and wives, the performance of employees before and after vacations, or the effects of a marketing test stimulus when persons were randomly assigned to groups and given pretests and posttests. Both parametric and nonparametric tests are applicable under these conditions.

Parametric Tests

The t-test for independent samples would be inappropriate for this situation because one of its assumptions is that observations are independent. This problem is solved by a formula in which the difference is found between each matched pair of observations, thereby reducing the two samples to the equivalent of a one-sample case—that is, there are now several differences, each independent of the other, for which one can compute various statistics.

In the following formula, the average difference $\overline{D}$ corresponds to the normal distribution when the α difference is known and the sample size is sufficient. The statistic t with $(n - 1)$ degrees of freedom is defined as

$$t = \frac{\overline{D}}{S_D/\sqrt{n}}$$

where

$$\overline{D} = \frac{\Sigma D}{n}$$

$$S_D = \sqrt{\frac{\Sigma D^2 - \frac{(\Sigma D)^2}{n}}{n - 1}}$$

To illustrate, we use two years of *Forbes* sales data (in millions of dollars) from 10 companies, as listed in Exhibit 17-9.

1. *Null hypothesis.*

   H_0: $\mu = 0$; there is no difference between year 1 and year 2 sales.

   H_A: $\mu \neq 0$; there is a difference between year 1 and year 2 sales.

2. *Statistical test.* The matched- or paired-samples t-test is chosen because there are repeated measures on each company, the data are not independent, and the measurement is ratio.

>**Exhibit 17-9** Sales Data for Paired-Samples t-Test (dollars in millions)

Company	Sales Year 2	Sales Year 1	Difference D	D²
GM	126932	123505	3427	11744329
GE	54574	49662	4912	24127744
Exxon	86656	78944	7712	59474944
IBM	62710	59512	3198	10227204
Ford	96146	92300	3846	14791716
AT&T	36112	35173	939	881721
Mobil	50220	48111	2109	4447881
DuPont	35099	32427	2672	7139584
Sears	53794	49975	3819	14584761
Amoco	23966	20779	3187	10156969
			$\Sigma D = 35821$	$\Sigma D^2 = 157576853$

>Exhibit 17-10 SPSS Output for Paired-Samples *t*-Test (dollars in millions)

```
                         ---t-tests for paired samples---

                Number                          Standard    Standard
Variable        of Cases      Mean              Deviation     Error

Year 2 Sales      10        62620.9             31777.649   10048.975
Year 1 Sales      10        59038.8             31072.871    9836.104


(Difference   Standard    Standard  |           2-tail  |   t    Degrees of  2-tail
  Mean)       Deviation     Error   |  Corr.     Prob.  | Value   Freedom    Prob.

3582.1000     1803.159    570.209   |  .999      .000   | 6.28      9         .000
```

3. *Significance level.* Let $\alpha = .01$, with $n = 10$ and d.f. $= n - 1$.
4. *Calculated value.*

$$t = \frac{\overline{D}}{S_D/\sqrt{n}} = \frac{3582.10}{570.98} = 6.27 \qquad \text{d.f.} = 9$$

5. *Critical test value.* Enter Appendix D, Exhibit D-2, with d.f. = 9, two-tailed test, $\alpha = .01$. The critical value is 3.25.

6. *Interpretation.* Since the calculated value is greater than the critical value (6.27 > 3.25), reject the null hypothesis and conclude there is a statistically significant difference between the two years of sales.

A computer solution to the problem is illustrated in Exhibit 17-10. Notice that an **observed significance level** is printed for the calculated *t* value (highlighted). With SPSS, this is often rounded and would be interpreted as significant at the .0005 level. The correlation coefficient, to the left of the *t* value, is a measure of the relationship between the two pairs of scores. In situations where matching has occurred (such as husbands' and wives' scores), it reveals the degree to which the matching has been effective in reducing the variability of the mean difference.

Nonparametric Tests

The *McNemar test* may be used with either nominal or ordinal data and is especially useful with before-after measurement of the same subjects. Test the significance of any observed change by setting up a fourfold table of frequencies to represent the first and second set of responses:

Before	After	
	Do Not Favor	Favor
Favor	A	B
Do Not Favor	C	D

Since $A + D$ represents the total number of people who changed (*B* and *C* are no-change responses), the expectation under a null hypothesis is that $1/2\,(A + D)$ cases change in one direction and the same proportion in the other direction. The McNemar test uses a transformation of the χ^2 test:

$$\chi^2 = \frac{(|A - D| - 1)^2}{A + D} \text{ with d.f.} = 1$$

The "minus 1" in the equation is a correction for continuity since the χ^2 is a continuous distribution and the observed frequencies represent a discrete distribution.

To illustrate this test's application, we use survey data from SteelShelf Corporation, whose researchers decided to test a new concept in office seating with employees at the company's headquarters facility. Managers took a random sample of their employees before the test, asking them to complete a questionnaire on their attitudes toward the design concept. On the basis of their responses, the employees were divided into equal groups reflecting their favorable or unfavorable views of the design. After the campaign, the same 200 employees were asked again to complete the questionnaire. They were again classified as to favorable or unfavorable attitudes. The testing process is:

1. *Null hypothesis.*

$$H_0: P(A) = P(D)$$
$$H_A: P(A) \neq P(D)$$

2. *Statistical test.* The McNemar test is chosen because nominal data are used and the study involves before-after measurements of two related samples.

3. *Significance level.* Let $\alpha = .05$, with $n = 200$.

4. *Calculated value.*

$$\chi^2 = \frac{(|10 - 40| - 1)^2}{10 + 40} = \frac{29^2}{50} = 16.82 \qquad \text{d.f.} = 1$$

	After	
Before	**Do Not Favor**	**Favor**
Favor	$A = 10$	$B = 90$
Do Not Favor	$C = 60$	$D = 40$

5. *Critical test value.* Enter Appendix D, Exhibit D-3, and find the critical value to be 3.84 with $\alpha = .05$ and d.f. $= 1$.

6. *Interpretation.* The calculated value is greater than the critical value (16.82 > 3.84), indicating one should reject the null hypothesis, and conclude that the new concept had a significant positive effect on employees' attitudes. In fact, χ^2 is so large that it would have surpassed an α of .001.

k-Independent-Samples Tests

We often use **k-independent-samples tests** in research when three or more samples are involved. Under this condition, we are interested in learning whether the samples might have come from the same or identical populations. When the data are measured on an interval-ratio scale and we can meet the necessary assumptions, analysis of variance and the *F* test are used. If preliminary analysis shows the assumptions cannot be met or if the data were measured on an ordinal or nominal scale, a nonparametric test should be selected.

As with the two-samples case, the samples are assumed to be independent. This is the condition of a completely randomized experiment when subjects are randomly assigned to various treatment groups. It is also common for an ex post facto study to require comparison of more than two independent sample means.

Parametric Tests

The statistical method for testing the null hypothesis that the means of several populations are equal is **analysis of variance (ANOVA)**. *One-way analysis of variance* is described in this section. It uses a single-factor, fixed-effects model to compare the effects of one *treatment* or *factor* (brands of coffee, varieties of residential housing, types of retail stores) on a continuous dependent variable (coffee consumption, hours of TV viewing, shopping expenditures). In a fixed-effects model, the levels of the factor are established in advance, and the results are not generalizable to other levels of treatment. For example, if coffee were Jamaican-grown, Colombian-grown, and Honduran-grown, we could not extend our inferences to coffee grown in Guatemala or Mexico.

To use ANOVA, certain conditions must be met. The samples must be randomly selected from normal populations, and the populations should have equal variances. In addition, the distance from one value to its group's mean should be independent of the distances of other values to that mean (independence of error). ANOVA is reasonably robust, and minor variations from normality and equal variance are tolerable. Nevertheless, the analyst should check the assumptions with the diagnostic techniques previously described.

Analysis of variance, as the name implies, breaks down or partitions total variability into component parts. Unlike the *t*-test, which uses sample standard deviations, ANOVA uses squared deviations of the variance so that computation of distances of the individual data points from their own mean or from the grand mean can be summed (recall that standard deviations sum to zero).

In an ANOVA model, each group has its own mean and values that deviate from that mean. Similarly, all the data points from all of the groups produce an overall *grand mean*. The total deviation is the sum of the squared differences between each data point and the overall grand mean.

The total deviation of any particular data point may be partitioned *into between-groups variance* and *within-groups variance.* The between-groups variance represents the effect of the treatment, or factor. The differences of between-groups means imply that each group was treated differently, and the treatment will appear as deviations of the sample means from the grand mean. Even if this were not so, there would still be some natural variability among subjects and some variability attributable to sampling. The within-groups variance describes the deviations of the data points within each group from the sample mean. This results from variability among subjects and from random variation. It is often called *error.*

Intuitively, we might conclude that when the variability attributable to the treatment exceeds the variability arising from error and random fluctuations, the viability of the null hypothesis begins to diminish. And this is exactly the way the test statistic for analysis of variance works.

The test statistic for ANOVA is the **F ratio.** It compares the variance from the last two sources:

$$F = \frac{\text{between-groups variance}}{\text{within-groups variance}} = \frac{\text{mean square}_{between}}{\text{mean square}_{within}}$$

where

$$\text{Mean square}_{between} = \frac{\text{sum of squares}_{between}}{\text{degrees of freedom}_{between}}$$

$$\text{Mean square}_{within} = \frac{\text{sum of squares}_{within}}{\text{degrees of freedom}_{within}}$$

To compute the *F* ratio, the sum of the squared deviations for the numerator and denominator are divided by their respective degrees of freedom. By dividing, we are computing the variance as an average or mean; thus the term **mean square.** The degrees of freedom for the numerator, the mean square between groups, are one less than the number of groups $(k - 1)$. The degrees of freedom for the denominator, the mean square within groups, are the total number of observations minus the number of groups $(n - k)$.

If the null hypothesis is true, there should be no difference between the population means, and the ratio should be close to 1. If the population means are not equal, the numerator should manifest this difference, and the *F* ratio should be greater than 1. The *F* distribution determines the size of ratio necessary to reject the null hypothesis for a particular sample size and level of significance.

To illustrate one-way ANOVA, consider *Travel Industry Magazine*'s reports from international travelers about the quality of in-flight service on various carriers from the United States to Asia. Before writing a feature story coinciding with a peak travel period, the magazine decided to retain a researcher to secure a more balanced perspective on the reactions of travelers. The researcher selected passengers

>**Exhibit 17-11** Data Table: Analysis of Variance Examples*

	Flight Service					Flight Service			
	Rating 1	Rating 2	Airline†	Seat Selection‡		Rating 1	Rating 2	Airline†	Seat Selection‡
1	40	36	1	1	31	52	65	2	2
2	28	28	1	1	32	70	80	2	2
3	36	30	1	1	33	73	79	2	2
4	32	28	1	1	34	72	88	2	2
5	60	40	1	1	35	73	89	2	2
6	12	14	1	1	36	71	72	2	2
7	32	26	1	1	37	55	58	2	2
8	36	30	1	1	38	68	67	2	2
9	44	38	1	1	39	81	85	2	2
10	36	35	1	1	40	78	80	2	2
11	40	42	1	2	41	92	95	3	1
12	68	49	1	2	42	56	60	3	1
13	20	24	1	2	43	64	70	3	1
14	33	35	1	2	44	72	78	3	1
15	65	40	1	2	45	48	65	3	1
16	40	36	1	2	46	52	70	3	1
17	51	29	1	2	47	64	79	3	1
18	25	24	1	2	48	68	81	3	1
19	37	23	1	2	49	76	69	3	1
20	44	41	1	2	50	56	78	3	1
21	56	67	2	1	51	88	92	3	2
22	48	58	2	1	52	79	85	3	2
23	64	78	2	1	53	92	94	3	2
24	56	68	2	1	54	88	93	3	2
25	28	69	2	1	55	73	90	3	2
26	32	74	2	1	56	68	67	3	2
27	42	55	2	1	57	81	85	3	2
28	40	55	2	1	58	95	95	3	2
29	61	80	2	1	59	68	67	3	2
30	58	78	2	1	60	78	83	3	2

*All data are hypothetical.
†Airline: 1 = Lufthansa; 2 = Malaysia Airlines; 3 = Cathay Pacific
‡Seat selection: 1 = economy; 2 = business.

who had current impressions of the meal service, comfort, and friendliness of a major carrier. Three airlines were chosen and 20 passengers were randomly selected for each airline. The data, found in Exhibit 17-11,[11] are used for this and the next two examples. For the one-way analysis of variance problem, we are concerned only with the columns labeled "Flight Service Rating 1" and "Airline." The factor, airline, is the grouping variable for three carriers.

>**Exhibit 17-12** Summary Tables for One-Way ANOVA Example*

Model Summary†					
Source	**d.f.**	**Sum of Squares**	**Mean Square**	**F Value**	**p Value**
Model (airline)	2	11644.033	5822.017	28.304	0.0001
Residual (error)	57	11724.550	205.694		
Total	59	23368.583			

Means Table				
	Count	**Mean**	**Std. Dev.**	**Std. Error**
Lufthansa	20	38.950	14.006	3.132
Malaysia Airlines	20	58.900	15.089	3.374
Cathay Pacific	20	72.900	13.902	3.108

Scheffè's S Multiple Comparison Procedure‡				
	Vs.	**Diff.**	**Crit. Diff.**	**p Value**
Lufthansa	Malaysia	19.950	11.400	0.0002 S
	Cathay	33.950	11.400	0.0001 S
Malaysia	Cathay	14.000	11.400	0.0122 S

*All data are hypothetical.
†Factor: airline; dependent: flight service rating 1.
‡S = significantly different at the .05 level; significance level: .05.

Again, we follow the procedure:

1. *Null hypothesis.*

   H_0: $\mu_{A1} = \mu_{A2} = \mu_{A3}$

   H_A: $\mu_{A1} \neq \mu_{A2} \neq \mu_{A3}$ (The means are not equal.)

2. *Statistical test.* The F test is chosen because we have k independent samples, accept the assumptions of analysis of variance, and have interval data.

3. *Significance level.* Let $\alpha = .05$, and d.f. = [numerator $(k - 1) = (3 - 1) = 2$], [denominator $(n - k) = (60 - 3) = 57$] = $(2, 57)$.

4. *Calculated value.*

$$F = \frac{MS_b}{MS_w} = \frac{5822.017}{205.695} = 28.304 \qquad \text{d.f. } (2, 57)$$

   See summary in Exhibit 17-12.

5. *Critical test value.* Enter Appendix D, Exhibit D-8, with d.f. $(2, 57)$, $\alpha = .05$. The critical value is 3.16.

6. *Interpretation.* Since the calculated value is greater than the critical value $(28.3 > 3.16)$, we reject the null hypothesis and conclude there are statistically significant differences between two or more pairs of means. Note in Exhibit 17-12 that the p value equals .0001. Since the p value $(.0001)$ is less than the significance level $(.05)$, we have a second method for rejecting the null hypothesis.

The ANOVA model summary in Exhibit 17-12 is a standard way of summarizing the results of analysis of variance. This table contains the sources of variation, degrees of freedom, sum of squares, mean squares, and calculated F value. The probability of rejecting the null hypothesis is computed up to 100 percent α—that is, the probability value column reports the exact significance for the F ratio being tested.

A Priori Contrasts

When we compute a t-test, it is not difficult to discover the reasons why the null is rejected. But with one-way ANOVA, how do we determine which pairs are not equal? We could calculate a series of t-tests, but they would not be independent of each other and the resulting Type I error would increase substantially. This is not recommended. If we decided in advance that a comparison of specific populations was important, a special class of tests known as **a priori contrasts** could be used after the null was rejected with the F test (it is *a priori* because the decision was made before the test).[12]

A modification of the F test provides one approach for computing contrasts:

$$F = \frac{MS_{CON}}{MS_{W}}$$

The denominator, the within-groups mean square, is the same as the error term of the one-way's F ratio (recorded in the summary table, Exhibit 17-12). We have previously referred to the denominator of the F ratio as the error variance estimator. The numerator of the contrast test is defined as

$$MS_{CON} = SS_{CON} = \frac{\left(\sum_{j} C_{j}\bar{X}_{j}\right)^2}{\sum_{j}\frac{C_{j}^2}{n}}$$

where

C_{j} = the contrast coefficient for the group j

n_{j} = the number of observations recorded for group j

A contrast is useful for experimental and quasi-experimental designs when the researcher is interested in answering specific questions about a subset of the factor. For example, in a comparison of coffee products, we have a factor with six levels. The levels, blends of coffee, are meaningfully ordered. Assume we are particularly interested in two Central American—grown blends and one Colombian blend. Rather than looking at all possible combinations, we can channel the power more effectively by stating the comparisons of interest. This increases our likelihood of detecting differences if they really exist.

Multiple Comparison Tests

For the probabilities associated with the contrast test to be properly used in the report of our findings, it is important that the contrast strategy be devised ahead of the testing. In the airline study, we had no theoretical reason for an *a priori* contrast. However, when we examine the table of mean ratings (Exhibit 17-12), it is apparent that the airline means were quite different. Comparisons after the results are compared require *post hoc* tests or pairwise **multiple comparison tests** (or *range tests*) to determine which means differ. These tests find homogeneous subsets of means that are not different from each other. Multiple comparisons test the difference between each pair of means and indicate significantly different group means at an α level of .05, or another level that you specify. Multiple comparison tests use group means and incorporate the MS_{error} term of the F ratio. Together they produce confidence intervals for the population means and a criterion score. Differences between the mean values may be compared.

There are more than a dozen such tests with different optimization goals: maximum number of comparisons, unequal cell size compensation, cell homogeneity, reduction of Type I or Type II errors, and so forth. The merits of various tests have produced considerable debate among statisticians, leaving the researcher without much guidance for the selection of a test. In Exhibit 17-13, we provide a general guide. For the example in Exhibit 17-12, we chose Scheffé's S. It is a conservative test that is robust to violations of assumptions.[13] The computer calculated the critical difference criterion as 11.4; all the differences between the pairs of means exceed this. The null hypothesis for the Scheffé was tested at the .05 level. Therefore, we can conclude that all combinations of flight service mean scores differ from each other.

>Exhibit 17-13 Selection of Multiple Comparison Procedures

Test	Pairwise Comparisons	Complex Comparisons	Equal *n*'s Only	Unequal *n*'s	Equal Variances Assumed	Unequal Variances Not Assumed
Fisher LSD	X			X	X	
Bonferroni	X		X	X		
Tukey HSD	X		X		X	
Tukey-Kramer	X			X	X	
Games-Howell	X			X		X
Tamhane T2	X			X		X
Scheffé *S*		X		X	X	
Brown-Forsythe		X		X		X
Newman-Keuls	X		X		X	
Duncan	X		X		X	
Dunnett's T3						X
Dunnett's C						X

While the table in Exhibit 17-12 provides information for understanding the rejection of the one-way null hypothesis and the Scheffé null, in Exhibit 17-14 we use plots for the comparisons. The means plot shows relative differences among the three levels of the factor. The means by standard deviations plot reveals lower variability in the opinions recorded by the hypothetical Lufthansa and Cathay Pacific passengers. Nevertheless, these two groups are sharply divided on the quality of in-flight service, and that is apparent in the plot.

Exploring the Findings with Two-Way ANOVA

Is the airline on which the passengers traveled the only factor influencing perceptions of in-flight service? By extending the one-way ANOVA, we can learn more about the service ratings. There are

>Exhibit 17-14 One-Way Analysis of Variance Plots

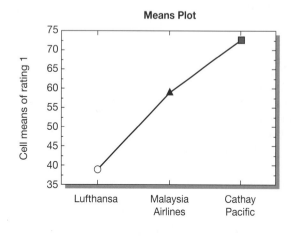

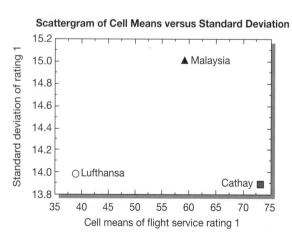

>**Exhibit 17-15** Summary Table for Two-Way ANOVA Example*

Model Summary†					
Source	**d.f.**	**Sum of Squares**	**Mean Square**	**F Value**	**p Value**
Airline	2	11644.033	5822.017	39.178	0.0001
Seat selection	1	3182.817	3182.817	21.418	0.0001
Airline by seat selection	2	517.033	258.517	1.740	0.1853
Residual	54	8024.700	148.606		

Means Table Effect: Airline by Seat Selection				
	Count	**Mean**	**Std. Dev.**	**Std. Error**
Lufthansa economy	10	35.600	12.140	3.839
Lufthansa business	10	42.300	15.550	4.917
Malaysia economy	10	48.500	12.501	3.953
Malaysia business	10	69.300	9.166	2.898
Cathay economy	10	64.800	13.037	4.123
Cathay business	10	81.000	9.603	3.037

*All data are hypothetical.
†Dependent: Flight service rating 1.

many possible explanations. We have chosen to look at the seat selection of the travelers in the interest of brevity.

Recall that in Exhibit 17-11, data were entered for the variable seat selection: economy and business-class travelers. Adding this factor to the model, we have a *two-way* analysis of variance. Now three questions may be considered with one model:

- Are differences in flight service ratings attributable to airlines?

- Are differences in flight service ratings attributable to seat selection?

- Do the airline and the seat selection interact with respect to flight service ratings?

The third question reveals a distinct advantage of the two-way model. A separate one-way model on airlines averages out the effects of seat selection. Similarly, a single-factor test of seat selection averages out the effects of the airline choice. But an interaction test of airline by seat selection considers them *jointly*.

Exhibit 17-15 reports a test of the hypotheses for these three questions. The significance level was established at the .01 level. We first inspect the interaction effect, airline by seat selection, since the individual *main effects* cannot be considered separately if the factors interact. The interaction was not significant at the .01 level, and the null is accepted. Now the separate main effects, airline and seat selection, can be verified. As with the one-way ANOVA, the null hypothesis for the airline factor was rejected, and seat selection was also rejected (statistically significant at .0001).

Means and standard deviations listed in the table are plotted in Exhibit 17-16. We note a band of similar deviations for economy-class travelers and a band of lower variability for business class—with the exception of one carrier. The plot of cell means confirms visually what we already know from the summary table: there is no interaction between airline and seat selection ($p = .185$). If an interaction had occurred, the lines connecting the cell means would have crossed rather than displaying a parallel pattern.

Analysis of variance is an extremely versatile and powerful method that may be adapted to a wide range of testing applications. Discussions of further extensions in *n*-way and experimental designs may be found in the list of suggested readings.

>Exhibit 17-16 Two-Way Analysis of Variance Plots

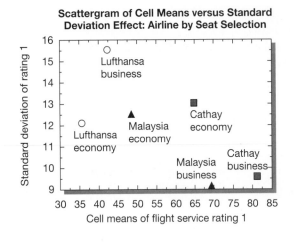

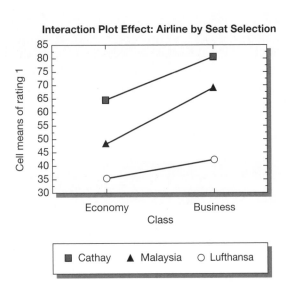

Nonparametric Tests

When there are *k* independent samples for which nominal data have been collected, the chi-square test is appropriate. It can also be used to classify data at higher measurement levels, but metric information is lost when reduced. The *k*-samples χ^2 test is an extension of the two-independent-samples cases treated earlier. It is calculated and interpreted in the same way.

The Kruskal-Wallis test is appropriate for data that are collected on an ordinal scale or for interval data that do not meet *F*-test assumptions, that cannot be transformed, or that for another reason prove to be unsuitable for a parametric test. Kruskal-Wallis is a one-way analysis of variance by ranks. It assumes random selection and independence of samples and an underlying continuous distribution.

Data are prepared by converting ratings or scores to ranks for each observation being evaluated. The ranks range from the highest to the lowest of all data points in the aggregated samples. The ranks are then tested to decide if they are samples from the same population. An application of this technique is provided in Appendix C.

k-Related-Samples Tests

Parametric Tests

A ***k*-related-samples test** is required for situations where (1) the grouping factor has more than two levels, (2) observations or subjects are matched or the same subject is measured more than once, and (3) the data are at least interval. In test marketing experiments or ex post facto designs with *k* samples, it is often necessary to measure subjects several times. These repeated measurements are called **trials.** For example, multiple measurements are taken in studies of stock prices, products evaluated by reliability, inventory, sales, and measures of product performance. Hypotheses for these situations may be tested with a univariate or multivariate general linear model. The latter is beyond the scope of this discussion.

The repeated-measures ANOVA is a special type of *n*-way analysis of variance. In this design, the repeated measures of each subject are related just as they are in the related *t*-test when only two measures are present. In this sense, each subject serves as its own control requiring a within-subjects variance effect to be assessed differently than the between-groups variance in a factor like airline or seat selection. The effects of the correlated measures are removed before calculation of the *F* ratio.

This model is an appropriate solution for the data presented in Exhibit 17-11. You will remember that the one-way and two-way examples considered only the first rating of in-flight service. Assume a second rating was obtained after one week by reinterviewing the same respondents. We now have two trials for the dependent variable, and we are interested in the same general question as with the one-way ANOVA, with the addition of how the passage of time affects perceptions of in-flight service.

Following the testing procedure, we state:

1. *Null hypotheses.*

   (1) Airline: H_0: $\mu_{A1} = \mu_{A2} = \mu_{A3}$

   (2) Ratings: H_0: $\mu_{R1} = \mu_{R2}$

   (3) Ratings $\times$ airline: H_0: $(\mu_{R2A1} - \mu_{R2A2} - \mu_{R2A3}) = (\mu_{R1A1} - \mu_{R1A2} - \mu_{R1A3})$

   For the alternative hypotheses, we will generalize to the statement that not all the groups have equal means for each of the three hypotheses.

2. *Statistical test.* The F test for repeated measures is chosen because we have related trials on the dependent variable for k samples, accept the assumptions of analysis of variance, and have interval data.

3. *Significance level.* Let $\alpha = .05$ and d.f. = [airline (2, 57), ratings (1, 57), ratings by airline (2, 57)].

4. *Calculated values.* See summary in Exhibit 17-17.

>**Exhibit 17-17** Summary Tables for Repeated-Measures ANOVA*

Model Summary†					
Source	**d.f.**	**Sum of Squares**	**Mean Square**	**F Value**	**p Value**
Airline	2	35527.550	17763.775	67.199	0.0001
Subject (group)	57	15067.650	264.345		
Ratings	1	625.633	625.633	14.318	0.0004
Ratings by air	2	2061.717	1030.858	23.592	0.0001
Ratings by subj	57	2490.650	43.696		

Means Table Ratings by Airline				
	Count	**Mean**	**Std. Dev.**	**Std. Error**
Rating 1, Lufthansa	20	38.950	14.006	3.132
Rating 1, Malaysia	20	58.900	15.089	3.374
Rating 1, Cathay	20	72.900	13.902	3.108
Rating 2, Lufthansa	20	32.400	8.268	1.849
Rating 2, Malaysia	20	72.250	10.572	2.364
Rating 2, Cathay	20	79.800	11.265	2.519

Means Table Effect: Ratings				
	Count	**Mean**	**Std. Dev.**	**Std. Error**
Rating 1	60	56.917	19.902	2.569
Rating 2	60	61.483	23.208	2.996

*All data are hypothetical.
†Dependent: flight service ratings 1 and 2.

>Exhibit 17-18 Repeated-Measures ANOVA Plot

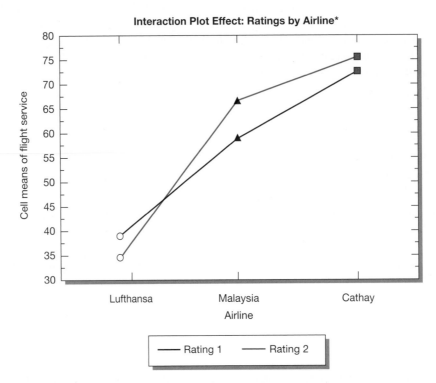

*All data are hypothetical.

5. *Critical test value.* Enter Appendix D, Exhibit D-8, with d.f. (2, 57), $\alpha = .05$ and (1, 57), $\alpha = .05$. The critical values are 3.16 (2, 57) and 4.01 (1, 57).

6. *Interpretation.* The statistical results are grounds for rejecting all three null hypotheses and concluding there are statistically significant differences between means in all three instances. We conclude the perceptions of in-flight service were significantly affected by the different airlines, the interval between the two measures had a significant effect on the ratings, and the measures' time interval and the airlines interacted to a significant degree.

The ANOVA summary table in Exhibit 17-17 records the results of the tests. A means table provides the means and standard deviations for all combinations of ratings by airline. A second table of means reports the differences between flight service ratings 1 and 2. In Exhibit 17-18, there is an interaction plot for these data. Note that the second in-flight service rating was improved in two of the three groups after one week, but for the third carrier, there was a decrease in favorable response. The intersecting lines in the interaction plot reflect this finding.

Nonparametric Tests

When the *k* related samples have been measured on a nominal scale, the Cochran *Q* test is a good choice.[14] This test extends the McNemar test, discussed earlier, for studies having more than two samples. It tests the hypothesis that the proportion of cases in a category is equal for several related categories.

When the data are at least ordinal, the Friedman two-way analysis of variance is appropriate. It tests matched samples, ranking each case and calculating the mean rank for each variable across all cases. It uses these ranks to compute a test statistic. The product is a two-way table where the rows represent subjects and the columns represent the treatment conditions.[15] See Appendix C for additional nonparametric tests.

>summary

1 In classical statistics we make inferences about a population based on evidence gathered from a sample. Although we cannot state unequivocally what is true about the entire population, representative samples allow us to make statements about what is probably true and how much error is likely to be encountered in arriving at a decision. The Bayesian approach also employs sampling statistics but has an additional element of prior information to improve the decision maker's judgment.

2 A difference between two or more sets of data is statistically significant if it actually occurs in a population. To have a statistically significant finding based on sampling evidence, we must be able to calculate the probability that some observed difference is large enough that there is little chance it could result from random sampling. Probability is the foundation for deciding on the acceptability of the null hypothesis, and sampling statistics facilitate acquiring the estimates.

3 Hypothesis testing can be viewed as a six-step procedure:

    a Establish a null hypothesis as well as the alternative hypothesis. It is a one-tailed test of significance if the alternative hypothesis states the direction of difference. If no direction of difference is given, it is a two-tailed test.

    b Choose the statistical test on the basis of the assumption about the population distribution and measurement level. The form of the data can also be a factor. In light of these considerations, one typically chooses the test that has the greatest power efficiency or ability to reduce decision errors.

    c Select the desired level of confidence. While $\alpha = .05$ is the most frequently used level, many others are also used. The α is the significance level that we desire and is typically set in advance of the study. Alpha or Type I error is the risk of rejecting a true null hypothesis and represents a decision error. The β or Type II error is the decision error that results from accepting a false null hypothesis. Usually, one determines a level of acceptable α error and then seeks to reduce the β error by increasing the sample size, shifting from a two-tailed to a one-tailed significance test, or both.

    d Compute the actual test value of the data.

    e Obtain the critical test value, usually by referring to a table for the appropriate type of distribution.

    f Interpret the result by comparing the actual test value with the critical test value.

4 Parametric and nonparametric tests are applicable under the various conditions described in the chapter. They were also summarized in Exhibit 17-6. Parametric tests operate with interval and ratio data and are preferred when their assumptions can be met. Diagnostic tools examine the data for violations of those assumptions. Nonparametric tests do not require stringent assumptions about population distributions and are useful with less powerful nominal and ordinal measures.

5 In selecting a significance test, one needs to know, at a minimum, the number of samples, their independence or relatedness, and the measurement level of the data. Statistical tests emphasized in the chapter were the Z and t-tests, analysis of variance, and chi-square. The Z and t-tests may be used to test for the difference between two means. The t-test is chosen when the sample size is small. Variations on the t-test are used for both independent and related samples.

    One-way analysis of variance compares the means of several groups. It has a single grouping variable, called a factor, and a continuous dependent variable. Analysis of variance (ANOVA) partitions the total variation among scores into between-groups (treatment) and within-groups (error) variance. The F ratio, the test statistic, determines if the differences are large enough to reject the null hypothesis. ANOVA may be extended to two-way, n-way, repeated-measures, and multivariate applications.

    Chi-square is a nonparametric statistic that is used frequently for cross-tabulation or contingency tables. Its applications include testing for differences between proportions in populations and testing for independence. Corrections for chi-square were discussed.

>keyterms

>**discussion**questions

Terms in Review

1 Distinguish between the following:

   a Parametric tests and nonparametric tests.

   b Type I error and Type II error.

   c Null hypothesis and alternative hypothesis.

   d Acceptance region and rejection region.

   e One-tailed tests and two-tailed tests.

   f Type II error and the power of the test.

2 Summarize the steps of hypothesis testing. What is the virtue of this procedure?

3 In analysis of variance, what is the purpose of the mean square between and the mean square within? If the null hypothesis is accepted, what do these quantities look like?

4 Describe the assumptions for ANOVA, and explain how they may be diagnosed.

Making Research Decisions

5 Suggest situations where the researcher should be more concerned with Type II error than with Type I error.

   a How can the probability of a Type I error be reduced? A Type II error?

   b How does practical significance differ from statistical significance?

   c Suppose you interview all the members of the freshman and senior classes and find that 65 percent of the freshmen and 62 percent of the seniors favor a proposal to send Help Centers offshore. Is this difference significant?

6 What hypothesis testing procedure would you use in the following situations?

   a A test classifies applicants as accepted or rejected. On the basis of data on 200 applicants, we test the hypothesis that ad placement success is not related to gender.

   b A company manufactures and markets automobiles in two different countries. We want to know if the gas mileage is the same for vehicles from both facilities. There are samples of 45 units from each facility.

   c A company has three categories of marketing analysts: (1) with professional qualifications but without work experience, (2) with professional qualifications and with work experience, and (3) without professional qualifications but with work experience. A study exists that measures each analyst's motivation level (classified as high, normal, and low). A hypothesis of no relation between analyst category and motivation is to be tested.

   d A company has 24 salespersons. The test must evaluate whether their sales performance is unchanged or has improved after a training program.

   e A company has to evaluate whether it should attribute increased sales to product quality, advertising, or an interaction of product quality and advertising.

7 You conduct a survey of a sample of 25 members of this year's graduating marketing students and find that the average GPA is 3.2. The standard deviation of the sample is 0.4. Over the last 10 years, the average GPA has been 3.0. Is the GPA of this year's students significantly different from the long-run average? At what alpha level would it be significant?

8 You are curious about whether the professors and students at your school are of different political persuasions, so you take a sample of 20 professors and 20 students drawn randomly from each population. You find that 10 professors say they are conservative and 6 students say they are conservative. Is this a statistically significant difference?

9 You contact a random sample of 36 graduates of Western University and learn that their starting salaries averaged $28,000 last year. You then contact a random sample of 40 graduates from Eastern University and find that their average starting salary was $28,800. In each case, the standard deviation of the sample was $1,000.

   a Test the null hypothesis that there is no difference between average salaries received by the graduates of the two schools.

   b What assumptions are necessary for this test?

10 A random sample of students is interviewed to determine if there is an association between class and attitude toward corporations. With the following results, test the hypothesis that there is no difference among students on this attitude.

	Favorable	Neutral	Unfavorable
Freshmen	100	50	70
Sophomores	80	60	70
Juniors	50	50	80
Seniors	40	60	90

11 You do a survey of marketing students and liberal arts school students to find out how many times a week they read a daily newspaper. In each case, you interview 100 students. You find the following:

$$\bar{X}_m = 4.5 \text{ times per week}$$
$$S_m = 1.5$$
$$\bar{X}_{la} = 5.6 \text{ times per week}$$
$$S_{la} = 2.0$$

Test the hypothesis that there is no significant difference between these two samples.

12 One-Koat Paint Company has developed a new type of porch paint that it hopes will be the most durable on the market. The R&D group tests the new product against the two leading competing products by using a machine that scrubs until it wears through the coating. One-Koat runs five trials with each product and secures the following results (in thousands of scrubs):

Trial	One-Koat	Competitor A	Competitor B
1	37	34	24
2	30	19	25
3	34	22	23
4	28	31	20
5	29	27	20

Test the hypothesis that there are no differences between the means of these products ($\alpha = .05$).

13 A computer manufacturer is introducing a new product specifically targeted at the home market and wishes to compare the effectiveness of three sales strategies: computer stores, home electronics stores, and department stores. Numbers of sales by 15 salespeople are recorded here:

> Electronics store: 5, 4, 3, 3, 3
>
> Department store: 9, 7, 8, 6, 5
>
> Computer store: 7, 4, 8, 4, 3

a Test the hypothesis that there is no difference between the means of the retailers ($\alpha = .05$).

b Select a multiple comparison test, if necessary, to determine which groups differ in mean sales ($\alpha = .05$).

From the Headlines

14 Researchers at the University of Aberdeen found that when people were asked to recall past events or imagine future ones, the participants' bodies subliminally acted out the metaphors we commonly conceptualized with the flow of time. With past years, the participants leaned backward, while when imagining the future, they leaned forward. The leanings were small, but the directionality was clear and dependable. Using this research as a base, if you have two groups (group A holds a cup of hot coffee, and group B holds iced coffee), what statistical hypothesis would you propose to test the groups' perceptions of the personality of an imaginary individual holding coffee based on its temperature?

>cases*

Inquiring Minds Want to Know—NOW!	Proofpoint: Capitalizing on a Reporters Love of Statistics
Mastering Teacher Leadership	Yahoo!: *Consumer Direct* Marries Purchase Metrics to Banner Ads
NCRCC: Teeing Up a New Strategic Direction	

* You will find a description of each case in the Case Abstracts section of the textbook. Check the Case Index to determine whether a case provides data, the research instrument, video, or other supplementary material. Written cases are downloadable from the text website (www.mhhe.com/cooper11e). All video material and video cases are available from the Online Learning Center.

>chapter 18

Measures of Association

>learningobjectives

After reading this chapter, you should understand . . .

1 How correlation analysis may be applied to study relationships between two or more variables.

2 The uses, requirements, and interpretation of the product moment correlation coefficient.

3 How predictions are made with regression analysis using the method of least squares to minimize errors in drawing a line of best fit.

4 How to test regression models for linearity and whether the equation is effective in fitting the data.

5 The nonparametric measures of association and the alternatives they offer when key assumptions and requirements for parametric techniques cannot be met.

> “The invalid assumption that correlation implies cause is probably among the two or three most serious and common errors of human reasoning.”
>
> Stephen Jay Gould,
> American paleontologist and science writer

Sara arrives for an analysis meeting with Jason and finds a round, bald little man sitting at Jason's desk, studying the screen of a laptop computer, stroking his gray beard and smiling broadly.

"Sara," says Jason, "meet Jack Adams, rising political consultant."

Jack, who seems to be caressing his laptop, grins broadly. "Hello, Sara," says Jack. "I wanted Jason to know this little computer has made me the marketing kingpin of the Boca Beach political scene."

"Jack sold his painting business on Long Island to his three boys and moved to Boca Beach after his wife passed away," offers Jason in explanation.

"For three months I played golf in the morning and sat by the pool and played cards in the afternoon. For three months, seven days, I did this. I was going crazy. Then my next-door neighbor Marty died and his wife gave me his MindWriter."

"Jason came through Boca Beach and stopped for a visit. He downloaded a statistical program, free from the Internet. I must say, statistics in college never generated as much excitement as they have recently," grins Jack. "We had a wise guy, Sandy Plover, a former electrical contractor in Jersey, who got himself into local politics. Being a natural-born troublemaker, he waited for his chance to agitate. As it happens, the sheriff released data to the newspaper that the incidence of arrests resulting from police calls to Oceanside—the richer of the two neighborhoods where the sheriff happens to live—is higher than in Gladeside."

Jack types the following:

Research hypothesis: Oceanside residents get special treatment when it comes to solving crimes and thus live in a safer environment due to their higher incomes and greater political power.

Null hypothesis: Gladeside and Oceanside receive the same attention from the police.

	Gladeside	Oceanside
Police calls without arrest	46	40
Police calls resulting in arrest	4	10
Total calls	50	50

"I doubt that Sandy would have paid attention, except that in both neighborhoods the total number of police calls happened to be 50, which made it easy for him to see that in Oceanside the rate of arrests was twice that in Gladeside."

"Actually," says Sara, "I'm surprised there would be any police calls in such an upscale community."

"We are old," says Jack, "but not dead."

"In any case, Sandy's finely honed political instincts told him he was going nowhere by trying to turn the community against the sheriff. It would be much, much better to turn voters of Oceanside against those in Gladeside. So he complained about the disparate impact of arrests. While both the communities are roughly the same size, in Oceanside folks are mostly from Brooklyn, and in Gladeside folks come from the Bronx."

"But the ethics . . ."

". . . meant nothing to Sandy. He told me, 'I think I'm gonna kick some butt and make a name for myself down here.'"

"The trouble with the police calls as an issue is that sheriffs' offices nowadays are well staffed with statistically educated analysts who know very well how to rebut oddball claims," interrupts Jason.

"Although I personally miss the old days, I punched the numbers into this MindWriter here to double-check the stats. I did the obvious first, just what I supposed a police analyst would have done. I ran a cross-tabulation and a chi-square test of the hypothesis that the arrests in Oceanside were disproportionate to those in Gladeside."

"To an untrained observer it would appear that they are," contributes Sara as she peers over Jack's shoulder. "But then I'm not so easily hoodwinked."

"Good for you, Sara!" exclaims Jack. "What you have here is the 'eyeball' fallacy, as my dear old professor called it almost 50 years ago. As I explained to Sandy, 100 police encounters resulting in a few arrests is nothing, nada, not a large enough sample to trust a quick peek and a leap to a conclusion. You run it through the computer, and, sure enough, although the ratios seem to be out of whack, the difference is not statistically significant. You cannot support 'disparate impact.' No way."

"Granting that 10 arrests per 50 is bigger than 4 per 50," observes Jason, "Jack saw that a statistician would say that it is not disproportionate enough to convince a scientist that the police were acting differently in the two neighborhoods. A statistician would say, Wait and see, let the story unfold, collect a bigger sample."

"How did Sandy accept your explanation, Jack?"

"He was ready to shoot the messenger, very much bothered, at first, that I would not support his political strategy. But I was pretty sure the sheriff would come roaring back with a statistical analysis to throw cold water over Sandy."

"Did you bring him around?"

"That jerk, come around? Never. He ran to the papers, and spilled his numbers and accusations in a letter to the editor that was printed on a Monday, and Tuesday the sheriff came back with his experts and made Sandy look like a fool—on page one, if you can believe it. So Sandy was washed up, but he mentioned to the reporter that I had provided the same interpretation before he went to the paper, so I now have a new career: resident political genius. What I do is look at the opponents' polling results and deny their validity for the newspapers and TV. If the opposing party is ahead by a few poll points, I scoff at the thinness of the margin. If their lead is wide, I belittle the size of the sample and intimate that any statistician would see through them."

"Jack is colorful, amusing, and good-natured in debunking his opponents' polls, and the newspaper writers have never challenged him to substantiate his claims or interpretations," contributes Jason. "What he learned from me is that statistics is so complicated, and scares so many people, that you can claim or deny anything. And he is usually right to debunk the polls, since, for a preelection political poll to be taken seriously, there has to be a large enough sample to produce significant results. And there has to be a big enough spread between winners and losers to protect against a last-minute shift in voter sentiment. In the small, closely contested voting precincts of condominium politics, hardly any poll can meet two such stringent criteria."

"So now I sit in my condo's clubhouse and people come over and want to know what I think about the Middle East, campaign reform, everything." Jack, rising, extends his hand to Sara, "I can tell you have things to do, so I'll move along. It was nice meeting you, Sara."

Sara watches Jack Adams give Jason a bear hug and then walk out the door.

"So, Sara, what did you think of Jack's knowledge of statistics?"

> Introduction

In the previous chapter, we emphasized testing hypotheses of difference. However, management questions frequently revolve around the study of relationships between two or more variables. Then, a *relational hypothesis* is necessary. In the research question "Are U.S. kitchen appliances perceived by American consumers to be of better quality than foreign kitchen appliances?" the nature of the relationship between the two variables ("country of origin" and "perceived quality") is not specified. The implication, nonetheless, is that one variable is responsible for the other. A correct relational hypothesis for this question would state that the variables occur together in some specified manner without implying that one causes the other.

Various objectives are served with correlation analysis. The strength, direction, shape, and other features of the relationship may be discovered. Or tactical and strategic questions may be answered by predicting the values of one variable from those of another. Let's look at some typical management questions:

- In the mail-order business, excessive catalog costs quickly squeeze margins. Many mailings fail to reach receptive or active buyers. What is the relationship between mailings that delete inactive customers and the improvement in profit margins?

- Medium-size companies often have difficulty attracting the cream of the MBA crop, and when they are successful, they have trouble retaining them. What is the relationship between the candidate's rank based on an executive interview and the rank obtained from testing or managerial assessment?

- Cigarette company marketing allocations shifted a few years ago as a result of multistate settlements eliminating outdoor and transit advertising. More recently, advertising in magazines with large youth readerships came under scrutiny. During a given period, what is the relationship between point-of-sale expenditures and net profits?

- Aggressive U.S. high-tech companies have advertised heavily in the European chip market, and their sales have grown 20 percent over sales of the three largest European firms. Can we predict next year's sales based on present advertising?

All these questions may be evaluated by means of measures of association. And all call for different techniques based on the level at which the variables were measured or the intent of the question. The first three use nominal, ordinal, and interval data, respectively. The last one is answered through simple linear regression.

With correlation, one calculates an index to measure the nature of the relationship between variables. With regression, an equation is developed to predict the values of a dependent variable. Both are affected by the assumptions of measurement level and the distributions that underlie the data.

Exhibit 18-1 lists some common measures and their uses. The chapter follows the progression of the exhibit, first covering bivariate linear correlation, then examining simple regression, and concluding with nonparametric measures of association. Exploration of data through visual inspection and diagnostic evaluation of assumptions continues to be emphasized.

> Bivariate Correlation Analysis

Bivariate correlation analysis differs from nonparametric measures of association and regression analysis in two important ways. First, parametric correlation requires two continuous variables measured on an interval or ratio scale. Second, the coefficient does not distinguish between independent and dependent variables. It treats the variables symmetrically since the coefficient r_{xy} has the same interpretation as r_{yx}.

Pearson's Product Moment Coefficient *r*

The **Pearson** (product moment) **correlation coefficient** varies over a range of $+1$ through 0 to -1. The designation *r* symbolizes the coefficient's estimate of linear association based on sampling data. The coefficient ρ represents the population correlation.

Correlation coefficients reveal the magnitude and direction of relationships. The *magnitude* is the degree to which variables move in unison or opposition. The size of a correlation of $+.40$ is the same as one of $-.40$. The sign says nothing about size. The degree of correlation is modest. The coefficient's sign signifies the *direction* of the relationship. Direction tells us whether large values on one variable are associated with large values on the other (and small values with small values). When the values correspond in this way, the two variables have a positive relationship: as one increases, the other also increases. Family income, for example, is positively related to household food expenditures. As income increases, food expenditures increase. Other variables are inversely related. Large values on the first variable are associated with small values on the second (and vice versa). The prices of products and services are inversely related to their scarcity. In general, as products decrease in

>Exhibit 18-1 Commonly Used Measures of Association

Measurement	Coefficient	Comments and Uses
Interval and Ratio	**Pearson (product moment) correlation coefficient**	For continuous linearly related variables.
	Correlation ratio (eta)	For nonlinear data or relating a main effect to a continuous dependent variable.
	Biserial	One continuous and one dichotomous variable with an underlying normal distribution.
	Partial correlation	Three variables; relating two with the third's effect taken out.
	Multiple correlation	Three variables; relating one variable with two others.
	Bivariate linear regression	Predicting one variable from another's scores.
Ordinal	**Gamma**	Based on concordant-discordant pairs: $(P - Q)$; proportional reduction in error (PRE) interpretation.
	Kendall's tau *b*	$P - Q$ based; adjustment for tied ranks.
	Kendall's tau *c*	$P - Q$ based; adjustment for table dimensions.
	Somers's *d*	$P - Q$ based; asymmetrical extension of gamma.
	Spearman's rho	Product moment correlation for ranked data.
Nominal	**Phi**	Chi-square (CS) based for 2×2 tables.
	Cramer's *V*	CS based; adjustment when one table dimension > 2.
	Contingency coefficient *C*	CS based; flexible data and distribution assumptions.
	Lambda	PRE-based interpretation.
	Goodman & Kruskal's tau	PRE-based with table marginals emphasis.
	Uncertainty coefficient	Useful for multidimensional tables.
	Kappa	Agreement measure.

available quantity, their prices rise. The absence of a relationship is expressed by a coefficient of approximately zero.

Scatterplots for Exploring Relationships

Scatterplots are essential for understanding the relationships between variables. They provide a means for visual inspection of data that a list of values for two variables cannot. Both the direction and the shape of a relationship are conveyed in a plot. With a little practice, the magnitude of the relationship can be seen.

Exhibit 18-2 contains a series of scatterplots that depict some relationships across the range *r*. The three plots on the left side of the figure have their points sloping from the upper left to the lower right of each *x-y* plot.[1] They represent different magnitudes of negative relationships. On the right side of the figure, the three plots have opposite patterns and show positive relationships.

>**Exhibit 18-2** Scatterplots of Correlations between Two Variables

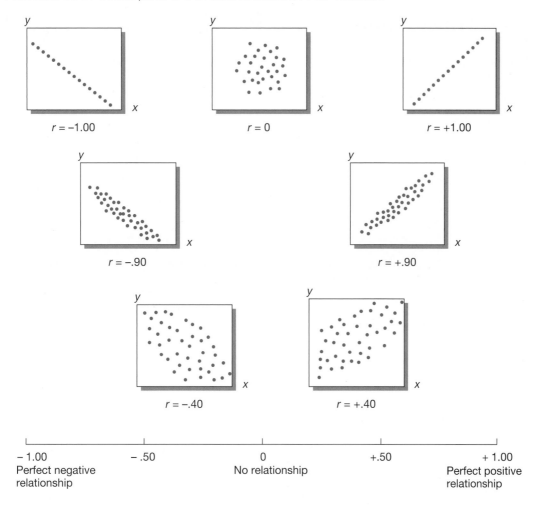

When stronger relationships are apparent (for example, the ±.90 correlations), the points cluster close to an imaginary straight line passing through the data. The weaker relationships (±.40) depict a more diffuse data cloud with points spread farther from the line.

The shape of linear relationships is characterized by a straight line, whereas nonlinear relationships have curvilinear, parabolic, and compound curves representing their shapes. Pearson's r measures relationships in variables that are linearly related. It cannot distinguish linear from nonlinear data. Summary statistics alone do not reveal the appropriateness of the data for the model, which is why inspecting the data is important.

The need for data visualization is illustrated with four small data sets possessing identical summary statistics but displaying strikingly different patterns.[2] Exhibit 18-3 contains these data, and Exhibit 18-4 plots them. In Plot 1 of the figure, the variables are positively related. Their points follow a superimposed straight line through the data. This example is well suited to correlation analysis. In Plot 2, the data are curvilinear in relation to the line, and r is an inappropriate measure of their relationship. Plot 3 shows the presence of an influential point that changed a coefficient that would have otherwise been a perfect +1.0. The last plot displays constant values of x (similar to what you might find in an animal or quality control experiment). One leverage point establishes the fitted line for these data.

We will return to these concepts and the process of drawing the line when we discuss regression. For now, comparing Plots 2 through 4 with Plot 1 suggests the importance of visually inspecting correlation data for underlying patterns to ensure linearity. Careful analysts make scatterplots an integral part of the inspection and exploration of their data. Although small samples may be plotted by hand, statistical software packages save time and offer a variety of plotting procedures.

>Exhibit 18-3 Four Data Sets with the Same Summary Statistics

S_s	X_1	Y_1	X_2	Y_2	X_3	Y_3	X_4	Y_4
1	10	8.04	10	9.14	10	7.46	8	6.58
2	8	6.95	8	8.14	8	6.77	8	5.76
3	13	7.58	13	8.74	13	12.74	8	7.71
4	9	8.81	9	8.77	9	7.11	8	8.84
5	11	8.33	11	9.26	11	7.81	8	8.47
6	14	9.96	14	8.10	14	8.84	8	7.04
7	6	7.24	6	6.13	6	6.08	8	5.25
8	4	4.26	4	3.10	4	5.39	19	12.50
9	12	10.84	12	9.13	12	8.15	8	5.56
10	7	4.82	7	7.26	7	6.42	8	7.91
11	5	5.68	5	4.74	5	5.73	8	6.89
Pearson's r	0.81642		0.81624		0.81629		0.81652	
r^2	0.66654		0.66624		0.66632		0.66671	
Adjusted r^2	0.62949		0.62916		0.62925		0.62967	
Standard error	1.2366		1.23721		1.23631		1.2357	

>Exhibit 18-4 Different Scatterplots for the Same Summary Statistics

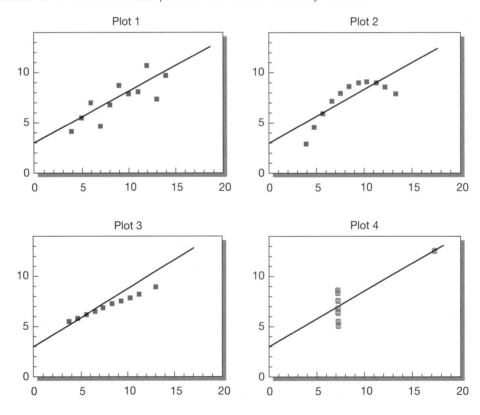

The Assumptions of r

Like other parametric techniques, correlation analysis makes certain assumptions about the data. Many of these assumptions are necessary to test hypotheses about the coefficient.

The first requirement for r is **linearity.** All of the examples in Exhibit 18-2 with the exception of $r = 0$ illustrate a relationship between variables that can be described by a straight line passing through the data cloud. When $r = 0$, no pattern is evident that could be described with a single line. Parenthetically, it is also possible to find coefficients of 0 where the variables are highly related but in a nonlinear form. As we have seen, plots make such findings evident.

The second assumption for correlation is a **bivariate normal distribution**—that is, the data are from a random sample of a population where the two variables are normally distributed in a joint manner.

Often these assumptions or the required measurement level cannot be met. Then the analyst should select a nonlinear or nonparametric measure of association, many of which are described later in this chapter.

Computation and Testing of r

The population correlation coefficient is

$$\rho = \frac{\text{Cov}(X, Y)}{\sigma_X \sigma_Y} \qquad (1)$$

Because population parameters are usually not known to us, we estimate from the random sample of (X, Y) observation pairs.

With the sample estimator of $\text{Cov}(X, Y)$ being $\text{SS}_{XY}/(n - 1)$, an estimator of σ_X is

$$\sqrt{\text{SS}_X/(n - 1)}$$

and an estimator of σ_Y is

$$\sqrt{\text{SS}_Y/(n - 1)}$$

We can substitute these estimators for their population counterparts in equation (2), giving us the sample correlation coefficient designated by r.

$$r = \frac{\text{SS}_{XY}}{\sqrt{\text{SS}_X \text{SS}_Y}} \qquad (2)$$

Another common formula for calculating Pearson's r is

$$r = \frac{\Sigma(X - \overline{X})(Y - \overline{Y})}{(n - 1)S_x S_y} \qquad (3)$$

where

n = the number of pairs of cases

S_x, S_y = the standard deviations for X and Y

A variation known as the reflective correlation, used when the data are not centered on their mean values, is:

$$r = \frac{\Sigma xy}{\sqrt{(\Sigma x^2)(\Sigma y^2)}} \qquad (4)$$

since

$$S_x = \sqrt{\frac{\Sigma x^2}{N}} \qquad S_y = \sqrt{\frac{\Sigma y^2}{N}}$$

If the numerator of equation (4) is divided by n, we have the *covariance*, the amount of deviation that the X and Y distributions have in common. With a positive covariance, the variables move in unison; with a negative one, they move in opposition. When the covariance is 0, there is no relationship. The

>Exhibit 18-5 Computation of Pearson's Product Moment Correlation

(1)	(2) Net Profits ($, millions)	(3) Cash Flow ($, millions)	(4) Deviations from Means	(5)	(6)	(7)	(8)
Corporation	X	Y	$(X - \bar{X})x$	$(Y - \bar{Y})y$	xy	x^2	y^2
1	82.6	126.5	−93.84	−178.64	16763.58	8805.95	31912.25
2	89.0	191.2	−87.44	−113.94	9962.91	7645.75	12982.32
3	176.0	267.0	−0.44	−38.14	16.78	0.19	1454.66
4	82.3	137.1	−94.14	−168.04	15819.29	8862.34	28237.44
5	413.5	806.8	237.06	501.66	118923.52	56197.44	251602.56
6	18.1	35.2	158.34	−269.94	42742.3	25071.56	72867.60
7	337.3	425.5	160.86	120.36	19361.11	25875.94	14486.53
8	145.8	380.0	−30.64	74.86	−2293.71	938.81	5604.02
9	172.6	326.6	−3.84	21.36	82.02	14.75	456.25
10	247.2	355.5	70.76	50.36	3563.47	5006.98	2536.13

$\bar{X} = 176.44$ $\bar{Y} = 305.14$ $\Sigma xy = 224777.23$
$s_x = 216.59$ $s_y = 124.01$

$\Sigma x^2 = 138419.71$

$\Sigma y^2 = 422139.76$

denominator for equation (4) represents the maximum potential variation that the two distributions share. Thus, correlation may be thought of as a ratio.

Exhibit 18-5 contains a random subsample of 10 firms of the Forbes 500 sample. The variables chosen to illustrate the computation of r are cash flow and net profits. Beneath each variable is its mean and standard deviation. In columns 4 and 5 we obtain the deviations of the X and Y values from their means, and in column 6 we find the product. Columns 7 and 8 are the squared deviation scores.

Substituting into the formula, we get

$$r = \frac{224777.23}{\sqrt{138419.71} * \sqrt{422139.76}} = .9298$$

In this subsample, net profits and cash flow are positively related and have a very high coefficient. As net profits increase, cash flow increases; the opposite is also true. Linearity of the variables may be examined with a scatterplot such as the one shown in Exhibit 18-6. The data points fall along a straight line.

Common Variance as an Explanation

The amount of common variance in X (net profits) and Y (cash flow) may be summarized by r^2, the **coefficient of determination.** As Exhibit 18-7 shows, the overlap between the two variables is the proportion of their common or shared variance.

The area of overlap represents the percentage of the total relationship accounted for by one variable or the other. So 86 percent of the variance in X is explained by Y, and vice versa.

Testing the Significance of r

Is the coefficient representing the relationship between net profits and cash flow real, or does it occur by chance? This question tries to discover whether our r is a chance deviation from a population p of zero. In other situations, the researcher may wish to know if significant differences exist between two or more r's. In either case, r's significance should be checked before r is used in other calculations or

>**Exhibit 18-6** Plot of Forbes 500 Net Profits with Cash Flow

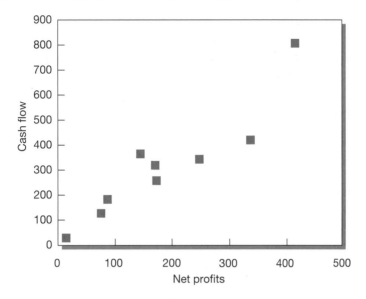

>**Exhibit 18-7** Diagram of Common Variance

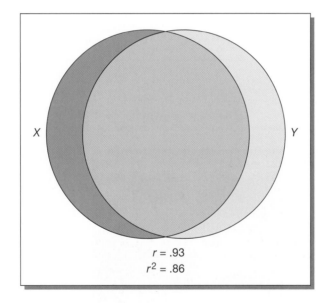

$$r = .93$$
$$r^2 = .86$$

comparisons. For this test, we must have independent random samples from a bivariate normal distribution. Then the Z or t-test may be used for the null hypothesis, $p = 0$.

The formula for small samples is

$$t = \frac{r}{\sqrt{\dfrac{1 - r^2}{n - 2}}}$$

where

$r = .93$
$n = 10$

Substituting into the equation, we calculate t:

$$t = \frac{.93}{\sqrt{\dfrac{1 - .86}{8}}} = 7.03$$

With $n - 2$ degrees of freedom, the statistical program calculates the value of t (7.03) at a probability less than .005 for the one-tailed alternative, $H_A: p > 0$. We reject the hypothesis that there is no linear relationship between net profits and cash flow in the population. The preceding statistic is appropriate when the null hypothesis states a correlation of 0. It should be used only for a one-tailed test.[3] However, it is often difficult to know in advance whether the variables are positively or negatively related, particularly when a computer removes our contact with the raw data. Software programs produce two-tailed tests for this eventuality. The observed significance level for a one-tailed test is half of the printed two-tailed version in most programs.

Interpretation of Correlations

A correlation coefficient of any magnitude or sign, whatever its statistical significance, does not imply causation. Increased net profits may cause an increase in market value, or improved satisfaction may cause improved performance in certain situations, but correlation provides no evidence of cause and effect. Several alternate explanations may be provided for correlation results:

- *X* causes *Y*.
- *Y* causes *X*.
- *X* and *Y* are activated by one or more other variables.
- *X* and *Y* influence each other reciprocally.

Ex post facto studies seldom possess sufficiently powerful designs to demonstrate which of these conditions could be true. By controlling variables under an experimental design, we may obtain more rigorous evidence of causality.

This ad captures data analysis accurately: "While data give answers in black and white, it's the subtleties of the gray areas that give you the big picture." Although a dominant answer to a variable might give you insight to the majority of responses, studying the less prevalent responses will likely give you a richer understanding of your relevant population.
www.burke.com

>Exhibit 18-8 Artifact Correlations

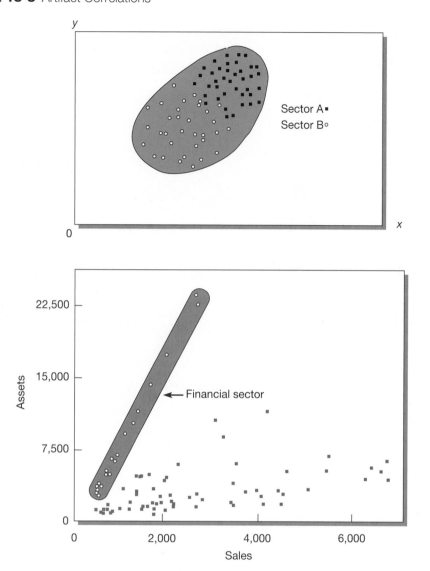

Take care to avoid so-called **artifact correlations,** in which distinct groups combine to give the impression of one. The upper panel of Exhibit 18-8 shows data from two business sectors. If all the data points for the *X* and *Y* variables are aggregated and a correlation is computed for a single group, a positive correlation results. Separate calculations for each sector (note that points for sector A form a circle, as do points for sector B) reveal *no* relationship between the *X* and *Y* variables. A second example, shown in the lower panel, contains a plot of data on assets and sales. We have enclosed and highlighted the data for the financial sector. This is shown as a narrow band enclosed by an ellipse. The companies in this sector score high on assets and low in sales—all are banks. When the data for banks are removed and treated separately, the correlation is nearly perfect (.99). When banks are returned to the sample and the correlation is recalculated, the overall relationship drops to the middle .80s. In short, data hidden or nested within an aggregated set may present a radically different picture.

Another issue affecting interpretation of coefficients concerns practical significance. Even when a coefficient is statistically significant, it must be practically meaningful. In many relationships, other factors combine to make the coefficient's meaning misleading. For example, in nature we expect rainfall and the height of reservoirs to be positively correlated. But in states where water management and flood control mechanisms are complex, an apparently simple relationship may not hold. Techniques like partial and multiple correlation or multiple regression are helpful in sorting out confounding effects.

Envirosell: Studies Reveal Left-Hand Retail

World retailers collect and subscribe to numerous data sources, but they need knowledge from the data to craft their merchandising, staffing, and promotion strategies, as well as their store designs. Retail giants (e.g., The Gap, Limited, Starbucks, Radio Shack, McDonald's) turn to consultant Paco Underhill when they want to know how consumers buy what they do and what barriers prevent or discourage buying. Underhill describes himself as a "commercial researcher, which means I am part scientist, part artist, and part entrepreneur." His company, Envirosell, has offices in the United States, Milan, Sidney, and São Paulo. Envirosell concentrates on the third segment of retail information, drawn from observation (segment 1 is register data, and segment 2 is communication studies). In an ABC News live e-chat, Underhill said, "The principal differences in 1st world shopping patterns are governed more by education and income than by ethnicity . . . but the Brits and Aussies [do] tend to walk as they drive. This sets up some very peculiar retail [shopping] patterns, because their walking patterns set up a left-hand dominance, whereas in the U.S. and much of the rest of the world, our walking patterns set up a right-hand dominance."

www.envirosell.com

If you were Gap and about to design a store to open in London, how would you design a study to verify Paco Underhill's conclusions about left-hand dominance?

With large samples, even exceedingly low coefficients can be statistically significant. This "significance" only reflects the likelihood of a linear relationship in the population. Should magnitudes less than .30 be reported when they are significant? It depends. We might consider the correlations between variables such as cash flow, sales, market value, or net profits to be interesting revelations of a particular phenomenon whether they were high, moderate, or low. The nature of the study, the characteristics of the sample, or other reasons will be determining factors. *A coefficient is not remarkable simply because it is statistically significant.*

By probing the evidence of direction, magnitude, statistical significance, and common variance together with the study's objectives and limitations, we reduce the chances of reporting trivial findings. Simultaneously, the communication of practical implications to the reader will be improved.

> Simple Linear Regression[4]

In the previous section, we focused on relationships between variables. The product moment correlation was found to represent an index of the magnitude of the relationship, the sign governed the direction, and r^2 explained the common variance. Relationships also serve as a basis for estimation and prediction.

>**Exhibit 18-9** Comparison of Bivariate Linear Correlation and Regression

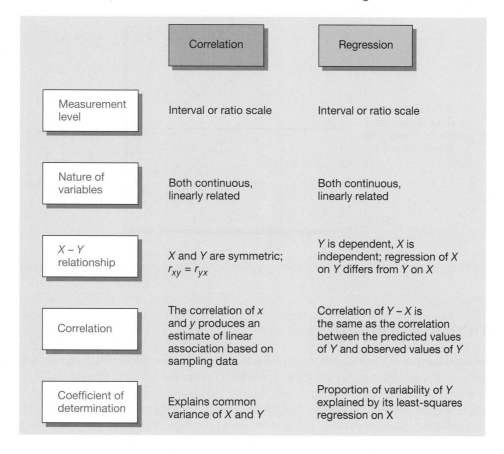

	Correlation	Regression
Measurement level	Interval or ratio scale	Interval or ratio scale
Nature of variables	Both continuous, linearly related	Both continuous, linearly related
X – Y relationship	X and Y are symmetric; $r_{xy} = r_{yx}$	Y is dependent, X is independent; regression of X on Y differs from Y on X
Correlation	The correlation of x and y produces an estimate of linear association based on sampling data	Correlation of Y – X is the same as the correlation between the predicted values of Y and observed values of Y
Coefficient of determination	Explains common variance of X and Y	Proportion of variability of Y explained by its least-squares regression on X

When we take the observed values of X to estimate or predict corresponding Y values, the process is called **simple prediction.**[5] When more than one X variable is used, the outcome is a function of multiple predictors. Simple and multiple predictions are made with a technique called **regression analysis.**

The similarities and differences of correlation and regression are summarized in Exhibit 18-9. Their relatedness would suggest that beneath many correlation problems is a regression analysis that could provide further insight about the relationship of Y with X.

The Basic Model

A straight line is fundamentally the best way to model the relationship between two continuous variables. The bivariate linear regression may be expressed as

$$Y = \beta_0 + \beta_1 X_i$$

where the value of the dependent variable Y is a linear function of the corresponding value of the independent variable X_i in the ith observation. The slope and the Y intercept are known as **regression coefficients.** The **slope,** β_1, is the change in Y for a 1-unit change in X. It is sometimes called the "rise over run." This is defined by the formula

$$\beta_1 = \frac{\Delta Y}{\Delta X}$$

This is the ratio of change (Δ) in the rise of the line relative to the run or travel along the X axis. Exhibit 18-10 shows a few of the many possible slopes you may encounter.

The **intercept,** β_0, is the value for the linear function when it crosses the Y axis; it is the estimate of Y when $X = 0$. A formula for the intercept based on the mean scores of the X and Y variables is

$$\beta_0 = \overline{Y} - \beta_1 \overline{X}$$

>Exhibit 18-10 Examples of Different Slopes

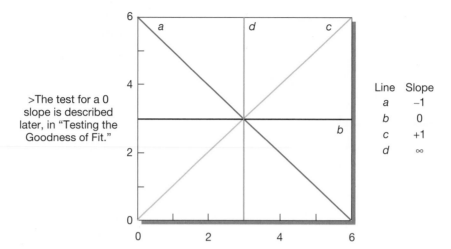

>The test for a 0 slope is described later, in "Testing the Goodness of Fit."

Line	Slope
a	−1
b	0
c	+1
d	∞

Concept Application

What makes Generation X-ers all over the world select a glass of wine rather than a beer, Jack Daniels and Coke, or Bacardi Breezer? A research report from Australia highlights Generation X attitudes toward wine. The results suggest the top influencers are friends and family, wine reviews, and visits to wineries.[6] From the winery's perspective, tasting from the barrel is not only a widespread sales tool but also a major determinant of market *en primeur* or futures contracts, which represent about 60 percent of the harvest.

Weather is widely regarded as responsible for pronouncements about a wine's taste and potential quality. A Princeton economist has elaborated on that notion. He suggested that just a few facts about local weather conditions may be better predictors of vintage French red wines than the most refined palates and noses.[7] The regression model developed predicts an auction price index for about 80 wines from winter and harvest rainfall amounts and average growing-season temperatures. Interestingly, the calculations suggested that the 1989 Bordeaux would be one of the best since 1893. French traditionalists reacted hysterically to these methods yet agreed with the conclusion.

Our first example will use one predictor with highly simplified data. Let X represent the average growing-season temperature in degrees Celsius and Y the price of a 12-bottle case in euros. Take, for example, a famous French burgundy such as Romanáe Conti St. Vivant, which sells for $340 per bottle (times 12 bottles per case or $4,080). This would be approximately 3,060 euros. The data appear here:

X Average Temperature (Celsius)	Y Price per Case (EUR)
12	2,000
16	3,000
20	4,000
24	5,000
$\bar{X} = 18$	$\bar{Y} = 3,500$

The plotted data in Exhibit 18-11 show a linear relationship between the pairs of points and a perfect positive correlation, $r_{yx} = 1.0$. The slope of the line is calculated:

$$\beta_1 = \frac{Y_i - Y_j}{X_i - X_j} = \frac{4,000 - 3,000}{20 - 16} = \frac{1,000}{4} = 250$$

>**Exhibit 18-11** Plot of Wine Price by Average Growing Temperature

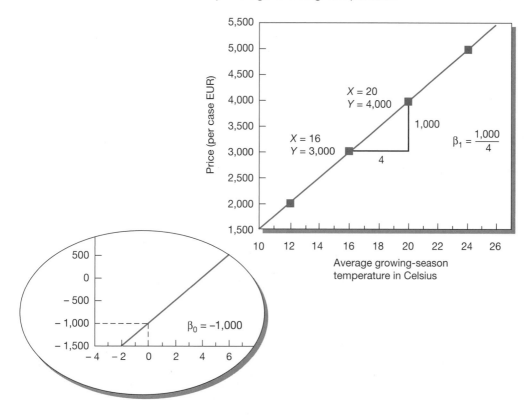

where the X_iY_i values are the data points (20, 4,000) and X_jY_j are points (16, 3,000). The intercept β_0 is $-1,000$, the point at which $X = 0$ in this plot. This area is off the graph and appears in an insert on the figure.

$$\beta_0 = \overline{Y} - \beta_1\overline{X} = 3,500 - 250(18) = -1,000$$

Substituting into the formula, we have the simple regression equation

$$Y = -1,000 + 250X_i$$

We could now predict that a warm growing season with 25.5°C temperature would bring a case price of 5,375 euros. $\hat{Y}$ (called *Y-hat*) is the predicted value of Y:

$$\hat{Y} = -1,000 + 250(25.5) = 5,375$$

Unfortunately, one rarely comes across a data set composed of four paired values, a perfect correlation, and an easily drawn line. A model based on such data is *deterministic* in that for any value of X, there is only one possible corresponding value of Y. It is more likely that we will collect data where the values of Y vary for each X value. Considering Exhibit 18-12, we should expect a distribution of price values for the temperature $X = 16$, another for $X = 20$, and another for each value of X. The means of these Y distributions will also vary in some systematic way with X. These variabilities lead us to construct a *probabilistic* model that also uses a linear function.[8] This function is written

$$Y_i = \beta_0 + \beta_1X_i + \varepsilon_1$$

where ε symbolizes the deviation of the ith observation from the mean, $\beta_0 + \beta_1X_i$.

As shown in Exhibit 18-12, the actual values of Y may be found above or below the regression line represented by the mean value of Y ($\beta_0 + \beta_1X_i$) for a particular value of X. These deviations are the error in fitting the line and are often called the **error term.**

>Exhibit 18-12 Distribution of Y for Observations of X

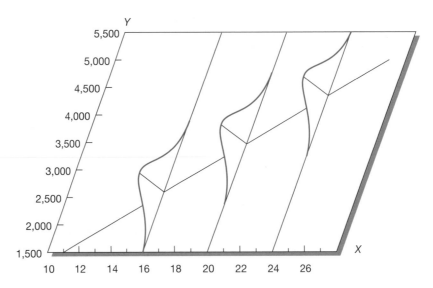

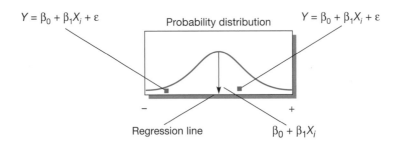

Method of Least Squares

Exhibit 18-13 contains a new data set for the wine price example. Our prediction of Y from X must now account for the fact that the X and Y pairs do not fall neatly along the line. Actually, the relationship could be summarized by several lines. Exhibit 18-14 suggests two alternatives based on visual inspection—both of which produce errors, or vertical distances from the observed values to the line. The **method of least squares** allows us to find a regression line, or line of best fit, that will keep these errors to a minimum. It uses the criterion of minimizing the total squared errors of estimate. When we predict values of Y for each X_i, the difference between the actual Y_i and the predicted $\hat{Y}$ is the error. This error is squared and then summed. The line of best fit is the one that minimizes the total squared errors of prediction.[9]

$$\sum_{i=1}^{n} e_i^2 \text{ minimized}$$

Regression coefficients β_0 and β_1 are used to find the least-squares solution. They are computed as follows:

$$\beta_1 = \frac{\sum XY - \frac{(\sum X)(\sum Y)}{n}}{\sum X^2 - \frac{(\sum X)^2}{n}}$$

$$\hat{\beta}_0 = \overline{Y} - \hat{\beta}_1 \overline{X}$$

>**Exhibit 18-13** Data for Wine Price Study

	Price (EUR) Y	Temperature (C) X	XY	Y²	X²
1	1,813	11.80	21,393.40	3,286,969.00	139.24
2	2,558	15.70	40,160.60	6,543,364.00	246.49
3	2,628	14.00	36,792.00	6,906,384.00	196.00
4	3,217	22.90	73,669.30	10,349,089.00	524.41
5	3,228	20.00	64,560.00	10,419,984.00	400.00
6	3,629	20.10	72,942.90	13,169,641.00	404.01
7	3,886	17.90	69,559.40	15,100,996.00	320.41
8	4,897	23.40	114,589.80	23,980,609.00	547.56
9	4,933	24.60	121,351.80	24,334,489.00	605.16
10	5,199	25.70	133,614.30	27,029,601.00	660.49
Σ	35,988	196.10	748,633.50	141,121,126.00	4,043.77
Mean	3,598.80	19.61			
s	1,135.66	4.69			
Sum of squares (SS)	11,607,511.59	198.25	42,908.82		

>**Exhibit 18-14** Scatterplot and Possible Regression Lines Based on Visual Inspection: Wine Price Study

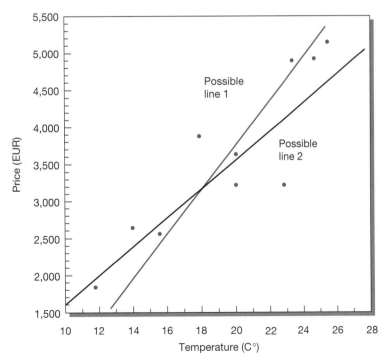

Substituting data from Exhibit 18-13 into both formulas, we get

$$\beta_1 = \frac{748{,}633.5 - \dfrac{(196.1)(35{,}988)}{10} = 216.439}{4{,}043.77 - \dfrac{(196.1)^2}{10}}$$

$$\hat{\beta}_0 = 3{,}598.8 - (216.439)(19.61) = -645.569$$

The predictive equation is now $\hat{Y} = -645.57 + 216.44\, X_i$.

>**pic**profile

Constellation Wines used both qualitative and quantitative research to design its "Count On It" campaign for its Blackstone brand. The recent recession caused wine buyers to change their behavior, so rather than purchase based on the adventure of discovery, today's buyers rely on the reduced risk associated with established brands. To take advantage of that change in behavior, Constellation Wines launched a multistage research project. First, positioning research used six focus groups—three each in Chicago and Los Angeles, half with women and half with men—to reveal how Blackstone wine compared to and contrasted with its nearest competitors. These guided discussions included word sorts. "We chose words we thought might be relevant, as well as those we thought were definitely not relevant," shared the Constellation Wines' marketing director. One unexpected word, masculine, kept surfacing among both men and women. Probing by the moderator revealed this was not masculine as macho or threatening, but rather masculine as strength. The focus groups revealed that several other words and phases were associated with Blackstone Wine: "unpretentious quality," "unassuming hero," "engaging," as well as "staple that's going to deliver." Amazon Advertising developed three different ad approaches and tested each to be sure it was true to the updated brand positioning. "Given the research findings, we wanted to be sure that our new campaign didn't come across quite as feminine as our last campaign." Gallup and Robinson then tested multiple ad executions using 20-minute Web-based interactive interviews, showing the ad against comparative run-of-press ads in targeted print media and capturing prospect recall, reaction, and understanding. The ad featured here is one of two ads that research helped Constellation Wines choose to promote Blackstone Wine. **www.cbrands.com**; **www.gallup-robinson.com**; **www.amazonadv.com**

What's a Business Education without Wine?

What do Harvard, Yale, UCLA, Columbia, the Kellogg School of Management at Northwestern, Pennsylvania's Wharton Business School, and Berkeley's Hass School of Business have in common? They are among a growing number of B-schools where wine clubs have flourished. Some have even added wine education to the business curriculum.

Although medical research has shown that moderate drinking can reduce the risk of heart disease, that's not the appeal for students who believe that it can be an effective tool for shaping positive business relationships. Brian Scanlon of Harvard's Wine & Cuisine Society summed it up this way: "Wine knowledge is an indispensable skill in today's business environment. If you're at a crucial business dinner and you want to pick the perfect wine to create the right atmosphere, you need to know the vintages, the regions and the best winemakers."

Vineyard owners couldn't be more supportive. Jack Cakebread of Cakebread Cellars, on a promotional tour at business schools around the country, reported the relationship between age and visitation frequency at Cakebread's tasting room. Almost 70 percent of visitors are in their 20s and 30s. Although wine industry research forecasts a drop in wine enthusiasm by Generation X, the future corporate executives represent a radically different segment.

David Mogridge is on a student team at Berkeley that brings in lecturers on a wide range of topics like growing, shipping, legal issues, branding, and strategy. In an interview with Eric Zelko of *Wine Spectator*, Mogridge said playfully, "When I think about it, everything I learned in business school, I learned in wine class."

www.winespectator.com

Drawing the Regression Line

Before drawing the regression line, we select two values of X to compute. Using values 13 and 24 for X_i, the points are

$$\hat{Y} = -645.57 + 216.44(13) = 2,168.15$$

$$\hat{Y} = -645.57 + 216.44(24) = 4,548.99$$

Comparing the line drawn in Exhibit 18-15 to the trial lines in Exhibit 18-14, one can readily see the success of the least-squares method in minimizing the error of prediction.

Residuals

We now turn our attention to the plot of standardized residuals in Exhibit 18-16. A **residual** is what remains after the line is fit or $(Y_i - \hat{Y}_i)$. When standardized, residuals are comparable to Z scores with a mean of 0 and a standard deviation of 1. In this plot, the standardized residuals should fall between 2 and −2, be randomly distributed about zero, and show no discernible pattern. All these conditions say the model is applied appropriately.

In our example, we have one residual at −2.2, a random distribution about zero, and few indications of a sequential pattern. It is important to apply other diagnostics to verify that the regression assumptions (normality, linearity, equality of variance, and independence of error) are met. Various software programs provide plots and other checks of regression assumptions.[10]

Predictions

If we wanted to predict the price of a case of investment-grade red wine for a growing season that averages 21°C, our prediction would be

$$\hat{Y} = -645.57 + 216.44(21) = 3,899.67$$

>Exhibit 18-15 Drawing the Least-Squares Line: Wine Price Study

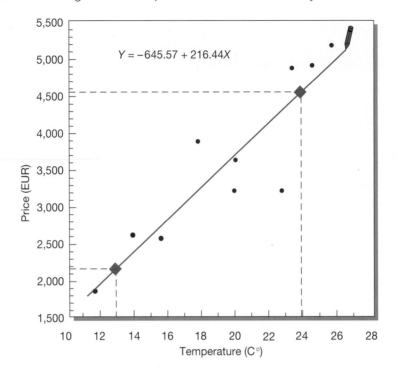

>Exhibit 18-16 Plot of Standardized Residuals: Wine Price Study

Case	−3.0	0.0	3.0	Y Price	Predicted Price	Residual
1				1,813	1,908.4112	−95.4112
2				2,558	2,752.5234	−194.5234
3				2,628	2,384.5771	243.4229
4				3,217	4,310.8844	−1,093.8844
5				3,228	3,683.2112	−455.2112
6				3,629	3,704.8551	−75.8551
7				3,886	3,228.6893	657.3107
8				4,897	4,419.1039	477.8961
9				4,933	4,678.8307	254.1693
10				5,199	4,916.9137	282.0863

This is a *point prediction* of Y and should be corrected for greater precision. As with other confidence estimates, we establish the degree of confidence desired and substitute into the formula

$$\hat{Y} \pm t_{\alpha/2} s \sqrt{1 + \frac{1}{10} + \frac{(X - \overline{X})^2}{SS_x}}$$

where

$t_{\alpha/2}$ = the two-tailed critical value for t at the desired level (95 percent in this example)

s = the standard error of estimate (also the square root of the mean square error from the analysis of variance of the regression model) (see Exhibit 18-19).

SS_x = the sum of squares for X (Exhibit 18-13).

$$3{,}899.67 \pm (2.306)(538.559) \sqrt{1 + \frac{1}{10} + \frac{(21 - 19.61)^2}{198.25}}$$

$$3{,}899.67 \pm 1{,}308.29$$

We are 95 percent confident of our prediction that a case of investment-quality red wine grown in a particular year at 21°C average temperatures will be initially priced at 3,899.67 ± 1,308.29 euros, or from approximately 2,591 to 5,208 EUR. The comparatively large bandwidth results from the amount of error in the model (reflected by r^2), some peculiarities in the Y values, and the use of a single predictor.

It is more likely that we would want to predict the average price of *all* cases grown at 21°C. This prediction would use the same basic formula but omitting the first digit (the 1) under the radical. A narrower *confidence* band is the result since the average of all Y values is being predicted from a given X. In our example, the confidence interval for 95 percent is 3,899.67 ±411.42, or from 3,488 to 4,311 EUR.

The predictor we selected, 21°C, was close to the mean of X (19.61). Because the **prediction and confidence bands** are shaped like a bow tie, predictors farther from the mean have larger bandwidths. For example, X values of 15, 20, and 25 produce confidence bands of ±565, ±397, and ±617, respectively. This is illustrated in Exhibit 18-17. The farther one's selected predictor is from X, the wider is the prediction interval.

Testing the Goodness of Fit

With the regression line plotted and a few illustrative predictions, we should now gather some evidence of **goodness of fit**—how well the model fits the data. The most important test in bivariate linear regression is whether the slope, β_1, is equal to zero.[11] We have already observed a slope of zero in Exhibit 18-10, line *b*. Zero slopes result from various conditions:

- Y is completely unrelated to X, and no systematic pattern is evident.
- There are constant values of Y for every value of X.
- The data are related but represented by a nonlinear function.

>**Exhibit 18-17** Prediction and Confidence Bands on Proximity to X

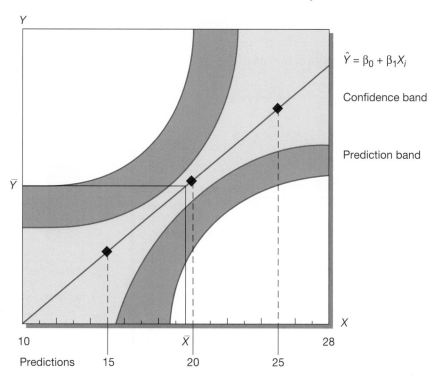

The *t*-Test

To test whether $\beta_1 = 0$, we use a two-tailed test (since the actual relationship is positive, negative, or zero). The test follows the t distribution for $n - 2$ degrees of freedom:

$$t = \frac{b_1}{s(b_1)} = \frac{216.439}{34.249} = 5.659$$

where

b_1 was previously defined as the slope β_1

$s(b_1)$ is the standard error of β_1[12]

We reject the null hypothesis, $\beta_1 = 0$, because the calculated t is greater than any t value for 8 degrees of freedom and $\alpha = .01$. Therefore, we conclude that the slope is not equal to zero.

The *F* Test

Computer printouts generally contain an analysis of variance (ANOVA) table with an F test of the regression model. In bivariate regression, t and F tests produce the same results since t^2 is equal to F. In multiple regression, the F test has an overall role for the model, and each of the independent variables is evaluated with a separate t-test. From the last chapter, recall that ANOVA partitions variance into component parts. For regression, it comprises explained deviations, $\hat{Y} - \bar{Y}$, and unexplained deviations, $Y - \hat{Y}$. Together they constitute the total deviation, $Y - \bar{Y}$. This is shown graphically in Exhibit 18-18. These sources of deviation are squared for all observations and summed across the data points.

In Exhibit 18-19, we develop this concept sequentially, concluding with the F test of the regression model for the wine data. Based on the results presented in that table, we find statistical evidence of a linear relationship between variables. The null hypothesis, $r^2 = 0$, is rejected with $F = 32.02$, d.f. $(1, 8)$, $p < .005$. The alternative hypothesis is accepted. The null hypothesis for the F test had the same effect as $\beta_1 = 0$ since we could select either test. Thus, we conclude that X and Y are linearly related.

Coefficient of Determination

In predicting the values of Y without any knowledge of X, our best estimate would be $\bar{Y}$, its mean. Each predicted value that does not fall on Y contributes to an error of estimate, $Y - \bar{Y}$. The total squared

>Exhibit 18-18 Components of Variation

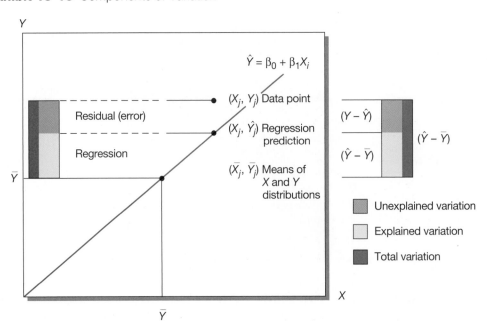

>**Exhibit 18-19** Progressive Application of Partitioned Variance Concept

General Concept

$(\hat{Y} - \bar{Y})$	+	$(Y - \hat{Y})$	=	$(Y - \bar{Y})$
Explained Variation (the regression relationship between X and Y)		Unexplained Variation (cannot be explained by the regression relationship)		Total Variation

ANOVA Application

$\sum\limits_{i=1}^{n} (\hat{Y} - \bar{Y})^2$	$\sum\limits_{i=1}^{n} (Y - \hat{Y})^2$	$\sum\limits_{i=1}^{n} (Y - \bar{Y})^2$
SS_r Sum of Squares Regression	SS_e Sum of Squares Error	SS_t Sum of Squares Total

Contents of Summary Table

Source	Degrees of Freedom	Sum of Squares	Mean Square	F Ratio
Regression	1	SS_r	$MS_r = \dfrac{SS_r}{1}$	$\dfrac{MS_r}{MS_e}$
Error	$n - 2$	SS_e	$MS_e = \dfrac{SS_e}{n-2}$	
Total		SS_t		

ANOVA Summary Table: Test of Regression Model

Source	Degrees of Freedom	Sum of Squares	Mean Square	F Ratio
Regression	1	9,287,143.11	9,287,143.11	32.02
Residual (error)	8	2,320,368.49	290,046.06	
Total		11,607,511.60		

Significance of F = .0005

error for several predictions would be $\Sigma(Y_i - Y)^2$. By introducing known values of X into a regression equation, we attempt to reduce this error even further. Naturally, this is an improvement over using $\bar{Y}$, and the result is $(\hat{Y} - \bar{Y})$. The total improvement based on several estimates is $\Sigma(\hat{Y}_i - \bar{Y})^2$, the amount of variation explained by the relationship between X and Y in the regression. Based on the formula, the *coefficient of determination* is the ratio of the line of best fit's error over that incurred by using Y. One purpose of testing, then, is to discover whether the regression equation is a more effective predictive device than the mean of the dependent variable.

As in correlation, the coefficient of determination is symbolized by r^2.[13] It has several purposes. As an index of fit, it is interpreted as the total proportion of variance in Y explained by X. As a measure of linear relationship, it tells us how well the regression line fits the data. It is also an important indicator of the predictive accuracy of the equation. Typically, we would like to have an r^2 that explains

80 percent or more of the variation. Lower than that, predictive accuracy begins to fall off. The coefficient of determination, r^2, is calculated like this:

$$r^2 = \frac{\sum_{i=1}^{n} (\hat{Y} - Y)^2}{\sum_{i=1}^{n} (Y - \bar{Y})^2} = \frac{SS_r}{SS_e} = 1 - \frac{SS_e}{SS_t}$$

For the wine price study, r^2 was found by using the data from the bottom of Exhibit 18-19:

$$r^2 = 1 - \frac{2,320,368.49}{11,607,511.60} = .80$$

27 The percent of students using a credit card for college costs due to convenience.

Eighty percent of the variance in price may be explained by growing-season temperatures. With actual data and multiple predictors, our results would improve substantially.

> Nonparametric Measures of Association[14]

Measures for Nominal Data

Nominal measures are used to assess the strength of relationships in cross-classification tables. They are often used with chi-square or may be used separately. In this section, we provide examples of three statistics based on chi-square and two that follow the proportional reduction in error approach.

There is no fully satisfactory all-purpose measure for categorical data. Some are adversely affected by table shape and number of cells; others are sensitive to sample size or marginals. It is perturbing to find similar statistics reporting different coefficients for the same data. This occurs because of a statistic's particular sensitivity or the way it was devised.

Technically, we would like to find two characteristics with nominal measures:

- When there is no relationship at all, the coefficient should be 0.
- When there is a complete dependency, the coefficient should display unity, or 1.

This does not always happen. In addition to being aware of the sensitivity problem, analysts should be alert to the need for careful selection of tests.

Chi-Square-Based Measures

Exhibit 18-20 reports a 2 × 2 table showing the test of an advertising campaign involving 66 people. The variables are success of the campaign and whether direct mail was used. In this example, the observed significance level is less than the testing level ($\alpha = .05$), and the null hypothesis is rejected. A correction to chi-square is provided. We now turn to measures of association to detect the strength of the relationship. Notice that the exhibit also provides an approximate significance of the coefficient based on the chi-square distribution. This is a test of the null hypothesis that no relationship exists between the variables of direct mail and campaign success.

The first **chi-square-based measure** is applied to direct mail and campaign success. It is called **phi (ϕ).** Phi ranges from 0 to +1.0 and attempts to correct χ^2 proportionately to N. Phi is best employed with 2 × 2 tables like Exhibit 18-20 since its coefficient can exceed +1.0 when applied to larger tables. Phi is calculated

$$\phi = \sqrt{\frac{\chi^2}{N}} = \sqrt{\frac{6.616257}{66}} = .3056$$

>**Exhibit 18-20** Chi-Square-Based Measures of Association

		Marketing Campaign Success		
	Count	Yes	No	Row Total
Direct Mail	Yes	21	10	31
	No	13	22	35
	Column Total	34	32	66

Chi-Square	Value	d.f.	Significance
Pearson	6.16257	1	.01305
Continuity correction	4.99836	1	.02537

Minimal expected frequency 15.030

Statistic	Value	Approximate Significance
Phi	.30557	.01305[*]
Cramer's V	.30557	.01305[*]
Contingency coefficient C	.29223	.01305[*]

[*]Pearson chi-square probability.

Phi's coefficient shows a moderate relationship between marketing campaign success and direct mail. There is no suggestion in this interpretation that one variable causes the other, nor is there an indication of the direction of the relationship.

Cramer's V is a modification of phi for larger tables and has a range up to 1.0 for tables of any shape. It is calculated like this:

$$V = \sqrt{\frac{\chi^2}{N(k-1)}} = \sqrt{\frac{6.616257}{66(1)}} = .3056$$

where k = the lesser number of rows or columns. In Exhibit 18-20, the coefficient is the same as phi.

The **contingency coefficient C** is reported last. It is not comparable to other measures and has a different upper limit for various table sizes. The upper limits are determined as

$$\sqrt{\frac{k-1}{k}}$$

where k = the number of columns. For a 2 × 2 table, the upper limit is .71; for a 3 × 3, .82; and for a 4 × 4, .87. Although this statistic operates well with tables having the same number of rows as columns, its upper-limit restriction is not consistent with a criterion of good association measurement. C is calculated as

$$C = \sqrt{\frac{\chi^2}{\chi^2 + N}} = \sqrt{\frac{6.616257}{6.616257 + 66}} = .2922$$

The chief advantage of C is its ability to accommodate data in almost every form: skewed or normal, discrete or continuous, and nominal or ordinal.

Proportional Reduction in Error

Proportional reduction in error (PRE) statistics are the second type used with contingency tables. Lambda and tau are the examples discussed here. The coefficient **lambda** (λ) is based on how well the frequencies of one nominal variable offer predictive evidence about the frequencies of another. Lambda is asymmetrical—allowing calculation for the direction of prediction—and symmetrical, predicting row and column variables equally.

The computation of lambda is straightforward. In Exhibit 18-21, we have results from an opinion survey with a sample of 400 shareholders in publicly traded firms. Of the 400 shareholders, 180 (45 percent) favor capping executives' salaries; 220 (55 percent) do not favor doing so. With this information alone, if asked to predict the opinions of an individual in the sample, we would achieve the best prediction record by always choosing the modal category. Here it is "do not favor." By doing so, however, we would be wrong 180 out of 400 times. The probability estimate for an incorrect classification is .45, $P(1) = (1 - .55)$.

Now suppose we have prior information about the respondents' occupational status and are asked to predict opinion. Would it improve predictive ability? Yes, we would make the predictions by summing the probabilities of all cells that are not the modal value for their rows [for example, cell (1, 2) is 20/400, or .05]:

$$P(2) = \text{cell } (1, 2) \ .05 + \text{cell } (2, 1) \ .15 + \text{cell } (3, 1) \ .075 = .275$$

>Exhibit 18-21 Proportional Reduction of Error Measures

What is your opinion about capping executives' salaries?				
	Cell designation Count Row Pct.	Favor	Do Not Favor	Row Total
	Managerial	1,1 90 82.0	1,2 20 18.0	110
Occupational Class	White collar	2,1 60 43.0	2,2 80 57.0	140
	Blue collar	3,1 30 20.0	3,2 120 80.0	150
	Column Total	180 45.0%	220 55.0%	400 100.0%

Chi-Square	Value	d.f.	Significance
Pearson	98.38646	2	.00000
Likelihood ratio	104.96542	2	.00000

Minimum expected frequency 49.500

Statistic	Value	ASEI	T Value	Approximate Significance
Lambda:				
Symmetric	.30233	.03955	6.77902	
With occupation dependent	.24000	.03820	5.69495	
With opinion dependent	.38889	.04555	7.08010	
Goodman & Kruskal tau:				
With occupation dependent	.11669	.02076		.00000[*]
With opinion dependent	.24597	.03979		.00000[*]

[*]Based on chi-square approximation.

Lambda is then calculated:

$$\lambda = \frac{P(1) - P(2)}{P(1)} = \frac{.45 - .275}{.45} = .3889$$

Note that the asymmetric lambda in Exhibit 18-21, where opinion is the dependent variable, reflects this computation. As a result of knowing the respondents' occupational classification, we improve our prediction by 39 percent. If we wish to predict occupational classification from opinion instead of the opposite, a λ of .24 would be secured. This means that 24 percent of the error in predicting occupational class is eliminated by knowledge of opinion on the executives' salary question. Lambda varies between 0 and 1, corresponding with no ability to eliminate errors to elimination of all errors of prediction.

Goodman and Kruskal's **tau** (τ) uses table marginals to reduce prediction errors. In predicting opinion on executives' salaries without any knowledge of occupational class, we would expect a 50.5 percent correct classification and a 49.5 percent probability of error. These are based on the column marginal percentages in Exhibit 18-21.

Column Marginal		Column Percent		Correct Cases
180	*	45	=	81
220	*	55	=	121
Total correct classification				202

Correct classification of the opinion variable = .505 = $\frac{202}{400}$

Probability of error, $P(1) = (1 - .505) = .495$

When additional knowledge of occupational class is used, information for correct classification of the opinion variable is improved to 62.7 percent with a 37.3 percent probability of error. This is obtained by using the cell counts and marginals for occupational class (refer to Exhibit 18-21), as shown below:

Row 1	$\left(\frac{90}{110}\right) 90 + \left(\frac{20}{110}\right) 20$ =	73.6364 + 3.6364 =	77.2727
Row 2	$\left(\frac{60}{140}\right) 60 + \left(\frac{80}{140}\right) 80$ =	25.7143 + 45.7142 =	71.4286
Row 3	$\left(\frac{30}{150}\right) 30 + \left(\frac{120}{150}\right) 120$ =	6.0 + 96.0 =	102.0000

Total correct classification (with additional information on occupational class) 250.7013

Correct classification of the opinion variable = .627 = $\frac{250.7}{400}$

Probability of error, $P(2) = (1 - .627) = .373$

Tau is then computed like this:

$$\tau = \frac{P(1) - P(2)}{P(1)} = \frac{.495 - .373}{.495} = .246$$

Exhibit 18-21 shows that the information about occupational class has reduced error in predicting opinion to approximately 25 percent. The table also contains information on the test of the null hypothesis that tau = 0 with an approximate observed significance level and asymptotic error (for developing confidence intervals). Based on the small observed significance level, we would conclude that tau is significantly different from a coefficient of 0 and that there is an association between opinion on executives' salaries and occupational class in the population from which the sample was selected. We can also establish the confidence level for the coefficient at the 95 percent level as approximately .25 ± .04.

Advanced Statistics Increase Satisfaction and Release More Funds through ATMs

The Navy Federal Credit Union (NFCU) is the world's largest credit union, with $40 billion in assets, 3.3 million members, 178 branch offices, and 7,100 employees worldwide. Its clientele represent all Department of Defense military and civilians and their families. According to Alan Payne, Navy's manager of member research and development, it regularly surveys members' satisfaction with lending, savings and checking, and investments and insurance programs using various products from SPSS PASW statistical, modeling, and text analysis modules.[a] Through a combination of statistical techniques NFCU discovered that members phoning the call center for account information also wanted to know about enhanced services and were receptive to cross-servicing promotions. Payne added that by discovering voice-of-customer insights on satisfaction levels, NFCU realized 15.3 times return on technological investment over a two-month period, creating almost $1.5 million benefit annually. NFCU was the recipient of a 2009 Technology ROI Award from Nucleus Research—one of just 10 Technology ROI Award winners from among 300 applications.[b]

Boeing Employees' Credit Union (BECU) is another proactive organization using sophisticated analytics. As a top financial cooperative in the United States with 625,000 members, two full-service centers, and more than 45 locations, Boeing recently launched an ambitious companywide research project to improve customer satisfaction. The project focused on whether to allow larger ATM withdrawals and more provisional credit for checks deposited. BECU hypothesized that allowing members to access cash more conveniently would improve retention and generate revenue. Additional objectives were to optimize response rates in direct marketing campaigns, lower per-unit acquisition costs, and identify new branch locations.

Calvin Bierley, market research analyst, in talking about its use of SPSS said, "A risk score model was embedded in the daily transactions processing system to automatically determine how much cash each member can withdraw from an ATM or receive when making deposits."[c] Then through other modeling statistical techniques, BECU identified receptive customers for marketing campaigns (achieving a 20 to 30 percent response rate on direct mail), saved $1 million annually in staffing by automating provisional credit decisions, increased revenue by $600,000 from new member acquisition and retention, and successfully identified new branch locations.

www.becu.org; www.navyfcu.org; www.spss.com

Measures for Ordinal Data

When data require **ordinal measures,** there are several statistical alternatives. In this section we will illustrate:

- Gamma.
- Kendall's tau *b* and tau *c*.
- Somers's *d*.
- Spearman's rho.

All but Spearman's rank-order correlation are based on the concept of concordant and discordant pairs. None of these statistics require the assumption of a bivariate normal distribution, yet by incorporating order, most produce a range from -1.0 (a perfect negative relationship) to $+1.0$ (a perfect positive one). Within this range, a coefficient with a larger magnitude (absolute value of the measure) is interpreted as having a stronger relationship. These characteristics allow the analyst to interpret both the direction and the strength of the relationship.

Exhibit 18-22 presents data for 70 managerial employees of KeyDesign, a large industrial design firm. All 70 employees have been evaluated for coronary risk by the firm's health insurer. The management levels are ranked, as are the fitness assessments by the physicians. If we were to use a nominal measure of association with these data (such as Cramer's V), the computed value of the statistic would be positive since order is not present in nominal data. But using ordinal measures of association reveals the actual nature of the relationship. In this example, all coefficients have negative signs; therefore, lower levels of fitness are associated with higher management levels.

>**Exhibit 18-22** Tabled Ranks for Management and Fitness Levels at KeyDesign

	Count	Management Level			
		Lower	Middle	Upper	
Fitness	High	14	4	2	20
	Moderate	18	6	2	26
	Low	2	6	16	24
		34	16	20	70

Statistic	Value*
Gamma	−.70
Kendall's tau b	−.51
Kendall's tau c	−.50
Somers's d	
Symmetric	−.51
With fitness dependent	−.53
With management-level dependent	−.50

*The t value for each coefficient is −5.86451.

The information in the exhibit has been arranged so that the number of concordant and discordant pairs of individual observations may be calculated. When a subject that ranks higher on one variable also ranks higher on the other variable, the pairs of observations are said to be **concordant.** If a higher ranking on one variable is accompanied by a lower ranking on the other variable, the pairs of observations are **discordant.** Let P stand for concordant pairs and Q stand for discordant. When concordant pairs exceed discordant pairs in a $P - Q$ relationship, the statistic reports a positive association between the variables under study. As discordant pairs increase over concordant pairs, the association becomes negative. A balance indicates no relationship between the variables. Exhibit 18-23 summarizes the procedure for calculating the summary terms needed in all the statistics we are about to discuss.[15]

Goodman and Kruskal's **gamma** (γ) is a statistic that compares concordant and discordant pairs and then standardizes the outcome by maximizing the value of the denominator. It has a proportional reduction in error (PRE) interpretation that connects nicely with what we already know about PRE nominal measures. Gamma is defined as

$$\gamma = \frac{P - Q}{P + Q} = \frac{172 - 992}{172 + 992} = \frac{-820}{1164} = .70$$

For the fitness data, we conclude that as management level increases, fitness decreases. This is immediately apparent from the larger number of discordant pairs. A more precise explanation for gamma takes its absolute value (ignoring the sign) and relates it to PRE. Hypothetically, if one was trying to predict whether the pairs were concordant or discordant, one might flip a coin and classify the outcome. A better way is to make the prediction based on the preponderance of concordance or discordance; the absolute value of gamma is the proportional reduction in error when prediction is done the second way. For example, you would get a 50 percent hit ratio using the coin. A PRE of .70 improves your hit ratio to 85 percent $(.50 \times .70) + (.50) = .85$.

With a γ of $-.70$, 85 percent of the pairs are discordant and 15 percent are concordant.[16] There are almost six times as many discordant pairs as concordant pairs. In situations where the data call for a 2×2 table, the appropriate modification of gamma is Yule's Q.[17]

Kendall's **tau b** (τ_b) is a refinement of gamma that considers tied pairs. A tied pair occurs when subjects have the same value on the X variable, on the Y variable, or on both. For a given sample size, there are $n(n - 1)/2$ pairs of observations.[18] After concordant pairs and discordant pairs are removed,

>Exhibit 18-23 Calculation of Concordant (*P*), Discordant (*Q*), Tied (T_x,T_y), and Total Paired Observations: KeyDesign Example

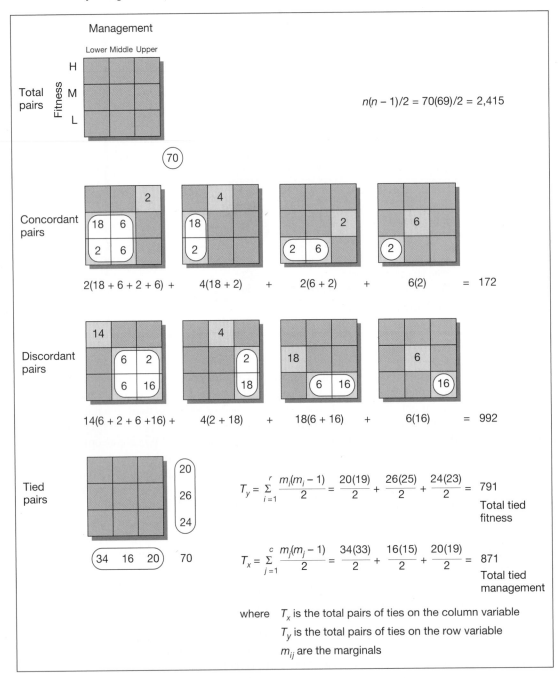

the remainder are tied. Tau *b* does not have a PRE interpretation but does provide a range of +1.0 to −1.0 for square tables. Its compensation for ties uses the information found in Exhibit 18-23. It may be calculated as

$$\tau_b = \frac{P - Q}{\sqrt{\left(\frac{n(n-1)}{2} - T_x\right)\left(\frac{n(n-1)}{2} - T_y\right)}}$$

$$= \frac{172 - 992}{\sqrt{(2{,}415 - 87-)(2{,}415 - 791)}} = \boxed{-.51}$$

Kendall's **tau** c (τ_c) is another adjustment to the basic $P - Q$ relationship of gamma. This approach to ordinal association is suitable for tables of any size. Although we illustrate tau c, we would select tau b since the cross-classification table for the fitness data is square. The adjustment for table shape is seen in the formula

$$\tau_c = \frac{2m(P - Q)}{N^2(m - 1)} = \frac{2(3)(172 - 992)}{(70)^2(3 - 1)} = -.50$$

where m is the smaller number of rows or columns.

Somers's d rounds out our coverage of statistics employing the concept of concordant-discordant pairs. This statistic's utility comes from its ability to compensate for tied ranks and adjust for the direction of the dependent variable. Again, we refer to the preliminary calculations provided in Exhibit 18-23 to compute the symmetric and asymmetric d's. As before, the symmetric coefficient (equation 1) takes the row and column variables into account equally. The second and third calculations show fitness as the dependent and management level as the dependent, respectively.

$$d_{sym} = \frac{(P - Q)}{n(n - 1) - T_x T_y/2} = \frac{-820}{1,584} = -.51 \tag{1}$$

$$d_{y-x} = \frac{(P - Q)}{\dfrac{n(n - 1)}{2} - T_x} = \frac{-820}{2,415 - 871} = -.53 \tag{2}$$

$$d_{x-y} = \frac{(P - Q)}{\dfrac{n(n - 1)}{2} - T_y} = \frac{-820}{2,415 - 791} = -.50 \tag{3}$$

The **Spearman's rho** (ρ) correlation is another ordinal measure. Along with Kendall's tau, it is used frequently with ordinal data. Rho correlates ranks between two ordered variables. Occasionally, researchers find continuous variables with too many abnormalities to correct. Then scores may be reduced to ranks and calculated with Spearman's rho.

As a special form of Pearson's product moment correlation, rho's strengths outweigh its weaknesses. First, when data are transformed by logs or squaring, rho remains unaffected. Second, outliers or extreme scores that were troublesome before ranking no longer pose a threat since the largest number in the distribution is equal to the sample size. Third, it is an easy statistic to compute. The major deficiency is its sensitivity to tied ranks. Ties distort the coefficient's size. However, there are rarely too many ties to justify the correction formulas available.

To illustrate the use of rho, consider a situation where KDL, a media firm, is recruiting account executive trainees. Assume the field has been narrowed to 10 applicants for final evaluation. They arrive at the company headquarters, go through a battery of tests, and are interviewed by a panel of three executives. The test results are evaluated by an industrial psychologist who then ranks the 10 candidates. The executives produce a composite ranking based on the interviews. Your task is to decide how well these two sets of ranking agree. Exhibit 18-24 contains the data and preliminary calculations. Substituting into the equation, we get

$$r_s = 1 - \frac{6\Sigma d^2}{n^3 - n} = \frac{6(57)}{(10)^3 - 10} = .654$$

where n is the number of subjects being ranked.

The relationship between the panel's and the psychologist's rankings is moderately high, suggesting agreement between the two measures. The test of the null hypothesis that there is no relationship between the measures ($r_s = 0$) is rejected at the .05 level with $n - 2$ degrees of freedom.

$$t = r_s \sqrt{\frac{n - 2}{1 - r_s^2}} = \sqrt{\frac{8}{1 - .4277}} = 2.45$$

>Exhibit 18-24 KDL Data for Spearman's Rho

Applicant	Rank by Panel x	Rank by Psychologist y	d	d²
1	3.5	6.0	−2.5	6.25
2	10.0	5.0	5.0	25.00
3	6.5	8.0	−1.5	2.25
4	2.0	1.5	0.5	0.25
5	1.0	3.0	−2.0	4.00
6	9.0	7.0	2.0	4.00
7	3.5	1.5	2.0	4.00
8	6.5	9.0	−2.5	6.25
9	8.0	10.0	−2.0	4.00
10	5.0	4.0	1.0	1.00
				57.00

Note: Tied ranks were assigned the average (of ranks) as if no ties had occurred.

>summary

1 Management questions frequently involve relationships between two or more variables. Correlation analysis may be applied to study such relationships. A correct correlational hypothesis states that the variables occur together in some specified manner without implying that one causes the other.

2 Parametric correlation requires two continuous variables measured on an interval or ratio scale. The product moment correlation coefficient represents an index of the magnitude of the relationship: Its sign governs the direction and its square explains the common variance. Bivariate correlation treats X and Y variables symmetrically and is intended for use with variables that are linearly related.

 Scatterplots allow the researcher to visually inspect relationship data for appropriateness of the selected statistic. The direction, magnitude, and shape of a relationship are conveyed in a plot. The shape of linear relationships is characterized by a straight line, whereas nonlinear relationships are curvilinear or parabolic or have other curvature. The assumptions of linearity and bivariate normal distribution may be checked through plots and diagnostic tests.

 A correlation coefficient of any magnitude or sign, regardless of statistical significance, does not imply causation. Similarly, a coefficient is not remarkable simply because it is statistically significant. Practical significance should be considered in interpreting and reporting findings.

3 Regression analysis is used to further our insight into the relationship of Y with X. When we take the observed values of X to estimate or predict corresponding Y values, the process is called simple prediction. When more than one X variable is used, the outcome is a function of multiple predictors. Simple and multiple predictions are made with regression analysis.

 A straight line is fundamentally the best way to model the relationship between two continuous variables. The method of least squares allows us to find a regression line, or line of best fit, that minimizes errors in drawing the line. It uses the criterion of minimizing the total squared errors of estimate. Point predictions made from well-fitted data are subject to error. Prediction and confidence bands may be used to find a range of probable values for Y based on the chosen predictor. The bands are shaped in such a way that predictors farther from the mean have larger bandwidths.

4 We test regression models for linearity and to discover whether the equation is effective in fitting the data. An important test in bivariate linear regression is whether the slope is equal to zero (i.e., whether the predictor variable X is a significant influence on the criterion variable Y). In bivariate regression, t-tests and F tests of the regression produce the same result since t^2 is equal to F.

5 Often the assumptions or the required measurement level for parametric techniques cannot be met. Nonparametric measures of association offer alternatives. Nominal measures of association are used to assess the strength of relationships in cross-classification tables. They are often used in conjunction with chi-square or may be based on the proportional reduction in error (PRE) approach.

 Phi ranges from 0 to +1.0 and attempts to correct chi-square proportionately to N. Phi is best employed with 2 × 2 tables. Cramer's V is a modification of phi for larger tables and has a range up to 1.0 for tables of any configuration. Lambda, a PRE statistic, is based on how well the frequencies of one nominal variable offer predictive evidence about the frequencies of another. Goodman and Kruskal's tau uses table marginals to reduce prediction errors.

Measures for ordinal data include gamma, Kendall's tau *b* and tau *c*, Somers's *d*, and Spearman's rho. All but Spearman's rank-order correlation are based on the

concept of concordant and discordant pairs. None of these statistics require the assumption of a bivariate normal distribution, yet by incorporating order, most produce a range from −1 to +1.

>**key**terms

artifact correlations 501

bivariate correlation analysis 493

bivariate normal distribution 497

chi-square-based measures 514

    contingency coefficient *C* 515

    Cramer's *V* 515

    phi (ϕ) 514

coefficient of determination (r^2) 498

concordant 519

discordant 519

error term 505

goodness of fit 511

lambda (λ) 516

linearity 497

method of least squares 506

ordinal measures 518

    gamma (γ) 519

    Somers's *d* 521

    Spearman's rho (ρ) 521

    tau (τ) 517

    tau *b* (τ_b) 519

    tau *c* (τ_c) 521

Pearson correlation coefficient 493

prediction and confidence bands 511

proportional reduction in error (PRE) 516

regression analysis 503

regression coefficients 503

    intercept (β_0) 503

    slope (β_1) 503

residual 509

scatterplot 494

simple prediction 503

>**discussion**questions

Terms in Review

1 Distinguish between the following:

  a Regression coefficient and correlation coefficient.

  b $r = 0$ and $\rho = 0$.

  c The test of the true slope, the test of the intercept, and $r^2 = 0$.

  d r^2 and r.

  e A slope of 0.

  f F and t^2.

2 Describe the relationship between the two variables in the four plots.

(a)

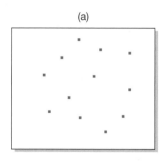

(b)

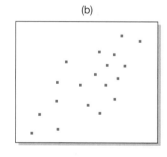

(c)

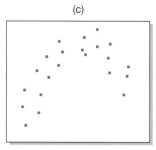

(d)

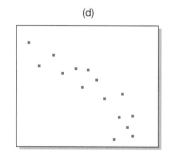

Making Research Decisions

3 A polling organization collected data on a sample of 60 registered voters regarding a tax on the market value of equity transactions as one remedy for the budget deficit.

Opinion about	Education		
Market Tax	High School	College Grad.	MBA
Favorable	15	5	0
Undecided	10	8	2
Unfavorable	0	2	18

  a Compute gamma for the table.

  b Compute tau *b* or tau *c* for the same data.

  c What accounts for the differences?

  d Decide which is more suitable for these data.

4 Using the table data in question 3, compute Somers's *d* symmetric and then use opinion as the dependent variable. Decide which approach is best for reporting the decision.

5 A research team conducted a study of soft-drink preferences among residents in a test market prior to an advertising campaign for a new cola product. Of the participants, 130 are teenagers and 130 are adults. The researchers secured the following results:

	Cola	Noncola
Teenagers	50	80
Adults	90	40

Calculate an appropriate measure of association, and decide how to present the results. How might this information affect the advertising strategy?

Bringing Research to Life

6 What would the numbers of "police calls resulting in arrest" for Gladeside and Oceanside need to change to in order to support the conclusion of "disparate impact."

From Concept to Practice

7 Using the following data,

X	Y
3	6
6	10
9	15
12	24
15	21
18	20

  a Create a scatterplot.

  b Find the least-squares line.

  c Plot the line on the diagram.

  d Predict: *Y* if *X* is 10.
           Y if *X* is 17.

8 A home pregnancy test claims to be 97 percent accurate when consumers obtain a positive result. To what extent are the variables of "actual clinical condition" and "test readings" related?

  a Compute phi, Cramer's *V*, and the contingency coefficient for the following table. What can you say about the strength of the relationship between the two variables?

  b Compute lambda for these data. What does this statistic tell you?

Actual Clinical Condition Test Readings of In-Vitro Diagnostic Cross-Tabulation

Count Actual Clinical Condition	Test Readings of In-Vitro Diagnostic		Total
	Positive	Negative	
Pregnant	451 accurate	36 inaccurate	487
Not pregnant	15 inaccurate	183 accurate	198
Total	466	219	685

9 Fill in the missing blocks for the ANOVA summary table on net profits and market value used with regression analysis.

ANOVA Summary Table

	d.f.	Sum of Squares	Mean Square	F
Regression	1	11,116,995.47	☐	☐
Error	☐	☐	116,104.63	
Total	9	12,045,832.50		

  a What does the *F* tell you? (alpha = .05)

  b What is the *t* value? Explain its meaning.

(See table on next page for data.)

		Forbes 500 Random Subsample ($, millions)			
Assets	**Sales**	**Market Value**	**Net Profit**	**Cash Flow**	**Number of Employees (thousands)**
1,034.00	1,510.00	697.00	82.60	126.50	16.60
956.00	785.00	1,271.00	89.00	191.20	5.00
1,890.00	2,533.00	1,783.00	176.00	267.00	44.00
1,133.00	532.00	752.00	82.30	137.10	2.10
11,682.00	3,790.00	4,149.00	413.50	806.80	11.90
6,080.00	635.00	291.00	18.10	35.20	3.70
31,044.00	3,296.00	2,705.00	337.30	425.50	20.10
5,878.00	3,204.00	2,100.00	145.80	380.00	10.80
1,721.00	981.00	1,573.00	172.60	326.60	1.90
2,135.00	2,268.00	2,634.00	247.20	355.50	21.20

10 Secure Spearman rank-order correlations for the largest Pearson coefficient in the matrix from question 9. Explain the differences between the two findings.

11 Using the preceding matrix data (Forbes 500), select a pair of variables and run a simple regression. Then investigate the appropriateness of the model for the data using diagnostic tools for evaluating assumptions.

12 For the following data,

X	Y
25	5
19	7
17	12
14	23
12	20
9	25
8	26
7	28
3	20

a Calculate the correlation between X and Y.

b Interpret the sign of the correlation.

c Interpret the square of the correlation.

d Plot the least-squares line.

e Test for a linear relationship:

(1) $\beta_1 = 0$.

(2) $r = 0$.

(3) An F test.

From the Headlines

13 The head of New York City's teachers' union has a theory that every time there is something that could be construed as bad news for the city's Department of Education, the city leaks a salacious story about teacher misconduct to draw attention away from the real bad news.

- December 8, 2009: federal test scores were released showing that the city's fourth- and eighth-graders made no notable improvement on federal math exams between 2007 and 2009.

- December 9, 2009: the *Daily News* reported on a high school in Brooklyn where unnamed sources told the paper that a janitor had caught two young female teachers undressed in a classroom, while students attended a talent show in the auditorium.

- December 10, 2009: the *Daily News* reported that a 31-year-old female social studies teacher was under investigation for having an inappropriate relationship with a male student.

Numerous such sequences have occurred.

a Which measure(s) of association would you use to test this theory?

b What would you need to know that is not presented in this scenario?

>cases*

Mastering Teacher Leadership	NCRCC: Teeing Up and New Strategic Direction

* You will find a description of each case in the Case Abstracts section of the textbook. Check the Case Index to determine whether a case provides data, the research instrument, video, or other supplementary material. Written cases are downloadable from the text website (www.mhhe.com/cooper11e). All video material and video cases are available from the Online Learning Center.

>chapter 19

Multivariate Analysis: An Overview

>learningobjectives

After reading this chapter, you should understand . . .

1 How to classify and select multivariate techniques.

2 How multiple regression predicts a metric dependent variable from a set of metric independent variables.

3 How discriminant analysis classifies people or objects into categorical groups using several metric predictors.

4 How multivariate analysis of variance assesses the relationship between two or more metric dependent variables and independent classificatory variables.

5 How structural equation modeling explains causality among constructs that cannot be directly measured.

6 How conjoint analysis assists researchers to discover the most important attributes and levels of desirable features.

7 How principal components analysis extracts uncorrelated factors from an initial set of variables and how (exploratory) factor analysis reduces the number of variables to discover underlying constructs.

8 How cluster analysis techniques identify homogenous groups of objects or people using a set of variables to compare their attributes and/or characteristics.

9 How perceptions of products or services are revealed numerically and geometrically by multidimensional scaling.

> **" Wonder, connected with a principle of rational curiosity, is the source of all knowledge and discovery . . . but wonder which ends in wonder, and is satisfied with wonder, is the quality of an idiot. "**
>
> Samuel Horsley, scientist and fellow
> Royal Society

Parker drapes his arm across Sara's shoulder, before bending in close to breathe his greeting in her face. "Saw some of my favorite people and just had to stop by for a 'friendly hello.'"

Jason takes pity on Sara, drawing Parker's attention as Sara tries to shrug off his arm. "How's business, Henry?" Jason inquires, although he already knows Parker's firm lost a proposed project to them just that morning. He stands and extends his hand for a handclasp he really doesn't want, with a quick smile thrown Sara's way that says, "You owe me!"

Parker clasps Jason's extended hand and puts a lock on his right bicep as well. Now it is Sara's turn to commiserate the invading of Jason's personal space.

It was Parker's annoying practice, while holding you in his firm grip, to make amazingly improbable comparisons between people, groups, institutions, products, services, practices—anything and everything—by declaring the likes of "All things being equal, Mercury would seem to be a more congenial planet on which life might emerge than Earth." Meaning, if you allowed for its atmosphere being nonexistent, and its temperature being 1,380 degrees Fahrenheit, there was presumably something about its gravitational fields or length of day that fitted Parker's preferred cosmology. You cannot argue against that kind of pseudoscientific blather.

Now Parker is lecturing Jason about a project he is doing with the governing board of the public housing authority. "The best tenants are the Pantamarians," he declares. "All things being equal, they are the most law-abiding and hard-working tenants. These folks are from Pantamarie, all English-speakers from a little island in the Caribbean. Never heard of Pantamarie before I started this project, but, I tell you, they are the most law-abiding tenants…"

"…all things being equal," echoes Jason ironically, as the very same words slip from Parker's mouth. Sara sees signs of Jason's increasing impatience, as he struggles to free himself from Parker's grasp.

"Do be more specific," urges Jason, yanking his arm from Parker's grasp none too gently. "Are you telling me that the Pantamarians have the lowest crime rate in the housing authority? You must have data—your project's funded by federal funds, right? So you must have data."

"Well," says Parker, evasively, "you have got to allow for these Pantamarians having very large families. And they did not get much schooling, back home."

"So what is not equal is their family size and education. What else is not equal?" Jason leans forward into Parker's space and stares icily into Parker's eyes.

Unbeknownst to Parker, he is saved from Jason's impending verbal attack by the arrival of the waiter carrying a loaded lunch tray.

"Well, I see lunch has arrived…nice to see you all…enjoy," smiles Parker as he turns and walks away.

"Parker wouldn't know how to prove his Pantamarian theory if we ran the numbers for him," shares Jason to the table at large. "You can be sure that the authority staff has been keeping really good records—family size, education, age—the Federal Housing and Urban Development people won't give Parker's firm a penny without it. But I'm equally sure he hasn't accessed those data.

"So, David, what would you do to prove or disprove Parker's theory?"

David, a doctoral student interning for the semester, pauses in lifting the fork to his lips. "I'd set crime rate as the dependent variable and country of origin as the independent variable and apply *analysis of covariance*, correcting for the effects of education, age, household size, whatever."

"Or maybe he could do a *factor analysis* that includes Caribbean country of origin, the population count for 2005, GDP per capita, teacher ratios, female life expectancy, births and deaths, the infant mortality rate per 1,000 of the population, radios and phones per 100 people, hospital beds, age, and family size. Then he'd know which variables are worth studying."

"Better yet," contributes Sara, joining into the spirit of the exercise Jason has started for his intern, "Parker could take the results of your factor analysis and run a *multiple regression* with crime rate as the dependent variable and the new factors that we output from the factor analysis as predictors."

"What about this," Jason contributes with a grin. "Parker could take his famous Pantamarians and the same data for their neighboring countrymen and see if he could correctly classify them with a *discriminant analysis.* Voilà! His Pantamarians could be proved to be the most law-abiding tenants," Jason pauses for effect. "Or not—all things being equal!"

Jason grins at Sara. "I completely forgot to congratulate him on landing the public authority contract and losing the more lucrative one—to us!"

After pausing for effect, Sara asks, "Now, David, what was that you were saying about your *multidimensional scaling* problem before Parker interrupted?"

> Introduction

In recent years, multivariate statistical tools have been applied with increasing frequency to research problems. This recognizes that many problems we encounter are more complex than the problems bivariate models can explain. Simultaneously, computer programs have taken advantage of the complex mathematics needed to manage multiple-variable relationships. Today, computers with fast processing speeds and versatile software bring these powerful techniques to researchers.

Throughout business, more and more problems are being addressed by considering multiple independent and/or multiple dependent variables. Sales managers base forecasts on various product history variables; researchers consider the complex set of buyer preferences and preferred product options; and analysts classify levels of risk based on a set of predictors.

One author defines **multivariate analysis** as "those statistical techniques which focus upon, and bring out in bold relief, the structure of simultaneous relationships among three or more phenomena."[1] Our overview of multivariate analysis seeks to illustrate the meaning of this definition while building on your understanding of bivariate statistics from the last few chapters. Several common multivariate techniques and examples will be discussed.

Because a complete treatment of this subject requires a thorough consideration of the mathematics, assumptions, and diagnostic tools appropriate for each technique, our coverage is necessarily limited. Readers desiring greater detail are referred to the suggested readings for this chapter.

> Selecting a Multivariate Technique

Multivariate techniques may be classified as **dependency** and **interdependency techniques.** Selecting an appropriate technique starts with an understanding of this distinction. If criterion and predictor variables exist in the research question, then we will have an assumption of dependence. Multiple regression, multivariate analysis of variance (MANOVA), and discriminant analysis are techniques in which criterion or dependent variables and predictor or independent variables are present. Alternatively, if the variables are interrelated without designating some as dependent and others independent, then interdependence of the variables is assumed. Factor analysis, cluster analysis, and multidimensional scaling are examples of interdependency techniques.

Exhibit 19-1 provides a diagram to guide in the selection of techniques. Let's take an example to show how you might make a decision. Every other year since 1978, the Roper organization has tracked public opinion toward business by providing a list of items that are said to be the responsibility of

>**Exhibit 19-1** Selecting from the Most Common Multivariate Techniques

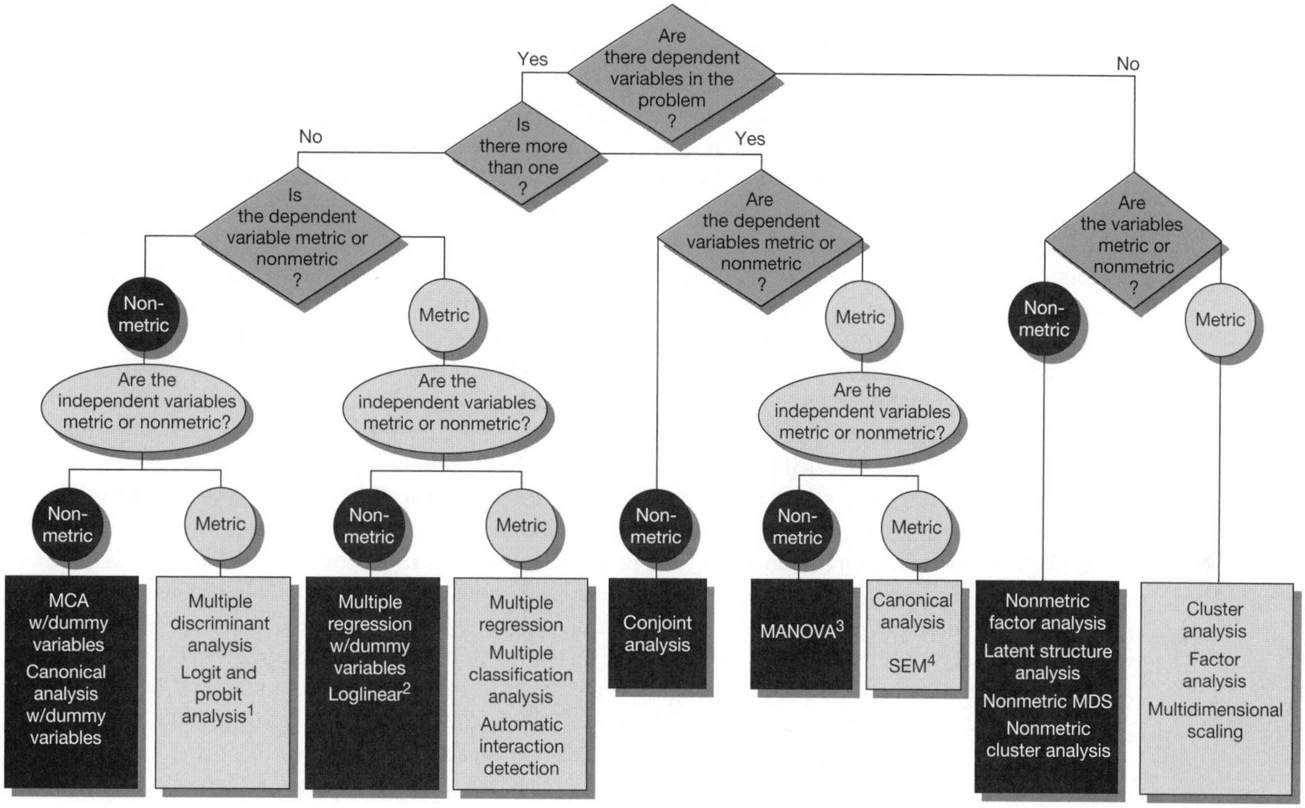

[1]The independent variable is metric only in the sense that a transformed proportion is used.
[2]The independent variable is metric only when we consider that the number of cases in the cross-tabulation cell is used to calculate the logs.
[3]Factors may be considered nonmetric independent variables in that they organize the data into groups. We do not classify MANOVA and other multivariate analysis of variance models.
[4]SEM refers to structural equation modeling for latent variables. It is a family of models appropriate for confirmatory factor analysis, path analysis, time series analysis, recursive and nonrecursive models, and covariance structure models. Because it may handle dependence and interdependence, metric and nonmetric, it is arbitrarily placed in this diagram.

Source: Partially adaxpted from T. C. Kinnear and J. R. Taylor, "Multivariate Methods in Marketing: A Further Attempt at Classification," *Journal of Marketing,* October 1971, p. 57; and J. F. Hair Jr., Rolph E. Anderson, Ronald L. Tatham, and Bernie J. Grablowsky, *Multivariate Data Analysis* (Tulsa, OK: Petroleum Publishing Co., 1979), pp. 10–14.

business. The respondents are asked whether business fulfills these responsibilities "fully, fairly well, not too well, or not at all well." The following issues make up the list:[2]

- Developing new products and services.
- Producing good-quality products and services.
- Making products that are safe to use.
- Hiring minorities.
- Providing jobs for people.
- Being good citizens of the communities in which they operate.
- Paying good salaries and benefits to employees.
- Charging reasonable prices for goods and services.
- Keeping profits at reasonable levels.
- Advertising honestly.

- Paying their fair share.
- Cleaning up their own air and water pollution.

You have access to data on these items and wish to know if they could be reduced to a smaller set of variables that would account for most of the variation among respondents. In response to the first question in Exhibit 19-1, you correctly determine there are no dependent variables in the data set. You then check to see if the variables are **metric** or **nonmetric measures.** In the exhibit, *metric* refers to ratio and interval measurements, and *nonmetric* refers to data that are nominal and ordinal. Based on the measurement scale, which appears to have equal intervals, and preliminary findings that show a linear relationship among several variables, you decide the data are metric. This decision leads you to three options: multidimensional scaling, cluster analysis, or factor analysis. *Multidimensional scaling* develops a perceptual map of the locations of some objects relative to others. This map specifies how the objects differ. *Cluster analysis* identifies homogeneous subgroups or clusters of individuals or objects based on a set of characteristics. *Factor analysis* looks for patterns among the variables to discover if an underlying combination of the original variables (a factor) can summarize the original set. Based on your research objective, you select factor analysis.

Suppose you are interested in predicting family food expenditures from family income, family size, and whether the family's location is rural or urban. Returning to Exhibit 19-1, you conclude there is a single dependent variable, family food expenditures. You decide this variable is metric because dollars are measured on a ratio scale. The independent variables, income and family size, also meet the criteria for metric data. However, you are not sure about the location variable because it appears to be a dichotomous nominal variable. According to the exhibit, your choices are automatic interaction detection (AID), multiple classification analysis (MCA), and multiple regression. You recall from Chapter 16 that AID was designed to locate the most important predictors in a set of numerous independent variables and create a treelike answer. MCA handles weak predictors (including nominal variables), correlated predictors, and nonlinear relationships. Multiple regression is the extension of bivariate regression. You believe that your data exceed the assumptions for the first two techniques and that by treating the nominal variable's values as 0 or 1, you could use it as an independent variable in a multiple regression model. You prefer this to losing information from the other two variables—a certainty if you reduce them to nonmetric data.

In the next two sections, we will extend this discussion as we illustrate dependency and interdependency techniques.[3]

> Dependency Techniques

Multiple Regression

Multiple regression is used as a descriptive tool in three types of situations. First, it is often used to develop a self-weighting estimating equation by which to predict values for a criterion variable (DV) from the values for several predictor variables (IVs). Thus, we might try to predict company sales on the basis of new housing starts, new marriage rates, annual disposable income, and a time factor. Another prediction study might be one in which we estimate a student's academic performance in college from the variables of rank in high school class, SAT verbal scores, SAT quantitative scores, and a rating scale reflecting impressions from an interview.

Second, a descriptive application of multiple regression calls for controlling for confounding variables to better evaluate the contribution of other variables. For example, one might wish to control the brand of a product and the store in which it is bought to study the effects of price as an indicator of product quality.[4] A third use of multiple regression is to test and explain causal theories. In this approach, often referred to as **path analysis,** regression is used to describe an entire structure of linkages that have been advanced from a causal theory.[5] In addition to being a descriptive tool, multiple regression is also used as an inference tool to test hypotheses and to estimate population values.

Method

Multiple regression is an extension of the bivariate linear regression presented in Chapter 18. The terms defined in that chapter will not be repeated here. Although **dummy variables** (nominal variables coded 0, 1) may be used, all other variables must be interval or ratio. The generalized equation is

$$Y = \beta_0 + \beta_1 X_1 + \beta_2 X_2 + \cdots + \beta_n X_n + \varepsilon$$

where

β_0 = a constant, the value of Y when all X values are zero

β_i = the slope of the regression surface (The β represents the regression coefficient associated with each X_i.)

ε = an error term, normally distributed about a mean of 0 (For purposes of computation, the ε is assumed to be 0.)

The regression coefficients are stated either in raw score units (the actual X values) or as **standardized coefficients** (X values restated in terms of their standard scores). In either case, the value of the regression coefficient states the amount that Y varies with each unit change of the associated X variable when the effects of all other X variables are being held constant. When the regression coefficients are standardized, they are called **beta weights** (β), and their values indicate the relative importance of the associated X values, particularly when the predictors are unrelated. For example, in an equation where $\beta_1 = .60$ and $\beta_2 = .20$, one concludes that X_1 has three times the influence on Y as does X_2.

Example

In a Snapshot later in this chapter, we describe an e-business that uses multivariate approaches to understand its target market in the global "hybrid-mail" business. SuperLetter's basic service enables users to create a document on any PC and send it in a secure, encrypted mode over the Internet to a distant international terminal near the addressee, where it will be printed, processed, and delivered. Spread like a "fishnet" over the world's major commercial markets, the network connects corresponding parties, linking the world's "wired" with its "nonwired." The British Armed Forces and several U.S. military organizations have used it to speed correspondence between families and service members in Afghanistan and Iraq.

We use multiple regression in this example to evaluate the *key drivers* of customer usage for hybrid mail. Among the available independent or predictor variables, we expect some to better explain or predict the dependent or criterion variable than others (thus they are *key* to our understanding). The independent variables are customer perceptions of (1) cost/speed valuation, (2) security (limits on changing, editing, or forwarding a document and document privacy), (3) reliability, (4) receiver technology (hard copy for receivers with no e-mail or fax access), and (5) impact/emotional value (reducing e-mail spam clutter and official/important appearance). We have chosen the first three variables, all measured on 5-point scales, for this equation:

Y = customer usage

X_1 = cost/speed valuation

X_2 = security

X_3 = reliability

SPSS computed the model and the regression coefficients. Most statistical packages provide various methods for selecting variables for the equation. The equation can be built with all variables or specific combinations, or you can select a method that sequentially adds or removes variables (forward selection, backward elimination, and stepwise selection). **Forward selection** starts with the constant and adds variables one at a time that result in the largest R^2 increase. **Backward elimination** begins with a model containing all independent variables and removes the variable that changes R^2 the least. **Stepwise selection,** the most popular method, combines forward and backward sequential approaches.

>Exhibit 19-2 Multiple Regression Analysis of Hybrid-Mail Customer Usage, Cost/Speed Valuation, Security, and Reliability

Model Summary

Model	R	R^2	Adjusted R^2	Std. Error of the Estimate	Change Statistics R^2 Change	F Change	d.f.1	d.f.2	Sig. F Change
1	.879	.772	.771	.6589	.772	612.696	1	181	.000
2	.925	.855	.854	.5263	.083	103.677	2	180	.000
3	.935	.873	.871	.4937	.018	25.597	3	179	.000

1 Predictors: (constant), cost/speed.
2 Predictors: (constant), cost/speed, security.
3 Predictors: (constant), cost/speed, security, reliability.

Coefficients

Model		Unstandardized Coefficients B	Std. Error	Standardized Coefficients Beta	t	Sig.	Collinearity Statistics VIF
1	(Constant)	.579	.151		3.834	.000	
	Cost/speed	.857	.035	.879	24.753	.000	1.000
2	(Constant)	9.501E-02	.130		.733	.464	
	Cost/speed	.537	.042	.551	12.842	.000	2.289
	Security	.428	.042	.437	10.182	.000	2.289
3	(Constant)	−9.326E-02	.127		−.734	.464	
	Cost/speed	.448	.043	.460	10.428	.000	2.748
	Security	.315	.045	.321	6.948	.000	3.025
	Reliability	.254	.050	.236	5.059	.000	3.067

Dependent variable: customer usage.

The independent variable that contributes the most to explaining the dependent variable is added first. Subsequent variables are included based on their incremental contribution over the first variable and on whether they meet the criterion for entering the equation (e.g., a significance level of .01). Unlike forward selection and backward elimination, stepwise selection allows variables to be added or deleted at each subsequent step in the method. Variables may be removed if they meet the removal criterion, which is a larger significance level than that for entry.

The standard elements of a stepwise output are shown in Exhibit 19-2. In the upper portion of the exhibit there are three models. In model 1, cost/speed is the first variable to enter the equation. This model consists of the constant and the variable cost/speed. Model 2 adds the security variable to cost/speed. Model 3 consists of all three independent variables. In the summary statistics for model 1, you see that cost/speed explains 77 percent of customer usage (see the "R^2" column). This is increased by 8 percent in model 2 when security is added (see "R^2 Change" column). When reliability is added in model 3, accounting for only 2 percent, 87 percent of customer usage is explained.

The other reported statistics have the following interpretations.

1. Adjusted R^2 for model 3 = .871. R^2 is adjusted to reflect the model's goodness of fit for the population. The net effect of this adjustment is to reduce the R^2 from .873 to .871, thereby making it comparable to other R^2's from equations with a different number of independent variables.

2. Standard error of model 3 = .4937. This is the standard deviation of actual values of Y about the estimated Y values.

3. Analysis of variance measures whether or not the equation represents a set of regression coefficients that, in total, are statistically significant from zero. The critical value for F is found in Appendix D (Exhibit D-8), with degrees of freedom for the numerator equaling k, the number of independent variables, and for the denominator, $n - k - 1$, where n for model 3 is 183 observations. Thus, d.f. $= (3, 179)$. The equation is statistically significant at less than the .05 level of significance (see the column labeled "Sig. F Change").

4. Regression coefficients for all three models are shown in the lower table of Exhibit 19-2. The column headed "B" shows the unstandardized regression coefficients for the equation. The equation may now be constructed as

$$Y = -.093 + .448X_1 + .315X_2 + .254X_3$$

5. The column headed "Beta" gives the regression coefficients expressed in standardized form. When these are used, the regression Y intercept is zero. Standardized coefficients are useful when the variables are measured on different scales. The beta coefficients also show the relative contribution of the three independent variables to the explanatory power of this equation. The cost/speed valuation variable explains more than either of the other two variables.

6. Standard error is a measure of the sampling variability of each regression coefficient.

7. The column headed "t" measures the statistical significance of each of the regression coefficients.

Again compare these to the table of t values in Appendix D, Exhibit D-2, using degrees of freedom for one independent variable. All three regression coefficients are judged to be significantly different from zero. Therefore, the regression equation shows the relationship between the dependent variable, customer usage of hybrid mail, and three independent variables: cost/speed, security, and reliability. The regression coefficients are both individually and jointly statistically significant. The independent variable cost/speed influences customer usage the most, followed by security and then reliability.

Collinearity, where two independent variables are highly correlated—or **multicollinearity,** where more than two independent variables are highly correlated—can have damaging effects on multiple regression. When this condition exists, the estimated regression coefficients can fluctuate widely from sample to sample, making it risky to interpret the coefficients as an indicator of the relative importance of predictor variables. Just how high can acceptable correlations be between independent variables? There is no definitive answer, but, as a rule of thumb, correlations at a .80 or greater level should be addressed. Because high intercorrelations between predictor variables suggest that they are measuring the same construct, the presence of multicollinearity can be dealt with in one of two ways:

1. Retain the variable that best captures the concept/construct you want to measure and delete the other.

2. Create a new variable that is a composite of the highly intercorrelated variables and use this new variable in place of its components.

However, making a decision to delete or alter variables based on the findings contained within the correlation matrix alone is not always advisable. In the example just presented, Exhibit 19-2 contains a column labeled "Collinearity Statistics" that shows a *variable inflation factor (VIF)* index. This is a measure of the effect of the other independent variables on a regression coefficient as a result of these correlations. Large values, usually 10.0 or more, suggest collinearity or multicollinearity. For the three predictors in the hybrid-mail example, multicollinearity is not a problem. However, there may be instances when you determine that the predictor variables are, in fact, conceptually distinct (precluding deletion) yet are nevertheless highly correlated (such as income and education level). In this situation, you must acknowledge the possible impact of multicollinearity on the unique effects of each predictor variable.

The last step in the multiple regression technique is to evaluate (validate) how well the regression equation predicts beyond the sample used originally to calculate it. A practical solution is to set aside a portion of the data (from one-fourth to one-third) called a **holdout sample.** One uses the equation with the holdout data to calculate a new R^2 and compare its similarity to the original R^2 to determine if the results are generalizable to the population.

Discriminant Analysis

Researchers often wish to classify people or objects into two or more distinct and well-defined groups. One might need to classify persons as either buyers or nonbuyers, good or bad credit risks, or to classify superior, average, or poor products in some market. The objective of discriminant analysis is to establish a classification method, based on a set of attributes, in order to correctly predict the group membership of these subjects. With this objective, it is easy to understand why discriminant analysis is frequently used in market segmentation research.

Method

As a dependency technique, **discriminant analysis** joins a nominally scaled criterion or dependent variable with one or more independent variables that are interval- or ratio-scaled. Once the discriminant equation is determined, it can be used to predict the classification of a new observation. This is done by calculating a linear function of the form

$$D_i = d_0 + d_1X_1 + d_2X_2 + \cdots + d_pX_p$$

where

D_i is the score on discriminant function i.

The d_i's are weighting coefficients; d_0 is a constant.

The X's are the values of the discriminating variables used in the analysis.

A single discriminant equation is required if the categorization calls for two groups. If three groups are involved in the classification, it requires two discriminant equations. If more categories are called for in the dependent variable, one needs $N - 1$ discriminant functions. Of note, each of the discriminant groups are both collectively exhaustive and mutually exclusive, in that each entity belongs to a group and to only one group.

While the most common use for discriminant analysis is to classify persons or objects into various groups, it can also be used to analyze known groups to determine the relative influence of specific factors for deciding into which group various cases fall. Assume we have MindWriter service ratings that enable us to classify postpurchase service as successful or unsuccessful on performance. We might also be able to secure test results on three measures: motivation for working with customers (X_1), technical expertise (X_2), and accessibility to repair status information (X_3). Suppose the discriminant equation is

$$D = .06X_1 + .45X_2 + .30X_3$$

Since discriminant analysis uses standardized values for the discriminant variables, we conclude from the coefficients that motivation for working with customers is less important than the other two in classifying postpurchase service.[6]

Example

An illustration of the method takes us back to the problem in the last chapter where KDL, a media firm, is hiring MBAs for its account executives program. Over the years the firm has had indifferent success with the selection process. You are asked to develop a procedure to improve the firm's current selection process. It appears that discriminant analysis is the most appropriate technique to fulfill this task. You begin by gathering data on 30 MBAs who have been hired by KDL in recent years. Fifteen of these new hires have become successful employees, while the other 15 were unsuccessful. The files provide the following information that can be used to conduct the analysis:

X_1 = years of prior work experience

X_2 = GPA in graduate program

X_3 = employment test scores

>**Exhibit 19-3** Discriminant Analysis Classification Results at KDL Media

A.

Actual Group		Number of Cases	Predicted Success	
			0	1
Unsuccessful	0	15	13	2
			86.70%	13.30%
Successful	1	15	3	12
			20.00%	80.00

Note: Percent of "grouped" cases correctly classified: 83.33%.

B.

	Unstandardized	Standardized
X_1	.36084	.65927
X_2	2.61192	.57958
X_3	.53028	.97505
Constant	12.89685	

Discriminant analysis determines how well these three independent variables will correctly classify those who are judged successful from those judged unsuccessful. The classification results are shown in Exhibit 19-3. This indicates that 25 of the 30 $(30 - 3 - 2 = 25)$ cases have been correctly classified using these three variables. In interpreting the discriminant function, it is also important to examine the misclassified cases for additional attributes or relationships that may improve the accuracy of the equation.

The standardized and unstandardized discriminant function coefficients are shown in part B of Exhibit 19-3. These results indicate that X_3 (the employment test) has the greatest discriminating power of the three attributes or independent variables used to assess the differences between these groups. Of the several significance tests that may be computed, Wilk's lambda has a chi-square transformation for testing the significance of the discriminant function. If computed for this example, it indicates that the equation is statistically significant at the $\alpha = .0004$ level. Using the discriminant equation,

$$D = .659X_1 + .580X_2 + .975X_3$$

you can now predict with a greater level of certainty whether future candidates are likely to be successful account executives.

MANOVA

Multivariate analysis of variance, or **MANOVA,** is a commonly used multivariate technique. MANOVA assesses the relationship between two or more continuous dependent variables and categorical variables or factors. In business research, MANOVA can be used to test differences among samples of employees, customers, manufactured products, production parts, and so forth.

Method

MANOVA is similar to the univariate ANOVA described earlier, with the added ability to handle several dependent variables. If ANOVA is applied consecutively to a set of interrelated dependent variables, erroneous conclusions may result (e.g., Type I error). MANOVA can correct this by simultaneously testing all the variables and their interrelationships. MANOVA uses special matrices

>Exhibit 19-4 MANOVA Techniques Show These Three Centroids to Be Unequal
in the CalAudio Study

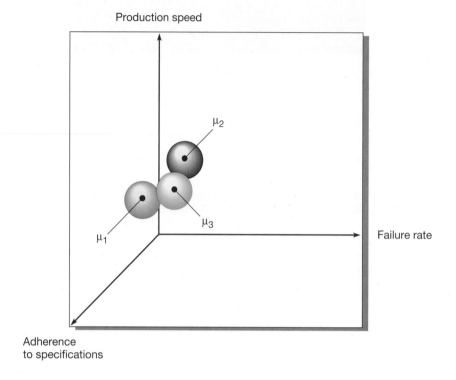

[sums-of-squares and cross-products (SSCP) matrices] to test for differences among groups. The variance between groups is determined by partitioning the total SSCP matrix and testing for significance. The F ratio, generalized to a ratio of the within-group variance and total-group variance matrices, tests for equality among groups. MANOVA examines similarities and differences among the multivariate mean scores of several populations. The null hypothesis for MANOVA is that all of the **centroids** (multivariate means) are equal, $H_0: \mu_1 = \mu_2 = \mu_3 = \cdots \mu_n$. The alternative hypothesis is that the vectors of centroids are unequal, $H_A: \mu_1 \neq \mu_2 \neq \mu_3 \neq \cdots \mu_n$. Exhibit 19-4 shows graphically three populations whose centroids are unequal, allowing the researcher to reject the null hypothesis. When the null hypothesis is rejected, additional tests are done to understand the results in detail. Several techniques may be considered in proceeding from a significant effect in MANOVA:

1. Univariate F tests can be run on the dependent variables (multiple univariate ANOVAs).

2. Simultaneous confidence intervals can be produced for each variable.

3. Stepdown analysis, like stepwise regression, can be run by computing F values successively. Each value is computed after the effects of the previous dependent variable are eliminated.

4. Multiple discriminant analysis can be used on the SSCP matrices. This aids in the discovery of which variables contribute to the MANOVA's significance.[7]

Before using MANOVA to test for significant differences, you must first determine that MANOVA is appropriate, that is, that the assumptions for its use are met.

Example

To illustrate how these assumptions are assessed and how MANOVA is performed, let's look at CalAudio, a firm that manufactures MP3 players. The manager is concerned about brand loyalty and fears that the quality of the manufactured players may be affecting customers' repurchase decisions. The closest competitor's product appears to have fewer repair issues and higher satisfaction ratings. Two measures are used to assess quality in this example: adherence to product specifications and time before failure. Measured on a 0-to-100 scale, with 100 meeting all product specifications, the specification variable is averaging approximately 90. The mean time before failure is calculated in weeks; it is approximately 159 weeks, or three years.

Management asks the industrial engineering department to devise a modified manufacturing procedure that will improve the quality measures but not change the production rate significantly. A new method is designed that includes more efficient parts handling and "burn-in" time, when MP3 players are powered up and run at high temperatures.

Engineering takes a sample of 15 MP3 players made with the old manufacturing method and 15 made with the new method. The players are measured for their adherence to product specifications and are stress-tested to determine their time before failure. The stress test uses accelerated running conditions and adverse environmental conditions to simulate years of use in a short time.

Exhibit 19-5 shows the mean and standard deviation of the dependent variables (failure, specifications, and manufacturing speed) for each level of method.[8] Method 1 represents the current manufacturing process, and method 2 is the new process. The new method extended the time before failure to 181 weeks, compared to 159 weeks for the existing method. The adherence to specifications is also improved, up to 95 from 90. But the manufacturing speed is slower by approximately 30 minutes (.473 hour).

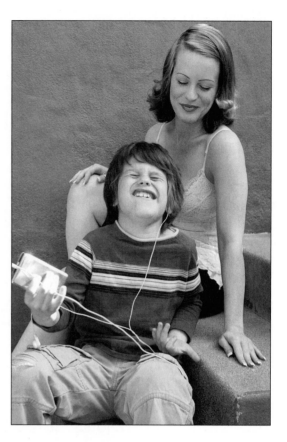

We have used diagnostics to check the assumptions of MANOVA except for equality of variance. Both levels of the manufacturing method variable produce a matrix, and the equality of these two matrices must be determined (H_0: variances are equal). Exhibit 19-6 contains homogeneity-of-variance tests for separate dependent variables and a multivariate test. The former are known as *univariate tests.* The multivariate test is a comparable version that tests the variables simultaneously to determine whether MANOVA should proceed.

The significance levels of Cochran's *C* and Bartlett-Box *F* do not allow us to reject any of the tests for the dependent variables considered separately. This means the two methods have equal variances in each dependent variable. This fulfills the univariate assumptions for homogeneity of variance. We then consider the variances and covariances simultaneously with Box's *M,* also found in Exhibit 19-6. Again, we are unable to reject the homogeneity-of-variance assumption regarding the matrices. This satisfies the multivariate assumptions.

>**Exhibit 19-5** MANOVA Cell Means and Standard Deviations in CalAudio Study

VARIABLE	FACTOR	LEVEL	MEAN	STD. DEV.
FAILURE				
	METHOD	1	158.867	4.998
	METHOD	2	181.067	5.994
	For entire sample		169.967	12.524
SPECIFICATIONS				
	METHOD	1	89.800	2.077
	METHOD	2	94.800	2.178
	For entire sample		92.300	3.292
SPEED				
	METHOD	1	2.126	.061
	METHOD	2	2.599	.068
	For entire sample		2.362	.249

>Exhibit 19-6 MANOVA Homogeneity-of-Variance Tests in the CalAudio Study

```
VARIABLE              TEST                         RESULTS
─────────────────────────────────────────────────────────────────────
FAILURE

           Cochran's C (14,2) =          .58954, P = .506 (approx.)
           Bartlett-Box F (1,2352) =     .44347, P = .506

SPECIFICATIONS

           Cochran's C (14,2) =          .52366, P = .862 (approx.)
           Bartlett-Box F (1,2352) =     .03029, P = .862

SPEED

           Cochran's C (14,2) =          .55526, P = .684 (approx.)
           Bartlett-Box F (1,2352) =     .16608, P = .684
─────────────────────────────────────────────────────────────────────
      Multivariate Test for Homogeneity of Dispersion Matrices

           Box's M =                     6.07877
           F with (6,5680) DF =          .89446, P = .498 (approx.)
           Chi-Square with 6 DF =        5.37320, P = .497 (approx.)
```

>Exhibit 19-7 Bartlett's Test of Sphericity in the CalAudio Study

```
Statistics for WITHIN CELLS correlations

Log (Determinant) =                  -3.92663
Bartlett's test of sphericity =     102.74687 with 3 D.F.
Significance =                         .000

F(max) criterion =                  7354.80161 with (3,28) D.F.
```

>Exhibit 19-8 Multivariate Tests of Significance in the CalAudio Study

```
Multivariate Tests of Significance (S = 1, M = 1/2, N = 12)

Test Name      Value       Exact F    Hypoth. DF   Error DF   Sig. of F

Hotelling    51.33492    444.90268       3.00        26.00       .000
Pillai         .98089    444.90268       3.00        26.00       .000
Wilks          .01911    444.90268       3.00        26.00       .000
```

Note: F statistics are exact.

When MANOVA is applied properly, the dependent variables are correlated. If the dependent variables are unrelated, there would be no necessity for a multivariate test, and we could use separate F tests for failure, specifications, and speed, much like the ANOVAs in Chapter 18. Bartlett's test of sphericity helps us decide if we should continue analyzing MANOVA results or return to separate univariate tests. In Exhibit 19-7, we will look for a determinant value that is close to 0. This implies that one or more dependent variables are a linear function of another. The determinant has a chi-square transformation that simplifies testing for statistical significance. Since the observed significance is below that set for the model ($\alpha = .05$), we are able to reject the null hypothesis and conclude there are dependencies among the failure, specifications, and speed variables.

We now move to the test of equality of means that considers the three dependent variables for the two levels of manufacturing method. This test is analogous to a t-test or an F test for multivariate data. The sums-of-squares and cross-products matrices are used. Exhibit 19-8 shows three tests, including the Hotelling T^2. All the tests provided are compared to the F distribution for interpretation. Since the observed significance level is less than $\alpha = .05$ for the T^2 test, we reject the null hypothesis that

>**Exhibit 19-9** Univariate Tests of Significance in the CalAudio Study

```
Univariate F Tests with (1,28) D.F.

Variable   Hypoth. SS   Error SS   Hypoth. MS   Error MS         F   Sig. of F

FAILURE    3696.30000   852.66667   3696.30000   30.45238   121.37967      .000
SPECS       187.50000   126.80000    187.50000    4.52857    41.40379      .000
SPEED         1.67560      .11593      1.67560     .00414   404.68856      .000
```

Note: F statistics are exact.

said methods 1 and 2 provide equal results with respect to failure, specifications, and speed. Similar results are obtained from the Pillai trace and Wilks's statistic.

Finally, to detect where the differences lie, we can examine the results of univariate *F* tests in Exhibit 19-9. Since there are only two methods, the *F* is equivalent to t^2 for a two-sample *t*-test. The significance levels for these tests do not reflect that several comparisons are being made, and we should use them principally for diagnostic purposes. This is similar to problems that require the use of multiple comparison tests in univariate analysis of variance. Note, however, that there are statistically significant differences in all three dependent variables resulting from the new manufacturing method. Techniques for further analysis of MANOVA results were listed at the beginning of this section.

Structural Equation Modeling[9]

Since the late 1980s, researchers have relied increasingly on structural equation modeling to test hypotheses about the dimensionality of, and relationships among, latent and observed variables. **Structural equation modeling (SEM)** implies a structure for the covariances between observed variables, and accordingly it is sometimes called *covariance structure modeling*. More commonly, researchers refer to structural equation models as LISREL (linear structural relations) models—the name of the first and most widely cited SEM computer program.

SEM is a powerful alternative to other multivariate techniques, which are limited to representing only a single relationship between the dependent and independent variables. The major advantages of SEM are (1) that multiple and interrelated dependence relationships can be estimated simultaneously and (2) that it can represent unobserved concepts, or *latent variables,* in these relationships and account for measurement error in the estimation process. While the details of SEM are quite complex, well beyond the scope of this text, this section provides a broad conceptual introduction.

Method

Researchers using SEM must follow five basic steps:

1. *Model specification.* The first step in SEM is the *specification,* or formal statement, of the model's *parameters.* These parameters, constants that describe the relations between variables, are specified as either *fixed* or *free.* Fixed parameters have values set by the researcher, and are not estimated from the data. For example, if there is no hypothesized relationship between variables, the parameter would be fixed at zero. When there is a hypothesized,

Harris Interactive is one of the world's largest research firms. It is known for its sophisticated data analysis, as well as for its newsworthy Harris Poll. This ad stresses the importance of insight formation in solving strategic questions. **www.harrisinteractive.com**

but unknown, relation between the variables, the parameters are set free to be estimated from the data. Researchers must be careful to consider all the important predictive variables to avoid **specification error,** a bias that overestimates the importance of the variables included in the model.

2. *Estimation.* After the model has been specified, the researcher must obtain estimates of the free parameters from the observed data. This is often accomplished using an *iterative method,* such as *maximum likelihood estimation (MLE).*

3. *Evaluation of fit.* Following convergence, the researcher must evaluate the goodness-of-fit criteria. *Goodness-of-fit tests* are used to determine whether the model should or should not be rejected. If the model is not rejected, the researcher will continue the analysis and interpret the path coefficients in the model. Most, if not all, SEM computer software programs include several different goodness-of-fit measures, each of which can be categorized as one of three types of measures.

4. *Respecification of the model.* Model respecification usually follows the estimation of a model with indications of poor fit. Sometimes, the model is compared with competing or *nested* models to find the best fit among a set of models, and then the original model is respecified to produce a better fit. Respecifying the model requires that the researcher fix parameters that were formerly free or free parameters that were formerly fixed.

5. *Interpretation and communication.* SEM hypotheses and results are most commonly presented in the form of **path diagrams,** which are graphic illustrations of the measurement and structural models. The main features of path diagrams are ellipses, rectangles, and two types of arrows. The ellipses represent latent variables. Rectangles represent observed variables, which can be indicators of latent variables in the measurement model or of independent variables in the structural model. Straight arrows are pointed at one end and indicate the direction of prediction from independent to dependent variables or from indicators to latent variables. Curved arrows are pointed at both ends and indicate correlations between variables.

In a research report, the path diagrams should illustrate the model originally specified and estimated by the researcher; the portion of the model for which parameter estimates were significant; and a model that resulted from one or more modifications and reestimations of the original model. The researcher should also take care to include the method of estimation, the fit criteria selected, and the parameter estimates.

Example

A research consultant, hired by MindWriter, investigated the relationship between customer satisfaction and service quality, as well as the degree to which customer satisfaction and service quality predict customer purchase intention. The researcher used the *competing models strategy,* and proposed three possible relations among the variables. In model 1, satisfaction was proposed as an antecedent of service quality, and only service quality had a direct effect on purchase intention. In model 2, service quality was proposed as an antecedent of satisfaction, and only satisfaction had a direct effect on purchase intention. And in model 3, service quality and satisfaction were correlated, and both had a direct effect on purchase intention.

To collect the data, the researcher added three assumedly valid batteries of questions to the company's product and service warranty card. As soon as a large enough sample was obtained, the researcher specified the parameters of the proposed models and compared the implied structure with the covariance matrix of the data using maximum likelihood estimation as the iterative process.

The researcher finds that of the three proposed models, none of them have a satisfactory goodness of fit. However, of the three, model 2 seemed the most promising in that it yielded the lowest chi-square value and the highest value for the adjusted-goodness-of-fit index. After examining the second model's residual matrices and modification index, the researcher finds that the model could achieve a better fit if relation between service quality and purchase intention were not fixed. Accordingly, the researcher respecifies the model, freeing that parameter, and the implied matrix yields an acceptable goodness of fit. The implications of the results are that good service quality leads to customer satisfaction and that both variables have a direct effect on purchase intention (see Exhibit 19-10).

>**Exhibit 19-10** Measurement Models Relative to the Full Structural Equation Model

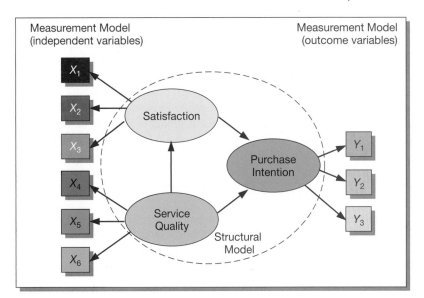

The example in Exhibit 19-10 illustrates the three measurement models, one for each latent variable, relative to the full structural model. The three latent variables are satisfaction, service quality, and purchase intention, and each latent variable has three indicators. The direction of the single-pointed arrows from service quality and satisfaction to purchase intention denotes that purchase intention is a dependent variable in its relation to both service quality and satisfaction. However, although satisfaction is independent in its relation to purchase intention, it is dependent in its relation to service quality. The ability to model all three relations simultaneously is one of the foremost advantages of using SEM over other multivariate techniques.

Conjoint Analysis

The most common applications for conjoint analysis are market research and product development. Consumers buying a MindWriter computer, for example, may evaluate a set of attributes to choose the product that best meets their needs. They may consider brand, speed, price, educational value, games, or capacity for work-related tasks. The attributes and their features require that the buyer make trade-offs in the final decision making.

Method

Conjoint analysis typically uses input from nonmetric independent variables. Normally, we would use cross-classification tables to handle such data, but even multiway tables become quickly overwhelmed by the complexity. If there were three prices, three brands, three speeds, two levels of educational values, two categories for games, and two categories for work assistance, the model would have 216 decision levels ($3 \times 3 \times 3 \times 2 \times 2 \times 2$). A choice structure this size

As this Booth Research Services ad suggests, the researcher's role is to make sense of numerous data displays and thus assist the research sponsor in making an appropriate decision. Great data exploration and analysis will distill mountains of data printouts into insightful and supportable conclusions.
www.boothresearch.com

poses enormous difficulties for respondents and analysts. Conjoint analysis solves this problem with various optimal scaling approaches, often with loglinear models, to provide researchers with reliable answers that could not be obtained otherwise.

The objective of conjoint analysis is to secure **utility scores** (sometimes called *part-worths*) that represent the importance of each aspect of a product or service in the subjects' overall preference ratings. Utility scores are computed from the subjects' rankings or ratings of a set of cards. Each card in the deck describes one possible configuration of combined product attributes.

The first step in a conjoint study is to select the attributes most pertinent to the purchase decision. This may require an exploratory study such as a focus group, or it could be done by an expert with thorough market knowledge. The attributes selected are the independent variables, called *factors*. The possible values for an attribute are called *factor levels*. In the MindWriter example, the speed factor may have levels of 1.5 gigahertz and 3 gigahertz. Speed, like price, approaches linear measurement characteristics since consumers typically choose higher speeds and lower prices. Other factors like brand are measured as discrete variables.

After selecting the factors and their levels, a computer program determines the number of product descriptions necessary to estimate the utilities. SPSS procedures build a file structure for all possible combinations, generate the subset required for testing, produce the card descriptions, and analyze results. The command structure within these procedures provides for holdout sampling, simulations, and other requirements frequently used in commercial applications.[10]

Example

Watersports enthusiasts know the dangers of ultraviolet (UV) light. It fades paint and clothing; yellows surfboards, skis, and sailboards; and destroys sails. More important, UV damages the eye's retina and cornea. Americans spend more than $1.3 billion on 189 million pairs of sunglasses, most of which fail to provide adequate UV protection. Manufacturers of sunglasses for specialty markets have improved their products to such a degree that all of the companies in our example advertised 100 percent UV protection. Many other features influence trends in this market. For this example, we chose four factors from information contained in a review of sun protection products.[11]

Brand	Bolle	Hobbies	Oakley	Ski Optiks
Style*	A	A	A	A
	B	B	B	B
	C	C	C	C
Flotation	Yes	Yes	Yes	Yes
	No	No	No	No
Price	$100	$100	$100	$100
	$72	$72	$72	$72
	$60	$60	$60	$60
	$40	$40	$40	$40

*A = multiple color choices for frames, lenses, and temples.
 B = multiple color choices for frames, lenses, and straps (no hard temples).
 C = limited colors for frames, lenses, and temples.

This is a 4 (brand) × 3 (style) × 2 (flotation) × 4 (price) design, or a 96-option full-concept study. The algorithm selected 16 cards to estimate the utilities for the full concept. Combinations of interest that were not selected can be estimated later from the utilities. In addition, four holdout cards were

>**Exhibit 19-11** Concept Cards for Conjoint Sunglasses Study

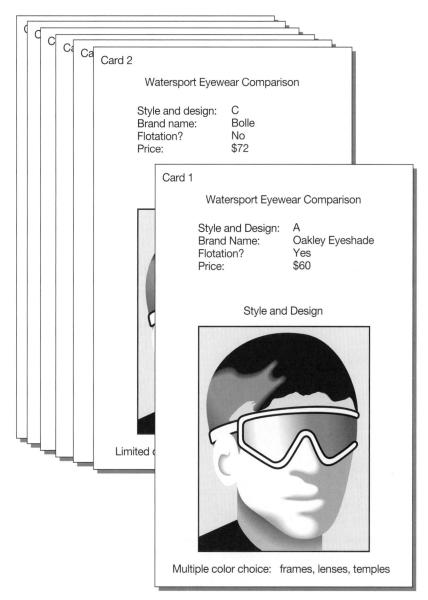

Card 2

Watersport Eyewear Comparison

Style and design: C
Brand name: Bolle
Flotation?   No
Price: $72

Card 1

Watersport Eyewear Comparison

Style and Design: A
Brand Name: Oakley Eyeshade
Flotation?   Yes
Price: $60

Style and Design

Multiple color choice: frames, lenses, temples

administered to subjects but evaluated separately. The cards shown in Exhibit 19-11 were administered to a small sample ($n = 10$). Subjects were asked to order their cards from most to least desirable. The data produced the results presented in Exhibits 19-12 and 19-13.

Exhibit 19-12 contains the results of the eighth participant's preferences. This individual was an avid windsurfer, and flotation was the most important attribute for her, followed by style and price and then brand. From her preferences, we can compute her maximum utility score:

$$\text{(Style B) } 3.46 + \text{(Oakley brand) } 1.31 + \text{(flotation) } 20.75$$
$$+ \text{(price @ \$40) } 5.90 + \text{(constant) } - 8.21 = 23.21$$

If brand and price remain unchanged, a design that uses a hard temple with limited color choices (style C) and no flotation would produce a considerably lower total utility score for this respondent. For example:

$$\text{(Style C) } - 2.04 + \text{(Oakley brand) } 1.31 + \text{(no float) } 10.38$$
$$+ \text{(price @ \$40) } 5.90 + \text{(constant) } - 8.21 = 7.34$$

>**Exhibit 19-12** Conjoint Results for Participant 8, Sunglasses Study

Subject name: 8

Importance	Utility (s.e.)	Factor	Level *
23.86	−1.4167(.3143) 3.4583(.3685) −2.0417(.3685)	STYLE	Style and design A B C
11.93	−1.4375(.4083) .3125(.4083) 1.3125(.4083) −.1875(.4083)	BRAND	Brand Name Bolle Hobbies Oakley Ski Optiks
45.01	10.3750(.4715) 20.7500(.9429) B = 10.3750(.4715)	FLOAT	Flotation? No Yes
19.20	1.4750(.2108) 2.9500(.4217) 4.4250(.6325) 5.9000(.8434) B = 1.4750(.2108)	PRICE	Price * $100 $72 $60 $40
	−8.2083(.9163)	CONSTANT	

Pearson's r = .994   Significance = .0000
Pearson's r = .990 for 4 holdouts   Significance = .0051

Kendall's tau = .967   Significance = .0000
Kendall's tau = 1.000 for 4 holdouts   Significance = .0208

*Subject reversed decision once.

We could also calculate other combinations that would reveal the range of this individual's preferences. Our prediction that respondents would prefer less-expensive prices did not hold for the eighth respondent, as revealed by the asterisk next to the price factor in Exhibit 19-12. She reversed herself once on price to get flotation. Other subjects also reversed once on price to trade off for other factors.

The results for the sample are presented in Exhibit 19-13. In contrast to individuals, the sample placed price first in importance, followed by flotation, style, and brand. Group utilities may be calculated just as we did for the individual. At the bottom of the printout we find Pearson's r and Kendall's tau. Each was discussed in Chapter 18. In this application, they measure the relationship between observed and estimated preferences. Because holdout samples (in conjoint, regression, discriminant, and other methods) are not used to construct the estimating equation, the coefficients for the holdouts are often a more realistic index of the model's fit.

Conjoint analysis is an effective tool used by researchers to match preferences to known characteristics of market segments and design or target a product accordingly. See your student Online Learning Center for a MindWriter example of conjoint analysis using Simalto+Plus.

60

The percent of workers on four continents who trust their organization's senior leaders.

>**Exhibit 19-13** Conjoint Results for Sunglasses Study Sample ($n = 10$)

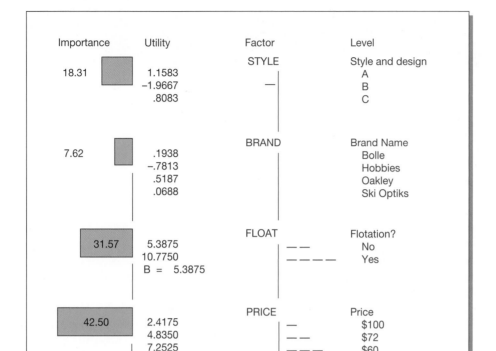

Importance	Utility	Factor	Level
18.31	1.1583	STYLE	Style and design
	−1.9667		A
	.8083		B
			C
7.62	.1938	BRAND	Brand Name
	−.7813		Bolle
	.5187		Hobbies
	.0688		Oakley
			Ski Optiks
31.57	5.3875	FLOAT	Flotation?
	10.7750		No
	B = 5.3875		Yes
42.50	2.4175	PRICE	Price
	4.8350		$100
	7.2525		$72
	9.6700		$60
	B = 2.4175		$40
	−3.4583	CONSTANT	

Pearson's r = .995   Significance = .0000
Pearson's r = .976 for 4 holdouts   Significance = .0120

Kendall's tau = .950   Significance = .0000
Kendall's tau = 1.000 for 4 holdouts   Significance = .0208

> Interdependency Techniques

Factor Analysis

Unlike the predictor-criterion relationship present in dependence techniques, the variables used for interdependence techniques, like factor analysis, are not classified as dependent or independent. Because these variables are considered interrelated, they are analyzed simultaneously in order to identify an underlying structure. **Factor analysis** is a general term for several specific computational techniques used to examine patterns of relationships amongst select variables. The objective of these techniques is to create a more manageable number variables (data reduction) from a larger set of variables based on the nature and character of these relationships. For example, one may have data on 100 employees with scores on six attitude scale items.

Method

Factor analysis begins with the task of reducing the number of variables in order to simplify subsequent analyses. The data reduction process is based on the relationships or intercorrelations among the variables within the correlation matrix. Although this can be done in a number of ways, the most

The Mail as a "Super" E-Business

From 2000 to 2030, the United Nations estimates that the world's urban population will grow at 1.8 percent, resulting in an urban population that will double in 38 years. Urbanized populations increase demand for postal services and attract competition from nonpostal operators. With the world's postal system growing at a rate of 4 percent, according to the Universal Postal Union, hybrid mail will account for more than 6 percent or approximately 35 billion of the world's 550 billion pieces of physical mail by the mid-2000s.

SuperLetter.com is an e-business success story in the hybrid-mail sector. According to founder Christopher Schultheiss, "SuperLetter Hybrid Mail is secure, encrypted mail from point of origin to delivery to recipient, transported electronically to a print point closest to the addressee. Hybrid mail begins as a unique, serial-numbered encrypted data record and ends as a sealed letter delivered to the recipient. It is secure, tamper-proof and CBR-free from end to end." This is one of the reasons it has been successful with rapid mail delivery to the British Armed Forces and U.S. Marine Corps in Iraq, Afghanistan, and other parts of the world. As the world's first global "hybrid mail" network, it enables users to create letters, documents, and photos on their personal computers and send them like e-mail over the Internet to remote printers near the recipients, where they are printed, folded, enveloped, and delivered.

Using a variety of multivariate statistical techniques, SuperLetter identified target markets as government/military organizations, professional and financial service firms, not-for-profit organizations, and cruise ship and yacht mail. SuperLetter also draws business from the $100 billion worldwide international courier market, like FedEx, UPS, and DHL, now experiencing strong growth rates. By bridging the gap between conventional door-to-door postal services, which take from 5 to 10 days for overseas delivery, and private express/courier services, which may take from two to three days, SuperLetter's basic international service delivers a letter from desk to door in two to three days for about one-tenth of private courier costs and under one-half of the courier costs for same-day service.

www.superletter.com

frequently used approach is **principal components analysis.** This method transforms a set of variables into either a smaller number of variables that represent those in the original set or a completely new set of composite variables or principal components that are not correlated with each other. These linear combinations of variables, called **factors,** account for the variance in the data as a whole. The first principal component, or first factor, is comprised of the best linear function of the original variables as to maximize the amount of the total variance that can be explained. The second principal component is defined as the best linear combination of variables for explaining the variance *not* accounted for by the first factor. In turn, there may be a third, fourth, and kth component, each being the best linear combination of variables not accounted for by the previous factors.

The process continues until all the variance is accounted for, but as a practical matter, it is usually stopped after a small number of factors have been extracted. It is important to note that principal components, or factors, will always be produced in a factor analysis. However, the quality and usefulness of the derived factors are dependent upon the types, number, and conceptual basis of variables selected for inclusion during the initial research design. The output of a principal components analysis might look like the hypothetical data shown in Exhibit 19-14.

>Exhibit 19-14 Principal Components Analysis from a Three-Variable Data Set

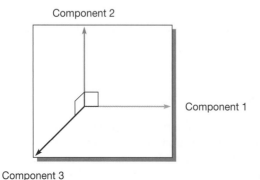

Extracted Components	% of Variance Accounted For	Cumulative Variance
Component no. 1	63%	63%
Component no. 2	29%	92%
Component no. 3	8%	100%

>**Exhibit 19-15** Factor Matrices

Variable	A Unrotated Factors			B Rotated Factors	
	I	II	h2	I	II
A	0.70	−.40	0.65	0.79	0.15
B	0.60	−.50	0.61	0.75	0.03
C	0.60	−.35	0.48	0.68	0.10
D	0.50	0.50	0.50	0.06	0.70
E	0.60	0.50	0.61	0.13	0.77
F	0.60	0.60	0.72	0.07	0.85
Eigenvalue	2.18	1.39			
Percent of variance	36.3	23.2			
Cumulative percent	36.3	59.5			

Numerical results from a factor study are shown in Exhibit 19-15. The values in this table are correlation coefficients between the factor and the variables (.70 is the r between variable A and factor I). These correlation coefficients are called **loadings.** The higher the loading, the greater the contribution of the variable in defining the particular factor. Two other elements in Exhibit 19-15 need explanation. **Eigenvalues** are the sum of the variances of the factor values (for factor I the eigenvalue is $.70^2 + .60^2 + .50^2 + .60^2 + .60^2$). When divided by the number of variables, an eigenvalue yields an estimate of the amount of total variance explained by the factor. For example, factor I accounts for 36 percent of the total variance. If a factor has a low eigenvalue, then it adds little to the explanation of variances in the variables and may be disregarded. The column headed "h^2" gives the **communalities,** or estimates of the variance in each variable that is explained by the two factors. With variable A, for example, the communality is $.70^2 + (−.40)^2 = .65$, indicating that 65 percent of the variance in variable A is statistically explained in terms of factors I and II.

As displayed in column A, the unrotated factor loadings are not informative because there are no definitive "drivers" for either of the two factors within the current structure. What one would like to find is some pattern in which factor I would be heavily loaded (have a high r) on some variables and factor II on others. Such a condition would suggest rather "pure" constructs underlying each factor. You attempt to secure this less ambiguous condition between factors and variables by **rotation.** This procedure allows choices between orthogonal and oblique methods. (When the factors are intentionally rotated to result in no correlation between the factors in the final solution, this procedure is called *orthogonal*; when the factors are not manipulated to be zero correlation but may reveal the degree of correlation that exists naturally, it is called *oblique*.) We illustrate an orthogonal solution here.

To understand the rotation concept, consider that you are dealing only with simple two-dimensional rather than multidimensional space. The variables in Exhibit 19-15 can be plotted in two-dimensional space as shown in Exhibit 19-16. Two axes divide this space, and the points are positioned relative to these axes. The location of these axes is arbitrary, and they represent only one of an infinite number of reference frames that could be used to reproduce the matrix. As long as you do not change the intersection points and keep the axes at right angles, when an orthogonal method is used, you can rotate the axes to find a better solution or position for the reference axes. "Better" in this case means a matrix that makes the factors as pure as possible (each variable loads onto as few factors as possible to simplify the structure). After performing the rotation as shown in Exhibit 19-16, the factor solution is improved substantially. Returning to Exhibit 19-15, column B, Rotated Factors, suggests that the measurements from six scales may be summarized by two underlying factors. Variables A, B, and C load primarily on factor I, whereas variables D, E, and F load heavily on factor II.

In this hypothetical example, the rotation resulted in the variables loading unambiguously onto only one of the two derived factors. In practice, however, the results displayed in the factor matrix are not always as clear, prompting the researcher to consider changes to the factor model such as using another rotation method, selecting a solution with either a greater or lesser number of factors, or deleting

>Exhibit 19-16 Orthogonal Factor Rotations

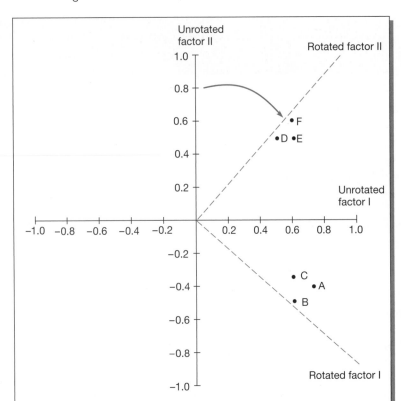

variables that lack significant loadings on any of the factors. Once this process is complete, the ultimate interpretation of factor loadings is largely subjective. There is no way to calculate the meanings of factors; they are what one sees in them, taking into consideration, as noted previously, the nature and conceptual basis of the variables included in the analysis. For this reason, factor analysis is largely used for exploration, allowing one to detect patterns in latent variables, discover new concepts, and reduce data.

Example

Student grades make an interesting example to illustrate the use of factor analysis. The chairperson of Metro U's MBA program has been reviewing grades for the first-year students and is struck by the patterns in the data. His hunch is that distinct types of people are involved in the study of business, and he decides to gather evidence for this idea.

Suppose the chairperson selects a sample of 21 grade reports from 10 of the program's courses for first-year students whose GPAs fall within the middle range. His analysis involves the following three steps:

1. Calculate a correlation matrix between the grades for all pairs of the 10 courses for which data exist.

2. Factor-analyze the matrix by the principal components method.

3. Select a rotation procedure to clarify the factors and aid in interpretation.

Exhibit 19-17 shows a portion of the correlation matrix. These data represent correlation coefficients between the 10 courses. For example, grades secured in V1 (Financial Accounting) correlated rather well (0.56) with grades received in course V2 (Managerial Accounting). The next best correlation with V1 grades is an inverse correlation ($-.44$) with grades in V7 (Production).

After the calculation of correlation matrix, the extraction of components is shown in Exhibit 19-18. Although the program will produce a table with as many as 10 factors, you choose, in this case, to stop

>**Exhibit 19-17** Correlation Coefficients, Metro U MBA Study

Variable	Course	V1	V2	V3	V10
V1	Financial Accounting	1.00	0.56	0.17	−.01
V2	Managerial Accounting	0.56	1.00	−.22	0.06
V3	Finance	0.17	−.22	1.00	0.42
V4	Marketing	−.14	0.05	−.48	−.10
V5	Human Behavior	−.19	−.26	−.05	−.23
V6	Organization Design	−.21	−.00	−.56	−.05
V7	Production	−.44	−.11	−.04	−.08
V8	Probability	0.30	0.06	0.07	−.10
V9	Statistical Inference	−.05	0.06	−.32	0.06
V10	Quantitative Analysis	−.01	0.06	0.42	1.00

>**Exhibit 19-18** Factor Matrix Using Principal Factor with Iterations, Metro U MBA Study

Variable	Course	Factor 1	Factor 2	Factor 3	Communality
V1	Financial Accounting	0.41	0.71	0.23	0.73
V2	Managerial Accounting	0.01	0.53	−.16	0.31
V3	Finance	0.89	−.17	0.37	0.95
V4	Marketing	−.60	0.21	0.30	0.49
V5	Human Behavior	0.02	−.24	−.22	0.11
V6	Organization Design	−.43	−.09	−.36	0.32
V7	Production	−.11	−.58	−.03	0.35
V8	Probability	0.25	0.25	−.31	0.22
V9	Statistical Inference	−.43	0.43	0.50	0.62
V10	Quantitative Analysis	0.25	0.04	0.35	0.19
Eigenvalue		1.83	1.52	0.95	
Percent of variance		18.30	15.20	9.50	
Cumulative percent		18.30	33.50	43.00	

the process after three factors have been extracted. Several features in this table are worth noting. Recall that the communalities indicate the amount of variance in each variable that is being "explained" by the factors. Thus, these three factors account for about 73 percent of the variance in grades in the financial accounting course. It should be apparent from these communality figures that some of the courses are not explained well by the factors selected.

The eigenvalue row in Exhibit 19-18 is a measure of the explanatory power of each factor. For example, the eigenvalue for factor 1 is 1.83 and is computed as follows:

$$1.83 = (.41)^2 + (.01)^2 + \cdots + (.25)^2$$

The percent of variance accounted for by each factor in Exhibit 19-18 is computed by dividing eigenvalues by the number of variables. When this is done, one sees that the three factors account for about 43 percent of the total variance in course grades.

>Exhibit 19-19 Varimax Rotated Factor Matrix, Metro U MBA Study

Variable	Course	Factor 1	Factor 2	Factor 3
V1	Financial Accounting	0.84	0.16	−.06
V2	Managerial Accounting	0.53	−.10	0.14
V3	Finance	−.01	0.90	−.37
V4	Marketing	−.11	−.24	0.65
V5	Human Behavior	−.13	−.14	−.27
V6	Organization Design	−.08	−.56	−.02
V7	Production	−.54	−.11	−.22
V8	Probability	0.41	−.02	−.24
V9	Statistical Inference	0.07	0.02	0.79
V10	Quantitative Analysis	−.02	0.42	0.09

In an effort to further clarify the factors, a varimax (orthogonal) rotation is used to secure the matrix shown in Exhibit 19-19. The largest factor loadings for the three factors are as follows:

Factor 1		Factor 2		Factor 3	
Financial Accounting	0.84	Finance	0.90	Marketing	0.65
Managerial Accounting	0.53	Organization Design	−.56	Statistical Inference	0.79
Production	−.54				

Interpretation

The varimax rotation appears to clarify the relationship among course grades, but as pointed out earlier, the interpretation of the results is largely subjective. We might interpret the above results as showing three kinds of students, classified as the accounting, finance, and marketing types.

However, a number of problems may affect the interpretation of these results. Among the major concerns are:

1. The sample is small and any attempt at replication, such as using a split sample, might produce a different pattern of factor loadings. Factor stability is affected by both the sample size and number of cases per variable.

2. Altering your decision to extract a different number of factors (rather than three) can result in variables loading to different degrees or onto different factors.

3. Even if the findings are replicated, the variance in the data may be due to the varying influence of professors or the way they teach the courses, rather than to the subject content or types of students.

4. The labels or classifications may not truly reflect the latent construct that underlies any factors we extract.

Factor analysis is a powerful technique that can be used to identify underlying dimensions for a set of variables. However, as this simple example illustrates, issues regarding research design, derived factors, and interpretation must be addressed with great care.

Cluster Analysis

Unlike techniques for analyzing the relationships between variables, **cluster analysis** is a set of interdependence techniques for grouping similar objects or people. Originally developed as a classification device for taxonomy, its use has spread because of classification work in medicine, biology, and other sciences. Its visibility in those fields and the availability of high-speed computers to carry out the extensive calculations have sped its adoption in business. Understanding one's market very often involves segmenting customers into homogeneous groups that have common buying characteristics or behave in similar ways. Such segments frequently share similar psychological, demographic, lifestyle, age, financial, or other characteristics.

Cluster analysis offers a means for segmentation research and other business problems, such as understanding buyer behaviors, where the goal is to identify similar groups. It shares some similarities with factor analysis, especially when factor analysis is applied to people (Q-analysis) instead of to variables. However, cluster analysis treats correlations as similarity (distance) measures whereas Q-analysis takes into account control variables (as in a general linear model). It differs from discriminant analysis in that discriminant analysis begins with a well-defined group composed of two or more distinct sets of characteristics in search of a set of variables to separate them. In contrast, cluster analysis starts with an undifferentiated group of people, events, or objects and attempts to reorganize them into homogeneous subgroups.

Method

Five steps are basic to the application of most cluster studies:

1. Selection of the sample to be clustered (e.g., buyers, medical patients, inventory, products, employees).
2. Definition of the variables on which to measure the objects, events, or people (e.g., market segment characteristics, product competition definitions, financial status, political affiliation, symptom classes, productivity attributes).
3. Computation of similarities among the entities through correlation, Euclidean distances, and other techniques.
4. Selection of mutually exclusive clusters (maximization of within-cluster similarity and between-cluster differences) or hierarchically arranged clusters.
5. Cluster comparison and validation.

Different clustering methods can and do produce different solutions. It is important to have enough information about the data, as well as the various clustering algorithms and stopping rules, to know when the derived groups are real and not merely imposed on the data by the method. In addition, issues such as variable scaling and intercorrelations can influence the final cluster solution.

The example in Exhibit 19-20 shows a cluster analysis of individuals based on three dimensions: age, income, and family size. Cluster analysis could be used to segment the car-buying population into distinct markets. For example, cluster A might be targeted as potential minivan or sport-utility vehicle

>**Exhibit 19-20** Cluster Analysis on Three Dimensions

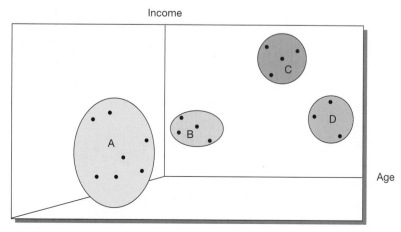

Income

Age

Family size

buyers. The market segment represented by cluster B might be a sports and performance car segment. Clusters C and D could both be targeted as buyers of sedans, but the C cluster might be the luxury buyer. This form of clustering or a hierarchical arrangement of the clusters may be used to plan marketing campaigns and develop strategies.

Example

The entertainment industry is a complex business. A huge number of films are released each year internationally with some notable financial surprises. Paris offers one of the world's best selections of films and sources of critical review for predicting an international audience's acceptance. Residents of New York and Los Angeles are often surprised to discover their cities are eclipsed by Paris's average of 300 films per week shown in over 100 locations.

We selected ratings from 12 cinema reviewers using sources ranging from *Le Monde* to international publications sold in Paris. The reviews reputedly influence box-office receipts, and the entertainment business takes them seriously.

The object of this cluster example was to classify 19 films into homogeneous subgroups. The production companies were American, Canadian, French, Italian, Spanish, Finnish, Egyptian, and Japanese. Three genres of film were represented: comedy, dramatic comedy, and psychological drama. Exhibit 19-21 shows the data by film name, country of origin, and genre. The table also lists the clusters for each film using the **average linkage method.** This approach considers distances between all possible pairs rather than just the nearest or farthest neighbor.

The sequential development of the clusters and their relative distances are displayed in a diagram called a *dendogram*. Exhibit 19-22 shows that the clustering agglomerative procedure begins with 19 films and continues until all the films are again an undifferentiated group. The solid vertical line shows the point

>**Exhibit 19-21** Film, Country, Genre, and Cluster Membership

Film	Country	Genre	Case	Number of Clusters			
				5	4	3	2
Cyrano de Bergerac	France	DramaCom	1	1	1	1	1
Il y a des Jours	France	DramaCom	4	1	1	1	1
Nikita	France	DramaCom	5	1	1	1	1
Les Noces de Papier	Canada	DramaCom	6	1	1	1	1
Leningrad Cowboys . . .	Finland	Comedy	19	2	2	2	2
Storia de Ragazzi . . .	Italy	Comedy	13	2	2	2	2
Conte de Printemps	France	Comedy	2	2	2	2	2
Tatie Danielle	France	Comedy	3	2	2	2	2
Crimes and Misdem . . .	USA	DramaCom	7	3	3	3	2
Driving Miss Daisy	USA	DramaCom	9	3	3	3	2
La Voce della Luna	Italy	DramaCom	12	3	3	3	2
Che Hora E	Italy	DramaCom	14	3	3	3	2
Attache-Moi	Spain	DramaCom	15	3	3	3	2
White Hunter Black . . .	USA	PsyDrama	10	4	4	3	2
Music Box	USA	PsyDrama	8	4	4	3	2
Dead Poets Society	USA	PsyDrama	11	4	4	3	2
La Fille aux All . . .	Finland	PsyDrama	18	4	4	3	2
Alexandrie, Encore . . .	Egypt	DramaCom	16	5	3	3	2
Dreams	Japan	DramaCom	17	5	3	3	2

>**Exhibit 19-22** Dendogram of Film Study Using Average Linkage Method

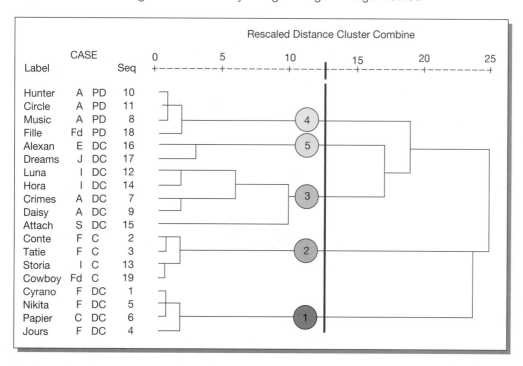

at which the clustering solution best represents the data. This determination was guided by coefficients provided by the SPSS program for each stage of the procedure. Five clusters explain this data set.

The first cluster shown in Exhibit 19-22 has three French-language films and one Canadian film, all of which are dramatic comedies. Cluster 2 consists of comedy films. Two French and two other European films joined at the first stage, and then these two groups came together at the second stage. Cluster 3, composed of dramatic comedies, is otherwise diverse. It is made up of two American films with two Italian films adding to the group at the fourth stage. Late in the clustering process, cluster 3 is completed when a Spanish film is appended. In cluster 4, we find three American psychological dramas combined with a Finnish film at the second stage. In cluster 5, two very different dramatic comedies are joined in the third stage.

Cluster analysis classified these productions based on reviewers' ratings. The similarities and distances are influenced by film genre and culture (as defined by the translated language). Comparison of the derived clusters reveals their particular characteristics, allowing the researcher to assign a descriptive label to each cluster. More importantly however, this examination assists in determining how the final cluster solution compares with those suggested by either prior research or by practical experience.

Because the optimal number of clusters formed is often at the discretion of the researcher, assessing the validity of the cluster solution is important to ensure that the process and methods are not inadvertently misapplied. There are several approaches that assist in validating the clusters, including utilizing a separate sample, splitting the existing sample into two groups, or selecting variables not included in the original analysis but known from prior research to vary across the clusters. For each of these methods, the results of cluster analysis are compared with the original findings.

Multidimensional Scaling

Multidimensional scaling (MDS) creates a special description of a respondent's perception about a product, service, or other object of interest on a *perceptual map*. This often helps the researcher to understand difficult-to-measure constructs such as product quality or desirability. In contrast to variables that can be measured directly, many constructs are perceived and cognitively mapped in different ways by individuals. With MDS, items that are perceived to be similar will fall close together on the perceptual map, and items that are perceived to be dissimilar will be farther apart.

Method

We may think of three types of attribute space, each representing a multidimensional map. First, there is *objective space,* in which an object can be positioned in terms of its measurable attributes: its flavor, weight, and nutritional value. Second, there is *subjective space,* where perceptions of the object's flavor, weight, and nutritional value may be positioned. Objective and subjective attribute assessments may coincide, but often they do not. A comparison of the two allows us to judge how accurately an object is being perceived. Individuals may hold different perceptions of an object simultaneously, and these may be averaged to present a summary measure of perceptions. In addition, a person's perceptions may vary over time and in different circumstances; such measurements are valuable to gauge the impact of various perception-affecting actions, such as advertising programs.

With a third map we can describe respondents' preferences using the object's attributes. This represents their ideal; all objects close to this ideal point are interpreted as preferred by respondents to those that are more distant. Ideal points from many people can be positioned in this preference space to reveal the pattern and size of preference clusters. These can be compared to the subjective space to assess how well the preferences correspond to perception clusters. In this way, cluster analysis and MDS can be combined to map market segments and then examine products designed for those segments.

Example

We illustrate multidimensional scaling with a study of 16 restaurants in a resort area.[12] The restaurants chosen represent medium-price family restaurants to high-price gourmet restaurants. We created a metric algorithm measuring the similarities among the 16 restaurants by asking patrons questions on a 5-point metric scale about different dimensions of service quality and price. The matrix of similarities is shown in Exhibit 19-23. Higher numbers reflect the items that are more dissimilar.

We might also ask participants to judge the similarities between all possible pairs of restaurants; then we produce a matrix of similarities using (nonmetric) ordinal data. The matrix would contain ranks with 1 representing the most similar pair and *n* indicating the most dissimilar pair.

A computer program is used to analyze the data matrix and generate a perceptual map.[13] The objective is to find a multidimensional spatial pattern that best reproduces the original order of the data. For example, the most similar pair (restaurants 3, 6) must be located in this multidimensional space closer together than any other pair. The least similar pair (restaurants 14, 15) must be the farthest apart. The computer program presents these relationships as a geometric configuration so that all distances between pairs of points closely correspond to the original matrix.

Determining how many dimensions to use is complex. The more dimensions of space we use, the more likely the results will closely match the input data. Any set of *n* points can be satisfied by a

>Exhibit 19-23 Similarities Matrix of 16 Restaurants

	1	2	3	4	5	6	7	8	9	10	11	12	13	14	15	16
1	0															
2	3.9	0														
3	4.7	6.7	0													
4	4.4	2.8	4.7	0												
5	14.0	12.4	18.5	15.2	0											
6	4.9	6.9	0.2	4.9	18.7	0										
7	0.8	3.7	4.1	3.7	14.5	4.3	0									
8	6.0	2.1	8.5	4.0	11.8	8.7	5.8	0								
9	4.3	6.9	1.1	5.3	18.3	1.2	3.8	8.9	0							
10	8.2	4.9	8.5	4.1	15.3	8.6	7.6	3.9	9.3	0						
11	8.6	8.7	4.7	5.9	21.1	4.5	7.8	9.7	5.7	7.7	0					
12	2.2	3.7	6.9	5.5	11.8	7.1	2.8	5.5	6.5	8.5	10.5	0				
13	8.4	9.8	3.7	7.2	22.0	3.5	7.8	11.2	4.5	10.0	2.9	10.6	0			
14	12.8	13.4	8.2	10.6	25.8	8.1	12.1	14.4	9.1	12.0	4.7	14.9	4.6	0		
15	19.1	18.2	23.8	21.0	6.2	24.0	19.7	17.8	23.4	21.5	26.9	16.9	27.4	31.5	0	
16	2.6	5.2	2.1	4.0	16.5	2.3	2.0	7.2	1.9	8.0	6.3	4.8	5.8	10.3	21.7	0

>**Exhibit 19-24** Positioning of Selected Restaurants

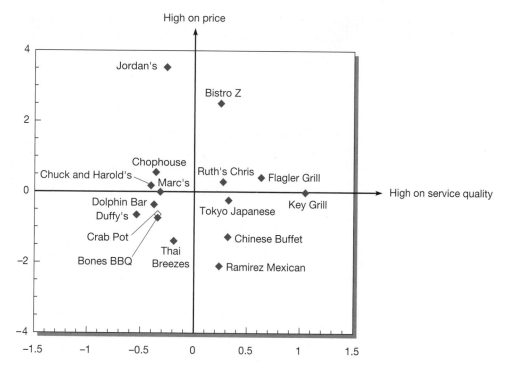

configuration of $n - 1$ dimensions. Our aim, however, is to secure a structure that provides a good fit for the data and has the fewest dimensions. MDS is best understood using two or at most three dimensions.

Most software programs include the calculation of a **stress index** (S-stress or Kruskal's stress) that ranges from the worst fit (1) to the perfect fit (0). This study, for example, had a stress of .001. Another index, R^2, is interpreted as the proportion of variance of transformed data accounted for by distances in the model. A result close to 1.0 is desirable.

In the restaurants example, we conclude that two dimensions represent an acceptable geometric configuration, as shown in Exhibit 19-24. The distance between Crab Pot and Bones BBQ (3, 6) is the shortest, while that between Ramirez Mexican and Jordan's (14, 15) is the longest. As with factor analysis, there is no statistical solution to the definition of the dimensions represented by the X and Y axes. The labeling is judgmental and depends on the insight of the researcher, analysis of information collected from respondents, or another basis. Respondents sometimes are asked to state the criteria they used for judging the similarities, or they are asked to judge a specific set of criteria.

Consistent with raw data, Jordan's and Bistro Z have high price but service quality close to the sample mean. In contrast, Flagler and Key Grills generated a price close to the sample's average while providing higher service quality. We could hypothesize that the latter two restaurants may be run more efficiently—are smaller and less complex—but that would need to be confirmed with another study. The clustering of companies in attribute space shows that they are perceived to be similar along the dimensions measured.

MDS is most often used to assess perceived similarities and differences among objects. Using MDS allows the researcher to understand constructs that are not directly measurable. The process provides a spatial map that shows similarities in terms of relative distances. It is best understood when limited to two or three dimensions that can be graphically displayed.

Exhibit 19-25 concludes our coverage of multivariate analysis with sample articles representing each technique described.

>Exhibit 19-25 Research Articles that Illustrate Each Multivariate Technique

Multivariate Method	Journal Article References
Multiple regression	Baker, T., Cronin, J. & Hopkins, C. (2009). The impact of involvement on key service relationships. *Journal of Services Marketing, 23*(2), 115–124.
	Lambrecht, K., Kaefer, F. & Ramenofsky, S. (2009). Sportscape factors influencing spectator attendance and satisfaction at a professional golf association tournament. *Sport Marketing Quarterly, 18*(3), 165–172.
Discriminant analysis	Li, P. (2010). Effects of individual differences on choice strategy in goal-directed online shopping. *The Journal of American Academy of Business, 15*(2), 186–192.
	Kuruvilla, S., Joshi, N. & Shah, N. (2009). Do men and women really shop differently? An exploration of gender differences in mall shopping in India. *International Journal of Consumer Studies, 33*(6), 715–723.
MANOVA	Meyer-Waarden, L. & Benavent, C. (2009). Grocery retail loyalty program effects: Self-selection or purchase behavior change? *Journal of the Academy of Marketing Sciences, 37*(3), 345–358.
	Smith, S. & Costello, C. (2009). Culinary tourism: Satisfaction with a culinary event utilizing importance-performance grid analysis. *Journal of Vacation Marketing, 15*(2), 99–110.
SEM	Kilic, C. & Dursun, T. (2010). The effect of organizational culture on customer orientation. *Journal of American Academy of Business, 15*(2), 1–7.
	Botonaki, A., Natos, D. & Konstadinos, M. (2009). Exploring convenience food consumption through a structural equation model. *Journal of Food Products Marketing, 15*(1), 64–79.
Conjoint analysis	Rokka, J. & Uusitalo, L. (2009). Preference for green packaging in consumer product choices—Do consumers care? *International Journal of Consumer Studies, 32*(5), 516–525.
	Han, H. (2010). The investigation of country-of-origin effect-using Taiwanese consumers' perceptions of luxury handbags as example. *Journal of American Academy of Business, 15*(2), 66–72.
Factor analysis	Krystallis, A. & Chryssochoidis, G. (2009). Does the country of origin (COO) of food products influence consumer evaluations? An empirical examination of ham and cheese. *Journal of Food Products Marketing, 15*(3), 283–303.
	Lu, C. & Yang, C. (2010). Logistics service capabilities and firm performance of international distribution center operators. *The Service Industries Journal, 30*(2), 281–298.
Cluster analysis	Thomas, H. & Li, X. (2009). Mapping globally branded business schools: A strategic positioning analysis. *Management Decision, 47*(9), 1420–1440.
	Boo, S. & Jones, D. (2009). Using a validation process to develop market segmentation based on travel motivation for major metropolitan areas. *Journal of Travel & Tourism Marketing, 26*(1), 60–79.
Multidimensional scaling (MDS)	Bao, J. & Sweeney, J. (2009). Comparing factor analytical and circumplex models of brand personality in brand positioning. *Psychology & Marketing, 26*(10), 927–949.
	Jin, Y. & Kelsay, C. (2008). Typology and dimensionality of litigation public relations strategies: The Hewlett-Packard board pretexting scandal case. *Public Relations Review, 34*(1), 66–69.

>summary

1 Multivariate techniques are classified into two categories: dependency and interdependency. When a problem reveals the presence of criterion and predictor variables, we have an assumption of dependence. If the variables are interrelated without designating some as dependent and others independent, then interdependence of the variables is assumed. The choice of techniques is guided by the number of dependent and independent variables involved and whether they are measured on metric or nonmetric scales.

2 Multiple regression is an extension of bivariate linear regression. When a researcher is interested in explaining or

predicting a metric dependent variable from a set of metric independent variables (although dummy variables may also be used), multiple regression is often selected. Regression results provide information on the statistical significance of the independent variables, the strength of association between one or more of the predictors and the criterion, and a predictive equation for future use.

3 Discriminant analysis is used to classify people or objects into groups based on several predictor variables. The groups are defined by a categorical variable with two or more values, whereas the predictors are metric. The

effectiveness of the discriminant equation is based not only on its statistical significance but also on its success in correctly classifying cases to groups.

4 Multivariate analysis of variance, or MANOVA, is one of the more adaptive techniques for multivariate data. MANOVA assesses the relationship between two or more metric dependent variables and classificatory variables or factors. MANOVA is most commonly used to test differences among samples of people or objects. In contrast to ANOVA, MANOVA handles multiple dependent variables, thereby simultaneously testing all the variables and their interrelationships.

5 Researchers have relied increasingly on structural equation modeling (SEM) to test hypotheses about the dimensionality of, and relationships among, latent and observed variables. Researchers refer to structural equation models as LISREL (linear structural relations) models. The major advantages of SEM are (1) that multiple and interrelated dependence relationships can be estimated simultaneously and (2) that it can represent unobserved concepts, or latent variables, in these relationships and account for measurement error in the estimation process. Researchers using SEM must follow five basic steps: (1) model specification, (2) estimation, (3) evaluation of fit, (4) respecification of the model, and (5) interpretation and communication.

6 Conjoint analysis is a technique that typically handles nonmetric independent variables. Conjoint analysis allows the researcher to determine the importance of product or service attributes and the levels or features that are most desirable. Respondents provide preference data by ranking or rating cards that describe products. These data become utility weights of product characteristics by means of optimal scaling and loglinear algorithms.

7 Principal components analysis extracts uncorrelated factors that account for the largest portion of variance from an initial set of variables. Factor analysis also attempts to reduce the number of variables and discover the underlying constructs that explain the variance. A correlation matrix is used to derive a factor matrix from which the best linear combination of variables may be extracted. In many applications, the factor matrix will be rotated to simplify the factor structure.

8 Unlike techniques for analyzing the relationships between variables, cluster analysis is a set of techniques for grouping similar objects or people. The cluster procedure starts with an undifferentiated group of people, events, or objects and attempts to reorganize them into homogeneous subgroups using a set of variables as the basis for their similarity.

9 Multidimensional scaling (MDS) is often used in conjunction with cluster analysis or conjoint analysis. It allows a respondent's perception about a product, service, or other object of attitude to be described in a spatial manner. MDS helps the business researcher to understand difficult-to-measure constructs such as product quality or desirability, which are perceived and cognitively mapped in different ways by different individuals. Items judged to be similar will fall close together in multidimensional space and are revealed numerically and geometrically by spatial maps.

>**key**terms

>discussionquestions

Terms in Review

1 Distinguish among multidimensional scaling, cluster analysis, and factor analysis.

2 Describe the differences between dependency techniques and interdependency techniques. When would you choose a dependency technique?

Making Research Decisions

3 How could discriminant analysis be used to provide insight into MANOVA results where the MANOVA has one independent variable (a factor with two levels)?

4 Describe how you would create a conjoint analysis study of off-road vehicles. Restrict your brands to three, and suggest possible factors and levels. The full-concept description should not exceed 256 decision options.

5 What type of multivariate method do you recommend in each of the following cases and why?

  a You want to develop an estimating equation that will be used to predict which applicants will come to your university as students.

  b You would like to predict family income using such variables as education and stage in family life cycle.

  c You wish to estimate standard labor costs for manufacturing a new dress design.

  d You have been studying a group of successful salespeople. You have given them a number of psychological tests. You want to bring meaning out of these test results.

6 Sales of a product are influenced by the salesperson's level of education and gender, as well as consumer income, ethnicity, and wealth.

  a Formulate this statement as a multiple regression model (form only, without parameter estimation).

  b Specify dummy variables.

  c If the effects of consumer income and wealth are not additive alone, and an interaction is expected, specify a new variable to test for the interaction.

7 What multivariate technique would you use to analyze each of the following problems? Explain your choice.

  a Employee job satisfaction (high, normal, low) and employee success (0–2 promotions, 3–5 promotions, 5+ promotions) are to be studied in three different departments of a company.

  b Consumers making a brand choice decision among three brands of coffee are influenced by their own income levels and the extent of advertising of the brands.

  c Consumer choice of color in fabrics is largely dependent on ethnicity, income levels, and the temperature of the geographic area. There is detailed areawide demographic data on income levels, ethnicity, and population, as well as the weather bureau's historical data on temperature. How would you identify geographic areas for selling dark-colored fabric? You have sample data for 200 randomly selected consumers: their fabric color choice, income, ethnicity, and the average temperature of the area where they live.

From Concept to Practice

8 An analyst sought to predict the annual sales for a home-furnishing manufacturer using the following predictor variables:

X_1 = marriages during the year

X_2 = housing starts during the year

X_3 = annual disposable personal income

X_4 = time trend (first year = 1, second year = 2, and so forth)

Using data for 24 years, the analyst calculated the following estimating equation:

$$Y = 49.85 - .068X_1 + .036X_2 + 1.22X_3 - 19.54X_4$$

The analyst also calculated an $R^2 = .92$ and a standard error of estimate of 11.9. Interpret the above equation and statistics.

9 You are working with a consulting group that has a new project for the Palm Grove School System. The school system of this large county has individuals with purchasing, service, and maintenance responsibilities. They were asked to evaluate the vendor/distribution channels of products that the county purchases. The evaluations were on a 10-point metric scale for the following variables:

Delivery speed—amount of time for delivery once the order has been confirmed.

Price level—level of price charged by the product suppliers.

Price flexibility—perceived willingness to negotiate on price.

Manufacturer's image—manufacturer or supplier's image.

Overall service—level of service necessary to preserve a satisfactory relationship between buyer and supplier.

Sales force—overall image of the manufacturer's sales representatives.

Product quality—perceived quality of a particular product.

The data are found on the text website.

Your task is to complete an exploratory factor analysis on the survey data. The purpose for the consulting group is twofold: (a) to identify the underlying dimensions of these data and (b) to create a new set of variables for inclusion into subsequent assessments of the vendor/distribution channels. Methodology issues to consider in your analysis are:

a Desirability of principal components versus principal axis factoring.

b Decisions on criteria for number of factors to extract.

c Rotation of the factors.

d Factor loading significance.

e Interpretation of the rotated matrix.

Prepare a report summarizing your findings and interpreting your results.

10 A researcher was given the assignment of predicting which of three actions would be taken by the 280 employees in the Desota plant that was going to be sold to its employees. The alternatives were to:

a Take severance pay and leave the company.

b Stay with the new company and give up severance pay.

c Take a transfer to the plant in Chicago.

The researcher gathered data on employee opinions, inspected personnel files and the like, and then did a discriminant analysis. Later, when the results were in, she found the results listed here. How successful was the researcher's analysis?

	Predicted Decision		
Actual Decision	A	B	C
A	80	5	12
B	14	60	14
C	10	15	70

From the Headlines

11 Nokia is the world's leader in cell phones. At the Consumer Electronics Show, Nokia president and CEO, Olli-Pekka Kallasvuo, discussed the company's strategy for reaching the world's developing markets. He wants Nokia to "do good business and do good at the same time." The company's program, "Calling All Innovators," aspires to change people's lives through mobile phones. He described a contest called the "Nokia Growth Economy Venture Challenge" that provides $1 million in funding to a company that create products that improve people's lives. He hopes the venture will promote upward mobility to cell phone users in markets where the average income is less than $5 a day. This year's theme is "Connecting Apps That Make a Difference." What multivariate technique or combination of techniques would you use to investigate mobile applications that, when connected, improve quality of life?

>cases*

Mastering Teacher Leadership	Proofpoint: Capitalizing on a Reporter's Love of Statistics
NCRCC: Teeing Up and New Strategic Direction	

* You will find a description of each case in the Case Abstracts section of the textbook. Check the Case Index to determine whether a case provides data, the research instrument, video, or other supplementary material. Written cases are downloadable from the text website (www.mhhe.com/cooper11e). All video material and video cases are available from the Online Learning Center.

>chapter 20

Presenting Insights and Findings: Written Reports

>learningobjectives

After reading this chapter, you should understand . . .

1 That a quality presentation of research findings can have an inordinate effect on a reader's or a listener's perceptions of a study's quality.

2 The contents, types, lengths, and technical specifications of research reports.

3 That the writer of a research report should be guided by questions of purpose, readership, circumstances/limitations, and use.

4 That while some statistical data may be incorporated in the text, most statistics should be placed in tables, charts, or graphs.

> Accurate information, sound logic, and the facts are necessary, of course, but truly effective leaders in any field—including technical ones—know how to tell "the story" of their particular research endeavor.
>
> Robert McKee, author,
> Story: Substance, Structure, Style and the Principles of Screenwriting

"Has it occurred to you that your draft of the MindWriter report has not been touched in the last two days? The stack of marked-up pages is right there on your desk, and you have been working around it."

Jason frowns and momentarily flicks his eyes to the stack of marked pages.

Sara plunges ahead with her complaint. "It's no big deal, you know. You promised to chop out three pages of methodology that nobody will care about but your fellow statistics jocks . . ."—Jason shoots her an aggrieved look— ". . . and to remove your recommendations and provide them in a separate, informal letter so that Myra Wines can distribute them under her name and claim credit for your 'brilliance.'"

"I think I have writer's block."

"No. Writer's block is when you can't write. You can't unwrite; that's the problem. You have unwriter's block. Look, some people do great research and then panic when they have to decide what goes in the report and what doesn't. Or they can't take all the great ideas running around in their heads and express their abstractions in words. Or they don't believe they are smart enough to communicate with their clients, or vice versa. So they freeze up. This isn't usually your problem. There is some sort of emotional link to this MindWriter report, Jason; face it."

"I love the MindWriter project."

"Ah, there's the problem," she says. "Jason, I have heard you say that you hate projects for other clients, and I have heard you say that you like projects. But this is the first time I have heard you say you love a project. There comes a time when, after you have nurtured something, you have to let go. Then it isn't yours. It is someone else's, or it is its own thing, but it is not yours."

"I guess you're right," Jason smiles sheepishly. "I'm a little too invested. This MindWriter project was my baby—well, yours and mine. If I chop three pages out of the report, it is finished. Then it belongs to Myra. I don't own it anymore. I can't implement my recommendations. I can't change anything. I can't have second thoughts."

"Fix it, then. Send MindWriter an invoice. Write a proposal for follow-up work. Do something, Jason. Finish it. Let go and move on." Sara smiles and pauses as she is about to leave Jason's office. Jason has pulled the report to the center of his desk, a very good sign.

"By the way, Custom Foods just called. It awarded us the contract for its ideation work. I'd hate to work on that project without you, but . . ."

> Introduction

As part of the research proposal, the sponsor and the researcher agree on what types of reporting will occur both during and at the end of the research project. Depending on the budget for the project, a formal oral presentation may not be part of the reporting. A research sponsor, however, is sure to require a written report. Exhibit 20-1 details the reporting phase of the research process.

> The Written Research Report

It may seem unscientific and even unfair, but a poor final report or presentation can destroy a study. Research technicians may ignore the significance of badly reported content, but most readers will be influenced by the quality of the reporting. This fact should prompt researchers to make special efforts to communicate clearly and fully.

The research report contains findings, analyses of findings, interpretations, conclusions, and sometimes recommendations. The researcher is the expert on the topic and knows the specifics in a way no one else can. Because a written research report is an authoritative one-way communication, it imposes a special obligation for maintaining objectivity. Even if your findings seem to point to an action, you should demonstrate restraint and caution when proposing that course.

Reports may be defined by their degree of formality and design. The formal report follows a well-delineated and relatively long format. This is in contrast to the informal or short report.

Short Reports

Short reports are appropriate when the problem is well defined, is of limited scope, and has a simple and straightforward methodology. Most informational, progress, and interim reports are of this kind: a report of cost-of-living changes for upcoming labor negotiations or an exploration of filing "dumping" charges against a foreign competitor.

Short reports are about five pages. If used on a website, they may be even shorter. At the beginning, there should be a brief statement about the authorization for the study, the problem examined, and its breadth and depth. Next come the conclusions and recommendations, followed by the findings that support them. Section headings should be used.

A letter of transmittal is a vehicle to convey short reports. A five-page report may be produced to track sales on a quarterly basis. The report should be direct, make ample use of graphics to show trends, and refer the reader to the research department for further information. Detailed information on the research method would be omitted, although an overview could appear in an appendix. The purpose of this type of report is to distribute information quickly in an easy-to-use format. Short reports are also produced for clients with small, relatively inexpensive research projects.

The letter is a form of a short report. Its tone should be informal. The format follows that of any good business letter and should not exceed a few pages. A letter report is often written in personal style *(we, you)*, although this depends on the situation.

Memorandum reports are another variety and follow the *To, From, Subject* format.

These suggestions may be helpful for writing short reports:

- Tell the reader why you are writing (it may be in response to a request).
- If the memo is in response to a request for information, remind the reader of the exact point raised, answer it, and follow with any necessary details.
- Write in an expository style with brevity and directness.
- If time permits, write the report today and leave it for review tomorrow before sending it.
- Attach detailed materials as appendices when needed.

>**Exhibit 20-1** Written Presentation and the Research Process

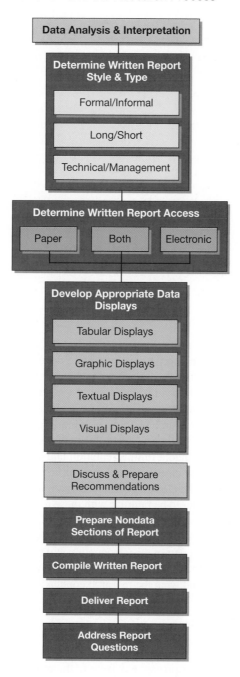

Long Reports

Long reports are of two types, the technical or base report and the management report. The choice depends on the audience and the researcher's objectives.

Many projects will require both types of reports: a **technical report,** written for an audience of researchers, and a **management report,** written for the nontechnically oriented manager or client. Although some researchers try to write a single report that satisfies both needs, this complicates the task and is seldom satisfactory. The two types of audiences have different technical training, interests, and goals.

E-Speed or No Speed

The Internet has forever transformed a decision maker's expectations relating to speed of data results. The Internet has given marketers a taste of "e-time"—data tabulated and synthesized in real time. "While some marketer's realize that e-speed may sacrifice quality in research," shared Darcy Zwetko, manager–research services, Opinion Search, Inc. (Ottawa, Canada), "knowing the speed available with online surveys encouraged us to make our CATI survey results accessible in real time, directly via each client's computer." Opinion Search calls this industry first *dataCAP* for "Data Control and Access Portal." Among other opportunities, dataCAP provides:

- Real-time frequencies.
- Real-time cross-tabulation.
- Real-time open-ended verbatim responses.
- Real-time quota status.
- Daily status of your projects.
- Daily call disposition reports.

Besides being fast, dataCAP delivers encrypted information to protect data privacy. Speed without safety won't win a firm any clients. And speed that sacrifices quality won't have them coming back.

www.opinionsearch.com

The Technical Report

This report should include full documentation and detail. It will normally survive all working papers and original data files and so will become the major source document. It is the report that other researchers will want to see because it has the full story of what was done and how it was done.

Although completeness is a goal, you must guard against including nonessential material. A good guide is that sufficient procedural information should be included to enable others to replicate the study. This includes sources of data, research procedures, sampling design, data gathering instruments, index construction, and data analysis methods. Most information should be attached in an appendix.

A technical report should also include a full presentation and analysis of significant data. Conclusions and recommendations should be clearly related to specific findings. Technical jargon should be minimized but defined when used. There can be brief references to other research, theories, and techniques. Although you expect the reader to be familiar with these references, it is useful to include some short explanations, perhaps as footnotes or endnotes.

The short technical report covers the same items as the long technical report but in an abbreviated form. The methodology is included as part of the introduction and takes no more than a few paragraphs. Most of the emphasis is placed on the findings and conclusions. A memo or letter format covers only the minimum: what the problem is and what the research conclusions are.

The Management Report

In contrast to the technical report, the management report is for the nontechnical client. The reader has little time to absorb details and needs a prompt exposure to the most critical findings; thus the report's sections are in an inverted order. After the prefatory and introductory sections, the conclusions with accompanying recommendations are presented. Individual findings are presented next, supporting the conclusions already made. The appendices present any required methodological details. The order of the management report allows clients to grasp the conclusions and recommendations quickly, without much reading. Then, if they wish to go further, they may read on into the findings. The management report should make liberal use of visual displays.

2.3

The number of gallons of fuel, in billions, that people burn while sitting in traffic.

Sometimes the client has no research background and is interested in results rather than in methodology. The major communication medium in this situation is the management report. It is still helpful to have a technical report if the client later wishes to have a technical appraisal of the study.

The style of the report should encourage rapid reading and quick comprehension of major findings, and it should prompt understanding of the implications and conclusions. The report tone is journalistic and must be accurate. Headlines and underlining for emphasis are helpful; pictures and graphs often replace tables. Sentences and paragraphs should be short and direct. Consider liberal use of white space and wide margins. It may be desirable to put a single finding on each page. It also helps to have a theme running through the report and even graphic or animated characters designed to vary the presentation.

> Research Report Components

Research reports, long and short, have a set of identifiable components. Usually headings and subheadings divide the sections. Each report is individual; sections may be dropped or added, condensed or expanded to meet the needs of the audience. Exhibit 20-2 lists four types of reports, the sections that

>**Exhibit 20-2** Research Report Sections and Their Order of Inclusion

Report Modules	Short Report		Long Report	
	Memo or Letter	Short Technical	Management	Technical
Prefatory Information		1	1	1
Letter of transmittal		✓	✓	✓
Title page		✓	✓	✓
Authorization statement		✓	✓	✓
Executive summary		✓	✓	✓
Table of contents			✓	✓
Introduction	1	2	2	2
Problem statement	✓	✓	✓	✓
Research objectives	✓	✓	✓	✓
Background	✓	✓	✓	✓
Methodology		✓	✓	3
Sampling design				✓
Research design				✓
Data collection				✓
Data analysis				✓
Limitations		✓	✓	✓
Findings		3	4	4
Conclusions	2	4	3	5
Summary and conclusions	✓	✓	✓	✓
Recommendations	✓	✓	✓	✓
Appendices		5	5	6
Bibliography				7

are typically included, and the general order of presentation. Each of these formats can be modified to meet the needs of the audience.

Prefatory Items

Prefatory materials do not have direct bearing on the research itself. Instead, they assist the reader in using the research report.

Letter of Transmittal

When the relationship between the researcher and the client is formal, a **letter of transmittal** should be included. This is appropriate when a report is for a specific client (e.g., a company officer) and when it is generated for an outside organization. The letter should refer to the authorization for the project and any specific instructions or limitations placed on the study. It should also state the purpose and the scope of the study. For many internal projects, it is not necessary to include a letter of transmittal.

Title Page

The title page should include four items: the title of the report, the date, and for whom and by whom it was prepared. The title should be brief but include the following three elements: (1) the variables included in the study, (2) the type of relationship among the variables, and (3) the population to which the results may be applied.[1] Redundancies such as "A Report of" and "A Discussion of" add length to the title but little else. Single-word titles are also of little value. Here are three acceptable ways to word report titles:

Descriptive study:	The Five-Year Demand Outlook for Consumer Packaged Goods in the United States
Correlation study:	The Relationship between Relative National Inflation Rates and Household Purchases of Brand X in International Markets
Causal study:	The Effect of Various Motivation Methods on Retail Sales Associates' Attitudes and Performance

Authorization Letter

When the report is sent to a public organization, it is common to include a letter of authorization showing the authority for undertaking the research. This is especially true for reports to federal and state governments and nonprofit organizations. The letter not only shows who sponsored the research but also delineates the original request.

Executive Summary

An **executive summary** can serve two purposes. It may be a report in miniature (sometimes called a *topline report*), covering all the aspects in the body of the report but in abbreviated form. Or it may be a concise summary of the major findings and conclusions, including recommendations. Two pages are generally sufficient for executive summaries. Write this section after the rest of the report is finished. It should not include new information but may require graphics to present a particular conclusion. Expect the summary to contain a high density of significant terms since it is repeating the highlights of the report.

Table of Contents

As a rough guide, any report of several sections that totals more than 6 to 10 pages should have a table of contents. If there are many tables, charts, or other exhibits, they should also be listed after the table of contents in a separate table of illustrations.

Forrester Research: Finding the Dramatic Story Line

In an earlier Snapshot we introduced you to Forrester Research, a firm that does issue-driven research in numerous industries and sells many of its reports by subscription. Forrester takes a modular approach to report writing, whether it's a "brief" drafted in a few hours or a report that might take as many as 30 hours. Each report has three main sections. The "Market Overview" section describes the data collected from interviews, surveys, and secondary searches. It starts by revealing simpler problems and moves on to more complex ones. It doesn't rehash information the audience knows but provides only those data that are new. The "Analysis" section interprets the findings. And the "What It Means" section speculates on the implications of the findings and the analysis.

In one such study, the Market Overview would relate the finding that "40 percent of the time auto dealers have the wrong cars." In the Analysis section, the report would relate that with all the data car manufacturers have about what cars—and features within cars—are selling, a dealer with access to this information should be able to improve his or her inventory mix. Senior analyst Mark Bunger relates that the What It Means section is speculative.

"We develop the W-I-M chain—if 'a' was found, then isn't 'b' likely? Or if 'b,' then 'c'; and if 'c,' then 'd.' A lot of deduction and conjecture based on solid knowledge and experience within the industry ends up in the last section of the report. So if 40 percent of the time dealers have the wrong cars, and the manufacturers have the information dealers need, then dealers could improve the inventory to reduce that rate to say 20 percent. And for those prospects who still can't find the car they want? They might be likely to custom build to order to achieve satisfaction." This speculative section is the smallest section of the report.

And when it comes to writing reports, Forrester researchers take the time to find the right words to relay their information. The title takes on special significance, as subscribers often choose the reports they access based on the title. "We'll get more people reading a report if we title it something intriguing like 'Will ad skipping kill television?' than if we call it something drier like 'The implications of technology on viewer control activities in television ad exposure.'"

www.forrester.com

Introduction

The introduction prepares the reader for the report by describing the parts of the project: the problem statement, research objectives, and background material.[2] In most projects, the introduction can be taken from the research proposal with minor editing.

Problem Statement

The problem statement contains the need for the research project. The problem is usually represented by a management question. It is followed by a more detailed set of objectives.

Research Objectives

The research objectives address the purpose of the project. These objectives may be research questions and associated investigative questions. In correlational or causal studies, the hypothesis statements are included. As we discussed in Chapter 2, hypotheses are declarative statements describing the relationship between two or more variables. They state clearly the variables of concern, the relationships among them, and the target group being studied. Operational definitions of critical variables should be included.

Background

Background material may be of two types. It may be the preliminary results of exploration from an experience survey, focus group, or another source. Alternatively, it could be secondary data from the literature review. A traditional organizational scheme is to think of the concentric circles of a target. Starting with the outside ring, the writer works toward the center. The bull's eye contains the material directly related to the problem. Resources and means for securing this information are presented in Chapter 5 and on your text website.

Previous research, theory, or situations that led to the management question are also discussed in this section. The literature should be organized, integrated, and presented in a way that connects it logically to the problem. The background includes definitions, qualifications, and assumptions. It gives the reader the information needed to understand the remainder of the research report.[3]

Background material may be placed before the problem statement or after the research objectives. If it is composed primarily of literature review and related research, it should follow the objectives. If it contains information pertinent to the management problem or the situation that led to the study, it can be placed before the problem statement (where it is found in many applied studies).

Methodology

In short reports and management reports, the methodology should not have a separate section; it should be mentioned in the introduction, and details should be placed in an appendix. However, for a technical report, the methodology is an important section, containing at least five parts.

Sampling Design

The researcher explicitly defines the target population being studied and the sampling methods used. For example, was this a probability or nonprobability sample? If probability, was it simple random or complex random? How were the elements selected? How was the size determined? How much confidence do we have, and how much error was allowed?

Explanations of the sampling methods, uniqueness of the chosen parameters, or other points that need explanation should be covered with brevity. Calculations should be placed in an appendix instead of in the body of the report.

Research Design

The coverage of the design must be adapted to the purpose. In an experimental study, the materials, tests, equipment, control conditions, and other devices should be described. In descriptive or ex post facto designs, it may be sufficient to cover the rationale for using one design instead of competing alternatives. Even with a sophisticated design, the strengths and weaknesses should be identified and the instrumentation and materials discussed. Copies of materials are placed in an appendix.

Data Collection

This part of the report describes the specifics of gathering the data. Its contents depend on the selected design. Survey work generally uses a team with field and central supervision. How many people were involved? What was their training? How were they managed? When were the data collected? How much time did it take? What were the conditions in the field? How were irregularities handled? In an experiment, we would want to know about participant assignment to groups, the use of standardized procedures and protocols, the administration of tests or observational forms, manipulation of the variables, and so forth.

Typically, you would include a discussion on the relevance of secondary data that guided these decisions. Again, detailed materials such as field instructions should be included in an appendix.

Data Analysis

This section summarizes the methods used to analyze the data and describes data handling, preliminary analysis, statistical tests, computer programs, and other technical information. The rationale for the choice of analysis approaches should be clear. A brief commentary on assumptions and appropriateness of use should be presented.

Limitations

This topic is often handled with ambivalence. Some people wish to ignore the matter, feeling that mentioning limitations detracts from the impact of the study. This attitude is unprofessional and possibly unethical. Others seem to adopt a masochistic approach of detailing everything. The section should be a thoughtful presentation of significant methodology or implementation problems. An evenhanded approach is one of the hallmarks of an honest and competent investigator. All research studies have their limitations, and the sincere investigator recognizes that readers need aid in judging the study's validity.

Findings

This is generally the longest section of the report. The objective is to explain the data rather than draw interpretations or conclusions. When quantitative data can be presented, this should be done as simply as possible with charts, graphics, and tables.

The data need not include everything you have collected. The criterion for inclusion is, Is this material important to the reader's understanding of the problem and the findings? However, make sure to show findings unfavorable to your hypotheses as well as those that support them, because this reinforces the bond of trust that has developed between researcher and sponsor.

It is useful to present findings in numbered paragraphs or to present one finding per page with the quantitative data supporting the findings presented in a small table or chart on the same page (see Exhibit 20-3). Although this arrangement adds to the bulk of the report, it is convenient for the reader.

>**Exhibit 20-3** Example of a Findings Page in Central City Bank Market Study

Findings:	1. In this city, *commercial banks are not the preferred savings medium.* Banks are in a weak third place behind money market accounts.
	2. Customers of the Central City Bank have a *somewhat more favorable attitude toward bank savings* and less of a preference for government bonds.
Question:	Suppose that you have just received an extra $1,000 and have decided to save it. Which of the savings methods listed would be your preferred way to save it?
	❐ Government bonds
	❐ Savings and loan
	❐ Bank savings
	❐ Credit union
	❐ Stock
	❐ Other

Savings Method	Total Replies	Central City Bank Customers	Other Bank Customers
Government bonds	24%	20%	29%
Savings and loan	43	45	42
Bank	13	18	8
Credit union	9	7	11
Stock	7	8	5
Other	4	2	5
Total	100%	100%	100%
	n = 216	*n* = 105	*n* = 111

Conclusions

Summary and Conclusions

The summary is a brief statement of the essential findings. Sectional summaries may be used if there are many specific findings. These may be combined into an overall summary. In simple descriptive research, a summary may complete the report, because conclusions and recommendations may not be required.

Findings state facts; conclusions represent inferences drawn from the findings. A writer is sometimes reluctant to make conclusions and leaves the task to the reader. Avoid this temptation when possible. As the researcher, you are the one best informed on the factors that critically influence the findings and conclusions. Good researchers don't draw conclusions that go beyond the data related to the study.

Conclusions may be presented in a tabular form for easy reading and reference. Summary findings may be subordinated under the related conclusion statement. These may be numbered to refer the reader to pages or tables in the findings sections.

Recommendations

Increasingly, researchers are expected to offer ideas for corrective actions. In applied research the recommendations will usually be for managerial action, with the researcher suggesting one or several alternatives that are supported by the findings. Also, researchers may recommend further research initiatives. In basic or pure research, recommendations are often suggestions for further study that broaden or test the understandings of a subject area.

Appendices

The appendices are the place for complex tables, statistical tests, supporting documents, copies of forms and questionnaires, detailed descriptions of the methodology, instructions to field workers, and other evidence important for later support. The reader who wishes to learn about the technical aspects of the study and to look at statistical breakdowns will want a complete appendix.

Bibliography

The use of secondary data requires a bibliography. Long reports, particularly technical ones, require a bibliography. A bibliography documents the sources used by the writer. Although bibliographies may contain work used as background or for further study, it is preferable to include only sources used for preparing the report.

> Writing the Report

Students often give inadequate attention to reporting their findings and conclusions. This is unfortunate. A well-presented study will often impress the reader more than a study with greater scientific quality but with a weaker presentation. Judging a report as competently written is often the key first step to a manager's decision to use the findings in decision making and also to consider implementation of the researcher's recommendations. Report-writing skills are especially valuable to the junior executive or researcher who aspires to rise in an organization. A well-written study frequently enhances career prospects.

Prewriting Concerns

Before writing, one should ask again, What is the purpose of this report? Responding to this question is one way to crystallize the problem.

The second prewriting question is, Who will read the report? Thought should be given to the needs, temperament, and biases of the audience. You should not distort facts to meet these needs and biases but should consider them while developing the presentation. Knowing who will read the report may suggest its appropriate length. Generally, the higher the report goes in an organization, the shorter it should be.

Another consideration is technical background—the gap in subject knowledge between the reader and the writer. The greater the gap, the more difficult it is to convey the full findings meaningfully and concisely.

The third prewriting question is, What are the circumstances and limitations under which I am writing? Is the nature of the subject highly technical? Do you need statistics? Charts? What is the importance of the topic? A crucial subject justifies more effort than a minor one. What should be the scope of the report? How much time is available? Deadlines often impose limitations on the report.

Finally, How will the report be used? Try to visualize the reader using the report. How can the information be made more convenient? How much effort must be given to getting the attention and interest of the reader? Will the report be read by more than one person? If so, how many copies should be made? What will be the distribution of the report?

The Outline

Once the researcher has made the first analysis of the data, drawn tentative conclusions, and completed statistical significance tests, it is time to develop an outline. A useful system employs the following organizational structure:

I. Major Topic Heading

  A. Major subtopic heading

    1. Subtopic

      a. Minor subtopic

        (1) Further detail

          (a) Even further detail

Software for developing outlines and visually connecting ideas simplifies this once-onerous task. Two styles of outlining are widely used—the topic outline and the sentence outline. In the **topic outline,** a key word or two are used. The assumption is that the writer knows its significance and will later remember the nature of the argument represented by that word or phrase or, alternatively, the outliner knows that a point should be made but is not yet sure how to make it.

The **sentence outline** expresses the essential thoughts associated with the specific topic. This approach leaves less development work for later writing, other than elaboration and explanation to improve readability. It has the obvious advantages of pushing the writer to make decisions on what to include and how to say it. It is probably the best outlining style for the inexperienced researcher because it divides the writing job into its two major components—what to say and how to say it.

Here is an example of the type of detail found with each of these outlining formats:

Topic Outline	Sentence Outline
I. Demand	I. Demand for refrigerators
A. How measured	A. Measured in terms of factory shipments as reported to the U.S. Department of Commerce.
1. Voluntary error	1. Error is introduced into year-to-year comparisons because reporting is voluntary.
2. Shipping error	2. A second factor is variations from month to month because of shipping and invoicing patterns.
a. Monthly variance	a. Variations up to 30 percent this year depending on whether shipments were measured by actual shipment data or invoice date.

The Bibliography

Style manuals provide guidelines on form, section and alphabetical arrangement, and annotation. Proper citation, style, and formats are unique to the purpose of the report. The instructor, program, institution, or client often specifies style requirements. The uniqueness of varying requirements makes detailed examples in this chapter impractical, although the endnotes and references in this book provide an example. As cited in Appendix A on the research proposal, we recommend the *Publication Manual of the American Psychological Association;* Kate L. Turabian, *A Manual for Writers of Term Papers, Theses, and Dissertations;* and Joseph Gibaldi, *MLA Handbook for Writers of Research Papers.*

Bibliographic retrieval software allows researchers to locate and save references from online services and translate them into database records. Entries can be further searched, sorted, indexed, and formatted into bibliographies of any style. Many retrieval programs are network-compatible and connect to popular word processors.

Writing the Draft

Once the outline is complete, decisions can be made on the placement of graphics, tables, and charts. Each should be matched to a particular section in the outline. Although graphics might be added later or tables changed into charts, it is helpful to make a first approximation of the graphics before beginning to write. Choices for reporting statistics will be reviewed later in this chapter.

Each writer uses different mechanisms for getting thoughts into written form. Some will write in longhand, relying on someone else to transcribe their prose into word-processed format. Others are happiest in front of a word processor, able to add, delete, and move sections at will. Whichever works for you is the best approach to use.

Computer software packages check for spelling errors and provide a thesaurus for looking up alternative ways of expressing a thought. A CD-ROM can call up the 20-volume *Oxford English Dictionary,* believed to be the greatest dictionary in any language. Common word confusion (*there* for *their, to* for *too,* or *effect* for *affect*) will not be found by standard spelling checkers. Advanced programs will scrutinize your report for grammar, punctuation, capitalization, doubled words, transposed letters, homonyms, style problems, and readability level. The style checker will reveal misused words and indicate awkward phrasing. Exhibit 20-4 shows sample output from a commercial package used on one of this text's vignettes. The program shown writes comments to a text file, prepares a backup copy of the original, and generates a statistics report. The statistics summarize the program's evaluation of readability, grade level, and sentence structure. Comparisons to "reference" documents, or documents that you submit for comparison, may be made. The software cannot guarantee an error-free report but will greatly reduce your time in proofreading and enhance the style of the completed product.[4]

Readability

Sensitive writers consider the reading ability of their audience to achieve high readership. You can obtain high readership more easily if the topic interests the readers and is in their field of expertise. In addition, you can show the usefulness of the report by pointing out how it will help the readers. Finally, you can write at a level that is appropriate to the audience's reading abilities. To test writing for difficulty level, use a standard **readability index.** The Flesch Reading Ease Score gives a score between 0 and 100. The lower the score, the harder the material is to read. The Flesch-Kincaid Grade Level and Gunning's Fog Index both provide a score that corresponds with the grade level needed to easily read and understand the document. Although it is possible to calculate these indexes by hand, some software packages will do it automatically. The most sophisticated packages allow you to specify the preferred reading level. Words that are above that level are highlighted to allow you to choose an alternative.

>**Exhibit 20-4** Grammar and Style Proofreader Results

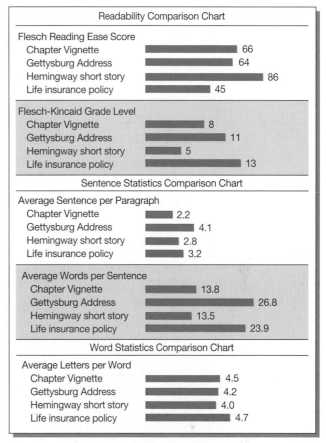

Statistics

Statistics for: Chapter Vignette	Problems marked/detected: 8/8

Readability Statistics

Flesch Reading Ease: 66	Flesch-Kincaid Grade Level: 8
Gunning's Fog Index: 11	

Paragraph Statistics

Number of paragraphs: 25	Average length: 2.2 sentences

Sentence Statistics

Number of sentences: 55		Passive voice:	4
Average length:	13.8 words	Short (< 12 words) :	39
End with "?" :	2	Long (> 28 words) :	7
End with "!" :	0		

Word Statistics

Number of words:	759	Average length:	4.58 letters

Document Summary for: Chapter Vignette	Problems detected: 8

Readability Statistics	Interpretation
Grade level: 8 (Flesch-Kincaid)	Preferred level for most readers.
Reading ease score: 66 (Flesch)	This represents 6 to 10 years of schooling.
Passive voice: 331	Writing may be difficult to read or ambiguous for this writing style.
Average sentence length: 13.8 words	Most readers could easily understand sentences of this length.
Average word length: 1.50 syl.	Vocabulary used in this document is understandable for most readers.
Average paragraph length: 2.2 sentences	Most readers could easily follow paragraphs of this length.

Comparisons

Readability Comparison Chart

Flesch Reading Ease Score
- Chapter Vignette — 66
- Gettysburg Address — 64
- Hemingway short story — 86
- Life insurance policy — 45

Flesch-Kincaid Grade Level
- Chapter Vignette — 8
- Gettysburg Address — 11
- Hemingway short story — 5
- Life insurance policy — 13

Sentence Statistics Comparison Chart

Average Sentence per Paragraph
- Chapter Vignette — 2.2
- Gettysburg Address — 4.1
- Hemingway short story — 2.8
- Life insurance policy — 3.2

Average Words per Sentence
- Chapter Vignette — 13.8
- Gettysburg Address — 26.8
- Hemingway short story — 13.5
- Life insurance policy — 23.9

Word Statistics Comparison Chart

Average Letters per Word
- Chapter Vignette — 4.5
- Gettysburg Address — 4.2
- Hemingway short story — 4.0
- Life insurance policy — 4.7

Advocates of readability measurement do not claim that all written material should be at the simplest level possible. They argue only that the level should be appropriate for the audience. They point out that comic books score about 6 on the Gunning scale (that is, a person with a sixth-grade education should be able to read that material). *Time* usually scores about 10, while *The Atlantic* is reported to have a score of 11 or 12. Material that scores much above 12 becomes difficult for the public to read comfortably. Such measures obviously give only a rough idea of the true readability of a report. Good writing calls for a variety of other skills to enhance reading comprehension.

Comprehensibility

Good writing varies with the writing objective. Research writing is designed to convey information of a precise nature. Avoid ambiguity, multiple meanings, and allusions. Take care to choose the right words—words that convey thoughts accurately, clearly, and efficiently. When concepts and constructs are used, they must be defined, either operationally or descriptively.

Words and sentences should be carefully organized and edited. Misplaced modifiers run rampant in carelessly written reports. Subordinate ideas mixed with major ideas make the report confusing to readers, forcing them to sort out what is important and what is secondary when this should have been done for them.

Finally, there is the matter of pace. **Pace** is defined as:

The rate at which the printed page presents information to the reader . . . . The proper pace in technical writing is one that enables the reader to keep his mind working just a fraction of a second behind his eye as he reads along. It logically would be slow when the information is complex or difficult to understand; fast when the information is straightforward and familiar. If the reader's mind lags behind his eye, the pace is too rapid; if his mind wanders ahead of his eye (or wants to) the pace is too slow.[5]

If the text is overcrowded with concepts, there is too much information per sentence. By contrast, sparse writing has too few significant ideas per sentence. Writers use a variety of methods to adjust the pace of their writing:

- Use ample white space and wide margins to create a positive psychological effect on the reader.
- Break large units of text into smaller units with headings to show organization of the topics.
- Relieve difficult text with visual aids when possible.
- Emphasize important material and deemphasize secondary material through sentence construction and judicious use of italicizing, underlining, capitalization, and parentheses.
- Choose words carefully, opting for the known and short rather than the unknown and long. Graduate students, in particular, seem to revel in using jargon, pompous constructions, and long or arcane words. Naturally, there are times when technical terms are appropriate. Scientists communicate efficiently with jargon, but the audiences for most applied research are not scientifically trained and need more help than many writers supply.
- Repeat and summarize critical and difficult ideas so that readers have time to absorb them.
- Make strategic use of service words. These are words that "do not represent objects or ideas, but show relationship. Transitional words, such as the conjunctions, are service words. So are phrases such as 'on the other hand,' 'in summary,' and 'in contrast.'"[6]

Integrated office suite software like Microsoft Office has made it infinitely easier, and more challenging, to craft the research report. Research sponsors expect articulate and well-organized reports and the software can deliver. However, they also expect perfection. Only with careful editing and rewriting, coupled with skilled use of the software, is the researcher capable of meeting that expectation.

Tone

Review the writing to ensure the tone is appropriate. The reader can, and should, be referred to, but researchers should avoid referring to themselves. One author notes that the "application of the 'you' attitude . . . makes the message sound like it is written to the reader, not sent by the author. A message prepared for the reader conveys sincerity, personalization, warmth, and involvement on the part of the author."[7] To accomplish this, remove negative phrasing and rewrite the thought positively. Do not change your recommendations or your findings to make them positive. Instead, review the phrasing. Which of the following sounds better?

> End users do not want the Information Systems Department telling them what software to buy.

> End users want more autonomy over their computer software choices.

The messages convey the same information, but the positive tone of the second message does not put readers from the Information Systems Department on the defensive.

Final Proof

It is helpful to put the draft away for a day before doing the final editing. Go to the beach, ride a bicycle in the park, or see a movie—do anything that is unrelated to the research project. Then return to the report and read it with a critical eye. Does the writing flow smoothly? Are there transitions where they are needed? Is the organization apparent to the reader? Do the findings and conclusions adequately meet the problem statement and the research objectives? Are the tables and graphics displaying the proper information in an easy-to-read format? After assuring yourself that the draft is complete, write the executive summary.

Presentation Considerations

The final consideration in the report-writing process is production. Reports can be typed; printed on an ink-jet, laser, color, or other printer; or sent out for typesetting. Most student and small research reports are typed or produced on a computer printer. The presentation of the report conveys to the readers the professional approach used throughout the project. Care should be taken to use compatible fonts throughout the entire report. The printer should produce consistent, easy-to-read letters on quality paper. When reports are photocopied for more than one reader, make sure the copies are clean and have no black streaks or gray areas.

Overcrowding of text creates an appearance problem. Readers need the visual relief provided by ample white space. We define "ample" as 1 inch of white space at the top, bottom, and right-hand margins. On the left side, the margin should be at least 1¼ inches to provide room for binding or punched holes. Even greater margins will often improve report appearance and help to highlight key points or sections. Overcrowding also occurs when the report contains page after page of large blocks of unbroken text. This produces an unpleasant psychological effect on readers because of its formidable appearance. Overcrowded text, however, may be avoided in the following ways:

- Use shorter paragraphs. As a rough guide, any paragraph longer than half a page is suspect. Remember that each paragraph should represent a distinct thought.
- Indent parts of text that represent listings, long quotations, or examples.
- Use headings and subheadings to divide the report and its major sections into homogeneous topical parts.
- Use vertical listings of points (such as this list).

Inadequate labeling creates another physical problem. Each graph or table should contain enough information to be self-explanatory. Text headings and subheadings also help with labeling. They function as signs for the audience, describing the organization of the report and indicating the progress of discussion. They also help readers to skim the material and to return easily to particular sections of the report.

> Presentation of Statistics[8]

The presentation of statistics in research reports is a special challenge for writers. Four basic ways to present such data are in (1) a text paragraph, (2) semitabular form, (3) tables, or (4) graphics.

Text Presentation

This is probably the most common method of presentation when there are only a few statistics. The writer can direct the reader's attention to certain numbers or comparisons and emphasize specific points. The drawback is that the statistics are submerged in the text, requiring the reader to scan the entire paragraph to extract the meaning. The following material has a few simple comparisons but becomes more complicated when text and statistics are combined:

> Walmart regained its number-1 rank in the Forbes 500 due to its strong sales performance (11% increase; $351.1 billion). Although Walmart surpassed number-2-ranked ExxonMobil in sales, Walmart's profitability ($11.2 billion) was far below the oil giant ($39.5 billion). Some credit several challenging public relations problems with the lower-than-expected level. Number-6-ranked General Electric also outperformed Walmart in profits with $20.8 billion. GE's robust sales growth (27.4%) is an indication that it will likely challenge both Walmart and ExxonMobil in the future.

This section continues on p. 586

MindWriter Written Report

A written report is the culmination of the MindWriter project, which has illustrated the research process throughout the book. The contract for the CompleteCare project requires a report about the size of a student term project. Although repetitive portions have been omitted to conserve space, it should give the reader some idea of how an applied project of this size is summarized. Descriptive statistics and simple graphics are used to analyze and present most of the data. References to chapters where specific details may be reviewed are shown in the marginal comments.

The presentation of findings follows the content specifications of Exhibit 20-2 for short reports. It falls between a memo/letter and a short technical report. The objective was to make it available quickly for feedback to the CompleteCare team. It was therefore set up as a PDF e-mail attachment.

The fax cover sheet acts as a temporary transmittal letter until the plain paper copies are sent.

It provides all necessary identification and contact information. The writer's and recipient's relationship makes using first names appropriate.

Authorization for the study. Scope of findings (month). Specific instructions for process issues.

Request for follow-up by the client to reduce the study's limitations.

Progress update and feedback on improvements.

To:	Myra Wines	**From:**	Jason Henry
Company:	MindWriter Corp.	**Company:**	Henry and Associates
Location:	Austin, TX Bldg 5	**Location:**	Palm Beach, FL
Telephone:	512.555.1234	**Telephone:**	407.555.4321
Fax:	512.555.1250	**Fax:**	407.555.4357

Total number of pages including this one: 11

January 5, 2011

Dear Myra,

This fax contains the CompleteCare December report requested by Mr. Malraison. You may expect the plain paper copies tomorrow morning for distribution.

We hope that the Call Center will complete the nonrespondent surveys so that we can discover the extent to which these results represent all CompleteCare customers.

This month's findings show improvements in the areas we discussed last week by telephone. The response rate is also up. You will be delighted to know that our preliminary analysis shows improvements in the courier's ratings.

Best regards,

Jason

>closeupcont'd

Title contains reference to a known survey and program. Descriptions of variables, relationships, and population are unnecessary.

The recipient of the report, corporation, and date appear next.

The report's preparer, location, and telephone number facilitate contact for additional information.

The information level identifies this as a restricted circulation document for in-house use only.

CompleteCare Customer Survey Results for December

Prepared for Myra Wines
MindWriter Corporation
January 2011

Henry and Associates
200 ShellPoint Tower
Palm Beach, Florida 33480

407.555.4321

e-mail: info@henry&assoc.com
www.henry&assoc.com

MindWriter CONFIDENTIAL

Title repeated.

Section headings are used.

Introduction contains period of coverage for report, management question, and secondary research objective.

An overview of the report's contents allows readers to turn to specific section of interest.

The executive summary provides a synopsis of essential findings. It is the report in miniature—six paragraphs.

Both positive and negative results are capsulized.

Criteria for indexes are provided as reminders.

MindWriter CompleteCare December Results

Introduction

This report is based on the December data collected from the MindWriter Complete-Care Survey. The survey asks customers about their satisfaction with the Complete-Care repair and service system. Its secondary purpose is to identify monthly improvement targets for management.

The findings are organized into the following sections: (1) an executive summary, (2) the methods used, (3) the Service Improvement Grid, (4) detailed findings for each question, and (5) patterns in the open-ended questions.

Executive Summary

The highest degrees of satisfaction with CompleteCare were found in the categories of "delivery speed" and "pickup speed." Average scores on these items were between 4.2 and 4.4 on a 5-point scale. "Speed of repair," "condition on arrival," and "overall impression of CompleteCare's effectiveness" also scored relatively well. They were above the *met all expectations* level (see appropriate charts).

Several questions were below the *met all expectations* level. From the lowest, "Call Center's responsiveness," to "Call Center's technical competence," and "courier service's arrangements," the average scores ranged from 2.0 to 3.9. In general, ratings have improved since November with the exception of "condition on arrival."

The three items generating the most negative comments are (1) problems with the courier's arrangements, (2) long telephone waits, and (3) transfer among many people at the Call Center. These same comments carry over for the last two months.

CompleteCare's criteria for Dissatisfied Customers consist of negative comments in the Comments/Suggestions section or ratings of less than three (3.0) on questions one through eight. Forty-three percent of the sample met these criteria, down from 56 percent last month. By counting only customers' comments (positive/negative or +/−), the percentage of Dissatisfied Customers would be 32 percent.

The ratio of negative to positive comments was 1.7 to 1, an improvement over November's ratio (2.3 to 1).

>**close**up**cont'd**

The methodology, reported in brief, reminds the readers of the data collection method, nature and format of the questionnaire, scales used, and target measurement issues.

The sample, a self-selecting nonprobability sample, and the response rate are shown. With respondents' data from the postcards and the Call Center's files on nonrespondents, a future study on nonresponse bias is planned.

This section begins the Findings section. Findings consist of the action planning grid and detailed results sections. The headings were specified by the client.

The method for creating the planning grid and the grid's contents are highlighted.

When the expectation-based satisfaction scores are adjusted for perceived importance, "Call Center responsiveness," "Call Center technical competence," and "courier arrangements" are identified as action items. "Repair speed" and "problem resolution" maintained high importance scores and are also rated above average.

Methodology

The data collection instrument is a postage-paid postcard that is packed with the repaired product at the time the unit is shipped back to the customer.

The survey consists of 12 satisfaction questions measured on 5-point scales. The questions record the degree to which the components of the CompleteCare process (arrangements for receiving the customer's computer through return of the repaired product) meet customers' *expectations.* A final categorical question asks whether customers will use CompleteCare again. Space for suggestions is provided.

Sample

The sample consisted of 175 customers who provided impressions of CompleteCare's effectiveness. For the four-week period, the response rate was 35 percent with no incentive given. Nothing is yet known about the differences between respondents and nonrespondents.

Service Improvement Grid

The grid on page three compares the degree to which expectations were met along with the *derived importance* of those expectations. The average scores for both axes determine the dividing lines for the four quadrants. The quadrants are labeled to identify actionable items and to highlight those that bear watching for improvement or deterioration.

The **Concentrate Efforts** quadrant is the area where customers are marginally satisfied with service but consider service issues important. Question 1a, "Call Center's responsiveness," Question 1b, "Call Center's technical competence," and Question 2a, "courier arrangements," are found here. "Technical competence" was similarly rated last month. Its perceived importance was rated higher in previous months. "Courier arrangements" has increased in perceived importance over previous reports.

The statistical technique for producing the grid is correlation. A modification of scatterplots was used to create a plot with reference lines (see Chapter 18).

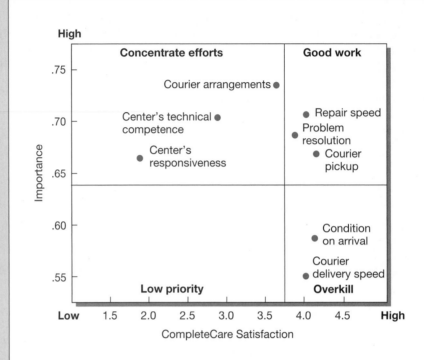

Note: Satisfaction scores are in the range of 1.0 to 5.0 and importance is in the range of 0 to 1.0.

The contents of each quadrant are described. Comparisons and connections to the next section are previewed.

In the **Good Work** quadrant, CompleteCare has, on average, *met all expectations* with the "repair speed" and "courier pickup" questions. Their mean scores are greater than 4.0 and considered important by respondents. "Problem resolution" has improved but remains a borderline concern.

There are no items in the **Low Priority** quadrant.

Overkill, the last quadrant, contains two questions. Question 5, "condition on arrival," has improved its ratings over last month but has dropped slightly on the importance scale because the average of importance scores (horizontal line) moved upward. Question 2c, "courier delivery speed," has a high satisfaction rating, but respondents considered this item to have lower importance than most issues in CompleteCare.

>**close**up**cont'd**

Detailed findings show the results of individual questions. This section announces the two-part content and presents, briefly and in a direct style, the most pertinent outcomes.

This graphic gives the reader a three-month view of all the questions at a glance. Vertical bars are the simplest and easiest to read for the amount of space allocated. Horizontal grid lines guide the eye from the bar tops to the closest value on the mean score axis.

Charts similar to these may be produced by the same spreadsheet that handles data entry. Charting programs offer other options and will import the data from spreadsheets.

Detailed Findings

The figures that follow provide (1) a comparison of the mean scores for each of the questions for the last three months and (2) individual question results. The latter contains frequencies for the scale values, percentages for each category, mean scores, standard deviations, and valid cases for each question. (See Appendix for question wording and placement.)

The three-month comparison (October, November, December) shows results for all scaled questions. December data bars (in dark blue) reveal improvements on all average scores (vertical axis) except Question 5, "condition on arrival." Most aspects of the service/repair process have shown improvement over the three-month period.

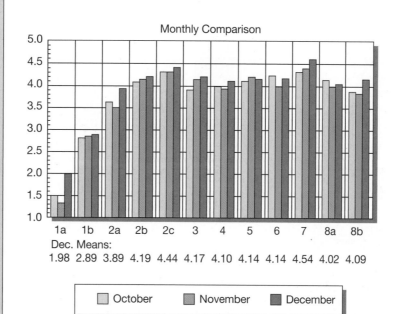

Monthly Comparison

Dec. Means:
1.98 2.89 3.89 4.19 4.44 4.17 4.10 4.14 4.14 4.54 4.02 4.09

October   November   December

The first individual item is reported with mean scores, percentages, and recommendations for improvement.

Question 1a. Call Center's Responsiveness. This question has the lowest mean score of the survey. Using a top-box method of reporting (combining the top two categories), 11 percent of the respondents felt that the Call Center met or exceeded their expectations for service responsiveness. This has improved only marginally since November and has significant implications for program targets. Based on our visit and recent results, we recommend that you begin immediately the contingency programs we discussed: additional training for Call Center operators and implementation of the proposed staffing plan.

This chart conveys the message of low responsiveness rather well but does not have a label for the vertical axis. It is easy to confuse percentages with the number of respondents (which it is supposed to represent).

Similar reporting formats are skipped.

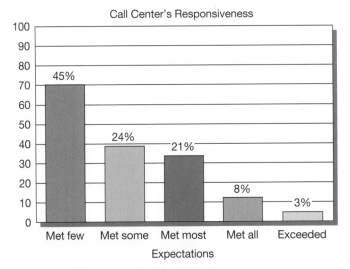

Call Center's Responsiveness

Met few	Met some	Met most	Met all	Exceeded
45%	24%	21%	8%	3%

Expectations

Mean score: 1.98   Standard deviation: 1.09   Valid cases: 159

>closeupcont'd

Question 6 shows the respondents' overall impression of CompleteCare. It would be an ideal dependent variable for a regression study in which questions 1 through 5 were the independent variables (see Chapters 18 and 19).

Question 6. Overall Impression of CompleteCare's Effectiveness. CompleteCare has increased the number of truly satisfied respondents with 46 percent (versus 43 percent in November) in the *exceeded expectations* category. The top-box score has increased to 75 percent of respondents (against 70 percent in November).

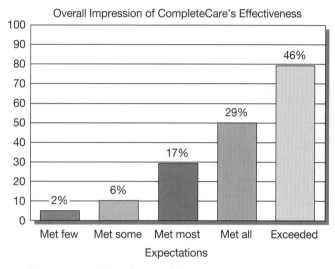

Overall Impression of CompleteCare's Effectiveness

Mean score: 4.14   Standard deviation: 0.98   Valid cases: 169

Question 8a is another question for more detailed research. It allows the researcher to connect the variables that describe the service/ repair experience with repurchase intentions.

Question 8a. Likelihood of Repurchasing MindWriter Based on Service/Repair Experience. Respondents' average scores (4.02) for this likelihood scale are the highest this month since measurement began. Improvement of the courier service's arrangements with customers and the resolution of the problem that prompted service appear to be the best predictors of repurchase at this time.

>**close**up**cont'd**

Using regression made it possible to identify two key influences for this question.

Question 8b (not shown) is similar, asking about the relation of product performance to repurchase intention.

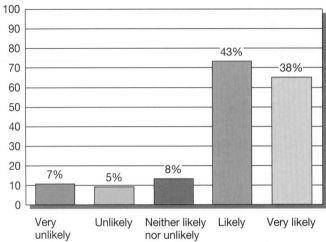

Likelihood of Repurchasing MindWriter
Based on Service/Repair Experience

Mean score: 4.02   Standard deviation: 1.10   Valid cases: 165

Patterns in the Open-Ended Questions

The questionnaire has one open-ended question that encourages respondents to make comments or suggestions.

Content analysis is used to distill the responses (see Chapter 15).

The following categories were found when the comments and suggestions were analyzed. The ratio of negative to positive comments was 1.7 to 1. Pickup problems continue to be "courier only" problems and coordination between MindWriter's telephone support and the courier. Customers complain of holding on the phone for long periods and being transferred between support people. Problems with service are split between large problems that have not been fixed and small, nuisance problems that customers are prepared to live with. Positive comments commend turnaround and service and also praise specific technical operators.

># **close**up**cont'd**

Although content analysis produces more than frequency counts of recurring themes, it is a labor-intensive process. The project's restrictive budget and the needs of the audience made this section of the report adequate for its purpose.

Negative Comments	Count
Shipping	19
Pickup problems (15)	
Delivery problems (2)	
Box damage (1)	
The courier charged customer (1)	
Call Center	19
Too long on hold (9)	
Transferred call too frequently/confusion (8)	
Untrained/hard to understand (2)	
Service	13
Problem continues (5)	
Small things not fixed/damaged (6)	
Took too long (2–7 weeks) (2)	
Product	6
Multiple repairs needed (3)	
Paint wears off (2)	
General dislike of product (1)	
Positive Comments	
General positive comment about the process	13
Quick response	12
Great service	7
Helpful phone personnel	6
Other Comments	
MindWriter shouldn't need to be repaired	4
Provide more information on what was done	2
Offer extended warranty	1
Won't use MindWriter Call Center again	1

>**close**up**cont'd**

This report's appendix contains a copy
of the questionnaire.

Appendix Contents
Sample Questionnaire

MindWriter personal computers offer you ease of use and maintenance. When you need service, we want you to rely on **CompleteCare,** wherever you may be. That's why we're asking you to take a moment to tell us how well we've served you.	Met **few** expectations 1	Met **some** expectations 2	Met **most** expectations 3	Met **all** expectations 4	**Exceeded** expectations 5

1. Telephone assistance with your problem:
   - a. Responsiveness — 1 2 3 4 5
   - b. Technical competence — 1 2 3 4 5
2. The courier service's effectiveness:
   - a. Arrangements — 1 2 3 4 5
   - b. Pickup speed — 1 2 3 4 5
   - c. Delivery speed — 1 2 3 4 5
3. Speed of the overall repair process. — 1 2 3 4 5
4. Resolution of the problem that prompted service/repair. — 1 2 3 4 5
5. Condition of your MindWriter on arrival. — 1 2 3 4 5
6. Overall impression of CompleteCare's effectiveness. — 1 2 3 4 5
7. Likelihood of using CompleteCare on another occasion.
   (**1 = very unlikely   3 = neither likely nor unlikely   5 = very likely**) — 1 2 3 4 5
8. Likelihood of repurchasing a MindWriter based on:
   (**1 = very unlikely   3 = neither likely nor unlikely   5 = very likely**)
   - a. Service/repair experience — 1 2 3 4 5
   - b. Product performance — 1 2 3 4 5

Comments/Suggestions: _____

_____

_____

How may we contact you to follow up on any problems you have experienced?

_____	_____	(_____) _____
Last Name	First Name	Phone

_____		
City	State	Zip

Service Code

Semitabular Presentation

When there are just a few figures, they may be taken from the text and listed. Lists of quantitative comparisons are much easier to read and understand than embedded statistics. The following is an example of a semitabular presentation is shown:

> Although Walmart regained the top spot in the Fortune 500, its performance shows signs of weakness in profitability.

- Walmart is the largest business in the Fortune 500 with sales increasing more than 11% over last year's performance.

- Oil giant and energy exploration leader ExxonMobil is the most profitable company in the Fortune 500 due to record crude oil prices increasing its profits to $39.5 billion, compared to $11.2 billion for Walmart.

- ExxonMobil's profits jumped 9% on a 2% increase in sales, while Walmart's profits increased a mere 0.5% on an 11% increase in sales.

- General Electric provided a 27.4% increase in profits on a 7.1% increase in sales, and outperformed Walmart on profits ($20.8 billion to $11.2 billion).

Tabular Presentation

Tables are generally superior to text for presenting statistics, although they should be accompanied by comments directing the reader's attention to important figures. Tables facilitate quantitative comparisons and provide a concise, efficient way to present numerical data.

Walmart regained its number one rank in 2007 by increasing its sales 11 percent over its prior year's sales. But it still trails in profitability.

How Walmart Compares	Rank	Revenues ($, millions)	Revenue Growth over Prior Year	Profits ($, millions)	Profit Growth over Prior Year
Walmart	1	$351,139.0	11.2%	11,284.0	0.5%
ExxonMobil	2	$347,254.0	2.2%	39,500.0	9.3%
General Electric	6	$168,307.0	7.1%	20,829.0	27.4%

Source: 2007 Forbes 500, http://money.cnn.com/magazines/fortune/fortune500/2007/.

Tables are either general or summary in nature. General tables tend to be large, complex, and detailed. They serve as the repository for the statistical findings of the study and are usually in the appendix of a research report.

Summary tables contain only a few key pieces of data closely related to a specific finding. To make them inviting to the reader (who often skips them), the table designer should omit unimportant details and collapse multiple classifications into composite measures that may be substituted for the original data.

Any table should contain enough information for the reader to understand its contents. The title should explain the subject of the table, how the data are classified, the time period, or other related matters. A subtitle is sometimes included under the title to explain something about the table; most often this is a statement of the measurement units in which the data are expressed. The contents of the columns should be clearly identified by the column heads, and the contents of the stub should do the same for the rows. The body of the table contains the data, while the footnotes contain any needed explanations. Footnotes should be identified by letters or symbols such as asterisks, rather than by numbers, to avoid confusion with data values. Finally, there should be a source note if the data do not come from your original research. Exhibit 20-5 illustrates the various parts of a table.

Graphics

Compared with tables, graphs show less information and often only approximate values. However, they are more often read and remembered than tables. Their great advantage is that they convey quantitative values and comparisons more readily than tables. With personal computer charting programs, you can easily turn a set of numbers into a chart or graph.

There are many different graphic forms. Exhibit 20-6 shows the most common ones and how they should be used. Statistical explanation charts such as boxplots, stem-and-leaf displays, and histograms were discussed in Chapter 16. Line graphs; area, pie, and bar charts; and pictographs and 3-D graphics receive additional attention here.

>**Exhibit 20-5** Sample Tabular Finding

Internet Access and Usage, Percent of Adults 18+			Have Internet Access				Title / Banner
	Total Adults	Any Online/ Internet Usage*	Home/ Work/ Other	Home	Work	Used the Internet in the last 30 days	Column Headers
	216,971	143,262	175,569	140,062	79,121	141,284	
Percent Distribution							
Men	48.2	48.0	48.3	49.1	49.4	48	
Women	51.8	52.0	51.7	50.9	50.6	52.0	
Education							
Graduated College Plus	25.2	35.1	29.9	34.4	46.3	35.4	
Attended College	27.2	33.1	30.5	31.8	31.3	33.3	
Did not Attend College	47.6	31.8	39.6	33.8	22.4	31.3	
Age							
Age 18-34	31.1	36.4	33.6	31.8	33.3	36.6	
Age 35-54	39.3	44.0	42.2	44.7	52.3	44.0	
Age 55+	29.6	19.7	24.2	23.5	14.4	19.4	
Employment							
Employed Full-time	52.9	62.7	58.4	60.6	87.1	63.0	
Employed Part-time	11.5	12.9	12.4	12.7	12.4	12.9	
Occupation							
Professional	13.3	19.0	16.1	18.4	31.1	19.3	
Mgmt./Bus/Finan./Ops.	9.5	13.1	11.4	12.8	20.8	13.2	
Sales/Office Occs.	16.1	20.9	18.7	19.0	29.3	21.0	
Nat. Res./Constr./Maint.	6.9	6.0	6.4	6.4	5.4	5.9	
Other Employed	18.6	16.7	18.1	16.7	13.9	16.5	
Household Income							
$150,000 or more	7.9	10.9	9.6	11.5	15.1	11.0	
$75,000–149,999	24.7	33.0	29.2	33.8	40.6	33.2	
$50,000–74,999	19.9	22.8	22.2	23.5	23.0	22.8	
Less than $50,000	47.5	33.3	39.1	31.1	21.3	33.0	
Marital Status							
Never Married	24.8	26.5	25.4	22.8	22.9	26.5	
Now Married	56.4	60.1	59.1	64.1	64.8	60.2	
Other	18.7	13.4	15.5	13.1	12.4	13.3	
Household Size							
1–2 Persons	46.6	41.9	43.2	41.0	41.1	41.8	
3–4 Persons	37.9	42.3	40.8	43.2	44.5	42.5	
5+ Persons	15.5	15.8	16	15.9	14.4	15.7	
Any Child in Household	41.1	45.6	44.2	45.0	48.1	45.7	

(Stub) (Body)

*Any online/Internet usage is net of those who looked at or used the Internet or any online service at home, work, or another place in the last 30 days. — Footnote

Source: MRI CyberStats, Spring 2006 (March 2005–May 2006) (http://www.siia.net/software/pubs/usage_06.pdf). Copyright 2006, Mediamark Research Inc. — Source Note

>Exhibit 20-6 Guide to Charts for Written Reports

For Components of a Whole or Frequency.

Pie Shows relationship of parts to the whole. Wedges are row values of data.

Exploded Pie Draws attention to critical component within the whole.

Simple Bar Places categories on the Y axis and amounts or percentages on the X axis.

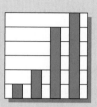

Simple Column Places categories on the X axis and amounts or percentages on the Y axis.

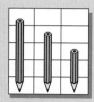

Pictograph Represents values as pictures; either bar or column.

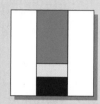

Stacked Bar Shows amounts of component variables; either bars or columns.

For Relationships or Comparisons

Bar Compares different entities on the same variable or component of a variable.

Bullet Bar Compares different entities on the same variable or component of a variable.

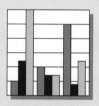

Column Compares different entities on the same variable or component of a variable.

Deviations (Bar or Column) Positions categories on X axis and values on Y axis. Deviations distinguish positive from negative values.

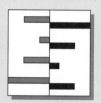

Mirror Image Bar Positions categories on Y axis and values on X axis as mirror images for different entities.

Area (surface) Like line chart, compares changing values but emphasizes relative value of each series.

Bubble Used to introduce third variable (dots of different sizes). Axes could be sales, profits; bubbles are assets.

Line Compares values over time to show changes in trends.

Filled Line Similar to line chart, but uses fill to highlight series.

Boxplots Displays distribution(s) and compares characteristics of shape (Chapter 17).

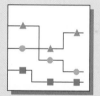

Step Compares discrete points on the value axis with vertical lines showing difference between points. Not for showing a trend.

Side-by-Side Stacked Bar Compares components of two or more items of interest.

Column with Line Item of most interest is presented in bars and compared to items represented by lines; categories on X axis and values on Y axis.

Stacked Pie Same as pie but displays two or more data series.

Multiple Pie Uses same data as stacked pie but plots separate pies for each column of data without stacking.

Scatter Shows if relationship between variables follows a pattern. May be used with one variable at different times.

Spider (and Radar) Radiating lines are categories; values are distances from center (shows multiple variables—e.g., performance, ratings, progress).

Line Graphs

Line graphs are used chiefly for time series and frequency distribution. There are several guidelines for designing a line graph:

- Put the time units or the independent variable on the horizontal axis.
- When showing more than one line, use different line types (solid, dashed, dotted, dash-dot) to enable the reader to easily distinguish among them.
- Try not to put more than four lines on one chart.
- Use a solid line for the primary data.

It is important to be aware of perceptual problems with line diagrams. The first is the use of a zero baseline. Since the length of the bar or distance above the baseline indicates the statistic, it is important that graphs give accurate visual impressions of values. A good way to achieve this is to include a zero baseline on the scale on which the curves are plotted. To set the base at some other value is to introduce a visual bias. This can be seen by comparing the visual impressions in parts A and B of Exhibit 20-7. Both are accurate plots of cable television systems in the United States from 1985 through 2007. In part A, however, using the baseline of zero places the curve well up on the chart and gives a better perception of the relation between the absolute size of cable systems and the changes on a five-year interval. The graph in part B, with a baseline at 35 million, can easily give the impression that the growth was at a more rapid rate. When space or other reasons dictate using shortened scales, the zero base point should still be used but with a break in the scale as shown in part C of Exhibit 20-7. This will warn the reader that the scale has been reduced.

The balance of size between vertical and horizontal scales also affects the reader's impression of the data. There is no single solution to this problem, but the results can be seen by comparing parts B and C in Exhibit 20-7. In part C, the horizontal scale is twice that in part B. This changes the slope of the curve, creating a different perception of growth rate.

>**Exhibit 20-7** Cable Subscribers, 1985–2007

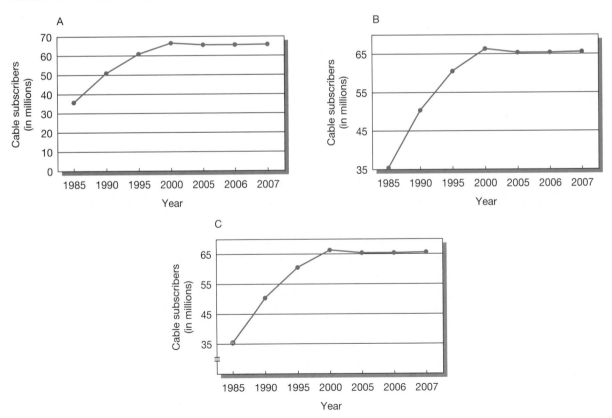

>**Exhibit 20-8** U.S. Truck Sales 1975–2005 (in thousands)

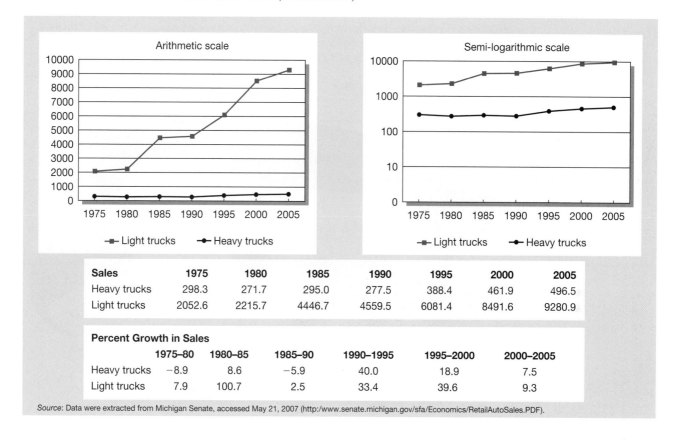

Sales	1975	1980	1985	1990	1995	2000	2005
Heavy trucks	298.3	271.7	295.0	277.5	388.4	461.9	496.5
Light trucks	2052.6	2215.7	4446.7	4559.5	6081.4	8491.6	9280.9

Percent Growth in Sales						
	1975–80	1980–85	1985–90	1990–1995	1995–2000	2000–2005
Heavy trucks	−8.9	8.6	−5.9	40.0	18.9	7.5
Light trucks	7.9	100.7	2.5	33.4	39.6	9.3

Source: Data were extracted from Michigan Senate, accessed May 21, 2007 (http://www.senate.michigan.gov/sfa/Economics/RetailAutoSales.PDF).

A third distortion with line diagrams occurs when relative and absolute changes among two or more sets of data are shown. In most charts, we use arithmetic scales, where each space unit has identical value. This shows the absolute differences between variables, as in part A of Exhibit 20-8, which presents the light-and heavy-truck sales in the United States from 1975 to 2005. This is an arithmetically correct way to present these data; but if we are interested in rates of growth, the visual impressions from a semi-logarithmic scale are more accurate. A semi-logarithmic scale uses a logarithm along one axis (usually the vertical or Y axis) and an arithmetic scale along the other axis (usually the horizontal or X axis). The Y axis shows quantity, and the X axis shows time. Arithmetic data are converted to natural logs by spreadsheet or statistical software and plotted. Semi-logarithmic graphics preserve percentage relationships across the scale.

A comparison of the line diagrams in parts A and B of Exhibit 20-8 shows how much difference a semi-logarithmic scale makes. Each is valuable, and each can be misleading. In part A, notice that sales of both light and heavy trucks have grown since 1970 but heavy-truck sales are only a small segment of U.S. sales of trucks and have a much flatter growth curve. One can even estimate what this proportion is. Part B gives insight into growth rates that are not clear from the arithmetic scale. It shows that while light trucks had a major growth spurt between 1980 and 1985, a spurt not shared by heavy trucks, since then their growth patterns have been more consistent with each other. From the calculated growth rate, in two of the last four five-year periods examined, the growth in heavy-truck sales actually exceeded the growth in light-truck sales, even while light-truck sales far exceeded heavy-truck sales.

Area (Stratum or Surface) Charts

An **area chart** is also used for a time series. Consisting of a line that has been divided into component parts, it is best used to show changes in patterns over time. The same rules apply to stratum charts as to line charts (see Exhibit 20-9).

>Exhibit 20-9 Examples of Area Charts: A Stratum Chart and Two Pies

Notice that the two pie charts seem to indicate a decrease in the "under 25" category relative to the stratum chart. The "under 25" category did in fact decrease (from 40 to 33 percent) but not as dramatically as the stratum to pie comparison would suggest. Also note that the sample size changed from 100 to 180 units between 1975 and 2005. It is important not to use a pie chart alone in a time series, to avoid giving erroneous impressions.

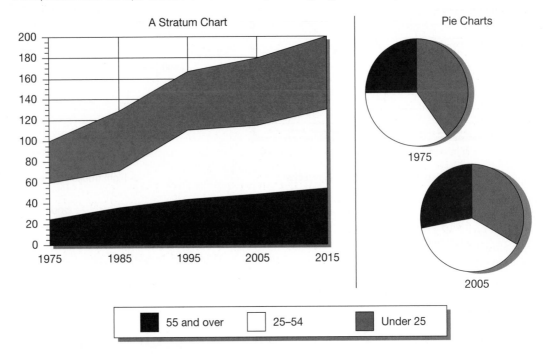

Pie Charts

Pie charts are another form of area chart. They are often used with business data. However, they can easily mislead the reader or be improperly prepared. Research shows that readers' perceptions of the percentages represented by the pie slices are consistently inaccurate.[9] Consider the following suggestions when designing pie charts:

- Show 100 percent of the subject being graphed.
- Always label the slices with "call-outs" and with the percentage or amount that is represented. This allows you to dispense with a legend.
- Put the largest slice at twelve o'clock and move clockwise in descending order.
- Use light colors for large slices, darker colors for smaller slices.
- In a pie chart of black and white slices, a single red one will command the most attention and be memorable. Use it to communicate your most important message.[10]
- Do not show evolution over time with pie charts as the only medium. Since pie charts always represent 100 percent, growth of the overall whole will not be recognized. If you must use a series of pie charts, complement them with an area chart.

As shown in Exhibit 20-9, pie charts portray frequency data in interesting ways. In addition, they can be stacked to show relationships between two sets of data.

Bar Charts

Bar charts can be very effective if properly constructed. Use the horizontal axis to represent time and the vertical axis to represent units or growth-related variables. Vertical bars are generally used for time series and for quantitative classifications. Horizontal bars are less often used. If neither variable is time-related, either format can be used. A computer charting program (e.g., Excel, the newest version of SPSS) easily generates charts. If you are preparing a bar chart by hand, leave space between the bars equal to at least half the width of the bar. An exception to this is the specialized chart—the histogram—in which continuous data are grouped into intervals for a frequency distribution (see Chapter 17). A second exception is the multiple-variable chart, in which more than one bar is located at a particular time segment. In this case, the space between the groups of bars is at least half the width of the group. Bar charts come in a variety of patterns. In Chapter 17, Exhibit 17-3 shows a standard vertical bar graph. Variations are illustrated in Exhibit 20-6.

Pictographs and Geographs

These graphics are used in popular magazines and newspapers because they are eye-catching and imaginative. *USA Today* and a host of imitators are often guilty of taking this to the extreme, creating graphs that are incomprehensible. A **pictograph** uses pictorial symbols (an oil drum for barrels of oil, a stick figure for numbers of employees, or a pine tree for amount of wood). The symbols represent data volume and are used instead of a bar in a bar-type chart. It is proper to stack same-size images to express more of a quantity and to show fractions of an image to show less. But altering the scale of the symbol produces problems. Since the pictures represent actual objects, doubling the size will increase the area of the symbol by four (and the volume by more). This misleads the reader into believing the increase is larger than it really is. The exception is a graphic that is easily substituted for a bar, such as the pencils in Exhibit 20-6.

Geographic charts use a portion of the world's map, in pictorial form, to show variations in regional data. They can be used for product sales, distribution status, media consumption, promotional response rates, per capita rates of consumption, demographics, or any of a number of other geographically specific variables.

Stacked data sets produce variables of interest that can be aligned on a common geographic referent. The resulting pictorial display allows the user to "drill" through the layers and visualize the relationships. With better Windows-based software and government agencies providing geo-codes and reference points, geographic spatial displays are becoming a more common form of graphic.

3-D Graphics

With current charting techniques, virtually all charts can now be made three-dimensional. Although a **3-D graphic** adds interest, it can also obscure data. Care must be used in selecting 3-D chart candidates (see Exhibit 20-10). Don't confuse pie and bar charts that have achieved dimensionality simply by adding depth to the graphics; this is not 3-D. A 3-D column chart allows you to compare three or

>**Exhibit 20-10** 3-D Charts

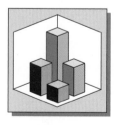  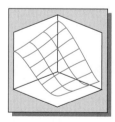 

3-D Column
A variation on column charts, they compare variables to each other or over time. Axes: X = categories, Y = series, Z = values. Other variations include 3-D area charts and connect-the-dots scatter charts.

3-D Ribbon This example is a one-wall plot showing columns of data (series) as ribbons. One or more columns are used. Axes: X = categories, Y = series, Z = values.

3-D Wireframe A variation of a contour or response surface; suitable for changes in time and multivariate data. Axes: X = categories, Y = series, Z = values.

3-D Surface Line Handles three columns of data and plots XYZ coordinates to show a response surface. Helpful for multivariate applications.

more variables from the sample in one bar chart–type graph. If you want to display several quarters of sales results for Hertz, Avis, Budget, and National, you have 3-D data. Surface charts and 3-D scatter charts are helpful for displaying complex data patterns if the underlying distributions are multivariate. Finally, be careful about converting line charts to ribbon charts, and area charts to 3-D area charts; these can be hard for a novice to read and your primary objective in graphical presentation is always data clarity.

>summary

1 A quality presentation of research findings can have an inordinate effect on a reader's or a listener's perceptions of a study's quality. Recognition of this fact should prompt a researcher to make a special effort to communicate skillfully and clearly.

2 Research reports contain findings, analysis, interpretations, conclusions, and sometimes recommendations. They may follow the short, informal format typical of memoranda and letters, or they may be longer and more complex. Long reports are of either a technical or a management type. In the former, the problem is presented and followed by the findings, conclusions, and recommendations. In the management report, the conclusions and recommendations precede the findings. The technical report is targeted at the technically trained reader; the management report is intended for the manager-client.

3 The writer of research reports should be guided by four questions:
   - What is the purpose of this report?
   - Who will read it?
   - What are the circumstances and limitations under which it is written?
   - How will the report be used?

   Reports should be clearly organized, physically inviting, and easy to read. Writers can achieve these goals if they are careful with mechanical details, writing style, and comprehensibility.

4 There is a special challenge to presenting statistical data. While some of these data may be incorporated in the text, most statistics should be placed in tables, charts, or graphs. The choice of a table, chart, or graph depends on the specific data and presentation purpose.

>keyterms

area chart 591	line graph 590	readability index 572
bar chart 592	management report 563	sentence outline 571
executive summary 566	pace 574	technical report 563
geographic chart 593	pictograph 593	3-D graphic 593
letter of transmittal 566	pie chart 592	topic outline 571

>discussionquestions

Terms in Review

1 Distinguish between the following:
   a Technical report and management report.
   b Topic outline and sentence outline.

Making Research Decisions

2 What should you do about each of these?
   a Putting information in a research report concerning the study's limitations.
   b The size and complexity of tables in a research report.

   c The physical presentation of a report.
   d Pace in your writing.

3 What type of report would you suggest be written in each of the following cases?
   a The president of the company has asked for a study of the company's pension plan and its comparison to the plans of other firms in the industry.
   b You have been asked to write up a marketing experiment, which you recently completed, for submission to the *Journal of Marketing Research*.

c Your division manager has asked you to prepare a fore-cast of promotional budget needs for the division for the next 12 months.

d The National Institutes of Health has given you a grant to study the relationship between advertising of prescription drugs and subsequent sales of those drugs.

4 There are a number of graphic presentation forms. Which would you recommend to show each of the following? Why?

a A comparison of changes in average annual per capita income for the United States and Japan from 1995 to 2010.

b The percentage composition of average family expenditure patterns, by the major types of expenditures, for families whose heads are under age 35 compared with families whose heads are 55 or older.

c A comparison of the changes in charitable giving between December 31, 2006, and December 31, 2010.

5 Use Exhibit 20-2 and plan the structure of your course project or of a research study you have read about in one of the Snapshots in this text.

6 Choose any case containing data from the text website and prepare a findings page, similar to the one in Exhibit 20-3.

From the Headlines

7 Executives at Warner Brothers believe that Ellen DeGeneres is the heir apparent to Oprah Winfrey in daytime TV. In a recent research report, the findings revealed that *The Ellen DeGeneres Show* was, for the first time, on par with *The Oprah Winfrey Show* in viewers' minds. Implementing the findings, Warner Brothers announced that NBC's 10 owned-and-operated stations would keep broadcasting DeGeneres's show through 2014.

The written report revealed that DeGeneres's hour-long show is upbeat and inspirational—traits that appeal to daytime's female audience; she is seen as relaxed and relatable; and she is more likable than Winfrey, according to the Q Scores Company. Even though the DeGeneres show lags behind the Winfrey show in the treasured Nielsen ratings, on emotional issues DeGeneres was in a virtual tie with Winfrey.

a What other questions should the report address?

b How would you advise the networks to "franchise" DeGeneres based on your study's results?

>cases*

Inquiring Minds Want to
Know—WOW!

 Ohio Lottery: Innovative Research
Design Drives Winning

Mastering Teacher Leadership

Proofpoint: Capitalizing on a
Reporter's Love of Statistics

NCRCC: Teeing Up and New
Strategic Direction

* You will find a description of each case in the Case Abstracts section of the textbook. Check the Case Index to determine whether a case provides data, the research instrument, video, or other supplementary material. Written cases are downloadable from the text website (www.mhhe.com/cooper11e). All video material and video cases are available from the Online Learning Center. The film reel icon indicates a video case or video material relevant to the case.

>chapter 21

Presenting Insights and Findings: Oral Presentations

>learningobjectives

After reading this chapter, you should understand . . .

1 How the oral research presentation differs from and is similar to traditional public speaking.

2 Why historical rhetorical theory has practical influence on business presentation skills in the 21st century.

3 How to plan for the research presentation.

4 The frameworks and patterns of organizing a presentation.

5 The uses and differences between the types of materials designed to support your points.

6 How proficiency in research presentations requires designing good visuals and knowing how use them effectively.

7 The importance of delivery to getting and holding the audience's attention.

8 Why practice is an essential ingredient to success and how to do it; and, what needs to be assembled and checked to be certain that arrangements for the occasion and venue are ready.

66 Thanks to the vast improvements in technology, the time is right for companies to include completely virtual meeting options as part of their overall meetings strategy. 99

Chris Gaia, vice president of marketing-travel division,

Maritz

Jason Henry and Sara Arens, partners in Henry & Associates, are just wrapping up a Web-based briefing on the MindWriter project. Jason and Sara are in Boca Raton, Florida. Myra Wines, MindWriter's director of consumer affairs is participating from Atlanta, as are others, including Jean-Claude Malraison, MindWriter's general manager, who joined from Delhi, India, and Gracie Uhura, MindWriter's marketing manager, and her staff, who joined from a conference room in their Austin, Texas, facility.

"Based on the poll results that are on your screen, you have reached a strong consensus on your first priority. The research strongly supports that you should be negotiating stronger courier contracts to address the in-transit damage issues. Congratulations," concluded Jason.

"That wraps up our briefing, today. Sara and I are happy to respond to any e-mail questions any of you might have after reading the summary report that has been delivered to your e-mail. Our e-mail address is on screen, and it is also on the cover of the report. Myra, I'm handing control of the meeting back to you."

As Myra started to conclude the meeting, Sara was holding up a sign in front of Jason that read. "Turn off your microphone." Jason gave a thumbs-up sign and clicked off his mic.

"Thank you, Jason," stated Myra. "The research has clarified some critical issues for us and you have helped us focus on some probable solutions. This concludes the meeting. I'll be following up soon with an e-mail that contains a link to the recorded archive of this presentation, allowing you to share it with your staff. You will also be asked to participate in a brief survey when you close the Web-presentation window. I'd really appreciate your taking the three minutes it will take to complete the survey. Thank you all for attending."

As soon as the audience audio was disconnected, Myra indicated, "That went well, Jason. The use of the Q&A tool to obtain their pre-report ideas for action was a stroke of genius. When you posted the results as a poll and had them indicate their first priority, they were all over the board. It helped them understand that one purpose of the research and today's meeting was to bring them all together."

"Sara gets the credit for that stroke of genius," claimed Jason after removing his microphone and clicking on his speakerphone. "She is a strong proponent of interaction in our briefings. And she continually invents new ways to get people involved and keep them engaged."

"Kudos, Sara," exclaimed Myra. "Who gets the credit for simplifying the monthly comparison chart?"

"Those honors actually go to our intern, Sammye Grayson," shared Sara. "I told her while it was a suitable graph for the written report; it was much too complex a visual for the presentation. She did a great job. I'll pass on your praise."

"Well," asked Myra, "where do we go from here?"

"Jason and I will field any questions for the next week from you or your staff," explained Sara. "Then we will consider this project complete—until you contact us again."

"About that," Myra paused, "I've just received an e-mail from Jean-Claude. He wants to meet with you both about a new project he has in mind. He asks if he could pick you up at the Boca airport on Friday, about 2:30 P.M. He says his flying office will have you back in time for an early dinner."

Sara looked at her BlackBerry and indicated she was available. Jason looked at his own calendar and smiled across the desk at Sara. "Tell Jean-Claude we'll meet him at the airport. Any idea what this new project is about?"

"Not a clue!"

> Introduction

Researchers frequently present their findings orally. Exhibit 21-1 introduces the process and indicates its fit with research process model.

A research presentation has some unique characteristics that distinguish it from other kinds of public speaking but with which it shares similarities. A small group of people is normally involved; statistics often constitute an important portion of the topic; the audience members are usually managers with an interest in the topic, but they want to hear only the data and conclusions that will help them make critical decisions; speaking time will often be as short as 20 minutes but may run longer than an hour; and

>**Exhibit 21-1** Oral Presentations and the Research Process

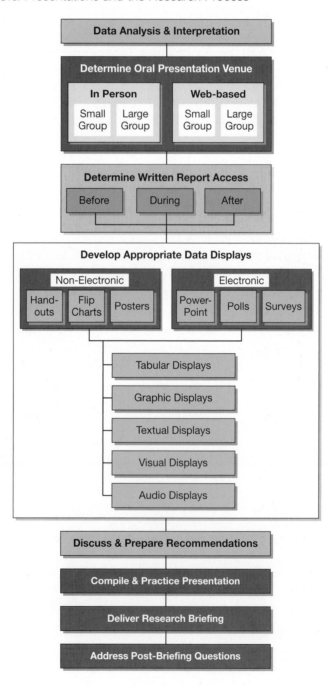

>**Exhibit 21-2** A Model for Presentation Planning

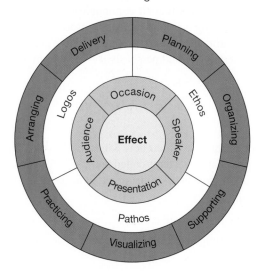

the presentation is normally interspersed with questions and discussion. In this chapter, we cover the essential ingredients for a successful presentation or briefing: how to plan, organize, support, visualize, deliver, practice, and arrange your presentation.

A successful presentation requires condensing a lengthy and complex body of information. Speaking rates should not exceed 100 to 150 words per minute; thus, a 20-minute presentation limits you to about 2,000 to 3,000 words. If you are to communicate effectively under such conditions, you must plan carefully. Begin by asking two questions. First, how long should you plan to talk? Usually the research sponsor indicates the acceptable presentation length. Following organizational custom, an organization may allot a given amount of time for such briefings. If the time is severely limited, then the need for topical priorities is obvious. This leads to the second question: What is the purpose? Is it to raise concern about problems that have been uncovered? Is it to add to the knowledge of audience members? Is it to give them conclusions and recommendations for their decision making? This chapter answers these questions and leads to a plan for your success. In Exhibit 21-2 you will note that the outer ring of the concentric circles coincides with the organization of this chapter. The next ring represents the type of proofs that are required in all presentations, as described by Aristotle. Finally, the dynamics of the speaker, speech, occasion, and audience lead to the effect that the presenter seeks.

> Aristotle's Three Principles of Persuasive Communication

Most readers recognize Aristotle as the authority who developed a comprehensive theory of rhetoric. Does a Greek philosopher, born in 384 BC, still have influence on business presentation skills in the 21st century? We think so. Aristotle considered rhetoric as the ability to see persuasive possibilities in every presentational situation and gave us a method to discover all the means of persuasion on any topic whatsoever. "Aristotle is important precisely because the rhetoric he taught was *inventional,* concerned with developing the best possible story, rather than aiming at being elegant, or ornamental, or passionate or beautiful or even at being a post-modernist rhetoric of giving voice to marginal people."[1] Aristotle's advice is as relevant today as during his time and should be the basis of developing and improving our presentational skills.

The basis of persuasion was defined by Aristotle with his three principles of proof: *ethos, pathos,* and *logos.* He associated communication with persuasion and identified communication as the ability to discover, in any given case, the available means to achieve persuasion.[2] If we think of persuasive discourse on a continuum from a conscious attempt to modify thinking to influencing the behavior and actions of the listener, then it is clear that all communication is persuasion, or at least includes a persuasive component. Understanding the communication process from this perspective seems more practical than artificially categorizing the types of presentations we give in business settings by purpose (informational, ceremonial, entertaining, and persuasive)—because more than one purpose is inevitably involved.

Ethos

Our perception of a presenter's character affects how believable or convincing we find that person. The projection of credibility via personal character is called the speaker's **ethos.** A strong research presentation relies on a researcher's ability to convince his or her audience of the following:

1. That he or she is credible.
2. That the findings from the research are credible.
3. That the audience should act upon the findings, as well as conclusions and recommendations drawn from these findings.

Ethos relies on how well the audience believes that the presenter is qualified to speak on the particular subject.[3] To inspire confidence in the speaker, Aristotle says that three things move us to belief apart from any proof: good sense, goodwill, and good moral character. Revealing these personal characteristics in your delivery can play a large role in gaining credibility for your ideas. People whose education, experience, and previous performance qualify them to speak on a certain issue earn the special extrinsic ethos of authority when their reputation is known ahead of time.[4] However, without prior experience, research presenters must borrow it by linking their methodology and procedures to credible sources with experience. In a culture where outward appearances have virtually taken over from the inner appeals of character (moral and intellectual), the appeal from *ethos* can be both problematic and advantageous.

Pathos

Rhetoricians over the centuries consider *pathos* the strongest of the appeals. **Pathos** relies on an emotional connection between the speaker and his or her audience. It involves an appeal to an audience's sense of identity, self-interest, and emotions. These appeals take advantage of common biases: we naturally move in the direction of what is advantageous, what serves our interests, or the interests of any group we are a part of.

People hear messages based on their state of mind. If their emotional disposition is positive, they are more likely to be receptive to the message; if it is negative, they will be less receptive to the message.[5] The research presenter must arouse emotions exactly because they have the power to modify the audience's predispositions and, thus, its judgments. Knowing the audience's predisposition (e.g., resistance or skepticism or receptivity) and predetermining a desired emotional response encourages the presenter to build the content and delivery of a presentation to stimulate a desired emotional state. Open-mindedness is the most important desired pre-presentation emotional state for any audience, and receptivity is the most desired post-presentation emotional state.

Logos

Finally, with **logos,** the logical argument, we find the explicit reasons that the speaker needs to support a position. This translates into supporting evidence and analytical techniques that reveal and uphold the researchers' findings and conclusions (described in more detail later in this chapter).

Appeals to *logos* most often use a variation of the syllogism called an enthymeme. The syllogism is a formal method of deductive reasoning (described in Chapter 3). You may recognize the **enthymeme** as a truncated syllogism where one or more minor premises are left unstated. This is done because people do not naturally speak in syllogistic form. The presenter gives the primary premise and expects

>**Exhibit 21-3** The Role of Aristotle's Proofs in Persuasive Communication

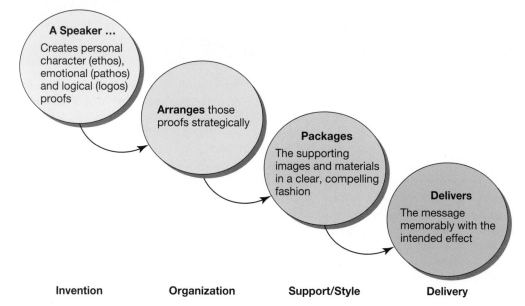

Source: Adapted from Raymie McKerrow, Bruce E. Gronbeck, Douglas Ehninger, and Alan H. Monroe, *Principles and Types of Speech,* 14th ed. (Boston, MA: Allyn & Bacon, 1999).

that the audience will supply the missing knowledge (premises) in order to reach the conclusion. In a research presentation, this planning is done in the audience analysis stage when estimating the audience's knowledge, predisposition, and attentiveness. However, most research presentations use the enthymeme to move from data to interpretations to conclusions. For example: "We do not have a sufficient advertising budget to improve consumers' perceptions of our second tier brand. The brand may falter and hinder our ability to remain competitive. We should divert resources to remain competitive."

Logos is the core of most research presentations; it is normally used to describe facts and findings that support the speaker's contentions about research results but it should not be the only content of the presentation. Since data are not likely to be manipulated by a trusted source, *logos* may sway cynical listeners. But, data can also be misleading, inaccurate, or unethically applied thereby eroding the goodwill and credibility previously established by the presenter. Researchers prone to build their presentations solely on *logos* reduce the likelihood that they will achieve their desired result—implementation of recommended actions inherent in the research findings. The role of Aristotle's three proofs is summarized in Exhibit 21-3.

> Plan

Where do we start to prepare for the research presentation? This is the dilemma faced by beginners and seasoned experts. Perhaps the more pertinent question is *how* do we start? From a Zen perspective, if we start from a beginner's mind we can see things more clearly, enthusiastically, and unburdened by fixed views. As Garr Reynolds, in *Presentation Zen,* advises, "If your state of mind is coming from a place of fear and risk avoidance, then you will always settle for the safe solutions—the solutions already applied many times before."[6] Some research companies use templates that can be modified for specific presentations. But if multiple presentations are made to the same audience of managers using such a template, presentations may fail to hold attention and communicate persuasively. Thus, an attitude of openness produces a fresh approach to planning your presentation.

Authors with similar viewpoints ask us to consider spending most of our time in thinking, sketching, and scripting. We are counseled to have a story to tell before even thinking of opening PowerPoint, and have a 90-to-1 ratio of preparation to delivery time; in other words, plan in analog. Planning in analog involves all the things we should do outside the digital domain. A three-step process,

The Culture of Reporting

One of the few universally followed rules in presenting research results is to craft the message to fit the client. When the Team One/Lexus team ventured to Japan to share their early research findings, they knew they had to deliver any negatives with a polite, highly sensitive approach. The news was good. But to engineers who had crafted the Lexus SC 430 to be twice as good as the Jaguar XK8— more comfortable, quieter, and easier to handle— some of the findings would be puzzling. The team had held three static product clinics—where more than 250 luxury buyers were assembled to compare, but not drive, the Lexus SC 430 and its competitors. Shortly thereafter they had conducted numerous focus groups of the top tier of these interested luxury buyers, known as acceptors. Among the early findings the team learned that buyers expected the car to growl when the accelerator was depressed, to show exhaust, and to handle more like a sports car, "Culturally, Japanese engineers have come to see themselves— and with justification—as entitled to make a car the way a car should be made," shared Arian Barrow, account manager for Lexus at Team One Advertising. This made telling them what they would consider negatives somewhat difficult. For example, buyers' expectations were that the car would zoom from zero to 60 in under five seconds, not arrive there in eight or nine seconds. "So we found ourselves sharing results in a less hard-hitting way than we would with a different client." How did they deliver the unexpected news? "People loved the car! But they would love it even more if it would go from zero to 60 in five seconds!"

www.teamoneadv.com; www.lexus.com.

writing–sketching–producing requires us to plot the story like a movie script. Using paper and pen to sketch ideas in the analog world leads to greater creativity and clarity for the finished product.[7] The consultant behind Al Gore's global warming documentary, *An Inconvenient Truth,* suggests that the speaker should plan to spend as much as 90 hours to create a 1-hour presentation containing 30 slides.[8] Our general checklist, which starts the planning process with five critical W's, accentuates the audience's role in the planning process.

- Who makes up the audience?
- What do they want to learn about?
- Why is this presentation occurring and how does it connect to the larger picture?
- When will the presentation take place and what are the time-of-day considerations?
- Where will the presentation take place—including nature of the venue and travel?[9]

Audience Analysis[10]

You have already noticed that most of these questions are audience-centered. So, let's look at some ways we can analyze the audience more effectively. First, good speakers understand that the primary purpose of their presentation is to gain a desired response from their listeners. The ultimate success of their presentation depends on the speaker's ability to anticipate audience response. An analysis of the expected attendees at a presentation or **audience analysis** is accomplished by keeping three questions in mind:

1. Who will I be addressing?
2. Why should my listeners really care about the information I present?
3. What do I want the audience to know, believe, and or do because of my presentation?

The answers to these first two questions help develop the *pathos* of your presentation. Your most important understanding about audiences is that they are egocentric; they pay attention to messages that affect them directly. Their mantra is "Why should I care?" Elements of *pathos* can be discovered by collecting past impressions from prior associations; interviewing critical members of the intended audience; or, often less feasibly, surveying a sample of the invitees regarding agreement with a series of statements about issues (to determine predispositions).[11] The answers to the third question help develop the *logos* of your presentation. Your research findings represent the core of the *logos* of your presentation.

Answers to these questions come from understanding the psychology of the audience. Several psychological principles have important implications for speakers.

- An audience member comes to the presentation venue with past knowledge of the speaker's topic and will judge the presentation based on selective perception (what they know and believe).

- As the audience listens to the speech and hears threads of information consistent with accumulated knowledge, their processed meanings will fluctuate between agreement/disagreement and clarity/confusion.

- As the speaker addresses an audience, he or she must attempt to imaginatively construct how the audience will interpret the message.

- Each audience member organizes his or her unique construct of the content presented, which is dependent on listener experience and openness to change.[12]

Demographic and dispositional audience characteristics also play an important role in assessing the answer to the first question. Audience composition in business now reflects a different mix than that of a few years ago. Speakers must adapt to the age of the group because generational similarities in experience and value affect receptivity. Gender can have a strong influence on audience response. In a multicultural and multiracial society, every audience will have a slightly different response to the speaker—just as religious views and cultural sensitivity need to be considered in a more narrow range of business situations. Finally, education, economic status, position in the organization, and group membership provide additional clues as to interest and attitude. The remote audience for a presentation (using Web services to present and connect) requires more, not less analysis, as the presenter has to work doubly hard to establish and maintain a connection.

The second question considers the disposition of the audience and their needs and attitudes. Targeting your presentation to fulfill appropriate needs differentiates successful presentations from those that fail. Knowing the needs of key audience members either through informal, advance conversations with the sponsor or psychological profiling can be critical to success. For example, once known, you are able to tailor your presentation to such need orientations as physiological, knowledge, social, or ego. And, you can have a good idea about the predispositions of decision makers regarding the importance they attach to achievement, status, career, recognition, or adherence to organizational norms.

General features of the presentation situation and unique features of the audience are also considerations of audience analysis. What is the physical setting of the presentation? The room size, seating arrangement, and temperature will all affect listeners. A large audience size may require a more formal presentation, or affect your language choice and visual aides. Presenting to an individual or a small group may dictate an informal briefing rather than a formal presentation. Although we will cover staging and arrangements in a later section, the audience affects these issues and should be part of your analysis. In Exhibit 21-4, we pose seven important questions to help you understand the nature of your audience.

Types of Learners

In planning for your presentation, it is wise to also consider that the audience is composed of three types of learners; the proportionate composition of learner types will vary based on topic and age group. Speakers can make an emotional connection with their audiences to the extent that they recognize the differences among visual, auditory, and kinesthetic learners. Audience members are more likely to act on information they have a connection with, but they cannot connect with anything that they have not internalized.

- **Visual learners.** About 40 percent of us are visual learners, people who learn through seeing. This group retains information that is highly visual. To address visual learners, avoid cramming too much text on visual aids. Build aids that have few words and key dominant images. As many visual aids used in research presentations employ graphs and charts, research presentations already appeal to visual learners. Visual learners connect through visual imagery.

>Exhibit 21-4 Seven Questions to Understand Your Audience

❶	**Who are they?**	Demographics and psychographics are a great start, but connecting with your audience means understanding them on a personal level.
❷	**Why are they here?**	Why did they come to hear you? Are they willing participants or mandatory attendees? What do they think they're going to get out of this presentation?
❸	**What keeps them up at night?**	Everyone has a fear, a pain point. Let your audience know you empathize— and offer a solution.
❹	**Why should they care?**	What's in it for the audience? How are you going to make their lives better?
❺	**What do you want them to do?**	Make sure there's clear action for your audience to take.
❻	**Should you expect resistance?**	What will keep them from adopting your message and carrying out your call to action?
❼	**How can you best reach them?**	People vary in how they prefer to receive information. This can include everything from the setup of the room to the availability of materials after the presentation. Give the audience what they want, how they want it.

Source: Adapted from Nancy Duarte, *slide:ology: The Art and Science of Creating Great Presentations.* (Sebastopol, CA: O'Reilly Media, 2008), p. 15.

- **Auditory learners.** Auditory learners represent about 20 to 30 percent of your audience. These people learn through listening and benefit from verbal and rhetorical techniques. Tell personal stories or use vivid examples to support your key messages. Research presenters can incorporate actual participant experiences related during the research to enrich the presentation for this type of listener. Auditory learners connect through stories.
- **Kinesthetic learners.** These people learn by doing, moving, and touching. In short, they are "hands-on." They get bored listening for long periods. Including activities in your presentation keeps kinesthetic listeners engaged. Pass around objects (as Steve Jobs did with the aluminum frame of a new laptop), conduct writing exercises, or have them participate in demonstrations.[13] Research presenters can use examples of the types of exercises used with research participants, showcasing how research data were collected, to make a methodology come alive for this type of listener. Kinesthetic learners connect through activities.

Keep Your Audience from Checking Out

The ability for an audience to recall critical information and to avoid boredom is not, but should be, factored into the planning of presenters. There is experimental support for the finding that recall accuracy varies as a function of an item's position on a list or an argument's sequence, referred to as the Audience Memory Curve[14] and otherwise known as the *serial position effect.* When asked to recall a list of items in any order (free recall), people recall best those items they hear at the end of the list (**recency effect**). Items at the end of the list seem to reside in short-term memory at the time of recall. Among earlier list items, or arguments, the first item in a list is initially distinguished as important (**primacy effect**) and may be transferred to long-term memory by the time of recall. The first few items are recalled more frequently than those in the middle of the presentation.[15] The implication for research presenters is that arguments presented first or last will be highly influential to understanding and motivation to act.

Once thought of as a "20-minute fatigue factor," audiences are now believed to become bored in 10 minutes—not 11 but 10.[16] According to recent research in molecular biology, the brain appears to be making choices according to a timing pattern influenced by genetics and environment.[17] Research presenters should observe the **10-minute rule** by varying their content by interspersing straight talk with graphs, videos, demonstrations, questions, and other means that allow the brain to seek new stimuli.

As technology advances, the Internet has become a medium for oral presentations and videoconferences. As with other presentations, you need to be cautious with equipment and look for software glitches. Have a backup copy of your presentation on your laptop or your company's server. Test your external mouse as well as the one that is connected to your computer. Be certain that your screensavers are disabled. And most important, be prepared to give your presentation even if the technology fails.

Planning and the Web-Delivered Presentation

With travel budgets reduced, managers interested in research projects often located in far-flung parts of the world, and the advance of Web-based technologies, web-delivered presentations are increasing. A **Web-delivered presentation** involves the use of a Web presentation platform (e.g., Live Meeting, WebEx, etc.), a presenter who remotely controls the delivery of the presentation visual aids to the audience's computer while he or she speaks to the audience via computer or a controlled-access phone line, and an invited audience who participates via the Web from their office or a Web-equipped room. The presentation platform builds in various participation opportunities—most notably the ability of the audience to type in questions throughout the presentation and the ability of the presenter to respond to questions, or to use intermittent survey questions to poll the audience on their understanding of material or their consensus on a conclusion or recommendation. Some platforms offer the ability of audience members to ask questions of the presenter through a phone connection. Most presentations can be archived for later viewing, but without the opportunity to participate. The biggest problems in planning for a Web-delivered presentation are the lower level of audience rapport affecting the pathos of the presentation and the longer time frame needed for planning, as is noted in Exhibit 21-5. Such a presentation format does, however, permit the audience to be large and offers built-in processes for pre-contact (all attendees must register, which is useful for audience analysis) and follow-up (useful for determining the effectiveness of the presentation). Web-delivered research presentations often use post-presentation surveys to query the audience's understanding, solicit additional questions, and deliver copies of the written report. These are actions the face-to-face presentation does not often duplicate.

We close this section with a quote from noted presenter Nancy Duarte that reminds us of the need to treat your audience as your first priority: "They didn't come to your presentation to see you. They came to find out what you can do for them. Success means giving them a reason for taking their time, providing content that resonates, and ensuring that it's clear what they are to do."[18]

> Organize

Presentations have an organizational structure. Without a framework, it is difficult to visualize and organize your content and impossible for an audience to follow and understand you. In this section, we review a variety of organizational strategies.

The research literature on speech organization covers (1) optimal order of arguments, (2) one-sided versus two-sided arguments, and (3) the effects of organized versus disorganized messages. Studies, however, do not support the conclusion of one overall superior method for organizing. Instead, presentations are organized into many patterns and tailored to the speaker, content, audience, occasion and venue, and intended effect. The pattern you choose will depend upon the purpose of your presentation.

>Exhibit 21-5 Timeline for a Web-Based Oral Research Presentation

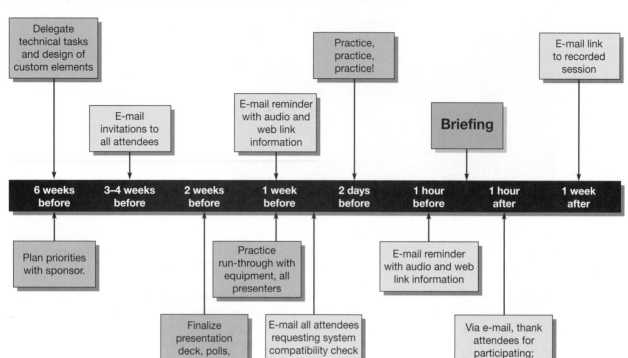

Traditional Patterns of Organization

- *Topical:* there are several ideas to present, but one idea seems naturally to precede the others in order. In a research presentation on survey research, the presenter could organize according to topical areas of the questionnaire.

- *Spatial:* material is organized by physical space. In a research presentation about skiing accidents in Colorado resorts, the presentation might be arranged by each specific ski area within Colorado.

- *Classification:* puts ideas, objects, or arguments into categories. In a presentation about what potential customers revealed in testing prototype iPads, the order of the presentation would be arranged by iPad features.

- *Climax order:* material is organized from the least important information to the most important. In a research presentation, elements are ordered to lead from the foundation findings to the key finding to the recommended solution.

- *Problem/solution:* first part of a speech describes a problem, the middle presents research findings, and the second presents a solution. In research presentations, you start with the management problem, proceed to the research problem and methodology, and conclude with the findings and recommendations.

- *Chronological:* uses time sequence for a framework. In a research presentation on plant safety issues, the order would be determined by when each research activity (focus group, survey, experiment) occurred.

- *Past/present/future:* first part section discusses the past, the second the covers the present, and the third predicts the future. In a research presentation using predictive modeling of inventory patterns, the organization starts with the data patterns of the past, then the present, then models the future.

- *Cause/effect/solution:* first part describes the cause of a problem, the second describes its effect, and the third presents a solution. In a research presentation about the effectiveness of Toyota's solution for accelerator pedal malfunction, the presentation starts with the discovery of the engineering defect, describes the effect on sales, brand image, and customer loyalty; then presents information on what research discovered about solutions which might resonate with the auto-buying public.

- *Pros/cons/recommendation:* benefits, disadvantages, how benefits are superior are discussed. In a research presentation, what the researcher discovered about benefits of e-books, their perceived disadvantages, and what Amazon might do to enhance the advantage of the Kindle DX would be presented.

- *Research briefing:* a **research briefing** is another term for the oral presentation; it starts with a brief statement that sets the stage for the body of the findings and explains the nature of the project, how it came about, and what it attempted to do. This is followed by a discussion of the findings that support it. Where appropriate, recommendations are stated in the third stage.

The Motivated Sequence Organization

One specialized pattern of organization applicable to all types of presentations is called the **motivated sequence** and is defined as "the sequence of ideas which, by following the normal processes of human thinking, motivates an audience to respond to the speaker's purpose."[19] The rationale, based on psychological principles, requires that the structure be designed to correspond to the way people habitually arrive at a decision despite individual differences. It consists of five steps:

- *Attention:* draw attention to the need for change.
- *Need:* call for change in existing conditions by creating dissatisfaction with them.
- *Satisfaction:* satisfy the need or address the dissatisfaction with an explanation, logical demonstration, or practical experience, or plan to meet objections.
- *Visualization:* picture the benefits the proposed action will bring.
- *Action:* detailed recommendation of what is needed to bring about the specified action.

When research presentations are designed to be persuasive rather than merely informative, this organization is powerful because it has as its goal stimulating overt action. In presentations that are more informative in nature, steps can be modified or deleted.

The Narrative Organization

The narrative pattern of presentation, or what is called *narrative imaging* by cognitive psychologists, is discussed in greater detail in the context of "stories" in the next section. The **narrative pattern** is an organizational framework that involves the use of stories as the primary vehicle for communicating the presenter's message.

We recognize that narration of stories alone may be the *sole organizing mechanism* for a presentation. Later in this chapter, you will see how a single story may be woven into the presentation as one means of supporting a point. A legend in the speech communication field once remarked, "The only possible way you can undermine a conviction is to tell a story with a point. . . . [it will be effective] when no other type of discourse can begin to do the job—argument won't do it, description can't do it, exposition won't do it. Narration is the only thing that can . . . tell a story. People will listen to stories."[20] In his book, Reynolds reminds us that we are "wired" to tell and listen to stories from the time we were kids. Unfortunately, the use of stories in business became marginalized as synonymous with fiction.[21] The story's resurrection with speakers such as Steve Jobs of Apple, Howard Schultz of Starbucks, and John Chambers of Cisco Systems not only makes it a credible tool but opens opportunities for new presenters to observe how the "pros" use it effectively. See the elements for constructing a story in Exhibit 21-6.

>**Exhibit 21-6** Constructing a Story

Story telling is a time-honored technique of engaging audiences. Author Cliff Atkins, in his book *Beyond Bullet Points,* suggests crafting such stories as three-act plays. Here is his format translated for a research project and its oral presentation.

- Act I: Sets up the key story elements: setting, characters, conflict, desired outcome

Affinity Bases for Athletic Alumni	
Presenter:	
Act I: Set up the story	
The Setting	Indicate the problem or stimuli that led to the research in *full sentence form using active tense, using conversational tone, limiting sentence length.* "It's important today for colleges to connect with their alumni."
The Protagonist	The protagonist is your audience, always. "Campus-wide efforts in fund raising need to enhance and maintain affinity."
The Imbalance	Define what is no longer as it used to be . . . why is audience here? "Economic and cultural conditions threaten donations."
The Balance	What do we want to see happen? "Customized affinity programs generate stronger alumni donations."
The Solution	How do we get there from here? "Use annual online surveys to discover an understanding of affinity connectors with athletic alumni and other alumni groups."

- Act II: Develops the conflict through actions and reactions of the characters in response to changing conditions

Act II: Develop the Action		
5-Minute Column:	**15-Minute Column:**	**45-Minute Column:**
Some of the things we do don't strengthen affinity.	Exhibit 1	Quote from … Quote from … Quote from …
	Exhibit 2	Quote from … Quote from … Quote from …
Athletic alumni affinity should be consistent across sports.	Exhibit 3	Quote from … Quote from … Quote from …
	Exhibit 4	Quote from … Quote from … Quote from …
Some new ideas to strengthen athletic alumni affinity.	Exhibit 5	Quote from … Quote from … Quote from …
	Exhibit 6	Quote from … Quote from …
	Exhibit 7	Quote from …
Turning Point	We can do things differently and affect contributions.	

> **Exhibit 21-6** Constructing a Story (*Continued*)

- Act III: ends the story, frames the resolution (climax and decision), reveals something about his/her character

Act III: Frame the Resolution	
The crisis	If we don't continually discover what motivates affinity, donations will continue to be stagnant or decline.
The solution	Use online surveys to discover an understanding of affinity connectors with athletic alumni and other alumni groups.
The climax	Survey results reveal we should change everything we do—from reunion weekends to logo merchandise in the bookstore and online.
The resolution	Customize an affinity program for each major alumni segment.

Research evidence on the effectiveness of the narrative organization versus the motivated sequence organization is informative. While the motivated sequence produces superior immediate recall, the narrative pattern of organization results in significantly more favorable attitudes toward the presentation and the speaker and may contribute to long-term recall.[22]

The Rule of Three and the Three-Point Speech

In the list of traditional patterns of organization, described at the beginning of this section, the last five examples used trios, triplets, or triads—the **rule of three.** This rhetorical device abounds in Western culture across many disciplines. It is found in religion (Three Wise Men with their *gold, frankincense, and myrrh*), movies *(Sex, Lies, and Videotape),* nursery rhymes *(Three Little Pigs* or *Goldilocks and the Three Bears),* government *(Executive, Judicial, and Legislative),* mottos (Fire safety: *Stop, Drop, and Roll*), and memorable speeches from Julius Caesar to Barack Obama *("We must pick ourselves up, dust ourselves off, and begin again the work of remaking America").*[23] The favorite metaphor of a three-act play is a proven formula and extensively used in storytelling and screenwriting. By applying the rule of three as an organizing device, one is able to use any form of support, including narration. The result is that your presentation "gains warmth, familiarity, and understandability. With the three-part outline framing your ideas, your speech will be easier to follow and remember."[24]

Is there empirical support for the rule? In 1956, Bell Labs scientist George Miller summarized studies that showed that individuals have difficulty retaining more than seven to nine digits in short-term memory.[25] Recent studies put the number closer to three or four; that is, working memory has a capacity of about four chunks in young adults and somewhat less in children and older adults.[26] It is, therefore, no coincidence that Steve Jobs outlines a "roadmap" for his audience that is almost always divided into three sets: a product description with three features or a demonstration in three parts.[27]

There are many variations on the **three-point speech** in addition to the ones listed earlier; some of which you are already familiar: introduction–body–conclusion; tell them what you are going to tell them–tell them–then tell them what you told them (overview–body–recap); introduction–three best supporting points–conclusion; surprising introduction–three stories (each with points)–a memorable conclusion tying the stories together. Good advice about the power of repetition as a speech construction technique is offered by Dlugan: "Take inspiration from Lewis Carroll in *The Hunting of the Snark*: 'I have said it thrice: What I tell you three times is true.'"[28]

> Support

Supporting materials are the leaves on the branches of your organizational framework. After selecting an organizational strategy, your efforts center on compiling supporting materials to develop and validate the points you are presenting for your listener's consideration or action. In a research presentation, this not only means the actual data and its interpretation but also the stories or demonstrations that

>Exhibit 21-7 A Checklist for Better Supporting Material

☐ **Relevant** — Each piece of support should be relevant to the point it is supporting and consistent with the topical theme.

☐ **Appropriate** — Each item of support should fit the needs and style of the receivers, meet the demands of that particular audience, and fit the occasion.

☐ **Believable** — The material must be accurate, ethically sourced, and fairly presented.

☐ **Timely** — The material must be workable within time limits.

☐ **Variety** — The presentation should not rely excessively on one type of support, but should instead use a number of different forms of support.

☐ **Balanced** — The presentation should include adequate amount of support but show a balance between quantity and variety, while not overburdening the case.

☐ **Speaker Specific** — The material should be selected to enhance the speaker's style of delivery as well as the message.

☐ **Stylistic** — The presentation should benefit from the power of analogies and metaphors.

☐ **Simplicity** — The presentation's statistics should be conveyed in understandable terms or through comparisons.

☐ **Detail** — Each piece of support needs to be developed to the point that audience members can understand and visualize how the item fits the point it is used for.

Source: Adapted from Thomas Leech, *How to Prepare, Stage, and Deliver Winning Presentations* (New York: AMACOM, 2004), pp. 98–102; and the Speech Department at Maui Community College, http://www.hawaii.edu/mauispeech/html/supporting_materials.html, downloaded January 27, 2010.

corroborate the data. Supporting materials create interest, clarify the presenter's point, provide emphasis to a point, and offer proof that results in belief. Without supporting materials, an oral presentation is nothing more than a series of claims without evidence. See the checklist in Exhibit 21-7 for criteria you may use to evaluate your own materials.

The following list presents examples of frequently used materials for supporting your presentation's arguments:

- **Facts** are verifiable data about situations that exist or events that are known to have occurred. Facts often involve statistical data that can be demonstrated to be true. If true, they are not in dispute and thus provide powerful backing. Facts are the foundation of many research presentations.

- **Statistics** are numerical data used in the collection, analysis, and interpretation of data, but also found in data collection planning, measurement, and design. Statistics are useful and expected for research presentations. To be a credible source of support, the listener needs to know if a statistic is valid and reliable, used correctly, properly interpreted, and relevant to the point. Statistics used sparingly reduce audience fatigue. Visuals are essential in research presentations to facilitate understanding of statistics.

- **Specific instance** refers to a single and often critical incident selected to prove an overarching claim whereby specifics are translated into more general principles. These are brief rather than detailed stories. An instance used in the research presentation of a survey might relate the responses of an individual respondent.

- **Examples** include a single instance used to clarify a complex concept. These are often less developed than a specific instance but have a similar advantage of helping listeners visualize the point. Examples may be true or hypothetical; the latter make use of a fictitious situation. In a research presentation, an example might relate the impact of a recommended action based on the responses of a single respondent or group of respondents.

- **Testimony/Expert opinion** is the perspective of recognized experts on a topic. Experts project credibility with your audience when used properly on the topic with which they have expertise. When used as testimonials, opinions of credible third-party endorsers allow the audience to absorb success stories. This is often in the form of a video clip, a quote, or participation of a recognized expert. These opinions represent an excellent source of support because they enhance *ethos*.

- **Analogy** is the use of reasoning or is used to explain parallel cases; it is a comparison between two different things to highlight a point of similarity. An analogy is not offered as conclusive proof for an argument, but a good analogy may be useful to clarify the argument or presenter's position.

   Greek philosophers Plato and Aristotle had a wider view of analogy. They saw it as a *shared abstraction*.[29] They believed analogous objects did not share necessarily a relation, but an idea, pattern, regularity, an attribute, an effect, or a function; for example, "Being obsessed with deficit reduction when the economy has suffered its largest setback since the Depression is like being obsessed with water conservation when your house is on fire—an admirable impulse, poorly timed."[30]

- **Metaphor** is an implicit comparison between two unlike things that actually have something important in common. A metaphor expresses the unfamiliar in terms of the familiar, achieving its effect via association, comparison, and resemblance. Metaphors "carry" meaning from one word, image, or idea to another. Students know that when Dr. Gregory House (in the TV series *House, M.D.*) says, "I'm a night owl, Wilson's an early bird. We're different species," he's speaking metaphorically.[31]

   Despite similarities, an analogy is not the same as a metaphor. The analogy "is a figure of language that expresses a set of like relationships among two sets of terms. In essence, the analogy does not claim total identification, which is the property of the metaphor. It claims a *similarity* of relationships."[32]

Conveying Personal Experience through Stories

In the previous section we introduced the power of the narrative form of organizing; now we emphasize individual stories *as a specific type of supporting material*. **Stories** tell the particulars of an act or occurrence or course of events. They are most powerful when involving personal experience. "Stories are who we are, and we are our stories. Good stories have interesting, clear beginnings; provocative, engaging content in the middle; and a clear conclusion."[33]

Personal experience, especially in a research presentation, links your topic to the audience and helps them connect with you. In a presentation, describing your experience with the study lends a real-life impression that cannot be achieved through facts or statistics. A personal experience helps the audience create a natural, emotional response.

Examples from your world are more powerful than those you borrow. They are easier to remember and deliver because of their familiarity. Work, home, travel, or daily encounters provide a rich set of experiences and also some of the most humorous anecdotes. Professors often use self-effacing humor because students see themselves mirrored in our weaknesses. They are also some of the most memorable lessons for students (see Exhibit 21-8).

Take the example of Steve Jobs's 2005 Commencement Address at Stanford University, where he used the rule of three to convey three personal anecdotes about himself: "connecting the dots, love and loss, and a story about death." By also finding a way to inject humor into a very serious subject, he created a memorable speech and one that is still frequently watched on YouTube.[34] But more important than the humor was that his story was authentic; it was from his gut and his heart. Unlike his other performances, this one was from a manuscript, yet his stories were not memorized because they were real to him and consequently real to the students and families in attendance.

Demonstrations

A good **demonstration** teaches. It is a variation of speech with informative intent using visual aids. It appeals to visual and kinesthetic learners, especially if there is an opportunity to handle the object. In a research presentation, the audience, through listening, watching, or participating, learns something new. It may be showing a new design for corporate identity or demonstrating a product that has resulted

>Exhibit 21-8 Ten Steps to a Good Story

1. Use audience analysis to match the story to your audience and topic.
2. Select language that reflects the characteristics of the audience.
3. Center your story on a point and state that point clearly.
4. Use the story as a mechanism to show passion and excitement about your topic.
5. Learn your stories. If you forget an element, be prepared to improvise and go on.
6. True facts from your life are far superior to someone else's story.
7. Keep humorous stories short to capture the punch line quickly.
8. Write the story out to eliminate needless diversions and unnecessary wordiness.
9. Use the principle of "tweets"—140 characters or less—to keep your sentences dramatic and punchy.
10. Emphasize adjectives and verbs to make your stories sound more vivid.

Source: Adapted from Advanced Public Speaking Institute, "Public Speaking Storytelling Do's," downloaded January 15, 2010 (http://www.public-speaking.org/public-speaking-storydo-article.htm).

from your research. As the audience's guide, you will take them through a *show and tell* process, revealing each step from start to finish. In presenting marketing and advertising research, a good demo informs your audience about your product, shows the benefits of ownership, and inspires them to take action.[35] Here is an example of the criteria for a great demonstration using an iPhone 3G:

- *Short:* The EDGE versus 3G demo was less than two minutes.
- *Simple:* Showed two websites loading on a smartphone.
- *Sweet:* A head-to-head comparison of 3G with competitor EDGE.
- *Swift:* Kept the demo moving but remained silent at key points to build drama.
- *Substantial:* Demo resolved the problem of waiting for graphically rich sites to load.[36]

> Visualize

Proficiency in your research presentation requires the ability to create good visuals and know how to use them. Because visuals are so fundamental to business presentations, we use the graphics concept of *visualization* to present the material in this section.

Eighty percent of the information humans receive comes through their eyes. For technical information, like research presentations, this number is probably higher.[37] Rick Altman, author of *Why Most PowerPoint Presentations Suck* and host of the PowerPoint Live User Conference, believes the real culprit of visually poor presentations is presenters who organize their thoughts with PowerPoint or other design software rather than away from the computer.[38]

15 The percent of reduced information that is delivered verbally when using a Power-Point presentation.

Edward Tufte, the guru of displaying quantitative information says, "The PowerPoint style routinely disrupts, dominates, and trivializes content."[39] Another author in this chorus urges presenters to remember that there are three parts of a presentation: slides, notes, and handouts. Remember the difference between take-away documents (handouts) and slides. An attempt to merge the two results in what Reynolds calls "slideuments"—or badly detailed PowerPoint documents masquerading as slides. Presentations constructed this way result in the presenter supplying the verbal content of a document ineffectually because the audience reads faster than he or she can speak.[40]

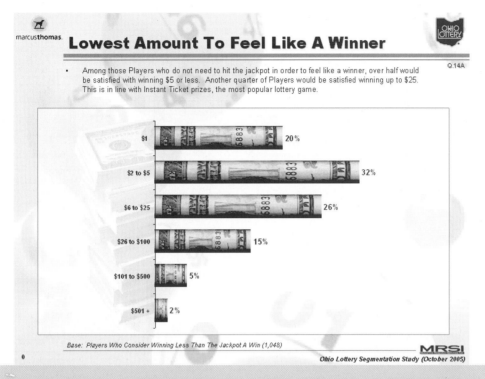

Psychological and Physical Foundations[41]

In his book *Clear and to the Point*, author Stephen Kosslyn argues that audience members of any presentation "should not have to search through a visual or conceptual haystack to find the needle you are talking about." Thus the process of **visualization** involves developing and organizing support materials that help the audience share in your understanding of the data. The composition and knowledge of the audience, the venue, and amount of time all influence choices in visualization.

Several psychological principles influence your audience's understanding of your findings. The **principle of relevance** infers that only information critical to understanding should be presented. Information that is presented verbally along with visual support will be perceived as more relevant than that mentioned only verbally without visual support. But the principle also indicates that we do not want to overwhelm the audience with too much information.

In the process of exploring your data, prior to developing a research presentation, you developed numerous tables, graphs, and textual summaries. Not all of these support materials, whether you use handouts, flip charts, or slides, can or should be used in most presentations due to time constraints. Any limitations in your audience's knowledge level (**principle of appropriate knowledge**) or their inability to process large amounts of information at one time (**principle of capacity limitations**) reduces the complexity of your support. In your attempt to share an understanding of the data, some support materials—for example, graphing techniques like box plots with which your audience may be unfamiliar—may instead create confusion or obscure the points you are trying to convey. A familiar visualization technique—a bar or column chart or table—would always convey information more quickly than an unfamiliar one. However, you can design even appropriate and familiar techniques in too complex a fashion by including unnecessary information. Your audience, after all, has only moments to digest visually what you may have been studying for days or weeks. Exhibit 21-9 summarizes data graphing techniques that are appropriate for oral presentations.

>Exhibit 21-9 Graph Selection for Oral Presentations

For components of a whole or frequency.

Pie: Shows relationship of parts to the whole. Wedges are row values of data.

Exploded Pie: Draws attention to critical component within the whole.

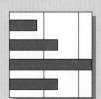

Simple Bar: Places categories on the Y axis and amounts or percentages on the X axis.

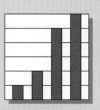

Simple Column: Places categories on the X axis and amounts or percentages on the Y axis.

Pictograph: Represents values as pictures; either bar or column.

For relationship or comparisons

Stacked Bar: Shows amounts of component variables; either bars or columns.

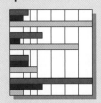

Bar: Compares different entities on the same variable or component of a variable.

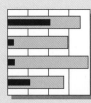

Bullet Bar: Compares different entities on the same variable or component of a variable.

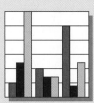

Column: Compares different entities on the same variable or component of a variable.

Mirror Image Bar: Positions categories on Y axis and values on X axis as mirror images for different entities.

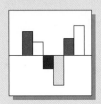

Deviations (Bar or Column): Positions categories on X axis and values on Y axis. Deviations distinguish positive from negative values.

Pareto Diagram: Item of interest is presented in bars and compared to aggregate represented by lines.

Side-by-Side Stacked Bar: Compares components of two or more items of interest.

Multiple Pie: Uses same data as stacked pie but plots separate pies for each column of data without stacking.

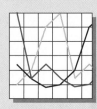

Line: Compares values over time to show changes in trends.

Scatter with Trend Line: Shows if pattern exist for a variable; X axis and values on Y axis.

Multiple Item Scatter: Multiple items are represented by different lines, with distinct markers for values; categories on X axis and values on Y axis.

Bubble: Used to introduce third variable (dots of different sizes). Axes could be sales, profits; bubbles are assets.

According to the **principle of informative changes,** your audience will expect anything you speak about or show in your presentation to convey important information. Therefore, it is critical for your presentation to convey what is new or a change with a separate slide or handout, a new property presented on a slide or handout (e.g., flow aid change), or a new design format. Demonstrations or exercises relate to this principle; your audience will automatically pay more attention when you do something different to convey new information.

Several additional psychological principles should also influence the visualization of your presentation.

- **Principle of salience.** Your audience's attention is drawn to large perceptible differences. Thus you should choose charting and graphing techniques that naturally showcase such differences. An exploding pie or a bar chart can often serve this purpose.

- **Principle of discriminability.** Two properties must differ by a large amount to be discerned. This means that if an important difference exists in your data but the difference is not large enough to be visually discernable, you must use techniques—a single highlight color, a supersized component, or breakouts—for the item that is important. You should also note whether the difference presented is statistically significant in order to establish importance.

- **Principle of perceptual organization.** Your audience will automatically group items together, even if you do not give them such groupings. This is a mechanism they use to allow them to absorb and store large amounts of information. Thus, if you are trying to establish associations or correlations between key findings, your support materials should group themselves (in your organization plan, put them in proximity to each other or put them together with the same flow aid) and title them as a group.

Design Principles

In addition to selecting the right visual elements to convey your findings and conclusions, overriding concepts should guide the design of visual support materials.[42] All are achieved by what Reynolds describes as "careful reduction of the nonessential"[43]—give the audience only what they need to understand your findings and conclusions, not everything you used to reach that level of understanding. Ideas reduced to their most simplistic tend to "stick" in the mind of the audience.[44]

Using the collective ideas of Reynolds, Duarte, Kosslyn, and Altman, several principles and guidelines for powerful visual design emerge:[45]

- **Visual preparation**. The presenter should conceptualize the visual support materials on paper before composing the digital versions.
  - A storyboard of slides, digital-camera documents, flip-chart ideas, or handouts allows the presenter to visually plot their argument and choose the appropriate visualization techniques.
  - Paper or sticky notes can be used to storyboard a presentation.
- **Flow aids.** Visual techniques, such as those shown in Exhibit 21-10, convey to the audience where the presenter is within the overall presentation.
  - Arrow or other flow symbols or diagrams are good at denoting location and direction within the presentation.
  - Images and diagrams should point toward slide content or center, not to the area beyond the screen.
  - Most animations draw attention away from the message incorporated into the support material; use animations sparingly.
  - Animation within charts (building a chart in PowerPoint or on a flip chart) can draw audience attention to a desired element.
- **Visibility.** The audience should be able to see the visual aids.
  - The bigger the room, the more likely you will need to use electronic visual aids.
  - Even small rooms need large visual aids to be seen.
  - The greater the distance between the audience and the visual aid, the larger the text and visual size you will need.

>Exhibit 21-10 Flow Aids for Structuring Presentations

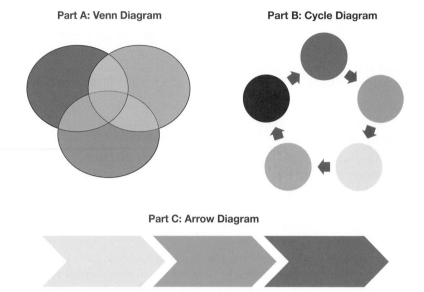

Part A: Venn Diagram

Part B: Cycle Diagram

Part C: Arrow Diagram

- A screen should be at least as wide as one-sixth of the distance between the screen and the farthest viewer from the screen.
- Individual copies of support materials can replace the need for supersizing your visual aids.
- **Whitespace.** Leave empty, uncluttered space surrounding important key visuals and text.
  - The audience should be able to achieve a visual focus.
  - Fewer but more compelling visual elements on each slide help achieve focus.
  - Bulleted keywords or phrases rather than sentences on a slide help achieve focus.
- **Picture supremacy.** According to research findings, graphics and photographic images are more memorable than text and oral presentation.[46] In one study, 10 percent of information presented orally was remembered 72 hours after presentation, with an increase to 65 percent if a picture was inserted.
  - Add pictures and reduce text to improve impact.
  - Allow pictures to dominate research presentations that are less statistical.
  - When using photographs, select situations that happen in real life; realism is appreciated by the audience more than staged images.
- **Photographic framing.** Create a focal point for all visuals.
  - By dividing a viewfinder by the **rule of thirds,** photographers compose their shots with real or imaginary cross-hairs that divide the field of view into thirds, vertically and horizontally. The cross-hairs form nine cells with four intersecting crossing points. These crossing points, also called *power points,* may be used to line up the image, creating a balanced, arresting visual, as well as a photograph.
  - The focal point of the image is off center—leaving whitespace around the visual.
  - Visual elements seem to present a better and more artistic sense of balance and flow.
  - The primary object is not on center, thereby avoiding predictability and redundancy and attracting attention.
- **Contrast.** Use high contrast to quickly draw audience attention to the main point.
  - Busy backgrounds detract from text and images or graphs.
  - Choosing high-contrast colors (e.g., black on white, black on yellow, red on white) for text, data, and background or colors on charts enhances readability and denotes change.
  - Highlighting text in a list or numbers on a table creates more contrast than dimming out elements you want to recede.

- By varying the thickness of a line, you add to its contrast.
- By adding color to an element, you add to its contrast.
- Using too many colors for graph elements diminishes contrast; highlight what helps make your point.

- **Compatibility.** The form of the message should be compatible with its content and the meaning of that content.
  - Organizational graphics can convey the overall presentation structure or illustrate sequences of steps.
  - Maps can be used to show location related information.
  - Data graphs can be used to reveal relative amounts.
  - Pie graphs and exploding pie graphs are used to show approximate, not absolute, proportions.
  - Tables convey impressions of relative amounts.
  - Line graphs can be used to convey trends over time.
  - Step graphs illustrate trends among two or more entities that vary along a noncontinuous scale.
  - Adjusting the size of elements (e.g., width of bars in bar chart or step graph) does not convey precise quantities.
  - An image or picture should be consistent with what it represents in a pictograph.
  - Photos or clipart can be used to define context, introduce abstract ideas, evoke emotion, or represent a finding or a conclusion.

- **Relationship.** The audience should be able to see the relationships between elements and sense what information goes together.
  - The presentation organization structure should make the hierarchy obvious.
  - Plotting different types of data in the same display only conveys meaning if the two are highly related.
  - Plotting two types of data when they are unrelated on the same graph to serves to confuse or clutter.
  - Keeping X and Y axis titles the same in comparative graphs facilitates the ability to see relationships.
  - Headers, titles, and colors can be used to group items.
  - Organizational diagrams that overlap, cluster elements, or radiate connecting elements can be used to group items.
  - Decreasing the space between bars or other graphing elements makes them easier for the audience to group in their mind.

- **Simplicity.** Reduce clutter and use only the information and visual techniques necessary to convey the data, idea, or conclusion (see Exhibit 21-11).
  - Only familiar graphs, symbols, images, and jargon should be used to enhance the transition of information.
  - Only the part of a graph that makes your point should be used.
  - Numerical labels are only necessary on graphs if precision is important.
  - Graph legends should be eliminated if element labels are used.
  - Background grids (horizontal or vertical) should be removed if value labels are used.
  - Graphic or pictorial backgrounds make quick understanding of a graph impossible by providing too much visual stimulation.
  - Graphical elements (wedges in a pie, bars on a chart) should be arranged in a simple progression (most to least, least to most), and this arrangement should be used consistently from graph to graph.
  - Corresponding bars, from graph to graph, should be marked in the same way (same color, same order).
  - Graphics or images should always help make the presenter's point or direct the audience's attention, not be included solely for appearance.
  - Numbered lists should be used to convey order; bulleted lists can be used when no order is implied.
  - Unnecessary borders (around legends, titles, axis titles) separate, rather than unify, elements.

>Exhibit 21-11 Simplifying Visuals

Part A

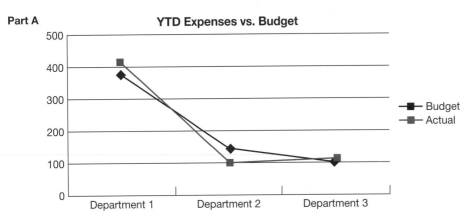

Inappropriate technique because departments are not related. Line graphs are most effectively used to show trends over time, not relationships at a point in time.

Part B

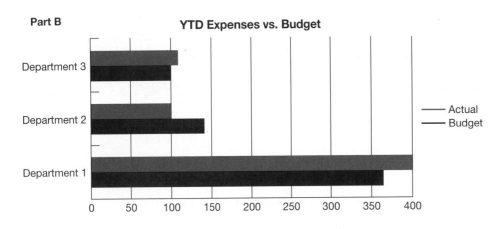

Appropriate technique, but differences do not stand out as quickly due to need for Department 1's bars to be on the same plane as Department 2 and Department 3, which have smaller budgets.

Part C

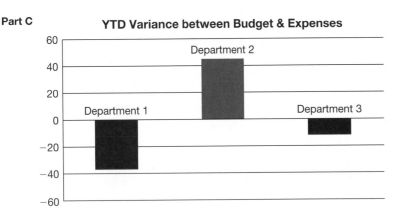

Appropriate technique and the differences—which departments are exceeding their budgets (Departments 1, 3) and which aren't (Department 2)—are quickly discerned, both by the chart type and by the color that separates the positive from the negative.

- **Clarity.** The audience should be able to perceive meaning from the location of elements. Simplicity leads to clarity and is obtained by reducing nonessential elements. Find balance between communicating too many research findings and being too simple. In general, however, think in terms of subtracting not adding.
  - Larger elements will be perceived to be more important than smaller ones.
  - Elements with color will be perceived as more important than those without color.
  - Fewer bullet points improve understanding.
  - Support materials should attach desired interpretation or meaning to data.
  - Mixed-media displays (e.g., bar graph overlaid with a line graph) are difficult to interpret during a presentation because different media do not form simple visual patterns.

>**Exhibit 21-12** Prescriptions for Better Slides

Rx for Better Slides
• Low word count.
• Slideuments defeat you.
• Keep it simple.
• The 10–20–30 rule.
• Font size = oldest age ÷ 2

Source: Based on an example from Nancy Duarte, *slide:ology: The Art and Science of Creating Great Presentations* (Sebastopol, CA: O'Reilly Media, 2008), p. 151.

Prescriptions for Better Slides

In summary, let us review some simple ideas for getting and holding your audience's attention (see Exhibit 21-12). Go for a very low word count on your slides. The default template for PowerPoint promotes a two-level title and numerous subpoints. This is a *slideument,* which defeats the presentation's purpose; therefore, consider using a title only. Then heed the bullet law: if you have to use bullets at all, use them in moderation, and remember they should represent keywords or brief headlines only. Sentences should be discouraged because they take your audience's attention away from the speaker while they read the sentence. Slide titles should be no more than one sentence (or a 140-character, memorable, Twitter-like statement). As Einstein said, "Everything should be as simple as possible but not simpler." Language and visuals that are simple to parse by the audience are memorable.

Use the good sense design ideas presented earlier to compose your slide. Venture capitalist, author, and noted public speaker Guy Kawasaki also promotes the idea that presenters always need to simplify their message. After being the audience for numerous funding proposals by entrepreneurs, he developed his *10–20–30 rule:* use no more than 10 slides, no more than 20 minutes (even if you have been allotted more time), and never use text on a slide smaller than 30 points.[47] Finding a good font is an art because each creates its own impression: serious or playful. But, finding its proper size is common sense: (1) not smaller than 30 points; (2) put your slides in the sorter option and view them at 66 percent—"if you can still read them, so can your audience"[48]; and (3) divide the oldest audience member's age by 2 and use that font size.[49] Following these suggestions, as shown in Exhibit 21-12 will lead to simpler visuals.

> Deliver

Although the content of a presentation is a major priority, how the speaker delivers the message is very important. A polished presentation adds to the receptiveness of the audience, but there is always danger that style may overpower the message. Fortunately, the typical research audience knows why it is assembled, has a high level of interest, and does not need to be entertained. Even so, the speaker faces a real challenge in communicating effectively. In research presentations, the delivery should be more restrained than in those that seek action or behavioral change. Demeanor, posture, dress, and total appearance should be appropriate for the occasion. Speed of speech, clarity of enunciation, pauses, and gestures all play a part. Voice pitch, tone quality, and inflections are proper subjects for concern. Rapport-developing techniques are essential so that the speaker can get and hold the audience's attention.

Modes of Delivery

What will be the mechanism by which you communicate your message to the audience? Will your presentation be memorized, read from a manuscript, or given extemporaneously? We rule out the impromptu briefing because **impromptu speaking** does not involve preparation. Your reputation and the research effort should not be jeopardized by "winging it."

Memorization is a risky and time-consuming course to follow. Any memory slip during the presentation can be a catastrophe, and the delivery sounds stilted and distant. Memorization virtually precludes establishing rapport with the audience members and adapting to their reactions while you speak. It produces a self- or speaker-centered syndrome and is not recommended.

Manuscript reading is also not advisable. The verbatim delivery of a presentation script sounds dull and lifeless because most people are not trained to read aloud, and therefore they do it badly. They become focused on the manuscript to the exclusion of the audience. This heads-down preoccupation with the text is clearly inappropriate for research presentations. If you are a trained reader with access to a teleprompter, this mode might work for you; most researchers do not have the skill or the equipment for such delivery.

The **extemporaneous presentation** is audience-centered and made from minimal notes. This mode permits the speaker to be natural, conversational, and flexible. Clearly, it is the best choice for an organizational setting. Preparation for this mode consists of writing a draft along with a complete sentence outline and converting the main points to notes. In this way, you can try lines of argument, experiment with various supporting materials, and develop memorable phraseology. Along the way, the main points are fixed sequentially in your mind, and supporting connections are made.

Scripts and Notes

Ditch the script! Manuscripts are often required for ceremonial speeches but are inappropriate for the majority of business presentations. They have no place in research presentations where audience members want to engage in information exchange, not to be read to. Imagine the audience asking itself why they should not be conversing with the person who wrote the script rather than the one who is reading it poorly to them.

Scripts are important in the planning phase but should be shelved by the time you get to practice. Here are one author's suggestions for evolving from ideation and organizing to becoming scriptless:

- Write the script in full sentences in the notes section of PowerPoint—no more than four to five sentences.
- Do not script every word; just rework your material removing filler words from sentences, leaving only key words.
- Highlight key words and use them without regard to details to get key points into memory.
- Memorize the one key idea for each slide: ask, "What is my audience's take-home message from this slide?"
- Practice the presentation without notes using the slide's keywords, graph, or visual as the prompter.[50]

Audiences accept **speaker note cards,** and their presence does wonders in allaying speaker fear. Even if you never use them, they are there for psychological support. Many prefer to use cards for their briefing notes. Card contents vary widely, but here are some general guidelines for their design:

- Place preliminary remarks on the first card.
- Use the remaining cards to carry a major section of the presentation. The amount of detail depends on the need for precision and the speaker's memory but should not become a mini-manuscript containing, for example, the details of supporting information.
- If using PowerPoint, match cards to slides.
- Include keywords and phrases, illustrations, statistics, dates, and a pronunciation guide for difficult words. Include quotations and ideas that bear repeating.
- Along the margin, place instructions or cues, such as SLOW, FAST, EMPHASIZE, SLIDE, TURN CHART, and BACK TO CHART 3.
- Sequentially number your cards or notes, so you can return them quickly to order if they are accidentally shuffled.

>Exhibit 21-13 Using Key Word Prompts as a Substitute for Notes

Key Word – Number	Presentation Script
22,000 jobs	The estimated number of jobs generated between 2003 and 2008 in preparation for the Vancouver Winter Games
2,500 athletes	About 2,500 athletes competed in the Vancouver Games
258 athletes	The number of athletes from 16 nations that competed in 1924 at the first Winter Olympic Games in Chamonix, France
67.8 mph skier	Antoine Deneriaz's average speed; winner of the men's downhill in 2006 at Torino, Italy
$1 million bonus	The amount of money Speedo gave Michael Phelps as a bonus after the Beijing Olympics for tying Mark Spitz's gold medal record

Source: Material adapted from "By the Numbers: The Olympics," *Sky* (January 2010), p. 25; www.deltaskymag.com.

When cards are not suited to the occasion, you might consider the example in Exhibit 21-13, which uses the previous advice on how a slide's keyword can serve as the prompter. In this example, the speaker is presenting, among other things, numerical information on the Winter Olympics in Vancouver, British Columbia.

Details Make a Difference

"Success is in the details" is our variation on German-born architect Ludwig Mies van der Rohe's (1886–1969) attributed remark that "God is in the details." In this section, we provide examples from often overlooked features of a presentation in a search for insights from the details.

Clutter

Careful language usage leads to clarity of your presentation and helps to establish one aspect of *ethos*, competence. **Clutter** in a speech includes repetition of fillers such as "ah," "um," "you know," "like," "basically," or "exactly." Clutter in a research presentation gives the impression of hesitancy and lack of competence. Caroline Kennedy was reported by *Time* to have botched her first interview with the New York press with "ums" and "you knows," cluttering the landscape of her comments with 144 "you knows" in an 8,500-word transcript.

> Asked to justify her candidacy—after days spent with handlers advising her on how to fill Hillary Clinton's vacant New York Senate seat—she began in a dull monotone: "Um, this is a fairly unique moment both in our, you know, in our country's history, and, and in, in, you know, my own life, and um, you know, we are facing, you know, unbelievable challenges, our economy, you know, healthcare, people are losing their jobs here in New York obviously um, arh, you know . . ."[51]

Jargon

Jargon, language specific to a profession or academic discipline, is considered meaningless and generally unintelligible to people outside of that group. Using jargon is a particular danger in delivery of a research presentation where your audience may not be schooled in the techniques of research or of statistical analysis. Jargon adds clumsy language and reduces the simplicity of the message, ultimately confusing all but the insiders to the "code." Jargon often needs to be defined for the audience.

Unfortunately, you often learn of this only at the end of the presentation when questions are asked and you learn that several key points eluded the audience due to the jargon you embedded in your presentation. There are many types of business jargon or buzz words (see BuzzWhack.com) to avoid; here are a few examples:[52]

Jargon	Clearer Meaning	Jargon	Clearer Meaning
conceptualize	imagine	output	results
downsizing	laying off	parameters	limits
infrastructure	framework	strategize	plan
interface	talk with	utilization	use
operational	working	viable	possible

Nonverbal Communication

Nonverbal communication is meaning conveyed through other than verbal means; it encompasses clothing and bodily characteristics, physical environment (physical space and time), movement and body position (including kinesics, posture, gesture, touch), eye gaze, and paralanguage (nonverbal cues of the voice).

Nonverbal, a significant component of the speaker's presentation, represents approximately 50 to 60 percent of communication meaning. Some studies cite as high as 93 percent. Nonverbal communication is a complex medium that can regulate the pace of your presentation, may be ambiguous, is sometimes more believable than verbal communication, and reinforces or contradicts the spoken message. Albert Mehrabian found a 7–38–55 rule, supposedly reflecting the percentages of how much communication was attributed to words, tone, and body language. Mehrabian's research showed that the receiver will accept the dominant form of communication, nonverbal (38 percent + 55 percent), rather than the literal meaning of the words (7 percent) under conditions where a communicator is talking about their feelings or attitudes.[53]

While a researcher making a presentation can use nonverbal communication to his or her advantage, it is equally important that he or she minimize distracting or contradictory nonverbal messages that interfere with achieving the purpose of the presentation. The complexity of this topic is such that we can only focus on four admonitions for the presenter.

- **Eye contact.** Do you focus above people's heads or on a wall when you present? Lack of eye contact is particularly bothersome to listeners and is common with inexperienced presenters. An important aspect of interpersonal communication is eye contact, which can also help regulate the flow of communication with your audience. The frequency of eye contact with the audience helps to establish rapport and comfort, thereby increasing the speaker's approachability. Presenters who make eye contact show concern, warmth, and authenticity. If you find eye contact difficult, practice using the drama coaches' advice: scan the room slowly, tracing an X or Z with your eyes, but varying the pattern size to avoid looking predictable. Stop and look at individuals long enough to communicate with them personally before moving on to another.

- **Gestures.** If you do not gesture while speaking, you may be perceived as unanimated, especially if you keep your hands at your sides. A speaking style that is animated and lively gains audience attention, facilitates learning, and makes your content more interesting. If you think consciously about your gestures, you are likely to gesture too late and as a result you will look stiff, awkward, and coached. In addition to hand gestures, facial expression (particularly smiling) is a powerful cue that transmits happiness, friendliness, warmth, liking, and affiliation. When you smile often, you will be perceived as more friendly, warm, and approachable. Luckily for the research presenter, gesturing to visual aids is almost mandatory and gets you started in the right direction. But a caution, you can overgesture in a presentation, distracting the audience with your body language.

- **Posture and body orientation.** You communicate numerous messages by the way you walk and stand. Standing erect, but not rigid, and leaning slightly forward communicates that you are approachable, receptive, engaged, and friendly. Interpersonal closeness results when you and your audience face each other and nothing blocks the audience's view, such as a lectern. Speaking with your back turned or looking too long at a slide communicates disinterest. In some rooms, there is too much distance between you and your audience. To offset this, moving about the room increases interaction with your audience. Proximity enables you to make better eye contact and reveals your confidence. A research presenter needs to know what is on his or her visual aids so that the aid does not demand his or her full attention; the audience should have that.

- **Paralanguage.** This facet of nonverbal communication includes such vocal elements as tone, pitch, rhythm, pause, timbre, loudness, and inflection. Practice varying these seven elements of your voice. One of the major criticisms is of presenters is speaking in a monotone. The audience perceives this as boring and dull. Modulate your voice to accentuate key words for impact.[54] Vary volume, tone quality, and rate of speaking. Any of these can be used successfully to add interest to the message and engage audience attention. Speakers should not let their words trail off as they complete a sentence. Do you speak so softly that someone cannot hear you well? It is helpful to have someone in the back of the room signal if your voice is not carrying far enough. Do you speak too rapidly? Remind yourself to slow down. Make deliberate pauses before sentences. Speak words with precision without exaggerating. However, some people talk too slowly, and this can make the audience restive.

> Practice and Arrange

Rehearsal Is Essential

What do super achievers and star performers have in common? Practice. Malcolm Gladwell, in his best-selling book, *Outliers,* presents the case for the "The 10,000-Hour Rule," claiming that the key to success is repeated practice of a specific task for 10,000 hours. He asserts that greatness or mastery in any field requires massive amounts of time. With examples from the Beatles and Bill Gates, he showed how the Beatles performed live in Hamburg, Germany, more than 1,200 times from 1960 to 1964, accruing more than 10,000 hours of playing time. For Gates, it was access to a high school computer in 1968, at age 13, and then spending 10,000 hours programming on it.[55] Whether you practice 60 hours or 6 hours, the time you spend rehearsing is the difference between a mastery performance and a disappointment. Here are some suggestions for recreating the presentational setting as you practice. The value obtained will pay off in preventing embarrassment, allowing you to check your ratio of material versus available time, uncovering holes in your supporting material, and preparing for the unexpected.

- Practice early and often, leaving time for revision.
- Simulate the actual setting and facilities.
- Stand and move (reading from your computer screen does not give you realistic voice projection or allow you to practice movement).
- Rehearse with props and visual aids.
- Practice with an audience from your organization or people on your team who have backgrounds similar to the key people in the real audience.
- Start by reading your notes or using your cue cards/slide cues to familiarize yourself with the flow of the presentation.
- Stop yourself during the rehearsal to write both content and stylistic ideas as they come to mind. You will want to note awkward phrases that were not edited and self-conscious movements that were better avoided.

- Experiment with different aspects of paralanguage (as previously discussed), gestures, or staging of the environment.
- Mark your speaker note cards or the practice script as to when to pause, either for a breath or to stress an important point.
- Time your presentation at least three times, or have an audience member time you.
- Rehearse contingency plans to counter things that might go wrong.

Now that you have had initial practice, it is time for video recording. A video of yourself speaking is an amazingly potent tool. Your habits—both good and bad—are captured. As you watch the video, look for:

- *Eye contact.* What is the proportion of direct contact versus reading from notes? Have you used a simple slide cue to maintain your focus on the audience and not the slide? You should have a minimum of 75 percent eye contact in practice to obtain a higher goal in the presentation.
- *Body language.* Are there frequent unconscious gestures like touching hair, touching your face, standing awkwardly, pulling at your clothes? Are gestures unsynchronized with your words or unvaried? Do you detect body sway? If using a visual aid, demo, or a prop, are your transitions smooth?
- *Vocal characteristics.* Watch for irregular breathing with long sentences, pauses in the wrong places, dropping or raising your voice at the end of sentences, repeated phrases (e.g., "and then I," "now," or "next") as transitions, rapid pace of delivery, repeated fillers words, and negligible variation in tone or pace.
- *Energy level.* Does delivering the presentation excite you? Are you enthusiastic, inspired, or bored? Do not underestimate the energy level necessary to generate enthusiastic listeners. One famous speech coach asks his clients, "On a scale of 1 to 10—1 being fast asleep and 10 being wildly pumped up like motivational speaker Tony Robbins—where you are right now?" Most place themselves at 3 to 6, leaving sufficient room to raise the level.[56]

Watching yourself on video for the first time can be traumatic. In itself, the experience should help you overcome many problems. But if you are serious about improvement, ask the observers for feedback on your performance as you watch the video together. To get honest feedback, stick with open-ended questions such as the following: (1) Which supporting evidence was most effective? Why? Which supporting evidence with ineffective? Why? (2) Did the order of findings or arguments help support the conclusion? Why/Why not? (3) What was the most powerful element in the presentation? Why? (4) What would improve the presentation?[57]

Controlling Performance Anxiety

Performance anxiety, or stage fright, is a fear produced by the need to make a presentation in front of an audience or before a camera. In public speaking, it arises in anticipation of a performance or accompanies the event and causes negative effects in presentational quality. In extreme cases, the fear is persistent phobia, which makes the individual dysfunctional in a presentation.

Performance anxiety has numerous physical symptoms: fluttering or pounding heart, tremor in the hands and legs, stomach cramping or nausea, facial nerve tics, flushing, hives, and dry mouth. More than 56 million citations on a Google search of "fear public speaking" give credence to the pervasiveness of such anxiety. Performance anxiety at various levels occurs to people of all experience levels and backgrounds, from students to seasoned professionals.[58]

Research found five causal common denominators among individuals who experience performance anxiety—all based in negative self-perception:

1. I perceive or imagine the presence of significant others who are able to judge me.
2. I consider the possibility of my visible failure at a task.
3. I feel a need to do well to avoid failure.
4. I feel uncertain as to whether I will do well.
5. I focus on my own behavior and appearance.[59]

>**snap**shot

Overcoming the Jitters

The fear of public speaking ranks up there with the fear of death and/or public nudity. Whether you are a seasoned pro or this is your first speech, stage fright, the illogical fear of facing an audience, can be a paralyzing emotion. How do you handle those times when your mind starts going blank and your stomach is turning? Patricia Fripp, an award-winning keynote speaker and speech coach, provides some answers. She suggests that you "need to anticipate your speech mentally, physically, and logistically." Mental preparation is key and should be a six-to-one ratio: Invest three hours of preparation for a 30-minute speech. There is no substitute for rehearsal. Spend some time memorizing your opening and closing—three or four sentences each. Although you may speak from notes, knowing your opening and closing helps your fluency, allowing you to make the vital connection in rapport with your audience when you are likely to be most nervous.

Logistically, know the room. Go there as early as possible to get comfortable in the environment. Practice using the microphone and check the equipment. A quick review of your visual aids is also helpful. Then, during the presentation, you can focus on your audience and not be concerned with the environment.

The physical part of overcoming nervousness is varied and may be constrained by your setting. In a small-group setting, shake hands, exchange greetings, and make eye contact with everybody beforehand. In a larger meeting, at least connect with the people in the front row. Do so sincerely, and they'll be cheering for your success. They are not waiting for you to fail—they are far too worried about themselves—and they are there to listen to you. If possible, avoid sitting while you're waiting to speak. Find a position in the room where you can stand occasionally.

The presenter's physical appearance often reveals performance anxiety with perspiration, blank stares, and facial nerve tics.

The rear of the room gives you access to the bathroom and drinking fountain.

If your anxiety level is still high, then you need an outlet for your energy. Comedians and actors find that doing light exercises in their dressing rooms or in another private area can relieve the excess energy. Fripp adds, "Find a private spot, and wave your hands in the air. Relax your jaw, and shake your head from side to side. Then shake your legs one at a time. Physically shake the tension out of your body." The object is to release enough nervous energy to calm your anxieties—without becoming so stress-free that you forget your purpose and audience.

www.fripp.com

According to the authors, optimal strategies for coping with performance anxiety include (1) reduce the imagined power of others by increasing the sense of one's own power; (2) eliminate the imagination of negative possibilities, and think about the positive outcomes of a successful presentation; (3) hold the performance in perspective by seeing its outcome as insignificant in relation to the totality of one's life; (4) remember that one cannot control other's reactions or judgments, but only one's own performance; and (5) refocus one's attention away from self and increase one's awareness of others, without considering them as judges. In short, focus on "process rather than results, the moment of experience rather than the future, positive approach goals rather than negative avoidance goals, and self-acceptance rather than self doubt."[60] See Exhibit 21-14 for strategies to reduce performance anxiety.

Some readers will say, I understand the psychology, but what can you suggest that is really practical? The best thing you can do is to be overwhelmingly, painstakingly, and totally prepared. After that, exercise. Presenters need regular exercise to reduce tension and stress. Desensitize with relaxation

>Exhibit 21-14 Addressing Performance Anxiety

Suggested Strategy	Anxiety Reducing Actions
Reduce the imagined power of others.	• Remind yourself that you know the methodology and the findings far better than anyone in the audience. • Remind yourself that you have new information and new insights that could help resolve the manager's problem. • See yourself as the audience's partner in solving their problem. • Wear clothing that increases your power (suits win out over causal apparel).

Eliminate imagining negative possibilities.	• Remind yourself of the positive outcomes of the sponsor adopting your recommendations… their company grows, avoids layoffs, etc.
	• Plan for contingencies
	  • Create a disaster kit with extra power cords, projection bulbs, and laptop.
	  • Burn your presentation to CD, as well as to a USB thumb drive.
	  • Make multiple copies of your script note cards or slide note pages, put them in different places (luggage, backpack, car).
	  • Have multiple copies of handouts of your slides as a backup to a PowerPoint malfunction.

Hold the performance in perspective.	• Think of the presentation as an opportunity for career-enhancing experience. • Remind yourself of what you'll be doing later today or tomorrow that will provide you great joy. • Plan a dinner with friends the evening following the presentation. • Plan a celebration with your teammates for after the presentation.
Control your own performance.	• Get some exercise to burn off your nervous energy. • Eat a couple of hours before you go onstage to avoid low blood sugar (can make you feel light-headed) or too much undigested food (can make you nauseous). • Craft your support materials with great care. • Develop strong examples, exercises, slides, and handouts. • Practice, Practice, Practice. • Apply the visualization techniques that the professionals use. • Rest shaking hands on the podium to hide trembling.
Increase your awareness of others without considering them judges.	• Meet your audience (all or at least some) before your presentation. • Learn something personal about a few audience members that makes them appear more human . . . they have kids who eat bark, they like cherry Kool-Aid, they hate sunshine (or snow), they have a chihuahua named Brutus, etc.

techniques (meditation, yoga, Tai Chi, Qi Gong, or EFT, as many entertainers do). If possible, talk with a few audience members before you speak to build your confidence and audience rapport. Before the presentation, or while being introduced, sit calmly and breathe slow, deep breaths.

Arrangements for Facilities and Equipment

Arrangements for the presentation occasion and venue, sometimes referred to as *staging,* involve detailed management of facilities, operational problems, equipment (lecterns, lights, projectors, cords, controls, sound systems, video, Internet conferencing, electronic boards, racks for charts, displays/models/props). Staging requires attention to the meeting room, seating arrangement, screens and lighting, testing of virtually everything, along with preparation/backup for disasters. Refer to Exhibit 21-15 for a detailed checklist of the activities involved in perfecting the arrangements.

The objectives of the meeting, the room, the technology, and the size and composition of the audience should all significantly influence the researcher's oral presentation.

>**Exhibit 21-15** Facilities and Equipment Checklist A and B

Checklist A		
Source	**Item**	**Considerations**
☐ **Facilities**	Meeting room	• On-site vs. off-site • Adjacent facilities and noise • Plain walls: distraction avoidance • Clock placement • Ingres-egress opposite speaker • Barriers between presenter and audience
	Lighting	• Rheostats • Screen proximity and wash-out • Access to bulbs and fixtures
	Electrical power	• Outlets: location • Power extensions
	Lectern	• Moveable vs. fixed vs. podium • Location and visibility • Size adequate for presenter's equipment
	Temperature	• Adjustable vs. central • Effect on audience
	Seating	• Theater vs. conference style • Conference table for small group: about 10 to 15 • Individual tables for larger group: 5 to 6 per table • U-shape for visibility and interaction
☐ **Projection Screens**	Size Visibility Projection Interfering barrier Brightness	• 1/6 distance from screen to last viewer • Side angle and elevation • 4 feet above floor level; keystoning • Columns, hanging fixtures, lighting • Reflectivity: black and white vs. color • Dim vs. dark room

>Exhibit 21-15 Facilities and Equipment Checklist A and B (*Continued*)

Checklist B		
Source	**Item**	**Considerations**
☐ Sound System	Microphone	• Need for professional sound specialist • System control access • Handheld: 6 to 10 inches vertical from chin • Fixed-handheld vs. wireless • Feedback proximity • Desirability of portable systems
☐ AV Equipment	LCD projector	• Portable vs. installed in room • Projector-PC compatibility • Computer power • Operating location in room • Wireless controller/mouse • Wireless keyboard (meeting-related)
	Video	• DVD/camcorder/VCR • Web streaming • Teleprompter • Playback monitor size • System tests
	Video conferencing/Webinars	• PC vs. Mac requirements • VoIP • Speaker systems • One broadcast vs. two-way interaction • Supported browsers
	Flipcharts/posters	• Size and visibility • Support systems—racks
	Electronic whiteboards	• Simulation of PC desktop • Create video files • Digital story telling • Brainstorming • Port over to PowerPoint • Use for review/repetition

Source: adapted in part from Thomas Leech, *How to Prepare, Stage, and Deliver Winning Presentations* (New York: AMACOM, 2004), pp. 167–87.

>summary

1 An oral research presentation has unique characteristics that distinguish it from public speaking but with which it shares similarities. A small group of people is normally involved; statistics often constitute an important portion of the topic; the audience members are usually managers with an interest in the topic, but they want to hear only the data and conclusions that will help them make critical decisions; speaking time will often be as short as 20 minutes, but may run longer than an hour; and the presentation is normally interspersed with questions and discussion.

2 Aristotle's rhetorical influence on business presentation in the 21st century acquaints us with persuasive possibilities in every presentational situation. The basis of persuasion has three principles of proof: *ethos, pathos,* and *logos.* Our perception of a presenter's character affects how believable or convincing we find that person. This is called the speaker's *ethos. Pathos* relies on an emotional connection between the speaker and his or her audience. It is an appeal to an audience's sense of identity, self-interest, and emotions. With *logos,* the logical argument, we find the explicit reasons

that the speaker needs to support a position. This translates into supporting evidence and analytical techniques that reveal and uphold the researchers' findings and conclusions.

3   We start to plan for the research presentation by accentuating the audience's role: Who is the audience? What do they want to learn? Why is this presentation occurring? When will it occur? Where will the presentation take place? The most important question is about the audience's mind-set: Why should I care? Demographic and dispositional characteristics of the audience also play a role. An audience is composed of three types of learners: visual, auditory, and kinesthetic—all with different needs and learning styles. To keep the audience attentive, research presenters should observe the 10-minute rule by varying their content. They should also understand that arguments presented first or last will be highly influential to understanding and motivate others to take action.

4   Presentations have a wide variety of organizational structures that the presenter can use to construct a framework, thereby assisting the audience to follow and understand the presentation. Numerous traditional patterns of organization (topical, spatial, classification, climax order, problem/solution, chronological, past/present/future, cause/effect/solution, pros/cons/recommendation, and research briefing) are viable options, although the motivated sequence, the narrative style of development, the rule of three, and the three-point speech are preferred organization strategies.

5   Supporting materials are leaves on the branches of the organizational framework. They include facts, statistics, specific instances, examples, testimony/expert opinion, analogy and metaphor, conveying personal experience through story, and demonstrations.

6   Proficiency in research presentation requires creating good visuals and knowing how to use them. The culprit of visually poor presentations is often presenters who create and organize their message with PowerPoint or other design software (which disrupts, dominates, and trivializes content) rather than in analog, away from the computer. Visualization involves developing and organizing supporting materials that help the audience understand your findings. Several psychological principles influence the visualization of your presentation: the principles of relevance (only information critical to understanding should be presented), appropriate knowledge (limitations in your audience's knowledge level), capacity limitations (inability to process large amounts of information at one time), informative changes (convey what is new with a separate slide or handout), salience (the audience's attention is drawn to large perceptible differences), discriminability (two properties must differ by a large amount to be discerned), and perceptual organization (when establishing associations or correlations between key findings, your supporting materials should group in proximity to each other).

In addition to selecting the right visual elements to convey your findings and conclusions, design principles should guide the design of visual support materials. They include visual preparation, flow aids, visibility, whitespace, picture supremacy, contrast, compatibility, relationship, simplicity, and clarity.

7   How the speaker delivers the message is very important. Demeanor, posture, dress, and total appearance should be appropriate for the occasion. Speed of speech, clarity of enunciation, pauses, and gestures all play their part. Voice pitch, tone quality, and inflections are proper subjects for concern. Rapport-developing techniques are essential so that the speaker can get and hold the audience's attention. The modes of delivery by which you communicate your message to the audience include impromptu speaking, memorization, manuscript reading, or extemporaneous presentation. We rule out the impromptu briefing, because it does not involve preparation, and discourage memorization and manuscript reading due to lack of audience connection. Scripts have no place in research presentations, where audience members want to engage in information exchange, but are important in the planning phase. Audiences accept the use of speaker notes, which are consistent with extemporaneous presentations.

Details make a difference in effective delivery, including reducing clutter, which gives the impression of hesitancy and lack of competence (repetition of fillers such as "ah," "um," "you know," "like,"). Using jargon is a particular danger when your audience may not be schooled in the techniques of research or of statistical analysis. Jargon adds clumsy language and reduces the simplicity of the message. Nonverbal communication accounts for approximately 50 to 93 percent of communication meaning and, because it is sometimes more believable than verbal communication, deserves careful attention. Major categories include eye contact, gestures, posture and body orientation, and paralanguage.

8   Practice is the critical ingredient that super achievers and star performers have in common. It serves to recreate the presentational setting as you practice, prevent embarrassment later, check your ratio of material versus available time, uncover holes in your supporting material, and prepare for the unexpected. A video rehearsal helps overcome many problems, especially with feedback from your practice audience. Stage fright occurs to people of all experience levels and backgrounds, from students to seasoned professionals. While we suggest several means of coping, the best thing you can do is to be overwhelmingly, painstakingly, and totally prepared.

Arrangements for the presentation occasion and venue, sometimes referred to as staging, involve detailed management of facilities, operational problems, equipment (lecterns, lights, projectors, cords, controls, sound systems, video, Internet conferencing, electronic boards, racks for charts, displays/models/props). Furthermore, arrangements require attention to the meeting room, seating, screens and lighting, testing of virtually everything, along with preparation/backup for disasters.

>**key**terms

>**discussion**questions

Terms in Review

1 Distinguish between the following:

  a Impromptu speaking and an extemporaneous presentation.

  b The motivated sequence and the cause/effect/solution pattern of organization.

  c The *rule of three* in organizing and the *rule of thirds* in visualizing.

  d Clutter and jargon in the delivery of a presentation.

2 Describe the differences among *logos, ethos,* and *pathos* and their uses for the research presentation.

3 What are the three types of learners, and how is the presentation different for each of these groups in your audience?

Making Research Decisions

4 The day before your presentation, you are suffering from pounding heart, a slight tremor in your hands, and stomach problems. What specific measures can you take to build your confidence and reduce performance anxiety?

5 Outline a set of visual aids that you might use in an oral presentation on these topics:

  a How to write a research report.

  b The outlook for the economy over the next year.

  c A major analytical article in the latest issue of *BusinessWeek.*

6 Your class team in research methods has completed a field project for a financial institution on branch location effectiveness. What questions about audience analysis should you answer as you plan your presentation?

Bringing Research to Life

7 Every presentation has its purpose. What was the purpose of Henry & Associates presentation to MindWriter?

8 How did the Henry & Associates presentation:

  a Perform an audience analysis?

  b Engage the audience?

From Concept to Practice

9 In your presentation to a venture capital company, you are pitching your research plan for a smartphone application that does short-term cash flow forecasts. Describe how you would use each type of supporting material to create interest, clarify your point, provide emphasis to a point, and offer proof that results in belief.

10 Using Exhibit 21-9, choose an appropriate graphing technique to show the difference between men's and women's attitudes on the top five Super Bowl ads. (You can find this listing on http://adbowl.com.)

11 You are creating slides for a presentation that is being given to seek a research contract with a leading toy manufacturer. Considering the following aspects of your presentation (introduction, problem to be solved, market opportunity, technology, manufacturing/production, financials, conclusion), create slides representing four of these areas using Exhibit 21-13.

From the Headlines

12 You are preparing to give a research presentation about the effectiveness of Toyota's advertising to restore public confidence in the wake of their delays in solving the accelerator pedal malfunction and antilock braking problems for high-tech hybrid vehicles. Which of the patterns of organization would be appropriate for your purpose? Why?

13 At an Apple press event, Apple CEO Steve Jobs announces the iPad, a new mobile device that is a half-inch thin and weighs 1.5 pounds; plays movies, music, and TV shows; and acts as an e-reader. It is powered with a 1-GHz Apple chip and comes with Wi-Fi and Bluetooth connectivity. Here are some quotes from his presentation:

"iPad is an awesome way to enjoy your music collection"

"You can discover music, you can purchase it, iTunes university . . . everything!"

"YouTube. You can watch YouTube on it!"

"It's awesome to watch TV and movies on."

"It's so much more intimate than a laptop, and so much more capable than a smart phone."

a What rhetorical devices is Jobs using in his presentation?

b How would you prepare the informational content and slides to announce the price?

>cases*

Inquiring Minds Want to Know—NOW!

Mastering Teacher Leadership

NCRCC: Teeing Up and New

Strategic Direction

Ohio Lottery: Innovative Research

Design Drives Winning

Proofpoint: Capitalizing on a Reporter's Love of Statistics

* You will find a description of each case in the Case Abstracts section of this textbook. Check the Case Index to determine whether a case provides data, the research instrument, video, or other supplementary material. Written cases are downloadable from the text website (www.mhhe.com/cooper11e). All video material and video cases are available from the Online Learning Center.

>case index

Case	Type	Ch 01	Ch 02	Ch 03	Ch 04	Ch 05	Ch 06	Ch 07	Ch 08	Ch 09	Ch 10	Ch 11	Ch 12	Ch 13	Ch 14	Ch 15	Ch 16	Ch 17	Ch 18	Ch 19	Ch 20	Ch 21
A GEM of a Study	W, T					X	X															
AgriComp	W, D															X						
Akron Children's Hospital	W, V		X		X	X		X	X		X		X	X	X							
Calling Up Attendance	W, I				X	X	X						X	X	X							
Campbell-Ewald Pumps Awareness into the American Heart Association	W, V						X				X				X							
Campbell-Ewald: R-E-S-P-E-C-T Spells Loyalty	W			X								X	X	X	X							
Can Research Rescue the Red Cross?	W										X		X	X	X							
Covering Kids with HealthCare	VC				X		X	X			X											
Cummins Engines	VC		X										X									
Data Development, Inc	VC	X									X	X										
Donatos: Finding the New Pizza	W, V				X	X	X				X		X									
Envirosell	VC								X													
Goodyear's Aquatred	VC				X	X	X								X							
HeroBuilders.com	W	X		X	X																	
Inquiring Minds Want to Know—Now!	W, I				X	X	X				X	X	X	X	X	X		X			X	X
Lexus SC430	VC				X			X			X											
Mastering Teacher Leadership	W, I, D				X	X					X		X	X		X	X	X	X	X	X	X
McDonald's Tests Catfish Sandwich	W									X												
NCRCC: Teeing Up a New Strategic Direction	W, I, T, D				X	X		X			X	X	X	X	X	X	X	X	X	X	X	X
NetConversions Influences Kelley Blue Book	W, T								X	X		X				X						
Ohio Lottery: Innovative Research Design Drives Winning	W, Q, T, V	X			X	X	X	X			X	X	X	X	X			X	X	X	X	X
Open Doors: Extending Hospitality to Travelers with Disabilities	W			X			X	X														
Pebble Beach Co.	VC											X		X	X							
Proofpoint: Capitalizing on a Reporter's Love of Statistics	W, T		X				X				X	X	X	X		X	X	X	X	X	X	
Ramada Demonstrates Its *Personal Best*™	W				X	X		X				X	X									
Starbucks, Bank One, and Visa Launch Starbucks Card Duetto™ Visa	VC						X	X			X			X	X							
State Farm: Dangerous Intersections	W				X	X	X		X				X		X							
The Catalyst for Women in Financial Services	W, T										X	X			X							
USTA: Come Out Swinging	W, I, VC				X	X					X	X	X	X	X							
Volkswagen's Beetle	VC						X						X	X	X			X				
Yahoo!: *Consumer Direct* Marries Purchase Metrics to Banner Ads	W											X	X									

LEGEND:

W = Written Case
D = Data File
T = Some table/graphed data

I = Instrument
Q = Some Measurement Instruments

VC = Video Case
V = Some video material

> A GEM of a Study

The Global Entrepreneurship Monitor Entrepreneurial Assessment, a joint project of the Kauffman Center for Entrepreneurship Leadership at Babson College and the London Business School, has undertaken a long-term, large-scale project to prove the causal links between a government's economic policies and initiatives, the resulting entrepreneurial activity, and subsequent economic growth. This case describes multiple-stage research, including thousands of interviews in several countries by established research firms.

> AgriComp

AgriComp, a supplier of computer systems for farmers, has surveyed its dealers on whether to change its procedure for settling warranty claim disputes. Currently local dealers handle warranty services for customers via local repair followed by a reimbursement claim to AgriComp. Denied claims follow an internal company appeal process. Dealers have been complaining about the fairness of the appeal process and in a recent survey were asked to respond to an alternative process, an impartial mediator. The student is asked to review survey results and determine whether the costly external mediator process would be worth implementing to keep the dealers happy.

> Akron Children's Hospital

Northeastern Ohio is a highly competitive health care market, especially for the care of seriously ill children. With powerhouse health care institutions like the Cleveland Clinic venturing into the children's care segment, Akron Children's needed a way to differentiate itself. The research profiled in this case helped develop the positioning of Akron Children's hospital and its promotional approach and resulted in an increase in its bed-occupancy rate, a key metric in the health care industry. **www.akronchildrens.org; www.marcusthomasllc.com**

> Calling Up Attendance

This case examines a study by Prince Marketing for TCS Management Group. TCS Management Group, Inc., part of Aspect Communications, is the leading provider of workforce management software, especially related to call center management. The study discusses measures of customer satisfaction and aims to predict attendance at a two-day educational event, Users Forum. **www.aspect.com**

> Campbell-Ewald Pumps Awareness into the American Heart Association

You wouldn't think that an organization that does as much good as the American Heart Association would have low awareness, but at the start of the described research program its unaided awareness level was just 16 percent. For a company reliant on contributions, low awareness is a major problem. This case profiles the research behind the American Heart Association's first-ever paid advertising campaign. **www.campbell-ewald.com; www.americanheart.org**

> Campbell-Ewald: R-E-S-P-E-C-T Spells Loyalty

Campbell-Ewald, the Detroit-based marketing communications company, part of the global Interpublic Group of Companies, is an award-winning consultancy. This case describes the research behind its effort to measure and improve customer loyalty and the development of its five respect principles that lead to enhanced customer commitment. **www.campbellewald.com**

> Can Research Rescue the Red Cross?

The American Red Cross seemed in its true element following September 11, 2001. It was flooded with donations to do its highly needed and regarded work. Most of those donations went to its Liberty Fund. But shortly after it started to disperse the funds, the media began asking questions. And the American Red Cross soon wore a patina of tarnish. Learn about the research that evaluated Americans' perception of the Red Cross and how research by Wirthlin Worldwide helped craft a new and highly effective donation solicitation process. **www.wirthlin.com; www.redcross.org**

> Covering Kids with Health Care

This video case describes the research done to increase enrollment in the federal government's SCHIP program. Managed at the state level, the State Children's Health Insurance Program provides basic health coverage for the children of the nation's working poor. Research by Wirthlin Worldwide revealed why families weren't enrolling, and findings were used by GMMB, Inc., to develop a major advertising and public relations initiative to increase enrollment. The research and campaign were sponsored by the Robert Wood Johnson Foundation. (Video duration: 16 minutes) **www.rwjf.org; www.wirthlin.com; www.gmmb.com**

> Cummins Engines

Cummins Engines makes advanced, fuel-efficient diesel power systems and engine-related components and specializes in customized diesel engine production. Shipping more than 1,000 engines per day to customers and dealers on every continent, Cummins has a long history of innovation, from winning performances at the Indianapolis 500 to the first natural gas–fueled engine to pass California's tough emissions regulations. This case focuses on the Signature 600 engine, the newest and most advanced diesel engine on the market. (Video duration: 14 minutes) **www.cummins.com**

> Data Development Corporation

This video case profiles Data Development Corporation (DDC), a leader in in-home and office personal interviewing. DDC has fielded more than 20,000 studies since 1960; it currently has four offices in the United States, with global capabilities in 80 countries worldwide. DDC WATS centers have 170 CATI (computer-assisted telephone interviewing) stations. The company offers a network of CAPI (computer-assisted personal interviewing) in more than 180 mall locations, as well as interactive software (STORE) simulations of store shelving, buildings, and so on, to develop and evaluate logos, signage, packaging, and the like. DDC's Internet Survey Group offers Web-based studies. (Video duration: 11 minutes) **www.datadc.com**

> Donatos: Finding the New Pizza

The pizza segment of the fast-food industry is very aggressive. As people's tastes change and new diets become the rage, restaurant chains must decide if and how to respond. This case focuses on the research behind the introduction of Donato's low-carbohydrate pizza and how the company collapsed its normal product-development research process to take advantage of a current trend. **www.donatos.com**

> Envirosell

Envirosell specializes in behavioral research, specifically in the retail environment. It has done this for Fortune 500 companies including banks, stores, and restaurant chains, as well as consumer product companies. In this video case, the managing director, research director, and senior analyst share information from several observational studies done in banks, as well as music, general-merchandise, and other retail environments. Envirosell, which has offices in the United States, Europe, Brazil, Japan, Mexico, and Turkey, strives to understand what people buy and how to get them to buy more. (Video duration: 10 minutes) **www.envirosell.com**

> Goodyear's Aquatred

This video case profiles the genesis of the Goodyear Aquatred tire. In 1993, the Aquatred tire, winner of more than a dozen awards, including Japan's prestigious Good Product Design Award, reached more than 2 million units in sales in the United States. This revolutionary tire pumps away more gallons of water per second as you drive at highway speeds. And a new tread rubber compound provides road-hugging traction and extends the tread life. The Aquatred tire segmented the market in a way that had not been done before. (Video duration: 14 minutes) **www.goodyear.com**

> HeroBuilders.com

Emil Vicale, president of BBC Design Group, used rapid prototyping technology (RPT) to build wax or plastic three-dimensional prototypes of his clients' designs. But this same technology can be used to custom-manufacture dolls. Shortly after September 11, 2001, Vicale Corporation, BBC's parent company, purchased an e-commerce toy company. Vicale's first action figure was made to honor the heroes who emerged from that event. Using RPT, he crafted a doll with the head of George W. Bush and the body of Arnold Schwarzenegger. Other figures followed. This case is about a design firm that used exploratory research to define a niche in the action-figure business. **www.herobuilders.com**

> Inquiring Minds Want to Know—NOW!

This case describes a multistage communication study undertaken by the research department of Penton Media, a publisher of business trade magazines, to determine the long-term viability of a reader and advertiser service, the *reader service card*, a postcard-size device used by readers to request additional information from a particular advertiser. **www.penton.com**

> Lexus SC 430

This video case follows the research used to develop the newest Lexus, the SC 430, the line's hard-top convertible. From auto show interviews to qual-quant clinics and positioning analysis, learn about how Team One Advertising, Lexus's U.S. agency of record, used research to position this latest entry into the crowded sport coupe category. (Video duration: 8 minutes) **www.teamoneadv. com; www.lexus.com**

> Mastering Teacher Leadership

This case is about a multistage communication study of teachers by Wittenberg University's Department of Education to determine the viability of starting a Master of Education program for Ohio-certified teachers working within school districts serving a five-county area. **www.wittenberg.edu**

> McDonald's Tests Catfish Sandwich

This case describes the test marketing for McDonald's catfish sandwich in the southeastern United States. It asks students to assume they are the new product development team and to assess the research design described.

> NCRCC: Teeing Up a New Strategic Direction

The NCR Country Club started out as a benefit for thousands of National Cash Register employees. By the late 1990s, those employees were aging rapidly and the core membership needed to be increased. NCRCC offers two golf courses. One is an award-winning, championship-hosting course on the PGA tour. But the club wasn't attracting new members, especially younger families. This case is about a membership study done as part of a larger management initiative to evaluate several strategic directions the club might take to expand its membership. **www.ncrcountryclub.com**

> NetConversions Influences Kelley Blue Book

Kelley Blue Book (KBB) is one of the most visited automotive sites on the Web. Visitors flock there to estimate the price of a car they might buy or sell. KBB needed to enhance its site's performance for advertisers, who had become a major source of revenue as sales of the printed *Kelley Blue Book* had declined. NetConversions is one of the new Web analytic services to evaluate website performance. This case reveals how websites are evaluated so that new design elements can be developed and tested. **www.netconversions.com; www.kelleybluebook.com**

> Ohio Lottery: Innovative Research Design Drives Winning

The Ohio Lottery was originally developed as an additional source of public school funding. Today proceeds from lottery games annually provide approximately 7 percent of the public educational budget. This research was originally undertaken because the lottery director wanted a deeper understanding of lottery players and insight into nonplayers. The research design described in this case is multistage and incorporates the use of both qualitative and quantitative research. This case reveals the research that guides the current Ohio Lottery promotional program that encourages play of its various games. **www.marcusthomasllc.com; www.mrsi.com; www.ohiolottery.com**

> Open Doors: Extending Hospitality to Travelers with Disabilities

Eric Lipp started the Open Doors Organization (ODO) to help travelers with disabilities. In order to get the attention of the travel and hospitality industries, and to effect changes desired by people with disabilities, ODO undertook a major research project to estimate the expenditures of persons with disabilities and the accommodations that would be necessary to get them to travel more. Harris Interactive was chosen to field the multimethod survey. This case describes the methodology and the effects of the first round of a multiphase study. **www.opendoorsnfp.org**

> Pebble Beach Co.

This case profiles the Pebble Beach Company, a 5,300-acre complex in Monterey, California, that offers three lodging options (Casa Palmero opened in September 1999, The Inn at Spanish Bay opened in 1989, and the Lodge at Pebble Beach opened in 1919), four golf courses, plus a new five-hole "golf links," eight restaurants, and an oceanside Beach and Tennis Club. Pebble Beach has repeatedly won awards as America's best travel resort and was host to the 2004 AT&T Pro-Amateur championship, the U.S. Open in 2000, the Callaway Golf Pebble Beach Invitational in 2004, and the newest tournament on the 2005 PGA Champions tour (First Tee Open). In January of 1999 The Inn at Spanish Bay was granted the coveted Mobil Five-Star Award from the 1999 *Mobil Travel Guide*. Pebble Beach achieves its quality status by focusing on seven core values. The company is land-locked, so it must develop ever-creative ways to make the facilities it has more intensively profit-generating. (Video duration: 11 minutes) **www.pebblebeach.com**

> Proofpoint: Capitalizing on a Reporter's Love of Statistics

Proofpoint provides antispam software and e-mail security software solutions for large enterprises. Their software products stop spam, protect against e-mail viruses, ensure that outbound e-mail messages comply with both corporate policies and external regulations, and prevent leaks of confidential information via e-mail and other network protocols like blogs and text-messaging. Proofpoint knew from its customer inquiries that the IT professional was increasingly concerned with outbound information privacy compliance issues. Believing that painting this broader picture would earn them valuable space and airtime in the business, IT, and mainstream media, Proofpoint sponsored a series of surveys among IT professionals. This case is about those surveys. **www.proofpoint.com**

> Ramada Demonstrates Its *Personal Best*™

This case describes syndicated research in the hospitality industry that revealed trends in customer satisfaction and Ramada's proprietary research leading to the development of the *Personal Best*™ employee hiring, training, and motivation program. **www. ramada.com**

> Starbucks, Bank One, and Visa Launch Starbucks Card Duetto™ Visa

In the very mature financial services industry, it is rare for a new financial product to garner much attention, let alone be named one of *BusinessWeek*'s outstanding products of the year. But what started as a way for Starbucks to add value to its existing Starbucks Card program developed into a financial product that many other institutions are interested in exploring. This case reveals the research that was done to develop this new payment option for Starbucks customers. (Video duration: 11 minutes) **www.starbucks.com; www.bankone.com; www.visa.com**

> State Farm: Dangerous Intersections

State Farm, the nation's largest auto insurer, distributed a list of the 10 most dangerous intersections in the United States based on crashes resulting in claims by its policyholders. What started as a study to reduce risk turned into an ongoing study that directs a major public relations effort: State Farm provides funds for communities to further research their dangerous intersections and initiate improvements based on the research. This case tells how the State Farm Dangerous Intersections initiative got started and how it is done. **www.statefarm.com**

> The Catalyst for Women in Financial Services

Smith Barney (now Morgan Stanley Smith Barney) was ordered by the court, in settling the landmark sexual harassment case, to evaluate the climate for personal development and advancement through promotion not only in Smith Barney but, as a comparative, in other financial services firms. The case describes the methodology used to sample both men's and women's beliefs and attitudes, as well as reveals some of the basic findings. **www.catalystwomen.org; www.smithbarney.com**

> USTA: Come Out Swinging

The United States Tennis Association funded one of the most aggressive surveys ever undertaken about a single sport in order to revitalize tennis in the minds of consumers. The survey results were supplemented with qualitative research by Vigilante, a specialist in urban communication campaigns. What resulted was a full-scale marketing initiative involving the establishment of Tennis Welcome Centers and the Come Out Swinging advertising, merchandising, and public relations campaigns. This case reveals the research and how the marketing initiative developed. (Video duration: 11 minutes) **www.usta.com; www.vigilantenyc.com; www.thetaylorgroup.com**

> Volkswagen's Beetle

This video case profiles the history of the original Beetle in the U.S. market from its introduction in 1949 to its demise in 1979 and then follows the initial two years of the New Beetle's rebirth, 1998 and 1999. The Beetle became a symbol of the 1960s rebelliousness, but it lost the love of a generation when it stressed engineering over style and low-cost operation, two factors that baby boomers considered crucial in the 1970s. By 1974, the Beetle had lost ground to its aggressive Japanese rivals for the value segment of the U.S. automobile market. In 1998, when the Beetle was reintroduced in the United States, it surpassed all sales estimates. The second year it doubled its sales. Historically, the Beetle is the world's best-selling car, having sold in more countries than any other automobile, with 21 million cars sold in its lifetime. (Video duration: 16 minutes) **www.vw.com**

> Yahoo!: *Consumer Direct* Marries Purchase Metrics to Banner Ads

As little as two years ago, many advertising pundits were bemoaning the inevitable demise of the banner ad on the Internet. But maybe they were too quick to judge. This case reveals how Yahoo!, in combination with ACNielsen's *Homescan®*, has developed a methodology *(Consumer Direct)* to evaluate the true effectiveness of banner ads, from ad exposure to shopping cart. It also reveals the role Dynamic Logic played in conducting postexposure ad evaluation. **www.yahoo.com; www.acnielsen. com; www.dynamiclogic.com**

>appendices

>appendixa

Business Research Requests and Proposals (with Sample RFP)

Proposing Research

Many students and some business researchers view the proposal process as unnecessary work. In actuality, the more inexperienced a researcher is, the more important it is to have a well-planned and adequately documented proposal. The proposal process, Exhibit a-1, uses two primary documents: *the request for proposal (RFP)* and the *research proposal*. When the organization has research specialists on the payroll, the internal research proposal is often all that is needed. Often, however, companies do not have adequate capacity, resources, or the specialized talents in-house to execute a project, so they turn to outside research suppliers (including research specialists, universities, research centers, and consulting firms). We will explore the second scenario first.

The Request for Proposal (RFP)

The **request for proposal (RFP)** is the formal document issued by a corporate research department, a decision maker, or some other sponsor to solicit services from research suppliers. Developing a well-written RFP takes time and planning. However, the benefit to the sponsoring organization is an opportunity to formalize the process of documenting, justifying, and authorizing the procurement of research. RFPs also provide a chance to evaluate different solutions and offer the means of establishing, monitoring, and controlling the performance of the winning supplier.

The researcher invites a qualified supplier to submit a proposal in accordance with a specific, detailed format—delivered by a deadline. Prescribing a common format makes comparison of competing proposals much easier. Each firm has its own requirements, and these are reflected not only in the form of the RFPs but in how they're distributed. The government, for example, is required by law to publicly announce RFPs. Private firms may limit supplier invitations to bidders that they have solicited before, to vendors that have provided past services, or to a single bidder (sole source). Both technical merit and the supplier's estimate of project cost determine how contracts are awarded.

Research suppliers consider RFPs an important source of future business. Thus, they must be vigilant to retain credibility with current and past clients and must seek to achieve positive word of mouth. Professional guides or business listing services promote the supplier's visibility. Companies sometimes avoid the formal RFP as a means of contacting suppliers. They may invite you to propose a project during a conversation and later ask you to formalize it in writing. Moreover, not all projects are conducive to the RFP process. However, in the next section, we will discuss how an organization requests state-of-the-art proposals for dealing with complex research problems.

Creating the RFP

The first step is to define and understand fully the problem being addressed. In formal RFP processes, internal experts define the problem. They may be brand managers, new product specialists, or representatives from other functions. Alternatively, an expert or a group of experts may be retained to assist in defining the problem and then writing the RFP. In the tourism study, members of the commerce department and experts in the hospitality, travel, advertising, and entertainment fields would have participated at the request of the governor. Once the problem is defined, the technical section of the RFP can be written.

>**Exhibit a-1** The Research Proposal Process

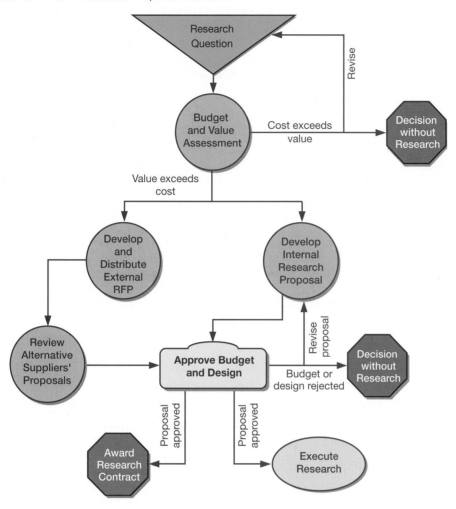

Besides a definition of the technical requirements of the desired research, critical components of the RFP include project management, pricing, and contract administration. These sections allow the potential research supplier to understand and meet the expectations of the sponsoring management team for the contracted services. Also, a section on proposal administration, including important dates, is included.

An important activity that precedes this is qualifying potential suppliers. Sponsors must determine which vendors have the capability to complete the project on time. When the process is not open to all bidders, criteria such as industry experience, reputation, geographic location, quality of previous work, size of staff, and strategic alliances with other vendors determine which bidders will be eligible to receive the RFP.

Although RFPs differ somewhat from firm to firm, the general components are:

- Proposal administration information.
- Summary statement of the problem.
- Technical section.
- Management section.
- Contracts and license section.
- Pricing section.

Proposal Administration   This section is an overview of important information on the administration of the project itself. It establishes the dates of the RFP process—when the RFP is released, when the RFP team is available for questions, the date the proposal is expected, and the dates of the evaluation and supplier selections. It includes all requirements for preparing the proposal and describes how proposals will be evaluated. Contact names, addresses, and relevant telephone and fax numbers are listed.

Summary Statement of the Problem   The summary statement can be an abstract of the technical section, or it can be included as the first page of the technical section. It often takes the form of a letter introducing the organization that issued the RFP and explaining its needs. As an example, let's use a problem statement from MindWriter that deals with a customer satisfaction issue:

> The call center in MindWriter's new CompleteCare facility currently operates without an automated recording and monitoring process. We have 10 dedicated reviewers sustaining this function. In addition, our call center supervisors spend six hours per month monitoring the quality of our reviewers. The reviewers rely on a manually generated schedule to select representatives and times for monitoring. When representatives are on active calls during the monitoring schedule, it is problematic to trace them. However, reviewers have access to the online scheduling software. Thus, they can view the account screens selected by the representative using our own software tool.
>
> The quality of our customer service and the resulting satisfaction are of vital importance to MindWriter. We need to significantly increase the efficiency of our customer call monitoring through automation and a recorded database for agent review. We also need to discover the extent to which these technical changes to our process improve customer perceptions of service.

Technical Section   Technical information needed by the supplier to create the proposal is presented in this section. It begins by describing the problem(s) to be addressed and the technical details of each requirement. It loosely describes the services to be performed and the equipment, software, and documentation required. This section should be neither too specific nor too general to allow the suppliers reasonable flexibility and creativity in research design but should also restrict them in meeting the needs of the sponsor. Typically, the following would be included:

- Problem statement.
- Description of functional requirements (what actual phases will be included in the research).
- Identification of constraints (what might limit research design creativity).

The sponsor's functional requirements assist suppliers in testing the comprehensiveness of their proposed solutions. Often, sponsors ask the proposed researcher to answer questions. In MindWriter's RFP, the writers have considered a wide range of functional issues:

Recording

- What proportion of calls does your proposed solution record?
- To what degree is your proposed system scalable?
- Can the representatives detect that they are being recorded?

System Integration and Retrieval

- Can you integrate multiple sources of information to the recording platform?
- Does your proposed solution offer redundancy in the event of a failure?
- Does your proposed solution store conversations along with their corresponding call-tag data in a single database?
- Can the recorded calls be replayed immediately?
- How does your proposed solution search calls for replay?
- What volume of long-term archived storage is available?

Evaluation and Analysis

- Can call data be displayed visually for analysis?
- How are calls selected for evaluation/scoring?
- Can values be assigned to each question and "rep performance" or "rep skill" category?
- Does your solution offer data mining capabilities?
- In what ways does your solution support managerial analysis of operations and business performance?
- How does your solution support the CompleteCare customer satisfaction philosophy at MindWriter?

Strategies for dealing with constraints include specifying what is anticipated. If the sponsor requires that the supplier offer creative solutions, the RFP describes the constraints within which solutions must work.

A client of Jason Henry's provides an example, below, of sampling constraints in its RFP. The client is interested in using the benchmarks from previous studies and thus needs consistency in its current project.

- The sample sizes and breakdowns for various markets are:
    - Europe: 500 completed surveys.
    - Asia: 500 completed surveys.
    - United States: 300 completed surveys.
        ◦ Regional differences.
        ◦ Differentiation by segment and brand.
- Proposed sample proportion for distributors/resellers:
    - Resellers = 90–95% of respondents.
    - Distributors = 5–10%.

Building technical quality control into the RFP will subsequently strengthen the project. When the technical section contains thorough specifications and clear criteria for evaluating proposals, even low bidders must provide the requisite quality for consideration. In addition, when the RFP requires that the supplier provide technical reports during the project, project management is less costly for the firm. When a thorough understanding of the constraints is unknown, sponsors may schedule a planning meeting with possible researchers prior to their RFP response to clarify and examine options.

Management Section   Each project requires some level of management. The sponsor's timing on schedules, plans, and reports is included in this section. The management section also lists the requirements for implementation schedules, training and reporting schedules, quality control, and other documentation. If specific supplier qualifications are needed, they should be shown here. References from the supplier's customers may also be requested. Increasingly, detailed documentation websites are used to provide additional information to those invited to submit proposals. These website URLs are documented in the RFP.

Contracts and License Section   The types of contracts the supplier is expected to sign and any nondisclosure agreements are included in this section. The supplier of research is often privy to a firm's strategies and tactics long before such competitive moves are undertaken. The supplier is also aware of challenges facing the firm and actions being considered to address those challenges. Nondisclosure of such information is therefore critical. It is in this context that the sponsor should discuss the safeguarding of intellectual property and the use of copyrights. Terms of payment and required benchmarks are also set forth here. Typically, a sample purchase contract would be included. Since the RFP document is usually a part of the final contract, it should be worded precisely to avoid problems of interpretation. If a task is not described in the RFP or during contract negotiations, the firm may not be able to require that the supplier complete it.

Pricing Section   To cost the proposal, suppliers must receive all needed information. A format that lists all anticipated activities helps the sponsor compare the cost of proposals with different approaches. The following list shows examples of items that could be included:

- Services.
- Data collection.
- Data analysis.
- Meetings with client.
- Travel.
- Respondent survey incentives.
- Mail and telephone costs.
- Design meetings.
- Internet design and activation.
- Facilities and equipment.
- Extensions to work agreements.
- Pilot tests.
- Report preparations.
- Computer models.
- Project management.
- Questionnaire and reproduction costs.
- Manpower costs.
- Deliverables:
    - Training.
    - Brochures/literature.
    - Videotapes.
    - Reports.
    - Promotionals.

Ethical standards are integral to designing the pricing section. For example, a sponsor would not send a vendor an RFP to (1) help the sponsor plan its project budget, (2) estimate costs and ideas for a project the sponsor intends to execute in-house, or (3) create the impression of a competitive bid when the sponsor intends to sole-source the project.

Format   The format requirements for RFPs differ widely. The sections above reflect informational requirements rather than an RFP outline. A typical format might contain the following elements:

- Instructions to bidders.
- Background.
  - Overview or profile of the buyer's company.
  - Project overview.
  - Project requirements.
- Vendor information.
  - Company profile.
  - History and description.
  - Legal summary (active lawsuits or pending litigation).
  - Partnerships and alliances.
  - References.
- Proposed solution.
- Services and support.
- Cost proposal.
  - Services pricing.
  - Maintenance pricing.
  - Contractual terms and conditions.

Because each research project is often unique, industry practices suggest that careful consideration should be used when qualifying potential research suppliers. Exhibit a-2 offers a checklist developed from recommendations of industry practitioners and associations.

To recap, the manager, research department, or research sponsor should achieve several objectives in the RFP process: qualify potential vendors, write and distribute the RFP eight to ten weeks before the requested date, be available to answer supplier questions or hold prebidding conferences, evaluate submissions on known criteria, award contracts and start the project on published dates, and provide a critique to all suppliers who submitted proposals. The latter will help unsuccessful bidders become competitive in the future and maintain your goodwill for future projects.

A well-written RFP allows an organization to request high-quality proposals for dealing with complex problems. When not done properly, the RFP process will take longer, cost more, and not provide a complete long-term solution. Therefore, when a manager decides to put a research project to bid using an RFP, it is essential that time and effort be invested at the beginning.

Now, let's say as a researcher you have received an RFP. What is next? First, you decide if creating a proposal is worth your investment of time and effort. Even if you are not responding to the RFP, becoming familiar with proposals can be helpful. As a researcher, you might consider producing all of your projects using a structure or template similar to the proposal format.

The Research Proposal

A **proposal** is an individual's or company's offer to produce a product or render a service to a potential buyer or sponsor. The purpose of the research proposal is:

1. To present the management question to be researched and relate its importance.
2. To discuss the research efforts of others who have worked on related management questions.
3. To suggest the data necessary for solving the management question and how the data will be gathered, treated, and interpreted.

>**Exhibit a-2** Checklist for Qualifying Research Suppliers

Research Supplier

❏ Research experience and industry status including appropriate accreditation.

  ❏ Scope/type of research performed (quantitative vs. qualitative vs. both; advertising creative development, product testing, site location, etc.).

    ❏ Knowledge of specific research methodologies (e.g. research with children, visual ethnography, conjoint analysis).

  ❏ Types of clients.

    ❏ Knowledge of specific markets.

      ❏ International links or associations, if needed.

  ❏ No conflicts of interest.

❏ Code of ethical performance.

Research Supplier's Staff

❏ Skill and experience to manage the project.

❏ Skill and experience to conduct desired research.

  ❏ Specialist skills, when needed (psychologists, anthropologists, Internet technologists, etc.).

❏ Understanding of the various business functions.

Research Supplier's Facilities, Procedures, and Quality Management

❏ Compatible project management system.

❏ Compatible contractual arrangements, including billing.

❏ Compatible client complaint and satisfaction handling procedures.

❏ Desired quality assurance procedures.

❏ Desired organization, procedures, and appropriate facilities.

  ❏ Data collection (interviewers, interviewer training, CATI, CAPI, proprietary methodologies, etc.).

    ❏ Field operations.

    ❏ Lab settings (taste testing, product testing, etc.).

  ❏ Data handling (internal or subcontracted, software used, etc.).

  ❏ Developing/drawing samples.

❏ Compatible standard reporting procedures and guidelines.

❏ Desired results presentation practices.

Source: This checklist was developed from recommendations of industry practitioners and material on the ESOMAR website: http://www.esomar.nl/guidelines/CommissioningResearch.htm.

In addition, a research proposal must present the researcher's plan, services, and credentials in the best possible way to encourage the proposal's selection over competitors. In contract research, the survival of companies depends on their ability to develop winning proposals.[1] A proposal is also known as a work plan, prospectus, outline, statement of intent, or draft plan.[2] The proposal tells us what, why, how, where, and to whom the research will be done. It must also show the benefit of doing the research.[3]

The research proposal is essentially a road map, showing clearly the location from which a journey begins, the destination to be reached, and the method of getting there. Well-prepared proposals include potential problems that may be encountered along the way and methods for avoiding or working around them, much as a road map indicates alternate routes for a detour.

Sponsor Uses

All research has a sponsor in one form or another. The student researcher is responsible to the class instructor. In a corporate setting, whether the research is being done in-house by a research department or under contract to an external research firm, management sponsors the research. University-, government-, or corporate-sponsored (grant) research uses grant committees to evaluate the work.

A research proposal allows the sponsor to assess the sincerity of the researcher's purpose, the clarity of his or her design, the extent of his or her relevant background material, and the researcher's fitness for undertaking the project. Depending on the type of research and the sponsor, various aspects of a standard proposal design are emphasized. The proposal displays the researcher's discipline, organization, and logic. It thus allows the research sponsor to assess both the researcher and the proposed design, to compare them against competing proposals on current organizational, scholastic, or scientific needs, and to make the best selection for the project. A poorly planned, poorly written, or poorly organized proposal damages the researcher's reputation more than the decision not to submit a proposal.

Comparison of the research project results with the proposal is also the first step in the process of evaluating the overall research. Comparing the final product with the stated objectives makes it is easy for the sponsor to decide if the research goal—a better decision on the management question—has been achieved.

Another benefit of the proposal is the discipline it brings to the sponsor. Many managers, requesting research from an in-house departmental research project, do not adequately define the problem they are addressing. The research proposal acts as a catalyst for discussion between the person conducting the research and the manager. The researcher translates the management question, as described by the manager, into the research question and outlines the objectives of the study. Upon review, the manager may discover that the interpretation of the problem does not encompass all the original symptoms. The proposal, then, serves as the basis for additional discussion between the manager and the researcher until all aspects of the management question are understood. Parts of the management question may not be researchable, or at least not subject to empirical study. An alternate design, such as a qualitative or policy analysis study, may need to be proposed. Upon completion of the discussions, the sponsor and researcher should agree on a carefully worded research question. As Exhibit a-3 reveals, proposal development can work in an iterative fashion until the sponsor authorizes the research to proceed.

>Exhibit a-3 Proposal Development

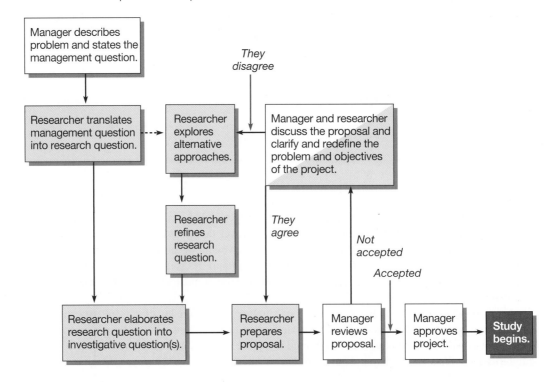

Researcher Benefits

A proposal is even more beneficial for the researcher than for the sponsor. The process of writing a proposal encourages the researcher to plan and review the project's logical steps. Related management and research literature should be examined in developing the proposal. This review prompts the researcher to assess previous approaches to similar management questions and revise the research plan accordingly. Additionally, developing the proposal offers the opportunity to spot flaws in the logic, errors in assumptions, or even management questions that are not adequately addressed by the objectives and design.

The in-house or contract researcher uses the approved research proposal as a guide throughout the investigation. Progress can be monitored and milestones noted. At completion, the proposal provides an outline for the final research report.[4]

Like any other business, a contract researcher makes his or her profit from correctly estimating costs and pricing the research project appropriately. A thorough proposal process is likely to reveal all possible cost-related activities, thus making cost estimation more accurate. Because many of these cost-associated activities are related to time, a proposal benefits a researcher by forcing a time estimate for the project. These time and cost estimates encourage researchers to plan the project so that work progresses steadily toward the deadline. Since many people are inclined to procrastinate, having a schedule helps them work methodically toward the completion of the project. Researchers often develop Gantt charts of the logical research steps, similar to the one in Exhibit 5-11 in Chapter 5, as working documents when developing responses to RFPs.

Types of Research Proposals

In general, research proposals can be divided between those generated for internal and those generated for external audiences. An internal proposal is done by staff specialists or by the research department within the firm. External proposals sponsored by university grant committees, government agencies, government contractors, not-for-profit organizations, or corporations can be further classified as either solicited or unsolicited. With few exceptions, the larger the project, the more complex the proposal. In public sector work, the complexity is generally greater than in a comparable private sector proposal.

There are three general levels of complexity: exploratory studies, small-scale studies, and large-scale studies. These are noted in Exhibit a-4. The exploratory study generates the most simple research proposal. More complex and common in business is the small-scale study—either an internal study or an external contract research project. The large-scale professional study, worth up to several million

>**Exhibit a-4** Proposal Complexity

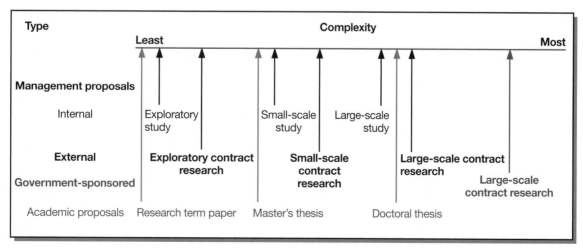

>**Exhibit a-5** Modules to Include in Proposals: A Comparison of Management-Oriented Proposals and Student Proposals

Proposal Modules	Management Internal — Exploratory Study	Management Internal — Small-Scale Study	Management Internal — Large-Scale Study	Management External — Exploratory Contract	Management External — Small-Scale Contract	Management External — Large-Scale Contract	Government — Large-Scale Contract	Student — Term Paper	Student — Master's Thesis	Student — Doctoral Thesis
Executive summary		✔	✔	✔	✔	✔	✔			
Problem statement	✔	✔	✔	✔	✔	✔	✔	✔	✔	✔
Research objectives	✔	✔	✔	✔	✔	✔	✔	✔	✔	✔
Literature review			✔			✔	✔		✔	✔
Importance/ benefits of study			✔	✔	✔	✔	✔			✔
Research design	✔	✔	✔	✔	✔	✔	✔		✔	✔
Data analysis						✔	✔			✔
Nature and form of results		✔	✔		✔	✔	✔		✔	✔
Qualification of researchers				✔	✔	✔	✔			
Budget		✔	✔	✔	✔	✔	✔			
Schedule	✔	✔	✔	✔	✔	✔	✔			✔
Facilities and special resources			✔	✔	✔	✔	✔		✔	✔
Project management			✔			✔	✔			
Bibliography			✔			✔	✔	✔	✔	✔
Appendices/ glossary of terms			✔			✔	✔		✔	✔
Measurement instrument			✔			✔	✔			✔

dollars, is the most complex proposal we deal with here. Government agency large-scale project RFPs usually generate proposals running several hundred pages and use the same modules that we discuss next. However, each agency has unique requirements, making generalized coverage beyond the scope of this text.

Exhibit a-5 displays a set of modules for building a proposal. Their order can represent an outline for a proposal. Based on the type of proposal you are writing, you may choose the appropriate modules for inclusion. This is a general guide, and sometimes more or less than what is shown here is appropriate for a specific purpose. For example, most small-scale studies do not require a glossary of terms. Terms are defined within the body of the proposal. However, if the proposal deals with an esoteric subject that is not familiar to management, it is appropriate to add a glossary. For a solicited study, the RFP will indicate both the content headings and their order.

Internal Proposals

Internal proposals are more succinct than external ones. At the least complex end of the continuum in Exhibit a-4, a one- to three-page memo from the researcher to management outlining the problem statement, study objectives, research design, and schedule is enough to start an exploratory study. Privately and publicly held businesses are concerned with how to solve a particular problem, make a decision, or improve an aspect of their business. Seldom do businesses begin research studies for other reasons. Regardless of the intended audience, in the small-scale proposal, the literature review and bibliography are consequently not stressed and can often be stated briefly in the research design. Since management insists on brevity, an executive summary is mandatory for all but the most simple of proposals (projects that can be proposed in a two-page memo do not need an executive summary). Schedules and budgets are necessary for funds to be committed. For the smaller-scale projects, descriptions are not required for facilities and special resources, nor is there a need for a glossary. Since managers familiar with the problem sponsor small projects, the associated jargon, requirements, and definitions should be included directly in the text. Also, the measuring instrument and project management modules are not required. Managers will typically leave this detail for researchers.

External Proposals

An external proposal is either solicited or unsolicited. A **solicited proposal** is often in response to an RFP. The proposal is likely competing against several others for a contract or grant. An **unsolicited proposal** represents a suggestion by a contract researcher for research that might be done. For an example, a consulting firm might propose a research project to a client that has retained the consultancy for other purposes. As another example, a research firm might propose an omnibus study to a trade association to address problems arising from a change in the cultural or political-legal environments. The unsolicited proposal has the advantage of not competing against others but the disadvantage of having to speculate on the ramifications of a management dilemma facing the firm's management. In addition to being an outsider assessing an internal problem, the writer of an unsolicited proposal must decide to whom the document should be sent. Such proposals are often time-sensitive, so the window of opportunity might close before a redirected proposal finds its appropriate recipient.

The most important sections of the external proposal are the objectives, design, qualifications, schedule, and budget. In contract research, the results and objectives sections are the standards against which the completed project is measured. The executive summary of an external proposal may be included within the letter of transmittal. As the complexity of the project increases, more information is required about project management and the facilities and special resources. As we move toward government-sponsored research, particular attention must be paid to each specification in the RFP. To ignore or not meet any specification is to automatically disqualify your proposal as "nonresponsive."[5]

We offer a sample of an external proposal on the Online Resource Center.

Structuring the Research Proposal

Consider again Exhibit a-5. Using this reference, you can put together a set of modules that tailors your proposal to the intended audience. Each of the following modules is flexible, so its content and length may be adapted to specific needs.

Executive Summary

The **executive summary** allows a busy manager or sponsor to understand quickly the thrust of the proposal. It is essentially an informative abstract, giving executives the chance to grasp the essentials of the proposal without having to read the details.[6] The goal of the summary is to secure a positive evaluation by the executive who will pass the proposal on to the staff for a full evaluation. As such, the executive summary should include brief statements of the management dilemma and management question, the research objectives/research question(s), and the benefits of your approach. If the proposal is unsolicited, a brief description of your qualifications is also appropriate.

Problem Statement

This section needs to convince the sponsor to continue reading the proposal. You should capture the reader's attention by stating the management dilemma, its background, its consequences, and the resulting management question. The importance of answering the management question should be emphasized here if a separate module on the importance/benefits of study is not included later in the proposal. In addition, this section should include any restrictions or areas of the management question that will not be addressed.

Problem statements too broadly defined cannot be addressed adequately in one study. It is important that the management question distinguish the primary problem from related problems clearly. Be sure your problem statement is clear without the use of idioms or clichés. After reading this section, the potential sponsor should know the management dilemma and the question, its significance, and why something should be done to change the status quo.[7]

Research Objectives

This module addresses the purpose of the investigation. It is here that you lay out exactly what is being planned by the proposed research. In a descriptive study, the objectives can be stated as the research question. Recall that the research question can be further broken down into investigative questions. If the proposal is for a causal study, then the objectives can be restated as a hypothesis.

The objectives module flows naturally from the problem statement, giving the sponsor specific, concrete, and achievable goals. It is best to list the objectives either in order of importance or in general terms first, moving to specific terms (i.e., research question followed by underlying investigative questions). The research question(s) (or hypotheses, if appropriate) should be separated from the flow of the text for quick identification.

The research objectives section is the basis for judging the remainder of the proposal and, ultimately, the final report. Verify the consistency of the proposal by checking to see that each objective is discussed in the research design, data analysis, and results sections.

Literature Review

The **literature review** section examines recent (or historically significant) research studies, company data, or industry reports that act as a basis for the proposed study. Begin your discussion of the related literature and relevant secondary data from a comprehensive perspective, moving to more specific studies that are associated with your problem. If the problem has a historical background, begin with the earliest references. A literature review might reveal that the sponsor can answer the management question with a secondary data search rather than the collection of primary data.

Avoid the extraneous details of the literature; do a brief review of the information, not a comprehensive report. Always refer to the original source. If you find something of interest in a quotation, find the original publication and ensure you understand it. In this way, you will avoid any errors of interpretation or transcription. Emphasize the important results and conclusions of other studies, the relevant data and trends from previous research, and particular methods or designs that could be duplicated or should be avoided. Discuss how the literature applies to the study you are proposing; show the weaknesses or faults in the design, discussing how you would avoid similar problems. If your proposal deals solely with secondary data, discuss the relevance of the data and the bias or lack of bias inherent in it.

The literature review may also explain the need for the proposed work to appraise the shortcomings and/or informational gaps in secondary data sources. This analysis may go beyond scrutinizing the availability or conclusions of past studies and their data, to examining the accuracy of secondary sources, the credibility of these sources, and the appropriateness of earlier studies.

Close the literature review section by summarizing the important aspects of the literature and interpreting them in terms of your problem. Refine the problem as necessary in light of your findings.

Importance/Benefits of the Study

In this section you describe explicit benefits that will accrue from your study. The importance of "doing the study now" should be emphasized. Usually, this section is not more than a few paragraphs. If you find it difficult to write, then you have probably not adequately clarified the management dilemma. Return to the analysis of the problem and ensure, through additional discussions with your sponsor or your research team or by a reexamination of the literature, that you have captured the essence of the problem.

This section also requires you to understand what is most troubling to your sponsor. If it is a potential union activity, you cannot promise that an employee survey will prevent unionization. You can, however, show the importance of this information and its implications. This benefit may allow management to respond to employee concerns and forge a linkage between those concerns and unionization.

The importance/benefits section is particularly important to the unsolicited external proposal. You must convince the sponsoring organization that your plan will meet its needs.

Research Design

Up to now, you have told the sponsor what the problem is, what your study goals are, and why it is important for you to do the study. The proposal has presented the study's value and benefits. The design module describes what you are going to do in technical terms. This section should include as many subsections as needed to show the phases of the project. Provide information on your proposed design for tasks such as sample selection and size, data collection method, instrumentation, procedures, and ethical requirements. When more than one way exists to approach the design, discuss the methods you have rejected and why your selected approach is superior.

Data Analysis

A brief section on the methods used for analyzing the data is appropriate for large-scale contract research projects and doctoral theses. With smaller projects, the proposed data analysis would be included within the research design section. It is in this section that you describe your proposed handling of the data and the theoretical basis for using the selected techniques. The object of this section is to assure the sponsor you are following correct assumptions and using theoretically sound data analysis procedures.

This module is often an arduous section to write. You can make it easier to write, read, and understand your data analysis by using sample charts and tables featuring "dummy" data.

The data analysis section is so important to evaluating contract research proposals that the researcher should contact an expert to review the latest techniques available for use in the particular research study and compare these to the proposed techniques. When there is no statistical or analytical expertise in the company, sponsors are more likely to hire professional help to interpret the soundness of this section.

Nature and Form of Results

Upon finishing this section, the sponsor should be able to go back to the statement of the management question and research objectives and discover that each goal of the study has been covered. One should also specify the types of data to be obtained and the interpretations that will be made in the analysis. If the data are to be turned over to the sponsor for proprietary reasons, make sure this is reflected. Alternatively, if the report will go to more than one sponsor, that should be noted.

This section also contains the contractual statement telling the sponsor exactly what types of information will be received. Statistical conclusions, applied findings, recommendations, action plans, models, strategic plans, and so forth, are examples of the forms of results.

Qualifications of Researchers

This section should begin with the principal investigator and then provide similar information on all individuals involved with the project. Two elements are critical:

1. Professional research competence (relevant research experience, the highest academic degree held, and memberships in business and technical societies).
2. Relevant management experience.[8]

With so many individuals, research specialty firms, and general consultancies providing research services, the sponsor needs assurance that the researcher is professionally competent. Past research experience is the best barometer of competence, followed by the highest academic degree earned. To document relevant research experience, the researcher provides concise descriptions of similar projects. Highest degree usually follows the person's name (e.g., S. Researcher, PhD in Statistics). Society memberships provide some evidence that the researcher is cognizant of the latest methodologies and techniques. These follow the relevant research experience as a string or bulleted list, with organization name followed by term of membership and any relevant leadership positions.

Researchers are increasingly in the business of providing advice, not just research services. And businesses are looking for quality advice. Comparatively, the researcher who demonstrates relevant management or industry experience will be more likely to receive a favorable nod to his or her proposal. The format of this information should follow that used for relevant research experience. The entire curriculum vitae of each researcher need not be included unless required by the RFP. However, researchers often place complete vitae information in an appendix for review by interested sponsors.

Research companies often subcontract specific research activities to firms or individuals that specialize or offer specific resources or facilities. This is especially true for studies involving qualitative research techniques such as in-depth personal interviews and focus groups. Usually brief profiles of these companies are provided in this section only if their inclusion enhances the credibility of the researcher. Otherwise, profiles of such subcontractors are included in an appendix of the final report, rather than in the proposal.

Budget

The budget should be presented in the form the sponsor requests. For example, some organizations require secretarial assistance to be individually budgeted, whereas others insist it be included in the research director's fees or the overhead of the operation. In addition, limitations on travel, per diem rates, and capital equipment purchases can change the way in which you prepare a budget.

Typically, the budget should be no more than one to two pages. Exhibit a-6 shows one format that can be used for small contract research projects. Additional information, backup details, quotes from vendors, and hourly time and payment calculations should be put into an appendix if required or kept in the researcher's file for future reference.

The budget statement in an internal research proposal is based on employee and overhead costs. The budget presented by an external research organization is not just the wages or salaries of its employees but the person-hour price that the contracting firm charges.

The detail the researcher presents may vary depending on both the sponsors' requirements and the contracting research company's policy. Some research companies, particularly in database and computerized analysis areas, quote on the basis of "man-machine hours" involved in a project. The man-machine hour is the hourly fee charged for a person with computer hardware and organizational resources. Here, rather than separating the "other costs," Exhibit a-6 shows these costs embedded in a combined rate. One reason why external research agencies avoid giving detailed budgets is the possibility that disclosures of their costing practices will make their calculations public knowledge, reducing their negotiating flexibility. Since budget statements embody a work strategy depicted in financial terms that could be used by the recipient of the proposal to develop a replicate research plan, vendors are often doubly careful.

The budget section of an external research contractor's proposal states the total fee payable for the assignment. When it is accompanied by a proposed schedule of payment, this is frequently

>**Exhibit a-6** Sample Proposal Budget for a Research Program

Budget Items	Rate	Total Days	Charge
A. Salaries			
1. Research director, Jason Henry	$200/hr.	20 hours	$ 4,000
2. Associate	100/hr.	10 hours	1,000
3. Research assistants (2)	20/hr.	300 hours	6,000
4. Secretarial (1)	12/h.	100 hours	1,200
Subtotal			$12,200
B. Other costs			
5. Employee services and benefits			
6. Travel			$ 2,500
7. Office supplies			100
8. Telephone			800
9. Rent			
10. Other equipment			
11. Publication and storage costs			100
Subtotal			$ 3,500
C. Total of direct costs			$15,700
D. Overhead support			$ 5,480
E. Total funding requested			$21,180

detailed in a purchase order. Like other large-ticket-price services delivered over time in stages (e.g., building a home), payments can be paid at stages of completion. Sometimes a retainer is paid at the beginning of the contract, then a percentage at an intermediate stage, and the balance on completion of the project.

It is extremely important that you retain all information you use to generate your budget. If you use quotes from external contractors, get the quotation in writing for your file. If you estimate time for interviews, keep explicit notes on how you made the estimate. When the time comes to do the work, you should know exactly how much money is budgeted for each particular task.[9]

Some costs are more elusive than others. Do not forget to build the cost of proposal writing into your fee. Publication and delivery of final reports can be a last-minute expense that may be easily overlooked in preliminary budgets.

Schedule

Your schedule should include the major phases of the project, their timetables, and the milestones that signify completion of a phase. For example, major phases may be (1) exploratory interviews, (2) final research proposal, (3) questionnaire revision, (4) field interviews, (5) editing and coding, (6) data analysis, and (7) report generation. Each of these phases should have an estimated time schedule and people assigned to the work.

It may be helpful to you and your sponsor if you chart your schedule. You can use a Gantt chart, shown in Chapter 5, Exhibit 5-11. Alternatively, if the project is large and complex, a **critical path method (CPM)** of scheduling may be included.[10] In a CPM chart, the nodes represent major milestones, and the arrows suggest the work needed to get to the milestone. More than one arrow pointing to a node indicates all those tasks must be completed before the milestone has been met. Usually a number is placed along the arrow showing the number of days or weeks required for that task to be completed. The pathway from start to end that takes the longest time to complete is called the *critical path,* because any delay in an activity along that path will delay the end of the entire project. An example of a CPM chart is shown in Exhibit a-7. Software programs designed for project management simplify scheduling and charting the schedule. Most are available for personal computers.

>**Exhibit a-7** CPM Schedule

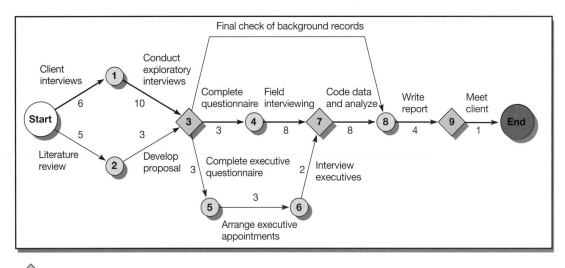

Milestones:

3 Proposal approval
7 Interviews completed
9 Final report completed

Critical Path:
S–1–3–4–7–8–9–E

Time to Completion:
40 working days

Facilities and Special Resources

Often, projects will require special facilities or resources that should be described in detail. For example, a contract exploratory study may need specialized facilities for focus group sessions. Computer-assisted telephone or other interviewing facilities may be required. Alternatively, your proposed data analysis may require sophisticated computer algorithms, and therefore you need access to an adequate system. These requirements will vary from study to study. The proposal should carefully list the relevant facilities and resources that will be used. The costs for such facility use should be detailed in your budget.

Project Management

The purpose of the **project management** section is to show the sponsor that the research team is organized in a way to do the project efficiently. A master plan is required for complex projects to show how all the phases will be brought together. The plan includes:

• The research team's organization.

• Management procedures and controls for executing the research plan.

• Examples of management and technical reports.

• The research team's relationship with the sponsor.

• Financial and legal responsibility.

• Management competence.

Tables and charts are most helpful in presenting the master plan. The relationships between researchers and assistants need to be shown when several researchers are part of the team. Sponsors must know that the director is an individual capable of leading the team and acting as a useful liaison to the sponsor. In addition, procedures for information processing, record control, and expense control are critical to large operations and should be shown as part of the management procedures.

The type and frequency of progress reports should be recorded so that the sponsor can expect to be kept up to date and the researchers can expect to be left alone to do research. The sponsor's limits on control during the process should be delineated.

This section also discusses any details such as printing facilities, clerical help, or information processing capabilities to be provided by the sponsor rather than the researcher. In addition, rights to the data, the results, and authority to speak for the researcher and for the sponsor are included.

Payment frequency and timing are also covered in the master plan. Finally, proof of financial responsibility and overall management competence is provided.

Bibliography

For all projects that require a literature review, a bibliography is necessary. Use the bibliographic format required by the sponsor. If none is specified, a standard style manual will provide the details necessary to prepare the bibliography.[11] Many of these sources also offer suggestions for successful proposal writing.

Appendices

Glossary   The researcher should include a glossary of terms whenever there are many words unique to the research topic and not understood by the general management community. This is a simple section consisting of terms and definitions, similar in format to the glossary in this textbook. Also, the researcher should define any acronyms used, even if they are defined within the text (e.g., *CATI* for "computer-assisted telephone interviewing").

Measurement Instrument   For large projects, it is appropriate to include samples of the measurement instruments if they are available when you assemble the proposal. This allows the sponsor to discuss particular changes in one or more of the instruments. If the proposal includes the development of a custom-designed measurement instrument, omit this appendix section.

Other   Any detail that reinforces the body of the proposal can be included in an appendix. This includes researcher vitae, profiles of firms or individuals to which work will be subcontracted, budget details, and lengthy descriptions of special facilities or resources.

To see how some of these elements were incorporated in the MindWriter research proposal, see Exhibit a-8.

Evaluating the Research Proposal

Proposals are subject to either formal or informal reviews. *Formal reviews* are regularly done for solicited proposals. The formal review process varies but typically includes:

- Development of review criteria, using RFP guidelines.
- Assignment of points to each criterion, using a universal scale.
- Assignment of a weight for each criterion, based on importance of each criterion.
- Generation of a score for each proposal, representing the sum of all weighted criterion scores.

The sponsor should assign the criteria, the weights, and the scale to be used for scoring each criterion before the proposals are received. The proposal then should be evaluated with this checklist of criteria in hand. Points are recorded for each criterion reflecting the sponsor's assessment of how well the proposal meets the company's needs relative to that criterion (e.g., 1 through 10, with 10 being the largest number of points assigned to the best proposal for a particular criterion). After the review, the weighted criterion scores are added to provide a cumulative total. The proposal with the highest number of points wins the contract.

>Exhibit a-8 Proposal for MindWriter CompleteCare Satisfaction Research

In preparing a proposal for Gracie Uhura, product manager at MindWriter Corporation, Jason and Sara decided to exclude the "executive summary" for two reasons: The proposal is short and the essentials will be contained in the cover letter. The proposal follows the components discussed in this chapter. It is an appropriate adaptation for an internal, small-scale study. The module "qualification of researcher" was not needed because MindWriter's employee solicited the proposal, thus had prejudged the researcher's qualifications.

Repair Process Satisfaction Proposal
MindWriter Corporation CompleteCare Program

Problem Statement

MindWriter Corporation has recently created a service and repair program, CompleteCare, for its portable/laptop/notebook computers. This program promises to provide a rapid response to customers' service problems.

MindWriter is currently experiencing a shortage of trained technical operators in its telephone center. The package courier, contracted to pick up and deliver customers' machines to CompleteCare, has provided irregular execution. MindWriter has also experienced parts availability problems for some machine types.

Recent phone logs at the call center show complaints about CompleteCare; it is unknown how representative these complaints are and what implications they may have for satisfaction with MindWriter products.

Management desires information on the program's effectiveness and its impact on customer satisfaction to determine what should be done to improve the CompleteCare program for MindWriter product repair and servicing.

Research Objectives

The purpose of this research is to discover the level of satisfaction with the CompleteCare service program. Specifically, we intend to identify the component and overall levels of satisfaction with CompleteCare. Components of the repair process are important targets for investigation because they reveal:

(1) How customer tolerance levels for repair performance affect overall satisfaction, and

(2) Which process components should be immediately improved to elevate the overall satisfaction of those MindWriter customers experiencing product failures.

We will also discover the importance of types of product failure on customer satisfaction levels.

Importance/Benefits

High levels of user satisfaction translate into positive word-of-mouth product endorsements. These endorsements influence the purchase outcomes for (1) friends and relatives and (2) business associates.

Critical incidents, such as product failures, have the potential to either undermine existing satisfaction levels or preserve and even increase the resulting levels of product satisfaction. The outcome of the episode depends on the quality of the manufacturer's response.

An extraordinary response by the manufacturer to such incidents will preserve and enhance user satisfaction levels to the point that direct and indirect benefits derived from such programs will justify their costs.

This research has the potential for connecting to ongoing MindWriter customer satisfaction programs and measuring the long-term effects of CompleteCare (and product failure incidents) on customer satisfaction.

Research Design

Exploration: Qualitative. We will augment our knowledge of CompleteCare by interviewing the service manager, the call center manager, and the independent package company's account executive. Based on a thorough inventory of CompleteCare's internal external processes, we propose to develop a mail survey.

Questionnaire Design. A self-administered questionnaire (postcard size) offers the most cost-effective method for securing feedback on the effectiveness of CompleteCare. The introduction on the postcard will be a variation of MindWriter's current advertising campaign.

Some questions for this instrument will be based on the investigative questions we presented to you previously, and others will be drawn from the executive interviews. We anticipate a maximum of 10 questions. A new five-point expectation scale, compatible with your existing customer satisfaction scales, is being designed.

Although we are not convinced that open-ended questions are appropriate for postcard questionnaires, we understand that you and Mr. Malraison like them. A comments/suggestions question will be included. In addition, we will work out a code block that captures the call center's reference number, model, and item(s) serviced.

>**Exhibit a-8** Proposal for MindWriter CompleteCare Satisfaction Research *(concluded)*

Logistics. The postal arrangements are: box rental, permit, and "business reply" privileges to be arranged in a few days. The approval for a reduced postage rate will take one to two weeks. The budget section itemizes these costs.

Pilot Test. We will test the questionnaire with a small sample of customers using your tech-line operators. This will contain your costs. We will then revise the questions and forward them to our graphics designer for layout. The instrument will then be submitted to you for final approval.

Evaluation of Nonresponse Bias. A random sample of 100 names will be secured from the list of customers who do not return the questionnaire. Call center records will be used for establishing the sampling frame. Nonresponders will be interviewed on the telephone and their responses compared statistically to those of the responders.

Data Analysis

We will review the postcards returned and send you a weekly report listing customers who are dissatisfied (score a "1" or "2") with any item of the questionnaire or who submit a negative comment. This will improve your timeliness in resolving customer complaints. Each month, we will provide you with a report consisting of frequencies and category percentages for each question. Visual displays of the data will be in bar chart/histogram form. We propose to include at least one question dealing with overall satisfaction (with CompleteCare and/or MindWriter). This overall question would be regressed on the individual items to determine each item's importance. A performance grid will identify items needing improvement with an evaluation of priority. Other analyses can be prepared on a time and materials basis.

The open-ended questions will be summarized and reported by model code. If you wish, we also can provide content analysis for these questions.

Results: Deliverables

1. Development and production of a postcard survey. MindWriter employees will package the questionnaire with the returned merchandise.
2. Weekly exception reports (transmitted electronically) listing customers who meet the dissatisfied customer criteria.
3. Monthly reports as described in the data analysis section.
4. An ASCII diskette with each month's data shipped to Austin by the fifth working day of each month.

Budget

Card Layout and Printing. Based on your card estimate, our designer will lay out and print 2,000 cards in the first run ($500). The specifications are as follows: 7-point Williamsburg offset hi-bulk with one-over-one black ink. A gray-scale layer with a MindWriter or CompleteCare logo can be positioned under the printed material at a nominal charge. The two-sided cards measure 4¼ by 5½.

This allows us to print four cards per page. The opposite side will have the business reply logo, postage paid symbol, and address.

Cost Summary

Interviews	$ 1,550.00
Travel costs	2,500.00
Questionnaire development	1,850.00
Equipment/supplies	1,325.00
Graphics design	800.00
Permit fee (annual)	75.00
Business reply fee (annual)	185.00
Box rental (annual)	35.00
Printing costs	500.00
Data entry (monthly)	430.00
Monthly data files (each)	50.00
Monthly reports (each)	1,850.00
Total start-up costs	$11,150.00
Monthly run costs	$ 1,030.00*

*An additional fee of $0.21 per card will be assessed by the post office for business reply mail. At approximately a 30 percent return rate, we estimate the monthly cost to be less than $50.

Several people, each of whom may be assigned to a particular section, typically review long and complex proposals. The formal method is most likely to be used for competitive government, university, or public sector grants and also for large-scale contracts.

Small-scale contracts are more prone to informal evaluation. In an *informal review,* the project needs, and thus the criteria, are well understood but are not usually well documented. In contrast to the formal method, a system of points is not used and the criteria are not ranked. The process is more qualitative and impressionistic. Exhibit a-9 shows Sara Arens's informal review of a proposal presented to her as a member of her county's Economic Development Council.

In practice, many factors contribute to a proposal's acceptance and funding. Primarily, the content discussed above must be included to the level of detail required by the sponsor's RFP. Beyond the required modules, other factors can quickly eliminate a proposal from consideration or improve the sponsor's reception of the proposal, among them:

- Neatness.
- Organization in terms of being both logical and easily understood.
- Completeness in fulfilling the RFP's specifications, including budget and schedule.
- Appropriateness of writing style.
- Submission within the RFP's timeline.

Although a proposal produced on a word processor and bound with an expensive cover will not overcome design or analysis deficiencies, a poorly presented, unclear, or disorganized proposal will not get serious attention from the reviewing sponsor. Given that multiple reviewers may be evaluating only a given section, the reviewer should be able to page through the proposal to any section of interest.

In terms of the technical writing style of the proposal, the sponsor must be able to understand the problem statement, the research design, and the methodology. The sponsor should clearly understand why the proposed research should be funded and the exact goals and concrete results that will come from the study.

The proposal also must meet specific RFP guidelines set by the sponsoring company or agency, including budgetary restrictions and schedule deadlines. A schedule that does not meet the expected deadlines will disqualify the proposal. A budget that is too high for the allocated funds will be rejected. Conversely, a low budget compared to competing proposals suggests that something is missing or there is something wrong with the researchers.

Finally, a late proposal will not be reviewed. Although current project disqualification due to lateness may appear to be the worst result here, there is a possible longer-term effect created. Lateness communicates a level of disrespect for the sponsor—that the researcher's schedule is more important than the sponsor's. A late proposal also communicates a weakness in project management, which raises an issue of professional competence. This concern about competence may continue to plague the researcher during future project proposal reviews.

>**Exhibit a-9** Informal Proposal Review

Sara Arens

200 ShellPoint Tower
Palm Beach, Florida 33480

Mr. Harry Shipley, President
Economic Development Council
1800 ShellPoint Tower
Palm Beach, Florida 33480

Dear Harry,

I have reviewed Robert Buffet's proposal for an investigation of the job creation practices of local companies and, in short, I am very much concerned with several aspects of the "proposal." It is not really a proposal at all, because it lacks sufficient detail.

First, let me mention that I shared Buffet's proposal with Mr. Jason Henry, my partner. Mr. Buffet and his organization may one day represent competition for us, and you must therefore be aware of a potential conflict of interest and perhaps discount the opinions stated here. Since I am delivering this letter to you in two days rather than the two weeks you requested, you may wish to discuss my comments with others.

What you and Mr. Buffet gave me is an abbreviated research plan for our county, but since it lacks many features found in a comprehensive proposal, I immediately saw it was not the full proposal that had been funded by the state commerce secretary. I called Tallahassee and reached a young woman who hemmed and hawed and refused to say if she was authorized to mail me the full proposal. Finally, I gave up arguing and gave her your address and told her she could mail it to you.

I then made several calls to people in Tallahassee whom I know. Did you know that this research idea is being floated by our senior U.S. senator, who is eager to throw a monkey wrench into the president's tax incentives plan? The senator whispered it to the governor and the governor whispered it to her commerce secretary, and here we are.

The problem statement is rather long and convoluted, but, in short, it poses the questions, Are new high-tech companies creating jobs for residents of our county? Or are they bringing technical and manufacturing workers from outside the state and bypassing the local work force? Or are they doing research in these companies with a low level of manufacturing job creation? Or are they investing in 'smart' capital equipment that does not create jobs? If you cut through the verbiage, I think you can see the project is dead on the mark with its questions.

The research objectives section is fairly straightforward. Buffet's people are going to identify all the companies in this county in the NAICS code groups associated with "high tech" and collect information on the number of locally hired employees in various job categories, chiefly in production, and also collect data on capital investments, debt, and other financial data, which Jason says makes good sense to collect and ought to be easy to do.

There is a section called Importance of the Study, which is full of platitudes and does not get around to mentioning the pending tax legislation. But at least the platitudes are brief.

I become nervous in the Design section. It calls for Mr. Buffet's group to go on site with a "team" and conduct in-depth interviews with the chief operating officer (COO), treasurer, and comptroller of each company and enter the data into a spreadsheet. I have double-checked this with Jason and also with a banker friend, and both of them assure me that a simple questionnaire might be mailed to the COO. There is no need whatsoever to send in a team to conduct open-ended interviews. Although there might be a noncompliance problem associated with filling out a form, this might appropriately be attended to by pointing out the auspices—the state commerce secretary and your Economic Development Council—with an interview request as a last resort.

The proposal contains no budget and no specific list of researchers who will comprise the team. The firm would have carte blanche to go in with anyone on their payroll and try to induce the subjects to stray beyond the stated research objectives to talk about anything at all. Obviously such license would be a marketing tool and might allow the researchers to collect a list of researchable problems not related to the secretary's needs, as stated in the problem section.

I strongly advise you to tell Mr. Buffet to collect the information through a simple mail survey. Offer to send it out under your council's letterhead, or see if you can get the commerce office or even the governor's office to send it out. But do not subject your local business community to unstructured, free-ranging visits, which are clearly not justified by the research objectives.

Sincerely,

Sara

Covering Kids RFP

Wirthlin Worldwide earned the Ogilvy Research Award for creative and effective research instrumental in the development of the Covering Kids advertising campaign. This RFP from sponsor Robert Wood Johnson Foundation started the process that resulted in enrolling more than one million additional children for a health insurance initiative.

March 13, 20xx

Name
Firm
Address
City, State Zip code

Dear XXXX:

As you know, we are working with GMMB&A to support the national Covering Kids Initiative (CKI). We appreciate your recent response to a proposal to support this effort's marketing research requirements. Since that time, we have further refined our requirements. We hope that you will be willing to review this request, and revise your previous proposal in any ways needed to meet these altered needs.

The Covering Kids Initiative is a $47 million national program of the Foundation that works to enroll eligible children in Medicaid and the Federal-state Children's Health Insurance Programs (SCHIP). Three-year grants for the Covering Kids Initiative support coalitions in 49 states and the District of Columbia. These coalitions conduct outreach initiatives and work to simplify and coordinate the enrollment processes for health coverage programs for low-income children. In its first two years of activity, the CKI has focused largely on simplifying the enrollment process. During the second year, in addition to continuing a focus on simplification and coordination, there will be target marketing campaigns to encourage adults to enroll eligible children in both the SCHIP and Medicaid programs.

The Foundation will work with its Covering Kids communications contractor to support these CKI coalitions in marketing, advertising, public relations, coalition building, and cause-related partnerships at the national and state levels. The tasks described here will help provide direction for the strategic development of communications and provide support for testing and measuring communications campaigns in six markets prior to introduction nationwide.

Background

There are approximately five million uninsured children in the US eligible for either SCHIP or Medicaid. While income eligibility requirements in the federally funded SCHIP programs vary from state-to-state, they all generally cover children in households of four with incomes up to $33,400 (higher in some states). About half of the eligible-uninsured Americans are non-Hispanic white, about 30% are African-American, another 20% are Hispanic/Latino. Although the numbers are much smaller, a large proportion of Native-Americans are also eligible but not covered.

There are many reasons why so many eligible children are not enrolled. Some primary barriers to enrollment are: lack of awareness of the availability of health programs, especially SCHIP; lack of knowledge of eligibility criteria for these programs; complicated/onerous application processes; a stigma attached to government-funded health care programs (especially for working parents); the lack of outreach experience and expertise (most states have never conducted outreach for programs like Medicaid).

The primary challenge for this project is to create a nationwide campaign to enroll children—yet the "fulfillment mechanisms" (the state SCHIP and Medicaid programs) vary from state to state. Many states have developed their own distinct marketing and branding campaigns, so that the SCHIP programs in Connecticut (HUSKY B) and in Georgia (PeachCare) and in Illinois (KidsCare) resemble traditional private health plans more than they do government programs based on income eligibility. A national 1-877-KIDS-NOW phone number is in use that seamlessly routes calls through to the appropriate state program office. We will likely use that toll-free number as a marketing and fulfillment mechanism for this effort.

The communications campaign will target specific groups of parents and other adults who could play a key role in enrolling eligible children in existing programs. Specific messages will be tested for use with subsets of low income Americans, including African-Americans, Hispanic/Latino, Native Americans and others. The Campaigns will first be tested and measured in six regional markets before national advertising begins. Ad buys and other communications activities will be coupled with local enrollment events. Communications activities and enrollment events will likely intensify twice annually, during the back-to-school and winter cold and flu seasons.

Contractual Needs

Requirements for market research and evaluation support are described in the two tasks below.

Task 1. MARKET RESEARCH. Design, conduct, analyze, and provide conclusions relevant to communications planning.

Task 1a. Develop an in-depth comprehensive profile (through a series of in-depth interviews) of the families of eligible-but-uninsured children—who are they, where are they, why are they not enrolled, the most effective messages/concepts to move individuals in specific groups to enroll in SCHIP/Medicaid, what messages/words/concepts are definite turn-offs among specific groups, etc.

Of particular interest:

- Hispanic/Latino rural/urban
- African-American rural/urban
- Native-American rural/urban
- White rural/urban
- Parents of children enrolled in SCHIP
- Parents of children enrolled in Medicaid
- Parents of uninsured children eligible for SCHIP and/or Medicaid who haven't applied
- Parents of uninsured children eligible for SCHIP and/or Medicaid who have applied but are not enrolled

Level of effort: approximately 120 in-depth interviews. [Alternative suggestions invited.]

Task 1b. Qualitative research among opinion leaders: their perceptions of SCHIP; their definition of success/failure, etc. These might include federal and state legislative staff, regulatory staff, child health advocates, constituency group leaders, and media gatekeepers.

Level of effort: approximately 25 in-depth interviews. [Alternative suggestions invited.]

Evaluation Task

Task 1. A comprehensive national survey. This survey will: help direct communications development; provide content for news placement; provide a pre-campaign benchmark (baseline data). We anticipate repeating this survey in the future to help gauge change and progress. However, at this time we are interested only in one benchmark survey.

We are considering two options for survey sampling: a) a national sample including oversamples of lower-income families as described above, or b) a sample consisting of lower-income families with sufficient subsets (described above) to be statistically reliable. We are interested in receiving recommendations regarding which option to pursue as well as a description of how this work would be done.

Task 2. An evaluation of the media campaign in 6 test markets. Because the national advertising and public relations components of the communication campaign will be large in scope and level of effort, this test market phase will be used to test and refine media messages, techniques, and decisions. The test market evaluation is critical to decision making for this effort.

Six mid-sized media markets will be selected to obtain a mix of the targeted demographic groups and geographic diversity. The Foundation will provide the list of selected sites to the contractor. The advertising and public relations test phase will span 4–6 weeks, planned for late-August–early-September 2000. The market test will be planned and executed through close collaboration with the communications contractor, the Covering Kids National Program Office and coalitions in the target markets, and the Foundation. It will be designed to gauge heightened awareness, perceptions of target audiences, willingness to apply, and impact of campaign on overcoming any attitudinal barriers to applying.

This market test will include

Task 2a. Benchmark survey—a random sample telephone survey with oversamples of target audiences. To include both benchmarking questions (such as awareness, attitude, intention measures) and message development questions (such as questions about message concepts, language).

Task 2b. Post-campaign survey—a brief telephone follow up survey using same sampling; to include questions to assess recall/awareness, attitudes, intentions.

Task 2c. Tracking of callers to the promoted toll-free number—the Foundation/National Program Office will provide a liaison to the toll-free manager(s). At this time it is not clear whether this will include only the national toll-free number or/and some state operated numbers. This task will include both compiling and analyzing call data and identifying ways to re-contact callers to assess further actions.

Task 2d. Follow-up with callers—brief telephone survey to identify any questions taken. Phone numbers will be provided through the liaison described above. [Alternative method of assessment may be needed.]

Alternative suggestions for test market evaluation, with approximately the same level of effort required, are acceptable.

Anticipated Time Schedule

April 20xx	contract awarded begin development of all tasks
May 20xx	conduct national survey
June 20xx	conduct research with potential beneficiaries, opinion leaders conduct benchmark survey in 6 test markets
August 20xx	begin ads in test markets begin telephone tracking
September 20xx	conduct testing market post-test surveys begin follow-up with telephone callers
October 20xx	present findings of national survey present findings from caller callbacks

Proposal Instructions

We invite you to submit a proposal addressing one or both of the tasks described above. Your proposal should address:

- your approach to conducting the work
- any alternative methods or procedures you would like to suggest for accomplishing the work described (optional)
- a discussion of any anticipated challenges to completing these tasks, and how you would propose handling the challenges
- comments on methodology and other recommendations for producing the needed information
- specific work to be performed, description of the deliverables to be provided, and all costs (included out-of-pocket costs), by task
- relevant experience and expertise
- references

The Foundation is not seeking lengthy or elaborate proposals. Rather proposals should succinctly provide information that will permit a review using the criteria listed below.

Review Criteria

In reviewing proposals, we will consider:

- your approach to the needs and tasks described here, including recommended methodology
- anticipated problems and how these would be handled
- company and staff experience in conducting similar market research and evaluation
- company and staff experience in conducting qualitative and quantitative research with a similar population
- company and staff experience with a health insurance or similar health care issue
- personnel, task and time line, project management
- proposed budget
- ability to respond to time schedule.

In addition we will expect that your company has no conflicts of interest with the Foundation.

Proposals will be due no later than COB Monday, March 27, delivered to

Stuart Schear (Four Copies)
Senior Communications Officer
The Robert Wood Johnson Foundation
Address
City, State Zip code
Phone

Kristine Hartvigsen (Three Copies)
Covering Kids National Program Office
Address
City, State Zip code
Phone

David Smith (Four Copies)
GMMB&A
Address
City, State Zip code
Phone

Elaine Bratic Arkin (One Copy)
Address
City, State Zip code
Phone

We anticipate notifying those who submit proposals of our decision no later than April 1, 2000. I am available by e-mail @ smr@rwjf.org to answer any questions you might have. The following websites offer a wealth of information as well:

<**http://www.coveringkids.org**>—the website for "Covering Kids," the RWJF-funded initiative that these tasks will support
<**http://www.insurekidsnow.gov**>—the HHS/HCFA website for the CHIP programs
<**http://www.cbpp.org**>the Center on Budget and Policy Priorities

Thank you for your thoughtful consideration of this request.

If you wish to speak with someone about this project, please call me at 609-951-5799. Either Elaine Arkin, a consultant to the Foundation, or I would be happy to speak with you.

Sincerely

Stuart Schear
Senior Communications Officer

Focus Group Discussion Guide*

Background

What if your firm manufactures cleansing products in multiple forms—deodorant bar, beauty bar, cream body wash, gel body wash—and your customers are not using the best form for their skin types and activity levels? You might use exploratory focus groups to determine what drivers motivate customers to select the *form* they choose. Given the dramatic growth in this market, you want to hear from women aged 16 to 50 and also from men aged 16 to 25. Also, you need to understand their trade-offs when choosing a specific form.

You turn to a research specialist to conduct focus groups in three cities representative of the category market. Prior to meeting the six groups (two groups in each city; two consisting only of teens), researchers ask each participant to prepare two visual collages using pictures cut from magazines. One collage is to reflect the participant's perceptions and experiences with each form (regardless of personal use experience). A second collage is to depict a month in the participant's life. The Intro and Forms segments of the discussion guide below reference these creative exercises.

Personal Cleansing Form Drivers   Atlanta, Seattle, Phoenix

INTRO (15 min)

    A. ALL ABOUT ME—name, family info, work, play, activities, interests. SHOW LIFE IN THE MONTH COLLAGE

    B. AT SOME POINT ASK: How often shower / bathe?

                                  Use fragrances / perfume? How often?

                                  Use scented or unscented deodorant, lotions, etc?

FORMS (60 min)

    A. LISTED ON EASEL "DEODORANT BAR, BEAUTY BAR, CREAM BODY WASH, GEL BODY WASH"

        Here are the different forms of soaps available that we want to learn about.

        How many have ever used _____? Still using or moved on / rejected?

    B. EASEL RESPONSES (BE SURE PICTURES ARE LABELED) Show and describe your picture collage (from homework), as you tell what you like / not, what **associate** w/_____ form.

        What else **like? / why use?**

        What **not like** about _____? Why not using (more often)?

        How compare to other forms—advantages / disadvantages?

        What **wish for** this form . . . what would make it **better / perfect** for you?

---

*This discussion guide was developed by Pam Hay, an independent qualitative consultant for more than 24 years with a career focused on consumable goods (personal care products, health and beauty aids, and OTC drugs). Her experiences include conducting focus groups, individual depth interviews, ethnography home visits, and multifunctional consumer direct processes for the purposes of concept development, advertising evaluation, insight exploration, consumer segmentation, and product development.

How / why **begin** to use? Specifically, what **remember** about _____ form then?

How find out about it? (ads, TV commercial, friends) What details remember about the ad—what show, who in it?

REPEAT FOR ALL FORMS

C. LINE UP THE FORMS—When you think about these different forms, are they **basically the same**—just a different form or do you think of these as different products with **different results**? Describe.

D. EXPLAIN CHART—Line these attributes up in the order you think is **best to worst for each of the attributes** listed on the paper.

CLEANLINESS / SKIN CARE / GERM KILL / DEODORANCY / LATHER / SCENT / VALUE

Why put in this order? What experience / notice with this form for (*attribute above*)?

What about the form makes that difference?

How much do you care about (*attributes above*)? Why / not? Affect whether you'd buy it?

E. SHOW EXAMPLES OF BRANDS WITH BOTH BAR AND BODY WASH—

Oil of Olay / Dove / Lever 2000 / Dial

So to summarize with some specific brands, whether you have tried or not, what would you **expect to be the difference,** if any, when using the bar of _____ brand vs. the body wash?

What difference, if any, in how they make you feel emotionally after bathing with the bar vs. body wash?

BRANDS (30 min)

A. Now let's focus on different brands. Write your favorite on your name card.

LINE UP EXAMPLES OF THOSE COMMONLY USED.

B. How many of you have used _____ ? How often / long ago?

Why **use / choose** (at store)? What like (better) about _____ .

Why **NOT** use (more often)?

C. How many have **tried Oil of Olay / Dove / Lever 2000 / Dial?** Why / not (more recently)?

What associate with (brand above)? What stand for? What makes it different / unique vs. other brands?

SUMMARY (15 min)

A. There are 3 basic considerations when choosing a soap—**brand, form, price.** Put them in order of what matters most, 2nd, 3rd. For example, you go to the store to buy, and your usual form isn't available in your usual brand, etc. What would you buy?

MAKE A CHART OF RESPONSES

B. Now think about 3 benefits we've discussed—**skin care, scent, cleanliness.** Put these in order of importance. Describe order.

Why is _____ more important than _____ ?

(MISC—TIME PERMITTING)

C. What do you see / notice in the store when shopping this aisle? New things? Switch around?

ADULTS—How many of you buy soap for other family members? Who? How do you decide which form / brand to choose for your husband / teen?

D. TEENS ONLY—Let's talk a bit more about how you learn about new types brands or versions of soaps. Where have you seen ads?

(Mall / locker room / Channel 1/ dressing rooms / etc.)

What do you remember about it? What show / say / what was the main idea?

What think of celebrity endorsements?

CONCLUSION

Nonparametric Significance Tests

This appendix contains additional nonparametric tests of hypotheses to augment those described in Chapter 17.

One-Sample Test

Kolmogorov-Smirnov Test

This test is appropriate when the data are at least ordinal and the research situation calls for a comparison of an observed sample distribution with a theoretical distribution. Under these conditions, the Kolmogorov-Smirnov (KS) one-sample test is more powerful than the χ^2 test and can be used for small samples when the χ^2 test cannot. The KS is a test of goodness of fit in which we specify the *cumulative* frequency distribution that would occur under the theoretical distribution and compare that with the observed cumulative frequency distribution. The theoretical distribution represents our expectations under H_0. We determine the point of greatest divergence between the observed and theoretical distributions and identify this value as D (maximum deviation). From a table of critical values for D, we determine whether such a large divergence is likely on the basis of random sampling variations from the theoretical distribution. The value for D is calculated as follows:

$$D = \text{maximum} \left| F_0(X) - F_T(X) \right|$$

in which

$F_0(X) = $ the observed cumulative frequency distribution of a random sample of n observations. Where X is any possible score, $F_0(X) = k/n$, where $k = $ the number of observations equal to or less than X.

$F_T(X) = $ the theoretical frequency distribution under H_0.

We illustrate the KS test, with an analysis of the results of the dining club study, in terms of various class levels. Take an equal number of interviews from each class, but secure unequal numbers of people interested in joining. Assume class levels are ordinal measurements. The testing process is as follows (see accompanying table):

	Freshman	Sophomore	Junior	Senior	Graduate
Number in each class	5	9	11	16	19
$F_0(X)$	5/60	14/60	25/60	41/60	60/60
$F_T(X)$	12/60	24/60	36/60	48/60	60/60
$\left\| F_0(X) - F_T(X) \right\|$	7/60	10/60	11/60	7/60	0
$D = 11/60 = .183; n = 60$					

1. *Null hypothesis.*

    H_0: There is no difference among student classes as to their intention of joining the dining club.

    H_A: There is a difference among students in various classes as to their intention of joining the dining club.

2. *Statistical test.* Choose the KS one-sample test because the data are ordinal measures and we are interested in comparing an observed distribution with a theoretical one.

3. *Significance level.* $\alpha = .05$, $n = 60$.

4. *Calculated value.* $D = \text{maximum}\,|F_0(X) - F_T(X)|$.

5. *Critical test value.* We enter the table of critical values of D in the KS one-sample test (see Appendix d, Exhibit d-5) and learn that with $\alpha = .05$, the critical value for D is

$$D = \frac{1.36}{\sqrt{60}} = .175$$

6. *Interpretation.* The calculated value is greater than the critical value, indicating we should reject the null hypothesis.

Two-Samples Tests

Sign Test

The sign test is used with matched pairs when the only information is the identification of the pair member that is larger or smaller or has more or less of some characteristic. Under H_0, one would expect the number of cases in which $X_A > X_B$ to equal the number of pairs in which $X_B > X_A$. All ties are dropped from the analysis, and n is adjusted to allow for these eliminated pairs. This test is based on the binomial expansion and has a good power efficiency for small samples.

Wilcoxon Matched-Pairs Test

When you can determine both *direction* and *magnitude* of difference between carefully matched pairs, use the Wilcoxon matched-pairs test. This test has excellent efficiency and can be more powerful than the *t*-test in cases where the latter is not particularly appropriate. The mechanics of calculation are also quite simple. Find the difference score (d_i) between each pair of values, and rank-order the differences from smallest to largest without regard to sign. The actual signs of each difference are then added to the rank values, and the test statistic T is calculated. T is the sum of the ranks with the less frequent sign. Typical of such research situations might be a study where husband and wife are matched, where twins are used, where a given subject is used in a before-after study, or where the outputs of two similar machines are compared.

Two types of ties may occur with this test. When two observations are equal, the d score becomes zero, and we drop this pair of observations from the calculation. When two or more pairs have the same d value, we average their rank positions. For example, if two pairs have a rank score of 1, we assign the rank of 1.5 to each and rank the next largest difference as third. When $n < 25$, use the table of critical values (see Appendix d, Exhibit d-4). When $n > 25$, the sampling distribution of T is approximately normal with

$$\text{Mean} = \mu_T = \frac{n(n+1)}{4}$$

$$\text{Standard deviation} = \sigma_T \sqrt{\frac{n(n+1)(2n+1)}{24}}$$

The formula for the test is

$$z = \frac{T - \mu_T}{\sigma_T}$$

Suppose you conduct an experiment on the effect of brand name on quality perception. Ten subjects are recruited and asked to taste and compare two samples of a product, one identified as a well-known drink and the other as a new product being tested. In truth, however, the samples are identical. The subjects are then asked to rate the two samples on a set of scale items judged to be ordinal. Test these results for significance by the usual procedure.

1. *Null hypothesis.*

   H_0: There is no difference between the perceived qualities of the two samples.

   H_A: There is a difference in the perceived quality of the two samples.

2. *Statistical test.* The Wilcoxon matched-pairs test is used because the study is of related samples in which the differences can be ranked in magnitude.

3. *Significance level.* $\alpha = .05$, with $n = 10$ pairs of comparisons minus any pairs with a d of zero.

4. *Calculated value.* T equals the sum of the ranks with the less frequent sign. Assume we secure the following results:

Pair	Branded	Unbranded	d_i	Rank of d_i	Rank with Less Frequent Sign
1	52	48	4	4	
2	37	32	5	5.5*	
3	50	52	−2	−2	2
4	45	32	13	9	
5	56	59	−3	−3	3
6	51	50	1	1	
7	40	29	11	8	
8	59	54	5	5.5*	
9	38	38	0	*	
10	40	32	8	7	$T = 5$

*There are two types of tie situations. We drop out the pair with the type of tie shown by pair 9. Pairs 2 and 8 have a tie in rank of difference. In this case, we average the ranks and assign the average value to each.

5. *Critical test value.* Enter the table of critical values of T with $n = 9$ (see Appendix d, Exhibit d-4) and find that the critical value with $\alpha = .05$ is 6. Note that with this test, the calculated value must be smaller than the critical value to reject the null hypothesis.

6. *Interpretation.* Since the calculated value is less than the critical value, reject the null hypothesis.

Kolmogorov-Smirnov Two-Samples Test

When a researcher has two independent samples of ordinal data, the Kolmogorov-Smirnov (KS) two-samples test is useful. Like the one-sample test, this two-samples test is concerned with the agreement between two cumulative distributions, but both represent sample values. If the two samples have been drawn from the same population, the cumulative distributions of the samples should be fairly close to each other, showing only random deviations from the population distribution. If the cumulative distributions show a large enough maximum deviation D, it is evidence for rejecting the H_0. To secure the maximum deviation, one should use as many intervals as are available so as not to obscure the maximum cumulative difference.

The two-samples KS formula is

$$D = \text{maximum} \left| F_{N1}(X) - F_{N2}(X) \right| \text{ (two-tailed test)}$$

$$D = \text{maximum} \left| F_{N1}(X) - F_{N2}(X) \right| \text{ (one-tailed test)}$$

D is calculated in the same manner as before, but the table for critical values for the numerator of D, K_D (two-samples test) is presented in Appendix d, Exhibit d-6, when $n_1 = n_2$ and is less than 40 observations. When n_1 and/or n_2 is larger than 40, D from Appendix d, Exhibit d-7, should be used. With this larger sample, it is not necessary that $n_1 = n_2$.

Here we use a different sample from a tobacco industry advertising study. Suppose the smoking classifications represent an ordinal scale (heavy smoker, moderate smoker, non-smoker), and you test these data with KS two-samples test for young and old age groups. Proceed as follows:

1. *Null hypothesis.*

   H_0: There is no difference in ages of smokers and nonsmokers.

   H_A: The older the person, the more likely he or she is to be a heavy smoker.

2. *Statistical test.* The KS two-samples test is used because it is assumed the data are ordinal.

3. *Significance level.* $\alpha = .05$. $n_1 = n_2 = 34$.

4. *Calculated value.* See the one-sample calculation (KS test) and compare with the table below.

5. *Critical test value.* We enter Appendix d, Exhibit d-6, with $n = 34$ to find that $K_D = 11$ when $p \leq .05$ for a one-tailed distribution.

	Heavy Smoker	Moderate Smoker	Nonsmoker
$F_{n1}(X)$	12/34	21/34	34/34
$F_{n2}(X)$	4/34	10/34	34/34
$d_i = K_{D/n}$	8/34	11/34	0

6. *Interpretation.* Since the critical value equals the largest calculated value, we reject the null hypothesis.

Mann-Whitney *U* Test

This test is also used with two independent samples if the data are at least ordinal; it is an alternative to the *t*-test without the latter's limiting assumptions. When the larger of the two samples is 20 or less, there are special tables for interpreting U; when the larger sample exceeds 20, a normal curve approximation is used.

In calculating the U test, treat all observations in a combined fashion and rank them, algebraically, from smallest to largest. The largest negative score receives the lowest rank. In case of ties, assign the average rank as in other tests. With this test, you can also test samples that are unequal. After the ranking, the rank values for each sample are totaled. Compute the U statistic as follows:

$$U = n_1 n_2 + \frac{n_1(n_1 + 1)}{2} - R_1$$

or

$$U = n_1 n_2 + \frac{n_2(n_2 - 1)}{2} - R_2$$

in which

n_1 = number in sample 1

n_2 = number in sample 2

R_1 = sum of ranks in sample 1

With this equation, you can secure two U values, one using R_1 and the second using R_2. For testing purposes, use the smaller U.

An example may help to clarify the U statistic calculation procedure. Let's consider the sales training example with the t distribution discussion. Recall that salespeople with training method A averaged higher sales than salespeople with training method B. Although these data are ratio measures, one still might not want to accept the other assumptions that underlie the t-test. What kind of a result could be secured with the U test? While the U test is designed for ordinal data, it can be used with interval and ratio measurements.

1. *Null hypothesis.*

    H_0: There is no difference in sales results produced by the two training methods.

    H_A: Training method A produces sales results superior to the results of method B.

2. *Statistical test.* The Mann-Whitney U test is chosen because the measurement is at least ordinal, and the assumptions under the parametric t-test are rejected.

3. *Significance level.* $\alpha = .05$ (one-tailed test).

4. *Calculated value.*

Sales per Week per Salesperson			
Training Method A	**Rank**	**Training Method B**	**Rank**
1,500	15	1,340	10
1,540	16	1,300	8.5
1,860	22	1,620	18
1,230	6	1,070	3
1,370	12	1,210	5
1,550	17	1,170	4
1,840	21	1,770	20
1,250	7	950	1
1,300	8.5	1,380	13
1,350	11	1,460	14
1,710	19	1,030	2
	$R_1 = 154.5$		$R_2 = 98.5$

$$U = (11)(11) + \frac{11(11 + 1)}{2} - 154.5 = 32.5 \qquad U = (11)(11) + \frac{11(11 + 1)}{2} - 98.5 = 88.5$$

5. *Critical test value.* Enter Appendix d, Exhibit d-9, with $n_1 = n_2 = 11$, and find a critical value of 34 for $\alpha = 0.5$, one-tailed test. Note that with this test, the calculated value must be smaller than the critical value to reject the null hypothesis.

6. *Interpretation.* Since the calculated value is smaller than the critical value ($34 > 32.5$), reject the null hypothesis and conclude that training method A is probably superior.

Thus, one would reject the null hypothesis at $\alpha = .05$ in a one-tailed test using either the t- or the U test. In this example, the U test has approximately the same power as the parametric test.

When $n > 20$ in one of the samples, the sampling distribution of U approaches the normal distribution with

$$\text{Mean} = \mu_U = \frac{n_1 n_2}{2}$$

$$\text{Standard deviation } \sigma_U = \sqrt{\frac{(n_1)(n_2)(n_1 + n_2 + 1)}{12}}$$

and

$$z = \frac{U - \mu_U}{\sigma_U}$$

Other Nonparametric Tests

Other tests are appropriate under certain conditions when testing two independent samples. When the measurement is only nominal, the Fisher exact probability test may be used. When the data are at least ordinal, use the median and Wald-Wolfowitz runs tests.

k-Samples Tests

You can use tests more powerful than χ^2 with data that are at least ordinal in nature. One such test is an extension of the median test mentioned earlier. We illustrate here the application of a second ordinal measurement test known as the Kruskal-Wallis one-way analysis of variance.

Kruskal-Wallis Test

This is a generalized version of the Mann-Whitney test. With it we rank all scores in the entire pool of observations from smallest to largest. The rank sum of each sample is then calculated, with ties being distributed as in other examples. We then compute the value of H as follows:

$$H = \frac{12}{N(N + 1)} \sum_{j=1}^{k} \frac{T_j^2}{n_j} - 3(N + 1)$$

where

T_j = sum of ranks in column j

n_j = number of cases in jth sample

$N = \Sigma w_j$ = total number of cases

k = number of samples

When there are a number of ties, it is recommended that a correction factor (C) be calculated and used to correct the H value as follows:

$$C = 1 - \left\{ \frac{\sum_{i}^{G} (t_i^3 - t_i)}{N^3 - N} \right\}$$

where

G = number of sets of tied observations

t_i = number tied in any set i

$$H' = H/C$$

To secure the critical value for H', use the table for the distribution of χ^2 (see Appendix d, Exhibit d-3), and enter it with the value of H' and d.f. = $k - 1$.

To illustrate the application of this test, use the price discount experiment problem. The data and calculations are shown in Exhibit c-1 and indicate that, by the Kruskal-Wallis test, one again barely fails to reject the null hypothesis with $\alpha = .05$.

>**Exhibit c-1** Kruskal-Wallis One-Way Analysis of Variance (price differentials)

One Cent		Three Cents		Five Cents	
X_A	Rank	X_B	Rank	X_C	Rank
6	1	8	5	9	8.5
7	2.5	9	8.5	9	8.5
8	5	8	5	11	14
7	2.5	10	11.5	10	11.5
9	8.5	11	14	14	18
11	14	13	16.5	13	16.5
	$T_j = 33.5$		60.5		77.0

$T = 33.5 + 60.5 + 77.0$

$\quad = 171$

$$H = \frac{12}{18(18+1)}\left[\frac{33.5^2 + 60.5^2 + 77^2}{6}\right] - 3(18+1)$$

$$\quad = \frac{12}{342}\left[\frac{1,122.25 + 3,660.25 + 5,929}{6}\right] - 57$$

$$\quad = 0.0351\left[\frac{10,711.5}{6}\right] - 57$$

$H = 5.66$

$$C = 1 - \left\{\frac{3[(2)^3 - 2] + 2[(3)^3 - 3] + 4[(4)^3 - 4]}{18^3 - 18}\right\}$$

$$\quad = 1 - \frac{18 + 48 + 60}{5814}$$

$$\quad = .978$$

$$H' = \frac{H}{C} = \frac{5.66}{.978} = 5.79$$

$d.f. = k - 1 = 2$

$p > .05$

>appendixd

Selected Statistical Tables

>**Exhibit d-1** Areas of the Standard Normal Distribution

	Second Decimal Place in z									
z	0.00	0.01	0.02	0.03	0.04	0.05	0.06	0.07	0.08	0.09
0.0	0.0000	0.0040	0.0080	0.0120	0.0160	0.0199	0.0239	0.0279	0.0319	0.0359
0.1	0.0398	0.0438	0.0478	0.0517	0.0557	0.0596	0.0636	0.0675	0.0714	0.0753
0.2	0.0793	0.0832	0.0871	0.0910	0.0948	0.0987	0.1026	0.1064	0.1103	0.1141
0.3	0.1179	0.1217	0.1255	0.1293	0.1331	0.1368	0.1406	0.1443	0.1480	0.1517
0.4	0.1554	0.1591	0.1628	0.1664	0.1700	0.1736	0.1772	0.1808	0.1844	0.1879
0.5	0.1915	0.1950	0.1985	0.2019	0.2054	0.2088	0.2123	0.2157	0.2190	0.2224
0.6	0.2257	0.2291	0.2324	0.2357	0.2389	0.2422	0.2454	0.2486	0.2517	0.2549
0.7	0.2580	0.2611	0.2642	0.2673	0.2704	0.2734	0.2764	0.2794	0.2823	0.2852
0.8	0.2881	0.2910	0.2939	0.2967	0.2995	0.3023	0.3051	0.3078	0.3106	0.3133
0.9	0.3159	0.3186	0.3212	0.3238	0.3264	0.3289	0.3315	0.3340	0.3365	0.3389
1.0	0.3413	0.3438	0.3461	0.3485	0.3508	0.3531	0.3554	0.3577	0.3599	0.3621
1.1	0.3643	0.3665	0.3686	0.3708	0.3729	0.3749	0.3770	0.3790	0.3810	0.3830
1.2	0.3849	0.3869	0.3888	0.3907	0.3925	0.3944	0.3962	0.3980	0.3997	0.4015
1.3	0.4032	0.4049	0.4066	0.4082	0.4099	0.4115	0.4131	0.4147	0.4162	0.4177
1.4	0.4192	0.4207	0.4222	0.4236	0.4251	0.4265	0.4279	0.4292	0.4306	0.4319
1.5	0.4332	0.4345	0.4357	0.4370	0.4382	0.4394	0.4406	0.4418	0.4429	0.4441
1.6	0.4452	0.4463	0.4474	0.4484	0.4495	0.4505	0.4515	0.4525	0.4535	0.4545
1.7	0.4554	0.4564	0.4573	0.4582	0.4591	0.4599	0.4608	0.4616	0.4625	0.4633
1.8	0.4641	0.4649	0.4656	0.4664	0.4671	0.4678	0.4686	0.4693	0.4699	0.4706
1.9	0.4713	0.4719	0.4726	0.4732	0.4738	0.4744	0.4750	0.4756	0.4761	0.4767
2.0	0.4772	0.4778	0.4783	0.4788	0.4793	0.4798	0.4803	0.4808	0.4812	0.4817
2.1	0.4821	0.4826	0.4830	0.4834	0.4838	0.4842	0.4846	0.4850	0.4854	0.4857
2.2	0.4861	0.4864	0.4868	0.4871	0.4875	0.4878	0.4881	0.4884	0.4887	0.4890
2.3	0.4893	0.4896	0.4898	0.4901	0.4904	0.4906	0.4909	0.4911	0.4913	0.4916
2.4	0.4918	0.4920	0.4922	0.4925	0.4927	0.4929	0.4931	0.4932	0.4934	0.4936
2.5	0.4938	0.4940	0.4941	0.4943	0.4945	0.4946	0.4948	0.4949	0.4951	0.4952
2.6	0.4953	0.4955	0.4956	0.4957	0.4959	0.4960	0.4961	0.4962	0.4963	0.4964
2.7	0.4965	0.4966	0.4967	0.4968	0.4969	0.4970	0.4971	0.4972	0.4973	0.4974
2.8	0.4974	0.4975	0.4976	0.4977	0.4977	0.4978	0.4979	0.4979	0.4980	0.4981
2.9	0.4981	0.4982	0.4982	0.4983	0.4984	0.4984	0.4985	0.4985	0.4986	0.4986
3.0	0.4987	0.4987	0.4987	0.4988	0.4988	0.4989	0.4989	0.4989	0.4990	0.4990
3.1	0.4990	0.4991	0.4991	0.4991	0.4992	0.4992	0.4992	0.4992	0.4993	0.4993
3.2	0.4993	0.4993	0.4994	0.4994	0.4994	0.4994	0.4994	0.4995	0.4995	0.4995
3.3	0.4995	0.4995	0.4995	0.4996	0.4996	0.4996	0.4996	0.4996	0.4996	0.4997
3.4	0.4997	0.4997	0.4997	0.4997	0.4997	0.4997	0.4997	0.4997	0.4997	0.4998
3.5	0.4998									
4.0	0.49997									
4.5	0.499997									
5.0	0.4999997									
6.0	0.499999999									

>**Exhibit d-2** Critical Values of *t* for Given Probability Levels

	Level of Significance for One-Tailed Test					
	.10	.05	.025	.01	.005	.0005
	Level of Significance for Two-Tailed Test					
d.f.	.20	.10	.05	.02	.01	.001
1	3.078	6.314	12.706	31.821	63.657	636.619
2	1.886	2.920	4.303	6.965	9.925	31.598
3	1.638	2.353	3.182	4.541	5.841	12.941
4	1.533	2.132	2.776	3.747	4.604	8.610
5	1.476	2.015	2.571	3.365	4.032	6.859
6	1.440	1.943	2.447	3.143	3.707	5.959
7	1.415	1.895	2.365	2.998	3.499	5.405
8	1.397	1.860	2.306	2.896	3.355	5.041
9	1.383	1.833	2.262	2.821	3.250	4.781
10	1.372	1.812	2.228	2.764	3.169	4.587
11	1.363	1.796	2.201	2.718	3.106	4.437
12	1.356	1.782	2.179	2.681	3.055	4.318
13	1.350	1.771	2.160	2.650	3.012	4.221
14	1.345	1.761	2.145	2.624	2.977	4.140
15	1.341	1.753	2.131	2.602	2.947	4.073
16	1.337	1.746	2.120	2.583	2.921	4.015
17	1.333	1.740	2.110	2.567	2.898	3.965
18	1.330	1.734	2.101	2.552	2.878	3.922
19	1.328	1.729	2.093	2.539	2.861	3.883
20	1.325	1.725	2.086	2.528	2.845	3.850
21	1.323	1.721	2.080	2.518	2.831	3.819
22	1.321	1.717	2.074	2.508	2.819	3.792
23	1.319	1.714	2.069	2.500	2.807	3.767
24	1.318	1.711	2.064	2.492	2.797	3.745
25	1.316	1.708	2.060	2.485	2.787	3.725
26	1.315	1.706	2.056	2.479	2.779	3.707
27	1.314	1.703	2.052	2.473	2.771	3.690
28	1.313	1.701	2.048	2.467	2.763	3.674
29	1.311	1.699	2.045	2.462	2.756	3.659
30	1.310	1.697	2.042	2.457	2.750	3.646
40	1.303	1.684	2.021	2.423	2.704	3.551
60	1.296	1.671	2.000	2.390	2.660	3.460
120	1.289	1.658	1.980	2.358	2.617	3.373
∞	1.282	1.645	1.960	2.326	2.576	3.291

Source: Abridged from Table III of Fisher and Yates, *Statistical Tables for Biological, Agricultural, and Medical Research,* 6th ed., published by Oliver and Boyd Ltd., Edinburgh, 1963. By permission of the publishers.

>Exhibit d-3 Critical Values of the Chi-Square Distribution

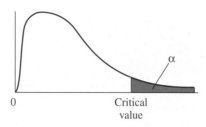

			Probability		
d.f.	**.10**	**.05**	**.02**	**.01**	**.001**
1	2.71	3.84	5.41	6.64	10.83
2	4.60	5.99	7.82	9.21	13.82
3	6.25	7.82	9.84	11.34	16.27
4	7.78	9.49	11.67	13.28	18.46
5	9.24	11.07	13.39	15.09	20.52
6	10.64	12.59	15.03	16.81	22.46
7	12.02	14.07	16.62	18.48	24.32
8	13.36	15.51	18.17	20.09	26.12
9	14.68	16.92	19.68	21.67	27.88
10	15.99	18.31	21.16	23.21	29.59
11	17.28	19.68	22.62	24.72	31.26
12	18.55	21.03	24.05	26.22	32.91
13	19.81	22.36	25.47	27.69	34.53
14	21.06	23.68	26.87	29.14	36.12
15	22.31	25.00	28.26	30.58	37.70
16	23.54	26.30	29.63	32.00	39.29
17	24.77	27.59	31.00	33.41	40.75
18	25.99	28.87	32.35	34.80	42.31
19	27.20	30.14	33.69	36.19	43.82
20	28.41	31.41	35.02	37.57	45.32
21	29.62	32.67	36.34	38.93	46.80
22	30.81	33.92	37.66	40.29	48.27
23	32.01	35.17	38.97	41.64	49.73
24	33.20	36.42	40.27	42.98	51.18
25	34.38	37.65	41.57	44.31	52.62
26	35.56	38.88	42.86	45.64	54.05
27	36.74	40.11	44.14	46.96	55.48
28	37.92	41.34	45.42	48.28	56.89
29	39.09	42.56	46.69	49.59	58.30
30	40.26	43.77	47.96	50.89	59.70

Source: Abridged from Table IV of Fisher and Yates, *Statistical Tables for Biological, Agricultural, and Medical Research,* 6th ed., published by Oliver and Boyd Ltd., Edinburgh, 1963. By permission of the publishers.

>**Exhibit d-4** Critical Values of *T* in the Wilcoxon Matched-Pairs Test

	Level of Significance for One-Tailed Test		
	.025	**.01**	**.005**
	Level of Significance for Two-Tailed Test		
n	**.05**	**.02**	**.01**
6	0	–	–
7	2	0	–
8	4	2	0
9	6	3	2
10	8	5	3
11	11	7	5
12	14	10	7
13	17	13	10
14	21	16	13
15	25	20	16
16	30	24	20
17	35	28	23
18	40	33	28
19	46	38	32
20	52	43	38
21	59	49	43
22	66	56	49
23	73	62	55
24	81	69	61
25	89	77	68

Source: Adapted from Table 1 of F. Wilcoxon, *Some Rapid Approximate Statistical Procedures* (New York: American Cyanamid Company, 1949), p. 13, with the kind permission of the publisher.

>**Exhibit d-5** Critical Values of *D* in the Kolmogorov-Smirnov One-Sample Test

	Level of Significance for $D = $ Maximum $|F_0(X) - S_N(X)|$				
Sample Size n	**.20**	**.15**	**.10**	**.05**	**.01**
1	.900	.925	.950	.975	.995
2	.684	.726	.776	.842	.929
3	.565	.597	.642	.708	.828
4	.494	.525	.564	.624	.733
5	.446	.474	.510	.565	.669
6	.410	.436	.470	.521	.618
7	.381	.405	.438	.486	.577
8	.358	.381	.411	.457	.543
9	.339	.360	.388	.432	.514
10	.322	.342	.368	.410	.490
11	.307	.326	.352	.391	.468
12	.295	.313	.338	.375	.450
13	.284	.302	.325	.361	.433
14	.274	.292	.314	.349	.418
15	.266	.283	.304	.338	.404
16	.258	.274	.295	.328	.392
17	.250	.266	.286	.318	.381
18	.244	.259	.278	.309	.371
19	.237	.252	.272	.301	.363
20	.231	.246	.264	.294	.356
25	.21	.22	.24	.27	.32
30	.19	.20	.22	.24	.29
35	.18	.19	.21	.23	.27
Over 35	$\dfrac{1.07}{\sqrt{N}}$	$\dfrac{1.14}{\sqrt{N}}$	$\dfrac{1.22}{\sqrt{N}}$	$\dfrac{1.36}{\sqrt{N}}$	$\dfrac{1.63}{\sqrt{N}}$

Source: F. J. Massey Jr., "The Kolmogorov-Smirnov Test for Goodness of Fit," *Journal of the American Statistical Association* 46, p. 70. Adapted with the kind permission of the publisher.

>**Exhibit d-6** Critical Values of K_D in the Kolmogorov-Smirnov
Two-Samples Test (small samples)

	One-Tailed Test		Two-Tailed Test	
n	α = .05	α = .01	α = .05	α = .01
3	3	—	—	—
4	4	—	4	—
5	4	5	5	5
6	5	6	5	6
7	5	6	6	6
8	5	6	6	7
9	6	7	6	7
10	6	7	7	8
11	6	8	7	8
12	6	8	7	8
13	7	8	7	9
14	7	8	8	9
15	7	9	8	9
16	7	9	8	10
17	8	9	8	10
18	8	10	9	10
19	8	10	9	10
20	8	10	9	11
21	8	10	9	11
22	9	11	9	11
23	9	11	10	11
24	9	11	10	12
25	9	11	10	12
26	9	11	10	12
27	9	12	10	12
28	10	12	11	13
29	10	12	11	13
30	10	12	11	13
35	11	13	12	
40	11	14	13	

Source: One-tailed test—abridged from I. A. Goodman, "Kolmogorov-Smirnov Tests for
Psychological Research," *Psychological Bulletin* 51 (1951), p. 167, copyright (1951) by the
American Psychological Association. Reprinted by permission. Two-tailed test—derived from
Table 1 of F. J. Massey Jr., "The Distribution of the Maximum Deviation between Two Sample
Cumulative Step Functions," *Annals of Mathematical Statistics* 23 (1951), pp. 126–27, with
the kind permission of the publisher.

>**Exhibit d-7** Critical Values of D in the Kolmogorov-Smirnov Two-Samples Test
for Large Samples (two-tailed)

Level of Significance	Value of D So Large as to Call for Rejection of H_0 at the Indicated Level of Significance, Where $D = \text{Maximum } \lvert S_{n1}(X) = S_2(X)\rvert$
.10	$1.22\sqrt{\dfrac{n_1 + n_2}{n_1 n_2}}$
.05	$1.36\sqrt{\dfrac{n_1 + n_2}{n_1 n_2}}$
.025	$1.48\sqrt{\dfrac{n_1 + n_2}{n_1 n_2}}$
.01	$1.63\sqrt{\dfrac{n_1 + n_2}{n_1 n_2}}$
.005	$1.73\sqrt{\dfrac{n_1 + n_2}{n_1 n_2}}$
.001	$1.95\sqrt{\dfrac{n_1 + n_2}{n_1 n_2}}$

Source: Adapted from N. Smirnov, "Table for Estimating the Goodness of Fit of Empirical Distribution,"
Annals of Mathematical Statistics 18 (1948), pp. 280–81, with the kind permission of the publisher.

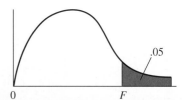

>**Exhibit d-8** Critical Values of the F Distribution for $\alpha = .05$

		Degrees of Freedom for Numerator								
n_2	1	2	3	4	5	6	7	8	9	
1	161.40	199.50	215.70	224.60	230.20	234.00	236.80	238.90	240.50	
2	18.51	19.00	19.16	19.25	19.30	19.33	19.35	19.37	19.38	
3	10.13	9.55	9.28	9.12	9.01	8.94	8.89	8.85	8.81	
4	7.71	6.94	6.59	6.39	6.26	6.16	6.09	6.04	6.00	
5	6.61	5.79	5.41	5.19	5.05	4.95	4.88	4.82	4.77	
6	5.99	5.14	4.76	4.53	4.39	4.28	4.21	4.15	4.10	
7	5.59	4.74	4.35	4.12	3.97	3.87	3.79	3.73	3.68	
8	5.32	4.46	4.07	3.84	3.69	3.58	3.50	3.44	3.39	
9	5.12	4.26	3.86	3.63	3.48	3.37	3.29	3.23	3.18	
10	4.96	4.10	3.71	3.48	3.33	3.22	3.14	3.07	3.02	
11	4.84	3.98	3.59	3.36	3.20	3.09	3.01	2.95	2.90	
12	4.75	3.89	3.49	3.26	3.11	3.00	2.91	2.85	2.80	
13	4.67	3.81	3.41	3.18	3.03	2.92	2.83	2.77	2.71	
14	4.60	3.74	3.34	3.11	2.96	2.85	2.76	2.70	2.65	
15	4.54	3.68	3.29	3.06	2.90	2.79	2.71	2.64	2.59	
16	4.49	3.63	3.24	3.01	2.85	2.74	2.66	2.59	2.54	
17	4.45	3.59	3.20	2.96	2.81	2.70	2.61	2.55	2.49	
18	4.41	3.55	3.16	2.93	2.77	2.66	2.58	2.51	2.46	
19	4.38	3.52	3.13	2.90	2.74	2.63	2.54	2.48	2.42	
20	4.35	3.49	3.10	2.87	2.71	2.60	2.51	2.45	2.39	
21	4.32	3.47	3.07	2.84	2.68	2.57	2.49	2.42	2.37	
22	4.30	3.44	3.05	2.82	2.66	2.55	2.46	2.40	2.34	
23	4.28	3.42	3.03	2.80	2.64	2.53	2.44	2.37	2.32	
24	4.26	3.40	3.01	2.78	2.62	2.51	2.42	2.36	2.30	
25	4.24	3.39	2.99	2.76	2.60	2.49	2.40	2.34	2.28	
26	4.23	3.37	2.98	2.74	2.59	2.47	2.39	2.32	2.27	
27	4.21	3.35	2.96	2.73	2.57	2.46	2.37	2.31	2.25	
28	4.20	3.34	2.95	2.71	2.56	2.45	2.36	2.29	2.24	
29	4.18	3.33	2.93	2.70	2.55	2.43	2.35	2.28	2.22	
30	4.17	3.32	2.92	2.69	2.53	2.42	2.33	2.27	2.21	
40	4.08	3.23	2.84	2.61	2.45	2.34	2.25	2.18	2.12	
60	4.00	3.15	2.76	2.53	2.37	2.25	2.17	2.10	2.04	
120	3.92	3.07	2.68	2.45	2.29	2.17	2.09	2.02	1.96	
∞	3.84	3.00	2.60	2.37	2.21	2.10	2.01	1.94	1.88	

Degrees of Freedom for Denominator (row label, left margin)

Source: Reprinted by permission from *Statistical Methods* by George W. Snedecor and William G. Cochran, 6th edition, © 1967 by Iowa State University Press, Ames, Iowa.

				Degrees of Freedom for Numerator (cont'd)						
n_2	10	12	15	20	24	30	40	80	120	∞
1	241.90	243.90	245.90	248.00	249.10	250.10	251.10	252.20	253.30	243.30
2	19.40	19.41	19.43	19.45	19.45	19.46	19.47	19.48	19.49	19.50
3	8.79	8.74	8.70	8.66	8.64	8.62	8.59	8.57	8.55	8.53
4	5.96	5.91	5.86	5.80	5.77	5.75	5.72	5.69	5.66	5.63
5	4.74	4.68	4.62	4.56	4.53	4.50	4.46	4.43	4.40	4.36
6	4.06	4.00	3.94	3.87	3.84	3.81	3.77	3.74	3.70	3.67
7	3.64	3.57	3.51	3.44	3.41	3.38	3.34	3.30	3.27	3.23
8	3.35	3.28	3.22	3.15	3.12	3.08	3.04	3.01	2.97	2.93
9	3.14	3.07	3.01	2.94	2.90	2.86	2.83	2.79	2.75	2.71
10	2.98	2.91	2.85	2.77	2.74	2.70	2.66	2.62	2.58	2.54
11	2.85	2.79	2.72	2.65	2.61	2.57	2.53	2.49	2.45	2.40
12	2.75	2.69	2.62	2.54	2.51	2.47	2.43	2.38	2.34	2.30
13	2.67	2.60	2.53	2.46	2.42	2.38	2.34	2.30	2.25	2.21
14	2.60	2.53	2.46	2.39	2.35	2.31	2.27	2.22	2.18	2.13
15	2.54	2.48	2.40	2.33	2.29	2.25	2.20	2.16	2.11	2.07
16	2.49	2.42	2.35	2.28	2.24	2.19	2.15	2.11	2.06	2.01
17	2.45	2.38	2.31	2.23	2.19	2.15	2.10	2.06	2.01	1.96
18	2.41	2.34	2.27	2.19	2.15	2.11	2.06	2.02	1.97	1.92
19	2.38	2.31	2.23	2.16	2.11	2.07	2.03	1.98	1.93	1.88
20	2.35	2.28	2.20	2.12	2.08	2.04	1.99	1.95	1.90	1.84
21	2.32	2.25	2.18	2.10	2.05	2.01	1.96	1.92	1.87	1.81
22	2.30	2.23	2.15	2.07	2.03	1.98	1.94	1.89	1.84	1.78
23	2.27	2.20	2.13	2.05	2.01	1.96	1.91	1.86	1.81	1.76
24	2.25	2.18	2.11	2.03	1.98	1.94	1.89	1.84	1.79	1.73
25	2.24	2.16	2.09	2.01	1.96	1.92	1.87	1.82	1.77	1.71
26	2.22	2.15	2.07	1.99	1.95	1.90	1.85	1.80	1.75	1.69
27	2.20	2.13	2.06	1.97	1.93	1.88	1.84	1.79	1.73	1.67
28	2.19	2.12	2.04	1.96	1.91	1.87	1.82	1.77	1.71	1.65
29	2.18	2.10	2.03	1.94	1.90	1.85	1.81	1.75	1.70	1.64
30	2.16	2.09	2.01	1.93	1.89	1.84	1.79	1.74	1.68	1.62
40	2.08	2.00	1.92	1.84	1.79	1.74	1.69	1.64	1.58	1.51
60	1.99	1.92	1.84	1.75	1.70	1.65	1.59	1.53	1.47	1.39
120	1.91	1.83	1.75	1.66	1.61	1.55	1.50	1.43	1.35	1.25
∞	1.83	1.75	1.67	1.57	1.52	1.46	1.39	1.32	1.22	1.00

Degrees of Freedom for Denominator

>Exhibit d-9 Partial Table of Critical Values of *U* in the Mann-Whitney Test

Critical Values for One-Tailed Test at $\alpha = .025$ or Two-Tailed Test at $\alpha = .05$											
$n_1 \backslash n_2$	9	10	11	12	13	14	15	16	17	18	19	20
1												
2	0	0	0	1	1	1	1	1	2	2	2	2
3	2	3	3	4	4	5	5	6	6	7	7	8
4	4	5	6	7	8	9	10	11	11	12	13	13
5	7	8	9	11	12	13	14	15	17	18	19	20
6	10	11	13	14	16	17	19	21	22	24	25	27
7	12	14	16	18	20	22	24	26	28	30	32	34
8	15	17	19	22	24	26	29	31	34	36	38	41
9	17	20	23	26	28	31	34	37	39	42	45	48
10	20	23	26	29	33	36	39	42	45	48	52	55
11	23	26	30	33	37	40	44	47	51	55	58	62
12	26	29	33	37	41	45	49	53	57	61	66	69
13	28	33	37	41	45	50	54	59	63	67	72	76
14	31	36	40	45	50	55	59	64	67	74	78	83
15	34	39	44	49	54	59	64	70	75	80	85	90
16	37	42	47	53	59	64	70	75	81	86	92	98
17	39	45	51	57	63	67	75	81	87	93	99	105
18	42	48	55	61	67	74	80	86	93	99	106	112
19	45	52	58	65	72	78	85	92	99	106	113	119
20	48	55	62	69	76	83	90	98	105	112	119	127

Critical Values for One-Tailed Test at $\alpha = .05$ or Two-Tailed Test at $\alpha = .10$											
$n_1 \backslash n_2$	9	10	11	12	13	14	15	16	17	18	19	20
1											0	0
2	1	1	1	2	2	2	3	3	3	4	4	4
3	3	4	5	5	6	7	7	8	9	9	10	11
4	6	7	8	9	10	11	12	14	15	16	17	18
5	9	11	12	13	15	16	18	19	20	22	23	25
6	12	14	16	17	19	21	23	25	26	28	30	32
7	15	17	19	21	24	26	28	30	33	35	37	39
8	18	20	23	26	28	31	33	36	39	41	44	47
9	21	24	27	30	33	36	39	42	45	48	51	54
10	24	27	31	34	37	41	44	48	51	55	58	62
11	27	31	34	38	42	46	50	54	57	61	65	69
12	30	34	38	42	47	51	55	60	64	68	72	77
13	33	37	42	47	51	56	61	65	70	75	80	84
14	36	41	46	51	56	61	66	71	77	82	87	92
15	39	44	50	55	61	66	72	77	83	88	94	100
16	42	48	54	60	65	71	77	83	89	95	101	107
17	45	51	57	64	70	77	83	89	96	102	109	115
18	48	55	61	68	75	82	88	95	102	109	116	123
19	51	58	65	72	80	87	94	101	109	116	123	130
20	54	62	69	77	84	92	100	107	115	123	130	138

Source: Abridged from D. Auble, "Extended Tables from the Mann-Whitney Statistic," *Bulletin of the Institute of Educational Research at Indiana University* 1, no. 2, reprinted with permission. For tables for other-size samples, consult this source.

>**Exhibit d-10** Random Numbers

97446	30328	05262	77371	13523	62057	44349	85884	94555	23288
15453	75591	60540	77137	09485	27632	05477	99154	78720	10323
69995	77086	55217	53721	85713	27854	41981	88981	90041	20878
69726	58696	27272	38148	52521	73807	29685	49152	20309	58734
23604	31948	16926	26360	76957	99925	86045	11617	32777	38670
13640	17233	58650	47819	24935	28670	33415	77202	92492	40290
90779	09199	51169	94892	34271	22068	13923	53535	56358	50258
71068	19459	32339	10124	13012	79706	07611	52600	83088	26829
55019	79001	34442	16335	06428	52873	65316	01480	72204	39494
20879	50235	17389	25260	34039	99967	48044	05067	69284	53867
00380	11595	49372	95214	98529	46593	77046	27176	39668	20566
68142	40800	20527	79212	14166	84948	11748	69540	84288	37211
42667	89566	20440	57230	35356	01884	79921	94772	29882	24695
07756	78430	45576	86596	56720	65529	44211	18447	53921	92722
45221	31130	44312	63534	47741	02465	50629	94983	05984	88375
20140	77481	61686	82836	41058	41331	04290	61212	60294	95954
54922	25436	33804	51907	73223	66423	68706	36589	45267	35327
48340	30832	72209	07644	52747	40751	06808	85349	18005	52323
23603	84387	20416	88084	33103	41511	59391	71600	35091	52722
12548	01033	22974	59596	92087	02116	63524	00627	41778	24392
15251	87584	12942	03771	91413	75652	19468	83889	98531	91529
65548	59670	57355	18874	63601	55111	07278	32560	40028	36079
48488	76170	46282	76427	41693	04506	80979	26654	62159	83017
02862	15665	62159	15159	69576	20328	68873	28152	66087	39405
67929	06754	45842	66365	80848	15262	55144	37816	08421	30071
73237	07607	31615	04892	50989	87347	14393	21165	68169	70788
13788	20327	07960	95917	75112	01398	26381	41377	33549	19754
43877	66485	40825	45923	74410	69693	76959	70973	26343	63781
14047	08369	56414	78533	76378	44204	71493	68861	31042	81873
88383	46755	51342	13505	55324	52950	22244	28028	73486	98797
29567	16379	41994	65947	58926	50953	09388	00405	29874	44954
20508	60995	41539	26396	99825	25652	28089	57224	35222	58922
64178	76768	75747	32854	32893	61152	58565	33128	33354	16056
26373	51147	90362	93309	13175	66385	57822	31138	12893	68607
10083	47656	59241	73630	99200	94672	59785	95449	99279	25488
11683	14347	04369	98719	75005	43633	24125	30532	54830	95387
56548	76293	50904	88579	24621	94291	56881	35062	48765	22078
35292	47291	82610	27777	43965	31802	98444	88929	54383	93141
51329	87645	51623	08971	50704	82395	33916	95859	99788	97885
51860	19180	39324	68483	78650	74750	64893	58042	82878	20619
23886	01257	07945	71175	31243	87167	42829	44601	08769	26417
80028	82310	43989	09242	15056	48250	04529	96941	48190	69644
83946	46858	09164	18858	12672	55190	02820	45861	29104	75386
00000	41586	25972	25356	54260	95691	99431	89903	22306	43863
90615	12848	23376	29458	48239	37628	59265	50152	30340	40713
42003	10738	55835	48218	23204	19188	13556	06610	77667	88068
86135	26174	07834	17007	97938	96728	15689	77544	89186	41252
54436	10828	41212	19836	89476	53685	28085	22878	71868	35048
14545	72034	32131	38783	58588	47499	50945	97045	42357	53536
43925	49879	13339	78773	95626	67119	93023	96832	09757	98545

Source: The Rand Corporation, *A Million Random Digits with 100,000 Normal Deviates* (Glencoe, IL: Free Press, 1955), p. 225.

>referencesandreadings

chapter 1

Reference Notes

1. Ian Davis and Elizabeth Stephenson, "Ten Trends to Watch in 2006," *The McKinsey Quarterly: The Online Journal of McKinsey & Co.* (January 2006) (http://www.mckinseyquarterly.com/article_page. aspx?ar=1734&L2=21&L3=114&srid=190&gp . . .).

2. http://www.haagen-dazs.com, downloaded August 23, 2002.

3. Peter D. Bennett, ed., *Dictionary of Marketing Terms,* 2d ed. (Chicago: American Marketing Association, 1995).

4. Presentation by Larry Stanek, vice president, consumer and mar-ketplace knowledge, Minute Maid, at AMA's Marketing Research Conference, Chicago, September 9, 2002.

5. See, for example, Elizabethann O'Sullivan and Gary R. Rassel, *Research Methods for Public Administration* (New York: Longman, 1999).

References for Snapshots, PicProfiles, Captions, PulsePoints, and Pull Quotes

Snausages

Hoag Levins (producer), "How Del Monte Social-Media Strategy Created a New Pet Food: Case Study From the IAB Conference," *Advertising Age,* May 25, 2009, accessed May 28, 2009 (http://adage.com/ brightcove/single.php?title=24149973001); http://www.snausages. com/snack-shack/breakfast-bites.htm; http://www.snausages.com/ snack-shack/breakfast-bites-ingredients.htm.

Mary Kay Inc.

Interview with Teri Burgess, director of marketing analysis, Mary Kay Inc., September 10, 2002.

PullQuote

"Bill Gates quotes," ThinkExist.com, accessed June 14, 2009 (http:// thinkexist.com/quotation/this_is_a_fantastic_time_to_be_entering_ the/147292.html).

PulsePoint

"The Problem with Social Media in the Office," *eMarketer,* May 27, 2009, accessed May 28, 2009 (http://www.emarketer.com/Article. aspx?R=1007109).

Yahoo!

"ACNielsen Homescan," ACNielsen, downloaded February 17, 2004 http://www.acnielsen.com/products/reports/homescan/).

Ken Mallon, director, Insights Products, Yahoo, interviewed February 17, 2004. SRI-Knowledge Networks, Media Scan—Spring 2003, shows that among women age 25 to 54, Internet consumption rose from 10 to 13% from Fall 2000 to Spring 2003. Forrester Research, September 2003, shows decreases in radio (10%), newspaper (16%), TV (21%), and magazines (13%) by women 25 to 54 since going online.

Phil Cara, "Online Market Research: Trends and Technology," American Marketing Association: WebEx event, February 5, 2004.

Classic and Contemporary Readings

Berry, Michael J. A., and Gordon Linhoff. *Data Mining Techniques: For Marketing, Sales, and Customer Support.* New York: Wiley, 1997. This is a practical guide to mining business data to help business managers focus their marketing and sales strategies.

Blattberg, Robert C., Rashi Glazer, and John D. C. Little, eds. *The Marketing Information Revolution.* Boston, MA: Harvard Business School Press, 1994.

Converse, Jean M. *Survey Research in the United States: Roots and Emergence 1890–1960.* Berkeley: University of California Press, 1987.

Haas, Peter J., and J. Fred Springer. *Applied Policy Research: Concepts and Cases.* New York: Garland Reference Library of Social Science, No. 1051, 1998. Chapter 2 discusses policy research strategies and contributions.

Kimball, Ralph, et al. *The Data Warehouse Lifecycle Toolkit: Expert Methods for Designing, Developing, and Deploying Data Ware-houses.* New York: Wiley, 1998. A definitive work on the business dimensional life-cycle approach and data warehouse architecture.

Miller, Thomas W., and Dana H. James. *Marketing Research and Information Services: 2003 Industry Report.* Madison, WI: Research Publishers, 2003.

Porter, Michael. *Competitive Strategy.* New York: Free Press, 1980. The seminal work in strategy development.

Random, Matthew. *The Social Scientist in American Industry.* New Brunswick, NJ: Rutgers University Press, 1970. A research report of experiences of social scientists employed in industry. Chapter 7 presents a summary of findings.

Remenyi, Dan, et al. *Doing Research in Business and Management: An Introduction to Process and Method.* Thousand Oaks, CA: Sage Publications, 1998. Chapters 1 and 2 establish the business research perspective for management students.

Sutton, Howard. *Competitive Intelligence.* New York: The Conference Board, 1988.

appendix 1a

Reference Notes

1. Portions are adapted from a presentation by Larry P. Stanek, "Getting and Keeping a Seat at the Executive Table," 23d Annual AMA Marketing Research Conference, Chicago, September 9, 2002.

2. *INformed* 4, no. 2 (April 2001) http://www.arfsite.org/webpages/ informed/vol4-no2/page2.html).

3. Ibid.

4. Philip Kotler, "Bringing Marketing Research into the Board Room," 23d Annual AMA Marketing Research Conference, Chicago, September 9, 2002.

5. CASRO, http://www.casro.org.

6. NFO WorldGroup website, downloaded November 9, 2002 (http://www.nfow.com/default2.asp).

7. TNSI website, downloaded November 9, 2002 (http://www. intersearch.tnsofres.com/custom/).

8. Ibid.

9. Curt Coffman and Gabriel Gonzalez-Molina, *Follow This Path: How the World's Greatest Organizations Drive Growth by Unleashing Human Potential* (New York: Warner Books, October 2002); interviews with Larry Emond, CMO, The Gallup Organi-zation, October 15–17, 2002.

10. Context-Based Research Group website, downloaded November 9, 2002 (http://www.contextresearch.com/context/index.cfm; http:// www.contextresearch.com/context/clients_recent.cfm).

11. "About MORI" and "Employee Opinion Research," MORInsight, accessed December 29, 2004 (http://www.mori.com/about/index.shtml; http://www.mori.com/employee/).

12. "Employee Opinion Survey Research," Mercer Human Resources Consulting, accessed December 29, 2004 (http://www.mercerhr.com/service/list.jhtml/dynamic/idCategory/140100018;jsessionid=JNOG5VRPDIFTUCTGOUFCHPQKMZ0QUI2C).

13. Gail Hohner, John Rich, Ed Ng, Grant Reid, Andrew Davenport, Jayant Kalagnanam, Ho Soo Lee, and Chae An, "Combinatorial and Quantity-Discount Procurement Actions Benefit Mars, Incorporated and Its Suppliers," *Interfaces* 33, no. 1 (January–February 2003), pp. 23–35, accessed December 29, 2004 (http://pubsonline.informs.org/feature/Edelman/1526-551X-2003-33-01-0023R.pdf).

14. Survey Sampling Inc. website, downloaded November 9, 2002 (http://www.surveysampling.com/ssi_products.html).

15. Greenfield Online website, downloaded November 9, 2002 (http://www.greenfield.com/sampling/panel.htm; http://www.greenfield.com/sampling/msn.htm).

16. Qualtrics Labs materials from the AMA Marketing Research Conference, Chicago, September 9, 2002; interview with CIO, Qualtrics Labs, Chicago, September 9, 2002.

17. Training Technologies Inc. website (http://www.surveytracker.com).

18. Information Resources Inc. website, downloaded November 9, 2002 (http://www.infores.com/public/global/aboutiri/glo_abt_history.htm).

19. NOP World website, downloaded November 9, 2002 (http://www.nop.co.uk/omnibus/hp_omnibus.shtml).

20. Medical Marketing Research Inc. website, downloaded November 9, 2002 (http://www.mmrx.com/mmrx/sld026.htm); TNS Intersearch website, downloaded November 9, 2002 (http://www.tnsofres.com/consumeromnibus/phonebus/index.cfm).

21. "Data Dump," *e-Marketer,* e-Marketer.com, March 8, 2007, accessed March 9, 2007 (http://www.emarketer.com/Article.aspx?1004659&src=article1_newsltr).

chapter 2
Reference Notes

1. This paragraph is based on a comparison of two studies: "Survey Documents State of Ethics in the Workplace," Ethics Resource Center: Press Release, October 12, 2005, accessed January 29, 2007 (http://www.ethics.org/research/2005-press-release.asp); "Major Survey of America's Workers Finds Substantial Improvement in Ethics," Ethics Resource Center, press release, May 21, 2003 (http://www.ethics.org/research/2003-press-release.asp).

2. Elizabethann O'Sullivan and Gary R. Rassel, *Research Methods for Public Administrators* (New York: Longman, 1999).

3. American Psychological Association, *Ethical Principles of Psychologists and Code of Conduct* (Washington, DC: APA, 1997).

4. Exhibit 2-2 shows the standard procedures used for informed consent in surveys conducted by the Indiana University Center for Survey Research. Wording and protocol by CSR IU.

5. Robert A. Baron and Donn Byrne, *Social Psychology: Understanding Human Interaction* (Boston: Allyn and Bacon, 1991), p. 36.

6. Floyd J. Fowler Jr., *Survey Research Methods,* rev. ed. (Beverly Hills, CA: Sage Publications, 1988), p. 138.

7. Jim Thomas, "Introduction: A Debate about the Ethics of Fair Practices for Collecting Social Science Data in Cyberspace," *Information Society* 12, no. 2 (1996).

8. "FAQs—Kroger Plus Shopper's Card," The Kroger Co., 2001 (http://www.kroger.com/faqs_shopperscard.htm).

9. "European Online Privacy Measures Up," *eMarketer,* October 26, 1998 (http://www.estats.com/news/102698_europri.html).

10. Robert O'Harrow, "Privacy Rules Send U.S. Firms Scrambling," *Washington Post,* October 20, 1998.

11. Fowler, *Survey Research Methods,* p. 139.

12. See Thomas, "Introduction." The Belmont Report was produced by the National Commission for the Protection of Human Subjects of Biomedical and Behavioral Research under the title, *Ethical Principles and Guidelines for the Protection of Human Subjects of Research* (Washington, DC: Department of Health, Education, and Welfare, 1979). The other source of ethical standards was the *Federal Register,* Part II, "Federal Policy for the Protection of Human Subjects: Notices and Rules" (Washington, DC: U.S. Government Printing Office, 1991).

13. R. Gorlin, ed., *Codes of Professional Responsibility,* 3d ed. (Washington, DC: BNA Books, 1994).

14. Jeff Allen and Duane Davis, "Assessing Some Determinant Effects of Ethical Consulting Behavior: The Case of Personal and Professional Values," *Journal of Business Ethics* (1993), p. 449.

15. Paul Davidson Reynolds, *Ethics and Social Science Research* (Englewood Cliffs, NJ: Prentice Hall, 1982), pp. 103–8.

16. The Nuremberg Code is a set of 10 moral, ethical, and legal principles for medical experimentation on humans. It comes from the judgment of the Nuremberg Military Tribunal against doctors and scientists who committed World War II Nazi atrocities. For a full listing of the Nuremberg Code, see Jay Katz, *Experimentation with Human Beings* (New York: Russell Sage Foundation, 1972), pp. 305–6. See also Allan J. Kimmel, *Ethics and Values in Applied Social Research* (Newbury Park, CA: Sage Publications, 1988), pp. 54–56.

17. Reynolds, *Ethics and Social Science Research,* pp. 103–8.

18. The Center for Business Ethics, Bentley College (Waltham, MA) (http://ecampus.bentley.edu/dept/cbe/).

19. http://www.ethicsandbusiness.org/index3.htm.

20. Adapted from stories in the *Palm Beach Post* during September 1992.

References for Snapshots, PicProfiles, Captions, PulsePoints, and Pull Quotes
Foundation for Transparency in Offshoring

"Help End the Market Research Professions' Secret," November 19, 2009, accessed January 24, 2010 (http://www.tomhcanderson.com/2009/11/19/help-end-the-market-research-professions-final-dirty-little-secret/).

"Recent Survey Data about Offshoring." Study conducted by Foundation for Transparency in Offshoring, November 2009, accessed January 24, 2010 (http://www.offshoringtransparency.org/images/charts/ngmr4.jpg).

Google

Danny Sullivan, "Searches Per Day," Search Engine Watch, April 20, 2006, accessed January 29, 2007 (http://searchenginewatch.com/showPage.html?page=2156461).

Ken Cessar, "The Other 95 Percent of Our Time," *Neilsen/NetRatings Reporter,* Neilsen/NetRatings, January 2007, accessed January 28, 2007 (http://www.netratings.com/press.jsp?section-newsletter&nav=2).

"2006 What's Hot," Google Inc., accessed January 29, 2007 (http://www.google.com/intl/en/press/zeitgeist2006/whatshot.html).

"2006 Year-End Google Zeitgeist," Google, Inc. accessed January 29, 2007 (http://www.google.com/intl/en/press/zeitgeist2006.html).

PullQuote

Humphrey Taylor, "Most People Are 'Privacy Pragmatists' Who, While Concerned about Privacy, Will Sometimes Trade It Off for Other Benefits," March 19, 2003, accessed June 14, 2009 (http://www.harrisinteractive.com/harris_poll/index.asp?PID=365).

PulsePoint

Deborah Stead, "Profiles in Pilfering," *BusinessWeek,* October 13, 2009, p. 16.

Online Professional Communities

Matthew D. Lees, "Building Professional Peer Communities," *eNEWS,* Patricia Seybold Group Inc., January 11, 2007, accessed January 26, 2007 (http://www.psgroup.com/detail.aspx?ID=787). Excerpts reprinted with permission of Patricia Seybold Group Inc.

Trust Trumps Privacy?

"Data Privacy: Business Week Survey," March 20, 2000, Center for Democracy and Technology, accessed January 29, 2007 (http://www.cdt.org/privacy/survey/findings/).

"Is Privacy Overrated?" *eMarketer.com,* eMarketer Inc., January 12, 2007, accessed January 29, 2007 (http://www.emarketer.com/Articles/Print.aspx?1004458&src=print_article_graybar_article).

Humphrey Taylor, "Most People Are "Privacy Pragmatists" Who, While Concerned about Privacy, Will Sometimes Trade It Off for Other Benefits," Harris Interactive: The Harris Poll #17, March 19, 2003, accessed January 28, 2007 (http://www.harrisinteractive.com/harris_poll/index.asp?PID=365).

TRUSTe

"The TRUSTe Program: How It Protects Your Privacy," TRUSTe, downloaded October 30, 2003 (http://www.truste.org/consumers/users_how.html).

Classic and Contemporary Readings

National Academy of Sciences. *On Being a Scientist: Responsible Conduct in Research.* 2d ed. Washington, DC: National Academy Press, 1995. Written for beginning researchers, this source describes the ethical foundations of scientific practices; personal and professional issues; and research applications for industrial, governmental, and academic settings.

Rosnow, Ralph L., and Robert Rosenthal. *People Studying People: Artifacts and Ethics in Behavioral Research.* New York: Freeman, 1997. A potent source of analysis and advice; particularly appropriate for Chapters 9 and 11 on observation and experimentation.

Stanley, Barbara H., et al., eds. Research Ethics: *A Psychological Approach.* Lincoln: University of Nebraska Press, 1996. Addresses important issues such as the discovery and neutralization of bias; sensitivity to the interests of experimental participants; and the counterweighing factors in rules, regulations, and enforcement.

Stern, Judy E., and Deni Elliott, eds. *Research Ethics: A Reader.* Hanover, NH: University Press of New England, 1997. An insightful review of ethical issues for managers and researchers.

Weisstub, David N., ed. *Research on Human Subjects: Ethics, Law, and Social Policy.* Oxford, England: Pergamon Press, 1998. Comprehensive exploration of challenges in research ethics for policymakers and institutions, with coverage of international perspectives.

chapter 3

Reference Notes

1. *Merriam-Webster's Collegiate Dictionary,* 10th ed. (Springfield, MA: Merriam-Webster, 1999) (http://www.m-w.com/cgi-bin/dictionary).

2. Fred N. Kerlinger, *Foundations of Behavioral Research,* 3d ed. (New York: Holt, Rinehart & Winston, 1986), pp. 436–37.

3. Kenneth R. Hoover, *The Elements of Social Scientific Thinking,* 5th ed. (New York: St. Martin's Press, 1991), p. 71.

4. Bruce Tuckman, *Conducting Educational Research* (New York: Harcourt Brace Jovanovich, 1972), p. 45.

5. William Stephens, *Hypotheses and Evidence* (New York: Thomas Y. Crowell, 1968), p. 5.

6. Based on Roger A Kerin, Eric N. Berkowitz, Steven W. Hartley, and William Rudelius, *Marketing,* 7th ed. (Burr Ridge, IL: Irwin/McGraw-Hill, 2003), pp. 294–302.

7. Ibid., p. 298.

8. Scott M. Smith and William R. Swinyard, *Introduction to Marketing Models* (Internet Text, 1999), Chap. 1 (http://marketing.byu.edu/htmlpages/courses/693r/modelsbook.html).

9. Ibid., Chap. 6 (http://marketing.byu.edu/htmlpages/courses/693r/modelsbook/airjordan.html).

10. P. M. Miller and M. J. Wilson, eds., *A Dictionary of Social Sciences Methods* (New York: Wiley, 1983), p. 27. Also see Benjamin B. Wolman, ed., *Dictionary of Behavioral Science* 2d ed. (New York: Academic Press, 1989).

11. Thomas S. Kuhn, *The Structure of Scientific Revolutions* (Chicago: University of Chicago Press, 1970).

12. Based on John Dewey, *How We Think* (Boston: Heath, 1910), and John R. Platt, "Strong Inference," *Science,* October 16, 1964, pp. 347–53.

13. Howard Kahane, *Logic and Philosophy,* 2d ed. (Belmont, CA: Wadsworth, 1973), p. 3.

14. Dewey, *How We Think,* p. 79.

References for Snapshots, PicProfiles, Captions, PulsePoints, and Pull Quotes

Business and Battlefield

a. G. P. Hodgkinson, J. Langan-Fox, and E. Sadler-Smith, "Intuition: A Fundamental Bridging Construct in the Behavioural Sciences," *British Journal of Psychology* 99 (2008), pp. 1–27.

b. Ibid.

c. Benedict Carey, "In Battle, Hunches Prove to Be Valuable," *New York Times,* July 27, 2009, accessed July 29, 2009 (http://www.nytimes.com/2009/07/28/health/research/28brain.html?pagewanted=3&th&emc=th).

d. Tony Perry, "Some Troops Have a Sixth Sense for Bombs," *Los Angeles Times,* October 28, 2009), accessed December 19, 2009 (http://www.latimes.com/news/nationworld/world/la-fg-bombs-vision28-2009oct28,0,36980.story).

e. Carey, "In Battle."

f. Ibid.

g. National Academy of Sciences (2008), Science, Evolution, and Creationism states: "In everyday language a theory means a hunch or speculation. Not so in science. In science, the word theory refers to a comprehensive explanation of an important feature of nature supported by facts gathered over time."

h. Randall Fitzgerald, "How Does Science Support 'Gut Hunches?'" *Toronto Examiner,* December 1, 2009, accessed December 19, 2009 (http://www.examiner.com/x-27763-Skepticism-Examiner~y2009m12d1-How-doesscience-support-gut-hunches).

i. Ibid.

j. See also the book by Malcolm Gladwell, *Blink: The Power of Thinking Without Thinking* (Boston: Little, Brown and Company, 2005).

k. Fitzgerald, "How Does Science."

l. R. A. Rensink, "Visual Sensing without Seeing," *Psychological Science* 15 (2004), pp. 27–32.

m. Fitzgerald, "How Does Science."

n. S. J. Gould, *The Mismeasure of Man* (New York: W. W. Norton, 1981), pp. 52–53.

Forrester Research

Mark Bunger, senior analyst, Forrester Research, interviewed January 22, 2004.

"Making Auto Retail Lean," *TechStrategy Report,* Forrester Research, accessed January 5, 2004 (http://www.forrester.com/ER/Research/Report/Summary/0,1338,32782,00.html).

PullQuote

Tom H. C. Anderson, "Judit Nagy of MySpace & Tom H. C. Anderson Discuss Social Media & Market Research," Anderson Analytics, June 15, 2009, accessed June 16, 2009 (http://www.tomhcanderson.com/2009/06/12/judit-nagy-of-myspace-tom-h-c-anderson-discuss-social-media-research/).

PulsePoint

"The Problem with Social Media in the Office," *eMarketer,* May 27, 2009, accessed May 28, 2009 (http://www.emarketer.com/Article.aspx?R=1007109).

Scientific Definitions

http://www.americanprogress.org/issues/2007/03/defining_problem.html.

Center for American Progress. *The Defining Problem: Defining Scientific Terms for Political Reasons Is Bad for Both Sides of the Debate.* Sam Berger and Jonathan D. Moreno, March 1, 2007.

www.kumc.edu; www.kslegislature.org.

Radio Chips

Arlene Weintraub and Janet Ginsburg, "A High-Tech Race to Corral Mad Cow," *BusinessWeek,* March 1, 2004, Issue 3872.

www.usda.gov; www.optibrand.com; www.swiftbrands.com; www.startupjournal.com.

Classic and Contemporary Readings

Beardsley, Monroe. *Practical Logic.* Englewood Cliffs, NJ: Prentice Hall, 1969. A lucid discussion of deduction and induction as well as an excellent coverage of argument analysis.

Browne, M. Neil, and Stuart M. Keeley. *Asking the Right Questions: A Guide to Critical Thinking.* Upper Saddle River, NJ: Prentice Hall, 1997. Addresses question-asking skills and techniques necessary for evaluating different types of evidence.

Hoover, Kenneth R., and Todd Donovan. *The Elements of Social Scientific Thinking.* 6th ed. New York: St. Martin's Press, 1995. A brief but highly readable treatise on the elements of science and scientific thinking.

Kaplan, Abraham. *The Conduct of Inquiry.* San Francisco: Chandler, 1964. A classic source for the philosophy of science and logical reasoning.

chapter 4

Reference Notes

1. Albert Einstein and L. Infeld, *The Evolution of Physics* (New York: Simon & Schuster, 1938), p. 95.

2. Walter B. Wentz, *Marketing Research: Management, Method, and Cases* (New York: Harper & Row, 1979), p. 35.

3. Robert D. Buzzell, Donald F. Cox, and Rex V. Brown, *Marketing Research and Information Systems* (New York: McGraw-Hill, 1969), p. 595.

4. Dik Warren Twedt, "What Is the 'Return on Investment' in Marketing Research?" *Journal of Marketing* 30 (January 1966), pp. 62–63.

5. Paul D. Leedy, *How to Read Research and Understand It* (New York: Macmillan, 1981), pp. 67–70.

6. Roger Cohen, "For U.S. Publishers, Awash in Red Ink, the Moment of Truth Looms," *International Herald Tribune,* March 6, 1990, p. 6.

7. Walter B. Reitman, "Heuristic Decision Procedures, Open Constraints, and the Structure of Ill-Defined Problems," in *Human Judgments and Optimality,* ed. Maynard W. Shelly II and Glenn L. Bryan (New York: Wiley, 1964), p. 285.

8. Carl M. Moore, *Group Techniques for Idea Building,* 2d ed. (Thousand Oaks, CA: Sage Publications, 1994).

9. Fred N. Kerlinger, *Foundations of Behavioral Research,* 3d ed. (New York: Holt, Rinehart & Winston, 1986), pp. 436–37.

References for Snapshots, PicProfiles, Captions, PulsePoints, and Pull Quotes

Covering Kids

"About Us," Robert Wood Johnson Foundation, downloaded July 22, 2002 (http://www.rwjf.org/aboutRwjf/index.jhtml).

Bureau of Labor Statistics, Household Data, 3. Employment Status of the Civian Noninstitutional Population by Age, Sex, and Race, 2008.

"Call for Proposals, Covering Kids: A National Health Access Initiative for Low-Income Uninsured Children," Robert Wood Johnson Foundation.

"Call for Proposals, Covering Kids and Families," Robert Wood Johnson Foundation.

"Covering Kids Communication Campaign—Target Market Summary: Phase I Market Research and Short-Term Evaluation Plans," Robert Wood Johnson Foundation, September 7, 2000.

Elaine Arkin, consultant to Robert Wood Johnson Foundation, interviewed October 4, 2002.

"Employment and Unemployment Among Youth—Summer 2008," Bureau of Labor Statistics, August 28, 2008, accessed June 26, 2009 (http://www.bls.gov/news.release/pdf/youth.pdf).

James Challenger, "Teens Face Uphill Battle in Summer Job Search," Midwest Business.com, June 8, 2009, accessed June 26, 2009 (http://wistechnology.com/articles/6163).

Stuart Schear, senior communication officer, Robert Wood Johnson Foundation, interviewed July 23, 2002.

Hiring Teens

"Are They Really Ready To Work: Employers' Perspectives on the Basic knowledge and Applied Skills of New Entrants to the 21st Century U.S. Workforce," The 21st Century Skills.org, September 29, 2006. Accessed March 9, 2007 (http://www.21stcenturyskills. org/documents/FINAL_REPORT_PDF9-29-06.pdf)

"Why Teens Aren't Finding Jobs, and Why Employers Are Paying the Price," *Knowledge@Wharton,* March 07, 2007. Accessed March 9, 2007 (http://knowledge.wharton.upenn.edu/article.cfm?articleid= 1681&CFID=3615973&CFTOKEN=98758842#).

Kraft

"Cheese Please! Kraft Singles Talks to Moms about Kids and Calcium," *American Demographics,* March 2000, pp. s6–s7.

PullQuote

Anthony Robbins, "How to Change the Quality of your Life," accessed June 14, 2009 (http://tonyrobbinstraining.com/119/ power-of-questions/).

PulsePoint

Dan Macsai, ". . . And I Invented Velcro," *BusinessWeek,* August 4, 2008, p. 15.

Classic and Contemporary Readings

Fox, David J. *The Research Process in Education.* New York: Holt, Rinehart & Winston, 1969. Chapters 1 and 5 include a research process model to compare with the one in this chapter.

Leedy, Paul D. *Practical Research: Planning & Design.* 6th ed. Englewood Cliffs, NJ: Prentice Hall, 1996. Practical and readable sections guide students through the research process.

Murdick, Robert G., and Donald R. Cooper. *Business Research: Concepts and Guides.* Columbus, OH: Grid, 1982. A supplementary text with a strong emphasis on problem identification and formulation.

Selltiz, Claire, Lawrence S. Wrightsman, and Stuart M. Cook. *Research Methods in Social Relations.* 3d ed. New York: Holt, Rinehart & Winston, 1976. Chapters 1 and 2 present a good research process example and discussion of formulating a research problem.

Tull, Donald S., and Del I. Hawkins. *Marketing Research: Meaning, Measurement, and Method.* 6th ed. New York: Macmillan, 1992. The authors provide good coverage of the valuation of research information through a Bayesian decision theory approach.

chapter 5
Reference Notes

1. "About This Encyclopedia," *TDM Encyclopedia,* Victoria Transport Policy Institute, accessed February 2, 2007 (http://www.vtpi. org/tdm/tdm12.htm).

2. "Encyclopedia of Private Equity and Venture Capital," VC Experts Inc, accessed February 2, 2007 (http://vcexperts.com/vce/library/ encyclopedia/).

3. Occupational Outlook Handbook, U.S. Bureau of Labor Statistics, accessed February 2, 2007 (http://www.bls.gov/oco/ocoiab.htm).

4. Joseph B. Sieczka and Robert E. Thornton, eds., "Potato Association of American Handbook," Potato Association of America, accessed February 2, 2007 (http://cropandsoil.oregonstate.edu/ classes/CSS322/Cppina.htm).

5. North American Industry Classification System (NAICS), U.S. Census Bureau. Accessed May 2, 2009 (http://www.census.gov/ eos/www/naics/). According to the Federal Register notice, NAICS 2007 plans to be published in January 2007. Accessed February 2, 2007 (http://www.census.gov/epcd/naics07/index.html).

6. *Associations Unlimited,* Gale Inc., accessed February 2007 (http:// www.gale.com/servlet/ItemDetailServlet?region=9&imprint= 000&titleCode=GAL7&type=4&id=110996).

7. *Green Book: A Guide for Buyers of Marketing Research Services,* New York AMA Communication Services Inc., accessed February 2, 2007 (http://www.greenbook.org/).

8. R. Srikant and R. Agrawal, "Mining Sequential Patterns: Generalizations and Performance Improvements," Proceedings, 5th International Conference on Extending Database Technology, Paris, France, March 1996.

9. B. DePompe, "There's Gold in Databases," *CMP Publications,* January 8, 1996 (http://techweb.cmp.com/iwk).

10. Table adapted from DIG White Paper 95/01, "An Overview of Data Mining at Dun & Bradstreet," Data Intelligence Group, Pilot Software, Cambridge, MA, September 1995.

11. "Data Mining: Plumbing the Depths of Corporate Databases," *Computer World Customer Publication,* insert to *ComputerWorld,* April 21, 1997, p. 12.

12. DePompe, "There's Gold in Databases."

13. "Data Mining: Plumbing the Depths," pp. 6, 18.

14. SAS Institute Inc., "Data Mining" (http://www.sas.com).

15. Exhibit 5-5 was adapted from ibid.

References for Snapshots, Picprofiles, Captions, PulsePoints, and Pull Quotes
Blogs

Lee Rainie, "The State of Blogging," *PEW Internet and American Life Report,* January 2005, accessed February 10, 2007 (http://www. pewinternet.org/pdfs/PIP_blogging_data.pdf).

"State of the Blogosphere, August 2006," Sifry's Alerts, accessed February 10, 2007 (http://www.sifry.com/alerts/archives/000436.html).

"State of the Blogosphere, February 2006 Part 1: On Blogosphere Growth," Sifry's Alerts, accessed March 7, 2007 (http://www.sifry. com/alerts/archives/000419.html).

Amanda Lenhart and Susannah Fox, "Bloggers: A Portrait of the Internet's New Storytellers," PEW Internet and American Life Project, July 19 2006, accessed March 7, 2007 (http://www.pewinternet.org/ pdfs/PIP%20Bloggers%20Report%20July%2019%202006.pdf).

Deception Line

Eamon Javers, "Spies, Lies, and KPMG," *BusinessWeek,* February 26, 2007, p. 86–88.

Deep Web

"About Us," About.com, accessed March 5, 2007 (http://advertise. about.com/about/index.html).

Chris Sherman, "The Invisible Web," Free Pint, no. 64, June 8, 2000, accessed March 5, 2007 (http://www.freepint.com/issues/080600. htm#feature).

"CompletePlanet Wins Award from Search Engine Watch," BrightPlanet. com press release, December 21, 2000, accessed March 5, 2007 (http:// www.brightplanet.com/news/prs/completeplanet-wins-award.html).

Robert J. Lackie, "Those Dark Hiding Places: The Invisible Web Revealed," Rider University, accessed March 5, 2007 (http://www. robertlackie.com/invisible/index.html#searchable).

Wendy Boswell, "The Invisible Web," About.com, accessed March 5, 2007 (http://websearch.about.com/od/invisibleweb/a/invisible_web. htm).

How Will Cloud Computing Affect Research?

a.   Agam Shah, "Dell Attempts to Copyright 'Cloud Computing,'" Techworld.com, August 4, 2008, accessed June 1, 2009 (http://www.techworld.com/opsys/news/index.cfm?newsid=102279).

b.   "Amazon Elastic Compute Cloud (Amazon EC2)," Amazon.com, accessed June 1, 2009 (http://aws.amazon.com/ec2/).

c.   James Staten, "Leveraging Cloud Computing for New Business Enablement," May 8, 2009, accessed June 1, 2009 (http://blogs.zdnet.com/forrester/?p=202).

d.   "What Is Force.com, anyway?" Salesforce.com, accessed June 1, 2009 (http://www.salesforce.com/platform/).

e.   Nancy Gohring, "Microsoft Offers Live Mesh to More Users," Techworld.com, July 17, 2008, accessed June 1, 2009 (http://www.techworld.com/mobility/news/index.cfm?newsid=102173).

f.   Bill Synder, "Cloud Computing: Tales from the Front," *CIO UK Magazine,* May 2, 2008, accessed June 1, 2009 (http://www.cio.co.uk/article/663/cloud-computing-tales-from-the-front/).

"Cloud Computing: Managing a Hybrid Services Environment," Hewlett-Packard, accessed June 1, 2009 (http://h71028.www7.hp.com/enterprise/us/en/technologies/cloud-computing.html).

David Spark, "Innovation Will Be Driven by the Adoption of Cloud Computing," June 10, 2008, accessed June 1, 2009 (http://enterprise2blog.com/2008/06/innovation-will-be-driven-by-the-adoption-of-cloud-computing/).

Laurianne McLaughlin, "Eleven Cloud Computing Vendors to Watch," *CIO UK Magazine,* May 6, 2008, accessed June 1, 2009 (http://www.cio.co.uk/article/665/eleven-cloud-computing-vendors-to-watch/).

Mining the Web

a.   Alex Wright, "Mining the Web for Feelings, Not Facts," *New York Times,* August 23, 2009, accessed August 24, 2009.

b.   Ibid.

c.   Ibid.

d.   Bo Pang and Lillian Lee, *Opinion Mining and Sentiment Analysis* (Hanover, MA: Now Publishers, 2008).

e.   Bo Pang and Lillian Lee, "Seeing Stars: Exploiting Class Relationships for Sentiment Categorization with Respect to Rating Scales," *Proceedings of the Association for Computational Linguistics* (ACL), 2005, pp. 115–24; and Benjamin Snyder and Regina Barzilay, (2007). "Multiple Aspect Ranking using the Good Grief Algorithm," *Proceedings of the Joint Human Language Technology/North American Chapter of the ACL Conference* (HLT-NAACL), 2007, pp. 300–77.

f.   See, for example, Scout Labs' approach to market intelligence (http://www.scoutlabs.com/); and Jodange's program on *Engaging Influentials with Twitter and Beyond* (http://jodange.com/news.html).

Netflix

a.   Netflix Investor Relations, Corporate Fact Sheet, accessed December 20, 2009 (http://ir.netflix.com/).

b.   Steve Lohr, "Netflix Competitors Learn the Power of Teamwork," *New York Times,* July 27, 2009, accessed December 20, 2009 (www.nytimes.com/2009/07/28/technology/internet/28netflix.html); Steve Lohr, "And the Winner of the $1 Million Netflix Prize (Probably) Is . . ." *New York Times,* June 26, 2009, accessed December 20, 2009 (http://bits.blogs.nytimes.com/2009/06/26/and-the-winner-of-the-1-million-netflix-prize-probably-is/?th&emc=th); and Steve Lohr, "A $1 Million Research Bargain for Netflix, and Maybe a Model for Others," *New York Times,*

September 21, 2009, accessed December 20, 2009 (http://www.nytimes.com/2009/09/22/technology/internet/22netflix.html?_r=1&th=&adxnnl=1&emc=th&adxnnlx=1258657308-i8o2aJa/xD5VRxcA2SELvQ).

c.   Lohr, "A $1 Million Research Bargain."

d.   Steve Lohr, "Netflix Challenge Ends, but Winner Is in Doubt" *New York Times Blog,* July 27, 2009, accessed December 20, 2009 (http://bits.blogs.nytimes.com/2009/07/27/netflix-challenge-ends-but-winner-is-in-doubt/?th&emc=th).

e.   Lohr. "And the Winner of the $1 Million."

Professional Community

Matthew Lees, "Building Professional Peer Communities: An Interview with Vanessa DiMauro, Principal, Leader Networks," Patricia Seybold Group, January 11, 2007, accessed February 9, 2007 (http://www.psgroup.com/detail.aspx?ID=787).

PullQuote

"KDnuggets Data Mining Guru Gregory Piatetsky-Shapiro and Tom H. C. Anderson Talk about Data Mining, Text Mining, Web 2.0, and Market Research," Anderson Analytics, March 29th, 2008, accessed June 11, 2009 (http://www.tomhcanderson.com/2008/03/29/kdnuggets-data-mining-guru-gregory-piatetsky-shapiro-and-tom-h-c-anderson-talk-about-data-mining-text-mining-web-20-and-market-research-%E2%80%93-anderson-analytics-round-table-discussion-3/).

PulsePoint

"Survey: Financial Institutions Confidence Shaken by Economic Crisis; Drastic Risk Management Reform Underway," SAS press release, March 6, 2009, accessed May 30, 2009 (http://www.sas.com/news/preleases/ERMsurveyserieslondon.html).

Classic and Contemporary Readings

Berry, Michael J. A., and Gordon Linoff. *Mastering Data Mining: The Art and Science of Customer Relationship Management.* New York: Wiley, 1999.

Fayyad, Usama M., Gregory Piatetsky-Shapiro, Padhraic Smyth, and Ramasamy Uthurusamy. Advances in Knowledge Discovery and Data Mining: 10th Pacific-Asia Conference, PAKDD 2006, Singapore, April 9–12, 2006, Proceedings. New York: Springer, 2006. Papers on classification, clustering, text and document mining, web mining, graph and network mining, association rule mining, biodata mining, outlier and intrusion detection, relational database, multimedia mining, and innovative applications.

Fox, David J. *The Research Process in Education.* New York: Holt, Rinehart & Winston, 1969. Chapter 2 includes a research process model to compare with the one in this chapter.

Leedy, Paul D., and Jeanne Ellis Ormrod. *Practical Research: Planning & Design.* 8th ed. Upper Saddle River: NJ, 2004. Practical and readable sections guide students through the research process.

Janes, Joseph. *Introduction to Reference Work in the Digital Age.* New York: Neal-Schuman Publishers, 2003. Focus on how the digital world has changed reference services and searching.

Katz, William A. *Introduction to Reference Work.* 7th ed. New York: McGraw-Hill, 1997.

Selltiz, Claire, Lawrence S. Wrightsman, and Stuart M. Cook. *Research Methods in Social Relations.* 3d ed. New York: Holt, Rinehart & Winston, 1976. Chapters 1 and 2 present a good research process example and discussion of formulating a research problem.

Thomson Gale, ed. *Encyclopedia of Business Information Sources.* 22nd ed. Farmington Hills, MI: Thomson Gale, 2007.

Appendix 5a

1. Good sources for Web size estimates are the studies by Steve R. Lawrence and C. Lee Giles, "Searching the World Wide Web," *Science* 280 (April 1998, pp.98–100, and "Accessibility of Information on the Web," *Nature* 400 (July 8, 1999), pp. 107–109, with updated summary data at www.wwwmetrics.com.

2. Michael Dahm, "Counting Angels on a Pinhead: Critically Interpreting Web Size Estimates," *Online* 24 (January-February 2000), pp.35–44. This article further interprets the pioneering research by authors Steve R. Lawrence and C. Lee Giles (op cit.).

3. The May-June 1999 issue of *Online* focuses on search engine technology. See, for example, Danny Sullivan, "Crawling under the Hood: An Update on Search Engine Technology," *Online* 23 (May-June 1999), pp. 30–38. See also Danny Sullivan's "Search Engine Watch" (http://searchenginewatch.com/) and Greg Notess's "Search Engine Showdown" (www.notess.com/search/) for current information about search engines and their features.

4. Greg R. Notess, "Duplicative Databases: Yellow Pages from infoUSA," *Database* 22 (February-March 1999), pp. 73–36.

5. See for example, the June 22, 1999 issue of *PC Magazine* for a special report detailing "Ten Trends That Are Defining the Future" (Introduction. p. 100).

6. "Federal Register Online via GPO Access," http://www.access.gpo.gov/su_docs/aces/aces140.html.

7. "About the Code of Federal Regulations," http://www.access.gpo.gov/nara/about-ctr.html#page1.

chapter 6

Reference Notes

1. Reprinted with permission of Macmillan Publishing from *Social Research Strategy and Tactics,* 2d ed., by Bernard S. Phillips, p. 93. Copyright © 1971 by Bernard S. Phillips.

2. Fred N. Kerlinger, *Foundations of Behavioral Research,* 3d ed. (New York: Holt, Rinehart & Winston, 1986), p. 279.

3. Ibid.

4. The complexity of research design tends to confuse students as well as writers. The latter respond by forcing order on the vast array of design types through the use of classification schemes or taxonomies. Generally, this is helpful, but because the world defies neat categories, this scheme, like others, may either include or exclude too much.

5. Kerlinger, *Foundations of Behavioral Research,* p. 295.

6. Abraham Kaplan, *Conduct of Inquiry* (San Francisco: Chandler, 1964), p. 37.

7. W. Charles Redding, "Research Setting: Field Studies," in *Methods of Research in Communication,* ed. Philip Emmert and William D. Brooks (Boston: Houghton Mifflin, 1970), pp. 140–42.

8. John Van Maanen, James M. Dabbs Jr., and Robert R. Faulkner, *Varieties of Qualitative Research* (Beverly Hills, CA: Sage Publications, 1982), p. 32.

9. Catherine Marshall and Gretchen B. Rossman, *Designing Qualitative Research* (Newbury Park, CA: Sage Publications, 1989), pp. 78–108.

10. This classification is suggested in Claire Selltiz, Lawrence S. Wrightsman, and Stuart W. Cook, *Research Methods in Social Relations,* 3d ed. (New York: Holt, Rinehart & Winston, 1976), pp. 99–101.

11. A comprehensive and detailed presentation may be found in Richard A. Krueger, *Focus Groups: A Practical Guide for Applied Research,* 2d ed. (Thousand Oaks, CA: Sage Publications, 1994), and David L.

Morgan, *Successful Focus Groups: Advancing the State of the Art* (Thousand Oaks, CA: Sage Publications, 1993). Also see Thomas L. Greenbaum, "Focus Group Spurt Predicted for the '90s," *Marketing News* 24, no. 1 (January 8, 1990), pp. 21–22.

12. "How Nonprofits Are Using Focus Groups,"*Nonprofit World* 14, no. 5 (September–October 1996), p. 37.

13. As stated in William J. Goode and Paul K. Hatt, *Methods in Social Research* (New York: McGraw-Hill, 1952), p. 75.

14. From *Methods in Social Research* by William J. Goode and Paul K. Hatt. Copyright (c) 1952, McGraw-Hill Book Company. Used with permission of McGraw-Hill Book Company.

15. Morris R. Cohen and Ernest Nagel, *An Introduction to Logic and Scientific Method* (New York: Harcourt, Brace, 1934), Chap. 13; and Blalock, *Causal Inferences,* p. 14.

16. Morris Rosenberg, *The Logic of Survey Analysis* (New York: Basic Books, 1968), p. 3.

References for Snapshots, Picprofiles, Closeups, Captions, PulsePoints, and Pull Quotes

Cheskin

Cheskin ad: "What Will Spark Your Next Evolution?" *American Demographics,* December 2001, p. 30.

"Kids Are Our Future," Cheskin, downloaded February 4, 2005 (http://www.cheskin.com/p/basic.asp?mlid=11).

"Pepsi Case Study," Cheskin, downloaded January 7, 2003 (http://www.cheskin.com/p/basic.asp?mlid_52).

Ohio Lottery

Cincinnati-based Marketing Research Services Inc. (MRSI), established in 1973, is a full-service research firm offering quantitative and qualitative business-to-business and business-to-consumer research that supports strategic planning, product development, advertising and promotion, and more. "History," MRSI, accessed February 19, 2007 (http://www.mrsi.com/history.html).

Jennifer Hirt-Marchand, vice president and director of research, Marcus Thomas LLC; interviewed February 23, 2007.

Marcus Thomas LLC is an integrated marketing communications agency that offers full service advertising, public relations, interactive and research for business-to-business, business-to-consumer and nonprofit organizations (http://www.marcusthomasllc.com/).

Ohio Lottery Segmentation Study, "Final Report" Marcus Thomas LLC and MRSI, October 2005.

PullQuote

Rajat Gupta and Jim Wendler, "Leading Change: An Interview with the CEO of P&G," *The McKinsey Quarterly,* July 2005, accessed June 12, 2009 (http://www.mckinseyquarterly.com/Organization/Change_Management/Leading_change_An_interview_with_the_CEO_of_P_G_1648?gp=1).

PulsePoint

Tomi T. Ahonen, "3 Billion Use SMS—What Does That Mean?" *Socially Minded,* March 6, 2009, accessed June 14, 2009 (http://www.sociallyminded.co.uk/2009/03/3-billion-use-sms-what-does-that-mean/).

Smith Barney

"Before You Ask Smith Barney to Manage Your Assets, Listen to These Sexual Harassment and Sex Discrimination Allegations," National Organization for Women (http://www.now.org/issues/wfw/smith-barney.html).

Paulette Gerkovich, project director, Catalyst, interviewed August 2001. "NOW Issues Reaffirmation of Support for Proposed Smith Barney Settlement," National Organization for Women, April 8, 1998 (http://www.now.org/press/04-98/04-08-98.html).

"Smith Barney Bias Deal Nears OK," *Record Online (Times Herald Record,* a division of Ottaway Newspapers, Inc.), April 10, 1998 (http://www.th-record.com/1998/04/04-10-98/smithb.htm).

"Smith Barney's Woman Problem," *BusinessWeek,* 1996 (http://www. businessweek.com/1996/23/b348154.htm).

"Statement of NOW President Patricia Ireland on Proposed Smith Barney Settlement," National Organization for Women, November 18, 1997 (http://www.now.org/press/11-97/11-18-97.html).

Peter Truell, "A Revised Pact Is Approved in Smith Barney Bias Case," *The New York Times,* July 25, 1998.

"Women in Financial Services: The Word on the Street: Executive Summary," Catalyst, Catalyst Publication Code R47, ISBN#0-89584-219-X, ©2001.

United States Tennis Association

Scott Staniar, independent marketing consultant to United States Tennis Association, interviewed April 27, 2004.

Danny Robinson, chief creative officer, Vigilante, interviewed April 30, 2004. Through Its *Urban Think Tank,* Vigilante has a number of cutting-edge proprietary products such as "Street Spies" and "Urban Passport" that keep the agency and its clients plugged into urban consumers (http://www.vigilantenyc.com/), downloaded April 30, 2004.

Wildcat Surveys

Jeffrey C. Adler, president, Centrac DC Marketing Research, email interview July 2, 2009 and December 5, 2009.

Josh Mendelsohn, vice president, Chadwick Martin Bailey, Inc., email interview July 6, 2009.

Postings to the Marketing Research SIG, American Marketing Association, June 2009.

Ruth Stanat, president and CEO, SIS International Research, email interview July 2, 2009.

Sharon Starr, director of market research, IPC, Inc., email interview July 2, 2009.

Classic and Contemporary Readings

Babbie, Earl R. *The Practice of Social Research.* 9th ed. Belmont, CA: Wadsworth, 2000. Contains a clear and thorough synopsis of design.

Creswell, John W. *Qualitative Inquiry and Research Design.* 5th ed. Thousand Oaks, CA: Sage Publishing, 1997. A creative and comprehensive work on qualitative research methods.

Krathwohl, David R. *Social and Behavioral Science Research: A New Framework for Conceptualizing, Implementing, and Evaluating Research Studies.* San Francisco: Jossey-Bass, 1985. Chapter 9 on causality is insightful, well reasoned, and highly recommended.

Mason, Emanuel J., and William J. Bramble. *Understanding and Conducting Research.* 2d ed. New York: McGraw-Hill, 1989. Chapter 1 has an excellent section on causation; Chapter 2 provides an alternative classification of the types of research.

Morgan, David L., and Richard A. Kruger, eds. *The Focus Group Kit.* Thousand Oaks, CA: Sage Publishing, 1997. A six-volume set including an overview guidebook, planning, developing questions, moderating, involving community members, and analyzing results.

Selltiz, Claire, Lawrence S. Wrightsman, and Stuart M. Cook. *Research Methods in Social Relations.* 3d ed. New York: Holt, Rinehart &

Winston, 1976. Chapters 4 and 5 discuss various types of research designs.

Strauss, Anselm, and Juliet Corbin. *Basics of Qualitative Research.* 2d ed. Thousand Oaks, CA: Sage Publishing, 1998. A step-by-step guide with particularly useful sections on coding procedures.

chapter 7

Reference Notes

1. John Van Maanen, "Reclaiming Qualitative Methods for Organizational Research: A Preface," *Administrative Science Quarterly* 24 (December 1979), pp. 520–24.

2. Judith Langer, *The Mirrored Window: Focus Groups from a Moderator's Point of View* (Ithaca, NY: Paramount Market Publishing, 2001), p. 26.

3. Jennifer Mason, *Qualitative Researching,* 2d ed. (London: Sage Publications, 2002).

4. This list was developed from numerous sources including David Carson, Audrey Gilmore, Chad Perry, and Kjell Gronhaug, *Qualitative Marketing Research* (Thousand Oaks, CA: Sage Publications, 2001), pp. 67–68, which references Norman Denzin and Y. Lincoln, *Handbook of Qualitative Research* (London: Sage Publications, 1994); Y. Lincoln and E. Guba, *Naturalistic Inquiry* (Newbury, CA: Sage Publications, 1985); M. Q. Patton, *Qualitative Evaluation and Research Methods,* 2d ed. (Newbury Park, CA: Sage Publications, 1990); A. M. Pettigrew, "On Studying Organizational Cultures," *Administrative Science Quarterly* 24 (1979), pp. 570–81; Mellanie Wallendorf, Russel Belk, and John Sherry, "The Sacred and the Profane in Consumer Behavior: Theodicy on the Odyssey," *Journal of Consumer Research* 16 (June 1989), pp. 1–38.

5. Carson et al., *Qualitative Marketing Research,* p. 65.

6. Adrian Holliday, *Doing and Writing Qualitative Research* (London: Sage Publications, 2002), pp. 71–72, 99, 105.

7. Ibid.

8. Hy Mariampolski, *Qualitative Market Research: A Comprehensive Guide* (Thousand Oaks, CA: Sage Publications, 2001), p. 79.

9. *Making Connections,* AT&T (video).

10. Mariampolski, *Qualitative Market Research,* pp. 31, 85.

11. Developed from material in Christine Daymon and Immy Holloway, *Qualitative Research Methods in Public Relations and Marketing Communications* (London: Sage Publications, 2002), pp. 223–25; and Mariampolski, *Qualitative Market Research,* pp. 206–19.

12. Langer, *The Mirrored Window,* p. 41

13. "Services: Research: Case Studies: Cracking the Low-Involvement Ceiling," Primary Insights, downloaded January 1, 2003 (http://www.primaryinsights.com/services.cfm?cid=15&cscont=CrackingCeiling.cfm).

14. Dennis W. Rook, "Out-of-Focus Groups," *Marketing Research* 15, no. 2 (Summer 2003), p. 13.

15. P. Hawe, D. Degeling, and J. Hall, *Evaluating Health Promotion: A Health Worker's Guide* (Artarmon, N.S.W.: MacLennan & Petty, 1990).

16. Rook, "Out-of-Focus Groups," pp. 10–15.

17. "Shoppers Speak Out in Focus Groups," *Discount Store News* 36, no. 5 (March 3, 1997), pp. 23–26.

18. Martin Bauer and George Gaskell, eds., *Qualitative Researching with Text, Image, and Sound: A Practical Handbook* (London: Sage Publications, 2000), pp. 48–51.

19. "How Nonprofits Are Using Focus Groups," *Nonprofit World* 14, no. 5 (September–October 1996), p. 37.

20. Carson et al., *Qualitative Marketing Research,* pp. 114–15.

21. Ibid., pp. 91–94, 100–06.

22. Tom Peters and Robert Waterman, *In Search of Excellence: Lessons from America's Best Run Companies* (New York: HarperCollins, 1982).

23. Carson et al., *Qualitative Marketing Research,* pp.159–63.

24. Uwe Flick, *An Introduction to Qualitative Research,* 2d ed. (London: Sage Publications, 2002), pp. 262–63.

References for Snapshots, PicProfiles, Captions, PulsePoints, and Pull Quotes

Anderson Analytics

Tom Anderson, founder and president, Anderson Analytics, interviewed March 8, 2006.

Focus Group Problems

Robert W. Kahle, *Dominator, Cynics, and Wallflowers* (Ithaca, NY: Parmount Market Publishing, Inc., 2006), pp. 22–33.

FocusVision

Debbie Robinson, senior account director, VideoMarker™ Services, FocusVision, interviewed September 10, 2002.

VideoMarker materials distributed at AMA Marketing Research Conference, Chicago, September 10, 2002.

Hallmark

"Cards Reflect Hispanic Culture and Heritage," Hallmark press release, downloaded January 7, 2003 (http://pressroom.hallmark.com/ Caminos_al_alma.html).

"Facts about Hallmark en Español," Hallmark press release, downloaded January 7, 2003 (http://pressroom.hallmark.com/en_espanol_facts. html).

"Facts about Sinceramente Hallmark," Hallmark press release, downloaded July 29, 2004 (http://pressroom.hallmark.com/Sinceramente_ Hallmark_facts.html).

Alison Wellner, "The Census Report," *American Demographics,* January 2002, p. S3.

Hamilton Beach

"The Company," Hamilton Beach/Proctor Silex, downloaded January 19, 2003 (http://www.hamiltonbeach.com/company/hbpsbio.html).

Joseph Rydholm, "Seeing the Right Mix," *Quirk's Marketing Research Review,* November 2001 (http://www.quirks.com/articles/article. asp?arg_ArticleID 728).

IBM

Steve Lohr, "Big Blue's Big Bet: Less Tech, More Touch," *The New York Times on the Web,* January 25, 2004, downloaded January 27, 2004 (http://www.nytimes.com/2004/01/25/business/yourmoney/ 25ibm.html).

Performance Review

a. Ajit Nair, "The Importance of Networking in Recruitment and Job Hunting," Kenexa Connection, April 3, 2009, accessed June 2, 2009 (http://events.kenexa.com/newsletter/2009043. asp?uid=1&tbl=news5).

b. Wendy Kaufman, "Online Tool Offers Honest, Anonymous Feedback," NPR, March 9, 2009, accessed June 2, 2009 (http://www. npr.org/templates/story/story.php?storyId=101281162).

c. Ibid.

d. Ibid.

"Employees Take to Cyberspace to Vent," NPR, February 9, 2009, accessed June 2, 2009 (http://www.npr.org/templates/story/story. php?storyId=100463251).

"Twitter," Wikipedia, accessed June 2, 2009 (http://en.wikipedia.org/ wiki/Twitter)

PullQuote

"David Meerman speaks to Tom H. C. Anderson about PR," February 7, 2009, accessed June 11, 2009 (http://www. tomhcanderson.com/2009/02/07/david-meerman-scott-speaks- to-tom-h-c-anderson-about-pr/).

PulsePoint

"The New High-end Consumer: 'Please Put My Bottega Veneta Wallet in a Plain Bag,'" *Knowledge@Wharton,* May 27, 2009, accessed May 28, 2009 (http://knowledge.wharton.upenn.edu/article. cfm?articleid=2248).

Classic and Contemporary Readings

Feagin, J. R. *A Case for the Case Study.* Chapel Hill: University of North Carolina Press, 1991. This book discusses the nature, characteristics, and basic methodological issues of the case study as a research method.

Kahle, Robert W. *Dominator, Cynics, and Wallflowers.* Ithaca, NY: Parmount Market Publishing Inc., 2006. This book offers not only insight into the types of problems that a moderator might experience, but also offers corrective actions the moderator might take.

Langer, Judith. *The Mirrored Window: Focus Groups from a Moderator's Point of View.* Ithaca, NY: Paramount Market Publishing, 2001. This book is written from the perspective of the moderator and thus lets you get a perspective on focus groups you won't get elsewhere.

Mariampolski, Hy. *Qualitative Market Research: A Comprehensive Guide.* Thousand Oaks, CA: Sage Publications, 2001. This is a wonderful overview of qualitative research techniques, providing extensive detail on many methodologies that are only mentioned elsewhere.

A bibliography relating to the case study methodology can be found at http://writing.colostate.edu/references/research/casestudy/pop2e.cfm.

chapter 8

Reference Notes

1. K. E. Weick, "Systematic Observational Methods," in *The Handbook of Social Psychology,* vol. 2, ed. G. Lindzey and E. Aronson (Reading, MA: Addison-Wesley, 1968), p. 360.

2. R. Bales, *Interaction Process Analysis* (Reading, MA: Addison-Wesley, 1950).

3. Weick, "Systematic Observational Methods," p. 381.

4. Louise H. Kidder and Charles M. Judd, *Research Methods in Social Relations,* 5th ed. (New York: Holt, Rinehart & Winston, 1986), p. 292.

5. Kenneth D. Bailey, *Methods of Social Science,* 2d ed. (New York: Free Press, 1982), pp. 252–54.

6. Donald F. Roy, "'Banana Time,' Job Satisfaction, and Informal Interaction," *Human Organization* 18, no. 4 (Winter 1959–60), pp. 151–68.

7. Robert F. Bales, *Personality and Interpersonal Behavior* (New York: Holt, Rinehart & Winston, 1970).

8. Kidder and Judd, *Research Methods in Social Relations,* pp. 298–99.

9. Ibid., p. 291.

10. E. J. Webb, D. T. Campbell, R. D. Schwartz, L. Sechrest, and J. B. Grove, *Nonreactive Measures in the Social Sciences,* 2d ed. (Boston: Houghton Mifflin, 1981).

11. W. L. Rathje and W. W. Hughes, "The Garbage Project as a Non-reactive Approach: Garbage In . . . Garbage Out?" in *Perspectives on Attitude Assessment: Surveys and Their Alternatives,* ed. H. W. Sinaiko and L. A. Broedling (Washington, DC: Smithsonian Institution, 1975).

12. William Grimes, "If It's Scientific, It's 'Garbology,'" *International Herald Tribune,* August 15–16, 1992, p. 17.

References for Snapshots, PicProfiles, Captions, PulsePoints, and Pull Quotes

Akron Children's Hospital

This snapshot and the accompanying case were developed with the assistance of Akron Children's Hospital and Marcus Thomas LLC. We thank them for their participation.

"2005 Child Magazine Ranking," *Child,* accessed September 22, 2006 (http://www.rainbowbabies.org/AboutRainbow/ChildMagazineRanking/tabid/717/Default.aspx).

"2005's 10 Best Children's Hospitals," *Child,* accessed September 22, 2006 (http://www.child.com/child/story.jhtml?storyid=/templatedata/child/story/data/1130522345565.xml).

"2005's 10 Best Children's Hospitals: Specialty Honors," *Child,* accessed September 22, 2006 (http://www.child.com/child/story.jhtml?storyid=/templatedata/child/story/data/1130522345565.xml&categoryid=/templatedata/child/category/data/1131546614395.xml&page=13).

"A Continuing Legacy of Caring for Children," *Child,* accessed September 22, 2006 (http://www.rainbowbabies.org/AboutRainbow/tabid/301/Default.aspx).

"About Akron Children's," Akron Children's hospital, accessed September 22, 2006 (http://www.akronchildrens.org/cms/site/14908a4d74b348d5/index.html).

Akron Children's Hospital TV and radio spots provided by Marcus Thomas LLC via DVD.

"Akron Children's Hospital," Wikipedia.com, accessed September 22, 2006 (http://en.wikipedia.org/wiki/Akron_Children%27s_Hospital).

"America's Best Hospitals 2006 Methodology," RTI international, accessed September 22, 2006. (http://health.usnews.com/usnews/health/best-hospitals/methodology_report.pdf)

"Best Hospitals 2006: Honor Roll," *U.S. News & World Report,* accessed September 22, 2006 (http://www.usnews.com/usnews/health/best-hospitals/honorroll.htm).

"Case Study: Akron Children's Hospital: Renewing a Brand Promise," Marcus Thomas LLC, provided by e-mail, September, 2006.

"Cleveland Clinic Children's Hospital for Rehabilitation," *U.S. News & World Report,* accessed September 22, 2006 (http://www.usnews.com/usnews/health/hospitals/directory/glance_6410650.htm).

Jennifer Hirt-Marchand, vice president, director of research, Marcus Thomas LLC, phone interviews, August 20 and September 15, 2006, and numerous e-mails.

"Methodology: What It Means to Be Best," *U.S. News & World Report,* accessed September 22, 2006 (http://www.usnews.com/usnews/health/best-hospitals/methodology.htm).

"Rainbow Babies and Children's Hospital, Cleveland," *U.S. News & World Report,* accessed September 22, 2006 (http://www.usnews.com/usnews/health/best-hospitals/directory/glance_6410920.htm).

Robin Segbers, manager of planning, Marcus Thomas LLC, phone interview, August 20, 2006.

www.akronchildrens.org; www.marcusthomasllc.com.

Best Buy observation Jena McGregor, "At Best Buy, Marketing Goes Micro," *BusinessWeek,* May 26, 2008, p. 52.

New Mexico

Barbara F. Chatterjee and Isaac Romero, "Seatbelt Observation Studies—The New Mexico Approach and Validation," New Mexico Department of Health, Office of Injury Prevention. 30th International Traffic Records Forum, Nashville, Tennessee, July 27, 2004.

www.atsip.org/oldsite/forum2004/Sessions/Tuesday_13-24/S19/s19_chatterjee.PPT.

People Meters

"Arbitron and Nielsen Report Progress in Portable People Meter (PPM) Response Rate Testing," Arbitron, October 21, 2003 (http://www.arbitron.com/portable_people_meters/home.htm).

"Nielsen Families," Nielsen Media Research (http://www.nielsenmedia.com/FAQ).

"NY Local People Meter 2003: A Super-Q Audit Process," Nielsen Media Research, March 29, 2004 (NY_LPM_Report_Nielsen.pdf).

"Our Research & Products," Nielsen Media Research (http://www.nielsenmedia.com/FAQ).

"Universe Estimates," Nielsen Media Research (http://www.nielsenmedia.com/FAQ).

"U.S. Market Trial Status," Arbitron, downloaded April 1, 2004 (http://www.arbitron.com/portable_people_meters/us_trial_status2.htm).

PullQuote

"Jonah Lehrer and Tom H. C. Anderson Discuss *How We Decide,*" Anderson Analytics, March 27, 2009, accessed June 11, 2009 (http://www.tomhcanderson.com/2009/03/27/market-researchers-are-neuroscientists-too/).

PulsePoint

Maggie Jackson, "May We Have Your Attention, Please?" *BusinessWeek,* June 23, 2008 pp. 55–56.

SizeUSA

"Background," SizeUSA, downloaded February 24, 2004 (http://www.sizeusa.com/background.html).

"Business Getting Squeezed due to Poor Fitting Garments?" TechExchange, downloaded February 24, 2004 (http://www.techexchange.com/thelibrary/bmsades.html).

Rebecca Gardyn, "The Shape of Things to Come," *American Demographics* 25, no. 6 (July–August 2003), pp. 25–30.

"An Introduction to the Body Measurement System of Mass Customized Clothing," TechExchange, downloaded February 24, 2004 (http://www.techexchange.com/thelibrary/bmsdes.html).

Teri Ross, "A Fitting Solution," *Apparel,* August 2003, downloaded February 24, 2004 (http://www.utexas.edu/centers/infic/NewCenNews/archives/2003/Oct.2003.ncn.html).

Dave Scheiber, "Whole Girth Catalog," *St. Petersburg Times,* October 18, 2003 (http://www.sptimes.com/2003/10/18/news_pf/Floridian/Whole_girth_catalog.shtml).

"SizeUSA—The Consumer's Perspective," TC2, downloaded February 24, 2004 (http://www.tc2.com/what/sizeusa/consumer.html).

"Sponsors," SizeUSA, downloaded February 24, 2004 (http://www.sizeusa.com/sponsors.html).

The US National Survey, TC2.com, downloaded February 24, 2004 (http://www.tc2.com/what/sizeusa/index.html).

Walmart

Vivek Agarwal, "Assessing the Benefits of Auto-ID Technology in the Consumer Goods Industry," Auto-ID Center, 2001 (http://www.autoidcenter.org/research/CAM-WWH-003.pdf).

Katherine Albrecht, "Supermarket Cards: The Tip of the Retail Surveillance Iceberg," *Denver University Law Review* 79, no. 4 (Summer 2002), pp. 534–39, 558–65.

Gerry Khermouch and Heather Green, "Bar Codes Better Watch Their Backs," *BusinessWeek Online,* July 14, 2003 (http://www.aol.businessweek.com/magazine/content/03_28/b3841063.htm).

"Goodyear Works with Wal-Mart to Bring RFID Supply Chain Technology to the Tire Industry," Goodyear Tire and Rubber Company press release, March 11, 2004 (http://www.goodyear.com/media/pr/22861ms.html).

"Overview of CASPIAN," CASPIAN, downloaded March 11, 2004 (http://www.nocards.org/press/overview.shtml).

"Press Releases," Trolley Scan (Pty) Ltd. (http://www.trolleyscan.com/pressrel.html).

"Radio Frequency ID: A New Era for Marketers?" *Consumer Insight,* ACNielsen, 2001 (http://www.acnielsen.com/pubs/ci2001/q4/features/radio.htm).

Classic and Contemporary Readings

Bailey, Kenneth D. *Methods of Social Research.* 4th ed. New York: Free Press, 1994. Includes a thorough discussion of observational strategies.

Bales, Robert F. *Personality and Interpersonal Behavior.* New York: Holt, Rinehart & Winston, 1970. From a pioneer in interaction process analysis, a model for structured observation, checklists, and coding schemes.

Denzin, Norman K., and Yvonna S. Lincoln. *Handbook of Qualitative Research.* 2d ed. Thousand Oaks, CA: Sage Publications, 2000. Of particular interest are Part 3 on strategies of inquiry and Part 4 on methods of collecting and analyzing empirical materials.

Hoyle, Rick H., Monica J. Harris, and Charles M. Judd. *Research Methods in Social Relations.* 7th ed. Belmont, CA: Wadsworth Publishing, 2001. Good overview of observational types and sampling plans.

Webb, Eugene J., Donald T. Campbell, Richard D. Swartz, and Lee B. Sechrest. *Unobtrusive Measures.* Thousand Oaks, CA: Sage Publications, 1999. The revised edition of the classic source of information on all aspects of unobtrusive measures. Excellent examples and ideas for project planning.

chapter 9

Reference Notes

1. Bibb Latane and J. M. Darley, *The Unresponsive Bystander: Why Doesn't He Help?* (New York: Appleton-Century-Crofts, 1970), pp. 69–77. Research into the responses of bystanders who witness crimes was stimulated by an incident in New York City, where Kitty Genovese was attacked and killed in the presence of 38 witnesses who refused to come to her aid or to summon authorities.

2. This section is largely adapted from Julian L. Simon and Paul Burstein, *Basic Research Methods in Social Science,* 3d ed. (New York: Random House, 1985), pp. 128–33.

3. For a thorough explanation of this topic, see Helena C. Kraemer and Sue Thiemann, *How Many Subjects? Statistical Power Analysis in Research* (Beverly Hills, CA: Sage Publications, 1987).

4. Kenneth D. Bailey, *Methods of Social Research,* 2d ed. (New York: Free Press, 1982), pp. 230–33.

5. The concept of a quota matrix and the tabular form for Exhibit 10–3 was adapted from Earl R. Babbie, *The Practice of Social Research,* 5th ed. (Belmont, CA: Wadsworth, 1989), pp. 218–19.

6. Donald T. Campbell and Julian C. Stanley, *Experimental and Quasi-Experimental Designs for Research* (Chicago: Rand McNally, 1963), p. 5.

7. Thomas D. Cook and Donald T. Campbell, "The Design and Conduct of Quasi-Experiments and True Experiments in Field Settings," in *Handbook of Industrial and Organizational Psychology,* ed. Marvin D. Dunnette (Chicago: Rand McNally, 1976), p. 223.

8. For an in-depth discussion of many quasi-experimental designs and their internal validity, see ibid., pp. 246–98.

9. Frederick J. Herzberg, "One More Time: How Do You Motivate Employees?" *Harvard Business Review* (January–February 1968), pp. 53–62.

10. William J. Paul Jr., Keith B. Robertson, and Frederick Herzberg, "Job Enrichment Pays Off," *Harvard Business Review* (March–April 1969), pp. 61–78.

References for Snapshots, PicProfiles, Captions, PulsePoints, and Pull Quotes

Best Buy

Stuart Elliot, "Best Buy Calls for New Venture," *The New York Times,* January 8, 2007, accessed January 17, 2007 (http://www.nytimes.com/2007/01/08/business/media/08adco_column.html?ex=1169182800&en=1b1d63baef279f9c&ei=5070).

bestbuymobile.com.

Hill Top Research

Good Morning America, ABC News, March 3, 2000 (http://www.hilltop.com/consumer.html).

Online Dating

a. DNA testing through Genepartner.com promotional: "Based on the genetic profile of the client, the GenePartner formula determines the level of genetic compatibility with the person they are interested in. The probability for successful and long-lasting romantic relationships is greatest in couples with high genetic compatibility." Accessed on December 17, 2009 (http://genepartner.com/index.php/aboutgenepartner).

b. Chart based on "Remember Online Dating?" *eMarketer.com* (from Piper Jaffray survey), accessed on December 12, 2009 (http://www.emarketer.com/Article.aspx?R=1006880).

c. Alina Tugend, "Blinded by Science in the Online Dating Game," *New York Times,* July 17, 2009, accessed July 24, 2009 (http://www.nytimes.com/2009/07/18/technology/internet/18shortcuts.html?pagewanted=1&th&emc=th).

d. See www.helenfisher.com/about.html; and http://www.chemistry.com/drhelenfisher/, ,accessed December 12, 2009.

e. Carl Bialik, "Marriage-Maker Claims Are Tied in Knots," *The Wall Street Journal,* July 29, 2009, accessed December 16, 2009 (http://online.wsj.com/article/SB124879877347487253.html).

f. Tugend, "Blinded by Science."

g. Bialik, "Marriage-Maker Claims;" IAC Press Release: http://iac.mediaroom.com/index.php?s=43&item=875, http://www.match.com; and http://weddingchannel.com.

h. Bialik, "Marriage-Maker Claims," p. 2.; and http://download.eharmony.com/pdf/eHarmony-Harris-2007-Marriages.pdf, accessed December 16, 2009.

i. Tugend, "Blinded by Science."

j. Psychology professor Jeffrey Lohr and two psychology graduates analyzed leading dating websites and found that promotional claims were more self-serving opinion than legitimate psychological science. See Physorg.com, "Researchers Skeptical of Claims by Online Dating Sites," June 15, 2009, accessed December 16, 2009 (http://www.physorg.com/news164292891.html); alumni Austin-Oden and King were students in an applied psychology research course with Lohr. Austin-Oden and King wrote papers about online dating and using the critical analysis techniques that Lohr taught. Lohr asked them to continue the research and he would collaborate in compiling the data. It took two years to complete the project.

PullQuote

"Richard Buckminster Fuller quotes," ThinkExist.com, accessed June 14, 2009(http://thinkexist.com/quotation/there_is_no_such_thing_as_a_failed_experiment/185928.html).

PulsePoint

Matthew Boyle, "Snap, Crackle, Pop at the Food Giants," *BusinessWeek,* October 6, 2008, p. 48.

Subject Line

www.rocketsciencegroup.com; www.mailchimp.com.

Ben Chestnut, partner, Rocket Science Group, LLC, interviewed February 12, 2007. "Email Marketing Subject Line Comparison," MailChimp, accessed February 12, 2007 (http://www.mailchimp.com/resources/subject-line-comparison.phtml).

T.G.I. Friday's

Video: T.G.I. Friday's[R] Restaurants Take Leadership Role with Portion Control, March 25, 2007 (http://www.prnewswire.com/cgi-bin/stories.pl?ACCT=ind_focus.story . . .; http://prnewswire.com/mnr/fridays/27066/).

www.fridays.com.

Classic and Contemporary Readings

Campbell, Donald T., and M. Jean Russo. *Social Experimentation.* Thousand Oaks, CA: Sage Publications, 1998. The evolution of the late Professor Campbell's thinking on validity control in experimental design.

Campbell, Donald T., and Julian C. Stanley. *Experimental and Quasi-Experimental Designs for Research.* Chicago: Rand McNally, 1963. A universally quoted discussion of experimental designs in the social sciences.

Cook, Thomas D., and Donald T. Campbell. "The Design and Conduct of Quasi-Experiments and True Experiments in Field Settings." In *Handbook of Industrial and Organizational Psychology,* 2d ed. Marvin D. Dunnette and Leaetta M. Hough. Palo Alto, CA: Consulting Psychologists Press, 1990. *Quasi-Experimentation: Design and Analysis Issues for Field Settings.* Chicago: Rand McNally, 1979. Major authoritative works on both true and quasi-experiments and their design. Already classic references.

Edwards, Allen. *Experimental Design in Psychological Research.* 4th ed. New York: Holt, Rinehart & Winston, 1972. A complete treatment of experimental design with helpful illustrative examples.

Green, Paul E., Donald S. Tull, and Gerald Albaum. *Research for Marketing Decisions.* 5th ed. Englewood Cliffs, NJ: Prentice Hall, 1988. A definitive text with sections on the application of experimentation to marketing research.

Kirk, Roger E. *Experimental Design: Procedures for the Behavioral Sciences.* 3d ed. Belmont, CA: Brooks/Cole, 1994. An advanced text on the statistical aspects of experimental design.

Krathwohl, David R. *Social and Behavioral Science Research: A New Framework for Conceptualizing, Implementing, and Evaluating Research Studies.* San Francisco: Jossey-Bass, 1985. Chapters 3, 4, and 5 present a convincing argument for reformulating internal and external validity into broader concepts. A conceptually refreshing approach.

appendix 9b

Reference Notes

1. Consumer Insight, Fifth Annual ACNielsen Consumer and Market Trends Report, 2001 (http://www.acnielsenbases.com/news/New%20Product%20Introductions.pdf).

2. http://www.iaea.or.at/icgfi/documents/dairy-queen.pdf.

3. Amy Forliti, "Shell Test Markets the First Robotic Gas Pump," Associated Press, March 9, 2000 (http://www.canoe.ca/TechNews0003/09_pumps.html).

4. http://www.acnielsen.com/.

5. http://www.infores.com/public/us/prodserv/factsheet/us_fact_btnewproduct.htm.

6. http://www.infores.com/public/us/news/us_new_102901.htm.

7. Ibid.

8. Joseph Willke, "The Future of Simulated Test Markets: The Coming Obsolescence of Current Models and the Characteristics of Models of the Future," ESOMAR Conference Proceedings, September 2002, excerpted by permission of ACNielsen (http://www.acnielsenbases.com/news/news%2009092002.html).

9. http://www.marcresearch.com/main.html.

10. Raymond R. Burke, "Virtual Shopping: Breakthrough in Marketing Research," *Harvard Business Review* 74, no. 2 (March–April 1996), p. 125.

11. Reg. No. 1,881,580, February 28, 1995, Allison Hollander Corporation of Atlanta, now Allison Research Technologies.

12. http://www.artechnology.com/.

13. Ely Dahan and V. "Seenu" Srinivasan, "The Predictive Power of Internet-Based Product Concept Testing Using Visual Depiction and Animation," *Journal of Product Innovation Management,* March 2000 (http://faculty-gsb.stanford.edu/ssrinivasan/rp1502.pdf).

14. John Gaffney, "How Do You Feel about a $44 Tooth-Bleaching Kit? Procter & Gamble Discovers What the Web Is Really Good For—Test Marketing," http://www.business2.com/articles/mag/0,1640,16977,FF.html (October 2001 issue).

15. Ibid.; Niall McKay, "What Test-Marketing? Why E-Tailers Are Testing the Waters after Jumping In," http://www.redherring.com/mag/issue78/mag-marketing-78.html (May 2000 issue).

References for Snapshots and Captions

Shell SmartPump

Amy Forliti, "Shell Test Markets the First Robotic Gas Pump," *Canoe CNews,* downloaded May 22, 2004 (http://www.canoe.ca/TechNews0003/09_pumps.html).

Test Marketing

Jack Neff, "White Bread, USA" *AdAge.com,* July 9, 2001 (http://adage.com/news.cms?newslID_33487).

chapter 10

Reference Notes

1. Floyd J. Fowler Jr., *Survey Research Methods* (Beverly Hills, CA: Sage Publications, 1988), p. 111.

2. B. W. Schyberger, "A Study of Interviewer Behavior," *Journal of Marketing* Research, February 1967, p. 35.

3. B. S. Dohrenwend, J. A. Williams Jr., and C. H. Weiss, "Interviewer Biasing Effects: Toward a Reconciliation of Findings," *Public Opinion Quarterly,* Spring 1969, pp. 121–29.

4. One of the top research organizations in the world is the Survey Research Center of the University of Michigan. The material in this section draws heavily on the *Interviewer's Manual,* rev. ed. (Ann Arbor: Survey Research Center, University of Michigan, 1976), and Fowler, *Survey Research Methods,* Chap. 7.

5. Robert L. Kahn and Charles F. Cannell, *The Dynamics of Interviewing* (New York: Wiley, 1957), pp. 45–51.

6. D. Wallace, "A Case for and against Mail Questionnaires," *Public Opinion Quarterly,* Spring 1954, pp. 40–52.

7. Jon Krosnick, "The Art of Asking a Question: The Top 5 Things Researchers Need to Know about Designing Questionnaires," a seminar sponsored by SPSS and American Marketing Association, March 30, 2004.

8. Ibid.

9. Mary Madden, "Internet Penetration and Impact, April 2006," PEW Internet & American Life Project, April 26, 2006, p. 1, accessed March 30, 2007 (http://www.pewinternet.org/pdfs/PIP_Internet_Impact.pdf).

10. John Horrigan, "Wireless Internet Access, February 2007," PEW Internet & American Life Project Data Memo, PEW Internet & American Life Project, February 25, 2007, p. 1, accessed March 30, 2007 (http://www.pewinternet.org/pdfs/PIP_Wireless.Use.pdf).

11. "How Women and Men Use the Internet," PEW Internet & American Life Project, December 28, 2005, pp. iv–v, accessed March 30, 2007 (http://www.pewinternet.org/pdfs/PIP_Women_and_Men_online.pdf).

12. Edith de Leeuw and William Nicholls II, "Technology Innovations in Data Collection: Acceptance, Data Quality, and Costs," *Sociological Research Online* 1, no. 4 (1996) (http://www.socresonline.org.uk/1/4/leeuw.html).

13. Personal experience of the author, November 2002.

14. de Leeuw and Nicholls, "Technology Innovations in Data Collection."

15. Don A. Dillman, *Mail and Telephone Surveys* (New York: Wiley, 1978), p. 6.

16. de Leeuw and Nicholls, "Technology Innovations in Data Collection."

17. Dillman, *Mail and Telephone Surveys,* pp. 160–61.

18. Ibid., pp. 12, 22–24.

19. "Total Design Method," February 4, 2000 (http://survey.sesrc.wsu.edu/tdm.htm). Don Dillman is professor of sociology and rural sociology and deputy director of research and development of the Social and Economic Sciences Research Center at Washington State University.

20. Leslie Kanuk and Conrad Berenson, "Mail Surveys and Response Rates: A Literature Review," *Journal of Marketing Research,* November 1975, pp. 440–53; Arnold S. Linsky, "Stimulating Responses to Mailed Questionnaires: A Review," *Public Opinion Quarterly* 39 (1975), pp. 82–101.

21. Kanuk and Berenson, "Mail Surveys," p. 450. Reprinted from the *Journal of Marketing Research,* published by the American Marketing Association.

22. Nelson King, "[Web-Based Surveys] How They Work," *PC Magazine,* January 18, 2000 (http://www.pcmag.com).

23. Robert M. Groves and Robert L. Kahn, *Surveys by Telephone* (New York: Academic Press, 1979), p. 223.

24. Institute for Social Research, *ISR Newsletter* (Ann Arbor: University of Michigan, 1991–92), p. 3.

25. Michael J. Havice, "Measuring Nonresponse and Refusals to an Electronic Telephone Survey," *Journalism Quarterly,* Fall 1990, pp. 521–30.

26. "2003 CMOR Respondent Cooperation and Industry Image Study Topline Report," CMOR, downloaded November 23, 2003 (http://www.cmor.org/resp_coop_news1003_2.htm). CMOR, founded in 1992 as the Council for Marketing and Opinion Research, tries to improve access to consumers for its more than 150 member trade associations and research companies, to increase respondent awareness of the value of research, and to increase respondent cooperation rates.

27. See, for example, J. H. Frey Jr., *Survey Research by Telephone* (Beverly Hills, CA: Sage Publications, 1989).

28. "Chart 3-8: Percent of U.S. Households with a Telephone by Income by Rural, Urban, Central City Areas, and Total U.S.," downloaded December 15, 2003 (http://www.ntia.doc.gov/ntiahome/net2/presentations/slide5.html through slide8.html). See also U.S. Census Bureau, Census 2000 Summary File 3, Matrices H6 and H43.

29. U.S. Census Bureau, Census 2000 Summary File 3, Matrices H6 and H43.

30. J. Michael Brick, J. Waksberg, D. Kulp, and A. Starer, "Bias in List-Assisted Telephone Samples," *American Association of Public Opinion Research*, May 14, 1994 (http://www.genesys-sampling.com/reference/bias.htm).

31. The Cellular Telecommunications and Internet Association's annualized wireless industry survey results, June 1985–June 2002, downloaded February 15, 2003 (http://www.wowcom.com/images/survey/june2002/annual_Table_slide_3.gif).

32. "Wireless Quick Facts, December 2006," CTIA, accessed March 30, 2007 (http://www.ctia.org/media/industry_info/index.cfm/AID/10323).

33. "VocalTec Unveils Surf & CallTM Network Services," TechSourceNJ.com (http://www.techsourcenj.com/feature_articles/apr00/vocaltec.shtml).

34. "Wireless Local Number Portability," Federal Communications Commission, downloaded May 22, 2004 (http://www.fcc.gov/cgb/consumerfacts/wirelessportability.html).

35. A *block* is defined as an exchange group composed of the first four or more digits of a seven-digit number, such as 721-0, 721-1, and so forth.

36. G. J. Glasser and G. D. Metzger, "National Estimates of Nonlisted Telephone Households and Their Characteristics," *Journal of Marketing Research,* August 1975, p. 360.

37. G. J. Glasser and G. D. Metzger, "Random Digit Dialing as a Method of Telephone Sampling," *Journal of Marketing Research,* February 1972, pp. 59–64; Seymour Sudman, "The Uses of Telephone Directories for Survey Sampling," *Journal of Marketing Research,* May 1973, pp. 204–07.

38. Personal participation by the author, October 2002.

39. Seymour Sudman, *Reducing the Costs of Surveys* (Chicago: Aldine, 1967), p. 65.

40. J. J. Wheatley, "Self-Administered Written Questionnaires or Telephone Interviews," *Journal of Marketing Research,* February 1973, pp. 94–95.

41. Robert M. Groves and Robert L. Kahn, *Surveys by Telephone* (New York: Academic Press, 1979), p. 223.

42. Peter S. Tuckel and Barry M. Feinberg, "The Answering Machine Poses Many Questions for Telephone Survey Researchers," *Public Opinion Quarterly,* Summer 1991, pp. 200–17.

43. Paul J. Lavrakas, *Telephone Survey Methods: Sampling, Selection, and Supervision,* 2d ed. (Thousand Oaks, CA: Sage Publications, 1993), p. 16.

44. Marilyn Geewax, "FTC Scrubs Do-Not-Call Start Date," Cox News Service, posted September 27, 2003 (http://www.dfw.com/mld/dfw/news/nation/6875595.htm).

45. "Annual Report to Congress for FY 2005 Pursuant to the Do Not Call Implementation Act on Implementation of the National Do Not Call Registry," Federal Trade Commission: National Do Not Call Registry, July 2006, p. 9, accessed March 6, 2007 (http://www.ftc.gov/os/2006/07/P034305FiscalYear2005NationalDoNotCallRegistryReport.pdf).

46. There are a number of sources for research services, some of which are annotated. For current listings, consult the latest edition of the *Marketing Services Guide* and the *American Marketing Association Membership Directory* (Chicago: American Marketing Association); *Consultants and Consulting Organizations Directory* (Detroit: Gale Research Corporation); or the research section of *Marketing News.*

47. A list of panel vendors is provided by Duane Davis, *Business Research for Decision Making,* 4th ed. (Belmont, CA: Wadsworth, 1996), p. 283. See also our Exhibit A1–4 on omnibus studies and Exhibit A1–3 on syndicated data providers in Appendix A.

References for Snapshots, PicProfiles, Captions, PulsePoints, and Pull Quote

Aleve

"Bayer HealthCare Ends 2006 on High as Schering Buyout Boosts Q4 Sales 75.3%," Global Insight, accessed March 30, 2007 (http://www.globalinsight.com/SDA/SDADetail8663.htm).

Sara Eckel, "Road to Recovery," *American Demographics,* March 2001, p. s8.

Anderson Analytics-BigEars

"New Survey Technology allows you to 'listen' to the voice of the customer: A third of college students say their mobile phone is an extension/reflection of themselves," Anderson Analytics press release, November 9, 2006.

Topline Report, Anderson Analytics, November 2006 (http://www.andersonanalytics.com/reports/AndersonAnalyticsBigEars.ppt).

Cell Phones

Andy Peytchev, survey methodologist, Research Triangle Institute, interviewed June 8, 2009.

David Chartier, "More Americans snipping landlines in favor of cell phones," ARS Technica, May 14, 2008, accessed June 8, 2009 (http://arstechnica.com/business/news/2008/05/more-americans-snipping-landlines-in-favor-of-cell-phones.ars).

Stephen J. Blumberg, and Julian V. Luke, "Wireless Substitution: Early Release of Estimates From the National Health Interview Survey, July–December 2007," National Center for Health Statistics, May 13, 2008, accessed June 9, 2009 (http://www.cdc.gov/nchs/data/nhis/earlyrelease/wireless200805.htm).

Stephen J. Blumberg, and Julian V. Luke, "Wireless Substitution: Early Release of Estimates From the National Health Interview Survey, July–December 2007-Tables," National Center for Health Statistics, May 13, 2008, accessed June 9, 2009 (http://www.cdc.gov/nchs/data/nhis/earlyrelease/wireless200805_tables.htm#T2).

Harris Interactive

The Harris Poll, September 4, 2003.

Humphrey Taylor, "Do Not Call Registry Is Working Well," HarrisInteractive: The Harris Poll #10, February 13, 2004, accessed April 8, 2007 (http://www.harrisinteractive.com/harris_poll/index.asp?PID=439).

PullQuote

"Fiona Shaw quotes," ThinkExist.com, accessed June 17, 2009 (http://en.thinkexist.com/quotation/there-once-was-a-demographic-survey-done-to/400408.html).

PulsePoint

Jena McGregor, "Making Every Hour Count," *BusinessWeek,* August 25/September 1, 2008, pp. 67–68.

Radio

Lee Ann Obringer, "How Top 40 Radio Works," HowStuffWorks.com: Entertainment, downloaded May 21, 2004 (http://entertainment.howstuffworks.com/top-40.htm).

RTI International

Tim Gabel, director of computing, RTI International, interviewed December 17, 2001.

Starwood Hotels

Tom Anderson, managing partner, Anderson Analytics, interviewed January 16, 2006.

Tom Anderson, Girish Punj, and Rebecca Gillan, "Mining Text in Guest Satisfaction Surveys: Do Ratings Truly Reveal Future Intentions?" White paper delivered at the SPSS Directions User Conference, November 16, 2005.

"Improve Business Results with Text Mining," SPSS ©2005, accessed January 16, 2006 (http://www.spss-sa.com/sites/54/images/TEXT%20MINING%203%20FOR%20CLEM.pdf).

Classic and Contemporary Readings

Arksey, Hilary, and Peter T. Knight. *Interviewing for Social Scientists: An Introductory Resource with Examples.* Thousand Oaks, CA: Sage Publications, 1999. Covers design, improvisation, success rates, specialized contexts, and transforming findings into results.

Dexter, Louis A. *Elite and Specialized Interviewing.* Evanston, IL: Northwestern University Press, 1970. Discusses the techniques and problems of interviewing "people in important or exposed positions."

Dillman, Don A. *Mail and Internet Surveys: The Tailored Design Method.* New York: Wiley, 1999. The Tailored Design Method, which expands on the Total Design Concept of Dillman's classic work, takes advantage of computers, electronic mail, and the Internet to better our understanding of survey requirements.

Dillman, Don A. *Mail and Telephone Surveys.* New York: Wiley, 1978. A classic on mail and telephone surveys.

Fowler, Floyd J., Jr. *Survey Research Methods.* 2d ed. Thousand Oaks, CA: Sage Publications, 2001. An excellent overview of all aspects of the survey process.

Groves, Robert M., et al. *Telephone Survey Methodology.* New York: Wiley, 2001. An important reference on telephone data collection techniques.

Lavrakas, Paul J. *Telephone Survey Methods: Sampling, Selection, and Supervision.* 2d ed. Thousand Oaks, CA: Sage Publications, 1993. This specialized work takes an applied perspective of interest to students and managers. Chapters 3, 5, and 6 on supervision are particularly useful.

Nesbary, Dale K. *Survey Research and the World Wide Web.* Needham Heights, MA: Allyn & Bacon, 2000. Screen shots from Windows and FrontPage, e-mail survey construction, and Internet orientation for survey research.

Groves, Robert M., et al. *Survey Nonresponse.* New York: Wiley, 2001. A compendium of up-to-date research in survey nonresponse.

chapter 11

Reference Notes

1. Fred N. Kerlinger, *Foundations of Behavioral Research,* 3d ed. (New York: Holt, Rinehart & Winston, 1986), p. 396; S. Stevens, "Measurement, Statistics, and the Schemapiric View," *Science,* August 1968, p. 384.

2. W. S. Torgerson, *Theory and Method of Scaling* (New York: Wiley, 1958), p. 19.

3. S. S. Stevens, "On the Theory of Scales of Measurement," *Science* 103 (1946), pp. 677–80.

4. We assume the reader has had an introductory statistics course in which measures of central tendency such as arithmetic mean, median, and mode have been treated. Similarly, we assume familiarity with measures of dispersion such as the standard deviation, range, and interquartile range. For a brief review of these concepts, refer to Chapter 15, Appendix 15a: "Describing Data Statistically" or see an introductory statistics text.

5. Although this might intuitively seem to be the case, consider that one might prefer *a* over *b*, *b* over *c*, yet *c* over *a*. These results cannot be scaled as ordinal data because there is apparently more than one dimension involved.

6. Parametric tests are appropriate when the measurement is interval or ratio and when we can accept certain assumptions about the underlying distributions of the data with which we are working (normality, independence, constant variance). Nonparametric tests usually involve much weaker assumptions about measurement scales (nominal and ordinal), and the assumptions about the underlying distribution of the population are fewer and less restrictive. More on these tests is found in Chapters 17 and 18 and Appendix C.

7. *Statistical power* is the probability of detecting a meaningful difference if one were to occur. Studies should have power levels of 0.80 or higher (i.e., an 80% chance or greater of discerning an effect if one was really there).

8. See Chapters 17 and 18 for a discussion of these procedures.

9. To learn more about Swatch's BeatTime, visit http://www.swatch.com/internettime/internettime.php3.

10. The exception involves the creation of a dummy variable for use in a regression or discriminant equation. A nonmetric variable is transformed into a metric variable through the assignment of a 0 or 1 and used in a predictive equation.

11. Claire Selltiz, Lawrence S. Wrightsman, and Stuart W. Cook, *Research Methods in Social Relations,* 3d ed. (New York: Holt, Rinehart & Winston, 1976), pp. 164–69.

12. Robert L. Thorndike and Elizabeth Hagen, *Measurement and Evaluation in Psychology and Education,* 3d ed. (New York: Wiley, 1969), p. 5.

13. Examples of other conceptualizations of validity are factorial validity, job-analytic validity, synthetic validity, rational validity, and statistical conclusion validity.

14. Thomas D. Cook and Donald T. Campbell, "The Design and Conduct of Quasi Experiments and True Experiments in Field Settings," in *Handbook of Industrial and Organizational Psychology,* ed. Marvin D. Dunnette (Chicago: Rand McNally, 1976), p. 223.

15. *Standards for Educational and Psychological Tests and Manuals* (Washington, DC: American Psychological Association, 1974), p. 26.

16. Wayne F. Cascio, *Applied Psychology in Personnel Management* (Reston, VA: Reston Publishing, 1982), p. 149.

17. Thorndike and Hagen, *Measurement and Evaluation,* p. 168.

18. Cascio, *Applied Psychology,* pp. 135–36.

19. Emanuel J. Mason and William Bramble, *Understanding and Conducting Research* (New York: McGraw-Hill, 1989), p. 268.

20. A problem with this approach is that the way the test is split may influence the internal consistency coefficient. To remedy this, other indexes are used to secure reliability estimates without splitting the test's items. The Kuder-Richardson Formula 20 (KR20) and Cronbach's coefficient alpha are two frequently used examples. Cronbach's alpha has the most utility for multi-item scales at the interval level of measurement. The KR20 is the method from which alpha was generalized and is used to estimate reliability for dichotomous items (see Exhibit 11–7).

21. Thorndike and Hagen, *Measurement and Evaluation,* p. 199.

References for Snapshots, PicProfiles, Captions, PulsePoints, and Pull Quotes

Copyright Infringement

John Fetto, "Americans Voice Their Opinions on Intellectual Property Rights Violations," *American Demographics,* September 2000, p. 8.

Measurement instrument prepared by TaylorNelson Sofres Intersearch.

Data tabulation generated by TaylorNelson Sofres Intersearch.

PullQuote

"George Bernard Shaw quotes," ThinkExist.com, accessed June 14, 2009 (http://thinkexist.com/quotation/the_only_man_who_behaved_sensibly_was_my_tailor/206884.html).

PulsePoint

Steve Hamm, "IBM Reaches For the Clouds," *BusinessWeek,* April 6, 2009, p. 34.

TiVo Households

a. Alex Midlin, "Drilling Down; Hit TV Shows Have Most-Skipped Ads," *New York Times,* September 29, 2009, accessed December 24, 2009 (http://query.nytimes.com/gst/fullpage.html?res=9C06E3D9143FF93BA1575AC0A96F9C8B63&scp=1&sq=research+measurement&st=nyt).

b. Ibid.

c. Stephanie Olsen, "Watching the Watchers: TiVo Tracks Ad Viewing," *Cnet News: Digital,* July 30, 2008, accessed December 24, 2009 (http://news.cnet.com/8301-1023_3-10002634-93.html).

d. Stuart Elliot, "Advertising; Late-Game Scores for Spots, Too," *New York Times,* February 3, 2009, accessed December 24, 2009 (http://query.nytimes.com/gst/fullpage.html?res=9D01E4DD1F38F930A35751C0A96F9C8B63&sec=&spon=&pagewanted=1).

e. Ibid.

Classic and Contemporary Readings

Cascio, Wayne F. *Applied Psychology in Personnel Management.* 4th ed. Englewood Cliffs, NJ: Prentice Hall, 1990.

Cook, Thomas D., and Donald T. Campbell. "The Design and Conduct of Quasi Experiments and True Experiments in Field Settings." In

Handbook of Industrial and Organizational Psychology, ed. Marvin D. Dunnette. Chicago: Rand McNally, 1976, Chap. 7.

Embretson, Susan E., and Scott L. Hershberger. *The New Rules of Measurement.* Mahwah, NJ: Lawrence Erlbaum Associates, 1999. Bridges the gap between theoretical and practical measurement.

Guilford, J. P. *Psychometric Methods.* 2d ed. New York: McGraw-Hill, 1954.

Kelley, D. Lynn. *Measurement Made Accessible: A Research Approach Using Qualitative, Quantitative, and TQM Methods.* Thousand Oaks, CA: Sage Publications, 1999. Sections on bias, reliability, and validity are appropriate for this chapter.

Kerlinger, Fred N., and Howard B. Lee. *Foundations of Behavioral Research.* 4th ed. New York: HBJ College & School Division, 1999.

Newmark, Charles S. *Major Psychological Assessment Instruments.* 2d ed. Boston: Allyn and Bacon, 1996.

Nunnally, J. C., and Ira Bernstein. *Psychometric Theory.* 3d ed. New York: McGraw-Hill, 1994.

Thorndike, Robert M. *Measurement and Evaluation in Psychology and Education.* 6th ed. Upper Saddle River, NJ: Prentice Hall, 1996.

chapter 12

Reference Notes

1. E. Aronson, D. Wilson, and R. Akert, *Social Psychology* (Upper Saddle River, NJ: Prentice Hall, 2002); Robert J. Sternberg, *Cognitive Psychology,* 3d ed. (Reading, MA: Wadsworth Publishing, 2002); Richard E. Petty and John T. Cacioppo, *Attitudes and Persuasion: Classic and Contemporary Approaches* (Boulder, CO: Westview Press, 1996); Gordon W. Allport, "Attitudes," in *A Handbook of Social Psychology,* vol. 2, ed. C. A. Murchison (New York: Russell, 1935), 2 vols.

2. See, for example, Robert A. Baron and Donn Byrne, *Social Psychology,* 10th ed. (Boston: Pearson Allyn & Bacon, 2002), and David G. Myers, *Social Psychology,* 7th ed. (New York: McGraw-Hill, 2002).

3. Bernard S. Phillips, *Social Research Strategy and Tactics,* 2d ed. (New York: Macmillan, 1971), p. 205.

4. J. P. Guilford, *Psychometric Methods* (New York: McGraw-Hill, 1954), pp. 278–79.

5. H. H. Friedman and Taiwo Amoo, "Rating the Rating Scales," *Journal of Marketing Management* 9, no. 3 (Winter 1999), pp. 114–23.

6. Donald R. Cooper, "Converting Neutrals to Loyalists," unpublished paper prepared for the IBM Corporation, New York, 1996.

7. G. A. Churchill and J. P. Peter, "Research Design Effects on the Reliability of Rating Scales: A Meta-Analysis," *Journal of Marketing Research* 21 (November 1984), pp. 360–75.

8. See, for example, H. H Friedman and Linda W. Friedman, "On the Danger of Using Too Few Points in a Rating Scale: A Test of Validity," *Journal of Data Collection* 26, no. 2 (1986), pp. 60–63, and Eli P. Cox, "The Optimal Number of Response Alternatives for a Scale: A Review," *Journal of Marketing Research* 17, no. 4 (1980), pp. 407–22.

9. A study of the historic research literature found that more than three-fourths of the attitude scales used were of the 5-point type. An examination of more recent literature suggests that the 5-point scale is still common but there is a growing use of longer scales. For the historic study, see Daniel D. Day, "Methods in Attitude Research," *American Sociological Review* 5 (1940), pp. 395–410. Single- versus multiple-item scaling requirements are discussed in Jum C. Nunnally, *Psychometric Theory* (New York: McGraw-Hill, 1967), Chap. 14.

10. Guilford, *Psychometric Methods.*

11. P. M. Synonds, "Notes on Rating," *Journal of Applied Psychology* 9 (1925), pp. 188–95.

12. This is adapted from Pamela L. Alreck and Robert B. Settle, *The Survey Research Handbook* (Burr Ridge, IL: Irwin, 1995), Chap. 5.

13. One study reported that the construction of a Likert scale took only half the time required to construct a Thurstone scale. See L. L. Thurstone and K. K. Kenney, "A Comparison of the Thurstone and Likert Techniques of Attitude Scale Construction," *Journal of Applied Psychology* 30 (1946), pp. 72–83.

14. Allen L. Edwards, *Techniques of Attitude Scale Construction* (New York: Appleton-Century-Crofts, 1957), pp. 152–54.

15. Ibid., p. 153.

16. Charles E. Osgood, G. J. Suci, and P. H. Tannenbaum, *The Measurement of Meaning* (Urbana: University of Illinois Press, 1957).

17. Ibid., p. 49. See also James G. Snider and Charles E. Osgood, eds., *Semantic Differential Technique* (Chicago: Aldine, 1969).

18. Louis Guttman, "A Basis for Scaling Qualitative Data," *American Sociological Review* 9 (1944), pp. 139–50.

19. John P. Robinson, "Toward a More Appropriate Use of Guttman Scaling," *Public Opinion Quarterly* 37 (Summer 1973), pp. 260–67.

References for Snapshots, PicProfiles, Captions, PulsePoints, and Pull Quotes

Campbell-Ewald

David Lockwood, senior vice president and director of account planning, Campbell-Ewald, interviewed February 9, 2004.

Nortel Networks

Christin Nowakowski, senior manager of marketing communications, Informative Inc., interviewed August 20, 2001.

Open Doors

"About Harris Interactive," Harris Interactive, downloaded March 20, 2004 (http://www.harrisinteractive.com/about/).

Laura Light, research director for public policy and public relations, Harris Interactive, interviewed March 10, 2004.

"Research among Adults with Disabilities: Travel and Hospitality," final report prepared by Harris Interactive for Open Doors Organization, delivered January 2002.

Eric Lipp, executive director, Open Doors Organization, interviewed March 4, 2004.

Steve Struhl, Harris Interactive, interviewed March 10, 2004. Headquartered in Rochester, New York, Harris Interactive combines proprietary methodologies and technology with expertise in predictive, custom, and strategic research. The company conducts international research through wholly owned subsidiaries—London-based HI Europe (www.hieurope.com) and Tokyo-based Harris Interactive Japan—as well as through the Harris Interactive Global Network of local market- and opinion-research firms.

PullQuote

"Jeanette Winterson quotes," ThinkExist.com, accessed June 14, 2009 (http://thinkexist.com/quotation/any_measurement_must_take_into_account_the/212869.html).

PulsePoint

"Loyalty in the Workplace: Executive Summary," September 2007, accessed June 1, 2009 (http://www.walkerinfo.com/pics/wlr/Employee_ExecSumm_07.pdf).

Classic and Contemporary Readings

Aiken, Lewis. *Attitudes and Related Psychosocial Constructs: Theories, Assessment, and Research.* Thousand Oaks, CA: Sage Publications, 2002. An overview for those involved in measuring, evaluating, and attempting to modify attitudes, especially Chapters 2 and 3.

Edwards, Allen L. *Techniques of Attitude Scale Construction.* New York: Irvington, 1979. Thorough discussion of basic unidimensional scaling techniques.

Kerlinger, Fred N., and Howard B. Lee. *Foundations of Behavioral Research.* 4th ed. New York: HBJ College & School Division, 1999.

Krebs, Dagmar, and Peter Schmidt, eds. *New Directions in Attitude Measurement.* Chicago: Walter De Gruyter, 1993.

Miller, Delbert C. *Handbook of Research Design and Social Measurement.* 5th ed. Thousand Oaks, CA: Sage Publications, 1991. Presents a large number of existing sociometric scales and indexes as well as information on their characteristics, validity, and sources.

Osgood, Charles E., George J. Suci, and Percy H. Tannenbaum. *The Measurement of Meaning.* Urbana: University of Illinois Press, 1957. The basic reference on SD scaling.

chapter 13

Reference Notes

1. "Technical Report: The How's and Why's of Survey Research," SPSS Inc., October 16, 2002.

2. Dorwin Cartwright, "Some Principles of Mass Persuasion," *Human Relations* 2 (1948), p. 266.

3. "What America Eats 2003," *Parade,* November 16, 2003. This is the ninth biennial survey of the food habits of the United States; 2,080 men and women, aged 18 to 65, were interviewed in March 2003 by Mark Clements Research.

4. More will be said on the problems of readability in Chapter 20, "Presenting Insights and Findings: Written and Oral Reports."

5. S. A. Stouffer et al., *Measurement and Prediction: Studies in Social Psychology in World War II,* vol. 4 (Princeton, NJ: Princeton University Press, 1950), p. 709.

6. An excellent example of the question revision process is presented in Stanley Payne, *The Art of Asking Questions* (Princeton, NJ: Princeton University Press, 1951), pp. 214–25. This example illustrates that a relatively simple question can go through as many as 41 different versions before being judged satisfactory.

7. Robert L. Kahn and Charles F. Cannell, *The Dynamics of Interviewing* (New York: Wiley, 1957), p. 132.

8. Hadley Cantril, ed., *Gauging Public Opinion* (Princeton, NJ: Princeton University Press, 1944), p. 31.

9. "The World Factbook: United States," Central Intelligence Agency, accessed April 16, 2007 (https://www.cia.gov/cia/publications/factbook/print/us.html).

10. "The Ohio State University," Wikipedia, accessed April 16, 2007 (http://en.wikipedia.org/wiki/Ohio_State_University).

11. Jon A. Krosnick and Duane F. Alwin, "An Evaluation of a Cognitive Theory of Response-Order Effects in Survey Measurement," *Public Opinion Quarterly* 51, no. 2 (Summer 1987), pp. 201–19.

12. Jean M. Converse and Stanley Presser, *Survey Questions: Handcrafting the Standardized Questionnaire* (Beverly Hills, CA: Sage Publications, 1986), pp. 50–51.

13. Ibid., p. 51.

14. Jane Sheppard, "Telephone Survey Practices Study 2000," ResearchInfo.com, June 01, 2000, accessed March 19, 2004 (http://www.researchinfo.com/docs/library/telephone_survey_practices_study_2000.cfm).

15. Frederick J. Thumin, "Watch for These Unseen Variables," *Journal of Marketing* 26 (July 1962), pp. 58–60.

16. F. Cannell and Robert L. Kahn, "The Collection of Data by Interviewing," in *Research Methods in the Behavioral Sciences,* ed. Leon Festinger and Daniel Katz (New York: Holt, Rinehart & Winston, 1953), p. 349.

17. Cantril, *Gauging Public Opinion,* p. 28.

18. The MindWriter questionnaire used in this example is based on a pilot instrument by Cooper Research Group Inc., 1993, for an unidentified client who shares the intellectual property rights. No part of the format, question wording, sequence, scale, or references to MindWriter © 2007 may be produced or transmitted in any form or by any means, electronic or mechanical, including photocopy, recording, or any information storage and retrieval system, without permission in writing from Cooper Research Group Inc. Reprinted with permission.

19. Converse and Presser, *Survey Questions,* p. 52.

References for Snapshots, PicProfiles, Captions, PulsePoints, and Pull Quotes
Cupid

Kerry Sulkowicz, "In Cupid's Cubicle," *BusinessWeek,* February 26, 2007, p. 18.

"Be My Valentine? Nearly 40 Percent of Workers Have Had a Workplace Romance, According to Latest Spherion Survey," Spherion Corporation press release: January 29, 2007, accessed February 24, 3007 (http:www.spherion.com/press/releases/2007/workplace-romance.jsp).

"QuickQuery Frequently Asked Questions," Harris Interactive, accessed February 24, 2007 (http://www.harrisinteractive.com/services/pubs/HI_QuickQuery_FAQ_Sheet.pdf).

"Consulting on the Psychology of Business," Boswell Group Inc., accessed February 24, 2007 (http://www.boswellgroup.com).

Dynamic Survey

"Dynamic Survey," Invoke Solutions, accessed October 15, 2004 (http://www.invoke.com/solutions_survey.html). "Invoke Solutions Now Offers Elegant Answer to Order Bias Challenges," Invoke Solutions press release, London Calling PR, September 20, 2004. Melissa London, London Calling PR, agent of Invoke Solutions, e-mail contact from October 4, 2004, to November 5, 2004. Peter MacKey, Invoke Solutions, interviewed October 22, 2004.

Ice Storm

"The North Carolina Ice Story: Who Lost What and for How Long," RTI International press release, January 8, 2003 (http://www.rti.org/page.cfm?objectid=D3AF52E9-56E4-4478-875008F15123275F).

"The North Carolina Ice Storm: Lost Time at Work and Other Impacts," RTI International press release, January 16, 2003 (http://www.rti.org/printpg.cfm?objectid=D3AF52E9-56E4-4478-875008F15123275F).

InsightExpress

Doug Adams and Bob Ferro, "Not as Easy as It Looks: Best Practices for Online Research," InsightExpress, March 11, 2004. This presentation was part of the American Marketing Association Online Seminar Series.

PullQuote

"Al Ries Talks to Tom H. C. Anderson about Marketing," Anderson Analytics, January 29th, 2009, accessed June 11, 2009 (http://www.tomhcanderson.com/2009/01/29/al-ries-talks-to-tom-h-c-anderson-about-marketing/).

PulsePoint

TrendMicro ad, *BusinessWeek,* March 23 & 30, 2009, inside cover.

Travel

"Deloitte Survey: Travelers Are Essentially Uninterested in Registered Traveler Program, Despite Frustration with Long Airport Security Lines; Privacy Concerns Cited; Cost Only a Minor Issue," *Hotels,* April 4, 2007. Accessed April 16, 2007 (http://www6.lexisnexis.com/publisher/EndUser?Action=UserDisplayFullDocument&orgld=616&topicId=12552&docld=1:593960847&start=10).

VOVICI

www.vovici.com

Classic and Contemporary Readings

Converse, Jean M., and Stanley Presser. *Survey Questions: Handcrafting the Standardized Questionnaire.* Beverly Hills, CA: Sage Publications, 1986. A worthy successor to Stanley Payne's classic. Advice on how to write survey questions based on professional experience and the experimental literature.

Dillman, Don A. *Mail and Internet Surveys: The Tailored Design Method.* New York: Wiley, 1999. A contemporary treatment of Dillman's classic work.

Fink, Arlene, and Jaqueline Kosecoff. *How to Conduct Surveys: A Step-by-Step Guide.* Thousand Oaks, CA: Sage Publications, 1998. Emphasis on computer-assisted and interactive surveys and a good section on creating questions.

Kahn, Robert L., and Charles F. Cannell. *The Dynamics of Interviewing.* New York: Wiley, 1957. Chapters 5 and 6 cover questionnaire design.

Payne, Stanley L. *The Art of Asking Questions.* Princeton, NJ: Princeton University Press, 1951. An enjoyable book on the many problems encountered in developing useful survey questions. A classic resource.

Sudman, Seymour, and Norman N. Bradburn. *Asking Questions: A Practical Guide to Questionnaire Design.* San Francisco: Jossey-Bass, 1982. This book covers the major issues in writing individual questions and constructing scales. The emphasis is on structured questions and interview schedules.

appendix 13a
Reference Notes

1. Sam Gill, "How Do You Stand on Sin?" *Tide,* March 14, 1947, p. 72.
2. Stanley L. Payne, *The Art of Asking Questions* (Princeton, NJ: Princeton University Press, 1951), p. 18.
3. Unaided recall gives respondents no clues as to possible answers. Aided recall gives them a list of radio programs that played last night and then asks them which ones they heard. See Harper W. Boyd Jr. and Ralph Westfall, *Marketing Research,* 3d ed. (Homewood, IL: Irwin, 1972), p. 293.
4. Gideon Sjoberg, "A Questionnaire on Questionnaires," *Public Opinion Quarterly* 18 (Winter 1954), p. 425.
5. Robert L. Kahn and Charles F. Cannell, *The Dynamics of Interviewing* (New York: Wiley, 1957), p. 108.
6. Ibid., p. 110.
7. Payne, *The Art of Asking Questions,* p. 140.
8. Ibid., p. 141.
9. Ibid., p. 149.
10. Gertrude Bancroft and Emmett H. Welch, "Recent Experiences with Problems of Labor Force Measurement," *Journal of the American Statistical Association* 41 (1946), pp. 303–12.
11. National Opinion Research Center, Proceedings of the Central City Conference on Public Opinion Research (Denver, CO: University of Denver, 1946), p. 73.
12. Hadley Cantril, ed., *Gauging Public Opinion* (Princeton, NJ: Princeton University Press, 1944), p. 48.
13. Payne, *The Art of Asking Questions,* pp. 7–8.
14. Barbara Snell Dobrenwend, "Some Effects of Open and Closed Questions on Respondents' Answers," *Human Organization* 24 (Summer 1965), pp. 175–84.

appendix 13b
Reference Notes

1. The sections on methods and purposes of pretesting have been largely adapted from Jean M. Converse and Stanley Presser, *Survey Questions: Handcrafting the Standardized Questionnaire* (Beverly Hills, CA: Sage Publications, 1986), pp. 51–64, and Survey Research Center, *Interviewer's Manual,* rev. ed. (Ann Arbor: Institute for Social Research, University of Michigan, 1976), pp. 133–34. For an extended discussion of the phases of pretesting, see Converse and Presser, *Survey Questions,* pp. 65–75.
2. W. R. Belson, *The Design and Understanding of Survey Questions* (Aldershot, England: Gower, 1981), pp. 76–86.
3. Perceival White, *Market Analysis* (New York: McGraw-Hill, 1921).

chapter 14
Reference Notes

1. United States Department of Commerce, Press Release CB99-CN.22, June 2, 1999 (http://www.census.gov/Press-Release/www/1999/cb99.html).
2. W. E. Deming, *Sample Design in Business Research* (New York: Wiley, 1960), p. 26.
3. Henry Assael and John Keon, "Nonsampling versus Sampling Errors in Survey Research," *Journal of Marketing Research* (Spring 1982), pp. 114–23.
4. A. Parasuraman, *Marketing Research,* 2d ed. (Reading, MA: Addison-Wesley, 1991), p. 477.
5. Proportions are hypothetical. *Advertising Age* recognized Serta's "Counting Sheep 'Penalty'" ad as one of the campaign's most effective for brand recall. Serta ranked eighth, using rankings from more than 2.6 million surveys of TV viewers from January 2 to April 1, 2003. This same campaign won a prestigious Gold Effie award in June 2002. Serta spends $20 million annually on the sheep campaign. "Counting Sheep Scheme to Win Back Clients in Serta's New TV Commercials," Serta press release, downloaded November 23, 2003 (http://www.serta.com/pressrelease/press_r2.pdf); "Ad Age Recognizes Serta," *Furniture Today* press release, downloaded November 23, 2003 (http://www.furnituretoday.com/cgi-bin/v2/showArchive.cgi?num=942&news=Ad%20Age%20recognizes%20Serta); *Advertising Age,* April 21, 2003.
6. Fred N. Kerlinger, *Foundations of Behavioral Research,* 3d ed. (New York: Holt, Rinehart & Winston, 1986), p. 72.
7. Amir D. Aczel, *Complete Business Statistics* (Burr Ridge, IL: Irwin, 1996), p. 180.
8. N. L. Rynolds, A. C. Simintiras, and A. Diamantopoulus, "Theoretical Justification of Sampling Choices in International Marketing Research: Key Issues and Guidelines for Researchers," downloaded May 28, 2004 (http://www.questia.com/PM.qst?a[H11005]o&d[H11005]5001902692).
9. Family Health International, "Sampling Approaches," and "Weighting in Multi-Stage Sampling," in *Guidelines for Repeated Behavioral Surveys in Populations at Risk of HIV* (Durham, NC: FHI, 2000), Chaps. 4 and 5, pp. 29–65.
10. Standard international sampling systems are based on standards such as ISO 2859 and ISO 3951.

11. All estimates of costs are hypothetical.

12. Leslie Kish, *Survey Sampling* (New York: Wiley, 1965), p. 188.

13. Ibid., pp. 76–77.

14. Typically, stratification is carried out before the actual sampling, but when this is not possible, it is still possible to stratify after the fact. Ibid., p. 90.

15. W. G. Cochran, *Sampling Techniques,* 2d ed. (New York: Wiley, 1963), p. 134.

16. Ibid., p. 96.

17. Kish, *Survey Sampling*, p. 94.

18. For detailed treatment of these and other cluster sampling methods and problems, see ibid., pp. 148–247.

19. J. H. Lorie and H. V. Roberts, *Basic Methods of Marketing Research* (New York: McGraw-Hill, 1951), p. 120.

20. Kish, *Survey Sampling,* p. 156.

21. For specifics on these problems and how to solve them, the reader is referred to the many good sampling texts. Two that have been mentioned already are Kish, *Survey Sampling,* Chaps. 5, 6, and 7, and Cochran, *Sampling Techniques,* Chaps. 9, 10, and 11.

References for Snapshots, PicProfiles, Captions, PulsePoints, and Pull Quotes

Alliance Research/Catalina Marketing

Jim Lane, senior vice president, Alliance Research, interviewed September 8, 2002.

Materials presented at the AMA Marketing Research Conference, Chicago, September 8–11, 2002.

Chinese Phone Use

"China's Cell Phone Industry (March 2009), " *TMCnet.com,* March 10, 2009, accessed June 23, 2009 (http://next-generation-communications. tmcnet.com/news/2009/03/10/4042685.htm).

"China's Cell Phone Users Top 670 Mil," *People's Daily Online,* May 21, 2009., accessed June 23, 2009 (http://english.people.com.cn/ 90001/90781/90877/6663007.pdf).

"New Cell Phone Users Far Outpace New Fixed-Line Phone Users," *Shanghai Daily,* March 22, 2007, accessed April 20, 2007 (http://english.eastday.com/eastday/englishedition/business/ userobject1ai2699467.html).

Ford David Kiley, "The Fight for Ford's Future," *BusinessWeek,* August 11, 2008, pp. 40–43.

Keynote

"About Us," Keynote Systems, accessed August 11, 2006 (http://www. keynote.com/about_us/about_us_tpl.html).

Danny Sullivan, "Hitwise Search Engine Ratings," SearchEngineWatch. com, August 23, 2006, accessed April 20, 2007 (http:// searchenginewatch.com/showPage.html?page=3099931).

Keynote_SES_Deck.ppt, PowerPoint presentation presented by Lance Jones, senior research analyst, Keynote Systems to Search Engine Strategies 2006 Conference and Expo, New York, February 27, 2006.

Lance Jones, "How Online Consumers Use and View Search Engines," web seminar presented by American Marketing Association, July 26, 2006.

Lance Jones, senior research analyst, Keynote Systems, interviewed August 11, 2006.

PullQuote

"Miguel de Cervantes Saavedra quotes," ThinkExist.com, accessed June 14, 2009 (http://thinkexist.com/quotation/the_proof_of_the_ pudding_is_in_the_eating-by_a/153068.html).

PulsePoint

Katie Hafner, "Texting May Be Taking a Toll," *The New York Times,* May 26, 2009, accessed June 1, 2009 (http://www.nytimes.com/ 2009/05/26/health/26teen.html).

SSI: Sampling

Linda Piekarski, senior vice president of database and research, Survey Sampling Inc., interviewed June 10, 2002.

Classic and Contemporary Readings

Deming, W. Edwards. *Sample Design in Business Research.* New York: Wiley, 1990. A classic by the late author, an authority on sampling.

Kalton, Graham. *Introduction to Survey Sampling.* Beverly Hills, CA: Sage Publications, 1983. An overview with particular attention to survey applications.

Kish, Leslie. *Survey Sampling.* New York: Wiley, 1995. A widely read reference on survey sampling, recently updated.

Namias, Jean. *Handbook of Selected Sample Surveys in the Federal Government.* New York: St. John's University Press, 1969. A unique collection of illustrative uses of sampling for surveys carried out by various federal agencies. Of interest both for the sampling designs presented and for the information on the methodology used to develop various government statistical data.

Yates, F. *Sampling Methods for Censuses and Surveys.* 4th ed. New York: Oxford University Press, 1987. A readable text with emphasis on sampling practices.

appendix 14a

Reference Notes

This appendix was built from two examples developed for *Business Research Methods,* 8th ed. (New York: McGraw-Hill, 2003), by Donald Cooper and Pamela Schindler.

1. A proportion is the mean of a dichotomous variable when members of a class receive the value of 1, and nonmembers receive a value of 0.

chapter 15

Reference Notes

1. Jean M. Converse and Stanley Presser, *Survey Questions: Handcrafting the Standardized Questionnaire* (Beverly Hills, CA: Sage Publications, 1986), pp. 34–35.

2. B. Berelson, *Content Analysis in Communication Research* (New York: Free Press, 1952), p. 18.

3. Klaus Krippendorff, *Content Analysis: An Introduction to Its Methodology* (Beverly Hills, CA: Sage Publications, 1980), p. 22.

4. Based on the operation of the SPSS Inc., product TextSmart.

5. Hans Zeisel, *Say It with Figures,* 6th ed. (New York: Harper & Row, 1985), pp. 48–49.

6. "Technology Overview," TraxUK, downloaded March 11, 2003 (http//www.trax-uk.co.uk./technology).

7. Ibid.

8. "Office XP Speaks Out: Voice Recognition Assists Users," Microsoft press release, April 18, 2001, downloaded March 11, 2003 (http://www.microsoft.com/presspass/features/2001/ apr01/04-18xpspeech.asp).

9. Adapted from a history of bar-code development: http://www. lascofittings.com/BarCode-EDI/bc-history.htm.

References for Snapshots, PicProfiles, Captions, PulsePoints, and Pull Quotes

CBS

"ACNielsen Entertainment Partners with CBS for Real-Time Audience Research," ACNielsen news release, April 18, 2001 (http://www.acnielsen.com/news/corp/2001/20010418.html).

Author's experience, September 9, 2005.

"CBS Television City Research Center," Vegas.com, downloaded April 16, 2004 (http://www.vegas.com/attractions/on_the_strip/televisioncity.html?f_m0at&t_stripa).

"GES Builds Television City for CBS Television Network; Ambitious Research Facility Ingeniously Captures Opinions amidst Las Vegas Excitement," Viad Corp. news release, September 5, 2001 (http://www.businesswire.com/webbox/bw.090501/212480444.htm).

"Tech Week: Entertainment's Creative Online Testing with Andy Wing, President, ACNielsen Entertainment," *Washington Post.com,* Friday, May 18, 2001 (http://discuss.washingtonpost.com/wp-srv/zform/01/washtech_wing0518.html).

Dirty Data

a.   "Dirty Data," Wikipedia, October 15, 2008, accessed June 9, 2007 (http://en.wikipedia.org/wiki/Dirty_data).

b.   Ibid.

c.   Craig Focardi, "Data Quality: the Cost of Dirty Data in the Secondary Market," *Mortgage Banking,* February 1, 2008, accessed June 2, 2009 (http://www.allbusiness.com/banking-finance/banking-lending-credit-services/8886090-1.html).

d.   Ibid.

e.   John Wilmes, "Defeating Dirty Data," *Destination CRM.com,* May 13, 2009, accessed June 2, 2009 (http://www.destinationcrm.com/Articles/Web-Exclusives/Viewpoints/Defeating-Dirty-Data-53828.aspx).

f.   Dan Tynan, "The Perils of Dirty Data," *InfoWorld,* October 29, 2007, accessed June 2, 2009 (http://www.infoworld.com/d/developer-world/perils-dirty-data-585).

g.   Nelson King, "Dealing with Dirty Data," March 1, 2003, *ComputerUser,* accessed June 2, 2009 (http://www.computeruser.com/articles/2203,3,6,1,0301,03.html).

h.   Mitch Betts, "Dirty Data," December 17, 2001, *ComputerWorld,* accessed June 9, 2009 (http://www.computerworld.com/action/article.do?command=viewArticleBasic&articleId=66618).

i.   "'Dirty Data' is a Business Problem, Not an IT problem, says Gartner," Gartner news release, March 2, 2007, accessed May 21, 2009 (http://www.gartner.com/it/page.jsp?id=501733).

j.   Nicole Kobie, "Firms Full of Dirty Data: As Much as 30 Percent of Data Held by Companies Could Be 'Dirty' in Some Way, According to a BCS Award Winner," *ITPro.com,* December 9, 2008, accessed June 2, 2009 (http://www.itpro.co.uk/609057/firms-full-of-dirty-data).

k.   Betts, "Dirty Data."

l.   Ibid.

m.   Kobie, "Firms Full of Dirty Data."

n.   "Dirty Data," Wikibooks, March 9, 2009, accessed June 9, 2009 (http://en.wikibooks.org/wiki/The_Computer_Revolution/Security/Dirty_Data).

o.   Betts, "Dirty Data."

Netnography Data

Douglas Gantenbein, "Good Reasons to Post Customer Reviews on Your Site," Microsoft Mid-size Business Center, accessed May 21, 2007 (http://www.microsoft.com/midsizebusiness/businessvalue/onlinereviews.mspx).

Zhilin Yang and Robin T. Peterson, "Web-Based Product Reviews Provide a Wealth of Information for Marketers," *Marketing Research,* Winter 2003, pp. 26–31.

PullQuote

"Carly Fiorina quotes," ThinkExist.com, accessed June 14, 2009 (http://thinkexist.com/quotation/the_goal_is_to_transform_data_into_information/346980.html).

PulsePoint

Michelle Conlin, "How to Get a Life and Do Your Job," *BusinessWeek,* August 25/September 1, 2008, pp. 37–40.

XSight

John Woolcott, vice president, American operations, QSR International, interviewed June 4, 2004.

"XSight," QSR International, demo software, © 2007.

"XSight: Your Intuition. Our Software," QSR International, product literature, © 2004.

Classic and Contemporary Readings

Aczel, Amir D., and Jayauel Sounderpandian. *Complete Business Statistics.* 5th ed. Burr Ridge: Irwin/McGraw-Hill, 2002. Chapter 1 on descriptive statistics and Chapter 4 on the normal distribution.

Bux, William E., and Kenneth L. Gorman. *Data Entry Activities for Micro Computers.* Cincinnati, OH: SouthWestern, 1995.

Zeisel, Hans. *Say It with Figures.* 6th ed. New York: Harper & Row, 1985. The entire book is worth reading for its excellent discussion of numerical presentation.

chapter 16

Reference Notes

1.   David C. Hoaglin, Frederick Mosteller, and John W. Tukey, eds., *Understanding Robust and Exploratory Data Analysis* (New York: Wiley, 1983), p. 2.

2.   John W. Tukey, *Exploratory Data Analysis* (Reading, MA: Addison-Wesley, 1977), pp. 2–3.

3.   Frederick Hartwig with Brian E. Dearing, *Exploratory Data Analysis* (Beverly Hills, CA: Sage Publications, 1979), pp. 9–12.

4.   The exhibits in this section were created with statistical and graphic programs particularly suited to exploratory data analysis. The authors acknowledge the following vendors for evaluation and use of their products: SPSS Inc., 233 S. Wacker Dr., Chicago, IL 60606; and Data Description, P.O. Box 4555, Ithaca, NY 14852.

5.   Paul F. Velleman and David C. Hoaglin, *Applications, Basics, and Computing of Exploratory Data Analysis* (Boston: Duxbury Press, 1981), p. 13.

6.   John Hanke, Eastern Washington University, contributed this section. For further references to stem-and-leaf displays, see John D. Emerson and David C. Hoaglin, "Stem-and-Leaf Displays," in *Understanding Robust and Exploratory Data Analysis,* pp. 7–31, and Velleman and Hoaglin, *Applications,* pp. 1–13.

7.   This section is adapted from the following excellent discussions of boxplots: Velleman and Hoaglin, *Applications,* pp. 65–76; Hartwig, *Exploratory Data Analysis,* pp. 19–25; John D. Emerson and Judith Strenio, "Boxplots and Batch Comparison," in *Understanding Robust and Exploratory Data Analysis,* pp. 59–93; and Amir D. Aczel, *Complete Business Statistics* (Homewood, IL: Irwin, 1989), pp. 723–28.

8.   Tukey, *Exploratory Data Analysis,* pp. 27–55.

9.   Hoaglin et al., *Understanding Robust and Exploratory Data Analysis,* p. 2.

10. Several robust estimators that are suitable replacements for the mean and standard deviation we do not discuss here—for example, the trimmed mean, trimean, the M-estimators (such as Huber's, Tukey's, Hampel's, and Andrew's estimators), and the median absolute deviation (MAD). See Hoaglin et al., *Understanding Robust and Exploratory Data Analysis,* Chap. 10, and SPSS Inc., *SPSS Base 9.0 User's Guide* (Chicago: SPSS, 1999), Chap. 13.

11. The difference between the definitions of a hinge and a quartile is based on variations in their calculation. We use Q_1, *25th percentile,* and *lower hinge* synonymously; and Q_3, 75th percentile, and *upper hinge,* similarly. There are technical differences, although they are not significant in this context.

12. R. McGill, J. W. Tukey, and W. A. Larsen, "Variations of Box Plots," *The American Statistician* 14 (1978), pp. 12–16.

13. See J. Chambers, W. Cleveland, B. Kleiner, and John W. Tukey, *Graphical Methods for Data Analysis* (Boston: Duxbury Press, 1983).

14. Harper W. Boyd Jr. and Ralph Westfall, *Marketing Research,* 3d ed. (Homewood, IL: Irwin, 1972), p. 540.

15. SPSS Inc., *SPSS Tables 8.0* (Chicago: SPSS, 1998), with its system file: Bank Data.

References for Snapshots, PicProfiles, Captions, PulsePoints, and Pull Quotes

Closeup: Tables

Sally Bigwood and Melissa Spore. *Presenting Numbers, Tables, and Charts.* Oxford: Oxford University Press, 2003.

Excel

This snapshot was developed from participating in numerous "Marketing Engineering with Excel" Web seminars provided by the authors, and using the downloaded plug-ins provided for Excel. The website (www.mktgeng.com) is rich with information for both instructors and students.

Internet-Age Researchers

a. Steve Lohr, "For Today's Graduate, Just One Word: Statistics," *New York Times,* August 5, 2009, accessed August 10, 2009 (http://www.nytimes.com/2009/08/06/technology/06stats.html?_r=1&th&emc=th).

b. IDC Technology Advice by Industry, accessed August 11, 2009 (http://www.idc.com/home.jhtml).

c. James Manyika, "Hal Varian on How the Web Challenges Managers," *The McKinsey Quarterly,* 2009, accessed July 4, 2009 (http://www.mckinseyquarterly.com/Hal_Varian_on_how_the_Web_challenges_managers_2286).

d. Ian Ayers, "The Value of Statistics" (http://freakonomics.blogs.nytimes.com/2009/08/13/the-value-of-statistics/).

PullQuote

"Seth Godin Talks to Tom H. C. Anderson about Marketing," Anderson Analytics, January 16, 2009, accessed June 11, 2009 (http://www.tomhcanderson.com/2009/01/16/seth-godin-talks-to-tom-h-c-anderson-about-marketing/).

PulsePoint

SAS Business Analytics ad, *BusinessWeek,* June 1, 2009, p. 12.

Media Outlook

Deborah Scruby, marketing director, PricewaterhouseCoopers, interviewed September 10, 2002.

Starbucks

Colette Courtion, director of Starbucks Global Card Services, interviewed April 26, 2004.

"Fast Facts," Duetto Card Press Kit jointly issued by Starbucks, Bank One, and Visa, October 2003 (http://www.duettopressroom.com).

"Starbucks Coffee Company, Bank One and Visa Team Up to Develop the Next Evolution of the Starbucks Card," press release, February 21, 2003 (http://www.shareholder.com/one/news/20030221-102404.cfm?category).

This snapshot and the accompanying case were developed with the assistance of numerous people from Bank One: Jessica Iben; Hugh Bleemer, executive vice president of programming; Mike Bordner, relationship manager on the Starbucks account; and Ajay Gupta, primarily in charge of the research. All the above were interviewed by phone, with conversations supplemented by e-mail, during Spring 2004.

Classic and Contemporary Readings

Aczel, Amir D. *Complete Business Statistics*. 6th ed. New York: Irwin/McGraw-Hill, 2006. Thorough coverage of exploratory and confirmatory data analysis.

Bigwood, Sally, and Melissa Spore. *Presenting Numbers, Tables, and Charts*. Oxford: Oxford University Press, 2003.

DeMers, Michael. *Basics of Geographic Information Systems*. New York: Wiley, 2004. Methodical coverage of basic input requirements, data management, reporting concepts, and ample depth in explaining spatial analysis issues. Highly regarded by students for its readability.

Hoaglin, David C., Frederick Mosteller, and John W. Tukey, eds. *Understanding Robust and Exploratory Data Analysis*. New York: Wiley, 2000. A complete and advanced treatment by influential writers in this field. Especially well-organized topical coverage.

Pallant, Julie. *SPSS Survival Manual*. Maidenhead, England: Open University Press, 2004.

Zeisel, Hans. *Say It with Figures*. 6th ed. New York: Harper & Row, 1985. The entire book is worth reading for its excellent discussion of numerical presentation.

chapter 17

Reference Notes

1. A more detailed example is found in Amir D. Aczel and Jayauel Sounderpandian, *Complete Business Statistics,* 5th ed. (New York: Irwin/McGraw-Hill, 2001).

2. The standardized random variable, denoted by Z, is a deviation from expectancy and is expressed in terms of standard deviation units. The mean of the distribution of a standardized random variable is 0, and the standard deviation is 1. With this distribution, the deviation from the mean by any value of X can be expressed in standard deviation units.

3. Procedures for hypothesis testing are reasonably similar across authors. This outline was influenced by Sidney Siegel, *Nonparametric Statistics for the Behavioral Sciences* (New York: McGraw-Hill, 1956), Chap. 2.

4. Marija J. Norusis/SPSS Inc., *SPSS for Windows Base System User's Guide,* Release 6.0 (Chicago: SPSS, 1993), pp. 601–06.

5. For further information on these tests, see ibid., pp. 187–88.

6. F. M. Andrews, L. Klem, T. N. Davidson, P. M. O'Malley, and W. L. Rodgers, *A Guide for Selecting Statistical Techniques for Analyzing Social Science Data* (Ann Arbor: Institute for Social Research, University of Michigan, 1976).

7. Statistical Navigator™ is a product from The Idea Works, Inc.

8. Exhibit 17–7 is partially adapted from Siegel, *Nonparametric Statistics,* flyleaf.

9. See B. S. Everitt, *The Analysis of Contingency Tables* (London: Chapman and Hall, 1977).

10. The critiques are represented by W. J. Conover, "Some Reasons for Not Using the Yates' Continuity Correction on 2 × 2 Contingency Tables," *Journal of the American Statistical Association* 69 (1974), pp. 374–76, and N. Mantel, "Comment and a Suggestion on the Yates' Continuity Correction," *Journal of the American Statistical Association* 69 (1974), pp. 378–80.

11. This data table and the analysis of variance tables and plots in this section were prepared with SuperANOVA™.

12. See, for example, Roger E. Kirk, *Experimental Design: Procedures for the Behavioral Sciences* (Belmont, CA: Brooks/Cole, 1982), pp. 115–33. An exceptionally clear presentation for step-by-step hand computation is found in James L. Bruning and B. L. Kintz, *Computational Handbook of Statistics,* 2d ed. (Glenview, IL: Scott, Foresman, 1977), pp. 143–68. Also, when you use a computer program, the reference manual typically provides helpful advice in addition to the setup instructions.

13. Kirk, *Experimental Design,* pp. 90–115. Alternatively, see Bruning and Kintz, *Computational Handbook of Statistics,* pp. 113–32.

14. For a discussion and example of the Cochran Q test, see Sidney Siegel and N. J. Castellan Jr., *Nonparametric Statistics for the Behavioral Sciences,* 2d ed. (New York: McGraw-Hill, 1988).

15. For further details, see ibid.

References for Snapshots, PicProfiles, Captions, PulsePoints, and Pull Quotes

Burrelle's

Sharon Miller, account executive, Burrelle's Information Services (Burrelle'sLuce), interviewed February 2003.

"Report on the Full Extent of Your Media Coverage," Burrelle's Media Analysis brochure, Burrelle's Information Services, Burrelle'sLuce, downloaded April 16, 2004 (http://www.burellesluce.com/images/mm/Bro_mediaana.pdf).

Drug Use in Movies

"New Study Looks at Drugs in Movies and Songs," America Cares Inc., April 1999 (http://www.americacares.org/drugs_in_movies.htm).

"Substance Use in Popular Movies and Music," Office of National Drug Control Policy, April 1999 (http://www.mediacampaign.org/publications/movies/movie_partIV.html).

PharmTrends

"Ad Aware Consumers Are Purchasing More Prescription Drug Scripts Than Those Not Aware of Direct-to-Consumer Advertising," Ipsos-NPD press release, June 27, 2002, downloaded July 12, 2002 (http://www.ipsos-npd.com/index_news.cfm?release=02_0626).

"Consumers Are Responding to Advertising for Prescription Medications," Ipsos-NPD press release, June 13, 2002, downloaded July 12, 2002 (http://www.ipsos-npd.com/index_news.cfm?release=02_0613).

Stuart Elliott, "The Fight to Keep Direct-to-Consumer Ads," *The New York Times*, July 12, 2002, downloaded July 12, 2002 (http://www.aef.com/06/news/data/2002/2069).

"PharmTrends," Ipsos-NPD, downloaded July 12, 2002 (http://www.ipsos-npd.com/index_pharm.cfm).

PullQuote

"Martin H. Fischer quotes," ThinkExist.com, accessed June 14, 2009 (http://thinkexist.com/quotes/martin_h._fischer/).

PulsePoint

Ad for Visa commercial, *BusinessWeek,* June 23, 2008, pp. 64–65.

Toyota Prius

"2010 Toyota Prius," Cars of the Year, June 4, 2009, accessed June 23, 2009 (http://socoolcars.blogspot.com/2009/06/2010-toyota-prius.htm).

Intermark Group (http://ebrochure.interx2.net/pdfengine/generate.pdf)

"Toyota Prius," Hybridcars.com, April 6, 2006, accessed June 23, 2009 (http://www.hybridcars.com/compacts-sedans/toyota-prius-overview.html).

www.toyota.com.

Classic and Contemporary Readings

Aczel, Amir D. *Complete Business Statistics.* 6th ed. New York: Irwin/McGraw-Hill, 2006. This excellent text is characterized by highly lucid explanations and numerous examples.

Cohen, Jacob. *Statistical Power Analysis for the Behavioral Sciences.* Mahwah, NJ: Lawrence Erlbaum Associates, 1990. A key reference on conducting power analysis.

DeFinetti, Bruno. *Probability, Induction, and Statistics.* New York: Wiley, 1972. A highly readable work on subjective probability and the Bayesian approach.

Kanji, Gopal K. *100 Statistical Tests,* 3d ed., Thousand Oaks, CA: Sage Publications, 2006. Coverage of the most commonly used statistics that students will encounter.

Kirk, Roger E. *Experimental Design: Procedures for the Behavioral Sciences.* 3d ed. Belmont, CA: Brooks/Cole, 1995. An advanced text on the statistical aspects of experimental design.

Levine, David M., Timothy C. Krehbiel, and Mark L. Berenson. *Business Statistics: A First Course,* 4th ed. Upper Saddle River, NJ: Prentice Hall, 2005. For students or managers without recent statistical coursework, this text provides an excellent review.

Siegel, Sidney, and N. J. Castellan Jr. *Nonparametric Statistics for the Behavioral Sciences.* 2d ed. New York: McGraw-Hill, 1988. The classic book on nonparametric statistics.

Winer, B. J. *Statistical Principles in Experimental Design.* 2d ed. New York: McGraw-Hill, 1971. Another classic source. Thorough coverage of analysis of variance and experimental design.

chapter 18

Reference Notes

1. Typically, we plot the *X* (independent) variable on the horizontal axis and the *Y* (dependent) variable on the vertical axis. Although correlation does not distinguish between independent and dependent variables, the convention is useful for consistency in plotting and will be used later with regression.

2. F. J. Anscombe, "Graphs in Statistical Analysis," *American Statistician* 27 (1973), pp. 17–21. Cited in Samprit Chatterjee and Bertram Price, *Regression Analysis by Example* (New York: Wiley, 1977), pp. 7–9.

3. Amir D. Aczel, *Complete Business Statistics*, 2d ed. (Homewood, IL: Irwin, 1993), p. 433.

4. This section is partially based on the concepts developed by Emanuel J. Mason and William J. Bramble, *Understanding and Conducting Research* (New York: McGraw-Hill, 1989), pp. 172–82, and elaborated in greater detail by Aczel, *Complete Business Statistics*, pp. 414–29.

5. Technically, estimation uses a concurrent criterion variable whereas prediction uses a future criterion. The statistical procedure is the same in either case.

6. Roz Howard and Jenny Stonier, "Marketing Wine to Generation X" for the 2000–2001 NSW Wine Press Club Fellowship. Reported in Murray Almond's "From the Left Island," May 25, 2002 (http://www.wineoftheweek.com/murray/0205genx.html).

7. Peter Passell, "Can Math Predict a Wine? An Economist Takes a Swipe at Some Noses," *International Herald Tribune*, March 5, 1990, p. 1; Jacques Neher, "Top Quality Bordeaux Cellar Is an Excellent Buy," *International Herald Tribune,* July 9, 1990, p. 8.

8. See Alan Agresti and Barbara Finlay, *Statistical Methods for the Social Sciences* (San Francisco: Dellen Publishing, 1986), pp. 248–49. Also see the discussion of basic regression models in John Neter, William Wasserman, and Michael H. Kutner, *Applied Linear Statistical Models* (Homewood, IL: Irwin, 1990), pp. 23–49.

9. We distinguish between the error terms $\varepsilon_i = Y_i - EY_i$ and the residual $e_i = (Y_i - \hat{Y}_i)$. The first is based on the vertical deviation of Y_i from the true regression line. It is unknown and estimated. The second is the vertical deviation of Y_i from the fitted Y on the estimated line. See Neter et al., *Applied Linear Statistical Models,* p. 47.

10. For further information on software-generated regression diagnostics, see the most current release of software manuals for SPSS, MINITAB, BMDP, and SAS.

11. Aczel, *Complete Business Statistics*, p. 434.

12. This calculation is normally listed as the standard error of the slope (SE B) on computer printouts. For these data it is further defined as

$$s(b_i) + \frac{8}{\sqrt{SS_x}} = \frac{538.559}{\sqrt{198.249}} = 38.249$$

where

s = the standard error of estimate (and the square root of the mean square error of the regression)

SS_x = the sum of squares for the X variable

13. Computer printouts use uppercase (R^2) because most procedures are written to accept multiple and bivariate regression.

14. The table output for this section has been modified from SPSS and is described in Marija J. Norusis/SPSS Inc., *SPSS Base System User's Guide* (Chicago: SPSS, 1990). For further discussion and examples of nonparametric measures of association, see S. Siegel and N. J. Castellan Jr., *Nonparametric Statistics for the Behavioral Sciences,* 2d ed. (New York: McGraw-Hill, 1988).

15. Calculation of concordant and discordant pairs is adapted from Agresti and Finlay, *Statistical Methods for the Social Sciences,* pp. 221–23.

16. We know that the percentage of concordant plus the percentage of discordant pairs sums to 1.0. We also know their difference is −.70. The only numbers satisfying these two conditions are .85 and .15 (.85 + .15 = 1.0, .15 − .85 = −.70).

17. G. U. Yule and M. G. Kendall, *An Introduction to the Theory of Statistics* (New York: Hafner, 1950).

18. M. G. Kendall, *Rank Correlation Methods,* 4th ed. (London: Charles W. Griffin, 1970).

References for Snapshots, PicProfiles, Captions, PulsePoints, and Pull Quotes

Advanced Statistics

a. Bob Reczek, "Navy Federal Credit Union Capitalizes on Predictive Analytics Software from SPSS Inc., Wins 2009 Technology ROI Award," *News Blaze,* September 1, 2009, accessed September 1, 2009 (http://newsblaze.com/story/2009090106065100001.bw/topstory.html).

b. "Navy Federal Credit Union Capitalizes on Predictive Analytics Software from SPSS Inc., Wins 2009 Technology ROI Award,"

SPSS press release, September 1, 2009, accessed November 4, 2009 (http://www.spss.com/press/template_view.cfm?PR_ID=1114).

c. Calvin Bierley, "Boeing Employees' Credit Union," SPSS, accessed November 20, 2009 (http://www.spss.com/success/pdf/Boeing%20Employees%20Credit%20Union%20Customer%20Story.pdf).

Business School Wine Clubs

E. Zelko, "Graduates of Wine," *Wine Spectator* 24, no. 15 (January 2000), pp. 88–90.

Constellation Wines

Natasha Hayes, Group Marketing Director, Ravenswood, Blackstone & Toasted Head, Constellation Wines US. Interviewed August 12, 2009; August 17, 2009; and September 19, 2009.

Stuart Elliot, "In Wine We Trust,' Ads Suggest," *New York Times,* August 10, 2009, accessed August 10, 2009 (http://www.nytimes.com/2009/08/10/business/media/10adnewsletter1.html?_r=1&adxnnl=1&8ad=&emc=seiaa1&adxnnlx=1266177729-WbcjIygTDT1As/PYF44/mw).

Envirosell

Live e-chat with Paco Underhill, July 8, 1999 (http://www.abcnews.go.com/sections/politics/DailyNews/chat_990511underhill.html).

PullQuote

"Stephen Jay Gould quotes," ThinkExist.com, accessed June 18, 2009 (http://en.thinkexist.com/quotation/the_invalid_assumption_that_correlation_implies/166237.html).

PulsePoint

Jessica Silver-Greenberg, "Getting Smarter School Loans," *BusinessWeek,* August 25/September 1, 2008, pp. 25–26.

Classic and Contemporary Readings

Aczel, Amir D. *Complete Business Statistics.* 6th ed. New York: Irwin/McGraw-Hill, 2006. The chapter on simple regression/correlation has impeccable exposition and examples and is highly recommended.

Agresti, Alan, and Barbara Finlay. *Statistical Methods for the Social Sciences.* 3d ed. Upper Saddle River, NJ: Prentice Hall, 1997. Very clear coverage of nonparametric measures of association.

Chatterjee, Samprit, and Ali S. Hadi. *Regression Analysis by Example.* 4th ed. New York: Wiley-Interscience, 2006. Updated version of widely used examples textbook.

Cohen, Jacob, and Patricia Cohen. *Applied Multiple Regression/Correlation Analysis for the Behavioral Sciences.* 2d ed. Mahwah, NJ: Lawrence Erlbaum Associates, 1983. A classic reference work.

Kutner Michael H., Christopher J. Nachtsheim, John Neter, and William Li. *Applied Linear Statistical Models.* 5th ed. Burr Ridge, IL: Irwin, 2004. Chapters 1 through 5 provide an excellent introduction to regression and correlation analysis.

Siegel, S., and N. J. Castellan Jr. *Nonparametric Statistics for the Behavioral Sciences.* 2d ed. New York: McGraw-Hill, 1988.

chapter 19

Reference Notes

1. Jagdish N. Sheth, ed., *Multivariate Methods for Market and Survey Research* (Chicago: American Marketing Association, 1977), p. 3.

2. William Schneider, "Opinion Outlook," *National Journal,* July 1985.

3. This chapter was revised for the 11th edition by Edye Cleary, School of Public Administration, Florida Atlantic University.

4. Benson Shapiro, "Price Reliance: Existence and Sources," *Journal of Marketing Research*, August 1973, pp. 286–89.

5. For a discussion of path analysis, see Elazar J. Pedhazur, *Regression in Behavioral Research: Explanation and Prediction,* 2d ed. (New York: Holt, Rinehart & Winston, 1982), Chap. 15, and Brian S. Everitt, Graham Dunn, and G. Dunn, *Applied Multivariate Data Analysis,* 2d ed. (London: Arnold Publishers, 2001).

6. Fred Kerlinger, *Foundations of Behavioral Research,* 3d ed. (New York: Holt, Rinehart & Winston, 1986), p. 562.

7. Joseph F. Hair Jr., Rolph E. Anderson, Ronald L. Tatham, and William C. Black, *Multivariate Data Analysis with Readings* (New York: Macmillan, 1992), pp. 153–81.

8. This section is based on the SPSS procedure MANOVA, described in Marija J. Norusis/SPSS Inc., *SPSS Advanced Statistics Users Guide* (Chicago: SPSS, 1990), pp. 71–104.

9. This section was prepared by Jeff Stevens, School of Public Administration, Florida Atlantic University. For further information, see Joseph F. Hair, Bill Black, Barry Babin, and Rolph E. Anderson, *Multivariate Data Analysis* 6th ed. (Upper Saddle River, NJ: Prentice Hall, 2005); J. Scott Long, *Covariance Structure Models: An Introduction to LISREL* (Thousand Oaks, CA: Sage Publications, 1984); J. Scott Long, *Confirmatory Factor Analysis: A Preface to LISREL* (Thousand Oaks, CAL Sage Publications, 1983); and Barbara M. Byrne, *A Primer of LISREL: Basic Applications and Programming for Confirmatory Factor Analytic Models* (New York: Springer-Verlag, 1989).

10. SPSS Inc., *SPSS Categories* (Chicago: SPSS, 1990).

11. Product specifications adapted from Lewis Rothlein, "A Guide to Sun Protection Essentials," *Wind Rider*, June 1990, pp. 95–103.

12. The data for this example are hypothetical.

13. See the ALSCAL procedure in Marija J. Norusis/SPSS, Inc., *SPSS Base System User's Guide* (Chicago: SPSS, 1990), pp. 397–416.

References for Snapshots, PicProfiles, Captions, PulsePoints, and Pull Quotes

PullQuote

"Samuel Horsley quotes," ThinkExist.com, accessed June 14, 2009 (http://thinkexist.com/quotation/wonder-connected_with_a_ principle_of_rational/169134.html).

PulsePoint

"Employees Trust Managers More Than Top Brass," *HR Magazine,* October 2008, accessed June 14, 2009 (http://findarticles.com/p/ articles/mi_m3495/is_10_53/ai_n30913769/).

SuperLetter.com

Christopher Schultheiss, founder and CEO, SuperLetter.com, interviewed June 2007.

Classic and Contemporary Readings

Hair, Joseph F., Bill Black, Barry Babin, and Rolph E. Anderson. *Multivariate Data Analysis.* 6th ed. Upper Saddle River, NJ: Prentice Hall, 2005. A very readable book covering most multivariate statistics.

Sage Series in Quantitative Applications in the Social Sciences. Thousand Oaks, CA: Sage Publications. This monograph series includes papers on most multivariate methods.

Schumacker, Randall E., and Richard G. Lomax. *A Beginner's Guide to Structural Equation Modeling.* Mahwah, NJ: Lawrence Erlbaum Associates, 2004. An introduction to structural models.

Stevens, James P. *Applied Multivariate Statistics for the Social Sciences.* 4th ed. Mahwah, NJ: Lawrence Erlbaum Associates, 2001. Comprehensive coverage with computer examples.

chapter 20

Reference Notes

1. Paul E. Resta, *The Research Report* (New York: American Book Company, 1972), p. 5.

2. John M. Penrose Jr., Robert W. Rasberry, and Robert J. Myers, *Advanced Business Communication* (Boston: PWS-Kent Publishing, 1989), p. 185.

3. Ibid.

4. Most word processors contain dictionaries. All-purpose word processors such as MS Word, WordPerfect, WordPro, or Macintosh products contain a spelling checker, table and graphing generators, and a thesaurus. For style and grammar checkers, programs such as Grammatik, RightWriter, Spelling Coach, and Punctuation + Style are available. New programs are reviewed periodically in the business communication literature and in magazines devoted to personal computing.

5. Robert R. Rathbone, *Communicating Technical Information* (Reading, MA: Addison-Wesley, 1966), p. 64. Reprinted with permission.

6. Ibid., p. 72.

7. Penrose, Rasberry, and Myers, *Advanced Business Communication,* p. 89.

8. The material in this section draws on Stephen M. Kosslyn, *Elements of Graph Design* (San Francisco: Freeman, 1993); DeltaPoint Inc., *DeltaGraph User's Guide 4.0* (Monterey, CA: DeltaPoint, 1996); Gene Zelazny, *Say It with Charts* (Homewood, IL: Business One Irwin, 1991); Jim Heid, "Graphs That Work," *MacWorld,* February 1994, pp. 155–56; and Penrose, Rasberry, and Myers, *Advanced Business Communication,* Chap. 3.

9. Marilyn Stoll, "Charts Other Than Pie Are Appealing to the Eye," *PC Week*, March 25, 1986, pp. 138–39.

10. Stephen M. Kosslyn and Christopher Chabris, "The Mind Is Not a Camera, the Brain Is Not a VCR," *Aldus Magazine*, September–October 1993, p. 34.

References for Snapshots, PicProfiles, Captions, PulsePoints, and Pull Quotes

DataCAP

dataCAP, Opinion Search, downloaded June 1, 2004 (http://www. opinionsearch.com/en/services/index.asp?subsection= 6&subsubsection=4).

Darcy Zwetko, director of research and systems, Opinion Search, interviewed June 2003.

Forrester Research

Mark Bunger, senior analyst, Forrester Research, interviewed January 22, 2004.

"Making Auto Retail Lean," TechStrategy report, Forrester Research, downloaded January 5, 2004 (http://www.forrester.com/ER/ Research/Report/Summary/0,1338,32782,00.html).

PullQuote

"Robert KcKee on the Power of Story," PresentationZen.com, July 19, 2008, accessed June 11, 2009 (http://www.presentationzen.com/presentationzen/2008/07/robert-mckee-on-the-power-of-story.html).

PulsePoint

IBM ad, *BusinessWeek,* March 16, 2009, p. 47.

Classic and Contemporary Readings

Campbell, Steve. *Statistics You Can't Trust.* Parker, CO: Think Twice Publishing, 2000. An enjoyable and entertaining approach to interpreting statistical charts and arguments.

Kosslyn, Stephen M. *Elements of Graph Design.* San Francisco: Freeman, 1993. Fundamentals of graph and chart construction.

Lesikar, Raymond V., Marie E. Flatley, and John D. Pettit. *Lesikar's Basic Business Communication.* 8th ed. Burr Ridge, IL: Irwin/McGraw-Hill, 1999. Practical guidance for writing and presenting reports.

Penrose, John M., Robert W. Rasberry, and Robert J. Myers. *Advanced Business Communication.* 3d ed. Cincinnati, OH: SouthWestern Publishing, 1997. A presentation of all aspects of business communications from organization through final writing and oral presentation.

Strunk, William, Jr., and E. B. White. *The Elements of Style.* New York: Macmillan, 1959. A classic on the problems of writing style.

Bigwood Sally, and Melissa Spore, *Presenting Numbers, Tables, and Charts.* Oxford: Oxford University Press, 2003. Great tips on tables and chart.

Tufte, Edward R. *The Visual Display of Quantitative Information.* New Haven, CT: Graphics Press, 1992. The book that started the revolution against gaudy infographics.

Tufte, Edward R. *Visual Explanations: Images and Quantities, Evidence and Narrative.* New Haven, CT: Graphics Press, 1997. Uses the principle of "the smallest effective difference" to display distinctions in data. Beautifully illustrated.

chapter 21

Reference Notes

1. Bernard E. Jacob, Lecture: "Aristotle and Rhetoric," Hofstra University School of Law, September 24, 2001, downloaded February 2, 2010 (http://people.hofstra.edu/Bernard_E_Jacob/lecturenotes1.pdf) p. 1.

2. Aristotle's *Rhetoric,* translated by Rhys Roberts (New York: Random House, 1954), Book I, Chapter 2.

3. Aristotle's *Rhetoric,* Stanford Encyclopedia of Philosophy, first published May 2, 2002, downloaded December 29, 2009 (http://plato.stanford.edu/entries/aristotle-rhetoric/#4.4).

4. From the essay by Jeanne Fahnestock "The Appeals: Ethos, Pathos, and Logos," downloaded January 7, 2010 (http://otal.umd.edu/~mikej/supplements/ethoslogospathos.html).

5. Aristotle's *Rhetoric,* Stanford Encyclopedia of Philosophy.

6. Garr Reynolds, *Presentation Zen: Simple Ideas on Presentation Design and Delivery* (Berkeley, CA: Pearson/New Riders, 2008), p. 33.

7. Cliff Atkinson, *Beyond Bullet Points* (Redmond, WA: Microsoft Press, 2008) p. 14.

8. Nancy Duarte, *slide:ology: The Art and Science of Creating Great Presentations* (Sebastopol, CA: O'Reilly Media, 2008).

9. Thomas Leech, *How to Prepare, Stage, and Deliver Winning Presentations* (New York: AMACOM, 2004), p. 29.

10. Portions of this section adapted from: http://www.smsu.edu/Academics/ChallengeProgram/Speech%20110/Audience%20Analysis%20(4).doc, downloaded January 7, 2010.

11. Mary Munter and Dave Paradi, *Guide to PowerPoint* (Upper Saddle River, NJ: Pearson/Prentice Hall, 2009), p. 6.

12. Doug Losee, "An Adaptation of Constructive Alternativism as Theory for Audience Analysis," presented at the Annual Meeting of the Western Speech Communication Association (Albuquerque, NM, February 19–22, 1983), downloaded January 7, 2010 (http://www.eric.ed.gov/ERICWebPortal/custom/portlets/recordDetails/detailmini.jsp?_nfpb=true&_&ERICExtSearch_SearchValue_0=ED229800&ERICExtSearch_SearchType_0=no&accno=ED229800).

13. Carmine Gallo, *The Presentation Secrets of Steve Jobs: How to Be Insanely Great in Front of Any Audience* (New York: McGraw-Hill, 2010), p. 147.

14. J. Deese and R. A. Kaufman, "Serial Effects in Recall of Unorganized and Sequentially Organized Verbal Material," *Journal of Experimental Psychology* 54, no. 3 (1957), pp. 180–7; B. B. Murdock Jr., "The Serial Position Effect of Free Recall," *Journal of Experimental Psychology* 64 (1962), pp. 482–88.

15. Ibid.

16. Gallo, *The Presentation Secrets,* p. 83.

17. John Medina, *Brain Rules* (Seattle: Pear Press, 2008), p. 74.

18. Duarte, *slide:ology,* p. 253.

19. A. H. Monroe and D. Ehninger, *Principles and Types of Speech,* 6th ed. (Glenview, IL: Scott, Foresman and Co., 1967), pp. 264–65.

20. Ralph Nichols, "The Greatest Sales Pitch," *Proceedings of the 30th Annual Rocky Mountain Speech Conference,* Denver, February, 1961, p. 17.

21. Reynolds, *Presentation Zen,* p. 16.

22. Donald R. Cooper, "An Experimental Study to Determine the Relative Effectiveness of the Motivated Sequence Versus the Narrative Pattern of Organizational Development in a Persuasive Speech," Unpublished Master's Thesis, 1968.

23. Andrew Dlugan, "Why Successful Speech Outlines Follow the Rule of Three," June 2009 downloaded January 7, 2010 (http://sixminutes.dlugan.com/speech-outline-rule-of-three/).

24. Ibid.

25. G. A. Miller, "The Magical Number Seven, Plus or Minus Two: Some Limits on Our Capacity for Processing Information," *Psychological Review* 63, no. 2 (1956), pp. 81–97.

26. N. Cowan, "The Magical Number 4 in Short-Term Memory: A Reconsideration of Mental Storage Capacity," *Behavioral and Brain Sciences* 24 (2001), pp. 87–185.

27. Gallo, *The Presentation Secrets,* pp. 50–51.

28. Dlugan, "Why Successful Speech."

29. C. Shelley, *Multiple Analogies in Science and Philosophy* (Amsterdam/Philadelphia: John Benjamins Publishing Company, 2003).

30. Daniel Gross, "A Birder's Guide to D.C.," *Newsweek,* November 16, 2009, downloaded January 20, 2010 (http://www.newsweek.com/id/221272).

31. This example is from http://grammar.about.com/od/qaaboutrhetoric/f/faqmetaphor07.htm, downloaded January 26, 2010.

32. Bradford Stull, *The Elements of Figurative Language* (New York: Longman Publishing Group, 2002) p. 37.

33. Reynolds, *Presentation Zen,* p. 80.

34. Gallo, *The Presentation Secrets,* pp. 216–17; see also http://www.youtube.com/watch?v=UF8uR6Z6KLc, downloaded December 28, 2009.

35. Guy Kawasaki, *The Macintosh Way* (New York: HarperCollins, 1990), p. 149.

36. See criteria at Kawasaki, *The Macintosh Way,* p. 149; and application at Gallo, *The Presentation Secrets,* p. 139.

37. David Adamy, *Preparing and Delivering Effective Technical Presentations,* 2d ed. (Boston, MA: Artech House, 2000), p. 12.

38. Rick Altman, *Why Most PowerPoint Presentations Suck: And How You Can Make Them Better* (Pleasanton, CA: Harvest Books Rick Altman: 2009), p. 31.

39. Edward Tufte, "PowerPoint Is Evil: Power Corrupts. PowerPoint Corrupts Absolutely," *Wired,* September 2003, downloaded February 6, 2010 (http://www.wired.com/wired/archive/11.09/ppt2.html).

40. Reynolds, *Presentation Zen,* pp. 67–68.

41. This section was developed using some of the principles presented by Stephen Kosslyn, *Clear and to the Point: 8 Principles for Compelling PowerPoint Presentations* (New York: Oxford Press, 2007), pp. 3–12.

42. Reynolds, *Presentation Zen* p. 43.

43. Ibid., p. 117.

44. Ibid., p. 97.

45. Ideas in this bullet list were developed by applying concepts presented by the following authors to research presentations: Duarte, *slide:ology,* p. 92; Reynolds, *Presentation Zen;* Kosslyn, *Clear and to the Point,* pp. 52–59, 127–59; Altman, *Why Most PowerPoint Presentations Suck;* and Munter and Paradi, *Guide to PowerPoint,* pp. 6–12, 61–68.

46. Medina, *Brain Rules,* p. 234.

47. Guy Kawasaki, "The 10/20/30 Rule of PowerPoint," December 30, 2005, accessed February 5, 2010 (http://blog.guykawasaki.com/2005/12/the_102030_rule.html).

48. Duarte, *slide:ology,* p. 152.

49. Kawasaki, "The 10/20/30 Rule of PowerPoint."

50. Adapted from Gallo, *The Presentation Secrets,* p. 202.

51. "Caroline Kennedy Botches Debut Interview with 'You Know' Attitude," *Timesonline,* December 30, 2008, downloaded January 30, 2010 (http://www.timesonline.co.uk/tol/news/world/us_and_americas/article5416006.ece).

52. "How to Say It," seagateteparuk.freetoasthost.com/files/Project4_How_to_Say_It.pdf; http://buzzwhack.com/, both downloaded January 20, 2010.

53. A. Mehrabian, *Silent Messages* (Belmont, CA: Wadsworth, 1971).

54. Mark L. Hickson, Don W. Stacks, and Nina-Jo Moore, *Nonverbal Communication: Studies and Applications,* 4th ed. (Boston, MA: Roxbury Publishing, 2004); "Six Ways to Improve Your Nonverbal Communications," downloaded December 16, 2009 (http://wimvdd.blogspot.com/2006/12/six-ways-to-improve-your-nonverbal.html).

55. Malcolm Gladwell, *Outliers: The Story of Success* (New York: Little, Brown and Company, 2008).

56. Gallo, *The Presentation Secrets,* p. 188.

57. Andrew Dlugen, "Why Practice? Does Practice Make Perfect?" downloaded January 8, 2010 (http://sixminutes.dlugan.com/speech-preparation-8-practice-presentation/).

58. Blair Tindall, "Better Playing Through Chemistry," *New York Times,* October 17, 2004, downloaded January 8, 2010 (http://www.nytimes.com/2004/10/17/arts/music/17tind.html?_r=1&ex=1270785600&en=37bef79604f97228&ei=5090&partner=rssuserland).

59. J. J. Barrell, D. Medeiros, J. E. Barrell, and D. Price, "The Causes and Treatment of Performance Anxiety: An Experimental Approach," *Journal of Humanistic Psychology* 25, no. 2 (1985), pp. 106–22.

60. Ibid.

References for Snapshots, PicProfiles, Captions, PulsePoints, and Pull Quotes

Lexus/Team One Advertising

Mark Miller, associate director, strategic planning, Team One Advertising, interviewed July 9 and October 5, 2002.

PullQuote

Ohio Lottery Segmentation Study: Final Report, Marcus Thomas, LLC, October 2005.

Public Speaking Jitters

Patricia Fripp, CSP, CPAE, award-winning keynote speaker and speech coach, author of *Get What You Want!,* and past president of the National Speakers Association (http://www.fripp.com/).

PullQuote

Chris Gaia, vice president of marketing-travel division, Maritz, "Corporate Meetings and Events Step in the Next Real-Total Virtual Environment," Maritz press release, May 20, 2009, accessed June 11, 2009 (http://www.maritz.com/Press-Releases/2008/InXpo-Release.aspx?intPage=0&Pagesize=10).

PulsePoint

April Savoy, Robert W. Proctor, and Gavriel Salvendy, "Information Retention from PowerPoint™ and Traditional Lectures," *Computers & Education* 52, no. 4 (2009), pp. 858–67, DOI: 10.1016/j.compedu.2008.12.005 (http://www.shockmd.com/2009/03/05/powerpoint-in-education/)

Classic and Contemporary Readings

Aristotle's *Rhetoric,* translated by Rhys Roberts. New York: Random House, 1954.

Atkinson, Cliff. *Beyond Bullet Points.* Redmond, WA: Microsoft Press, 2008.

Duarte, Nancy. *slide:ology:* The Art and Science of Creating Great Presentations. Sebastopol, CA: O'Reilly Media, 2008.

Gallo, Carmine. *The Presentation Secrets of Steve Jobs: How to Be Insanely Great in Front of Any Audience.* New York: McGraw-Hill, 2010.

Kosslyn, Stephen. *Clear and to the Point: 8 Principles for Compelling PowerPoint Presentation.* New York: Oxford Press, 2007.

Leech, Thomas. *How to Prepare, Stage, and Deliver Winning Presentations.* New York: AMACOM, 2004.

Reynolds, Garr. *Presentation Zen: Simple Ideas on Presentation Design and Delivery.* Berkeley, CA: Pearson/New Riders, 2008.

a priori **contrasts** a special class of tests used in conjunction with the *F* test that is specifically designed to test the hypotheses of the experiment or study (in comparison to post hoc or unplanned tests).

accuracy the degree to which bias is absent from the sample—the underestimators and the overestimators are balanced among members of the sample (i.e., no systematic variance).

action research a methodology with brainstorming followed by sequential trial-and-error to discover the most effective solution to a problem; succeeding solutions are tried until the desired results are achieved; used with complex problems about which little is known.

active factors those independent variables (IV) the researcher can manipulate by causing the subject to receive one treatment level or another.

activity analysis see **process analysis**.

administrative question a measurement question that identifies the participant, interviewer, interview location, and conditions (nominal data).

alternative hypothesis (H_A) that a difference exists between the sample parameter and the population statistic to which it is compared; the logical opposite of the null hypothesis used in significance testing.

ambiguities and paradoxes a projective technique (imagination exercise) in which participants imagine a brand applied to a different product (e.g., a Tide dog food or Marlboro cereal), and then describe its attributes and position.

analogy a rhetorical device that compares two different things to highlight a point of similarity.

analysis of variance (ANOVA) tests the null hypothesis that the means of several independent populations are equal; test statistic is the *F* ratio; used when you need *k*-independent-samples tests.

applied research research that addresses existing problems or opportunities.

arbitrary scales universal practice of ad hoc scale development used by instrument designers to create scales that are highly specific to the practice or object being studied.

area chart a graphical presentation that displays total frequency, group frequency, and time series data; a.k.a. *stratum chart* or *surface chart*.

area sampling a cluster sampling technique applied to a population with well-defined political or natural boundaries; population is divided into homogeneous clusters from which a single-stage or multistage sample is drawn.

argument statement that explains, interprets, defends, challenges, or explores meaning.

artifact correlations occur when distinct subgroups in the data combine to give the impression of one.

association the process used to recognize and understand patterns in data and then used to understand and exploit natural patterns.

asymmetrical relationship a relationship in which we postulate that change in one variable (IV) is responsible for change in another variable (DV).

attitude a learned, stable predisposition to respond to oneself, other persons, objects, or issues in a consistently favorable or unfavorable way.

audience characteristics and background of the people or groups for whom the secondary source was created; one of the five factors used to evaluate the value of a secondary source.

audience analysis an analysis of the attendees at a presentation through advance conversations or psychological profiling of age, size, education/knowledge level, experience, gender, diversity, company culture, decision-making roles, and individual attitudes, needs, and motivations.

auditory learners audience members who learn through listening; represent about 20 to 30 percent of the audience; implies the need to include stories and examples in research presentations.

authority the level of data and the credibility of a source as indicated by the credentials of the author and publisher; one of five factors used to evaluate the value of a secondary source.

authority figure a projective technique (imagination exercise) in which participants are asked to imagine that the brand or product is an authority figure and to describe the attributes of the figure.

automatic interaction detection (AID) a data partitioning procedure that searches up to 300 variables for the single best predictor of a dependent variable.

average linkage method evaluates the distance between two clusters by first finding the geometric center of each cluster and then computing distances between the two centers.

backward elimination sequentially removing the variable from a regression model that changes R^2 the least; see also *forward selection* and *stepwise selection*.

balanced rating scale has an equal number of categories above and below the midpoint or an equal number of favorable/unfavorable response choices.

band see **prediction and confidence bands**.

bar chart a graphical presentation technique that represents frequency data as horizontal or vertical bars; vertical bars are most often used for time series and quantitative classifications (histograms, stacked bar, and multiple-variable charts are specialized bar charts).

bar code technology employing labels containing electronically read vertical bar data codes.

basic research see **pure research**.

Bayesian statistics uses subjective probability estimates based on general experience rather than on data collected. (See "Decision Theory Problem" at the Online Learning Center.)

benefit chain see **laddering**.

beta weights standardized regression coefficients in which the size of the number reflects the level of influence *X* exerts on *Y*.

bibliography (bibliographic database) a secondary source that helps locate a book, article, photograph, etc.

bivariate correlation analysis a statistical technique to assess the relationship of two continuous variables measured on an interval or ratio scale.

bivariate normal distribution data are from a random sample in which two variables are normally distributed in a joint manner.

blind when participants do not know if they are being exposed to the experimental treatment.

boxplot an EDA technique; a visual image of the variable's distribution location, spread, shape, tail length, and outliers; a.k.a. *box-and-whisker plot.*

branched question a measurement question sequence determined by the participant's previous answer(s); the answer to one question assumes other questions have been asked or answered and directs the participant to answer specific questions that follow and skip other questions; branched questions determine question sequencing.

brand mapping a projective technique (type of semantic mapping) where participants are presented with different brands and asked to talk about their perceptions, usually in relation to several criteria. They may also be asked to spatially place each brand on one or more semantic maps.

buffer question a neutral measurement question designed chiefly to establish rapport with the participant (usually nominal data).

business intelligence system (BIS) a system of ongoing information collection about events and trends in the technological, economic, political and legal, demographic, cultural, social, and competitive arenas.

business research a systematic inquiry that provides information to guide business decisions; the process of determining, acquiring, analyzing and synthesizing, and disseminating relevant business data, information, and insights to decision makers in ways that mobilize the organization to take appropriate actions that, in turn, maximize organizational performance.

callback procedure involving repeated attempts to make contact with a targeted participant to ensure that the targeted participant is reached and motivated to participate in the study.

cartoons or empty balloons a projective technique where participants are asked to write the dialog for a cartoonlike picture.

case the entity or thing the hypothesis talks about.

case study (case history) a methodology that combines individual and (sometimes) group interviews with record analysis and observation; used to understand events and their ramifications and processes; emphasizes the full contextual analysis of a few events or conditions and their interrelations for a single participant; a type of preexperimental design (one-shot case study).

categorization for this scale type, participants put themselves or property indicants in groups or categories; also, a process for grouping data for any variable into a limited number of categories.

causal-explanatory study a study that is designed to determine whether one or more variables explain the causes or effects of one or more outcome (dependent) variables.

causal hypothesis see **explanatory hypothesis**.

causal-predictive study a study that is designed to predict with regularity how one or more variables cause or affect one or more outcome (dependent) variables to occur.

causal study research that attempts to reveal a causal relationship between variables. (A produces B or causes B to occur.)

causation situation where one variable leads to a specified effect on the other variable.

cell in a cross-tabulation, a subgroup of the data created by the value intersection of two (or more) variables; each cell contains the count of cases as well as the percentage of the joint classification.

census a count of all the elements in a population.

central limit theorem the sample means of repeatedly drawn samples will be distributed around the population mean; for sufficiently large samples (i.e., $n = 30+$), approximates a normal distribution.

central tendency a measure of location, most commonly the mean, median, and mode.

central tendency (error of) an error that results because the participant is reluctant to give extreme judgments, usually due to lack of knowledge.

centroid a term used for the multivariate mean scores in MANOVA.

checklist a measurement question that poses numerous alternatives and encourages multiple unordered responses; see *multiple-choice, multiple-response scale.*

chi-square-based measures tests to detect the strength of the relationship between the variables tested with a chi-square test: phi, Cramer's V, and contingency coefficient C.

chi-square (χ^2) test a test of significance used for nominal and ordinal measurements.

children's panel a series of focus group sessions in which the same child may participate in up to three groups in one year, with each experience several months apart.

chronologic interviewing see **sequential interviewing**.

clarity a design principle that advocates the use of visual techniques that allow the audience to perceive meaning from the location of elements.

classical statistics an objective view of probability in which the hypothesis is rejected, or not, based on the sample data collected.

classification question a measurement question that provides sociological-demographic variables for use in grouping participants' answers (nominal, ordinal, interval, or ratio data).

closed question/response a measurement question that presents the participant with a fixed set of choices (nominal, ordinal, or interval data).

cluster analysis identifies homogeneous subgroups of study objects or participants and then studies the data by these subgroups.

cluster sampling a sampling plan that involves dividing the population into subgroups and then draws a sample from each subgroup, a single-stage or multistage design.

clustering a technique that assigns each data record to a group or segment automatically by clustering algorithms that identify the similar characteristics in the data set and then partition them into groups.

clutter verbal behaviors in a presentation that distract the audience; includes repetition of fillers such as "ah," "um," "you know," or "like."

code of ethics an organization's codified set of norms or standards of behavior that guide moral choices about research behavior; effective codes are regulative, protect the public interest, are behavior-specific, and are enforceable.

codebook the coding rules for assigning numbers or other symbols to each variable; a.k.a. *coding scheme.*

coding assigning numbers or other symbols to responses so that they can be tallied and grouped into a limited number of categories.

coefficient of determination (r^2) the amount of common variance in X and Y, two variables in regression; the ratio of the line of best fit's error over that incurred by using the mean value of Y.

collinearity occurs when two independent variables are highly correlated; causes estimated regression coefficients to fluctuate widely, making interpretation difficult.

communality in factor analysis, the estimate of the variance in each variable that is explained by the factors being studied.

communication approach a study approach involving questioning or surveying people (by personal interview, telephone, mail, computer, or some combination of these) and recording their responses for analysis.

communication study the researcher questions the participants and collects their responses by personal or impersonal means.

comparative scale a scale in which the participant evaluates an object against a standard using a numerical, graphical, or verbal scale.

compatibility a design principle that encourages matching visual techniques that comprise the form of the message to its content and the meaning of that content.

component sorts a projective technique in which participants are presented with flash cards containing component features and asked to create new combinations.

computer-administered telephone survey a telephone survey via voice-synthesized computer questions; data are tallied continuously.

computer-assisted personal interview (CAPI) a personal, face-to-face interview (IDI) with computer-sequenced questions, employing visualization techniques; real-time data entry possible.

computer-assisted self-interview (CASI) computer-delivered survey that is self-administered by the participant.

computer-assisted telephone interview (CATI) a telephone interview with computer-sequenced questions and real-time data entry; usually in a central location with interviewers in acoustically isolated interviewing carrels; data are tallied continuously.

concealment a technique in an observation study in which the observer is shielded from the participant to avoid error caused by observer's presence; this is accomplished by one-way mirrors, hidden cameras, hidden microphones, etc.

concept a bundle of meanings or characteristics associated with certain concrete, unambiguous events, objects, conditions, or situations.

conceptual scheme the interrelationships between concepts and constructs.

concordant when a participant that ranks higher on one ordinal variable also ranks higher on another variable, the pairs of variables are concordant.

confidence interval the combination of interval range and degree of confidence.

confidence level the probability that the results will be correct.

confidentiality a privacy guarantee to retain validity of the research, as well as to protect participants.

confirmatory data analysis an analytical process guided by classical statistical inference in its use of significance and confidence.

confounding variables (CFV) two or more variables that are confounded when their effects on a response variable cannot be distinguished from each other.

conjoint analysis measures complex decision making that requires multiattribute judgments; uses input from nonmetric independent variables to secure part-worths that represent the importance of each aspect of the participant's overall assessment; produces a scale value for each attribute or property.

consensus scaling scale development by a panel of experts evaluating instrument items based on topical relevance and lack of ambiguity.

constant-sum scale the participant allocates points to more than one attribute or property indicant, such that they total to 100 or 10; a.k.a. *fixed-sum scale.*

construct a definition specifically invented to represent an abstract phenomenon for a given research project.

construct validity see **validity, construct**.

content analysis a flexible, widely applicable tool for measuring the semantic content of a communication—including counts, categorizations, associations, interpretations, etc. (e.g., used to study the content of speeches, ads, newspaper and magazine editorials, focus group and IDI transcripts); contains four types of items: syntactical, referential, propositional, and thematic; initial process is done by computer.

content validity see **validity, content**.

contingency coefficient C a measure of association for nominal, nonparametric variables; used with any-size chi-square table, the upper limit varies with table sizes; does not provide direction of the association or reflect causation.

contingency table a cross-tabulation table constructed for statistical testing, with the test determining whether the classification variables are independent.

contrast a design principle that advocates using high-contrast techniques to quickly draw audience attention to the main point.

control the ability to replicate a scenario and dictate a particular outcome; the ability to exclude, isolate, or manipulate the influence of a variable in a study; a critical factor in inference from an experiment, implies that all factors, with the exception of the independent variable (IV), must be held constant and not confounded with another variable that is not part of the study.

control dimension in quota sampling, a descriptor used to define the sample's characteristics (e.g., age, education, religion).

control group a group of participants that is not exposed to the independent variable being studied but still generates a measure for the dependent variable.

control variable a variable introduced to help interpret the relationship between variables.

controlled test market real-time test of a product through arbitrarily selected distribution partners.

controlled vocabulary carefully defined subject hierarchies used to search some bibliographic databases.

convenience sample nonprobability sample in which element selection is based on ease of accessibility.

convenience sampling nonprobability sampling in which researchers use any readily available individuals as participants.

convergent interviewing an IDI technique for interviewing a limited number of experts as participants in a sequential series of IDIs; after each successive interview, the researcher refines the questions, hoping to converge on the central issues in a topic area; sometimes called convergent and divergent interviewing.

correlation the relationship by which two or more variables change together, such that systematic changes in one accompany systematic changes in the other.

correlational hypothesis a statement indicating that variables occur together in some specified manner without implying that one causes the other.

Cramer's *V* a measure of association for nominal, nonparametric variables; used with larger than 2×2 chi-square tables; does not provide direction of the association or reflect causation; ranges from zero to $+1.0$.

creativity session qualitative technique in which an individual activity exercise is followed by a sharing/discussion session, in which participants build on one another's creative ideas; often used with children; may be conducted before or during IDIs or group interviews; usually consists of drawing, visual compilation, or writing exercises.

criterion-related validity see **validity, criterion-related**.

criterion variable see **dependent variable**.

critical incident technique an IDI technique involving sequentially asked questions to reveal, in narrative form, what led up to an incident being studied; exactly what the observed party did or did not do that was especially effective or ineffective; the outcome or result of this action; and why this action was effective or what more effective action might have been expected.

critical path method (CPM) a scheduling tool for complex or large research proposals that cites milestones and time involved between milestones.

critical value the dividing point(s) between the region of acceptance and the region of rejection; these values can be computed in terms of the standardized random variable due to the normal distribution of sample means.

cross-sectional study the study is conducted only once and reveals a snapshot of one point in time.

cross-tabulation a technique for comparing data from two or more categorical variables.

cultural interview an IDI technique that asks a participant to relate his or her experiences with a culture or subculture, including the knowledge passed on by prior generations and the knowledge participants have or plan to pass on to future generations.

cumulative scale a scale development technique in which scale items are tested based on a scoring system, and agreement with one extreme scale item results also in endorsement of all other items that take a less extreme position.

custom-designed measurement questions measurement questions formulated specifically for a particular research project.

custom researcher crafts a research design unique to the decision maker's dilemma.

data information (attitudes, behavior, motivations, attributes, etc.) collected from participants or observations (mechanical or direct) or from secondary sources.

data analysis the process of editing and reducing accumulated data to a manageable size, developing summaries, looking for patterns, and applying statistical techniques.

data case see **record**.

data entry the process of converting information gathered by secondary or primary methods to a medium for viewing and manipulation; usually done by keyboarding or optical scanning.

data field a single element of data from all participants in a study.

data file a set of data records (all responses from all participants in a study).

data mart intermediate storage facility that compiles locally required information.

data mining applying mathematical models to extract meaningful knowledge from volumes of data contained within internal data marts or data warehouses; purpose is to identify valid, novel, useful, and ultimately understandable patterns in data.

data preparation the processes that ensure the accuracy of data and their conversion from raw form into categories appropriate for analysis; includes editing, coding, and data entry.

data visualization the process of viewing aggregate data on multiple dimensions to gain a deeper, intuitive understanding of the data.

data warehouse electronic storehouse where vast arrays of collected integrated data are stored by categories to facilitate retrieval, interpretation, and sorting by data-mining techniques.

database a collection of data organized for computerized retrieval; defines data fields, data records, and data files.

debriefing explains the truth to participants and describes the major goals of the research study and the reasons for using deception.

deception occurs when participants are told only part of the truth or the truth is fully compromised to prevent biasing participants or to protect sponsor confidentiality.

decision rule the criterion for judging the attractiveness of two or more alternatives when using a decision variable.

decision support system (DSS) numerous elements of data organized for retrieval and use in decision making.

decision variable a quantifiable characteristic, attribute, or outcome on which a choice decision will be made.

deduction a form of reasoning in which the conclusion must necessarily follow from the reasons given; a deduction is valid if it is impossible for the conclusion to be false if the premises are true.

demonstration presentation support technique using a visual presentation aid to show how something works.

dependency techniques those techniques in which criterion or dependent variables and predictor or independent variables are present (e.g., multiple regression, MANOVA, discriminant analysis).

dependent variable (DV) the variable measured, predicted, or otherwise monitored by the researcher; expected to be affected by a manipulation of the independent variable; a.k.a. *criterion variable*.

descriptive hypothesis states the existence, size, form, or distribution of some variable.

descriptive statistics display characteristics of the location, spread, and shape of a data array.

descriptive study attempts to describe or define a subject, often by creating a profile of a group of problems, people, or events, through the collection of data and the tabulation of the frequencies on research variables or their interaction; the study reveals who, what, when, where, or how much; the study concerns a univariate question or hypothesis in which the research asks about or states something about the size, form, distribution, or existence of a variable.

deviation scores displays distance of an observation from the mean.

dichotomous question a measurement question that offers two mutually exclusive and exhaustive alternatives (nominal data).

dictionary secondary source that defines words, terms, or jargon unique to a discipline; may include information on people, events, or organizations that shape the discipline; an excellent source of acronyms.

direct observation occurs when the observer is physically present and personally monitors and records the behavior of the participant.

directory a reference source used to identify contact information (e.g., name, address, phone); many are free, but the most comprehensive are proprietary.

discordant when a subject that ranks higher on one ordinal variable ranks lower on another variable, the pairs of variables are discordant; as discordant pairs increase over concordant pairs, the association becomes negative.

discriminant analysis a technique using two or more independent interval or ratio variables to classify the observations in the categories of a nominal dependent variable.

discussion guide the list of topics to be discussed in an unstructured interview (e.g., focus group); a.k.a. *interview guide*.

disguised question a measurement question designed to conceal the question's and study's true purpose.

disk-by-mail (DBM) survey a type of computer-assisted self-interview, in which the survey and its management software, on computer disk, are delivered by mail to the participant.

disproportionate sampling see **stratified sampling, disproportionate**.

distribution (of data) the array of value counts from lowest to highest value, resulting from the tabulation of incidence for each variable by value.

"don't know" (DK) response a response given when a participant has insufficient knowledge, direction, or willingness to answer a question.

double-barreled question a measurement question that includes two or more questions in one that the participant might need to answer differently; a question that requests so much content that it would be better if separate questions were asked.

double blind study design in which neither the researcher nor the participant knows when a subject is being exposed to the experimental treatment.

double sampling a procedure for selecting a subsample from a sample; a.k.a. *sequential sampling or multiphase sampling*.

"dummy" table displays data one expects to secure during data analysis; each dummy table is a cross-tabulation between two or more variables.

dummy variable nominal variables converted for use in multivariate statistics; coded 0, 1, as all other variables must be interval or ratio measures.

dyad (paired interview) a group interview done in pairs (e.g., best friends, spouses, superior-subordinate, strangers); used often with children.

EDA see **exploratory data analysis**.

editing a process for detecting errors and data omissions and correcting them when possible; certifies that minimum data quality standards are met.

eigenvalue proportion of total variance in all the variables that is accounted for by a factor.

electronic test market test that combines store distribution, consumer scanner panel data, and household-level media delivery.

empiricism observations and propositions based on sense experience and/or derived from such experience by methods of inductive logic, including mathematics and statistics.

encyclopedia a secondary source that provides background or historical information on a topic, including names or terms that can enhance your search results in other sources.

enthymeme a truncated syllogism where one or more minor premises are left unstated. The presenter gives the primary premise and assumes that the audience will supply the missing knowledge in order to reach the conclusion.

environmental control holding constant the physical environment of the experiment.

equal-appearing interval scale an expensive, time-consuming type of consensus scaling that results in an interval rating scale for attitude measurement; a.k.a. *Thurstone scale*.

equivalence when an instrument secures consistent results with repeated measures by the same investigator or different samples.

error discrepancy between the sample value and the true population value that occurs when the participant fails to answer fully and accurately—either by choice or because of inaccurate or incomplete knowledge.

error of central tendency see **central tendency (error of)**.

error of leniency see **leniency (error of)**.

error term the deviations of the actual values of Y from the regression line (representing the mean value of Y for a particular value of X).

ethics norms or standards of behavior that guide moral choices about research behavior.

ethnographic research see **ethnography**.

ethnography interviewer and participant collaborate in a field-setting participant observation and unstructured interview; typically takes place where the behavior being observed occurs (e.g., participant's home).

ethos how well the audience believes that the presenter is qualified to speak on the particular subject; determined by the perception of a presenter's character, his or her past experience, or the credibility and experience of those the presenter evokes.

event sampling the process of selecting some elements or behavioral acts or conditions from a population of observable behaviors or conditions to represent the population as a whole.

ex post facto design after-the-fact report on what happened to the measured variable.

example a true or hypothetical instance used to a clarify complex idea.

executive summary (final report) this document is written as the last element of a research report and either is a concise summary of the major findings, conclusions, and recommendations or is a report in miniature, covering all aspects in abbreviated form.

executive summary (proposal) an informative abstract providing the essentials of the proposal without the details.

experience survey (expert interview) semistructured or unstructured interviews with experts on a topic or dimension of a topic; an exploratory technique in which knowledgeable experts share their ideas about important issues or aspects of the subject and relate what is important across the subject's range of experience; usually involves a personal or phone interview.

experiment (experimental study) study involving intervention (manipulation of one or more variables) by the researcher beyond that required for measurement to determine the effect on another variable.

experimental treatment the manipulated independent variable.

expert group interview group interview consisting of individuals exceptionally knowledgeable about the issues or topics to be discussed.

expert interview a discussion with someone knowledgeable about the problem or its possible solutions.

expert opinion (testimony) opinions of recognized experts who possess credibility for your audience on a topic; used as support or proof.

explanatory (causal) hypothesis a statement that describes a relationship between two variables in which one variable leads to a specified effect on the other variable.

explanatory study attempts to explain an event, act, or characteristic measured by research.

explicit attitude an expressed positive or negative evaluation.

exploration the process of collecting information to formulate or refine management, research, investigative, or measurement questions; loosely structured studies that discover future research tasks, including developing concepts, establishing priorities, developing operational definitions, and improving research design; a phase of a research project where the researcher expands understanding of the management dilemma, looks for ways others have addressed and/or solved problems similar to the management dilemma or management question, and gathers background information on the topic to refine the research question; a.k.a. *exploratory study* or *exploratory research*.

exploratory data analysis (EDA) patterns in the collected data guide the data analysis or suggest revisions to the preliminary data analysis plan.

exploratory research see **exploration**.

exploratory study see **exploration**.

exposition statement that describes without attempting to explain.

extemporaneous presentation an audience-centered, preplanned speech made from minimal notes; generates a presentation that is natural, conversational, and flexible to audience interests.

external validity occurs when an observed causal relationship can be generalized across persons, settings, and times.

extralinguistic behavior the vocal, temporal, interactive, and verbal stylistic behaviors of human participants.

extraneous variable (EV) variable to assume (because it has little effect or its impact is randomized) or exclude from a research study.

extranet a private network that uses the Internet protocols and the public telecommunication system to share a business's information, data, or operations with external suppliers, vendors, or customers.

eye contact a meeting of the eyes between two people that expresses meaningful nonverbal communication revealing concern, warmth, and authenticity.

F **ratio** *F* test statistic comparing measurements of *k* independent samples.

fact a piece of information about a situation that exists or an event known to have occurred; it takes the form of a statement about verifiable data that support the presenter's argument.

factor denotes an independent variable (IV) in an experiment; factors are divided into treatment levels for the experiment.

factor analysis a technique for discovering patterns among the variables to determine if an underlying combination of the original variables (a factor) can summarize the original set.

factor scales types of scales that deal with multidimensional content and underlying dimensions, such as scalogram, factor, and cluster analyses, and metric and nonmetric multidimensional scaling.

factors in factor analysis, the result of transforming a set of variables into a new set of composite variables; these factors are linear and not correlated with each other.

field conditions the actual environmental conditions in which the dependent variable occurs.

field experiment a study of the dependent variable in actual environmental conditions.

filter question see **screen question**.

findings nondisclosure a type of confidentiality; the sponsor restricts the researcher from discussing the findings of the research project.

five-number summary the median, the upper and lower quartiles, and the largest and smallest observations of a variable's distribution.

fixed-sum scale see **constant-sum scale**.

flow aids a design principle that provides a visual aid that reveals to the audience where the presenter is within the overall presentation.

focus group the simultaneous involvement of a small number of research participants (usually 8 to 10) who interact at the direction of a moderator in order to generate data on a particular issue or topic; widely used in exploratory studies; usually lasts 90 minutes to two hours; can be conducted in person or via phone or videoconference.

forced-choice rating scale requires that participants select from available alternatives.

forced ranking scale a scale in which the participant orders several objects or properties of objects; faster than paired comparison to obtain a rank order.

formal study research question–driven process involving precise procedures for data collection and interpretation; tests the hypothesis or answers the research questions posed.

format how the information is presented and how easy it is to find a specific piece of information within a secondary source; one of five factors used to evaluate the value of a secondary source.

forward selection in modeling and regression, sequentially adds the variables to a regression model that results in the largest R^2 increase; see also *backward elimination and stepwise selection.*

free-response question a measurement question in which the participant chooses the words to frame the answer; a.k.a. *open ended question* (nominal, ordinal, or ratio data).

frequency distribution ordered array of all values for a variable.

frequency table arrays category codes from lowest value to highest value, with columns for count, percent, valid percent, and cumulative percent.

full-service researchers a firm with both quantitative and qualitative methodology expertise that conducts all phases of research from planning to insight development, often serving as both research firm and consultant.

funnel approach a type of question sequencing that moves the participant from general to more specific questions and is designed to learn the participant's frame of reference while extracting full disclosure of information on the topic (nominal, ordinal, interval, or ratio data).

gamma (γ) uses a preponderance of evidence of concordant pairs versus discordant pairs to predict association; the gamma value is the proportional reduction of error when prediction is done using preponderance of evidence (values from -1.0 to $+1.0$).

geographic chart uses a map to show regional variations in data.

gestures a form of nonverbal communication made with a part of the body, used instead of or in combination with verbal communication; allows presenters to express a variety of feelings and thoughts, positive and negative.

goodness of fit a measure of how well the regression model is able to predict Y.

graphic rating scale a scale in which the participant places his or her response along a line or continuum; the score or measurement is its distance in millimeters from either endpoint.

grounded theory an IDI technique in which analysis of the data takes place simultaneously with its collection, with the purpose of developing general concepts or theories with which to analyze the data.

group interview a data collection method using a single interviewer who simultaneously interviews more than one research participant.

halo effect error caused when prior observations influence perceptions of current observations.

handbook a secondary source used to identify key terms, people, or events relevant to the management dilemma or management question.

heterogeneous group participant group consisting of individuals with a variety of opinions, backgrounds, and actions relative to a topic.

histogram a graphical bar chart that groups continuous data values into equal intervals with one bar for each interval; especially useful for revealing skewness, kurtosis, and modal pattern.

holdout sample the portion of the sample (usually ⅓ or ¼) excluded for later validity testing when the estimating question is first computed; the equation is then used on the holdout data to calculate R^2 for comparison.

homogeneous group participant group consisting of individuals with similar opinions, backgrounds, and actions relative to a topic.

hypothesis a proposition formulated for empirical testing; a tentative descriptive statement that describes the relationship between two or more variables.

hypothetical construct construct inferred only from data; its presumption must be tested.

ill-defined problem one that addresses complex issues and cannot be expressed easily, concisely, or completely.

imaginary universe a projective technique (imagination exercise) in which participants are asked to assume that the brand and its users populate an entire universe; they then describe the features of this new world.

imagination exercises a projective technique in which participants are asked to relate the properties of one thing/person/brand to another.

implicit attitude an attitude about one object that influences the attitude about other objects.

impromptu speaking a speech that does not involve preparation, and evolves spontaneously in response to some stimulus, such as a question.

incidence the number of elements in the population belonging to the category of interest, divided by the total number of elements in the population.

independent variable (IV) the variable manipulated by the researcher, thereby causing an effect or change on the dependent variable.

index secondary data source that helps identify and locate a single book, journal article, author, etc., from among a large set.

indirect observation occurs when the recording of data is done by mechanical, photographic, or electronic means.

individual depth interview (IDI) a type of interview that encourages the participant to talk extensively, sharing as much information as possible; usually lasts one or more hours; three types: structured, semistructured, and unstructured.

induction (inductive reasoning) to draw a conclusion from one or more particular facts or pieces of evidence; the conclusion explains the facts.

inferential statistics includes the estimation of population values and the testing of statistical hypotheses.

informed consent participant gives full consent to participation after receiving full disclosure of the procedures of the proposed survey.

interaction effect the influence that one factor has on another factor.

intercept (β_0) one of two regression coefficients; the value for the linear function when it crosses the Y axis or the estimate of Y when X is zero.

intercept interview a face-to-face communication that targets participants in a centralized location.

interdependency techniques techniques in which criterion or dependent variables and predictor or independent variables are not present (e.g., factor analysis, cluster analysis, multi-dimensional scaling).

internal consistency characteristic of an instrument in which the items are homogeneous; measure of reliability.

internal database collection of data stored by an organization.

internal validity the ability of a research instrument to measure what it is purported to measure; occurs when the conclusion(s) drawn about a demonstrated experimental relationship truly implies cause.

interquartile range (IQR) measures the distance between the first and third quartiles of a data distribution; a.k.a. *midspread*; the distance between the hinges in a boxplot.

interval estimate range of values within which the true population parameter is expected to fall.

interval scale scale with the properties of order and equal distance between points and with mutually exclusive and exhaustive categories; data that incorporate equality of interval (the distance between one measure and the next measure); e.g., temperature scale.

intervening variable (IVV) a factor that affects the observed phenomenon but cannot be seen, measured, or manipulated; thus its effect must be inferred from the effects of the independent and moderating variables on the dependent variable.

interview phone, in-person, or videoconference communication approach to collecting data.

interview guide see **discussion guide**.

interview schedule question list used to guide a structured interview; a.k.a. *questionnaire*.

interviewer error error that results from interviewer influence of the participant; includes problems with motivation, instructions, voice inflections, body language, question or response order, or cheating via falsification of one or more responses.

intranet a private network that is contained within an enterprise; access is restricted to authorized audiences; usually behind a security firewall.

investigative questions questions the researcher must answer to satisfactorily answer the research question; what the manager feels he or she needs to know to arrive at a conclusion about the management dilemma.

item analysis scale development in which instrument designers develop instrument items and test them with a group of participants to determine which highly discriminate between high and low raters.

jargon language unique to a profession or discipline; when unknown by the audience can reduce the clarity of the message.

judgment sampling a purposive sampling in which the researcher arbitrarily selects sample units to conform to some criterion.

k-independent-samples tests significance tests in which measurements are taken from three or more samples (ANOVA for interval or ratio measures, Kruskal-Wallis for ordinal measures, chi-square for nominal measures).

k-related-samples tests compares measurements from more than two groups from the same sample or more than two measures from the same subject or participant (ANOVA for interval or ratio measures, Friedman for ordinal measures, Cochran Q for nominal measures).

kinesics the study of the use of body motion communication.

kinesthetic learners people who learn by doing, moving, and touching.

kurtosis measure of a data distribution's peakedness or flatness (ku); a neutral distribution has a ku of 0, a flat distribution is negative, and a peaked distribution is positive.

laboratory conditions studies that occur under conditions that do not simulate actual environmental conditions.

laddering (benefit chain) a projective technique in which participants are asked to link functional features to their physical and psychological benefits, both real and ideal.

lambda (λ) a measure of how well the frequencies of one nominal variable predict the frequencies of another variable; values (vary between zero and 1.0) show the direction of the association.

leading question a measurement question whose wording suggests to the participant the desired answer (nominal, ordinal, interval, or ratio data).

leniency (error of) a participant, within a series of evaluations, consistently expresses judgments at one end of a scale; an error that results when the participant is consistently an easy rater.

letter of transmittal the element of the final report that provides the purpose of, scope of, authorization for, and limitations of the study; not necessary for internal projects.

level of significance the probability of rejecting a true null hypothesis.

life history an IDI technique that extracts from a single participant memories and experiences from childhood to the present day regarding a product or service category, brand, or firm.

Likert scale a variation of the summated rating scale, this scale asks a rater to agree or disagree with statements that express either favorable or unfavorable attitudes toward the object. The strength of attitude is reflected in the assigned score, and individual scores may be totaled for an overall attitude measure.

limiters database search protocol for narrowing a search; commonly include date, publication type, and language.

line graph a statistical presentation technique used for time series and frequency distributions over time.

linearity an assumption of correlation analysis, that the collection of data can be described by a straight line passing through the data array.

linguistic behavior the human verbal behavior during conversation, presentation, or interaction.

literature review recent or historically significant research studies, company data, or industry reports that act as the basis for the proposed study.

literature search a review of books, articles in journals or professional literature, research studies, and Web-published materials that relate to the management dilemma, management question, or research question.

loadings in principal components analysis, the correlation coefficients that estimate the strength of the variables that compose the factor.

logos the logical argument; requires supporting evidence and analytical techniques that reveal and uphold the researcher's findings and conclusions.

longitudinal study the study includes repeated measures over an extended period of time, tracking changes in variables over time; includes panels or cohort groups.

mail survey a relatively low-cost self-administered study both delivered and returned via mail.

main effect the average direct influence that a particular treatment of the IV has on the DV independent of other factors.

management dilemma the problem or opportunity that requires a decision; a symptom of a problem or an early indication of an opportunity.

management question the management dilemma restated in question format; categorized as "choice of objectives," "generation and evaluation of solutions," or "troubleshooting or control of a situation."

management report a report written for the nontechnically oriented manager or client.

management–research question hierarchy process of sequential question formulation that leads a manager or researcher from management dilemma to measurement questions.

manuscript reading the verbatim reading of a fully written presentation.

mapping rules a scheme for assigning numbers to aspects of an empirical event.

marginal(s) a term for the column and row totals in a cross-tabulation.

matching a process analogous to quota sampling for assigning participants to experimental and control groups by having participants match every descriptive characteristic used in the research; used when random assignment is not possible; an attempt to eliminate the effect of confounding variables that group participants so that the confounding variable is present proportionally in each group.

MDS see **multidimensional scaling**.

mean the arithmetic average of a data distribution.

mean square the variance computed as an average or mean.

measurement assigning numbers to empirical events in compliance with a mapping rule.

measurement questions the questions asked of the participants or the observations that must be recorded.

measures of location term for measure of central tendency in a distribution of data; see also *central tendency*.

measures of shape statistics that describe departures from the symmetry of a distribution; a.k.a. *moments, skewness*, and *kurtosis*.

measures of spread statistics that describe how scores cluster or scatter in a distribution; a.k.a. *dispersion* or *variability* (variance, standard deviation, range, interquartile range, and quartile deviation).

median the midpoint of a data distribution where half the cases fall above and half the cases fall below.

memorization the act of committing to memory all details of a presentation.

metaphor a figure of speech in which an implicit comparison is made between two unlike things that actually have something important in common.

metaphor elicitation technique an individual depth interview that reveals participants' hidden or suppressed attitudes and perceptions by having them explain collected images and each image's relation to the topic being studied.

method of least squares a procedure for finding a regression line that keeps errors (deviations from actual value to the line value) to a minimum.

metric measures statistical techniques using interval and ratio measures.

mini-group a group interview involving two to six people.

missing data information that is missing about a participant or data record; should be discovered and rectified during data preparation phase of analysis; e.g., miscoded data, out-of-range data, or extreme values.

mode the most frequently occurring value in a data distribution; data may have more than one mode.

model a representation of a system that is constructed to study some aspect of that system or the system as a whole.

moderating variable (MV) a second independent variable, believed to have a significant contributory or contingent effect on the originally stated IV-DV relationship.

moderator a trained interviewer used for group interviews such as focus groups.

monitoring a classification of data collection that includes observation studies and data mining of organizational databases.

motivated sequence a presentation planning approach that involves the ordering of ideas to follow the normal processes of human thinking; motivates an audience to respond to the presenter's purpose.

multicollinearity occurs when more than two independent variables are highly correlated.

multidimensional scale a scale that seeks to simultaneously measure more than one attribute of the participant or object.

multidimensional scaling (MDS) a scaling technique to simultaneously measure more than one attribute of the participant or object; results are usually mapped; develops a geometric picture or map of the locations of some objects relative to others on various dimensions or properties; especially useful for difficult-to-measure constructs.

multiphase sampling see **double sampling**.

multiple-choice, multiple-response scale a scale that offers the participant multiple options and solicits one or more answers (nominal or ordinal data); a.k.a. *checklist*.

multiple-choice question a measurement question that offers more than two category responses but seeks a single answer.

multiple-choice, single-response scale a scale that poses more than two category responses but seeks a single answer, or one that seeks a single rating from a gradation of preference, interest, or agreement (nominal or ordinal data); a.k.a. *multiple-choice question*.

multiple comparison tests compare group means following the finding of a statistically significant *F* test.

multiple rating list scale a single interval or ordinal numerical scale where raters respond to a series of objects; results facilitate visualization.

multiple regression a statistical tool used to develop a self-weighting estimating equation that predicts values for a dependent variable from the values of independent variables; controls confounding variables to better evaluate the contribution of other variables; tests and explains a causal theory.

multivariate analysis statistical techniques that focus upon and bring out in bold relief the structure of simultaneous relationships among three or more phenomena.

multivariate analysis of variance (MANOVA) assesses the relationship between two or more dependent variables and classificatory variables or factors; frequently used to test differences among related samples.

narrative see **oral history**.

narrative pattern a presentation organizational pattern that involves the use of stories as the primary vehicle for communicating the presenter's message.

negative leniency (error of) an error that results when the participant is consistently a hard or critical rater.

nominal scale scale with mutually exclusive and collectively exhaustive categories, but without the properties of order, distance, or unique origin.

noncontact rate ratio of noncontacts (no answer, busy, answering machine, and disconnects) to all potential contacts.

nondisclosure various types of confidentiality involving research projects, including sponsor, findings, and purpose nondisclosures.

nonexpert group participants in a group interview who have at least some desired information but at an unknown level.

nonmetric measures statistical techniques using ordinal and nominal measures (nonparametric).

nonparametric tests significance tests for data derived from nominal and ordinal scales.

nonprobability sampling an arbitrary and subjective procedure in which each population element does not have a known nonzero chance of being included; no attempt is made to generate a statistically representative sample.

nonresistant statistics a statistical measure that is susceptible to the effects of extreme values; e.g., mean, standard deviation.

nonresponse error error that develops when an interviewer cannot locate the person with whom the study requires communication or when the targeted participant refuses to participate; especially troublesome in studies using probability sampling.

nonverbal behavior human behaviors not related to conversation (e.g., body movement, facial expressions, exchanged glances, eyeblinks).

nonverbal communication meaning conveyed through other than verbal means; encompasses clothing and bodily characteristics, physical environment (physical space and time), movement and body position (including kinesics, posture, gesture, touch), eye gaze, and paralanguage (nonverbal cues of the voice).

nonverbal observation observation of human behavior without the use of conversation between observers and participants.

normal distribution a frequency distribution of many natural phenomena; graphically shaped like a symmetrical curve.

normal probability plot compares the observed values with those expected from a normal distribution.

null hypothesis (H_0) assumption that no difference exists between the sample parameter and the population statistic.

numerical scale a scale in which equal intervals separate the numeric scale points, while verbal anchors serve as labels for the extreme points.

objects concepts defined by ordinary experience.

observation the full range of monitoring behavioral and nonbehavioral activities and conditions (including record analysis, physical condition analysis, physical process analysis, nonverbal analysis, linguistic analysis, extralinguistic analysis, and spatial analysis).

observation checklist a measurement instrument for recording data in an observation study; analogous to a questionnaire in a communication study.

observation playgroup an observation technique that involves observing children at play, often with targeted objects (toys or materials); observers are usually behind one-way mirrors.

observation study a monitoring approach to collecting data in which the researcher inspects the activities of a subject or the nature of some material without attempting to elicit responses from anyone; a.k.a. *monitoring*.

observed significance level the probability value compared to the significance level (e.g., .05) chosen for testing and on this basis the null hypothesis is either rejected or not rejected.

observer drift a source of error affecting categorization caused by decay in reliability or validity of recorded observations over time.

OCR see **optical character recognition**.

omnibus researcher fields research studies, often by survey, at regular, predetermined intervals.

omnibus study combines the questions of several decision makers who need information from the same population.

one-sample tests tests that involve measures taken from a single sample compared to a specified population.

one-tailed test a test of a null hypothesis that assumes the sample parameter is not the same as the population statistic, but that the difference is in only one direction.

online focus group a type of focus group in which participants use the technology of the Internet, including e-mail, websites, Usenet newsgroups, or an Internet chat room, to approximate the interaction of a face-to-face focus group.

open-ended question see **free-response question**.

operational definition a definition for a variable stated in terms of specific testing criteria or operations, specifying what must be counted, measured, or gathered through our senses.

operationalized the process of transforming concepts and constructs into measurable variables suitable for testing.

optical character recognition (OCR) software programs that transfer printed text into a computer file in order to edit and use the information without rekeying the data.

optical mark recognition (OMR) software that uses a spreadsheet-style interface to read and process data from user-created forms.

optical scanning a data entry process whereby answers are recorded on computer-readable forms and then scanned to form a data record; reduces data handling and the errors that accompany such data handling.

oral history (narrative) an IDI technique that asks participants to relate their personal experiences and feelings related to historical events or past behavior.

ordinal measures measures of association between variables generating ordinal data.

ordinal scale scale with mutually exclusive and collectively exhaustive categories, as well as the property of order, but not distance or unique origin; data capable of determining greater-than, equal-to, or less-than status of a property or an object.

outliers data points that exceed $+1.5$ the interquartile range (IQR).

p **value** probability of observing a sample value as extreme as, or more extreme than, the value actually observed, given that the null hypothesis is true.

pace the rate at which the printed page presents information to the reader; it should be slower when the material is complex, faster when the material is straightforward.

paired-comparison scale the participant chooses a preferred object between several pairs of objects on some property; results in a rank ordering of objects.

paired interview see **dyad**.

panel a group of potential participants who have indicated a willingness to participate in research studies; often used for longitudinal communication studies; may be used for both qualitative and quantitative research.

paralanguage nonverbal communication that includes such vocal elements as tone, pitch, rhythm, pause, timbre, loudness, and inflection.

parametric tests significance tests for data from interval and ratio scales.

Pareto diagram a graphical presentation that represents frequency data as a bar chart, ordered from most to least, overlaid with a line graph denoting the cumulative percentage at each variable level.

participant the subject, respondent, or sample element in a research study.

participant-initiated response error error that occurs when the participant fails to answer fully and accurately—either by choice or because of inaccurate or incomplete knowledge.

participant observation when the observer is physically involved in the research situation and interacts with the participant to influence some observation measures.

participants' perceptual awareness the subtle or major changes that occur in participants' responses when they perceive that a research study is being conducted.

path analysis describes through regression an entire structure of linkages that have been advanced by a causal theory.

path diagram presents predictive and associative relationships among constructs and indicators in a structural model.

pathos an appeal to an audience's sense of identity, self-interest, and emotions, which relies on an emotional connection between the presenter and his or her audience.

Pearson correlation coefficient the *r* symbolizes the estimate of strength of linear association and its direction between interval and ratio variables; based on sampling data and varies over a range of $+1$ to -1; the prefix $(+, -)$ indicates the direction of the relationship (positive or inverse), while the number represents the strength of the relationship (the closer to 1, the stronger the relationship; $0 =$ no relationship); and the *p* represents the population correlation.

performance anxiety (stage fright) a fear produced by the need to make a presentation in front of an audience or before a camera.

permission surveying the act of surveying prospects or customers who have given permission for such engagement, usually through panel membership.

personification a projective technique (imagination exercise) in which participants are asked to imagine inanimate objects with the traits, characteristics and features, and personalities of humans.

phi (ϕ) a measure of association for nominal, nonparametric variables; ranges from zero to $+1.0$ and is used best with 2×2 chi-square tables; does not provide direction of the association or reflect causation.

photographic framing the practice of creating a focal point for all visuals used in presentations.

physical condition analysis the recording of observations of current conditions resulting from prior decisions; includes inventory, signs, obstacles or hazards, cleanliness, etc.

physical trace a type of observation that collects measures of wear data (erosion) and accretion data (deposit) rather than direct observation (e.g., a study of trash).

pictograph a bar chart using pictorial symbols rather than bars to represent frequency data; the symbol has an association with the subject of the statistical presentation and one symbol unit represents a specific count of that variable.

pie chart uses sections of a circle (slices of a pie) to represent 100 percent of a frequency distribution of the subject being graphed; not appropriate for changes over time.

pilot test a trial collection of data to detect weaknesses in design and instrumentation and provide proxy data for selection of a probability sample; see also *pretesting*.

point estimate sample mean; our best predictor of the unknown population mean.

population the elements about which we wish to make some inferences.

population element the individual participant or object on which the measurement is taken; a.k.a. *population unit, sample element, sample unit*.

population parameter a summary descriptor of a variable of interest in the population; e.g., incidence, mean, variance.

population proportion of incidence the number of category elements in the population, divided by the number of elements in the population.

portal a Web page that serves as a gateway to more remote Web publications; usually includes one or more directories, search engines, and other user features such as news and weather.

posture and body orientation communication of nonverbal messages by the way you walk and stand.

power of the test 1 minus the probability of committing a Type II error (1 minus the probability that we will correctly reject the false null hypothesis).

practical significance when a statistically significant difference has real importance to the decision maker.

practicality a characteristic of sound measurement concerned with a wide range of factors of economy, convenience, and interpretability.

PRE see **proportional reduction in error**.

precision one of the considerations in determining sample validity: the degree to which estimates from the sample reflect the measure taken by a census; measured by the standard error of the estimate—the smaller the error, the greater the precision of the estimate.

precoding assigning codebook codes to variables in a study and recording them on the questionnaire; eliminates a separate coding sheet.

predesigned measurement questions questions that have been formulated and tested by previous researchers, are recorded in the literature, and may be applied literally or be adapted for the project at hand.

prediction and confidence bands bow-tie-shaped confidence intervals around a predictor; predictors farther from the mean have larger bandwidths in regression analysis.

predictive study is used to determine if a relationship exists between two or more variables. When causation is established, one variable can be used to predict the other. In business research, studies conducted to evaluate specific courses of action or to forecast current or future values.

predictor variable see **independent variable**.

pretasking a variety of creative and mental exercises to prepare participants for individual or group interviews, such as an IDI or focus group; intended to increase understanding of participants' own thought processes and bring their ideas, opinions, and attitudes to the surface.

pretesting the assessment of questions and instruments before the start of a study; an established practice for discovering errors in questions, question sequencing, instructions, skip directions, etc.; see also *pilot test*.

primacy effect order bias in which the participant tends to choose the first alternative; a principle affecting presentation organization in which the first item in a list is initially distinguished as important and may be transferred to long-term memory; implies an important argument should be first in your presentation.

primary data data the researcher collects to address the specific problem at hand—the research question.

primary sources original works of research or raw data without interpretation or pronouncements that represent an official opinion or position; include memos, letters, complete interviews or speeches, laws, regulations, court decisions, and most government data, including census, economic, and labor data; the most authoritative of all sources.

principal components analysis one method of factor analysis that transforms a set of variables into a new set of composite variables; these variables are linear and not correlated with each other; see also *factor analysis*.

principle of appropriate knowledge only information compatible with your audience's knowledge level should be used in a presentation.

principle of capacity limitations the audience cannot process large amounts of information at one time.

principle of discriminability two properties must differ by a large amount for the difference to be discerned by your audience.

principle of informative changes your audience will expect anything you speak about, demonstrate, or show in your presentation to convey important information.

principle of perceptual organization your audience will automatically group items together, even if you don't give them such groupings; this facilitates their absorbing and storing large amounts of information.

principle of relevance only information critical to understanding should be presented.

principle of salience your audience's attention is drawn to large perceptible differences.

probability sampling a controlled, randomized procedure that ensures that each population element is given a known non-zero chance of selection; used to draw participants that are representative of a target population; necessary for projecting findings from the sample to the target population.

probing techniques for stimulating participants to answer more fully and relevantly to posed questions.

process (activity) analysis observation by a time study of stages in a process, evaluated on both effectiveness and efficiency; includes traffic flow within distribution centers and retailers, paperwork flow, customer complaint resolution, etc.

project management the process of planning and managing a detailed project, through tables and charts with detail responsibilities and deadlines; details relationship between researchers, their assistants, sponsors, and suppliers; often results in a Gantt chart.

projective techniques qualitative methods that encourage the participant to reveal hidden or suppressed attitudes, ideas, emotions, and motives; various techniques (e.g., sentence completion tests, cartoon or balloon tests, word association tests) used as part of an interview to disguise the study objective and allow the participant to transfer or project attitudes and behavior on sensitive subjects to third parties; the data collected via these techniques are often difficult to interpret (nominal, ordinal, or ratio data).

properties characteristics of objects that are measured; a person's properties are his or her weight, height, posture, hair color, etc.

proportion percentage of elements in the distribution that meet a criterion.

proportional reduction in error (PRE) measures of association used with contingency tables (a.k.a *cross-tabulations*) to predict frequencies.

proportionate sampling see **stratified sampling, proportionate**.

proposal a work plan, prospectus, outline, statement of intent, or draft plan for a research project, including proposed budget.

proposition a statement about concepts that may be judged as true or false if it refers to observable phenomena.

proprietary methodology a research program or technique that is owned by a single firm; may be branded.

proxemics the study of the use of space; the study of how people organize the territory around them and the discrete distances they maintain between themselves and others.

proximity an index of perceived similarity or dissimilarity between objects.

pure research (basic research) designed to solve problems of a theoretical nature with little direct impact on strategic or tactical decisions.

purpose the explicit or hidden agenda of the authors of the secondary source; one of five factors in secondary source evaluation.

purpose nondisclosure a type of confidentiality; occurs when the sponsor camouflages the true research objective of the research project.

purposive sampling a nonprobability sampling process in which researchers choose participants arbitrarily for their unique characteristics or their experiences, attitudes, or perceptions.

Q-sort participant sorts a deck of cards (representing properties or objects) into piles that represent points along a continuum.

qualitative research interpretive techniques that seek to describe, decode, translate, and otherwise come to terms with the meaning, not the frequency, of certain phenomena; a fundamental approach of exploration, including individual depth interviews, group interviews, participant observation, videotaping of participants, projective techniques and psychological testing, case studies, street ethnography, elite interviewing, document analysis, and proxemics and kinesics; see also *content analysis*.

qualitative techniques nonquantitative data collection used to increase understanding of a topic.

quantitative research the precise count of some behavior, knowledge, opinion, or attitude.

quartile deviation (*Q*) a measure of dispersion for ordinal data involving the median and quartiles; the median plus one quartile deviation on either side encompasses 50 percent of the observations and eight cover the full range of data.

questionnaire an instrument delivered to the participant via personal (intercept, phone) or nonpersonal (computer-delivered, mail-delivered) means that is completed by the participant.

quota matrix a means of visualizing the matching process.

quota sampling purposive sampling in which relevant characteristics are used to stratify the sample.

random assignment a process that uses a randomized sample frame for assigning sample units to test groups in an attempt to ensure that the groups are as comparable as possible with respect to the DV; each subject must have an equal chance for exposure to each level of the independent variable.

random dialing a computerized process that chooses phone exchanges or exchange blocks and generates numbers within these blocks for telephone surveys.

random error error that occurs erratically, without pattern; see also *sampling error*.

randomization using random selection procedures to assign sample units to either the experimental or control group to achieve equivalence between groups.

range the difference between the largest and smallest scores in the data distribution; a very rough measure of spread of a dispersion.

range tests see **multiple comparison tests**.

ranking question a measurement question that asks the participant to compare and order two or more objects or properties using a numeric scale.

ranking scale a scale that scores an object or property by making a comparison and determining order among two or more objects or properties; uses a numeric scale and provides ordinal data; see also *ranking question*.

rating question a question that asks the participant to position each property or object on a verbal, numeric, or graphic continuum.

rating scale a scale that scores an object or property without making a direct comparison to another object or property; either verbal, numeric, or graphic; see also *rating question*.

ratio scale a scale with the properties of categorization, order, equal intervals, and unique origin; numbers used as measurements have numeric value; e.g., weight of an object.

reactivity response the phenomenon that occurs when participants alter their behavior due to the presence of the observer.

readability index measures the difficulty level of written material; e.g., Flesch Reading Ease Score, Flesch Kincaid Grade Level, Gunning's Fog Index; most word processing programs calculate one or several of the indexes.

recency effect order bias occurs when the participant tends to choose the last alternative; in presentations, people remember what they hear at the end of the list of arguments in a speech, recalling those items best; implies an important argument should be the last in your presentation.

reciprocal relationship occurs when two variables mutually influence or reinforce each other.

record a set of data fields that are related, usually by subject or participant; represented by rows in a spreadsheet or statistical database; a.k.a. *data case, data record*.

record analysis the extraction of data from current or historical records, either private or in the public domain; a technique of data mining.

recruitment screener semistructured or structured interview guide designed to ensure the interviewer that the prospect will be a good participant for the planned research.

refusal rate ratio of participants who decline the interview to all potential/eligible contacts.

region of acceptance area between the two regions of rejection based on a chosen level of significance (two-tailed test) or the area above/below the region of rejection (one-tailed test).

region of rejection area beyond the region of acceptance set by the level of significance.

regression analysis uses simple and multiple predictions to predict *Y* from *X* values.

regression coefficients intercept and slope coefficients; the two association measures between *X* and *Y* variables.

relational hypothesis describes the relationship between two variables with respect to some case; relationships are correlational or explanatory.

relationship a design principle that encourages the use of visual techniques that allow the audience to perceive the relationships between elements and sense what information goes together.

relevant population those elements in the population most likely to have the information specified in the investigative questions.

reliability a characteristic of measurement concerned with accuracy, precision, and consistency; a necessary but not sufficient condition for validity (if the measure is not reliable, it cannot be valid).

reliability, equivalence a characteristic of measurement in which instruments can secure consistent results by the same investigator or by different samples.

reliability, internal consistency a characteristic of an instrument in which the items are homogeneous.

reliability, stability a characteristic of measurement in which an instrument can secure consistent results with repeated measurements of the same person or object.

replication the process of repeating an experiment with different subject groups and conditions to determine the average effect of the IV across people, situations, and times.

reporting study provides a summation of data, often recasting data to achieve a deeper understanding or to generate statistics for comparison.

request for proposal (RFP) a formal bid request for research to be done by an outside supplier of research services.

research briefing another term for the oral presentation; starts with a brief statement that sets the stage for the body of the findings and explains the nature of the project, how it came about, and what it attempted to do. This is followed by a discussion of the findings that support it. Where appropriate, recommendations are stated in the third stage.

research design the blueprint for fulfilling research objectives and answering questions.

research process a sequence of clearly defined steps within a research study.

research question(s) the hypothesis that best states the objective of the research; the answer to this question would provide the manager with the desired information necessary to make a decision with respect to the management dilemma.

research report the document that describes the research project, its findings, analysis of the findings, interpretations, conclusions, and, sometimes, recommendations.

research variable see **variable**.

residual the difference between the regression line value of Y and the real Y value; what remains after the regression line is fit.

resistant statistics statistical measures relatively unaffected by outliers within a data set; e.g., median and quartiles.

respondent a participant in a study; a.k.a. *participant* or *subject*.

response error occurs when the participant fails to give a correct or complete answer.

return on investment (ROI) the calculation of the financial return for all organizational expenditures.

right to privacy the participant's right to refuse to be interviewed or to refuse to answer any questions in an interview.

right to quality the sponsor's right to an appropriate, value-laden research design and data handling and reporting techniques.

right to safety the right of interviewers, surveyors, experimenters, observers, and participants to be protected from any threat of physical or psychological harm.

rotation in principal components analysis, a technique used to provide a more simple and interpretable picture of the relationships between factors and variables.

rule of thirds the method by which photographers compose their shots in the viewfinder using real or imaginary cross-hairs that divide field of view into thirds, vertically and horizontally to create a balanced visual.

rule of three a presentation organizing device that uses trios, triplets, or triads in organizing support for an argument.

sample a group of cases, participants, events, or records consisting of a portion of the target population, carefully selected to represent that population; see also *pilot test, data mining*.

sample frame list of elements in the population from which the sample is actually drawn.

sample statistics descriptors of the relevant variables computed from sample data.

sampling the process of selecting some elements from a population to represent that population.

sampling error error created by the sampling process; the error not accounted for by systematic variance.

scaling the assignment of numbers or symbols to an indicant of a property or objects to impart some of the characteristics of the numbers to the property; assigned according to value or magnitude.

scalogram analysis a procedure for determining whether a set of items forms a unidimensional scale; used to determine if an item is appropriate for scaling.

scatterplot a visual technique that depicts both the direction and the shape of a relationship between variables

scientific method systematic, empirically based procedures for generating replicable research; includes direct observation of phenomena; clearly defined variables, methods, and procedures; empirically testable hypotheses; the ability to rule out rival hypotheses; and statistical rather than linguistic justification of conclusions.

scope the breadth and depth of topic coverage of a secondary source (by time frame, geography, criteria for inclusion, etc.); one of the five factors for evaluating the quality of secondary sources.

screen question question to qualify the participant's knowledge about the target questions of interest or experience necessary to participate.

script a written version of the introduction, arguments, conclusion, and recommendations used in preparing for a presentation.

search query the combination of keywords and connectors, operators, limiters, and truncation and phrase devices used to conduct electronic searches of secondary data sources; a.k.a. *search statement*.

search statement see **search query**.

secondary data results of studies done by others and for different purposes than the one for which the data are being reviewed.

secondary sources interpretations of primary data generally without new research.

self-administered survey an instrument delivered to the participant via personal (intercept) or nonpersonal (computer-delivered, mail-delivered) means that is completed by the participant without additional contact with an interviewer.

semantic differential (SD) scale measures the psychological meanings of an attitude object and produces interval data; uses bipolar nouns, noun phrases, adjectives, or nonverbal stimuli such as visual sketches.

semantic mapping a projective technique in which participants are presented with a four-quadrant map in which different variables anchor the two different axes; they then spatially place brands, product components, or organizations within the four quadrants.

semistructured interview an IDI that starts with a few specific questions and then follows the individual's tangents of thought with interviewer probes; questions generally use an open-ended response strategy.

sensitive attitude one that a holder feels uncomfortable sharing with others.

sensory sorts participants are presented with scents, textures, and sounds, usually verbalized on cards, and asked to arrange them by one or more criteria as they relate to a brand, product, event, etc.

sentence completion a projective technique in which participants are asked to complete a sentence related to a particular brand, product, event, user group, etc.

sentence outline report planning format; uses complete sentences rather than key words or phrases to draft each report section.

sequential interviewing an IDI technique in which the participant is asked questions formed around an anticipated series of activities that did or might have happened; used to stimulate recall within participants of both experiences and emotions; a.k.a. *chronologic interviewing*.

sequential sampling see **double sampling**.

simple category scale a scale with two mutually exclusive response choices; a.k.a. *dichotomous scale*.

simple observation unstructured and exploratory observation of participants or objects.

simple prediction when we take the observed values of X to estimate or predict corresponding Y values; see also *regression analysis*.

simple random sample a probability sample in which each element has a known and equal chance of selection.

simplicity a design principle that emphasizes reducing clutter and advocates using only the information and visual techniques necessary to convey the data, idea, or conclusion.

simulated test market (STM) test of a product conducted in a laboratory setting designed to simulate a traditional shopping environment.

simulation a study in which the conditions of a system or process are replicated.

skewness a measure of a data distribution's deviation from symmetry; if fully symmetrical, the mean, median, and mode are in the same location.

skip interval interval between sample elements drawn from a sample frame in systematic sampling.

skip pattern instructions designed to route or sequence the participant to another question based on the answer to a branched question.

slope (β_1) the change in Y for a 1-unit change in X; one of two regression coefficients.

snowball sampling a nonprobability sampling procedure in which subsequent participants are referred by current sample elements; referrals may have characteristics, experiences, or attitudes similar to or different from those of the original sample element; commonly used in qualitative methodologies.

solicited proposal proposal developed in response to an RFP.

Somers's *d* a measure of association for ordinal data that compensates for "tied" ranks and adjusts for direction of the independent variable.

sorting participants sort cards (representing concepts or constructs) into piles using criteria established by the researcher.

sound reasoning the basis of sound research, based on finding correct premises, testing connections between facts and assumptions, and making claims based on adequate evidence.

source evaluation the five-factor process for evaluating the quality and value of data from a secondary source; see also *purpose, scope, authority, audience*, and *format*.

spatial behavior how humans physically relate to one another.

spatial observation the recording of how humans physically relate to each other; see also *proxemics*.

spatial relationships study an observation study that records how humans physically relate to each other (see also *proxemics*).

speaker note cards a brief version of a presentation, in outline or keyword form; may be written on index cards; used for reminding the presenter of the organization of the presentation.

Spearman's rho correlates ranks between two ordered variables; an ordinal measure of association.

specialty researcher establishes expertise in one or a few research methodologies; these specialties usually are based on methodology, process, industry, participant group, or geographic region; often assists other research firms to complete projects.

specific instance a critical incident selected to prove an overarching claim whereby specifics are translated into more general principles; not as detailed as stories; a form of inductive reasoning.

specification error an overestimation of the importance of the variables included in a structural model.

sponsor nondisclosure a type of confidentiality; when the sponsor of the research does not allow revealing of its sponsorship.

spreadsheet a data-entry software application that arranges data cases or records as rows, with a separate column for each variable in the study.

stability characteristic of a measurement scale if it provides consistent results with repeated measures of the same person with the same instrument.

standard deviation (*s*) a measure of spread; the positive square root of the variance; abbreviated *std. dev.;* affected by extreme scores.

standard error of the mean the standard deviation of the distribution of sample means.

standard normal distribution the statistical standard for describing normally distributed sample data; used with inferential statistics that assume normally distributed variables.

standard score (Z score) conveys how many standard deviation units a case is above or below the mean; designed to improve compatibility among variables that come from different scales yet require comparison; includes both linear manipulations and nonlinear transformations.

standard test market real-time test of a product through existing distribution channels.

standardized coefficients regression coefficients in standardized form (mean = 0) used to determine the comparative impact of variables that come from different scales; the *X* values restated in terms of their standard deviations (a measure of the amount that *Y* varies with each unit change of the associated *X* variable).

Stapel scale a numerical scale with up to 10 categories (7 positive, 7 negative) in which the central position is an attribute. The higher the positive number, the more accurately the attribute describes the object or its indicant.

statistical significance an index of how meaningful the results of a statistical comparison are; the magnitude of difference between a sample value and its population value; the difference is statistically significant if it is unlikely to have occurred by chance (represent random sampling fluctuations).

statistical study a study that attempts to capture a population's characteristics by making inferences from a sample's characteristics; involves hypothesis testing and is more comprehensive than a case study.

statistics (in presentations) numerical data used in the collection, analysis, and interpretation of data, but also found in of the data collection planning, measurement, and design; expected in research presentations.

stem-and-leaf display a tree-type frequency distribution for each data value, without equal interval grouping.

stepwise selection in modeling and regression, a method for sequentially adding or removing variables from a regression model to optimize R^2; combines *forward selection* and *backward elimination* methods.

stories a type of supporting material used in a presentation that tells the particulars of an act or occurrence or course of events; is most powerful when involving personal experience.

strategy the general approach an organization will follow to achieve its goals.

stratified random sampling probability sampling that includes elements from each of the mutually exclusive strata within a population.

stratified sampling, disproportionate a probability sampling technique in which each stratum's size is not proportionate to the stratum's share of the population; allocation is usually based on variability of measures expected from the stratum, cost of sampling from a given stratum, and size of the various strata.

stratified sampling, proportionate a probability sampling technique in which each stratum's size is proportionate to the stratum's share of the population; higher statistical efficiency than a simple random sample.

stress index an index used in multidimensional scaling that ranges from 1 (worst fit) to 0 (perfect fit).

structural equation modeling (SEM) uses analysis of covariance structures to explain causality among constructs.

structured interview an IDI that often uses a detailed interview guide similar to a questionnaire to guide the question order; questions generally use an open-ended response strategy.

structured response participant's response is limited to specific alternatives provided; a.k.a. *closed response*.

summated rating scale category of scales in which the participant agrees or disagrees with evaluative statements; the Likert scale is most known of this type of scale.

supergroup a group interview involving up to 20 people.

survey a measurement process using a highly structured interview; employs a measurement tool called a *questionnaire, measurement instrument,* or *interview schedule.*

survey via personal interview a two-way communication initiated by an interviewer to obtain information from a participant; face-to-face, phone, or Internet.

symmetrical relationship occurs when two variables vary together but without causation.

syndicated data provider tracks the change of one or more measures over time, usually in a given industry.

synergy the process at the foundation of group interviewing that encourages members to react to and build on the contributions of others in the group.

systematic error error that results from a bias; see also *systematic variance.*

systematic observation data collection through observation that employs standardized procedures, trained observers, schedules for recording, and other devices for the observer that mirror the scientific procedures of other primary data methods.

systematic sampling a probability sample drawn by applying a calculated skip interval to a sample frame; population (*N*) is divided by the desired sample (*n*) to obtain a skip interval (*k*). Using a random start between 1 and *k*, each *k*th element is chosen from the sample frame; usually treated as a simple random sample but statistically more efficient.

systematic variance the variation that causes measurements to skew in one direction or another.

t **distribution** a normal distribution with more tail area than that in a *Z* normal distribution.

t-**test** a parametric test to determine the statistical significance between a sample distribution mean and a population parameter; used when the population standard deviation is unknown and the sample standard deviation is used as a proxy.

tactics specific, timed activities that execute a strategy.

target population those people, events, or records that contain the desired information for the study that determine whether a sample or a census should be selected.

target question measurement question that addresses the core investigative questions of a specific study; these can be structured or unstructured questions.

target question, structured a measurement question that presents the participant with a fixed set of categories per variable.

target question, unstructured measurement question that presents the participant with the context for participant-framed answers; a.k.a. *open-ended question, free-response question* (nominal, ordinal, or ratio data).

tau (τ) a measure of association that uses table marginals to reduce prediction errors, with measures from 0 to 1.0 reflecting percentage of error estimates for prediction of one variable based on another variable.

tau b (τ_b) a refinement of gamma for ordinal data that considers "tied" pairs, not only discordant and concordant pairs (values from -1.0 to $+1.0$); used best on square tables (one of the most widely used measures for ordinal data).

tau c (τ_c) a refinement of gamma for ordinal data that considers "tied" pairs, not only discordant and concordant pairs (values from -1.0 to $+1.0$); useful for any-size table (one of the most widely used measures for ordinal data).

technical report a report written for an audience of researchers.

telephone focus group a type of focus group in which participants are connected to the moderator and each other by modern teleconferencing equipment; participants are often in separate teleconferencing facilities; may be remote-moderated or -monitored.

telephone interview a study conducted wholly by telephone contact between participant and interviewer.

telephone survey a structured interview conducted via telephone.

10-minute rule varying a presentation's content on 10-minute intervals with videos, demonstrations, questions, and other means to allow the brain to avoid boredom/fatigue and seek new stimuli.

tertiary sources aids to discover primary or secondary sources, such as indexes, bibliographies, and Internet search engines; also may be an interpretation of a secondary source.

testimony (expert opinion) opinions of recognized experts who possess credibility for your audience on a topic; used as support or proof.

test market a controlled experiment conducted in a carefully chosen marketplace (e.g., website, store, town, or other geographic location) to measure and predict sales or profitability of a product.

test unit an alternative term for a subject within an experiment (a person, an animal, a machine, a geographic entity, an object, etc.).

Thematic Apperception Test a projective technique in which participants are confronted with a picture (usually a photograph or drawing) and asked to describe how the person in the picture feels and thinks.

theoretical sampling a nonprobability sampling process in which conceptual or theoretical categories of participants develop during the interviewing process; additional participants are sought who will challenge emerging patterns.

theory a set of systematically interrelated concepts, definitions, and propositions that are advanced to explain or predict phenomena (facts); the generalizations we make about variables and the relationships among variables.

3-D graphic a presentation technique that permits a graphical comparison of three or more variables; types: column, ribbon, wireframe, and surface line.

three-point speech variations on the *rule of three* in speech organization that may include introduction–body–conclusion; introduction–three best supporting points–conclusion; three stories; or, other devices in threes.

time sampling the process of selecting certain time points or time intervals to observe and record elements, acts, or conditions from a population of observable behaviors or conditions to represent the population as a whole; three types include time-point samples, time-interval samples, and continuous real-time samples.

topic outline report planning format; uses key words or phrases rather than complete sentences to draft each report section.

treatment the experimental factor to which participants are exposed.

treatment levels the arbitrary or natural groupings within the independent variable of an experiment.

triad a group interview involving three people.

trials repeated measures taken from the same subject or participant.

triangulation research design that combines several qualitative methods or qualitative with quantitative methods; most common are simultaneous QUAL/QUANT in single or multiple waves, sequential QUAL-QUANT or QUANT-QUAL, sequential QUAL-QUANT-QUAL.

truncation a search protocol that allows a symbol (usually "?" or "*") to replace one or more characters or letters in a word or at the end of a word root.

two-independent-samples tests parametric and nonparametric tests used when the measurements are taken from two samples that are unrelated (Z test, t-test, chi-square, etc.).

two-related-samples tests parametric and nonparametric tests used when the measurements are taken from closely matched samples or the phenomena are measured twice from the same sample (t-test, McNemar test, etc).

two-stage design a design in which exploration as a distinct stage precedes a descriptive or causal design.

two-tailed test a nondirectional test to reject the hypothesis that the sample statistic is either greater than or less than the population parameter.

Type I error error that occurs when one rejects a true null hypothesis (there is no difference); the alpha (α) value, called the level of significance, is the probability of rejecting the true null hypothesis.

Type II error error that occurs when one fails to reject a false null hypothesis; the beta (β) value is the probability of failing to reject the false null hypothesis; the power of the test $1 - \beta$ and is the probability that we will correctly reject the false null hypothesis.

unbalanced rating scale has an unequal number of favorable and unfavorable response choices.

unforced-choice rating scale provides participants with an opportunity to express no opinion when they are unable to make a choice among the alternatives offered.

unidimensional scale instrument scale that seeks to measure only one attribute of the participant or object.

unobtrusive measures a set of observational approaches that encourage creative and imaginative forms of indirect observation, archival searches, and variations on simple and contrived observation, including physical traces observation (erosion and accretion).

unsolicited proposal a suggestion by a contract researcher for research that might be done.

unstructured interview a customized IDI with no specific questions or order of topics to be discussed; usually starts with a participant narrative.

unstructured response participant's response is limited only by space, layout, instructions, or time; usually free-response or fill-in response strategies.

utility score a score in conjoint analysis used to represent each aspect of a product or service in a participant's overall preference ratings.

validity a characteristic of measurement concerned with the extent that a test measures what the researcher actually wishes to measure; and that differences found with a measurement tool reflect true differences among participants drawn from a population.

validity, construct the degree to which a research instrument is able to provide evidence based on theory.

validity, content the extent to which measurement scales provide adequate coverage of the investigative questions.

validity, criterion-related the success of a measurement scale for prediction or estimation; types are predictive and concurrent.

variability term for measures of spread or dispersion within a data set.

variable (research variable) a characteristic, trait, or attribute that is measured; a symbol to which values are assigned; includes several different types: continuous, control, decision, dependent, dichotomous, discrete, dummy, extraneous, independent, intervening, and moderating variables.

variance a measure of score dispersion about the mean; calculated as the squared deviation scores from the data distribution's mean; the greater the dispersion of scores, the greater the variance in the data set.

videoconferencing focus group a type of focus group in which researchers use the videoconference facilities of a firm to connect participants with moderators and observers; unlike telephone focus groups, participants can see each other; can be remotely moderated, and in some facilities can be simultaneously monitored by client observers via Internet technology.

virtual test market a test of a product using a computer simulation of an interactive shopping experience.

visibility the design principle that visual support materials must be sized and placed in the presentation setting to facilitate the audience's ability to see and read the content.

visitor from another planet a projective technique (imagination exercise) in which participants are asked to assume that they are aliens and are confronting the product for the first time; they then describe their reactions, questions, and attitudes about purchase or retrial.

visual aids presentation tools used to facilitate understanding of content (e.g., chalkboards, whiteboards, handouts, flip charts, overhead transparencies, slides, computer-drawn visuals, computer animation).

visual learners people who learn through seeing; about 40 percent of the audience; implies the need to include visual imagery, including graphs, photographs, models, etc., in research presentations.

visual preparation the design principle that a presenter should conceptualize the visual support materials on paper before composing the digital versions.

visualization the process of developing and organizing support materials that help the audience share in your understanding of the data.

voice recognition computer systems programmed to record verbal answers to questions.

Web-based questionnaire a measurement instrument both delivered and collected via the Internet; data processing is ongoing. Two options currently exist: proprietary solutions offered through research firms and off-the-shelf software for researchers who possess the necessary knowledge and skills; a.k.a. *online survey, online questionnaire, Internet survey.*

Web-delivered presentation one that involves the use of a Web presentation platform, a presenter who remotely controls the delivery of the presentation, and an invited audience who participates via the Web from their office or a Web-equipped room.

Web-enabled test market test of a product using online distribution.

whitespace a design principle of leaving empty, uncluttered space surrounding important key visuals and text; permits audience to achieve a visual focus.

word or **picture association** a projective technique in which participants are asked to match images, experiences, emotions, products and services, and even people and places to whatever is being studied.

Z distribution the normal distribution of measurements assumed for comparison.

Z score see **standard score**.

Z test a parametric test to determine the statistical significance between a sample distribution mean and a population parameter; employs the Z distribution.

>photocredits

Note: locators with n indicate note.

A

Aczel, Amir D., 705n7, 707, 707n7, 708, 708n1, 709, 709n3, 710, 710n11
Adams, Doug, 207, 704
Adams, Jack, 491–492
Adamy, David, 713n37
Adler, Jeffrey C., 149
Agarwal, Vivek, 697
Agrawal, R., 692n8
Agresti, Alan, 710, 710n8, 710n15
Aiken, Lewis, 703
Akert, R., 702n1
Albaum, Gerald, 699
Albrecht, Katherine, 198, 697
Allen, Jeff, 689n14
Allport, Gordon W., 702n1
Almond, Murray, 710n6
Alreck, Pamela L., 703n12
Altman, Rick, 612, 615, 713n38, 713n45
Alwin, Duane F., 704n11
Amoo, Taiwo, 703n5
An, Chae, 689n13
Anderson, Rolph E., 529, 711, 711n7, 711n9
Anderson, Tom, 167, 247, 261, 696, 701
Anderson, Tom H. C., 45, 428, 691, 693, 696, 697, 704, 708
Andrews, F. M., 708n6
Anscombe, F. J., 709n2
Aristotle, 599–601, 611, 628, 712n2–3, 712n5, 713
Arkin, Elaine Bratic, 84, 691
Arksey, Hilary, 701
Aronson, E., 696n1, 702n1
Assael, Henry, 705n3
Athanasiou, Robert, 337
Atkinson, Cliff, 608, 712n7, 713
Auble, D., 686
Ayers, Ian, 708

B

Babbie, Earl R., 695, 698n5
Babin, Barry, 711, 711n9
Bailey, Kenneth D., 696n5, 698, 698n4
Baldia, Sonia, 45
Bales, R., 96, 191, 696n2
Bales, Robert F., 696n7, 698
Bancroft, Gertrude, 705n10
Barker-Motley, Constance, 145
Baron, Robert A., 689n5, 702n2
Barrell, J. E., 713n59–60
Barrell, J. J., 713n59–60
Barrow, Arian, 602
Barzilay, Regina, 693
Bauer, Martin, 696n18
Bearden, William, 337
Beardsley, Monroe, 691
The Beatles, 623
Belk, Russel, 695n4
Belson, W. R., 705n2
Bennett, Peter D., 688n3
Berelson, B., 706n2
Berenson, Conrad, 700n20–21
Berenson, Mark L., 709
Berger, Sam, 691
Berkowitz, Eric N., 66, 690n6–7

Bernstein, Ira, 702
Berry, Michael J. A., 688, 693
Betts, Mitch, 707n h, 707n k–l, 707n o
Bialik, Carl, 698n e, 698n g–h
Bierley, Calvin, 518, 710n a
Bigwood, Sally, 434, 435, 708, 712
Black, Bill, 711, 711n9
Black, William C., 711n7
Blattberg, Robert C., 688
Bleemer, Hugh, 708
Bolton, Brian, 65
Bordner, Mike, 708
Boswell, Wendy, 692
Bowers, Diane, 39
Bowlus, George, 239
Boyd, Harper W., Jr, 705n3, 708n14
Boyle, Matthew, 699
Bradburn, Norman N., 705
Bramble, William J., 695, 702n19, 709n4
Brick, J. Michael, 700n30
Broedling, L. A., 696n11
Brokaw, Tom, 174
Brooks, William D., 694n7
Brown, Rex V., 691n3
Browne, M. Neil, 691
Bruner, Gordon, 337
Bruning, James L., 709n12–13
Bryan, Glenn L., 691n7
Bunger, Mark, 61, 567, 691, 711
Burgess, Teri, 10, 688
Burke, Raymond R., 699n10
Burnett, Steven, 69
Burstein, Paul, 698n2
Bush, George W., 637
Bux, William E., 707
Byrne, Barbara M., 711n9
Byrne, Donn, 689n5, 702n2

C

Cacioppo, John T., 702n1
Caesar, Julius, 609
Cakebread, Jack, 509
Campbell, Donald T., 696n10, 698, 698n6–7, 699, 702, 702n14
Campbell, Steve, 712
Cannell, Charles F., 246, 699n5, 704n7, 705, 705n5–6
Cannell, F., 704n16
Cantril, Hadley, 355, 356, 704n8, 704n17, 705n12
Cara, Phil, 688
Carey, Benedict, 69, 690
Carroll, Lewis, 609
Carson, David, 163, 174, 695n4–5, 696n20–21, 696n23
Cartier-Bresson, Henri, 4
Cartwright, Dorwin, 704n2
Cascio, Wayne F., 702, 702n16, 702n18
Castellan, N. J., Jr., 709, 709n14, 710, 710n14
Cervantes Saavedra, Miguel de, 362, 706
Cessar, Ken, 689
Chabris, Christopher, 711n10
Chambers, J., 708n13
Chambers, John, 607
Champion, Sam, 363
Chatterjee, Barbara F., 194, 697
Chatterjee, Samprit, 710
Chen, Jesse, 261
Chesley, David, 401

Chestnut, Ben, 215, 699
Churchill, G. A., 703n7
Cleveland, W., 707n13
Clinton, Hillary, 621
Coblenz, Edith, M. D., 239–240
Cochran, William G., 487, 537, 684, 705n15–16, 706n21
Coffman, Curt, 688n9
Cohen, Jacob, 709, 710
Cohen, Morris R., 694n15
Cohen, Patricia, 710
Cohen, Roger, 691n6
Conlin, Michelle, 707
Conover, W. J., 708n10
Converse, Jean M., 688, 704, 704n12–13, 704n19, 705n1, 706n1
Converse, Philip E., 337
Cook, Stuart W., 692, 694, 694n10, 695, 702n11
Cook, Thomas D., 698n7, 699, 702, 702n14
Cooper, Donald R., 38, 692, 700n13, 703n6, 706, 712n22
Corbin, Juliet, 174, 695
Courtion, Colette, 708
Covey, Stephen M. R., 710
Cowan, N., 712n26
Cox, Donald F., 691n3
Cox, Eli P., 703n8
Creswell, John W., 695

D

Dabbs, James M., Jr., 694n8
Dahan, Ely, 699n13
Dahm, Michael, 694
Damasio, Antonio, 69
Darley, J. M., 698n1
Davenport, Andrew, 689n13
David, Ian, 688n1
Davidson, T. N., 708n6
Davis, Duane, 689n14, 701n47
Day, Daniel D., 703n9
Daymon, Christine, 695n11
De Leeuw, Edith, 700n12, 700n14, 700n16
Dearing, Brian E., 707n3
Deerfield, Eddie T., 174
Deese, J., 712n14–15
DeFinetti, Bruno, 709
Degeling, D., 695n15
DeGeneres, Ellen, 595
Dellarocas, Chrysanthos, 420
DeMers, Michael, 708
Deming, W. Edwards, 365, 705n2, 706
Deneriaz, Antoine, 621
Denzin, Norman K., 695n4, 698
DePompe, B., 692n9, 692n12
Dewey, John, 73, 690n12, 690n14
Dexter, Louis A., 701
Diamantopoulus, A., 705n8
Dillman, Don A., 700n15, 700n17–19, 701, 704
DiMauro, Vanessa, 116, 693
Dlugan, Andrew, 609, 712n23–24, 712n28, 713n57
Dobrenwend, Barbara Snell, 699n3, 705n14
Donovan, Todd, 691
Dotson, Jean D., 337
Drucker, Peter F., 132
Duarte, Nancy, 604, 605, 615, 619, 712n8, 712n18, 713, 713n45, 713n48
Dunn, Graham, 711n5
Dunnette, Marvin D., 698n7, 699, 702, 702n14